The Full Monty

VOLUME I

NIGEL HAMILTON

The Full Monty

VOLUME I:
MONTGOMERY OF ALAMEIN,
1887–1942

ALLEN LANE
THE PENGUIN PRESS

ALLEN LANE
THE PENGUIN PRESS

Published by the Penguin Group
Penguin Books Ltd, 80 Strand, London WC2R 0RL, England
Penguin Putnam Inc., 375 Hudson Street, New York, New York 10014, USA
Penguin Books Australia Ltd, Ringwood, Victoria, Australia
Penguin Books Canada Ltd, 10 Alcorn Avenue, Toronto, Ontario, Canada M4V 3B2
Penguin Books India (P) Ltd, 11, Community Centre, Panchsheel Park, New Delhi – 110 017, India
Penguin Books (NZ) Ltd, Private Bag 102902, NSMC, Auckland, New Zealand
Penguin Books (South Africa) (Pty) Ltd, 24 Sturdee Avenue, Rosebank 2196, South Africa

Penguin Books Ltd, Registered Offices: 80 Strand, London WC2R 0RL, England

First published 2001
1

Maps drawn by Nigel Andrews

Set in 10/13.5 pt Adobe Sabon
Typeset by Rowland Phototypesetting Ltd, Bury St Edmunds, Suffolk
Printed and bound in Great Britain by The Bath Press, Bath
Cover repro and printing by Concise Cover Printers

A CIP catalogue record for this book is available from the British Library

ISBN 0-713-99334-0

For Julia Briggs, who believed

Contents

BOOK III
ALAMEIN

'The hero was as daring as they thought him,
But his peculiar boyhood missed them all;
The angel of a broken leg had taught him
The right precautions to avoid a fall.'

W H Auden, 'The Quest'

Illustrations

The author would like to thank members of the Montgomery family and friends, once again, for their kindness in making available private photographs. Photographic acknowledgements are given in brackets. The publishers will be happy to make good in future editions any errors or omissions brought to their attention.

Maps

Preface

Robert Skidelsky, chronicler of the lives of Oswald Mosley and John Maynard Keynes, noted some time ago that it is the private life of an individual which now enthrals us in biography. 'The life is the achievement', Skidelsky commented on the changing face of biography; 'what used to be called the achievement is now only one accompaniment, possibly a minor one, of living.'[1]

How does such a view square with the life of an individual such as Field Marshal Montgomery, whose battlefield achievements are still the stuff of such historical controversy among British and American historians of World War II? Is the private life an aid to historical reconstruction and understanding?

In the late 1970s I was asked to become Monty's official biographer, and faced this very question. His reputation, since the late 1950s, had been trashed by a growing cohort of British and American military historians who disliked the man, and permitted their bias to pervert their historianship. Using Monty's personal papers and diaries for the first time, and conducting several thousand interviews across the world, I attempted to re-balance military historiography in a three-volume study, without concealing Monty's many warts.[2]

I did not, at that time, peer too closely into Monty's strange sexuality, not only because I had a larger task in hand, but because I wasn't ready, as a young biographer, to enter those dark waters. My father, who had served under Monty (and had been decorated by him in the field as a young battalion commander in 1944), and who had later serialized Monty's controversial memoirs in the London *Sunday Times*, would have been aghast at the thought, as would many of those who co-operated and assisted in compiling the opus.

The dark waters did not recede, however. After publication of the first volume of *Monty* in 1981, I received a letter from a Swiss gentleman, offering to show me more than a hundred love-letters from the Field Marshal to himself, from the age of twelve. Mercifully for me, my second volume only took Monty's life story up to 1944: two years before the 'affair' with the little 'Swiss boy' began. I was thus able to put the letters – which Monty's son David courageously handed over to me to use as I saw fit – out of sight and out of mind in a drawer marked 'Volume 3', and before I could publish the volume, the Swiss gentleman's story had independently hit the newsstands.

'Was Monty Gay?' The headline that appeared in the British tabloid press in the summer of 1985 was, thankfully, not inspired by me but by one of Monty's former wartime liaison officers, Major T. E. B. Howarth, who had become headmaster of Monty's old school, St Paul's. He had decided to collect and publish a series of personal reminiscences by members of Monty's staff and friends – including an essay by Dr Lucien Trueb: Monty's 'little Swiss friend'. In this, Dr Trueb chronicled the genesis and development of Monty's extraordinary infatuation with him, including his insistence that Lucien stay with him in his special chalet at Gstaad after World War II, where Monty personally bathed the boy, and towelled him dry 'so I wouldn't catch a cold'.[3]

I interviewed Dr Trueb, who had lived for many years in America and had later become a senior science journalist in Zürich. He assured me nothing 'untoward' had ever taken place; yet Monty's predilection for young men – and, increasingly, boys – was something that was replicated many, many times over in Monty's later life. Clearly it was not a facet I could entirely overlook as a serious biographer – the more so since I had personal knowledge of it.

Like Dr Trueb, I also had been twelve when I first met the Field Marshal; I also had stayed with him in his home, and over the years had got to know him as well as, or perhaps better than, anyone of my generation. I also had received over a hundred affectionate, loving letters from him, which I had kept and, indeed, treasured. I did not use them in my official biography lest they compromise my integrity as an historical biographer, and of Lucien's many letters I decided to use only a few token lines to instance this quirk in Monty's character, while setting it within the context of his life at that time: an exhausted, world-renowned soldier who, by his total dedication to the art of modern democratic warfare, had saved the democracies in their hour of need and was struggling once again to protect democracy in Europe in the difficult postwar years.

Today, however, we inhabit a different world from that of Monty's lifetime, or the decades immediately after his death. The infamous British law on homosexuality – the Labouchère Amendment of 1885 – was finally repealed as part of the Sexual Offences Act legislation in 1967. Gay rights were asserted throughout the Western world, and in a remarkably short time – given the punitive treatment meted out to gays since the Wilde trial of 1896 – gay relationships became accepted within society. More recently, a momentous change has taken place in military as well as social law in the West: the decision by the British government in January 2000 to bring British military regulations into line with Britain's EU counterparts and permit gays in the military.

That ruling must – given the intimate co-operation between US, British, European and other democratic nations in global peacekeeping and UN military duties – inevitably be replicated one day in the United States, where it is already tacitly accepted ('Don't ask, don't tell').

Gay recruits, whether men or women, cadets, officers or GIs, are and will inevitably be subjected to vilification and abuse as 'the military' adjusts to this change. Yet, as proved to be the case with racial integration, the adjustment will not only come to pass in time, but will prove beneficial in a world where the military forces of democratic nations require the support and approval of their citizens to carry out their often difficult assignments. Homophobic behaviour, or misbehaviour, will not be tolerated, any more than racism.

Who will such recruits look up to as their heroes, though? Their exemplars and predecessors in sexual nature or preference, however repressed? Alexander the Great? Frederick the Great? Baron von Steuben – the great trainer of the Continental Army during the American Revolution? Lawrence of Arabia? Not the least dereliction resulting from late-Victorian and post-Victorian homophobia has been the failure of military historians and biographers to take up Sigmund Freud's crusading biographical torch[4] – though it must be admitted that, given the severities of criminal law, social taboo and military regulations over the past century, it is not hard to understand why.

Pondering the question, I do not think I would be tempted to revisit a character and a military saga I have already told at such inordinate length, were it not for three further factors that impel me to do so.

First, an abundance of new documentary material, published and archival, has become available to historians since the publication of my original Monty volumes in the 1980s: material which not only casts fresh light on Monty's involvement in military operations such as the Dieppe raid of 1942, but which gives us far richer opportunities for comparison with his counterparts and contemporaries, such as Field-Marshal Haig, T. E. Lawrence and Basil Liddell Hart.

Second, given the rumours and stories that have circulated in increasing number in recent times,[5] if the official biographer of the field marshal, who knew the man intimately in the final twenty years of his life, will not undertake to clarify the position and incorporate a fresh view of Monty's sexuality when looking at his military life, who will?

Third – and perhaps most important – is it not time that the question of 'gayness' – of affection and love, even passion for members of one's own sex – be reconsidered as a primary factor in military effectiveness in a democracy? Monty, for himself, never ceased to regard 'morale' as a 'battle-winning factor' in World War II. He personally transformed the morale of a defeated 8th Army at Alamein in the summer of 1942 – a transformation which was considered, at the time, to mark the 'turning of the tide' in the Allied struggle against Nazism. *How did he do it?* How did that small, beaky-nosed, obsessive, unphotogenic, dedicated soldier with white knees imprint himself so unmistakably, unshakeably, unforgettably upon the hardened as well as novice fighting men of the 8th Army – men drawn from the forces of Britain, Australia, New Zealand, India, South Africa, Rhodesia, France, Belgium, Greece, Poland, Canada – even America? Upon officers, NCOs, privates, GIs alike; ambulance drivers, airmen, artillerymen, pioneers, payclerks . . .

Moreover, how did Monty then go on to revive the morale of a flagging Home Army in Britain in the early months of 1944 – a democratic army crushed at Dunkirk, and again at Dieppe? How did he raise its fighting skills and spirit, and lead the four British, Canadian and American armies to victory in France in the summer of 1944 – from the D-Day beaches to the breakout to the Seine and the recapture of Paris? Was it solely a matter of superior tactical generalship, under the inter-service stewardship of General Eisenhower? Or did Monty manage, for the first time in the twentieth century – in a British-commanded group of armies at least – to bridge the gulf that had existed in World War I between the leader and the led?

Did Monty, in other words, have a weapon more powerful even than his revolutionary approach to training in a democracy? Did he somehow come to combine the greatest professionalism ever achieved by an Allied field commander in the twentieth century with something else – something difficult to define, yet which we must try to articulate if we are ever to understand its genesis and significance?

Jealous, narrow-minded military historians on both sides of the Atlantic have tended to play down Monty's effect on morale, or to ascribe it simply to PR; so much so that one is tempted to ask whether such historians are guilty – consciously or unconsciously – of homophobia. For the underlying, revolutionary ingredient in Monty's leadership was, to all intents and purposes, homosocial. That is to say, from his earliest days as an infantry cadet at Sandhurst and officer on the North-West Frontier of India, Monty showed not the remotest interest in women or the female sex, beyond a passionate devotion to his tyrannical mother. Instead he devoted himself to the 'British soldier': to his welfare, his training, even his need for 'horizontal refreshment', as he called it, so that in war and in battle that soldier, fit and healthy, would not only carry out his orders, but know why he was doing so; moreover, would know how to do so with the best possible chance of succeeding – and surviving.

'In all people there are great emotional forces bottled up inside them,' Monty once reflected. 'I say "bottled up" purposely, because I believe that, as you take the cork out of the bottle, so there must be an outlet for the human emotions. It must be a constructive, positive outlet, which warms the heart and excites the imagination.' As a battlefield commander he found the outlet, which involved a new form of leadership through a new compact between commander and his troops. 'I made my soldiers partners with me in battle,' Monty later explained to an assembly of schoolboys. 'I have handled large numbers of men. Indeed in the War I was eventually in command of two million men – it's a terrific number if you think of it! In those men were great forces. If you get confidence and trust from two million men, there is nothing you cannot do, everything is in your power.'[6]

Monty's strange and absolute devotion to this compact with his men was noticed from the beginning, and it characterized his leadership from command of a platoon to a group of armies. Insofar as we know, he never had physical contact with any of his soldiers but, as one of his superiors had already noted in the early 1930s, he was 'really popular with his men who he regards and treats as if they were his children'.[7] When World War II came those soldiers, drawn from many lands, repaid that paternalistic devotion by an example of offensive fighting determination – a willingness to follow their new commander in battle in 1942, and if necessary to die for him – that stunned Stalin and silenced the doubters in Washington.

Monty's marriage in 1927 seems to have been an exception in this otherwise exclusively homosocial odyssey, yet all the more moving for its unexpected happiness. After the death of his wife, Monty would allow no woman near him, even in his headquarters; indeed, as we shall see, he would allow no wives or female relatives in the area of England where his men were stationed after Dunkirk. With his coterie of personally selected young staff officers and ADCs, he went about a re-invention of the art of modern command in the leading of largely civilian male (i.e., volunteer or conscripted, as opposed to regular army) soldiers.

Hitler's 'total' war licensed Monty to create, first in England, then in the Egyptian desert, a homosocial bond with his men – officers and other ranks – on a scale unequalled in British history: a bond that could, I am certain, have been created only by a man who loved men – young men – beyond all else, and was prepared to sweep aside any obstruction – traditional, military, political or social – in order to get the best out of them. 'In war too many generals move men about like pieces on a chessboard,' Monty once wrote to my father. 'I reckoned I was moving "human beings" and was out to get the quickest results with the least loss of life. To me, men were not just expendable. Each man mattered.'[8]

Both Churchill and King George VI came to fear the power of this bond, this compact, which at times went to Monty's head; without it, however, it is questionable whether Britain would have been able to compete against the indoctrinated and highly disciplined forces of Hitler's Third Reich on the field of battle, or carry out the D-Day landings successfully. Even Eisenhower, the Supreme Allied Commander, privately confided: 'I don't know if we could have done it without Monty. It was his sort of battle. Whatever they say about him, he got us there.'[9]

It is this homosocial bond I wish, in particular, to re-examine while retelling Monty's life story, at the start of a new millennium in which gay servicemen and servicewomen – at least in Britain and Europe – may legitimately now fight for their country and for the free world. Much has been written about the warrior poets of World War I and the extent to which homosocial/repressed-homosexual feelings of love and responsibility for one's comrades and men motivated officers such as Wilfred Owen, Siegfried Sassoon and Robert Graves to return to the trenches of the Western Front and almost certain death. (The life expectancy of a front-line subaltern in 1916 was two weeks.) 'Given this association between war and sex', writes Paul Fussell in his literary compendium *The Great War and Modern Memory*, it was not surprising to find 'front-line experience replete with what we can call the homoerotic'. Fussell pointed out how, in World War I, the 'object' of such 'temporary homosexuality' was not physical sex – a recourse that was relatively rare – but a passionate intensity of emotion, expressed in 'mutual affection, protection, and admiration' between frightened men, as they faced the possibility, even inevitability of their own deaths. As at British boarding schools, 'such passions were antidotes against loneliness and terror' – and they were responsible, in turn, for the deepest emotions felt by soldiers.[10]

Recognizing the 'emotional forces' bottled up in his men, as well as their need for self-respect, affection, purpose and protection, Monty used his own sublimated passions to lead a great army to victory in the desert, and great Allied armies to victory in Europe in World War II. I believe it is time, therefore, to recount his unique life history in terms of those sublimated passions and that homosocial bond; for upon it, in the great battles of World War II, rested the fortunes of democracy in its struggle against the Nazis.

In short, it is a story that is not merely of intrinsic interest, given our increasing fascination with human sexuality, but of historic significance in understanding the winning of World War II by the democracies of the West at a critical moment in human history. In retelling this story I have sought to bring to bear the fruits of much recent social, literary and military scholarship, including many publications and documents: books, articles, diaries, letters, memoirs, papers. In this way I hope *The Full Monty* will offer a fresh account, told from a fresh perspective, for a fresh readership. Robert Skidelsky's analysis of the trend in biography in the 1980s was not wrong – indeed, it was all too correct. But the virtue of early twenty-first-century biography, to my mind, will be the incorporation of a franker, more open-minded interest in human sexuality in the equation between individuality and performance – something of which Dr Johnson, the founder of the modern approach to biography who insisted on the need to reconstruct a human life 'really as it was', would undoubtedly have welcomed.[11]

'It is not easy,' Johnson warned in *The Rambler* 250 years ago, 'for the most artful writer to give us an interest in happiness or misery, which we think ourselves never likely to feel, and with which we have never yet been made acquainted.' As he memorably added, 'the most artful writer' was thus charged with a great test: how to move 'the man whose faculties have been engrossed by business, and whose heart never fluttered but at the rise or fall of stocks'; a man who 'wonders how the attention can be seized, or the affections agitated by a tale of love'.[12]

I hope, therefore, that this new 'tale of love' – the first of two volumes, the second of which will examine the impact of fame upon Monty's often tormented personality – will help enlarge our understanding of twentieth century military history, the unique role which Monty played in that history, and the man he really was.

Nigel Hamilton, October 2000

Acknowledgements

This book owes its genesis and existence to many people. In 1997 Simon Winder of the Penguin Press first raised the possibility of a new, updated version of my official Montgomery biography, published in the 1980s and out of print. The staff of the Imperial War Museum, where Monty's papers are archived, kindly offered me their facilities, and in 1998 I began work on a project that I did not, initially, imagine would take too much time. I therefore began looking at the many books, articles and documents which have become available to historians since the 1980s, and to condense the original three-volume text into a proposed single volume, for publication in 2000.

This plan did not eventuate. It is not given to many historical biographers to be permitted to rewrite their own work after the passage of two decades. My work as a university teacher of the history of twentieth-century biography had illustrated how each succeeding decade marked major shifts in the way biography has been undertaken in the West. With each era and each generation, the biographical perspective, approach, market and even medium altered. What was acceptable to one generation became inadequate for the next.

My original three-volume Monty opus now seems not only inadequate in terms of new material and sources, but in its very perspective – that of a young(ish) historian who had known Montgomery in the field marshal's later years, leading up to his death in 1976. This late-1970s/early-1980s perspective has now shifted, as has the readership for modern biography. My 1992 work on the life of President Kennedy – *JFK: Reckless Youth* – made painfully clear to me that a committed biographer cannot avoid controversy in the quest to make his work *actuel*. In the case of JFK, this entailed being honest about the President's dysfunctional family, his medical travails, sexual entanglements and struggle with his dominating father before entering politics in 1946. Unwelcomed by older members of the Kennedy family, it was mercifully received with enthusiasm by its younger members and by the American public. Today it is considered to be an important, if not defining, portrait of the making of the century's most charismatic President.

In Montgomery's case, happily, I have been blessed by an honest Montgomery family, open to historical and biographical inquiry, an Imperial War Museum staff similarly interested in historical truth, and an academic circle of colleagues, friends and students who saw in the enterprise a prime example of modern biography's delicate balancing act, combining psychological, social, sexual and professional understanding for a modern audience. My biographical journey to re-examine the origins of Montgomery's revolutionary impact on the British army has therefore been an enormous and abiding scholarly and artistic challenge. The resultant text is inevitably marred by its own internal faults of understanding, subjective bias and even biased scholarship; nevertheless, I would like to take this opportunity to thank all those who have made the work possible, *faute de mieux*.

First, I would like to thank Simon Winder, my editor, for commissioning the book, and for his encouragement and patience as it metamorphosed into something far larger and more ambitious than the work he had originally envisaged. His love of history, and his engagement with the issues of modern history and biography, have been a real and abiding inspiration to me.

Secondly, I would like to thank David, Viscount Montgomery of Alamein CMG CBE, for his long-standing friendship and support, even where we disagree or hold different opinions. His honesty, directness, courage and encouragement have made my biographical task immeasurably simpler, and more humanly rewarding. Viscount Montgomery has generously agreed to the use of materials in which he owns the copyright on the basis that a contribution will be made from the royalties to the Imperial War Museum Trust (Montgomery Appeal).

Thirdly, I would like to thank Robert Crawford, Director-General of the Imperial War Museum, who has been a stalwart friend and proponent of modern museum exhibition, archiving, and education, for the public benefit. The Imperial War Museum houses the majority of Monty's personal as well as military papers, as well as the complete papers relating to my original three-volume biography, including all the interviews conducted for the official biography.

I am indebted, also, to Jane Carmichael, the IWM's Director of Collections, Rod Suddaby, the Keeper of Documents, and all the staff of the Imperial War Museum for their unstinting help in the preparation of this volume. Over the years the Montgomery Collections Committee has met and helped extend the IWM's holdings of Montgomery material – from vehicles to manuscripts – into the richest of all military collections in Britain relating to a British field commander. During those years I have made many friends, not all of whom I can name here. Field-Marshal Bramall and Johnny Henderson have been inspirational. Ted Inman, Director of IWM Duxford, has been a pioneer, but it is in the Department of Documents, headed by the indefatigable and devoted Rod Suddaby, that I have worked on a daily basis, and to whose staff I owe a debt of gratitude I can never really repay, not only for archival help, but for the companionship, ribbing, and support of its members. To Rod Suddaby, Simon Robbins, Stephen Walton, Tony Richards, Wendy Lutterlock, my heartfelt thanks – as also to my fellow historians Malcolm Brown, Julian Thomson and Michael Carver, and Christopher Hunt, IWM Department of Printed Materials, and his unfailingly helpful colleagues. Grateful thanks are also due to the copyright holders in the many documents I have quoted and footnoted throughout. The provision of such unique source material for the use of scholars is a priceless bounty – and the work of the Department of Documents in obtaining, preserving, cataloguing and making such materials available to the public, is the foundation of military history that is practised today.

To undertake a radical re-examination of a major twentieth-century leader, and to re-explore his military development in part in terms of his sexuality, has required extensive reading and even more extensive discussion with fellow historians, scholars and biographers. I was particularly lucky, on returning from the USA in 1994, to start teaching in the history department of Royal Holloway, University of London, one of the best in Britain. Francis Robinson, Tony Stockwell, Roz Thomas, John Turner, Amanda Vickery, Nigel Saul, Lyndal Roper, Matthew Jones, Pam Pilbeam, Justin Champion, Penny Corfield, Hugo Blake, Claudia Liebeskind, Sarah Ansari, Sam Barnish, Greg Claeys, Vanessa Martin, Martin Francis, Caroline Barron, Pauline Croft, Emmett Sullivan, and Peter Dewey provided not only intellectual stimulation, but memorable goodwill and support. From Royal Holloway I moved in 1999 to De Montfort University, Leicester, as Professor of Biography – a post created by the Dean of the Faculty of Humanities, Judy Simons, with a pioneering interdisciplinary agenda. Again, the intellectual stimulus provided by Judy and her colleagues, especially David Sadler, George Rousseau, Julia Briggs, Peter Robinson, Wray Vamplew, Mark Sandle, Mike Hiley, Tony Mason, Dick Holt, Nigel Wood, Ray Sibbald, Margaret Baddley and colleagues in the Institute for the Study of War and Society was inspirational as well as challenging. My students, too, helped me to see more clearly the ways in which modern biographical approaches can not only allow us to better understand the past but – as Dr Johnson hoped would happen – to incorporate that understanding into our own personal lives. I hope the resultant work does not disappoint their individual and collective expectations.

In the United States and Canada a number of fellow military historians have discussed the project with me and provided encouragement over the years. They include Carlo D'Este, Roger Cirillo, Terry Copp, Paul Halpern, Paul Bookbinder and Marc Milner among many. To my fellow biographers of the Biography Club in London, under its founder Andrew Lownie, my thanks also for their companionship and support – most especially my colleagues Michael Holroyd and Christine Nicholls, who have helped guide our charitable British Institute of Biography through the difficult funding waters of recent years, and to develop its current biographical project for young people, on the internet, real-lives.com, led by my former student and content director, Garth Davies.

In rewriting a three-volume opus of the 1980s, meanwhile, I was reminded how very much I owed to the members of the Montgomery family, to professional colleagues and subordinates of the field marshal, and all those who contributed to the original biography and its 1987 BBC Television documentary version, *Monty – In Love and War*, directed by Jeremy Bennett. Sadly, though it is said that old soldiers never die, a number of these contributors have since passed away. Contributors included Brian Montgomery, 'Bunty' Montgomery, Lady Michelmore, John Carver, Jocelyn Carver, Richard Carver, Audrey Carver, G. R. H. Bailey, A. R. Barker, R. F. K. Belchem, Harry Broadhurst, P. B. I. O. Burge, Ian Calvocoressi, Michael Carver, Terry Coverdale, Alan Davidson, 'Kit' Dawnay, 'Freddie' de Guingand, Frances Denby, J. P. Duke, P. J. Gething, John Harding, 'Johnny' Henderson, Gwen Herbert, Otway Herbert, F. H. Hinsley, Neil Holdich, Brian Horrocks, Ian Jacob, H. G. James, Geoffrey Keating, Sidney Kirkman, Ronald Lewin, Betty Macdonald, R. C. Macdonald, Carol Mather, William Mather, M. St John Oswald, Robert Priestley, Tom Reynolds, Charles Richardson, 'Pip' Roberts, 'Simbo' Simpson, Eric Sixsmith, Ed Stevens, Gerald Templer, L. T. Tomes,

H. R. W. Vernon, Dudley Ward, 'Bill' Williams, and Douglas Wimberley. For their unstinting help, I can only restate my homage as an historian and biographer, and my lasting gratitude for so much assistance before their memories and insights could fade and became lost to history.

My agents, Bruce Hunter of David Higham Associates in England and Owen Laster of the William Morris Agency in America have both been wonderfully encouraging in terms of the project and its new perspective – if also concerned about the length of the manuscript in a commercial publishing market where size matters – usually negatively! Again, if the work disappoints them commercially because of its length, I hope they will nevertheless be reconciled to its potential importance in military biography today – and the importance to me of grounding my re-examination in an exacting and detailed military as well as personal inquiry.

On my own personal front, I enjoyed the continuing support of my wife, Outi, and my four sons, Alexander, Sebastian, Nicholas and Christian, as well as friends too numerous (and self-effacing) to list. I cannot, however, close without thanking Robin Whitby, my oldest friend from Cambridge days, and David Polstein and Emily Stavis, who took me into their hearts and home in the United States as the manuscript – and its author – reached its critical mass. To David and Emily, their children, Gus and Harry; to Richard and Judy Feldman; David and Liisa Chanoff; Paul and Alexandra Vozick-Hans; Ed Beard and my colleagues in the John W. McCormack Institute, University of Massachusetts at Boston; and all those who have helped, guided and encouraged me on this long biographical journey, I can only say again: Thank you.

Nigel Hamilton
De Montfort University, Leicester
McCormack Institute of Public Affairs, UMass Boston.

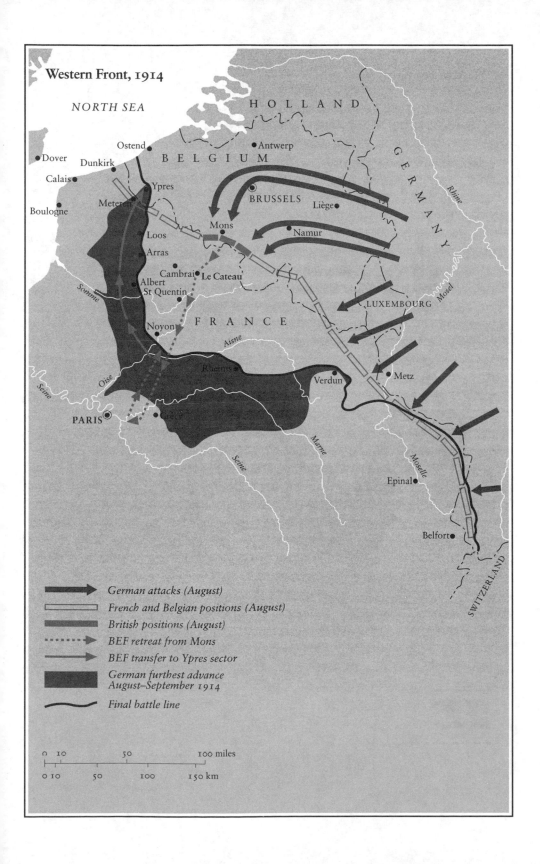

Western Front, 1914

NORTH SEA

HOLLAND

B E L G I U M

G E R M A N Y

•Dover
Dunkirk•
Calais•
Boulogne•
Ostend•
Ypres•
Meteren•
Loos
Arras
Cambrai•
Albert•
St Quentin•
Noyon•

•Antwerp
BRUSSELS
Liège•
Mons
Namur•
Le Cateau

LUXEMBOURG

F R A N C E

Rheims•
Verdun
•Metz

•Crecy
PARIS•

Epinal•

Belfort•

Rhine
Mosel
Moselle

Somme
Oise
Seine
Aisne
Marne
Seine

SWITZERLAND

German attacks (August)
French and Belgian positions (August)
British positions (August)
BEF retreat from Mons
BEF transfer to Ypres sector
German furthest advance
August–September 1914
Final battle line

0 10   50   100 miles
0 10   50   100   150 km

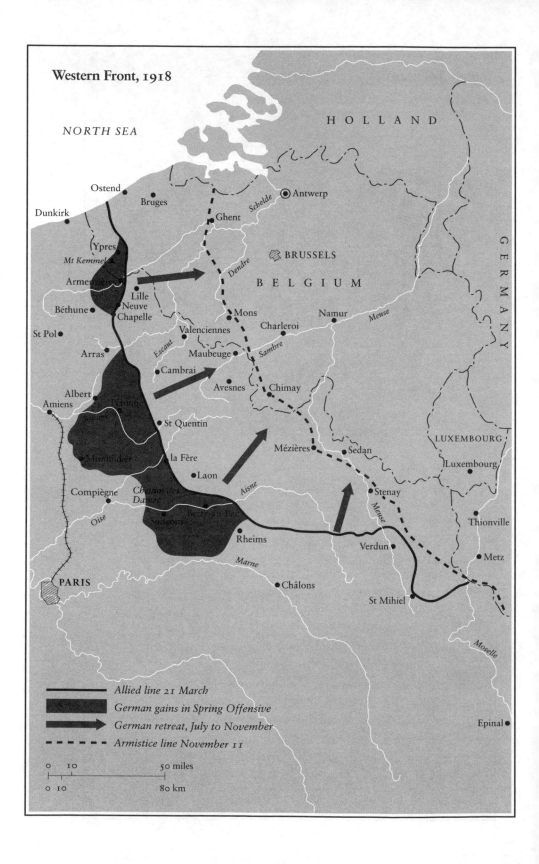

Western Front, 1918

NORTH SEA

HOLLAND

GERMANY

Dunkirk

Ostend

Bruges

Ghent

Schelde

Antwerp

Ypres

Mt Kemmel

Armentières

BRUSSELS

BELGIUM

Béthune

Lille
Neuve
Chapelle

Dendre

Mons

Namur

Meuse

St Pol

Valenciennes

Charleroi

Arras

Escaut

Maubeuge

Sambre

Chimay

Albert
Amiens

Cambrai

Avesnes

LUXEMBOURG

Péronne

Somme

St Quentin

Montdidier

la Fère

Mézières

Sedan

Luxembourg

Laon

Aisne

Stenay

Compiègne

Chemin des
Dames

Thionville

Oise

Soissons

Berry-au-Bac

Meuse

Rheims

Verdun

Metz

Marne

Châlons

St Mihiel

PARIS

Moselle

Epinal

Allied line 21 March

German gains in Spring Offensive

German retreat, July to November

Armistice line November 11

0   10   50 miles

0   10   80 km

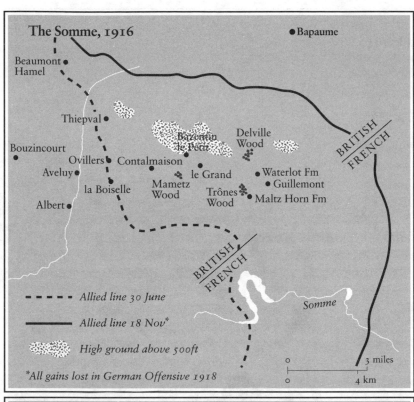

The Somme, 1916

Bapaume

Beaumont
Hamel

Thiepval

Bouzincourt

Bazentin
le Petit

Delville
Wood

Ovillers
Contalmaison
Aveluy
Mametz
Wood
le Grand
Waterlot Fm
Guillemont
la Boiselle
Trônes
Wood
Maltz Horn Fm
Albert

BRITISH
FRENCH

BRITISH
FRENCH

Somme

– – – – – Allied line 30 June

———— Allied line 18 Nov*

High ground above 500ft

*All gains lost in German Offensive 1918

0   3 miles
0   4 km

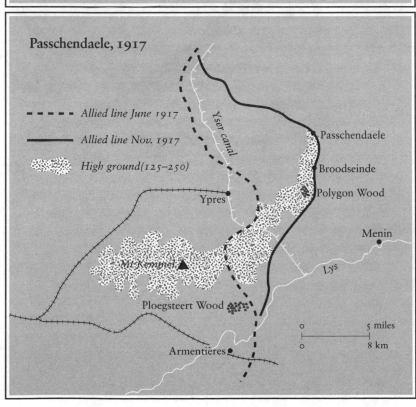

Passchendaele, 1917

– – – – Allied line June 1917

———— Allied line Nov. 1917

High ground(125–250)

Yser canal

Passchendaele

Broodseinde
Polygon Wood
Ypres

Menin

Mt Kemmel

Lys

Ploegsteert Wood

0   5 miles
0   8 km

Armentières

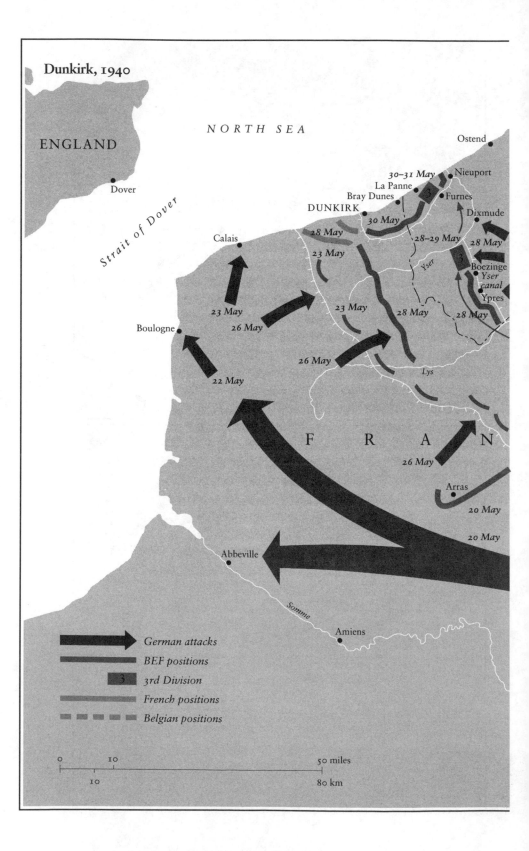

Dunkirk, 1940

NORTH SEA

ENGLAND

Dover

Strait of Dover

Ostend

30–31 May
La Panne
Bray Dunes
DUNKIRK
Nieuport
Furnes
Dixmude
28 May

28 May

28–29 May

30 May

28 May

Calais

23 May

Yser

Boezinge
Yser
canal
Ypres

23 May

23 May

23 May

26 May

28 May

28 May

Boulogne

22 May

26 May

Lys

26 May

F   R   A   N

26 May

Arras

20 May

20 May

Abbeville

Somme

Amiens

German attacks

BEF positions

3   3rd Division

French positions

Belgian positions

0   10   50 miles

10

80 km

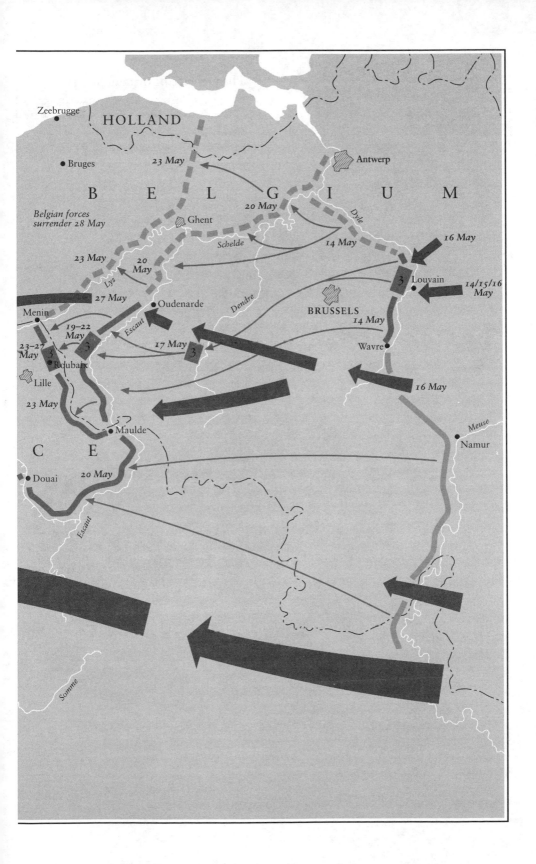

Zeebrugge

HOLLAND

Bruges

B   E   L   *23 May*   G   I   U   M

Antwerp

Belgian forces
surrender 28 May

Ghent

20 May

Dyle

16 May

Louvain

14/15/16 May

14 May

Schelde

23 May

20 May

Lys

27 May

Menin

Oudenarde

Dendre

BRUSSELS

14 May

Wavre

19–22 May

3

Escaut

17 May

3

23–27 May

3

Roubaix

Lille

16 May

23 May

Maulde

C   E

20 May

Douai

Meuse

Namur

Escaut

Somme

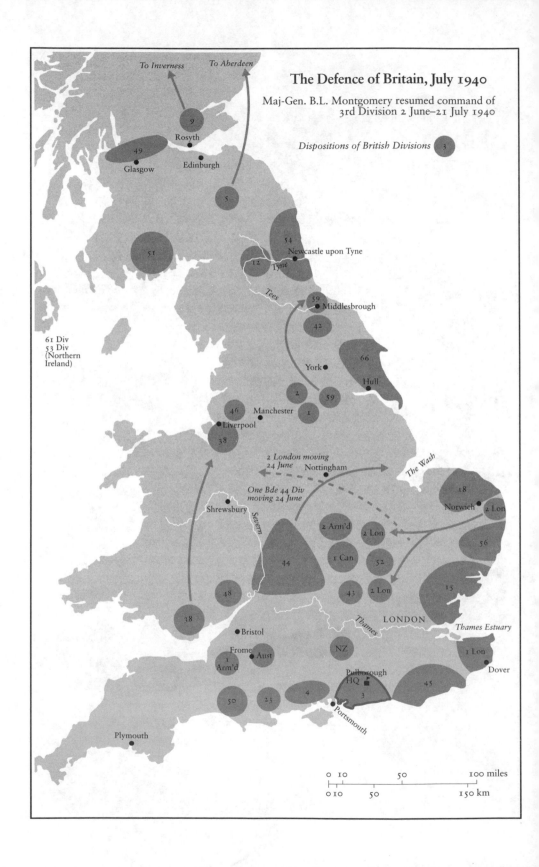

The Defence of Britain, July 1940

Maj-Gen. B.L. Montgomery resumed command of
3rd Division 2 June–21 July 1940

Dispositions of British Divisions

To Inverness

To Aberdeen

9

Rosyth

49

Glasgow

Edinburgh

5

51

54

Newcastle upon Tyne

12   Tyne

Tees

59   Middlesbrough

42

York

66

Hull

61 Div
53 Div
(Northern
Ireland)

2

59

46   Manchester

1

Liverpool

38

*2 London moving
24 June*   Nottingham

*One Bde 44 Div
moving 24 June*

Shrewsbury

Severn

18

Norwich   2 Lon

44

2 Arm'd

2 Lon

56

1 Can

52

48

43

2 Lon

15

38

Thames   LONDON

Thames Estuary

Bristol

NZ

Frome

Aust

1 Lon

Dover

1
Arm'd

Pulborough
HQ

50

23

4

3

45

Portsmouth

Plymouth

| 0 10 | | 50 | | 100 miles |
| 0 10 | 50 | | 150 km | |

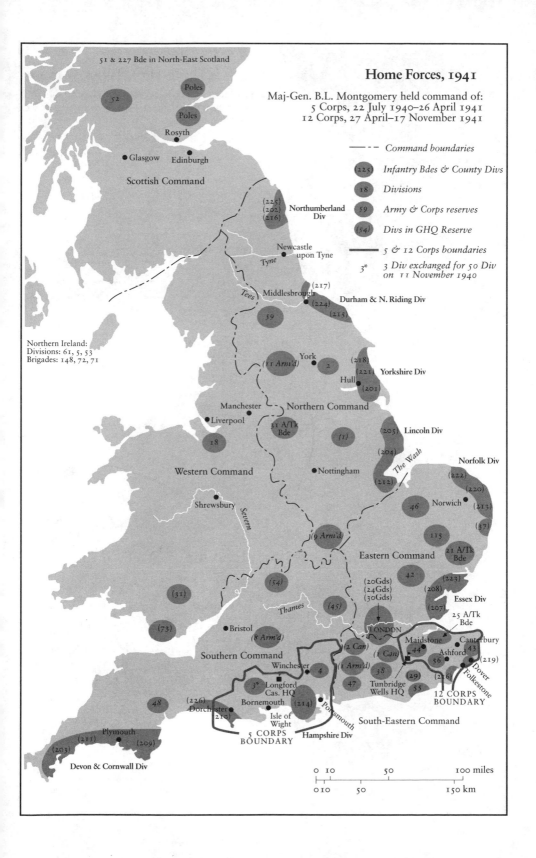

51 & 227 Bde in North-East Scotland

Home Forces, 1941

Maj-Gen. B.L. Montgomery held command of:
5 Corps, 22 July 1940–26 April 1941
12 Corps, 27 April–17 November 1941

Poles

Poles

(52)

Rosyth

Glasgow   Edinburgh

Scottish Command

– - – - – *Command boundaries*

(225) *Infantry Bdes & County Divs*

18 *Divisions*

59 *Army & Corps reserves*

(54) *Divs in GHQ Reserve*

5 & 12 Corps boundaries

3* *3 Div exchanged for 50 Div on 11 November 1940*

(225)
(202)   Northumberland
(216)   Div

Newcastle
upon Tyne

Tyne

Tees   Middlesbrough

(217)
(224)   Durham & N. Riding Div
(215)

59

Northern Ireland:
Divisions: 61, 5, 53
Brigades: 148, 72, 71

(11 Arm'd)   York   2

(218)
(221)   Yorkshire Div
Hull
(201)

Manchester

Liverpool

31 A/Tk
Bde

Northern Command

(11)

(205)   Lincoln Div

18

Nottingham

(204)   *The Wash*

Western Command

Shrewsbury

Severn

Norfolk Div

(222)
(220)
(212)   46   Norwich   (213)

(37)

(9 Arm'd)   115

21 A/Tk
Bde

Eastern Command

(54)   *Thames*   (20Gds)
(24Gds)
(30Gds)

42

(223)
(208)   Essex Div
(207)

(45)

(31)

(73)   Bristol

(8 Arm'd)   LONDON

25 A/Tk
Bde

Southern Command

Winchester

(2 Can)

Maidstone   Canterbury
44   43
(1 Can)   Ashford   56   (219)
4   (1 Arm'd)   38   (29)   Dover
47   Tunbridge   35   (216)   Folkestone
Wells HQ
3*   Longford
Cas. HQ
Bournemouth   (214)
Dorchester   Portsmouth
(226)   Isle of
(210)   Wight   12 CORPS
BOUNDARY

48   South-Eastern Command

Plymouth   Hampshire Div
(211)   (209)   5 CORPS
(203)   BOUNDARY

Devon & Cornwall Div

0   10   50   100 miles

0 10   50   150 km

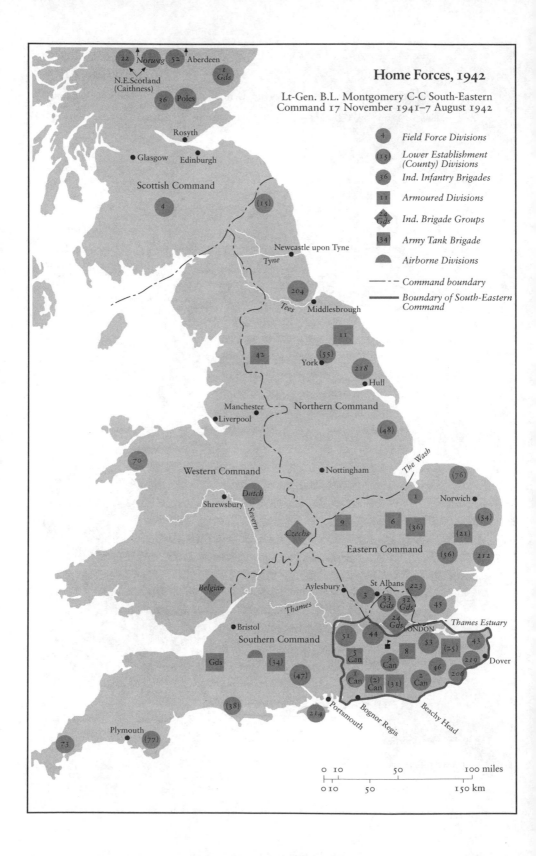

Home Forces, 1942

Lt-Gen. B.L. Montgomery C-C South-Eastern Command 17 November 1941–7 August 1942

4	*Field Force Divisions*
(15)	*Lower Establishment (County) Divisions*
36	*Ind. Infantry Brigades*
11	*Armoured Divisions*
Gds	*Ind. Brigade Groups*
34	*Army Tank Brigade*
	Airborne Divisions

— · — · — *Command boundary*

———— *Boundary of South-Eastern Command*

22 *Norweg* 52 Aberdeen

N.E. Scotland (Caithness)

1 Gds

36 Poles

Rosyth

Glasgow Edinburgh

Scottish Command

4

Newcastle upon Tyne

Tyne

204

Tees Middlesbrough

11

42 York (55)

218 Hull

Manchester
Liverpool

Northern Command

(48)

70 *The Wash*

Western Command Nottingham

(76)

Dutch
Shrewsbury 1 Norwich

Severn (54)

Czechs 9 6 (36) (21)

Eastern Command (56) 212

Belgian Aylesbury St Albans 223

3 33 Gds 32 Gds 45

Bristol *Thames* 24 Gds *Thames Estuary*

Southern Command 51 44 LONDON 53 43

Gds 5 Can 8 (25) 219 Dover

(34) (47) 3 Can 46 206

1 Can (2) Can (31) 2 Can *Beachy Head*

(38) Portsmouth *Bognor Regis*

214

73 Plymouth (77)

0 10   50   100 miles

0 10   50   150 km

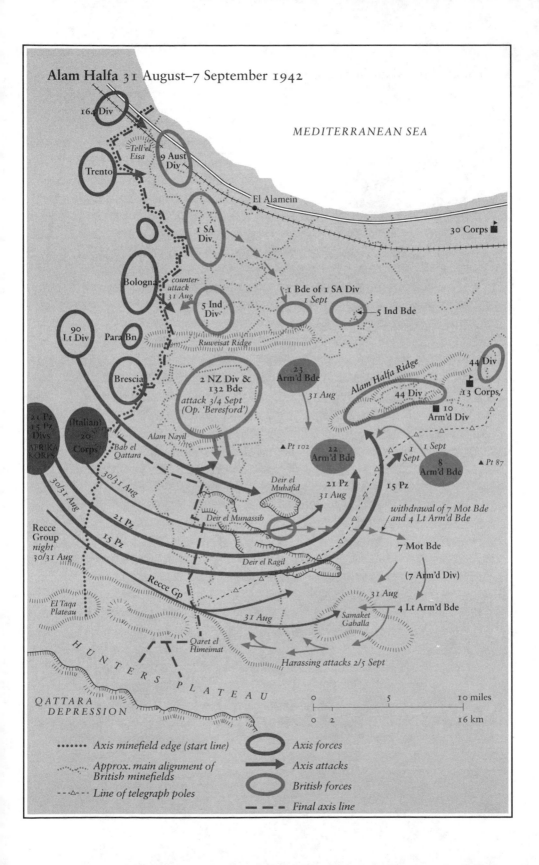

Alam Halfa 31 August–7 September 1942

MEDITERRANEAN SEA

164 Div

=Tell el
Eisa

9 Aust
Div

Trento

El Alamein

30 Corps

1 SA
Div

Bologna

*counter-
attack
31 Aug*

1 Bde of 1 SA Div

1 Sept

5 Ind
Div

5 Ind Bde

90
Lt Div

Para Bn

Ruweisat Ridge

44 Div

23
Arm'd Bde

Alam Halfa Ridge

44 Div

13 Corps

Brescia

2 NZ Div &
132 Bde

*attack 3/4 Sept
(Op. 'Beresford')*

31 Aug

10
Arm'd Div

21 Pz
15 Pz
Divs
AFRIKA
KORPS

(Italian)
20
Corps

Alam Nayil

*Bab el
Qattara*

▲ Pt 102

22
Arm'd Bde

1 Sept

1 Sept

8
Arm'd Bde

▲ Pt 87

*Deir el
Muhafid*

21 Pz
31 Aug

15 Pz

*withdrawal of 7 Mot Bde
/ and 4 Lt Arm'd Bde*

30/31 Aug

Deir el Munassib

7 Mot Bde

Recce
Group
night
30/31 Aug

21 Pz

15 Pz

Deir el Ragil

(7 Arm'd Div)

Recce Gp

31 Aug

4 Lt Arm'd Bde

*El Taqa
Plateau*

31 Aug

*Samaket
Gaballa*

*Qaret el
Himeimat*

Harassing attacks 2/5 Sept

H U N T E R S   P L A T E A U

QATTARA
DEPRESSION

0   5   10 miles

0   2   16 km

•••••• *Axis minefield edge (start line)*

⬭ *Axis forces*

⟶ *Axis attacks*

⬭ *British forces*

···△··· *Line of telegraph poles*

—— *Final axis line*

.... *Approx. main alignment of
British minefields*

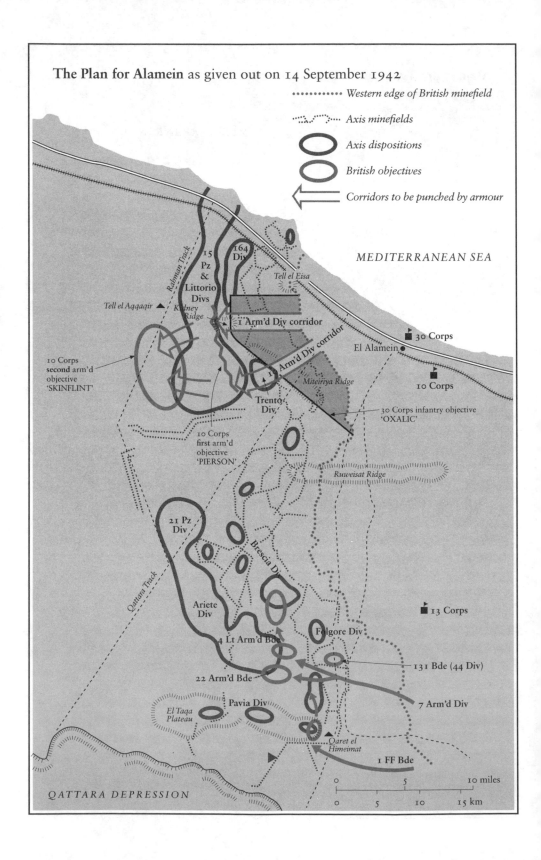

The Plan for Alamein as given out on 14 September 1942

- •••••••••• Western edge of British minefield
- Axis minefields
- Axis dispositions
- British objectives
- Corridors to be punched by armour

MEDITERRANEAN SEA

Rahman Track

15 Pz & Littorio Divs

164 Div

Tell el Eisa

Tell el Aqqaqir ▲

Kidney Ridge

1 Arm'd Div corridor

10 Corps second arm'd objective 'SKINFLINT'

10 Arm'd Div corridor

■ 30 Corps

El Alamein ●

▶ 10 Corps

Trento Div

Miteiriya Ridge

30 Corps infantry objective 'OXALIC'

10 Corps first arm'd objective 'PIERSON'

Ruweisat Ridge

21 Pz Div

Brescia Div

Qattara Track

Ariete Div

■ 13 Corps

4 Lt Arm'd Bde

Folgore Div

22 Arm'd Bde

131 Bde (44 Div)

Pavia Div

7 Arm'd Div

El Taqa Plateau

Qaret el Himeimat ▲

1 FF Bde

| 0 | | 5 | 10 miles |

| 0 | 5 | 10 | 15 km |

QATTARA DEPRESSION

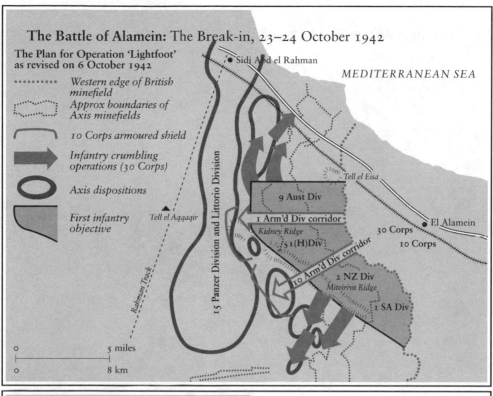

The Battle of Alamein: The Break-in, 23–24 October 1942

The Plan for Operation 'Lightfoot'
as revised on 6 October 1942

- Western edge of British minefield
- Approx boundaries of Axis minefields
- 10 Corps armoured shield
- Infantry crumbling operations (30 Corps)
- Axis dispositions
- First infantry objective

MEDITERRANEAN SEA

Sidi Abd el Rahman

Tell el Eisa

15 Panzer Division and Littorio Division

Tell el Aqqaqir

9 Aust Div

1 Arm'd Div corridor

Kidney Ridge

51 (H) Div

30 Corps
10 Corps

El Alamein

10 Arm'd Div corridor

2 NZ Div

Miteiriya Ridge

1 SA Div

Rahman Track

0   5 miles
0   8 km

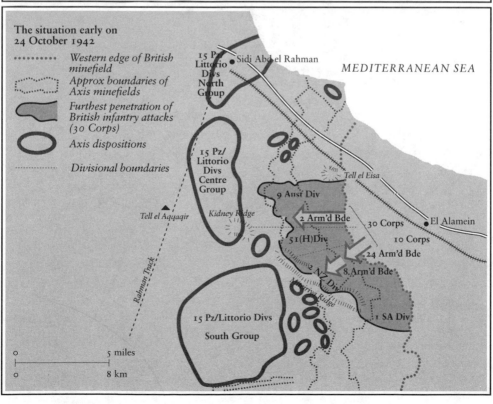

The situation early on 24 October 1942

- Western edge of British minefield
- Approx boundaries of Axis minefields
- Furthest penetration of British infantry attacks (30 Corps)
- Axis dispositions
- Divisional boundaries

MEDITERRANEAN SEA

15 Pz/Littorio Divs North Group

Sidi Abd el Rahman

15 Pz/Littorio Divs Centre Group

Tell el Eisa

Tell el Aqqaqir

Kidney Ridge

9 Aust Div

2 Arm'd Bde

51 (H) Div

30 Corps
10 Corps

El Alamein

24 Arm'd Bde

8 Arm'd Bde

2 NZ Div

Miteiriya Ridge

15 Pz/Littorio Divs South Group

1 SA Div

Rahman Track

0   5 miles
0   8 km

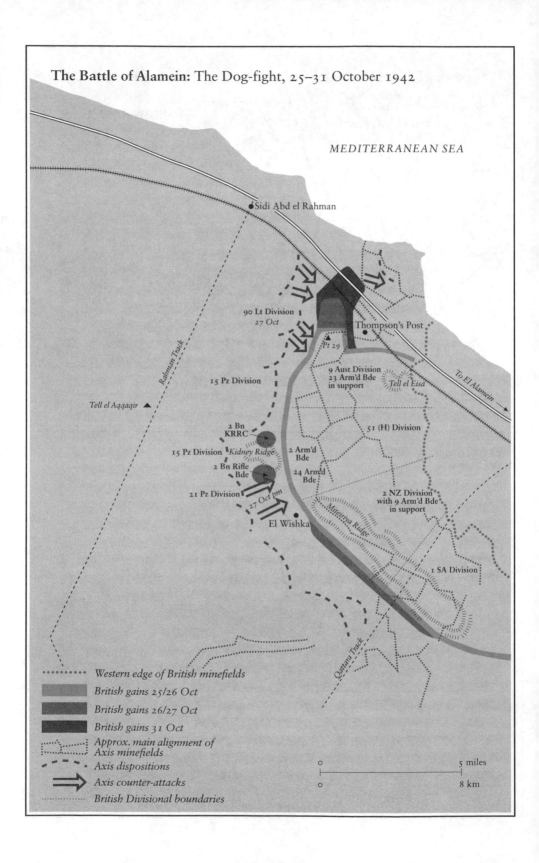

The Battle of Alamein: The Dog-fight, 25–31 October 1942

MEDITERRANEAN SEA

Sidi Abd el Rahman

Rahman Track

90 Lt Division
27 Oct

Thompson's Post

Pt 29

To El Alamein

15 Pz Division

9 Aust Division
23 Arm'd Bde
in support

Tell el Eisa

Tell el Aqqaqir

51 (H) Division

2 Bn
KRRC

15 Pz Division   Kidney Ridge

2 Arm'd
Bde

2 Bn Rifle
Bde

24 Arm'd
Bde

21 Pz Division

2 NZ Division
with 9 Arm'd Bde
in support

27 Oct pm

Miteiriya Ridge

El Wishka

1 SA Division

Qattara Track

········ Western edge of British minefields

▬▬▬ British gains 25/26 Oct

▬▬▬ British gains 26/27 Oct

▬▬▬ British gains 31 Oct

⌁⌁⌁ Approx. main alignment of
Axis minefields

▬ ▬ Axis dispositions

⇨ Axis counter-attacks

········ British Divisional boundaries

0 ────────── 5 miles
0 ────────── 8 km

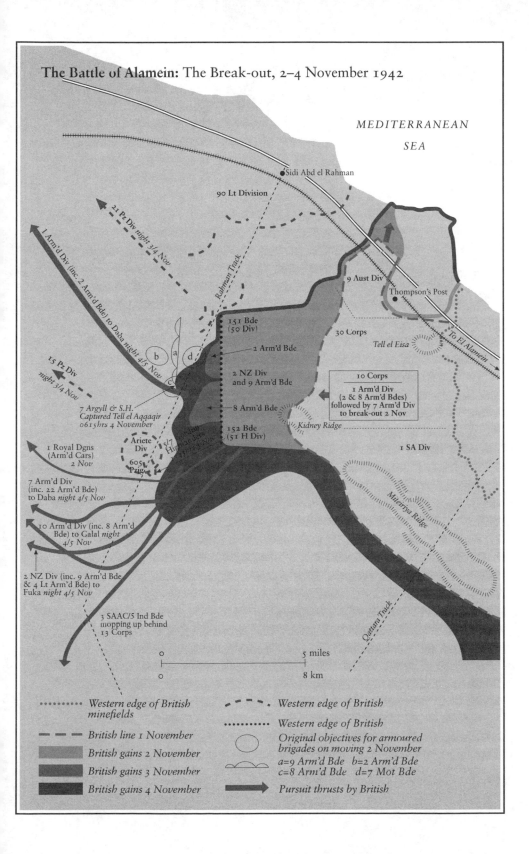

The Battle of Alamein: The Break-out, 2–4 November 1942

MEDITERRANEAN

SEA

Sidi Abd el Rahman

90 Lt Division

21 Pz Div *night 3/4 Nov*

1 Arm'd Div (inc. 2 Arm'd Bde) to Daba *night 4/5 Nov*

9 Aust Div

Thompson's Post

Rahman Track

151 Bde
(50 Div)

30 Corps

Tell el Eisa

15 Pz Div
night 3/4 Nov

2 Arm'd Bde

b   a   d

2 NZ Div
and 9 Arm'd Bde

10 Corps
1 Arm'd Div
(2 & 8 Arm'd Bdes)
followed by 7 Arm'd Div
to break-out 2 Nov

To El Alamein

c

8 Arm'd Bde

7 Argyll & S.H.
*Captured Tell el Aqqaqir
0615hrs 4 November*

152 Bde
(51 H Div)

Kidney Ridge

1 SA Div

1 Royal Dgns
(Arm'd Cars)
2 Nov

Ariete
Div

5/7
Gordon
Highlanders
21/22 Nov

605
Pzjg

7 Arm'd Div
(inc. 22 Arm'd Bde)
to Daba *night 4/5 Nov*

Mitewya Ridge

10 Arm'd Div (inc. 8 Arm'd
Bde) to Galal *night
4/5 Nov*

2 NZ Div (inc. 9 Arm'd Bde
& 4 Lt Arm'd Bde) to
Fuka *night 4/5 Nov*

3 SAAC/5 Ind Bde
mopping up behind
13 Corps

Qattara Track

| 0 | | 5 miles |
| 0 | | 8 km |

········· *Western edge of British
minefields*

– – – – *British line 1 November*

 British gains 2 November

 British gains 3 November

 British gains 4 November

– – · – *Western edge of British*

············ *Western edge of British*

◯ *Original objectives for armoured
brigades on moving 2 November*
⌢ *a=9 Arm'd Bde   b=2 Arm'd Bde
c=8 Arm'd Bde   d=7 Mot Bde*

➤ *Pursuit thrusts by British*

BOOK I

THE MAKING OF A GENERAL

I

Born Unto Trouble

The English vice

Bernard Law Montgomery was born on 17 November 1887, the year after the Labouchère Amendment, or 'Blackmailer's Charter', passed through Parliament at Westminster as part of a new Criminal Law Amendment Act – a legal act that forbade sexual relations between men (but not between women) for the following eighty years of British history.

The Labouchère clause, introduced on the back of the Purity League's laudable efforts to outlaw child prostitution and the white slave trade, outlawed not only the practice of sodomy, however, but *all* forms of physical intimacy or contact between males, in public or in private. It was the only such law in Europe. On its cross, as Hugh David has written, Oscar Wilde was in 1895 'nailed': the most celebrated victim of 'the English vice'.[1]

Was this tragedy inevitable, historically, or was it simply the product in Britain of a chance aberration during the passage of a bill designed to tackle female child prostitution? No one has satisfactorily explained Labouchère's sudden change of stance towards the impending Criminal Law Amendment Bill in August 1885, or his invention of the infamous Clause XI only the night before its first passage. Was it a spoof clause designed to ridicule the whole Act? Labouchère certainly anticipated the cost of his proposal to society, since he himself wrote that a Criminal Law Amendment Act would simply create a potential for blackmailing. Or was it possible that, as editor of the weekly *Truth*, Labouchère – like certain present-day tabloid editors – wished to pose publicly as an even more righteous, right-wing, populist lawmaker than his rival W. T. Stead, editor of the *Gazette*?

Either way, Clause XI of the Act, forbidding 'in public or in private . . . any act of gross indecency' between men, soon gave rise to the English term 'homosexual' for 'male persons' who were not primarily attracted to the opposite or second sex, or even those who were bisexual.

Some 'homosexuals', in their 'perverse' way, grew to like the label, as well as the illicit status of their newly coined sexuality, revelling in the word 'queer'. Most, however, had to repress their instincts and desires if they were to avoid legal or social exclusion, and the loss of their jobs. Wilde refused to, and his fate was symbolic: not only sentenced to prison with hard labour, but never able to create theatre again.

The lesson was clear. Apart from a few exceptions, most Englishmen who were bisexual or exclusively attracted to people of their own gender, whether writers, politicians or soldiers, were obliged by English law to conceal their sexuality after 1886 – often from themselves.

St Mark's, Kennington

Bernard Law Montgomery was the third son and fourth child of the Reverend Henry Montgomery and his young wife Maud, née Farrar. Both Henry and Maud came from distinguished Victorian families: Sir Robert Montgomery, Henry Montgomery's father, had been knighted for his service as an administrator in India during the Mutiny, or First War of Indian Independence; Canon Frederick Farrar, Maud's father, was even more celebrated, having become one of the most famous headmasters and preachers in England, and rector of St Margaret's Church, Westminster, opposite the Houses of Parliament. He not only wrote a popular *Life of Jesus*, but penned a series of morally edifying Victorian novels of rites-of-passage, such as *Eric, or Little by Little, Julian Home* and *St. Winifred's or The World of School*, that were as popular in their time as *Tom Brown's Schooldays*.

Henry – who had been a young curate in Canon Farrar's parish – had met Maud when he was twenty-nine, balding and bearded, she flat-chested and only eleven. They had become engaged when Maud was fourteen, and were married when Maud was still only sixteen.

Though not uncommon in Victorian England, the age gap between bride and bridegroom was mirrored in the gap between their educations, indeed in the gulf separating the sexes. Henry Montgomery had gone to Harrow School – a 'dung-hill' where '[every] boy of good looks had a female name, and was recognized either as a public prostitute or as some bigger fellow's "bitch",' as J. A. Symonds recorded. 'Here and there one could not avoid seeing acts of onanism, mutual masturbation, the sports of naked boys in bed together. There was no refinement, no sentiment, no passion; nothing but animal lust in these occurrences.'[2] Henry had then studied at Cambridge. 'God, who kept me from the temptations of school life, did not desert me at college', he claimed later.[3] But Maud Farrar had never been to school at all.

The difference in their educations – sexual as well as scholarly – was thus marked. Henry had taken holy orders under instruction from the notorious Dr C. J. Vaughan. According to J. A. Symonds, Dr Vaughan had publicly announced he would switch, or birch, a certain boy for indulging in sodomy or 'spooning', but was then found to indulge in the practice himself with one of Symonds' fellow pupils – a practice his wife was well aware of, flinging herself at the knees of Symonds' father when he compelled Vaughan to resign with the plea that 'Her husband was subject to this weakness, but it had not interfered with his usefulness in the direction of the school at Harrow'.[4] The disgraced headmaster of Harrow, who had been forced to turn down the offer of two bishoprics thereafter, had then become a simple teacher of divinity to young men such as Henry Montgomery.

Whether Henry himself was ever importuned by Vaughan is unknown, but Henry certainly attracted the passionate affection of the Dean of Westminster, Dean Stanley, whose secretary he had become, and who in 1879 got him his own living as vicar of St Mark's, Kennington: a large, sprawling parish in south London. It was as vicar of St Mark's that Henry was then able to marry his fiancée, whose engagement had been kept secret even from her sisters.

The wedding, in a chapel of Westminster Abbey, was marred by the sudden death of Dean Stanley, Henry's patron. Worse was to follow. Of their wedding nuptials in the Bull Hotel in Cambridge, in July 1881, Maud openly confided to her youngest son that 'she did not exactly enjoy that first night'.[5] Thereafter, in the turmoil of a busy Victorian parish, dedicated to religious conversion and the saving of more souls, she confessed she was 'not very happy'.[6]

It was hardly surprising. Maud had grown up as one of ten children – five boys and five girls. She missed them, and found the switch from the big, warm, affectionate Farrar family to the cold, formal Montgomerys as great a shock as sexual penetration. She hardly knew Henry; for two years before marriage, between the ages of fourteen and sixteen, she had been allowed to see her fiancé only twice per week, under strict supervision – and had no other suitors.[7] At the Montgomery family estate in Northern Ireland, overlooking Lough Foyle in County Donegal, where she spent her honeymoon, she was escorted each night to her bed – by Lady Montgomery. 'The men always came to bed later,' Maud recalled – lamenting that her husband took her for granted, never told her that he loved her or indeed had any feelings for her, but simply imposed on her, as the vicar's new sixteen-year-old wife, sexual obedience and awesome responsibilities: a parish of 14,000 people, administered by her husband, three curates, 250 church workers and 125 Sunday school teachers indoctrinating 1,500 Sunday school children.[8]

For this Maud would make her husband, and her children, pay.

Nothing to do

What went wrong in the Kennington vicarage will probably never be known. 'I was often very lonely at Kennington,' Maud later confided. 'My husband was out every evening, and I can remember sitting in the drawing room and crying bitterly because I had nothing to do and felt so lonely.'[9]

She was, one of her sons recorded, 'vivacious and high-spirited and a great tomboy, but not clever'.[10] Tennyson, the Brownings, Matthew Arnold, Lewis Carroll, Tom Hughes, Burne-Jones, Millais, Charles Darwin, William Gladstone – all the luminaries of Victorian England had peopled her father's living-room at Westminster when, as rector of St Margaret's and a canon of Westminster Abbey, Dr Farrar disputed the Anglican church's doctrine of eternal punishment.[11] For his arrogance Maud and her siblings had seen him rewarded by temporal punishment – being passed over for promotion for twenty years, despite being possibly the most popular preacher in Britain. (Even after twenty years at St Margaret's, he would only be made Dean of Canterbury Cathedral.)

Lonely and disappointed in marriage, Maud began, whether she liked it or not (and, according to her son Brian she did not), to people her own drawing room. Her first child was born four weeks after she turned eighteen. More followed in almost annual succession. Within eight years she had given birth to five. In addition, she was obliged to take in the three children of her husband's cousin, then in India. By her early twenties – and still in many respects a child herself – Maud was thus looking after eight children. It is difficult not to sympathize with Maud's plight, paying a high price for age disparity, gender disparity and rabid Christian fundamentalism in the 1880s.

What went on in the hearts and minds of the Reverend Montgomery and his young wife we cannot know, since their own recollections – published and private – avoid the question of sex and sexual compatibility. We know, however, from J. A. Symonds' long-unpublished memoirs something of the torment which Victorian wives underwent, when their husbands were sexually ignorant, indifferent, or more interested in men than women. According to Havelock Ellis, Symonds' wife Catherine, 'the member of a noble family, disliked sexual connection and hated pregnancy', though she 'begat 4 children'. Eventually, Symonds confessed his homosexual preference and 'wholly abandoned matrimonial connection. He did this with the full approval of his wife, to whom the step brought relief ', Ellis maintained in his famous *Sexual Inversion*.[12] According to Symonds himself Catherine was a victim of her own prudery: 'She shrinks from what men and women are, and what they must be, as from something common and unclean. "That vulgar and trivial way of coition," as Sir Thomas Browne puts it, has for her no attraction' – but it did bring Catherine 'the society of her daughters, whom she deeply loves', Symonds acknowledged – indeed, to his great gratitude she became lovingly *complaisante*, befriending Symonds' platonic lover Norman Moor 'like a son', and happily accepting her husband's later affairs with men in Venice and Switzerland.[13]

Maud Montgomery's response was very different: indeed it smacks, albeit at second hand, of punitive resentment, towards both Henry and the children he made her bear. Leaving Henry to his parish duties she, not Henry, became the family boss and tyrant queen. Monty's siblings accepted this change in parental authority without demur. Monty, for reasons that are still unclear, did not.

Missionary positions

In 1889, two years after the birth of his fifth child and third son, the Reverend Henry Montgomery was offered the chance to become the Right Reverend Montgomery: as first Bishop of Van Diemen's Land, or Tasmania. Unsure where exactly Van Diemen's Land was, Henry nevertheless accepted – and took his wife and five children with him, by steamship.

'I have no great gifts or talents,' Henry Montgomery confessed in Tasmania; 'I am neither a scholar, nor a preacher, nor a speaker.'[14] He was, however, an evangelical Christian – and in a church noted, like its Roman Catholic counterpart, for its self-serving rhetoric rather than the sincerity of its leaders, his missionary zeal stood out like a beacon. Tales of his conversions and confirmations in the wild outback of Tasmania and its many satellite islands made inevitable his later selection as the head of the Anglican church's missionary movement – but this missionary position, so to speak, did not impress or convert his young wife. Left at home while her husband toured the parishes, priests and parishioners of his vast diocese, she became more and more 'difficult', as the local doctor's son recalled: frustrated and increasingly tyrannical: an imperious young materfamilias, increasingly determined to root out and deal with 'sin'.

How little Bernard responded to such a dedicated, fugitive Christian missionary, on the one hand, and such a sin-obsessed Christian tyrant – physical as well as psychological – at home, on the other, was to be in many ways the inner story of his life: a misfit who was perpetually at war with himself as well as with others, and often driven to the very edge of madness.

Inheritance

Whether Bernard Montgomery – like General Gordon – inherited a streak of madness through his Montgomery ancestors, or whether, as in Symonds' case, his wildness or near-madness resulted from the repression of his profoundest instincts remains a matter of opinion. The 'Law' in his name derived from his grandfather's brother, Samuel Law Montgomery: a strange, misogynistic parson who never married, having backed out of an engagement at vast financial cost, and who mortgaged his Moville property heavily to finance a series of 'improvements' such as a railway, which never eventuated. As Bernard's brother Brian learned from the family archives, Samuel Law Montgomery was 'somewhat humpbacked', owing to 'a spinal defect',[15] but such physical disability aroused no sympathy in Bernard, who disliked the name he'd inherited from the humpback and his father. When Bernard was eventually bequeathed all the family portraits, including that of his namesake, he refused to hang the painting of his great uncle alongside the other stately portraits of his Montgomery ancestors in his Hampshire home. 'I won't have it hung in my house; the picture frame is the only part of it which I like,' he later told Brian when giving it away.[16]

Nor did Monty acknowledge any genetic debt to his celebrated maternal grandfather Canon (later Dean) Farrar, whose cultured home and prolific literary output Monty always found somehow threatening, and whose sons became involved in 'scandals' of a sexual nature – including pederasty. Referring proudly to the Montgomerys, as opposed to the Farrars, Monty asserted towards the end of his life: 'We have all kept on the rails. There have been no scandals in the family; none of us have appeared in the police courts or gone to prison.'[17] Yet, as even Monty acknowledged, there was a price to pay for such Victorian purity – 'an absence of affectionate understanding of the problems facing the young, certainly as far as the five elder children were concerned'.[18] For this he blamed one person alone: his mother.

The Tyrant Queen

Brian Montgomery, Monty's youngest brother, rejected Bernard's dire account of their mother Maud, and their unhappy childhood, unequivocally. 'Bernard did not', he later categorically asserted, 'grow up in an atmosphere of fear – of mother – or develop any inward-looking, withdrawn characteristic because of her.'[19]

Monty, however, remained adamant. In later years he would deliberately search the lives of other great military leaders, and find – perhaps for the very reasons that he was looking – the same unhappiness in their childhoods: most significantly in the lives of the dukes of Marlborough and Wellington.[20] His own early childhood he certainly regarded retrospectively as nothing less than outright war with his tyrannical mother: an almost fatal 'clash of wills'. 'Battle succeeded battle,' he recorded[21] – 'fierce battles, from which my mother invariably emerged the victor,' as he admitted – though 'the constant defeats and beatings with a cane, and these were frequent, in no way deterred me'.[22]

Maud's war on 'sin' became total, her rules absolute. Behind the colonial-style mansion in Hobart with its wrap-around veranda, overlooking the river Derwent, she arranged for a schoolhouse and dormitory to be built, importing male tutors from England. Under their tutelage the children 'rose at dawn, tidied their rooms, cleaned their shoes and chopped wood for the fires', Alan Moorehead learned when writing the first biography of Montgomery during Maud's lifetime, and after interviewing all members of the family. 'Lessons began at 7.30, followed by an inspection of the bedrooms (the children standing on parade at the doorways), and then chapel. After chapel, breakfast and then lessons again all morning.' There were games in the afternoon, while Maud rested. No one, not even the Bishop was permitted to disturb her sleep. 'Supper, the children prepared for themselves, and ate in the schoolroom. And finally the day closed at the appointed hour with family prayers.'[23]

On Sundays the regime became even stricter; there were no games and the whole day was 'devoted to religious readings and services. This was the fixed unalterable rule of the house and Maud Montgomery would allow no breaches of it.'[24] Brian, born at the end of Bishop Montgomery's stint in Tasmania, remembered that it was 'a strict rule of my mother that on Sundays her children should only read books classed by herself as "good" books, and preferably one of her father's stories', such as Farrar's goody-goody, didactic *Eric, Or Little by Little*.[25] 'We frankly loathed them!' Brian confessed.[26] Meanwhile the older children, at least, 'had to be tough. They learned that if they woke in the night with some possibly frivolous malaise they could not call on her; they must wait for the morning. If they wasted their pocket money they were beaten.'[27]

Why so many canings in a religious family? According to Moorehead none of this was 'exceptional' for a 'churchman's household' – save that the beatings were carried out by a woman. The Bishop 'never interfered with his wife's routine; she was the head of the domestic arrangements and the final authority in the children's lives'.[28]

Vain love

Monty later claimed that 'we were an average Victorian family', which in terms of size, attitudes and religiosity was true. But in terms of gender-roles it was not. Maud 'wore the trousers', as Monty put it, while his father slunk away in skirts. And as the only male in the Montgomery family willing to stand up to her, Monty was made to take down his own trousers and was flogged unmercifully, *pour mieux décourager les autres*. 'I was the bad boy of the family, the rebellious one,' Monty reflected, while the others 'were more amenable to the régime and gave no trouble'.[29]

In such an unwanted war, however, there was no hate on Monty's side. Rather, the reverse. He loved Maud: fiercely, fixedly, fixatedly, devotedly. It was a love that would haunt him to his dying days: for however much he tried, he could not get Maud to love him back.

Porcelain wives

Monty's Victorian childhood was not unique. 'The more one knows about Victorian society, the more one realizes the gap between its moral pretensions and realities,' wrote the historian A. L. Rowse, 'between the face put upon things and what went on underneath. The gap was all the wider because the standards supposed to be adhered to were, for average human nature, unattainable – even in many respects undesirable. The extent of the gap draws attention to the besetting sins of the Victorians – hypocrisy and humbug.'[30]

For T. E. Lawrence, born within a year of Monty, childhood involved the same inversion of traditional gender-roles between father and mother, and even more humbug. Lawrence's mother, though illegitimate herself, had run off, as a nanny, with an Irish baronet and produced three illegitimate sons; she also birched her boys and tyrannized them with a diet of impassioned religiosity and warnings about 'sin'. Meanwhile she concealed from T. E. and his brothers, until Lawrence was an adolescent, that she was herself living in sin, in the middle-class quarter of north Oxford.

Lawrence's brothers – two of whom would be killed in the Great War – survived their upbringing 'normally', but T. E. certainly did not. He had guessed anyway from the age of nine that he was illegitimate, and became a hoarder of grandiose dreams and desires: a brilliant but deeply sexually repressed individual who was driven to seek military glory on the margins of the British Empire, as he projected his love for his friend Salim Ahmed on to the Arabs and sought 'freedom for the race' as an 'acceptable present' for Salim.[31] He was also driven to fantasize about being raped and whipped by eastern potentates – indeed later *was* whipped, at his own request, by his fellow servicemen, riding instructors, swimming instructors and others, when he discarded his officer's uniform and 'joined the ranks'. Letters demonstrating the elaborate nature of Lawrence's desire for flagellation (usually involving an 'uncle' who demanded penance) continue to surface, seventy years after he gave rein to his 'perverse'[32] masochistic fantasies, usually pivoting on exposure of his illegitimacy, and a repetition of his mother's birching.[33] As his biographer John E. Mack noted, 'I believe that in insisting that the beatings be so severe and painful Lawrence was trying (short of emasculating or killing himself) to destroy his sexuality.'[34] Lawrence's most recent biographer, Michael Asher, pointed out that those writers who attempted to 'sanctify' Lawrence's 'flagellation disorder' were naïve: not only did Lawrence experience orgasm as a result of his floggings, but the insistence on flagellation of the bare buttocks was quite different from medieval whippings or service punishments administered to the bare back.[35] The famous Dara'a incident of *Seven Pillars of Wisdom* – involving whipping, rape and buggery – is now largely accepted by scholars to have taken place in Lawrence's mind rather than reality.[36] As Michael Asher has written, after retracing Lawrence's exploits by camel and examining Lawrence's diaries and the literature documenting his life, 'Lawrence was a masochist with a homosexual nature, who had from a very early age fantasized about being dominated by other men, especially in the ranks of the army.'[37] As he wrote to Mrs Charlotte Shaw, 'I long for people to look down upon me and despise me . . . I want to dirty myself outwardly, so that my person may properly reflect the dirtiness which it conceals', too afraid to 'go off stewing into the Lincoln or Navenby brothels with the fellows' because he 'wouldn't know what to do' with women.[38]

This confluence of repressed sexuality and empire was an aspect of British history that could not really be addressed or even acknowledged by historians until the repeal of the Criminal Law Amendment Act in 1967. In recent years, however, the subject has played a significant part in historical revisionism. Late-Victorian homophobia; late marriage for men; the pretence of female frigidity; the pseudo-scientific retitling of all sexual pleasure as 'perversion' – in the view of Ronald Hyam, the leading historian of British sexuality and empire, these by-products of the Victorian age were the cause of much human misery, the cost of which is difficult to tabulate yet which should not be forgotten in the table of British imperial history. 'In the twentieth century the cumulative result of these four peculiar features was a society with too many frigid wives (or at least "porcelain where pottery is wanted", as Burton put it), too many terrorized and desexualized children, and too many outcast men, stigmatized whenever they strayed into any variations from the supposed "norm",' Hyam concluded. 'In short, there resulted a generalized proliferation of needless anxiety and sexual starvation, with a diversion into outright eccentricities, such as flagellation (the "English vice"), and sympneumata [prolonged mutual masturbation].'[39]

Flagellation, prolonged mutual masturbation, even anal penetration were certainly eccentricities that would excite the tortured imaginations and longings of many of Monty's contemporaries, not only T. E. Lawrence. The Empire and Orient offered certain escape valves to tortured Puritans. As Lawrence described in *Seven Pillars of Wisdom*, 'thirsting to punish appetites they could not wholly prevent', his fellow nomads, far from the society of women, 'took savage pride in degrading the body, and offered themselves fiercely in any habit which promised physical pain or filth'.[40]

Monty's response to late-Victorian psychosexual tyranny would be different from that of Lawrence of Arabia – but just as strange. Both would seek the affection, loyalty, indeed adulation of their fellow men; both felt the hand of destiny on their dreams; both were 'loners' at war with themselves and the world; and both men were almost exclusively drawn to people of their own sex. But where Lawrence, having achieved fame and glory, would sublimate his sexual desires in masochistic flagellation, Monty would find a different release.

2

Bad Boy

Coitus interruptus

How much Maud was 'responsible' for the sexualities of her offspring, only a psychologist could say. She had, as one biographer has described, 'moved straight from childhood to womanhood without ever having been a girl, or what would have been called a young lady. Her life switched abruptly from cloistered seclusion to hard, unremitting drudgery, from which there was little prospect to escape.'[1] Small wonder, then, given her own frustrations, that she tyrannized and caned her children, while her husband, though more merciful, spread the words 'sin' and 'eternal damnation', in common with priests, missionaries and army chaplains working throughout the British Empire.

Hand in hand with religio-medical nonsense – such as the mortal sinfulness of masturbation – went an increasing imperial arrogance and racism towards other cultures, Hyam observed, as the ' "social distance" between rulers and ruled was remorselessly widened'. Thus for historians such as Hyam, 'the whole tone of the British empire' had, by World War I, become 'radically different from what it had been only thirty years before'. As Hyam and others have lamented, whatever economic, social and political advantages the British Empire conferred upon its colonies, toleration of sexual diversity was not among them. Indeed, the reverse was the case in the late nineteenth century, as sex was pseudo-scientifically catalogued, labelled and then damned by its missionary priests, save for the most missionary reproductive act. 'All was reduced to the exclusive promotion of reproductive adult marital sexuality,' Hyam noted – any deviation from that Victorian reproductive ideal being, by the latter 1880s, no longer sanctioned or tolerated, in particular 'juvenile masturbation', which became 'increasingly a matter for pious eradication'. The fear of resulting death or physical and mental disability was instilled into every Victorian middle-class child.

All earthly, especially earthy, delights were to be denied, in the service of a higher, evangelical cause. Middle-class women, especially women of the church, were expected to dislike sex, and merely do their duty – which was to bear children. 'Female orgasm was certainly not "respectable"', Hyam chronicled,[2] and it is unlikely Bishop Montgomery knew how to induce it, or Maud Montgomery to enjoy it, even wish it. At any event, after bearing five children by her mid-twenties, Maud seems to have called a halt, both to children and to the 'reproductive act' itself.

For 'young couples like Henry and Maud', their son Brian chronicled, 'children came from God and contraception would be a violation of their religious principles.'[3] Save perhaps for *coitus interruptus*, sexual abstinence thus provided the only legitimate way of avoiding childbirth, and it seems therefore likely that Maud declined or avoided sexual inter- course – at least intercourse leading him to orgasm – with her husband during their first seven years in Tasmania. Certainly Maud bore no further children for her first seven years there.

For his part Bishop Montgomery appears to have accepted abstinence with equanimity, sublimating his own sexual starvation in almost manic missionary endeavour – even chartering a sailing ship, the *Southern Cross*, to carry him to offshore islands, Fiji and the Solomons. If he 'was generally away from Hobart for one hundred and eighty days in the year, visiting every parish on the island', as Brian recorded, with a full year spent away in Melanesia, it was perhaps not really surprising.[4]

Death, too, may have played its part in Maud's Tasmanian transforma- tion into the partner who 'wore the trousers' and became a sort of Tyrant Queen. Maud's eldest daughter Sibyl – or 'Queenie' as her doting parents had called her – had died within a few weeks of their arrival in Hobart, aged nine. How deeply this affected Maud is unknown, but it is uncontested that her relationship with the older children was far less happy than with her later brood. 'We elder ones never became a united family,' Monty chronicled.[5]

Did the tragic death of Queenie disrupt Maud's emotional commitment as a mother towards Monty as an infant? Were the potentially mortal illnesses he suffered as a child a way of attracting her mourning attention? Whatever the psychosomatic truth, Monty grew up 'restless almost to the point of nervousness',[6] small in build and prone to serious, sometimes life-threatening illness, while Maud became more and more imperious. The local people found her aloof and 'aristocratic' – a 'difficult' woman, 'sweeping in with a rustle of black taffeta skirts, her children trailing in behind her'.

Tongues wagged. 'Frequently she startled the people on the holiday beaches by galloping along at breakneck speed, riding side-saddle in her dark blue habit. They wondered how it came about that this fiery woman had become the wife of the venerable Bishop, with his gentle unassuming manners. The Bishop usually walked.'[7]

Disobedience

It is impossible, at a century's remove, to know what was going on in Maud and Henry's hearts, but the concept of 'transgression' came increasingly to dominate Montgomery family life: monitored by Maud, punished by Maud. 'Rule was all', Moorehead described the atmosphere at Bishopscourt, Hobart. 'Sin had to be closely watched. It lay across a thin dividing line from virtue, and the safest thing was to observe a very definite code of behaviour.'[8]

For Monty this posed an insuperable problem. His mother wanted him to be a girl – even sent him, at one time, to a girls' school, and dressed him in girl's clothes. In his *Memoirs* he recorded how hard this was to cope with, for he obstinately declined the role, and thereby earned her punitive wrath: giving rise to a 'clash of wills' that was never to be resolved in their lifetime.

For Maud Montgomery, Bernard's pretty, pert-lipped mouth and rebellious blue eyes of a renegade girl bespoke femininity, not masculinity, and throughout his childhood Maud insisted on dressing her third son in satin and velvet, tight Fauntleroy-knickers, jackets with puff sleeves and slashed shoulders. Clearly she saw in Monty the girl he himself could not acknowledge – and when he rebelled she became relentlessly, ruthlessly determined to beat the boy out of him. ' "Go and find out what Bernard is doing, and tell him to stop it" ' was his mother's perpetual refrain '[i]f I could not be seen anywhere. *Whatever I was doing*!' Monty repeated with emphasis, sixty years afterwards. 'I hardly think that that was the right treatment for a high-spirited, strong-willed boy.'[9]

'Certainly I can say that my own childhood was unhappy,' Monty went on, for he was the only child to resist her tyranny, and thereby became, in a strange, almost addictive symbiosis, the family scapegoat for her fury. As Moorehead revealed, Monty actively *courted* her treatment, seeming to experience an erotic, even masochistic pleasure from his knowledge of imminent retribution. 'Sometimes, when he knew he had been naughty and that it would not be long before punishment overtook him, he would go coursing through the garden, and then, throwing himself down in the long grass he would whisper, "What have I done? What have I done?" '[10]

What he had done was to touch the nerve of sexual tension underpinning a large Victorian family – a family obsessed with righteous middle-class Anglican religious 'purity', and committed to persecution of those who transgressed.

The conflict would never give Monty any peace. 'He was the bad boy of the family,' his elder brother Donald recalled: 'trouble' as well as troubled. As such Monty constantly drove his mother to 'exasperation', forcing her to cane him – so often and so hard that one cannot avoid the conclusion that this physical abuse was what, at heart, Monty wished: the nearest thing to love. 'Standing at the head of the stairs she would call him, "Bernard, come here". He would walk up staunchly, and having taken his beating, would come down again, still in control of himself but with trembling lip.'[11]

A *frightful little boy*

'If my strong will and indiscipline had gone unchecked,' Monty later ruminated, 'the result might have been even more intolerable than some people have found me. But I have often wondered whether my mother's treatment for me was not a bit too much of a good thing: whether, in fact, it was a good thing at all. I rather doubt it,' he considered. 'I began,' he concluded, 'to know fear early in life, much too early.'[12]

These were Monty's words, and whether or not he exaggerated, he remained tormented by the memory to the end of his life. Visiting Monty in old age at his home, where he lay bed-ridden and seemingly unable to read or distract himself, Field-Marshal Carver once asked Monty what he did all day. 'I think.' Carver asked what Monty thought about. Perhaps his great battles, Alamein or Normandy? 'No,' Monty retorted. 'I think about my mother – and how beastly she was to me.'[13]

Was it fear of Maud's punishment that Monty meant in his *Memoirs*? Or did the fear lie deeper than the canings she administered: fears that his mother would abandon or emasculate him, did not love the boy he was?

A cousin later recalled Monty's 'straight hair and cool grey eyes, just as he is now, beret and all, only the beret was a scarlet one' – wearing 'knickers of black facecloth, with little buttons on the outside seam, and short covert' coat that 'seemed the height of elegance'.[14] Girlish or not, Monty would never lose his dress sense – though it was an area in which he was, characteristically, determined to dictate fashion, not follow it. Whether he ever understood the underlying dynamic of his relationship with his mother, however, is questionable – indeed, whether *we* can ever really understand it is unlikely. But one thing seems indisputable. Whatever Monty or Brian later said about Maud, Monty's entire early life was dominated by her – indeed, one may see his whole life, emotionally, as an extended bid to win her approval and compel her acceptance of his masculinity – a battle he seemed never to win.

At one level Monty knew this. After all, how could she love him when he was not only frightened but 'a frightful little boy', as he admitted. But at another, he could not understand her emasculating gaze, and ultimately did not, seeking acceptance, eventually, from others whom he could control.

In the meantime the entire family left Tasmania at the end of 1900, returning to London – where Bishop Montgomery, having swallowed his sense of loss in leaving his beloved Tasmania, glowed with pride at having been appointed a virtual 'foreign secretary' of Anglican missionary work around the world – 'a referee and guide in all Greater Britain questions'[15] of the Anglican church: Secretary of the Society for the Propagation of the Gospel, the SPG.

Leaving Tasmania

Alongside the obvious good which Bishop Montgomery and other missionaries intended in Tasmania and Melanesia, the socio-sexual damage for which the SPG was responsible is only now being unpicked by historians. The Protestant missionaries were guilty, among other things, of a 'fierce reordering of life in the Pacific islands', Hyam noted. 'In some societies, especially in the South Pacific, almost the entire range of social amusements and communal activities became interdicted. Victorian missionaries seldom stopped to enquire what structural function the practices they objected to so often performed in ensuring the cohesion of traditional societies.'[16]

Bishop Montgomery, sadly, was no exception, priding himself on having introduced cricket to Melanesian tribesmen, while weaning them from another team game, polygamy. But if the cost of such exported European missionary morality was high for the indigenous peoples of the South Pacific, it was not negligible in the homes of the missionaries themselves, where the children were not only forbidden to consort with natives but, in Monty's case, forbidden even to go to school with other Australian children. The Montgomery children were, according to Moorehead, caned if they pronounced any word with a local Australian accent: a 'distancing' that was, in its way, symbolic of the entire British Empire in its fin-de-siècle metamorphosis.

Brought up in the Colonies, yet segregated from the local inhabitants, the Montgomery children had now to adapt to an English urban environment. 'I had been educated at home, in Tasmania by tutors imported from England, and had never been to school,' Monty recorded inaccurately.[17] (In fact he was suppressing a term at a private girls' infants' school in Hobart, where he had once been sent with his sister Una, and a term at the King's School, Canterbury, when his father attended the 1897 Lambeth Conference of Bishops.) But in essence, Monty was recalling the truth for him, at age fourteen, faced with a new life in London.

Bishop Montgomery was clear that his eldest son Harold – who was not intellectually well-endowed – would probably go into the army, in fact into the cavalry, since he was an accomplished horseman. The Bishop's second son, Donald, was extremely clever at school, and destined to go to Oxford or Cambridge as a scholar, if all went well. This left Bernard, the Bishop's third son, over whom there hung a question-mark, given his frail health and his waywardness.

Taking a house in Chiswick, west London, as the new head of the SPG at the end of 1901, Bishop Montgomery waved goodbye to Harold as he set off to join the Imperial Yeomanry in South Africa in the last months of the Boer War. In the meantime it was decided to send Donald to the nearby St Paul's day school, and Bernard too – if the boys could get in.

'The entrance examination to St Paul's had to be passed and during the Christmas holiday I attended a class at Colet Court, took the examination, and passed,' Monty recalled. His brother Donald, however, did more than pass. 'He won a scholarship; he was immensely proud of the silver fish on his watch chain. No fishes came my way!'[18]

No watch did, either – for to his father and mother's consternation, on his first day home from school, in January 1902, Monty announced he had opted for the school's preparatory course for the army: 'the lowest army class – Class C'.[19]

Army Class 'C'

'But why the Army?' Monty's parents asked. 'Why did you choose that?'[20]

Monty could only reply, stubbornly, that he wanted to be a soldier – an ambition he had never entertained before in his life. 'Grieved and uneasy, the Bishop left the room', according to Moorehead[21] – just as, when Monty had been caught smoking in Tasmania, it had been his father who had knelt in prayer in the family chapel and had assured Bernard of God's forgiveness, only to leave him to the punitive mercies of Maud, who administered a caning the savagery of which he would never forget.

This time, having turned fourteen a few weeks before, Monty was too old to be caned. 'My father had always hoped that I would become a clergyman', he recounted in his *Memoirs* – adding that the Bishop 'never attempted to dissuade me; he accepted what he must have thought was the inevitable; and if he could speak to me today I think he would say that it was better that way'.[22]

Maud did attempt to dissuade her errant son, however. Harold, she pointed out, was eminently suited for imperial army duty – indeed for little else (he later became a chief native commissioner in Kenya, and an alcoholic); but even Harold had first obtained his parents' blessing in joining the army. Monty, by contrast, had not.

This latest act – opting in advance, at age fourteen, to become a soldier without Maud's knowledge or consent – seemed on the face of it to belong to Monty's repertoire of outrages. It was perhaps this that made Monty's father leave the room; Maud would deal with the matter, as she always did.

But Maud couldn't. The boy was too big to cane into submission. Indeed this was the ultimate confrontation between mother and son. Monty had always been frail – he had almost died of a mastoid infection aged eight – and was not cut out for a man's job – one which involved, inevitably, the subjugation of women. Not even her husband had managed that.

As Maud cross-examined her son, however, she realized she was heading, for the first time, for defeat. Bernard was adamant; her 'feminine' son was declaring his absolute intent to become a man in that most masculine of all the professions: the military.

Childhood and sexuality

What no one has ever satisfactorily explained is the conjunction of Monty's childhood and his same-sex love. While the majority of boys sent to all-boys schools sooner or later showed an interest in girls, Monty – like T. E. Lawrence – never did. He had two surviving sisters, but until his late thirties there was only one woman in his life: his mother. The resemblance to his contemporary T. E. Lawrence in this respect is remarkable. Arnold Lawrence, writing of his brother, once remarked: 'The strongest impression I have is that his life has been injured by his mother' – for, as John Mack has described, T. E. Lawrence's 'intense identification with her and with her conflicts made it almost inevitable that the imposition of her ambitions, emotional needs, guilt and demands upon him would ultimately have a devastating effect upon his personality.' Lawrence was condemned to a lifelong struggle to resist her 'influence, to become completely separate and distant from her . . . Discipline, according to Arnold [Lawrence], was administered in the form of severe whippings on the buttocks and was delivered by his mother because his father was "too gentle, too imaginative – couldn't bring himself to".' These beatings, Arnold believed, were distinctive in that they were 'given for the purpose of breaking T. E.'s will. Never losing her faith in such punishments, Mrs Lawrence once remarked in her later years that the reason Lord Astor's horses never won was because he wouldn't whip them.'[23]

Meanwhile, though Monty claimed never to have regretted his decision to become a soldier, he did regret the manner of its choosing – and the genesis of that decision. 'In my case, two matters cannot have been right,' he summarized his childhood, 'both due to the fact that my mother ran the family and my father stood back.'

The first matter was the 'fear' which Maud inspired in him and which caused him to withdraw 'into my own shell' and to battle on 'alone', as he described, an enemy of society rather than a confident insider.[24] Looking back, he could see this was not right – and that his decision to opt for the army represented a turning point in his young life. Somewhere in his fourteen-year-old psyche he'd known he must escape her psychological emasculation, or end in skirts like his frocked father. But how? In opting for an army career he was hurling himself into the unknown, since he was not strong and healthy like his eldest brother, nor had he any longstanding interest in the army or in things military. Stamp collecting and domestic escapades had been far more interesting than British military history or practice.

The whole experience of St Paul's school came, in this sense, as a shock to Monty's adolescent system – indeed, this was the mysterious 'second' problem to which he referred in recounting and analysing his childhood. Looking back half a century later, he felt he had been thrown into a major English boys' private – or 'public' – school, at the end of the Victorian era, without preparation – indeed without having really been to school before, and 'without having had certain facts of life explained to me'.[25]

The facts of life

Quite what Monty meant by this is uncertain, since he never really explained the statement. Clearly, however, he meant sexual facts – which in the context of Victorian public schools were startling: namely that, despite the Labouchère Amendment, and whatever morality the Bishop and his wife might propound at home, English public schools practised virtually tribal initiation rites concerning sex, puberty and adolescence, with ritualized systems of 'fagging' (young boys acting as servants to older boys), male–male love relationships and erotic, often sexually consummated relationships between boys, and between boys and 'masters'.

For Monty these sexual 'facts of life' were utterly new – and, given the manner in which his mother had enforced strict discipline and the policing of 'sin', it was to him extraordinary that the headmaster took no interest in what was going on under his nose. Sitting with his new Army Class C colleagues in the gallery at prayers, Monty fifty years later remembered the first, almost biblical apparition of Dr Walker. '[I]t was from that elevated position on my first morning at school that I saw the High Master, the great Dr Walker,' he recalled. 'If I had known any French I would have exclaimed "Mon Dieu"; to me, a savage from far off Australia, he was an amazing sight with his flowing beard.'

When passing Dr Walker in the corridor Monty, like other boys, averted his eyes. 'I learnt later that Walker was in his day the greatest of all British headmasters, and the school as we know it today was his creation.' Yet to Monty Dr Walker was simply too old, and too distant from his 'troops' – as would be the generals of World War I. 'I never got to know him, since he never spoke to me,' Monty recorded with retrospective amazement, given that he had spent five long years at the school – adding that Walker was a very old man, aged seventy-five, when he retired in 1905. (Almost the first thing Monty determined to do when he became a governor of the school was to 'insist that the High Master should depart after 15 years, or on reaching the age of 60 – whichever comes first'.)[26]

Meanwhile, since he never spoke to his boys, Dr Walker had no idea what went on in the school, either between boys or between masters and boys. L. D. Wainright, the classics master, 'was another teacher with whom Bernard was friendly, and on cold, wintry afternoon is they sometimes had tea together' a 1947 picture-biography recorded coyly, overlooking the usual connotations;[27] but whether Monty was molested, or whether he formed any close relationships with other boys, platonic or sexual, is equally undocumented. Yet he certainly felt retrospective concern over the way in which he was thrown into such a homosocial, even homosexual, arena without knowledge or warning of what lay ahead.

Would prior knowledge have made his belated schooldays easier? Would he have been protected against things which he could not later bring himself to describe, beyond a reference to the 'facts of life'? We will probably never know, and can only surmise. What is clear, however, is that the old clash of wills that had characterized Monty's upbringing at home in Tasmania was now repeated at St Paul's in a clash with new authority. Swotting was pansyish, and he would not be compelled to follow that path. By his own admission he did almost no work, spending his time challenging the patience and rule of his teachers, and fighting other boys: 'the Monkey' as he was nicknamed, not only because of his mischievousness, but the vicious way he behaved on the sports field.

Looking back, Monty felt his waywardness to be partly his own fault, but also partly the result of ignorance and innocence. On his arrival he had been assigned to D Club – one of the six houses for day boys. 'On the second evening of the term was the New Boys' Tea in the dining hall, at which the captains and officials of each club endeavoured to find out what the new entry was worth in the games line. I was asked whether I was a batsman or bowler, and my place in the field at rugger; my reply was that I had never played cricket or rugger in my life. Did I box? No, but I could fight. It was now the turn of the captain of the Club to say "Mon Dieu"; he clearly considered me the lowest possible form of animal life, and left me to enjoy the tea.'[28]

Starved of maternal affection, the Tasmanian savage had joined an even more loveless, rulebound community, though this time exclusively male – with still more licensed caning. (It was small wonder he loved the musical *Oliver!*, in later life, when he could look back with something approaching nostalgia at his harsh upbringing and, on a visit to Cheltenham School, could say, amidst laughter, that his early life was 'a pretty good struggle against adversities' – indeed, that he was 'sorry to hear there is no beating here by the prefects. That's a pity, I'm all for laying it on,'[29] – something his contemporary, T. E. Lawrence, had actually found a way of having laid on to himself.)

As in Tasmania Monty certainly courted caning at St Paul's. 'I must admit that I did practically no work,' he confessed; in fact the 'only school work at which I excelled' was scripture. His sharp, retentive mind had little difficulty memorizing biblical stories. 'My father was a bishop and I had been brought up in the shadow of the church. This skill led to my undoing,' he remembered, recalling his classroom ditty on the story of Uriah the Hittite – involving 'David on his palace roof / In his night attire' who sees 'a lady in her bath / Whose name was Mrs Uriah'. His form master, Captain C. H. Bicknell, was not amused. 'I reckoned it showed great powers of simplifying the somewhat difficult situation in which King David found himself. Bicknell did not,' Monty recalled. 'I was caned.'[30]

At least the caning was administered by males, now. At school, moreover, the misfit could vent his hyperactive, tormented personality in organized games, once he learned their rules. Donald, his 'amenable' elder brother, did not; he worked hard and went on to win a scholarship to Cambridge. But Monty seems to have responded to his sin-obsessed family by ignoring books and immersing himself in organized football – in which he became school captain – swimming and cricket, in which he also became school captain and scored 87 against the legendary W. G. Grace and his team. (He later questioned, however, whether in terms of his own ability he was 'worth' his place as captain of the school's First Eleven, 'but I was strong and could deal the ball a hefty swipe', he reflected, 'and maybe this helped'.)[31]

Having experienced a profound fear of emasculation in childhood, Monty had already learned to meet adversity without tears. Now, in adolescence, he earned the respect of his peers for doing so – becoming a prefect under the new system introduced by Walker's successor, 'and maybe the best known boy in the school', as he recalled.[32] It was fame, or notoriety of a sort: 'The Monkey is vicious, of unflagging energy, and much feared by the neighbouring animals owing to its tendency to pull out the top hair of the head. This it calls "tackling",' the school magazine reported. 'To foreign fauna it shows no mercy, stamping on their heads and twisting their necks, and doing many other inconceivable atrocities with a view, no doubt, to proving his patriotism . . . So it is advisable that none hunt the monkey.'[33]

Few did. Monty emerged after five years at St Paul's an uncultured, ill-educated, socially uncouth eighteen-year-old, but at least an unexpected games hero, and therefore acceptably 'masculine'. He was not liked, but was at least acknowledged as distinctive by his fellow pupils. He had, as he later put it, 'become self-sufficient, intolerant of authority and steeled to take punishment'.[34] In English his essays were 'sensible but he has no notion of style' his teacher had already noted in 1905,[35] and he had not greatly improved when the competitive exams for the Royal Military College, Sandhurst, took place in the autumn of 1906. Nevertheless, on the strength of his native intelligence and his prowess at games he passed in at number 72 of an intake of 170. In January 1907 the former 'Colonial' thus began life as a gentleman cadet.

Whether he could behave like a gentleman, however, was another matter.

Pyromanic outburst

At school, the rugby football coach, J. L. Phillips, noted how Monty would 'assemble the XV around him at half-time and carefully outline his policy for the rest of the game'.[36] As a natural leader Monty soon made his mark at Sandhurst also – indeed, in March 1907 he was promoted to cadet-lance-corporal, with the prospect, if all went well, of being made the next colour-sergeant of his company and graduating after only two terms into his chosen regiment.

But all was *not* well.

As at St Paul's, Monty remained impecunious and envious of other boys' affluence ('I doubt if many cadets were as poor as myself . . . Those were the days when the wrist watch was beginning to appear and they could be bought in the College canteen; most cadets acquired one. I used to look with envy at those watches, but they were not for me,' Monty could still recall wistfully fifty years later. 'Now I suppose every boy has one at the age of seven or eight'[37]). He had been 'lonely and unhappy' throughout his schooldays when at home in Chiswick, 'often silent for hours at a stretch. His mother scolded him. "You must talk. You must be agreeable and sociable." But he had', Moorehead reported, 'nothing to say' – at home.[38] Mischievous, often violent in behaviour and a natural leader at school and at military college, yet silent, morose, uncommunicative at home. What lay behind all this?

In Tasmania Monty had been hyperactive, but his 'nervousness' had not amounted to a 'visible neurosis', Moorehead considered.[39] At Sandhurst, however, Monty's inner volcano reached its eruption point. As he would often remark, in later talks to schools, 'In all people there are great emotional forces bottled up inside them. I say "bottled up" purposely, because I believe that, as you take the cork out of a bottle, so there must be an outlet for the human emotions. It must be a constructive, positive outlet, which warms the heart and excites the imagination.'[40]

At Sandhurst, it was more than Monty's heart that was warmed: it was a fellow cadet's backside.

Tempting fate

Pyromania is a mental disorder in which fire is repeatedly and deliberately set, not for monetary gain or for other benefit, but because an individual cannot resist the impulse to engulf something or someone in flames. The pyromaniac experiences tension before setting the fire and pleasure, relief, even erotic gratification afterwards. He or she is legally considered an arsonist. While pyromania can often be treated by psychotherapy today, there was no treatment available in December 1907 when, at the point of a poker, Monty forced a fellow cadet against the fire in his room, as he dressed for dinner, and set him alight.

Doubtless in the scale of the horrors of war in the twentieth century,

Monty's crime cannot be reckoned as too egregious; indeed, one is compelled, as biographer-historian, to consider whether, without the trials of his early life and their unpleasant outcomes, Monty could possibly have developed, over time, into the ruthless military leader, thriving on violence, which the Allies so desperately needed in World War II if they were to succeed in combat against the collective discipline and fire-power of indoctrinated Nazis. As Brigadier Sir Edgar Williams, Monty's famous chief of intelligence, later remarked: 'He wasn't a nice man – but nice men don't win wars!'[41]

The truth was, Monty wasn't nice, nor did he try to be. He *had* to be boss, to be in control, to give orders and seek release in aggressive action if he was to structure the violent, troubled emotions and disordered sexuality which his mother's tyrannical upbringing had stirred.

Possibly as a residential pupil or boarder at an English public school, he might have found the kind of adolescent boy-love that characterized the experiences of contemporaries such as Rupert Brooke or Hugh Dalton – the later Labour chancellor – at Cambridge University, to which his brother Donald matriculated. Cambridge was certainly famous for its 'homosocial' atmosphere at this period, in which intimate friendship, homoeroticism and sexual intimacy were not only tolerated in defiance of the Criminal Law Amendment Act, but talked up and widely practised – providing an escape from the impossible hypocrisies and tabloid taboos, policed by cane and worse, of a still largely Victorian middle-class society. But for Monty, still psychologically enslaved to his mother, there are no records of any such 'deep' male friendships, insofar as we know. Certainly neither his brothers nor his sisters could remember him having any intimate friends, though there was no shortage of cadets willing to follow his wild, almost demonic schemes.

Once, in fact, a Hobart contemporary confided to Moorehead, Monty had tied the hands of a group of children and made them each, in turn, climb a ladder on to the roof of Bishopscourt, then – still handcuffed – 'walk around it and come down again' under his escort, regardless of vertigo or the risk of serious injury, even death – 'fighting against this until the skin ate into' their skins. 'Parents on both sides were displeased', the contemporary had added.[42] On another occasion, Monty had terrified a little girl visiting his house by pursuing her with a carving knife – for which he had been ritually caned. Now, once again, at Sandhurst in December 1907, Monty had tempted fate, leading his 'Bloody B' company into another company's quarters, armed with pokers and bayonets, and holding an unpopular cadet's posterior against the coal-fire, igniting his shirt-tails as he dressed for dinner.

The cadet was 'a dreadful chap', as Monty told his brother Brian: a quiet, shy and studious boy who not only symbolized the sort of inner intellectual confidence the hyperactive Monty seemed unable to attain, but perhaps also the feminine self, in a man, that Monty dared not confront. Igniting his backside, at the point of a poker, said it all.

Badly burned and hospitalized, the cadet nobly refused to name his assailants. Monty was, however, identified as ringleader, 'despite there being no direct evidence'[43] against him at the subsequent court of inquiry set up by the commandant. As a result Monty was reduced to the ranks, sent home to Chiswick and denied the possibility of being commissioned into the regiment of his choice after only two terms. Meanwhile the commandant pondered Monty's military future. As his brother Brian put it, 'consideration was given, in the circumstances of this case, to his fitness to hold a commission in His Majesty's army'.[44]

In the event it was Monty's mother who rescued her delinquent third son – telegraphing the commandant and travelling straight to Surrey to stay the night and discuss the matter with Colonel Capper and his wife.

Saving grace

Whether Maud undertook her errand of mercy for Monty's sake or for the sake of the family honour (she performed a similar role when one of her brothers was tried in court for sexually harassing his secretary, and another was accused of homosexual paedophilia) is a matter of conjecture. What is significant is that, once again, it was Monty's father who took the back seat, Maud who acted. 'She was then forty-three and a very handsome woman with a look of great determination and resolve about her,' Brian Montgomery later described.[45] As a result of her intercession Monty was permitted to return to the college as a simple cadet, after the New Year, for a third term – losing not only his stripe but his seniority in the army lists.

For Monty it was a sobering experience. He had spent most of his boyhood attempting to prove his masculinity, under the emasculating gaze of an extraordinary and controlling woman, provoking her female anger, while in turn bossing and bullying others. His latest pyromanic performance, however, had led this time not to a flogging but to something worse: to near-disaster in terms of his career, after almost six years of preparation for the army.

Yet the episode underlined and achieved a psychic purpose. His mother had not colluded in his dismissal from Sandhurst and withdrawal from an army career; for whatever reasons, she had chosen to support him at the critical moment, thus affirming him, finally, in his choice of a 'masculine' career. Certainly the episode moved Monty to express gratitude to her, for perhaps the first time in his life. 'My mother was a most remarkable woman, with a strong and sterling character,' Monty would write later, in a moment of unusual magnanimity. 'She made me afraid of her when I was a child and a young boy. Then the time came when her authority could no longer be exercised. Fear then disappeared and respect took its place. From the time I joined the Army until my mother died, I had an immense and growing respect for her wonderful character.'[46]

As a result of the Sandhurst incident and its aftermath, Monty claimed, he had 'learnt my lesson, and this time for good'.[47] It was a characteristic exaggeration.

Passing out

Back at Sandhurst in January 1908 Monty began to work with great determination, hoping to improve his performance and perhaps gain entry into the famed Indian army, where a soldier could live on his pay and obtain guaranteed promotion at laid-down intervals.

The results, in the summer of 1908, 'bitterly' disappointed Monty,[48] who passed out thirty-sixth – not quite high enough to merit a commission in the Indian army. However, it was sufficiently good to merit a commission in his second choice, the Royal Warwickshire Regiment – which had a regiment stationed in India.

India was a vital posting both for the young subaltern and for his family, who would otherwise have to support him. Without a private income Monty's parents – who had been badly hit during the bank failures of the early 1890s in Tasmania – were still burdened by the £12,000 mortgage on the Moville property and faced understandable difficulty in privately educating the remainder of their eight surviving children on the church salary of a former bishop, however eminent. Monty's commission into the Royal Warwickshire Regiment on 19 September 1908 was therefore a financial blessing, allowing Monty to serve – and draw active-service pay – in the 1st Battalion, stationed south of the Khyber Pass in Peshawar, on the North-West Frontier.

Monty's mother was delighted, not least because it promised to erase the stain of Bernard's pyromanic misdemeanour, and would remove him from troublemaking in England or Ireland. She therefore arranged a special party for him at Moville – 'a very grand affair, with a band from Derry with all its trimmings', one contemporary recalled. Dancing went on until 4 a.m. 'I remember dancing the supper dances with Bernard, but found him rather stiff ... The others were more amusing,' she remembered.[49]

Monty, reading of this ball some sixty years later, could not recall the occasion or the girl. Girls were never on his agenda at that or any stage in his life, and the instance seemed to him unlikely. 'She says she danced with me at New Park in honour of my having "passed out" of Sandhurst. I certainly don't recall it,' he wrote dismissively to his brother Brian, 'and as you know, I was nearly pushed out instead of "passing out"!'[50]

While the relationship with his mother thereby took a turn for the better, the question-mark over Monty's 'masculinity' remained. His stand-offishness with girls would become legendary among the Montgomery family and their relatives and friends. Later it would be passed off as peculiar but unworthy of comment, since it was ascribed to Monty having married the army rather than a wife. For the moment, however, it was simply put down to shyness. India would, it was reckoned, provide him with a chance to 'grow up', and at last become a man.

Pathan boys

From the selfsame Peshawar the young Winston Churchill had, eleven years before, set out to participate in the Malakand campaign – a series of frontier skirmishes in which Dum-Dum bullets were used and no quarter given on either side.[51] Monty, too, was out to prove himself on the North-West Frontier, though for very different reasons. To his chagrin, however, thanks to his pyromanic outburst he arrived too late: the latest punitive Bazar valley and Mohmand expeditions of spring 1908 were already over.

What Monty learned in India, however, was something that was to be far more useful to him – and the free world – than the satisfaction of Victorian honour, for it was in India that Monty – like T. E. Lawrence in Carchemish – bumped up against the strengths and weaknesses of the British Empire in the clash of opposing civilizations. In particular, it revealed to him the sheer amateurism and social snobbery that would bring Britain, despite its amazing imperial network, to the very brink of disaster.

No sooner had Monty arrived in the ante-room of the Royal Warwick-shires officers' mess in Peshawar on his first day than he was offered a drink. 'It was mid-winter on the frontier of India, and intensely cold; I was not thirsty. But two whiskies and sodas arrived and there was no escape,' Monty recalled; 'I drank one, and tasted alcohol for the first time in my life.'[52]

The clergyman-manqué was appalled. Now twenty-one, he was entering a colonial world very different from Sandhurst, Chiswick or even Hobart, Tasmania. Drink, however, was not the only local temptation. At Pesha-war there was a licensed regimental brothel, subject to medical inspection – one of seventy-five such cantonment institutions across India (though the VD rate of infection still remained astonishingly high, at around 50 per cent for British troops, who often strayed beyond the regimental brothels). As only a tiny percentage of soldiers were permitted to have wives with them, and a maximum of only 10 per cent of married officers were allowed the luxury, prostitution was an established element of imperial rule, fixed at approximately one tart per forty-four men, whatever the Purity Movement's objections. The only alternative was 'situational homosexuality' in the regiments, as the Viceroy, Lord Elgin, had noted in 1894, when the Contagious Diseases Act and Purity Movement threatened the survival of the regimental brothels. Wellington had famously remarked that British soldiers were 'the scum of the earth, enlisted for drink'; it seemed unreasonable for Purity movers to expect soldiers to be suddenly transformed into paragons of virtue, as the commander-in-chief in India, Sir George White, had already pointed out in 1888.[53] Without reglemented regimental prostitutes there would be 'even more deplorable evils', Elgin reckoned, noting that 'there is already an increase in unnatural crimes'.[54]

Unnatural crimes meant sodomy. Pathan boys were readily available, with a range of intercourse on sale, from intercrural and fellatio to anal intromissive. When, four years later, E. M. Forster came to stay in Pesha-war with a young Queen's Own Royal West Kent officer, Captain Kenneth

Searight, Searight personally attested to the flourishing trade in carnality, mostly involving Pathan boys aged twelve to fourteen. These relationships were more personal than most soldiers' relations with Indian tarts, Searight made clear in his diary: meticulously noting his positions and emissions, with up to a hundred fornications per boy. As Ronald Hyam has commented, 'What is perhaps of principal interest to us in all this is the way in which India acted as the safe and effective catalyst or displacement channel for the pursuit of his dangerous ways in a way that had never been possible in Britain.'[55]

Empire, among other things, was thus a safety-valve for English sexual repression. The anonymous 'G.R.' in Havelock Ellis's *Studies in the Psychology of Sex*, for example, became promiscuously bisexual once away from England's shores. Such opportunities 'indicate in a vital way the range of sexual possibilities which could be pursued uninhibitedly and with impunity within the formal empire well into the twentieth century', Hyam considered, 'at least within the army'.[56] Lawrence, travelling to the Middle East the year after Monty was posted to India, then to Beirut and Aleppo in 1910, encountered 'the delicious free intimacy of the men of Carchemish'[57] – in particular that of the fourteen-year-old Dahoum, or Salim Ahmed, a Hittite Arab with whom he fell in love and to whose memory he later dedicated *Seven Pillars of Wisdom* – to the scandalization of Dahoum's village, given the 'intimacy of the friendship', which involved Dahoum posing naked for Lawrence.[58]

That Monty came to approve of heterosexual brothels for British soldiers stationed in Peshawar is more than likely, given his later emphatic insistence on the availability of 'horizontal refreshment', as he called it, for his troops in Egypt and northern France – both times to the point of endangering his career. Monty remained unrepentant; just as an army marched on its stomach, he later maintained, so it needed to be sexually healthy to march at all – and given the demands of human nature it was preferable, in his view, to have medically reglemented outlets for sexual desire than unreglemented. Yet the existence of such regimental brothels in Peshawar must initially have come as a distinct surprise to the bishop's son, raised – at the end of a cane – to fear 'sin'.

Whether Monty himself could gain release in this way is unknown, however, though it seems unlikely. Like Lawrence he was not only shy to the point of muteness with women but demonstrated no interest whatsoever in girls, his sole connection with the female sex being through his mother and sisters, and he made no bones about this.

As regards homosexual encounters, also prevalent in Peshawar, it is less easy to be sure. Monty's later fulminating outbursts at the passing of the Sexual Offences Bill – claiming that to license sodomy even between consenting adults was to 'condone the Devil and all his works' – suggests that sodomy, as an expression of sexual desire, disturbed him deeply. But other forms of physical contact with boys? His later relationships, and his fear of being arraigned for sexual harassment, and even of blackmail, suggest a certain fixation; but whether this was first aroused, or even explored, with Searight's Pathan tribal boys in Peshawar will probably never be known, and it would be presumptuous to speculate.

What seems clear, however, is that the officially tolerated existence of prostitution and regimental brothels in Peshawar enabled Monty, as a young subaltern, for the first time to glimpse beyond the evangelical, 'sin'-dominated, flagellatory regime in which he had been brought up, and to accept the importance of pleasurable, healthy sex in a healthy army – even if his understanding of copulation remained limited to the notion of 'horizontal refreshment' as he would always term it.

His own sexuality, however, was another matter.

An unmitigated nuisance

'I do remember I was amazed sometimes at Monty's energy and unabated keenness,' wrote his adjutant later, adding, 'but truth to tell he was sometimes a little argumentative and did not always do as he was told' in India.[59]

The fact was, socially and sexually, Monty was a misfit. 'He was five feet eight inches in height, under eleven stone in weight, his face was thin and pointed and there was already an air of tautness, a curiously quick and bird-like quality in the way he held himself,' Moorehead described him – 'wiry' as the majority of Monty's colleagues put it. Wary, too. Indeed, his whole manner expressed aggressive-defensiveness, an impression 'that there was something held back'.[60]

Monty hunted, played hockey and cricket, and from his nine pounds a month pay bought his own horse, Probyn; yet he never quite fitted the regimental 'sporting type', Moorehead commented after interviewing Monty's former colleagues. In the January 1909 Peshawar Vale Hunt Point-to-Point, for example, Monty fell off, remounted, won the race –

and fell off yet again as the judges declared him the winner. As Moorehead remarked, Monty not only lacked style but 'was spectacularly lacking in heartiness. In the early regimental photographs he sits among the jutting jaws and massively folded arms like an alert fox-terrier in the midst of a collection of bulldogs.'[61]

'One is hard put to it to think of anyone so peculiarly unfitted for this life as Second-Lieutenant Bernard Montgomery', Moorehead summarized.[62] Nevertheless, the young officer quickly passed his exams in heliography and mule-care (though slapped down for 'impertinence' when he dared question the importance of the nocturnal rate of urination, the first question in the examination, as he later humorously recalled); learned to observe arcane mess rituals (including full regimental mess silver laid out at dinner every evening, with junior officers having to sit 'while two old majors at the President's end of the table exchanged stories over their port far into the night').[63] However, he 'could not dance and he was not interested in betting', Moorehead described. Nor was Monty physically or socially attractive. 'Imagine a horse with blinkers staring straight ahead with searchlights instead of eyes. There you have Montgomery,' a Sandhurst-contemporary described him.[64]

Required to drink alcohol in every officers' mess in the Peshawar garrison – with a strict rule against non-alcoholic beverages – Monty was nonplussed by the insularity and indolence of British imperial soldiering – aspects which not only left him with a lifelong aversion to alcoholic excess, but to the Indian army itself. Of the science and conduct of war, on any scale, Monty learned to his disappointment next to nothing. In his eyes the Indian army was responsible for this: infecting the visiting English regiments with its own deplorable amateurism. 'The battalion thinks it's still in India,' Robert Graves would quote a fellow officer's description of his own regiment's second battalion on its return from India to the Western Front in 1915. 'The men treat the French civilians just like "niggers", kick them about, talk army Hindustani at them' – prompting Graves to protest: 'But all this is childish. Is there a war on here, or isn't there?'[65]

Class division at home was transformed into racism abroad. 'The basic trouble,' Monty later wrote, 'was the beastly climate and the absence of contact with Europe', with the result that the officers 'tended to age rapidly after about forty-five. An expression heard frequently was that so-and-so was a "good mixer". A good mixer of drinks, I came to believe, for it soon appeared to me that a good mixer was a man who had never been known to refuse a drink.'

Superenergetic and determined to prove his masculinity in a man's profession, Monty was deeply disappointed. 'Overall,' he concluded, 'by the time I left India in 1913 I was glad that fate had decided against my passing high enough out of Sandhurst to be elected for the Indian Army.'[66]

Devoted to the British soldier

'The average young officer,' Monty later summarized, 'went to India to drink gin, play polo and have a good time.'[67] In a new century, with the four great empires in Europe – British, French, German and Russian – hurtling towards war, this was potentially fatal. It was not 'fashionable to study war and we were not allowed to talk about our profession in the Officers' Mess,' Monty recalled with retrospective incredulity.[68]

'At this time there did seem to me,' Monty recollected frankly of his soldiering days in India, 'to be something lacking in the whole business, but I was not able to analyse the problem and decide what exactly was wrong; nor did I bother unduly about it.' The fact was, as he afterwards related, 'I was happy in the battalion and I had become devoted to the British soldier.'[69]

This was perhaps the crux of Monty's Indian experience: an experience that might well have been denied him had he gained admission to the Indian army, with its white officers and Indian troops. What drew him, though, to Wellington's 'scum of the earth', after years of private tutoring, private education and privileged officer-cadet instruction?

While the older officers were, in Monty's view, largely 'useless, quite useless',[70] the 'men' were 'splendid; they were natural soldiers and as good material as anyone could want', he later considered. Where his relationship with his fellow officers was tense, charged with argumentativeness and unyielding competitive drive, his relationship with his men was strangely affectionate, patient, and older-brotherly. 'He organizes the battalion sports,' Moorehead described Monty's time in Bombay, after the battalion moved down to the plains and Monty had been promoted to full lieutenant and regimental quartermaster. 'He lives almost entirely with the little section of men under his command, exploring with apparent fascination all the minutiae of musketry, shooting and drilling. Long after a more intellectual officer would be bored to extinction Lieutenant Montgomery is found on the parade ground instructing the recruit in the final nicety of grounding his rifle butt or presenting arms. Rarely has the Army so fascinated one of her children.'[71]

The truth was, Monty cared nothing for ceremonial, as such, at this or any later time in his military life. The fascination with drill and musketry was entirely one of officer-to-soldier, or master–servant. Fastidious in his habits, obsessively tidy, intrigued by dress and captivated by detail, Monty seemed impelled by some inner, unconscious force that made him want to share this love of basic soldiering, almost like a stamp collection, with his colleagues. And since such sharing of military matters was taboo in the officers' mess – 'You were not supposed to show keenness in soldiering'[72] – Monty shared his passion with 'the men', who had, at least on duty, to go along with it.

It is impossible to exaggerate the importance of this new, exploratory compact in Monty's life. It did not make him a better leader of men in an army where leadership was still synonymous with the gentlemanly quali- ties of a squire, not a professional commander. Monty did not fit the bill of squire at all. 'It was impossible not to notice his peculiarities,' Moorehead chronicled: especially Monty's manic 'over-concentration on his military duties'.[73] Yet his early fascination with 'the British soldier' in India would be a quality which the later poets and junior officers would also evince in World War I: a homosocial bond of caring and responsibility that, for example, made homosexual poets such as Wilfred Owen and Siegfried Sassoon, even the bisexual Robert Graves, return to the horror of the Western Front time and again, even when they could have remained in safety in England, a fascination with young men, male beauty, innocence and death that cannot simply be dismissed as 'camaraderie', for it sub- sumed a profound, Housman-like idealization, the suppression of sexual instincts, and above all a difference in rank that gave the bond its very special, erotic quality – intense, quasi-paternal, quasi-amorous. 'People', Lawrence later wrote to a young male friend, thinking of Dahoum, 'aren't friends till they have said all they can say, and are able to sit together, at work or rest, hour long without speaking.'[74]

In Greek times military love had furnished some of the noblest soldiers of the classical world: 'comrades-in-arms' in both senses. In the Hellenic world of Athens, affection and love – such as that of Achilles and Patroclus, Theseus and Pylades – were considered primary factors in producing and maintaining fighting spirit, rather than Spartan discipline through emotional deprivation and fear. As someone who had undergone a long childhood of fear, Monty had no intention of returning to the Spartan model. Instead, there was in him a deep well of loneliness, bitterness and repressed sexual energy that now sought an outlet not simply in activity and action but in the responsible, 'safe', caring daily interplay of male–male contact, however mundane or unintellectual. If this was incomprehensible to sexually active contemporaries such as John Masters ('Of those who tried sublimation,' Masters noted caustically, 'some chased polo balls and some chased partridge, some buried themselves in their work, and all became unmitigated nuisances'[75]) Monty took no notice. 'There was a barrier separating him from other people and that was that,' Moorehead summarized. 'The thought of kissing a girl was not so much ridiculous as a waste of time,' was how he attempted to explain Monty's heterophobia. Yet asexuality does not begin to describe Monty's condition, for he was far from asexual, as are men who withdraw from reality into inner dreamworlds of fantasy and thought. Monty did not withdraw; neither did he read. His military ignorance, indeed his educational ignorance, was a terrible indictment of the English public-school system, where science was not taught, and there were more playing fields in England than classrooms or laboratories. Monty tried, he confided to Moorehead, to read Clausewitz, but 'could make neither head nor tail of it'.[76]

Yet this lack of education and contempt for his superiors provided an instant point of common ground between Monty and his men – just as Lawrence set up an extraordinary bond with the Arabs of Carchemish. 'He became thoroughly conversant with the intricacies of their tribal and family jealousies, rivalries and taboos, their loves and hates, and their strengths and weaknesses. It was this carefully gathered knowledge', Mack recorded, including Lawrence's ability to identify with the 'emotions and concerns upon which their self-esteem, security, power and prestige were based, that enabled Lawrence to win the confidence and acceptance of the Arab peoples, both during the Carchemish years and afterwards during the war.'[77]

In Monty's case, he had been brought up during his formative years as an Australian, a 'Colonial', and had a lasting suspicion, even hatred, of authority, as many of the soldiers did. Like most of them he was not a reader, nor did he put on airs or graces. He had no grain of snobbery save in bravado; possessed an acute sense of irony; and exhibited a love of practical jokes, and an ebullient, irrepressible sense of fun, especially jests of the 'banana-skin' type, aimed at establishment figures and the pompous – especially older officers.

The truth was, had he not been born the son of a churchman who became a bishop, Monty would have made an excellent sergeant in the British army.

Le Petit Caporal

Monty's likeness to an army sergeant was precisely what most irritated his later critics. It was later said that in the British army an outstanding professional commander such as Rommel would have been kept down as a non-commissioned officer – as if this fate was beneath British middle- or upper-class contempt.

Such a view was deeply British and, as would become clear in both world wars, deeply misguided. As in every army, it was the NCOs of the British army, in fact, who led and represented the ordinary soldiers – and to understand and sympathize with those ordinary soldiers' concerns, to see their strengths and know their weaknesses, would turn out to be the key to successful high command on the battlefield, not table manners. Not for nothing was Napoleon known as Le Petit Caporal – or the Führer as Corporal Hitler. Knowing about ordinary soldiers was the key to soldiering – and without a knowledge of ordinary soldiers, brilliant tactics were useless.

Thus Monty learned in the mountains and then the plains of India about British soldiers – and, in his strange, repressed but passionate and devoted way, to love them, just as J. A. Symonds, once he moved to Davos for his health, found in the company of 'peasants of every description, postilions, drivers, carters, conductors of the diligence, carpenters, doctors, parsons, schoolmasters, porters in hotels, herdsmen on the alps, masons, hunters, woodmen, guides, hotelkeepers, shopkeepers, stableboys, artizans' the 'sturdy children of nature' that 'confirmed my belief in democracy'.[78]

For Monty, too, the bond with his soldiers would confirm his faith in democracy. Meanwhile, returning to Shorncliffe, near Folkestone, England, with his battalion at the end of 1912, Monty found nothing had changed socially, economically or even politically, save that there was a growing concern about possible war with Germany. Diplomatic relations with Berlin were now strained, and the Agadir incident had shown how easy it might be for a minor incident to precipitate a major European war.

With the money he'd saved in India Monty meanwhile bought himself a Ford motor car, in which he hurtled round Kent. He went on a musketry course as well as one in machine-gunning, and in recognition of his energies was promoted to assistant adjutant, aged twenty-six. Only when an older officer returned from a two-year course at the army's Staff College in Camberley in the summer of 1913 and befriended him did Monty begin to see that there were larger questions to be asked in terms of waging modern war: that grand strategy involved naval as well as ground-force considerations, and that fighting a modern continental nation, using modern artillery and machine-guns, might prove more difficult, even, than subduing the Boers – which had been hard enough.

In January 1914, however, Captain Lefroy departed for duties at the War Office and Monty was left to prepare for modern European combat without training or instruction of any relevant kind, as the international situation deteriorated in the summer of 1914.

The long afternoon of Edwardian England, with its tiffin and chota pegs, polo and prizes on the lawn, was coming to an end.

3

The Great War

Letters to Maud

Like all young officers in July 1914 Monty was eager to see combat. What sort of combat would that be, though? Would Britain be sucked in? And how would the experience change him?

Hitherto, Monty had simply been the errant son, the black sheep of the Montgomery family. His Boer War veteran eldest brother Harold, who had moved to South Africa, and his Cambridge scholar elder brother Donald, who had moved to Canada, had so far won all the family glory, but World War I was to change all that. As Monty noted humorously, in later years, though he 'began the First World War in a Workhouse'[1] he would end it a decorated lieutenant colonel, in control, if not command, of fifteen thousand men and an entire orchestra of his own weapons of mass destruction, from machine-guns and artillery to tanks. 'During those four years of war,' he added, 'I learnt much about war and men which was to prove of very great value to me in later years.'[2]

It would be of the greatest value to others, too. Re-examining what happened to the twenty-six-year-old in World War I is therefore important, not only in following Monty's life-thread, but in explaining the secret of his revolutionary approach to battle in a democracy.

'My darling Mother'

Perhaps the first thing to stress, as a biographer, is the closeness of Monty's bond with his mother in World War I. In a very real sense, his life had become a mission, to prove himself and his masculinity to that person who meant most to him in the world: 'My darling Mother' as each of his wartime letters is addressed.

Though she did not return his love in quite the way that Monty wished, Monty's mother remained his sole 'girlfriend'; indeed over the years 1914 to 1918 his letters to Maud would amount to a sort of love album, each addressed to her, with only an occasional letter to the Bishop – addressed, more formally, as 'Dear Father'. These letters, chronicling his career from platoon commander to chief of staff of a division, were kept by Maud, and given back to Monty by his eldest brother after her death. He cherished them, not only as a reminder of his first wartime service, but of the feelings he'd had for her. 'The letters are all in my own handwriting, mostly in pencil, and of tremendous interest – to me at any rate', he wrote when annotating them in old age, after sorting them out and Sellotaping them into a large red, leather-bound scrapbook. 'I suppose a skilled psychologist, or handwriting expert, would be able to judge from the letters the sort of person I was during the First World War.'[3]

The handwriting, certainly, was distinctive: each word clearly written and evenly spaced across the pages, characterized by bold upright letters, with a single flourish in crossing of his 't's. The instant impression is of a childlike, innocent clarity. It is an unmistakable script: emphatic, rhythmic as in a measured beat, self-confident, unguarded. There is no reason to doubt his sincerity, or the emotion he felt for Maud, which spills from every page. She was his light, the woman who'd given him life, to whom he owed his earthly existence, and to whom he was almost umbilically linked as he went to war. In the security of that innocent, devoted affection he was determined to do well, and be worthy of her; no longer to be beaten as the 'bad boy' of her family, but to be respected, finally, as the prodigal son.

Modern war

Monty's first experience of impending war began on 30 July 1914, five days before its declaration, when fetched from a game of tennis in Folkestone. At 'about 6 p.m.', he told his 'darling Mother', an officer 'rushed down to summon us all back to barracks'. From there, that night, he was sent by train to Sheerness and the Isle of Sheppey, 'right at the mouth of the Thames on the south bank', where a composite infantry battalion was assembled to guard the aviation sheds and prevent a possible German invasion. He had been appointed battalion adjutant and didn't know 'how long we shall be here; I don't think the whole army is mobilising although certain brigades certainly are. I think it is just a precautionary move so as to be not caught napping. They are very frightened of a hostile landing here, as the coast is very suitable for it all round here. Don't be anxious if I don't write,' he warned his mother who was in New Park, Moville, preparing to give a large garden party. 'I shall let you know if we are ordered abroad, but I don't think myself that the war will involve us.' If it did, he would, however, be one of the first to go into battle: 'we are relieved by Territorials [peacetime volunteers] & we return to Shorncliffe and go off from there. Best love to all at New Park from / yr loving son / Bernard.'[4]

The Isle of Sheppey was a strange place to start a war. 'The Colonel and I live in the work-house here,' Monty informed his mother in his next letter, three days later, '& ride around daily to see outposts etc. We have 550 with us here at Minster, & another 500 in various attached posts.' Numerous warships had appeared off Sheerness, including '4 large cruisers' with their 'decks cleared for action'; meanwhile to his amusement, on the ground, a 'young subaltern' mistook '2 men crawling on hands & knees through the long grass on the plain in front of the [aviation] sheds', and assumed they were enemy spies 'so we all rushed out with revolvers & rifles to capture them, & found they were 2 men picking up refuse from a refuse heap there'.

Thus, comically, war loomed; indeed, it was the very comedy masking something so potentially serious that tickled Monty's sense of humour. 'The people here seem quite a different race & know nothing about what is happening in the outside world. They imagine we are territorials out camping & don't in any way connect our presence with a landing of the Germans. I hope they won't have a rude awakening. The old parson here looks about 96 and looks as if he had been here 50 years. He gave us a parade service this morning at 9.30 a.m. & preached to us in a whisper from a pulpit a long way off, so I don't know what it was about. He is very deaf. I spoke to him in the vestry afterwards & thanked him for the service etc. I told him England was mobilising for war but he hadn't the least idea what I meant, or what war meant. He said "Yes, very interesting."'

This would, Monty felt, amuse his father, the Bishop. 'What are you doing in Moville; and have all the guests come yet?' he asked. 'I hope you will have it fine. We are lucky here, as it has'nt [*sic*] rained for a week. I will write again when I have time, but you will understand that we are very busy. I am especially so, being adjutant of a very large and scattered battalion. However it is good experience, as we are on active service to all intents & purposes. Best love from / yr loving son / Bernard.'[5]

Monty's letter epitomized the unpreparedness of Britain for a major European war in 1914. Even in the battalion there was no idea what lay ahead. 'It is hard to know what is really happening,' Monty confessed. 'I see from this morning's papers that Germany has declared war on Russia, so we are now pretty bound to be dragged in,' he accepted. He couldn't help thinking it would be a good thing, though, for 'the war is bound to come sooner or later & much better have it now & get done with it. A modern war would not last very long, & would be such an awful affair that there would be no more war for 50 years,' he predicted. 'The general opinion, which I share, is that Germany will get an awful hammering. Austria will be pretty well occupied by Servia & the Balkan states who will probably come in; Italy is trying to remain neutral. So Germany will be left on her own to take on Russia & France, one on each side of her, and England. Germany couldn't possibly do this; the trouble is that she may realise this and back out.'[6]

Germany, however, *did* countenance war on two fronts: indeed had a brilliant plan for moving before the stately British, nervous about invasion, could react: disposing of France in a lightning attack on Paris via Belgium, while holding off the Russians in the east, then dealing with them.

Had Germany succeeded, the course of twentieth-century history would have been very different, and Britain might never have needed a man like Monty.

War by timetable

Could Britain have stayed out of World War I in 1914, as did the USA? The British Cabinet was split upon the issue. News of Russian and German declarations of war came in, but it was only at 11 p.m. on 4 August 1914 that the British government's ultimatum ran out, and the Cabinet made its irrevocable decision.[7] Using the abrogation of Belgium's neutrality as its reason, involving an early nineteenth-century British guarantee, the British government joined France in declaring war on Germany: for a mere 'piece of paper', as the German Chancellor contemptuously derided Sir Edward Grey, the British Foreign Secretary.

There was sad truth in this. With hindsight, Germany's war aims were remarkably similar to its objectives eighty years later: a European customs union, dominated by Germany, which would become a confederation strong enough to compete in world markets with America.[8] Germany had, after all, invaded France in 1870, beaten the French army at Sedan, and exacted reparations which the French, enjoying a postwar boom, had been happy – and quick – to pay.

This time, however, Britain felt too threatened by the growing might of Germany – especially its navy – to stand idly by. The die was cast. Whether, as with the punitive treatment of the Afghan tribes on the North-West Frontier, it would be worth British blood, was uncertain. Honour would be satisfied, at least; Sir Edward Grey could then return to his beloved fly-fishing,[9] and Churchill, the First Lord of the Admiralty, to his political ambitions (once he had changed political party).

Certainly for Monty, aged twenty-six when war was declared, honour was at stake. Like millions of his fellow countrymen, and young men of other countries, he was the willing victim of nationalistic war rhetoric, fanned over the preceding decade. As Sir Michael Howard has pointed out, 'The children of Europe were being trained for war, and war was regarded as something natural and inevitable.' European philosophers, after all, preached that 'the highest morality of the individual lay in the service of the state' – even when such service was replicated by individuals in opposing countries serving *their* state, with potentially disastrous consequences. Howard pointed to 'popular "social Darwinism" with its creed of the survival of the fittest among nations as among species' as another explanation of the growing sense of inevitability of war, as well as 'the technical requirements of mass armies, which coincided conveniently with these philosophical trends'. Moreover there was, too, 'an upper class which, with its status rendered precarious by industrialization, found in military life the security, purpose and prestige increasingly denied it in civil' – and therefore welcomed war as a chance to legitimize its parasitical idleness – like the bored Count Vronsky rushing to war in *Anna Karenina*. Yet even among 'ordinary people' there was 'a great mass of uprooted proletariat and urbanized petty bourgeoisie, for whom the national pride provided a status and fulfilment lacking in their drab everyday lives' – a national pride that was now challenged by the invasion of Belgium and the deliberate flouting of Britain's solemn if now ancient guarantee, made in post-Napoleonic times. 'There was', too, as Howard pointed out, 'that disquieting strain of primitive savagery which composers and artists were beginning to tap during the first decade of the twentieth century. There were the frustrations of deepening class-war'[10] – in which real war against 'foreigners' offered an outlet or escape.

Thoughtful people were aware of this. Paul Crook has recorded the efforts of 'peace biologists' to avert war before 1914, pointing out that it was the growth of protectionism and nationalism that destroyed the hopes of free-traders and liberals that capitalism would flourish in burgeoning inter-state commerce and communications. Instead, 'nations seemed ready to fight each other for economic and geo-political leverage', he reflected, as the new protectionism 'allied itself in militarism, seeing war as a legitimate and profitable instrument of state policy'.[11]

State policy, in a twentieth-century industrialized context where millions of men could be mobilized, equipped, armed and put into battle in a matter of days, affected vast populations – and incorporated mass-psychological motives. Writing a few months before the outbreak of World War II, John Bowlby and E. F. M. Durbin made the socio-psychological point that 'appetitive frustration', in civilized adults, leads to displacement and projection, whether in religious, social or economic groups. 'And the greatest of all these groups – at least in the modern world – is the State. It is by identification of the self with the State and by the expression of aggression through it, that the individual has in recent times chiefly exhibited his aggressive impulses.' The state arbitrated over and controlled, through law and force, the behaviour of its citizens. 'Tendencies to civil war are successfully repressed. In such circumstance,' the authors considered, 'it is natural, in our view, that transformed aggression should be chiefly canalized by, and flow unimpeded through, the State organizations of common endeavour and military adventure. In the service of the State the rationalized and transferred impulses of men find their last remaining and freest outlet.'[12]

In such circumstances, continental war was a fearful but not unthinkable possibility – though Monty himself still found it difficult to believe that Britain would become involved, at least initially, on any significant military rather than naval scale. 'What I expect will happen is that we will mobilise and then wait, all ready, to come in when France wants us,' he had told his mother on 3 August 1914. 'Our fleet is what they chiefly need, & that is ready now.'[13]

The French Cabinet certainly agreed with Churchill, the First Lord of the British Admiralty, that French naval forces could best secure the Mediterranean while the British navy controlled the Atlantic and North Sea, and blockaded Germany. But, crucially, the French *also* wanted British soldiers to serve on land in France in any new war – which Churchill did not. Thus, as Niall Ferguson has pointed out, though Russo-German mobilization in the final days of July 1914 doomed continental Europe to war, given the exigencies of the German chiefs of staffs' 'war by timetable' (the historian A. J. P. Taylor's phrase), that war would in most likelihood have been over quickly, and with a minimum of casualties – had Britain not interfered.

For fear of letting in the Tories

It was, ironically, the British Liberal Cabinet's decision to go to war for 'fear of letting in the Tories'[14] that doomed the Germans to failure. Without the government's declaration of war and the British Expeditionary Force's intervention the German armies 'would almost certainly have succeeded in overwhelming the French defences within a matter of months', Niall Ferguson considered[15] – and most military historians agree. The intervention of the little BEF, shipped briskly across the Channel in ferryboats and performing miserably at Mons, would nevertheless tip the delicately balanced scales of war, bringing the German masterplan for a quick, pre-emptive strike to grief.

Monty's part in this world-historical cock-up would be brief, minimal and highly symbolic. It would result in his near-death – but also a profound and lasting determination to find a new approach to modern democratic war.

Destination unknown

On 6 August 1914 Monty's composite battalion on Sheppey was duly relieved by Territorials and he returned to Shorncliffe, whence he wrote to his mother on 7 August, as the German armies began to sweep through Belgium, that 'no one knows when we shall go as everything is being kept very secret. We are working night & day to get ready.'[16]

A series of novels and plays had, since the turn of the twentieth century, predicted a German invasion of the English coast – from Erskine Childers' *The Riddle of the Sands* through William Le Queux's *Invasion of 1910* to Saki's 1913 futuristic fiction *When William Came: A Story of London under the Hohenzollerns*. Thus, in spite of the navalist view that 'sea power alone could decide the war',[17] the British army did not trust its sister department, the Admiralty, to halt a German invasion force at sea. It had been secretly agreed with the French that, in the event of war, some six British divisions plus a cavalry division would be shipped to France within fifteen days, but thanks to the mythic threat of invasion, the British reneged. Instead, two of the promised BEF infantry divisions were withheld on the orders of the new Secretary of State for War, Field-Marshal Lord Kitchener, on 6 August 1914. Monty's division – the 4th Division – was one of them. As a consequence, the 1st Battalion of the Royal Warwickshire Regiment, having put its silver and paintings into store and stripped its mess tables down to bare boards, was sent not to France or Belgium but to the east coast of England.

Monty's mother had by then held her garden party, and intended to set off for London, where she hoped to say goodbye to Bernard in person before he left for France. Monty had warned her he'd probably be too busy to get up to London, but was keen to see her: 'you must come to Shorncliffe', he insisted. 'They will probably give us notice several days before, so you will have time to come over alright.'[18] There was no time, however. On the morning of 8 August he sent an urgent cable: 'Just had orders to go leaving Shorncliffe in two hours destination unknown'.[19]

The destination turned out to be Cromer, on the Norfolk coast. Though he could make neither head nor tail of army orders, he remained naïvely confident, though back on ordinary duty in command of a platoon. 'I have 67 men in it, they are under my sole charge and I am responsible to Major Day [the company commander] for it. He gives me a very free hand. My men are all very good fellows and are putting up with the present hardships & discomfort very well.'

Proud of his unit, his loyalty to his men brooked no interference. 'The people of England are all learning that they must each do their little to help. We are mobilised and a state of war exists and if you ask anyone for something & they refuse, we can take it,' he declared – inaccurately. 'Of course we ask nicely at first, & generally get it without going further. But twice at Sheerness I had to use force. I asked a farmer for some water to fill my men's water bottles with; he refused & said he was short of water.

So I brought my men in & took it. The second time I wanted breakfast for 8 officers at a hotel; they had had a lot of work & no food for over 24 hours. It was only a small inn & they refused & said they never provided meals. I said we must have it & I would lock them in one room while we took it, if they refused. We were willing to pay whatever they asked. We got it.'[20]

The dictatorial gang leader of Hobart, St Paul's and Sandhurst was re-emerging, licensed this time by the state, as Monty saw it, to take, take aim and to kill when the moment came. Aged twenty-six, he knew his mind in this respect: a mind focused almost entirely on his military responsibilities; indeed, in the context of amateur, sleepy, class-conscious England there was something strangely blinkered, almost psychopathic about Monty's focus as the son of a bishop: everything set out with clarity and simplicity, from the larger war-picture to the minutiae of his military life. 'The chocolate you sent was much appreciated & was just what I wanted; also the writing pad. They are packed in my field kit which we take with us. We are only allowed 35lbs of kit each; this includes the weight of the valise, so you can't take much. I have got 1 greatcoat, 1 blanket, 1 spare pair of boots, 1 spare suit, khaki, 2 changes underclothes, 6 pairs socks, 12 handkerchiefs, washing things, 1 bath towel, your chocolate & writing pad, a woolly Swiss hat for sleeping in at night, 2 spare shirts, 1 sweater. It is difficult to write in the train, but hope you can read this. Give my love to everyone, with lots to you and father from / yr very loving son / Bernard.'[21]

The coal yard

Unfortunately the train's destination was a bleak one. 'For the last 5 days we have been living in the coal yard at York station,' he reported to his mother on 14 August 1914, using the writing paper she'd sent. 'I never imagined I should ever live in a coal yard; you can't imagine how filthy it is. It was no good washing or having a bath, you were dirty again in 5 minutes.'[22]

The experience was, however, a foretaste of trials to come. 'We draw Government rations now just like the men and we officers live in messes by companies i.e. the officers of each company mess together. Our servants cook for us. In our company we bought a "Service Canteen" from the A.

& N. Stores and it is enough for all of us; we are 5 in all. It contains plates, knives, forks, cup etc, also saucepan, frying pan & stewing pot, & the whole thing packs into one big pot.' He himself had charge of the mess. Though he hoped orders would come to return to Shorncliffe and from there they would set off for France, he clearly revelled in the simple business of soldiering, and preparing to kill. 'We are of course all looking forward very much to fighting the Germans; but this war will be no small thing', he now warned, '& will demand all our endurance before it is over.'[23] He asked for – and got, by post – a clasp knife and a strong leather purse. He had insisted on taking the reservists down to the range for rifle-firing practice before leaving barracks, and once the battalion was let out of the coal siding he concentrated on getting his platoon fit for the rigours ahead. 'We have any amount of work to do as the reservists want a lot of polishing up in their work, also they are very soft and in bad condition. So every morning we go for a long route march to get their feet hard and finish up with some manoeuvres of sorts. Then every evening we inspect all the men's feet to see if they have'nt [sic] got blisters etc, & also to see that they wash them. If you left a man alone he would never wash his feet! But it is most important, as if your men can't march they are no use.'[24]

Monty was thus in his element: a dedicated young lieutenant who thought of no other issues than playing his part in the war and looking after his men, even down to their feet.

The last to go

Having returned to Shorncliffe from its trip to the coal yard, the 1st Battalion of the Royal Warwickshire Regiment finally received the order it had been waiting for. With officers' swords sharpened and Lee-Enfield rifles distributed, the battalion entrained on the night of 21 August 1914 for Southampton and embarked on the troopship *Caledonia*. At Southampton docks Monty learned from the chief engineer that four divisions had already gone, or 'about 100,000 men. We are the last to go, at any rate for the present. We were not meant to go yet, but they suddenly decided to send one more [division], so it looks as if we were wanted.'[25]

They were.

Disrupting the timetable

Mons – Monty's destination – would be the British army's first battle fought on European soil since 1815, almost a century before: an unplanned, shapeless battle in which the BEF would be completely routed – indeed the BEF would be so traumatized by its experience that within a mere week of fighting the army would be considered unfit to fight another battle, and its commander, Field-Marshal Sir John French, would beg permission to take the entire British force out of the line to rest, refit, and perhaps evacuate, via St Nazaire – as would be the case in 1940 at Dunkirk.

None the less, the hasty appearance of five British divisions on the western flank of the German advance, as the Kaiser's million-strong German steamroller swept from Belgium into France in order to roll up the French line, came as an unwelcome surprise to the German High Command, which had hoped to envelop the little BEF in its staging area before it was assembled.

Without the BEF's aggressive intervention, von Kluck's 1st German Army would, in all probability, have outflanked the French line and invested Paris from the west – indeed in expectation of this the government of France actually fled from the capital on 2 September 1914. Yet it was not the battlefield performance of the British army that worried the Germans, but the worrying *presence* of British soldiers in line, during a lightning campaign aimed only at the French. The more the Germans mauled the British, without managing to encircle and force them to surrender, the more likely was the British public to support the raising of vast numbers of volunteers to fight, and thus prolong the war – a war that could be won by Germany only in a quick, pre-emptive battle such as Schlieffen had planned.

General Foch had envisaged precisely this five years earlier, in 1909, in conversation with the British Director of Military Operations, who was on a visit from the War Office to the École de Guerre. General Wilson had asked what was the smallest BEF that would be of any practical assistance to the French in the event of war. 'One single private soldier,' Foch had replied, 'and we would take good care that he was killed.'[26]

Certainly neither the British nor the French had any clear idea of how to use the BEF – as was illustrated by the arguments in the British War Council on 5 August 1914, when no one could decide whether to send the BEF to Antwerp, Amiens or Maubeuge, a fortress town near Mons on the Franco-Belgian border. In the event, it was decided to ignore the Belgian port of Antwerp – which could easily be surrounded by the Germans – and to append the BEF to the western flank of the French armies, facing the Belgian border, under the overall French strategic direction of Maréchal Joffre. Maubeuge was the local railhead – and the subsequent battle near by, beginning on 23 August, at Mons, proved a disaster for all concerned. The German timetable for encircling Paris – a 400-kilometre march by almost a million men – was disrupted, while the British, having put up token resistance, ran. It was in this unprepossessing situation that Monty's battalion reached the front.

To *the limit of exhaustion*

Combat in August 1914 proved surprisingly little different from that of the eighteenth and nineteenth centuries. In fact, as Richard Holmes has commented, 'although the railways whisked men to concentration areas with a comfort their grandfathers would have envied, once they had detrained they were scarcely more mobile than the warriors of Agincourt or Crécy.'[27] As of old, the opposing armies were fronted by horsed cavalry, acting as reconnaissance scouts and advance guards, and even in infantry battalions, all company commanders were mounted on horses. Virtually all artillery was horse-drawn, and even the regulation two machine-guns per battalion were horse-drawn, on two-wheeler carts with two-wheeled ammunition tenders.

The performance of a million German soldiers, marching through Belgium and into France, was therefore nothing short of miraculous, an extraordinary testament to German discipline, tenacity and ruthlessness. Franc-tireurs were shot mercilessly, as were civilian hostages in communities harbouring such snipers. Louvain library, with its priceless collection of books and manuscripts, was torched. Several weeks later the German commander-in-chief, von Moltke, wrote to his wife: 'How much blood has been spilled and how much misery has come upon numberless innocent people whose houses have been burned and razed to the ground. Terror often overcomes me when I think about this, and the feeling I have is as if I must answer for this horror, and yet I could not act otherwise than as I have.'[28]

He could not. To spare a long drawn out war required ruthlessness of purpose and execution, once declared. Moltke's uncle had already warned the Kaiser in 1905 of the consequences of failure to win outright victory in the first few weeks, namely 'a war between peoples which is not to be concluded with a single battle but which will be a long, weary struggle with a country that will not acknowledge defeat until the whole strength of its people is broken; a war that even if we should be the victors will push our own people, too, to the limits of exhaustion.'[29]

Nothing more prophetic could have been stated a decade before the outbreak of the war – and it was von Moltke's very awareness of this responsibility for quick victory that would lead to his breakdown and dismissal when the Schlieffen plan fell apart.

Retreat from Mons

Why the German plan to surround Paris fell apart, indeed, whether it need have fallen apart, is a question that has vexed military historians ever since. Many reasons have been given, from the sheer impossibility of such a forced march by a million men to the individual performances of the German army commanders – particularly von Bülow; the remoteness of von Moltke, the commander-in-chief, at Coblenz; and the often misguided but rousing, on-the-spot leadership of Joffre on the French side. What is clear, however, almost a century later, is that the BEF's role in spoiling the Schlieffen plan was minimal, unintentional – and yet effective beyond all logic; indeed, one might liken the BEF's performance to that of a pebble causing a horse to stumble momentarily before being kicked out of the way, yet causing it thereby to lose the race.

Relations between the French and British commanders were more hostile than those between French and German. The inaptly named Field-Marshal Sir John French, commander-in-chief of the BEF, and General Lanrezac, the neighbouring French general, despised each other *dès le premier rencontre*. 'If we are beaten it will be thanks to you,' Lanrezac's chief of staff remarked to Sir John already on 17 August 1914, anxious about the German march through Belgium and the slowness of the BEF to move into line. In the face of Lanrezac's bitter entreaties Sir John agreed to accelerate British participation, with a view to meeting the right wing of the German attack on the Mons–Condé canal – sixty-eight feet wide, with only eighteen bridges – where his 100,000 British troops duly took up positions, spread along twenty-one miles.

That fresh British troops, arriving by train and backed by artillery, only managed to hold for a few hours on 23 August the tired wing of a German army that had already marched 340 kilometres was certainly nothing of which Britain could be proud – especially when the BEF promptly surrendered the line, after suffering only 1,600 casualties, and retreated.

Retreat was the order of the day, however, as the entire Franco-British line west of Verdun fell back. As would happen in 1940, however, no previous thought had been given to such a possibility, and the withdrawal itself, from a command point of view, was chaotic. Very often orders did not reach the front-line units, and even at the upper echelon of command Field-Marshal French's headquarters abrogated its responsibility, instructing the two British corps commanders – who had never worked together – to arrange details of the retreat between themselves.

Fortunately for the British, Field-Marshal French chose, as his line of retreat, a compass line running south-west rather than south-east to Maubeuge, which the Germans would have encircled the next day. Thus the five BEF divisions withdrew before General von Kluck's irresistible steamroller: the British retreat from Mons becoming a rout, yet miraculously avoiding an encirclement that would probably have won the war for Germany.

Every line of retreat, however, must take account of terrain. In the case of the BEF, Sir John French's chosen line necessitated retreating beyond the forest of Mormal, which was considered impenetrable. It was in this situation that French, as BEF commander, ordered his two corps commanders to split apart and retreat on either side of the forest. Separated from Haig's I Corps by the Mormal forest, II Corps, under General Smith-Dorrien, ended up in Le Cateau on 26 August 1914 – and Smith-Dorrien refused to retreat further until his men had rested.

It was a few miles from Le Cateau that Monty first saw battle.

Le Cateau

In her book *1914: The Days of Hope*, Lyn Macdonald described the retreat from Mons as a remarkable performance – the men of the British Expeditionary Force having 'retired in a series of carefully calculated moves, changing places methodically, turning to dig in on a new position to meet the enemy'.[30]

This was rubbish – and certainly not how Monty's unit encountered the retreat. What the Royal Warwickshire battalion saw when it finally reached Beaumont on 25 August, according to its War Diary, was no methodical army withdrawal but an amorphous mass straggling southwards: soldiers mixed with refugees, all fleeing the Germans.[31] Finally, at 6 p.m., a day and a half after detraining at Le Cateau, the Royal Warwicks came under German horse artillery gunfire. The battalion offered no resistance, for at 7 p.m. it too received orders to withdraw as soon as the 18th Brigade of their own 4th Division had passed through, in accordance with Sir John French's wishes.

Already the hot, sticky day had given way to thunder, lightning and heavy rain showers. No rations arrived. At 11 p.m. the battalion began its own night march south-westwards through Beauvois to Haucourt, about twelve miles away. Wet and exhausted, the men finally arrived there at 4.30 a.m. on 26 August, and bivouacked for a few hours in a cornfield.

Aircraft observations had correctly indicated a menacing series of German divisions, both infantry and cavalry, converging on the Le Cateau front; but according to the official historian (who was at the time senior general staff officer (GSO 1) of the 4th Division) 'this very accurate picture does not seem to have been communicated to the corps or divisions, or to the cavalry'.[32]

This was to prove disastrous. The brigadier of the 10th Brigade had already the day before reconnoitred the terrain where his battalions would rest for the night of 25 August, namely the reverse of the ridge above the Warnelle brook, protected from German artillery sights – but he seems to have given no thought to how they would face the Germans if attacked at dawn, which they were.

It had been intended by Sir John French that the British retreat would be continued at 7 a.m. on 26 August, to avoid encirclement. However, even a withdrawal requires good positioning of rearguards to delay the enemy. General Allenby, commander of the Cavalry Division, urged the corps commander, General Smith-Dorrien, to get his divisions away before daylight, as he had insufficient forces to recapture the high ground overlooking the line of retreat at Solesmes. But, told that his II Corps units were too exhausted and too scattered to move before 9 a.m., Smith-Dorrien made a fatal decision to make a stand for twenty-four hours – 'to strike the enemy hard and, after he had done so, continue the retreat.'[33]

This was moonshine, since troops too weary and uncoordinated to retreat were hardly likely to strike very hard at the enemy. None of them were properly entrenched, and their bivouac positions had been chosen for shelter rather than defence. Thus between the villages of Ligny and Haucourt, west of Le Cateau, dawn of 26 August 1914 marked for Monty the beginning of his education in the cock-ups of real warfare.

Had the battalion simply continued the retreat, as Sir John French had ordered, there would have been no problem. Instead, thanks to Smith-Dorrien's insubordination, the retreat was suspended. The single battalion posted on the ridge, as Monty noted candidly in his *Memoirs*, 'was forward on a hill, covering the remainder of the brigade in the valley behind; we could see the soldiers having breakfast, their rifles being piled. That battalion was suddenly surprised by the Germans and fire opened on it at short range; it withdrew rapidly down the hill in great disorder.'

Seeing the covering battalion running away from the Germans, the Royal Warwickshires had either to retrieve the situation or flee themselves. 'Our battalion was deployed in two lines; my company and one other were forward, with the remaining two companies out of sight some hundred yards to the rear. The CO galloped up to us forward companies and shouted to us to attack the enemy on the forward hill at once. This was the only order; there was no reconnaissance, no plan, no covering fire.'[34]

In a letter to his father some weeks after the battle, Monty described what happened. 'At about 7.30 a.m. we made an effort to retake the ridge; it was terrible work as we had to advance through a hail of bullets from rifles & machine-guns & through a perfect storm of shrapnel fire. Our men behaved very well, though they were knocked down like ninepins; we reached the top but could not stay there & had to retire. I wonder anyone came off the ridge alive; the whole air seemed full of bullets & bursting shells. I was not touched. We had 8 officers wounded, some very badly, and I should think 200 men killed & wounded; the exact numbers are not known. We retired & entrenched ourselves & the whole of the rest of the day we were heavily shelled by the Germans.'[35]

It was a bloodletting Monty would never forget. 'If this was real war it struck me as most curious and did not seem to make any sense against the background of what I had been reading,' he related in his *Memoirs* over forty years later. That modern war would be 'awful' he had already acknowledged in his letters; that the units would go into battle 'knowing absolutely nothing, not even where the enemy is until we bump up against him',[36] he had accepted. Yet he had trusted, in his innocence, that at a higher level the staff would know what the brigade was doing and why; and also, at a local level, that his battalion commander would use some tactical intelligence in the disposition of his forces, especially in attack.

They didn't. The performance of the British army at Le Cateau was characterized by both lack of communication and, where contact was made with higher HQs, a constant countermanding of orders. The 5th Division's artillery brigadier felt that to conceal one's field guns 'lacked gallantry'; most of them were hit by German gunfire or captured. Infantry battalions had few machine-guns, no training in modern continental warfare, and command by 'umpiring': issuing orders/directives, and leaving others to carry them out. The result at Le Cateau was a massacre. The 4th Division was stretched across a five-mile front, with 15,000 unsupplied and unfed troops, without divisional artillery, signal companies, engineers, ammunition or cavalry. It was small wonder they were pulverized.

This was hardly the calculated and methodical retreat Lyn Macdonald mythologized. Years later Monty confided his own comic contribution to the attack: 'Waving my sword I ran forward in front of my platoon, but unfortunately I had only gone six paces when I tripped over my scabbard, the sword fell from my hand (I hadn't wound that sword strap round my wrist in the approved fashion!) and I fell flat on my face on very hard ground. By the time I had picked myself up and rushed after my men I found that most of them had been killed.'[37] Behaving like Zulus the two forward companies had thus lost two-thirds of their officers on the first day of battle! In his *Memoirs* Monty recorded the end of his first brush with the enemy: 'My Company Commander was wounded and there were many casualties. Nobody knew what to do, so we returned to the original position from which we had begun the attack.'[38]

Nor was this suicidal charge the end of the affair; for having sent the two companies to their death, Lieutenant-Colonel Elkington now abandoned them! As Monty's letter to his father went on: 'The army began to retire about 3 p.m.; we were right up in the very front firing line & somehow (through bad staffwork) we received no orders.' Only when the truth dawned on them, after dark, and they heard the Germans advance, did the remnants of the two companies, plus some lost souls from the rest of the brigade, decide to withdraw. 'About 10 p.m. we suddenly realized that we were alone & we could hear the Germans advancing in large numbers. So we hastily formed up & retired.' Lieutenant-Colonel Elkington, far from ascertaining the fate of his forward companies, had meanwhile ridden fifteen miles to St Quentin where, at the behest of the mayor, he and the commander of the neighbouring Royal Dublin Fusiliers battalion agreed that evening to surrender to the Germans if they appeared. 'Middle-aged men, both of them looked utterly exhausted. From their appearance they were suffering severely from the sun,' wrote a medical officer who witnessed the scene. 'Without Staff, without maps or orders, without support from artillery or cavalry, what could the remnants of broken infantry do before the advance of a victorious army, whose cavalry could have mopped them up in an hour?'[39] Both were subsequently cashiered for cowardice.[40]

In such confusion – 'broken infantry' rather than 'carefully calculated moves' – it was hardly surprising that Monty was posted missing by the War Office, and his parents informed accordingly.

The 'Retreat from Moscow'

For two days and nights Major Poole, the senior officer, led the group of Royal Warwickshire survivors by compass to try to catch up the retreating British army. 'I shall never forget that march; we call it the "Retreat from Moscow",' Monty related to his father.

'We were behind our own army and in front of the Germans; we had several very narrow escapes from being cut up and at times had to hide in woods to escape being seen by Uhlan patrols. We had no food & no sleep, and it rained most of the time. We were dead tired when we started so you can imagine what we were like when we finished it. Our men fell out by the dozens & we had to leave them; lots were probably captured by the Germans, some have since rejoined. The chocolate Mother had sent me was invaluable, as of course we had no rations all the time and there was no food in the villages. The villagers were all fleeing before the advancing Germans. All our kit was burnt to make room in the wagons for wounded etc. so we had only what we stood up in. We had passed our kit burning on the wayside; altogether the outlook was black and we were in low spirits. When we retired on the 26th we had got split up into two parties; it was a very dark night & somehow we got separated. There were 300 of us in the party I was in and about 300 in the other party.'[41]

The days of route marching in Yorkshire, and the hardening of the men's feet, had paid off, at least. In the end, on 28 August, Monty's group 'caught up our division & they put us on the motor lorries of a supply column; they took us to Compiegne which we reached at 3 p.m. on the 29th.'[42]

Breaking nerves

Such was Monty's account of his first experience of battle. What he did not tell his father at the time – not only because of censorship, but because he was still unwilling to analyse the fiasco into which he had been pitched – was that the entire business had been characterized by a typically English mixture of amateurishness, confusion, gallantry, cowardice, desertion, tenacity and luck, as a result of which thousands of men died or were wounded and captured, and the battalion CO (who should by rights have been shot) was dismissed from the army.

Smith-Dorrien's so-called 'stand' at Le Cateau cost the British army more casualties (killed, wounded and predominantly captured) than Wellington's at Waterloo: 8,482 men on 26 August alone. Nevertheless, despite his mishap with his sword strap, Monty's courage in attempting to bring back a wounded superior on 26 August, and his performance in the 'Retreat from Moscow', as he called it, must have impressed Major Poole, the officer commanding his fleeing contingent, for when Poole was subsequently made CO of the 1st Battalion he immediately promoted Lieutenant Montgomery to temporary captain and put him in charge of a company of 250 men – usually a major's appointment, as Monty proudly informed his parents.

The débâcle at Mons and Le Cateau, however, had meanwhile broken Sir John French's nerve. By a miracle he had evaded the claws of the German army – and, like General Lord Gort three decades later, he wanted now to separate the BEF from their seemingly doomed French allies, leaving the line altogether to 'refit', either in Brittany or Britain. Only Lord Kitchener's trip to Paris on 1 September 1914 stopped him. Reckoning on German exhaustion after the long Schlieffen march, Joffre bravely struck back at von Bülow's 2nd German Army; and von Bülow appealed in turn to von Kluck, commander of the 1st German Army, which had successfully rolled back the British, to abandon his victorious advance and shift sideways to help him. Reacting to the new French threat, the Germans thus stood in danger of losing the initiative.

Von Moltke should have ordered his army commanders to press on regardless (as would be ordered in May 1940) but he was now too far from his ever-advancing front to form a clear judgement. With von Moltke's approval, von Kluck's 1st German Army relinquished its pressure on the retreating British and swung back south-eastwards: *north* of Paris, instead of an encircling movement south-west, around the capital. The military governor of Paris, Gallieni, recognizing what was happening, launched the French 6th Army under Maunoury into von Kluck's broad flank.

It was a brilliant counter-stroke, which caused the Germans to panic. To their shame the retreating British – whose transport staff had been preparing St Nazaire on the west coast of Brittany as the BEF's new port of evacuation or re-supply, according to the outcome of the battle for France – were told to turn about and fight.

Monty, with the remnants of the 1st Battalion, the Royal Warwickshire Regiment, was half-way to St Nazaire when the new orders came through. They had been driven by lorry to Compiègne (where the eventual armistice would be signed), and to all intents and purposes had left the French to fight the Germans. 'We left there at 9 a.m. on Sunday 30th [August] by train & went by train to LE MANS & had a good rest; we were far away from war there & we lunched & dined in restaurants daily,' he explained to his father. 'I had my last bath there on 4th September, over 3 weeks ago.'[43]

Lord Kitchener's trip to France and the reappearance of the BEF, dragged from its French restaurants back into line after much delay, proved crucial, however – for once the BEF strengthened the French counter-offensive east of Paris, on the Marne, the thinly held gap between von Kluck and von Bulow's armies was exposed. As a result the British did not have to do much fighting, as von Moltke, who had moved his headquarters from Coblenz to Luxembourg, now lost *his* nerve – and Schlieffen's grand strategy came irrevocably to grief. It was the turn of the German army to retreat to a more defensible line: and from a situation of complete British rout, Monty now witnessed the Germans retreating – albeit in good order – before the troops of the BEF: the battle of the Marne.

Though von Moltke feared the worst, von Kluck, in his memoirs, claimed that by withdrawing he had not only avoided the danger of envelopment by French forces, but had created a new chance to envelop the attacking French – recording how he had 'kept in mind also how the mighty genius of the Great and Unique Frederick displayed itself, in situations strategically hopeless, in a lightning succession of victories, with all their political consequences.'[44] Von Kluck was therefore disgusted by the timidity of the German Supreme Commander – whose chief of staff, a mere lieutenant colonel, interfered in the battle of the Marne and ordered von Kluck to retreat still further, just as he was, as he saw things, about to roll up the French and British line from the rear.[45]

Whatever the truth, it was heartening to British soldiers who'd recently been fleeing for their lives to be now chasing the Germans for theirs. On 4 September 1914 Montgomery's battalion moved from Le Mans to rejoin the battle for France at Crécy, 'where the Battle of Crécy was fought', Monty noted in his letter home of 27 September.[46] The advance was heartening. 'From 5th to the 13th September we marched hard all day, generally starting at 4 a.m. and not getting in till 7 or 8 p.m. [. . .] Every day we saw fresh signs of a retreating army, such as dead horses and men, discarded stores etc. We usually reached places in the evening which the Germans had left in the morning.'[47]

The Germans, however, were merely withdrawing to a more manageable line, to which they could bring up reinforcements.

No time for washing

'On the 13th Sept (a fortnight ago today) we came up to them & that is where we are now' Monty related on 27 September; 'I cannot name the place.'

The BEF had reached the Aisne, after hundreds of miles of gruelling marches. On 15 September 1914 Monty had related to his mother: 'We are all very hard & sleep & eat whenever possible; we sleep in the fields in all weather, & none of us have colds. We ought all to have pneumonia as it rains hard most nights, but I suppose we are all too hard. It is not pleasant being under fire, especially shrapnel fire, but you soon get used to it & treat it with indifference. I command my own company now as my major got his leg broken in our first fight; so I ride a horse, as all company commanders are mounted. I have a big beard. I have not washed my face or hands for 10 days; there is no means of washing & no time for it. The necessary things are sleep & food; washing is unnecessary. Don't forget the cigarettes, will you.'[48]

Had the Germans now decided to call a halt not only to their retreating armies but to the war in the west, many millions of lives would have been saved, for the Schlieffen plan had clearly failed, and there was no back-up plan. This, however, is to speak with hindsight, knowing the eventual extent of the losses in human life and destruction obstinately incurred over the following four years. At the time it remained a matter of honour. Thus the Germans persevered with their attempted conquest of France – and the holocaust of the Western Front unfolded.

Bearded and bombarded

So far the war in the west had been a contest of manoeuvre, but as the Germans entrenched themselves by the Aisne the conflict began to take on its ultimate character – a far more terrible one than skirmishing, retreating and route marching: trench warfare.

On 20 September 1914 Monty wrote again to his mother, thanking her for the first parcel he'd received from home, including some peppermint creams from his sister Winsome. 'We get letters in strange situations,' he described; 'I eat the peppermints with a dead man beside me in the trench. I have been awfully lucky so far as I have had some very narrow shaves; on two occasions the man standing up next to me has been shot dead. The weather is perfectly vile; they say Sept is a very wet month in France. It is getting cold too and they will have to send out warm things soon for our men if they are to keep well. Any warm things you like to send out for the men of my company would be very acceptable.'

The future scourge against smoking and drinking was getting through twenty-five cigarettes – Capstans Navy Cut Medium – in three days, smoking a pipe, and relying on spirits to keep out the cold. 'I had an awful night in the trenches last night,' he recounted; 'it poured with rain all night & the trenches became full of water. I had to go forward visiting sentries etc all night to see they kept alert. Some were very far out to the front towards the German trenches & I crawled about on my stomach in mud & slush & nearly lost myself. The advanced German trenches are only 700 yards from us, so I might easily have been captured by one of their patrols. But good luck pursues me & I am quite safe. My clothes are in an awful state of mud & of course wet through. But it doesn't seem to matter much as I haven't even a cold after it; I came straight in my wet clothes, threw myself down and slept as I was, without taking off anything. I find that rum is a great standby; they give us some every day.'[49]

Two days later he remarked: 'I keep extraordinarily fit & well, and really believe that if I washed I should get ill!' The battalion was echeloned in forward and supporting trenches, each company taking it in turns to man the front line. It was 'here that we get casualties. We have had none today so far; it is now 2 p.m. The firing on both sides is generally heaviest in the early morning from 5–9 a.m.; we can't get the wounded men away from the forward trenches as stretcher bearers coming up would at once get knocked out. So they have to lie there till it is dark, with just a field dressing on the wound. We can see the Germans coming out of their trenches at dawn, stretching themselves & rubbing their eyes; we wait until a few collect together & then fire on them. They tried a night attack the other night but we beat them off alright. What we really want is some fine weather to dry up the trenches & get all our clothes thoroughly dry. It would be fine I think but for the guns; this morning it was beautiful but as soon as the guns began it started raining. Our men are all very cheery indeed, in spite of hardships and living as they are at high pressure. Of course they get very good food. They get biscuits, bully beef, bacon, jam, cheese, everyday and of course we get the same.'[50]

Bearded and bombarded, Monty was living on adrenalin as much as food. 'I shall not shave again till this war is over,' he vowed; 'I wish you could see me. If possible I will be photographed before being shaved, it would be an interesting record. We have only had one officer killed so far; a very nice young fellow called Knapton who had only been with us about a year,' he informed his mother. 'And will you write as often as you have time; tell anyone how much we out here appreciate letters from home, and cigarettes too! There is no doubt that when you are fighting in a strange country letters from home are one of the chief things that keep you going. I cannot write as much as I should like to as I have lots to do even when off duty, as it were. It is no small responsibility being in command of 250 men on active service & within 600 yards of the German Army; it is really a major's command and I am lucky to have it. I have 2 officers under me but the responsibility rests on me, & I am glad it does.'[51]

As regards the general war picture on the Western Front, however, Monty still trusted to the Allied higher commanders. 'The two armies are sitting watching each other & have been doing so for 2 weeks,' he noted in his letter of 27 September to his father. 'Our object is I think to hold them here while the French get round behind them, or there may be some other reason; we are not told much of the strategic plans.'[52]

Of all the lessons of World War I, it was the lack of communication between commanders and their troops that would be the most serious, in retrospect, to Monty – and the one he would seek to reverse in World War II. First, however, he had to survive the impending bloodbath.

Lasting over Xmas

Waiting for a strategic decision that would break the stalemate, Monty meanwhile described life in the new trench systems. The German artillery was superior to the British 'as they have with them the big siege guns which they had brought up to besiege Paris with. They have given us a very bad time & we have had 1 officer & a number of men killed. They are numerically much stronger than us & occasionally they attack our line, by day and by night. A night attack is not pleasant as you cannot tell what is happening; a lot of wild firing goes on & you are just as likely to be fired on by your own people as by the Germans. I am writing this under cover in a shrapnel proof shelter in our most advanced trench, as my company is on duty there. I can see the Germans in their trenches & occasionally we exchange shots; I bagged one man this morning, and one horse. The shrapnel is screaming overhead and altogether it is rather different from a Sunday at home.'[53]

Letters took just over a week to arrive. On 29 September Monty learned of his cousin Pleasance's death – which 'upset me greatly', he confessed. 'She was one of the few girls I have ever cared for and I liked her better than any of the others' – a sentence which his mother struck out before having it copied for other members of the family. Several of the latter were joining up, including his cousins Aubrey and Valentine, and his brother Donald in Canada. 'I wonder if any of them will come out here or if it will all be over before they are fully trained. It looks to me as if the war will last over Xmas,' he gave his own opinion. 'I hope it won't; it is getting very cold here now and I should think a winter campaign in this country would be awful, and the troops would die like flies from the cold. I think it is too scientific a war for it to last long; Europe would not stand for it; and where is the money going to come from?' he asked.[54]

Others were asking the same thing – trusting that the politicians would sort things out. Conversely, the politicians trusted in the higher military commanders to resolve the issue. But they couldn't. The war on the Western Front was settling into a mode that would permit neither side to break through; literally, deadlock.

Going through untouched

Like T. E. Lawrence, stationed in the Middle East, Monty wrote home as often as he could, and was irritated when chided for not writing more. Regarding the local paragon of correspondence whom his mother quoted, he remarked: 'I don't know where Paddy is but if he has found time to write long letters home he must be behind somewhere at the base or on the lines of communication. I will write whenever I can as you know, and when you don't hear you will know it is because of duty & work which prevents me.'[55]

Nevertheless, in one sense Monty's dream had come true; he had at last got his mother's full attention. He knew by now of the War Office's telegram to his parents during the battle of Mons – 'Regret to inform you that Lieut. B. L. Montgomery Warwickshire Regt. is reported missing this does not necessarily mean that he is killed or wounded' – and though he scorned it, he was proud to have survived, and that they cared. Moreover, in terms of his own honour or self-respect, he had undergone his baptism of fire. 'I keep awfully well in spite of the cold & wet; we are living under high pressure too as you can judge,' he wrote to his father. 'The continued shelling is rather trying. But you very soon get used to it; this is in itself a danger as you are apt to get careless and expose yourself too much.'[56]

No letter of his in the long ensuing years of attrition and slaughter ever so much as hinted at fear – though it was perhaps evident at times, between the written lines and the real lines. 'The soldier can feel intense loneliness during moments in battle,' he wrote towards the end of his life. 'In the early stages of the 1914/18 war, as a young platoon commander on a patrol in no-man's land, I was several times cut off from my men. I was alone in the neighbourhood of the enemy, and I was frightened,' he confessed; 'it was my first experience of war. I got used to it of course. But in those days I came to realize the importance of the soldier knowing that behind him were commanders, in their several grades, who cared for him. The general who looks after his men and cares for their lives, and wins battles with the minimum loss of life, will have their confidence. All soldiers will follow a successful general.'[57]

Meanwhile, when he heard his sister Una's young husband, Andrew Holden, was about to enlist, he wrote he was glad: 'We will want everyone before it is over and you have to take your chance with the shells and bullets. Some go through untouched, others are not so lucky.'[58]

Combat suited Monty, he found; he could at last be a 'real' man, among real men: his masculinity at last acknowledged by his mother, in a war that ought to be over by Christmas.

Instead, for him, it was almost over by October.

Protestations of love

Only two new officers had arrived from England to replace the eight lost at Le Cateau and after. 'I had a youngster join my company yesterday', Monty recounted on 29 September; 'he only applied for a commission the day war broke out so has had no experience; but he is very keen & will do alright I think.' Such paternalistic concern turned to a wry amusement in his duties as censor of his men's letters home. 'The letters are all very much the same; full of protestations of love to their sweethearts & hoping they will remain true etc. They all ask to be sent cigarettes, and some say "Thanks to our officers we are still safe." '[59]

Occasionally a delicacy would be found with which to supplement the government rations – such as hare and vegetable stew. 'It was a tame Belgian hare which an old French woman had in a hutch in her garden, white with pink eyes, & she was only too pleased to sell it to us for 3 francs. She killed it herself in front of us!' he recorded with astonishment – despite the horrors of human death he'd witnessed over the past six weeks. 'The scarcity of eggs is rather interesting. There are plenty of chickens about but the French people say the sound of the guns upsets them & stops them from laying.' He even cherished the idea of bringing home some souvenirs – two 'German shell cases, in splendid condition; they will clean up & polish & look very nice on each side of the grate or fireplace.'[60] He had formed a close friendship with Second-Lieutenant E. V. Briscoe, 'a young officer in the battalion', as Monty later explained in his annotations. 'He was my greatest friend in those days, being about 2 years or so younger than me. He occasionally wore an eye glass and the

soldiers called him "tin eye" '.[61] To his mother he confided at the time: 'I
have a very great friend here called Briscoe, who joined us from Sandhurst
about 18 months ago. I don't see very much of Waker and Bretherton
now as they are in the other half battalion, but Briscoe is in my half and I
have got to know him really well. We were together too through all the
very hard time we have had, & helped each other on. I never knew him
well before.' Briscoe's parents lived in London, in Kensington, and Monty
urged his parents to meet them, taking his letter recounting the retreat
from Mons with them so that old Major Briscoe, a former artillery major,
could 'explain to you lots of things which you may not understand in it'.[62]

It was the first quasi-romantic friendship, with a younger man, that
Monty had ever formed outside his family, and it was significant he'd
asked his parents to meet the young man's: as if to validate it. But it was
doomed – for Monty's days in battle with the 1st Battalion of the Royal
Warwicks were coming to an end, and Briscoe himself would be killed six
months later at Ypres.

A kick in the balls

On 7 October 1914, eight weeks after the war broke out, Monty sent his
last letter from the Aisne trenches. A few days later it was decided to
withdraw the BEF, currently wedged between two French armies east of
Soissons, and transfer it further north, in an attempt to outflank the
Germans – later misnamed the 'Race for the Sea'.

Unfortunately the Germans, with copious divisions released by the fall
of Antwerp, did the same. Outnumbered seven to ten, the British were
thrown into battle once again. 'We moved from our Aisne positions and
were transferred by train round to Belgium,' Monty recorded in his later
annotation to his letters. 'We marched back for 2 days, then by train, and
then forward into battle at Meteren. On the 13th October, I was again
a Platoon Commander; a retired Captain had joined from England to
command my Company.'[63]

The first Battle of Ypres had begun the day before, on 12 October.
Despite his demotion Monty was more confident of success this time.
'Poole was in command, and there was a plan and there were proper
orders,' he related in his Memoirs.[64] '10. a.m. On reaching FLETRE enemy
were reported to be holding high ground along ridge in front of METEREN,'

66

the Battalion War Diary recorded.[65] Major Poole, deploying all four of the battalion's companies, forced the enemy to withdraw from the high ground to the edge of the village. But ousting them from Meteren itself was to prove a costly affair – as Monty was to discover.

The German trenches had been dug immediately in front of houses, hedges and walls, and the earth scattered, so that the British found it almost impossible to sight the defenders. The day was wet and misty, precluding artillery support – an excuse which held good for the British but did not stop the Germans from using the high church tower as an observation point from which to see clearly the whole of the British advance, and direct their sniping and shelling accordingly.

Despite Major Poole's more intelligent command, the battalion was ordered at 11 a.m. by the divisional commander to continue its advance and take the village without artillery support. The result was almost as deadly as on 26 August at Le Cateau. 'Dash and spirit shown by all concerned,' recorded the battalion diarist[66] – but not before over a hundred officers and men had fallen.

The forward companies having been held up, C and D Companies advanced, with Montgomery leading his platoon and brandishing his sword. This time he managed to avoid tripping over the scabbard; but no sooner had he stormed the outlying German trench than he found a German soldier aiming a rifle up at him. Apart from ceremonial drill, no sword training had ever been given; so, abandoning his weapon, Monty leaped 'and kicked him as hard as I could in the lower part of the stomach', as he related in his memoirs. 'I had read much about the value of surprise in war. There is no doubt that the German was surprised and it must have seemed to him a new form of war; he fell to the ground in great pain and I took my first prisoner.'[67]

The village being still full of Germans the divisional general called off the Royal Warwickshire assault at 1.30 p.m. The first formal British attack of World War I was then ordered; the entire III Corps was brought into action, advancing on a five-mile front, with the 12th and 10th Brigades delivering a two-pronged attack to envelop Meteren. According to Monty's own version, 'I made my platoon take up defensive positions behind a ditch and hedge about 100 yards from the village and went out myself in front to see what the positions looked like from the enemy point of view – in accordance with the book!'

This was foolhardy, to say the least – indeed, betrayed the very excess of self-assurance he had warned against in his earlier letters. 'It was then that I was shot by a sniper,' he afterwards related; 'the bullet entered at the back, which was towards the enemy, and came out in front, having gone through my right lung but broken no bones. I collapsed, bleeding profusely. A soldier from my platoon ran forward and plugged the wound with my field dressing: while doing so, the sniper shot him through the head and he collapsed on top of me. I managed to shout to my platoon that no more men were to come to me until it was dark. It was then 3 p.m. and raining. I lay there all the afternoon; the sniper kept firing at me and I received one more bullet in the left knee. The man lying on me took all the bullets and saved my life.'[68]

Digging Monty's grave

According to surgeons' reports, Monty had received two bullets through the lung, but it was nightfall before the Germans withdrew from the village, and his men could bring him in. For negligible losses the Germans had held up an entire British corps, and inflicted more than 700 casualties. The 1st Battalion of the Royal Warwickshires had alone sustained casualties of forty-two killed and eighty-five wounded. Brave Major Christie who had led the assault at Le Cateau was killed, as well as Monty's fellow subaltern, Lieutenant Gilliat. Monty seems to have escaped the same fate only by virtue of the dead soldier lying on top of him: locked in an embrace of death.

'No further attempts were made by my platoon to rescue us,' Monty recalled; 'indeed it was presumed we were both dead.' When it got dark 'a party from my platoon soon came to me'. The soldier lying across him seemed lifeless 'and I was in a bad way'. The party had no stretcher, 'so four of them carried me in an overcoat to the road, and down it they met some stretcher-bearers from the RAP [Regimental Aid Post] who took me over and carried me down the road to an advance dressing station manned by RAMC [Royal Army Medical Corps] personnel. I was barely conscious.' Blood was pouring from his chest; 'the doctor reckoned I could not live and, as the station was shortly to move, a grave was dug for me'.[69]

'When he was at last taken back to a dressing station after dark he was in a very poor state', his colleague, Captain Clement Tomes, also later recalled, 'and, indeed, we heard that they had begun to dig his grave!'[70]

Monty, however, had assured his mother he would come home alive, and he did – but only just.

4

The Somme and After

A matter of atonement

For five days and nights Monty lay between life and death in a French hospital at St Omer before he was considered well enough to be moved. He was then taken by train to England, where on 18 October he began his recovery at the Royal Herbert Hospital in Woolwich.

His survival astonished his colleagues, who attributed it to his strength of will more than anything: '– perhaps because he was Monty!' as his former adjutant, Captain Tomes, put it.[1] Yet the extended struggle with death had a lasting effect on his health, his psyche and his career. He would always feel the cold (initiating the British fashion for jerseys and sweaters), and fear catching a chill; but it was the very shock of his wounding that most affected him. Hitherto the war, with its promise of death, had been 'an awfully big adventure', in Barrie's famous phrase; Monty's letters had treated it as such, boasting of 'bagging' his first German, wanting to have photographs taken of his beard by which to remember the period, and polishable German shell cases to stand by the grate or fireplace at home – even a German *Pickelhaube*, according to Captain Tomes, who recalled a story circulating the battalion that Monty when shot had been arguing with a German prisoner in the captured trench at Meteren, demanding the captive hand over his helmet.[2]

The awfully big adventure had very nearly ended there – as Monty, lying helpless in hospital, was pitifully aware. The truth of his near-fatal wounding was prosaic, not heroic. His foolhardiness had cost a brave English soldier's young life, a fact that was confirmed to Monty as he recovered: one of his own men, whose welfare he had been at such pains to look after. War was suddenly no longer a game, an adventure, a proving ground of one's masculinity, irrespective of

69

the opponent or enemy, or even one's own men; now, it became – as it had after his pyromanic misbehaviour at Sandhurst – a matter of atonement.

Recovery

In a sense, the rest of Monty's life would be a sort of second life granted to him; one in which he searched for, and developed, a new purpose: no longer a young man, but a grown man.

The first medical board to assess Monty's progress was called on 5 November 1914, only two weeks after his admission. Captain B. L. Montgomery (he had been promoted to substantive captaincy by Colonel Poole in recognition of his leadership during the attack on Meteren, and was soon awarded the Distinguished Service Order) was reported to be 'suffering from gunshot wounds of the right side of the chest with effusion of blood into the right pleural cavity'. Miraculously the 'wounds are now almost healed and the right lung is now beginning to expand satisfactorily', the latest medical examination showed. In its opinion, however, the board considered the chest wounds to be of such severity that their effects were 'likely to be permanent'.[3]

If the board thought that Monty's military life was over, however, it had misjudged its man. A month later the board reconvened to re-assess Montgomery's case – for on 5 December 1914, only seven weeks since his wounding, Monty claimed he felt well enough to leave hospital! Permission was granted, and he was given three months' home leave, but it was made clear he would never be allowed to go back to his battalion as a fighting soldier.

For Monty this was disappointing, yet it probably saved his life, for it would lead to his volunteering to become – without ever having attended Staff College – a staff officer at home in England, at the very moment in the war when Britain needed to train a completely new army of civilian volunteers. In this capacity Monty would develop a talent for training civilians that would place him, a generation later, head and shoulders over any other Allied general in World War II.

The tragic irony, however, was that this skill, as a trainer of men, was developed in World War I against a backcloth of mass homicide prosecuted by a new British commander-in-chief whose relentless butchery would destroy his nation's will ever to bear arms again – indeed led in 1933 to a famous Oxford Union debate in which the majority of students recorded their refusal, in the event of another world war, to fight for King or Country.

Given such a tragedy it would, Monty found, be insufficient simply to train civilian soldiers to perform well in battle, for their sense of the futility of war when led by bad generals was too marked. If democracy was to survive, in such circumstances and in armed conflict with totalitarian regimes, it would be imperative to find a new way of inspiring men to fight, and if necessary to lay down their lives.

Only by learning these two lessons would Bernard Montgomery – the one-time Sandhurst bully, whose foolhardiness in battle had cost a brave young man in his platoon his life – be able to transform the pathetic performance of democracy in war from humiliating defeat into victory. How Monty learned those two lessons – what lay behind the learning, the mistakes he made, the tragedies associated with the process and the secrets of his success – constitutes the next part of our journey through his life story.

Kitchener's New Army

Having lost the flower of its pre-war regular army at Mons, the Aisne and Ypres, the British government was left in 1916 with three choices: to explore with France the prospects of peace with Germany, now that the German conquest of France had been thwarted; to try to hold on in the trenches of France while pursuing the war elsewhere (as in the Middle East); or to assist France in winning victory over the German army by smashing the German line somewhere along its 450-mile Western Front, stretching from Switzerland to the English Channel.

To have any chance of assisting in the last – or stopping German forces from achieving the reverse – Britain would have to raise fresh troops, not only to replace fallen regulars and reservists, but to create, for the first time in Britain – which had never in its history had compulsory military service (save for naval press gangs) – a national army numbering in millions: Kitchener's New Army.

Recruiting measures (such as Kitchener's famous 'Your country needs YOU!' posters) ensured by the early months of 1915 an extraordinary surge of civilian volunteers – 1.1 million men – for Kitchener's New Army, from all walks of life. This triumph of patriotic propaganda transformed modern war and modern society – as well as the expectations of that society. The war, once a distant event in the Balkans, Russia, France and Belgium, now became not a professional war but a people's war, with the whole British nation – and its dominions and colonies – participating, from the men in the trenches, to women in the factories.

As Correlli Barnett has written, in contrast to France and Germany which had vast standing armies, the traditionally tiny British army was wholly unprepared for the influx of so many volunteers. Instead of funnelling them as reinforcements into existing regular or Territorial (part-time volunteer) units, Kitchener insisted on New Army battalions created under the aegis of regular army regiments: the traditional two-battalion county regiments sprouting as many as thirteen, fourteen, fifteen and more battalions, grouped then in New Army brigades and divisions, with 'dug-outs' brought back from retirement to officer them. 'The volunteers lived in improvised rented camps and wore firstly their own clothes, and later an improvised blue uniform. Their weapons consisted of now-obsolete rifles or broomsticks. Their senior officers and non-commissioned officers consisted of Boer War or even pre-Boer War regulars, brought out of retirement. These "dug-outs" were out of touch with the professional modernization of the army since 1902, and with modern weapons and tactics, modern organization and methods,' Barnett chronicled. 'They were totally ignorant of trench warfare.'[4]

It was to a brigade of such Kitchener New Army volunteers, the 104th Brigade, that Captain Montgomery – who had insisted the War Office find him a position, even if he was not allowed to return to active service – was now posted as brigade major, or senior staff officer under the brigadier general. The post was normally that of a major, but the urgent need for more troops meant that a regular soldier who had already seen action on the Western Front – and had won the DSO in the field – was highly prized, even if he was only twenty-seven, recovering from severe wounds, had never been to Staff College, and had only ever been a platoon/ company commander – in fact had only really held the rank of captain for three months in an English hospital ward before going home to Chiswick.

The commander under whom Monty was deputed to serve was, however, even less qualified for modern brigade command in Flanders: a brigadier general of the Royal Inniskilling Fusiliers, 'dug out' of retirement:

G. M. Mackenzie – 'a very nice person' Monty later noted in the annotations to his letters, 'but quite useless, and it would be true to say that I really ran the Brigade and they all knew it'.[5]

Monty's happy life as a knight-adventurer in a regular army unit, living in intimate proximity to his beloved men, in pursuit of almost childlike adventure in combat as a proof of his masculinity, was now over, his transformation into an 'apparatchik' or efficient staff officer, training civilian volunteers for the business of modern mass slaughter, about to begin.

Brigade major

'Bernard was fortunate,' his brother Brian recorded, 'as from the outset General Mackenzie, who was a wise and tolerant man, full of common sense, fully appreciated his Brigade-Major's worth and gave him all the support he needed, without stint of any kind.'[6]

This was no less than the truth. The overenergetic young subaltern had had his wings clipped by the Germans, in close combat. He had had time to reflect on his life and near-death. He did not wish to resign from the army, but at the same time, he wanted his second lease on life to be worth more, perhaps, than that of mere sword-brandishing. Thus he warmed to the challenge of his new job, despite or perhaps because of the complete ignorance of war displayed by the five thousand young civilians under his care. War is often society's ritualistic way of imposing order on the chaos of existence; Monty had been imposing order on his own chaos of feelings since childhood in acts of aggression and violence; now he could legitimately impose it on civilians who were, in a sense, helpless and in his power. He would see that they were given a reasonable chance of succeeding in battle on the Western Front, in trench warfare. General Mackenzie, having seen no service since the Boer War, had little to offer in this respect. Thus it was left to Monty to exploit talents he did not know he had: an almost psychopathic clarity of mind and decision-making, as well as a gift for instruction. Among traditional regular army blimps he was and would always be at odds – argumentative and difficult, as Brigadier Tomes later recalled. But in a New Army, with no regimental bores, no class or caste distinctions to maintain and full freedom to act on behalf of his brigadier general, Monty could test and develop his own skills in command, communication and, above all, *training*. His 'Colonial' background, his lack of sophistication and his sheer love of soldiering – of taking responsibility for dozens, hundreds and now five thousand young men who looked to him for leadership – empowered him in a way that had not been true before the war, and would end with the Great War, once the New Army was disbanded and Britain returned to the Edwardian snobberies and professional amateurism of peacetime regular regimental and imperial soldiering.

In other words, the misfit outsider became, for a brief time in World War I, a model insider, as he would a generation later, once given an army to command: decorated for bravery, highly competent, uninterested in preserving the traditional army hierarchy and zealous in his determination in 1915 to turn a 5,000-strong brigade of civilian volunteers from the Lancashire area into effective soldiers.

To achieve this transformation the secret, Monty discovered, was simple: namely to place himself in the minds of his charges. Patriotic, enthusiastic and willing if necessary to die for their country, the men needed a clear idea of what was expected of them in modern trench combat, and how to live up to those expectations. Of Monty this required powers of organization, planning, communication and delegation; the giving out of clear orders; ensuring orders were received and understood; and the training of units under command, from battalion headquarters down to companies and platoons, to respond to what was instructed. Certainly no one who served under Monty from this moment on would ever ignore or forget him. In the 'fog of war' his instructions, like his letters home, would be unmistakable, unconfusable, and understandable by anyone.

Unfortunately, such talents were now placed at the service of arguably the most callous commander in British history: 'Butcher' Haig.

Back to France

'He ought to have a brilliant future in the Army, and rise to high rank' Brigadier-General Mackenzie predicted already on 29 January 1916 as the 104th Brigade left for the front: for, after ten months as brigade major, the twenty-eight-year-old Captain Montgomery seemed to Mackenzie not only a born administrator but an outstanding trainer of troops. 'Be my stay with this Brigade long or short,' Mackenzie assured Monty's father in a farewell letter, 'I shall not fail, before I leave it, to bring his admirable services to the notice of the authorities, and to do all I can to further his advancement with them'.[7]

General Mackenzie duly did his best, Monty later recalled. 'The Brigadier did recommend me for Brevet-Major, and promotion on the staff. But as he was himself given the sack and sent back to England the following week – nothing came of it!!!'[8]

By then the brigade had been in line for several months, and the limitations of its commander had become all too apparent to senior generals, in the run-up to Britain's great offensive battle, the battle of the Somme: the latest brainchild of Field-Marshal French's successor as commander-in-chief of the BEF, General Sir Douglas Haig.

'I went through the whole war on the Western Front, except during the period I was in England after being wounded,' Monty claimed later in his *Memoirs*; 'I never once saw the British Commander-in-Chief, neither French nor Haig, and only twice did I see an Army Commander.'[9]

Monty – sickened in retrospect by Haig's brutality and isolation from the suffering of his men – was forgetting his own part in Haig's offensive, and his own naïve attitude towards it indeed, was forgetting that he'd actually paraded his brigade before Haig while preparing to go up to the front. 'We were out route marching, and he watched us march past,' Monty related to his still 'darling Mother' in February 1916. 'His military secretary, the Duke of Teck [*sic*], was with him and I talked to him for about 10 minutes. He is I think a brother of the Queen; he is very deaf and you have to rather shout at him. Haig looks very worn and aged: of course he had a very harassing time at the beginning of the war in the retreat. That was when he made his great reputation. He has been out here all the time and been in all the big fights, and I suppose a man of his age (56) ages quicker and hasn't the same rebound as a younger man.'[10]

Haig had not; indeed he had the obstinacy of a very old man: certain, as a cavalryman, that 'victory' would come from horsed cavalry 'breakthrough'.

Only cads and cowards

'The organization of the Army out here is quite wonderful and one could write several books about it all,' Monty the New Army staff officer lauded Haig's transformation of the BEF. 'All that sort of thing has improved a lot since I was last out. We have over a million men out here now, which is not bad. Of course they are not all up at the front, but there are quite ½ a million up and we have huge reserves behind and at the bases.'[11]

Like almost all his colleagues, Monty trusted that this massive increase in the size of the BEF would lead to a coherent application of strength on the battlefield. In the meantime return to the battlefields held no ghosts – or if it did, he was keen to exorcize them by direct confrontation. On 22 February 1916 he had related to his 'darling Mother' how he'd borrowed a motor car and 'went with Tomes to see the place where I was wounded, Meteren. It was most interesting going over the ground again and I remembered it all quite well,' he reported. 'The trench I charged and captured has been used as a grave to bury the Germans we killed. I saw the exact spot where I lay for over 2 hours while they shot at me. The place is just the same except for one haystack which is not there now. All the fields about there are full of graves of our men; the graves of Major Christie and Gilliat are well kept and in quite good condition. If you have their addresses their family's [sic] might like to know that I visited the graves and that they are being well looked after.'[12]

Such lack of emotion, side by side with a concern over the way the graves of his former commanding officer and colleagues were being kept, was uncanny; almost as if he'd outgrown the experience of their and his own mortality and was a spectator. This strange, dissociative quality now characterized his correspondence, even where it related to members of his own family. On 7 March 1916, for example, he wrote to his mother that four officers in the brigade had now been killed in the front line, 'two of whom are in Valentine's Regt, the 17th Battalion Lancashire Fusiliers. I hope nothing will happen to him; if anything did I couldn't telegraph to you, as they wouldn't send it. I would write at once but Aunt May would probably hear first as the War Office would telegraph to her at once. The best thing would be for him to get wounded at once, not dangerously; a broken leg would mean he would be home for a year and Aunt May would be quite happy.'[13]

Was this a premonition? Valentine was Valentine Farrar, Monty's cousin; like so many other young subalterns on the Western Front, Valentine would be unlucky. 'On a route march the other day,' Monty had reported to his mother, 'I stopped and rode beside him for a short time and he said the life suited him very well'[14] but Monty, knowing the divisional commander's penchant for raids – or 'winter sports' as Haig called them – was more sanguine. 'After a few days in the line we were ordered to prepare and carry out a company raid against the enemy's trenches,' he recorded in his Brigade History[15] – and Valentine was duly killed.

To some extent Monty blamed himself. Despite 'very complete preparations' and continual practice 'over a model of the ground to be traversed', as Monty recorded in his Brigade History, and 'in spite of very gallant leading' the raid turned out a complete 'failure, probably owing to our inexperience in such matters'.[16] Valentine, shot in the head, died in military hospital shortly afterwards. He was, Monty recalled sadly in his annotation to his letters almost fifty years later, 'a very nice lad'.[17]

Such 'unsuccessful' raids – i.e., ones that killed no Germans or brought in no prisoners – won black marks for the battalion and brigade commanders, who were made to feel incompetent, or insufficiently courageous. Worse, however, was in store for the brigade. With spring the thick carpet of snow and the freezing cold that had kept the trenches firm thawed, turning the British lines into a rain-sodden quagmire. In the autumn of 1914 Monty had predicted a cold winter would kill the men off like flies, and that the European nations would never stand for the inevitable casualties. He had been wrong; the governments of the European nations *did* stand for them, largely on the recommendation of the generals. Indeed, the very success of Field-Marshal Kitchener's recruiting campaign in Britain, the New Army organization and administration, war propaganda, military build-up in Flanders, and the extraordinary patriotic loyalty and stoicism of the men permitted Sir Douglas Haig to sell to the British War Council in the spring of 1916 the war's most terrible idea to date: a massive, broad-front British infantry attack that would supposedly permit horsed cavalry to break through the German lines north of the Somme, as in some eighteenth-century pageant. Why no previous offensive had ever succeeded in achieving breakthrough on the Western Front in World War I, what this horsed cavalry would do once it broke through, or how the quadrupeds would be protected from machine-guns, rifles and artillery, Haig seems not to have considered. Nor would he permit mere politicians in England to pose such questions, though he took for granted the absolute

and obedient loyalty of the officers and men under his command. He had
lost no fewer than 50, 000 men in the battle of Loos the previous autumn,
yet had blamed the commander-in-chief, Sir John French, for being unable
to break through the German lines – and for wanting, as a result of the
abortive offensive, to conclude a peace with the Germans 'otherwise
England would be ruined!' as Haig disgustedly noted Field-Marshal
French's view.[18]

Haig was made of sturdier stuff, in his own opinion. If he was, as has
sometimes been maintained, homosocial by nature, he repressed all such
feelings in absolute rigidity of purpose. Inarticulate in speech and completely lacking in imagination, he made up for his deficiencies by obstinacy,
steadfastness of will and conspiracy in the cause of his own advancement,
which he considered synonymous with the good of the British army. He'd
married a lady-in-waiting to the Queen, in his forties, after only a few
days' acquaintance; then, once he'd connived with her and the King to
become commander-in-chief of the British armies on the Western Front
at the end of 1915, he'd brooked no criticism or disagreement with his
brutalist approach to war. Only 'cads and cowards stood in the way' of
British military 'victory', in his view.[19] The Minister of Munitions, Lloyd
George, and 'a fairly strong party in the Cabinet' were 'opposed to
offensive operations in the Spring or indeed at any other time',[20] Haig had
been warned in January 1916 by the new CIGS, General Robertson –
who had come up from the ranks – but Haig, a Scottish aristocrat, had
other ideas. He hated the idea of a settlement with Germany, and was
determined to show what British 'manliness' could do. He had surrounded
himself with a staff of mediocrities, judging them by whether they were
'gentlemen': i.e., loyal to him. Anyone who did not support his suicidal
policies, either in the field or at home, was damned as either disloyal or
left-wing, or both. The result was to be death on a scale unknown in
British history.

Tours in the trenches

Meanwhile, like millions of fellow British and imperial regulars and
volunteers, Monty remained dedicated to his country's cause, dependable,
and loyal to his commander-in-chief. His keenness might be an irritant
to traditional fellow regimental officers seeking an easy sporting life in

peacetime; but in modern war, with the brigade constantly being moved to different sectors of the line, his imperturbable efficiency was a boon both to the constituent battalions and to Brigadier-General Mackenzie, his brigade commander.

Mackenzie's dismissal came as no surprise to Monty. 'I am sorry to say that General Mackenzie is being sent back to England,' he confided to his mother. 'They say he is too old to command a Brigade out here; I think myself they are right. He is 56 and is old-fashioned and out of date in most things he does; a younger, more modern, man is really wanted. He is a very nice man, quite charming, but that of course is nothing to do with it! I expect you remember I wrote some time back and said this would probably happen. [. . .] If a younger and more modern man is sent it will mean that I shall not have so much work to do; up to date I have had to do lots of things which the general ought to do himself. Of course the above is quite private.'[21]

Hitherto Monty had – like most young men of his generation – assumed the right of older men to hold senior command positions, while younger men did the real work. Mackenzie's replacement by a younger brigadier general taught him an important, and lasting lesson: for it vividly illustrated the advantage of younger generals in war.

The new brigadier general, J. W. Sandilands, was sixteen years younger than Mackenzie – 'a first class officer from whom I learnt a great deal', Monty remarked of him in his annotations.[22] The transformation in morale in the brigade was immediate – and for Monty remained an indelible example of how a new commander could alter the whole tenor and performance of a military force. 'I have rather changed my habits since General Mackenzie left and since the summer began,' Monty soon wrote to his mother. 'I get up every day at 6.15 a.m. Breakfast at 7 a.m. Start out at 7.45 a.m. Sometimes I go with the General; at other times we go different ways. We come back in time for lunch at 1 p.m. In the afternoon we do the office work and after tea we go round some places near our Headquarters or go & see the gunners or the Engineers and arrange plans. Dinner at 8 p.m. Then more work and bed at 10 p.m. if lucky. This is a pretty lively place –' but the censor struck out the reference to Neuve Chapelle as indiscreet. 'There is always a fair amount of shelling going on by day; at night it is very lively indeed, rifle and machine-gun fire going on most of the night. Our casualties here have been wonderfully small considering the place we are in. I have been very lucky myself in escaping the places most shelled. There are 2 ways up to the trenches and they nearly always shell the particular one which I am not using at that time.'[23]

Given the strain both of work and of continuous shelling the confidence with which Monty wrote from the front remained remarkable. Of his regimental colleague Major Tomes, at that time brigade major of 106th Brigade, he reported to his mother: 'I had a long talk with him. I don't think he was looking very well; he worries over things more than most people.' By contrast Monty, despite his near fatal wounds, seemed in his element as a staff officer. He was appalled by the destruction of Neuve Chapelle, yet somehow emotionally untouched by it. The place was 'really a most extraordinary sight. At one time it must have been quite a pretty little village; now there is nothing to be seen there at all', he related. 'The whole village has been razed to the ground and is nothing but a heap of rubble; not even the walls of the houses are left standing. Our line goes about 200 yards in front of what was once the village,' he continued in his dispassionate prose – as if, in some strange way, the thrashings he had endured throughout his childhood and his near-death at Meteren had beaten out all sentimentality, leaving a repressed but imperturbable twenty-eight-year-old officer who relished responsibility, and could in war cut a cruelly straight line between his job and his feelings.[24]

A fish in water

Outside the army Monty was, increasingly, like a fish out of water; indeed, he had already become a caricature of the serious military officer: energetic and self-confident in the ordered society of the military, but lost when at home. Brian Montgomery later recalled how, prior to leaving for the front again in 1915, Monty had gone into Goringe's, a well-known department store in central London, to buy a new hat for his sister Winsome – and how literal crowds had collected outside, in Buckingham Palace Road, at the extraordinary sight of the captain inside, with his bright red lapels and red ribbon around his own hat, lost amidst myriad ladies' hats, pointing wildly with his new swagger-stick, clearly out of his depth in a ladies' fashion store for the first time in his life. His parents, out walking that day, had seen the commotion, and joined the crowd, only to see their son inside, like an exotic wild bird in a zoo. Among the Montgomerys and Farrars it became, through Maud's telling, another ludicrous example of Bernard's social ineptitude.

Yet on the battlefield, amidst constant shelling and machine-gunning, the situation was reversed: 'normal' men traumatized and terrified, lost in the metaphorical fog of war while Monty retained a clarity of mind that made him a superlative staff officer, able to plan ahead, direct and supervise other men with cool efficiency that marked him – as Brigadier-General Mackenzie had perceived – for the very highest rank in the army, over time. It was as if his nerve endings had been cauterized: leaving him almost without feelings save those of family and army loyalty: utterly fearless, self-contained, focused. In short, modern industrialized war – so horrific to those of poetic or even normal sensitivities – suited him, despite his rudimentary British education and early experience in India.

General Mackenzie had given Monty the freedom and encouragement to create his own position as quasi chief of staff. But it was General Sandilands who now began to *teach* Monty, by example, the proper nature of the brigade commander's job: in particular the relationship between the brigade commander and his artillery and engineer commanders. This was a lesson of paramount importance in young Captain B. L. Montgomery's career, and a lesson he would certainly never forget. In modern, largely static siege war between competing artilleries, with engineers responsible for all aspects of the terrain from wiring to entrenchments and mining, war on the Western Front had changed, shifting from skirmishing and the need for imaginative tactical initiative to the grim, professional reality of siege warfare and siege-defences. Because Monty had missed the battle of Ypres and the bloodbaths of Neuve Chapelle and Loos in 1915, and because he was so good at organizing the various elements of siege warfare, he did not yet think to question its ultimate futility. Until, that is, the summer of 1916 and the battle of the Somme.

Pâté d'homme gras

By May 1916 both the Germans and the French had suffered more than 100,000 casualties in the struggle for the forts of Verdun; by June approximately twenty million shells had been fired by opposing artilleries. Casualties reached 200,000 men per side – and the front line scarcely moved. Yet Haig drew no lessons from this. He was all against a negotiated peace, reassuring his wife that the French would go on fighting for another year, 'but there are some weaklings about Paris and the south away from the war who would of course welcome peace'.[25]

Though not a 'weakling', Haig himself was 'away from the war' in all but name. He had eventually chosen to live in a comfortable château by the sea at Montreuil, sixty miles away from the trenches, 'on a hill with jolly rolling country all round and the sea breezes'[26] – where he was treated to mixed fruits, turtle soup, fresh meat and fish and foie gras supplied by Siegfried Sassoon's cousin, Leopold Rothschild, and brought over by the King's Messenger.

In planning his own British offensive, Haig had already asked Robertson in January 1916 to re-open the recruiting campaign for horsed cavalry, as he hoped to 'unleash the horses' as soon as he had worn down the enemy opposing his forces, in order to smash a passage through the German lines. At a conference of army commanders in March he emphasized the cavalry's role in exploiting a breakthrough – and a few days later insisted that his Cavalry Corps commander and protégé, General Gough, 'spread the "doctrine" and get Cavalry Officers to believe in the power of their arm when acting in cooperation with guns and Infantry', as there were 'some officers who think that Cavalry are no longer required!!!'[27]

Haig's obtuseness and the mediocrity of his staff would now cost Britain and its imperial forces casualties on a scale never before countenanced – though he persistently lied about them and deliberately misled his own government. Haig had originally intended to attack at Ypres, in the northern part of the British sector, but had been compelled to plan for an assault alongside the French on the Somme, at the southern end of the sector. Instead of assisting the French, Haig proposed a major British effort, however – an offer that became all the more important as the French found themselves fighting a terrible *bataille d'usure* at Verdun.

What *was* Haig's intention at the Somme? Given that the battle was to be the most costly in British history, it is an almost incredible truth that neither in 1916, nor today, eight decades later, are we sure. Did he mean to break through the German lines and exploit such a breakthrough? Or did he wish to reciprocate the battle of attrition at Verdun, but on British terms, in order to wear out the German forces? Or did he wish the Somme to be the right-handed blow of a double-punch: first at the Somme, then – two weeks later – at Ypres? No one in France, Flanders or Britain was clear – leaving historians ever afterwards to speculate.[28]

Given the terrible losses being suffered by the French, Haig certainly accepted that the French role in his planned offensive near the Somme would be limited – but it did not cause him to reconsider its scope; indeed, he rejected his 4th Army commander's initial plan as being insufficiently ambitious. Haig wanted a 'hurricane' artillery bombardment, but had not the guns to achieve it – or the artillery organization to co-ordinate it. Only four weeks before the Somme offensive, the new chief artillery officer Major-General Noël Birch, found no 'list of the guns in France in the office and very few books of reference on artillery matters', indeed found that 'altogether there was no artillery office at GHQ'.[29] Nevertheless, since the French had 'worn down' the German Army at Verdun, Haig assured Joffre on 10 April 1916, his own Somme offensive would be 'decisive' in bringing the Germans to their knees in the west – whatever this meant.[30]

Lord Kitchener, as the Minister of War who had raised the New Army, was not so sure. Kitchener, like the 4th Army Commander, Lieutenant-General Rawlinson, had tried vainly to persuade Haig to undertake only small attacks to prompt German counter-attacks, and draw off German reserves from the Verdun sector, but Haig got his way. As the new commander-in-chief of the BEF, he insisted he be given the chance to prove himself: and the 'Big Push' – despite its nebulous aim – was given the green light for early July 1916.

Criminal fantasy

Henry Rawlinson, Haig's senior infantry general, was sceptical. In February he had thought the terrain 'capital country' with 'any amount of partridges which we are not allowed to shoot', and predicted that 'we ought to be able to avoid the heavy losses which infantry have suffered on previous occasions'.[31] As the months went on, he became less sure – especially when Haig overruled his plans for only a short advance, into the enemy's first line of defence. Rightly or wrongly, Haig was convinced he would only draw in German reserves – rather than local units – if he blew a hole deep enough to force the enemy to react. Joffre's reduction of the French contingent did not alter Haig's determination, for the continuing slaughter at Verdun would achieve the object of French participation in the Somme battle, and might even make a British cavalry breakthrough possible, if pushed through with sufficient courage, he reasoned. By this means, one biographer has argued, German reserves in Flanders would also be drawn into battle on the Somme, allowing the British army in Flanders to break through to the Belgian coast – complete with British amphibious landings in the German rear; but if this was his plan, no one other than Haig was aware of it, and it certainly did not eventuate. Moreover, he even despatched to the chief of the general staff, in London, a strong letter claiming that, as long as he was retained as commander-in-chief, he alone was 'responsible for the efficiency of the Armies in France', and was not answerable to the government, Parliament or the people of Britain over use of the men with whom he was supplied.

Had he been a military genius, Haig's hubris would have been in the national interest. Unfortunately for Britain's soldiery he was not. He had been horrified to hear that the King favoured reducing the number of cavalry divisions, remonstrating that 'in order to shorten the war and reap the fruits of any success, we must make use of the mobility of the cavalry',[32] and forcing Rawlinson to plan for a cavalry breakthrough on the Somme. He appeared to have drawn no significant tactical or technical lessons from the great bloodbaths of 1915 – especially the vulnerability of horsed cavalry, the difficulty of using artillery bombardment to cut barbed wire (adapted from American ranchers, who designed it to hold back whole herds of cattle) – and above all, the manner in which no-man's land was now dominated by the machine-gun.

First day of the Somme

Haig's cavalry-breakthrough plan on the Somme was in retrospect so ridiculous that General Rawlinson later gave orders for all mention of it in army war diaries and files to be called back and destroyed. Haig's plan for his infantry battle, however, was equally suicidal. At Rawlinson's insistence a major British artillery bombardment was to be laid on, following which, on Haig's orders, some 120,000 British infantrymen would *walk* across no-man's land, without any covering fire whatsoever, in broad daylight, in a linear attack aimed at the second line of German defences. Thirty per cent of these infantrymen would, it was reckoned, become casualties, but their places would be taken by succeeding waves. When the survivors had burst their way through the German trench systems, armed only with rifles and portable mortars, three British cavalry divisions and two reserve infantry divisions were to rush through the gap they made, under General Gough, and finally sweep the Germans out of Bapaume. Relieved by infantry reserves, they would then drive the Germans out of the Arras salient.[33]

No one dared question the purpose of the offensive, or its planning. Haig's subordinate generals had observed how Haig had connived to get rid even of his own superior, the BEF's first commander-in-chief, for showing 'weakness'; inevitably they feared to lose their own commands if they counselled caution. General Rawlinson, for example, thought Haig's Somme battle plan overambitious, yet promised 'to carry out his plan with as much enthusiasm as if it were my own'.[34]

There were certainly large numbers of sacrificial victims now on hand. The once tiny British Expeditionary Force was growing in leaps and bounds. Forced conscription of able-bodied men to the age of forty-one had finally been introduced in Britain on 1 April 1916, and by the summer of 1916 the strength of the BEF had reached forty-seven divisions – including Monty's 104th Brigade in the 35th Division. In these circumstances, Haig reckoned, he not only enjoyed local superiority in numbers in his sector of the Western Front, but could afford almost limitless losses – either ignoring the lesson of Verdun, namely that if the French, though numerically inferior, had withstood prolonged German attempts to smash through their defensive line, the Germans would be equally tenacious in holding on to their own line, north of the Somme, or not caring if they did, since a battle of attrition would be to Germany's disadvantage, having to fight the war on two fronts.

A devout Scottish Presbyterian, Haig had been encouraged by his chaplain to see himself as God's instrument on earth – 'We are merely tools in His hands, used for a special purpose.'[35] He moved his headquarters temporarily to Beauquesne, nearer to his army commanders for the battle, and informed his wife that 'The men are in splendid spirits.' He claimed that 'The [enemy's barbed] wire has never been so well cut', and that the British 'Artillery preparation' had never been 'so thorough'[36] – even though it was less than half that used for French offensive attacks, was technically poor, and employed less than 8 per cent high explosive shells – the only ammunition capable of either smashing the enemy wire or, in a direct hit, reaching German machine-guns, which were kept thirty feet below ground until required.

Contrary to Haig's assumption, the British artillery barrage failed to cut the enemy's barbed wire, failed to subdue the German defenders in their deep trenches, indeed failed to hit a single machine-gun. The barrage then stopped for a full two minutes *before* the British infantry start-whistle – allowing the German defenders time to leave their dug-outs and man their trenches. As the brave British soldiers climbed out of their own trenches and attempted to cross no-man's land in bright, silent morning sunlight, there was nothing to stop the Germans from bringing up their machine-guns from their deep shelters and massacring the British as they advanced.

The slaughter of 19,000 British infantrymen – killed outright or who died from their wounds – in a few hours of battle on the morning of 1 July 1916 was bloodier than any previous episode in British military history: a sort of infantry version of the doomed Charge of the Light Brigade – wave upon wave of innocent British junior officers and men going 'over the top' towards the German lines, once the British artillery bombardment had ended, into the jaws of German machine-guns. By the end of the day almost 60,000 casualties had been sustained.

The massacre was sickening – though Haig did not witness it, nor make any effort to do so. The British infantry – each man weighed down by a 60lb pack – were ordered to walk slowly, not to run, or follow cover, lest they lose cohesion, or direction, or courage. Thus, behaving like English redcoats in an age of flintlock musketry, they were mercilessly cut down in their tens of thousands by a weapon not available to earlier opponents of the redcoats. For the Germans it was like slaughtering natives.

Even French observers, who had looked forward to the British 'Big Push' to relieve pressure on their front, were amazed at the blind loyalty, bravery and stupidity of the British – as were the German machine-gunners, who could not believe their eyes; indeed, many of them were incredulous at what the British generals were doing, sacrificing men's lives so callously and to no purpose whatsoever. Ludendorff's famous phrase, 'lions led by donkeys', said it all.

The order to move slowly and offer virtually sitting targets to the Germans seemed especially criminal. 'We were surprised to see them walking,' one German machine-gunner recalled, 'we had never seen that before. The officers went in front. I noticed one of them walking calmly, carrying a walking stick. When we started to fire we just had to load and reload. They went down in their hundreds. We didn't have to aim, we just fired into them.'[37]

Stupidity characterized every aspect of Haig's undertaking. The British officers wore distinctive, tailored uniforms, with Sam Browne belts and jodhpurs, so that they would be easily seen by their men; in fact it made them particularly easy for the enemy to pick off, given the slow walking pace that had been ordered. Far from being severed, as Haig claimed, the thick, often coiled German barbed wire was invariably left intact: and the sight of those unfortunate souls who reached it 'strung out like wreckage washed up on a high water mark' was revolting to both sides. 'Quite as many died on the wire as on the ground, like fish caught in a net', one private recalled – though Haig himself refused to look. As one historian, Hugh L'Etang, has commented, 'Certainly never before, nor since, had such wanton, pointless carnage been seen, not even at Verdun, where in the worst month of all [June 1916] the total French casualty list barely exceeded what Britain lost on her *one* day.'[38]

At Ovillers, on the Somme, the British 8th Division lost 5,500 men out of 8,750 in two hours; the defenders lost only 300.[39] Haig, however, refused to believe he had made a terrible mistake. At 11 a.m. on 1 July he telegraphed his wife to tell of his 'Very successful attack this morning', that he hoped shortly 'to get the cavalry through', and that 'All went like clockwork'.[40]

Haig was clearly obsessed by clocks, however badly they were keeping time. Indeed, for the historian, it was Haig's distance from the battlefield, his psychological removal from reality, that makes his case so seminal. Was he simply a man of his time? Can he be blamed when no other commander on the Western Front was able to break through, either? Should he have foreseen the stalemate and counselled defensive warfare, even negotiated peace (as he began to do in the early months of 1918)? What *is* the dividing line between competence and inhumanity?

By nightfall Haig knew the battle had been an unmitigated disaster, with at least 40,000 casualties – a figure which was soon revised to 57,000 – almost a third of them dead! (It would rise to 59,000 once the fatally wounded were counted.) Thus Haig had lost half his attacking armies in a single day, for almost no advance in the line.

Instead of reconsidering, Haig ordered that the bloodbath continue; he had, after all, been aware of the heavy losses the British army would suffer – indeed, five weeks before the Somme battle started he'd announced to newspaper correspondents: 'Three years of war and the loss of one-tenth of the manhood of the nation is not too great a price to pay in so great a cause.'[41]

Cajoled by Joffre – whose French forces had done better than the British on the Somme, achieving all their targets for significantly fewer casualties – and in turn by Lord Kitchener, who wished to conform to Anglo-French strategy, Haig now abandoned his notion of a punch with his left fist at Ypres, in Flanders, and continued the futile Somme 'push' for another three months – by which time British and Commonwealth casualties had exceeded half a million.

Continuation of the Somme

Like so many officers waiting in reserve, Monty was deliberately misinformed by higher headquarters as to the magnitude of Haig's first-day losses. Four days after the start of the battle he wrote to his mother: 'We moved South and are now in Reserve behind the big offensive waiting to be used if required. Just at first the push didn't go so well as we hoped but now it has settled down more and is going on very well. We have any number of troops in Reserve and the thing should be a success.'[42]

'Going on very well' and a 'success' was certainly how Haig chose to cover up the disaster – even calling *The Times* on the telephone from his headquarters to ensure the deceit was effective. 'Sir Douglas Haig telephoned last night that the situation was favourable,' *The Times* duly reported on 3 July 1916, claiming 'effective, nay substantial progress'.[43]

This was a travesty of the truth, as Haig – and his senior commanders – well knew. 'Lies for the cabinet; candour for the generals on the spot,' was the way one biographer summed up Haig's approach to reports.[44] He had reckoned he had up to 700,000 troops on hand, in and behind the line. After the first week of battle he assured his wife 'that before long the enemy's resistance will break down',[45] and on 8 July wrote that 'In another fortnight, with Divine help, I hope some decisive results may obtain.'[46] There was no question of '*discussing* peace terms', he wrote to his wife on 17 July, 'we must *dictate* peace terms to the Germans'.[47]

Yet to lose up to 600,000 casualties over the three and a half months of the offensive, for virtually no advance in the line or evidence of the German morale cracking, or reserves committed that would facilitate breakthrough elsewhere, was not only brutal but, since it led to no breakthrough there or elsewhere, criminal. It was small wonder that by the end of 1917, after Passchendaele, the Prime Minister withheld reinforcements for the Western Front because he 'refused to be Haig's butcher'.[48]

Once it became apparent that the German lines had not been broken, nor were likely to be, Haig and General Rawlinson began nefariously to change their Somme battle story – Rawlinson even recalling his guidance notes, issued prior to the battle, and doctoring the 4th Army War Diary to conform to Haig's new lie. No longer was the Somme to be a blow with the right, drawing in German reserves in order to facilitate a British attack at Ypres, at least in any foreseeable future. Instead, the Somme was to be *the* battle of the Western Front, a battle of attrition, bringing the German army to virtual hand-to-hand combat in order to destroy its long-term ability to resist. As the official British historian – creator of MI5 – explained the retrospective agenda of government publications, 'I hope to show and prove from German sources that the Somme was the turning point of the war since most of the best of the Germans were killed off. This could not be done without losing the flower of our manhood.'[49]

If so, what was the point? Why was the British Parliament not warned? Haig's vague plan, transmuted by pride and obstinacy into a battle of attrition, thus doubly doomed the 'flower of the nation's manhood', since British casualties were never less than twice those of the Germans, and in some cases were eight times as severe.

This disparity was kept concealed from politicians and general public alike. By retrospectively changing the purpose of the battle, Haig was able to avoid disgrace or dismissal. It was a brilliant strategy for keeping his crown, but one which squandered the lives of British and Commonwealth soldiers on a scale never dreamed of before – 'one of the most elaborate perversions of historical truth that has come to light,' as B. H. Liddell Hart would write in 1930 in *The Real War 1914–18*, after Haig's death, when the risk of criminal libel was over.

Haig's Edwardian inhumanity was made all the worse by his distance from the front, as commander-in-chief of the British armies on the Continent. 'While Haig slept in a cosy bed in a quiet country château,' one of his biographers later wrote,

and dined on the best food Rothschild could provide, his men lived in muddy, noisy trenches, sharing their bully beef and biscuit with big, bloated rats. It apparently did not bother Haig that his war was so much more comfortable than that of the men he commanded. Nor did he see any injustice in using the Army transport system to send meat and dairy products from the Army's store to his wife so that she would not have to suffer the shortages at home. The luxuries were the privilege of his class and his high rank. The idea of denying himself simply because there was a war on was unthinkable. Britain had not gone to war to destroy the Edwardian social system and the privileges it implied, but to defend it.[50]

In this class-divided system it was easy to treat casualties as mere 'statistics', and the men of the New Army as laggards and cowards. 'I am inclined to believe that few of the 8th Corps left their trenches,' he gave his own opinion of what had happened on 1 July, and accused the men of being 'amateurs' – even though the Corps suffered 14,000 casualties on the first day![51] The artillery, he claimed, had let him down, and so had the soldiers of his New Army – causing him to insist not on new methods, but on more of the same: 'more energy, more time, more guns, more men, and, therefore, more casualties', as one biographer put it – quoting an anonymous missive from a 'fan' which Haig kept in his papers, urging him to shed yet more blood: 'You shall report 500,000 casualties, but the Soul of the empire will afford them. And you shall break through with the cavalry of England and France for the greatest victory that history has ever known . . . Drive on, Illustrious General!'[52]

The stoicism and loyalty of ordinary men in obeying such fanatical, obstinate and self-deceiving commanders was phenomenal. Even the Germans were awed by the courage and blind faith of the British fighting soldiers. 'All along the line, Englishmen could be seen throwing their arms into the air and collapsing, never to move again. Badly wounded rolled about in agony, while other casualties crawled into shell holes for shelter. But the British soldier has no lack of courage. His lines, though badly shaken with many gaps, now came on faster . . .'[53]

Monty, serving as a brigade major, first in reserve, then at the very heart of the battle of the Somme, would for the moment be as blindly loyal as his fellow-countrymen. He did not question his orders, but merely marvelled at the scenes of human and material destruction. Certainly he never dreamed, in the summer of 1916, that it would become his historical destiny to reverse such a monumental display of inhumanity almost three decades later.

Big casualties

For several days Monty waited behind the front with his brigade for the inevitable summons to participate in the 'Big Push', unaware of the increasing scale of the disaster: 100,000 casualties suffered in the first three days. Not even increasing signs of failure dimmed his optimism. Though he noted that the pouring rain had postponed resumption of the offensive for two days and the conditions 'must be very unpleasant for the troops actually attacking', it did not occur to him for the moment that the offensive itself was a mistake; he trusted in the commander-in-chief. 'It will be very bad luck if it goes on', he noted of the rain rather than the British attack – yet all around him the ominous indications of failure were becoming evident.[54]

'We have had big casualties,' he reported to his mother, 'motor ambulances with wounded go through our present village all day and night. I don't know our total losses but they must of course be very large.'[55] Haig had promised his political masters he would call off the offensive if it met with a serious reverse; but he was not a man to keep his word to politicians, whom he despised – particularly politicians who purported to represent the 'common' people, for whom he had an equal contempt.

Initial failure thus served to strengthen Haig's determination to continue the battle, rather than causing him to question his aim, and he deliberately lied to the War Office and to the government about the astronomical casualties. He had become 'a devotee both of spiritualist practices and of fundamentalist religion', John Keegan has written; 'as Commander-in-Chief he fell under the influence of a Presbyterian chaplain whose sermons confirmed him in his belief that he was in direct communication with God and had a major part to play in a divine plan for the world. His own simple religion, he was convinced, was shared by his soldiers, who were inspired thereby to bear the dangers and sufferings which were their part of the war he was directing.'[56]

Such hubris was the death-knell for a generation – yet even to this day Haig's supporters and defenders extoll his integrity, steadfastness and sterling leadership in a sort of tragic paradigm of Haig's own inhumanity.[57]

Such continuing Haigiography testifies to the power of British patriotism and loyalty into which, as a British general, Haig tapped. The asininity of his horsed cavalry convictions was exceeded only by his wilful obstinacy as commander-in-chief when faced by the evidence that his battle had failed – and his deceit in covering up the enormity of that failure. Thus the suicidal 'Push' went on, with Haig and the headquarter staffs concealing and ignoring their casualties, while reporting only the numbers of enemy troops captured.

Inevitably, though initially held in reserve for a supposed breakthrough, the 104th Brigade was sucked into the bloodbath. 'My darling Mother,' Monty wrote on 12 July 1916, 'I have had quite an extraordinary time since last writing; and have seen and done a great deal.' Indeed, so overwhelmed was Monty by his experience of the past few days that he now committed what, in his later annotation, he referred to as 'a truly monstrous breach of security regulations. It was lucky for me that the letters were not opened by the Censor!!' he added in his later annotation – for he would certainly have been court-martialled.[58] By separate post he sent his mother a numbered list of village names near the Somme, so that in a letter proper he could, using the numbers, describe to his mother the exact movements of his formation in the great battle.

They took us in motor buses to [Bouzincourt], which is about 3 miles West of [La Boiselle]. We are now at [Ovillers] being heavily shelled and expecting to be ordered to advance at any moment. I have been over the whole ground and seen all the recent battlefields including [Beaumont Hamel, Hamel, Thiepval, Ovillers, La Boiselle, Contal-Maison, and Mametz Wood]. It was all most interesting. Of course the whole place is a perfect shambles: villages [Thiepval] and [La Boiselle] exist no longer. When I first saw them I was on a hill, just behind them & they were pointed out to me. But I could see nothing except about a dozen tree stumps; there is nothing else to see as the whole of them has been reduced to dust. I now realize what it means for a place to be razed to the ground; but you have to see it to believe it.

It will be a long time before we get all the British and German dead cleared away. They are lying about as they fell. All the wounded have I think been got back. German prisoners come in every day and all day. One dead German I saw this morning must have been at least 65. We are living in a dug-out, and a very damp one too. However one is very cheerful; the men wonderfully so. We have the upper hand of the Bosche as regards artillery and our guns must be very annoying to him. The shelling goes on all day and all night and at times is intense; the noise is perfectly deafening and at times one has to put your hands to your mouth and shout, even across the table during meals.

Albert is a very pretty little place. There is a gilt figure of the Virgin on top of the church tower there; its supports have been shot away and the figure is leaning out at right angles to the tower. The French say that when the figure falls completely down the war will end and the Germans be beaten. I expect you have seen a picture of it. I am very well indeed. No more now from yr loving son, Bernard.[59]

The Virgin did not fall, however, and the Germans were nowhere near being beaten, as Haig confided to his senior army commanders on 2 August.[60] Haig's greatest flaw – the insistence on reinforcing his failures in the vain hope he was inflicting more enemy casualties than his own armies were suffering – now compounded his initial disaster, not merely once, but time and again. On 20 July, three weeks after the battle began, Monty's brigade was ordered to take part in another suicidal British so-called 'advance'. Still Monty showed no sign of emotion at the terrible loss of life. 'My darling Mother,' he wrote three days later, 'I enclose in a separate envelope a further list of places, numbered so that I can refer to them by numbers. We are at present holding the front line just east of [Trones Wood]. [Bazentin-le-Petit] and [Bazentin-le-Grand] are just to our N.W. and [Delville Wood] is just to our N. Facing us is [Guillemont] with [Waterlot Farm] to our left front. [Maltz Horn Farm] is in no man's land.'[61]

These names, not to be found on any ordinary map of France, would become monuments to wilful slaughter – the graveyard of Kitchener's volunteer army, and an indictment of Haig as the greatest serial murderer in British twentieth-century history: guilty of 'criminal stubbornness', as the French historian Marc Ferro judged.[62] Even the much-excoriated 'Bomber' Harris, of World War II fire-bombing notoriety, would become responsible for indiscriminate butchery of *enemy* civilians, rather than his own men. Haig's indifference to the death of his men defies belief. Shirkers were sentenced to death;[63] the rest were enticed, encouraged, inspired, cajoled and otherwise coerced into a form of mass suicide, in which 419,654 British and imperial BEF soldiers alone were killed or maimed in cold blood, gas and murderous machine-gun and artillery fire on the Somme, and 180,000 Frenchmen: a record that has been likened in its callousness to the barbaric cruelty of certain Nazis – indeed, one that prompted the Royal Engineer turned university reader in psychology Norman Dixon to liken Haig to Himmler: emotionless, devoid of compassion or concern for casualties; an anal-obsessive who considered it his duty not to visit casualty clearing stations because they made him physically sick.[64]

Even the Australian official historian wrote that Haig slaughtered 'the cream of the British population, the new volunteer army'. Worse still, the young men – officers, NCOs and soldiers – advanced to their deaths: 'Inspired by lofty altruistic ideals traditional in British upbringing, in high purity of aim and single-minded sacrifice it was probably the finest army that ever went to war.'[65]

Even though he doctored and withheld the true casualty figures (only giving the government his estimates of casualties above supposedly 'normal trench warfare' figures[66]), Haig could not prevent the seriousness of the casualties getting through to the representatives of the people at home. Even his indefatigably supportive chief of the imperial general staff in London, General Robertson, wrote to warn him, on 29 July 1916, that 'The powers-that-be are beginning to get a little uneasy with regard to the situation. The casualties are mounting up and they are wondering whether we are likely to get a proper return for them.'[67]

There *was* no return, save for a few razed hamlets in an area seven miles square, into which thirty million shells were fired until no blade of grass was left. Some men were simply buried in the trenches themselves and covered in quicklime; others were given pine coffins, while endless stretchers bore away those of the wounded that could be reached under fire. Thus Haig's 'Big Push' got nowhere: securing a 'wedge of muddy ground, at no point more than about nine miles deep on a front of some twenty miles or so – and of no strategic value', as Monty put it in his *History of Warfare*.[68]

In hell

Had Haig bothered to meet or to interview survivors of his Somme battle, he might have seen the human, or inhuman, consequences of his 'wearing down' decisions. One sergeant watching survivors of the 1st Division coming out of the line wrote home that 'Those who watched them will never forget it as long as they live. They looked like men who had been in hell. Almost without exception each man looked drawn and haggard and so dazed that they appeared to be walking in a dream.'[69]

Haig refused to visit forward field hospitals, or to speak to survivors as they came out of battle: only as they went in. Indeed, he seemed to get an unnatural *frisson* from seeing the men of his armies parading before battle, just as he had watched Monty's brigade march past earlier in the year. He admired the men's courage and bearing, knowing as they did that they were marching towards almost inevitable extinction. 'To many it meant certain death,' he confided frankly in his diary the following spring, after his first visit to the battlefield, 'and all must have known it before they started.'[70] He himself had certainly known it; indeed, he seemed almost to derive a sense of power and satisfaction at the mounting losses: not only criticizing divisional commanders whose casualties appeared to him to be too low, but berating his own government for daring to question the rightness of his sacrificial offering.

One Australian subaltern, shortly before his death at Pozières, just to the west of Monty's brigade on the Somme, wrote home, regardless of the military censor: 'I want to tell you, so that it may be on record, that I honestly believe that Goldie [a compatriot] and many other officers were murdered through the incompetence, callousness and personal vanity of those high in authority. I realize the seriousness of what I say, but I am so bitter, and facts so palpable, that it must be said.'[71]

Regardless of consequences

Why did the men not mutiny?

'The readiness of millions of men to spend four and a quarter years killing and being killed', as Niall Ferguson put it, is a puzzle that has exercised thinking World War I historians to this day, but there is still no real consensus.[72] As Sir Michael Howard pointed out, 'Once at war, British and Germans went for each other with the stubborn fury of berserkers, engaging in a long, slow, horrible death-grapple from which neither was fully to recover' – yet the rivalry between Britons and Germans had, before hostilities, never 'reached, let alone surpassed, the level which had been normal in Anglo-French relations – with rare intervals – between Waterloo and the *Entente Cordiale*'.[73]

Berserkism clearly characterized the British refusal to count the cost of continuing the battle of the Somme. Certainly the letters Monty sent to his mother in 1916 show no criticism regarding the prosecution of the war, or indeed of the Somme battle. 'The fighting here has been very fierce,' he acknowledged on 23 July 1916; 'we have lost heavily in the Brigade, particularly in Officers. However you can't take part in a show of this sort without losing.'[74]

In his seminal literary survey of World War I, Paul Fussell would remark on the widespread use of such theatrical parlance, once civilian soldiers became involved in the 'show'. The troops had a 'real life' back at home in their countries, whether as salesmen or artisans. 'If "real life" is "real,"' then military life must be pretense. The wearing of "costumes" not chosen by their wearers augments the sense of the theatrical. So does the availability of a number of generically rigid stage character-types, almost like those of Comedy of Humors: the hapless Private, the vainglorious Corporal, the sadistic Sergeant, the adolescent, snobbish Lieutenant, the fire-eating Major, the dotty Colonel. If killing and avoiding being killed are the ultimate melodramatic actions, then military training is very largely training in melodrama.'[75]

For Monty it certainly was. Fussell, examining the psychology of individual response to a melodrama involving one's own demise, considered it was the very 'unthinkableness' of one's own death that made participants convert it into theatre. 'The whole thing is too grossly farcical, perverse, cruel, and absurd to be credited as a form of "real life." Seeing warfare as theatre provides a psychic escape for the participant: with a sufficient sense of theatre he can perform his duties without implicating his "real" self and without impairing his innermost conviction that the world is still a rational place.'[76]

Monty would be a prime example of this psychic response: his vocabulary, his humour, his caricaturing eye all transforming the mad into the acceptable. 'We have put in 3 big attacks,' Monty recorded in his letter to his mother of 23 July,' and I expect one more will finish us for the time being. They will take us out to refit and collect ourselves, and will fill us up with fresh drafts. The whole country round about here is a perfect shambles; everything absolutely shelled to bits. We have an enormous amount of artillery here and we shell the Germans all day and all night. His artillery fire is also very intense as he too has amassed a lot of guns against us. I have come through untouched so far though I had a narrow escape this morning. I was out on an important reconnaissance with another officer and 4 big shells (8-inch) burst quite close to us; he was hit in the head and I was not touched at all. Goodbye with best love from Yr loving son, Bernard.'[77] In that week alone his 104th Brigade suffered almost a thousand casualties – a third of its front-line fighting strength. Others, however, suffered 100 per cent casualties – but were expected to go on fighting 'regardless of casualties'.

Haig appeared to draw no lessons from the continuing maelstrom – and no one appears to have been able to make him do so. 'A major problem in Britain was that the war was run by the generals,' Monty later wrote. 'It was not understood by the British people that the higher conduct of war must lie in political hands.'[78] This, however, was written in hindsight. At the time he merely did his job: providing cannon fodder. Far from being pushed back, or expending more lives than the enemy, let alone being shelled into submission, the German armies slaughtered their attackers; and on 27 July Monty wrote to his mother, 'I was returned as wounded yesterday, but am still doing duty. We have had an absolutely hellish time the last few days and yesterday morning I went up to Trones Wood to help extricate one of our Battalions which had had a particularly bad time. They were scattered about all over the place and very much shaken up. To collect them I had to run about the place in the open between Trones Wood and Guillemont,' he related, dropping the disguise of numbers-for-names in his obvious state of exhaustion; 'the latter place is strongly held by the Germans & we have so far failed to take it. Heavy shelling was going on and I was sniped at incessantly by the Bosches. However I escaped with the exception of a bit of high explosive shell which grazed the palm of my hand. It is quite alright and I am at work just the same. No time for more.'[79]

On the last day of July 1916 Monty's 104th Brigade was finally withdrawn from the Somme battle, decimated and exhausted. 'The chief lesson to be drawn from the operations referred to,' wrote Brigadier-General Sandilands in an appreciation deposited with the War Diary the next day, 'is the time required to develop an infantry attack against prepared trenches ... In my opinion the attacks referred to [...] had but little chance of success owing to the lack of time for proper organization although it is not for me to say that there were not very good reasons for attacking regardless of consequences.'[80]

'Regardless of consequences' would be the BEF's epitaph, as the battle of the Somme degenerated into utter futility. Either peace negotiations were required, or a completely new approach to battle; Haig, now relying on a process of methodical attrition of the enemy's forces in the hope that the Germans might at any moment 'crack', regardless of the cost to the Allies, counselled neither.

As the 104th Brigade counted the terrible price paid for its abortive efforts in the battle of the Somme, however, Monty finally began to share his commander's view. Could British 'civilization' survive such a deliberate holocaust? Would it not sap the morale and faith of the combatants – and through them, their families and loved ones at home? To successfully attack an enemy in solidly held positions, using officers and men from civilian backgrounds, it was not enough to make them rehearse old lines; a new script, surely, was required.

No *imagination*

At twenty-eight Monty was still too young and too junior in the military hierarchy to question the conduct of Haig and the BEF's army commanders, but without doubt it was Brigadier-General Sandilands who helped him to recognize that the men of a largely volunteer, non-professional army could simply not be expected to penetrate well-defended trenches and defensive systems, in the face of machine-guns, mortars and heavy artillery, unless new tactics were developed, and with a better rationale than mutual attrition.

This lesson, however, had still to sink into a mind and a conscience that had been rendered immune to pain: a young man unwilling and almost unable to *feel*. A week later, however, in the serenity of a 'beautiful house with a charming garden' about forty miles behind the lines, Monty recorded his memory of the battle for his mother. 'I don't suppose anyone can realize the awfulness of the show generally in this Somme push unless they have been in it. The French who are on our immediate right say that Verdun at its worst was as nothing compared to this.' As far as he could see the Germans were far from being defeated: 'The Germans have had time to mass a very large quantity of guns here now and use them well. The only consolation is that if it is bad for us it must be much worse for the Bosche, as we are far superior to him in men and especially in guns. The worst thing he uses are gas shells,' he recorded – but the censor tore out the next page in which he described the 'new kind' the enemy was using.[81]

Monty had hoped for a month's rest and retraining, 'But I expect they will only leave us here about 10 days,' he wrote on 6 August 1916, the day after they reached their rest billets.[82]

Even ten days' rest and retraining was more than Haig would allow, however. After only four days Monty wrote: 'My darling Mother, We have left our pleasant abode away behind the line, and are now back in the line again in our old haunts, where I was wounded the other day. We were of course very annoyed at only being given 4 days rest; it certainly does seem rather absurd taking us all the way back there for 4 days. However we have to go where they send us though it is very annoying. I hope we shall come out of it alright this time,' he added – the first note of personal anxiety ever to creep into his letters home. He was suffering from severe headaches, he confided, and had asked his aunt May to send aspirin from England.[83]

Certainly, given his near-fatal wounds of 1914, Monty's physical resilience was extraordinary. A week later, back in the heat of battle, he was his old self again, though, having recovered from his headaches and with his hand completely healed. It amused him to receive letters from members of the family who had seen his name in the casualty lists – he later wrote that he was only persuaded to report the wound for official purposes in case it went septic and he died as a result of gas gangrene or had to have the hand amputated. Meanwhile the news of his cousin Rosella's engagement he found incredible: 'I haven't seen Rosella for many years and can't imagine her as engaged,' he told his mother.[84] Love and marriage, like 'real life', seemed inconceivable in the carnage of the Somme. Even his cousin Hugh, who was a GSO 2 on the staff of Monty's own VIII Corps, had been withdrawn from the line, he was so worn out.

'The King has been round this way,' Monty continued, 'but I did not see him. The Prince of Wales [later Edward VIII/Duke of Windsor] is on the Administrative Staff of the Corps we are now in; he holds a very junior appointment of course and I can't imagine that he does much real work.' Even within the 104th Brigade staff itself there had been some 'weeding'. 'We have just turned out our old Staff Captain, the one whom Father met at Masham. He has been with us for a long time now but was really getting too old. I am now the only member of the Brigade Staff left who came out from England with the Brigade, as the Signalling Officer was wounded the other day.'[85]

The accelerated return of 104th Brigade to the Somme very nearly fatally completed the weeding process. At Haig's insistence the battle went on and on. 'We have been up in the fight again,' Monty wrote home on 27 August 1916, 'and there has been no time for anything. I can give you no details about what we did as the censor is strict these days. But I had the narrowest escape I have ever had. I was up in the most forward part of our line one morning at 5 a.m. with the General and two orderlies. An 8 inch shell burst on the ground 4 feet from us. I was blown in one direction and the General in another. The two orderlies were also blown off their feet. We were covered in dust and surrounded by black smoke and fumes from the explosive. Not one of us was in any way hurt or touched by the shell or pieces from it. What saved us was being so close to it. All the pieces of a high explosive shell go up into the air and descend several hundred yards away so the safest place is either very close or some way away. Of course we were all a bit shaken but we got up and went on. On our way back about half an hour later we ran right into a very heavy artillery barrage. There was no way out of it except to go straight on, which we did and by some extraordinary manner came through it untouched. It was a pretty hot morning's work.'[86]

Haig was still contemptuous of the BEF's showing – especially that of 49th Division, whose 'total losses' were 'under a thousand!' as Haig complained:[87] less than the 10 per cent he considered minimum for a 'good show'. Monty's narrative, however, must have moved his own audience, for his original letter was evidently passed around the Montgomery and Farrar relatives and only a fair copy in a juvenile hand remains. In particular, though, Monty was concerned with what his troops could and could not be expected to endure. 'We came out last night and it has begun to rain this morning. We shall probably be going right away behind somewhere to rest and refit. I don't think we shall be brought up into it again: the men could hardly stand three helpings of that sort of thing. We were once again on the extreme right of the British line and fought side by side with the French.'[88]

'Helpings' was another psychically evasive term for futile slaughter. Uninhibited by censors, however, the Brigade War Diary told how on 23 August new orders had been received to attack Falgemont Farm – with the brigade's left flank 'in the air'. 'We were informed that the operation must be carried out at all costs,' Monty recorded; but in the end, after various 'misfortunes', the attacking battalion was simply not ready to launch the assault on the morning of 24 August, and Sandilands made this clear to the general. 'The Divisional Commander came to Brigade HQ at 9.30 a.m. and these facts were pointed out to him,' the war diarist recorded. As a result the suicidal attack was cancelled, and new orders were given out. The 17th Lancashire Fusiliers advanced and 'only suffered about 60 casualties'.[89]

'Only'. For Monty's brigade, however, this, mercifully, was the end of their current bloodbath, the survivors being moved to the Arras front while Haig relentlessly continued his 'Push' on the Somme for a further two months, claiming the British were inflicting defeat after defeat on the enemy – though most of the hamlets no longer existed after the fighting. By November, over 400,000 British[90] and almost 200,000 French casualties had been sustained, but the Allied line had scarcely moved.

Pawn in a military blunder

Later, the truth would dawn on Monty, as upon millions of British soldiers, that he had been a pawn in a terrible, indeed criminal, military policy. His conscience would revolt at the way the Allied offensive had been continued, long after it had become clear it was achieving neither a breakthrough nor a significant wearing-down of the enemy's will or forces with which to resist. It betokened a new kind of war, one where commanders, if their initial plans were stymied, simply switched to battles of attrition, designed to 'wear down' the enemy by killing and wounding so many of his troops that he could no longer continue the war. However, to achieve this the attacker had necessarily to kill and maim *millions* of the enemy before the task could be accomplished; moreover, since to attack is inevitably more expensive in life than to defend, it entailed a greater loss in blood. In this way the attacker's own will to continue would be tested to the point of insurrection, relying entirely on men's patriotism, loyalty to their officers, stoicism and group courage.

The risk in pursuing such an inhumane policy was incalculable. Not only would the 'flower of the nation's manhood' thereby be sacrificed, but the soldiery and the public, once they became aware of the true magnitude and despicableness of the slaughter, might refuse to enter such a conflict ever again. This was a price more awful still than the appalling loss of life, for it would, as events were to show, render democracy vulnerable, indeed prostrate, before a dictator willing to countenance vast casualties by threatening to start a new war.

Retrospectively Monty thus became 'amazed' at the way millions of soldiers had submitted to a battle of yards and inches, under a commander-in-chief content to sacrifice 10 per cent of his country's – and the Commonwealth's – young manpower, without calculating the moral, political, economic and social cost of such futility. As Monty put it in retrospect, 'the method chosen was simple frontal bludgeoning in repeated assaults. It was a basic miscalculation to suppose that such a method could prevail: all commanders underestimated the power of the tactical defensive. If the Allied commanders had been serious students of history, and had been truly professional soldiers, they would have realized early in 1915 that such frontal assaults were not going to achieve positive results. But this did not happen. They decided to continue the same policy on a more massive scale for the next year – which was not war as I understand it.'[91]

The problem, as Monty later came to feel, was that Haig, like Joffre, Foch and other commanders, had no imagination. 'Maybe he was competent according to his lights,' Monty later wrote of Haig, 'but these were dim; confidence of divine approval appeared to satisfy him. Nothing can excuse the casualties of the Somme and Passchendaele' he concluded.[92]

This, however, was written with hindsight, when the enormity of Haig's inhumanity had become clear. Haig, who died in 1928, would not have agreed. He remained obstinately convinced, both in the war and later, of his own 'success' – and was determined, where necessary, to falsify the record to demonstrate his rightness.[93] Fewer and fewer witnesses agreed. Even Haig's own chief of staff confessed, after the war, that 'the latter stages of the fight were hardly justified'.[94] Bernard Shaw, after a visit to the front, wrote that Haig 'made me feel that the war would last thirty years, and that he would carry it on irreproachably until he was superannuated'.[95]

The only impressive results

Eventually, on 3 November 1916, three months into the battle of the Somme, even the British War Committee concluded that 'the offensive on the Somme, if continued next year, was not likely to lead to decisive results and that the losses might make too heavy a drain on our resources having regard to the results to be anticipated'. It therefore decided to look at whether 'a decision might not be reached in another theatre'.[96]

Alarmed, Haig ordered yet another suicidal 'Push' on the Somme on 13 November 1916. It advanced only one mile – and was, as Haig's chief staff officer later confided, deliberately contrived in the hope of providing 'a good effect at the approaching Paris conference'.[97] Five days later he finally abandoned the disastrous offensive, claiming 'victory'. As Monty later noted, however, there were no 'victories' on the Western Front. 'The only impressive results in the European theatre were the casualties.'[98]

Disproportionate slaughter

Haig's conduct, or misconduct, of high command has exercised historians for decades. Given the level of British casualties, how was he able to escape being sacked, as his predecessor Sir John French had been dismissed? Why did young men like Montgomery go on giving the commander-in-chief their support – and their lives?

Part of the reason was Haig's doctoring of British casualty figures and deliberate magnification of German losses. 'The enemy's losses have undoubtedly been very heavy – far heavier than those of the Allies',[99] Haig lied a week after the battle was called off, though he was rumbled by a few, almost from the start. For example, Winston Churchill, briefly a major commanding a battalion in the trenches on the Western Front in the spring of 1916, had already circulated a memorandum on 1 August 1916, a month into the battle, in which he 'viewed with the utmost pain, the terrible and disproportionate slaughter of our troops. We have not conquered in a month's fighting as much ground as we were expected to gain in the first two hours. Nor are we making for any point of strategic or political consequence. The open country towards which we are struggling by inches is capable of entrenched defence at every step and is utterly devoid of military significance.' The battle, he pointed out in a special plea circulated among members of the British Cabinet, had no earthly chance of 'inducing a general withdrawal of the German armies in the West. In personnel the results of the operation have been disastrous.'[100]

Churchill, however, was ignored – his right to criticize having been irremediably damaged by his own costly failure in the Dardanelles and resignation from the government. Haig, when he heard about it, was furious at being criticized, and damned Churchill with the assertion that 'Winston's judgment is impaired from taking drugs'.[101]

'The command structure was based on obedience to superiors and suspicion of subordinates,' the historian Niall Ferguson has written, in an attempt to explain the lack of imagination and the futile slaughter on the Western Front.[102] In continuing to pursue his suicidal offensive the commander-in-chief of the BEF had an important personal ally, however, through his wifely connections: King George V, who had not only ensured Haig became commander-in-chief, but made him a field marshal for his command of the battle of the Somme. Haig also had supporters in the War Office, where regular army generals were just as keen to stop 'mere' politicians from telling soldiers how to do their job. Thus neither the first wartime Prime Minister, Mr Asquith, nor his successor at the end of 1916, David Lloyd George, were willing, yet, to sack a commander-in-chief who enjoyed the continuing stoic loyalty of his generals and troops, and under whom there had still been no army insurrection (apart from isolated, muted protests by individuals who were sentenced to death), despite the terrible casualties.

Churchill, disgraced over the Gallipoli fiasco, was an example here. Determined to obtain another job in government he was, despite his passionate private protest, unwilling to publish his controversial memorandum, which would have been damned by his fellow countrymen as unpatriotic, and would have caused him to be sidelined to the very end of the war. Discretion became not the better part of valour, but of lack of moral courage – and in a climate of patriotism and lack of public criticism, only men and women of real independence of judgement dared speak out. Serving officers and soldiers who did so faced court-martial; civilians faced call-up, imprisonment and/or denigration by their fellow countrymen. As D. H. Lawrence wrote of his fellow conscripts, after appearing before a medical board for call-up, 'Yes, I liked the men. They all seemed so decent. And yet they all seemed as if they had chosen wrong . . . Their manliness all lies in accepting calmly this death, this loss of integrity. They must stand by their fellow man: that is the motto . . . This is what the love of our neighbour has brought us to, that, because one man dies, we all die.'[103]

Thus, although Haig's 'Big Push' had ended in failure – failing to draw enemy reserves so that the British armies could attack elsewhere, failing to wear down the enemy decisively, in terms of attrition, and failing to secure ground of any tactical or strategic significance, while bleeding the voluntary British and Commonwealth forces to the point of impotence – almost no one in Britain dared say so, for fear of aiding the enemy. Haig was able to go on claiming that the Germans were being worn down by their losses and would soon crack, as he had claimed every few weeks throughout the battle – and went on talking with impunity of yet another 'Big Push' in 1917.

Here then was the 'great betrayal', that would almost result in the demise of democracy in the aftermath of World War I, despite the so-called 'victory' of the Allies. Stoic loyalty from below had permitted senior officers to cover up the truth, with no loyalty downwards, by leaders on behalf of ordinary soldiers whose lives were being squandered. When, on behalf of the latter, the poet and infantry officer Siegfried Sassoon published his anti-war denunciation in 1917 he would simply be put in a mental hospital, while Bertrand Russell would be deprived of his Fellowship at Trinity College, Cambridge.

The death instinct

As is clear from his letters, Monty voiced no protest at such mass slaughter in 1916 – indeed, seemed to obtain a certain personal fulfilment through his intimate involvement in destruction and bloodshed on such a massive scale. Nor was he alone. Reflecting on 'The Death Instinct: Why Men Fought', Ferguson rejected the 'selfish gene' theory beloved of geneticists – since dead men not only tell no tales but beget no offspring. Ferguson himself preferred Freud's 'Eros and Thanatos' dialectic. The prospect of death in battle was frightening, it was true, yet offered 'Cool madness', in the words of the poet Robert Nicholas;[104] certainly those with repressed sexualities seemed the most enthralled, Ferguson commented. Robert Graves, in love still with a male schoolfriend, experienced a distinctively erotic thrill from combat, maintaining his chastity in quasi-knightly service of his 'Dick' at home, Ferguson pointed out, while the Catholic priest, Teilhard de Chardin, served as a stretcher bearer and experienced a form of inner orgasm: 'emerging from within yourself an underlying stream of clarity, energy and freedom that is to be found hardly anywhere in ordinary life' as de Chardin described.[105]

Was Monty drawn to battle by similar desires? Certainly his letters to his 'darling Mother' reveal a young man uncommonly drawn to death and obliteration. It was as if, for all the stresses and strains of the battlefield, he came most alive when being shelled or shot at, his emotional armour protecting him in battle, as it would go on protecting him against 'narrow shaves', despite taking part in almost all the great battles of World War I on the Western Front from 1916 to 1918: Arras, Passchendaele, the Lys, Chemin des Dames and Amiens.

By then, however, he had changed: for it was in the final stages of the suicidal bloodbath of Passchendaele that the penny, finally, began to drop. Not only could British military operations be more professionally conducted, he learned, but the very art of modern warfare, expressed through the purpose and conduct of battle, needed to be revised, as World War I drew to a climax.

Third Ypres

On 6 April 1917 the United States of America declared war on Germany and joined the entente Allies. Paradoxically, instead of waiting to concert the efforts of the three major entente powers on the Western Front, Haig launched the battle of Arras. Within three weeks casualties rivalled those of the early days of the Somme débâcle, reaching 120,000 killed, wounded and missing – for almost no appreciable advance in the line.

Notwithstanding this failure – and in direct opposition to the Prime Minister's wish that he limit operations to small attacks while waiting for the Americans – Haig then ordered another bloodbath, which would prove as tragic as the Somme: the so-called third battle of Ypres, or Passchendaele.

Rawlinson's 4th Army had been sidestepped to the north; 5th Army, commanded by Haig's fellow cavalryman General Sir Hubert Gough, had been given the 'decisive' role in the Passchendaele attack, with the aim, once again, of breaking out with horses, to recapture the Channel ports and clear the Belgian coast.

Gough's artillery was dispersed all along his line, however, and the new German technique of defence – holding the front line only thinly, while keeping artillery and reserves of troops further back, trained for counter-attack – proved too much for the British. Haig duly falsified the facts at a meeting of the British War Cabinet, insisting that the opening attack had been 'highly satisfactory and the losses slight'.[106] To his wife he boasted that 'on the whole it was a most successful day's work and such a good beginning promises well for the future'.[107] To the government he deliberately lied, reporting that the 'total of enemy casualties exceeds ours by as much as 100%', and that he could 'drive the enemy from any position,' he claimed, 'without undue loss'.[108]

He couldn't; he could only dislodge the enemy a few hundred yards at exorbitant human cost: human lives which had ceased to have any reality for him other than as false figures on a page he would wave at his government, leaving the politicians to try to find out the truth from others – while he himself claimed they were disloyal to distrust him by doing so!

Far from promising well for the future, the third Ypres battle promised from the beginning a reprise of the Somme: almost 35,000 casualties suffered in four days. The long weeks of preparatory barrage had ruined the natural drainage capacity of the area – as Haig had been warned in advance by his engineers – and the sector became a quagmire, impassable by tanks. Even the cavalry held out no hope of getting through – as Haig himself recognized when he read an officer's letter home, opened by the censor, that revealed the cavalryman's despondency. 'Cavalry commanders above all,' Haig expostulated to his wife, 'should be hopeful!' The British were 'beating the Enemy', he insisted, lamenting how difficult it was to make this clear to people at home 'unless one is actually in the front area where the battle is going on, and one can see the ground gained, state of enemy prisoners, etc.'.[109]

Had Haig or the 'people at home' witnessed the state of the British dead and wounded they would have thought twice about continuing. By the end of August British casualties had risen above 50,000 men killed or wounded: the size of an army. Yet it would have to reach eight times that figure in killed, wounded and captured before the suicidal 'Push' was finally abandoned.

The greatest power in the world

Haig should, like Nivelle, have been sacked; instead, he kept holding out the prospect of beating 'the Germans before Winter' if 'our Government would only stir themselves', as he complained to his wife. Constantly tempting the government with the prospect of imminent 'decisive' military victory in return for so much human and economic sacrifice, he kept his position as commander-in-chief of the British armies on the Western Front, even though his vision of war and the purpose of victory were becoming increasingly empty. If the Germans cracked before the American armies entered the field, he posited in a stunning confession, 'Great Britain would find herself not merely the greatest power in Europe, but in the World. The chief people to suffer would be the Socialists, who are trying to rule us all, at a time when the right minded of the Nation are so engaged in the country's battles that they (the Socialists) are left free to work their mischief.'[110]

Such 'mischief' was, ironically, only inflamed by the waste of human life on the Western Front. As the casualties mounted, they could not be kept from the public, and Haig's credit began to run low. He had used the young men of his nation, indeed of the British Empire, as a human battering ram, yet the German door had not opened. 'Success' had become a meaningless concept, save as wanton human attrition. Reluctantly Haig had to ask General Plumer, a non-cavalryman, to assume command of Gough's offensive, which had achieved nothing. Plumer ordered a pause of three weeks while more realistic plans were drawn up and training carried out, with the limited objective of capturing the high ground and thick woods west of Ypres, and it was in this endeavour that Monty's skills as a trainer became more widely known.

Duck's paradise

As part of its preparatory instructions for Plumer's new autumn offensive the British IX Corps issued a sixty-page training document in the unmistakable style of its new GSO 2 (Training), the first of many training manuals and notes on war which Monty would issue in his long career. A mind uncomplicated by subtlety and unhindered by self-consciousness transformed the complexity of command and administration into a clarity that still shocks today by its absolute freshness and unfolding simplicity.

What was remarkable in these preparatory instructions was not the originality of ideas but their crystal-clear narrative presentation. Point by point, Monty set out a doctrine that would guide the largely civilian battalions, brigades and divisions of IX Corps in the coming battle – sixty pages, together with forty pages of appendices and twelve pages of maps, that laid down the current Plumer principle of 'bite and hold': the creeping barrage that would precede the men; the leap-frogging of fresh units through the advancing front line (later known as the 'expanding torrent'); the preparations for German counter-attack; communications with spotter planes furnished with wireless; the training of specialist units; the use of aerial photographs and intelligence; the provision of ammunition dumps and so forth. The ground itself was considered unsuitable for tanks, but otherwise the instructions would hold largely true for a further generation – expressed in clear language that was understandable by regular officers, volunteers and conscripts alike.

On 3 September 1917 constituent units of IX Corps were told that 'all plans for the offensive will be based on the instructions contained in the following publication issued by the General Staff', namely Monty's 'Instructions for the training of Divisions for offensive action'.[111] Four days later Corps HQ ordered that 'a full dress rehearsal of the attack in every detail will be carried out by each assaulting brigade in the Berthen Training Area. The services of the GSO 2 Training, IX Corps, [Montgomery] are placed at the disposal of the GOC 19th Division for the purpose of assisting in the preparation of the ground.'[112]

There followed the step-by-step assaults, starting in the third week of September 1917, which proved that, if battlefield operations were properly prepared and rehearsed, with clear, achievable objectives and co-operation between artillery, infantry, engineers and spotter aircraft, even non-regular British divisions composed of civilian soldiers were capable of breaching the most heavily manned German defences – advances which helped hearten the French and to which Monty pointed with pride when writing to his father on 9 October 1917: 'Things are going very well here and we are entirely successful every time we attack,' he reported. 'We are of course learning many very valuable lessons and there are few, if any mistakes. The attacks delivered on 20th Sept (Polygon Wood), 26th Sept (Menin Road), 4th Oct (Broodseinde), and today are really masterpieces and could not have been better. I don't know when I shall have leave: it is impossible to say.'[113]

Plumer's three autumn attacks were indeed models of preparation, training and execution, the troops not only achieving all their objectives but holding on to them despite relentless German counter-attacks. At Broodseinde 2nd Army captured 100 officers and 4,000 men in a single day. Above all, however, the operations demonstrated that if civilian soldiers were trained for a specific battle, with clear planning, realistic targets and full artillery backing, they could force the enemy to respond, thereby gaining the initiative and imposing greater losses by wresting from him the advantage of defence. This lesson Monty would never forget, indeed, it would become the cornerstone of the battle of Alamein, a quarter of a century later.

Towards the end of October Monty was confirmed officially as GSO 2 (Operations) IX Corps: and from 1 November 1917 all general staff orders in the Corps were signed by him on behalf of the brigadier general (GSO 1). He was becoming an operations staff officer of repute.

The weather had now broken, however, and Plumer, recommending that offensive operations be closed down for the winter, was transferred to Italy. Instead of consolidating his hard-won gains, as Lloyd George wanted, Haig insisted that he knew better. The area around Passchendaele, from the very beginning, had been 'a duck's paradise', as one biographer of Haig put it;[114] nevertheless, Haig now demanded a winter offensive, and the former Gough-led disaster was renewed.

Field-Marshal French, in England, had been scathing all along. Decisive results could not be expected 'if the decisive numbers do not exist, if the decisive hour has not struck or if the decisive place is ill-chosen'.[115] Any suggestion that the German armies were not cracking was, however, treated with contempt by Haig – who pretended to the War Cabinet that the British were inflicting twice as many casualties on the Germans as they were themselves sustaining; indeed, Haig ridiculed General McDonough, Director of Military Intelligence at the War Office, for his pessimistic assessment of the battle's effect on German morale, claiming McDonough's work to be that of a 'Roman Catholic' using 'tainted (i.e., Catholic) sources'.[116]

Thus ignoring intelligence that contradicted his faith in 'decisive' victory, Haig – anti-Catholic, anti-socialist, anti-politicians – insisted on extending Plumer's three limited operations into a do-or-die battle for the ill-fated Passchendaele ridge – against Plumer's and Gough's advice, and against the warnings of the Prime Minister. Plumer's comparatively successful attacks were escalated into yet another of Haig's bloodmires. 'The enemy is faltering and . . . a good decisive blow might lead to decisive results,' Haig told his sceptical army commanders – having assured assembled press correspondents on 9 October that 'the enemy has only flesh and blood against us'.[117]

The whole art of war

Sadly, it was British and imperial flesh and blood that was expended at Passchendaele – for negligible gains. Once again the result was criminal in its futility: 324,000 casualties, of whom 70,000 gave their young lives. Haig had literally slaughtered his own army, for nothing.

'The cold weather has set in and I am collecting my winter kit together,' Monty noted wisely to his father. Soon the winter rains began to fall – 'our best ally' as Crown Prince Rupprecht of Bavaria, commanding the German group of armies, put it. What had been a salutary demonstration to the Germans of British offensive capacity while waiting for their new American allies had been squandered in the mud of Passchendaele, where so many brave Canadians were forced to give their lives – lives wasted by a crazed commander who wished Britain to win the war on the Western Front unilaterally and become again 'the greatest power in the World', before the Americans could take the credit.

In the two weeks between 26 October and 11 November 1917, when Haig finally closed down the Passchendaele offensive, his continuation of the Passchendaele folly cost the four divisions of the Canadian Corps no fewer than 15,634 Canadian casualties – more than a quarter of its troops killed, wounded or drowned in the quagmires and craters; it was almost precisely the figure that its corps commander, General Currie, had warned Haig the battle would cost, before it began. As John Keegan remarked of Haig: 'On the Somme he had sent the flower of British youth to death or mutilation; at Passchendaele he had tipped the survivors into the slough of despond.'[118]

It was the senseless continuation of the battle of Passchendaele in midwinter and the suicidal gallantry of the Canadians that finally caused Monty to question the British conduct of war on the Western Front. However much Haig might fantasize about people at home seeing the 'ground gained', there was no such ground to be seen, only a muddy quagmire. Nor were there any British army commanders to be seen. Haig's chief of staff, Brigadier-General Sir Launcelot Kiggell, for example, due to return to England at Christmas 1917 at the end of the battle of Passchendaele, asked if, before doing so, he might 'visit the Passchendaele Ridge and see the country. When he saw the mud and the ghastly conditions under which the soldiers had fought and died he was horrified and said: "Do you mean to tell me that the soldiers had to fight under such conditions?" And when he was told that it was so, he said: "Why was I never told?"'

Monty, hearing this story later, was disgusted. As he remarked, the fact that 'the Chief of Staff of the British Armies in Europe had no idea of the conditions under which the troops had to live, fight, and die, will be sufficient to explain the uncertainties that were passing through my mind when the war ended.'[119]

Belatedly, Monty began to see the senselessness of what was actually happening. He had recognized the value of General Plumer's step-by-step approach when using civilian-soldiers, and had admired its achievements within the context of tactical strategy. He had then seen the lessons of this new approach thrown away in a return to suicidal bravery, the men being asked to achieve the impossible. 'At plain straightforward fighting they are magnificent,' he remarked of the Canadian troops in a salutary letter home in December 1917, following a visit to his brother Donald's unit, 'but they are narrow-minded and lack soldierly instincts.' Boasting of their prowess, 'they seem to think they are the best troops in France and that we have to get them to do our most difficult jobs. I reminded them that the Ypres Battle began on 31st July and the only part they have taken is during the last 10 days', at Passchendaele. Then, in a sentence that would encapsulate the twenty-nine-year-old's military philosophy for the rest of his life, he added: 'They forget that the whole art of war is to gain your objective with as little loss as possible.'[120]

The German Spring Offensive

Despite the British disaster at Passchendaele, Haig refused to resign. The British commander-in-chief had become a law unto himself. Strengthened in resolve by his army chaplain, he had mastered the art not of beating the enemy, but of turning 'black into white', as one biographer judged.

The government in England, aware of increasing protests against the conduct of the war, became desperate. Afraid to dismiss the commander-in-chief lest this demoralize the country after so much sacrifice, it nevertheless insisted there must be a scapegoat. It duly got one: Haig's chief of intelligence, Brigadier-General Charteris, who had fed Haig the stories of waning German morale Haig had so wanted to hear, at the cost of so many of his own men's lives.[121]

Charteris's head was not enough. He was soon followed by Haig's equally poor chief of staff, Kiggell, and the quartermaster general, Maxwell. Meanwhile the Prime Minister sent Field-Marshal Smuts and Colonel Hankey, the Cabinet Secretary, to France to see whether there was another commander who might take Haig's place as British commander-in-chief.

They could find no one, for there was no 'victory' to be won on the Western Front – at least, not without such horrific loss of human life that the winning of 'victory' became pyrrhic. Controlling Haig – refusing him political authorization to mount another disastrous unilateral offensive before the American armies were deployed in the field – was therefore considered the best and only option for the moment, while increasing the output of British tanks to 4,000 – against Haig's vain opposition – and trying vainly to abolish the cavalry, against Haig's more successful machinations.

Such a defensive policy, while building up American, British and French strength, offered the political prospect of a negotiated peace on acceptable terms. Yet the very prospect of such a build-up of Allied strength by American reinforcements, after Russia's withdrawal from hostilities following the October Revolution, was bound to cause the German military to consider a pre-emptive solution – and it did. Aware that Haig had now killed or maimed the best contingents of his own armies on the Somme, at Passchendaele and at Cambrai, Ludendorff had decided to attack the British rather than the French or American front.

Launched on 21 March 1918, the German steamroller, or 'Spring Offensive', penetrated the British front as no British offensive had ever done in reverse: indeed, the battle soon resembled the retreat from Mons. Monty's IX Corps headquarters was suddenly ordered to prepare an English Hindenburg line, called the GHQ line, some fifty *miles* behind the former British front line. On 25 March, in conditions of near panic, a suitable defensive line was identified in the rear, and Lieutenant-General Gordon and his staff set about marking it out.

The new defence line ran right up to the old Channel Ports. In the next weeks it would consume over 23,000 tons of barbed wire and necessitate the digging of 5,000 miles of new trenches. Meanwhile, as the German 18th Army under von Hutier smashed through the Franco-British 5th Army, only Ludendorff's misguided decision to halt his southern thrust and redouble his vain efforts at Arras, further north, saved the Allies from the inter-Allied split which Pétain had feared; and by the time Ludendorff revived von Hutier's attack, the pace of his drive was lost.

Haig had always resisted the notion of a Supreme Allied Commander, but Ludendorff's offensive made such bigotry redundant. Foch, a Frenchman, was appointed. Instead of Douglas Haig the commander of the 5th Army, Sir Hubert Gough, was chosen as scapegoat and sacked on 27 March 1918, together with his general staff ('I decided that the public at home, whether right or wrong, demanded a scapegoat, and that the only possible ones were Hubert or me. I was conceited enough to think that the Army could not spare me,' Haig confessed to a colleague the following year).[122] General Rawlinson, the most experienced BEF infantry army commander and British Military Representative at Supreme Headquarters at Versailles, was recalled and put in Gough's place. It was just in time; though the German Somme offensive carried some forty miles into Allied territory and reached the suburbs of Amiens, it then ran out of steam, having inflicted 175,000 casualties on the British in a fortnight.

By now Monty had been made a temporary major, and on 1 April 1918, while laying out the new GHQ line, his IX Corps headquarters was ordered to proceed to the 2nd Army to relieve the Australian Corps, six days before the second great German Spring Offensive, known afterwards as the battle of the Lys, began. The fighting was terrible, mustard gas mixing with the early morning fog, and an artillery barrage so intense and tactically directed that British communications were once again totally disrupted. On the morning of 10 April 1918, having put a Portuguese division at Neuve Chapelle to flight and broken through as far as Estaires, the Germans extended their attack further north, in the XV and IX Corps sectors overlooking the Lys. By the evening of 11 April the XV Corps commander had been relieved of his command, with the Germans having pushed as far as Meteren, the scene of Monty's near-fatal wounding, on the XV Corps front. Monty's IX Corps was forced back in tandem, though holding fast to the XXII Corps at its northern boundary.

For Monty and his colleagues it was a nightmare ten days, for IX Corps held the all-important Kemmel ridge, overlooking the Lys basin, which, if it fell, would provide the key to German victory. Throughout the battle Monty issued – as he had since November 1917 – all corps operations orders, involving some six divisions. Though the corps front was pulled back, the Kemmel heights were held, and the Germans proved unable to bring up sufficient arms and men to break the British line.

The issue of the battle had passed out of Haig's hands, and he could only appeal to the survivors of the armies he had so mercilessly slaughtered over the previous four years. Thanks to the extraordinary tenacity of the British and Commonwealth troops, the line, for the moment, held. But there was still more to come.

Chemin-des-Dames

Following the battle of the Lys French troops took over Monty's sector, allowing IX Corps headquarters to be transferred to a quiet French sector, charged with command of decimated divisions withdrawn from the British front in the north, on their way to reserve duty behind the French. Work was begun on 24 April training the 8th, 21st and 50th Divisions near Soissons – with Monty the officer in charge – when at noon on 26 May 1918 an intelligence report warned that, according to an interrogated prisoner, the Germans were about to launch a new all-out offensive in that sector the next day: the third Spring Offensive!

After the nightmare battle of the Lys in April, it seemed too much to bear. Once again, Monty's corps bore the brunt of the renewed German attack. In the battle of the Lys the six divisions under IX Corps had already lost a staggering 27,000 casualties; and it was precisely because of this that the Germans decided to smash through the IX Corps in its 'resting' French sector near Soissons, and thus threaten Paris – a manoeuvre which would then allow their northern armies to deliver a knock-out blow on Hazebrouck early in July, and push the British back to the sea.

Once again the German assault achieved tactical surprise – despite the fact that from 4.30 p.m. on 26 May all units of IX Corps were at battle stations. The French 6th Army commander had ignored Pétain's new doctrine of elasticity, and had sited his artillery, his reserves and his supply dumps far too close to the front line. Thus when, at 1 a.m. on 27 May 1918, the greatest artillery concentration of the war opened, the two allied corps were instantly condemned: 3,719 guns bearing down on a chosen area of the front.

By evening the Germans had penetrated some twelve miles. An entire British battalion, the 2nd Devons, was 'exterminated almost to a man' according to Sir Alexander Gordon's subsequent account.[123] But by brilliant staffwork the 21st Division managed to hold arms with its neighbouring French division on the right and pull back its left through hilly wooded country so that Rheims was secure. Though the German offensive smashed through the junction of the French and British forces, putting German troops on the river Marne within four days, it remained a diversion, Pétain surrounding and sealing off the salient with ample reserve divisions.

For IX Corps the Battle of Chemin-des-Dames, however, was a second inferno within six weeks, and by 30 May 1918, when German soldiers reached the Marne, 'the British fighting troops were reduced to approximately the strength of a division, and all of them had been placed under a single command, that of the 19th Division', as the corps commander later reported.[124] Casualties were horrendous, but the 19th Division, though technically relieved on 30 May, continued to supply units for the front, and on 6 June distinguished itself again by counter-attacking the seemingly successful German attempt to take the high ground near Epernay, overlooking the Marne valley. Haig was contemptuous of the French, recording on 13 June that 'Petain ought to have shot 2,000 instead of only 30 when so many mutinied this time last year,' and mocking the French system of '"leave" and "repos"'.[125] Whatever Haig might say, however, the Anglo-French line held. Finally, on 19 June 1918, the 19th Division was relieved, and at the end of the month IX Corps began to move back north to the British lines.

Monty was exhausted, but alive. On 3 June, immediately after the main battle, he was promoted brevet major (entitling him both to the temporary rank and pay of major and to accelerated substantive promotion as soon as a vacancy occurred in the permanent lists). The corps commander, in understated British prose, paid tribute to the work of his staff in such 'unique, unexpected and complicated conditions', but the commander of the Groupe des Armées du Nord was more lyrical in his praise:

Avec une tenacité, permettez-moi de dire, toute Anglaise, avec les débris de vos divisions décimées, submergées par le flot ennemi, vous avez reformé, sans vous lasser, des unités nouvelles que vous avez engagées dans la lutte, et qui nous ont enfin permis de former la ligne, où ce flot est venu se briser – cela, aucun des témoins ne l'oubliera![126]

The lessons of German breakthrough

For Monty the experience of meeting a massive German breakthrough would be of crucial importance two decades later, when in May 1940 the German Wehrmacht launched its great Blitz invasion of Holland, Belgium and France, towards Dunkirk – and once again in December 1944 when almost thirty German divisions of the waning Third Reich smashed through American forces in the Ardennes. In the meantime, in the spring and summer of 1918 he was not only a witness but a participant in the *Gotterdämmerung* of the Second Reich – for once the German Spring Offensive had miscarried it was to be possible, with almost two million American soldiers swelling the Allied line,[127] to start bringing the drama – begun in 1914 with the invasion of Belgium – to a close. To do so, the Allies needed either to negotiate peace with Germany, or to force a military victory over the German armies. The Allies chose to pursue the latter.

Again, Monty would play his part, this time as a lieutenant colonel, and chief of staff of a division, the 47th (London) Division, under 'a bachelor and senior Major-General in the Army': Major-General G. F. Goringe.

Serving the 'bachelor general'

'All the Corps Commanders under whom he served were junior to him in service,' Monty later recorded of General Goringe. 'But he was very unpopular and Haig would not give him a Corps.'[128]

Haig's animosity to the 'bachelor general' was to Monty's advantage, for here was a highly experienced battlefield commander who liked and trusted his thirty-year-old bachelor appointee sufficiently to adopt the German system of a single chief of staff, acting as the commander's deputy, as well as being in overall charge of all headquarters staff departments – administrative officers, engineers, artillery, intelligence and operations. Thus, despite his young age, Monty now assumed complete responsibility, under General Goringe, for the running of a division – involving 15,000 troops including infantry, machine-gunners, field-gunners, heavy artillery gunners, tanks, engineers and cavalrymen.

As in the desert a quarter of a century later, Monty did not waste time in taking over the reins – in fact, he began issuing orders at 8 p.m. on the evening before his appointment began. Within four days, moreover, on 20 July 1918, he had sent out a major new document that would form the basic fighting policy of the division: 'Defence Scheme, III Corps Northern Sector, 47th (London) Division'. In his unmistakably clear style it set out the division's frontages, tactical features, the responsibility of the division, and the action to be taken if attacked – including code-signs and calls he would issue from Divisional HQ to alert his brigades, the disposition of reserves and, in a series of appendices, the infantry, artillery, machine-gun, tank and signals dispositions – a remarkable manual to be drawn up within so short a time.

What became increasingly clear was that Haig and Joffre/Foch had almost lost the war by bleeding their own forces to the point where they could not withstand a massive German onslaught. Yet with the American army now taking a significant sector of the Allied line, the Germans were risking everything on their spring gamble; if it failed, the Allies would eventually win by sheer force of numbers – and by 1 August 1918 the first signs of this appeared, as patrols reported that the Germans were withdrawing over the Ancre, and the BEF, reinforced by hundreds of thousands of fresh troops, began to contemplate an attack once again. In a telegram to his army commanders on the first night of his new BEF counter-offensive in August 1918, Haig called upon his armies to be bold, claiming that 'risks which a month ago would have been criminal to incur, ought now to be incurred as a duty'.

That Haig himself used the word 'criminal' was illuminating, given the risks he had taken with the BEF since 1915. By the time of the Spring Offensive in 1918 he had, however, become no more than a figurehead, as local commanders stemmed the German tide, and once again this proved to be the case as, in August, the lessons learned from four long years of failure on the Western Front were belatedly put into practice by army, corps, division and brigade commanders.

Even now, however, there was no 'breakthrough', despite the growing demoralization of the German armies following their failure in the spring. Churchill, as Minister of Munitions, spoke of the war continuing into the summer of 1920, and Lloyd George did so too. The War Cabinet, in other words, had lost faith in Haig's promises of 'decisive' breakthroughs and victory. For this Haig had no one to blame but himself: he had cried sheep too long.

The hundred days

Certainly Goringe was unwilling to risk another Somme or Passchendaele with unseasoned troops in his own sector. Goringe therefore resolutely declined to give targets beyond those that were within the compass of his largely raw and untried replacement troops – particularly after the poor showing of the sister 18th British Division in the corps, which had taken the 47th Division's place in the front line for the new offensive on 8 August.

Recognizing the necessity for clearly defined instructions for offensive operations, and proper preparation if the replacement troops were to have a reasonable chance of success, Monty issued, on behalf of General Goringe, a new series of his own 'Instructions for the Offensive' on 18 August insisting that the division's attack be practised on selected ground behind the front, which he ordered to be taped out and made as realistic as possible, using live ammunition, as under Plumer. By the time the final word came to relaunch the assault he had issued seven consecutive preparatory orders to the division to ensure co-ordination of all arms, and was confident the division would achieve its targets. As he wrote to his mother, 'The day generally commences with an organized attack at dawn, after which we continue to work slowly forward all day; then another organized attack is arranged for the next morning to carry us forward again, and so on. It means little sleep and continuous work; at night guns have to be moved forward, communications arranged, food and ammunition got up, etc. etc. The general and I work out the next day's plan and he tells me in outline what he wants. I then work out the detail and issue the orders. Then I send for all the heads of each branch of the staff tell them the plan and explain the orders. They tell me what they propose to do to fit in with the scheme. If I think it is bad I say so and tell them what I think is a better way to do it; there is often no time to refer to the general and I take the responsibility on myself. I know his ideas and thoughts well now and so far he has always backed me up and approved of everything,' he noted gratefully. 'The heads of the various branches are all Lt-Colonels, older and senior in rank (but not in position as I am Chief-of-Staff) to me and one is a Brigadier-General. But we all work in very well together and they do what I tell them like lambs.'[129]

From platoon commander with charge of sixty-seven men in battle the young army officer had become, in effect, deputy divisional commander, responsible for 15,000 combat troops – all in the space of four years. The lessons he had learned were to be crucial, once a second world war broke out, for the secret of success in such large-scale military operations was not tactical exploitation – for which there was almost no opportunity – so much as the marshalling of the division's inherent strength: the cohesion of artillery, engineers, infantry and specialist units. It was a lesson of which Monty was justly proud – and the basis for his re-creation of the British 8th Army after its terrible failure in 1942. The German history of the 120th Württemberg Regiment, for example, described how in 1918 Monty's 47th Division 'rolled forward behind a mighty curtain of fire and thoroughly smothered the very mixed up combatants, who had to defend themselves simultaneously against infantry, squadrons of tanks, cavalry and aircraft. What did it matter if here and there our guns blew up a tank, if our machine-guns shot an attacking cavalry detachment to pieces, if our fighter aeroplanes shot down several hostile machines?' it recorded. The result was the same.

On 3 September 1918 the BEF offensive was halted in Monty's sector, and on 6 September 1918 the division was withdrawn and moved to XIII Corps, 5th Army, for rest and further training. It had captured 1,463 enemy troops as well as some 200 machine-guns and artillery pieces, but Monty was far more interested in the lessons of the battle than in its material fruits. Four days later, he issued a pamphlet to all the divisional units: 'Lessons learnt in Operations undertaken in August and September 1918'.[130]

The pamphlet was divided into ten sections: Communications, Headquarters, Tanks, Artillery, Stokes Mortar, Mounted Troops, Machine-Guns, Employment of Royal Engineers, Supplies and General Remarks. It stressed the need to develop tactical initiative rather than 'toeing the line'; the necessity for special training in order to knock out enemy strong-points and machine-gun nests; the importance of merging infantry and artillery headquarters; the advantages of varying times of attack in order to achieve tactical surprise; and the significance of wireless communications.

Now that Monty was chief of staff, mobile communications seemed to him the crucial factor in modern war, since they permitted the commander to reinforce success and maintain flexibility wherever there was failure. 'I devoted much thought to the problem of how to get to Divisional Headquarters quickly the accurate information of the progress of the battle which is so vital, and which enables a general to adjust his dispositions to the tactical situation as it develops,' Monty later recorded of this time. 'We finally devised a system of sending officers with wireless sets up to the headquarters of the leading battalions and they sent messages back by wireless. The difficulty in those days was to get reliable sets which could be carried by a man and would give the required range. Our system was very much a make-shift and often broke down; but it also often worked, and overall it produced useful results.'[131]

This, as Monty made clear, was the germ of another idea that he would develop in World War II: sending trained young liaison officers in jeeps to the advanced headquarters of fighting units so that the C-in-C had the most accurate, up-to-date information possible; an innovation that would in large measure be responsible for Montgomery's ability to take over two American armies during the Battle of the Bulge in 1944/45, and thereby restore order out of chaos.

The 47th Division pamphlet on 'Lessons learnt' meanwhile accompanied new full-scale divisional training orders, which Monty issued on 11 September 1918. The general principle to be borne in mind, Monty stressed in these instructions, 'is that we must profit as much as possible by the experience gained in the recent fighting in which the Division has taken part' and that 'this experience must be imparted to any reinforcements which may be posted to units'.[132] Not only were fresh troops and junior officers to be indoctrinated: the young lieutenant colonel was adamant that all the battalion commanders should also take part in brigade training exercises together with their staff officers, adjutants and, most importantly, the artillery, Royal Engineer and machine-gun commanders in the brigade groups. Clear training plans were to be drawn up before the exercises, with programmes of training to reach Monty 'at least 24 hours before the training is to be carried out', and reports made out afterwards, recording and analysing their efficacy.[133] Week two was to be devoted to battle drill and tactical exercises, using the extensive manoeuvre area that had been made available, while a divisional signals school had been started to work on new wireless communications.

Aged thirty, Monty had finally found his real métier: no longer Hotspur, or even administrator, but the brilliant, tireless manager and trainer of civilians: rehearsing them to perform as professional fighting men on a world stage.

Armistice

'These are stirring times and everyone is being pushed to the limit of their endurance,' Monty had written to his mother on 3 September 1918. 'We really have got the Bosche on the hop, he is thoroughly disorganized and it looks as if we might get away beyond our old battle grounds and get into country as yet untouched by shells etc. It will be splendid if we do that as we shall get into good billets again. At present I live in a tent which I have carried on my motor car; I prefer a tent pitched on clean ground rather than some bosche hut or dugout full of bosche straw and smells and bugs.'[134]

Ironically, smells and bugs disturbed him, but cordite and high-explosive did not. Offensive battle both absorbed and inspired him. 'The Division has been wonderfully successful,' he wrote with pride, 'and we have never failed yet to do what we set out to do, and we have taken a lot of prisoners.' By the end of September 1918 the 1st, 3rd and 4th British Armies had pierced the Hindenburg line, and the writing, for the Kaiser's Second German Reich, was on the wall – Ludendorff having urged since August that the German government open diplomatic avenues to a negotiated peace.

On 6 October 1918 news duly leaked that the Germans were requesting an armistice based on President Wilson's Fourteen Points, and in mid-October 1918 Monty's division rode in triumph through the town of Lille, which it had liberated. 'I rode with the General at the head of the Division till we reached the Grande Place,' he reported to his parents, 'then we got off our horses and stood with the Mayor while the troops marched past; it took 2½ hours for them to go by and even then we had left out most of the transport. The whole Division with all its transport etc. takes up 14 miles of road. We reduced the column to 8 miles by leaving out several units and most of the transport.'[135] Winston Churchill, the Minister of Munitions, sat on the stand behind Monty, together with General Birdwood, the 5th Army commander.

Yet the fact was, the jubilation of the French population masked the failure by the Allied High Command – Foch, Pétain, Haig and Pershing – to punch an Allied hole through the new German defensive line and bring the war in the west to a decisive military conclusion, despite the naval blockade, lack of supplies and growing German despondency. The British and French had largely fought separate wars, and Pershing's American army also battled on its own, taking monstrous casualties through insistence upon learning its own lessons, rather than from the bitter experience of others. Thus, far from cracking, the German armies pulled back as the French and British had done in 1914 – but without being routed. Pershing's American forces were fought to a standstill in the Argonne Forest, the French nowhere breached the German line, and Haig was unable to exploit a Canadian breakout.

Such was the result of the fighting on the Western Front. As the Germans negotiated peace terms throughout October 1918, Lieutenant-General Braithwaite, commanding Monty's old IX Corps, became infuriated that 'our own Damned Government' was not congratulating Haig, the commander-in-chief;[136] but the soldiers themselves seldom saw anything for which to congratulate him. Braithwaite's own son had died in the futile battle of the Somme; Haig's constantly promised 'breakthrough' had never come then, and it had not come now, as Haig himself knew, though commanding officers were putting the men into battle with greater professionalism than ever before. In this sense, Haig had evinced no genius, merely a stoic ability to suffer casualties and to inflict them. By late October 1918 Haig's five British armies were barely twenty miles forward of their 1914 line, not even having reached Mons, where they had started. Haig warned the new CIGS, Sir Henry Wilson, that the enemy was resisting fiercely, and was not 'ready for unconditional surrender. In that case there would be no armistice, and the war would continue for another year.'[137]

Negotiating a reasonable peace was, as it had been all along, the only humane course.

Rotten terms

But would the Allies offer terms the German government could accept? For the moment, in October 1918, Monty remained proud of his division's performance, but sceptical about the future of the war. Impressed by German tenacity and professionalism, it seemed to him all too probable that Germany would fight to the bitter end. The conditions which the French and Americans were insisting upon were too stiff, he felt. 'I think Germany's allies will drop off one by one,' he wrote home on 28 October, awed by the way the Germans were staving off their pursuers, 'but that she will go on to the end, as she is going to get such rotten terms that she will fight it out unless a revolution does them in.'[138]

Revolution soon did. Haig, recognizing he would never defeat the Germans decisively in battle, said he would be content to accept an offer of withdrawal from occupied areas as the basis of peace. However, Haig himself had personally ensured that the cost of the war made generous peace terms impossible; the price in human life, suffering and destruction too high for statesmen to be magnanimous. The German government declined the harsh terms, and the political situation moved inexorably towards German political and social collapse.

On 3 November 1918 the German fleet at Kiel mutinied, and on 7 November a revolution in Munich initiated a Bavarian Republic. 'These are certainly great times,' Monty wrote to his father, 'and the next fortnight will I think either see the Bosche accept our terms or refuse them. Personally I can't help thinking he will refuse them.'[139]

He was wrong. The internal situation in Germany – as once in Russia – was now in free fall. Germany was clearly fighting both an internal and an external war. The German civilian population was near to starvation, and in such circumstances further military resistance was pointless. The war could not be won, it could only be lost, sooner or later, and at further cost in men and money – as had been the probability when the Schlieffen plan failed in 1914. Germany was back at square one, having lost

1,600,000 men killed in the process, and many millions more wounded, maimed and taken into captivity.

Belatedly the German government in Berlin now chose sooner, and on the morning of 10 November 1918, the Kaiser was compelled to abdicate and flee to Holland. The next day, following German capitulation in Foch's railway carriage at Compiègne, the armistice took effect, with detailed terms to be dictated to a republican German government at Versailles the following summer.

For Monty it was an extraordinary and sudden end to a quite extraordinary war.

5

Peace

War to end all wars

The Allies had won World War I – on points. Had 'victory' been worth the twenty million war dead, though, their names gradually inscribed on municipal and village memorials across the world? Why had neither side been able to break through? Was trench warfare on the Western Front the face of future industrial, sledgehammer war – war in which human beings were not simply cannon fodder, but rotting food for rats? Or would a League of Nations ensure such a thing never happened again – a war that had ended all wars?

The holocaust of World War I would raise many questions. It brought down kingdoms and empires, gave rise to revolutions, the revising of state borders, genocide, economic ruin. Each country, new or old, had to adjust, in its own way, according to its own culture, the pressures of its neighbours – and a changing twentieth-century world. Some societies, such as Britain, retrenched; some chose or were swept down the paths of radical political and social change.

For Monty the adjustment was to be historic, as it would be for Winston Churchill. Changing political party, at one time voted out of the House of Commons, it would be Churchill's destiny to back British imperialism of the most flagrantly nineteenth-century kind, yet also to perceive the rising threat of Nazi Germany in the 1930s – and, as a politician of enormous experience and energy, to prepare himself and those around him to counter it, once given the power to do so. It would be Monty's destiny as a soldier to do the same – held back, ironically, for two crucial war years by the selfsame Winston Churchill, who had taken a personal dislike to him.

In due course, we will have to examine the possibly homophobic reasons for this. Only when all other military options had been exhausted, and

Britain's performance as a fighting democracy in World War II had reached its nadir, would Churchill be persuaded to promote Monty to army command in the field, thus ensuring Britain won rather than lost World War II. In the meantime, however, let us briefly trace the course of Monty's years in the post-World War I wilderness, from the end of 1918 to World War II, for it was in those years that Monty, reduced to peacetime rank, slowly rose from brevet major to major-general, becoming in the eyes of his superiors the most unpopular general in the British army – though not in the eyes of professional-minded subordinates and his military disciples.

More importantly, in terms of Monty's biography, it was during this period that the shy, homosocial major, wedded to the army, chose a wife and found, to his own surprise, a new life as husband, father and paterfamilias – an experience which, though ended prematurely by tragedy, was to have a profound effect on Monty's character.

The people's century

Rescuing the fate of democracy from the hands of incompetent superiors would prove an almost insurmountable challenge for Monty in the modern military arena, as it would be for Churchill in the political, battling back from unemployment, the back benches of Parliament, and continued subordination to Prime Minister Neville Chamberlain for the first, disastrous year of World War II.

Chamberlain's years spent guiding the (mis)fortunes of Britain are well documented; those of Bernard Montgomery, struggling against the forces of reaction in the British army, are less so. Yet it was during these years that Monty endeavoured to transform the democratic approach to war, on lines we take for granted today: professional, highly trained military forces working in intimate inter-service co-operation; promotion based on merit; great emphasis on proper planning, training and rehearsal; clear aims understood by officers and other ranks; and a strict concern to mind the body-count. Indeed, the enshrinement of the greatest art of modern, democratic war – as Monty had written to his mother during the disastrous climax of the battle of Passchendaele – was the achieving of one's objectives with the minimum, not maximum, expenditure of human life.

How, though, could such an approach to modern war be developed in a modern democracy, after the disasters of the Somme and Passchendaele? Haig had demanded, and got, the men he needed to bludgeon the enemy, and bleed him to death – but his 'victory' was pyrrhic. No British troops had mutinied during World War I itself, but the survivors did in the aftermath, dissatisfied with the pace of demobilization. Haig was furious, and threatened executions, blaming Bolshevism – the catch-all culprit in the eyes of Edwardian conservatives. Haig's vision of war against Germany was founded on a personal determination to 'purify and strengthen Britain', as his biographer Gerard De Groot put it, and 'no price was too high for so sublime a prize'[1] – that prize being the further expansion of Britain's empire and the preservation of Victorian/Edwardian privileges. But was such an expansion of empire what the people of Britain actually wanted in 1918? As Lloyd George and others knew, Haig was completely out of touch with social reality, if not actually out of his mind. 'In the Victorian age,' his biographer concluded, Haig's tenacity and ultimate 'victory' over the Germans 'would have been enough for him to qualify as a hero.'[2] But times had changed; it was no longer the Victorian era, but was rapidly becoming what the historian Eric Hobsbawm would call 'the people's century'. For Haig, fantasizing from the time of the Somme about government 'prize money' for his 'victories' so that he might be able to buy the family seat at Bemersyde,[3] and resolutely opposed to social change, change was unimaginable; indeed, having recommended as Chief of the Home Army in 1919 that troops be issued with live ammunition to shoot unarmed civilians in a general strike, he was sacked.[4] 'When Britain became a people at war instead of simply an Army at war', Haig's biographer pointed out, 'there was a corresponding alteration in the definition of victory' – something Haig, as a British upper-class bigot, determined during the battle of the Somme to see that 'a grateful nation' should make him and his family 'well enough off to make ourselves comfortable', whatever the cost in other men's lives, seemed unable to recognize.[5]

'Well, Field Marshal, I know the private [British] soldier very well, and there are people he criticizes a good deal more strongly than General Nivelle!' Lloyd George once remarked when Haig pompously declared British soldiers would never serve under a French commander-in-chief. But Haig did not even understand the remark.[6] He was 'a dour, inarticulate and laconic Scotsman from the upper echelons of society for whom gentlemanly values were sancrosanct', his biographer noted; Lloyd George, by contrast, saw himself as the friend and champion of the common man. In a new, 'people's century' it was a vital distinction – and one which would have profound ramifications on Monty's career as 'the people's general'.

Class distinction

'Before the war,' Paul Fussell has written, 'the British exhibited the most conspicuous class system in Europe' – a society almost on a par with the caste system in Hindu India. As George Orwell observed, in Britain in 1910 'every human being in these islands could be "placed" in an instant by his clothes, manners and accent'.[7] Even army regiments were ranked, Fussell pointed out, 'in a strict hierarchy of class, from the Guards at the top to the Territorials at the bottom'.[8]

This British military hierarchy had swollen, in war, to a gargantuan size, but without serious revision of the class/caste system. *The Making of an Officer*, published in 1916 from articles in the London *Times*, was typical of its time. In the anonymous author's view, the 'regimental officers of the Old Regular Army' had proved at Mons that they were 'probably the finest officers the world has ever seen'.[9]

As Monty knew, this was ridiculous; the performance of the British army at Mons was pathetic, the use of swords by officers typical and comic, the lack of training for modern continental warfare a scandal. His own CO had even been cashiered, along with the CO of the neighbouring battalion, for cowardice. Yet the anonymous 1916 author extolled the keeping of a horse by every subaltern, lauded 'the utter horror with which an officer regarded any possible disgrace to his uniform',[10] and deplored the way the modern regimental mess, in war, was becoming 'the gathering together of a number of civilians'.[11] Nor did this attitude change after the war – some families even complaining that their dead sons and relatives, as officers, were being buried in the same part of the war cemeteries as 'other ranks'.

Monty, although a regular army officer, saw things differently, as we have seen. His sexuality, in terms of his exclusively homosocial interests, had marked him out from other officers from the start as an eccentric. In the grim business of war, however, his love and caring for his men, allied to an almost psychopathic clarity of mind in the stress and strain of battle, had led to his rapid promotion as a staff officer, and had given him, under

Goringe, the 'bachelor general', a vision of how a modern army should be organized, trained and led in wartime. Now peace had come, his ideas needed to be rethought and reflected upon. 'By the time the 1914–18 war was over,' he later wrote, 'it had become very clear to me that the profession of arms was a life-study, and that few officers seemed to realize this fact.'[12]

An uncertain future

Reduced to the rank of brevet major in March 1919, on demobilization of the 47th Division, Monty had been posted as a staff officer to the headquarters of the British Army of the Rhine in Cologne. One of his duties, on behalf of the commander-in-chief, was to take a distinguished visitor, Sir Peter Fryer, by car around Germany, and the French battlefields of the Western Front, including St Mihiel, Chemin-des-Dames and Verdun. ('A very nice round [trip] and over 1000 miles by car altogether; he is a rich man and I get all my expenses paid. It will be very interesting seeing Verdun and St Mihiel; Rheims & the Chemin des Dames of course I know.[13]) However, the summer of 1919 also brought the signing of the punitive Versailles treaty, and with it Monty's recognition that his own job at GHQ would be axed. 'My plans will be very uncertain for a bit,' he wrote to his mother on 18 August 1919. 'I shall get away from here about 1st September and will not come back again; the Army is being broken up and my job (Operations) ceases to exist. So I shall bring all my kit home and will ask the War Office what they propose to do with me. I shall try and get a good long leave out of them, a month or more.'[14]

Bearding the commander-in-chief

For many regular army officers the transition back to England and peacetime soldiering was a chance to pick up where they had left off in 1914. For Monty it was not. In the management of fighting forces in war he had finally found his *grand métier*. He was determined to build on that – and was mortified to discover that, despite his distinguished performance as a staff officer ever since the spring of 1915, his name did not figure on the list of students selected for entry to the army's Staff College at Camberley for the one-year course beginning in January 1920. Yet it was now, in the aftermath of a continental war which so shattered all preconceptions, that he urgently felt the need to study what had happened, and to consider the implications. Invited one day by the commander-in-chief of the British Army of Occupation in Germany to a tennis party at his house in Cologne, Monty therefore armed himself not only with a racquet but with the determination, if the moment appeared opportune, to put his problem before his host.

Sir William ('Wully') Robertson, like Lloyd George, was a man of the people: the first British field marshal to have started in the ranks as an ordinary soldier. He had been CIGS from 1915 to 1918, and had loyally backed Haig as commander-in-chief of the BEF, but like Kiggell and others had been sacrificed instead of the real culprit. Monty's keenness to learn more about the art of war and its better administration impressed Robertson; a few weeks after the tennis party, Monty heard that his name had been added to the 1920 Camberley student intake.

Robertson did more than send Monty to the Staff College, though. He promoted Monty once again to temporary lieutenant colonel as the new commanding officer, from 5 September 1919, of the 17th Battalion, the Royal Fusiliers – one of a number of battalions that had been detailed to maintain a presence in the Rhineland while peace terms were signed and put into effect. It was, as Monty nostalgically recalled in the annotations to his wartime letters 'a battalion of young soldiers, all under 20'.[15] As he told his brother Brian, he enjoyed the experience enormously as 'I had already seen so many examples of how not to command a battalion'.[16]

Monty's opportunity to lead such young men, however, was short lived. It would not come again for ten years. On 22 January 1920 he stepped back down in rank to brevet major, and after spending Christmas with his parents, he duly entered the army's Staff College in Camberley, ready to start studying the 'business of modern war'.

A bloody menace

The British army's Staff College came as a great disappointment to Monty. The dictates of war on the Western Front had given rise to a new professionalism by 1918, holding out the promise, as in the German army, of a new military meritocracy based on ability and hard work, rather than indolence, social snobbery and conniving for advancement.

Anxious to begin a thorough study of the military arts, past and present, Monty had certainly not banked on the Staff College returning to its pre-war preoccupation with hunting, socializing and cavalry concerns. 'I was critical and intolerant,' he confessed later[17] – an attitude that certainly did not endear him to the directing staff, who considered him a 'bloody menace', as his brother Brian remembered.[18]

This is borne out by an apocryphal story that circulated in his regiment, the Royal Warwickshires, thereafter. Colonel P. J. Gething recalled almost sixty years later how 'at the Staff College – this is only hearsay – one of the students was court-martialled. His sentence was to have breakfast beside Monty for a week!'[19] Contemporary records certainly bear this out. Under the heading 'Things we want to know' the Staff College magazine asked at Christmas 1920: 'If and where Monty spent two silent minutes on Armistice Day?'[20]

Most officers had had enough of killing, and talk about killing. Monty, however, *wanted* to talk about it, and discuss its ethics and implications. He had read Alan Herbert's 1919 novel *The Secret Battle* and had been deeply moved – 'the best story of front-line war I have read' he later remarked. 'This is the gist of it' Herbert's narrator had ended the novel; 'that my friend Harry was shot for cowardice – and he was one of the bravest men I ever knew.'[21] As John Terraine has remarked, though execution was comparatively rare on the Western Front (284 men shot for desertion and cowardice), the book's ending highlighted 'all the stupidities, the lack of perception and imagination, the wanton cruelty' which had 'blighted A. P. Herbert's war, and many others besides'.[22]

'Victory' had quickly become a shameful word. Battles such as the Somme, the historian A. J. P. Taylor later remarked, 'set the picture by which future generations saw the First World War: brave helpless soldiers; blundering, obstinate generals; nothing achieved'.[23] The 'betrayal' of higher commanders, Norman Dixon would write, 'terminated for all time the hitherto reverential and blind faith which troops had in their generals'.[24]

The ramifications of such post-war disillusion were potentially fatal for democracy, yet like many others, Gething thought Monty was 'all blah' at this time: opinionated, conceited, over-talkative. Doubtless this was true, as the keyed-up self-subordinating loyalty and growing personal disquiet at the senseless casualties incurred in the fighting on the Western

Front gave way to a new ambition: to help reshape Britain's regular army as a modern institution, founded upon professionalism and the end of class-divisiveness.

It was to be a losing battle in the 1920s and 30s. Monty had simply expected too much of the Staff College and its staff: namely, a chance for distinguished officers to set their recent experiences into the context of the history of modern warfare, and to prepare a common approach to future military and social tasks in a post-war democratic world.

Yet if Monty found the Staff College course unsatisfactory and the instructors deficient, it did not sour his belief in the need for such a college; rather, it increased his desire to see such an institution run properly. Idle at school and wild at Sandhurst, he had at last woken to the need for better *education* if the British army was to become a professional force in a post-war twentieth-century democratic world. Thereafter, to the end of his life Monty would preserve an unshakeable respect for schools and colleges, seeing them as fundamental structural supports of a modern, technological society. Cleverness for its own sake – especially intellectual snobbery – did not impress him; it was in the preparation and application of intelligence and knowledge to modern life that he saw the crucial value of education. As he put it later, he himself had no claim to 'cleverness' in any academic sense. 'I thought I had a certain amount of common sense, but it was untrained; it seemed to me that it was *trained* common sense which mattered', he reflected in a memorable insight.[25]

Thus, in a strange way, the Staff College's very inadequacy encouraged Monty at a turning point in his life, making him more vividly aware of, even in comparison with other, better-endowed officers, his own didactic talents, his almost forensic ability to analyse his experience of warfare, and to see his potential contribution as a teacher/trainer to the British army.

Though he was never told how well or badly he did during the year, Monty must certainly have made an impression, for whether in punishment or as a reward for his zeal, when he passed out of the college at the end of 1920 it was to find he had been given one of the toughest brigade-major appointments in the British army at that time: Ireland.

Troubles

In India, between 1908 and 1912, Monty had been part of British imperial defence forces that were used, effectively, to keep Indians down, as was the case also in Ireland. While British troops continued to 'keep order' in both countries, both nations had furnished significant numbers of troops for Britain's World War I struggle with the Kaiser's Germany – and in its aftermath, educated patriots in both India and Ireland naturally expected Britain to practise what it had preached; indeed, to allow what the British government had given leaders in both countries to believe would be granted after the Great War was won: self-rule. Instead, while seemingly every small state in Europe from Czechoslovakia to Estonia was granted self-determination in the Treaty of Versailles, India was denied it by a few hundred MPs sitting in Parliament in Westminster, and Ireland was offered a paltry form of partition under British rule.

The response was predictable. In India and Ireland violence escalated – the worst excess in India being the infamous Amritsar massacre of a thousand men, women and children by British troops under the command of General Dyer on 13 April 1919. In Ireland, however, similar violence took place in 1919 and 1920 – including that of 11 December 1920, when units of Churchill's 'Black and Tan' auxiliary policemen ran amuck in Cork, razing three hundred buildings in the centre of the town and murdering suspected Sinn Feiners.

If ever there was a propitious moment for complete independence from British rule it was now, most Irish leaders felt – a view with which the British, having conquered and forcibly settled the Catholic country with Protestants since the seventeenth century, were reluctant to comply. Fiercely loyal to the concept of 'Great' Britain, the largely Protestant population of the northern counties refused to have any truck with Irish independence, in which they would then be outnumbered by the Catholic majority.

Confronting this schism, Lloyd George thus had the awkward task of granting self-rule to Irish nationalists, permitting the Protestant North to remain part of Great Britain and keeping, if possible, overall diplomatic and military suzerainty over the two parts of the country as part of the ongoing, if floundering, British Empire. This compromise he attempted to achieve by pushing through Parliament the Irish Home Rule Bill in 1920, allowing for two subsidiary Irish parliaments, one in Ulster and one in Dublin. Sinn Fein, which had won almost all Irish constituencies in the December 1919 general election, refused, however, to go along with such a compromise 'divide-and-rule' policy. The result was arson, murder and reprisal, leading in December 1920 to the introduction of martial law throughout the South – and it was into this calamitous situation that Major Bernard Montgomery was cast, in January 1921: a moment when insurrection, far from being contained by the massive increase of British troops stationed in the country, was increasing to the point of civil war.

Martial law

Although the intellectual and political centre of the Irish revolt was Dublin, it was in the southern, rural counties that the British were hardest put to keep order. The countryside was poor in roads, while telephone and postal communications were in the pocket of the Irish Republican Army. Loyalists were few and isolated; assassination had become commonplace. The tighter the British clamped down on the 'rebels', the more unpopular the 'occupation' army became.

For Monty the Irish Revolution of 1919–22, as it has become known, posed grave problems of personal loyalty. He was Northern Irish by birth and ancestry. The Montgomery family estate was still at New Park, Moville, County Donegal, just outside the Six Counties of Ulster, and he still went there when on leave. Most upsetting of all, Lieutenant-Colonel Hugh Montgomery, Monty's first cousin, had been murdered in cold blood by the IRA in Dublin on 21 November 1920: one of eleven British intelligence officers assassinated that day – assassinations which in turn prompted a massacre among innocent civilians at Croke Park football ground that afternoon – 'Bloody Sunday' – by the Black and Tans.

Monty had been fond of Hugh, with whom he had kept close contact throughout the war in France and Flanders. In the circumstances it would have been natural for him to feel a personal sense of mission, even revenge, when he arrived at Cork on 5 January 1921. What he did not bargain for was the sheer size of the brigade he was expected to run, containing no fewer than seven battalions.

The 17th (Cork) Infantry Brigade was already the largest brigade in Ireland – and would get even bigger. It was originally intended to split the

17th Brigade into two; but at the critical moment early in 1921 'it was considered that the situation was so complex that a new Brigadier would take several months to pick up the threads', as Monty later explained to a colleague.[26] Thus the Cork Infantry Brigade was simply expanded, growing over ensuing months to some nine battalions – more than a tenth of all British troops in Ireland.[27]

Monty's brigade commander, Major-General Higginson, had been at Cork since November 1919, but urgently required a first-class chief of staff. In Monty he found one. 'I had 3 Staff Captains, in addition to a large "I" staff. But it was really too much,' Monty later confided, '– the work was fearfully hard.'[28]

Morale, when Monty arrived, was low – many vacancies in battalions and headquarters remaining unfilled, as officers were loath to serve in the campaign. The divisional commander, leading the 16th, 17th, 18th and Kerry Brigades, was Major-General Sir Peter Strickland – another decorated officer from the Western Front brought to Ireland in 1919, and a representative of the 'landed-gentry' school of officering. He evidently hated having to put his case before politicians ('I loathe that sort of thing,' he recorded of a Cabinet meeting which he was asked to attend on 29 December 1920[29]), and mourned the time when he had been able to shoot and fish in the beautiful countryside around his headquarters. On Saturday 1 January 1921 he lamented in his diary: 'Last year was bad enough, but nothing to this. We could move about, hunt etc. and personally I can now do neither ... What will be the end I can't say, but I hope and trust I won't be here 1.1.22. It's been one of the worst years I've known anywhere. Murder and crime seem so deep-rooted that one wonders how it can be stamped out.'[30]

It couldn't. Martial law was counter-productive. By February 1921, a month after Monty's arrival, Strickland was offering the GOC-in-C in Ireland, General Macready, his resignation, so weary and pessimistic did he feel – for the IRA, having pursued until then a policy aimed primarily at the Irish police constabulary, merely responded to martial law by switching their attacks to target the military.

Organizing themselves on similar lines (and in similar uniforms) as the British army, the IRA invented a new form of guerrilla tactics: flying columns that could move in specially trained units across large areas, calling upon local units to help in ambushes, concealment, re-supply and intelligence. This was to become a model for guerrilla warfare the world over – and it proved as difficult for the cumbersome British formations to counter in 1921 as for the Americans in Vietnam in the 1960s or Russian troops in Afghanistan in the 1980s and Chechnya in 1999 / 2000.

There was little or no real co-ordination between the 'authorities' in Ireland: the official Irish police, the hated auxiliary Black and Tan forces and the khaki-clad British army. Intelligence was unreliable, public hostility was whipped up by the seeming lack of control over the Black and Tans, and the higher military command itself was torn between those who thought it best to ride out the storm while politicians negotiated a settlement and others who advocated sterner measures designed to stamp out the IRA completely.

Monty's change of heart as a result of his experience in Ireland was to be of profound significance in his evolution into a modern 'people's' general.

A tiger for work

One Highlander, stationed at Queenstown in 1921, vividly recalled the return of a shocked colleague to the battalion following a short staff attachment at Cork Brigade headquarters. 'This subaltern, on reporting to me on his return to regimental duty, blurted out words somewhat as follows: "Our new Brigade-Major is certainly a little tiger for work, and by Jove you have to jump when he gives you any order, and he is also a martinet as regards punctuality." '[31]

A stream of orders continually issued from Monty's desk to the brigade battalions – so many that by June 1921 they were collected together into a small booklet, printed by 6th Division HQ in Cork, entitled: '17th Infantry Brigade: Summary of Important Instructions'. It was, as its author declared in the introduction, 'intended as a reference work to assist officers, when they first arrive in Ireland, in making themselves acquainted with the various instructions laid down for dealing with the situation obtaining in that country', and was soon issued to all 6th Division officers. It covered every aspect of an officer's duties in the martial law area with amazing conciseness and lucidity. The twenty-nine headings were arranged alphabetically, so that it was, in fact, an ABC of service in Ireland, with instructions for everything from Armoured Cars to Wireless. Arrests, Ciphers, Convoys, Operations, Patrols, Pigeons, Reprisals – all set out in Monty's crystal-clear language that no subaltern, no matter how inexperienced, could misunderstand. Despite its unprepossessing title it was in fact a model of its kind – and not least remarkable for its insistence on discretion as the better part of valour. 'The behaviour of the Army must be kept beyond reproach', it urged. Official reprisals, instituted when martial law was declared in December 1920, had backfired, since the IRA merely burned the houses of Loyalists in retaliation, and by early June 1921 the British government banned them – an edict Monty stressed in his booklet, adding that 'unofficial reprisals' were equally 'strictly prohibited', whether by troops or police. Instead, '"Precaution" and "cunning" are all important,' Monty declared in his instructions for operations.[32]

Did Monty, then, believe the IRA could be defeated?

Damned effort at peace

A special Cork City intelligence unit was set up in the city, and time after time Brigade-Major Montgomery organized large-scale manoeuvres or 'drives' in which the different brigades in the division co-operated, traversing the countryside and flushing out rebels. Meticulously planned and executed, these drives nevertheless failed to locate, let alone destroy, the IRA guerrilla columns. They miscarried, as Haig's offensives in 1916 and 1917 had miscarried – leading to the same three questions that had arisen in World War I: should the army be strengthened in numbers, in order to achieve its aims; should it rethink its tactics; or should a political settlement be reached?

In prolonged small wars throughout the century these same questions would arise, whether in Vietnam or Afghanistan. In Ireland in 1921, meanwhile, the higher military commanders merely appealed to Churchill, as Minister of War, and the Prime Minister, Lloyd George, for yet more weapons and troops, as Haig had done on the Western Front, as American commanders would do in Vietnam, and Russians in Afghanistan. Monty, by contrast, began to recognize the futility of the struggle. He could be uncompromisingly tough, even cruel, when it came to fighting. 'My whole attention was given to defeating the rebels and it never bothered me a bit how many houses were burned,' he later recorded.[33] 'Any civilian or Republican soldier or policeman who interferes with any officer or soldier *is shot at once*,' he wrote to his father after the truce;[34] yet behind the implacable mask he was increasingly sceptical about the long-term outlook.

Unlike Major-General Strickland, unlike the officers on the 6th Division staff, unlike his colleague Major Arthur Percival – the most ruthless of the English intelligence officers in his Cork Brigade – Monty came to see evacuation by the British as the only feasible solution to the Irish problem. In this he was completely at odds with his colleagues, who were determined to 'defeat' the 'rebels'. 'We had a perfect organization and had "them" beat,' General Strickland claimed in his diary of the summer of 1921 when the truce was declared.[35] 'At last it looked as if the government were going to deal drastically with the gangs of murderers', commented the 6th Division history, drawn up by its general staff, in view of the seven new battalions sent over to strengthen the division at the end of June 1921. 'The next two months were looked forward to eagerly by everyone except the IRA', the anonymous chronicler remarked.[36] 'A short time more would have completed it [the smashing of the IRA] thoroughly. But "they" knew this and got the politicians to negotiate – with the present result,' Strickland recorded in May 1922 as civil war loomed larger. '*Never* has the country been in such a state. No sort of order or authority in these parts. All our labour and energy have been thrown in the gutter, to say nothing of expense, and deprivation. It almost makes one wish one had never been concerned in the show at all.'[37]

Certainly the 'show' and the subsequent 'damned effort at peace', as Strickland called it,[38] were galling to British officers and troops who, as part of the truce, were confined to a role of all too vulnerable passivity for the following ten months, pending a final settlement on independence for southern Ireland between Griffith and Lloyd George. The 6th Division history was particularly scathing of the truce: 'As soon as all chance of immediate fighting was over, the scattered bands of desperados formed themselves into the Companies and Battalions to which they had always belonged *on paper*, and started to train, practise musketry, hold reviews, etc.'

Monty, however, did not take the same view.

Public opinion

Although the situation deteriorated towards winter 1921, when still no settlement was agreed and civil war between Republicans and Partitionists seemed likely, Monty's conviction that the British should leave Ireland only strengthened. 'It really is most degrading for us soldiers having to stay on here,' he wrote to his father in March 1922, when the truce was in its ninth month, 'and I shall be heartily glad to see the last of the people and the place. Our presence here undoubtedly acts as a deterrent on the more extreme of the IRA,' he acknowledged; but he was under no illusion that the South was anything but 'entirely ruled by the Irish Republican Army who publicly state by proclamation in the local papers that they owe no allegiance to the Provisional Government and that they adhere to the Republic'.[39]

Back in England the following year, and having had a chance to think through the lessons of the war in Ireland, Monty set down his personal conclusions for his colleague, Major Percival, who had subsequently gone as a student to the Staff College, Camberley and wished to deliver a series of lectures on guerrilla warfare in Ireland. 'My own view,' Monty wrote, taking issue with Strickland and Percival, 'is that to win a war of that sort you must be ruthless; Oliver Cromwell, or the Germans, would have settled it in a very short time. Nowadays public opinion precludes such methods; the nation would never allow it, and the politicians would lose their jobs if they sanctioned it. That being so I consider that Lloyd George was really right in what he did; if we had gone on we could probably have squashed the rebellion as a temporary measure, but it would have broken out again like an ulcer the moment we had removed the troops; I think the rebels would probably have refused battle, and hidden away their arms, etc. until we had gone. The only way therefore was to give them some form of self-government, and let them squash the rebellion themselves; they are the only people who could really stamp it out, and they are still trying to do so and as far as one can tell they seem to be having a fair amount of success . . . You probably will not agree.'[40]

Percival did not. He had made himself one of the most hated British names to Irish Republicans, leading his own mobile column against the IRA, and in his opinion 'our tactics of rapid movement and surprise had had such a demoralising effect on their nerves that in another few weeks,' had it not been for the Truce, 'the back of the Rebellion would have been broken,' he considered.[41] In his letter to Percival, Monty had said he had regarded 'all civilians as "shinners" [supporters of Sinn Fein]' – an attitude which Percival, in his eventual lecture, declared was 'fundamentally wrong', for 'in conditions of this nature, you must at all costs distinguish the sheep from the wolves. If you fail to do so, you drive the whole population into the hands of the enemy.'[42]

Whether Percival or Montgomery was right must be a matter of opinion: imperialist or republican. Yet it remains a fact that Percival is still remembered in Ireland as a vicious sadist, the man responsible for the 'Essex Battalion Torture Squad', a man who had personally taken 'a rifle with fixed bayonet from one of the troops and bayoneted one man ten times', as the IRA leader Tom Barry put it; whereas Montgomery was recognized by the IRA as an efficient 'enemy' staff officer who had behaved 'with great correctness'.[43] Moreover, though he was to become a respected battalion commanding officer, Percival was destined to undertake perhaps the most humiliating act of World War II, the surrender of Singapore to the Japanese, while the brigade major whose views he found so 'fundamentally wrong' on Ireland would go on to take in time the surrender of all the northern German armed forces at the conclusion of World War II in the west.

Quite a step

The truth was, the Victorian-Edwardian world had crumbled with the catastrophe of World War I, Monty recognized – and most of his superiors in the military were simply unable to adjust to the loss of their social and other privileges. Post-war democracy – with a huge increase in the electorate after partial female suffrage in 1918 – meant that 'public opinion' was no longer the preserve of *Times* readers – but *Times* readers were the slowest to acknowledge this. Thus most old-fashioned 'imperial' soldiers like Strickland and Percival saw the British government's handling of the Irish rebellion as a disgusting example of politico-military infirmity – much as 'imperial' German officers came to believe in the 'stab in the back' by politicians that had 'lost' them World War I.

Monty did not subscribe to such right-wing views. The revolution in Ireland finally taught him what World War I had failed to: namely to question his own and other people's political and ethical, as well as military, assumptions. It was not that he believed public opinion should lead politics, but leaders in a democracy *must*, he felt, be able to carry public opinion with them. In attempting to quash the 'rebellion' in southern Ireland, Monty saw, the military was running counter to the will of the nation, however many troops were brought over for the task. In the aftermath of the Great War public opinion in Britain would not tolerate Ireland becoming another killing ground. Legitimizing an Irish authority to impose its own order on the country was therefore the best democratic solution in his view. For a Northern Irish Protestant whose cousin had been assassinated by the IRA, it was quite a step.

Querulous opinions

What *was* the new art of democratic soldiering, meanwhile, in the post-World War I world – and how did one master it?

Another soldier who dreamed of high command was Basil Liddell Hart – the 'Captain Who Teaches Generals' as Yigal Allon later dubbed him.[44] As Liddell Hart's latest biographer has shown, Lieutenant B. L. Hart saw the briefest of service as second in command of a company on the Somme, where he was 'shelled, panicked and gassed, probably in that order, in a dark wood'.[45] Hart emerged with phosgene poisoning, anxieties about his own courage in action (he had understandably given way to his fear) – and manic delusions of military greatness. Though he never again commanded anything ('except in the trivial sense that adjutants and education officers may be said to fulfil that function' as his post-modern biographer caustically put it[46]), Hart nevertheless dreamed of holding high command. By 1920, the year when he first met Monty, Hart was fantasizing that 'given health and opportunity I could at the present time handle a brigade at least with distinction in battle and that with experience I could prove myself one of the "masters of war"'.[47]

Lieutenant Hart's delusions of grandeur did not end there. 'I believe that with more experience of the conditions and capabilities of the other arms I could command an army equally well,' he claimed, 'if given the chance.'[48] The chance of commanding an army, he acknowledged with the part of his brain still capable of realism, was, however, slim: 'under modern conditions it looks as if the opportunity, if it ever comes, will only come – under the rigid rules of seniority – when my intellectual keenness and agility is dulled by time'.[49]

The 'rules of seniority', in a post-war period of financial cutback, certainly made prospects of rapid promotion for Lieutenant Hart unlikely. He won wide notice in 1921 when, as a twenty-six-year-old staff captain, he rewrote the army's *Infantry Training Manual* as the designated author failed to carry out the task. Liddell Hart's critical and querulous opinions, however, incensed his hidebound superiors; in 1924 he was placed on half pay, and three years later discarded. Though he protested to his MP and got such influential figures as Colonel 'Boney' Fuller, the chief instructor at the Staff College, to complain on his behalf, there was no change of heart. Evicted from the army, he became a journalist by profession, concentrating on defence, tennis – and, as we shall see, ladies' corsetry.

Degeneration

By contrast, although he was not decorated for his service during the Troubles, Montgomery's performance in Ireland did not go unnoticed at the War Office. As a result he managed at least to survive the post-war 'Geddes Axe', which cut down Britain's military establishment to the minimal levels for a waning great power. As Monty later wrote, 'Opportunity was taken to get rid of a great deal of inefficient material in the lower ranks' – adding: 'in the higher ranks much dead wood was left untouched'.[50]

Such 'dead wood' would very nearly lose Britain the next great war. As Sir David Fraser would later write, the period after 1920 saw 'the decline in the British Army's quality, strength, and sense of direction'.[51] As in the United States, the very notion of renewed continental warfare was consigned to the waste-paper basket. In the wake of the notorious Ten-Year Rule' of July 1919 it was assumed that 'the British Empire will not be engaged in any great war during the next ten years, and that no Expeditionary Force is required for this purpose . . . The principal functions of the Military and Air Forces is to provide garrisons for India, Egypt, the new mandated territory, and all territory (other than self-governing) under British control, as well as to provide the necessary support to the civil power at home.'[52]

While this proved the case in factual terms, the Ten-Year Rule meant that Britain's defence forces were trained and maintained only for such 'imperial' policing work. Self-centred and devoted once again to pre-war pleasures, the 'higher ranks' abandoned any responsibility for preparing Britain for combat with a modern industrial power. Indeed, at one point in the dark days of 1940, having inherited a War Office in 1939 that was constitutionally and by its recent history of incumbents incapable of conducting modern defence against a first-class enemy, the CIGS General Sir Edmund Ironside would openly declare that his predecessors – especially Field-Marshals Milne and Massingberd – 'ought to be shot'.

Certainly the British army after World War I would gradually degenerate to the point in 1939 where, despite modern weapons, it was less effective than it had been two decades before, in 1918.

This was not, as so many maintained after the disaster of World War II, solely a matter of poor British government funding. The fact was, the 'people's army' or citizen-army that was disbanded after World War I had proved invincible in battle, even with Douglas Haig at its helm. With its demobilization in 1918/19, however, the old, Edwardian regular army revived, with its class snobberies and pre-war class distinctions unchanged. Not even the cavalry could be closed down.

Because senior officers wrote efficiency reports on their subordinates, rather than the other way round, subordination became the name of the army game in Britain – a development that would produce a new service, the Royal Air Force, entirely divorced from its former army parent, and an army completely unfitted in turn for future warfare against a modern enemy, whether Japanese or German. The British army would thus enter World War II having proved itself powerless, over the preceding twenty years as a primary global imperial power, to develop armoured and mechanized formations on any significant scale – despite having invented the tank; to develop tactics to use such armour; to develop close tactical air support (*Blitzkrieg*) by fighter-bombers; to co-ordinate combined naval, air and army forces; or even to develop the intimate, concentrated artillery support which had, effectively, enabled the Allies to win World War I in the west. It was, as General Fraser summarized, 'a tragedy indeed'.[53]

One by one junior and senior officers with futuristic views would be thrown out of the British army. Perhaps the miracle, in such a catalogue of inter-war failure, was that Monty himself survived without being dismissed or placed on half pay – though, as will be seen, he came very close to such a fate. Others, such as Fuller, Martel and Hobart, were not so fortunate.

Internal aggression

Abiding English social attitudes among the officer class were, at heart, the 'British problem'. Hunting, shooting, riding, fishing and club life remained, as before World War I, the passions of upper- and middle-class army personnel. In this respect, the 'public' (in fact private) schools had much to answer for. Intellect and thinking were still anathema, while clubby amateurism was *de rigueur*. As T. E. Lawrence noted in *Seven Pillars of Wisdom*, this had already led to a British army in World War I in which the 'men were often gallant fighters, but their generals as often gave away in stupidity what they had gained in ignorance'.[54]

Sadly, such wilful ignorance did not improve after World War I. To prescribed indolence and English social snobbery would be added, as the decade of the 1920s came to a close, the problems of world recession and unemployment. But the real culprit was the question-mark over the *role* of a modern British army. Was it the army's role to defend Britain and Britain's empire from outside threat – or from *internal* aggression?

'First shoot the socialists down, behead them, render them impotent – if necessary per bloodbath – and then war abroad!' Kaiser Wilhelm had written to his Chancellor, von Bülow, in 1905.[55] In a society nervous about the growing power of industrial workers and of women – who finally won the vote (for women over thirty) in 1918 – the establishment in post-war Britain was equally concerned to combat socialism, indeed saw the danger of socialism at home as more significant than threats to British rule abroad. Thus the majority of British battalions, including all Guards regiments, were deliberately kept in Britain or brought back to England in order to put down possible civil unrest or socialist revolution. The CIGS, Sir Henry Wilson (assassinated by the IRA), felt 'it was not wise to remove' his ten Guards battalions from England, as he put it, 'in view of the general industrial unrest'.[56] 'If 8 Battns were sent to Ireland we should have very little for our own internal troubles', Wilson challenged the Prime Minister, '& nothing for India, Egypt, C[onstantin]ople, etc.'[57] The CIGS's plea to be allowed to bring back thirteen battalions from Silesia and elsewhere in the spring of 1921 was, according to his diary, specifically 'to be able to hold both England and Ireland in the event of a Triple Strike . . . I asked L[loyd] G[eorge] if he wanted to be P. M. of England or of Silesia', Wilson recorded.[58]

Thus, having helped the Allies to win World War I, the British army undertook two deeply reactionary roles thereafter: policing (and denying independence to) an obsolescent empire abroad, while preparing to quell socialist unrest, even revolution, at home.

To the extent that Britain hung on to most of its decaying empire between 1919 and 1939, with the exception of the Republic of Ireland, and avoided social revolution in England itself, it succeeded; but it only did so by failing to address the need for social change, and permitting its old-fashioned army to bankrupt the country of any possibility of successfully challenging the rise of the dictators: for the citizenry – as became clear in the famous Oxford Union debate of 1933 – refused to countenance military service under such right-wing blimps ever again.

Haig's callous butchery in World War I had led to a population unwilling to consider such futile slaughter, while the failure of army officers to prepare for modern war doomed Britain to defeat if world war nevertheless became inevitable – as, inevitably, it did.

Musical chairs

Ireland taught Monty to question the wisdom of imperialist subjugation in a people's century. However, it was Monty's work in England thereafter that helped him hone his vision of a modern army in defence of modern democracy – despite the military incompetence and complacency of that democracy.

From an organization of 3.5 million in November 1918 the British army had reduced its numbers to 370,000 in 1920 – while policing an empire larger, by virtue of Britain's mandates in Palestine and Mesopotamia, than before the war. Financially the run-down was just as severe: overall defence expenditure being cut by almost 80 per cent, from £502 million to £75 million in 1919.[59]

Such necessary slimming in a democracy required a radical reorganization of defence forces under a combined Ministry of Defence, instead of three services (after creation of the RAF in 1918), with three political heads (First Sea Lord, Minister of War and Minister for Air) competing for diminishing defence funds; moreover, it needed forward-looking, flexible minds in its high-command structure instead of Victorian hangovers as generals, admirals and air marshals. It also needed professional soldiers who would not be 'geared to the pace of regimental soldiering as an agreeable occupation rather than a demanding profession', as the military historian of the inter-war period, Professor Brian Bond, put it.[60] Given these failings, and the 'confused amalgam of imperial responsibilities' as Field-Marshal Carver later phrased it,[61] the outlook for the British army, if challenged by a major enemy, was bleak. Officered by men anxious only to look after their own privileges and preserves, its reversals, in the early years of World War II, would be nothing if not merited.

Certainly it was not for want of trying, or protest, by certain younger officers that the requirements of modern democratic defence were ignored. Given the massive, accelerated reduction in the size of Britain's wartime army, however, middle-ranking and senior officers were, from the 1920s, subjected to a game of musical chairs, where the survivors were given fixed-term appointments dependent on their age and seniority, rather than their ability. Such musical-chair appointments were dictated by the War Office, under the Secretary of State, CIGS and Military Secretary. If any officer sat out too long on half pay, without an appointment, or as the result of a poor annual assessment by a jealous senior officer, he was compulsorily retired. This process virtually guaranteed the fossilization of Britain's army. As the historian of the army of this period noted, they 'resurrected a pre-1914 style of life' which 'later generations would find hard to understand'.[62]

Under the deadening burden of such senior officers, younger officers with any brains or interest in modern soldiering fared no better than antique ones, indeed often fared worse, and were driven out. Moreover, the atmosphere of competition in hanging on to one's commission at all costs meant that rivalry exceeded co-operation. Thus, meeting Monty for the first time in 1920, Lieutenant Liddell Hart later considered the bishop's son, with 'his perky manner, peaky face and small stature . . . did not show the natural signs of leadership, or a knack of handling men' that Hart believed he himself possessed – for all that Monty had, effectively, run a division of 15,000 men on the Western Front, and a brigade of 10,000 troops in Ireland.[63] Yet even Hart was awed by the fact that Monty was 'one of the most thoroughly professional soldiers in the army', leaving Hart all 'the more impressed because by then I was coming to realize, through widening experience, how amateurish most "professional soldiers" still were'.[64]

Certainly no one could be unaware of Monty's emerging gift for tactical training. At 8th Infantry Brigade, following his service in Ireland, Brigade-Major Montgomery ran 'masterclasses' for aspiring officers wishing to take the entrance exams to the Staff College, Camberley; at 49th (Territorial Army) Division, where he was appointed GSO 2 in the summer of 1923, he not only continued to run his 'masterclasses' for aspiring Staff College officers, but organized winter tactical training for part-time Territorial officers and NCOs, over a sand-table, so that they would be able to rehearse tactical leadership in summer-camp manoeuvres. 'It was not easy to get this going,' Monty explained in a private letter to Liddell Hart; 'there was no precedent for it and the Territorial Army is very conservative. However, once we got them to realize it was a good egg, they took it up and got down to it splendidly.'[65]

For Monty, the experience of teaching Territorial Army leaders – officers and NCOs – was his first such challenge since raising the volunteer Bantam brigade in 1915, and training largely civilian-soldiers in the four years thereafter. Though the reconstituted TA was nominally funded for home defence only, Monty refused to believe its leaders would not be required in time of war – indeed, that such a war could ever be won without them, as the war of 1914–18 had proved. For Monty this naturally suggested energetic training of the TA, and close links between regular and TA units – an approach that ill-suited the trend towards soldiering as a profession where 'many officers, so far from wishing to adapt to social and technical changes', as Professor Bond has remarked, 'looked to the Army as a haven where they could escape from them'.[66]

In this sense Monty's 'dynamism and determination',[67] as Liddell Hart described the brevet major's impact on those around him, meant that for the next twenty years Monty would be swimming against an unending tide of British social snobbery, complacency, myopia and indolence – with the threat, moreover, of losing his job if he objected, or became too outspoken.

Only one army

'I find the Territorial Army most interesting,' Monty confided at the time to Liddell Hart. 'The officers are very keen on the whole; they are very appreciative of assistance in improving their military knowledge ... I often wonder why they join the Territorial Army; they get nothing out of it, in fact it costs them money. It is really the old volunteer spirit still existing; some of our units are very old and have a tremendous esprit de corps.

'All this is of course excellent. The Regular Army should without doubt give of its best to the Territorial Army; unfortunately this is not always the case as service in the Territorial Army is regarded by many as a backwater. I always tell our Division that there is only one Army in England, and we all belong to it, whether we are in the Regulars, Territorials, or OTC [Officer Training Corps, in schools and universities].' For Monty there were thus only 'two categories' of soldiers: '1. Those who devote all their time to soldiering, i.e. the Regular Army. 2. Those whose main work is some other profession, and who only soldier in their spare time. Personally, I take my hat off to those in Category 2 every time.'[68]

If anyone, in the years to come, was to ask whence Monty's openness towards non-professional and 'civilian' soldiers in World War II – whether on his staff or in fighting units – derived, it was surely from his period with the TA in York from 1923 to 1924, following his experience in World War I. Haig had only employed regular army officers on his staff, and this went for most of the senior staffs of the BEF. It had merely led to an army of 'lions', as the German general Ludendorff quipped, 'led by donkeys'. Monty intended it to be otherwise.

Wine, women and gambling

Most of all, Monty saw in the challenge of teaching non-regular officers and men a challenge to his own skills as a communicator. Thus in seeking to instruct others he was himself all the time learning – particularly so in his 'astonishing "one-man" performance', as one of his masterclass pupils at York, young Freddie de Guingand, called it.

Monty was equally impressed by the wildly handsome twenty-two-year-old subaltern. 'Freddie was a 2nd Lieutenant on the Depot strength, and was O[fficer] i/c the training Cadre' of the West Yorkshire Regiment, Monty later recalled. 'I quickly spotted him as a very intelligent young officer, and made use of him and his Cadre to help me with the T.A. Division by giving demonstrations of platoon tactics. His life in those days revolved round wine, women and gambling – in all of which he excelled!! I reckon he was about 22; I was a Captain (Bt. Major), and about 35. We became great friends. We played a lot of golf together, and bridge most evenings in the Mess. When I saw his potentialities, I urged him to work for the Staff college – or rather to begin a serious study of his profession, and to read widely, because he was too young <u>then</u> to take the exam.'[69]

Monty's encouragement of de Guingand was to bear historic fruit, on a par with Napoleon and Berthier. In the meantime, running his masterclasses for entry to the Staff College, Monty lectured on all the subjects, set the papers and corrected them. 'He can have had little sleep during this period,' de Guingand reflected.[70]

Undeterred, Monty also began a five-part history of tactical warfare for his regimental magazine, the *Antelope*, examining infantry tactics from Gustavus Adolphus in 1611 up to the then-present day, 1924. His agenda was to extract the main lessons of the past four hundred years of infantry warfare, in order that he might critically assess the tragic battles of the Somme and of Passchendaele, and spur debate over the issues. Thus, in the very first article Monty made clear the axiom that would become his fundamental rule of tactical warfare. 'All through history, from the days of the great phalanx of the Roman Legion,' he set down his credo, 'the master law of tactics remains unchanged; this Law is that to achieve success you must be superior at the point where you intend to strike the decisive blow.'[71]

He would never make a clearer or more concise statement of his primary tactical policy.

Slanging matches

Monty's dictum at York, de Guingand later recalled, was that a dedicated officer could not make 'a good soldier and a good husband': soldiering was a full-time occupation.[72] Back at the Royal Warwickshire's barracks at Shorncliffe, where Monty was next sent, however, the dictum was ill-received.

The battalion commander's son, Major-General R. C. Macdonald, later vividly remembered Monty's arrival. 'I can remember Monty coming to the battalion in 1925 and spending about a year with us at Shorncliffe. Even in those days everybody recognized the fact that he would probably go to the top of his profession – a rare bird in that he was a chap who was not only very astute himself, but he'd really studied the business of soldiering, which not many people did in those days – not in the dedicated sense.'[73] Monty's quasi-messianic return to the regiment, armed with a four-month proposal for company training, caused uproar in such a traditional infantry unit, however. At that time pains were taken only to ensure good hunting in the area; few wished to be reminded of the realities of war after the devastations of the last one. 'There was much opposition in the mess to Bernard's attitude,' Monty's brother Brian later chronicled, 'and I recall witnessing some bitter slanging matches, with few holds barred.'[74] Fortunately the CO, in the words of his son, 'recognized the fact that he was himself lacking in tactical ability having spent the whole war in New Zealand. He was therefore glad to have Monty, and so handed over the training to him.'[75] By 12 March 1925 Monty's plans for training were finalized to the point where they could be printed and staple-bound. 'The idea that we aim at,' he declared in his preface, 'is that by the end of Company Training every officer, NCO and man will have a clear idea of the action of his unit in each of the various operations of war.'[76]

There had never been anything like it in the Royal Warwicks before. Aware, however, that Monty was in danger of alienating colleagues by his single-minded dedication to professionalism, it was wise Colonel Macdonald who thought to take him away for a holiday. Macdonald duly asked Monty to join him and his wife on a golfing vacation to France. Their destination was Dinard, on the Brittany coast: a popular, inexpensive haunt of families in the Civil Service or armed services – and their eligible daughters.

A madman

'We didn't go out very often,' one such eligible daughter, Betty Anderson, later recalled, 'but one night I was asked to join a party and we went down to the Kursaal, which is now a casino. I was dancing very happily, with the pro. I had this black taffeta dress on. I didn't have many dresses in those days, so this felt rather smart with roses down the side. I was suddenly called by the party to come up to the balcony, because there was a man who wanted to meet me. He seized my hand and rushed me back onto the floor. Oh dear, he wasn't a very good dancer and I very nearly tumbled over his feet. He was humming to himself out of tune "When you and I were 17". Well, of course I was seventeen and a-half, and thought to myself he's rather ancient – and discovered he was double my age!'

Monty was thirty-seven. Betty was horrified. However, 'he wouldn't let me go the whole of the rest of the evening, and I had to stick with him.

Very determined, he was. And towards the end of the evening he said, "Now we're going to sit out on the stairs." So we sat out on the stairs, and he began extolling my praises, and saying I had lovely golden hair, and I thought, dear me, it's rather strange all this. So then he said: "I've made up my mind this evening that I'm going to marry you." '

Horror turned to disbelief. 'I thought, dear me, I've met a madman. I really did think . . . I mean I'd never had anything happen like that before in my life. So I said: "I'm awfully sorry, but I'm not going to marry anybody. I'm studying music." '[77]

Though a decorated army officer, Monty had few if any graces with women, having all his adult life confined his deeper affections solely to his mother. As his brother Brian and sister Winsome recalled, he was simply not orientated towards women. 'He wasn't shy with girls,' his sister Winsome recalled. 'During the war, when on leave, he arranged parties for me. He didn't dance himself – he didn't like dancing – he'd just sit and watch.' To Winsome there was nothing perverse in this celibate self-distancing, and certainly not indicative of homosexual orientation. 'Oh, no, some men aren't [interested in women]!' she laughed.[78] Their brother Harold, ambitious to succeed as a colonial policeman and later administrator in Kenya, she pointed out, also married rather late.

Yet the suddenness of Monty's decision that he would marry Betty Anderson suggests something more complex than belated amorousness, or even strategic positioning for battalion command (for which marital status was usually a prerequisite): something that needs to be examined if his strange behaviour that spring is to be understood. It was something, after all, which would end, later, in a saga of outraged family feelings, even a refusal by Monty himself to attend his 'darling Mother's' funeral. 'Something went wrong,' Winsome subsequently acknowledged, puzzled by his later behaviour towards herself and his own family, 'and I cannot tell you what it was, I don't know'.[79]

In flagrante delicto

The fact was, until 1925 Monty had remained, in a personal sense, entirely under his mother's spell, not only because he so earnestly desired her affection – which he did – but also because of the domineering woman Maud was. 'Ooh, my word, she was strong minded!' Winsome later recalled.[80] To herself and to the outside world Maud presented a picture of absolute marital fidelity – 'a fierce and passionate devotion' to her husband 'that knew no bounds';[81] but Maud evidently missed a certain demonstrative affection from Henry – a disappointment she had come to sublimate in her energetic, even tyrannical domestic rule.

Growing older, Monty had seen into this vortex – and had fantasized he could perhaps take his father's place in her affections, perhaps by being more 'manly' than his 'saintly' father. His letters from the Western Front had been highly prized, and Maud had certainly become boastful of her son's medals. Yet all efforts at a more intimate, more mutually loving relationship had been rejected. 'Often he would lavish a gift on her to show his feeling – a cheque with which to "buy yourself a new coat" or something like that,' Winsome recollected, 'and all she did was to give the money to Belgian Refugees in the First War' – always 'brushing him off '.[82] 'She was too harsh with him,' Winsome felt in retrospect. 'I think it was her fault. I think Bernard had an image of her she wouldn't play up to . . .'[83]

Perhaps the simple fact was, as Winsome confided to one biographer, she 'simply did not love Bernard'.[84] Thus, in devoting himself to pleasing her, all Monty succeeded in doing was making himself ridiculous. And in a terrible repetition of that vain bid to be taken seriously by the only woman who figured in his bachelor life, he now behaved in the same 'mad' way with a total stranger: a blonde, innocent seventeen-year-old – perhaps hoping that Betty, a child in all but name, would be easier to control.

Perhaps, too, Monty chose Betty Anderson from the crowd of Kursaal dancers because she looked beautiful, virginal; and almost boyishly unblemished. After their return from Tasmania Monty's mother had given all her love to Monty's younger brother Desmond – 'a gifted and very good looking boy, with marked talents as a musician, particularly with the violin, at which he excelled', Brian recalled.[85] Monty himself once noted: 'My favourite brother was Desmond, who was born in May 1895 in Tasmania. He died in November 1909 at home in Chiswick from meningitis, after two serious operations; he was at that time a schoolboy at St Paul's School in London, and was 14. I was serving with my regiment in India at the time.'[86]

Did Betty remind Monty of Desmond – as, later in his life, certain teenage boys would do, evoking an outpouring of passionate feeling and strange filial/paternal tenderness? Pent up within him in 1925 there was, undoubtedly, a lifetime's emotion which, given the framework of his fear-filled childhood and his adult military dedication, he had never found a way of expressing save in barely controlled aggression. Dutifully, he attempted to 'prove' himself to his mother – indeed, some of his letters to her, from the Western Front, make sad reading, in terms of unrequited devotion. 'My darling Mother', he'd written in the midst of the battle of the Somme, 'I have just received your letter of the 24th August. I wrote yesterday in a great hurry saying how sorry I was to have missed your birthday but we were fighting hard from 19th to 26th August and I had no time for anything else. I enclose a cheque for £5 for you to get a birthday present for yourself with . . . There is only one condition I make and that is that it is not to be spent on <u>anyone</u> else. I should like you to reassure me on this point.'[87] Yet the more his mother had rejected his embarrassing advances ('I seem to have been insistent that the money is to be spent on herself and not on anybody else' Monty noted sadly in his annotation to the letter, half a century later[88]), the more he'd yearned to prove his capacity for love, not merely duty. He had lavished fraternal attention on his sister Winsome, but she was now married. He had paid for his brother Brian's schooling and got him into his own regiment. It was time, he knew, to move on.

Where to, though? He relished the comradeship of the army, where he could work and live with men. The army had enabled him to assert his 'masculinity' – with medals to prove it. But in a society where intimate male–male love dared not speak its name, indeed where its physical manifestation was a criminal offence and an incitement to blackmail, even when enacted in private, there was perhaps another reason for choosing a wife: to assert his 'normality'. As his brother Brian later chronicled, their mother was a devout and proud woman, but tormented by sexual fears. 'This is one of the few pictures in which she appears anxious or worried', Brian annotated a 1919 photograph. 'No doubt because at that time three of her brothers, who were of course our uncles (and children of the great Dean Farrar) had shattered all the generally accepted rules and conventions by conduct which, in those days, was held to be outrageous – legally, morally *and* socially.' Two of these conventions involved homo-sexual acts.

The Reverend Percival Farrar 'was chaplain to the Sovereign', Brian explained. 'But in his case, no one knew that Percival was a homosexual until he was caught in flagrante delicto with one of his own choir-boys! He had to leave the country immediately . . . Another brother, rector in a country parish, was also found to be homosexual.'[89]

Proposing to a woman was thus perhaps a final attempt to appease and please his mother: to prove he was not like her brothers, his uncles. Or if he was, by nature, then that he had the strength of will to control such urges, indeed to 'pass' as heterosexual in the most fundamental way of all: as a husband.

The proposal

'Where are you staying?' Monty had asked – 'he had a very sort of abrupt way of speaking,' Betty recalled Monty's manner.

'We're at the Madeleine Hotel.'

'I shall be round to see your parents in the morning,' Monty said.

'I did all I could not to laugh,' Betty later confessed. 'I thought I mustn't, because I realized he was serious, but I thought it was most peculiar. I rushed home to my mother, woke her up and said, "Hey, wake up, I've had a proposal from somebody! I think he must be a bit mad – I've only just met him! He's coming to see you in the morning."

'The next day he duly arrived, and to my astonishment my mother and father excluded me, taking him into a room to talk to him. I was left outside. When they came out my mother said: "This is a very interesting man, a most unusual man, and you've got to go for walks with him every day."'

Dutifully, Betty obeyed – 'In those days one didn't think of not doing what one's parents told one to do, at least I didn't. So he arrived very punctually, always on the dot when he said he was going to, and walk we did. Walk and walk. Round the walls of St Malo, across the pine woods, down to the sands at Dinard.'[90]

In the last of his multi-part series on the history of infantry tactics for his regimental magazine, the *Antelope* (published the following January), Monty had decided to adopt a new and much more questioning stance over the role of the tank in modern warfare. In the Great War and immediately afterwards he had regarded it as a form of mobile, heavily armoured field-artillery / machine-gun weapon, supporting infantry when-ever and in whichever way was required – but in an age of industrial mass production, he accepted, this role might well change. 'The present tank is too expensive to produce in large numbers,' he acknowledged of the Geddes-axe era of defence downsizing; but, if funding was found and tanks were mass produced, 'it will be for consideration whether infantry can still be called the chief arm, the arm which in the end wins the battle. It seems that the time is coming when the tanks will be the assault arm of the army, the artillery will be the arm which makes the assault possible, and the infantry the arm which occupies the conquered area. Some hard and clear thinking will be required before we are finally settled on the right road.'

'All he talked about was warfare,' Betty remembered of their walks at Dinard. 'He had this little cane he always used to carry with him, and one day he said: "Now, I'll tell you how I'm going to win the next war. I'm deploying my tanks like this" – and he drew on the sands, quite a big drawing. I mean, I didn't even know what a tank was! Never heard of a tank – nor had many people in those days. He drew this great thing with his little cane, and then said to me: "You know, I'm the youngest Major in the British Army."'

Betty was unimpressed. 'I am afraid that didn't interest me,' she recalled. 'I wasn't the least interested in war.' Nor did she like the way he took her for granted – as if her only task was to be impressed by him. 'I don't remember him talking about anything else really. He never asked me if I was interested in music or ballet. He never seemed to be worried about what I thought: it was just what he was thinking . . .'[91]

Such male chauvinism could only have worked if Monty had been sexually attractive to women. He wasn't.

'He couldn't have been nicer,' Betty commented politely, in retrospect. 'He was a charming chap, but not the sort of person that you fall for when you are 17. I mean if he'd been Clark Gable or somebody – dark, tall or handsome or something, one might have been swayed and have thought it would be rather nice to get married, but I was rather bored to tell the truth. He never discussed books or anything at all. It just seemed to be his whole mind was geared on how he was going to win this war and, I mean I never thought there'd be a war, I wasn't thinking of wars – I mean, one didn't. I'd been through the 1914 war when I was a child and to me that was the last war we were ever going to see, I hoped.'

Monty's lack of self-awareness, of how others might see him, was astounding to Betty. The difference in their ages seemed no bar to him for the simple reason that he did not see her: saw only a sort of idealized reflection of himself, transformed into beautiful adolescence, with luxuriant blond hair, like his lost brother. 'He was 37 and he'd been wounded badly in the first war, and he'd got rather thin and he wasn't very tall,'

Betty described. 'He always used to say to me, "Call me Bernard," but I never called him anything but Monty. He was really rather shy and he didn't show any signs of emotion at all. It seemed to me about a hundred years but I suppose it was just a few weeks.

'Eventually I told him "Quite truthfully, I told you I didn't want to marry you the first night and I don't want to marry you now. I don't want to marry anybody. So let's say goodbye."

' "Oh no," he said' – his response as childlike as his apparent infatuation – ' "you can come to Ireland and meet my mother and drive all her cars!" – quite an inducement as I'd only just learned to drive a car,' Betty recalled with a frankness that appealed to Monty. 'But I said, "No, thanks awfully, I don't want to do that."

'So then he said: "Well, I'll take you to a shop and you can buy something awfully nice for yourself." '

As in the past with his mother, Monty desperately hoped he could somehow buy Betty's affection, even if he could not win it. 'So he took me to the smartest shop in Dinard, he showed me these diamanté bags and things.'

The seventeen-year-old was unimpressed, finding Monty weird and manic. 'I said, "Quite honestly, I don't want anything. I'm not giving you anything. I'm really saying goodbye." So I went back to my mother and I said: "Look, I've done what you asked me, but I don't want to marry him and that's finished." '[92]

Monty's bid for normality – for the first truly heterosexual relationship in his life – was over. He had failed. Aged thirty-seven, he returned to his regiment the same strange bachelor as before: wedded still to the army rather than to a real wife.

6

Marriage

A trophy wife

How serious was Monty's proposal of marriage? Did he really think he could change his sexual orientation, his sexuality, overnight? How much derived from the need to impress his mother, or to untie himself from his mother? And how much was simply the desire to get command of a battalion of his regiment – for which he needed a trophy wife?

We will never know for sure, since Monty excluded the episode from his memoirs, and never alluded to his failed bid for the rest of his life. Yet the reversal of his well-known doctrine on marriage and soldiering, and his sudden wish to return to his beloved regiment a married man certainly signified an absolute determination to succeed within the army, whatever anybody thought – however stifling its hierarchy and establishment ethos. 'You are being decapitated. I am being strangled,' the legendary proponent of mechanization, Colonel J. F. C. ('Boney') Fuller, had written to Liddell Hart on hearing the news of the latter's reduction to half pay the year before.[1] Both would be forced to leave the army they loved – Fuller to become, in time, an impassioned pro-fascist, Liddell Hart an appeaser.

Monty, equally opinionated and ambitious, would also come very close to dismissal in the years ahead, but it says something for the moral background in which he had been raised that he recognized the danger of going too far in the advocacy of his own views. The more he felt himself to be an outsider, mentally, emotionally, even sexually, the more, para-doxically, he wished to remain part of the 'family' that was, for him, the army. His ambition, as Liddell Hart's had been until ousted, was to succeed as a military commander, not military critic: to lead great armies, not merely marshal them in fantasy.

To do so, Monty reasoned, he must make compromises, and ensure loyalties that would provide support in times of need. Whatever Liddell

Hart might feel about him as a leader of men, Monty had no qualms concerning his commanding ability. He did not suffer from depression, or undertake debilitating self-analysis. He had proved that in battle he had a cooler, clearer mind than most, and in peace the ability, energy and patience to impart his tactical doctrine in a way that every officer and soldier could understand. He had preached celibacy to his students in an effort to make them understand that soldiering was a full-time vocation, not a simple pastime. Now that he had proved his dedication to soldiering he felt ready to undertake the next stage of military advancement with a partner, and to know marital felicity and companionship, as his father had done, with a child bride. But he had not succeeded.

The key to command

For Monty it was quite a blow. However, the very emotional detachment that made him seem so 'mad' to Betty Anderson and to other women here came to his aid. The hopes he'd vested in the seventeen-year-old he now shelved in renewed dedication, even addiction, to his profession.

Brian Montgomery later recorded how dictatorial in his personal behaviour the bachelor major became at that time – as if redoubling his already manic application to his work and mission. Thus, for example, he arranged to take Brian and two other subalterns from the regiment on a bicycle tour of World War I battlefields. 'We crossed over from Folkestone to Boulogne and bicycled from there to Le Cateau and the retreat from Mons. We had to follow strict discipline, of course, and move in military formation under his orders and never dismount or mount until he gave us the order,' Brian recollected. He would tolerate no 'belly-aching', as he chose to call it. When one 'wretched chap got very ill' Monty showed no compassion. 'He had sand fly fever and diarrhoea and couldn't really keep up. So Bernard said, "Right, we are going on. Unless you come up and keep up within five minutes, I shall send you home in disgrace." That's the way he treated it! Of course he was right. The fellow did have to pedal on, and he was quite all right. But that was a good example of his determination, and his desire to ensure that young people knew something, got some experience of what war was really like, based on personal knowledge.'[2]

It was also evidence of a worrying fixation with discipline and control of others that made many people, not only Betty Anderson, wonder whether he was not 'a bit mad'.

Spurned by Betty Anderson, it was in 1925 that Monty realized how important it was to get himself across to his men if he was ever to convey his vision of modern tactical efficiency and effectiveness to his troops. The key to achieving this was to deal directly with the NCOs.

In some ways it was a revelation, for he had always abided by the army's hierarchical officer/men divide. Now, at Shorncliffe, he began to realize that the key to revolutionizing the British army might lie not in training officers, or not solely in training officers, but in directly training NCOs – who trained the men.

The revelation was chronicled, day by day, in a training diary he kept. 'The instruction given by the NCOs commanding No. 3 and No. 4 Platoons left much to be desired,' he recorded frankly at the end of the first day of company training with the Royal Warwicks – and made it his object, in himself taking command of one of the platoons, to teach the NCOs how, in turn, to teach and train their men. 'Before returning to barracks,' Monty recorded in the training diary, '4 hours' map reading was done with the NCOs. They were taught how to set a map; to locate their own position; and how to identify distant objects on the ground and on the map. They displayed a great lack of knowledge of this subject, and much attention will have to be given to it in the future.'[3]

In the German Wehrmacht, junior leading by NCOs was axiomatic; in the British army it was, sadly, discouraged – and once again, following his invaluable experience in training a Territorial Army division, Monty was able to see and redress, albeit in a local dimension, a major weakness in his country's armed forces in peacetime.

Lieutenant-Colonel Duke, Monty's later successor as battalion commander, still vividly remembered more than half a century later Monty's performance with his company on army manoeuvres. Duke was then serving as a staff captain in northern England, but in order to keep in touch with the regiment Duke came down to watch the exercises. 'Monty said to me: "Tonight we've got a night show. We're going out to do an attack at dawn. Now I've got a bivouack that takes two – so you'd better come with me!" '

'Whether Monty slept or not, I don't know,' Duke reflected. 'We got up in the middle of the night and stood-to in a lane, ready to attack at dawn. The attack took place across an open field, in which stood a number of stooks. Monty was commanding a company and took up his headquarters behind one of the stooks; the company was deployed behind other stooks. To my surprise I found he had trained his Company Sergeant Major to take down messages quickly; and runners were soon sent off very gallantly across the ground' – a model demonstration of officer–NCO rapport in mock-battle conditions. 'Monty was very orderly,' Duke described; 'it all worked very quietly.'[4]

Not the least impressive, though, was the way Monty insisted upon realism, not only in simulating battle conditions and co-operation with other arms, but the very scenario of battle.

To carry out training that made intellectual sense, he argued, the men must know 'the reason why': for whom, and against whom, they were fighting, as well as the circumstances. The Ten-Year Rule had led to the army reverting to its traditional role of imperial policing duties, but Monty was having none of that. 'Southland, an overseas power, declared war on England on 1st May 1925,' he explained to the men and to the watching 'dignitaries' in his preliminary scene-setting. 'Since the Great War of 1914–1918, England has been occupied with large agricultural schemes, to the detriment of armaments.' The result of such neglect was a possible 'Southland' invasion, Monty went on. The British Prime Minister was 'a naturalized Welshman, and under his guidance the Army & Navy had been reduced to dangerously low limits. The Army, though small, was, however, well trained. Southland, on the other hand, possessed a large army which was well equipped with the most modern inventions. She also had a powerful fleet. It was realized by the English C-in-C that with the forces at his disposal he would be unable to prevent hostile landings until such time as new armies could be raised and trained. Orders were therefore issued for a network of defences to be constructed in depth in the vicinity of the most likely landing places. The role of the garrisons of these places was to offer determined resistance to enemy movement inland, and to fight stubborn rearguard actions. In accordance with these orders, work on defensive positions was commenced early in May by the garrison of Shorncliffe . . .'[5]

Fifteen years before Operation Sealion, Hitler's proposed German invasion of England in 1940, Monty was not only ensuring that training exercises must have a realistic 'context' to make them meaningful to the participating officers and troops but – however tongue-in-cheek – was being prophetic.

Concentrated application

Ten years of combat, staff duties and study had given Monty a host of ideas about the sort of professional regular and Territorial armies Britain should have. However, it was only in the one-on-one conditions of company command in 1925 that Monty recognized the cardinal importance of communication between higher commanders and the ordinary soldiers – and that the key to this lay with the NCOs.

What started as an exercise in how to plan and carry out company tactical instruction thus became a model for training his whole battalion – with a two-way benefit. He organized not only an RAF officer to be attached for a week, during manoeuvres, but a section of pack artillery too. Real artillery shells were fired, and the platoon practised closing up 'as close as possible to the artillery fire before it lifted', he noted in the company diary on 6 May 1925, as senior officers in the brigade and division congregated to watch. He got the commanding officer of the local 5th Battery, Lieutenant-Colonel Bartholomew, to give a further demonstration the next day, followed by a lecture and 'many questions' being asked by the NCOs and men. The next day No. 2 Squadron of the RAF gave a demonstration 'showing the various ways in which aircraft can cooperate with infantry in war'. Night operations followed and, on 13 May, a 'scheme involving field entrenching, carried out in cooperation with 9th Field Company RE'.

It was not an easy time, and none of Monty's contemporaries would pretend that Monty, as superenergetic martinet, was suited to the microcosmic conditions of a company command in his late thirties, after holding such exalted staff positions. Even command of a battalion would, in the words of his successor as CO, be 'too small' a unit for Montgomery. Monty's sights were, in the end, on bigger horizons.

Yet even Monty's most vehement critics recognized that his zeal was not intrinsically egotistical. His military instruction might be resented by colleagues, but as example of professionalism it would never be forgotten, especially once war approached, a decade later.

Liddell Hart would later declare that Monty, lacking 'natural' talents for leadership, had studied military history books and biographies and thereby, as Hart put it, 'learned the methods by which Napoleon and the other "Great Captains" had impressed themselves on troops *en masse* and evoked an enthusiastic response from their armies'.[6] This, however, was to vastly overestimate the power of military historians and biographers. It assumed – as Hart's own fantasies of high command demonstrated – that popular leadership could be learned in such a literary way. Thinking back to Monty in the 1920s Liddell Hart was much closer to the mark when he observed that Monty was 'an outstanding example' of the self-made commander – and that Monty had achieved his success after 'concentrated application to the job and the problem'.[7]

Bloody good

Undoubtedly, in the Royal Warwickshire company exercises – conceived, planned and commanded by Monty himself – which Monty developed in 1925, the foundations were laid for the great training exercises Monty would later conduct – and which would gradually transform the British army in World War II from amateurism to professionalism. By the beginning of August 1925, his reputation as a teacher and trainer was meanwhile beginning to snowball. General Sir 'Tim' Harington had done Monty proud in his confidential report the previous October: 'An officer of very marked ability. An excellent instructor and lecturer – a student of his profession – considerably above average in professional ability and knowledge – recommended for Instructor at the Staff College.'[8]

Acting on this and other testimonials, the War Office not only authorized Monty's promotion to full and substantive major, but offered him a three-year appointment as instructor at the very Staff College he had attended five years previously as a student.

At last, after so much unstinting effort, Monty's talents were being rewarded. The teaching appointment at the Staff College was to begin on 26 January 1926. It 'put a hallmark on my career', Monty later described the moment, 'and my foot was now at last a little up the ladder'. Camberley, he knew, would allow him to assimilate as well as to instruct; 'I knew enough by then to realize that the teacher learns much more than his students. And these three years would be spent working closely with certain other instructors already there, ones who were known to me as some of the best officers in the Army' – men like Colonels Alan Brooke and Bernard Paget – grouped under General Sir Edmund Ironside, legendary commander of the Allied forces in northern Russia during the civil war in

1918–19. Such learning, Monty reasoned, would 'enable me to handle bigger jobs later on with confidence'.[9]

Yet even at this juncture, with his military life mapped out for the next decade (he had forecast to the Military Secretary at the War Office that he would become eligible for Royal Warwickshire battalion command 'in nine years, i.e. 1934, unless of course someone is brought in. I should then be 46'[10]), Monty still dreamed of having a life's companion at his side: someone whom he could spoil, cherish – and control. The memory of Betty Anderson, the attractive, virginal, tomboyish blonde suddenly stirred him to a quite uncharacteristic change of mind. At the last moment, without telling anyone, he therefore packed his things at Christmas and set off for Switzerland – to see if Miss Anderson would reconsider.

Washing her out

The Anderson family was staying in Lenk, in the Bernese Oberland, with a party of largely Indian civil service personnel and their children. Monty was now a brevet lieutenant colonel, appointed an instructor at the Staff College. He would be given a house if he wished, on campus. Who knew? Perhaps even the eyes of the blonde eighteen-year-old might yet be turned, if not by his advances, then by his advancement.

If this was how Monty reasoned – and we can only speculate – he received a brutal shock. Interviewed sixty years later, Betty Anderson recalled her horror when she saw Monty standing waiting in the foyer. 'We arrived at this hotel and who should I see in the lobby but Bernard Montgomery! I thought my goodness, here we go again! *Very* persistent man.

'He knew what he wanted,' Betty granted. Equally, she knew what she didn't want. Irritated by his presumption she decided to ridicule his expectations of a good army wife. There was going to be a fancy dress dance, 'so I said, I know, I'll just play the fool, I'll go as a newspaper boy and call out in cockney all evening – which I did.'[11]

Monty, Betty recalled with a laugh, went along dressed as Napoleon! (Whether the Emperor was still more entranced by his love-object dressing as a boy must remain conjecture.)

Still infatuated, Monty would certainly not relent. In the end Betty engineered a showdown. She was utterly determined. 'Well, do you realize now, I do mean I don't want to marry you?' she fired at the crestfallen colonel – and would never forget his response. '"Yes, I realize now. I shall wash you out of my life. You're the first thing I've not conquered."'

'So wash me out he did!' Betty reflected with a laugh.[12] For his part, Monty's brother Brian recalled the relief with which he learned from their mother at New Park that Monty had written 'to say he knew beyond doubt that Betty did not love him. His final words were "It is all over and I have to accept it."'[13]

Betty never rued her decision. Whether Monty did is unknown; he certainly washed her out of his autobiography, however.[14] On the rebound, meanwhile, he threw himself into his now habitual recourse, when baulked – instruction of those whom he *could* control, and who looked up to him. In this case, it was the children in the Wildstrubel winter sports party, whom he set about teaching to ski and skate. Then the party broke up and returned to England; the children to boarding school, the Andersons to India, and Monty to his new teaching post at Camberley.

Camberley

Monty had vowed he would wash Betty Anderson out of his life, and he did. At the Staff College, Camberley, he threw himself into his new job heart and soul – conceiving a lasting admiration for a man who would later play a profoundly important role in his life: the senior instructor, Colonel Alan Brooke.

Brooke was an artillery officer and, like Colonels Dill and Wavell, tipped in many quarters as a future CIGS. Three years older than Monty, Brooke had ended the Great War a brevet colonel with two DSOs and a reputation as an expert in the technique of rolling artillery barrages, pioneered by the French. Being bilingual – he had been educated in France until the age of eighteen – had helped, but Brooke was equally at home in German, and as dedicated to the business of soldiering as Monty, to the exclusion of almost all else, save ornithology. He possessed a keen, incisive and logical mind – which, like Monty and others, he was bringing to bear on the role of tanks, or mobile, armoured artillery, in future war.

In this way Monty found himself, in 1926, at the very centre of the debate over the future role of 'mechanicalization', and the use of armour in battle: a debate in which Brooke held views at complete variance with pioneers of mobile warfare such as Colonel Fuller.

The year before, Brooke had inadvertently caused the death of his Irish wife in a car accident while driving too fast; thereafter, his ribs and one leg broken, he had 'retreated behind a mask, seldom lowered', as his biographer, David Fraser, later described. 'He rarely spoke to anyone except and about work. He developed a pronounced stoop and rarely smiled. His gifts of wit and capacity for laughter seemed, at least for a while, to have gone as if for ever.'[15]

Whether because of Brooke's widowed demeanour or because of the very fierceness of his views, based upon unrivalled artillery experience, it would not be an exaggeration to say that Monty stood in awe of Alan Brooke from the moment they met – an awe that never diminished to the day Brooke died. Sternness, such as Maud Montgomery had shown all his childhood and youth, was something Monty was bound to fear; sternness allied to a penetrating intelligence and total dedication to the art of war were qualities Monty could not fail to admire. As Brooke's biographer later described, Brooke was 'forbidding', and could 'unnerve with his rapidity of thought, speech and action. His contempt for inadequacy was very apparent. He could be hot-tempered. He suffered fools not at all, and quick in everything, was quick to make judgments of men.'[16]

Brooke, however, could be appreciative also. He had been an instructor since 1923 and had become Director of Studies in 1925; he appears to have taken Monty under his wing, and introduced him to the wider horizons of larger-scale tactical exercises without troops, or TEWTs.

Backed by the Director of Studies, Monty proved a brilliant lecturer. The days of 1920 when he would mock the Staff College establishment were over as, with Colonels Brooke, Franklyn, Paget, Lindsell, Pownall and the other instructors, he approached the course with all the professionalism he could bring to bear.[17] Among the students he would teach in the ensuing three years were many of the most outstanding generals of the next war: from Harold Alexander to Miles Dempsey, from Oliver Leese to Archie Nye, John Harding, Gerald Templer, Humphrey Gale, John Kennedy and Richard McCreery. Other students included Sandy Galloway, Eric Dorman-Smith, 'Bubbles' Barker, D. N. Wimberley, V. C. Russell, G. C. Bucknall, 'Jock' Whiteley, Robert Bruce-Lockhart, Cam Nicholson and A. F. Christison.

Already a master of instruction over a sand-table and an imaginative presenter of tactical problems, Monty loved his time at Camberley. He liked the challenge of putting himself across as a lecturer – liked the limelight and also the rapt attention of a hall full of aspiring male students of warfare. He had, after all, been coaching students wishing to enter the Staff College since 1922, and his own experience as a brigade major – for which appointment the college attempted in the first instance to educate its students – was distinguished, both in war and civil strife, at home and overseas. He had seen service on the North-West Frontier of India, in the plains of southern India, in France, Belgium, Germany and Ireland, had become an expert in the co-ordination of all arms and technologies – infantry, artillery, engineers, tanks, wireless communications, intelligence – as well as co-operation with the RAF and Royal Navy. Other lecturers might show greater rhetorical skills, wider reading, even greater range of military imagination, but few if any could equal Monty's wide experience or his skill at vivid simplification in teaching infantry tactics and staff organization. Intent upon dispersing the fog of war he was determined to see that his students master the essential techniques of command, planning and organization before embarking on hare-brained attempts at original- ity. To Liddell Hart he had already explained his belief in teaching to a 'norm' in the first instance – and he was uncompromisingly forthright with those students, like the ill-fated 'Chink' Dorman-Smith, who allowed cleverness to precede thoroughness. To one student – a future field marshal – he remarked, when the latter gave his solution to a military problem Monty had set: 'Ah, that's interesting, very interesting. It would end in only one way: a scene of intense military confusion.'[18]

Monty's determination to keep things simple, and to take into account the difficulties inherent in asking civilian-soldiers to carry out complex military tasks, would be one of his chief claims to fame in the ensuing war; but it was not always appreciated in peacetime, when there was little apparent fog to disperse, or civilian-soldiers to take into account. Yet he was insistent; it was the responsibility of staff officers and future commanders, he declared, to be crystal clear in setting out their objectives and how they wished them to be achieved; any obfuscation or slapdashness would risk men's lives. He duly made enemies as well as converts. One poor student received the mark of nought for a military paper, out of a possible 500. When asked how the student could possibly have done so badly, Monty answered: 'Quite simple. It says clearly that you are not to write in the margin. This student wrote in the margin. If he can't obey a simple instruction like that, he's not fit to command others.'[19]

From the beginning of his instructorship in 1926, then, Monty's reputation as a brilliant, demanding but somewhat dictatorial and eccentric bachelor teacher grew. It was, however, soon to be tempered by something he had sought for a lifetime, yet never felt reciprocated: love.

Dirty bugger

Monty's failure to win Betty Anderson's hand in marriage in 1925/6 was, in retrospect, fortunate. Homosexual or strictly homosocial officers of his generation who tended towards misogyny were not always lucky when taking younger trophy wives. For example, a certain Claude Auchinleck married, at the age of thirty-six, a beautiful twenty-one-year-old while at the Staff College, Camberley – a marriage that would come to grief in the most humiliating way for Auchinleck, when she ran off with a more exciting air marshal. Lord Gort, too, married a twenty-year-old beauty while trying to enter the Staff College – a marriage which also came apart in scandalous circumstances, as Gort's young wife sought men better able to satisfy her sexual expectations, forcing Gort to divorce her in a highly publicized case. It is not unreasonable, therefore, to question whether, had Monty's pursuit of young Betty Anderson proved successful, he would have been able to keep her as a wife. In a post-Victorian era when women's behaviour could no longer be coerced and controlled through patriarchal laws, marriage between men and women of widely disparate ages and sexual orientation placed, in all too many cases, intolerable strains upon its success, unless both partners were exceptionally flexible – as proved the case between Lord Mountbatten and his heiress-wife Edwina Ashley.

Meanwhile, what *was* Monty's underlying sexual orientation? In the controversial debates in the House of Lords many years later Monty himself would pour scorn on the proposed bill to legalize homosexual intercourse between consenting adults, maintaining that to do so would be to remove a 'bulwark' against 'evil influences' that threatened to 'undermine the very foundations of our national character'. As historians of sexuality have observed, 'it is often noted that those who articulate hostility to homosexuals or bisexuals are in a panic of anxiety about their own ambivalence or repressions'.[20]

Monty certainly articulated hostility during the passage of the bill, and seemed unnaturally anxious about men's repressed desires – desires that were, in his view, held in check only by fear of the law. 'To condone unnatural offences in male persons over 21, or, indeed, in male persons of any age, seems to me utterly wrong,' he argued. 'One may just as well condone the Devil and all his works. I am entirely opposed to this Bill,' he would declare in 1965, when seventy-eight years old. 'My main reason is that a weakening of the law will strike a blow at all those devoted people who are working to improve the moral fibre of the youth of this country. And heaven knows! it wants improving,' he explained with a laugh to a packed chamber.

'I am not very expert on girls,' Monty then openly confessed. About boys and men, however, particularly in the armed services, he could speak with authority, he claimed. He had become, in his way, a twentieth-century equivalent of Mr Gladstone, who had spent his old age trying to get to know and reform prostitutes; had become involved, as he himself declared, with many organizations for boys, from the Church Lads' Brigade to the Mayflower Centre, and knew 'quite a lot' about helping them, while his concern for the welfare and efficiency of the army was legendary. Ignoring the fact that the bill did not cover behaviour in the armed forces, he was at pains to articulate its threat to military discipline. 'The fighting men of Britain have been my comrades-in-arms for over half a century,' he declared. 'If these unnatural practices are made legal, a blow is struck at the discipline of the British Armed Forces.' To give an example, he quoted the men of 'an infantry battalion. Suppose the men know that their officers, perhaps, are indulging in these practices, and it is legal and nothing can be done. Take a large aircraft carrier, with 2,000 men cooped up in a small area. Imagine what would happen in a ship of that sort if these practices crept in. No action could be taken; it is legal. How can good order – How can discipline and good order be maintained in such circumstances? Surely it must not be.' He ended with an impassioned plea to his fellow peers not to condone such 'practices', but to 'defy them'.[21]

Clearly the defying of homosexual desire, especially desire for younger men, was, even at age seventy-eight, still a problem for Monty. It was undoubtedly fear which propelled him to speak up as he did in the House of Lords, and which then prompted him, when he realized the new Sexual Offences Bill might well become law, to propose an extraordinary amendment. This would set the age of homosexual consent to eighty, when Monty felt he himself would at last be beyond temptation. (He wasn't.) Moreover, an added reason for postponing the age of consent beyond retirement age, he declared in an absurd but revealing non-sequitur, was that 'at least one has the old-age pension to pay for any blackmail which may come along'.[22]

Not content to let the matter rest there, he made a solemn declaration which made many peers and commentators feel he 'doth protest too much'. 'I regard,' Monty told the House of Lords with great solemnity, 'the act of homosexuality in any form as the most abominable bestiality that any human being can take part in and which reduces him almost to the status of an animal. The time will come when we shall have to choose a title for this Bill, and I think that instead of, "Sexual Offences Bill" the proper title should be, "A Charter for Buggery".'[23]

No statement could have more vividly portrayed the anxiety Monty felt, even at age seventy-eight. Meanwhile, aged thirty-eight in 1926, had Monty, in seeking to get married, struggled to defy 'the Devil and all his works' – i.e., his attraction to young men and boys?

About the trip he had paid to Lenk at Christmas 1925 Monty was, in his *Memoirs*, coy, neglecting to mention it had been made to see Betty Anderson. He did, however, mention a Mrs Carver and her two attractive boys: 'I soon made friends with the boys and with their mother, and the holiday passed pleasantly', he recalled.[24] So pleasantly that Monty, sometime during his first year as instructor at the Staff College, arranged a second Lenk holiday for the winter of 1926–7.

Was it the Carver boys who drew Monty – or their mother? Possibly Monty himself, anxious to find a wife but humiliatingly defeated at his first attempt, did not know. However, if his interest in Betty Carver's young boys was the initial attraction, in the manner of Thomas Mann's *Death in Venice*, then the word 'homosexuality' does not do justice to the complexity of Monty's emotions, desires, repressions and sublimations. As the Cambridge historian Ronald Hyam noted, the word 'homosexual' is 'an imprecise and dangerous word for historians, since it has become associated with a supposedly exclusive identity and with the "gay" cultural group of our own day'.[25] Another historian of sexuality, Richard Daven-port-Hines, noted how the 'outlawing of homosexuality' through the Labouchère Amendment to the Criminal Law Amendment Act of 1885, almost two years before Monty's birth, 'separated affection from sexuality, and increased the isolation and stylization of many men' – generally as 'queers' or 'buggers'.[26] One young man later recalled how, after falling in love with a sailor in World War I, he was derided as a 'dirty bugger' in the street. 'I couldn't believe that love and affection – which had brought me such happiness – were things to be ashamed of, and was incredulous when told I could be sent to prison.'[27]

Hyam certainly considered the word 'homosexuality' a particularly 'false and vulgar label when applied to individuals such as Kitchener and Montgomery'. The two field marshals were, he claimed, 'easily acquitted of any actual physical contact with other males. But in Montgomery's case there is a confusion: he was not in the least attracted by men,' he stated categorically though erroneously, 'but he was emotionally involved with small boys. Either way, much ink has been spilled on trying to find an answer to the question why some people are attracted to members of the same sex.'

Spilling a trifle more, Hyam reminded readers that Freud himself had puzzled as to why the majority of people become exclusively heterosexual, given that *all* human beings grow up with some homosexual feelings, of varying intensity. But whatever the reason for exclusive heterosexuality among the majority of adults, there was a terrible price paid by those who had therefore to conform to sexual norms, even when their own sexuality did not accord with such strict ruling. This price was repression, sublimation and compensation, often leading to 'some degree of maladjustment, to eccentricity and even mental illness'.[28]

Elements of all three outcomes would certainly be evident in Monty's tortured post-Victorian psyche, as will be seen. Did his lack of interest in the female sex, and severely disciplined but evident affections for, almost adoptions of, young men issue from the same sexuality as his Farrar uncles – or did it all go back to his sometimes vicious, domineering mother, and a psychosexual knot he simply could not untie? It is almost impossible to answer such a question with assurance. As far as Betty's eldest son, John Carver – who was now in his second year at Charterhouse School – was aware, no actual meeting took place between his mother and Monty during the year, yet he and his brother 'concluded something was up' by the summer, because 'we never had any money, and my mother said: "You liked Switzerland very much, didn't you?"' – followed by her suggestion, ' "Well, I think we ought to go back to Lenk again. But if we're going to afford to do this you'll have to fork out some of your savings." (A lot of the money she had was for us, in trust, you see.) So we all agreed to this. In fact we thought it was tremendous. It never occurred to us that there was any ulterior motive, because we wanted to go anyway, we were very keen. But it occurred to me later there might have been an ulterior motive!'[29]

The whiff of romance

For Betty the motive was simple: the shy brevet lieutenant colonel. There was no big party at the Wildstrubel when the Carvers arrived early in January 1927 – only Sir Edward and Lady Crowe, and the eccentric Staff College teacher.

Whatever the motive for Monty, the result was to alter his whole life. 'This time I saw a great deal of Betty Carver,' he related in his *Memoirs*, 'and by the time the holiday was over I had fallen in love: for the first and only time in my life,' he claimed – forgetting, it appeared, his passionate pursuit of Betty Anderson the year before.

But perhaps Monty was not forgetting. As Betty Anderson recalled, Monty had seemed to be wholly uninterested in who she really was, imagining he could simply impress her into submission with his rising rank and swagger-stick, even his mother's cars in Ireland. Betty Carver was in a very different category: indeed, one might say she was the first and only woman, apart from his mother, with whom Monty had a truly profound relationship in his life.

J. M. Barrie, author of *Peter Pan*, had likewise fallen deeply in love with the mother of some boys he'd met in Kensington Gardens twenty-seven years earlier. Revising his manuscript of *Tommy & Grizel* after meeting Sylvia Llewelyn Davies, their mother, Barrie had made new notes that Grizel, in line with Sylvia Llewelyn Davies, was now to have a 'nose uptilted (really more as if point cut off). She is a square-shouldered woman who will always look glorious as a mother, (so I think of her now, always so). A woman to confide in (no sex in this, we feel it in man or woman). All secrets of womanhood you feel behind these calm eyes & courage to face them. A woman to lean on in trouble.'[30]

Monty's growing affection for the widowed mother of the Carver boys, Betty Carver, mirrored Barrie's earlier infatuation with Sylvia Llewelyn Davies, and her children. It was to have a different outcome, however – for Betty Carver was not a 'safely' married lady but a single woman, a widow.

Adult women had, until this moment, always frightened Monty – as his mother had. Betty Carver, however, had a magical ability to make people feel comfortable. Certainly she was able to put Monty, the most threatened of men in the company of women, at his ease, and seemed delighted by the paternalistic attention he paid to her boys.

Betty had been deeply in love with her husband, who was killed at Gallipoli, and was not seeking another romance of that kind. She thus found Monty engagingly eccentric, even laughing at his 'Monty' parlance, which infuriated many people: a form of jocular, teasing inquisition during which key subjects or significant items of interest would be deliberately caricatured, with mocking yet affectionate relish. Thus Monty had questioned her closely on her '*château*' in Chiswick: ribbing Betty's rented accommodation, yet also genuinely interested in her habitat, since it was where the Montgomerys had settled on return from Tasmania.

Soon Monty found the company of the boys' mother wonderfully congenial – a discovery he found almost shocking, given his lifetime of misogyny. Betty was, in most respects, his opposite – for example 'the boys were taught to hate war and anything to do with soldiers', Monty recalled – but this opposition intrigued and challenged him. 'Betty Carver was about the same age as my brother, but otherwise utterly different from him in every conceivable way, except one,' Brian Montgomery later observed – namely her sense of humour; 'in fact she was always laughing, at people, events and life generally, and in a manner which was highly infectious'. In contrast to Bernard, however, Betty was an artist, a painter in oils and watercolour, and keen on sculpture. 'In appearance she was dark and vivacious,' Brian recalled, 'with a high forehead, wide-spaced grey eyes, a large nose and full mouth.'[31]

Though opposites in most respects – the misogynist soldier and the anti-war artist – Monty and Betty had in truth much more in common than their sense of humour. Her father, Robert Hobart, had come from Southern Ireland and, like Monty's grandfather Sir Robert Montgomery, had 'served the empire' by entering the Indian Civil Service as a young man. Having achieved a certain success by his forties he also had married a much younger Victorian bride, a seventeen-year-old girl from Northern Ireland. It was thus, as Betty's son John later put it, an almost identical family to the Montgomerys in its Irishness, its size, the age gap between the parents, the dominance of the religiously obsessed mother (a strict Calvinist), and the pattern of the children entering either the Indian Civil Service or the armed forces. Charles, the eldest son, went out to India as a civil servant; Frank, the second son, went into the navy; Patrick – known universally as 'Hobo' – became an army engineer, attending the Staff College, Camberley, the year before Monty, in 1919; and Stanley, another son, joined the army and attended the Staff College in the same year as Monty, 1920.

Betty herself had been sent to a finishing school in Lausanne, where she had made friends with a certain Alison Carver, whose father was a cotton-mill owner, said to be worth a quarter of a million pounds, and who kept twenty hunters in his stables. In due course Betty, invited to stay with the Carvers at their country seat in Cheshire, had met Alison's two brothers, who had both entered the cotton mill. One of these brothers was Waldo: a brilliant and handsome boy who had started rowing when at Cambridge University and within four years was representing his country at the Olympic Games.

Waldo Carver and Betty Hobart had fallen deeply in love. Curiously, it had not been opposition from the rich Carvers which had threatened their prospect of marriage, but the prejudice then rife in 'professional' families such as the Hobarts about 'marrying into trade'. 'You cannot imagine the opposition there was in those days,' Betty told John, her son, later, 'the feeling that the Hobarts would thereby demean themselves.' In the end Betty's father was persuaded to give his consent only on payment of the 'most enormous marriage settlement' – a fortunate agreement, since Robert Hobart, exhausted by his years in India, and recently retired from the ICS, died just a few days before the couple were wedded in 1910.

Though far from being a beauty, Betty was generous and kind by nature, had a profoundly artistic temperament, was highly intelligent, and possessed a lack of emotional inhibition which endeared her to people. When her husband Waldo was killed, she was incoherent with grief and, according to her son John, it took a long time before she got over the loss of both her husband and her father.[32] For a while she lived with her mother-in-law in Cheshire, together with her two small children and their nanny; but they did not get on well, she felt trapped and soon moved down to London where she did war work, riding her controversial motor cycle and sidecar, in which passengers travelled 'at their peril', John remembered.[33]

After the war Betty had made a number of not altogether successful attempts to achieve personal and financial independence. She took a job as an art and English mistress at a preparatory school in Norfolk so that her two children could be with her. However, the headmaster importuned her and she left after only a term. In the end she decided to enrol at the Slade as a student, under the famous Professor Tonks. Thus, relatively late in the day, she began her initiation into the artistic and bohemian world of London.

Betty had remained particularly close to her brother Hobo: a brilliant army officer who had transferred to the Royal Tank Corps and was currently an instructor at the Staff College, Quetta. It was, in fact, through Hobo that Betty had come to live in Chiswick, after meeting Hobo's close friends Gwen and Alan Herbert – author of *The Secret Battle*. The Herberts lived by the Thames; Gwen Herbert had taken such a liking to the widowed sister of their friend Hobo that she'd offered to rent Betty a house they owned in a neighbouring street, off Chiswick Mall.

Gwen Herbert still remembered this period clearly when in her eighties. Her husband Alan reckoned that Colonel Patrick 'Hobo' Hobart was destined to achieve great things in the army, for he had a fascinating and forceful mind, and was interested in as many things outside army life as in it. His sister Betty, though less dynamic, was just as intelligent, but also gay and lively in company, trusting and loyal in friendship. Because the Herberts too had children, they began to spend family holidays together in Cornwall, where Betty started to paint seriously.

It was in the spring of 1927 that the Herberts caught the first whiff of Betty's romance.

'Bring him in'

Betty called on the Herberts one morning to return something she'd borrowed. After a while, seeing that Betty was becoming nervous, if not agitated, Gwen said: 'Betty, what on earth's the matter?' 'I must go,' Betty blushed. 'There's someone waiting in the car.' 'Well, for heaven's sake, bring him in!' Gwen insisted. But Betty shook her head. 'Oh, no, I couldn't do that – he's far too shy!' she answered.[34]

Did the Herberts think the match a strange one, when finally they did meet Monty? Lady Herbert recalled that they did. It was not, she emphasized, because of Betty's anti-war convictions, but simply because they themselves found Monty, at that time, so 'unremarkable'! If he had achieved a certain reputation in the army, it was not one that had filtered through to the world outside. Monty's tactical doctrines of modern warfare, so carefully thought out and incomparably presented before junior officers and NCOs, made little sense to an outside world that, since the 1925 Treaty of Locarno, was intent upon disarmament and wished largely to forget war. Hobo Hobart was an exception because he was such an outspoken personality in his professional and private life, and held such futuristic ideas – ideas about mechanization and tanks which had a certain panache to a layman; Monty's theories, on the other hand, had little romantic appeal beyond the readers of the *Antelope* and the lower echelons of the Staff College. Certainly they were of scant interest in the cultured circles frequented by the Herberts – something they did not hide, and which caused Monty to be understandably shy of entering their bohemian house.

If her friends felt, privately, that the socially timid Staff College instructor was an inappropriate match for Betty, however, it does not seem to have inhibited Betty in the least. She and Monty began to meet more and more frequently in the spring of 1927; so frequently that, when Monty failed to propose to her, it became sufficiently embarrassing in her family circle for her brother Hobo to urge her to force Monty to 'declare his intentions'.[35] Did the brevet lieutenant colonel intend to marry her, or not?

The proposal

If, as Monty claimed in his *Memoirs*, he had fallen in love with Betty Carver already at Lenk in January 1927, why did it take him so long to propose?

The fact was that, like J. M. Barrie, Monty had befriended two attractive young boys, and had then become deeply attached to their warm, intelligent, laughing and loving mother. But Barrie, 'safely' married himself and not interested in the sexual side of marriage, could enjoy a familial yet idealized, platonic relationship with Sylvia Llewelyn Davies – even taking Sylvia away on holiday with one or several of her boys – given her own happy marriage to her husband Arthur, a promising barrister. Monty, by contrast, was not married. Nor was Betty.

Yet, if Monty wished to achieve command of a battalion in the army – the prerequisite to higher command posts – he still needed to have a wife. It was in this quandary that pressure from Betty's brother Hobo brought him to the crossroads of his life.

In other circumstances, Hobo might have ignored his sister's private affairs, but the spring of 1927 had proved the turning point in his own. 'Uncle P – as we called him – reckoned he was going to become a field marshal,' John Carver later recalled of his ambitious uncle, 'and there was a tacit understanding that later on my mother would keep house for him. I mean this was seriously considered.'[36] But early in 1927, as Hobart's biographer, Kenneth Macksey, recorded, Hobo's chances of becoming a field marshal plummeted, for he began a controversial affair with Dorothea Chater, the wife of a fellow army officer, which became a scandal throughout the British army, the two of them behaving 'like homing magnets' in Macksey's phrase.

Major Chater had been Hobo's brother officer in the Royal Engineers, before Hobo switched to the Royal Tank Corps; he then became a student at Quetta Staff College, where Hobart was the tank instructor – and began bedding the student's wife.

Rumours of the affair between Dorothea and Hobo not only spread like a forest fire in India, but soon had the telegraph wires between London and India overheating – indeed the War Office became so worried about potential disaffection in the army as a direct result of Hobart's scandalous affair that it sent out an official letter warning that any officer who 'disrupted' the marriage of a 'brother officer' in the same regiment would be expected to resign. This was a fortunate let-out for Hobart, given his 1923 transfer into the Royal Tank Corps – though the scandal did in effect ruin him.

Returning to England from Quetta, and having decided to marry Dorothea Chater if she could obtain a divorce, Hobo meanwhile realized he would not, after all, be requiring his sister's domestic or hostessing services. It was this, then, that caused him to redouble his concern about the 'intentions' of Betty's new beau.

Pressured, Betty decided she must be forthright with her boyfriend. Bernard had offered to drive her to her son John's school, Charterhouse, to which Betty's younger boy, Dick, was due to go that autumn. On arrival Betty told the boys to busy themselves, while she and Monty entered the fives courts to have a private conversation.

In later years Monty would often tell the story. His sense of humour was always tickled by life's incongruities: and the fives courts of a British boys' boarding school seemed to him a most incongruous place to propose. At any rate, once alone, Betty suggested they ought to stop seeing each other, at least for a while, as people were beginning to gossip about them. Monty, who ought to have told her much sooner what he felt about her, argued, finally expostulating: 'Don't be silly, Betty – I love you.' Betty then began to cry.

Tears were not part of Monty's emotional territory. He had learned to withhold them early in life; to take his beatings 'like a man'. He had never cracked in World War I, as a soldier, nor had he during the conflict in Ireland. Yet before Betty's womanly tears he felt helpless – and to his own surprise, triumphant.

'That finished it,' Monty would recount with wonder, remembering Betty's flood. 'We were engaged!'[37]

The wedding

The Carver boys, impatient to know 'what was going on', burst into the fives courts, and were told what had happened. Betty's younger son, Dick, was appalled. 'At that age one thought this was a nice friend who was great fun . . . I was shocked and upset,' Dick confessed candidly later. 'It had never occurred to me they might get married.'[38]

Perhaps it had not really occurred to Monty, as a reality. Certainly the couple did not rush to announce the news. The boys returned to school and only several months later, on 25 June 1927, did a formal announcement appear in *The Times*:

LIEUTENANT-COLONEL B. L. MONTGOMERY AND MRS CARVER The marriage arranged between Lieutenant-Colonel B. L. Montgomery, DSO, of the Staff College, Camberley, and Mrs E. A. Carver of 2, Riverside, Chiswick Mall, London W4 will take place very quietly in London on July 27.

'Arranged' was perhaps the operative word. Monty's family, colleagues and students were utterly amazed. 'WHICH IS IT TO BE, THE SOLDIER OR THE HUSBAND?' young Francis de Guingand, Monty's protégé in York, cabled immediately, referring to Monty's maxim.

Having given his word, though, Monty was determined to try his best. He was, however, nervous about his mother and her reaction – so much so that he secretly decided to avoid it. The wedding service, he arranged with his father, would be conducted by the aged Bishop himself, with Monty's brother Colin, a curate in a parish near Gravesend, assisting him. It would take place in the parish church of Chiswick, a few doors away from Betty's house. Meanwhile, his brother Brian was ordered to be best man. Beyond keeping the ring handy, Brian would have 'nothing else to do', Monty assured him at dinner on the eve of the wedding, which he spent with the Carver boys; 'don't make a muck of it,' he cautioned; 'put the ring in your pocket and be very careful not to drop it!'

Brian was most careful, he recalled. From the club where he was staying in London – the Junior United Service – Monty drove Brian, on the morning of 27 July 1927, to Betty's 'pretty little house' on Chiswick Mall, and together they went inside 'to see that everything was all right', as Monty put it. Brian was amazed.

We met Betty who was thereupon told by her fiancé not to be late at the church, where she was due at twelve noon. We then drove to Chiswick Parish Church where I remember Bernard gave me the wedding ring with a repetition of his previous injunction about it. He himself then went first, he said 'to tip the verger and see that he knows what he's about'; and secondly 'to the vestry to make sure that Father and Colin are there and that they are ready and know what to do'. Looking back, I have often thought it must have been an unusual event, even for a bishop of world-wide experience, to be tackled in the vestry by a bridegroom, whom he was about to marry, with a query as to his own ability to conduct the service! I then went into the church and at the steps met Hobo, Betty's brother, who was to give her in marriage. I remember we stood there chatting as the members of the family and close friends, perhaps some twenty-five in all, were arriving . . . When it was over we all followed the bride and bridegroom down the aisle to the West door, and beyond the porch into the street outside, where Bernard's car was parked . . . Father and Colin had also joined us, still in their robes, so there was now quite a crowd outside the church, opposite that wonderful old inn in the street leading down to the river, when Bernard and Betty got into their car. To our astonishment the bridegroom then turned to our parents and said: 'Goodbye, goodbye, we're off now, straight to our honeymoon'[39]

– the traditional reception having been deliberately excluded from Monty's plans.

This, then, was the beginning of the strangest metamorphosis, as the once-misogynistic bachelor, Lieutenant-Colonel Montgomery, drove off with his equally amazed bride, leaving their nonplussed families, friends and onlookers deliberately behind.

The honeymoon

Monty need not have worried; he had fallen into the very best of hands. Ruled throughout childhood by her puritan mother, deprived by death of her father and then, after only five years of marriage, of her first husband, there was for Betty real and lasting security in now finding a man who, by his willingness to shoulder responsibility, acted as a surrogate father as well as companion to her. He proved fiercely loyal – and profoundly devoted, too, to her two sons. Besides, if Monty was considered by most people to be eccentric and super-controlling, he was far less so than Betty's irascible and dictatorial brother Hobo.

But if Monty was this to Betty, how much more was Betty to Monty! Monty's pride of possession in bearing her triumphantly away like the spoils of war, said all. Approaching forty, rejected by the only girl to whom he had ever proposed, aware that he was talented and even, possibly, called upon to achieve great things in the course of time; yet lonely, often yearning to show love, to express love and affection towards surrogate sons, and to find a mother figure who would accept him . . . It is easy to see how, as the months went by, Monty's pride turned to joy as he began to recognize this was a much deeper relationship than ever his amour for Miss Anderson had been, or perhaps could have been. To him 'Betty I' had been an ideal, a trophy to be won; whereas 'Betty II' was real: a mature woman in flesh and blood; not beautiful but sensitive, intelligent, serious, experienced, artistically talented and a delight to be with. Had Miss Anderson said yes to his proposal, Monty might have spent his life vainly attempting to impress her, as he had done with his mother, whereas with Betty Carver he was able, it seems, to attain a naturalness, a (for him) relaxed and yet excited happiness that came almost unexpectedly in his life: something that seemed God-given and which undoubtedly restored his faith in the Almighty at a time when, as his brother Brian recalled, his religious faith, in the aftermath of World War I, had wavered to the point of agnosticism.

So, in retrospect, it would appear. Only Basil Liddell Hart, in the years to come, would ever dispute the impression that Monty and Betty formed an almost idyllic couple. 'You are a bully, Monty, a born bully. You bullied your wife unmercifully, as you bullied everyone else!' he once taunted Monty towards the end of his life, when staying as his guest at Bournemouth. Monty went pale and his face sharpened. 'Don't you *ever* mention Betty!' he rapped. 'Don't you ever mention her name!'

The wasp waist

Basil Liddell Hart was hardly one to talk. It is now known that his own relationship with his first wife Jessie, behind the façade of her bourgeois Stroud respectability, was deeply skewed. Jessie's father was a stock-broker; Hart had counted on her eventual inheritance – his love speaking 'more of sober calculation than grand passion', as his biographer has described.[40] Marrying her in 1918 Hart had soon conceived a passion for her underclothes that bordered on the manic. 'About the [female] waist, the wasp-waist, he exhibited a form of monomania,' Alex Danchev later revealed. 'The instrument of the wasp-waist, the totem of shapeliness, was the corset.'[41] In due course Hart became as tormented by the notion of corsetry as he was about military history and high command: 'his consuming interest in tight-lacing . . . outsailed the bounds of fashion and yawed into fetishism'.[42] This fetishism led in turn to exhibitionism – involving the vicarious pleasure of seeing his wife tightly corseted, then fawned over and even bedded by others. 'Smitten men fell at her feet . . . The impression she created was also the impression he created. He shaped her and he draped her. He veiled her and he unveiled her. He bought her clothes, not merely paying for them but selecting them personally' – the captain noting each purchase, each gift, in his minutely detailed diary entries: fawn kid gloves, satin shoes, taffeta petticoat, silk vests, six brassieres, fawn flared dresses, satin frock, silk jumper, red frock . . .

In pride of place, for Liddell Hart, however, were the corsets he designed for Jessie, made with nineteen-inch waists, detachable suspenders, 'special V shape contoured' and as 'strongly boned as possible'. The result, for Jessie, was a form of sexual bullying that would ultimately be catastrophic in its effect both on her and on their son. 'Hubby dear – I don't like these [?illegible] corsets,' she complained on one occasion, 'because I am uncomfortable and they make me feel sick.'[43] Nevertheless, she submitted to his para-exhibitionism, and on his apparent encouragement, if not open pimping, she took a number of lovers. 'Was he Captain or Captive?' his biographer asked.[44]

Hart's son, Adrian, was less generous. His father's exhibitionism, he claimed, involved transvestism, his mania for corsetry extending to designing and wearing wasp-waisted corsets himself, as well as designing them for Jessie to wear. Some might see him as a war invalid, betrayed by an increasingly adulterous, cantankerous and extravagant wife, but the other view, the one Adrian set out, was that Hart was a young man 'from a spoilt and sheltered home who had been introduced to his innocent young wife by a sex pervert in her home town . . . He continued the transvestite practices with which he was already engaging and required a submission, involving a degree of physical sadism as well as violent outbursts of temper; with this she long continued to put up, while helping him in his early struggles for success. Other men had been introduced by my father himself into this set-up and then my father, bored by his wife's companionship, had been enticed away, leaving her to live unhappily ever afterwards.'[45]

Though his son's version might be jaded by filial resentment, Liddell Hart certainly left among his voluminous papers notes of a private consultation with Jessie's gynaecologist, in which the doctor diagnosed Jessie's enlarged left ovary as the result of 'sex starvation' – a diagnosis seemingly compounded by Hart's own admission that he'd had 'no [sexual] connection for years'. Hart's shenanigans, the doctor warned, especially his 'indirect sexual excitation', had merely increased his wife's 'neurasthenia'.[46] The doctor prescribed a baby; Hart confined himself to writing about 'expanding torrents' in his publications on military tactics.

It is possible Hart had become, partly through his hypochondria, partly through the effects of his gassing and the trauma of his fears during the battle of the Somme, impotent. 'More than most men, Liddell Hart liked to look: to look and not to touch,' his biographer recorded.[47] At any event, instead of giving his wife another baby he simply gave her more corsets, before finally leaving her in 1938. (His corset-mania was then transferred to his second wife and her daughters – Hart threatening to go on hunger strike unless they did as he insisted, namely, abandon their country clothes and wear the high heels, stockings and the corsets he had measured them for. 'Corset conflict', as his biographer chronicled ruefully, 'continued, at varying intensity, for several years.'[48])

Set against Liddell Hart's perversion, then, as well as T. E. Lawrence's fetishistic fantasies (leading to the invention of 'the Old Man' who required him to be beaten and disciplined – his 'creative psychopathology' as his biographer John E. Mack described his addiction), or Hobo Hobart's scandalous affair with Dorothea Chater, the wife of his student, Monty's courtship, marriage and love for Betty Carver seem extraordinarily conventional and happy, for all the consternation that the marriage caused among their friends and relatives who thought him incapable of a heterosexual relationship, let alone marriage. 'The taboo against intimacy with women was,' as Mack has written of Lawrence, 'always intense for Law-rence. Lawrence was generally more comfortable with closeness among men, and could tolerate perhaps a perverse form of intimacy with certain men in a way that he could never have tolerated in a woman. Only in the link between the flagellation ritual and the childhood beatings at the hands of the mother does the never-resolved conflict over the attachment to her remain in evidence. Penitent rituals,' Mack pointed out, were not unusual in an era of repressed homosexuality; 'Typically, they recreate childhood scenes, relationships and conflicts that have been revived by the events and traumata of adult life.' Once Lawrence began to use his young 'macho' Scotsman, John Bruce, for his elaborate sexual scenarios, Mack posited, Lawrence knew he 'could no longer return to public life';[49] the private would have become too political.

In Monty's case, just as he had managed to stay within the military 'system' despite his difficult character, so too had he managed to stay within the bounds of conventional sexual mores despite his difficult sexu-ality. Beyond his relationship with his mother, his affections were reserved exclusively for men. Growing love and admiration for Betty, as a woman, a mother and an artist, had allowed him to avoid the psychopathological outrages, private or public, of his seemingly more brilliant contemporaries. Moreover, it was not that there was no truth in Liddell Hart's allegation of marital bullying, despite pot calling kettle black – Monty's angry response betraying his very vulnerability to such criticism – but it took no account of Betty's very real contentment at such controlling solicitude: a form of bullying she'd experienced and learned to manipulate to her own advantage since childhood and which, once again, she turned to her advantage in Monty. Tears might be a woman's most obvious weapon, but with a martinet like Monty they were extraordinarily effective. Monty had never in his life seen his mother cry, whereas he had often seen others weeping at her cruelty – indeed, he once offered to buy two replacements for a broken vase if she would refrain from beating his weeping cousin. In short, the martinet melted.

Thus, while the Herberts saw in Monty a relative nobody – a small, rather sharp-featured little officer who was quite unread, shy and with-drawn in their company, and of slightly dubious sexuality, and in Betty a gifted, artistic, sensitive woman who ought by rights to be the wife of a 'real' man – Betty herself saw better than they did, perceiving in the socially shy, unimposing brevet lieutenant colonel with the high voice and the habit of tugging his ear a talent that surpassed her own, even that of her brother Hobo. Years before, she'd written that a woman 'is essentially the sensitive transparent globe into which man pours the riches of his originality'. Far from taking the feminist stance of the Bloomsbury figures with whom she associated, Betty considered that any creative achievement by a woman was only a modified reflection, a reprocessing of the creativity she absorbed through the love of a man, and in Monty she recognized that man.

It was, to be sure, a very different love from the one she'd shared with her first husband Waldo, as her letters reveal, but no less important to her for that. Indeed, it was probably deeper and richer for the very experience she now had of life and of death. Instinct told her she had found the right man: a man whose genius perhaps she alone, outside the army, recognized and whom, despite his weird sexuality and his bossy, even tyrannical ways, she could love and . . . mother?

For the moment, however, they drove to Church Stretton in Shropshire for a few days – days so etched with happiness as they played golf together and read James Stephens's *Crock of Gold* to each other in the evenings that Monty would later insist on his stepson John doing the same when he got married. Lieutenant-Colonel and Mrs Montgomery then returned to London to check the boys were in good hands (they were to go to New Park in August); and continued their honeymoon where their romance had started: in Switzerland. They were, at last, a couple.

Married life

From the moment Monty and Betty returned from their honeymoon the new family of Lieutenant-Colonel B. L. Montgomery, with its two ready-made Carver sons, came into existence. Betty's son John had taken a somewhat materialistic point of view when the wedding was announced. 'Hurrah,' he'd shouted, 'we'll have a car at last!', rather than a motorcycle and side-car. They did indeed have a car now: 'an old Belsize – a wonderful thing. We thought this was marvellous. One of the greatest proofs of his love was that he allowed my mother to drive it – which was horrifying actually!'[50]

Monty had promised to bring up Betty's two boys. He proved as good as his word. Thus, once the 'shock' of their mother's marriage had worn off, the two boys found themselves leading a very different life in the school holidays. Gone was the old chaos in which Betty had run her domestic affairs. From now on Monty took charge of everything. When his sister Winsome met Betty for the first time in Ireland and asked how she was coping with being married to Bernard, Betty replied: 'It's absolute bliss after ten years battling with two small boys and bringing them up.' She then added, with a laugh: 'But I've had to give up many of my own ideas – he even engages the servants!'

'It was a bolt from the blue when he got married,' Winsome later reflected. 'His wife Betty was a lovely person. I suppose she was plain. She had a very interesting face, not pretty at all. We just took her to our hearts straight away . . . Monty did everything for her – everything. He just opened out, he was so thrilled to have somebody to love. She drew him out to express his affection and enter into family life. For her boys to have a step-father, that was the great thing for her.'[51] 'She just fitted in with us, you see,' Winsome recorded later. 'She was a darling, and my mother adored her – we all loved her, for she made Bernard so transparently happy.'[52]

Relations with Maud, as Dick Carver recalled of the summer, were by no means as easy as Winsome assumed. Betty was actually 'a bit chary' of Maud – as indeed everyone was, including Monty, who battled with her as of yore. In New Park, the year before, he'd caused a memorable stir when insisting that the dairy was unhygienic (a sewer ran through the yard) but then ordering that the family cow be put down after he had accidentally lost the vet's thermometer in the animal's behind – a decision that had led to Maud's understandable wrath! Looking back, John Carver was also reminded of the tension between Monty and the Hobart-Carver family, even at this period. 'I think Monty did feel people didn't love him as he ought to be loved. He did have a thing about his relations – I don't remember him saying anything really very pleasant about any of his relations, except his father, for whom he had the highest regard. He didn't get on with his mother at that time. Under my mother's influence he did his best to be on friendly terms, but I think he always felt that his mother hadn't appreciated him, and that she had this feeling against him.'[53]

At their new home at the Staff College, Camberley, however, Monty was master – and for the Carver boys the change was significant. 'He took over everything . . . he couldn't bear to see anything that wasn't well run, efficiently run according to his ideas, so he ran the whole place according to military principles, on military lines,' Dick Carver recalled. Yet this was far from anathema to Dick's mother, 'who was terribly disorganized really and artistic, and was only too glad to let him'. Moreover in matters of any real importance to her it was Betty's will that prevailed. Monty might say no to her in public: but once she tackled him 'in camera', so to speak, she always had her way. 'They were indeed complete opposites in character,' Dick acknowledged, but it was 'an attraction of opposites, and there was no doubt how deeply Monty was in love with my mother'. According to Dick, neither really understood the other's world, perhaps respecting each other so profoundly because of this, for there could be no rivalry in spheres – military and artistic – so alien to each other.

Perhaps, too, this attraction of opposites represented, for each of them, the attraction of the very areas they denied in themselves. Just as Betty's bohemianism betrayed a certain need for order, so too Monty's total self-discipline belied a yearning for disorder, for the unplanned, for naked emotion. 'He was at heart a romantic,' Dick Carver later confided. Even the children, irritated at first by Monty's authoritarian home-management, and his inability to admit that he was ever wrong, accepted that he was doing his best. Not only that, but accepted that this 'best', really, was the product of his love for their mother. 'Everyone sympathized with my mother,' Dick remembered, 'for there was no doubt that Monty was a very difficult person, and they used to ask "How do you do it?" But we managed.'[54]

Dick's elder brother agreed. 'I think he went into [the courtship] to start with in a fairly cold-blooded manner. But to be quite honest I think he became very much in love and got carried away more than he intended to! I don't think he intended that his wife would be an influence on him – which she was, of course! I'm sure it was a happy marriage. A lot of people said it couldn't be – you know: "Your poor mother, what she had to put up with!" But I don't think she ever looked on it in that light, quite honestly. Although she allowed Monty a lot of rope to play with and he may have given the impression that he was the boss and his word went on every occasion, I think she was quite confident that if she really wanted something done, she could persuade Monty to do it.' On Monty's assumption of paternal authority John Carver commented, 'Naturally there was a slight uphill struggle, because we'd been very spoilt and hadn't had any male discipline at all. "Discipline at home" was a great cry – of which there hadn't been any, to be more or less honest. So naturally there was a certain amount of resistance to this, but it went well . . . the family existed as a unit at this period.'[55]

In fact, the Montgomery family now existed, at Camberley, in a markedly coherent way, with more opportunities for the children to be with their mother and enjoy themselves during the holidays than ever before. 'Monty organized riding for us on the Sandhurst horses. There was also a lake on which we could take out a boat, and a swimming pool about fifty yards from the Staff College bungalow in which we lived. There were woods for bicycling and walking – compared with where we'd been before we were very well placed,' John recalled appreciatively.[56]

For his part, Monty tried hard to fit into Betty's world, just as she was doing for him. He unfailingly allowed himself to be introduced to her 'bohemian' friends, sitting silently while they talked of art and lacerated one another's works and reputations – though he was not perhaps quite as shy as some have made out. If he found Alan Herbert a 'bit daunting' at first, and the atmosphere in the Chiswick salons *'un peu formidable'*, he was not entirely lost for words. When asked what he made of Eric Kennington, then a popular draughtsman whose portraits of Liddell Hart and Hobo Hobart would become celebrated, he remarked with mock seriousness: 'Dreadful fella! Eats peas off his knife' – which was taken as rather a witty *bon mot* that exactly captured Kennington's awkwardness and lack of ease.

There was no doubt, too, that Betty's 'strange' assembly of friends helped to bring Monty out of his limited military sphere at just the right moment in his career: a moment when he was not holding a command, but was employed as a college instructor and reflecting deeply on the nature and history of war – especially the morality of battles like the Somme and Passchendaele, whose haunting vestiges he had toured with Brian and the group of subalterns.

What *was* the moral of such human sacrifice? Could democracy be defended without such bloodshed? Did Monty's own approach to war change as a result of his marriage? Douglas Haig had met and married the Honourable Dorothy ('Doris') Vivian, lady-in-waiting to Queen Alexandra, in the private chapel of Buckingham Palace, in 1905, following a lightning romance – the inveterate, homosocial forty-four-year-old woman-hater proposing to the Hon. Miss Vivian only two days after meeting her, and marrying her a month later. Although the marriage had enabled Haig to use royal influence to further his ambitions, it had remained a formal, stilted, utterly unemotional relationship which had not made Haig a more humane individual or commander – indeed, the opposite might be said, as Haig became steadily more authoritarian, more ambitious, more obsessive, and more obstinate. By contrast, Monty seemed transformed by marriage. 'My love was returned in full measure, although I was a soldier,' Monty recorded – aware of Betty's principles and the way she had compromised them for him. Moreover, he became profoundly grateful to her for the world she introduced him to – and there is little question but that Monty's later enjoyment and encouragement of interesting company in his tactical HQ, even in the midst of historic battles, went back to this golden time with Betty and her friends. However he might deprecate them afterwards in conversation, he *enjoyed* meeting them, and was certainly not unappreciative of their intellects and talents, however little he could understand them as artists – a fact which may go some way towards explaining his almost unique willingness, in the British army, to employ highly talented 'amateur' soldiers during the ensuing war – a willingness that made Haig's 'regular army' headquarters, in World War I, seem unbelievably mediocre by comparison.

Monty was, in fact, developing an eye for character and ability outside the army that would stand him in good stead over the years; and the very brilliance of some of Betty's circle of artists and writers – such as Augustus John, A. P. Herbert and Jack Squire – served to make Monty doubly aware of the dullness and stupidity of many of his army colleagues. 'Silly old bugger, he's no use anyway,' Freddie de Guingand recalled Monty, as a major, saying of a brigadier who objected to Monty hustling him on the golf green, during his time at 49th Division at York. Now, in the relative tranquillity and security of the Staff College, as a brevet lieutenant colonel and happily married man, Monty began to further loosen his uncomfortably outspoken tongue, enjoying a certain delight in flouting convention, and in upsetting the complacent. His step-son Dick remembered quite clearly the pleasure with which Monty would walk across forbidden lawns at Sandhurst, beside the Staff College – he who laid down such strict laws about behaviour and domestic management at home. Or later, when watching a passing-out parade at the RMA at Woolwich, Betty commented that the cadet receiving the Sword of Honour would surely become a general. 'What? You'll never hear of him again, never hear of him again!' Monty responded, so loudly everyone in the stand could hear – silenced only by the cadet's mother turning round in the front row and glaring at him.[57] Equally, Monty's rivalry with his new brother-in-law Hobo Hobart was given full rein. 'Mother gave a priceless description at this period,' John Carver later recalled, 'with their horns locked. They were giving Uncle P[atrick] a lift in Monty's car, and Uncle P was saying "It's very stuffy in here, we want the window open, let in some air." Monty said, "My car – windows stay shut!" This childish argument went on throughout the whole journey, neither giving an inch – neither at all used, in fact, to not having their wishes respected.'[58]

Procreation

'I was then thirty-eight years old and a confirmed bachelor,' Monty wrote candidly of his courtship of Betty. 'Women had never interested me and I knew very few; I disliked social life and dinner parties. My life was devoted almost entirely to my profession and I worked at it from morning to night, sometimes taking exercise in the afternoon. I believe some ribald officer once said that the army was my wife and I had no need for another!'[59]

Now that he had a real wife, the army became for Monty a second wife – and this bigamous scenario did him nothing but good. Moreover, Betty was as much mother to him as wife: the sort of mother Monty had never had, in the sense of a woman who loved him unreservedly, who was kind and patient, encouraging and affectionate, tolerant and forgiving. Maud's second name had been pain; now, in Betty, Monty experienced for the first time in his life real mutual affection, amounting to love. As a result his heart, like a cup, overflowed, as did his very being – and with a significant consequence. In January 1928 he and the boys once again travelled to Lenk.

'We went out as a family,' John Carver remembered – the journey made notable because Betty became 'desperately sick' on the way.[60] It was not, however, from the Channel crossing. Monty had always been solicitous in looking after Betty; now, however, he began to fuss over her like a hen. No need of hers went unanswered, no whim unfulfilled, for Betty was going to bear him a child!

Paterfamilias

Six months later, on 18 August 1928, attended by numerous nurses and doctors, Betty Montgomery gave birth in the instructor's bungalow at Camberley to a boy, whom the proud parents named David.

Betty was no longer young; she had passed forty and had to be careful with her health. As Monty later wrote, Betty 'was never very strong afterwards', but this was no impediment to their life together – in fact, it proved the opposite. Monty's mother had refused to let Bernard spoil her, had given his gifts to charity and spurned his gestures of affection – 'brushed him off,' as Winsome put it. Betty did not. 'It had never before seemed possible,' Monty later related, 'that such love and affection could exist.'[61]

He was not exaggerating. 'He organized everything for her – everything,' Winsome recalled – even the breastfeeding. 'I went up to see this new baby,' she related. 'Betty was in bed – they used to stay in bed longer in those days after having a baby – and she said to me: "Oh, Bernard is wonderful. I'm nursing David, and I can never remember which side to feed him from." She'd told Bernard this. "Oh, we'll soon fix that," he'd said – you can imagine him saying it in his quick, high voice: "We'll soon fix that!"' There was a china rabbit on a shelf over the bed. 'He picked up the rabbit and said: "Now – you're feeding him with the right breast this side, so we'll put the rabbit over his head. You'll be feeding him on the left side next time and the rabbit goes over that side!" She thought that was great!'[62]

The birth of a son, however, did not in any way lessen Monty's affection for, and sense of responsibility towards, his step-sons. Perhaps remembering his own unhappy childhood, Monty insisted the older boys should not feel left out because of the new arrival. A nanny was employed to help Betty and when Christmas 1928 approached, as John Carver recalled, Monty announced: ' "These boys must keep up their skiing." And so my mother was left behind with the baby, while Monty took us again to Lenk.'[63]

Monty was in his element: licensed, as it were, to love children and, like Barrie, enjoy the miracle of their company, with its extraordinary, almost dreamlike intimacy. 'We all three shared a room – and all the beds were in one line. I can remember this very clearly,' John Carver recalled. 'We all ploughed up the mountain every day. Funnily enough, the thing I can remember him saying is: "You boys are very uncivilized. You must stand up to use a chamber-pot, you mustn't kneel down!" The thing was, we'd never been brought up with a father to tell us these things.'[64]

Again, like Barrie, it was the emotional need of the boys for him which moved Monty. As always, the day was planned in advance. 'Things didn't always pan out quite as expected,' Dick Carver later recollected, 'and we did rather pull his leg about this' – a sort of joshing Monty took in good spirit. He was, in his awkward, Monsieur-Hulot-like way, reliving his own childhood – but with love and affection as its theme, not fear and retribution. With adults he always seemed threatened, holding tight to the role of infallible officer: teaching, training, commanding – unable to make mistakes. With the boys he was curiously unguarded, fascinated by their responses to life, and anxious to learn from them, as much as they from him. Thus he loved them in the manner of a paternalistic elder brother, with whom he shared a mother: *their* mother, now his wife. 'Keep to your own partums!' was a constant injunction in the dormitory-style room, reflecting Monty's almost obsessive tidiness; yet he was equally determined they should enjoy themselves to the full. 'He was a rather cautious skier, but he fancied himself somewhat as a skater, at which he was very good, particularly waltzing on ice,' Dick recalled. 'He also loved music hall songs' – his favourite limerick beginning:

> There was a young curate of Kidderminster
> Who very severely chid-a-spinster
> When she on the ice
> Used words far from nice
> When he quite accidentally slid against her![65]

If the holiday was memorable for Monty's step-sons, however, it was also a chance for Monty to get away from England and reflect on his career – for at the end of 1928 his three-year post as a lecturer at the Staff College expired. His honeymoon – military and marital – was finally over.

Shortly after New Year, 1929, the bungalow at Camberley was surrendered, and Brevet-Lieutenant-Colonel Montgomery was sent back to his regiment where, at the Inkerman Barracks in Woking, the 1st Battalion of the Royal Warwickshires was commanded by his old friend and mentor, Clement Tomes.

The ripples of his fame as a trainer, however, soon reached Whitehall, and it was at Woking, in the summer of 1929, that Monty received word from the War Office asking him to revise the army's *Infantry Training Manual*, Volume II. The soldier would finally become author.

Author, author!

In truth, the appointment was to be secretary of an authoring committee, charged with revising the army's *Infantry Training Manual* on tactics, not sole author – and Monty hated committees.

'Attached' to the War Office for six months from 15 October 1929, at the special salary of an additional five shillings per day, Monty consulted absolutely no one in the preparation of his first draft. He reckoned he probably possessed more experience in producing training instructions than any other officer in the British army. His brief, as he put it the next year to Liddell Hart, was to assemble 'a complete handbook on tactics for the regimental officer, regular and territorial', and he was determined to do that in the widest possible sense. 'I decided to make the book a comprehensive treatise on war for the infantry officer,' he wrote later in his *Memoirs* – revising the pamphlets, booklets, and lectures he had been writing and giving since World War I in a new and at last official form that would, if well done, become British army doctrine for the next five years.

Monty's revision of the *Infantry Training Manual* was to be his one and only appointment in the War Office before he became head of the British army some seventeen years later – though in truth most of his work was done at home, at the Inkerman Barracks where he lived with Betty, baby David, and his step-sons John and Dick whenever they came home from school. 'The book when published was considered excellent,' he later wrote, 'especially by its author.'[66]

Others did not agree. When Monty showed his first draft to the committee there were 'heated arguments'. The committee went through the manual chapter by chapter. Monty thought their criticisms were 'nit picking' ones, and the committee 'ga-ga'.[67] Numerous amendments were made, which Monty would not accept, and for a while it looked as if there would be no new edition of the *Manual*.

The fault was not entirely that of the committee, chaired by Sir David Campbell, the General Officer Commanding, Aldershot Command. If the text was to be 'official', it must reflect War Office views rather than personal ones – something Monty was unwilling to consider. The terms of reference were clearly for a handbook on infantry tactics; Monty intended it to be a personal treatise, in his own clear style. The twain would not meet, causing Monty to suggest the committee be disbanded and that he should complete the manuscript in his own unpaid time, incorporating their amendments. Weary of arguing and aware of the cost-consciousness in the War Office, the committee agreed. As Monty wrote in his *Memoirs*, this was the signal for Nelsonian tactics: 'I produced the final draft, omitting all the amendments the committee had put forward.'[68]

This was, as the archives reveal, all too true! A letter addressed to Liddell Hart from the Inkerman Barracks in September 1930, and preserved in Liddell Hart's voluminous papers, illustrates how Monty fielded inevitable criticism – and carried on regardless. Though Liddell Hart (to whom it had been surreptitiously passed) praised certain sections of Monty's draft, his essential verdict was a thumbs-down. He acknowledged that Monty had reduced 'some of the superfluous verbiage' of the previous volume, written by Lord Gort, VC, but felt it was written now for too high a level of officer – 'brigade or battalion commander' – rather than the 'company and platoon commander – who really need its guidance'. In particular, Liddell Hart bewailed the omission of exploitation in attack: 'It drops out the passages which explained exactly how reserves could exploit weak points and be passed through to "expand the torrent." '[69]

Here was the crux of their differences – both at this time and in the historical arguments that blossomed after the next war. Ever since Liddell Hart had overcome his innocent faith in the higher staff in World War I, he had searched for a theory that would breach the stalemate of trench warfare. This, for him, was exploitation; a theory at first based on infantry breakthrough, and later adapted to mean armoured breakthrough supported by infantry. Surprise, the exploitation of weak spots, the breakthrough: these were the principles which, increasingly, Liddell Hart felt would bring victory in future warfare; and which he consolidated in his own unofficial primer, *The Future of Infantry*, published in 1931.

Monty agreed on notepaper, but disagreed in practice and in the printed text – a disagreement that was fundamental to his personality as well as to his military philosophy. For Liddell Hart it was this 'blind spot' in Monty's tactical perception that would explain Monty's later failure to fully exploit his great victory at Alamein and subsequent World War II battles; whereas Monty would always feel it was Haig's fantasies of breakout and cavalry exploitation that had doomed his citizen-army to so many millions of unnecessary casualties in World War I. For Monty it was, in a citizen-army, the body-count that counted – and Hart's theories of exploitation were beyond the capabilities of most citizen-soldiers.

Both men were right, according to their lights – though Liddell Hart's theories were best suited to Nazi troops – where obedience and initiative, especially among trained NCOs of Hitler's vast, standing armies, provided a bedrock upon which imaginative German commanders could 'exploit' enemy weaknesses – or to commanders like George S. Patton, who would kick, curse and drive his 'cavalry' units into mobile action on a scale and with speed and opportunism that thrived on the 'can do, will do' American spirit of adventure, unrestrained by divisions of class, caste or snobbery. In the British army, characterized by deliberate officer amateurism and indolence, debilitating class-division, distrust between different arms and services, as well as obstructionism, even bloody-mindedness among the ranks, such an approach invited – and almost invariably produced, when fighting a first-class enemy – failure and even disaster. The British army would never produce, at least among its civilian-soldiers, exploiters and expanding torrenters, Monty felt; but the army could produce professional officers and NCOs who 'knew their stuff' and trained their common sense to ensure they would 'pull together' as a team on the battlefield.

The objections of the War Office committee, and of Liddell Hart in particular, were therefore disregarded by Monty – and the general reception given to the new *Infantry Training Manual* was distinctly favourable, as Monty foresaw, and Liddell Hart had enviously to acknowledge.

Monty had reason, then, to be proud of his work: the literary seal on his three years at the Staff College, Camberley. Flushed with success at getting his own way over the *Infantry Training Manual*, and confident that he would succeed Tomes as CO of the 1st Battalion of the Royal Warwicks, Monty was now irrepressible: determined to have fun at last, in tandem with the serious business of soldiering.

Blasted little pipsqueak

The happier Monty was with Betty, the more he began to see fun and seriousness as two sides of the same professional coin: recreation acting as a stimulus to wholehearted professional soldiering. He had always 'disliked social life and dinner parties'; now he actually began to give them, with dancing to boot, as Brian, on leave from East Africa, recalled. 'I shall always recall how some of those present found it rather disconcerting when, not infrequently, he climbed on to a table and, in ringing tones, gave everyone orders to "change partners",' – orders which neither the colonels present nor the subalterns dared disobey. As Brian commented, it was 'clear evidence of Betty's growing influence on him.'[70]

At Moville, in the summer that year, Monty was much the same; family and guests would come down to breakfast after chapel in the morning to find Bernard's 'Orders of the Day' pinned to the dining-room door, including dicta such as 'Betty will paint', and 'Colin will write sermon'; at noon 'Girls will pick flowers for the house', at '1300 hours' lunch ('Don't be late'), and at 1430 hours 'All to golf course at Greencastle, less Winsome and Wangy [Holderness] who will prepare tea and convey it to Golf course'.[71] The once errant bachelor son had come home a married man – brimming with excitement and pride.

However much inspired by his marital happiness, though, Monty's bossiness did not always find favour. When he ordered the gardener to cut down the ivy in front of the New Park windows, for example, there was – perhaps appropriately in the house of an evangelical missionary bishop – 'hell to pay'. Henry Montgomery had in 1928 been made an honorary KCMG, or Knight Commander of the Cross of St Michael and St George, which did not entitle prelates to use the title 'Sir' in front of their name, nor permit their wives to use the title 'Lady'. Typically, this proved no obstruction to Monty's mother, who thenceforth called herself – and insisted others call her – 'Lady' Montgomery. 'Lady' Montgomery having given specific orders that the ivy was *not* to be cut down, there was a great row, as John Carver remembered later. 'You've no right to do that!' declared Maud. 'No right at all – it's my house.' 'Well, I was getting rather blinded, you see,' retorted Monty, rather apologetically – though, as John recalled, he was absolutely determined to get his own way, and in this case – the ivy having already been removed – did.[72]

There were similar contretemps in the regiment, too. Brigadier Tomes later recorded that although Monty was 'very loyal and efficient' as second-in-command, he could cause problems too. The trouble, he explained, was that 'Aldershot Command continually demanded him for such jobs as umpire or as a staff officer on schemes. In this he did not always please. I well remember one infuriated General coming to my HQ on a scheme and demanding the blood of "that blasted little pipsqueak – Montgomery!"'[73]

Marriage thus emboldened Monty, rather than changed his essential character. After a lifetime of being a social outsider, he was now socially as well as in military terms an insider; indeed, the next step would be command of his regiment – leading, hopefully, to command of a brigade and then, as a general, of a division. The once pyromaniacal cadet had, at last, made good.

7

In Command

To the Holy Land

As 1930 came to a close Colonel Tomes was posted to the War Office, and Monty was duly confirmed as the 1st Battalion's next commanding officer. The eccentric, brilliant but difficult subordinate had, at forty-three, finally achieved his goal – commanding a battalion of his own regiment – with orders to take the unit abroad for a tour of duty first in Palestine, then Egypt, and finally India.

Bishop Montgomery was delighted to hear that his rebel son, who had insisted on opting for the army as a career rather than the church, would now be taking his battalion to the Holy Land. Betty, too, was delighted – though because her eldest son John was seriously ill she would have to follow later. Early in January 1931, therefore, the 1st Battalion, the Royal Warwickshire Regiment, set sail from Southampton, bound for Port Said, whence they would travel by train to Jerusalem. Colonel Tomes, Betty and baby David waved goodbye from the quay as Her Majesty's Troopship *Neuralia* drew away, and Lieutenant-Colonel Montgomery – his rank made substantive on 17 January 1931 – assumed formal command of a battalion for the first time since the autumn of 1919, more than a decade before. But his stewardship of the Royal Warwicks was to be far from plain sailing.

Promotion by merit

Since the Great War the 1st Battalion, the Royal Warwickshire Regiment, had been extremely lucky in its COs. Monty's first company commander, C. R. Macdonald, was the soul of honesty and discretion; Monty's first adjutant, Clement Tomes, who succeeded Macdonald, was also a man of the highest principles, known as 'Old Smoulder' in the regiment owing to the eternal pipe in his mouth. Under Tomes the battalion had formed part of the Aldershot experimental brigade, with new company organization and even mechanized carriers for its machine-gun company. Pat Burge, then a subaltern, felt the battalion was distinctive for the courtesy and quiet efficiency of Tomes' leadership, with a strong body of warrant officers and a happy spirit throughout the unit, both in barracks and on exercises. 'All this was to change under Montgomery,' Burge recollected.

The problem was, a battalion's tour of service overseas lasted twenty-one *years*, so those NCOs and soldiers with two years or less to serve before retirement were excluded from the move. For Monty, this was the perfect chance to refashion the battalion with new, younger NCOs, promoted by merit – at least, his merit – and the result was unexpectedly bitter. As Liddell Hart went so far as to claim of Monty, in his *Memoirs*: 'When he was eventually given command of a battalion, after sixteen years on the staff, he brought it to the verge of mutiny by misjudged handling.'[1]

Uproar in the sergeants' mess

Monty certainly misjudged the moment to introduce new rules on promotion. In order to bring the battalion up to its full active-service establishment of about 950 officers and men, a draft of young soldiers from the 2nd Battalion, returning from the Sudan after many years abroad, had also to be inducted into the 1st Battalion. Tensions between the two contingents were bound to arise – and did. The 1st Battalion had been kitted out in generally ill-fitting, standard-size brown drills, while the draft from the returning 2nd Battalion had a very different appearance. 'Frankly we looked pretty beastly,' Burge remembered; 'whereas the draft from the Sudan arrived in tailor-made green suits and looked bloody good. At once there was a "them" and "us" atmosphere.'

The task of welding these two contingents into a happy and efficient battalion, Burge recalled, was one that required great tact and understanding – neither of which Monty possessed. Instead, Monty bulled ahead with his new plans on promotion, without reference to the War Office, the Colonel of the Regiment at home, or the elderly senior officers, or indeed any of the older soldiers under his command. The proof of the

pudding would come in the eating, Monty was certain; the newly promoted, keener, younger NCOs would be encouraged to try harder, as in
the German army, and as a result the energy and professionalism of the
battalion would not be levelled down, but up.

The order defied gravity, going against centuries of tradition in the
regiment – indeed, Monty's new system backfired almost immediately;
'there was uproar in the sergeants' mess', Colonel Burge later confided, as
a result of which 'a number of those sergeants have never been to a
regimental reunion since'.[2]

Stopping fights and squabbles

Monty ignored the disquiet in the regiment, since the disquiet in Palestine
was to him far more important than the sensitivities of old-fashioned
NCOs and soldiers used to promotion by long service. Because the GOC
British troops in Egypt and Palestine, General Sir John Burnett-Stuart,
was based in Cairo, Monty found he was required to act as military
governor of the entire country, indeed responsible not only for commanding all British troops in Palestine, but for meeting and maintaining contact
with the various military forces stationed in neighbouring Syria, Trans-
jordan and the Lebanon. Thus, immediately on his arrival in January
Monty became a virtual brigadier, taking under command a battalion of
the King's Own at Haifa as well as his own Warwickshire battalion. 'I
was at Haifa last night,' he wrote to his mother and father on 11 January
1931 from Mr R. Grossman's Hotel Tiberias on the shores of Lake Galilee,
'& inspected the garrison there this morning. Tomorrow I carry out
inspections round here & to the north, and also see the Arab cavalry who
garrison the Jordan valley. I have covered many miles by car since I
have been out here & have been practically all over Palestine. It is very
interesting but is hard work. Early next month I shall go up to Syria, to
see the French general who commands there and discuss mutual problems
with him. I shall see Beyrouth [Beirut] and Damascus and also want to
inspect the Foreign Legion, of which they keep one Bn. in Syria. The hotel
here is vile. No time for more. Yr loving son, Bernard.'[3]

'Life is very strenuous,' he reported in his next letter from Jerusalem,
dated 5 February 1931, 'as I have taken over command of all the British
troops in Palestine and have much work & travelling to do.' The town,

however, was 'a wonderful place. In the new city and shopping areas outside the old walled city you have hotels that would not disgrace New York, & you can buy anything you want from a Singer sewing machine to a Rolls Royce car. Then you go through the Jaffa Gate into the old walled city and you pass at once into an eastern city of 1000 years ago or more; little narrow streets, donkeys camels & humans all jostling each other, brilliant colours in the bazaars, & many smells.'

For the bishop's son, raised in a family obsessed by Christianity and the stories of the Bible, it was breathtaking to see the sources of such myth-ology. 'Parts of the walls are of Herod's time,' he wrote. 'I saw on Sunday the entrance gate to Pilate's hall, & the court-yard outside where the soldiers sat & played, & the paved street up which Jesus walked with his Cross. It is all underground as it has been excavated recently. But it is said to be the most authentic site in Palestine. The Dome of the Rock (or Mosque of Omar) is really beautiful. And the view from the Mt of Olives across the garden of Gethsemane towards Jerusalem is wonderful . . . All very interesting.'[4]

Political conditions in Palestine, however, upset Monty's plans to visit his French neighbours. Early in March he wrote to say, 'My visit to Syria had to be postponed; things have looked rather troublesome in Palestine recently & the High Commissioner does not want me to leave the country just at present.' Nevertheless, he managed to visit the great crusader castle at Acre – 'a perfect example of late 18th century fortress . . . The town has never been sacked or destroyed and is exactly the same as it was in the days of Richard Coeur de Lion in 1190 AD. I saw the place where Richard pitched his tent in 1190 and from the same place Napoleon directed operations when he besieged the town in 1799 AD.' Betty and David, he hoped, were now 'settled at Camberley & I hope they will stay there until they come out here'.[5]

As the Turks had found over previous centuries, the problem for the British occupiers, was to keep the peace among competing 'believers'. On 10 March Monty gave his mother his impressions of Bethlehem, which he had only just got to see properly. The Church of the Nativity 'is supposed to be the oldest church in the world; its date is 300 AD,' he wrote. 'The pathetic thing is that by the manger a policeman in uniform sits all day & all night, his task being to stop fights and squabbles between the various religions when processions through the stable take place'. The irony was patent. 'It is the same wherever you go; the various religions fight over who shall have the custody of this place or that and are very jealous of their own privileges. It is the same with the Jews & Arabs,' he recorded, giving as example the custody of Rachel's tomb, outside Bethlehem. 'The Jews have the custody of the tomb. But the local Moslems have the right to wash their dead in the courtyard of the tomb. This they like to do just when the Jews are having some ceremony inside the tomb, out of sheer devilry of course. Result: much trouble & friction. It is all very curious. I must stop now. I am glad Father is keeping well.'[6]

As spring came, the tension in Palestine rose. He had been 'fearfully busy lately with Easter,' Monty wrote to his mother on 10 April from Jerusalem, 'and the precautions we have to take in case riots should break out.' The spectacle of religious rivalry as something requiring military intervention never ceased to amaze him, involving 'a diversity of religious pageantry which you would see nowhere else in the world. For instance on Good Friday the Christians (RCs) in enormous crowds process up the Via Dolorosa, the way Christ went with His Cross. The Jews wail all day at the Wailing Wall. The Moslems hold uproarious processions all round the town. The difficulty is to keep them from clashing. I have had troops out in the town for the last 10 days & have escaped trouble so far. After tomorrow I hope to be able to dispense with them.'[7]

It was a peacekeeping role – keeping believers in the so-called love of God from murdering each other – that would characterize much of the business of soldiering at the end of the twentieth century and the start of the twenty-first – as thanklessly then as now.

Ideas of grandeur

In June 1931, however, Monty's wife Betty arrived with baby David, as well as Betty's son John Carver. The Armstrong-Siddeley motor car that Monty had arranged to be shipped out went 'magnificently' and the Montgomerys travelled together as a family as far as Petra, Jerash, Damascus and Baalbec, armed with topographical, historical, political, religious and military literature – as well as Betty's easel.

'It was just his cup of tea,' John Carver, who had joined the Royal Engineers, recalled later. 'He was in his element; in fact, I remember he got definite ideas of grandeur. He filled up a whole page of my passport. I wanted to go down to Egypt and there was something about my not having a visa, so he wrote in his own fair hand in my passport: "On duty

in Egypt", signed "B. L. Montgomery". He thought that was good enough
– that you could go round the world on his signature!'[8]

Betty, meanwhile, loved her stay in the Holy Land. Her watercolour
depicting Palestinians drawing water by the steps of a mosque in Jerusalem
remains one of her most charming works. It was in Palestine, too, that she
met – and later painted – the great explorer and Arabist, 'Jack' Philby, at
whose marriage, as a distant cousin, Monty had acted as best man in India
almost a quarter of a century before – and whose son Kim would become
one of the most infamous British traitors of the twentieth century.

At the end of 1931, however, the Royal Warwickshire battalion was
posted to Egypt – and it was there, thanks to sex, that trouble, for
Lieutenant-Colonel Montgomery really began.

Trouble in the brothels

Alongside a detachment of horsed cavalry in Alexandria the 1st Battalion,
Royal Warwicks, assumed its garrison duties, as part of the Suez Canal
Brigade, commanded by Brigadier Frederick Pile.

'Rumbles and unwelcome reports began to emerge from Alexandria
soon after Montgomery's battalion settled in,' wrote Monty's first biographer, Alan Moorehead, who had interviewed Sir Frederick Pile. 'Senior
officers were sent down from Cairo and were frankly annoyed by what
they saw.'[9]

What they saw was a battalion commander uninterested in drill, auto-
cratically ordering German-style promotion of NCOs by merit, contemptuous of the still-horsed cavalry next door – and taking extraordinary
and unilateral measures to ensure the sexual health of his men.

The Alexandria of the early nineteen-thirties, Moorehead wrote a
decade later, was

a maze of sweltering streets teeming with every nationality in the Levant. Most of
the coloured population was gripped by a garish and amoral poverty and immersed
in the sordid struggle to escape from it by any method they could. Backsheesh.
Piastres. These were the governing inspirations of life. In commerce there were no
holds barred. Sell – sell anything so long as you sell – bathtub gin, poisonous
shellfish, fake jewellery, raddled women, drugs; ask ten times the market price,
bargain for everything down to a toothpick. In that generous and foetid heat,

obscure cafés and saloons with broken-down gramophones, women flourished along every other street, the residence of innumerable flies by day and innumerable pimps by night.

This wasn't, as Moorehead pointed out, the Alexandria that tourists saw, but it was, unfortunately, 'the Alexandria into which the soldier penetrated on his night out and inevitably he ran into trouble. A very great deal of the trouble originated in the brothels.'[10]

Penetration and unclean brothels made for a sick unit. Alarmed at the VD rate, Monty quickly decided to take the matter in hand. A battalion 'knocking shop' was set up, monitored, as then Lieutenant Pat Burge recalled, by the garrison adjutant, 'an ex-RFC pilot who was an excellent administrator and a decent, honourable man'. As Burge remembered, 'the ladies were inspected by our own MO. The soldiers gave only their army number, no name, and signed a chitty saying they had used the prescribed prophylactic. As a result, our VD rate was extremely low. I mean, you have to remember that Alexandria was the most remarkable place. Everything was there! Racing, tennis, duck-shooting – you name it, it was there. You couldn't stop the men getting a woman; you could ensure it was healthy.'

Monty was completely unjudgemental. Heterosexual desire was a fact of life, and for those soldiers without wives – even those with wives – sexual release was natural. 'In fact he regarded it as a huge joke – he used to joke with the soldiers about what he called "horizontal refreshment".'[11]

Monty's unilateral action in setting up such a regimental brothel, however, was anathema to GHQ Cairo, which became alarmed about possible 'questions' at home. Monty, by contrast, was supremely indifferent to 'political' repercussions in England. His sole concern was the professional efficiency of the battalion. The lure of unprotected sex was all too real, threatening the battalion's 'proficiency', as Brian Montgomery – who knew Alexandria well – described.

Alexandria at that time was the playground of the wealthy Pashas in Cairo, including a very rich Greek colony, and the standards of luxury and good living, all readily available to healthy young men, were hard to resist. Also of course all the spurious attractions of a large Eastern city and sea port, with the innumerable bars and brothels and drugs and general invitations for self-indulgence on a massive scale, were there for all to see. More sinister were the temptations and often dire results which stemmed from the much advertised offers to take part in pornographic and homosexual activities.[12]

Sinister or not, it was the latter which exercised Monty's deepest fears. Given the continuing provisions of the 1885 Criminal Law Amendment Act in Britain, and strict army regulations relating to homosexual behaviour, temptations in Alexandria meant a risk, for officers especially, of blackmail – a risk of which the CO was well aware. Monty therefore interrogated each of his officers in turn – an approach which did not always go down well. 'Young officers who were apt to give up their leisure hours to the more earthly and exotic pleasures of Alexandria were suddenly finding themselves on the mat in front of the Colonel, their private lives most rudely exposed and the most unusual punishments forced upon them,' Moorehead chronicled. Feeling that a soldier's private life was his own, they complained; Monty took the converse view: that if a soldier's 'private habits made him unfit for duty then he must be corrected'.[13]

Certainly in carpeting young officers, warning them against indiscretion and punishing them where they took unwise risks, Monty meant well – indeed was speaking, in part, to his own deepest tendency. Perhaps his revived faith in Christ added to his conviction that homosexual temptation, in its physical manifestation, *must* be defied, not condoned. His recent experience of the Holy Land, though it had caused him to laugh at the ridiculousness of competing religious bigotries, had certainly made his own Christian religion more vivid and real – Christianity which, though centred in compassion for human weakness, also urged a continual battle with sin. 'Place your faith in God . . . you come from a family of gentlemen . . . remember that you must always be responsible for your actions . . . undiluted hell fire has done me a great deal of good . . . whatever you do place God first in your life',[14] Monty's father's letters to him in Palestine had exhorted, according to Moorehead – and the bishop's words did not fall on stony ground. Instead, they encouraged Monty to sublimate his own tendencies in an increasingly noble endeavour: looking after the welfare and professional training of his charges. 'He is really popular with his men who he regards and treats as if they were his children,' Brigadier Pile would write in Monty's confidential report.[15]

Monty's paternalistic devotion to his men mirrored the same, very real paternalism evident at home. His happiness and excitement at being married and a real father suffused his command of the battalion: an eccentric in his absolute devotion to soldiering as a profession, though never unapproachable or distant, or lacking in humour. He himself followed an increasingly ordered existence, rising early, reading the Bible, and eating at strict times. 'More and more he was subduing his life to a strict and minute routine; half an hour for breakfast, so many minutes for dealing with reports and correspondence, so many hours for inspections. A light and very limited diet,' Moorehead described – but such a regime was not designed as a model for others, only to ensure he himself could accomplish what, increasingly, he saw as his life's task. 'He had his career all mapped out and allowed nothing to interfere with his plan,' recalled Colonel Burge. 'When he was commanding the battalion on army manoeuvres in Egypt he was offered a staff job, I think DAQMG, which he turned down. I made the remark "Is that wise, sir? That is the second staff job you have refused, you won't be offered another perhaps." He replied: "What! I'll go home and thump the table in the War Office. Look! At the end of the year I shall take this battalion to India. I shall then become a brigadier and after that I shall take command of a division, ending up as CIGS." '[16]

Was this megalomania – or the ambition of a man with a vision of transforming Britain's desperately moribund military defence forces into a modern, professional organization?

Time would tell.

A *devoted couple*

Now that wives were permitted and their passage to Egypt paid, Betty was found by the other officers and their wives to be a very good colonel's lady: kind and helpful, absolutely sincere, and not in the least showy. 'I was invited often to dine,' recalled Captain Bailey, Monty's machine-gun company commander, 'and found Betty Montgomery a charming person. Though artistic – she was both a sculptress and painted – she was in no way eccentric in her dress or appearance, but wore plain sensible clothes. I found her full of fun and a lively person to talk to, with a great deal of humour. She often poked fun at Monty – I'm sure they were a devoted couple.'[17]

The same picture emerges from all who knew Betty at this time. Monty drank and smoked in moderation, gambled occasionally, played bridge frequently – and well. Alan and Gwen Herbert travelled out from Chiswick to stay with the Montgomerys in Alexandria. 'Well, I must go and command my regiment now,' Monty would say, absenting himself from their company.[18]

Among the soldiers of the 1st Battalion there was certainly a growing respect for the new colonel, and his wife – especially after the 'pigeon affair'.

A dispute having arisen between a corporal and the quartermaster over the ownership of a pigeon, the entire Royal Warwickshire battalion collected to watch Monty's solution to the problem. 'I encouraged hobbies of every kind, and one of these was the keeping of pigeons; this was very popular and we kept some ourselves,' Monty recalled. He asked both the corporal and quartermaster if they agreed that 'a pigeon when released would always fly direct to its own loft'. They did. Monty thereupon ordered the disputed pigeon to be kept for a day and a night in the battalion orderly room, then to be released.

The 'whole battalion had heard of the incident and some 800 men watched from vantage points to see what would happen'.[19] To Betty's considerable amusement – and the applause of the battalion – the pigeon flew into her loft!

Monty's less classical solution was required in the instance of Captain Nicholson. To the end of his days Monty would tell the story of the 'emergency', when Captain Nicholson telephoned to ask to be released from his undertaking.

'Nicholson was a bachelor,' recalled Major-General R. C. Macdonald (Monty's successor many years later as Colonel of the Regiment), 'an officer who liked his booze, and every so often "fell by the wayside" over women. Eventually he began to show signs of wear and was had up before Monty. Monty, who had something of a soft spot for Nicholson, didn't sack him, but elicited the truth and made him promise to lead a blameless life thenceforward. "No booze. And understand, Nicholson, no women! If you must have a woman, tell me first."'

Nicholson promised. But one evening, at a dinner party, 'the telephone rang at Monty's house (he always kept a telephone by his place at the head of the table).

'"Who is it?" Monty asked.

'"Sir, it's Nicholson."

'"What is it, Nicholson?"

'"Sir, I've got to have a woman."

'"Hum. Well, all right"' he responded, with Betty listening to every word, '"– but just one, mind!"'

Training by night

But Monty's ultimate mission was not battalion entertainment, nor safe sex, nor – as when he abolished ceremonial church parade on Sundays – the unregimented worship of God: it was the training of his troops for combat. In this realm he was determined to make his real mark, and in this respect he was anxious to get into the desert outside Alexandria, which stretched through Tripolitania towards Libya – little suspecting it would, a decade later under his own army command, be the scene of the first great Allied triumph against the Nazis in World War II: a battle that would prove to be the 'turning of the tide'.

Captain Bailey, the battalion's machine-gun company commander, was emphatic on the subject of training. '[Monty] was the finest trainer of troops I think I've ever known,' he related. 'I mean to say, he behaved in a way no other CO had ever behaved. When it came to your company training he'd say: "Go back to your office and make out a full programme. I want you to clear miles out of Alexandria, anywhere you like. Go and reconnoitre the place, see that there's plenty of water supply there, and everything else. Take the quartermaster along with you if you like. Make all your own arrangements and submit to me your training programme for the next month." And there you were – you were left with that! You went out into the Blue [desert], tents and all, you know! And he said: "Most of the training's got to be done by night. Not less than forty-eight hours at a time away from camp."

'Well, no other CO had ever done it like that. I mean to say, the footling little Company exercises we did around Aldershot which were nothing. It was simply marvellous working under him. He said: "I'll come out and see you from time to time" – he didn't say when, of course. He might turn up in the middle of the night or the daytime.

'His great thing was this training by night. It was really at the back of his mind more than anything else. The soldier, he'd say, must be trained to exercise his skills in the dark, especially with machine-guns and support guns.'[20]

Company training led then to the training of the whole battalion as a cohesive unit. Having avoided massacre only by tripping over his sword-strap on his first day in battle in World War I, Monty was adamant that the battalion rehearse the business of war before war arrived. He therefore insisted the battalion train away from the distractions of Alexandria.

When GHQ Cairo turned down his request for transport to the desert, he simply ordered the battalion to march there, heat or no heat. Bailey vividly recalled one such training week at Idku, 'a day and night march from Alexandria, among the sand hills of the Nile delta. Those were pretty strenuous days and nights, and by the time they ended the Battalion did not relish a day and night march back to barracks. Nevertheless we started the march back, and unknown to all but a few Monty had arranged for a train to be waiting in a siding about half-way back, to take us the rest of the way. I can well remember how the men cheered and laughed at this well-kept secret!'[21]

Ironically, not even Bailey knew the real truth. P. J. Gething came out as a major to Egypt in 1932, convinced it would be the end of his career. 'I thought, this is where I get a bowler hat because Monty and I don't see eye to eye. He doesn't like me, and I don't like him.' Nor was Gething far wrong, as he later found out. When Monty learned that, having got rid of one incompetent company commander, he was to be given Major Gething as a replacement he thumped the table and said he wouldn't have him. 'Africa isn't big enough for the two of us,' he is reported to have said of the somewhat obstinate, punctiliously correct Gething who had so often opposed his will at Chatham in 1925. 'Well, Gething, I'm giving you my worst company,' he said, when Gething reported to him in Alexandria. 'Thank you very much, Sir,' replied Gething. But when Monty saw Gething's performance on company exercises he soon overcame his personal antipathy. 'Men will always work well if they're well led,' he extolled Gething's company command at the first post-mortem. 'After that we made friends,' Gething recalled. 'I learned more tactics under Monty in that one winter than in all the years before. Underneath all the blah he was really good.'

According to Gething, Monty's original request to take the battalion to Idku was turned down categorically by Brigade HQ. 'Brigade said no, the rains are coming and we don't agree. They had a row about it – and Monty took us! He marched us all the way there – it took us two days. We bivouacked at night and marched by day.' Once in the desert, Gething recalled, Monty ordered a series of infantry manoeuvres based on realistic battle scenarios he wrote out himself. 'This was the kind of thing he'd do,' Gething recalled. 'It was a new idea, and I think it was very useful: he made a scheme out. He got his intelligence officer and made him the enemy. We'd either got to go out for a couple of days and blast the enemy village, or defend some place. Monty was the judge. And to encourage us, when we came back [to camp] every few days, he'd hold a concert party competition. Each company would have to put on a show, and the best one would be allowed two days' leave in Alexandria. Well, Monty was right – the rains *did* hold off. But Brigade HQ was furious, and ordered Monty back! – I knew this from the adjutant, Catherall. But Monty didn't let on [to the men]. At the last concert party one night he got up and said to the battalion: "I've got a bit of good news for you. You've done so well while you were here that I'm taking you home tomorrow!"' – by troop trains provided by a much-miffed Brigade HQ.[22]

Such was the background to General Burnett-Stuart's laudatory report, though one advising greater tact:

Lt-Col B. L. Montgomery. He is clever, energetic, ambitious, and a very gifted instructor. He has character, knowledge, and a quick grasp of military problems. But if he is to do himself full justice in the higher positions to which his gifts should entitle him he must cultivate tact, tolerance, and discretion. This is a friendly hint as I have a high opinion of his ability.[23]

The report of the commander of the Canal Brigade, Brigadier 'Tim' Pile, was similarly concerned on this score. In his confidential report the following spring he noted: 'He is definitely above the average of his rank and should attain high rank in the Army. He can only fail to do so if a certain high-handedness which occasionally overtakes him becomes too pronounced.'[24]

High-handedness was anathema to a caste of English 'gentlemen' – men who would, unfortunately, soon be at world war with non-gentlemen.

Night operations

Whatever personal cautions Monty's commanding general or brigadier might append to their confidential reports, however, both fell silent before Monty the tactician – as Gething witnessed during army manoeuvres.

'This was the kind of thing that happened,' Gething recalled. 'The battalion was attacked by tanks and we were out of action for six hours to reorganize before the tanks came and strafed us [again]. A conference was then held in our lines. As a matter of fact I had my company lying down resting, just outside a mess tent in which the generals held this conference. I couldn't see anything, but I could hear. The generals and the brigadier were holding forth about what they would do the next day. And they turned to Monty – and he was only a lieutenant colonel – and asked: "What do you think of that, Monty?" "Nonsense!" Monty answered – and all the three brigadiers and the generals there too. "Look!" he said – and he gave his plan for the next day. And they followed it – and it worked. Not often a general has his plans called "nonsense" by a lieutenant colonel!'[25]

Liddell Hart's claim, in his memoirs, that it was he who converted Montgomery – via Tim Pile, the brigadier – to night operations would appear typically specious, both on Captain Bailey's and Major Gething's evidence. Fighting by moonlight was very much the area in which Monty felt training could produce significant results, and the night operations he practised with his battalion on both company and full battalion exercises certainly went on to prove the key to Monty's success in army manoeuvres in 1933 – as was instanced when Monty was tried out in the role of brigadier, with a young brigade major deputed by Cairo. That brigade major proved to be none other than Freddie de Guingand.

Desert manoeuvres

Encouraged by Betty's affectionate devotion, Monty was at this stage of his life a very different commander from the cautious, iron-willed general he would become during World War II; and the very 'Monty' qualities which romantic military historians have so scorned – such as the insistence on overwhelmingly favourable odds before embarking on schemes – were in reality much more an iron mask Monty forced himself later to wear, while commanding citizen-armies. With trained, professional soldiers Monty was all for imaginative tactics. Far from planning a conventional daytime desert confrontation in 1933, for example, Monty insisted on a pre-emptive night attack, based on his own tactical assumptions about the enemy's likely bivouac site, without first confirming their precise location. 'Monty was going to make a balls of it,' de Guingand candidly recalled after Monty's death. 'He was too eager and I was having to hold him down and hold him down, saying "Now wait, sir, we haven't got enough information. You can't say we know where the enemy forces are . . ." I got on to some friends of mine at the RAF at Cairo and I said,

"Can you do a flight in a certain area, taking photographs?" They came back very rapidly, showing exactly where the enemy were laagered in the desert . . . We then marched off and surrounded them by dawn. For this Monty got a very good mark,' de Guingand remembered; 'but, if he'd done what he originally wanted, it would have counted against him.'[26]

It was thus de Guingand who, as Monty's brigade major for the annual army manoeuvres in Egypt, acted as a cautionary brake on Monty's impetuousness, as well as providing brilliantly imaginative support for his commander's boldness and skill in nighttime operations. Together they made a battle-winning team that augured well for the future. Brigadier Pile was certainly impressed. 'It is a positive pleasure to watch him commanding his unit on manoeuvres,' Brigadier Pile wrote in his confidential report of March 1933[27] – omitting to say that Monty's exposition of his battalion's intended operations on the sand-table was so spellbinding that Brigade HQ actually went off with the sand-table afterwards![28]

Too big for his boots

It was, as Colonel Gething later put it, Monty's clarity of presentation that doubly impressed onlookers and participants. After every scheme a conference was held, and Monty's summings-up, as commander, were so accurate and so decisive that there was often little remaining for Brigadier Pile or General Burnett-Stuart – the actual umpires – to add, as Gething remembered. 'He'd get up and hold forth about what he'd done. He'd say: "I realize now that that was a mistake – I ought to have done this, that and the other. So he took the wind out of all their sails. When he'd finished there was nothing left to say!'[29]

In fact no one – save Liddell Hart – could fault Monty as a tactical instructor and commander. By March 1933 General Burnett-Stuart was writing in his confidential report: 'I have a very high opinion of, and a great liking for, Lt-Col Montgomery. He has been an outstanding Battalion Commander and I hope soon to see him employed in a higher capacity.'[30]

Brigadier Pile even recommended Monty as 'an admirable chief instructor at the Staff College' that same March – leaving just the slightest suspicion that both Burnett-Stuart and Pile were anxious for a quieter life.

Perhaps, too, Burnett-Stuart and Pile – both contenders to become CIGS in the next few years, once the disastrously reactionary General Sir

Archibald Massingberd had served his time – were genuinely anxious that Monty's talents should not be spurned by senior officers who were blind to the importance of modern training and tactical rehearsal. In an age when the British army was still loath to mechanize its twenty British cavalry regiments, and with a CIGS determined to silence surviving 'brains' within the army ('character is more important than brains' Massingberd insisted to Liddell Hart[31]), Monty's modern approach to military professionalism might possibly prove his undoing, they reckoned.

They were, as will be seen, very nearly right. Certainly Lieutenant Neil Holdich, who joined the battalion as a subaltern in September 1933, found a situation in which Monty had outgrown his usefulness. It was not, Holdich emphasized, that Monty was getting too big for his boots, but that his boots were perhaps becoming too small for him. From a tactical point of view, the battalion was excellent, he recalled some forty-five years later. 'Even the lance corporals had begun to think tactically as they would in the field. But, when you've said that, you've said the best part about it. The company commanders, though gentlemen and very decent people, were not particularly bright. And, with these rather average officers, Montgomery had centralized everything on himself.' Determined to impart his revolutionary approach to training, 'There was no arguing with him, he decided everything. No men could be moved from one platoon to another without Montgomery's approval. The second-in-command, the adjutant, and the quartermaster were all yes-men, his mouthpieces. Montgomery decided all the promotions himself – haphazard promotion by so-called "merit" that did nothing to help morale among the ranks. Nobody knew where they stood, and Montgomery wasn't, frankly, all that popular as a result. It was a regular, somewhat rigid pre-war army battalion; and Montgomery's methods didn't always go down well.

'It was the same outside the battalion. The brigadier, Sir Frederick Pile, was really an artilleryman. Very smooth; but he didn't really get on very well with Monty. Montgomery told him what he should do – that he didn't know his infantry stuff. And he didn't tell him very tactfully.

'Nor were we popular with the Coldstream Guards, who were stationed in Cairo, and came down to Alexandria either socially, to bathe, or on manoeuvres. Monty was pretty rude to them. Except for the 12th Lancers, the cavalry was in those days still horsed – and Monty thought they were a nonsense, not serious soldiers, just there for hunting, polo, and fishing. And told them so.

'When we left, at the end of 1933, to go to Poona, in India, Brigadier Pile saw us off at Suez. He said we left with our reputation second to none. But we think he wrote differently to India; because, when we got there in January 1934, the reception we got was distinctly chilly.'[32]

The 1st Battalion of the Royal Warwicks might be fit and ready for modern war, the brigadier and general in Egypt conceded, but was it fit for peace?

To the 'Sloth Belt'

Autocratic commander, super-efficient administrator, brilliant instructor, a master of infantry tactics – Lieutenant-Colonel Montgomery was indeed, as Sir Frederick Pile put it, 'definitely a strong character', who had his sights on the very pinnacle of the British army. But would he survive peacetime protocols to get there?

On 25 November 1932, Monty's father had died at Moville, at the august age of eighty-five, leaving 'Lady' Montgomery the titular as well as de facto head of the family. Where Monty later obtained the idea that better nursing by his mother might have prolonged his father's already long life, as he claimed in his *Memoirs* ('Poor dear man, I never thought his last few years were very happy; he was never allowed to do as he liked and he was not given the care and nursing which might have prolonged his life. My mother . . . was not a good nurse'[33]) is a mystery; but there can be little doubt Monty was distressed his father did not live to witness his rise to fame; and, in the wake of widowerhood, bitter that his mother should have taken so long to acknowledge his right to it.

For the moment, however, the presence and affection of Betty warded off such thoughts. On Christmas Eve 1933 he personally supervised the boarding of HM Troopship *Worcester* at Suez, having a line of soldiers stationed the length of the gangplank passing up babies to their waiting mothers. Thereafter he sailed off to Bombay, determined that his next command should be that of a brigade.

For a mere lieutenant colonel, Monty was remarkably self-confident, indeed self-opinionated. Though no stickler for drill, he was known to be a fanatic for efficiency and training. He expected his orders to be obeyed instantly. He believed in promotion by merit, and had no use whatsoever for horsed cavalry. The only time he had ever paid any attention to ceremonial was when – in answer to a demonstration against the presence of the British – he marched the entire 1st Battalion of the Royal Warwicks with band, drums and regimental antelope through the centre of Alexandria. He was openly contemptuous of idle and amateur officers, and was known to have trained his battalion in exercises to function without officers – that is to say, entirely under its RSM and NCOs, with all officers as 'casualties'! Conversely, he was famous for running officers' tactical training exercises without troops (TEWTs), over a sand-table in the evening for aspiring young officers instead of the conventional cocktail parties.

Unfortunately the Indian station to which the Royal Warwicks had been posted was traditionally known as the 'Sloth Belt' – and it was not long before the master tactician met the master of ceremonies, General Sir George Jeffreys.

Trouble from the start

'Poona was absolutely ghastly,' Colonel Pat Burge related later. 'To a keen soldier I cannot think of any worse fate than to have to go there. We arrived well-trained, with a charitable description as being "adequate" in turnout and ceremonial from headquarters, Egypt, and we fell into the clutches of the GOC Southern India Command, General Sir George Jeffreys. He was a fine, indeed wonderful man – as second-in-command of a Grenadier Guards Battalion during the retreat from Mons he boasted they had not lost a single man – but he had no interest at all in training of any kind. He certainly didn't recover for a long time the first time he saw us!'[34]

There was a considerable irony in this confrontation, for General Jeffreys had written Volume I of the *Infantry Training Manual*, on drill, while Monty had written Volume II, on tactics. Thus if Monty was said to be 'mad' about tactical training, Jeffreys was equally obsessed by square-bashing. Though the story of General Jeffreys' first inspection of the battalion – in which Monty, having been told that he was seven paces too far to the left, simply swivelled on his saddle and ordered the whole battalion to move seven paces to the right – is apocryphal, it was not far from the truth. Lieutenant Holdich, in charge of a platoon at the time, vividly remembered the occasion. It took place in January 1934, in the early morning, on the race course at Poona. Jeffreys' reputation had preceded him, and Holdich made himself as inconspicuous as possible behind the large and portly figure of Captain Edlin, his company commander.

'"Good morning, Montgomery, you should be standing whatever-number-of-paces in front of your battalion. You are not standing the correct number of paces," Jeffreys said – the first thing, before Montgomery could get out "Present arms" or anything. After that everything went wrong. We were hopeless. It was one glorious muddle.'[35]

Nor did it stop there. Jeffreys insisted on seeing the battalion perform his favourite company drill – a complicated series of movements in which one company hinges neatly on the next. 'Monty should have given a series of orders of which he hadn't the slightest idea at all,' Colonel Burge later recollected, confirming Holdich's memory. 'As a result we got into the most almighty tangle. But what Montgomery did then say – this I can swear to, because I was there – was: "Royal Warwickshires – follow me in fours!" and steamed off on his horse. It was most unorthodox, but the soldiery disentangled themselves in some way, and followed him.'[36]

If Jeffreys humiliated the commander of the 1st Battalion, the Royal Warwickshire Regiment, on the parade ground, however, he certainly did not have things all his own way.

'Jeffreys regarded Montgomery as a bit of an upstart,' Major Holdich recalled, 'with new, advanced ideas; equally, Montgomery regarded Jeffreys as an out-of-date old fogey, and didn't conceal it. There was bound to be friction between them – and there was.'[37]

The rivalry between the two authors of the two volumes of the British army's *Infantry Training Manual* became a veritable sparring match. 'Montgomery undoubtedly sailed very close to the wind, from the instant he went out to India,' Burge remembered. 'It wasn't soldiering as we'd known it in Europe. There was a stack of "modifications for India" which negated everything the War Office was trying to do to modernize the army. And since the Indian government paid for the troops that were there, and since these troops were primarily for internal security and at most to meet a threat from Afghanistan, there was no new material of any kind – transport, tanks, aeroplanes: nothing. I can well imagine that that pile of "modifications for India" made Montgomery see red. My impression is that he wrote off the whole hierarchy there; and there was trouble from the start.'[38]

Almost immediately, HQ Southern India Command queried Monty's

Sunday church parade system. Because the Indian Mutiny of 1857 had broken out on a Sunday morning while the British were at church, the battalion must go to church armed with rifles, Southern Command still ordered, almost a century later. This, as Monty knew, necessitated endless paperwork, as every individual rifle had to be signed for and countersigned when returned. Headquarters insisted. In the end Monty sent a small armed platoon to stand outside church each Sunday 'in case the second mutiny should break out again!', as Monty sarcastically declared. Jeffreys was furious – as he was over the Kirkee controversy.

'Montgomery was told to provide a company and a half to guard the arsenal at Kirkee,' Burge related, 'and he wrote back to HQ asking for instructions as to the threat against which he was to defend it. I remember there was one sentence in it – it was a most impudent letter, but it was damned funny; he had started to itemize the possible threats, and he began at the top of the page with: "The Germans. Presumably we would have prior notice of this . . ." He was asking for trouble. He'd written off the hierarchy there and didn't take the slightest notice of it.'[39]

Missing the boat

Monty's attitude was tantamount to insubordination; thus it certainly seemed a good idea to all when he applied for leave to travel with his wife on the P & O Line annual six-week cruise to the Far East that spring, starting from Bombay and taking in Colombo, Penang, Singapore, Hong Kong and Shanghai before setting its passengers down for a fortnight in Japan.

Young David Montgomery, then aged five, had been sent back to England with a nanny – the first of a long train of such abandonments – and Monty and Betty looked forward to a complete break from barracks-style soldiering. Monty had now commanded the battalion for three years, with a single break for a month at home in August 1933. 'Nobody had any doubt that Montgomery was destined for higher things,' Lieutenant Burge – who also went on the voyage – was later to remember. 'But only if he didn't fall by the wayside in the meantime. One more year in Poona would have finished him, I'm sure.'[40]

The sea journey to Japan, chosen as a rest, was to be much more eventful than the Montgomerys imagined, though. For a start, General Jeffreys was also on board. Furthermore, a casual perusal of the passenger list revealed an even more surprising name: the architect of the new German army, General von Seeckt, whose book on modern German military methods, *Thoughts of a Soldier*, had been published in English.[41] In it, von Seeckt had emphasized training, particularly the training of NCOs; but he had also argued, like the British chief of staff of the army, that 'the days of the cavalry, if trained, equipped and led on modern lines, are not numbered, and that its lances may still flaunt their pennants with confidence in the wind of the future.'[42] 'Montgomery hadn't seen the passenger list for more than thirty seconds,' Burge recalled, 'before General von Seeckt found himself with his back against the wall! They used to have great talks together and the CO often used to have me up there with him, while the interpreting was done by a Colonel von Heinz.'[43]

Burge was equally surprised when, at every port of call, Monty went ashore, taking his wife and the young lieutenant with him, 'to survey the military situation. He always seemed to know somebody, the OC Troops or a senior officer presumably from his Staff College days.'[44] Indeed, it seemed as if Monty was more an inspecting officer than a tourist. Yet the biggest surprise came at the end of March 1934, when the liner arrived in Hong Kong. Amidst the mail for Lieutenant-Colonel Montgomery was a telegram from Army HQ Simla, offering him the post of chief instructor (GSO 1) at the Staff College, Quetta.

'What always reminds me of this,' recalled Colonel Burge nearly forty-five years later, 'is that I would have thought anybody receiving such a message would have leaped overboard. Not a bit of it. "I'll brood on this," he said.'[45]

The matter, however, was not as simple as young Lieutenant Burge imagined. Monty had assured Major Gething that he would next command a brigade, followed by a division, ultimately becoming CIGS. He was now forty-six; he already had experience of Staff College instructing and would be forty-nine when the proposed chief instructorship came to an end. Would this be a sideways step, depriving him of the chance of field command for three vital years? The War Office in London had cabled to the C-in-C India on 19 March 1934: 'No objection to offering Montgomery. But you should tell him that failing this he will probably be selected for staff appointment at home next year.'[46]

It was this rider that very likely prompted Monty to accept. To serve as chief instructor at Quetta might be a three-year side-step on the military command ladder. But to spend a further year at Poona under General

Jeffreys and his equally fogeyish brigadier before being posted back to England – if indeed he survived a year with Jeffreys – to a mere staff appointment at the War Office would be an even greater waste. The Chief of the Imperial General Staff – CIGS – was a widely acknowledged dolt, expansion of the Royal Tank Corps had been vetoed, the new Tank Brigade had been disbanded, and the horsed cavalry reprieved – despite Hitler's announcement that the German army would be expanded to thirty-six divisions! The great exponent of tank warfare, Major-General 'Boney' Fuller, had been forcibly retired in 1933, after being unemployed by the army for three years. All in all, for 'progressives' in the British army in England, the outlook was bleak.

After consultation with Betty, then, Monty cabled acceptance. It would mean he would be promoted to full colonel on commencement of his teaching duties in June 1934. They would have a comfortable house in the cantonment, several miles outside the picturesque city of Quetta: gateway to Afghanistan and Persia, perched 6,000 feet above sea level in the mountains of what is now Pakistan. The commandant had expressly asked for an infantry officer, as his other British service instructors were gunners and sappers. The college was far from the Sloth Belt, and its standard of instruction was second only to Camberley's, with students nominated not only from among officers serving in India but also from the dominions. Within reason, Monty would be his own boss. They would be able to have David out again, and would see Betty's sons John and Dick as soon as they finished their military training as sappers at Chatham and were posted to India.

Having made up his mind, Monty thought no more about it. But at least one of his students at Quetta remembers a fatalism in the new chief instructor's attitude, a feeling that he might have 'missed the boat' and would be too old to be given an active command when eventually war came – as Monty was convinced it must.[47]

A bad state

News of Monty's promotion provoked a mixed reaction in the Royal Warwickshire Regiment. The *Antelope* recorded that 'all those who have served with Colonel Montgomery will regret that the Regiment is to lose an officer who has done so much to instil into all ranks the modern theory of war, and on behalf of all our readers we wish him many more steps in promotion.'

At regimental-officer level, however, the loss went unmourned. Monty's successor, Lieutenant-Colonel J. P. Duke, was in the great mould of Royal Warwickshire colonels: tall, elegant, sincere, without pretension. Monty had told Duke how to plan his training course at Sandhurst in 1926 when Duke was put in charge of military training as chief instructor at the Royal Military College – 'one term characteristics of the arms, one term larger formations, third term company tactics – a system that proved highly successful and remained the protocol for many years', Duke recalled gratefully. For Montgomery as tactics expert and instructor, Duke had the highest regard; but, although he thought Monty would rise to higher command than lieutenant colonel, he did not believe Monty would become a commander-in-chief, 'because he could be so rude, and made himself unpopular'.[48]

The word was significant, for the fear of not being 'popular' among colleagues in one's club or regiment was the millstone of the British army, dooming it to disaster upon disaster in the next war, as one socially acceptably tall, elegant, or unpretentious gentleman-commander after another failed the test of modern war when pitched against the Nazis.

It is not without historical interest, then, to ask how 'popularity in the mess' could ever have infiltrated a profession so martial as soldiering as the basis for promotion. It was certainly no longer the case in Germany, whose army was now expanding rapidly under the direction of the Third Reich's new Führer. Was it, then, a disease of democracy? Or was it an unfortunate side-effect of the Geddes axe, which condemned the army to look backwards, not forwards; to save money rather than to modernize; to discard difficult personnel by any means possible, making subservience to higher, report-writing authority the basic criterion of survival – in other words, a recipe for mediocrity? 'He is very strongminded and I would advise him (and this is meant for advice, not adverse criticism) to bear in mind the frailties of average human nature and to remember that most others have neither the same energy, nor the same ability as himself,' Sir George Jeffreys warned in his final report on Monty at Poona.[49]

Duke was certainly intrigued by the state of the battalion when arriving to take over in June 1934. Monty was 'away when I arrived', Duke recalled, 'although he'd left a few notes on paper. The younger officers were content under him; but the senior officers were in a state of revolt. They said: "For God's sake take things easy, because the men are on the point of revolution."' As Duke recognized, they were speaking for themselves. 'They didn't like him, the senior officers. Monty thought they were a lot of dug-ins; but the mutiny story wasn't true,' Duke emphatically stated – 'that was balls, really. The senior officers were merely disgruntled.'[50]

What was clear was that the regiment was hamstrung by elderly majors and superannuated subalterns and that Southern India Command expected the turnout of a Guards battalion: a British unit which could carry out ceremonial duties and carry the flag – while Monty wished to fashion a modern weapon of war. 'I was sent for by the brigade commander and the army commander, Jeffreys,' Duke recalled, 'and they said: "Your battalion is in a bad state. They don't drill properly and they don't turn out properly." So I had to set out to re-drill the Battalion and get that side right. But their tactics I found were good. The truth is,' Duke reflected half a century later, 'there wasn't enough for Monty to do, commanding a battalion. Not in Poona – Poona was a very fashionable social place – and Monty didn't care for that much.'[51]

Relieved of such ceremonial and social expectations Monty meanwhile departed, leaving Lieutenant-Colonel Duke to restore the jaded ceremonial reputation of the battalion and improve its drill. As of 29 June 1934, Colonel B. L. Montgomery assumed the post of chief instructor, Quetta Staff College.

Public speaking

Monty's three-year period in the Himalayas now rescued him from the Sloth Belt of Poona, and the frustrations of a War Office in London refusing to modernize – indeed, in which the CIGS, Field-Marshal Milne, at a conference in January 1933 to review the lessons of World War I in the light of the secret Kirke Report had declared 'it is very unlikely that in your lifetime, or in the lifetime of younger officers, we shall be engaged in a national campaign on the continent of Europe'.[52]

Quetta thus gave Monty the chance to set his recent experience of battalion command against his previous experience as a staff officer, and to draw the lessons, not only for himself, but for his students: students not only of war, but of a war he was increasingly certain was inevitable, given Hitler's rise to power in Germany and Monty's own talks with General von Seeckt.

With great wisdom the commandant of the college, General Williams, had decided that, although Monty had been appointed to replace Colonel Paget, the chief instructor responsible for the second-year students, this would be to waste Monty's skills. 'Guy Williams – now he was the most wonderful man,' Major-General Eric Sixsmith remembered some forty-five years later. 'He handled Monty in the most remarkable way. He'd been the senior army instructor at the Imperial Defence College before, and he was a man of the very broadest outlook. He used Monty to the full. You learned the technique of battle in your first year and you went on to broader issues – internal security problems, imperial problems, grand strategy, all that you went on to in your second year. So anyone who had Monty in his hands would obviously see that he was the man to teach the Junior Division [first-year students] the technique of battle command and staff duties.'[53] Monty was therefore made chief instructor of the Junior Division with a directing staff of five officers.

Brigadier 'Tochi' Barker later recalled Montgomery's impact on the students in 1934 – and what Monty was up against. 'There were a lot of old stiffs in our year – all the old stiffs of the First World War whose last chance it had been to get into the Staff College.' For these men Montgomery's arrogance was beyond the pale. As a junior officer, how-ever, Barker was awed by Monty's ability to simplify the complexities of modern warfare. Looking back, he recalled that Monty, too, was learning new skills, as well as the students. Hitherto, Monty had applied himself to the demanding business of analysis: reducing the complexities of modern war to their essentials. In doing so he had lectured either from a prepared text, broken down into themes and sections, or from extensive notes. Now, in 1934, he became determined to master the art of speaking without notes at all.

'I remember he invented a new method of lecturing there,' Barker recounted. 'He'd come in with his notes, read to himself one page – taking three or four minutes reading them while one sat waiting. And then he'd walk to the front of the stage and talk splendidly, absolutely right . . . Then he'd go back to his desk and study his notes for another three or four minutes. And then he'd give us another ten minutes or so, straight off, and damned good it was – in my opinion. And afterwards, when I got to know Monty very well, I rather ragged him; I said: "Now, Sir, I enjoy your talks . . . My only point is: you take such frequent pauses in your progress. You go and you leave us sitting for four or five minutes while you study your notes."'

Monty was apparently unabashed. '"I'll tell you what I'm doing. I'm training myself to think as I speak, and not read out from a script. So I like to refresh my memory with the facts, and then I like to go and give it as I think, to speak out." And he was damned good.'[54]

Verbal communication thus became Monty's next priority, after tactics and training. Thousands of miles from England, 6,000 feet up in the mountains of Baluchistan, east of the border with Afghanistan, Monty developed the art which he would perfect as no other Allied or even Axis general in World War II: learning to simplify not only the vision he wished to convey to his officers, but the means by which to convey it.

Some historians would be as contemptuous of this ability as the 'old stiffs' of Quetta, feeling that 'public relations' skills were somehow inappropriate to a military commander – one historian, Correlli Barnett, even deriding Monty for projecting himself on his army in 1942 'like a politician or a crooner'.[55] Those like Brigadier Barker who witnessed Monty's painstaking attempt to improve his speaking skills in the mid-1930s, felt, by contrast, that such historians were obtuse: defenders of the very failures of communication that would bedevil Britain's armies for the first three years of World War II. Barnett extolled, as did other British writers, Field-Marshal Rommel as a commander who did not need 'public relations' skills to raise the morale of his troops – ignoring the fact that German soldiers were subject to the most powerful 'public relations' efforts ever invented by modern propaganda professionals, including newspapers, newsreels and radio broadcasts. Inspired by Hitler, well trained and led by a new breed of NCOs and officers who were unencumbered by the sort of social snobberies, pretensions, inertia and indolence that characterized so much of the British officer class, Wehrmacht troops would prove the most formidable soldiers of the twentieth century, with or without Rommel.

By contrast Britain, like other European democracies, laboured under the burden of military 'victory' in World War I: complacency, class-consciousness and class-division, lack of funding, and a bigoted amateurism making it almost impossible for the nation to modernize. It said a great deal for Monty's genius, Brigadier Barker maintained, that Monty recognized already in 1934, only a year after Hitler's accession to power in Germany, the need of British military commanders to learn the techniques of modern communication. Moreover, these techniques, so distrusted by the likes of Correlli Barnett, were not those of massaging media, but relied on a much profounder perception, namely the challenge of personal projection: of putting oneself and one's message across to others in a manner that made people sit up, pay attention, and respond. As Barker put it: 'I used to sit there and think: that's always what I've thought, this is quite right, but I haven't got enough wit to say it, the language.' In other words, Barker felt, Monty was striving to develop a new language of command: a way of visualizing the problems of war, breaking them down into components, and presenting them and their solutions in a manner that helped people both to understand them and feel confidence in themselves in dealing with them. To achieve this with maximum effectiveness, Monty had recognized, it was not sufficient merely to write clearly; it was imperative also to speak clearly – directly, without looking down, or interrupting the psychic link between instructor and students. It was a talent which Britain's senior generals in the early years of the coming war would neglect to the point of imperilling Britain's military survival.

In Monty's case, the result of so much effort, once he had mastered the art, was electric – and in this respect Monty would have no equal as an army commander in twentieth-century warfare, whether land, sea or air. Where Haig (who was unable to string two sentences together in oral communication with his staff or commanders) and his senior commanders in World War I had failed ever to project their ideas and tactical vision to their subordinate officers or men with clarity or vibrance, Monty made it his new aim to master the technique of oral presentation five years before World War II began, while still a colonel, knowing how crucial it would prove: an ability which, although incomparably important in war, would often be deeply resented by certain jealous colleagues, rivals, subordinates and, later, historians, most of whom had no idea or interest in its genesis or purpose, but simply confused it with his rising egomania.

An immense privilege

Meanwhile, although he was uncompromisingly forthright about those students whom he considered to be 'useless' ('a great improvement – thoroughly bad', he marked on one recalcitrant student's paper[56]), Monty would take infinite pains over those who, he felt, showed promise.

In one of the two British army battalions stationed in the Quetta district was Captain Francis de Guingand (known as 'Wizz-Bang' for his ever-fertile brain). Anxious lest a young officer of de Guingand's calibre be lost to the army by failure to advance him in the service ('He had qualified for the Staff College in the exam; but he had left it rather late and could not sit again', Monty later explained[57]), Monty personally wrote to the War Office in London to back de Guingand's candidacy for a place at the Staff College, Camberley. From Quetta, on 30 July 1934, Monty then wrote to de Guingand, who had thanked him the moment he heard he had got in:

My dear Freddie,

Thank you for your letter. I heard from the D[irector] S[taff] D[uties] some days ago. His letter was dated 27th June and I gathered from it that as far as he was concerned all would be well. I did not tell you, as accidents sometimes happen.

I am not used to backing the wrong horse when it comes to asking favours of people in high places; it would result only in one's own undoing!! You ought to do well at Camberley. I know many of the instructors there, and some of them very well; one of them – Nye – is in my Regt. I will write and commend you to them in due course.

We are coming to your dance on 14 Aug. and are dining first with the Army Comdr.

Yrs ever, B. L. Montgomery[58]

Monty's sponsorship of de Guingand was to be an investment that would repay him incalculably in the course of time. De Guingand, however, was not the only young protégé Monty backed at this time, for that winter he arranged – and even paid for – the still incompletely cured Lieutenant Burge, who had fallen ill with polio, to come and stay with him at Quetta. The following year he would make a personal visit to the War Office in London to see that a gifted lieutenant from his first-year course be given accelerated promotion – Dudley Ward, a future army commander. And if Monty could not bring himself to approve of inefficiency or shoddy work, his happy marriage nevertheless seems to have softened him. 'Don't you think you ought to give so-and-so another chance?' Betty was often heard to say. 'She was dark and vivacious, always cheerful and frequently laughing,' one young officer recalled. 'Both she and Monty shared a keen sense of humour and loved pulling one another's legs. They were good and generous hosts, and I was asked to join their dinner parties on several occasions. At one of these, just before a week's spell in camp on outdoor exercises, at the end of dinner, she said: "Ladies, do come with me and we'll discuss what we are going to do whilst Monty and the men go away to camp to play soldiers." Monty loved it. They were devoted to one another and didn't mind showing it.'[59]

There would always be those like Liddell Hart who felt Betty had a hard time, bossed about by her egocentric spouse. But those who really knew them – Monty's brother Brian, Betty's sons John and Dick, officers from the Royal Warwickshire Regiment in Palestine, Alexandria and Poona, students at Quetta – all testify to the opposite. Alongside Monty's prickly egoism was a genuine respect and love of young men that made Monty a curious but rather touching mix of martinet and mentor. Rather than resent this, or question the extent of Monty's fondness for such young men, Betty accepted it and rewarded him with her own loyal affection and confidence in her husband's sincerity and purpose. Perhaps the ultimate proof of how well the marriage worked, from Betty's point of view, lay in the artistic work she was able to do in India.

However bossy he might be in running their household, Monty had always insisted upon ensuring she had freedom to paint and sculpt. This she did, from Palestine to India, in ever-increasing amounts. Even guests were required to help – Lieutenant Burge, for example, when staying with the Montgomerys at Quetta, being asked by Monty to organize a number of Indian soldiers from different regiments and backgrounds to model for a series of military portraits she wished to do. Indeed, Betty produced so many canvases and figures at this time that she was able to give away a considerable number when returning to England, as Brigadier Barker recalled.

'Betty – she was charming, and a good artist. I've got several of her pictures still. Before she went home in 1935, in her drawing room she hung all the pictures she'd painted – quite a lot – and invited her friends, including me and Mrs Barker – and said, "Come along and pick anything you like and take it." So I arrived there. And Monty said: "Ah, yes, Tochi, I'll show you the picture you should have." I said, "No, no, I want to choose my own." Monty was insistent. "No, no, I'll show you" – and he took me to a picture of some flowers, irises. He said: "That's the one!" I objected. "No, no, I shall go around and choose." So I did. But of course I chose the one that Monty had said – it was easily the best!' Years later, 'after the war, I heard that Monty had lost all his pictures at Portsmouth [during a German air raid]. So I wrote to him and said, "Now I have several of Betty's pictures," I named them, "and you can have them all or any one you like to pick." And Monty wrote back straight away – he had a memory like an elephant – and said: "I will have the 'Irises'!" '[60]

Monty's admiration for Betty's work and his respect for her as a woman, a mother, a wife and a companion were transparently genuine. 'Looking back it is difficult to understand the astonishment we all felt at the marriage, an astonishment that still seems to haunt biographers,' commented her son John many years later.[61] After Cheshire, 'the world of her brother Patrick, A. P. Herbert and the Café Royal *literati* was heady stuff and she enjoyed every minute. The Herberts were unfailingly kind, Arnold Bennett told her she was a very intelligent woman and she had lots of exciting acquaintances; nevertheless – and this is the point – she was never more than half in and of this world; she was never entirely at ease with its rather lax moral standards and many of her closest friends were outside it . . . Monty's world was not to her such an alien one as is sometimes implied. "I am reverting to type," she would say to her astonished Chiswick friends when explaining her engagement and in a fundamental sense this was true, though she could never be a typical army wife any more than her remarkable husband was a typical army officer.'[62]

'Montgomery fussed over, looked after her devotedly,' remembered Colonel Burge of his stay there. 'She took his mind off soldiering; she made him giggle, able to laugh at himself. There was a lightness in the house, and a great deal of amusing chit-chat, gossip and talk quite apart from military discussion. Betty didn't know the difference between a corporal and a corps commander – or behaved as if she didn't, which was quite superb – and very good for Monty.'[63]

Monty's brother Brian, at this time stationed in India, thought so too. 'My brother and his wife lived in a pleasant bungalow, with a large garden, on Hanna Road, where they were very comfortable and were able to do all the entertaining expected of a senior officer on the directing staff.'[64] Brian, who was serving with the Baluch Regiment at Karachi and often visited Monty in Quetta, recollected 'dinner parties which were always great fun and most amusing'. With students from the British army, Indian army and dominion forces, including Australia, Canada, New Zealand and South Africa, there was a wide mix of backgrounds and talent. 'During dinner, and afterwards over the port and coffee (there was always plenty to drink), Bernard would deliberately introduce a problem for discussion, and, if necessary (which it generally wasn't), follow it up by some perfectly outrageous statement calculated to provoke someone into counter-argument. Betty's own gaiety and charm, and her skill as a hostess, created a relaxed atmosphere and made everyone feel at home.'[65]

This was a Monty unknown to later observers: indeed the period at

Quetta was 'among the happiest times of his life,' Brian judged,[66] for Monty was in his element: enjoying a happy marriage, being a doting father, heading up a team of army instructors, surrounded by keen young men, and with a commanding vision of modern warfare predicated upon clear tactical ideas, high-class staffwork and the intimate co-operation of all arms. Both Brian Montgomery and General Sir Dudley Ward felt, in retrospect, that Monty's concept of war had now fully matured. Though the detailed classes were taken by the various G2 instructors, the course was entirely as laid down by the chief instructor himself. 'At Quetta the whole of the instructing staff was under his charge,' General Sir Dudley Ward – then a lieutenant – remembered, 'and I think they learned as much from Monty as we students did. There's no doubt we all felt immensely privileged to be taught the higher aspects of our profession by someone of Monty's calibre. Indeed, any later development of one's own military ability came from Monty at Quetta, and his tactical doctrines.'

These military doctrines were, like politics, founded on the art of the possible. It was not enough, Monty argued, to have bright ideas about 'rolling torrents' and 'exploitation'. 'People like Liddell Hart I think are vastly overrated,' Ward considered. 'They were obsessed by mobility – which is fine if you can have it. But it isn't often so; and the only way you can win battles is to defeat the enemy who wants to deprive you of that mobility. It was Monty who taught us how to do this. He could be very chaffing and had a strong sense of humour. But at other times he could be deadly serious. I remember him saying the last time he addressed us: "You gentlemen must now get on with the business of making yourselves professionals in your chosen profession – because we only have the time it takes Germany to become what she considers to be sufficiently re-armed." '[67]

Recommended for early command

Major-General Williams certainly held the highest opinion of his chief instructor, and within a year – in April 1935 – was recommending Monty for 'early command of a Regular Brigade or Brigadier, General Staff'.

Colonel Montgomery, Williams wrote in his confidential report, was 'a forceful personality, widely read and with practical experience in the field, he is a fine trainer and a convincing teacher. He demands a high standard of conduct and of work. I am grateful to him for his wise and constructive help in all matters connected with the College.'[68]

Williams' report, together with Monty's now growing file of testimonials, did not go unnoticed at the War Office in London; and on 8 May 1935 the War Office Selection Board approved the appointment of Colonel B. L. Montgomery to command a regular infantry brigade as soon as one became available.

When that would happen, however, in an army where mediocrity, good manners, turnout and likeableness in the mess counted for more than professionalism, was left open.

The white topee

Monty, who was always so careful to compute in advance his chances of promotion, cannot have failed to be aware that, aged forty-seven, he would be nearing fifty if no vacancy for brigade command occurred before the end of his instructorship at Quetta. By the time he got the next higher command – that of a general commanding a division – he would be fifty-four, still a very long way from becoming CIGS, the cut-off age for which was sixty. Although he was more than ever convinced there would be another war again between Britain and Germany, he began to doubt whether it would come within the period of his active career – a fact which seems to have added fuel to his exhortations to his students. Against the background of polo playing, of regimental parties and colonial life with servants and abundant drink in India he warned: 'Remember it will be your show, and you will neglect the study of your profession at your peril.'[69]

According to Major-General Sixsmith, who was a student at Quetta, 'there is no doubt about it that he was considered to be out on a limb in the army, one who took his own line'.[70] Yet, if Monty sometimes wondered whether he would ever be given the opportunity to reach the high command to which he aspired, he never ceased preparing himself. Whatever lengths he went to in order to help talented students, he himself never relaxed his own example of command. When the new Junior Division students assembled before him in February 1935 he made it quite clear what 'the form' was. 'I remember he talked to us,' Major-General Sixsmith recalled his first meeting with the chief instructor. 'He said: "Well, you'll all ask me to dinner. Of course I shan't come. But I shall ask all of you to dinner. I couldn't possibly go out with thirty of you! I couldn't possibly spare the time for that. But you'll all come to my house." And of course we all did. The other thing I'll always remember about that first lecture – which showed how his mind worked – he said: "Now after the outdoor [tactical] exercises we'll all come home as we wish. Those people who've got motor cars I hope will take out those who've not got motor cars. We go in plain clothes. Once the exercise is over, we'll all go home, quick as you like – as long as no one gets in front of me!"'

There was also the matter of headgear – 'his white "stationmaster's hat" as we called it', Sixsmith recalled, 'while we all wore Bombay bowlers.'[71] Monty 'wore a white topee – an old one,' 'Tochi' Barker remembered. 'This was very unfashionable, but was very popular with us students because on all the schemes – and Quetta is wide-open spaces – you could always tell where Monty was! You could see this topee, bobbing about. We were all in plain clothes, mufti, for exercises, but you could always spot Monty. Later on I ragged him and I said, "Sir, why do you wear this white topee, it's very unfashionable. We don't object of course, but it's very old-fashioned." This was 1935. And Monty said: "Well, people like wearing unusual hats, it stamps their personality. Winston Churchill always goes in for unusual hats – so do I!" And it's extraordinary that, because Churchill was rather in the doldrums then.'[72]

Monty's three-year period as chief instructor at Quetta seemed to be passing uneventfully and happily. David had been brought out from England by a nanny late in 1934 and Dick had joined his parents for the Christmas holiday. On the last day of May 1935, however, not long after Monty heard of his green light for promotion to brigade command if a vacancy arose, and two weeks after the death of T. E. Lawrence in a motorcycle accident in England, there occurred at Quetta a disaster which, in its horror, presaged not only a personal disaster in the Montgomery family but horrors on an almost incalculable global scale to come: an earthquake which in a single night accounted for the lives of half the population of the city.

The suffering was as concentrated and grotesque as anything Monty can have witnessed in the Great War; indeed, the scale of the disaster was so great and the danger of typhoid so acute that the army commander reluctantly ordered the entire city be ringed with barbed wire and sealed off, like an amputated, infected limb. '30,000 people were killed in five minutes,' Monty later recorded. He, Betty and little David were spared, though the house 'was badly shaken'.[73]

The Staff College, mercifully situated on a different stratum of rock, also escaped destruction. As long as its clock tower continued to stand it would carry on its business, Major-General Williams cabled in answer to the sister college at Camberley, which had offered to take the students and staff.

Two days after the quake, however, further tremors were felt in the Quetta valley; and the college clock struck seventeen.

Family matters

Though the Quetta Staff College was kept going, the quake left permanent scars. For Monty himself it entailed an eight-month separation from his wife who, after rendering night-and-day help with the injured and homeless in the Quetta cantonment, returned to England with seven-year-old David on the P & O evacuation ship *Karanja*. Moreover, according to Monty, the earthquake 'had an effect on his [David's] nervous system which took many years to wipe out, though he himself would probably not realise that'.[74]

More than forty years later David still recalled the crumbling and shaking, followed by confusion and departure from Quetta. 'I came back to England with Mama and we went to live with the Mathers [friends of the Carver family from Cheshire] in Roehampton, on the outskirts of London. We then moved into a residential hotel [the Carlton] on Putney Hill, not far from them, and I was sent to school [Chopes] there from September to December. In January 1936 I went to prep school [Amesbury], and my mother returned to India.'[75]

Monty, who had joined Betty and David for Christmas, flew back to Quetta, while Betty travelled back to India by sea. It was on this passage that Betty befriended a young captain, Alan Davidson, who was about to enter the Staff College, Quetta. Davidson well recalled the trip. 'I was to be one of the students in the two-year course starting there in Feb. Hearing of this, she was kind enough to ask me up to the first-class lounge on several occasions (needless to say, as a captain in the Fourth Gurkhas, I was saving my passage account by travelling second!), and put me into the picture of the Staff College from a wife's point of view, both socially and also partly professionally in general terms of the programme, besides mentioning individual instructors and the staff. I remember so well when referring to Monty, she told me not to be apprehensive of him: "He is really a very human person." Her very sound advice to me on the whole course was: "be natural" – words echoed by Monty himself during his opening lecture to us.'[76]

The Montgomery 'family unit', however, was beginning to show fissures. Left behind in England, still somewhat traumatized by the earthquake, little David now found himself in school vacations like an unwanted parcel, posted from one place to another. 'I was really rather miserable,' he recollected of this period. 'One was going to and from these strange places. It must have been quite obvious that I was unhappy, for towards the end of 1936 my brother Dick saved me by coming and rescuing me from one particularly unpleasant institution [Crowthorne].'[77] Even Monty later admitted that the 'holiday home at Crowthorne, Berkshire' was 'a dreadful place'.[78]

David's holiday accommodation was not the only difficulty, however. Betty's eldest son John, having trained as an army engineer and gone up to Cambridge, fell in love with an admiral's daughter aged twenty – then below the age of consent. When it proved impossible, according to contemporary convention, for the girl to be invited with John to Lenk, where Monty wished the family to assemble for a winter holiday, John had caused uproar in the Montgomery family by refusing to go.

Monty was furious at their Christmas plans being dislocated. 'Thank God I have no daughters,' he apparently wrote to the admiral; 'but if I had I'd keep them under control!'[79] – a typical Monty caricature of a complex and emotive situation. Admiral Sir Hugh Tweedie was equally put out; he forbade John Carver to see his daughter, Jocelyn. Once Betty arrived in Quetta, however, Monty softened, and on 16 June 1936 he wrote to John at Chatham:

I've heard again from the Admiral giving me the latest situation. I've written to him again by mail to the following effect:

1) That as you are 24 and Jocelyn nearly 21 and you've fallen in love I can see no possible point in preventing you from meeting since you're both quite desirable people.

2) The best thing is to get you to declare definitely your intentions.

3) If your intention is to become engaged now, to go to India in October and return in 2 years' time and marry Jocelyn, then I recommend him to agree and remove all restrictions as to meeting.

4) In 2 years' time you'll be 26 and Jocelyn 23 and there can be no possible objection to your getting married . . . He regards two years as important and so do I in order to make sure it is not a passing infatuation. If you approach him now, as in para 3 above, you will win.

Such a letter revealed Monty's simplistic attitude towards affairs of the heart – like politics, a region he never really understood, and which he sought to 'bring to order' by an almost comic resort to military parlance and tactical approach. Yet there is no doubt, as his other step-son Dick reflected, that Monty was at heart a decidedly sentimental, even romantic person, and that his ruthless dedication to his profession went hand in hand with an almost childlike reverence for the notion of love. To fall in love was, to him, a God-inspired thing; and if he insisted, like the admiral, on a two-year separation, it was with the best of intentions. Nor can he be said to have been wrong. 'It was absolutely heartbreaking! *Two years!* They seemed like monsters, those parents, on both sides, my own as well as John's,' Jocelyn said later.[80] Yet her marriage to John was to prove as deep, as happy and as devoted as that of Betty and Monty.

Limited liability

Monty would certainly have relished the chance of a brigade command, anywhere, had he been offered one. Significantly, he was not: a square peg in a round hole. In Quetta, however, he continued to receive the most glowing confidential reports from the commandant of the Staff College. He had brought to the college new horizons in its training: the use of the sand-table; exercises in the field without troops; and insistence that all students learn to integrate in their headquarters staff work the various branches of their profession, including artillery, engineers, armour – and air. More and more Monty was impressed by the potential of air power, and ground-to-air co-operation.[81] Years before, in his appreciation of the 1921 British campaign in Ireland for Major Percival, Monty had considered the use of aeroplanes futile 'except as a quick and safe means of getting from one place to another. Even the landing grounds were few and far between. The pilots and observers knew nothing whatever about the war, or the conditions under which it was being fought, and were not therefore in a position to be able to help much.'[82] Now he began to teach the importance of intimate liaison between the two services – a policy which was at that very moment being enacted by anti-Republican forces in the Spanish Civil War, which had broken out on 16 July.

That year, 1936 was indeed the turning point in modern European history. On 7 March Hitler had invaded the Rhineland and in early May Mussolini had conquered Abyssinia – both without opposition from European nations. By summer Italian and German munitions and men were being sent to Spain – opposed only by Stalin, for his own nefarious reasons. It proved impossible to move the National Government in Britain, with its disastrously obstinate and short-sighted Chancellor, Neville Chamberlain, into a more urgent frame of mind. Besotted by the scandalous love of their young king for an American divorcee, the British public either wanted no mention of possible war (military officers were asked not to speak publicly about planning for a British Expeditionary Force[83]), or felt the confrontation between fascist-nationalism and communism to be a continental and entirely un-British affair.

Although Liddell Hart did not feel the latter, he was adamant that the British should not get sucked, once again, into a continental military commitment beyond its imperially overstretched means. His book *The British Way in Warfare*, published in 1931, excoriated the whole idea of British army commitment on French or Belgian soil, preferring naval blockade and only 'limited liability' in terms of military intervention. The Chancellor, Neville Chamberlain, likewise approved the concept of 'limited liability' on grounds of expense, having propounded the view, in 1934 and 1935, that the RAF could be entrusted to constitute a cheap and effective deterrent to the threat of German military attack. 'The consequences,' as the historian of the inter-war period, Brian Bond, has written, 'were unfortunate in that the period from July 1935 to May 1937 witnessed a drift toward "limited liability".'[84]

Sadly, Monty's commander in Egypt, General Burnett-Stuart – who left Egypt in 1934 to become GOC Southern Command in England for two crucial years while mechanization was being debated and rehearsed, and became the main candidate to succeed General Massingberd as CIGS – similarly felt that a continental British commitment was unwise. Burnett-Stuart thus hobbled all armoured exercises in order to keep down tank-enthusiasts such as Hobart, Martel, Lindsay and other exponents of armoured divisions who thought that a war between Germany and France/Britain could be won by mobility.

Here, despite the many thousands of miles between England and Quetta, was a controversy of the very highest importance for any thinking officer. What, then, was Monty's attitude towards a British Expeditionary Force – in whose potential compass he might command an infantry brigade, if a vacancy could be found?

In his memoirs, twenty years later, Monty was quite emphatic. 'It had for long been considered that in the event of another war with Germany the British contribution to the defence of the West should consist mainly of the naval and air forces,' he wrote. 'How any politician could imagine that, in a world war, Britain could avoid sending her Army to fight alongside the French passes all understanding.'[85]

In the mid-1930s, Monty was far from being so uncomprehending. If French forces proved unable to defend their territory in Europe after winning a world war, he had grave reservations about throwing good men after bad; moreover, he greatly admired General Burnett-Stuart who, he thought, ought to have become CIGS already in 1933 instead of Massingberd.

Such strategic controversy, however, did not overly concern Monty as, at Quetta, he concentrated on the tactical instruction of his first-year students. He enjoyed the company of his students and would often, as Alan Davidson remembered, 'turn up at one's quarter in the afternoon, and ask one to go for a longish walk out into the Quetta countryside' where, rather than discussing European politics, he would more likely talk about 'subjects such as the then topical Simon Report on future government of India and revision of the Prayer Book'.[86]

It was a time, above all, for personal reflection before his re-immersion in the world of military command. In November 1936 Betty's son John arrived in India to be met by his parents at Karachi; the Montgomerys were now reconciled to an informal engagement, and arrangements were made to meet young Jocelyn when they stayed in London after Christmas. But first there must be a further sentimental visit to Lenk in Switzerland. On 19 December therefore the Montgomerys left by Imperial Airways for London, collected David from his school at Amesbury, and arrived with Dick Carver at the Wildstrubel Hotel on Christmas Day. There they remained for almost a month, returning to London only on 19 January – troubles on the North-West Frontier having necessitated cancellation of the annual Quetta College tour of the frontier and permitting Monty to take extended leave until mid-February.

It would be Monty's last winter-skiing holiday with Betty. In London they stayed in a service apartment. Both were in good form, as General

Ward later remembered with amusement. 'Monty wanted to look at what I had married, so my wife and I were summoned to his service flat. Betty was absolutely charming – they complemented each other. They took us out for dinner at the Rag [Junior Army & Navy Club], then on a busman's honeymoon, then back to Piccadilly to dance. Betty was a very good dancer. It was a charming evening . . . Later on I went to Dorset to see my parents. When I got back there was a telegram from my father "Many Congratulations". As we weren't having another child this was a bit puzzling – until I got a signal from Monty. In it he said: "I've been to the War Office. You are being offered accelerated promotion into the King's Regiment. You will of course accept!" '[87]

Mrs Ward was not the only wife to be looked over. Young Jocelyn Tweedie was also summoned, with her parents, to an introductory luncheon at the Rag. Monty and her father, mercifully, got on well and soon the conversation developed into a name-by-name critical summary of the members of their families and mutual acquaintances. 'It was the first time I'd set eyes on either of them,' Jocelyn recollected later of Betty and Monty. Monty and her father talked 'hammer and tongs – discussed everyone's careers. When Betty's brother Frank came up, Monty said, "That chap's no good – useless." He was rather apt to strike people off the list in those days. But he didn't by any means get his own way with John's mother. Actually Monty was then rather being teased and being told what to do by her. He was saying, "No, you're not going to have the car, you're not going there this afternoon." And she said: "Oh well, I am actually." And she did! Monty took it very well. The whole atmosphere was very happy. She got her own way all the time.'[88]

John Carver concurred. 'Oh, yes, we knew the form pretty well, which was that if he laid down "This or that will take place" we'd have a colloquy with Mama and she'd have a word with him. And the next day he'd say, "I've changed my mind . . ." '[89]

Betty was a shrewd and perceptive observer of people, and could even be cruel in the way she teased Monty. 'Monty's conversation, you know, consists in asking questions,' she once said of him – which was strikingly true. Betty was, in fact, a proud, intelligent and firm woman whom Monty not only loved but deeply respected. 'She could always get her way if she felt the matter was of sufficient importance,' John Carver recollected. 'She expected a fairly high standard of everyone around her,' he also maintained.[90] Far from being an ideological pacifist, she was very much a moral realist. She rejected her brother-in-law Dick Shepherd's famous

Peace Pledge Movement, saying: 'It's no use crying Peace! Peace! when there is no peace in the world'; and, when Jocelyn wrote to her saying she was having second thoughts about marrying a soldier, she responded without hesitation:

War is a ghastly process, mad indeed, but inevitable for many a decade to come. We are no more civilized really than our ancestors. For us women, we can only hope that our own beloved ones remain untouched because our motives are personal. Many is the time I have thought as you do that to remain immune, untouched by love is to be outside life and one would rather have the pain than not feel it at all. We have to pay the price and be prepared to pay. Certainly nothing is actually worth having without the will to pay.[91]

These were prescient words – for Betty was soon to pay the ultimate price herself.

Promotion to brigadier

Throughout his time in Quetta Monty had been thinking about the nature of high command in a modern army. After so many years of self-preparation he was chafing to try out his new ideas. In the whole of the Great War, he told Lieutenant Burge, he had only once seen Douglas Haig, the commander-in-chief – and he had recognized him only because he had an escort of Lancers. 'Any future C-in-C has got to be well known, not only to the soldiers, but to their wives and mothers,' he insisted.[92]

But did he have the wherewithal – or even the opportunity – to become well known? On 20 February 1937, only a few days after his return to Quetta, the War Office cabled to India to offer Colonel Montgomery command of the 9th Infantry Brigade at Portsmouth, England, due to fall vacant on 5 August that year.

Delighted, Monty cabled back his acceptance – never dreaming that the move would result in his wife's death. He would be given the temporary rank of brigadier on commencement of his new command; meanwhile from 29 June, when his current appointment at Quetta ceased, he was to be reduced to half pay!

Such parsimony was characteristic of the Paymaster General's office. Meanwhile, Lieutenant-General Williams's final confidential report in

March that year must have amply compensated. 'Colonel Montgomery's work as GSO 1 and instructor at the Staff College has had a marked influence on the course, and the students who have passed through his hands have been fortunate in learning from so experienced and convincing a trainer,' General Williams began. After a fulsome tribute, at the bottom of his commendation, he added an additional note: 'He is about to take command of a Regular Infantry Brigade. Fitted now for promotion to Major-General and for employment in command and on the staff in that rank.'

As if this were not enough, General W. H. Bartholomew, the Chief of General Staff in India, added his own remarks before forwarding the report to Whitehall: 'I agree with the opinion of the Commandant of the Staff College. Colonel Montgomery has been a great asset at the Staff College and his work invaluable.'[93]

The Deputy Chief of General Staff, however, would not be drawn. 'I do not know Colonel Montgomery well enough to be able to report on him,' he wrote – and signed his name: 'Major-General C. J. Auchinleck.'[94]

Auchinleck's correct but cool refusal to comment on Monty was, sadly, the start of a terrible hostility that would simmer in England, become inflamed in Egypt, and end almost in the law courts in 1958, when both men were field marshals.

In the meantime, having accumulated a certain amount of leave over the past years, Monty left the Staff College, Quetta, on 6 May 1937, making his way south to Bombay, where he embarked on the P & O steamship *Viceroy of India*. It would be his last sight of India and its ocean before becoming head of the British army a decade later – and he was not sorry to leave. As the *Viceroy of India* made its stately passage from India he seized the chance to shed the slothful, polo-marked shadow of the subcontinent. Using the enforced calm of the voyage, he considered the European realities towards which he was heading, and while other passengers played deck-quoits, the impending brigadier sat penning a new article, which General Williams then suggested he submit to the *Journal of the Royal Engineers*: 'The Problem of the Encounter Battle'.

Europe in arms

'My dear Liddell Hart,' Monty wrote from Port Said on 22 May 1937, 'I am on my way home to command the 9th Inf Bde at Portsmouth. In Bombay I bought a copy of your new book *Europe in Arms*[95] and I have been reading it during the voyage. I should like to say how much I have enjoyed it – it is a masterpiece of clear and logical reasoning and should be read by all soldiers.'[96]

This was the first correspondence Monty had had with Liddell Hart since preparation of the new *Infantry Training Manual* seven years before. Monty had continued to read Hart's books, however, and even gave copies to his step-son John to read during the latter's military training at Chatham. Moreover, Monty 'loved to gossip', as John Carver recalled; he cannot therefore have been unaware, even at Quetta, that the new Prime Minister's Secretary of State for War, Mr Leslie Hore-Belisha, boasted of a new if unpaid military adviser: Captain B. H. Liddell Hart. The military correspondent of the London *Times*, in other words, had become the power behind the military throne.

As Liddell Hart's biographer, Alex Danchev, later described, Hart wanted to 'protect Western civilization from the catastrophe of total war', and obtain a knighthood for himself in doing so – something which his burgeoning relationship with Hore-Belisha now put 'within his grasp'. 'They were Tweedledum and Tweedledee,' Danchev characterized Hart and Hore-Belisha;[97] or as Correlli Barnett memorably described, 'a strategic Jeeves to Hore-Belisha's political Bertie'.[98]

This was one of the strangest episodes in British politico-military history. Hore-Belisha had never been near a battle-front, having served in the Army Pay Corps in World War I. As Transport Minister in the National Government he had recently introduced driving tests and pedestrian crossings. He 'knew nothing of the Army and said so', Danchev summarized.[99] Tweedledee, by contrast, said he knew a lot about the army – though he also, in truth, had scant knowledge of front-line warfare, having seen only the briefest of service in the field in the rank of lieutenant.

In his new proto-knightly capacity as *éminence grise*, however, Hart had already set to work – not only providing the new minister with the material for his first Commons speech as Secretary of State for War but initiating, as he later boasted, some sixty-two military reforms, from divisional restructuring to accelerated mechanization and earlier retirement age. More importantly for Monty and for Britain, however, Hart swayed, indeed often determined, the selection of senior army officers: in particular, the promotion of the fifty-one-year-old English simpleton, Major-General Lord Gort, VC, three DSOs, MC, in July 1937, to be Military Secretary in the rank of lieutenant general.

Backing the promotion of Lord Gort was one thing; deciding Britain's strategic defence policy, however, was another. Hart's isolationism reflected, sadly, his admiration for Mussolini and fascism, and his concomitant conviction that Britain should leave them, and Europe, well alone. In this respect he had already had an uncomfortably strong influence on Chamberlain – for, on becoming British Prime Minister in May 1937, Neville Chamberlain had not only appointed Hore-Belisha Minister of War but had urged him to read Hart's *Europe in Arms*, which Hart had sent to Chamberlain as an inscribed gift. In particular, Chamberlain recommended the chapter on the future role of the British army.

Hart, though an exponent of modern mobile warfare, argued that Britain should not go beyond an air force commitment to the European continent in the event of war, but should concentrate instead on an imperial reserve, or field force. This reserve should be 'for the reinforcement of the overseas garrisons, the mobile defence of the overseas territories, and for such expeditions, truly so-called, as may be needed to fulfil our historic strategy under future conditions.' This did not include the continent of Europe, however – for the simple reason that the British army was no good at offensive battles. 'Since Marlborough the British Army has rarely shone in the offensive,' Hart argued, 'not through want of courage, but from lack of aptitude. It has been superb in defence, and unrivalled as an agent in maintaining order.' All in all, he warned that 'the balance seems to be heavily against the hope that a British field force on the Continent might have a military effect commensurate with the expense and the risk.'[100]

Chamberlain enthusiastically concurred. 'I found your articles in *The Times* on the role of the Army extremely useful and suggestive. I am quite sure we shall never again send to the Continent an Army on the scale of that which we put into the field in the Great War,' Chamberlain assured Hart.[101]

Monty, en route from India, certainly seemed as swayed by Hart's imperial-defence rhetoric as Chamberlain and Hore-Belisha had been. 'Regarding the Field Force,' Monty continued in his letter from Port Said. 'I feel myself that the nature of our Empire demands that we should have available as a reserve a small force of say 4 divisions, properly equipped, and available to be sent anywhere at any time. It need not necessarily be kept in England; Palestine would probably be quite a good place for it, over & above the troops we shall keep in the Canal area under the new treaty. I would avoid getting this reserve committed on the continent of Europe.'[102]

But if the imperial mobile reserve was kept for duties abroad, outside Europe, could Britain avoid being sucked into the continental war Monty himself saw coming? If there was war in Europe, Britain would have to field an army, and such an army would, in all likelihood, have to be prepared to meet the German armies once again in France or Flanders, however much the politicians sought to 'avoid' a continental commitment.

'I would much like to discuss this and other questions with you some time, and I hope we may meet in England,' Monty suggested to Hart – mentioning also his current preoccupation, namely 'the problem of the encounter battle as affected by modern British establishments'. The burning question in his mind was leadership in battle: where the commander should best position himself to direct the battle when advancing armies collide. 'The army has got to learn a new technique and this will involve a change of tactics – I feel there is a grave danger that we shall carry on with the old tactics, relying on the material solution to solve our difficulties. I shall be interested to have your views on the article when it appears in September.'[103]

The rise of Lord Gort

Lord Gort, as Hart and Hore-Belisha were eventually to discover when it was too late, was beset by feelings of inferiority, having been nicknamed 'Fatboy' at Harrow. He had become a Grenadier Guards officer after Sandhurst, but while hunting in Canada in 1910 had mistakenly shot dead his Indian guide instead of a moose.

The following year Gort had married his brilliant and beautiful second cousin, Corinna Vereker. As even Gort's fawning biographer, John Colville, remarked, Gort was 'more notable for brawn than for brain'; worse still, in a marriage to a highly intelligent and beautiful woman there was the distressing fact that 'she was highly sexed which he was not'.[104] Though a widely respected and decorated young battalion commander in World

War I, Gort had been mercilessly cuckolded by his wife, prompting him to divorce her in a 'lurid' and sensational court case in 1925. Corinna had 'showed no signs of regret or remorse', and had thereafter 'flitted from lover to lover', while Gort, deeply humiliated, settled for the affection of his 'fanatically' devoted daughter Jacqueline, as well as platonic friendship with the motherly wife of a fellow officer, Lady Marjorie Dalrymple-Hamilton, née Coke, of Holkham in Norfolk – a non-sexual relationship rendered definitive by the contraction of mumps in 1931 'in a most delicate area'.[105]

As his biographer noted, Gort's 'least attractive characteristics' included not only 'a certain lack of humanity' but a lack of pity for any person 'he judged to have failed in their duty' and a 'rigidity of outlook on matters he did not understand'.[106] The latter included almost everything beyond battalion infantry tactics and drill. As his commanding officer in China wrote of him in 1927, 'It may be the result of his domestic troubles, but if he was like this before I can quite imagine his wife leaving him.'[107]

Gort's courage under fire was legendary (he had won the Victoria Cross, three Distinguished Service Orders and the Military Cross in the trenches in World War I), but his limited brain, obsession with detail and World War I mindset were ample reasons why his sudden advancement in 1937 was a mistake, which even Gort himself knew in his heart of hearts. As he confessed to Liddell Hart when the serving CIGS, Sir Cyril Deverell, was summarily dismissed that autumn, he did not wish it to be said 'that I had pushed out Deverell and then Liddell Hart had made me CIGS'.[108] This was, however, the case: one cuckold paving the way for another.

Gort's mind was not only small and obstinate, but mean. Sir Cyril Deverell had refused to delay Gort's appointment in 1936 as the new commandant of the Staff College, Camberley, by the necessary week in order to allow Gort a major tax concession on his past year abroad; as a result, as Military Secretary in 1937 and Hore-Belisha's closest official adviser on appointments, Gort was able not only to oust Sir Cyril Deverell as CIGS with Hart's help but to pen a humiliating letter of dismissal and ensure 'shabby financial treatment' for the outgoing general: a worrying example of Gort's displacement of sexual resentment, with ominous ramifications for army colleagues who in any way upset his *amour propre* or aroused feelings of intellectual inferiority – as, unfortunately, Monty had already done in India. 'Your friend Pandit Montgomery Karnel Sahib is once more holding forth pontifically on the rostrum while the poor students below catch an odd forty winks,' Gort had written sarcastically to his daughter in India, after the Quetta earthquake. 'He fancies himself more than ever now, I expect.'[109]

Gort's own abilities in communication, however, were as poor as Haig's had been. General Bertie Fisher, Commandant of the RMA Sandhurst, found Gort incapable of summing up a discussion when Gort was commandant at the Staff College next door, and Gort proved no better on paper. The documents which Gort presented to Hore-Belisha once he became CIGS were generally rendered hopelessly unclear by his preoccupation with detail, and within months Hore-Belisha would be ruing Liddell Hart's recommendation of the 6th Viscount.[110]

Gort's meteoric elevation to CIGS, however, would not take place until December 1937. In the meantime, Monty had perhaps the greatest personal trial of his own life to face. Arriving back in England on 31 May 1937, he was determined to spend his entire two months' accumulated leave with Betty, motoring in the Lake District and visiting their relatives and friends in Cheshire, before taking over as brigadier of 9th Infantry Brigade and Portsmouth Garrison commander on 5 August. Since the brigade would be going into summer training camp near Salisbury in late August and the brigadier's residence at Portsmouth needed redecoration, it was therefore arranged that, following their motoring trip, Betty and David would stay at New Park with Monty's mother from the end of July until the third week in August; they would then go to a seaside hotel at Burnham-on-Sea, near Weston-super-Mare, for the rest of David's holiday, before setting up their new home in Ravelin House, the official residence of the Portsmouth Garrison commander, in September.

But it was not to be.

8

The Death of Betty

Burnham-on-Sea

Had Betty stayed at New Park with Monty's mother Maud for the rest of the summer of 1937 she would, ironically, have lived; but she could not see her way to staying so long with 'Lady' Montgomery, who was now a widow in her seventies, and even more domineering than ever.

Burnham-on-Sea was chosen because it was the village where one of Betty's closest friends lived, the artist Nancy Nicholson, former wife of Robert Graves. Compared with New Park, Burnham-on-Sea would also be comparatively near to Monty's 9th Brigade training camp near Salisbury, just over fifty miles away. David could play on the sands and Betty, who was on a special diet after a long bout of laryngitis, would take life easy.

So solicitous was Monty about Betty's health, in fact, that he had forbidden her to meet Jocelyn at Sheerness in late July 'as even if we get there I must use my voice as sparingly as possible', Betty explained her husband's edict to her future daughter-in-law. 'I am already much better & its so quiet & peaceful here that I should be quite well before I leave,' she had written from Ullswater on 7 July. 'I expect to be at Burnham-on-Sea with David for the last week of August and into September & perhaps you could come over & see us – it does not look far from Wraxhall . . .'[1]

It was not. But in inviting Jocelyn, Betty had no inkling that her strange but happy marriage was now coming to an end: that she would shortly be greeting Jocelyn not on the beach but on her deathbed.

No drifting aimlessly into battle

While Betty stayed first at New Park, then travelled to Burnham, Monty took command of 9th Infantry Brigade.

Whether the brigade would be part of Liddell Hart's 'Imperial Reserve' or a new British Expeditionary Force on the Continent, Monty's task now was to make it the the the best-trained force in the regular army.

If the BEF was reconstituted, Monty insisted, there would be no more helter-skelter retreats, as from Mons. The article he'd written for the *Royal Engineers Journal* went to the very heart of his current preoccupation: command in battle. Thanks to mechanization of transport and fast reconnaissance aircraft there would be no 'footling around' with mounted cavalry acting as advance guards, as General von Seeckt still believed – the term itself ought to be abolished, Monty declared in his article. 'We have got to develop new methods, and learn a new technique,' he insisted; and the main plank of this new technique lay in the command posts of the brigade and divisional commanders themselves. It was vital, in modern warfare, that a good start be obtained. 'If the start is a bad one either through a bad plan, or faulty dispositions, or loss of time when time is very precious, or for any cause whatsoever – then the battle can be pulled out of the fire only by the gallantry of the troops, and they are bound to suffer heavy casualties in the process ... Although information may be lacking or incomplete, he [the commander] must still make a plan and begin early to force his will on the enemy ... If he has no plan he will find that he is being made to conform gradually to the enemy's plan.'[2]

This concentration on forward planning was the latest tenet of Monty's military thinking. He simply did not agree that modern battle would ever revert to the static trench warfare of World War I; and his insistence on fighting to a definite 'masterplan' went back to the bitter days in late August 1914, when his brigade was thrown into line against the Germans without either a plan or the most elementary attempt to choose tactically advantageous ground. 'Success in the initial encounters will go to the commander who knows what he wants, has a plan to achieve it, does not allow his formation or unit to drift aimlessly into battle, but puts it into the fight on a proper plan from the beginning,' he argued in words that would later become characteristic or 'quintessential Monty'. Thus, well before World War II began, he insisted that aspiring generals take reponsibility for tactical battle-planning, rather than leaving plans to their staffs – or to the enemy.

In the early stages of the encounter battle the commander must have his HQ, Monty emphasized, 'well forward – he will then gain the earliest possible information, see the ground, and be able to plan ahead and issue orders to subordinates before their units arrive'. Thereafter the HQ should be pulled back so as never to become 'unduly influenced by local situations on the battle front', while himself remaining mobile, with adequate mobile communications. Thus, during the battle itself, the commander 'must be prepared to go forward at critical periods when important decisions may be required; he must take with him the necessary means to exercise command. To remain at his HQ at such times, waiting for information that may never arrive, may be fatal.' He must have his Royal Artillery commander alongside him at his HQ, and his chief engineer; must plan to fight at night rather than at time-honoured dawn; and be prepared to command his mobile, armoured forces himself rather than leaving this up to a specialized 'cavalry' commander.

This was a conception of modern battle presented with far more clarity and insight than Lord Gort, the aspiring CIGS, would ever credit, until, in the aftermath of his disastrous command of the BEF, the penny would drop: namely, that Britain had almost no field commanders capable of fighting the Germans in modern war. To its shame the nation had, moreover, made no real attempt to train such commanders – indeed, where they did emerge, in men like Hobo Hobart, they were got rid of using one excuse or another: as unpopular in the mess, or 'difficult', or socially beyond the pale – guilty of divorce or adultery (or both).

In this saddest of ways a once-mighty imperial power, administering the largest empire in human history, tottered towards military ruin, with Winston Churchill kept on the back benches of its parliament, while a new Prime Minister sat on the front bench, devoid of any understanding of military power or strategy or modern warfare; and beside him sat a Minister of War proficient at transport matters – epitomized in the Belisha beacon pedestrian crossing – but unable and unwilling to prepare his country for continental hostilities.

Liddell Hart, reading Monty's article as unpaid adviser to the Minister of War, was, however, strangely impressed – for Monty's concern with generalship went far beyond Liddell Hart's current 'reforms'. 'I have read the article with great interest and much agreement,' he wrote back, scoring it in the margin with lines and ticks of approval.[3]

In the meantime, before the article had even appeared in the *Royal Engineers Journal*, Monty decided there was not a moment to lose. As the brigade prepared to move to St Giles Camp to take part in the summer exercises which Monty's predecessor, G. T. Raikes, had arranged, he therefore made the article the basis of his first policy document issued at 9th Infantry Brigade HQ on 14 August 1937, through the brigade major, Major F. E. W. Simpson. The 9th Infantry Brigade would not 'drift into battle' but would plan ahead, Monty declared. 'He was among the relatively few who at that time saw clearly the certainty of war, and he intended that his command, at least, should be ready for it,' Simpson later recalled. 'His conception of training was consequently far removed from some of the "social" peacetime exercises then prevailing, and came as a distinct shock to some of the units subjected to it.'[4]

Gun-catching

'Simbo' Simpson, posted to the 9th Infantry Brigade only eight months previously from the Military Secretary's department at the War Office, had been warned what was in store. 'There was no lack of sympathetic friends to tell me that I would never stand him, or would never last,' Simpson later recorded, 'but I was immediately captured by his efficiency and dedication to training.'[5]

Monty's new brigade comprised four battalions,[6] and belonged to the regular army's 3rd Division, commanded since 1936 by Major-General D. K. Bernard, who still wore spurs and liked to see his men drilling in pre-war fours.[7] The GOC Southern Command was General Burnett-Stuart, who had been Monty's army commander in Egypt and was, until Gort's overpromotion, tipped to be the next CIGS.

'Raikes was a good trainer of troops, but his approach to the training was entirely different to that of Monty,' Simpson recalled. 'Monty seized hold of the training programme and said: "This won't do. I see no purpose in having several exercises lasting only one day. I will merely have four big exercises which will each last for three days and the brigade will have three nights out in the field. Troops have got to be accustomed to working by night."'

Such an approach was welcomed by the regular infantry battalions. 'His ideas were made very clear and I had little trouble in producing a revised programme incorporating these much bigger exercises. I was quite sure that, though some of the troops of the brigade might grumble at being kept out so long, they would really fall in with Monty's plans because it was good training,' Simpson recalled.[8]

Though the infantry commanders fell into line with Monty's proposals, however, the cavalry did not – leading to outright farce.

No British CIGS had been able to eradicate or even reduce the British army's love affair with cavalry, or 'affection for the horse' as Sir David Fraser later called it;[9] indeed, the tragic Charge of the Light Brigade only seemed to add lustre to the notion of British cavalry rather than mocking its irrelevance to modern twentieth-century war. The army's 136 infantry battalions were, in terms of their brigaded strengths, still 'supported' in the 1930s by no fewer than eighteen horsed cavalry regiments, with a mere four battalions of tanks and two regiments of armoured cars as the only concession to the twentieth century. 'Britain spent the twenty-one years between 1918 and 1939 with an army in India and an army at home, neither seriously designed, trained, equipped or organized for major war and neither in the least ready for it', as Sir David Fraser summed up[10] – while in Germany Hitler introduced twelve months' conscription and military training for every able-bodied German from 1935 onwards, creating fifty-two active divisions and fifty-one reserve divisions by 1939: a potential three and a half million *already trained* troops on mobilization.

At Wimborne St Giles, meanwhile, the cavalry baulked at Monty's training plan. 'An unexpected problem then arose,' Simpson recorded.

We had been told that to be included in the brigade camp was a Territorial Army regiment, the Wiltshire Yeomanry, who were horsed, and a very fine horsed cavalry regiment indeed. It was run like so much of the TA in those days on rather feudal lines. The officers were the bigger farmers and some landowners. The men themselves came from jobs working for the same officers, and when they heard that we were going to have those tremendous exercises – three nights out at a time – they jibbed violently. They said that they gave up their time and sometimes their work voluntarily to come and learn to be soldiers, but they also wanted a bit of fun while in camp. Most of them had their own cars of sorts and they had looked forward to exercises all day and then going for a bit of jollity at night to places like Bournemouth before returning about two or three in the morning.

All this would be knocked on the head if they had to spend three nights out in the field every week. So they asked: 'Please could we be excused from taking part in the lengthy exercises.'

This got Monty on the raw at once. He said: 'I am not going to have these people coming back into the camp at two in the morning, probably drunk, making a noise, disturbing all my hardworking troops. If they won't play over our exercises, I don't want them in the camp.'

It was no good my arguing that the War Office had directed that they should attend the camp, and there looked to be quite a problem raising its head. However, after a bit of negotiation – which gave me quite a lot of trouble – it was arranged that the Wiltshire Yeomanry could have their own camp on the other side of a small hill. This would let the War Office feel that they were in the area of the 9th Infantry Brigade Camp . . .

This worked admirably. The infantry battalions of the 9th Infantry Brigade and their attached troops did not get disturbed at all by the Wiltshire Yeomanry, who at the same time looked on rather curiously at what the 9th Infantry Brigade was doing.

After a bit they came to the conclusion that there was some sense in these big exercises, and they came to me and said: 'Would the Brigade Commander mind if we are incorporated on the last one?' They were prepared to forgo their nightly jaunts, away from their wives, to Bournemouth and would join wholeheartedly with the infantry of the brigade.

This gave great pleasure to Monty, who felt that at last these soldiers had seen the light and they were duly incorporated in the big exercise at the end of the second week.

Seeing the light did not, however, mean seeing sense – indeed, the upshot would encapsulate the fatuousness of horsed cavalry better than any other incident in this period. As Simpson recalled, the final exercise 'involved an approach march with its cavalry spearhead onto what was a prepared enemy position on a small ridge. It all went very well until the umpires stopped the cavalry – commanded by a subaltern named Brown – and told him that he could not go on because he was being fired on by an enemy machine-gun from a copse about 1,200 yards to the front.'

Simpson would never forget the scene.

I was there myself as assistant to the Brigade Commander, who was controlling the exercise, and it so happened that at the moment when he appeared in his car to see what was going on and while he was being told about the position – he was waiting to see what action the subaltern would take – up came the CO of the Wiltshire Yeomanry, cantering on his horse, to ask what the hell the subaltern was delaying over.

The subaltern turned to him and said: 'Sir, I am told that I am being fired on somewhat heavily by a machine-gun in yonder copse and that I cannot advance from here.'

The CO bellowed with rage and said: 'Damn it, boy, you have a horse, go and catch the bloody gun!'[11]

Sheer stupidity

'Tell the umpires,' Monty said, having witnessed the episode, 'that the whole of the cavalry troop has been slaughtered by machine-gun and let the others decide what they had best do in the circumstances.'[12]

In retrospect it seems incredible that such a conflict between the *ancien régime* and the new could still exist in 1937. Sadly, it was so, and the inevitable outcome would be witnessed two years later, in Poland. Worse still, such stupidity was fuelled not merely by ignorance of what was going on in Spain or Germany, since this was well known, but reflected, at heart, a profound upper- and middle-class English snobbery over soiling one's hands. There remained at this time, Sir David Fraser described, a fundamental and incurably English 'prejudice between those regarded by their opponents as greasy mechanics on the one hand and as snobbish amateurs on the other', a struggle between armoured warfare proponents and horsed cavalry diehards which perhaps only war could cure.[13]

Monty could only shake his head: knowing what was in store for such blimps – who now 'withdrew from the exercise because Monty had been so rude to them', as Simpson recalled.[14]

John Brown's body

The exercise over, Monty was surprised to receive an invitation to attend 'the big guest-night of the camping period': a party thrown by the Wiltshire Yeomanry in their camp on the other side of the hill.

As Simpson recollected,

We went [although] I was feeling slightly apprehensive considering what had happened previously. But they were the most charming hosts . . . even Monty had a glass or two of wine. All was going very well indeed until after dinner – after the port had been brought round – and then the band changed from its usual cheerful tunes into a sort of funeral dirge and several of the officers carried in a stretcher on which was the body of the subaltern.

They then sang 'John Brown's Body' in a very mournful way and put a notice on his chest that he had been killed by order of the umpires.

He had been made to look a ghastly corpse, his face all grey and blood coming out of his ears and mouth.

All looked at the brigade commander – who roared with laughter. There was a sigh of relief. 'It was a great success. Monty took the whole thing in wonderful heart and the party ended extremely well,' Simpson recalled.[15]

The brigadier had, at all events, a sense of humour.

Seeds of Alamein

The Wiltshire Yeomanry guest-night proved a salutary test of Monty's patience and humour, for the next test was fast approaching: a mock battle with a competing brigade, the 7th Infantry Brigade. On the results of the exercise would depend Monty's promotion prospects for command of a division, as a general.

The Divisional Commander was going to control this exercise, testing out the two brigadiers and their staffs; it seemed certain to involve two nights out and perhaps two whole days as well.

So Monty said to the Yeomanry, did they want to come on this final exercise against the 7th Infantry Brigade? They said, yes, they would like to, as that was going to be the climax of the camp.

I was given the task by Monty of preparing beforehand an appreciation and plan for that particular operation, and I suppose my appreciation and plan was very much on the lines I was taught at the Staff College. It was more or less an orthodox one. We were making three feints and putting in the strongest attack behind one of them.

Monty went through it and said: 'This won't do at all. This is too orthodox. You want to do something that surprises Platt [the opposing brigadier]. I know him well and if you do anything too orthodox he will expect it and counter it. If you attack him from a totally unexpected direction you will get him cold.'

So he told me what he wanted to do, which was a complete flank attack in a direction I had not believed possible, and I doubted whether we would be able to get into a position to carry out that attack without the 7th Infantry Brigade discovering it, and being given plenty of time to counter it.

Still, Monty was determined to do it, but he said: 'I will do something else he does not expect. I will attack before he thinks the battle has even started.'

The exercise was planned to commence at midnight on the first day and the general assumption was that no one would really get going until daylight had come. However, Monty had said he was determined to get going at midnight as soon as the exercise had started. 'All the troops will be ordered to go to sleep from teatime until 11 p.m. beforehand, and they can then be roused ready to start marching at midnight.'

The seeds of Alamein were already being planted, as Simpson later recognized. In the meantime,

orders were issued and operations started accordingly. We certainly got into a very favourable position on the first day without being detected. There were a lot of very highly placed senior officers taking an interest in this exercise, and I can remember being visited on that first day by the CIGS of the day [Deverell] and the Army Commander in Southern Command [Burnett-Stuart], and almost everybody else in high places in the south of England.

The battle proceeded, very favourably from the point of view of the 9th Infantry Brigade.

The result of all this was that by the next morning Monty was in a very good position indeed. He took advantage of the fact that the weather had improved and put in a forced march to reach his objective in the middle of Salisbury Plain. The Divisional Commander [Major-General Bernard] then called the exercise to a halt.

Monty drove over to see his opposite number, Platt. He came back with a grin on his face and said to me: 'Platt did not seem to want to see me, even to say what a good fight we had had. I think you will find he is going to sack his Brigade-Major.'

Monty took good care to see that very good reports were put up on his own staff – I know I myself was made within a few months a brevet Lt-Colonel, so he had done me very well.[16]

The divisional commander and GOC Southern Command were equally impressed by Monty's performance, and in their confidential reports that autumn both recommended Monty for promotion. Major-General Denis Bernard, the 3rd Division commander, wrote: 'Brigadier Montgomery has already shown himself a good Brigade Commander. He assumed command at a most awkward time – just before Bde Training – but soon took hold and trained his Bde very well. He has a quick brain and a clear head – knows what he wants to do, and does it. He is very keen and seems to have the power of conveying his keenness to his units . . . I have no doubt that when his turn comes he will be in every way fitted for promotion to Major-General.'[17]

'Buggins' turn' was still, however, Britain's way of preparing for possible war with Germany. General Burnett-Stuart, the Southern Command C-in-C, was more urgent: 'He is most capable. He is full of ideas, can express them and pass them on. He studies his profession with vision and understanding. A rather imperious commander who at once impressed his personality on his Bde. I have known him well for some years. I have no hesitation in saying that he is fitted for promotion in any Major-General's command or employment. Especially fitted for a Regular Divisional Command.'[18]

Whether a vacancy for divisional command would come Monty's way, no one could predict, but the outstanding testimonials he earned by his performance in the summer manoeuvres on Salisbury Plain certainly left Monty 'well placed' for the next round of senior army command appointments. He had demonstrated the dynamism with which he could take over and transform a military formation as its new commander, and had roundly defeated his opposing commander: a harbinger of things to come in real battle. But the next test was to face defeat himself.

The insect bite

To Monty it was important that the redecoration of Ravelin House, the official home of the Portsmouth Garrison brigadier, be completed as soon as possible after summer camp, so that he and Betty could move in. Before travelling to Ireland he'd had Betty choose the curtain material and carpets. After years of bungalow life it was going to be their first real home in England, decorated to their own taste, and – more importantly – a real home for young David, who had had to spend so many of his vacations in holiday camps since the earthquake at Quetta. John and Dick Carver would be able to stay there on leave from their stations in India. It would, in sum, be Monty's answer to New Park: his own 'château', shared with his own wife, and his own son; perhaps a chance, too, as a brigadier, to impress her Chiswick and bohemian friends who had once thought him so uninteresting.

Betty was meanwhile still at New Park on 19 August, for she wrote from Ireland to her son John – a chatty but revealing letter that gives a vivid idea of her intelligence, her gentle snobbery, human understanding, and the seriousness with which she thought about larger issues. 'Darling John,' she wrote as the rain fell over Lough Foyle,

Sweet of you to remember David & send him £1 – he was so thrilled. He had a lovely birthday, lots of presents and a jolly party of 9 children for tea and then sat up for supper. His little friend Peter is a dear little chap but rather young for David as is also Gardner, the son & heir of the Montgomerys & the 'apple' of Lady M's eye – a jolly little chap but definitely above himself at times.

[Monty's brother Colin] looks 'prosperous' & well fed but seems to me to have developed a good deal ... [Colin's wife Margaret is] a real good sort even if definitely 'of the people'. Have been reading a good deal about India lately & suppose that now I am away from it safely I have more sense of perspective as well as the interest of having you & Dick there. 'Legacy to India' by Garratt is good & concise & also the old novel 'Passage to India'. Wonder if you can get hold of these books or if you would like me to send them ...

We (Lady M) are reading out in the evening a book about Ireland in the days of Elizabeth – most interesting as it brings in Greencastle & Rougham of the O'Neills, which was where my mother came from & the old castle was standing in the grounds which I well remember. I read an article too about officers from India who save to come home instead of spending their leave in the country & that this was to be deplored as we would thus be losing touch with native life – this is as may be. Travelling facilities will increase & so will the 'coming home' & that may be one of the reasons towards 'self government'. India is not a white man's country & inevitably to my mind, one day we shall withdraw, though whether India will ever withstand the penetration of another white nation is a surmise. I am glad to think of you & Dick together & that you have managed to meet I hope. This place is lovely as ever, but the weather has broken & now we are getting it very 'soft'.

Much love, my dear, from Mother.

It was one of the last letters she would ever write. She and Monty both felt that, in pursuance of the Simon Report, India should be granted full autonomy and ultimately independence. Certainly Betty never foresaw personal danger at home, having survived the Quetta earthquake and safely avoided the many diseases prevalent in Palestine, Egypt and India.

A few days after writing the letter to her son John, Betty left New Park with David, and after spending a few days with her husband on Salisbury Plain 'near where the 9th Infantry Brigade was in camp',[19] made her way to Burnham-on-Sea, near Bristol, as planned. Almost immediately, on the beach, she was bitten on the foot by some insect. 'She could not say what sort of insect it was,' Monty recorded ruefully in his memoirs, 'and this was never known. That night her leg began to swell and became painful; a doctor was called in and he put her at once into the local Cottage Hospital and sent for me.'[20]

For Betty it was the beginning of the end. She would never watch her son David grow up, nor witness Indian independence, nor be the life-companion Monty could cherish in his rise to military greatness as the heir to Wellington; but her influence on Monty would not be in vain.

The death of Betty

The memory of Betty's terrible, lingering death would scar Monty for the rest of his life. Yet the sudden infection, late in August 1937, was initially treated as a mere inflammation, painful but not fatal. Whether it derived from the insect bite, or being trodden on by a horse while in Ireland, or even from rheumatism was still unclear to the doctor at Burnham. Monty, so deeply committed to making his first brigade exercises on Salisbury Plain a success, was loath to hand over to others. So, with Betty's agreement, he rang young Jocelyn Tweedie's father and asked the admiral if Jocelyn could come and stay in the hotel at Burnham to look after David until Betty was recovered.

Half a century later Jocelyn still remembered the telephone call: 'Father: "She's never stayed in a hotel by herself!" Monty: "Well, it's about time that she did!" '[21]

Thus while the innocent twenty-one-year-old fiancée of John Carver came to look after her young future brother-in-law, aged only nine, at the hotel in Burnham, Monty returned to Salisbury Plain and Betty lay in increasing pain in the cottage hospital.

'He was an absolute terror!' Jocelyn recalled of David Montgomery.

Though they got on very well, she found she 'couldn't control him at all. He was very devoted to his mother. He had his "rules" . . . Every night he would read a chapter of the Bible – partly so that he would have an excuse to keep his light on, partly because his mother had told him to. He was a very bossy little boy. He used to shout and say: "You're nothing to do with me. You're only going to get married to my brother. You can't give orders to me!" We used to go every day to see John's mother. She got worse and worse. In the end she couldn't speak to David at all. He was terribly upset. He knew.'[22]

Time, fortunately, would erase David's memory of this; and from the moment he returned to Amesbury School Monty kept him well out of the way. 'Perhaps I did wrong,' Monty wrote in his memoirs, 'but I did what I thought was right.'[23]

The little nine-year-old, however, saw more clearly than his father where all this was leading. He was, after all, on the spot, whereas Monty, according to Jocelyn, hardly appeared at all in the fortnight she was there. 'Yes, he came to lunch once. And he came to pack all David's things, and get his suits clean and respectable – I think it was Betty who asked for this. I don't think Monty believed it was anything much. There was nothing showing on the outside of her skin, it was inside.'

By the time David took his leave of her, Betty was, however, unable to speak for pain. 'Gradually she became worse,' Jocelyn recalled, 'and when I took David to say goodbye before going back to school, she tossed restlessly and couldn't speak to him. He had bought her a present of a little gold sword brooch, and he just left it on her sheet, and went back to the hotel to write her a letter, which he told me to read to her after he had gone. He was only nine years old, but he seemed to know it was really goodbye.'

At times Betty's condition improved, and she rallied, though still too weak to read or write. What struck Jocelyn – who would read to her each day from *The Times* – as strangest of all was the virtual secrecy with which Betty's illness was handled by Monty, who asked Jocelyn to stay on until Betty's cousin Katie took over. 'Nobody came while I was there. I remember Monty telling me on no account must Aunt Zillah [Betty's sister] know that she was ill. I thought the whole thing was rather extraordinary. I talked to Matron – she didn't know what the illness really was. There was certainly no specialist called down while I was there. She was very ill again when I last saw her – so ill she couldn't speak to me. That was in late September.'[24]

By this time the summer manoeuvres on Salisbury Plain were over, and Monty was in Portsmouth. Jocelyn had stayed on for a further week, overlapping with Katie Hobart. No one else was summoned or even allowed to be present as Betty fought for her life, alternately critical and then seemingly on the mend. On 9 October 1937, several weeks after Jocelyn's departure, Betty asked her cousin Katie to thank Jocelyn on her behalf for the flowers she'd sent.

'It's difficult to say anything definite about Betty,' Katie Hobart added to her thank-you letter. 'There's no straightforward progress, it's a very up & down business, & tho' today she is ever so much better than she has been since Monday, she is not so well as she was a week ago! It's very disappointing, as she did improve a lot last weekend & one did hope the corner was turned. I think it's really the poison in her system that is retarding recovery, also all the different serum injections which she gets have strange effects . . .'

This led Katie to reflect on Monty, about whom she had always had ambivalent feelings. 'Poor Monty – his cut & dried plans miscarry,' she noted. 'He had "timetabled" that she was to be moved to Portsmouth last week, then it was to be today. I was quite certain that she would not be fit for this & the Dr forbade it. Monty, I fear, has still to learn that in serious illness things do not work out according to plan like ordering an advance at dawn! He came over yesterday & left today, as he has some big Corporation affair with the Mayor tomorrow. David is to be there. Won't the other boys at school feel mere worms on Monday! . . .'[25]

For Monty it was a 200-mile round trip each time he visited Betty, and natural that he should want her transferred to Portsmouth, where she would also receive more expert attention. However, David's pride at being able to witness a ceremonial occasion in Portsmouth alongside his father was tainted by the knowledge that his mother still lay in the little cottage hospital, almost two months since they first went on holiday there.

The hours of Betty's life were indeed ticking away. On 15 October Katie Hobart was again writing to Jocelyn: 'I am terribly sorry to say that poor Betty is much worse. Her lungs are now affected by the poisoning & she has great difficulty in breathing. She is being given oxygen which eases her a little. Without hearing anything officially I thought she was terribly ill on Wednesday & she became so bad that night that the Dr sent for Monty who arrived yesterday. She is no worse today – in fact pulse & temperature a shade better, but she is very seriously ill & we are all very anxious & worried. One can only hope & pray she has enough strength left to pull through. I'm sorry to give such depressing news but things are very serious at present . . .'[26]

They were indeed. Despite the primitive facilities of the cottage hospital major surgery on her infected limb seemed the only possible recourse, if that was the source of the poisoning. 'Then came the day when the doctors decided that the only hope was to amputate the leg,' Monty wrote in his memoirs; 'I agreed and gained hope.'[27] He wrote immediately to David, telling him that his mother would henceforth be an invalid, but that this was not the end of the world. He must learn to do things for her, as they would all have to do. Everything, in fact, was to run as before, David later remembered.[28] 'A life could be made for a cripple,' Alan Moorehead described the moment. 'There were special wheeled chairs. There had been tremendous improvements in artificial limbs. They would work and practise together until she walked again. The rooms at Portsmouth were to be altered immediately. By rearranging things Betty should have a room that would catch the sun all day. There must be new furniture, bright and cheerful. The boy would be there. He [Monty] would be there. He planned at a frantic pace . . .'[29]

Doubtless Monty believed his own post-operative scenario. Had he not fussed over Betty since the day they married, husbanding her health and physical resources to the point of tyranny? Katie Hobart had certainly told Jocelyn, during the week they were together at Burnham-on-Sea, that whenever she came to stay with her cousin, the time she would be permitted to be with Betty as a visitor was strictly allotted by Monty in advance, lest she overtire her.

However, there was little opportunity in which to organize Betty's new invalid life, for the amputation was a medical gesture of despair. To the very end the doctors had no idea what was really the cause of Betty's blood-poisoning, and once it had infected other parts of her body, surgery was not only futile, but a final drain on her remaining strength. She had battled for more than six weeks. Though she survived the operation itself, she quickly succumbed to pneumonia. As the end drew near Monty read to her from the Bible: 'Yea though I walk through the valley of the shadow of death, I will fear no evil: for Thou art with me; Thy rod and Thy staff they comfort me.'

'Betty died on the 19th October 1937, in my arms,' Monty re-counted in his memoirs some twenty years later.[30] The big house at Portsmouth would never see its intended mistress; David would be motherless. 'Covers were placed over the furniture and the bright new carpets were rolled up,' Moorehead recorded. 'He locked the doors of the unwanted rooms.'[31]

9

Post-Mortem

The funeral

Perhaps the death of any close relative changes us; most of all the death of a spouse. Monty, hardened in childhood, had developed a persona able to withstand machine-gun fire, shelling, the death of others around him, even by his side. He was inured to physical pain or injury, seemed not to allow emotion a purchase on his inner heart, lest it get the better of him and result in a humiliation he would not allow. Locked in a lifelong battle to prove himself – his masculinity, his normality, his talent – he had sought a wife both to impress Maud and to escape from her parental vice. He had failed to win the seventeen-year-old Betty Anderson, but had then won, on the rebound, the love of a mature, patient, intelligent, understanding and artistic woman who believed in him, and accepted him as he was, with all his peccadilloes – even his affection for men, and boys.

At first he could not credit what had happened. The law in England, where the death was not from natural causes at home, required a post-mortem and an inquest. Septicaemia was duly recorded, after which the body was authorized to be interred or cremated.

In a strange panic Monty decided – without consulting his step-sons, or Betty's family or any member of his own, that Betty's body should not only be buried, but laid to rest in the church cemetery at Burnham-on-Sea, where she'd died. Moreover, he wanted no witnesses. There was thus only one mourner at the graveside: Monty. He was accompanied by his chief of staff, a staff captain and a driver, none of whom had ever met Betty.

This was Monty's personal wish, which no one in his family ever really understood. Why exclude all members of Betty's family and his own, not to speak of friends who had known and loved her?

Not even their own son David was allowed to attend the funeral; equally, Betty's older sons, John and Dick Carver, were not permitted to fly from India. No relatives were invited from Ireland or England, whether Montgomerys or Hobarts, and certainly there was no question of Monty's mother – who had, after all, just had Betty and David to stay for an entire month in July / August – attending. Even more quietly than he had married the thirty-nine-year-old widow, Monty now took his leave of her as the priest – Canon Dick Sheppard – commended the departed to the mercy of Almighty God.

Utter darkness

Monty's misery, and his refusal to share it with any human being, appalled his brigade major, watching his normally self-possessed, energetic and undauntable commander break down and weep uncontrollably. 'It was the only time during our long friendship that I ever saw him less than in control of himself,' related General Simpson more than forty years later. 'As he faced a sixty-mile drive home alone, I urged him to come back with me in the staff car. Nothing would persuade him.'[1]

Why? What fears preyed upon Monty? Was it simply a refusal to let others – his family, Betty's – see his distress, humiliation, loss?

'I was utterly defeated,' Monty described his pain. After breaking the news to David at his school in Amesbury he returned to Ravelin House 'which was to have been our home; I remained alone for many days and would see no one'.[2]

Alan Moorehead remarked that 'If there is any mystery in Montgomery's life it probably lies here in these dark months in the winter of 1937. No one quite knows what he thought or did during the long hours when he was entirely alone in his house with his son. Clearly it was no ordinary struggle for reconciliation with life.'[3]

But David was not in the house; indeed he would spend less and less time with his father, who seemed consumed not only by grief now, but by something else too: some new struggle, at once personal and yet public, too, that excluded David.

At first Monty blamed himself. 'I began to search my mind for anything I had done wrong that I should have been dealt such a shattering blow,' he described in his memoirs, 'I could not understand it; my soul cried out in anguish against this apparent injustice. I seemed surrounded by utter darkness; all the spirit was knocked out of me. I had no one to love except

David and he was away at school. I suppose it was good for me,' he added in words reminiscent of his childhood traumas, 'but it seemed hard.'[4]

'Hard' was an understatement.

In every knocking a thief

Afterwards, his family would all agree that Betty's death transformed Monty – though each saw the change in a different light.

His sister Winsome felt that Monty sublimated his grief in a renewed but now total dedication to soldiering: the winning of the next war. Yet even Winsome felt that something else changed in her brother, that Betty's death altered his entire relation to the 'outside world'. 'Something went wrong,' Winsome acknowledged, puzzled by his later behaviour towards her, her family and his own family, 'and I cannot tell you what it was, I don't know.'[5]

Brian Montgomery was also puzzled. Betty's death and Monty's 'intense loneliness' thereafter proved the turning point in Monty's life, inspiring not only renewed military dedication but a new 'streak of intolerance', the striking of 'unreasonable attitudes' which had as their basis 'his anger with fate, call it a form of jealousy if you like, that had suddenly and brutally deprived him of the wonderful happiness and partnership he had so enjoyed during his marriage years'. Worst of all, from Brian's perspective, was Monty's subsequent pattern of personal rejection, as the embittered widower turned 'against certain close relatives and friends of very long standing' – behaviour that would have been avoided had Betty lived.[6]

Monty's step-son John agreed; indeed, he felt in retrospect that Betty's role in his step-father's life had been crucial in 'humanizing' the misogynist. Her death had put a sudden end to that; it was as if the most precious thing in his life had been snatched away and, like a man burgled of his proudest possession, he had installed locks on every point of entry to his heart, and heard in every knocking a thief.

A *tendency to paranoia*

Monty's tendency towards paranoia was, in John Carver's view, the aspect of his character Betty had miraculously balanced – most especially by her sense of humour, and her acceptance of him, with all his eccentricities and foibles. One night, at a fancy-dress dinner, she had worn his evening clothes, with a moustache painted over her upper lip – and, imitating his clipped speech, had toasted 'the ladies – God bless 'em', thus mocking Monty's well-known 'aversion to women, or at least the idea of a woman controlling his life'. Everyone present had 'glanced apprehensively at Montgomery to see how he would take it'.[7]

Betty alone, wearing Monty's clothes, pastiching even his moustache, had thus dared to switch and mock their gender-roles, as he – engaging servants, ordering groceries, arranging the furniture – had so often assumed hers. Did she go further, though, implying through an assumed masculinity, that they were both men, twins almost, since Monty had refused to wear fancy dress? Did she thus legitimize, through her under-standing, loving affection for him and her acceptance of his strange, threatened sexuality, his essentially misogynist, homosocial nature?

Whatever the truth, the depth of their companionship and affection was uncontested – leading people to wonder, in the aftermath of her death, how Monty would cope, she had become so much a part of his life, as he of hers. 'People speculate on what might have happened if my mother had lived,' John Carver later reflected. 'To my mind a more interesting speculation concerns what would have happened if he and my mother had never met. I think there might have been real danger that those schizoid tendencies engendered by his upbringing which were always latent might have become dominant in his personality; I mean a single-mindedness progressing to narrow-mindedness, a detachment leading to lack of human feeling and suspicion of the motives of others, and that such characteristics might have developed to such an extent as to have rendered him unsuitable for high command. It may not be entirely fanciful to suggest that the country owes something at least to my mother.'[8]

This was a bold claim for a son to make – namely that Betty had kept her latently schizoid spouse sane during the critical years between forty and fifty.

Fanciful or not, however, it was certainly true that Brigadier Mont-gomery, despite his arrogance, rashness and eccentricities, had reached the eve of fifty without major mishap, was currently judged a 'character' in the British army, but not mentally unbalanced – something which could certainly not be said for his brother-in-law, the irascible Major-General Patrick Hobart, who, not long afterwards, was dismissed from his divisional command (and ultimately the army) for being 'self-opinionated and lacking in stability'.[9] Nor could it be said for Liddell Hart, the ending of whose marriage in 1938 and whose increasing mania for tight corsetry, at this time, went hand-in-hand with a mental and physical breakdown: leading to the loss not only of his wife but of his unpaid post as Hore-Belisha's *éminence grise*, at the very core of the British military establishment. Indeed, Liddell Hart would even be sacked from his job as defence correspondent of *The Times* – his writing becoming so erratic in the summer and autumn of 1939 that his contract was terminated amid speculation he had gone mad – the editor deploring Hart's 'pessimism' and rejecting his excuse that 'neither his health nor his conscience would allow him to do any work'; the deputy editor, meanwhile, finding Hart 'a monolith of egotism and vanity', in the weeks before his dismissal.[10]

That Monty had survived, John Carver considered, was a testament to his mother's influence. But Betty was now dead, Monty was alone, and his own breakdown was approaching.

A marriage of convenience

'I never left her for the last 24 hours and it was heart breaking to watch her slowly dying,' Monty meanwhile confided in a letter that Dick, Betty's younger son, would treasure all his life. 'The final end was very peaceful, just one deep sigh; and she had no pain the last few days. She knew me up to about one hour before she died, after which she never opened her eyes or spoke . . . I think she knew she could not live. This morning when the doctor had left the room she whispered to me to go after him and ask him what he thought. And later when he came in again she gasped "Is there any hope?" Poor darling – she had a ghastly time during the last 6 weeks and had fought most bravely to live. I used to tell her she must fight for our sakes. But it was too much for her.'[11]

From Ravelin House two days later Monty described for Dick her burial in the 'pretty little cemetery' at Burnham-on-Sea that morning – omitting to mention the paucity of mourners.

The funeral is over and I am back at Ravelin House. It was a lovely day & brilliant sun. Dick Sheppard came and took the service most beautifully.

I sat [. . .] in the room at the hospital until they came to screw the lid on the coffin. She looked too wonderful – utterly calm and peaceful . . .

I kissed her dear face for the last time just before the lid was put on. The room was full of the most lovely flowers sent by all our friends. All my battalions in the Bde sent wreaths, and I was very touched to see one from the men of the Queens. I tried hard to bear up at the service and at the graveside. But I could not bear it and I am afraid I broke down utterly. Dick [Sheppard] was too wonderful & when everyone had gone away we knelt down together at the graveside and he said a very intimate family prayer, and we knelt there in silence. I said I could not believe it was God's will that she should have all that pain & suffering, and then die after it; surely if she had to die it should have been before all the pain. He said that God's ways of working are very mysterious, and I suppose that is true.

But, oh Dick, it is hard to bear and I am afraid I break into tears whenever I think of her. But I must try to bear up. I have come back alone to this big empty house for good now. And I get desperately lonely and sad. I suppose in time I shall get over it, but at present it seems that I never shall.[12]

The light of his life had gone out – Betty with her slightly breathless, husky voice, who thanks to her intelligence and perception brought excitement into everything she did, no matter how trivial; Betty with her sense of fun, who alone could pull Monty's leg, who was not irked by his eccentricities, who had made an inveterate bachelor, a man who had no social graces and was only comfortable with men or boys, the most happily married spouse. They had sparked each other off; had been married for ten years and been at the end as loving to each other as on the day of their wedding. It was not a marriage of convenience; and yet it certainly was not inconvenient either, Betty's son John and his wife would both later consider. It was a marriage which suited both parties, was good for the children – for everyone. Betty, who was apt to get nervy, to get in a flap, was cared for by someone who had a natural if exaggerated sense of order, who loved and respected her enough to see that she had time to paint, the freedom and financial security to be herself, while he took responsibility for her boys, and their son David. And in return she had looked beyond his gaucheness, his schoolboy innocence, his constant need to assert himself, to boss others; had given the two things which Monty's mother had always refused: her uninhibited love and her belief in his ability. She was the only person who had ever – would ever – put her arms around him, comfort him, even make love with him.

As with Liddell Hart, however, the ending of his marriage posed for Monty profound questions regarding his sexuality – questions which a relationship of the depth and mutuality he had experienced with Betty had simply set aside for a decade. Alan Moorehead puzzled over the dilemma Monty faced in the days and weeks after Betty's death; yet the truth is, in the loneliness of Ravelin House, in October 1937, he was forced to confront the man he had been before he married Betty: Monty the misogynist. Following Betty's death Monty would hate even to be touched by a woman. He himself was candid on this point. Friends, he later wrote, 'said that I would marry again. They little knew what they were saying.'[13]

They did not. The fact was, marriage to Betty had papered over not only the cracks in Monty's psyche, but his sexuality. By nature he was exclusively drawn to members of his own sex – a fact which his happy marriage had conveniently masked. But in 1937, the closet was not somewhere out of which a man might come – unless he wished to destroy himself and his career, as Wilde had done, and T. E. Lawrence, too, in his way. Betty's death thus brought Monty back, with a jolt he would never forget or, as his brother Brian noted, never quite forgive, to a homophobic society in which 'homosexuality' – indeed any expression of physical tenderness to a member of one's own sex – was still a criminal offence. It was small wonder he felt angry with his God.

Yet there was at least one consolation. Betty's death had robbed him of marital happiness, and without her his efforts at paternal responsibility over the following years would be, he himself admitted, dire. But as a soldier he inhabited a special world in which misogyny drew no special attention – especially in a widower or divorcé. As Betty had 'reverted to type' in marrying a soldier, so Monty now reverted to type in terms of his fear of women, and his exclusive tenderness towards men and boys. 'A male servant was engaged to look after David,' Moorehead chronicled. 'No woman was ever allowed to come into that house.'[14] Widowerhood would thus confer, in a still homophobic age, a valid mask for an attitude towards women that now bordered on allergy.

Back in business

Liddell Hart's path, after the breakdown of his marriage, would be one of defensive-mindedness leading towards defeatism (he would move to Devon to escape the bombing of south-east England, and openly counsel appeasement with Hitler), while on the personal front he would retreat, according to his latest biographer, into a mid-life crisis marked by besottedness with male constructs of 'femininity'.

Monty's post-marital path, however, would be very, very different. Until his marriage, he had been 'irrevocably married to his profession', as his brother Brian put it; 'he had virtually no other interests'.[15] In the aftermath of Betty's death he would revert to that heterophobic condition: with profound consequences for the outcome of World War II.

First, however, he would have to pull himself together and ensure he became a general. 'At 1 a.m. on the night after the funeral,' his brigade major later recalled, 'I was wakened in bed by the telephone. "That you, Simbo?" said the caller. "I'm afraid I've left things rather to you these last few days. Tomorrow I want all the papers on my desk at 9 a.m. and we'll get down to work." I went to sleep happy,' Simpson recalled. 'We were back in business.'[16]

Study week

After almost two decades of peace and pacifism in England the business of soldiering was, at last, becoming more serious. No longer was it a question of hores-for-courses; even the most myopic of military blimps could see, in Germany's manoeuvres and its intercession in the Spanish Civil War, the signs of things to come.

Britain's response, under the prime ministership of Neville Chamberlain, left much to be desired. In December 1937, as has been noted, Lieutenant-General Lord Gort, the Military Secretary and arguably the most small-minded general in the British army, was made CIGS by the Secretary of State for War, Leslie Hore-Belisha – with Liddell Hart's connivance. Given Gort and Monty's mutual dislike this meant that Monty's chances of promotion to general in command of a division in peacetime now plummeted.

It was not only Gort, however, who was opposed to Monty's promotion. As Field-Marshal Wavell later recalled: 'Monty's name had come up several times in front of the selection board; everyone always agreed that he ought to be promoted, but every other commander who had a vacancy for a major-general had always excellent reasons for finding someone else more suitable than Monty.'[17]

Fortunately, Monty's higher ambition was tempered, in a professional sense, by his determination to succeed at every task he undertook; and, while there were some who said Wavell was tiring, and had passed his peak when, in the early 1930s, he commanded an infantry brigade at Blackdown, the opposite could be said of Monty. Monty's Salisbury Plain training exercises and manoeuvres in the late summer of 1937 were only the first items in a whole new programme of retraining for modern war, which he carried out in the winter of 1937/8. His sense of urgency was manifest: 'The introduction of new weapons, mechanisation, the increase in armoured fighting vehicles, progress in gas, air power, and scientific inventions generally, have all combined to complicate the modern battle,' he began his first Individual Training Memorandum for his brigade officers in the autumn of 1937. 'It will be equally obvious that as a result of these new aids to warfare we shall have to overhaul our tactics – we must in fact develop a new technique. If we enter the next war using the old methods we shall lose the first round,' he warned. 'All commanders, in their several grades, must have a good knowledge of the technique of staging the many and varied operations that their unit may be called on to undertake in war, whether offensive or defensive – they must understand the stage-management of the battle ... With a view to studying some of the many problems involved the Brigade Commander will conduct a study week for officers at Portsmouth from 15th to 19th November 1937.'[18]

If he was emotionally crushed by the sudden excision of Betty from his domestic life, Monty allowed no sign of this to show in his professional performance; indeed, it was as if he had, in some almost psychotic way, put her memory, like a framed photograph, into a compartment of his mind where no one but he could commune with her. Moreover it was as if, rather than continuing to grieve in any introspective way after the funeral, he would make someone pay. That someone was the enemy – indeed, anyone who stood in his way.

Attack by night, the use of reserves, organization of defence, the role of artillery, night withdrawal, river crossing under fire: all were considered in Monty's infectiously fresh, lucid and wonderfully straightforward style.

Liddell Hart's work might be stimulating in a controversial way for historians and thinkers – but Monty was concerned to guide his colleagues and subordinates towards professional preparations for actual battle – an approach that was, as the divisional commander's chief of staff, Colonel Morgan, remarked, the precursor of later wartime exercises 'of which Monty made himself so great a master and from which so many people have benefited so greatly over the years that followed'. Small wonder that Morgan recorded, 'at the end of the course even Monty' – who had run the entire study week single-handedly after Lieutenant-Colonel Simpson suffered burns – 'began to wilt a little'.[19]

Atmosphere of gloom

Monty had tried to put Betty's death to the back of his mind by an almost manic dedication to his work, and to his vision of the military future. To those he liked or respected, however, he remained as avuncular as always. He would not at first permit a replacement for Simpson – who had inadvertently set himself alight with a box of matches in his pocket. When the wound festered and Simpson got steadily worse in the Netley Hospital at Portsmouth, Monty even arranged for him to be 'kidnapped' – bundled through a window and taken in his car to the King Edward VII Hospital in London, where the famous plastic surgeon Archibald MacIndoe operated on him.

Come Christmas 1937, however, there could be no distraction. David duly came home from school. 'David had been handled in his early years almost entirely by his mother and he had at times resented any interference on my part in this procedure. He had a strong will and his mother was always defeated by him,' Monty wrote many years later in his *Memoirs*. 'Remembering my own boyhood, it was our plan that I should become the predominant partner in his upbringing when he went to his preparatory school. We had just started on this plan and the sparks used to fly when I insisted on obedience; then suddenly his mother died.' In this retrospective version, Betty's death chastened both father and son, and gave rise to a new relationship. 'He and I now had to make a new life together and became close friends; he was nine when his mother died and I was fifty.'[20]

This was not how David remembered their story. 'It was a dreadful Xmas, with just bereaved father and son,' David recalled, despite the new model railway his father had bought him; and he went off to school with relief again in January 1938.[21] Soon afterwards John Carver's fiancée Jocelyn came to stay, along with her father, Admiral Sir Hugh Tweedie. Monty had insisted that the engagement be formally announced, as planned, the week after Betty's death. For the moment, at least, he treated John's fiancée as a daughter – though with faintly macabre undertones. 'There was a frightful atmosphere of gloom,' Jocelyn vividly recalled. 'I remember he produced some jewellery that had belonged to Betty, and I had to choose some. We went out in the evening with the Portsmouth admiral and Monty brought down Betty's coat and said, "You're to wear this," and I argued and there was quite a tussle in the hall. I remember I had to wear it in the end. He seemed to want to project – he was terribly lonely, and he talked quite a lot about Betty.'[22]

Privately, Monty afterwards admitted his failure in these years – and the unfortunate effect on David. 'I think few boys have had to lead such a difficult life in their early years,' he confided – difficulties which began with the Quetta earthquake. 'Two years later, in October 1937 when he was nine, his mother died. He did not see her at the end and I did not take him to the funeral. I thought it best not to do so. In those days he was very highly strung,' Monty reflected – concluding, after a holiday-by-holiday tabulation of David's years in domestic wilderness, that David 'had a rotten life as a boy' – and blaming himself for not having been able to give his son the quality of loving care that would have made up for Betty's absence. 'Without my wife by my side during the war years it was really not possible for me to look after David properly,' he concluded. 'The loss of his mother was a shattering blow to us both.'[23]

Killing two birds with one stone

If social intercourse was funereal after Betty's funeral, the challenge of rebuilding his brigade into a modern army formation, capable of undertaking any task in modern war, seemed at least to offer Monty the semblance of a 'normal' life – though it would never be more than that, for the rest of his career. His vision of modern war, two years before Britain reluctantly delared war, was, however, stunning: in fact, as Colonel Morgan noted, Monty's training methods formed the blueprint of those he would later use to transform the British army in World War II. His single-handed 9th Infantry Brigade officers' week instruction was, moreover, only the start of his reshaping of his brigade, from toe to top. Quoting from intelligence reports about German company training, he was insistent that battalion commanders begin to train their junior officers to take command of larger units, even the battalion itself, in preparation for the day when there would be heavy casualties. 'The junior officer of today is the commanding officer of tomorrow and, adequately to insure the future, some small sacrifice has to be made,' he laid down. 'Therefore the CO with the long view welcomes any opportunities of sending his more senior officers on duties away from the unit, such as umpiring, liaison, etc., during collective training. This policy kills two birds with one stone; it widens the outlook of the more senior officer by giving him a change of environment, and it gives the junior officer the opportunity to practise command and to study his manuals carefully so as to do himself justice. When war comes senior officers may become casualties and this system repays itself ten-fold.'[24]

As the political situation in Europe deteriorated even the most obtuse of British officers began to take note. By the middle of February 1938, Lord Halifax, the Foreign Secretary, was denying war was 'imminent' – itself an acknowledgement of public unease. Despite – or as a result of – this reassuring British political neutralism, Hitler, having dismissed his army chiefs and made himself head of the German Reichswehr, ordered on 11 March the invasion and annexation of Austria, gateway to Czechoslovakia. It was obvious that Liddell Hart's policy of a field force uncommitted to Europe and trained and equipped only for imperial duties was bankrupt. All eyes turned towards Hitler's enlarged Third Reich, and its burgeoning 'defence' – in reality assault – forces.

It was in this context that Monty proposed a combined air–sea–land exercise that was to have historic repercussions: the precursor of landings that Britain would have to conduct in Norway after the German invasion of April 1940, and, on a vastly larger scale, in the Mediterranean in 1942 and 1943, and finally on the coast of France in 1944: D-Day.

D-Day rehearsal

Although many hundreds of books and articles have been written about the development of armoured warfare and the tank during the inter-war years, there was probably no more visionary exercise carried out in Britain in the pre-war period, nor one that would have greater significance in the outcome of World War II, than 9th Infantry Brigade's combined forces assault landing at Slapton Sands, south Devon, in the summer of 1938.

'The object of the exercise was to investigate the tactical and technical aspects of an approach from seaward, and the landing of a force on an enemy coast; the provision and distribution of fire from ships in company supporting the landing force; and the co-operation of aircraft,' Major-General D. K. Bernard explained the nature of the 9th Infantry Brigade exercise to the press and military observers in July 1938.[25]

Royal Navy support was significant: a battleship, two cruisers, an aircraft carrier and a flotilla of destroyers. The joint navy, army and air command was headed by Brigadier Montgomery, and his 'Eastland army' of two corps (represented by three battalions from 9th Infantry Brigade). The battalions were landed from the troopships *Lancashire* and *Clan MacAlister* before dawn on 6 July, ostensibly to be supported by 150 light tanks. Engineers constructed landing piers and beach tracks for the armoured vehicles, and Brigadier Montgomery, once ashore, took command of the invasion, which had taken the 'Wessex' defences totally by surprise.[26]

The Times recorded that 'the landing of an Infantry Brigade on Slapton Sands was carried out with great success this morning, under ideal weather conditions. The three regiments concerned, the KOSBS, the Lincolns and the East Yorks were brought ashore in Naval cutters and whalers and in transports' lifeboats between one-thirty and four o'clock; and when dawn broke, the guns, tanks and lorries, accompanied by numerous stores, were landed in special flat-bottomed craft. The troops will be re-embarked this evening.'

It was only the second operation of its kind since Gallipoli. Together with the naval C-in-C at Portsmouth, Admiral-of-the-Fleet Lord Cork and Orrery – subseqently naval commander of the Anglo-French landings in Norway in 1940 – Monty had organized the whole exercise. 'As one would anticipate,' the GSO 1 of the 3rd Division acknowledged later, 'the invasion was meticulously organized, the expenditure of foolscap paper by 9th Infantry Brigade amounting, as I recall, to 30,000 sheets for which I subsequently got the bill.'[27]

Colonel Morgan may have been surprised by the immense organization involved – Monty's step-son Dick was even detailed, on his leave from India, to make a complete fifteen-foot model of the Slapton shoreline – and by the bill, but few of the 30,000 sheets of foolscap paper relating to this visionary exercise would survive, sad to say, and to all intents and purposes the exercise was allowed by the three services to pass into utter obscurity.[28]

For Monty it was real enough, however. Using tanks and mortars, his brigade rehearsed 'fighting' its way inland, supported by twelve Fleet Air Arm Swordfish 'bombers' from the carrier *Courageous* and the heavy guns of the *Revenge*, the *Southampton* and the *Sheffield*, and five destroyers. Hopes of easy re-embarkation, however, began to fade when the weather broke in the afternoon. The navy, anxious about being blown on to a lee shore, decided not to wait for the army or the end of the exercise – and left some 1,200 officers and men without tents and in driving rain.

'All were wet through and hungry, and most of the troops had spent the previous day being seasick . . . such scenes can never have been seen here before,' the magazine of the Royal Naval College, Dartmouth, recorded. 'The quarterdeck, gunrooms, boot and changing rooms, Drake annexe and cinema rooms were all used to hold the troops who were packed like sardines in a tin. A pleasant change from the normal routine, it gave us a chance of seeing how the Army fare during "war time," and an opportunity to practise the very necessary organization of inter-Service co-operation,' it remarked – only two years before British disasters in Norway and Dunkirk. 'We may well be grateful,' it concluded.[29]

If so, few in the military hierarchy showed any gratitude at the time, or later.

Inter-service co-operation

Part of the problem was the way in which Monty's exercise – the first since the 1920s, off the east coast – had shown up Britain's hopelessly inadequate preparations for inter-service co-operation, or combined operations. Monty was understandably proud of the performance, but the distinguished observers were shocked into silence: especially by the sight of men being rowed ashore in lifeboats as in Nelson's time. The new CIGS, General Lord Gort, had come by car to watch the landing. He said nothing. Nor did General Wavell, who had had recently returned from Palestine and had succeeded Sir John Burnett-Stuart as C-in-C Southern Command.

Wavell had watched the day's activities with a critical eye from the naval C-in-C's yacht, and had braved the storm that night at sea. The next day he landed, 'to be greeted', as Wavell's biographer John Connell recorded, 'by a Montgomery who was bubbling over with enthusiasm and full of explanations of the course of the exercise. Wavell said, "I see," and stumped on up the hill to the car' and drove back to Salisbury.[30]

Wavell had nothing against Monty's handling of the exercise, which he admired; it was the ramifications that depressed him. The situation in Czechoslovakia was critical; it was more than possible that Britain might be involved in a continental war that year – an eventuality which, in contrast to his fellow area commanders in Britain, Wavell was inclined to welcome, since he feared, rightly, that Germany would use additional peacetime to better military advantage than would Britain. But Monty's ambitious and amphibious assault provided a most unwelcome illustration of Britain's unpreparedness – 'a pitiful exposition of our complete neglect of landing operations', he wrote later. 'There was one so-called landing craft, an experimental one made many years before and dug out of some scrap-heap for this exercise, in which I rather think it sank. For the rest the troops landed in open row-boats as they had done for the last 200 years and more.'[31]

Wavell's despondency was well founded, but he did nothing about it. Indeed, his response reflected an attitude that was to become all too prevalent in the years ahead – the tendency to blame equipment to the point of losing sight of the human factor, and the need for imaginative training. After all, the German army had re-created itself illegally, using wooden rifles and wooden tanks; why should British commanders not concentrate on leadership, tactics and training while waiting for equipment? As British – and later, American – factories would demonstrate, equipment could be produced very quickly if need be; trained personnel – especially soldiers, airmen and sailors trained to co-operate – could not.

Such co-operation would be crucial to Britain's attempts to help win World War II, and it would be in this area that Monty's character was at once brilliantly inspiring and yet a potentially disastrous liability. 'I remember,' recalled Morgan 'asking the Brigadier, for my own edification, for some amplification of his ideas on this business of inter-service co-operation – to which I got the simple answer, "Co-operation, my dear chap, no problem there. I tell them what to do and they do it." '[32]

The fur flies

High-handedness had always dogged Monty's performance as a commander – as it would the career of George S. Patton. In a defence force such as the Wehrmacht, this would not have been a problem; Monty and Patton, however, were servants of democracy. Both men were determined to impose an approach to training and to modern combat that would enable the democracies to fight a fascist, militaristic enemy on equal terms, but both men found themselves on repeated collision course with the bumbling 'powers that be', threatening their very careers.

In Monty's case, he had often sailed close to the wind in terms of antagonizing his superiors – especially in Egypt and India. Now, in the summer of 1938, with war imminent and the need for adequate military preparation becoming dire, Monty suddenly found himself being investigated by the War Office for unauthorized use of government funds and property!

Monty had no one to blame but himself. In conjunction with the Mayor of Portsmouth, he had cut a rash deal: the illegal leasing of War Office military property for an August Bank Holiday fairground. This deal had netted £1,000 for the garrison's married families' welfare fund, with a further £500 to the Mayor for a pet local scheme. 'The fur then began to fly,' Monty recorded in his *Memoirs*.[33] A senior administrative officer from the War Office arrived at Portsmouth to ask what had happened to the money. 'I replied that the £1,500 had been spent; £500 had been used to bribe the Lord Mayor, and £1,000 had been spent on the welfare of the married families; I produced all the receipts.'[34]

Bribery and corruption did not go down well, despite the good causes. 'The Major-General i/c Administration Southern Command, Salisbury, came to see me,' Monty later recalled, 'and said that this incident had ruined my chances of promotion in the Army.'[35] General Wavell managed to keep the case fluid by passing the relevant file backwards and forwards between Whitehall and Salisbury; but it was, as Monty recognized, 'growing rather large'.[36]

Undeterred, Monty concentrated on his new winter training programme – including a winter study period for which the 'Campaign in Egypt and Palestine from the outbreak of war with Germany to June 1917' was selected. 'Probably the most interesting operation during the period,' Monty wrote in his Instruction No. 4 of 7 October 1938, addressed to all officers of the 9th Infantry Brigade, 'is the 1st Battle of Gaza in March 1917, for the following reasons:

'a) It was fought by just such a force as might be employed during the early stages of a future war in Europe or the Middle East.

'b) It is prolific in lessons in command, staff duties, and organization. The personality of the commanders played an interesting part in the battle. The fog of war was more than usually a deciding factor in the conduct of the battle by the commanders of both sides.

'c) The plan for battle was sound.
The execution of the plan by a large part of the troops was faultless.
The battle was at one time to all intents and purposes won.
And yet it was a failure.'

As Monty pointed out, 'There are many advantages in studying an operation which was a failure. The 1st Battle of Gaza failed, among other things, owing to a number of accidents and to the almost incredible lack of information available.'[37]

When writing this, Monty had no inkling that, in the course of a few years, Allied commanders would be privileged to receive through 'Ultra' – the decrypting of Germany's highest-grade secret signals – information about the enemy that dwarfed that of any campaign in the history of war since ancient times. Meanwhile, however, each battalion in 9th Infantry Brigade was to furnish a specialist six-man study syndicate under a major, and the lessons of every step in the Palestine campaign were to be clarified and demonstrated on the brigade model. COs were to form 'a Criticism Syndicate for the purpose of deducing lessons for our future guidance; they will also consider the effect present day armament and organization would have on the operations, and how the same problem would be tackled in 1939'.[38]

Few if any brigade commanders in the British army had paid such personal attention to teaching, but Monty's winter study scheme was the last he would ever run in that rank. Four days after issuing these training instructions he received the offer for which he was waiting: command of an infantry division, in the field, as a major-general. After a lifetime's preparation he had made it. He had lost a beloved wife, but he was, finally, a general.

10

Breaking Down

The powder keg

The new division Monty was assigned to command was the 8th Division in Palestine – one of two new military formations set up to quell growing Arab insurrection. On 28 October 1938 Monty therefore set sail for Haifa, 'to fight the Arabs in Palestine', as he later recorded.

Whether the Arabs deserved such treatment is a matter of historical debate. The Turks had ruled the country with an iron fist for centuries until Allenby, Lawrence and the Arabs had collectively evicted them. The Turks had at least been fellow Muslims, however, if much resented by the Palestinians. Now, with Versailles/League of Nations backing, it was the Christian-British who, since 1918, ruled; and with the British had come – or come back, as Zionists preferred to see it – Jews in ever-increasing numbers. Thus what had seemed like a country that would one day achieve Arab self-government and independence – indeed, had been promised such a future in return for helping the British fight the Turks – began to look like a powder keg.

David, now ten years old, was meanwhile 'handed over to the care of Major and Mrs Carthew-Yarstoun – the Portsmouth Garrison adjutant and his wife – who lived at Bedhampton near Portsmouth. The Carthew-Yarstouns would look after David in the holidays for the following three years, while Monty made himself first a general, then – when denied command of a promised division in England – a general nuisance.

Meanwhile, no sooner had Monty arrived in Haifa to form the 8th Division than he received a further communication from the Military Secretary – namely that, at a selection board held on 8 November 1938, it had been decided he would be offered the post of his former divisional commander, Major-General Denis Bernard, on his retirement in December the following year, 1939. Monty would, in other words, command the famous 3rd (Iron) Division – which was bound to be in the vanguard of the BEF, if one was formed, as in 1914.

Monty accepted with alacrity.

A steely glint

The appointment to succeed General D. K. Bernard was entirely Wavell's doing as C-in-C Southern Command. In his confidential report of October 1938 Wavell had written:

I have known Brigadier Montgomery for a number of years. He is one of the clearest brains we have in the higher ranks, an excellent trainer of troops, and an enthusiast in all he does. His work this year in the Combined Operations Exercise and Gas Trials was of a very high order. He has some of the defects of the enthusiast, in an occasional impatience and intolerance when things cannot be done as quickly as he would like or when he meets brains less quick & clear than his own.[1]

Days later, Wavell was asked by the selection board 'whom I wanted to succeed Bernard in the 3rd Division. I replied at once – "Monty". There was something like a sigh of relief from the other Army Commanders and instant acquiescence.'[2] No one, bar Wavell, wanted 'that damned pipsqueak' under his command – imminent war or no war.

War, however, was bound to come in Europe within the next two years, Monty was certain, and the 3rd Division would be in the thick of it from the start, he reckoned, since it was by tradition one of the primary component divisions of a British Expeditionary Force. He was delighted. No longer would he be taking part in battles under commanders who had neither trained nor rehearsed their troops for modern combat, but would himself be a field general, able to train the troops of his division, before time, and to lead them into modern battle with, he hoped, distinction.

First, however, he must command the 8th Division in Palestine. The appointment thus offered a tremendous opportunity to rehearse command of a division on active service, and it was the poor Arabs in Palestine who were used as guinea-pigs – for they, not the Germans, were to be Monty's enemy *pro tempore*.

A tragedy for the Arabs

'Dealing with the rebellion was a very unsatisfactory and intangible business' was all Wavell – who had briefly been GOC in Palestine, from 1937 to 1938, but had failed to quell rising Palestinian insurgency, stemming from the Balfour declaration of 1917 and the increased settling of foreign Jews in kibbutzim and enclaves – would commit himself to say. 'I don't think I produced any better answers than anyone else. But I think I kept it within bounds and did as much as I could with the troops available.'[3] (It was very much what he would say about his period as Viceroy in India.)

Monty, however, was a very different character, and even those Arabs who had known him as Officer Commanding the Holy Land in 1931 were stunned by the contrast. In 1931 he had been a highly professional soldier, but also a happily married man, with a wife and children, who spent his spare time visiting and exploring the biblical and classical sites, Baedeker in hand. Seven years later he was a changed person. He had no wife or children with him, only the steely glint of a ruthless military commander who would brook no opposition. He had visited China and Japan in 1934, and was aware how frail was Britain's imperial necklace, stretching from Cairo to Hong Kong. It could be snatched at any moment – which was why the complacency of both the Indian army and the British army at home so worried him. Aware that Palestine would be a key territory in defending the Suez Canal – Britain's gateway to India, its Far East colonies, and the dominions of Australia and New Zealand – Monty had recommended to Liddell Hart that a four-division British Imperial Reserve be stationed in Palestine, from which units could be despatched with speed to any location. Palestine, therefore, must be kept secure – for the British.

For the Arabs this was historically disastrous. For them a great tragedy would now unfold, as their rightful national aspirations were submerged by a growing Zionist agenda, innocently compounded by a ruthless British commander who would stop at nothing to quell their insurrection.

Smashing the Arab revolt

The GOC in Palestine was Lieutenant-General 'Bob' Haining, the former Director of Military Operations and Intelligence at the War Office. Haining had been Monty's predecessor as instructor at the Staff College, Camberley, but was not in Monty's league as a commander who knew what he wanted, and would get it. Commanding the 7th Division in the south of Palestine was Major-General 'Dick' O'Connor, who had also been an instructor at Camberley: a shy but brilliant officer who deferred to Monty's clarity of purpose and military zeal. It was clear to both Haining and O'Connor, once Monty arrived, who would be running the campaign against the Arab guerrillas.

A royal commission under Lord Peel had already recommended partition of the country in 1937. The British Partition Commission of 1938 decided, however, in their wisdom, that this would be unworkable – inadvertently dooming the notion of an independent Palestinian-Arab nation, in the manner of neighbouring Jordan, Syria or Saudi Arabia. Meanwhile, pending the only workable solution – which would have been a ban on further Jewish immigration – the British army was expected to deal with rising civil violence before it reached the point of civil war – as, tragically, it would in 1948.

Concerned with other matters Lord Gort, the CIGS, paid little attention either to Palestine or to Monty. However, Monty was fortunate to have one important friend in the War Office: Lieutenant-General Sir Ronald ('Bill') Adam, the deputy CIGS. On 8 November 1938, while still en route to Palestine, Monty had written to Adam to give his views on army training at home; Adam had thanked him and indicated he would be grateful for Monty's observations on the situation in Palestine. Early in December Monty's first unofficial report arrived. He had, he said, 'toured the whole Div[isiona]l area and studied the situation and the problem' before deciding how to tackle the Arab insurrection. 'This area includes Samaria, Galilee, and the whole of the frontier district. During my tour I visited every single military garrison, detachment and post in the area; interviewed every civil servant; and talked to every single British policeman. It was an immense task and it took me one week. I got up at 5.0 a.m. each morning and went to bed at midnight. My division is in 35 garrisons and detachments, but it was well worth while, and enabled me to take over operational control with a definite and formed policy.'

It was, in other words, Monty's policy – and not that of the commanding general in Palestine, Lieutenant-General Haining. He had been completely open about this. 'Before leaving Jerusalem I said to Force HQ that I wanted the answer to the following question: Is the campaign that is being waged against us a National movement, or is it a campaign that is being carried on by gangs of professional bandits?'

This was the question he had asked himself in Ireland – concluding that Irish insurrection had been a national movement, which could only be tackled by an Irish government. Haining felt the same in Palestine: 'Force HQ was quite clear that the campaign was definitely a national movement.'

Alas for the Arabs! Monty was sceptical, and was determined to see for himself. It did not take him long.

When I had got about halfway on my tour it began to be clear to me that the campaign was not a national movement. I am certain now that this view is correct. The campaign against us is being waged by gangs of professional bandits; these constitute an Army, with a definite though somewhat crude organization. There are three 'Army' commanders and they take their orders from Damascus; there is little cohesion in the rebel forces and the esprit-de-corps is a 'gang' one.

A gang is anything from 50 to 150 men, and each 'Army' commander controls the gangs in his area by means of subarea commanders. There is no higher organization than the gang as far as is known.

The 'Army' commanders are very elusive and it will be difficult to catch them; we know where they keep their women, and that is about all. The gangs operate in the country and live in the hill areas. They move about from place to place and conscript the local peasants – against their will – and force them to take up arms against us; the peasants have to comply, since refusal means death and the destruction of their houses. The gang leaders also have agents in the towns, and by means of them they carry out assassinations and commit other acts of terrorism; this is very difficult to combat, especially in a large place like Haifa with a population of over 100,000.

The net result is that the British Army in Palestine is at war with a rebel army which is one hundred per cent Arab.

If you now examine the feelings of the general public, including the peasantry, you find it is as follows:

The bulk of the Arab population of the country are 'fed up' with the whole thing; they are very short of food and are hustled about by both sides i.e. the British and rebel armies; they would like to see law and order restored; they would be quite content to live under the British mandate so long as Jewish immigration is limited to a fixed total (say of 500,000).

The Jewish population go on with their work as if there was no war on but they defend their own colonies stoutly with arms which we allow them to have for the purpose; the colonies are all protected by wire obstacles, powerful searchlights operate all night long, and there is a regular system of sentries and patrols in each colony by day and night.

The above gives a brief picture of the situation and having read so far I think it is important to realize that we are definitely at war. British soldiers are being killed and wounded in battle with the rebels every day. The enemy army wears uniform when operating by gangs and for movement about the country it resorts to civilian dress. The normal uniform in the North is a high neck polo sweater of a saffron colour, with riding boots and khaki trousers or breeches.

I think that what has been lacking out here has been any clear cut statement, defining the situation and saying what was to be done about it. I decided that I must issue such a statement of policy at once in my division so that all efforts would be directed along the same lines. Having briefly defined the situation as it appeared to me, I went on to give the tasks on which we would concentrate. They were as follows, in order of importance:

a) To hunt down and destroy the rebel armed gangs. They must be hunted relentlessly; when engaged in battle with them we must shoot to kill. We must not be on the defensive and act only when attacked; we must take the offensive and impose our will on the rebels. The next few weeks, before the winter rains set in, is an opportunity and during them we may well smash the rebel movement given a little luck. We must put forward our maximum effort now and concentrate on killing armed rebels in battle; this is the surest way to end the war.

b) To get the dwellers in urban areas, and the peasantry, on our side. To do this we must be scrupulously fair in our dealings with them. We want them to realize that they will always get a fair deal from the British army; but if they assist the rebels in any way they must expect to be treated as rebels; and anyone who takes up arms against us will certainly lose his life.

c) To prepare the police force to take over from us when the rebellion is crushed.

The police are working as soldiers. Large reinforcements are coming in and these are practically all ex-soldiers; they are fitted out in Jerusalem and then drafted straight out to their districts (I am referring to the British police, of whom there are to be some 3000).

It is the British police who will form the backbone of the future Palestine Police

Force. They are now being used like soldiers, but we cannot stay here for ever and when we have restored law and order we shall want to hand over control to the police; we have therefore got to help them to get back gradually to their duties as 'police'. They are under our orders and so we have a definite responsibility in the matter. In order to do this they must receive training; they require instruction in police duties and they must be able to speak Arabic.

The British police are now concentrated in the larger towns and on the Northern frontier; as their numbers increase we must aim at getting them out into the country areas working with our military detachments; it is the British police who will form the backbone of the mounted gendarmerie that will eventually be organized for the control of rural areas, and we must begin to fit them for this role.

I started off with this policy in the North and Dick O'Connor is doing much the same in the South. He and I are great personal friends and we are keeping in the closest touch. During the last week in my area the rebels have been brought to battle twice and dealt two smashing blows. On 28th November we cornered a gang of about 60 in the Carmel Range and killed fifty of them; they fought like wild beasts, knowing that they were 'for it' and in one case there was a hand-to-hand conflict between a Corporal of the Irish Fusiliers and an Arab in which the Arab was finally killed. All the killed men were armed and dressed in uniform. Present with the gang was ABU DORRAH, the 'Rebel Army' Commander in the North; it is reported he was killed but we cannot definitely confirm this; the action took place in the afternoon and in the broadcast from Beyrouth that night it was stated he had been killed. This is the real way to end the war, i.e. to kill the rebels and particularly their leaders. To do this we must take the offensive and hunt them relentlessly.[4]

For the Arabs, the arrival of Monty had thus been like a desert storm; for the Jews, a godsend – for, in the wake of *Kristallnacht* and Hitler's growing pogrom in Nazi Germany, they had understandably no intention of agreeing to a cap on the total size of Jewish population in Palestine. Monty had meant to ensure peace, fairness and goodwill in a multi-racial country for the next ten years of the League of Nations mandate, when Arab independence would be granted; but by deciding to smash the Arab insurrection as banditry, while failing to see increasing Jewish immigration as the real threat to peace in Palestine, he inadvertently robbed the Arabs of their nationhood for the rest of the century while paving the way for a Jewish one. On top of the Zionist 'Special Night Squads' organized by Orde Wingate under General Wavell the year before, it was, in Arab eyes, the rawest of deals.

Utterly and completely useless

In London the Palestinian war was completely overshadowed by darkening events in Europe. In Haifa, however, having either killed or captured almost the entire Arab 'army' in the north, Monty found he was having to release one detainee for every new captive.

Overcrowding in the camps had led, as he reported to Sir Ronald Adam, to 'an amazing picture'.

We rope in all rebels and enemies and lock them up; the detention camps then get full; we then have to start letting them out; if I put in 50 I must let out 50.

I have no doubt that as the time for the London conference approaches we shall be ordered to let out a good many in order to create a good 'atmosphere' for the talks. We adopted this policy during the Shinn [*sic*] Fein war in Ireland in 1920/1; it produced the most dreadful repercussions and prolonged the war for many months.

There is no doubt that we British are an amazing people. We never seem to learn from past mistakes. I went up to Beyrouth last week to liaise with the French and had lunch with the French C-in-C, General Cailloux. The French of course think we are quite mad as regards our conduct of the war in Palestine. They are expecting trouble themselves in Syria and have everything ready to stamp it out in one day; and they will be quite ruthless; they have 28,000 troops in the country and can cope with any situation.[5]

For the moment he accepted such inconsistency. As he put it, 'we seem to win our wars in the end and one must, I suppose, preserve a sense of humour'.[6] But would he, under greater stress, be able to curb his critical tongue? After Dunkirk, the following year, its sharpness and candour would cost him the chance of corps or army command in the field for two long years. In the meantime, emboldened by his direct line of communication with the deputy CIGS, Monty launched into a bitter attack on the force that would have to take over the occupation of Palestine once the army's role was over: the enlarged Palestine Police Force. 'The Secretary of State *himself* should know the facts,' he urged General Adam, 'and he should know them at once. He should also be told that when we hand over to the police and the civilian government finds that they (the police) are no use, they must never say that we soldiers did not tell them that their police force was useless or that we never gave them our advice as to how to remedy this state of affairs. I give below an outline of the situation. A large British police force is being recruited for Palestine; it will be nearly 3000 strong. This will form the backbone of the Palestine police force, which will have to contain Arabs and Jew personnel as well.'

Recruits for this multi-ethnic British police force 'are coming in fast. They are nearly all ex-soldiers,' Monty noted with approval. 'They are magnificent material and from it a really fine police force could be formed. I have spoken personally to nearly every British constable in the North of Palestine and I see a lot of their work, and I am not speaking without knowledge.' However, 'This magnificent material is slowly sliding down the hill. The men are badly looked after and badly housed. Their officers take no interest in them. They (the men) are drinking very heavily.'

Monty blamed the senior personnel – indeed, his criticism was excoriating, as it would be when he took over the defeated 8th Army at Alamein, and 21 Army Group prior to the D-Day landings.

The real trouble is that the senior officers in the Palestine police are utterly and completely useless. Furthermore the organisation is basically unsound; there is no proper chain of command which enables responsibility to be fixed when things go wrong; everyone is imbued with the spirit of 'passing the baby' to someone else. The organisation could of course be put right if the senior officers were any good.

The basic root of the whole trouble is the senior officers. If the Colonial Office want to have a proper and efficient police force in Palestine they will have to make a clean sweep of the present senior officers and bring in some really good men.

Nothing else will be of any use.

If they do not do so the Police Force will continue to deteriorate, and there will always be rows and troubles in Palestine.

The matter is urgent. Strong action requires to be taken at once. There is therefore in my opinion, only one solution to the problem. The present Inspector General of Police should be removed, and Sir Charles Tegart should be made Inspector General in his place.

The latter is a really good man and he must be given a free hand, and a mandate to push out any officers he likes.[7]

This was quintessential Monty, in the aftermath of Betty's death: wildly oversimplifying complex situations, and suggesting simple, draconian solutions that an ailing imperial democracy such as Britain was unfitted to implement, even if the authorities agreed with Monty – which they didn't. Yet the letter – one of a series sent by Monty to General Adam from Palestine – was also a vivid example of Monty's clarity of approach, and his concern with the welfare of ordinary soldiers. He might not be willingly accountable to his superiors – indeed, insubordination would become his second name – but he *was* devoted to his men: and in the coming war, it would be that loyalty and downwards accountability that would make him the most popular field commander in English history. For all his eccentricities and boastful ego, he *cared* about them, ordinary soldiers felt – and in a nation still racked by class-division and snobbery, this would be the sword that cut through the Gordian knot British battle-field failure, and transformed the nation's army.

Breakdown

On 15 March 1939, meanwhile, Hitler's troops marched into Prague and annexed the remainder of the newly independent state of Czechoslovakia. It was clear that, despite Chamberlain's much-vaunted Munich Agreement, the Prime Minister's piece of paper guaranteeing 'peace in our time' was no more than that: a piece of paper. War with Germany was now inevitable.

In April 1939, the Military Secretary at the War Office, Lieutenant-General Brownrigg, wrote to Monty telling him he would be required to take command of the 3rd Division earlier than anticipated, as Major-General Bernard had now been appointed the next governor of Bermuda and was expected to take up his post early that autumn, instead of in December. Four days later Monty wrote back from HQ, 8th Division, Haifa:

My dear Brownie,

Thank you for your letter of 15 April. I had seen that [General] Bernard was to go to Bermuda. I shall be quite ready to come home at any time that you order me; the rebellion out here as an organized movement is smashed; you can go from one end of Palestine to the other looking for a fight and you can't get one; it is very difficult to find Arabs to kill; they have had the stuffing knocked right out of them.

I shall be sorry to leave Palestine in many ways as I have enjoyed the 'war' out here.

But I feel there is a sterner task awaiting me at home.

Next winter's individual training season in England will be a fearfully important time; it will have to be carefully organized on a sound plan. Quite confidentially, between ourselves, I do not think Podge [Bernard] will bother about it; the programme for the winter has to be issued to the troops in August so that all can think ahead and make their plans.

Possibly Podge will take 2 months leave in July. I should like to come home in July and take over the 3rd Division then, so that I can organize and launch the winter training. I could be on leave from here and my successor need not take over here till September. I do not want any leave myself. I am very fit and well and thrive on plenty of work.[8]

These were famous last words – for a week later Monty began to suffer sudden nausea and vomiting, followed by slight gastric symptoms. He ignored them for the moment, and on 19 May 1939 Brownrigg sent him official War Office orders to assume command of 3rd Division in England 'on or about 1st October. It is not possible to state the exact date of the vacancy as that depends on the date that [General] Bernard leaves the United Kingdom for Bermuda.' However, Brownrigg had taken the com-mander-elect's point about winter training, and in the most tactful way he suggested how Montgomery might effect it: '[General] Bernard will probably go on leave for about 2 months before he embarks, and during this period the Division will be commanded by his senior Brigadier. Perhaps if you wish to interest yourself in the affairs of the Division before you take over, you will arrange it unofficially with [General] Bernard. Yours ever, W. D. S. Brownrigg, Lt-General.'[9]

This was a strange way to prepare for war in Europe, but par for the British course. From now on, however, things began to go badly wrong for Monty. On 24 May 1939, after two days of 'dull persistent headache, rising fever and growing weakness in the legs', Major-General Mont-gomery was admitted to the military hospital in Haifa. He was paralysed.

For eleven days Monty lay in hospital while tests were done. There was then a lull, Monty writing to his sister Winsome at Moascar, suggesting he travel to Egypt and spend a week with her and her husband in absolute quiet to recuperate. However, the fever then recurred, with pain in the chest, on 14 June, 'and definite signs of pleurisy on the 18th'. He was treated with M & B (a well-known medication of the time) for thirty-six hours and a series of X-rays were taken of his chest – the fear being that he had collapsed with tuberculosis. On 19 June, the radiologist tendered his report, maintaining that there was 'evidence of tubercular infiltration in the mid-zone of the left lung, with minimal pleural effusion at the base'.[10]

Tuberculosis would, if confirmed, rule out command of the 3rd (Iron) Division in England. At a medical board meeting summoned the next day the senior consultant physician to the British forces in Palestine was called upon to diagnose the case. Despite Monty's fever and the difficulty he had in breathing – he found it impossible (or unwise) even to bring up enough sputum to be analysed for TB – Monty now pulled rank on the lieutenant colonel. Talk of tuberculosis was ridiculous, he said; it was very likely his old war wound that was playing up in the hot, humid climate of Haifa. It was imperative he get home to England to take over the 3rd Division's training programme; he was certain that the sea passage would restore his health.

If Lieutenant-Colonel Marsh was won over it was not on medical grounds – for Monty's war wound had been in his right lung, not his left! Marsh was sceptical, acknowledging in his report that the 'general clinical picture of the case, coupled with X-ray results, are strongly suspicious of the causal organism of the whole illness being the tubercular bacillus, but unless TB are found in the sputum I do not consider tuberculosis should be diagnosed'.[11]

Monty had won. Lieutenant-Colonel Marsh recommended the sick general be invalided back to the UK at once, as a stretcher case, accompanied by two nursing sisters and two male orderlies. The War Office was duly informed. A bed was reserved at the Queen Alexandra Military Hospital, Millbank, London, and permission given for Monty to travel home aboard the next available ship, the SS *Ranchi*, due to sail from Port Said on 3 July.

Sheer guts

How sick was Monty? It is difficult to say. In his own later words to his future daughter-in-law, he had fallen 'very ill in Palestine in April 1939'.[12] This was an admission Monty rarely, if ever, made. He was certainly considered too ill to move from his bed, even to cough up sputum. He had lost significant weight and looked a wreck, yet had persuaded the doctors to delay a definitive diagnosis.

In the event, Monty was considered too ill even to travel by rail to Egypt. He was therefore transported by air with his nursing entourage on 2 July from Haifa direct to Port Said. His sister Winsome was by chance booked to travel home on the same ship; she visited him immediately in the military hospital at Port Said, where she found him 'very white and ill and in bed, unable to walk'. Still finding it difficult to draw breath Monty explained the arrangements that had been made for his passage. He was to have a large cabin, and planned to admit no one during the voyage save Winsome, every morning at 10 a.m. 'The next day, aboard ship, we watched him being put in a carrying chair from the stretcher.'[13]

The journey to England began. 'The ship's doctor came up to me one day,' Winsome recalled, 'and said: "Mrs Holderness, I believe you're the general's sister?" I said, "Yes." "Well, may I have a few words with you?" We walked up and down the deck. He said: "I'm terribly worried about that brother of yours. His lung is in a very bad state. Now, do you mind me asking if anyone in your family has had TB?" And I said, "Yes, I have, very badly indeed and I'm completely cured now. And an aunt – that's all." Anyway, he said, "Well, he hasn't got TB, but his lung's in a very bad state and he thinks he's going to serve in the war that's coming. Well, he's not – he'll never see action."'

Winsome, who saw Monty every day during the voyage, felt her brother's response was simply an act of supreme will. 'I watched Bernard every day with the greatest of interest being carried up on deck, unable to walk; then he'd get out of the chair and he'd walk. He'd walk say the length of this room, and the next day the length of the deck, and in no time at all he was walking round it . . . Well, Bernard got better and better. He wouldn't mix with anyone – wouldn't let anyone come near his cabin. But I think he was beginning to get known, because when we stopped at Malta a launch came out to meet us, and some high official came aboard. When I asked Bernard the next day, he said, "Yes, that was the governor." It was the same at Gibraltar. He wouldn't leave the ship, not even when we got to Casablanca. We just used to sit and chat. It was just sheer guts, will power. He wasn't going to give in. There was the sea air, rest, good food. He had Betty's photographs in the cabin, and two very nice male nurses.

'And then when we got to Tilbury I packed my things and went up to the First Class and asked him, "What are you going to do now, Bernard?"

' "Well, I've got to attend a medical board – but that'll be all right," he said confidently. "I feel as fit as a fiddle."

'I've often wondered what that ship's doctor thought . . .'[14]

Like Lazarus from his bed

The authorities at the Queen Alexandra Military Hospital were equally mystified by Monty's crippling illness – and his apparition at Millbank: like Lazarus rising from his bed. The papers from Egypt had told them to expect a stretcher case; instead in walked a sprightly major-general on 14 July 1939 who 'looks fairly well, says he feels very fit, has no pain in the chest. Temperature normal. Tongue clean. Heart normal. Liver not enlarged.'[15]

Monty was kept at the Millbank hospital for five days while more tests were made; but on 19 July 1939, as no sign of any disability had been found, he was discharged. The pleurisy had vanished and there was no evidence of tubercular infection. In their records the hospital could only state that he had suffered from an 'infection – causal organism unknown'.[16] He was told to take another three weeks' sick leave, and to report for a final medical board on 10 August 1939.

Delighted, Monty went off to stay with his old commandant while at Quetta, Sir Guy Williams, who lived in retirement near Sevenoaks, Kent, while Mrs Carthew-Yarstoun kindly took David with her two children to Wengen in Switzerland for the summer holiday.

Monty was cured, whether of an undiagnosed infection or a psychosomatic breakdown, or both, no one would ever know. But he would live to fight again. If, that was, he could get to command his new division.

In the ranks of the unemployed

From Sevenoaks Monty now began to shell the War Office with letters and telegrams – urging that, in view of the deteriorating situation in Europe, and with German forces assembling on the border with Poland, he be given immediate command of the 3rd (Iron) Division in the absence of General Bernard – who was fishing, in Ireland!

Britain was not alone its unpreparedness. The condition of the United States military was in many ways as bad as that of Britain, as General Dwight D. Eisenhower later recorded. 'When the nation began, in 1939, first steps towards strengthening its military establishment,' he wrote, 'it started from a position as close to zero as a great nation could conceivably have allowed itself to sink': an army of 175,000 men spread across the globe from the Arctic Circle to Corregidor, and a mere 1,500 men in tank units.[17]

In Britain's case war was closer, however, and the day of reckoning was approaching. In March 1939 the Secretary of State for War had announced the doubling of the Territorial Army to 340,000 men, but the military clock which had been stopped in 1919 could not be so simply wound up again. Popular resentment over Haig's bloodletting and the failure of the military's officer class to tackle the need to modernize, and to create an army based on merit rather than class, meant that numbers alone would not suffice. The army was, save for a few exceptions, completely moribund.

Perhaps no incident in the summer of 1939 more typified the military state of the British nation than the muddle over Monty's command of the 3rd (Iron) Division. Monty's former brigade major, now Lieutenant-Colonel Simpson, had returned to the War Office as the new Assistant Military Secretary. He remembered the comic-opera situation well. General D. K. Bernard was busy getting himself 'fit for what he thought was going to be an arduous post', Simpson recalled sarcastically, by going off in July 1939 to Ireland 'on a two-month fishing holiday. So the 3rd Division with HQ at Portsmouth was left without a commander on the spot, and the war clouds were building up fast.' War hinged on Danzig, for, having integrated Austria and Czechoslovakia into the Third Reich, Hitler was determined to reclaim the contentious corridor between Danzig and East Prussia, through Poland. 'The situation,' Simpson related, 'worried Monty, who went down to Portsmouth, took up his quarters in a hotel, and started to run the Division although he was not in any position to do so. I used to get very humorous messages from my predecessor at the War Office, Colonel Morgan [still at Southern Command], as to how the Divisional Commander-to-be was going to upset all the orders given by the Divisional Commander of the day who was not present to argue about them.'

Monty, as Simbo Simpson recalled, 'used to ring me up to say: "This is a monstrous situation. Here we are, getting ready for war, and the man who ought to be getting the Division ready is quietly fishing in Ireland. Can't you get him out?" There was nothing I could do about getting him out. All I could do was to report Monty's wails to my general, the Military Secretary.'[18]

It was a tragi-comic farce in which, until war was actually declared, nothing would be done. General Haining was signalling from Jerusalem to ask whether he could appoint a successor to Montgomery, still technically the GOC 8th Division; Montgomery was busy preparing to retrain the 3rd Division, of which he was still not legally the commander; the former Military Secretary, General Brownrigg, had gone to take command of the TA; and General Bernard sat on a fishing stool in Ireland!

At 11 a.m. on 10 August, at a medical board at the Queen Alexandra Military Hospital, Millbank, Monty was at last declared fit for general duties – i.e. combat; but as the days passed, these duties became even more questionable – for if Britain mobilized, all pending appointments would, by long-standing War Office protocol, be 'frozen', and Monty would lose his promised command of 3 Division.

Mobilization certainly looked daily more inevitable. On 23 August 1939 Germany and Russia concluded their infamous 'non-aggression' pact (permitting both countries to dismember Poland, and Stalin to invade Finland). Having failed to conclude any agreement with Russia, despite the urging of France to do so, Britain, by virtue of its guarantee to Poland, was now left in much the same position as in August 1914, when its guarantee to Belgium, if honoured, necessitated its participation in continental war and débâcle.

Appeasement had manifestly failed. Instead of resigning as Prime Minister, however, Chamberlain decided to hang on to parliamentary power: imagining he could, in extremis, change his mantle, in his seventies, and become a war leader – thus dooming Britain to pay for his neglect of its army for a further year of his own catastrophic leadership.

In this way, on 25 August 1939 Britain duly confirmed its mutual assistance treaty with Poland, similar to its guarantee to Belgium in 1914. It was, in the short term, a meaningless threat which Hitler ridiculed; he merely postponed his military invasion, planned for 25 August, for a few days in order to summon a Polish plenipotentiary to Berlin to see whether Poland would surrender immediately or would fight and be conquered in short shrift. In the case of the latter, however, the two guarantors of Polish independence, France and Britain, would be dragged into world war with the Third Reich.

European hostilities now hung in the balance, but at Portsmouth there was great embarrassment. A successor – Brigadier A. R. Godwin Austen – had been appointed on 23 August to take over the 8th Division in Palestine; meanwhile, General D. K. Bernard was due to return from his fishing holiday and would find a usurper trying to take command of his division. Frantically Montgomery – officially now unemployed and on half pay – telephoned the War Office, as Simpson recalled.

Monty rang me up in a state of great perturbation from Portsmouth to ask what was going on. I had no difficulty about explaining the rule about cancellation of appointments [on mobilization], and he then asked what was to happen to himself. I replied that he would be put into the pool of Major-Generals for a future appointment, and I was certain a very good one would be found for him in due course.

Monty was incensed at this and said: 'Here is a Division getting ready for battle and it has no Divisional Commander at all. It is just drifting aimlessly at the moment. It has got a good staff but the Divisional Commander is enjoying himself in Ireland. I will get on to the GOC Southern Command [Lieutenant-General Alan Brooke] and tell him it is all nonsense.'

I went and reported all this at once to the new Military Secretary, who just grinned and said nothing – he felt he could do nothing about this particular appointment.

I discovered afterwards that Monty had got on to Alan Brooke. However, although Alan Brooke said that he would see what he could do, Monty was told to go away somewhere and stay in the [unemployed] pool.[19]

A near-run thing

Fortunately for Monty, General Brooke, as area or corps commander, was just as concerned as Monty over the poor state of readiness for war of the 3rd Division. General Bernard 'was on leave and had taken little interest in the training of the Division in those dark days prior to the War', Brooke later recalled.[20] It seemed the height of idiocy for the War Office to cancel Montgomery's appointment and recall Major-General Bernard. Brooke therefore called Sir George Giffard, the new Military Secretary.

'Giffard took Brooke's strictures very calmly and then said he wanted to sit down quietly and think for a period,' Simpson remembered.

He had a mischievous grin on his face and I wondered what he was thinking. I very soon discovered. He was, of course, well known in the Colonial Office (he had spent most of his military career serving in East and West Africa) and he decided he would go over and see them. He saw one or two of the very senior civil servants and I think the Colonial Secretary. He came back with a written request to the Secretary of State for War from the Colonial Secretary to say that they understood the reasons of the War Office for wanting General Bernard to take the 3rd Division to France; but the Colonial Secretary would like to feel that the interests of the Empire were more important than those of the British Army and that the Empire was unlikely to play its full part in the war unless this distinguished soldier, General Bernard, was allowed by the War Office to go to take up his post as Governor of Bermuda. General Giffard showed this to the Secretary of State for War [Hore-Belisha], who said, 'Of course we must allow that. Get someone else to command the 3rd Division at once.' I then had the great joy of ringing up Monty, who had just arrived at Sevenoaks [home of General Guy Williams], and ordering him on behalf of the Military Secretary to return to Portsmouth at once and take command of the 3rd Division.[21]

Brooke had got what he wanted, and so had Monty. Telegrams were despatched from the War Office ordering Major-General Montgomery to take command of the 3rd Division with effect from 28 August 1939.

It was a near-run thing. Only days later, on 1 September 1939, Hitler ordered his postponed invasion of Poland to proceed. The British army mobilized officially at 2 p.m. that day. After two further days of hesitation, the British government declared war on Germany at 11 a.m. on 3 September 1939, to be followed, at 5 p.m., by France. World War II had begun.

BOOK II

THE YEARS OF DEFEAT

11

Dunkirk

A nation on trial

In declaring war on Nazi Germany Britain had kicked off, belatedly and reluctantly, with men in power who were beyond their sell-by date, or who – like Liddell Hart – had lost faith in themselves and their ability to fight a first-class enemy bent on total war, with all its technologies of destruction.

But as Monty also knew from his time in Palestine, no matter how strong the Luftwaffe, how fearsome Hitler's armoured divisions and however inspiring the Nazis' racist ideology, Germany would not necessarily be able to win a prolonged second global war, any more than the Kaiser's Germany had been in 1914–18. Britain had a wealth of younger officers and men ('the war out here is the most magnificent training for the army and the RAF and we are producing seasoned fighting men who are second to none' he'd written from Palestine[1]) – who would fight well, if well led.

Monty the trainer was determined they would be. Whether Britain would lose the war before his turn came, was far less certain.

The Belgian ostrich

Whatever the guarantee given by the British government to Poland, there was never the remotest British intention to help the Poles by sending ground forces to the Baltic. As in 1914, the British Expeditionary Force was earmarked to cross the Channel and help France. Once there it would become part of the Anglo-French armies defending western, not central, Europe: indeed, it would be stationed on the Franco-Belgian border once again, in anticipation of another German invasion via the Low Countries.

This time, unfortunately, Belgium – ravaged in World War I – wanted no help or guarantees; in fact the Belgian government obstinately but understandably refused to enter into any military negotiations with the Western Allies that might irritate an irascible, even demented leader of Germany's Third Reich, and even declined to permit French or British military personnel to reconnoitre possible defence lines should the country be invaded by the Nazis.

Thus, ostrich-like, Belgium doomed itself either to a swift German juggernaut-conquest, or to a messy, unreconnoitred encounter battle between Germans and Franco-Belgian-British forces within its borders, if attacked and compelled belatedly to ask for Allied help. It was a recipe for defeat.

Britain's misfortune

Belgium's misfortune was thus to be a small nation on the most direct German path to the Channel seaports and north-west France, lacking the means to defend itself. Britain's misfortune was to be a once-'great' power, standing in Hitler's way to Nazi hegemony in Europe, but without the military means or ability to stop Hitler – and lacking a Prime Minister capable of inspiring confidence that Britain could ever do so.

First, however, Hitler had to crush Poland, before readying his forces for a decisive campaign in the west.

The fall of Poland

In the ensuing, tragic weeks Poland perished without a British shot being fired, leaving Hitler's forces free to deal with the 1.8 million Polish Jews (indeed, with any Polish 'subhumans', as Hitler called them) who posed an obstacle to the transformation of Poland into a slave state.

In France, meanwhile, the BEF was put in the hands of arguably the bravest but most incompetent British army commander of the twentieth century: Lord Gort VC – a general whose limitations were to be exceeded only by those of his French and Belgian counterparts, who proved not only as incompetent in command as Gort, but cowards into the bargain.

Monty's own iron determination as a British battlefield commander would be forged against the pitiful example of Lord Gort and so many British, French and Belgian officers over the following eight months leading up to the catastrophe of Dunkirk – indeed, it is impossible to understand Monty's performance in World War II without understanding both the run-up to Dunkirk and the evacuation itself. In his memoirs Monty later magnanimously gave credit to Gort for ordering the helter-skelter evacuation of the BEF in 1940, even without their weapons or equipment, rather than permitting the BEF to continue to remain a pawn in French military fantasyland; but in private he believed Gort's performance to have been a mockery of British army command in the field: an object lesson in how *not* to lead a modern army. To the very last days of World War II, the memory of Dunkirk would rankle. Together with his personal misfortune in losing his beloved Betty, it would be the desire to avenge the British army's utter and ignominious defeat at Dunkirk that made Montgomery become such a ruthless field commander, unwilling to take unwarranted risks. For him there would be no easy scapegoats, such as the weight of German armour, the failure of Britain's allies, or the paucity or inappropriateness of British arms. What he witnessed between September 1939 and June 1940 would be engraved for ever on his memory: a lamentable British army commander; appalling communications; complete mismanagement.

Dunkirk, in Monty's eyes, would come to signify the end of the road for British amateurism, the final catastrophe for a nation and an officer class that had been unwilling to take the conduct of modern warfare seriously.

Littering the roads of France

The story of the BEF in 1939–40 proved, behind the scenes, far worse than that of 1914. Already, on the morning of 3 September 1939, Monty had listened with disappointment to Chamberlain's broadcast to the nation, and his heart had sunk. 'I was not inspired,' he candidly recalled, 'nor would anyone have been who heard him. How differently would Churchill have spoken!'[2] Worse still, with Chamberlain's blessing, the Minister of War, Leslie Hore-Belisha, had summoned Lord Gort that day from his office as CIGS, and had asked him, with the Prime Minister's approval, to be the new BEF commander – indeed, had put him under the orders of the French commander-in-chief of the north-east theatre of operations.

Given Gort's limited intelligence and the incompetence and rivalries in the French high command, this was disturbing. 'One only has to read [Gort's] instructions signed by Hore-Belisha, and dated 3-9-39 to know what he was in for,' Monty later commented; 'that directive is a pretty fair commentary on the [Allied] command set-up and it required a much better brain than Gort's to deal with such a complicated problem'[3] – a problem compounded by the need for Gort to act both as administrative C-in-C of British forces in France and as army commander.

In the meantime, while Hitler's forces subdued the Poles, a series of trains bore the initial 10,000 men of the 3rd (Iron) Division and its officers to Southampton on the morning of 29 September 1939. Embarkation began at 10.30 a.m., and just before midnight the fleet sailed, arriving at Cherbourg the next morning. Monty had wisely taken a War Office Humber Snipe with him. This was fortunate, for hundreds of miles away the division's road transport was unloaded at Brest – and provided a sorry sight.

'We were short of drivers for our own vehicles, and more and more arrived every day, including requisitioned civilian trucks, laundry vans, etc.,' one officer remembered. 'They were all makes and sizes and still had "Swindon Steam Laundry" etc. painted on. We painted them all dark green ... [A] crash course was organized to train about one hundred drivers in a week. Very few men could drive in 1939, and so they had to start from square one.'[4]

Upon unloading in Brest it was found that French dockers had managed to open and pilfer every officer's locked car boot, as well as forcing open many of the doors of the division's impressed laundry vans. The chief problem, however, was not theft but the sheer variety of manufacturers, the age of the vehicles and the shortage of spare parts. 'Naturally, firms sent their own vehicles and the spare-part problem for so many types was beyond us. When we landed in France and drove to the Belgian border the roads of France were littered with these broken down vehicles.'[5]

It was an inauspicious beginning for Britain's 3rd (Iron) Motorized Division – though things would get far, far worse.

An amazing layout

On 3 October 1939, without road transport and having travelled in cattle-trucks as in 1914, the men of 3 Division arrived in the line equipped with only what they carried. It was very much how they would leave, at Dunkirk.

The 3rd Division's allotted sector was a defensive area south of Lille – the city Monty had liberated in 1918 – offering a single anti-tank ditch as its sole obstacle to enemy penetration. Had the Germans invaded France then, as Brooke noted in his diary, it would have been a walkover.[6]

Hitler had similar thoughts. In a conversation with the German army's chief of staff, General Halder, on 27 September 1939 (the last day of Polish resistance), Hitler – who had been stunned by the success of his own armoured divisions – urged an immediate assault on northern France, through Holland and Belgium, in the manner of the Schlieffen plan carried out in 1914, but on wheels and tracks, not trains and foot. Not only would this act as a pre-emptive strike, before the French could do the reverse and invade the Ruhr, but even if, as in 1914, it led to stalemate, it would ensure North Sea and Channel bases for German U-boats as well as aerodromes for the Luftwaffe. 'Essential that immediate plans for an attack against France be prepared,' Halder recorded in his diary that day.[7] Hitler's views were intuitive: 'Doubt the estimated French strength. No preparation for mobile war . . . French have less value than the Poles . . . The English are deciders.'[8]

Hitler was overestimating the English. The British official history skated over the 'phoney war' in France, devoting only a handful of pages to the eight-month war of waiting. Equally, many historians, including Lord Gort's biographer, have assumed that, in the absence of British armoured divisions, the BEF was doomed from the start – Gort himself declaring, when informed in the winter of 1939 that the Germans had ten armoured divisions poised for attack in the west: 'In that case we haven't an earthly chance.'[9]

Yet, for the officers and men who were seriously engaged in preparing the BEF for war, the result was by no means a foregone conclusion, and the war was by no means 'phoney'. Given trained and resourceful defensive tactics, tanks were not unstoppable; given skilful generalship the Germans could be lured on to unfavourable ground and exposed to a long campaign for which, as Hitler himself acknowledged, Germany was neither materially nor politically well suited. If the BEF and its allies could be trained to face both infantry and armoured assault, and be commanded by officers of adequate calibre, the chances of swift success for the Germans were not beyond question. It was this vital, eight-month respite (Hitler had quoted a maximum period of ten months to Halder) before German invasion that gave the Allies a chance to prepare for war in the west, in the manner of Wellington during the Peninsular War – a chance they had not had in 1914.

Yet, having virtually emptied the War Office of senior officers to serve with him at his headquarters in the BEF ('It is almost unbelievable that such a thing should have been allowed to happen,' Monty noted in his draft memoirs[10]) Gort loyally placed himself under overall command of the French; indeed, permitted himself to be given a subordinate role in the French military hierarchy not much superior to that of a junior corps commander. Worse still, he approved a French scheme, devised by the Supreme Allied Commander General Gamelin, whereby the entire British Expeditionary Force would, in the event of German invasion of Belgium, relinquish its own prepared defences on the French border and, with both its strategic armoured reserve (the 7th French Army) and the 1st French Army on the BEF's right flank, meet the Germans on unreconnoitred ground of the latter's choosing in Belgium – leaving the Germans to attack the Allied rear from the east!

Aware of Gamelin's plan to move deep into Belgium, this is exactly what the Germans, altering their autumn plans, would do: Operation Sichelschnitt.

Gort's two subordinate corps commanders, Lieutenant-Generals Brooke and Dill, both objected to the Gamelin plan, but were ignored by Gort. Moreover, in his anxiety over possible German aerial attack, Gort decided to split his headquarters at Arras into an untidy and incohesive bureaucracy with disparate messes, spread across '13 villages covering an area of some 50 square miles', as Monty noted with retrospective disgust. 'This dispersed system called for a cumbersome network of communications. It was difficult to know where anyone was and command from the top suffered from the very beginning. It was an amazing layout.'[11] Even verbal communication between British commanders was lacking, since Gort refused to discuss with Dill and Brooke the military tactics he would pursue once the planned advance into Belgium took place.

Most shocking of all, during the entire eight months Gort had in which to prepare his headquarters for the campaign, he never once conducted an administrative, signals, intelligence or even staff movement exercise! As Monty commented, 'the need for wireless silence was given as an excuse; but an indoor exercise on the model could easily have been held. The result was a total lack of any common policy or tactical doctrine throughout the BEF'[12] – a criticism which was fully supported by Gort's chief supply officer. 'What you have said about Lord Gort ... is to my mind absolutely fair,' Lieutenant-Colonel Bridgeman later wrote to Monty. 'And what you have said about his running no GHQ exercise strikes at the root of the whole of his relationship with Dill and Brooke. To have run such an exercise would have inevitably resulted in Gort's having to give his casting vote on some difference of opinion between those two Commanders and that, as I was well aware at the time, he did not want to do.'[13]

Gort's eventual performance in May 1940 would be played down and, to a large extent, excused by successive government apologists and even independent historians, who preferred to blame Britain's deficient arms, her disastrous allies and the brilliance of German strategic and tactical generalship. However, these excuses only serve, as they did in 1940, to obfuscate a simpler and more worrying truth: that Britain put into the field in Europe in 1939 an army that was not only ill equipped, but monstrously ill led, from Lord Gort down to individual battalion commanders and regimental officers – an army doomed to fail wherever it fought the Germans, irrespective of equipment or allies.

Gort's brain

'Monty despised Lord Gort,' Field-Marshal Templer later snarled, when asked, '– and I despised Monty for despising Lord Gort!'[14] Yet Monty did not despise Gort; he felt he had simply been promoted way above his capabilities. The price was paid in British blood – Gort's failure to prepare for modern battle proving fatal for many thousands of British soldiers. The fawning view of Gort's biographer Colville – who had been Neville Chamberlain's private secretary and proud admirer – that Lord Gort would have made a brilliant 8th Army commander in action against Rommel in the desert Monty found typical of the Establishment. Gort would, he was certain, have been trounced by Rommel in half a day. His appointment to command the BEF itself had been a farce – Hore-Belisha, in a bid to rid himself of the very CIGS he had himself appointed, personally making Lord Gort the commander-in-chief! 'He was unfitted for the job – and we senior officers all knew it,' Monty wrote later in *The Path to Leadership*; 'he loved detail and couldn't see the wood for the trees.'[15] Brooke was even more caustic at the time. 'Gort's brain has lately been compared with that of a glorified boy-scout!' he noted in his diary on 21 November 1939. 'Perhaps unkind, but there is a great deal of truth in it.'[16]

By contrast General Brooke, Monty's II Corps commander, had a magisterial capacity for seeing the wood, and Monty was undoubtedly immensely privileged to have him as his corps commander. Indeed, Brooke's example would in many ways be the model for his own conduct as a commander for the rest of the war: a strategist of decisive intellect and professionalism. Yet it is important also to stress their differences, since Brooke was later mortified – as General Marshall would be, in Washington – by Churchill and the War Cabinet's decision not to ask him to command the Allied armies for the D-Day landings in 1944.

Brooke was certainly an immensely professional corps commander in the field; however, he had no rapport with his men, and belonged very much to the World War I school of remote command. He had no gift of personal communication, was taciturn, private and unapproachable. Like General Marshall in the United States, he commanded men by earning respect among senior officers for his intellect and decisiveness, rather than for tactical originality, innovativeness, or ability to command offensive operations where leadership of men – of junior officers and soldiers – was required. Brooke would be knighted for his performance in the retreat to Dunkirk, asked to command the second BEF thereafter, was soon given command of all Home Forces in Britain, and eventually made CIGS under Churchill; but his gifts remained those of a strategist, administrator and astute critic of others: superiors, allies and subordinates. As a staff general in the highly professional German Wehrmacht, he would have made an excellent officer; but in the business of transforming the morale of amateurish democratic forces, especially citizen forces, of a decaying empire into battle-winning armies he belonged to a past era – and, for all his perspicacity, failed to recognize Monty's genius for field command until it was almost too late.

Putting cigarettes behind their ears

Already in October 1939 Brooke was worrying in his diary about 'the turnout' of Monty's men when visiting Lille – indeed, he immediately insisted Monty issue a personal memorandum on 'Discipline' to every officer in 3 Division above the rank of major, calling upon soldiers to salute military cars carrying senior officers, NCOs to be less slack in 'calling men to attention when a senior officer appears' and men to stop putting 'cigarettes behind their ears'.[17] From the desk of Field-Marshal Haig such an instruction would not have come amiss; but in a war against trained Nazi forces, the insistence on respect to be shown to superior officers smacked of Victorian-Edwardian privilege, not of the need for a new form of democratic leadership.

Monty thought such matters to be trivial compared with the urgent need to prepare proper defences, get down to battle training and ensure the assimilation of reservists. '[R]eservists had to be trained in the Bren gun, 2" and 3" mortar, carrier, and as M.T. drivers,' one infantry officer recalled; more 'specialists, assault pioneers, signallers, D.R.s etc.' were urgently required; also 'platoons and companies had to be worked up as teams, as old reservists with long service were mixed up with young soldiers from the Depot, many commanded by Officers and N.C.O.s they had never seen or served under before'.[18]

Brooke, an artilleryman, did not really understand the intricacies of infantry warfare. Worse still, he was a dreadful prude – a strict Northern-Irish Protestant, with a nineteenth-century outlook on sex. Thus when, in November 1939, Lord Gort complained about an order Monty had given to his division, Brooke as corps commander behaved like a maiden aunt: the so-called 'VD affair'.

An urgent tactical problem

George S. Patton would, in 1943, be removed from battle command for conduct unbecoming to a senior commander in the field: slapping and threatening with a pistol to shoot shell-shocked GIs in a forward field hospital. Such misconduct went to the root of democratic warfare – the accountability of senior officers, particularly towards their own men. But

Monty's near-removal from field command in the 'phoney war' in 1939 seems, when viewed sixty years later, something so comic it is hard to credit: particularly in the context of Hitler's imminent invasion of western Europe.

Hitler had intended to launch his initial attack through Holland and Belgium, on 12 November 1939. Owing to bad weather the attack was postponed to 26 November. ('The violation of Belgian and Dutch neutrality is unimportant,' Hitler had told his assembled generals *in camera*. 'Nobody will ask about such things after we have won.'[19] Expecting combat to begin at any moment, Monty's troops had therefore been put on three-hour *alerte*. Thus, when told of an urgent visit to be paid to him by General Brooke on 23 November, Monty thought he was to be let in on secret orders regarding the Allied move from prepared positions into unreconnoitred Belgium.

He received a rude awakening. 'I did not know about the storm which was blowing up,' Monty later recalled, 'and when I received a message that the Corps Commander was coming to see me, and I was to remain in until he arrived, I thought in my innocence that some urgent tactical problem was to be discussed. I was mistaken! He arrived, and I could tell by the look on his face and his abrupt manner that I was "for it" – and I was right. He let drive for about ten minutes, and I listened.'[20]

Favours in the beetroot fields

Brooke did not mince his words. Despite the likelihood of German invasion in the next hours or days 'I pointed out to Monty that his position as Commander of a Division had been seriously affected by the issue of such a document,' Brooke recorded in his diary on the night of 23 November, 'and could certainly not withstand any further errors of this kind.'[21]

Monty could scarcely believe the corps commander was being serious. Parties of 3 Division's men had been permitted for some time to go on weekend leave and enjoy 'horizontal refreshment' in Lille, where the brothels were clean and regularly inspected, but by 15 November more than forty new cases of VD had been reported – and the figure was rising sharply. On making enquiries Monty had found his men were subsidizing the local country girls for favours 'in the beetroot fields'; he had therefore promulgated a divisional order on the subject.

As Monty later confessed, he'd been rather proud of this effort which, in a time of continuing English sexual hypocrisy, struck a refreshingly modern, sensible and candid note. Perhaps Monty's exclusive interest in men made it possible for him to be candid and objective regarding their heterosexual needs; certainly there was no suggestion that the 3rd Division's commander was arguing from his own libertine motives, since he was known to be in all respects an abstemious and strictly moral individual.

Monty's 'mistake', however, was to issue the five-point order under his own name. Although operational messages often took days to get to the appropriate officer at GHQ, a copy of the VD order was passed immediately on 16 November to the senior BEF chaplain in Arras – who demanded Lord Gort take punitive action.

Gort, as has been seen, was envious of Monty. He had recently witnessed a major four-day exercise by 3 Division – but had declined to order a similar rehearsal either of movement or of communications at GHQ. As a result of the chaplain's complaint, however, he had swung into immediate action – insisting, via the adjutant-general of the BEF, that Monty publicly withdraw the document, just as Patton was forced later to apologize for his behaviour in Sicily before his own men.

Though commander-in-chief of the BEF, Gort was wary of disciplining a divisional commander directly, however. Brooke, as Monty's superior officer, was therefore told he must make Monty publicly withdraw the order. To do so, however, would have meant making Monty's position in the division impossible, Brooke felt. 'I should have been forced to withdraw Monty from his division and to send him home,' Brooke later noted.[22]

Given the impending German invasion, Brooke had therefore insisted that as corps commander he should be permitted to deal with the problem in his own way.

Could Monty's military career really have been put at risk over a VD document, in the middle of a world war – indeed when the Allied armies were on *alerte*? Monty decided it must be a joke, and assumed Brooke was merely speaking 'officially' on behalf of Lord Gort. As he later recalled the confrontation with Brooke: 'When he had run out of words he became calmer, and even smiled. I then plucked up courage and said I reckoned my circular letter was rather a good one, and extremely clear. That finished it; he began again and I received a further blasting.'[23]

If a man wants to have a woman

To Monty's incredulity, Brooke was in complete earnest. 'I informed him that I had a very high opinion of his military capabilities and an equally low one of his literary ones!' Brooke recorded in the published version of his diary;[24] the unpublished version reveals that he thought Monty's efforts downright 'obscene',[25] and in his 'Notes on My Life' written a decade later he still maintained that 'the language in which this document had been written had to be seen to be believed'.[26]

'My view is that if a man wants to have a woman,' Monty had written in the order, 'let him do so by all means: but he must use his common sense and take the necessary precautions against infection – otherwise he becomes a casualty by his own neglect, and this is helping the enemy.' Monty's solution was straightforward. The battalion COs must address the men frankly, condoms must be on sale in the NAAFI shop and sexual hygiene promoted. The cleaner brothels in Lille must be extolled, and the men taught the French for 'French letter' (*capot anglais*) in case they wished to buy one in a French shop. 'We must face up to the problem, be perfectly frank about it,' Monty had concluded his order 'and do all we can to help the soldier in this very difficult matter.'[27]

Brooke was and remained thereafter disgusted. From his point of view as an old-fashioned corps commander and deeply religious man, he could not understand how a promising and dedicated general could put at risk his whole military career for the sake of a matter that was the prerogative of the medical or even religious staff. He thus failed to recognize the very distinctiveness of Monty's approach to command: his genuine and personal sense of responsibility for every area of his men's welfare – military, spiritual and sexual.

Victorian attitudes

In this sense Brooke did not then understand, nor ever later understood, Monty's revolutionary style of command. After his first wife's death in a motoring accident, Brooke had remarried – choosing (like Monty) the widow of a Dardanelles victim, Lady Lees. Brooke's love for Benita Lees was every bit as devoted as Monty's had been for Betty, but it was far more seriously religious. Widow and widower read the Bible together, and tried to read the same passages simultaneously when apart.[28]

Monty could only puzzle over Brooke's Victorian attitudes. Betty had fully concurred with his own efforts, when commanding the Royal Warwickshire 1st Battalion in Alexandria, to ensure both the availability of 'horizontal refreshment' for officers and men in Alexandria and the monitoring of sexual hygiene. As Monty wrote in retrospect, however: 'I have since come to the conclusion that it is better to remain silent on such occasions and take all that comes to you.'[29]

What was coming, however, was far more serious than a carpeting over VD prevention.

General of love

In the event, Monty's reputation did not suffer – though a rude ditty circulated in 3 Division, referring to Monty as the 'General of Love'.[30] Monty did not mind; the important thing was that the incidence of venereal disease 'ceased',[31] so that he felt quietly vindicated. Brooke, casting his mind back to the occasion in his later 'Notes on My Life', was especially pleased at the outcome. 'I never ceased to thank Heaven that I saved Monty at this danger point in his career,' Brooke congratulated himself. 'I should never have had the opportunities that I had in 1940 to estimate his true value, and should probably have remained ignorant of them and consequently failed to recommend him for command of the 8th Army in the Middle East.'[32]

As will be seen, Brooke would be less than insistent in recommending Monty for command of the 8th Army. Meanwhile, that the military career of the finest trainer in the British army could be put on the line over a VD pamphlet is perhaps the ultimate reflection of Britain's inability to wage democratic war against a modern enemy in the autumn of 1939. As Brooke's biographer summarized, Brooke considered Monty a worrying eccentric, 'prone to egotism, to misjudgment in personal matters, as tending to say foolish and impetuous things'.[33] In this Brooke was wholly correct. But in 1939 Britain, where 'proper' behaviour by officers counted for a great deal more than professional ability in battle, Gort's and Brooke's attitude to the 'VD affair' typified all that was wrong about Britain and its armed forces. Politicians favoured pliable generals, while the generals themselves relied on an old-boy solidarity and old-fashioned values to see them through, rather than modern professionalism and a new approach to command of ordinary soldiers in a modern democracy – thus failing their subordinate officers and their men.

In this sense the antiquated British political and military class structure of the 1930s expressed itself all too shamefully in its army: an old-fashioned, privilege-obsessed imperial élite, pitted against an implacably rearming, anti-democratic enemy gearing itself for modern 'total war'. Worse still, the British officer élite continued to rely on its own version of 'natives' and 'navvies': working-class English soldiers, as in World War I, who would be willing to do as they were told, like sheep, even to the point of suicidal casualties in battle.

Times, however, had changed. While regular soldiers were obedient, the general citizenry from whom reservists, Territorials and conscripts would be drawn resented the suicidal sacrifices made to no purpose in World War I. The betrayal of the soldiers' right to expect good leadership, as Norman Dixon wrote, had 'terminated for all time the hitherto reverential and blind faith which troops had in their generals'.[34] In this final confrontation between modern militarism and an old-fashioned army structure based on class and respect, Monty's superiors seemed to miss the point – still unable or unwilling to credit the need for a new approach to the relationship between leader and the led in a democracy at war.

Inertia and class

Monty's own approach was very simple, yet it would be wholly ignored by every British official historian of the war, and by most military writers thereafter.

Though Brooke was disgusted by Monty's attitude to sex, he was impressed by Monty's secret weapon. In his retrospective 'Notes on My Life' he remarked that 'it was a matter of the greatest interest watching Monty improving every day as he found his feet as a commander'[35] as Monty inculcated a new professionalism among his men by practising and refining the art of rehearsal.

To beat the Germans, as Monty already knew from World War I, it was necessary to prepare troops for modern combat – as Germans had been doing for years. Young Germans were encouraged by the National Socialists to be obedient but also, in the armed forces under compulsory military service, to show initiative, especially at NCO level. Training was not a bad word, as in England, but the basis for all effective performance.

The British army, by contrast, remained dedicated to caste-distinction, avoidance of hard work, and 'bellyaching' as Monty called it – finding reasons for not doing as one is ordered. Not only was Monty's predecessor addicted to fly-fishing, but he had done almost nothing to train the 3rd Division – a division composed not only of regular troops, but of reservists who had to be assimilated. The key to making a British division into an effective orchestra of war was, he maintained, not athletic training, or small-arms training, but rehearsal: predicting what might happen in battle, and rehearsing the division for it, in advance.

To achieve this, a commander must write his own script: namely, how he intended to fight his future battle. After that he must rehearse his officers and men, until the equivalent of word-perfect. Some might baulk at this; others – jealous colleagues, allies, or, later, British and American military historians – might scoff, and accuse Monty of ponderousness in comparison with the *Fitzerspitzengefühle* of a Rommel or Patton. But neither Rommel nor Patton would be able to achieve battlefield success without well-trained, well-commanded troops, troops brought up to disregard class and who were able and willing to exercise initiative in the field. The problem in Britain was inertia and class: millstones of the British nation throughout the first three decades of the twentieth century, and ones that threatened to bring down its democracy altogether when threatened by a German Reich in which the various elements and strata of its society had been relentlessly indoctrinated by Nazi propaganda, welded to Hitler's task – and in which dissenting voices were silenced by force.

The formula for success

Monty, beginning World War II as a divisional commander in 1939, could not change Britain's disastrous social and political disability. What he *could* do was invent a new approach to democratic command that overcame the debilitating effects of English class and the British army's caste system – permitting each man to participate effectively in the output of the democratic orchestra in battle.

Thus, while it might be impossible to make 'lower-class' lions learn to show the kind of personal initiative that comes with a relatively classless or meritocratic society, it was possible, he believed, to retrain British donkeys – the officers – to become professionals: thinking officers. To achieve this, the first thing to do was to set down the rationale of battle and the objectives he hoped to achieve. The second was to explain clearly how such objectives were to be met – verbally and in writing. And thirdly, by training officers and men to work together towards common goals, Monty hoped to create a new social compact on the battlefield, a compact in which soldiers respected their leaders not as class-superiors but as professionally competent NCOs and officers: a compact in which soldiers would be, once again, willing to fight and if necessary to die – not out of blind obedience, as in World War I, but because their loyalty upwards was matched by modern professionalism and accountability downwards.

Monty's formula for inculcating such professionalism, honed over almost a quarter of a century, was thus to turn the concept of battle into a democratic challenge: deciding in advance those operations which a unit or formation would have to carry out in war, and rehearsing them at all stages from the initial sand-table to signals exercises, vehicle movement and full-scale manoeuvres involving artillery, engineers, mechanized cavalry, machine-gun companies and medics. By this method officers learned what worked and what did not, in mock-battle scenarios and conditions, while the soldiers practised those movements, co-operations and skills that they would be called upon to perform in actual combat.

Intelligent rehearsal – i.e., rehearsals which accurately and imaginatively predicted the form the battle would most likely take – thus became the cornerstone of Monty's command.

In the years that followed this formula would offer the British army a way of succeeding in battle that would, once implemented on a wider scale, overcome the inherent disadvantages of the army's hidebound caste structure as well as the ruinously class-divided, 'bolshie', indolent citizenry from which English soldiers came: a battle-winning formula which Monty invented and perfected for the democracies, yet a formula which, as will be seen, the élites within the democracies were, until the eleventh hour, loath to use.

Simulating future battle

Alone among divisional commanders on the Western Front, Monty used the 'phoney war' period to prepare his division for the battle it would actually have to fight. He objected fiercely to the new 'Gort Line' of concrete gun-emplacements, designed to stretch the Maginot line along the Franco-Belgian border – especially if, as the French plan decreed, the BEF was to move into Belgium once the Germans invaded. Forced to comply with the GHQ directive on pillbox construction (see below), Monty therefore focused the main attention of his division on rehearsals for the *real* battle that would take place in Belgium, if the Germans invaded. From the moment 3 Division took up its positions in France in October 1939, then, Monty began planning a series of divisional rehearsals and exercises to practise signal communications, vehicle movement, artillery support, seizing of key bridges and installations, leapfrogging of units, as well as infantry fighting by day, and movement by night – when the German air forces could not operate.

Because the front-line divisional area was too small for this, Monty sought and got permission to commandeer roads and waterlines to the rear of 3 Division. He sacked all officers he felt were too old or obstinate to cope with the sort of *blitzkrieg* war reported from Poland, and wrote the scenarios and training exercise orders entirely himself. His surviving notes for these exercises testify to the realism he was determined to cultivate, with units leapfrogging through each other, and officers and troops practising a 'proper system of adequate reliefs for rest and sleep'.

Both Gort and Brooke watched Monty's first four-day exercise at the end of October 1939, rehearsing motorized movement of the entire division by night, marches by day and even a 'telephone battle' simulating the progress reports and issuing of orders during the four-day period. Brooke was amazed by Monty's clarity and determination, he wrote later; but it would be March of the following year, six months later, before Brooke got his other division – General Johnson's 4th Division – to carry out its first exercise, the quality of which, Brooke noted, was lamentable.

Chamberlain's imbecility

Lord Gort was even less interested in replicating Monty's methods, either at his own headquarters or throughout the BEF, for he was increasingly involved in biting the hand that had fed him since 1937, rather than preparing to fight the Germans. In this respect he would be able to boast of one final victory before his own ignominious battlefield defeat: the dismissal of the Jewish Secretary of State for War, Leslie Hore-Belisha.

A thin-skinned, vain and egotistical politician, Leslie Hore-Belisha was aware – as he admitted to Liddell Hart – that he was making mistake after mistake, but he had no idea himself how to prepare an army for modern war, or what kind of war to expect, despite the examples of Spain and Poland. The lack of tanks – indeed the lack of a single British armoured division for the BEF, even by the spring of 1940 – was a terrible indictment both of Hore-Belisha and of the nation which had invented the tank; but the lack of effective anti-tank weapons (the two-pounder gun was unable to penetrate any but the thinnest armour) was even more depressing. Calling for more pillboxes – especially when the French were set upon a strategy of advancing deep into Belgium once Hitler invaded – was to hoist himself with his own petard.

Stupidly, after a visit to the BEF in France in December 1939, Hore-Belisha made a rash and completely unwarranted claim, in public and to the Army Council: that British troops were not building pillboxes as fast as the French, with the implication that the British were therefore less energetic in preparing to fight the Germans than their continental allies. This was statistically and morally untrue, and Gort decided to prove it so. Thus, thanks to Gort's protest, the very man who had given Gort command of the BEF was, within a few weeks of his visit to France, replaced by Oliver Stanley.

Hore-Belisha had none the less sensed that something was wrong; it was just that he was too ignorant, in military terms, to know what it was. The truth was, not only were the French not building pillboxes at a faster rate than the British, but the bulk of their armies, as General Brooke soon realized, had no real intention of fighting the Germans – in France or in Belgium. Not only were the French soldiers he saw 'disgruntled and insubordinate', but their anti-tank defences – ditches with no provision for covering fire – were scandalously poor. As Brooke's biographer Sir David Fraser noted, Hitler's estimate of the 'inertia and cowardice of the

French' was all too warranted.[36] World War I had ended for ever the reputation of Napoleon's armies and *les poilus*. The post-World War I political system, with its endless factions and musical chairs, was unable to match the revolutionary spirit and social, economic and military coercion of the dictators. The fact was, the continual change of French governments, the internecine sparring between ambitious generals, and the feeling among veterans and their families that the Great War had been a worthless sacrifice of human life, left very little hope that France would fight as hard or as cohesively as in World War I.

Whether the British soldiery would fight under a Prime Minister like Neville Chamberlain was equally questionable, however. On 16 December 1939, during a visit to the 3rd Division, Chamberlain murmured quietly to Monty: 'I don't think the Germans have any intention of attacking us, do you?'[37]

German plans

Chamberlain's obtuseness defies retrospective belief. Given his access to secret military intelligence – with ample evidence of Hitler's plans for an attack on the West, postponed only because of bad weather that would militate against full use of his air and armoured forces – Chamberlain's remark to Monty was extraordinary. It was all the more reprehensible in that it was made to a British general trying to prepare his division for imminent battle. Monty was contemptuous. 'In my view,' he retorted, 'the attack would come at the time of their [the Germans'] own choosing; it was now winter and we must get ready for trouble when the cold weather was over.'[38]

The Prime Minister's dimness – he would even crow in public the following spring, shortly before the German invasion of the West, that 'Hitler has missed the bus' – would assure him the worst reputation of any British Prime Minister in the twentieth century. Meanwhile, bowing to injured British army pride, he dismissed Hore-Belisha on 8 January 1940 over the 'pillbox row' – but made clear he had no intention of ceding his own place to a younger leader.

Chamberlain's appointment of a new Minister of War, Oliver Stanley, did no good. It was simply too late. On 10 January 1940 a German courier plane came down in Mechelen, Belgium, in thick fog; on board were found Hitler's clear-cut plans for invasion of Belgium. The Belgians were shocked; the British also. If Chamberlain had had any reason to question the seriousness of Hitler's offensive intentions, they were now void.

Rehearsal for retreat

Meanwhile, having warned Chamberlain of Hitler's real intent, Monty continued rehearsing his troops for the coming encounter battle. The object of his Number Two exercise was: 'a) To practise rapid movement in M/T to seize and hold a river line, pending the arrival of additional troops and b) To practise the staging and delivering of a counter-attack, supported by infantry tanks and air and artillery, to drive an enemy back over an obstacle over which he may have succeeded in establishing a bridgehead,' as the divisional war diary recorded.[39] The general situation, as Monty impressed on all COs before the exercise began, was 'Not too good; front may crack at any time. Speed of movement to secure the river line is very important; it may be a close thing as to who gets there first.' For this reason, the exercise would not rehearse a strictly laid-down plan, for it was 'a mistake to issue orders in advance for situations that may never arise';[40] it was only the *outline* situation that was important, within which the division must demonstrate its mobility, flexibility and expertise at combining movement, reconnaissance, signals, artillery, the work of the engineers, medical units and headquarters.

The exercise took place, despite bitterly cold weather, between 13 and 15 December for the majority of the division; it was then repeated from 19 to 21 December 1939 by the mechanized corps 'cavalry' (light tanks and Bren-gun carriers), as well as the divisional machine-gun battalion and the 9th Infantry Brigade, which had manned the front during the previous exercise.

This second divisional exercise did more than practise mobility and counter-attack, however. By directing the division westwards to defend a line on the river Canche above Amiens, Monty was rehearsing it for movement into Belgium, but in reverse (since Belgium would still not permit Allied troops or even staff officers across its borders); moreover, he even pictured the future German breakthrough in the division's rear area as part of the exercise, predicting the dire straits of a British Expeditionary Force in an Allied army, facing south, yet which had been outflanked by Germans attacking from the east. His 'opening situation' narrative ran: 'As it is possible that Jumboland [Allied] frontier defences of the Somme will be outflanked by a hostile move East of Amiens, BEF is, as a first step, to seize and hold the line of the R. CANCHE . . . ARRAS itself is strongly fortified. Jumboland Army is to withdraw to this position, if it finds itself unable to hold the line of the Somme . . .'[41]

This was, ironically, an accurate prediction to within several miles of what was actually to take place five months later when German armoured forces sliced through the Allied armies to Amiens, Boulogne and Calais. Sadly, Lord Gort did nothing to prepare for such an eventuality. As a result, the story of the BEF's southern and eastern flanks would be one of panic, confusion and disintegration.

Fears about the French army

In January 1940 Monty took the opportunity of visiting one of his brigades serving alongside a unit of the French army in an 'active' position in the Maginot line in the Saar. He spent 'a few days having a look round' – and what he saw worried him so deeply he became 'seriously alarmed and on my return I went to see my Corps Commander, and told him of my fears about the French Army and what we might have to expect from that quarter. Brooke had been down there and had formed the same opinion.'[42]

Shocked by what he'd seen, Monty now altered the entire tenor of his rehearsals. No longer would he only be rehearsing engagement with the enemy and staged, cohesive Allied withdrawal towards ground of the Allies' own choosing; he would prepare his troops for the collapse of the BEF's own allies too.

The 3rd Division's Exercise No. 3, carried out on 7 and 8 March 1940, thus rehearsed Monty's entire division advancing at night to a river some sixty miles away, followed by withdrawal. As he explained in his post-mortem conference of officers on 11 March, he had deliberately changed the orders half-way through the exercise in order to simulate battlefield reality – where nothing ever goes to plan. At six in the morning 'a situation arose which involved an immediate change of plan; our Allies in front had been driven in, our flanks were in danger of being turned and GHQ ordered a withdrawal to the St Pol line . . .' The problem involved was a tricky one: 'To disengage, and withdraw the Division back some

17 miles to a rear position. To get that rear position organized. To give the enemy no inkling that a withdrawal was to be carried out . . .'[43]

'Some said it was impossible to move a division sixty miles by night, deploying it in the dark and to be ready to fight at dawn,' Monty said prophetically to the hundreds of officers of the division who had assembled in a local cinema to examine the lessons of the exercise. 'I maintained that the 3rd Division could do it,' he declared, 'and it did.'[44]

It was precisely what the 3rd Division would be required to do, at a critical juncture in the Dunkirk campaign, six weeks later when Belgian resistance collapsed.

Smacking it about

Monty was determined that, whatever fate might befall the BEF, 3 Division would perform like clockwork. Dissatisfied by the way his 'cavalry' (light tanks and carriers) units typically focused on billets and messes rather than tactical positions he forced them to repeat Exercise No. 3 from 29 and 31 March (Exercise No. 4), then prepared Exercise No. 5: a four-day mock battle in April to seize an enemy-held river line, hold it and then retreat – with special emphasis on demolitions to delay the enemy.

Time was running out. On 9 April 1940, in order to forestall British naval moves to seal off Scandinavia and its vital iron-ore supplies, Hitler invaded Denmark and Norway, and a new, mini Franco-British Expeditionary Force was hastily thrown together to land on the coasts of central and northern Norway, repel the Germans and hold the iron-ore mines. Despite the snow and mountainous terrain, ideal for defence, it proved a catastrophe.

Meanwhile, in France the whole BEF went on to *alerte*. Then, to Brooke's consternation, on 18 April his fellow corps commander in the BEF, Sir John Dill, was sent back to London to back up General Ironside as deputy CIGS. In Brooke's view it was, for the BEF, 'the most serious loss since the beginning of the war' as he recorded in his diary[45] – for the man Gort accepted as Dill's successor, Lieutenant-General Michael Barker, was a nonentity, and would soon break down under the strain of combat.

While Brooke was deeply disturbed about the higher leadership of the BEF, however, Monty remained deeply concerned about leadership *within* the BEF – knowing how quickly the stresses and strains of combat could derail 'normal' individuals. One of the great merits of his large-scale divisional exercises was that they not only rehearsed the officers and men in duties they would have to perform in battle, but tested in mock battle the officers' breaking strains. Thus on 11 April 1940 Monty wrote at length to Brooke, complaining of the 'low standard of the Commanding Officers that have been appointed to my Division during the last few months. If the C.O.s that have been given to me are typical of what we are to expect,' he warned, 'then I suggest that the outlook is black.' His chief signaller, for example, was technically competent, 'But he is completely lacking in personality, energy and drive, and this comes out very clearly in exercises; he has no "fire"; he lacks that character and personality which inspires confidence in others, and he is not the one to "binge up" the show and keep it on its toes. He looks permanently tired.' The CRE, or chief engineer, was no better – 'a very charming person; he has a gentle disposition and is pleasant to deal with', but 'he does not grip hold of his show, "binge up" his engineers and generally "smack it about"'. The commander of the 33rd Field Artillery Regiment was even worse: 'a mouse-like creature' who was 'nervous of anyone senior to him' and 'definitely lacking in character and personality'. Such leaders were failing their men, Monty felt, and should be given jobs in rear areas – 'jobs removed from the hurly-burly of the battle, where rapid decisions and great drive are not essential, where life is generally is more ordered, and where men's lives are not directly at stake'. The same held true of some of his infantry battalion commanders. Having got rid of one, who possessed in Monty's view 'a depressing and dismal personality', the War Office had sent a replacement who lacked 'the infectious enthusiasm which I like to see in my unit commanders' – 'a nice person, but terribly dismal'. As Monty summarized to Brooke, 'I consider that in a front line fighting Division it is necessary to have commanders who have that character and personality that will inspire confidence in others; they must be mentally robust; and be possessed of initiative, energy and "drive"; they must in fact be officers who are capable of grasping a situation rapidly, doing something about it, and seeing that their subordinates do something about it also. They must possess enthusiasm, and be able to impart that enthusiasm to those under them.'

Monty's letter survives in a copy left among his papers hidden at the Abbey of St Sixtus in Belgium, during the retreat to Dunkirk, and only recently rediscovered. However, together with his training documents, it illustrates Monty's mission to reform the British army perhaps better than any other document from the 'phoney war' period. 'We shall not win this war,' Monty warned Brooke, his own commanding officer, 'unless we have commanders to lead our units in battle who are men of character, personality and drive – who have enthusiasm – and who will "smack it about" in difficult and unpleasant situations.' The answer, in Monty's view, was an army based on promotion by merit and performance, not seniority. 'We should do more than we appear to be doing in the way of picking the right man for the right job. Seniority might count less,' Monty proclaimed, 'and "suitability for the job" count more.'[46]

Brooke may well have wondered at Monty's arrogance in setting out a meritocratic agenda that was hardly the prerogative of a divisional general. Yet Monty was looking – as would become his hallmark as a field commander – at the battle beyond the immediate one: namely, the revamping of the British army into a wartime meritocracy, where modern professional skills and battle leadership would be developed as a first priority. Those who lacked such leadership qualities might do 'excellently in a less strenuous sphere, back behind somewhere – where conditions which are almost unendurable are not likely to arise'. But in fighting the Germans, Monty cautioned, 'the crux of the matter is leadership. A unit commander in a fighting Division must have his men "with him"; when the supreme test comes it is leadership that is going to count,' he predicted. 'An officer may know all about his job, and technically be very good,' he warned, 'but if he cannot get the last ounce out of his men when conditions are almost unendurable, then he is out of place in an active, fighting Division.'[47]

Like a piece of steel

Gwen Herbert had said of Monty to her husband in September 1939: 'Well, perhaps it's a good thing this war's begun. Horrible – but it's a chance for Monty to recover. At last he's got a real job to do.'[48] To the best of his ability, he had done it; as Hitler got ready to launch his invasion of the West the first part of Monty's job – the preparation of his division for combat – was over. The 'first clash' was about to begin.

Since September 1939 Monty had been weeding out officers, sending home or to the rear those who would not be able to stand the strain of modern combat. 'When the real test comes,' he added in his final memorandum to his senior officers before the German invasion, 'it is leadership that is going to pull us through. Our British soldiers are capable of anything if they are well led. We have got to see to it that our officers and NCOs are fit to lead, and are instructed in the essential details of training as affecting their commands. No officer is of any use as a leader unless he is mentally robust, and has that character and personality which will inspire confidence in his men. All officers who fail in this respect must be removed from the Division at once; if their names are reported to me I will do the rest.'[49]

He was as good as his word. On 4 May 1940 he met his fellow divisional commander, Major-General H. C. Lloyd of the 2nd Division – like Lieutenant-General Barker, an officer who would suffer a nervous break-down in the coming days. Monty was unimpressed. It was vital, he felt, that there be no weak links in the chains of command – it was simply not fair on the men. Within a short time the BEF would be ranged against the most proficient and highly indoctrinated army in modern times, encour-aged by its ruthless *blitzkrieg* conquest of Poland. Whichever way the larger battle swung, Monty was determined that the 3rd Division should prove itself the premier fighting division in the British Expeditionary Force. By May it was. 'There were no weak links,' Monty later considered; 'all the doubtful commanders had been eliminated during the previous six months of training. The division was like a piece of steel. I was immensely proud of it.'[50]

Lured into a trap

Under the notorious 'Allied Plan D', however, on news of German attack the 3rd (Iron) Division was to leave its prepared positions to spearhead the advance of II Corps into Belgium, with 4th and 50th Divisions follow-ing. The 3rd Division would seize a defensive line, as it had been trained to do, on the banks of the Dyle, from Wavre to Louvain, while the 600,000 troops of the Belgian army delayed the German invasion further north, on the Albert Canal, as well as to the west, along the Belgium–Luxembourg border – if all went well.

It did not. The Allies had done nothing to integrate their air forces with their ground forces – indeed the RAF's whole history from its metamorphosis into an independent service in 1917 had been devoted to fighting independently, in a separate corner from the army or the navy. It was a disastrous separation which RAF historiography would almost completely overlook and exonerate in later years, despite the ample opportunity which service personnel had in drawing lessons from German combined air and ground operations in Poland. As the German official history of the 1940 campaign commented, while the British had correctly assessed the strategic air threat from Germany in good time, and had similarly prepared fighter and bomber forces and their organization, they had utterly failed to see 'the need for tactical air support of the ground troops. Neither the British nor the French possessed an aircraft as wonderfully well gauged to this purpose as the Ju 87' – the Stuka dive-bomber. 'The example of Poland ought also to have made the Western powers aware that German strategy hinged upon bringing the enemy's air force to its knees by a surprise attack as the invasion kicked off. Indeed the opportunity to learn the lessons of the Polish campaign was completely missed.'[51]

The truth of this was to be seen on the ground. Early on the morning of 10 May 1940, the *Sitzkrieg* ended and *Blitzkrieg* began. Hitler's armies attacked in Holland and Belgium, luring the French and British into leaving their prepared positions to meet the threat. Such a move fatally ignored the possible threat to the Allied flank, should the Germans choose also to attack through the Ardennes – which they now did. Striking across the British lines of communication which stretched back to Le Mans, on the Loire, Hitler's 'Operation Sichelschnitt', in the words of General Sir David Fraser, proved 'one of the most swift, brilliant and decisive ever fought by German arms'.[52] The BEF, together with Gamelin's sole strategic reserve and his northern armies, was trapped – with the enemy closing the cage behind. Within five days the question would be not how long the British could hold off the advancing German forces through Belgium, as in 1914, but how could the BEF, surrounded on three sides, get out?

Allied and British military intelligence had performed abysmally. As one of 3 Division's artillery officers wrote on his return from Dunkirk, 'It will be interesting after the war to hear an account of the work of the British Intelligence Service in the early days of 1940.'[53] He never did hear; British official histories seldom rake over the failures.

Unaware that the BEF was moving into such a trap, however, not even the normally astute Brooke paused to wonder, at the time, why the

Germans failed to bomb his divisions racing forward across the Belgian border to the river Dyle on the afternoon of 10 May 1940. For the troops it was uncanny. 'A squadron of German bombers flew overhead but ignored us,' one artillery officer in 3 Division, Robin Dunn, noted in his diary. 'The road, the people, the buildings on either side were much like a by-pass near London at a summer's week-end.' In Brussels, crowds cheered 'and threw flowers and fruit and sweets at us, as the guns bumped and rattled over the cobbles . . . I thought of Wellington's Army moving out of that same city to Waterloo.'[54]

Dunn soon witnessed what the BEF was in for when he reached Louvain: not Waterloo, but Wagram. At 5.30 p.m. German Stukas attacked the main bridge. 'It was the most awe-inspiring sight I have ever seen. Calmly, unimpeded, the aeroplanes circled round, each one in turn diving with a high pitched whine, which was followed by the four crashes of the bombs. I did not like it!'[55]

Nor did Monty, as the leading divisional commander in the II Corps advance. He had for years called for close-support aircraft, able to co-operate effectively with infantry; the RAF had ignored all pleas. Meanwhile Monty's eyes were focused on the Dyle defences and Louvain city – which he found 'defended' by the Belgian 10th Division.

At first light on 11 May the Belgians had actually begun firing at the 3 Division cavalry troops. 'There was practically war between Britain and Belgium when dawn broke that morning,' remembered 'Kit' Dawnay, Monty's new intelligence officer, who acted as interpreter during the comic interviews and negotiations that followed.[56]

'There were a few small Pill Boxes,' one infantry officer recalled, 'but all our area was occupied by the Belgian Army! They appeared to have no artillery support except small mortars pulled by two dogs! What a to do! Montgomery ordered us disregard the Belgian Army, and dig in and prepare our defensive positions astride the river as if they were not there.'[57]

Messages began to fly between GHQ, corps HQs and divisional HQs, arguing over the proposed BEF–Belgian boundary lines, while further north German troops methodically seized the Belgian bridges over the Albert Canal and attacked the great fortress of Eban Emael – the Verdun of Belgium. Brooke went personally to see and plead with King Leopold, but Lord Gort was not similarly disposed. At 6 o'clock on the evening of 11 May, without bothering to ascertain the morale or genuine fighting power of the Belgians in Louvain, Gort simply ordered II Corps to squeeze the 3rd Division in to the right of the British line, alongside the left flank of the neighbouring I Corps, rather than risk dissension with the Belgians.

Monty, however, refused to budge. Louvain was the enemy's pathway to the Belgian capital, Brussels, he felt; the city and its high ground were too vital to be defended by a weak Belgian division with only horse-drawn transport. He therefore withdrew the main body of 3 Division west of Louvain and echeloned it as a second line of defence behind the Belgians rather than moving into the I Corps sector, informing the Belgian commander of this at 10 a.m. on 12 May. At lunch he told Brooke that all was now well.

'I expressed surprise,' Brooke recorded, 'and asked him how he had settled the matter. He then told me: "Well, I went to the Belgian Divisional Commander and said to him: '*Mon général*, I place myself and my Division unreservedly under your orders, and I propose to reinforce your front.'" He said that the Belgian Commander was delighted with this arrangement. I then asked Monty what he proposed to do if the Germans started attacking. He replied: "Oh! I then place the Divisional Commander under strict arrest and I take command."'[58]

One of the great moments of history

If Brooke was amused, Gort was not. Visiting Brooke's II Corps headquarters Gort insisted that his suggestion that 3 Division move into the I Corps area was an order. Monty again refused to obey it. In a tart, written reply, sent by a liaison officer to Brooke, he reiterated his determination to defend Louvain.

'Before my troops went into the line,' he wrote, 'the morale of the Belgian troops was very low. I go so far as to say that they would have retreated without fighting if attacked. Once my division began to move up to the line Belgians recovered. I am informed by liaison officer just arrived from Belgian GHQ (Needham Mission) that enemy armoured forces were reported this afternoon moving west . . . General Needham is worried about this and considers the Belgians will not stand and fight. In view of the poor state of morale of the Belgian troops as known to me and the possibility of a danger to the left flank of the BEF or to the right flank of the Belgian Army I consider that to move my division south from the high ground running west from Louvain is most inadvisable and might have very serious consequences. I discussed the whole problem with you this afternoon so you are in full possession of the facts . . . I will delay any move until I hear from you. I consider the best action would be for the 3rd Division to be in depth behind the 10th Belgian Division.'[59]

This was insubordination. The entire episode is absent from the British official history of the campaign, *The War in France and Flanders*, yet there can be no doubt that the 3rd Division's successful defence of Louvain in the days ahead avoided what General Needham, in his telephone message to Gort on 12 May, predicted might become 'a rout';[60] for on 13 May dawned the moment of truth, as the Germans pushed the retiring French and Belgian forces up to the river Dyle. Gort issued a message 'to all ranks', congratulating the BEF on its admirable advance to the river. 'We are now on the eve of one of the great moments of our history,' he declared. 'The struggle will be hard and long, but we can be confident of final victory.'[61]

In American parlance this was bullshit, for the Allied struggle in Belgium would be all too brief. As German pressure built up towards Louvain, the Belgian 10th Division decided, after all, not to fight – thus relieving Monty of the necessity of arresting its commander. The Belgian general maintained that he was moving out so that his 'tired troops could rally, rest and support our defence', as he explained to the signals officer of the 3rd Division who was taking over his HQ.[62]

Monty was contemptuous – and relieved. There was now no one between him and the enemy. Brooke found him 'quite happy and in great form',[63] ready to take on the Germans for the first time since 1918.

No confidence in Gort

According to German Army Group B instructions, the front between Louvain and Namur, barring access to Brussels, had to be smashed quickly before the French and Belgians could dig in. On the night of 14 May German patrols appeared to have penetrated into Louvain; the battle for Louvain seemed to have begun in earnest. However, a counter-attack by a battalion of the Grenadier Guards found next day that the enemy patrols had in fact been residual Belgians of the 10th Division who had got left behind and were now fleeing the ever-closer bursts of German gunfire. Finally, at mid-morning on 15 May, the Germans did indeed begin to push their way into the outskirts of Louvain.

A series of vicious local engagements followed – the Germans receiving a rude shock to find not Belgians but British troops in position and barring their assault towards Brussels.

Monty's assessment of the Belgian troops had meanwhile proved all too accurate, while Gort, according to Brooke, simply failed to recognize their 'poor fighting quality'.[64] Panic had spread throughout the Low Countries since the capitulation of the Dutch on 14 May – so much so that the British ambassador in Brussels packed precipitately that night, and fled secretly west without word to Brooke or the BEF – only to be captured, for his pains, a few days later by German armoured forces that had broken through at Sedan!

Brooke worried about his left flank ('I would not trust the Belgians a yard,' he confided to his diary on 15 May[65]); but Gort's days of field command were numbered. He had failed to rehearse his headquarters in either movement or communication in battle. Split into three echelons – GHQ at Arras, a forward command post at Wahagnies, and a third, indeterminate C-in-C command post, with inadequate or non-existent communication between them – leadership of the BEF began to disintegrate at the very moment when inter-allied communication and co-operation were essential.

Rumour fed rumour and Gort was soon summoned by his corps commanders to make decisions like a helpless captain whose ship is sinking. On 15 May the Belgians claimed that Louvain was in German hands; since GHQ had, incredibly, no contact with II Corps, it was impossible for them to know that Montgomery was still in firm possession of the town. Moreover, news from the French front to the right of the BEF was equally menacing, for it appeared – if reports were accurate – that German armoured columns had broken clean through the French lines. In his diary that night Brooke noted presciently that the BEF 'is likely to have both flanks turned, and will have a very unpleasant time extricating itself out of its present position';[66] yet Gort, the C-in-C, still failed to see what was happening, or the consequences. Instead of moving his reserve divisions into place to protect his flank and rear, as the German Army Group A smashed its way through towards the English Channel in the ensuing, critical days, Gort relied on an *ad hoc* collection of 'Macforces', 'Polforces', 'Petreforces', 'Woodforces', 'Frankforces' and 'Usherforces', each independently formed and locally led. Only Rundstedt and Hitler's incredible decision to halt dead their armoured forces at Calais on 22 May would save the BEF from total destruction.

Gort's 'boy-scout' brain, his lack of forward planning, his inability to train himself or his army for modern warfare, his chaotic command structure and his deference to his French superiors were the death-seal of the BEF. As Brooke noted later, reflecting on the first day of the German assault on 10 May, 'I had by now few illusions as to the fighting efficiency of the French. The Belgians still remained to be seen, but what I had heard about them was not promising. On top of all I had no confidence in Gort's leadership when it came to handling a large force. From all that I had seen of him during the last seven months he seemed at most times incapable of seeing the wood for the trees . . .'[67]

Without intelligence

Communications – or the lack of them – were only part of the problem, however. GHQ information about the enemy, Gort's allies, and his own forces, was risible – and was made unpardonably worse on 17 May, when Gort permitted both his Director of Military Intelligence and deputy DMI to abandon their intelligence-gathering and reporting function, on behalf of the entire BEF, and take command of local infantry units: Macforce. Thereafter Gort was utterly without intelligence – commanding 400,000 British troops in a fight that would be 'long and hard', and was supposed to result in 'final victory'!

In the event it would prove all too short – and end in utter defeat.

Administrative disaster

Gort's failure, as commander-in-chief of the BEF, to prepare for modern combat was a scandal, though subsequently covered up. Even the syco-phantic J. R. Colville, however, considered Gort's headquarters to be an 'administrative disaster'. '[A]s the days went by', Colville wrote, 'an already imperfect system of communications deteriorated to such an extent that the link between Gort and the nucleus of his staff was all but severed. Thus the special Operations Intelligence Section at Arras to which, by long arrangement, all reports of German movements were sent was often unable to pass the information to the Command Post' – and in the absence of Gort and his chief of staff there was no one at the main headquarters able to take authoritative decisions; 'in order to speak to Gort himself,' Colville noted, the main headquarters staff had to rely on 'an inefficient civilian telephone exchange from which, during air raids, the operators frequently fled'![68]

The administrative and operations chaos of the French headquarters was still worse, however: suffering from an absence of proper maps, provisions, and even air and ground protection. At General Blanchard's 1st Army HQ, to the right of the BEF, there was not even a system for recording incoming and outgoing messages! 'Incredible though it might be,' commented Colville, 'the professional staff of one of Europe's most professional armies was totally unorganized for war.'[69]

The Belgians were no better. Though some Belgian units eventually put up a fight, the majority surrendered their country to the Germans without a shot being fired at the enemy – and the same was pitifully true of the majority of the French. 'Nowhere was any resistance attempted,' Rommel recorded in his account of the campaign.[70] For Jews, political activists and minorities dependent on stout-hearted Allied resistance, this was frightening.

Monty's troops were a different matter. Robin Dunn, commanding a troop of the 7th Field Regiment in support of 3 Division's 8th Brigade, marked out on 13 May the registration lines for shelling German troops as they approached Louvain, 'and discussed things with the Infantry, who seemed absolutely confident'. The next day the Belgian batteries ran away from the battle 'at a brisk trot', he noted. 'So far,' however, 'all had gone according to plan. The Belgians had not held out as long as we had expected, but it had been exactly as we had practised countless times . . . I slept dreamlessly and well.'[71]

Monty's rehearsals had borne fruit. 'We had unbounded confidence in our Infantry,' Dunn recorded on 16 May, as the advancing Germans attempted again to infiltrate their way into Louvain, and 3 Division's infantry turfed them out. The Germans had 'complete air superiority' – 'We seldom saw a British fighter, and when a patrol went over, it was always at a time when there were no German machines about,' Dunn recorded, but the actual damage caused by German bombing was nominal. With strong, well-practised artillery able to bring down heavy shellfire wherever needed, Dunn was certain 3 Division could hold Louvain and the Dyle, however hard the Germans attacked. 'We expected the Germans to put in a terrific attack in a few days, in the meantime, we made our preparations confidently.'

That afternoon, however, Dunn received a telephone order to fire his artillery at twenty rounds per hour; then forty rounds. Soon he was instructed to fire his entire dumped ammunition – 600 rounds per gun. By 5 p.m. the guns were 'red hot' and 'the gunners working like slaves'. The battery major called from headquarters to explain: the Germans had broken through on the right flank of the BEF, and 3 Division was to withdraw in the night to the river Dendre, ten miles south of Brussels.

However disappointing, this was exactly the scenario Monty had set out as the basis for the division's exercises, though it stunned the men, whose morale was at its peak. The gunners 'could not understand it when I told them we were to retreat. "Why sir? Why don't we advance? If they leave us here nothing will ever get through this." I explained that nothing ever would but that it was elsewhere that things had gone wrong, and that unless we went we would be cut off.'[72]

This was no more than the truth. Not only had German forces broken through the 1st French Army front, forcing the whole army to retreat, but further south Hitler's armoured forces had smashed their way through the 9th French Army at Sedan and were racing towards Arras itself – the headquarters of the BEF – with only a British lieutenant colonel to organize its defence! Yet instead of bombing rail and road communications supporting the German breakthrough Churchill – who had become Prime Minister on 10 May, and had immediately made himself Minister of Defence, too – ordered the RAF to bomb the Ruhr!

The rout was becoming a fiasco.

A stark choice

Gort's deputy chief of operations staff, Brigadier Oliver Leese, now took stock. The failure of the French high command to command; the complete breakdown of General Billotte, the northern army group commander; the collapse of the French armies in the face of aerial, armoured and infantry attack; the refusal of the Belgian troops to fight; and the breakneck armoured breakthrough of the Germans towards the English Channel, north of the Somme – all pointed to a simple choice for the British. Either the BEF could evacuate, or it must fight its way across the German salient to the safety of the Somme.

Drawing his own conclusions from the darkening situation reports, and out of touch with Gort, Leese prepared a contingency plan for withdrawal of the BEF to Dunkirk, from which port it could be taken off by the navy. Late on 18 May Leese's plan was read out to Gort, his chief of staff General Pownall, and the quartermaster general and engineer-in-chief, at the Wahagnies command post – just as General Billotte, co-ordinator of the northern Allied armies, arrived to tell the unhappy story of French disintegration on the right of the BEF, fleeing madly to avoid bombing, mistaking their own tanks for Germans, even shooting one another.

Leese's plan, according to the GHQ war diary, was to move the BEF in the form of a hollow square with 50th Division providing a flank guard along the La Bassée Canal. It was then estimated that the reserves of one division would be sufficient to mount guard on every bridge from Raches to the sea.[73] In this way, not only would the integrity of the BEF be maintained, but with proper planning much of its matériel and most of its personnel could be saved in an orderly evacuation.

Had Gort been able or willing to act unequivocally on Leese's outline plan of 18 May, a well-administered British withdrawal and embarkation could have been effected. Politics and honour, however, militated against such a decision.

Hitler's tortoise

The new Prime Minister thought British counter-attack, not evacuation, was the answer, irrespective of French and Belgian military collapse. 'Referring to the rapid advance of the German army he said "The tortoise is thrusting his head very far beyond the carapace",' his private secretary recorded.[74]

This was a memorable metaphor, but all too redolent of Churchill's childhood battlegames with tin soldiers. Gort was torn. He had loyally accepted a subordinate position within the Allied military hierarchy that precluded him from making independent military decisions unless his government specifically ordered him otherwise. Aware that the moment had arrived for such specific political orders he therefore asked the British government to decide whether he was to 'retire to the sea, forming [a] bridgehead round Dunkirk or to fight his way south-eastwards, leaving the Belgians to their fate, in order to rejoin the French'.[75] Churchill's War Cabinet, meeting on the afternoon of 19 May, chose the second option – chaining Gort to his French allies and catastrophe. Although Gort allowed Leese on 19 May to continue to explore with the Admiralty the possible naval requirements for an eventual evacuation ('We are still going back – & are hoping against hope that the French will recover. If not, it all looks pretty gloomy. Even the Poles seem to have done better than the French', Leese scribbled in a note to his wife[76]), it was kept as quiet as possible, and few if any military provisions were made for the sea-lift of such a huge army.

Gort thus faced in all directions, attempting to conform to the wishes of all, without any clear view himself, as commander-in-chief of the BEF. To his allies he merely explained that the BEF was being forced to pull back, owing to the collapse of the 1st and 7th French armies, but not saying clearly where it was heading – while at a GHQ conference of corps commanders on 19 May, a strategy of withdrawal to the coast was privately agreed to be the best solution. 'If all goes wrong with the French, things will get difficult for the B.E.F.', Leese explained in coded language to his wife, 'but it does not necessarily mean that we lose the war.'[77]

Brooke, interestingly, favoured evacuation through the Belgian ports of Ostend and Zeebrugge, but was overruled on the grounds that the Belgians might collapse completely, and refuse to co-operate in such an evacuation; meanwhile neither the French nor the Belgians were informed of Gort's secret proposals. Thus, as late as 28 May, with the surrender of the Belgians and final evacuation of British troops beginning in earnest, the commander of the Allied northern army group would claim to have no idea the British intended to leave French soil![78]

Gort's tranquil evening

Gort's prevarication belied his 'honourable schoolboy' character. The idea that the French might accuse him of absconding from the field of battle gnawed at him; therefore in inter-allied councils he espoused a policy of waiting upon the French and upon events. Having permitted Leese to ask the Admiralty to draw up contingency evacuation plans on 19 May, neither he nor Pownall paid further attention to the air, naval and military requirements of such a huge evacuation, nor the need to appoint a commander to take charge of it – indeed, Gort considered his task as BEF commander was simply to show firm moral fibre, while his chief of staff, Pownall, actually began to think things might not be so bad when, on 19 May, having received the British War Cabinet instructions for the BEF to fight its way south and re-establish contact with the French forces on the far side of the German salient, on the Somme, the 1st French Army suddenly 'reappeared from somewhere. They would occupy a line – it fitted in with our arrangements. And the evening ended tranquilly,' Pownall noted obtusely in his own diary[79] as he and Gort retired to bed. In a postscript to his note to his wife, later that evening, Leese added: 'This morning things looked terribly glum, & it looked like another Namsos [i.e. evacuation]. Now the French seem to be taking a pull, & we are helping. If only we can stem this one rush, on which all is staked, we shall win! Courage – Formidable – Stickey!!'[80]

It was to be the sleep of fools. For Gort and his chief of staff to ignore the administrative and operational requirements of a possible major evacuation, involving up to 400,000 troops of Britain's primary field army, north of the Somme, was to fiddle while Rome burned. Nothing was done to examine the defences of Dunkirk port, or to prepare the beaches for the emergence of so many British troops, not to speak of other Allied personnel or armies. No naval beach personnel were brought over from England, no piers or landing jetties erected, no anti-aircraft guns sited, no HQ positions prepared, no proper field signals set up. Had the Germans not halted their panzers outside Dunkirk on 23 May, on Hitler and Rundstedt's orders, Gort would, without doubt, have lost the entire BEF.

Churchill at his least fine

Meanwhile, retreating in stages to the Scheldt, the original northern front of the BEF had now become the eastern flank of the Allied armies in Belgium also. Although General Barker, the I Corps commander, broke down, and though the commander of 2nd Division had to be dismissed in the field, the regular divisions fought as divisions, and there were no enemy penetrations.

However well the British regular divisions fought, the strategic situation remained the same. The Germans had successfully entrapped the northern Allied armies by cutting a great armoured swathe through their rear; they had only now to tighten the pincers of their two Army Groups A and B, like the strings of a sack, and Allied surrender in the north would be inevitable, they believed.

King Leopold III certainly saw matters this way, and was only persuaded to continue his country's 'struggle' by the orderliness of the British I and II Corps' retirement alongside the Belgian army's flight. As this retirement moved inexorably back from one river line to another, though, all leading towards the frontier of France, the argument for prolonged Belgian resistance became weaker and weaker. More Belgian troops would be killed by bombing and shelling, more Belgian roads, bridges, towns, villages, ports and property damaged. And for what? So that the remnants of a Belgian army could fight a doomed battle on French soil? Given the influence of the King's *éminence grise*, Colonel van Overstraeten, and the domino effect of events, it is altogether remarkable that the Belgians remained technically at war until 28 May 1940. (The word 'technically' must be used, since very few Belgians could be persuaded to fight; they either deserted or joined an ill-assorted mass fleeing from the German invasion, while the BEF withdrew south and west.) Inevitably the Belgian army would split off – and it was through the resultant gap that the Germans hoped to drive a wedge with their IV Corps, which would race south along the coast and cut off the eastern flank of the BEF from the sea.

Gort's attention, meanwhile, had shifted to his inland, south-eastern oriented flank. The CIGS, General Sir Edmund Ironside, had arrived at 6.15 a.m. on 20 May to insist, on behalf of the War Cabinet, that, in conjunction with a French attack northwards from the Somme, Gort must attack southwards, before the Germans reinforced the armour in their tortoise-head salient with infantry. Instead of planning the inevitable evacuation of the BEF, Gort therefore loyally committed himself to a doomed offensive against the German salient in order to appease both the French and the British War Cabinets.

This attack, using General Franklyn's 50th Division and General Martel's Tank Brigade on 21 May, certainly worried General Hoth's Panzergruppe (XV and XVI Corps), but it was easily repulsed, especially as it was not matched by a planned attack by the French from the Somme – the proposed attack delayed and then cancelled on the orders of the new French supreme commander, the seventy-three-year-old General Weygand. By then the German armour had reached Boulogne! Evacuation seemed inevitable, as even Churchill's private secretary, J. R. Colville, noted in his diary: 'The German advance is now really dangerous, and it is staggering that France should have so far put up less resistance to invasion than did Poland, Norway or Holland. Preparations are being made for the evacuation of the B.E.F. in case of necessity.'[81]

The Allied campaign was now bedevilled by domestic and international politics, orders and counter-orders, as the German and British leaders both made flawed decisions that prejudiced the outcome of the battle, Hitler refusing his panzer commanders permission to seize Dunkirk from the south, Churchill instructing Gort to attack southwards yet again – this time with 'eight Allied divisions and the Belgian cavalry corps'.

This was Churchill at his worst, for how he imagined Gort could disengage his two main fighting corps in the midst of heavy fighting against General Bock's Army Group B on the north-eastern flank and send them into a new offensive south-westwards said as little for Churchill's military sagacity as for that of French politicians.

As Arras itself was finally surrendered to the Germans, Gort began, belatedly, to realize that evacuation was the only solution. Thus the next day he 'gave instructions that his staff should again examine the arrangements for a withdrawal to the coast which he had first considered a wise precaution five days previously'.[82]

Five days in such a fast-moving campaign was an eternity. Was it already too late? If German armoured forces were already in Boulogne and, with Hitler's reluctant permission, heading north towards St Omer and Dunkirk, was evacuation even possible? On 25 May Gort decided yet again to give up the idea, and instead to fight his way southwards, across the German armoured salient, towards the main body of the French armies, south of the Somme.

The new 'escape' plan entailed abandoning the Belgians definitively, and was revealed to Brooke on the morning of 25 May. Brooke wasn't sorry. He felt the Belgians had put up a miserable fight, and that they could not last another twenty-four hours; he felt, too, that the idea of being crushed up against the Channel coast with only a single, unprepared port by which to evacuate or be reinforced was equally, if not more, hazardous than a breakout across the German lines to the south. 'I was then informed that the "rush for the sea" plan was abandoned,' Brooke wrote in his diary that night. 'I have always hated this plan. The new plan is to try to break through to the French forces south of the German penetration. It might be possible, but I should doubt it. I then went round 4 & 3 Divs to discuss our breakthrough plans with them.'[83]

Strangely this change of plan by General Gort was never publicly revealed in post-war accounts of Dunkirk. Gort did not mention it in his despatches, and it was not recorded by his biographer, J. R. Colville; Sir Arthur Bryant omitted the passage from Brooke's diary in his edited version, *The Turn of the Tide*, and even the British official history of the campaign did not disclose it. Yet, not only is the change of plan documented in Brooke's unpublished diary and Major Archdale's liaison officer's diary ('At 3 p.m. I was told [at Gort's HQ] that Winston Churchill had sent instructions to fight south, and that the C. in C. was determined now to do that with or without the French'[84]), it is also confirmed in Monty's diary of 3rd Division events on 25 May:

Corps Comdr visited me 1600 hrs with outline idea on how the BEF might abandon the Belgians and fight its way through to join the French.

Assembled my Brigadiers at 1800 hrs and ordered certain moves and recces as precaution; all B Echelon to join up with units.[85]

Avoiding the coup de grâce

Would such a breakthrough have succeeded? Brooke evidently doubted it, though he felt it would be more valiant than defeat and surrender on the beaches of northern France. Monty gave no indication in his diary of his own feelings on the subject, nor did he ever reveal the plan in later years. However, he did refer to it obliquely in his *Memoirs* when, at the end of his assessment of the BEF campaign and of Gort's performance, he remarked: 'A cleverer man might have done something different [than evacuating the BEF], and regained touch with the main French forces beyond the Somme. If he had done this,' Monty went on, 'the men of the BEF might have found themselves eventually in French North Africa – without weapons and equipment' – and unable to oppose a German invasion of Britain.[86]

Such a view presupposes that a mass BEF breakout would have been possible, if well commanded; but a study of the general situation map on the evening of 24 May/morning of 25 May 1940 lends no confidence to such a supposition. The tortoise-neck of the German salient was now 100 kilometres wide, and the salient itself contained no fewer than fourteen armoured or motorized German divisions, as well as numerous infantry divisions. To have detached itself cleanly from General Bock's Army

Group A in the north and the east, and fought its way southwards across this massive German salient was, as Brooke acknowledged, a very dubious proposition. Monty's units might have made it, given their training, but the majority would inevitably have been destroyed or captured. Capitulation or an armistice by the British government might thereafter have been inevitable: a Vichy Britain alongside Vichy France.

Plans for such a BEF breakthrough were, however, short lived. Monty had laid down a policy of offensive patrolling on his front which, although it resulted in a nasty encounter on 24 May when nine officers and almost a hundred men in the 8th Infantry Brigade were wounded (a 'raid' severely criticized in the British official history), paid off suddenly in the most spectacular way. One of the patrols pounced on a German staff car. The German driver was killed, but the staff officer escaped[87] – leaving a wallet containing not only the entire order of battle of the German army, but new tactical plans for a German VI Corps pincer movement designed to outflank the BEF at its northern extremity, towards Ypres, where the Belgian forces could be detached and the Germans race down the coast – thus rolling up the entire BEF from the north-east.

Faced with such advance warning of German plans, Brooke reluctantly pressed Gort to change his mind. The BEF would, in such circumstances, be unable to break away from Bock's forces, but would be forced to fight off the impending two-corps German attack in the north. With its back to the sea wall, the BEF could therefore only hope to evacuate from Dunkirk; any other possibility was ruled out. Ammunition, now that the lines of communication to the Loire, Cherbourg and Brest had been cut, was so low it was having to be parachuted in from England, and Gort had ordered the whole BEF to go on to half rations. The French army, south of the Somme, was showing itself incapable of the meanest offensive to re-establish contact with the northern 'armies'. If the Belgians surrendered shortly, as seemed highly likely, almost the entire German military machine in the north could be turned on the BEF and the remnant French forces.

Hitler's Sichelschnitt strategy of luring the BEF and the 1st and 7th French Armies into a Belgian sack and cutting them off from their supplies had succeeded. The only question was how to avoid the German *coup de grâce* by Bock's Army Group B.

Letting things slide

Two actions were now required to save the BEF: a definitive decision to pull the BEF back to Dunkirk in order to evacuate as many troops as possible and a concerted attempt to parry Bock's northern sickle. Gort reluctantly made the first decision; Brooke did the rest – switching Monty's 3rd Division from its old Franco-Belgian border positions near Lille, and using it to fight off Bock's northern pincer towards the Yser, east of Dunkirk.

Looking back, once he had had an opportunity to study the campaign in later years, Monty gave Gort 'full marks' in his memoirs, 'and I hope history will do the same. He saved the men of the BEF. And, being saved, they were able to fight again another day.'[88] Later still Monty wrote of Gort: 'when all is said and done, it must never be forgotten that in the supreme crisis of his military life, in May 1940, he acted with courage and decision – doing the right thing for Britain. If he had failed at that moment, disaster might well have overtaken British arms. He did not fail.'[89]

Such was the British view. The French, disintegrating before the German onslaught, were appalled by Gort's 'faithlessness'. According to Major Archdale, the British liaison officer to the co-ordinator of the Allied northern army group, despair among the French field commanders had led on 24 May to the French III Corps commander, General de Laurencie, actually 'begging Lord Gort to take command of 1st French Army' – where General Blanchard had broken down. 'Blanchard,' Archdale noted in his diary, 'appeared to be bereft of any power of action or improvisation and just let things slide.'[90]

A slave to events

That an incompetent but brave British commander-in-chief should be asked by the commander of the French III Corps to take command of their broken forces north of the Somme from an even more incompetent French commander was an indication of how desperate the situation for the democracies had become. But although Gort made the fateful decision to call off his southern 'sortie',[91] he himself was hardly the man to command large fighting formations; 'the most trivial things have always preyed on his mind', even his loyal chief of staff, Pownall, noted in his diary.[92] He had been, since 10 May, 'a slave to events'; Major Archdale, speaking to Gort at 5.30 p.m. on 25 May, found him 'at his table very silent, and looking rather bewildered and bitter. I felt most strongly that he was wishing that he could take an active physical part in this battle: that it was irking him terribly to be forced to sit there with nothing but weary Allies all round him: weary in body but oh! so terribly weary in mind.' From 'start to finish there had been no direction or information from the [French] High Command,' Gort complained – and gave way to a series of retrospective lamentations. '"Why" – he asked – "did they retreat to the Escaut when they knew of the great gap in the middle – why not retreat south and preserve a front and lines of communication?"'[93]

It was too late to deplore the successful German breakthrough, though. Gort himself had approved the BEF advance into Belgium – leaving the security of its prepared positions along the Franco-Belgian border. Having turned down any suggestion that he should now take command of the remnant northern French forces, Gort judged it important only to evacuate the British Expeditionary Force at Dunkirk, with whatever remaining French forces could be persuaded to accompany it – and to explain the reality of the battlefield situation to the elderly General Weygand in Paris, who had finally replaced the feckless General Gamelin on 20 May.

It is significant that to do this, Gort had to send his liaison officer, Major Archdale, first by sea from Dunkirk to Cherbourg, and then by car to Paris – a journey lasting twenty-three hours, in the middle of the critical battle for the West!

Major Archdale was seen first by Reynaud and then Maréchal Pétain, who at age eighty-four had joined Reynaud's French government as the vice-premier! To Archdale's consternation Pétain, too, asked if Gort would take command of French forces north of the German salient, in view of the breakdown of French command – just as Monty, four years later, would be asked to take command of the two American armies north of the German breakthough in the Ardennes, the so-called Battle of the Bulge! Monty would be only too delighted; but in May 1940 Major Archdale had to explain that Gort had more than enough on his plate commanding the BEF – at which point, the growing French need for scapegoats reasserted itself. By 9.30 p.m. on 26 May Archdale was having to defend British evacuation plans to General Georges, the C-in-C of the Allied north-eastern armies – who had never once visited the northern front since 13 May. Archdale explained that, although it was 'a fallacy' to assert that the British had been 'preparing for some time for a withdrawal of the B.E.F. to the coast', he wished, on behalf of the BEF commander, 'by every possible argument to extract a promise of full co-operation for a joint evacuation'. This remained now, Archdale assured General Georges – who had admitted the French had 'no strategical reserve' to undertake any offensive or even defensive action – the sole possibility other than surrender: 'the only military operation for us to perform'.[94]

Utter ignorance

Rarely a good picker or assessor of men, Winston Churchill had put his faith in four Frenchmen: Reynaud, Mandel, Pétain and Weygand.

Churchill's trust had been misplaced. Reynaud's mistress, Madame de Portes, favoured capitulation and co-operation with the Germans, while Reynaud's military adviser, Colonel Villelume, was 'fat and sly, pouring defeatism into his ears', in the words of Churchill's emissary, Major-General Spears. General Weygand was, at seventy-three, 'wizened and dried up'. He had been Foch's right-hand-man at the German armistice signed in Compiègne in 1918, but now the 'spirit was missing'. He blamed the inter-war politicians, not without reason: ' "we have gone to war with a 1918 army against a German Army of 1939" '. Pétain was in another world – the atmosphere at the octogenarian Maréchal's office in Les Invalides 'as dead, as somnolent as the chambers of a provincial lawyer's office on a Sunday afternoon', as Spears described. Unlike Weygand, Pétain 'seemed to accept catastrophe as if detached from the present, even from the world'.[95] In such an atmosphere of impending, catastrophic defeat there was no longer any real interest in fighting: only in blame.

Instead of attempting to lead the nation, Churchill's four esteemed Frenchmen now wallowed in recriminations and accusations – railing against Churchill for his refusal to commit to France the RAF fighters now needed to protect Britain, Lord Gort for not saving the day by offensive action or taking command of the remnant French forces, and the Belgians, whose territorial integrity France had risked its own national security to defend . . .

The utter ignorance of the political and military authorities in Paris regarding the true state of affairs on their own battlefront was a terrible indictment of French democratic government; however, the War Office and Churchill's War Cabinet in London were scarcely better informed, thanks to French mis-communications and to their own antiquated British organization. Democracy had proved itself too slow, feeble and pathetic when challenged by the charismatic dictator of a modern, fascist, militarist state.

In such circumstances, could the BEF be saved? And even if it could be saved, could the British army ever be refashioned to fight the Germans on equal terms – and win?

Night moves

For the men of the BEF the outlook on 26 May was bleak. Yet in the final days before evacuation, two figures stood out who were, in time, to effect a miraculous transformation of the British army: Generals Brooke and Montgomery. Monty was convinced he knew how to create and lead a modern British fighting army in battle against the Germans; Brooke would in due course demonstrate how to command a brilliant but difficult subordinate like Monty – and handle an even more brilliant but flawed political boss, in Winston Churchill. Had the Germans managed to out-flank and capture Brooke and Montgomery, it is highly doubtful, in retrospect, whether Britain could successfully have survived World War II.

Meanwhile the side-step movement by night to the Yser which Monty was asked to perform by Brooke was perhaps the most difficult manoeuvre a division can make in war. Not only had he to disengage his entire division – more than 14,000 troops – from contact with the enemy, during the battle for the Ypres–Comines Canal, but to cross the lines of communication of no fewer than three fellow divisions in total darkness, a few miles behind a fluctuating front line, and take up an unreconnoitred position before dawn. 'It was a task', Brooke later acknowledged, 'that might well have shaken the stoutest of hearts, but for Monty it might just have been a glorious picnic. He told me exactly how he was going to do it, and was as usual exuberant in confidence. There is no doubt that one of Monty's strong points is his boundless confidence in himself. He was priceless on this occasion, and I thanked Heaven to have a Commander of his calibre to undertake this march.'[96]

There was every reason, however, for Monty to feel his 3rd Division could perform such a night withdrawal. Movement by night had been rehearsed time and time again on 3 Division's exercises, before the battle had ever started; since 17 May the division had withdrawn its infantry, engineers and artillery successfully by night from the Dyle to the Dendre, from the Dendre to the Escaut, and from the Escaut to the French frontier defences, which had been the starting point from which they had first sallied forth into Belgium on 10 May. The art of rehearsal had been Monty's secret weapon – and had proven far more effective than turnout, courage, tenacity, or equipment.

Monty's intelligence officer, Kit Dawnay, still remembered the 'night march' nearly forty years later. Ever since hearing of the German break-through in the south Dawnay had surmised the BEF would have to evacuate 'from the beaches somewhere' or be forced to surrender. 'Monty, however, was completely calm,' he recalled, 'and gave no indication that he was at all worried. At one moment we had a very complicated night march, a retirement where we marched across the face of the enemy to take up positions further to the left. Monty treated it exactly the same as if it had been an exercise. The route was carefully marked, guides were put out all the way. Monty had studied movement to a very big extent, we were a very mobile division, we had wireless, he exercised very close control and it went extremely well.'[97]

So used to night movement had the men of the division become, in fact, that for the most part they were unaware how extraordinary a feat they had conducted in the midst of a critical battle. As the second-in-command of the 2nd Battalion, Lincolnshire Regiment, later recorded, the division had 'carried out endless night drives, with no lights, except a tiny light which lit up the rear axle of the truck in front showing the regimental number', and in many ways, the night move was 'no different to a 3 Div exercise'.[98]

Brooke was delighted. 'Found he had, as usual, accomplished almost the impossible,' Brooke entered in his diary on 28 May.[99] But if Brooke was relieved, Gort was increasingly despondent. Having made his fateful decision to evacuate, he was now no longer master of the BEF. Between the morning of 27 May and his final hours at La Panne beach near Dunkirk, Brooke never once saw Gort or a senior member of GHQ, and for long periods he was not even informed where GHQ was situated. The decisions he made, such as commandeering I Corps' artillery and units of Alexander's 1st Division under I Corps, as they withdrew, were made entirely on his own initiative. GHQ had estimated that no more than 25 per cent of the BEF would ever get away. That it managed to evacuate its entire personnel in the few days between 26 May and 2 June can largely be ascribed to Brooke's generalship – a fact which no officer involved in those critical days and hours has ever disputed, though Brooke himself ascribed it to the unbelievable resilience of the British soldier who, as in Rudyard Kipling's poem, kept his head while all about him were losing theirs.

Having been brought up in France and having admired the way France held firm in the Great War, Brooke was, by contrast, saddened by the complete disintegration of French morale, epitomized at his HQ on 29 May when élite French cavalrymen started killing their horses and throwing away their guns, although the Germans were more than twenty miles away.

However, it was the long-feared surrender of the Belgians which caused Brooke his biggest headache, for, at the very moment when Monty rushed his 3rd Division north of Ypres, King Leopold began unilaterally to sue for an armistice. Thus, no sooner had Monty arrived to take up his new sector at 7 a.m. on 28 May than he found there would be no Belgian troops between him and the sea at Nieuport – a gap of some fifteen miles.

'Here was a pretty pickle!' Monty recollected in his memoirs. In his *History of Warfare* he wrote: 'At dawn on 28th May I learned that the King of the Belgians had surrendered [without the authority of his own government] the whole of his army to the Germans. I decided in my own mind that it is not suitable in the mid-twentieth century for kings to command their national armies in battle. One thing was fortunate – there were so many Belgian soldiers between my division and the sea that the Germans would have some difficulty in getting through, thus giving me a little time to think about it!'[100]

It had been intended that 3 Division should dig in on the waterline running north from Ypres, and like a mantled arm shield the 4th Division as, in its turn, it retreated to the safety of the Dunkirk perimeter. But during the afternoon of 28 May, Monty's Signals HQ picked up wireless reports that German units, advancing down the Belgian coast, had got into Nieuport, where only a single regiment of cavalry (light armoured vehicles) was in place to stop them. Fortunately, heavy rain and low cloud kept the German air force from the scene, and this undoubtedly saved the day, since the roads were crammed with Allied troops and transport running nose to tail. By despatching 3 Division artillerymen and engineers with rifles and instructions to hold the Loon Canal until the night of 28/ 29 May, when units of the 4th Division could get up, Monty managed to seal off the gap.

There was, however, a personal tragedy. When he heard news of the German penetration in Nieuport Monty had immediately sent a messenger to Brooke's HQ – 'he knew enough about my plans to realize at once the importance of this new and unexpected development', as Brooke wrote later.[101] Anxious then to send Brooke the latest information on the 'gap', and what he was doing to fill it, Monty then sent his own chief of staff, Colonel 'Marino' Brown, to give Brooke an authoritative situation report. While Monty slept at his HQ in the Trappist monastery of St Sixtus, Brown made his way through the darkness to II Corps HQ. 'On his way there he was held up by a bad traffic block. He got out of his car to investigate and immediately afterwards he was shot, probably by a sentry,' the 3rd Division's war diary recorded the next day.[102]

Brown's death somehow symbolized the collapse of France – a once-proud nation whose soldiers were, in their shame and their panic-stricken flight, killing their allies rather than fighting the enemy, on their own soil. Certainly Brooke saw his death in this way – namely that Brown had been murdered by French deserters he had upbraided: 'he was known to have a hottish temper, and he may well have used the rough of his tongue on some of this rabble . . . It was a real tragedy as he had a brilliant future in front of him,' Brooke noted.[103]

Liquid refreshment

After the comparative orderliness of the 3rd Division's staged withdrawals up to 28 May, the last days of Dunkirk became a nightmare. Even for Lieutenant-Colonel Brian Horrocks, temporarily in command of the 3rd Division's two machine-gun battalions, it was 'a far more nerve-shattering experience than the vast battle in Normandy' in 1944, as the Germans shelled the division, and launched attack after attack.[104]

On 29 May the 3rd Division again withdrew, this time to be the central stop-gap at Furnes on the eastern perimeter of the Dunkirk bridgehead, while General von Bock moved into Monty's vacated quarters at the St Sixtus monastery to direct the final battle for Dunkirk.[105]

With four enemy divisions now concentrated upon Monty's front, and its withdrawal routes choked with abandoned lorries, equipment and troops, the battle became more and more savage – severe casualties being suffered as the Germans sniped, shelled, infiltrated and exploited every small gap that could be forced between retreating units. However, by dawn on 30 May the 3rd Division was in its final position, with its HQ in La Panne, overlooking the sea. '8 and 9 Inf Bdes got in very late, and all very tired. Spent morning organizing front,' Monty recorded in his diary.[106]

'This lack of sleep affected everyone, high and low,' Horrocks later recalled, 'with one exception – General Montgomery. During the whole of the withdrawal he insisted on having meals at regular hours and never missed his normal night's sleep. Consequently when we arrived at Dunkirk he was as fresh as when he started. And he was about the only one who was . . . I saw him every day, sometimes several times a day, and he was always the same; confident, almost cocky you might say, cheerful and apparently quite fresh. He was convinced that he was the best divisional commander in the British Army and that we were the best division. By the time we had reached Dunkirk I had come to the same conclusion!'[107]

Captain Gough, commanding the HQ company of the 2nd Lincolnshire Regiment, agreed. He later recalled having been sent back to 'recce' the position that his battalion was to hold north of Lille. Looking for a suitable headquarters he had 'noticed a small well concealed house more or less in the centre of our position, with a large 3 Div truck outside with several men loading files. It proved to be 3 Div HQ moving out, and I arranged for several signal lines to be left, as they might be useful for our own communications. After allocating Company areas and finding cover for vehicles and put[ing] out markers, I noticed there was a door, inside the house, which led, by a steep flight of stone steps, to a cellar full of wine. I selected three bottles and started up the steps when I saw a figure looking down at me from the cellar door. It was Monty! Knowing full well his views on drinking and smoking, the thought flashed through my mind of being placed under close arrest. However he only smiled and said something like this – "Well Gough, I see you are getting up a little liquid refreshment for your CO when he gets in, best of luck," and departed!'[108]

Certainly the 3rd Division, numbering still more than 13,000 men,[109] was the largest of Brooke's four divisions when Brooke toured their sectors on 30 May. 'Our casualties were not heavy compared with others,' Dawnay recorded. 'The division felt itself quite confident about seeing the

Germans off as far as it was concerned; it was a question of whether other people had let us down, put us in an impossible situation.'[110]

Retiring to Dunkirk, however, was one thing; successfully evacuating by sea was another.

Brooke's tears

At 11 o'clock on the morning of 30 May Lieutenant-General Brooke arrived at Monty's 3 Division HQ at La Panne. Since the previous day Brooke had known that he was to hand over command of his corps and go home to help 'reforming new armies', but he had told no one in France. 'After having struggled with the Corps through all its vicissitudes, and having guarded it to the sea, I felt like a deserter not remaining with it till the last,' Brooke later wrote.[111] He had used every minute of his final twenty-four hours trying to see that the left flank of the BEF was secure, and hoped to get Gort to agree that II Corps should embark first – not for selfish reasons, but because the western flank around the port of Dunkirk, currently held by I Corps, must obviously be defended to the bitter end.

The meeting with Monty was unexpectedly emotional. Brooke had managed almost single-handedly – as far as higher BEF command was concerned   to foil the German pincer movement from 25 to 30 May, when he finally met Gort again. Whether it was the tragedy of the BEF or the accumulated tension after so many days of unremittingly distinguished generalship, Brooke now gave way to his emotions. 'He arrived at my headquarters to say goodbye and I saw at once that he was struggling to hold himself in check,' wrote Monty later in his *Path to Leadership*; 'so I took him a little way into the sand hills and then he broke down and wept – not because of the situation of the BEF, which was indeed bad, but because he had to leave us all to a fate which looked pretty bad.'[112]

Brian Horrocks was a surprised witness. He had been summoned to 3rd Division HQ and 'as I approached I saw two figures standing in the sand-dunes. I recognized our corps commander, General Brooke, and my divisional commander, General Montgomery. The former was under a considerable emotional strain. His shoulders were bowed and it looked as though he were weeping. Monty was patting him on the back. Then they shook hands and General Brooke walked slowly to his car and drove away.'[113]

That General Brooke, so reserved, so austere and private, should break down in front of the commander of his division amazed Horrocks. To Monty, however, Brooke's breakdown signified something much deeper than a momentary lapse of self-control. 'When the reserve of the English heart is broken through, most of us like to be alone,' Monty wrote in his *Path to Leadership*. 'And so when Alanbrooke broke down and wept on my shoulder, I knew it meant his friendship was all mine – and I was glad to have it that way. That scene in the sand-dunes on the Belgian coast is one that will remain with me all my life.'[114]

The mark of intimacy

Whether Brooke's lowering of his impassive mask was quite the symbol of 'friendship' that Monty took it to mean is questionable. For Monty, however, tears were – as they had been the day he proposed to Betty Carver – the deepest measure of trust. Lonely, single-minded, suspicious or contemptuous of most contemporaries and seniors, unable to show tenderness now that Betty was no longer alive, and living in an exclusively homosocial world, Monty was moved beyond words by Brooke's gesture. Four years later, on the eve of D-Day, Churchill too would burst into tears in front of him, and thus cement a friendship for life, on Monty's part – for such tears represented the mark of intimacy Monty had most craved from his mother, and had only ever shared with his beloved Betty.

Meanwhile Horrocks 'remained a silent and interested spectator of this astonishing scene', as he recalled. Such sentimentality was swiftly shelved, however. 'Monty beckoned me over and said, "General Brooke has just received orders to hand over the 2nd Corps to me and go back to England."'[115] Brigadier Kenneth Anderson from the 4th Division would succeed Monty in command of 3rd Division, while Horrocks would take over Anderson's brigade. The last scene of Act I, World War II, was about to begin.

Stout hearts and cool heads

Monty had comforted Brooke 'saying that we would all get back to England somehow and join up with him again,' Monty himself recalled, 'but I must confess that at that moment it wasn't clear to me how it would be done, but it became clearer later that day when I had time to study the problem at Corps HQ.'[116]

The handover of command was due to take place that evening, after a conference at Gort's GHQ. Meanwhile, though the higher German commanders boasted that the encirclement and destruction of the BEF were almost complete (and dropped leaflets on the British and French troops, calling on them to surrender), all attacks were beaten off by 3 Division's infantry and artillery. At Furnes the Grenadier and Coldstream Guards and 4th Berkshires repulsed assault after assault. 'My admiration for the Guards, always high, became unbounded during that afternoon,' noted Robin Dunn in his diary, recording that 'the atmosphere of complete calm and self control was marvellous'.[117] The infantry felt the same about the artillery. Provided the perimeter defences were manned with resolution, and intelligent use of local reserves was made, the BEF had every chance of evacuating the larger part of its remaining troops, Monty considered – and for the most part his men felt the same. The adjutant of the 7th Field Artillery Regiment 'said that he expected we would have to stay for about five days', Dunn recalled, and no one demurred.[110] 'We have not quite finished our task yet,' Monty stated in a final order of the day, 'and the next two or three days may see some hard fighting. Provided we maintain our present positions, all will be well; if we fail to maintain them our difficulties will become enormous. During the next few days we shall need stout hearts and cool heads, and all must be prepared to uphold the good name of the 3rd Division by hard fighting. To our task, then, with determination and good British tenacity. The 3rd Division will stand firm and show the way; I have complete confidence in its ability to hold its own and prevent any enemy penetration of its front.'[119]

Having issued this final mesage as 3 Division commander, Monty walked to Gort's headquarters. Significantly it was the first time he had seen his commander-in-chief since the campaign began on 10 May.

A scene from Thucydides

The scene was worthy of Thucydides. Gort was now 'alone in the dining room of the house and looked a pathetic sight, though outwardly cheerful as always,' Monty recalled in his memoirs. 'His first remark to me was typical of the man: "Be sure to have your front well covered with fighting patrols tonight." '[120]

The conference had been called to give final evacuation orders for the BEF, in view of the paucity of naval vessels, and the War Cabinet's latest instructions regarding surrender. 'Our chances are being frittered away by the Navy,' Gort's new chief of staff, Brigadier Sir Oliver Leese, scribbled home to his wife. 'A wonderful day with low clouds, & not a single ship working. It will lose us a day – & we've not got many days to waste. In fact none.'[121]

Accounts of the conference vary. The British official history of the campaign, compiled by Major L. F. Ellis, skimmed over the evacuation period, as if embarrassed to have to tell the truth. Ellis thus recorded that when Churchill requested him to nominate a rearguard commander for the final evacuation, Lord Gort appointed Major-General Alexander as commander of I Corps.[122] Gort, in preparing his despatches, also covered up his appointment of Lieutenant-General Barker.[123] Monty, however, was there and knew better: that Gort assumed the rearguard would be forced to surrender to the Germans, and appointed the hapless Lieutenant-General Michael Barker to do this – a decision which, given Barker's breakdown, would have led to the wholesale surrender of I Corps. The GHQ War Diary for 30 May 1940, however, written by Lieutenant-Colonel Lord Bridgeman, confirmed Gort's decision to put Barker in charge of the final evacuation and surrender: 'C-in-C saw General Barker and told him he would be nominated as the Commander.'[124]

Monty, though only a temporary corps commander from 6 p.m., was appalled. His own handwritten diary for 30 May was caustic: 'C-in-C read out telegram from War Office ordering one Corps to be surrendered to enemy with the French at Dunkirk; Barker selected 1 Corps.' 'This was a very fateful conference, of GHQ,' he recognized in his diary, written that night. British surrender would go down in history – but was it actually necessary? 'The atmosphere was tense and those members of GHQ who were present were obviously out of touch with realities and lacked any sense of proportion. The C-in-C could make no constructive proposals and could give no quick and definite decisions. Barker (1st Corps) was excited and rattled; his BGS (Holden) was frightened and out of touch.'

Brooke's diary concurs, noting that he 'found Gort undecided as to how to continue evacuation',[125] but was himself called away to his waiting destroyer. 'Brooke (who had handed over 2 Corps to me) was present for the first ¼ hour & then left for England; he was first class and must play a big part in the future schemes of re-organization,' Monty noted in his own diary – having himself given 'my definite opinion as to what was, and was not, possible'.[126]

Gort's shilly-shallying was also covered up not only by the official historian but by his 1972 biographer, J. R. Colville – despite the fact that in a long, unpublished letter in 1952 Monty had given Colville a candid, no-holds-barred eyewitness account of the 'fateful' GHQ conference:

I arrived early at the conference as my HQ were on the outskirts of La Panne. Gort was in a house on the sea front.

He was alone when I arrived.

I don't think I have ever seen a more pathetic sight; the great and supposedly famous C-in-C of the British Army on the Continent, alone; the staff of GHQ was scattered to the four winds of Heaven; he had in La Panne two staff officers; one was first class (Oliver Leese); the other was useless (a 'Q' officer whose name I have forgotten for the moment, and who had lost his nerve).

Gort, in my opinion, was finished. He was incapable of grasping the military situation firmly, and issuing clear orders. He was incapable of instilling confidence or morale. He had 'had it' and I remember saying as much to Brooke, who was at the Conference and left for England from the beach immediately it was over.

Gort had a telegram in his hand.

He told us the gist of what he had been ordered to do; he finished by telling Barker he did not think the 1 Corps would be able to get away and that he (Barker) must stay with it and surrender to the Germans.

The effect on Barker was catastrophic; he was incoherent at first and then relapsed into silence.

I knew Gort very well, personally.

After we had broken up I got him alone and told him that we could not yet say it was impossible to get 1 Corps away; but that it would *never* get away if Barker was in control, and that the only sound course was to get Barker out of it as soon as possible and give 1 Corps to Alexander.[127]

In this letter Monty claimed that 'Gort agreed' and Barker – 'an utterly useless commander, who had lost his nerve by 30 May' – was 'sent away; he was never employed again and I have never heard anything of him, or seen him, since that Conference at La Panne on the evening of 30 May 1940'.[128]

No surrender

Whatever Monty urged, the truth is that Gort remained incapable of clear decision-making for a further critical day at Dunkirk. 'The whole place is full of panic,' Leese acknowledged in the scribbled note he sent to his wife, 'mostly French. A retreat is a terrible thing to see, & before long we'll have men fighting for boats and food. We have embarked many Rearward Services, but unless things go well, we shall lose all the good fighting troops.' Surrender seemed, in view of Gort's breakdown, to be inevitable. 'I must say I dread the thought of Germany,' Leese confided to his wife, while trying to show 'a cheerful face' to his colleagues.[129]

Thus the next morning, 31 May 1940, Barker was still in command of I Corps, which was to be surrendered to the Germans, as the GHQ war diary for 31 May, kept by Brigadier Oliver Leese, noted. The commander of 1st Division, Major-General Alexander, had called on Gort at 8.30 a.m, Leese recorded: 'He was told to thin out his division as it appeared probable that he would have to surrender the majority alongside the French in accordance with War Office instructions.'[130]

In fact, Churchill's instructions – whatever the gist given by Gort at the 'fateful' GHQ conference – were by no means categorical as to capitulation. Churchill's telegram had been sent at 2 p.m. on the afternoon of 30 May. Its final lines read that only when 'The Corps Commander chosen by you' felt 'no further organized evacuation is possible and no further proportionate damage can be inflicted on the enemy he is author-ized in consultation with the senior French Commander to capitulate formally to avoid useless slaughter'.[131]

That situation had not been reached; the weather was still calm, and the evacuation going ahead with miraculously light casualties, either from Göring's Luftwaffe, or German artillery shelling – since the sandy soil absorbed all but direct hits.

The truth was, the commander-in-chief was in a state of semi-paralysis.

Only at 1 p.m. on 31 May 1940 was Alexander finally summoned back to La Panne. Over lunch Gort told him, at last, on Monty's advice 'he was to command 1 Corps'. After lunch Alexander was given 'written orders by the C-in-C. He [Alexander] stated his intentions at all costs to extricate his command and not to surrender any part of it', the GHQ war diary recorded. 'Lt-General Barker was told to hand over 1 Corps to Major-General Alexander and to go back to England.'[132]

Monty was delighted. In his own diary for 31 May he was savagely laconic: 'Continued plans for embarking 2 Corps. Enemy attacked almost continuously but was held. C-in-C very pathetic sight, a defeated and disappointed man. He was to leave by destroyer at 1800 hrs.'

With the C-in-C gone, the fate of the BEF now lay in the hands of its two remaining corps commanders: Montgomery and Alexander.

Dunkirk

Monty's plan for the evacuation of II Corps was straightforward. The Germans were to be viciously counter-attacked whenever they attempted to cross the Nieuport–Furnes Canal, with as much artillery shelling as possible and air attack; then, under cover of darkness that night, the 3rd and 4th Divisions were to thin out and make for the beaches of La Panne and Bray Dunes, where they were to embark, using jetties that Monty's RE troops had been making all day from transport vehicles that were run out into the sea and covered.

Despite the squally weather that had brought beach evacuation almost to a standstill that morning, Monty still exuded confidence. 'Landing beaches were a sight worth seeing,' recorded the II Corps war diary. 'Thousands of troops, many ships large and small and numerous aircraft patrolling. Embarkation was difficult owing to the choppy seas and piers were built over the top of lorries. There were numerous air battles and bombing raids.'[133]

Monty had arranged that reception camps be set up in the dunes; soldiers were only to be sent down on to the more exposed beach for embarkation when the beach commander called them – a system that worked admirably, thanks to the redoubtable 3rd Division's signallers who managed during the retreat to bring back enough cable to link not only the perimeter with Divisional HQ but the reception camps with the beach commander. Despite the gloomy forecast, embarkation in the afternoon and evening went surprisingly well, with very few casualties despite heavy German shelling. At 9 p.m., after dark, the great exodus was stepped up. At 8.30 p.m. Monty had seen Alexander – 'We were both confident that all would be well in the end,' Monty later recalled.[134]

There was now an air of calm and complete authority. The two commanders agreed that if La Panne became unusable, II Corps would withdraw entirely via the beach at Bray Dunes; if that also became untenable, the port of Dunkirk itself would be closed to I Corps personnel until II Corps was safely evacuated.

This was a fortunate agreement, for after 11 p.m. on 31 May evacuation from both beaches became impossible – the culprit being the tide. Between 11 p.m. and 3 a.m. the next morning it was simply too low for the piers, constructed on lorries, to be usable, at either La Panne or Bray Dunes. At Bray Dunes Monty had the men redirected to Dunkirk itself – a march of over fifteen miles for the already exhausted troops of 4th Division. As Monty described in his diary: 'It was clearly impossible to continue embarkation at the beaches and I ordered the troops to move on to Dunkirk and embark there; this they were loath to do as they saw the ships lying off and hoped boats would come to the shore; but no boats came.'[135]

With the last of II Corps' perimeter defences withdrawing in the early hours of 1 June, it became imperative that the whole corps be within the Dunkirk port perimeter by dawn; therefore Monty remained at Bray Dunes until 3.30 a.m. At one point a shell landed in the sand near by, wounding his young ADC, Lieutenant Charles Sweeny. Monty told him he was a fool not to be wearing a helmet – at which the ADC remonstrated that his corps commander was not wearing one either!

Fortunately, Brooke had warned Admiral Ramsay at Dover that the greatest effort would be needed on the night of 31 May/1 June, and the weary men of II Corps, as they reached Dunkirk, were not disappointed. Altogether some 68,000 troops were evacuated on 31 May – almost 23,000 of these from the beaches, the remainder from the great mole at Dunkirk: a scene unparalleled in military history, and a figure equivalent to half the Allied troops that would be landed on the beaches of Normandy almost exactly four years later.

Leaving Bray Dunes at 3.30 a.m. on 1 June, Monty walked with his chief of staff Neil Ritchie and his wounded ADC down the beach towards Dunkirk. 'Enemy was shelling the beach but caused no casualties,' he noted in his diary. 'After one hour we struck inland and picked up a lorry which took us in to Dunkirk; the town was being shelled and bombed and was in a complete shambles. Found the naval shore station on the Mole and got sent off to a destroyer (HMS *Codrington*, Capt. Stevens-Guille, DSO, OBE). Heavy bombing attacks while lying at the Mole and on the journey to Dover. Arrived London 1500 hrs and reported to CIGS at War Office.'

He had survived to tell the tale. Whether Britain would do so, after the fall of France, was another matter.

12

In the Aftermath of Dunkirk

Battling Churchill

While Monty travelled to London to give his views to the War Office, General Alan Brooke was ordered back to France to take command of another BEF campaign. This was the second ill-fated attempt to assist the French armies: armies that were rapidly disintegrating before German attacks south of the Somme.

Britain's renewed military campaign in France proved even more disastrous than the first. The British and French governments agreed a plan to withdraw into an Allied 'redoubt' in Brittany, but General Georges and General Weygand admitted to Brooke in private (though not in Weygand's memoirs) that this was fantasy, with only four British divisions, a few French remnants, no reserves and no defensive preparations made.[1] Brooke thereupon counselled immediate evacuation of all remaining BEF and any Allied forces willing to leave France, through Brest and the Brittany ports.

Sir John Dill, who had succeeded General Ironside as the new CIGS, agreed wholeheartedly. Mr Winston Churchill, as Prime Minister and Minister of Defence, did not. 'What the hell,' demanded Brooke, exasperated, '*does* he want?'[2]

The Prime Minister, speaking on a bad telephone connection to Le Mans, then took the receiver, and told Brooke he wanted the 52nd Division to stay and fight to the end with the French – even though the entire 51st Highland Division had already been needlessly sacrificed at St Valéry on 11 June, where virtually the whole division had been captured by the Germans. Churchill told Brooke that he'd 'been sent to France to make the French feel that we were supporting them'. Brooke's riposte was, for a man educated and brought up in France, brutally tart. 'I replied that it was impossible to make a corpse feel, and that the French Army was, to all intents and purposes, dead.'[3]

Churchill was forced to think again. Brooke remained implacable. 'From my first interview with Weygand and Georges I saw it was quite hopeless and that the only thing was to extricate the remainder of the BEF as quick as possible if we wanted to avoid another Dunkirk. But it was not easy to get the Government [Churchill] to appreciate what was the situation, & I had some anxious moments,' Brooke confided to Monty on 24 June 1940.[4]

If Churchill was obtuse, it was because he could not credit the depths of French cowardice and defeatism. In truth, the eighty-four-year-old Pétain, who had succeeded Reynaud as Prime Minister of France on 16 June 1940, feared social unrest, even 'mutiny' in the armed forces and a socialist uprising in France. For the 'good' of the nation – i.e., to avoid socialism in his own country – Pétain was determined to surrender the nation to Hitler rather than fight on for democracy from North Africa.

Submission to Nazi domination thus seemed to Pétain better than another French Revolution and socialist experiment; besides, he was too old to play Napoleon, so he played Quisling instead. On 17 June 1940, on his orders, all French troops were ordered to stop fighting pending an armistice, and it was German tumbrils that sounded. The following day Brooke left St Nazaire aboard an armed trawler, sad and disgusted by the French performance. Democracy had willingly submitted to the fascist rule of force.

Useless generals

Meanwhile, Captain Robin Dunn, landing in Dover on the morning of 1 June 1940, recorded in his diary how he and other 3 Division survivors from Dunkirk were 'bundled into trains and by 10-30 were steaming through the Kentish countryside'. They 'stopped at a station and were given hot tea and bread and marmalade. Never have I enjoyed a meal more. After that things became embarrassing. At every station where we stopped a mass of women appeared with cigarettes, sweet biscuits, lemonade and other delicacies. At one station a woman got in and insisted on feeding us and thanking us. I sat in my corner with 24 hours growth on my beard longing for the train to start. It was astonishing to be treated thus, we had expected the population to turn their backs on us – a beaten army.'[5]

Monty, travelling by train to London from Dover the same evening, received the same English tea-cakes-and-cigarettes treatment. Not having slept the night before, he went directly to a hotel, but the next morning, 2 June 1940, he marched straight into the office of the new CIGS, General Sir John Dill.

Dill looked despondent. 'Do you realize that for the first time for a thousand years this country is now in danger of invasion?' he asked Monty.

To Dill's consternation Monty laughed aloud – a mad, almost manic laugh. 'I said that the people of England would never believe we were in danger of being invaded when they saw useless generals in charge of some of the Home Commands, and I gave him some examples,' Monty recalled.[6]

Monty might laugh, but he wasn't joking. Defeat at Dunkirk had not only laid Britain open to invasion, it had laid bare – to him at least – the utter incompetence of those in high command in Britain and the BEF. Monty's personal diary entry for that day (which he did not publish in his memoirs, having only found the diary 'in an old locked box in my attic box room' in 1963[7]) was cruelly frank. 'Visited War Office and demanded a private interview with CIGS,' he recorded in his own, clear and emphatic handwriting on 2 June. 'Informed him as to the condition of Gort and Barker at the final conference at La Panne on evening 30 May; said that the events of the past few weeks had proved that certain officers were unfit to be employed again and should be retired.' In describing Gort's final conference to Dill, Monty added that, in his view, 'the BEF had never been "commanded" since it was formed, and that for the next encounter we must have a new GHQ and a new C-in-C. I said that the only man to be C-in-C was Brooke.'[8]

Dill was alarmed. Having served under Gort for eight months in the BEF, the new CIGS knew Monty was telling the unvarnished truth, but it was not a truth he wished to be broadcast beyond his room. 'He could not but agree,' Monty wrote in his memoirs, 'but he ticked me off for speaking in such a way at such a time in our misfortunes, and said that remarks of that kind could only cause a loss of confidence.'[9] The British public must not be told the bitter truth.

Fashioning the legend of Dunkirk

Some days later Monty 'received a letter telling me to stop saying such things', he recalled in his memoirs.[10] He recalled correctly.

'My dear Montgomery,' Dill wrote in the manner of a headmaster admonishing a pupil who had told tales out of class. 'I learn that there is a certain amount of rather loose criticism going on among commanders of the B.E.F. regarding the manner in which their seniors, their equals and their juniors conducted the recent operations in France and Belgium. Such criticism is calculated to shake the confidence of the Army in its leaders of all ranks, and I need not emphasize its dangers, particularly at a time like the present. I look to you to put a stop to all this. Any failings of commanders or Staff officers should be submitted confidentially through the proper channels but on no account must they be discussed unofficially.'[11]

Dill was not the only one to silence dissenters. On 5 June 1940 a personal note from Lord Gort's chief of staff, Major-General Pownall, was also sent to Monty. 'Among the flood of stories and rumours that are being spread is one which has come to me, and to the C-in-C, that you have yourself been telling exaggerated stories!' Pownall complained from Buckingham Palace Road, where Lord Gort's fantasy account of the campaign was already being concocted by Pownall.[12] (When Brooke, for example, asked for Pownall as his chief of staff for BEF II, he was told that 'Pownall could not be spared, as Gort required him for the writing of despatches'.[13]

'After the strain & tension that we've all been through,' Pownall warned Monty, 'and nobody more than yourself, there is certainly a tendency for tongues to wag (I've found it myself) but it's a dangerous business and more likely to bring discredit than honour to the B.E.F. This would be a pity after the magnificent showing the B.E.F. have made. Of all the divisional commanders the C-in-C reckons you have come out either a good second or equal first,' he assured Monty, 'so I do hope that if there's any truth in the story I've heard you won't do anything to upset the tremendous opinion the C-in-C has formed of you.'[14]

Like Haig's versions of the 'success' of his 'Big Push' on the Somme and his Passchendaele battles, the legend of Dunkirk was thus being fashioned by the commander-in-chief and his loyal entourage, who not only controlled the writing up of the campaign in the form of official despatches, but who made the selection of those officers recommended for medals – including themselves. Lord Gort, who had won the VC in World War I, was made a Knight Grand Cross of the Order of the Bath (KGCB), while Pownall was also knighted as Sir Henry Pownall – despite arguably the worst British example of command since the Boer War! Churchill, however, loved a lord, and remained a stalwart admirer of Gort. In Parliament on 6 June 1940 he declared that Britain 'will have to reconstitute and build up the B.E.F. under its gallant Commander, Lord Gort';[15] indeed, Churchill never lost his respect for Gort as a field commander, even trying to get him sent out to North Africa as commander of the 8th Army two years later.[16]

Demotion

Monty was not alone in criticizing Lord Gort; Major-General Mason-Macfarlane, Gort's own Director of Military Intelligence, went about speaking of Gort's leadership 'with contempt', Gort's biographer noted frankly, while General Brooke told a fellow general, Andrew Thorne, that Gort was no better than ' "a lance-corporal"; others too began to whisper their denigrations in the clubs and the corridors'.[17]

Monty did not frequent clubs or corridors; he had not whispered, but had spoken confidentially and honestly to the head of the British army, the CIGS – and been ordered to shut up. Nevertheless, he did not and could not see that the BEF had performed 'magnificently' – on the contrary, he felt Gort's headquarters had been a discredit to the British army, and that Gort in particular should be removed as a senior commander if Britain wanted to stay in the war and save democracy. The BEF had suffered 69,000 casualties, left behind 2,472 guns, around 400 tanks, 63,879 vehicles and 415,000 tons of stores;[18] it was a catastrophe. Gort's 'ceiling was a Divisional Commander', he later told Gort's biographer, John Colville. 'This was well known to Brooke and myself, and we often discussed it privately. Dill knew it and admitted it to me when he was C.I.G.S.' The British army had been saddled at the start of World War II by 'bad leadership', thanks to Hore-Belisha's insistence on 'getting rid of' Gort by appointing him to command Britain's primary army in the field – a commander whose 'GHQ in the field was a thoroughly bad set up'. Gort had 'made no preparations for exercising effective command when the phoney war became a live war: which it did on 10 May. From that moment GHQ lost control, and never regained it.' To consider – as Churchill, Alexander, Colville and others did – that Gort would have made an effective opponent against Rommel in the desert in 1942 was, Monty felt, typical of the utter military ignorance characterizing Britain's 'old-boy-network' society. 'A good General,' he explained to Colville, 'will so organize his Headquarters and his staff that he can grip the battle, and he will not lose control even when the battle begins to go against him.'[19]

Monty was equally insulted by the suggestion that he had only come out 'a good second' among divisional commanders, given that the 3rd Division had rehearsed all its moves and operations before the start of the campaign, and was the only British division to return almost intact from Dunkirk. Leaving Gort and Pownall (across whose letter Monty later pencilled the words: 'Lieut-General Sir Henry Pownall, Chief of the General Staff of BEF, under Gort. He was completely useless') to 'honour' the BEF's mythical performance, however, Monty cut bait and returned to 3 Division's new headquarters at Frome in Somerset – having been demoted once again to divisional command, albeit still as a major-general, and without a knighthood.

Too old for this kind of war

With Allied defeat at Dunkirk Monty's military life had reached its nadir – and it was his own fault for not holding his tongue. To all intents and purposes he was the last professional battlefield commander left in Britain capable of successfully fighting the Nazis – yet, for the next two years, he would be kept from fighting the Germans in the field as a 'loose cannon'.

For Britain this was symptomatic of the unwillingness to question the social and military system that had led to the catastrophe of Dunkirk. Whatever Lord Gort might write in his despatches, the BEF had failed miserably, just as the French armies had done. General Barker, the I Corps commander, had proved to be a total 'dud',[20] and although General Brooke had been a tower of strength commanding II Corps, his breakdown at La Panne was revealing. After withdrawing BEF II from St Nazaire he would never fight again in the field – or dare to, when offered the chance. Although he was made C-in-C Southern Command, then C-in-C Home

Forces and ultimately CIGS, he remained a brilliant artillery officer and strategist, with no rapport whatever with ordinary men in a democracy. As Monty would later write in *The Path to Leadership*, 'I doubt if he would have been such a highly successful commander in the field as he was a national Chief of Staff – because I don't think he would have got himself over to the soldiers in the right way.'[21] Nor did Brooke have any ability to make British soldiers fight offensively – especially citizen-conscripts. His outrage over Monty's 'VD order' was all too indicative. Like the commanders of World War I – in which he had pioneered the 'creeping' artillery barrage – he relied on the British class system of respect for one's 'betters', in the hope that this pride in serving one's social superiors would motivate men to fight and, where necessary, give their lives for their country. They had done so at the Somme, and again at Passchendaele in vast numbers – but in truth they would never do so again. Haig and his generals, while imagining they were 'purifying' the British race by such deliberate bloodletting, had in fact ruined it.

Reflecting on the French collapse, Winston Churchill dimly recognized this, noting on 29 June 1940 that 'there had been a rot in France which had affected every class and stratum of the community; it was not merely the Generals and the politicians but the whole country'.[22] Was Britain any better, though? Secret surveys reported that women were twice as defeatist as men; moreover, although with his mastery of rhetoric and his love of (English) history Churchill was able to articulate a defiance of fascism that helped unite the British people after Dunkirk, exhorting them to fight on, it is widely recognized today – particularly in view of recently released files detailing the response of British nationals to the German occupation of the Channel Islands (Guernsey and Jersey) – that most Britons, if conquered, would have conformed to Nazi occupation exactly as did the French and other conquered European nations – willingly handing over their Jewish minorities and refuseniks. (A list of several thousand, the so-called Black Book, had already been prepared by the Reichskommissar charged with the occupation of Britain.[23])

Over this national demoralization, despite making himself Minister of Defence, Churchill simply had no power beyond his metaphors. Bob Boothby, an MP who had been Churchill's private secretary, wrote to warn his old boss that the country now needed 'drastic measures', perhaps even martial law. 'This is essentially a young man's war,' he pointed out to the ageing PM. 'It is this incredible conception of a movement (in Germany), young, virile, dynamic and violent, which is advancing irresistibly to overthrow a decaying old world, that we must continue to bear in mind,' Boothby went on; 'for it is the main source of the Nazi strength and power.' Churchill's Military Secretary had warned the Prime Minister already that Britain's leaders were 'past it'; Boothby reiterated the plain fact that 'our leaders (as Pug Ismay[24] said the other night), are too old for this kind of war and that there is growing discontent with the fact among younger officers'.[25]

In his heart of hearts Churchill knew this; indeed, he sent a personal note to Lord Beaverbrook, the Minister of Air Production, on 8 July 1940, confessing that Britain had 'no continental army which can defeat the German military power' and begging Beaverbrook to put everything into Britain's 'only sure path' to winning the war: 'heavy bombers' raining TNT 'upon the Nazi homeland. We must be able to overwhelm them by this means without which I do not see a way through.'[26]

Sadly, Churchill was wrong. As the Germans would shortly discover when ordering the *Blitzkrieg* on English cities, heavy bombing only hardened a country's resistance. Meanwhile the fact was, though he could order Britain's gentlemen-commanders to fight, and tell them where and for how long to fight, from Greece to Crete, Singapore to Burma, Benghazi to Tobruk, Churchill had no way of *making* British soldiers fight, for all his incomparable oratory.

The simple truth is, a nation gets the government it deserves. As a class-bound, traditional society the British had got not only the government it deserved, but also the army: an army that deserved to fail in modern battlefield combat against a first-class enemy.

For the next two years in the struggle against Nazi Germany, the British army fell prey to the same social divisiveness and inter-service bloody-mindedness that had bedevilled their forces since the end of World War I. Indeed, the very things which most defined modern democracy – respect for individual rights and freedom of speech – appeared most to doom it in modern combat, thanks to Haig's futile bloodletting in World War I, for no one relished the thought of a reprised battle of the Somme.

Times had changed. As the Roman Empire had collapsed before the depredations of the Visigoths, so Britain now seemed powerless to confront the ruthlessness and fighting skill of the Nazis. Even Churchill's own military adviser, General Spears, who had watched the French collapse, thought that if the Germans decided to invade Britain, Britain would be unable to deal either with a German aerial armada, or the landing of German tank formations.[27]

In short the problem, as in ancient Rome, was as much social as political or military. In World War I Britain had confronted a Prussian-style army run on not entirely dissimilar lines to that of its own Victorian-Edwardian class-divided society; in 1940, however, it faced an indoctrinated national-socialist enemy, tribally led: a society in which class no longer played a significant part, while co-operation in achieving new national goals, however fantastical, went unquestioned. Churchill could refer in Parliament and on the radio to Britain's traditions, to its history, empire and humanity, but in reality he had no forward-looking social vision to match that of Hitler's young Germany – and in Britain's lamentable military perform-ance it showed. German troops fought for their new Reich and its quasi-socialist aims; the British did not.

It would be Monty's historic role to change this dynamic: to demonstrate that Britain's army *could* fight and *would* fight – if he was permitted to become the team captain and coach. But, unattractive, rude and a social misfit in post-Edwardian England, he wasn't – thanks to Churchill.

Meeting his match

Monty would, of course, be himself to blame for his failure to get appointed again to field command in the two years after Dunkirk. He was not nature's diplomat, rather the reverse. He had not only criticized his commander-in-chief and dared to recommend that the CIGS sack almost the entire high command in Britain, but when he finally met Churchill for the first time, exactly a month later on 2 July 1940, he was similarly disparaging.

The Prime Minister had arranged to visit Monty's 3 Division in its invasion-defence role near Brighton, on the south coast, followed by dinner at a prominent hotel, the Royal Albion. Looking out of the window, Churchill had seen one of Monty's men demolishing an old wooden hut on Brighton pier to make way for a machine-gun post. Nostalgically he'd remarked 'that when at school near there he used to go and see the performing fleas in the kiosk'.[28]

Monty had never seen performing fleas; nor did he miss the sight. Picking up up on Churchill's throwaway remark, however, he ridiculed 3 Division's role. Should a regular army division, which had been until the evacuation at Dunkirk the only fully mobile regular British infantry

division, be squandered in static defence of Brighton pier? Ignoring protocol, Monty pointed out the fatuousness of permitting Britain's only fully
re-equipped division to be rendered fully immobile. 'Some other troops
should take on my task,' Monty complained; 'my division should be given
buses, and be held in mobile reserve with a counter-attack role. Why was
I immobile?'[29]

As the two men spoke, buses plied the Brighton parade. 'There were
thousands of buses in England,' Monty harangued the Prime Minister/
Minister of Defence; 'let them give me some, and release me from this
static role so that I could practise a mobile counter-attack role . . .'[30]

Not content with such criticism of government policy Monty challenged
the overweight, cigar-smoking, whisky-smelling epicurean Prime Minister
by saying – as General Ismay and Bob Boothby had already said, though
in confidence – that elderly commanders should be sacked, and only
younger, healthier men retained in command.

Churchill stopped Monty there. He 'asked me what I would drink at
dinner and I replied – water,' Monty remembered in his memoirs. 'This
astonished him. I added that I neither drank nor smoked and was 100 per
cent fit.'

Churchill's eyes narrowed. He resented the personal implication; taking
his glass in one hand and his cigar in the other, he replied 'that he both
drank and smoked, and was 200 per cent fit'.[31]

Confrontation with Churchill

The two men eyed each other: each a mountebank, resented by the diehards
of their respective professions; each aware that the current war would
make or break them.

It was not only King George VI who'd had reservations when calling
upon Winston Churchill to form a coalition government seven weeks
earlier, on 10 May 1940; most civil servants in Whitehall had trembled
at Churchill's penchant for rash, ill-considered ventures – such as the
Norwegian débâcle. 'Rab' Butler, a Conservative under-secretary in the
Foreign Office, who was a leading appeaser and supporter of Chamberlain
in the government, deplored Churchill, a once-Liberal turncoat, as the
enemy of 'the good clean tradition of English politics', indeed, called him
'the greatest adventurer of modern political history'. In Butler's widely

held view, Chamberlain and his right-hand men such as Lord Halifax and the Minister of War, Oliver Stanley, had 'weakly surrendered to a half-breed American'.[32]

This, however, was better than surrendering to a half-breed Austrian, as Chamberlain, Halifax and Butler would undoubtedly have done otherwise. Nevertheless, the 'half-breed American' was certainly a liability when combining the duties of Minister of Defence with his prime ministership: constantly proposing rash operations under impossible conditions, under flawed commanders whom he liked. Anyone Churchill disliked was passed over – as Monty was to find out.

Thus the two pugnacious characters – Punch and Judy – clicked, and yet did not click. Irritated by Monty's insubordinate, presumptuous self-confidence, Churchill listened to the little, beaky-nosed major-general's ideas on how to use mobile 3 Division reserves to repel a possible German invasion. On the one hand he was undoubtedly stimulated by Monty's offensive-mindedness (and bullied his staff, when he got back to London, to reshape British anti-invasion policy as a result), yet at the same time he was alarmed by Monty's literally offensive personality: his strange, over-energetic, weird, almost mad blue-grey eyes, his sharp, bony features, his lack of respect for the courtesies and proprieties of 'club gentlemen'; his openly critical tone when discussing colleagues and superiors; his clearly dictatorial and controlling character. Monty was, to Churchill, obnoxious.

If Monty despised Lord Gort professionally, as was claimed, then Churchill despised Monty socially. Monty had not been to the right school (Eton or Harrow) – and it showed. He had not the right manners for a 'Churchill-man': ideally men like the Hon. Sir Harold Alexander, son of an earl, or Lord Louis Mountbatten, son of a German prince. Monty, by contrast, was 'common': an obsessive soldier, uninterested in good food or drink. In terms of high command, moreover, despite Ismay's and Boothby's warnings, Churchill could not see how the qualities of this 'little man' might actually save Britain and the free world.

Churchill had, it was true, been impressed by 'Monty's leopards', as he called 3 Division's counter-attack troops. But that Monty himself held, in his approach to modern war in a democracy, the key to British military renaissance in World War II, Churchill could not see – indeed, to Churchill Monty came across that day (as he would, several years later to General Marshall) as nothing more than 'a little man on the make', as he is supposed to have remarked to a colleague.[33] The Prime Minister thus left the Royal Albion Hotel with his entourage of fawning assistants, and although Monty 'got my buses', as he recalled,[34] he was not promoted – indeed, on Churchill's orders he would deliberately be denied field command for a further two years of national military failure and disaster, until Britain's battlefield performance became an international disgrace, threatening Britain's alliance with the United States and the Soviet Union; until, in other words, necessity, not perspicacity, became the mother of military virtue.

The way to fame

Clearly, from the point of view of the real world, Monty's failure to achieve field command was his own fault. He would not and could not 'play the system'. As he later wrote, with a character like his own, 'The way to fame is a hard one. You must suffer, and be the butt of jealousy and ill-informed criticism; it is a lonely matter. One just has to go on doing what you think is right, and doing your duty: whatever others may say or think; and that is what I try to do.'[35]

How, then, did this 'little man on the make' make such history?

The answer is that he completely ignored the 'outer world' for the next two years, concentrating entirely on his *own* world – knowing that one day, despite Churchill's animosity, his hour would come, and attempting to prepare for it by developing and rehearsing his own unique style of command.

It is time, then, to peer more closely into this Monty-world, at its strengths, limitations and eccentricities, for almost everything that would happen between the summer of 1942, when Monty assumed command of the 8th Army at Alamein, and the surrender of the entire German armed forces in north-west Germany and Scandinavia to him at Lüneburg in 1945 was prefigured in those two 'wilderness' years in Home Command as, in the aftermath of defeat at Dunkirk, he slowly climbed back from major-general in command of a division to lieutenant general in command of a corps, then another corps, then of two corps as an area commander, and finally of an army on the field of battle. Around the periphery of this slow rise would be the bitterness and resentment he engendered through his insensitivity, arrogance, ruthlessness, prejudice, paranoia, indifference, bloody-mindedness and occasional malice; but at its heart, its centre, what we need to examine is an issue that has never been properly explained by military writers and historians: how an unattractive, unprepossessing little man learned to inspire the loyalty of a handful of young men, and transformed that devotion, little by little, into the loyalty of a corps, an army, a group of armies and ultimately a nation.

As we shall see, the temptation of most revisionist historians, even in Monty's own lifetime, would be increasingly to see this process as a matter of PR – as if PR ever won battles against German troops! The reality was very, very different, involving a strange, homosocial compact in which Monty became teacher/master first to a small coterie of disciples, then, step-by-step, to an entire army. The growing admiration and gratitude, indeed the quasi-love of these men for their commander, would become in part, for Monty, a wartime substitute – sometimes the sole substitute – for the love he'd sought as a child, the respect he'd courted as a young adult, and the ten-year acceptance he'd attained in marriage, and so tragically lost. In this strangest of ways the misogynist widower, a misfit alienating himself from his own son and family, would throw himself into a homosocial compact with his men that might pass for love, however weird – and vault thereby two centuries of English class-division.

If Churchill invented, in the trials of 1940, a new parliamentary rhetoric, rich and metaphorical, for his country's suffering and stoicism in war, Monty was to invent a new vocabulary and dress for battle – indeed, so stunned would Churchill be by the stirring simplicity and directness of Monty's new style and approach that he would insist on taking copies of Monty's first edicts in the Egyptian desert back to London in August 1942, even before Monty's first, defensive battle at Alamein, and distributing them among the Cabinet. It would be clear, Churchill's Military Secretary would note, 'who means to be master in the desert'; that Rommel had, finally, met his match in a British commander whose first and only love was the soldiery: young 8th Army men he would make into winners, not losers.

13

Home Forces

New family

So obsessed was Monty with the reformation of Britain's moribund army that his own son David received no visit from his father after Dunkirk. In an extraordinary catalogue of a sad boyhood, Monty himself later listed David's school holidays:

Easter 40	Hotel in Portsmouth
Summer 40	Hog, Swimbridge
Xmas 40	Edinburgh
Easter 41	Hog, Swimbridge
Summer 41	Hog, ditto, (broke leg)
Xmas 41	Bath (Whitehead) . . .

No Montgomery relatives were listed, even as ports of call during David's holidays. Like 'Lady' Montgomery, they too were now kept at arm's length – as if Monty wished not to have to 'owe' them any favours; indeed, in some strange way wanted none of them to peer too deeply into his post-Betty soul, heart – or perhaps even his sexuality. The ten years of happiness with Betty were thus idealized, or picture-framed in his own mind, with no relative allowed to own or share in her memory – or console him. Already as a major-general in 1938 he had begun to 'collect' young men as his ADCs on his personal staff as well as on his headquarters staff, their names carefully noted in pencil at the back of his pocket diary.[1] Each year the list had grown longer. It was these men who now became his 'family'.

As an artist and woman of independent mind Betty Montgomery had encouraged Monty to express his opinions and feelings without restraint. This improved confidence and latitude in Monty's intellectual make-up did not leave him after her death; rather, he became outspoken in a new, even more uncompromising way, as if personal happiness was a thing of the past, and only one thing now mattered: preparing himself, his men and his country for war.

In the course of his commands – of 9th Infantry Brigade, 7th Division in Palestine, 3rd Division and II Corps in France – Monty had developed his skills as a trainer of officers and men to the point where he was satisfied he'd found the secret of military success in modern democratic battle: training, rehearsal, clear-cut communications and strong command. Returning from Dunkirk he would not care what Gort, Pownall, Dill or others thought or said. With or without martial law he would now pursue military greatness with a single-mindedness bordering on madness; would ignore the whole rickety edifice of English class-bound 'society', crossing the great English divide between managers and workers, owners and servants, middle classes and lower classes; would appeal, as he had tried to do when taking command of his battalion in 1931, to the basic meritocratic instincts of his young men, convincing them that by learning the skills of their deadly trade they would succeed in battle, and earn thereby the best chance of surviving. And in doing so, he encouraged each man to believe his life mattered.

Such an approach was not, however, well received in an England that still hoped for miracles – indeed, when Monty assembled the men of 3 Division at Frome on their return from Dunkirk, and proudly announced they were to have the honour of going straight back to France as part of BEF II in Brittany, to fight the Germans south of the Somme, the men booed!

A miscalculation

Monty the widower general simply didn't 'get it', his 3 Division intelligence officer Kit Dawnay vividly recalled. 'His ADC had been slightly wounded in the final evacuation, so he took me round as his ADC. Monty decided that nobody was to have any leave. He went round the division and saw practically everybody. He made the same speech to them all: the 3rd Division had done magnificently, had been chosen to go back into the fight, was instantly to be re-equipped, what a great honour, etc. It was received extremely badly.'

This was an understatement, The Coldstream Guards, though the most disciplined of all British soldiers, 'went so far as to barrack him!' Dawnay remembered. 'Everybody, having got through the Dunkirk party, wanted at any rate just to show themselves to their families. To have no leave whatsoever was, to say the least, very frustrating.'[2]

It was more; it was poor leadership – which Monty realized when he got back to his headquarters that evening. He had miscalculated, had treated his men as if they shared the same dedication, obsession even, with war. Clearly, they didn't – even the regular soldiers. He would have to make allowances if he was to keep their loyalty, to temper his personal sense of mission with an understanding of ordinary men's hopes, dreams, desires – and fears. Where George S. Patton would several years later 'lose it' in Sicily, take out his pistol and slap and threaten shell-shocked American troops in a field hospital because he thought they were 'shirkers', Monty's realism came mercifully to his aid now, in the aftermath of Dunkirk in early June 1940, as he prepared his division to go back to France. Reconsidering the orders he'd given, he announced that night that, as 'supplies are not coming through as quickly as we thought', the 15,000 men of the division were 'to go on forty-eight hours' leave from midnight tonight!' As Dawnay remembered, 'He got a very high feeling of admiration from the division for being able to reverse his own decision like that.'[3]

A name for annoying people

'Total' war imposes strains and stresses that are, at the higher levels of command and power, almost impossible for 'normal' people to bear, and the biography of wartime leaders thus often becomes the record of necessarily unpleasant people driving themselves and others to super-human effort.

The CIGS who had told Monty to shut up, Sir John Dill, was himself broken by his nightly combat with Churchill, who nicknamed him 'Dilly-Dally', called him 'the dead hand of inanition' to his face and before the Cabinet, and when Dill died, damned him with faint praise – despite Dill having been Churchill's military representative in Washington throughout the crucial inter-allied years from December 1941 to November 1944.[4] Exhausted by years of difficult marriage to a mentally unstable, often hospitalized woman who finally died in 1940 following a long series of paralytic strokes, Dill had been doubly crushed. Overworked and stretched to the mental limit in his attempt in Washington to explain American strategy to the British and to excuse British imperial strategy to the Americans, Dill would pay the ultimate medical penalty, dying of aplastic anaemia in 1944 at the age of 62.[5]

Alan Brooke's way of coping with the stress of war, beyond outbursts of his famous temper, was to keep an illicit, nightly journal in which he could let off steam, as well as indulging a passion for birdwatching that went hand-in-hand, ironically, with a love of bird shooting – an outlet for his military frustration, and an escape valve from the daily purgatory of maintaining a demeanour of 'outer confidence' that 'is the function of every commander'. Beneath his 'powerful exterior' Brooke suffered 'a certain melancholy of disposition' or tendency to depression, his biographer chronicled.[6] A deep sense of loneliness and fear of failure made 'the load of responsibility almost unbearable', as Brooke himself confessed. It was 'a test of one's character the bitterness of which must be experienced to be believed'.[7]

Brooke's promotion to C-in-C Home Forces in mid-July 1940, however, was a godsend for Monty, given Churchill's active dislike. Brooke swiftly promoted Monty, in late July 1940, to V Corps command – but soon wrote personally, in his own hand, to warn Monty 'against doing wild things. You have got a name for annoying people at times with your ways,' he pointed out candidly, 'and I have found difficulties in backing you at times against this reputation.' Monty was not, he stressed, to 'let me down by doing anything silly'.[8]

Time and time again similar warnings and appeals would be made by Eisenhower to his best combat commander, Patton – who ignored them in the heat of the moment. Monty, likewise, had no ability to curb his military bark; indeed, he was like a pit-terrier, straining at the leash.

On 9 June 1940 he insisted in a letter to his area commander that the 3rd Division be renamed the 3rd (Iron) Division, and in the following weeks he prepared the division for a variety of madcap War Office schemes, from the seizure of the Azores to the Cape Verde Islands, even a plan to take Cork and Queenstown in the Republic of Ireland. 'I had already fought the Southern Irish once, in 1921 and 1922, and it looked as if this renewed contest might be quite a party – with only one division,' Monty later noted,[9] thankful that his area commander, General Thorne, had persuaded Churchill to abandon the idea.[10] On 30 June 1940, however, Monty called a divisional conference at which he outlined wholly new orders to senior 3 Division officers. All training and preparation for special War Office combined operations was to cease, Monty announced; secret War Office information had come through, suggesting the Germans would invade between 2 and 9 July. The 3rd Division was to dispose itself to meet this imminent enemy landing: prompting Monty to give a series of orders that shook the residents of the area to their bones – and for which Monty would never be forgiven by certain persons.

Wives and mistresses

Monty's edicts proved not dissimilar to those issued by the German military as an occupying power on the coasts of northern France. The United Kingdom Emergency Powers (Defence) Act had been passed on 22 May 1940, but it was still difficult, Monty explained to his senior officers, to get the troops or the local residents to realize England might be invaded within forty-eight hours, and for this Monty blamed 'the presence of women, children and evacuees in the beach area. Many schools were still open. It was necessary to tighten up everything,' the division's war diarist recorded. 'The Divisional Commander said we had now got to the stage where we must do what we like as regards upsetting private property. If a house was required as an HQ it must be taken. Any material required to improve the defences should be taken. On matters of this nature unit commanders must decide for themselves and must not decentralise. Kindness, firmness and politeness was all that was required.'[11]

It was not, though. Private property was the very taproot of British upper- and middle-class society, and therefore sacrosanct in southern England, enemy invasion or no. It is easy, therefore, to understand how unpopular Monty became as a result. Lieutenant-Colonel Brian Horrocks had been appointed by Monty to command the 9th Infantry Brigade on 17 June; even he was surprised. 'Monty used to pay constant visits,' Horrocks recalled. ' "Who lives in that house?" he would say pointing to some building which partly masked the fire from one of our machine-gun positions. "Have them out, Horrocks. Blow up the house. Defence must come first." '[12]

It was from this moment that stories abounded; some apocryphal, most real enough. To make matters worse, the 'mad general' was not content to stop at property; he wanted to ensure that officers, especially, kept their eyes on the enemy, not on women. 'Wives and families of officers and men were to leave the Div area on Monday 1 July and were not to return', the division's war diary records Monty's scandalous new edict.[13]

Many of those who lost their homes, wives or mistresses would never forgive him – 'a decision which provoked great bitterness, especially among the wives', as one biographer recorded.[14] Monty's later fame in battle only served to inflame their prejudice. More and more, among officers and their wives and womenfolk, he became a general who was either admired or detested.

The necessity to become infamous

To what extent Monty actually sought such a scandalous reputation is debatable. Certainly the general seemed to take an impish delight in these new emergency powers: the embittered, homeless widower – his worldly goods put into store in Portsmouth, his own son parked out of sight and mind at a country boarding school or in holiday homes – deliberately separating happy families and wives from their officer-menfolk, and turfing hitherto happy residents out of their homes.

Monty was, and remained, unabashed. The men should see that there were not two Englands: one for officers and the upper classes, another for the working classes and ordinary soldiers. In his memoirs Monty recorded proudly how 3 Division 'descended like an avalanche on the inhabitants of that area; we dug in the gardens of the seaside villas, we sited machine-gun posts in the best places . . . The protests were tremendous. Mayors, County Councillors, private owners, came to see me and demanded that we should cease our work; I refused and explained the urgency.'[15]

As Monty reflected, the 'real trouble in England in the early days after the fall of France was that the people did not yet understand the full significance of what *had* happened, and what *could* happen in the future. The fact that the B.E.F. had escaped through Dunkirk was considered by many to be a great victory for British arms. I remember the disgust of many like myself when we saw British soldiers walking about in London and elsewhere with a coloured embroidered flash on their sleeve with the title "Dunkirk". They thought they were heroes, and the civilian public thought so too. It was not understood that the British army had suffered a crushing defeat at Dunkirk and that our island home was now in grave danger. There was no sense of urgency.'[16]

Later, Monty's overblown ego and dictatorial ways would be ascribed by Americans, especially, to Monty's Britishness – his nationalistic pride, and his deeply irritating conviction that British officers and units could perform better than American ones. Those acquainted with Monty's life story, however, knew that this wasn't true, at least in the early days of World War II – indeed that Monty's greatest struggle from 1939 had not been to defeat the Germans, which he thought comparatively straightforward, but was with his own compatriots! Overcoming British amateurism, complacency, class division, indolence, distraction and lack of initiative became Monty's greatest life-task, whatever the cost in unpopularity. Long before he was famous, in short, it was necessary to become infamous – among his own people.

The British problem

If Monty was determined to give the British officer class a tremendous kick up the backside, it was not because he disliked officers, only that he thought they were not doing their job. And if the officers didn't do their job – which was to become professionals and learn to lead men in modern war – then, inevitably, the men would not do theirs, Monty argued.

There was ample evidence of the latter. General Brooke, having written off the French, found the British soldiery at home equally depressing. 'He was dissatisfied with what he regarded as the softness of the British Army, compared to its texture of only twenty years before against the same enemy,' his biographer noted[17] – though failing to identify the root cause: an antiquated English class system, in which amateurism among the upper and middle classes had, since late Victorian times, masqueraded as modernity. In an ever-expanding English-speaking empire public-school accents had come to count for more than brains or proficiency: a socio-economic conspiracy that kept the working classes – and subject peoples – not only servile and uneducated but, in a military sense, ineffective and utterly lacking in personal initiative.

One typical example of the 'British' problem may be given, among many: that of Private Samuel Gresty, whose job was to drive ammunition and stores up to the forward troops of Monty's 3 Division during the Dunkirk campaign. On 25 May 1940 Gresty had been ordered to take three vital vehicles, loaded with petrol, ammunition and food, to the 1/7th Middlesex Regiment, which had pulled back in stages to defend its old positions on the Franco-Belgian frontier near Roubaix. Gresty had been told to drive the trucks to a certain small town, and 'park on the Market Square' until a despatch rider from the Middlesex machine-gun battalion arrived to show him where to go.

Gresty had duly arrived at 11.30 on the morning of 25 May – and had remained there, doing nothing, for forty-eight hours in the midst of a critical battle! German shellfire got hourly closer while Gresty's fellow drivers became pleasantly drunk in the local café. Never once did Gresty or his colleagues seek further information or orders, or advice from an officer. Even after two days and nights they only agreed to move out of the town when a passing motorcyclist warned them the 3rd Division was withdrawing, and a Royal Engineers demolition officer confirmed that this was so: that the BEF was, in fact, now retreating to the beaches. 'You shower, we've had no supply of goods from you lot for 4 or 5 days', a major in the Middlesex Regiment shouted when by accident Gresty came upon the 2nd Battalion. 'That's not my fault, I deliver to the 1st/7th Middlesex and I've been waiting for one of the D.R.'s to contact me at a given point,' Gresty defended himself. 'I've been there from 11.30 am, 25th May till 10.05 today. This is now 27th May.'[18]

This was taking the injunction to remain loyally at one's post to extremes – and the example was repeated many thousands of times over, throughout the BEF. Monty did not blame the men for such obtuseness, but he did give thought to the problem of how unimaginative, indolent and blinkered British troops could ever be brought to fight the inspired, indoctrinated and well-trained Germans of the 1940s, and win. The 3rd (Iron) Division was a regular division, supposedly the core of Britain's professional army. In a wartime army that would have to rely more and more on Territorial battalions – in which there had been innumerable cases of French-style desertion and outright cowardice in the run-up to evacuation at Dunkirk – it was a problem that could only proliferate. Clearly, whatever Churchill might exhort in terms of fighting not only 'on the seas and oceans', nor simply 'on the beaches' and 'on the landing grounds', nor even in 'the fields and streets', but 'in the hills' of England also,[19] the average British conscript soldier was unlikely to perform any more successfully than the French had done.

The answer, Monty felt, was to refashion the whole army as an instrument of war: to kick out the 'dead wood' among the officers – senior and junior – and to start retraining formations and units along the lines of his inter-war and 3 Divisional programmes, with a clear idea of what, in a modern democracy, was required – and not required.

Sealion

As Monty had explained to Churchill, it was fatuous to try to defend the entire eastern and southern coasts of England with a handful of divisions, a few tanks and a few hundred guns in static roles; the Germans would simply bypass the majority of them – as they had done in breaking through the Maginot line, and intended to do under Hitler's Directive No. 16 of 7 June 1940, codenamed 'Sealion'.

The British army, Monty argued, must be reorganized as a series of mobile tactical reserve formations, trained to counter-attack any infiltration by sea and air, before the enemy could get properly established on English soil.

Unfortunately, Monty's new neighbouring corps commander, Lieutenant-General Auchinleck, did not agree – and the stage was set for a personal hostility that would go far deeper than Monty's feelings towards the Germans; one that has poisoned military historiography in Britain to this day.

In the front window

Like Brooke, Lieutenant-General Auchinleck – who had been in command of the ill-fated Anglo-French spring campaign in Norway – complained that his British troops lacked 'self-reliance and manliness generally. They give an impression of being callow and undeveloped, which is not reassuring for the future, unless our methods of man-mastership and training for war can be made more realistic and less effeminate.'[20] Auchinleck was equally dismissive of rumours there was to be a 'Dunkirk Medal'. 'We don't want to perpetuate the memory of that episode, surely?' he asked in a letter to the vice-CIGS on 29 June 1940. He also called for the removal of any distinction between regulars and Territorials – 'We shall not win this war so long as we cling to worn out shibboleths and snobberies. I am sure of this. Cobwebs want removing at once.'[21] Yet Auchinleck, like Brooke, had no idea how to remove the 'shibboleths and snobberies' of the British army.

Churchill (who invited Auchinleck to stay at Chequers as his guest in July 1940) liked, admired and trusted Auchinleck, indeed would promote him to replace General Wavell in Egypt the following year, to his own eventual embarrassment – for Auchinleck, like Wavell and Brooke, had no rapport with ordinary soldiers, was obstinate to the point of obtuseness, and was bereft of ideas how, in practice, to fight the Germans successfully, beyond giving orders to his subordinates where to attack or what to defend. His training abilities were nil, and his tactical plans to meet the threat of German invasion in July 1940 were, to Monty's mind, a complete 'dog's breakfast'. Confrontation between the two men became inevitable.

The first encounter took place on 27 June 1940, when Monty was still in command of 3 Division and Auchinleck the neighbouring V Corps commander. It went extremely badly. Throughout June Auchinleck had insisted, like the C-in-C Home Forces, General Ironside, that given the shortage of trained soldiers and equipment it was the 'right policy' to 'have all our goods in the front window': to defend Britain on the beaches, in other words.[22] But on 19 July 1940, General Ironside had been dismissed (he was made a field marshal and a peer, but given no further employment for the rest of the war). Lieutenant-General Alan Brooke became C-in-C Home Forces, Auchinleck took over Brooke's post as C-in-C Southern Command – and Monty took over Auchinleck's job as Commander of V Corps on 22 July, moving to the Melchett Court headquarters. He was a lieutenant general at last – but under the direct command of a general he did not admire.

Monty's arrogance

Monty had always had a problem with superior officers he did not respect. Brigadier Pile – a contender for the post of CIGS, and later still the commander-in-chief of British anti-aircraft defences in World War II – confessed he had wanted to get rid of Monty as a 'darned nuisance' in the Canal Zone, in 1932;[23] so had General Sir George Jeffreys in India in

1934; so had the War Office in 1938; and General Lord Gort in 1939 over the VD affair. It was not long before Auchinleck, too, was wishing to be rid of him.

For his part, Monty wished the British army could be rid of such old-fashioned, 'remote' officers. In particular Monty categorically disagreed with the idea of putting all Britain's goods in the front window. No sooner did he take command of Auchinleck's V Corps, then, than he cancelled all Auchinleck's orders – and sacked most of his staff too! By lunchtime on 22 July 1940 Monty's new policy was laid down, and by late afternoon the first officers to be 'bowler-hatted' were leaving his headquarters.

Auchinleck was amazed at Monty's arrogance.

A really pathetic sight

On his second day in command of V Corps, 23 July 1940, Monty inspected the 4th Division, which now came under his command. His uncompromising report on the division was typical of what would become Monty's 'new broom' approach to command.

Clearly, it was impossible to change British society, and thus its citizenry and soldiery; but it *was* possible to sack the officers who led the men – and to retrain the remainder to perform as professionals. The 4th Division's artillery was 'definitely below standard', Monty began his summary, with 'a lot of "dead wood" which must be cut out'. He proceeded to list the human timber to be felled, including the artillery commander, two field-regiment commanders and the deputy chief of staff of the division 'at once'.

'I have discussed the removal of the above with the Div Commander: he agrees and is taking action; he should have done so before,' Monty – himself only a divisional commander till the day before – reported. Not content with cross-examining the senior officers of the 4th Division, however, Monty moved on to the troops defending the Isle of Wight, under 4 Division. The 'CO of the 50th (Holding) Battalion, Hampshire Regiment, is far too old and quite unfit to command a battle with an operational role, or in fact any battle. He must be removed at once,' Monty stated. 'I have told the Divisional Commander to take action.' Nor was the divisional commander himself spared. 'Generally the 4th Division has gone back somewhat. It lacks that sure and firm guidance from the top; it lacks a strong commander who knows exactly what is wanted and exactly how to set about getting it.'[24]

Clearly, the new corps commander meant business. Yet in comparison with his report on the 4th Division, Monty's assessment of the Portsmouth area command was, if anything, even more damning. He spent the following days of 24 and 25 July visiting the sector – which included the Isle of Wight, the garrison at Portsmouth and the surrounding area – and he was appalled. 'After a whole day spent in close investigation of the situation in the Portsmouth Area,' he reported, 'I have no hesitation in saying that the Area Commander, and certain members of his staff, should be at once removed. The situation in Portsmouth itself is particularly bad. There are some 8000 armed men in the garrison,' he pointed out, 'which is ample for defence needs as there are a large number of armed sailors in addition. But the organisation and administration has been very sketchy; reserve supplies are all held centrally instead of each unit having two or three days of its own; medical arrangements are practically nil; the late Garrison Commander seems to have done nothing. The Area Commander has exercised no supervision and taken no steps to see that things were put on a proper basis.'

On the Isle of Wight, in the 8th Battalion of the Hampshire Regiment, the situation needed to be seen to be believed. 'The CO is 63. The 2nd i/c is 59. I interviewed several platoon commanders of 55.' Originally recruited as officers in the Home Guard, these men now commanded companies of young recruits – 'boys of 18 years old. I saw one of these companies at Stubbington. It is absurd to allow these companies of boys to be commanded by old men of between 50 and 60, and this matter should be taken in hand urgently,' the new corps commander (aged fifty-two) demanded. 'The CO is a really pathetic sight. He served in South Africa in 1899; he is very old, frail, and looks very ill. He should be removed from command at once, and sent away to end his life in peace somewhere. The 2nd i/c is old and decrepit, and should go at once. All the officers should be checked over, and the worst cases replaced by younger men.'

For this to happen, though, a new area commander was necessary. Although a 'nice person', the existing commander was 'quite unable to stand up to exacting cross-examination', Monty declared. 'He is ineffective, lacks initiative, energy and drive and is obviously extremely idle. He is quite unfit to be a Major-General, and should be relieved of his command at once and placed on retired pay.' The AA & QMG, or chief of admin, was similarly disparaged: 'An old retired officer of the 60th Rifles. Is idle and has taken to drink. He should never have been made the senior administrative staff officer of an important area. He is a director of a brewery, and farms his own estate. His services should be dispensed with at once and he should go back to his farm.'[25]

Such uncompromising language defied British military convention, but Monty didn't care. Britain was at total war: a war it was bound to lose unless action was taken – fast. In his sorry catalogue of British incompetence in V Corps, the commander of the Royal Engineers in the Portsmouth area also received his comeuppance: 'Completely and utterly useless. He has served many years in India and is prematurely aged; has also taken to drink. He is unable to explain anything clearly and gives the impression of being mentally deficient. He is a serving regular soldier and should be retired at once.'[26]

Returning from the Portsmouth area on 25 July 1940, Monty dictated his report and forwarded it, with his notes on the 4th Division, straight to General Auchinleck – who saw red.

Orders are orders

Such damning criticism of dozens of officers, from majors to major-generals, who had until a few hours before been under Auchinleck's operational command, was certainly undiplomatic. Three days later however, on 28 July, Monty produced yet another report for Auchinleck! This time it concerned the other division in V Corps, Major-General Martel's 50th Division. Although couched in more discreet language, complimenting the division on its high morale and 'amazing' work on beach defences, it was if anything an even more direct attack on Auchinleck's defensive strategy. 'The standard of training in the Division is low,' Monty began. 'All energies have been directed to work on the defences . . . The nett result is that all the finer arts of how to compete with the Germans in battle have been put in the background. There are men who have never in their lives fired more than 5 rounds with the rifle; there are men who have never fired the Bren gun; the use of carriers is not practised; the Headquarters of formations and units are untrained; the technique of observation and sniping as learnt from the Germans is untouched; and so on.' In Monty's view the division was no longer battleworthy.

'The result of concentrating entirely on defensive works and neglecting other matters is going to reflect adversely on the battle efficiency of the Division unless we are careful. I met companies who had been in the same place for one month, doing nothing but dig and work on defences. The men had done no drill, no PT, no training. The men did not seem to be on their toes; I did not see the light of battle in their eyes. The best defences in the world,' Monty warned, 'are in themselves of little value unless the troops in them are full of beans and mentally alert.' The division would 'fight well defensively, and would put up a dogged resistance,' he acknowledged, recollecting their plucky performance before Dunkirk. 'But it is on a front of over 80 miles; fluid fighting would develop and in its present state the Division has no hope of competing with the Germans in mobile war with any reasonable chance of success. I have discussed the matter with the Divisional Commander, and he agrees.'[27]

Auchinleck was furious, understandably. By return of messenger he thanked Monty for his notes and agreed with 'much of what you say'; but insisted that the work on beach defences continue. 'I want to make it quite clear, however, that I wish the instructions as to the urgent need for the completion of the defences so as to admit of the withdrawal of men for training, which I issued to the Corps just before I left (Operation Instruction No. 14) carried out,' Auchinleck obstinately declared as commander-in-chief. 'I intend to issue a Command Instruction to the same effect.' For Monty's benefit he emphasized that 'orders are orders and will, of course, be obeyed'.[28]

Such a response was, seen in retrospect, destined to create antagonism, for Auchinleck was no Alan Brooke. Having reached the rank of lieutenant general Monty no longer obeyed orders, he gave them – and by seeking to squash Monty, Auchinleck only enraged him. Worse still, Auchinleck must have complained to the new Home Forces C-in-C, for a few days later Brooke became alarmed enough to send his warning letter about 'doing wild things'.[29]

Aware of the source for this ticking-off, Monty only came to despise Auchinleck the more deeply. He certainly took no notice of Brooke's warning, for the following day he went up to London and, over Auchinleck's head, protested against the orders Auchinleck had given about certain officers being seconded or transferred from V Corps by the War Office. Auchinleck was forced yet again to remonstrate, complaining that 'I do not consider this is the proper manner in which this, or any other matter of this nature, should be handled. When orders are issued by these

Headquarters, whether they come from the War Office or direct from these Headquarters, and you wish to make a protest, from whatever point of view, against those orders, I wish such protests to be made to these Headquarters and not to War Office officials over my head.'[30] Monty took no notice. 'I note you say the Auk admires me,' Monty retorted when, years later, his chief of staff pointed out how much Auchinleck respected Monty for his 'great qualities'. 'But I don't admire him – and never have from the day I served under him in the Southern Command after Dunkirk. That experience was enough for me.'[31] 'I cannot recall that we agreed on anything,' Monty wrote candidly in his memoirs[32] – he and Auchinleck remaining at loggerheads all summer while, across the Channel, eleven German divisions were carrying out intensive training for Operation Sealion, targeted at the south coast of England from the North Foreland to the Isle of Wight.

History would prove, on the coast of Normandy in 1944, that not even the best-defended beaches can withstand concentrated air and seaborne assault by a well-trained invading army – and Auchinleck's sacrifice of mobile divisional counter-attack forces in favour of static beach defences that would be bypassed under the Sealion plan would almost certainly have jeopardized Britain's chances of repelling the German invasion.

Thanks to the Battle of Britain the Germans did not invade, however, and Monty was able to start retraining the men under his command, using his 'secret weapon': a series of training exercises that would gradually prepare the British army to fight again on the continent of Europe.

These historic exercises, carried out over the two years between the summers of 1940 and 1942, would transform the British army in England from an uncohesive collection of amateurs into an army of professionals. Yet Monty himself was not promoted to battlefield command, despite failure after failure by British forces in the field. The historian, like the biographer, must ask why.

A struggle over wives

Prophets are seldom recognized in their own country – as Churchill had best cause, in the 1930s, to know. Monty's prophetic approach to the need for first-class battlefield training in a democracy would one day be lauded by even the most hostile of his critics. As the American historian and Eisenhower-biographer Stephen Ambrose would later remark to a National Press Club audience in Washington, 'Everybody knows about what a supercilious prick Montgomery was. (Laughter.) But I'll tell you this – he was a great trainer of troops – not a very good general, but a great trainer of troops.'[33]

Monty's approach was to apply the training techniques he had used in 3 Division in France to each formation he was appointed to command in Home Forces, in succession, rehearsing officers and men in the sort of operations they would be likely to undertake in the field of battle. As Field-Marshal Sir Gerald Templer later reflected, 'it was Monty's achievement to rebuild the British army in England after Dunkirk. There is no doubt that, however much he was mocked outside V Corps, his methods were copied and in time became the accepted doctrine throughout the army, particularly in southern England.'[34]

Monty was, Templer recalled, immune to the mockery. A once-great nation was sliding towards defeat, and only leadership could halt the slide, backed by a new attitude to war. In politics it was Winston Churchill who, initially mocked by appeasers, now provided the inspiration necessary to overcome defeatism. In the military sphere, however, mocked and deplored by those who felt safe in their island haven, it was Monty who inspired a new approach to warmaking, based on absolute professionalism.

In order to achieve that professionalism in a democracy Monty had to make it clear that soldiering against German forces was a cold and deadly business, which required total dedication if the Nazis were to be defeated. Just as at 3 Division in Brighton, therefore, Monty immediately ruled in V Corps that all relatives of serving officers must be banned from the area as an unwarranted distraction. 'If an officer's wife and family were present with him in or near his unit area, and the attack came, an officer would be tempted to see to their safety, amid all the shelling and bombing of the battle, and his thoughts would be with them,' he argued, 'rather than on the priority task of defeating the Germans.'[35]

Certainly the example of the ex-King Edward VIII, who had recently fled, without authorization, from his post in the BEF in France to look after his wife, the ex-Mrs Simpson, was a vivid one. Was the Duke of Windsor typical, though? 'A struggle took place over wives,' reads Monty's quixotic version of this battle of the sexes. 'I was told that a good officer would never give a single thought to his wife and family in such conditions; his whole mind would be on the battle.' Don Quixote, however, remained adamant. 'I said that I did not believe it. Anyhow, human nature was weak and I was not prepared to let an officer be tempted to fail in his duty. The whole future of England, and indeed civilization, was at stake; I would remove temptation and then there would be no doubt. Moreover, since the men could not have their families with them, the officers shouldn't either. The wives must go. And they did.'[36]

England being England, many stayed – under assumed names! But the point was made: the corps commander was a misogynist, who demanded total concentration upon soldiering, in preparation for total war. Any officer who was too old, too unfit, or too idle, was 'out', and swiftly removed; those who stayed would be the backbone of a new army: an army trained to win. Such training was to be 'hard and tough; it must be carried out in all conditions of weather and climate; in rain, snow, mud, fair weather and foul, at any hour of the day or night – we must be able to do our stuff better than the Germans', as he laid down. All training 'was to be organized to lead up to exercises at the higher level, and all exercises were to be staged in an imaginative way. The large-scale exercises from the divisional level upwards must be designed to ensure that commanders, staffs and troops were capable of continuous and sustained operations over prolonged periods' – 'Commanders and staff officers at any level who couldn't stand the strain, or who got tired, were to be weeded out and replaced – ruthlessly.'[37]

This, as veterans would attest, was no less than the truth. In a lecture to the senior Staff College course at Minley Manor in October 1940 Monty explained, after analysing German battle technique, the rationale behind his own exercises. Conventional wisdom in Britain had it that officers and men must be first trained in platoon tactics, and then worked up to larger-scale exercises in a tedious progression. Such an approach might be appropriate, he pointed out, to peacetime, but not to war – when it was 'definitely dangerous'. The fact was, a military 'formation or unit has got to be able to operate against the enemy at any time – as a complete unit'. This 'may be tomorrow' – and time was therefore of the essence. The 'stage management of the battle must be practised & the machinery of the unit exercised; the unit comdr. must have practice in handling his command', Monty insisted. As a result, an 'untrained unit may do badly. That does not matter,' he explained ' – it will be experience which will save casualties when the operation has to be done in battle – possibly next week.' Moreover, by recognizing how small-unit operations fitted 'in to the final picture' the men 'will learn by trial and error that if the machine as a whole is to run smoothly at all times, a very high standard of individual and sub-unit efficiency is necessary'.[38]

Here, years before the great battle of Alamein, was the core of Monty's revolution in democratic warmaking: the attempt to make the soldier, NCO and officer, at each level from platoon upwards, understand how his task fitted into the 'big picture' – and how important it was for him to perform it efficiently. 'Therefore individual training must be sandwiched in with collective training,' Monty explained – 'it being remembered that the enemy may have to be met at any time.' He blamed the products of the Staff College, Camberley, who had produced bad plans that were beyond the competence of the formations. Thinking of Norway and France, he stated that 'It has become increasingly difficult to rectify initial mistakes – in fact you can't. If you start on the wrong leg you are done.' Basically, any battle fell into one of two categories: defensive and offensive. In a defensive battle 'layout must be good, artillery properly deployed, everything so balanced that you can always do something about it', while in attack the 'recce echelons properly positioned, technique of battle drill perfect, HQ in the right place, good arrangements for inter-communication, and so on'. Even so, good staff work and organized command were only half the battle. 'No good trying to fight a first class enemy unless the soldiers absolutely on their toes. They must have a "stomach for the fight". They must have light of battle in their eyes. They must look forward to a good fight. They must be full of "binge". Cannot be full of binge if you are not fit; must have that exhilaration that comes from physical well being; optomistic [sic] outlook on life; no good being pessimistic with a face like a piece of cheese. Physical fitness and powers of endurance are essentials for victory. PT drill & highest standards of smartness in the execution of duties; great aids. Cross country runs – get rid of all the smoke and gin. Cannot be full of "binge" if you are always "belly-aching". Too much of it in the Army. Stop it. Must have 100% binge – No belly-aching. Militarily fit – mentally fit – physically fit.'[39]

Such, in note form, was Monty's approach to training. Obtaining permission direct from General Brooke in September, he had overridden Auchinleck's beach defence policy and withdrawn both the divisions in V Corps into reserve, leaving only specialist beach defence battalions to guard the coast. His classic formula for training incorporated individual or sub-unit training; indoor training using a sand-table or battlefield model; brigade signal exercises; and collective training, in which battalion and brigade exercises were conducted once a week, 'with the complete Division moving out on exercise at least once a month'.[40]

Auchinleck, as C-in-C Southern Command, was invited to attend not only the exercises, but Monty's initial lectures, in which he explained the objects of the exercises, as well as his post-mortems, at which neither smoking nor coughing was allowed. 'I used to go and listen in to his lectures,' Auchinleck later recalled, '– no coughing no smoking, runs before breakfast – all very inspiring and made me feel a bit inadequate.'[41]

Had Auchinleck sought to learn from Monty's new approach, or developed – as Patton later did – his own approach to battlefield training he might have performed better in the desert against Rommel; but like Gort and Wavell before him, Auchinleck chose to rely upon the talents he had, and the officers he had, rather than learning new ones and appointing new ones. As result his army would be totally defeated in battle. To win total war, against indoctrinated and professional opponents like the Germans, meant total application to winning – and Monty, however much he might be resented or mocked, was determined to win.

Fringe warfare

Little by little the ripples of Monty's new approach to training spread. On 6 December 1940 the London *Times*, under the headline 'Forty Thousand Men in a Field Exercise', reported that the 'new British Army that has largely been created since Dunkirk has just carried out the most ambitious exercise in the field that has ever taken place in this country. Certainly nothing like it has ever been seen before in wartime conditions . . .' Brooke attended as C-in-C Home Forces, noting that the post-mortem conference 'was in the Odeon Cinema and absolutely packed, at least 800 officers! Monty gave a first-class discourse & I said a few words after him.'[42] General Auchinleck had in late October been appointed the new C-in-C in India, and it might have been expected that Monty would succeed him. However, it was not to be; indeed, it was to be another year before Monty was given anything beyond a corps command.

Quite why this was so is difficult to reconstruct with certainty. Brooke's mind, in December 1940, was still obsessed with the defence of Britain, rather than training an army to fight abroad; the CIGS, Sir John Dill, had his hands full with Churchill and the problems of fighting the Italians, rather than the Germans, in the Middle East. Thus the success of Wavell and O'Connor's brilliant operations against the Italians in Libya and Cyrenaica in the winter of 1940–41 lulled the War Office into thinking that Churchill's policy of fringe warfare – picking off the second-class forces of Hitler's weaker ally, while trying to bring the United States into the war – might indeed prove effective.

General Richard O'Connor certainly wreaked havoc with Graziani's army in North Africa. By 11 December 1940 O'Connor – Monty's fellow divisional commander in Palestine in 1938–9 – had taken Sidi Barrani, with 38,000 Italian prisoners; by 22 January 1941 Tobruk, with 25,000 Italian prisoners; and by 7 February 1941 virtually the entire Italian army in Libya surrendered to him at Beda Fomm, with a further 25,000 prisoners. Total prisoners taken by O'Connor amounted to 130,000 Italians, with 500 tanks and 800 guns – for the loss of fewer than 2,000 Commonwealth casualties, of whom only 500 were killed. Churchill was overjoyed, and O'Connor was knighted.

Pride in Britain's performance against the Italians, however, presaged a catastrophic fall – for the German way of making war was quite, quite different from the Italian. Within three weeks of German forces being committed in the spring of 1941, Greece was conquered, the Balkans were cleared of British troops, and Rommel, landing in Tripoli with the Deutsche Afrika Korps, had overrun Cyrenaica – capturing O'Connor! In eleven days, despite complete knowledge of German plans and dispositions through Ultra (decrypting of high-grade German signals to Hitler and the Wehrmacht High Command, the OKW) an inferior number of German parachutists succeeded in capturing Crete – a virtually impregnable, mountainous island defended by almost 30,000 British and Commonwealth troops, as well as two Greek divisions. Churchill, disappointed, sacked Wavell, and appointed General Auchinleck as C-in-C Middle East. Thus the stage was set for a series of further British defeats, despite unique Ultra intelligence and a vast preponderance of tanks and troops.

To run and die

For Monty the failure to be given a battlefield command was galling. Yet if he was disappointed by Churchill's failure to send him overseas to fight in battle, or even to promote him to a higher command than a corps at home, he did not show it. His simple, almost evangelical mission was to show how British troops under his command should and could be trained for successful battle against the Germans – and all his energies were directed to that one end. Thus in V Corps exercise followed exercise, each one becoming longer and more challenging than the previous one, with more troops, more weapons and more supporting forces involved, from parachute troops to armoured units and RAF close-support aircraft.

That Monty's fellow division commander from Dunkirk, General Alexander, had been appointed southern commander in the place of Auchinleck, rather than himself, did not worry him. Alexander did not interfere with his V Corps command; he was idle, charming and imperturbable – 'the only man, yes, the only man under whom any admiral, general or air marshal would gladly serve in a subordinate position', as Monty said admiringly of Alexander at the time.[43]

Alexander was astute enough to recognize, as Auchinleck did not, that having a live wire like Montgomery as a corps commander was a blessing, not a threat; he therefore did everything to help rather than hinder Monty's work – and the results were soon remarkable. 'It is interesting to note how the daily sick rate drops as the troops become fit and hard,' Monty noted in his summing up at the end of V Corps Exercise No. 5, in March 1941. 'The average daily admission to hospital in divisions of 5 Corps during the past winter has been 10 per day per division of 16,000 men'; or less than 0.1 per cent.[44]

Unfortunately, such extraordinary results were subsumed, outside Southern Command, in the growing stories about the mad martinet of V Corps. Not only had Monty ordered all wives and families out of the area, as at 3 Division, but he had insisted on greater physical fitness – not only on the part of the troops, but of the headquarters staff! It was this order that aroused the most vociferous criticism among officers. Auchinleck questioned whether 'runs before breakfast really produce battle winners, of necessity' – thereby completely failing to understand Monty's psychological as well as physical fitness aim. In World War I headquarters staffs, with their red tabs and hat-ribbons – wonderfully captured by William Roberts in his coloured drawing *General Staff*[45] – had become despised by the troops serving in the trenches. To help get rid of such 'them and us' resentment Monty made not only the fighting troops but every single officer and man serving at V Corps headquarters go out on weekly five-mile runs – refusing to listen to medical 'excuses'.

Stories quickly abounded of heart attacks and collapses, but Monty would give no quarter – indeed, he relished the chance to put portly or malingering staff officers on the spot. One colonel who wished to be excused was asked by Monty whether he thought that, if he did the run, he would die. When the colonel replied in the affirmative, Monty insisted he should run none the less, with the callous comment that 'if he was thinking of dying it would be better to do it now, as he could be replaced easily and smoothly; it is always a nuisance if officers die when the battle starts and things are inclined to be hectic. His state of health was clearly not very good, and I preferred him to do the run and die.'[46]

The officer did not die. Neither did the story, to the disgust of outraged HQ officers, but the delight of ordinary troops. Fighting morale in V Corps shot up.

Deep opprobrium

If Monty was becoming a character, indeed something of a hero to the ordinary soldiers of V Corps, the opposite was the case in Whitehall. There, Montgomery's name became synonymous – as it had done in 1937–8 – with military efficiency, but was viewed with deep personal opprobrium if not odium by the pen-pushers.

Finally, however, at the end of April 1941, Monty received notification that he was to move. Any hopes that he was to be promoted to command a larger formation, however, were soon dashed, for he learned he was merely being sidestepped to command another, neighbouring corps. This was General Thorne's XII Corps, in Kent, in order that 'Bulgy' Thorne could be promoted to take command of all troops in Scotland.

Bursting like a 15" shell

Monty was surprisingly unfazed. Satisfied with the state of training in V Corps, he was determined to raise the level of training among other troops in England, in whatever rank. He wanted also to rehearse the ability to take sudden command of a new formation – the essence of battlefield command.

Those who later professed amazement at the self-confidence with which

Monty took command of the defeated 8th Army at Alamein in 1942, or Allied land forces in England for the invasion of Europe in 1944, had clearly not studied Monty's career. 'I rather fancy I burst in Kent like a 15" shell,' Monty himself boasted to his old intelligence officer, Kit Dawnay, of his move to command XII Corps, 'and it was needed!! Wives are being evacuated by train loads; it is just a matter as to whether the railways will stand the traffic. A number of heads are being chopped off – the bag to date is 3 Brigadiers and 6 COs. The standard here was very low.'[47]

Like General Auchinleck, General Thorne had deeply impressed Churchill as XII Corps commander – but not Monty. Brooke, too, had never confided any dissatisfaction with General Thorne, or his dispositions, in his diary – indeed, had actually been responsible for his promotion to Scottish Command. Yet Thorne's plans for the defence of Kent were, in Monty's eyes, disastrously poor, and destined to fail in the event of German invasion – a view with which several historians of Hitler's proposed Sealion operation fully concurred.[48]

There was, in Monty's mind, no likelihood of a German invasion in 1941; but the threat, at least, would provide an excuse to explore the problems of meeting an enemy attack, of organizing a counter-attack, and thus examining the unfolding of a cross-Channel invasion – three lessons which were to be of immense importance in the coming years. Thus on 2 May 1941 – less than a week after arriving at his new headquarters at Tunbridge Wells – Monty issued his first corps instruction, damning the tactical doctrine of his predecessor. 'The very long frontages which have to be held,' he informed commanders, 'have led to a desire to defend every possible yard of the beach or coast; this has led to undue dispersion, and the principle of locality defence has been entirely disregarded.'

This principle, as Monty would demonstrate in Egypt the following year, was one of powerful reserves, held back and able to watch over well-sited and well-defended defensive positions. 'It must be realised, however, that isolated section posts have no possible hope of survival in the modern battle. Risks must be accepted in order to concentrate platoons, and where necessary companies, in strong, well-wired localities, capable of all-round defence and capable of holding out until our reserves get into action. There may often be gaps between platoon localities; that cannot be avoided when holding long fronts. The enemy may penetrate between platoon localities; that will not matter providing the localities themselves are mutually supporting, and are so strong they can hold out', he concluded. 'It is vital that the principles of true locality defence should be adhered to in our dispositions on the coast, and in fact anywhere. To ignore them is to lose the battle before it has even begun ... All defences on the coast, and elsewhere in the Corps Area, will be based on these principles. In cases where the existing defensive layout is at variance with these principles, the necessary steps will be taken at once to re-group sub-units conforming to the principles of locality defence outlined above.'[49]

This instruction is quoted at length because it so well demonstrates Monty's method of taking over command. As will be seen, a coterie of loyal Auchinleck supporters would later invent a version of events at Alamein in which Montgomery took over plans and dispositions laid down by his predecessor, General Auchinleck, and for which Monty unjustly took historical credit, indeed renown, from the noble figure of the 'Auk'. This was moonshine: out of character, contrary to method for Monty, and historically untrue. Monty had felt nothing but professional contempt for Auchinleck's approach to beach defence in 1940; on taking command of the neighbouring XII Corps, ten months later, he expressed the same contempt for Thorne's defensive layout, characterized by static beach defences and 'stop lines' to the rear, to which units and formations were to withdraw when pressed – exactly as Auchinleck was to order in the desert.

The truth was, Monty was neither by constitution nor by tactical reasoning a commander who happily took on anyone else's plans; indeed, no field commander in the British army in 1941 or 1942 possessed as clear an idea how he wished to fight defensively or offensively against the Germans, nor how, in either case, he aimed to position his forces. Any commander who was not 'up to it' was sacked, irrespective of his seniority in the 'Army Lists'; any talented protégé he believed in, he would fight to get promoted. 'I have got Horrocks here now, as a Major-General commanding 44 Div. This took a lot of doing and is a great triumph. He arrived yesterday,' Monty wrote to Kit Dawnay on 14 June 1941.[50]

Nor did Monty like others to do his thinking for him. On 16 May 1941 he issued a formal XII Corps 'Plan to Defeat Invasion'. The vital garrison towns of Dover, Folkestone, Ashford and Canterbury would be held as pivots. 'As long as they hold out and remain intact, then east Kent cannot be lost,' he declared in language that would be repeated in the desert the following summer. 'They must therefore hold out – and will do so.' Moreover divisions would not be fragmented, but kept as powerful reserves – reserves that 'will not be used to occupy defensive positions or to hold extended stop lines; they will be kept assembled so that they can act offensively and strike blows, and will be trained accordingly.'[51]

Six weeks later Monty summed up the lessons of his first XII Corps exercise: a fiasco.

Close investigation

'The army is not a mutual congratulation society; great issues are at stake,' Monty warned the 2,000 XII Corps officers present – and decried the failure of the reserve division in the exercise, noting stage by stage how the battle had been lost almost before it had begun.

To his consternation there seemed no understanding in the corps of the simplest problems of modern battlefield management and command: not only the marshalling and movement of large-scale formations, but how to confront the most elementary obstacles such as demolitions or mines. In particular, the use made of Royal Engineer (sapper, or pioneer) units, and the staff work needed for large-scale movement of combined arms were virtually non-existent. Yet if troops and artillery could not be properly launched into battle 'then you start the battle on the wrong leg; you are then easily thrown off balance by a good enemy'. It was essential that the 'dispositions of the fighting troops, employment and positioning of supporting arms, the arrangements for keeping communications open, the organization of supply services and so on – all must be good initially . . . If they *are* good, then the forward troops will have every chance to seize the tactical advantage early in the battle.'[52]

Monty's diagnosis of this exercise would be historically important, for in it he recognized the primary fault of the British army in the early years of World War II. This was not inferior weaponry – the commonest excuse for any defeated army – but the inevitable decline of military knowledge and expertise as the British army was expanded to meet its wartime commitments. There had been no conscription or enforced military service between the wars, as there had been in Germany once Hitler took power. Inevitably this meant that, while drawing on potentially excellent civilians, both as officers and men, the army might well get worse before it got better

It is in this context that Monty's desire to bring in some of his 'own' men to the corps, both on the staff and as commanders, must be understood. He had spent almost a year making V Corps the most battleworthy corps in England; if he was to raise XII Corps to the same standard in the minimum time possible, it was essential to introduce men who would help spread the new gospel of professionalism. The manner in which he absconded with V Corps officers and pressed the Military Secretary to obtain yet more of them for XII Corps may have smacked of arrogance, but his purpose was constructive, not vain: namely, to raise the fighting standards of the British army as a cohesive, modern army in war. To achieve such a standard the army must rehearse and practise large-scale movement, the co-operation of different arms, and the carrying out of a clear battle plan, laid down by the army commander.

Though Monty had still not been promoted to an army or even area command, thanks to Churchill's ill will, he remained utterly confident, despite the spate of recent German successes in Greece, the Mediterranean, Crete and North Africa. Not even the most daring of German army commanders could vanquish a British army, he believed, if only certain fundamental principles of modern war were recognized and observed. One of these was the basic doctrine of fighting in divisions. 'And so we see,' he addressed his audience on 30 June 1941, a few days after the Germans launched Operation Barbarossa against the Soviet Union, and at the very moment when General Sir Claude Auchinleck was arriving in Cairo to take over British military forces in the Middle East from Wavell (whose counter-offensive, Operation Battleaxe, against Rommel had come to grief), 'that the first essential – the proper launching of the formation – does not stand up to very close investigation. I consider that this is due to fighting in brigade groups on all occasions.'

Here was a cardinal issue which, despite his undoubted physical presence, moral authority and intelligence as a commander, General Auchinleck would singularly fail to put right in Egypt in the following fourteen months. Despite superior intelligence (particularly from Ultra), superiority in numbers of tanks, artillery, vehicles, RAF fighters, bombers and supplies, Auchinleck and his lieutenants would fritter away every advantage, resulting in a growing policy of despair, as Auchinleck lost faith in infantry divisions, and looked to 'Jock Columns' and brigade groups as 8th Army's only possible salvation.

Monty acknowledged there would be isolated cases in war when to fight in brigade groups *was* the correct procedure: but Exercise Binge, in which the fictional German invasion army was advancing through parts of Kent, was not one of them. 'The division is a fighting formation of all arms, and the way you fight it will vary with the problem,' Monty allowed. But from his own experience in the BEF he was convinced that the cohesive, crushing weight of a well-commanded modern fighting division was the backbone of the British army – and to split it into pieces was, given the British genius for muddle, a desperately misguided policy for the main battlefield, as Exercise Binge had demonstrated. 'I commanded a division in battle against the Germans in this war,' he reminded those officers in the audience who were not aware of his Dunkirk experience. 'I never fought it in brigade groups once; I was never embarrassed by the Germans – nor do I propose to be in the future.'[53]

This was no idle boast, as the world would one day see.

Promotion at last

Throughout 1941 Monty continued to mount major XII Corps exercises, such as Morebinge, and Superbinge, each of which rehearsed different operations of war on an increasingly ambitious and challenging scale. Finally, in November 1941, Dill was removed as CIGS and replaced by Brooke, General Paget took over from Brooke as C-in-C Home Forces, and on Brooke's recommendation Monty – finally – was promoted to South-Eastern Command, in place of Paget, and moved to his new head-quarters in Reigate, Surrey.

It had been a testing period, in all senses. It would become more testing still, for Monty made it his business not only to shake up his latest command, but to try and make it into something new in England: an army.

A bit mad

Without reference to the War Office, and to the horror of many diehards and blimps, Monty instantly retitled his new formation. 'South-Eastern Command' became, on his immediate orders, 'South-Eastern Army'; he himself changed his title from C-in-C, South-Eastern Command to 'Army Commander'.

To many men on his new staff, as well as on other staffs, such self-aggrandizing new nomenclature smacked of megalomania. 'Of course there's nothing wrong with Monty really. He's just a bit mad,' a senior officer at Home Forces GHQ would openly say of Monty by the following spring.[54] It was not hard to see why. 'Every day new rumours would circulate about his latest eccentricities,' a GHQ intelligence officer recalled. Those 'who cared for the dignity of their profession were often scandalized by the pretensions of the GOC-in-C, South-Eastern Army, while those who suffered from them directly, like his staff and his formation commanders, sometimes wondered, with a mixture of alarm and scepticism, whether they were playing a part in war or *opéra bouffe*'.[55]

But Monty wasn't interested in the 'dignity' of the military profession, only in modern military professionalism itself, if Britain was ever to defeat the Nazis in battle on the continent of Europe. In his new 'army' he now had two corps under his command: XII Corps and the Canadian Corps. Together they would constitute a field army of nine divisions – and it was essential to start rehearsing battlefield command of such large forces if they were to succeed in combat with the Germans in Europe.

Within ten days of making himself army commander Monty therefore issued his first 'Army Commander's Personal Memorandum', setting out his training programme for the winter – including *five* major exercises, the dates of which had already been devised and notified, he declared. Meanwhile, indoor exercises 'on the model' and outdoor manoeuvres would enable officers not only to study and practise the art of battlefield operations, but to learn how 'at the right moment, to break down the large-scale divisional battle and continue the fight by means of very hard-hitting smaller packets. The Germans,' he noted, 'are extremely good at this; and in the mobile and fluid operations on the modern battlefield it is this type of fighting that completes the success gained in the divisional battle ... Success in such fighting lies in the hands of our company commanders; the technique must be taught at Army, Corps and Divisional Schools.'[56]

Such schools were now proliferating throughout England, as the War Office woke up to the need for new approaches to military education and training in a largely citizen army. Schools for camouflage, raiding, driving, tank warfare, staff duties and all manner of specialisms abounded; what was needed more than ever, though, was leadership in seeing that these specialisms fitted into the bigger picture of battle. It was the responsibility of the commanding officer of any unit, Monty maintained, no longer just to 'lead' men into battle, but to train his officers. In Britain's old-fashioned regimental army – and even in the trenches of World War I, as Robert Graves brilliantly described in *Goodbye to All That* – COs had treated their younger officers as 'warts'. In World War II this was no longer tolerable; Monty would remove any CO who was unwilling or unable to train his officers. 'Well-trained officers soon produce a good unit,' Monty declared; 'if the officers are not well trained, nothing happens'.[57] Meritocracy was in, tradition out; education in, amateurism out. A major XII Corps study week was planned for December 1941, and Monty expected representatives from the Canadian Corps to attend; in turn, XII Corps representatives would attend the Canadian Corps study week in January 1942.

It was now, however, that Monty was rocked back upon what would become his Achilles heel: the business of dealing with allies. He had been brought up in Australia, and would always get on well with Australians and New Zealanders; but unlike his father, he had never been to the USA – or Canada.

Canadian musical chairs

In transforming the British approach to warfare Monty had discovered a masterkey that would unlock the fighting abilities of a so-called democratic but in truth deeply hierarchical and hidebound nation, crippled in its effectiveness by clubs and trade unions, often competing and at odds with each other. As Churchill had in 1940 found the key to popular anti-fascist support in appealing to a deep-seated national historical pride, so Monty had, without press publicity at this stage of his life, cut the vital latchkey to English military motivation by treating war as a modern educational and management experience, inspiring pride and positive motivation. In the wake of disasters such as Norway and Dunkirk this was man-management on a scale and in a manner never before attempted in Britain. However, it was a key that could only be turned if Monty possessed the power to see his orders were obeyed, that 'dead wood' was ruthessly cut out, and that he could then count on willing subordinates. Unfortunately none of theses premises was fulfilled in the case of the Canadian Corps in November 1941 – or thereafter.

Lieutenant-General Gammell, who succeeded Monty in command of XII Corps, proved no problem, being almost embarrassingly anxious to carry out Monty's directives as the new army commander. The Canadian Corps, however, was an entirely different matter. Its commander – Lieutenant-General McNaughton – had suffered a nervous breakdown in November,[58] so that when Monty arrived in Reigate the Canadian Corps was being temporarily commanded by a very 'gallant soldier' but one entirely lacking in 'brains', Monty considered: the commander of the 1st Canadian Infantry Division, Major-General Pearkes, VC, DSO, MC – a general who was quite 'unable to appreciate the essentials of a military problem', let alone 'formulate a sound plan'.[59]

To compound this disastrous situation, there was immediately a struggle for command of the Canadian Corps – with an even less appropriate Canadian general usurping command in December 1941: a man who had 'practically no experience in field command' at all.[60]

As in the high command appointments in the British army in September 1939, a calamitous game of musical chairs now took place in Canadian forces in Britain – with dire results for the Canadians, as Marx's dictum about history repeating itself first as tragedy then as farce was borne out.

A nightmare of amateurism

Since 1940 the Canadian chief of the general staff in Ottawa had been Lieutenant-General Harry Crerar, a pompous, obtuse and conniving general with a profound inferiority complex. In accepting the role of CGS, Crerar had extracted the promise of a divisional Canadian command in England. This he finally got, in 1941, but on arriving in England in December 1941 as a lieutenant general he had immediately considered himself senior to the acting commander of the Canadian Corps, Major-General Pearkes – and had insisted he displace Pearkes as temporary corps commander!

For Monty this charade was not the way to ensure battlefield success: indeed it was, as had proved the case with Lord Gort, a recipe for defeat in battle against the Germans. Worse still, Crerar, having held the top post in Canada, considered himself not only temporary Canadian Corps commander in England in the absence of McNaughton, but guardian of the Canadian national military interest – an attitude that brought him on to collision course with a new army commander who, instead of merely allowing the Canadian Corps to do its own thing, was determined both to give it orders and dictate its training policy and programme, as part of his newly christened South-Eastern Army.

On behalf of Canada and the Canadian Corps, Lieutenant-General Crerar immediately resisted Monty's right to give orders – indeed for months Crerar and his corps headquarters staff would refuse to address correspondence to Monty as 'Army Commander', only 'C-in-C, South-Eastern Command'. Moreover, when Monty attempted to draw up contingency plans in February 1942 for the use of GHQ reserves in South-Eastern Army area in the event of a German invasion, Crerar protested that Canadian reserves could only be allocated with the express consent of the Canadian government or its authorized representative. To Monty – who within months would be commanding Polish, French, Indian, Australian, New Zealand and South African forces as well as British – Crerar's pedantry was a form of 'belly-aching' more likely to lose the war than win it; and his relations with Crerar – as well as McNaughton (who, once recovered, was 'kicked upstairs' to become so-called 1st Canadian Army Commander on April 1942) never improved.

For the rest of the war, tragically – given the superlative volunteer fighting troops in the Canadian armed forces – McNaughton and Crerar, arguably the two worst generals in the forces of the dominions, remained the two most senior Canadian military commanders.

Monty, however, was stuck with them: a nightmare of bureaucratic obstructionism that mirrored the amateurism of the BEF in 1939 and 1940 under Lord Gort.

Magnificent material

General McNaughton had considered the Canadian Corps to be 'thoroughly prepared for battle' before he left to convalesce.[61] Monty did not. Fortunately the corps chief of staff, Brigadier Guy Simonds, was a generation younger than Crerar, and an officer of exceptional ability. As Simbo Simpson later recalled, Monty soon had the three chiefs of staff – of South-Eastern Army, XII Corps and Canadian Corps – closeted together in the evenings to co-ordinate their staff work. Dealing with Crerar, however, proved a continuing nightmare.

Monty's two highest priorities, as regards the new Canadian Corps, were training and planning, and in November 1941 he insisted the

Canadians adopt the same systematic approach to training as XII Corps, involving unit and sub-unit training, mobile HQ exercises at the end of December 1941, and full-scale corps exercises the following spring.

In the same way as he had in XII Corps, Monty simultaneously defined, as army commander, the tactical doctrine which he wished the Canadian Corps to adopt. However unlikely a German invasion, its 'threat' provided South-Eastern Army with the framework for making detailed defensive plans. As in V Corps and in XII Corps, Monty was determined to get rid of any Maginot or 'stop line' mentality. In a new South-Eastern Army Instruction on 'Locality Defence' on 2 December 1941, a few days before Pearl Harbor and the Japanese invasion of Malaya, he poured scorn on the notion of continuous defence lines. 'A system of linear defence based on isolated selection of posts is useless in modern war,' he mocked the Canadian defensive system from Beachy Head to Chichester, 'and will in all cases be avoided. The principle of LOCALITY DEFENCE will be applied throughout South-Eastern Army.' As he explained, 'LOCALITY DEFENCE implies the concentration of platoon and in some cases companies in strong, well-wired localities designed for all-round defence.' The 'considerable gaps between localities cannot be avoided,' he declared, nor was it necessary to worry on this account. 'Enemy penetration through these gaps is of no great importance so long as the localities can hold out till our counter-attacks can be launched . . .'[62]

These were not arcane matters. Following Japanese advances in Malaya and the fall of Hong Kong (with 2,000 fresh Canadian troops), Monty insisted on personally addressing the Canadian corps, division and unit headquarters staffs, to review the lessons of their first exercise, codenamed Beaver I. Again and again he hammered home the point that 'defensive mindedness' would result in failure against skilful opponents such as the Germans or the Japanese – indeed, he disliked the word defence altogether. 'In the invasion battle the enemy has the initiative,' he explained, after running through his eight-point 'Plan to Defeat Invasion'. 'Therefore initially our operations tend to have a defensive bias . . . But the successful defeat of invasion will never be achieved by defensive action,' he warned. 'Successful defeat of invasion will be achieved by offensive action. This being the case our worst enemy is "defensive mentality". We have got to develop the offensive spirit in our officers and men. As the enemy has the initiative and we may have to meet a great avalanche at any moment, we want to be clear as to what is meant by the "offensive spirit". It does not mean that we will knock our heads up against every snag that the enemy likes to prepare for us, regardless of the situation. It means that we are offensively minded. It means that although initially we may be forced to act on the defensive, we are on the watch all the time for opportunities to take *offensive action*, and when those opportunities occur we will be ready to seize them with both hands and get on with it. The opportunity when it does come may be fleeting; immediate advantage must be taken of it before the chance passes; any relapse to a purely defensive mentality, even when everything seems hopeless, must never be allowed. Nothing is ever hopeless so long as hearts are stout, and men have the weapons with which to fight. I therefore say that the first requirement in the successful defeat of invasion is proven, well-trained soldiery, who are mentally alert, skilled in field-craft, expert in the use of their weapons, and are offensively minded. Given such a soldiery, if put into battle properly, and well led in the battle by their junior leaders, then all will be well.' This brought him back to beach defences, and stop lines. 'There is a tendency to think that the only way to defeat invasion is to have good defences, with plenty of pill-boxes,' he remarked. 'Such defences will be of no avail if the men inside them are dull, with no fighting spirit and are defensively minded. If I were to choose between good defences and good men I am quite definite that I would sooner have the men,' he asserted, 'and *no* defences rather than have the best defences in the world manned by a soldiery with no fighting spirit.'[63]

What was crucial was to look forward, not backwards, and to see defensive positions as the springboard for offence, not standing still. 'I suggest that in preparing your schemes and plans,' he declared, 'you should not use the nomenclature or words "defence schemes". These words tend to give the impression of defence only. But the successful defeat of invasion is based on offensive action. I therefore recommend that your written schemes should be entitled "Plan to Defeat Invasion".' He then proceeded to bring out the most valuable lessons of the exercise: the proper positioning and defence of headquarters 'so that the divisional or brigade commander can give his whole attention to the battle going on in his area or sector'; the proper organization of command, with a clearly known hierarchy in which Home Guard and reserves would know the chain of command; the correct dispositions for units, following the principles of 'locality defence', avoiding 'undue dispersion which is strong nowhere'; and in the light of the exercise, assessing those major features which must be held 'at all costs'. In this case, the exercise had brought out the imperative need to hold the South Downs of Sussex, which had been shown to be poorly defended owing to their defences being thin and too dispersed. 'The problems need to be examined so that you hold very *strongly* the really good approaches on to the Downs and ignore the rest,' Monty declared of what, in essence was the problem he would tackle the following year at Alam Halfa.[64]

Commanders must learn to prioritize. Moreover, there was the question of road communications and demolitions. It was no good, he felt, simply blowing all bridges. Only in the front line, on the coast, was such a policy defensible; behind that line it was important that the chief engineer of the corps be in firm control, together with his corps commander. Certain bridges might be needed for counter-attack; and besides, to send out all the engineers in the corps in demolition parties was once again to invite defeat through undue dispersion, leaving the chief engineer empty-handed just when he might require his forces. There was also the crucial matter of signals ('if there is any lack of co-operation between staff and signals, then you're done'); the need to fight to kill 'without quarter asked or given', if the Germans dared to invade; and finally the paramount importance of air support. 'I mention this last not because it is least important – but because it is the most important of all the points I've touched on. I mention it last so that you are more likely to remember it.' Exercise Beaver had shown how little 'air-minded' was the Canadian Corps still – how, hours after the original report of a 'German invasion', the RAF support squadrons had still not been alerted, nor were they subsequently used in Canadian operations. 'It is very necessary you should cultivate an "air"-sense,' he emphasized. 'You must become air-support minded. The Germans have a system which gives extraordinary quick support . . . We must be satisfied with nothing less.'[65]

All this had emerged, as Monty pointed out, without a single soldier having been mobilized for the exercise! Training, he reiterated, was not playtime: *it was the intellectual and physical preparation for success in modern battle.* If the commanding officers ensured that they put their troops into battle on the right footing, if the junior leaders led with intelligence and resolution, and if the soldiery was hardened for 'a real rough house lasting for weeks', then success would be inevitable. 'Canadian officers and men have always been renowned for these qualities,' Monty concluded, 'and they possess that very great quality of being able to rise to the top of their form when all is not going well. A soldiery with these sterling qualities will always excel in battle. So for you the outlook is bright,' he ended. 'If you officers ensure you put properly into the fight the magnificent material you possess, then there is no Corps taking part in this worldwide war – of any nation – that will be able to compete with you.'[66]

Deserving to lose the Empire

Monty's address was a tour de force; indeed, such an address, at a time of unremitting Allied disaster against the Japanese and the Germans, was to younger officers all the more inspiring because its rhetoric was so clearly based upon a lifetime's study of the art of modern war – and professional battlefield experience. Moreover, it was an address given against a sorry backcloth of currrent British failure to meet enemy offensives. Having pulled back from Benghazi in December, General Rommel suddenly launched on 21 January 1942 a major counter-offensive from El Agheila – forcing the British 8th Army to reel back across the desert. In the Far East the Japanese, having already invaded the Philippines, Malaya and Hong Kong, were threatening Burma. Defensive mindedness and confused priorities soon led to catastrophic British defeat: Singapore surrendering with 60,000 troops to a mere 5,000 Japanese. 'Having failed to save Singapore,' Brooke's biographer Sir Arthur Bryant wrote, 'the British now proceeded to lose Burma.'[67] Despite a year and a half of world war, training had been appalling, and as Sir David Fraser noted in his history of the British army, 'there was little cohesion, and morale suffered as confidence waned'.[68] By 18 February 1942 Brooke was noting in his diary 'If the Army cannot fight better than it is doing at present we shall deserve to lose the Empire'[69] – indeed the British were now performing comparably to the French in 1940.

Exactly as Monty had warned the Canadians in his comments on Exercise Beaver, the retreating 17th Division's headquarters in Burma, for example, prematurely blew the only bridge over the Sittang – leading to the destruction of most of the division, who were drowned, killed or captured. General Chiang Kai-shek cabled Roosevelt to say he had never in his life seen such confusion, unpreparedness and degradation.[70]

Yet instead of welcoming Monty's professionalism and leadership, Crerar now did everything he could, on behalf of Canadian forces, to obstruct Monty's command! Far from being awed by Monty's address to Canadian officers at the end of Exercise Beaver, he raged – and telephoned the CIGS, General Brooke, who invited him to lunch to sort things out.

The Canadians revolt

With allies such as the senior Canadian generals, Britain did not need enemies. Alan Brooke had gained intimate knowledge about Canadian forces in World War I; the day after lunching with Crerar, Brooke wrote to warn Monty that a Canadian revolt was brewing. In the traditional green ink of the CIGS he began his handwritten letter by saying he was 'delighted that things are going so well with the Canadian Corps', as Monty had informed him in a recent letter. Yet he felt he must caution Monty not to underestimate what he was up against. 'They are grand soldiers, that I fully realized after spending 1½ years with them in the last war. But they are very touchy and childlike in many ways. You will therefore have to watch your steps with them *far* more than you would with British troops. I had Crerar to lunch, and he is delighted with all your help, and all out to play to the utmost. But he warned me of three dangers which I had not thought of:- a) The possibility that the umpires sent to assist formations [Monty had offered to send junior umpires to help] may be looked on as "spies" to report on efficiency and state of training. This will want watching by careful selection of umpires. b) The danger of the impression being created that you were trying to "drive" the Canadian Corps! c) The danger, in large conferences of all ranks, of criticizing senior officers in front of the juniors. As Canadians they are only too ready to criticize their own seniors, but they resent having their Brig & Div Commanders criticized by a British officer! Their tendency as Canadians will at once be to take [*sic*] pacts against the British officer & to resent his remarks. I pass these points on to you for what they are worth.'[71]

This was, unbeknown either to Brooke or to Monty, the first real salvo in Monty's greatest – and largely losing – battle of all: his struggle to keep his Allied colleagues sweet in the bitter, deadly business of fighting the Germans.

Senior officers the trouble

The Canadian revolt caused Monty to rethink the remark he'd made to his mother during the battle of Passchendaele. 'In point of fact the soldiers were far better than their senior officers!' he later remarked in an annotation to his November 1917 letter to his mother. 'It was those senior officers who were the trouble.' In particular, he reflected for posterity, Crerar's elevation to army commander in 1944 was a tragedy. 'I had great troubles with Crerar, the Commander of the Canadian Army in North-West Europe in 1944–45. He was utterly unfit to command an Army, and some of his Divisional Commanders were very poor. I complained to Alanbrooke (the CIGS) about it and he replied that I must somehow pull them along. He said he had the same trouble in the First World War when it was found necessary to replace Byng by Currie. However Alanbrooke did manage to get McNaughton kicked out; he was a useless commander, and was really a scientist.'[72]

It has become customary among historians to compare Montgomery with 'diplomatic' commanders such as Eisenhower or Alexander, who possessed the vital talents of charm and conciliatory manner so essential to inter-allied harmony. But Monty was not, nor ever would be, a diplomat in military matters: he was a fighting general, with a unique ability to train and lead modern citizen-soldiers of democratic countries in battle against the forces of the dictators. As such, among serious students of the twentieth century, he continues to hold an indisputable place as the foremost Allied commander of his kind in World War II, without whom the D-Day landings could simply not have been successfully mounted – with incalculable effects on twentieth-century history. Yet the problem of dealing with below-par allies was in many ways beyond him, demanding talents of conciliation that he did not possess, any more than 'Vinegar Joe' Stillwell or George S. Patton, for example (whose relations with his subordinate Free French commanders would be marred by strife).

Perhaps the two forms of generalship – diplomatic and fighting – could never co-exist in one man, given the superhuman requirements of each role. To turn amateur and amateurish soldiers almost overnight into professionals, capable of defeating the Germans in battle, but without the utterly inhumane sacrifice of troops made by the Russians, was a mission which Monty undertook of his own accord, and in his own manner, based on a lifetime's study and practice of training and command. He set and maintained standards of professional expectation, on a vast scale, which dwarfed the ambitions of any other commander on the Allied side – and he dedicated himself ceaselessly and tirelessly to achieving his aims. As a professional warrior he was determined to transform the Canadian Corps in the same manner that he had transformed V Corps and XII Corps – but the effort rendered him almost demented, given the obstacles that McNaughton, Crerar and others put in his path.

Tragically, Crerar – and later, in the same way, certain senior American generals – could not understand that Monty's criticisms of Canadian performances in Exercise Beaver were not made for self-glory or to humble Canadians, but were precisely the professional criticisms he made of all men serving under his command, and were designed solely to produce better results on the battlefield, where men's lives were at stake. His outspoken criticism of Gort, or Auchinleck, or a thousand subordinate officers he sacked in Home Forces, were expressions of ruthless profession-alism: the refusal to accept second best, if the British were to match and better the Germans in battle. British soldiers performed abysmally in offensive battle unless well officered; therefore the army must adopt new standards of officer performance, both junior and senior, field and staff. Canadian troops made significantly better battlefield soldiers than British – but these troops would be let down in real battle, and their lives squandered, unless their officers became more professional in their approach to war, and to training for war. An exercise such as Beaver thankfully drew attention to their deficiencies, prior to the ruder test of combat – deficiencies which Crerar and his colleagues, in Monty's view, did everything to mask rather than address.

To Monty this was a tragedy.

The finest war machine

Monty had taken a young Canadian officer, Captain Trumbull Warren, as his ADC, and to him Monty confided his almost endless frustrations. When Warren returned to Canada to enter the Canadian Staff College (at Monty's urging), Monty kept him 'up-to-date' with his struggle.

'I have to proceed very carefully and to be very tactfull [*sic*] – there is considerable jealousy in a certain quarter,' he lamented in March 1942 to Warren, who was studying in Kingston, Ontario. 'The [South-Eastern] Army has no direct control over the [Canadian] Corps; it is under me for training, operations, etc, etc, and is now beginning to become known as a good Corps (after 2½ years). When we meet again I can tell you some very interesting side-lights; meanwhile I have no doubt you can read between the lines.'[73]

Warren could – for throughout the spring of 1942 Monty had, by personal inspections and through the laying on of exercises at every level from the indoor model to battalion, brigade, division, corps and army, worked to separate the Canadian wheat from the chaff, visiting no fewer than twenty-seven Canadian infantry battalions. 'Your soldiers are coming on very well,' Monty wrote to Warren on 25 March 1942. The Canadians 'have got to the stage of large scale exercises now – inter divisional – and they're showing up certain weaknesses in the higher ranks. I spend practically all and every day out on the training area with them, trying to help them in the collective training as I did in the unit training and organization when you and I went round the Corps together visiting the C.O.'s. It is hard work, but I keep pegging away at it; one gets one's reward when they really do begin to progress, as is happening now. The work you and I did together was only the foundation, or groundwork. Having got that right we have got to get the whole show working smoothly as a team, and running like a well oiled machine . . . My objective is to make the Corps the finest war machine that we have ever had, and I am not going to fail.'[74]

To succeed, however, meant cutting out dead wood, as he had in every formation of which he had taken command since becoming a brigade commander in 1937. 'I hope to be sending Price back to you; he will be of great value in Canada where his knowledge of the milk industry will help on the national war effort,' he remarked, sarcastically.[75] Others went too. 'I hope to be sending you Pearkes, Potts, and Ganong back to Canada shortly; you will find them useful your side, I hope.' The net result would be 'a good deal of promotion; the good young chaps are now getting their chance and beginning to emerge'.[76]

Monty was constantly on the lookout for such younger officers. The 44th Division's commander, Brian Horrocks, later remarked that Monty would have made a 'first class talent spotter for any football club'. In general 'Army Commanders with many thousands of troops under their command tend to become remote God-like characters whom few know even by sight, yet in some extraordinary way Monty's influence permeated all strata of SE Command and his knowledge of the personalities under his command was uncanny. Often he would ring me in the evening and make the most searching inquiries about some young second-lieutenant whom he had noticed on training . . . The only way I could deal with these inquiries was to have a book containing details of every officer in the division handy beside the telephone.'[77]

Stephen Grenfell, serving under Montgomery in XII Corps, later wondered 'whether he got any sleep in those days, but he seemed to be everywhere. His appearances weren't visits; they were visitations. A couple of staff cars would erupt into your line of vision. A stringy, bird-like little man would jump out; there'd be a flurry of salutes and the General would be right amongst the pigeons. Striding on ahead, with his staff stumbling behind in the dunes, he'd make straight for the nearest private soldier. "Who are you? Where do you come from? What are you doing? Do you know what's going on? Are you in the picture? Can you see the coast of France today? Good; that's where the enemy is . . .'[78]

XII Corps' exercises Galahad, Conqueror, Victor and Lancelot took place in unremitting succession. Meanwhile, by April 1942 Canadian Corps was mounting its own five-day exercises: Beaver III and Beaver IV, in which operational staff work, administration, movement, integration of artillery, infantry and air support as well as mobile operations, were rehearsed.

Finally on 19 May 1942 Monty mounted Exercise Tiger: the largest military exercise ever held in Britain. As Monty wrote to Warren's wife, 'all your people over here took part; it lasted 11 days and some of the units marched and fought over 250 miles of country; many of the men had no soles to their boots and their powers of endurance were stretched to the limit'.[79] But to Warren himself Monty made clear it was not only the endurance of the 100,000 troops he was testing, but the commanding officers: 'Crerar v. Gammell, or Sussex v. Kent.'[80]

Offending amour propre

As Monty explained to the 2,000 senior officers in his two-hour summing up on 4 June 1942, he had been requested to try out the two new types of British division, armoured and infantry. His own view was that a modern corps commander must be able to handle both. 'Every commander has therefore got to understand fully the handling of armoured formations,' he stressed, 'and how to get the best value from the combined action of armoured and unarmoured units.' This led Monty to a mesmerizing reminder of the general principles of modern battlefield tactics.

The 'whole essence of modern tactical methods' could, Monty claimed, be reduced to three words: concentration, control and simplicity. Armoured divisions could most easily defeat their panzer opponent by 'forcing him to attack our own armour on previously selected and occupied ground. To ensure he attacks, possession of the ground selected must be vital to the enemy,' he maintained – in essence, the recipe he would put to use three months later in the battle of Alam Halfa. Equally, the role of an armoured division might be to punch a hole in the enemy defence, with infantry following 'closely to take over the ground gained and to hold the battlefield; indeed, if the infantry brigade of an armoured division could close right up behind the armour, complete with anti-tank guns, the armour would then be well placed 'with a view to drawing the enemy armoured units on to the infantry anti-tank defence' – the tactics Rommel was about to unleash upon the British 8th Army at Gazala, and the core tactic on which the battle of Alamein would be based, four months later.

Surprise, flexibility of grouping, intimate co-operation with artillery, concentration . . . Point by point Monty examined the lessons of the exercise, including the need for much greater co-ordination with air head-quarters. Without such co-ordination the battle plan might well fail. 'It involves the whole of the Air action – the employment of the fighter force for air superiority and protection at the right time and place; the employment of the heavy bomber force and careful selection of bombing objectives best calculated to assist the military aim; and not least the careful planning of air reconnaissance without which the close support squadrons for the attack of ground targets cannot operate with maximum efficiency.' Such an approach seemed eminently simple, yet Canadian Corps had been given seven fighter and two bomber squadrons to support them and 'never at any time were their demands for close support sufficient to employ fully four fighter squadrons, and the bomber squadrons were less than half fully employed'.[81]

Such criticism of the Canadian Corps was to ignore Brooke's warnings about their sensitivity, but for Monty the lessons were of life-or-death importance compared to Crerar's *amour propre*. The various tactical lessons would be tackled in a series of cloth-model discussions and signals exercises in June, Monty announced, together with more training exer-cises, this time using live ammunition.

If General Crerar was difficult to instruct, it was only a foretaste of what would happen with American colleagues, however – the first of whom were now arriving in Britain.

Periphery-pecking

As emissaries of General Marshall, the head of the US army in Washington, Major-Generals Dwight D. Eisenhower and Mark Clark had personally attended Exercise Tiger on 27 May, eight days into the eleven-day simulated battle. Asked to explain the manoeuvres, Monty – who disliked being 'interrupted' by social or political engagements in the midst of a mock battle – agreed to take time out to brief the two Americans personally. As Clark recalled, Monty was 'late, very late' but greeted them with the words 'I'm sorry I'm late, but I really shouldn't have come at all. I'll make it brief.'[82] Then, 'As he took up the pointer and was about to speak, Eisenhower lit up a cigarette. Montgomery sniffed the tobacco and said, "Who is smoking?"

'Eisenhower said, "I am, sir."

'"Stop it," Montgomery said. "I don't permit it."

'Eisenhower meekly put out his cigarette.'[83] In another account, Clark recorded that 'Ike dropped the cigarete on the floor, stepped on it, and looked at me, very red faced. Monty took a few minute more, then said, "That concludes my presentation. Sorry to be so abrupt." He shook hands, and out we went.'[84]

Learning this, Stephen Ambrose, Eisenhower's official biographer, was retrospectively offended by the apparent snub to a man who would become America's military – and later, political – idol. Already as a colonel, and chief of staff to 3rd US Army, Eisenhower had evinced 'an absolute genius at public relations' in Ambrose's account.[85] Reporters and subordinates loved his 'frankness, his facility for explaining things, no matter how technical, so that they could understand them, his easy informality, his jokes, and his honesty'.[86] He was six foot tall, his modesty was 'irresistibly appealing' and he was 'one of the most photogenic men in the country, even in the world'.[87]

Alas, Monty was not. As Ambrose described, 'Montgomery wore a field greatcoat which emphasized his own physical stature and tiny steps. He was, by nature, condescending, especially towards Americans, most of whom regarded him with extreme distaste.'[88]

Did this encounter poison the relationship between Monty and Ike thereafter? Whatever the damage to his *amour propre*, Eisenhower was – unlike Crerar – far too astute to allow his irritation either to show or to influence his estimation. He had never served on the field of battle, or even commanded large bodies of men on or off the field of battle. He had, however, a sharp, critical and intelligent mind behind the 'Aw, shucks' exterior, and had been chief of staff for the 'Louisiana' invasion manoeuvres the year before, on an even larger scale than Exercise Tiger. As a soldier he was impressed by Monty's professionalism and clarity of presentation – whereas his own kinsman, Major-General Chaney, who was the senior US military representative in Britain, was, in Eisenhower's view, a dud who deserved to go home 'on a slow boat, without escort'.[89] What was needed, if the Allies were to launch an invasion of Europe across the English Channel, was to 'get punch behind the job'.[90] Monty, in the words of one young officer who visited his headquarters at this time, gave the impression he might 'lead his army directly across the Channel in a personal campaign to liberate Europe'.[91] Such a man – whether or not he tolerated smoking in his own office – was sorely needed by the Allies, Eisenhower was the first to acknowledge.

Eisenhower's directive was to report, on behalf of the chief of the American general staff in Washington, on why plans for a second front, or cross-Channel invasion of Europe, in 1942 or '43 were not progressing faster. 'We've got to begin slugging with air at West Europe, to be followed by a land attack as soon as possible. We've got to quit wasting resources all over the world,' he'd jotted in his diary in January 1942;[92] given that in London the Americans saw the British as 'periphery-pecking'[93] rather than showing a genuine desire to start a second front across the Channel, Monty's greatcoat did not matter. He clearly believed British and Canadian troops could beat the Germans in battle, and that Monty was a trainer of genius – and in the brief meeting in Monty's office, whatever miffed historians might later concoct, an historic partnership was prefigured that would, only two years later, bring the Allies their greatest triumph of the war: the D-Day landings.

'General Montgomery,' Eisenhower reported back to Marshall in the Pentagon, 'explained the exercises to us. General Montgomery is a decisive type who appears to be extremely energetic and professionally able.'[94] Together – since Marshall immediately appointed Eisenhower the US commander of the European theatre of operations in place of Major-General Chaney – they could do business.

Rightly or wrongly, however, it would not be across the Channel for some considerable time, for there was much 'peripheral pecking' first to be accomplished.

14

Personal Relations

Butcher and run

To the profound suspicion, indeed despair, of American strategic planners, the second front in Europe was postponed for two years while Churchill pursued his peripheral strategy: securing North Africa and the Mediterranean, then invading Italy, the 'soft underbelly'.[1]

In the meantime, in order to give hope to the hard-pressed Russians and a sop to the Americans, who had generously agreed to a Europe-first, Pacific-second strategy, the Prime Minister urged that a raid be mounted on the French coast: the sort of 'butcher-and-run' operation he had first dreamed of in the wake of Dunkirk in 1940. It would make headlines, show British willingness (or mask British unwillingness) to fight in the field, perhaps even draw German divisions from the Eastern Front . . . or something.

Thus was concocted the disastrous British raid on Dieppe – in which the blood spilled would not, for the most part, be British, but Canadian.

A job in the dog-racing world

Monty's role in Churchill's Dieppe disaster would be controversial, and deserves to be re-examined in the light of recent evidence. But before this is done, and particularly in terms of Monty's failure to be selected for battlefield command overseas, it may be appropriate to examine, once again, Monty's personality between 1940 and 1942: professional and personal.

Goronwy Rees, who was an intelligence officer at General Paget's Home

Forces GHQ, left a memorable description of Montgomery in his book
A Bundle of Sensations, in which he described Monty's professional
reputation in Home Forces in 1942: namely, that of a commander of
awesome professionalism, but often outrageous pretensions of military
grandeur, and decided eccentricities.

One early instance of Monty's strange psychopathology, even paranoia,
in V Corps, had been that of 'the dog-racing adjutant', during Monty's
first, apocalyptic inspection of 4 Division and the Portsmouth Garrison in
the summer of 1940. The new corps commander's eagle eye had missed
nothing; indeed, it was clear to all that a completely new level of professionalism was going to be necessary. When, however, the new Portsmouth
Garrison commander confessed he had no idea what had happened to the
garrison's welfare funds – which had almost cost Monty his head as a
lowly infantry brigadier in 1938 – Monty became visibly alarmed. Had
the funds been plundered? Hearing that the garrison adjutant was 'a
reserve officer who had been called up from a job in the dog-racing world'[2]
and had been dismissed that very day – moreover was due to get on a train
at Portsmouth at that very moment – Monty brought the entire inspection
to a halt, insisting that military police be despatched forthwith to Portsmouth station to arrest the man.

The scene, as the hapless officer was 'caught' and brought back to HQ
(where it was found that the funds were safe and sound, in fact had
attracted useful interest, having lain untouched since 1938) was farcical.
'My good General Dudley Johnson never quite understood this episode.
He said nothing like that had ever happened to him,' Simpson remembered
with a smile.[3]

This was understandable – but it did raise further doubts about Monty's
sanity – doubts which proliferated throughout Monty's time in Home
Forces.

Churchill's guns

Another episode Simpson recalled was that of the 'very heavy guns stationed on the coast near Dover'. Churchill's private secretary had recorded
how, on 11 July 1940, the Prime Minister had been to inspect the new
gun site that was 'being prepared at considerable risk, and with immense
labour, for the purpose of bombarding the coast of France. It will require

three valuable and vulnerable cranes to put it in position and will only last 100 rounds: the military authorities call it a "pure stunt".'[4]

Inheriting these 14-inch guns as part of XII Corps, Monty had decided to see if they worked, writing to his old ADC, Charles Sweeny, on 29 May 1941 to invite Sweeny to 'stay here with me for 48 hrs, 7 days, or as long as you like. I will show you many things in Kent, and you can shell Germans in Calais.'[5]

'Shelling the Germans in Calais' was not a sport to which Sweeny was attracted. Three weeks later Monty had not given up, though complaining at Sweeny's 'long time' in answering his letter. The month of June 1941 was out, now, he explained. 'I have a big Corps Ex[ercise]. between 24 and 30 June so that is no good. In fact I am very full up till 5 July. After that I am free, and am going to move myself to Dover Castle for a week' – Dover being 'in the front line – you can see France and push shells over into Calais – the Germans shell Dover – air battles go on in the Channel all day – in fact it is all good fun – very different from your quiet life in the West of England!!'[6]

This was 'Monty parlance' – reducing the immense task facing the Allies to a sort of humorous caricature that would keep up the spirits of his junior staff when the picture in Nazi Europe – and further east – seemed alarmingly bleak. But firing 'Churchill's gun' was, as Simpson recalled, no laughing matter. As part of a special exercise, on Monty's orders, the guns were duly loaded. Unfortunately the RAF spotter plane which had been detailed to observe the falling of the shells began to run out of radio range in mid-Channel – confirming the verdict of the 'military authorities' that the guns, with their range of twenty-one miles plus, were a pure 'stunt'. Ordered by Monty to return to base, however, the Blenheim aircraft was promptly shot down in flames, before the very eyes of the corps commander and his young friend, by three Messerschmitts over St Margaret's Bay, with the loss of several British lives.[7] According to Major Rees, who was serving at Home Forces GHQ, Monty had then insisted the gun be fired, despite the gunnery officer's protest that the gun 'could only be fired on the direct command of the War Office. "Fire it," said the Army Commander. "No," said the subaltern. "Fire it," said the Army Commander. "*My* Army, *my* gun. Fire it." The gun was fired, with what effects were not known.'[8]

In fact, the effects *were* known, as Simpson recalled. 'With an enormous roar they were fired and the shells departed on their journey.'

Beyond sight or air survey, the shells duly landed in Calais. According to Simpson – who became the Deputy Director of Military Operations at the War Office – secret intelligence later revealed that the fired shells landed 'on a café . . . which was, fortunately for us, well patronized by German officers'. As he recalled 'many of these officers had been killed'. The Germans were not amused. As in some 1920s Keystone film they were 'incensed by this unexpected landing of shells in their midst', and 'decided to retaliate and launched a night raid on Dover the same night. There were over 20 casualties in Dover,' Simpson chronicled, 'all unfortunately to civilians, as a result.'[9]

When Churchill heard of the incident there was an even greater explosion – indeed 'its detonation', Rees remembered, 'reverberated throughout our headquarters'.[10] The 'guns were regarded as the Prime Minister's personal guns, not to be fired without an order from him', Simpson explained. 'We were given a pretty sharp instruction that never again was the corps commander or anybody similar to take upon himself the firing of these guns. If an invasion was going to take place the Prime Minister would order the firing.' As Simpson remarked, 'How all that was going to work with all the other preoccupations the Prime Minister would have if there was an invasion we never quite understood, but that was an order and we obeyed.'[11]

In Churchill's eyes, the episode was a further indication of Monty's arrogance as the Kent corps commander at the time – and the failure of Monty to obey Brooke's warning not to annoy people unnecessarily. Certainly Monty – who knew very well Churchill's embargo on firing the guns – had been amost childishly determined not only to see the guns fired in practice, but to demonstrate his authority over them, in competition with the Prime Minister. His plan had, one might say, misfired.

Yet behind the almost schoolboy competitiveness, there was a more serious issue at stake, which outsiders and later historians so often overlooked: Monty's insistence on rehearsing the whole business of firing the guns in a mock-operational scenario, in advance of an emergency, so that they could be brought into action swiftly and effectively when required in earnest. The rehearsal had, indeed, pointed up the ridiculousness of twenty-one-mile-range guns operating with spotter aircraft unable to monitor the fall of their shells more than half-way across the Channel. This was the disappointing lesson Monty drew from the exercise, and the reason why he had brought the whole exercise to an immediate halt. Churchill's irritated edict, after the firing, then took the guns out of Monty's control – but with fatal consequences, which cost forty men's lives and brought utter humiliation to the British navy and coastal command a few months later when, on Hitler's personal orders, Operation Cerberus was enacted: the escape from Brest of the German battleships *Scharnhorst* and *Gneisenau*, together with the heavy cruiser *Prinz Eugen*, on 12 February 1942, in broad daylight through the Straits of Dover.

On Simpson's personal order as Monty's chief of staff (Monty was away at the time) the guns *did* have to be fired – again without prime ministerial sanction. But with no spotter aircraft and only primitive radar to plot the moving targets, the guns completely missed the battleships, which escaped virtually unscathed to Kiel. As J. D. Potter narrated in his account of the episode, *Fiasco*, the Prime Minister called Admiral Ramsay, the hero of the Dunkirk evacuation, 'to know how they [the battleships] had got through'. The answer, as the radar officer said to Ramsay, was simple. 'It was simply due to the fact that there was no forethought, no co-ordination whatsoever.'[12]

It was Monty's historic role to provide that forethought and co-ordination – through the art of rehearsal.

Monty's warts

Monty's approach to the problem of professionalism – which would become standard practice in industry as in the armed services the world over, after World War II – was to teach large bodies of men to develop their professional skills through exercises which rehearsed not only combat operations in advance of real combat, but practised the whole business of communications, command and co-operation between all arms and all services.

With a recalcitrant ally in the Canadians, however, Monty's training task had become doubly challenging – and some of his personal actions clearly betrayed the growing strain he was under. He not only paid scant attention to his son David, but even rejected a private letter from his own step-son, John Carver, who was in hospital suffering from measles, with the words: 'Your letter has been received here. I ordered it to be burned immediately and I haven't read it.'[13] He also sacked a perfectly good junior intelligence officer at XII Corps, Henry Sherek, who had been a theatrical producer, because he was fat and had German connections about which GHQ had become anxious – 'Can't have that here,' Monty told his chief of staff. 'Get rid of him at once. He must leave the Corps area in three hours from now.'[14]

Yet, as Rees recorded, these were warts. Monty the military commander had high expectations of his men; if you satisfied them, and were young, he more than backed you; if you failed for any reason his exacting expectations, you were unlikely to survive in office.

In assessing the Canadian Corps, for example, Monty considered only half the brigade commanders worth keeping, seven of the battalion commanders unacceptable, and even fewer seconds-in-command. Of one battalion CO he remarked, 'This is the worst and most ignorant C.O. I have met in my service in the Army', who trained neither his officers or his NCOs. The failure to train NCOs in the Canadian Corps was, Monty considered, a scandal – while the paper-factories of their various headquarters were calamitous.[15]

As an inspector general, then, Monty had by the spring of 1942 earned an unenviable reputation. When Rees was ordered to appear at Monty's headquarters at Reigate in March 1942, for instance, his boss gave him 'a sympathetic look as if he were sentencing me to immediate execution,' Rees recalled. ' "You'd better be on your toes, or he'll have you back here in no time and then there'll be hell to pay. He'll be up here himself before you know." He spoke as if this were to be avoided at all costs. I had the feeling that I had been selected, for no very good reason, for a specially dangerous mission, with the particular objective of protecting GHQ Home Forces from this unknown but mysteriously terrifying general.'[16]

On meeting Monty, however, Rees was bowled over by the uncanny calm and orderliness that Monty exuded. 'The Army Commander occupied a comfortable villa on the hill overlooking Reigate . . . Through the open french-windows I could see a small, rather unimpressive figure walking on the lawn, head slightly bent and hands clasped behind its back . . . When he had received his ADC's message, the little figure turned and came into the study.' The little general, Rees saw, possessed a 'narrow foxy face, long-nosed, sharp and intelligent and tenacious, with very bright and clear blue eyes, and a small, light, spare body. The effect was not at all imposing, except for his eyes and an indefinable look in his face of extreme cleverness and sagacity, like a very alert Parson Jack Russell terrier. But what was impressive was an air he had of extraordinary quietness and calm, as if nothing in the world could disturb his peace of mind.'[17]

After the chaos and tension of General Paget's GHQ, characterized by

Paget's 'rudeness and bad temper' deriving from an old World War I war wound, Rees found himself appreciating the reason 'why Monty liked to have about him men who were physically well and whose nerves were relaxed by the physical sedative of physical exercise'.[18] Such men were often young, and their youth, and often good looks, aroused a certain degree of speculation – for Monty's relationships with them were often at complete variance with his martinet image.

It is time, now, to look more closely at some of them.

Friends for life

Young Kit Dawnay inspired in Monty feelings of intense affection, playfulness and loyalty. In encouraging Dawnay to move with him to V Corps in the summer of 1940 Monty had apologized: 'I am afraid I haven't asked you if want to come with me and it may be that you would sooner stay with the 3rd Division. Let me know. Charles [Sweeny] and I would like to have you with us; if they let you come you will become a Major and Charles will have to call you "Sir"', he joked.[19] Dawnay was also asked to stop addressing Monty so formally in his letters: 'Possibly you could manage General Monty. After all,' he pointed out to Dawnay, 'I regard you as one of my real friends.'[20]

Unfortunately, Lieutenant Sweeny had then been posted back to his regiment, in September 1940. To Dawnay Monty lamented: 'I have lost my Charles; I really do miss him terribly and life seems quite different without him. We have been through a good deal together and I have a very great and real affection for him; I had to let him go though. He is a dear lad and I hope and pray no harm will come to him in this war.'[21]

To Sweeny himself Monty confessed on 5 October 1940: 'I had got used to having you with me and I really do miss you terribly. But you know one thing Charles – you can count on me as a friend for life, and if there is I anything I can do for you, you have only to ask. I regard you and Kit as real friends, that I will always want to see.'[22]

That this relationship did not, however, extend beyond the bounds of contemporary propriety was touchingly evident from Monty's shy request: 'If you can bring yourself to do it, I would like you to call me General Monty, and I have no doubt you refer to me as such when I am not present!'[23]

Very great affections

What did Monty mean by friendship with such young men? Certainly, whatever Monty's own suppressed feelings or attraction, he never assumed or presumed that his wards were anything other than heterosexual in their own orientation. 'My dear Kit, I was delighted to see in *The Times* of the arrival of a son,' he wrote on 8 November 1940. 'I hope the lad is doing well – and his mother. He will I trust become a soldier in due course!' Having made this point, however, Monty added how much he looked forward to seeing Kit again. 'When are you coming to stay with me? There is a ducal bedroom here for you whenever you care to come along.'[24] He soon agreed to become a godfather to Dawnay's first son, and writing to Dawnay on Boxing Day, 1940, adopted the sort of jolly-hockey-sticks banter – larding euphemism with exaggeration – that passed for humour: expressing the baptismal hope that 'Rupert is none the worse for his cold bath on Monday last'.[25]

When transferred from V Corps to XII Corps, however, Monty reverted to unfettered emotion: 'One reason why I dislike going is that I shall not see so much of you. I have a very great affection for you Kit, and I count you as a real friend; I was very pleased when you asked me to be godfather to Rupert.'[26]

A succession of bright young men followed in Sweeny's and Dawnay's footsteps – most especially the young Canadian captain Monty took as an ADC, once Canadian Corps came under his aegis, if not command, in November 1941. It is in these relationships that we may go some way towards understanding Monty's lonely heart, as well as the personal key to his beckoning greatness as a modern democratic military commander.

A kind of stillness

Had Monty sought to make 'real friends' of his senior colleagues in the armed services, even of women on his staff, as for example Dwight D. Eisenhower did, then many of Monty's high-command, inter-service and inter-allied problems would have been eased. But in this respect Monty had clearly made a decision, after Dunkirk, not only to avoid all contact with women, but as far as possible to avoid any but professional and necessary contact with his peers. The Parson Jack Russell terrier would operate as a ruthlessly professional commander, but would centre his private life on the company and affection of young officers, whom he would push up the military ladder.

Monty's letters to Trumbull Warren, his Canadian ADC, betrayed the same need for young male company, loyalty and intelligence as with his English officers, Sweeny and Dawnay. 'You need to have no fear as to how you did your work here,' Monty wrote to assure Warren on 11 March 1942 when Warren was posted back to Staff College in Canada; 'you are far and away the best A.D.C. I have ever had and you are a real loss to my mess. As for myself personally, I miss you more than I can say; I had got used to having you around me, you were exactly what I wanted, and I had become very attached to you. So much so that I used to discuss confidential matters that I would never have done with any A.D.C. before, and probably will never do again. I knew I could trust you and I had complete confidence in you. I would like you to look on me now as a real friend – not as the British General that you served with over in England, but as a friend you have made. *Real* friends are rather scarce; I would like to feel that we are now real friends, and for keeps. That is why I want you to write to me and tell me what you are doing; and I will write to you. And when the war is over I will come and stay with you in Canada. All my friends call me Monty. If you feel you can hardly do this, then call me General Monty.' And to close he added, as he so often did in such letters, 'If there is anything I can do for you in this world, you have only to ask. It will be done at once.'[27] Though sometimes he might sign himself Monty, such letters were generally signed 'Yrs sincerely, B. L. Montgomery'.

Whether or not such relationships involved repressed homosexual affection on Monty's side, they now became a distinct, indeed unique feature of Monty's command method. T. E. Lawrence had sought the company of 'ordinary' men in the ranks of the army and RAF, and submission to NCOs and officers, even inventing stern old men and 'uncles' to give orders that he be whipped or made to swim in cold water, in order to expiate his repressed feelings and guilt. Monty's method of dealing with such issues was different, and deserves to be looked at more closely than has been done hitherto. Often half-crazed in his determination to develop and demonstrate the art of command in modern war in a democracy, it was the efficiency and youthful gaiety that young men brought to his headquarters which kept Monty on the right side of sanity, permitting him to create a sort of male family around himself, which in turn allowed him to unbend and relax – relatively speaking – in the security of his headquarters, away from women. 'But what was impressive,' young Major Rees recorded in his impressions of Monty at his headquarters villa in Reigate in the spring of 1942,

was an air he had of extraordinary quietness and calm, as if nothing in the world could disturb his peace of mind. He spoke in a quiet voice and his manner, though incisive, was quiet also; one had the feeling that with him everything was in order, like a good housewife whose domestic arrangements are always ready for any conceivable emergency . . . That air of calm and peace which he carried with him was so strong that after a moment my panic and alarm began to die away; it was something which one felt to be almost incongruous in a soldier. He made me sit in a window seat with my back to the garden, so that my face was in shadow and the evening light streamed in on his and I had the opportunity to see how very finely it was moulded, with the kind of fineness one sees in in some animals that are very highly bred and trained for the particular purpose they have to fulfil. And as one talked to him, one was aware all the time of the stillness and quietness that reigned all around him, in the study itself, in the entire household, in the garden outside, as if even the birds were under a spell of silence; it was a kind of stillness one would associate more easily with a priest than a general. And indeed our conversation itself had something of the same character; it was very onesided and I had to speak nearly all the time, as it took the form of a long, precise, patient interrogation . . . In the small polite man who had listened so attentively to my report on myself I could see no sign of the disagreeable and pretentious exhibition-ist who was the subject of so much rumour and gossip or anything to justify his reputation as a 'terror'.[28]

Clearly, Monty's relations with such young men were different from the tense, formal contact he had with other generals, such as Eisenhower. These young officers were Monty's eyes and ears, his window on the real world of young adults in war, all of them volunteers rather than regulars: their hopes, fears, expectations. If he could win their trust, he recognized instinctively, he would be on the right path to military success in battle – something that would outweigh all the difficulties of pride and pomposity he experienced with senior officers.

As such, these young men proved of profound importance to Monty's mission as a new kind of commander, whose meritocratic professionalism required a new relationship between the leader and the led, between a general and his men: one that ignored the chasms of rank and class distinction. As Rees put it, 'after experience of many senior officers, though none so exalted as him, he was extremely polite, so that one almost forgot his rank, and this could have been dangerous, except that not for one moment could one forget that one was in the presence of a very remarkable person'.[29]

In providing welcome relief from the tension of his command mission, Monty's young staff allowed the strange widower general to live vicariously, through their stories and escapades. As will be seen, Monty meant exactly what he said in his letters to them: indeed, he proved more fiercely loyal to them than to members of his own family, and would allow no one to criticize or threaten such personal disciples. Later, when some were accused of looting in Normandy, for example, he would have the whole matter hushed up, his chosen staff exonerated, the accusing officer sent home – and he purloined the official file when he himself became CIGS!

Not only did such young men serve, relax and entertain Monty at his battlefield court, as in a Shakespearean drama, but the special affection, even devotion, Monty felt towards them was, increasingly, the basis of his devotion to all 'his' troops – many of whose commanding officers, even when an army group commander far removed from such matters, he hand-picked. Modern war, on the battlefield at least, demanded youth and vitality. No matter how much bad blood it might cause among the pompous older officers, Monty was determined to bring on younger officers, remove the 'dead wood' and ensure the army improve its fighting edge. As he would write to Trumbull Warren, years later, of a young field officer he had promoted, 'I gave him command of an armoured regiment, and he commanded it when we landed in Normandy in June 1944. In July 1944 I gave him command of an Armoured Brigade; he was then only 28 . . . He now commands the 3rd Division, my old Division, and goes to the War Office as Director of Staff Duties in September next. He is very clever, brilliant in fact. He could become C.I.G.S. But he has enemies and does not suffer fools gladly!!'[30]

Monty's interest in young officers, then, may be seen as a continuum: his devotion to his personal staff being replicated, professionally, in his devotion to 'his' army. He was never impressed by servility, 'yes-men', men who were inarticulate, or who could not state their preferences or personal views honestly and straightforwardly. Warren's replacement as ADC in the early spring of 1942 was a young French-Canadian; when he was recalled to his battalion, Monty wasn't sorry, though he did rec-

ommend him for the Canadian Staff College. 'I was glad really,' he told
Warren, 'as he never quite fitted in here; in his favour of course one has
to admit that you had set rather a high standard.'[31]

What Monty wanted – and got – were handsome, effective, go-getting,
uncomplicated individuals, without side, willing and able to tell the unvarnished truth. In return Monty gave them his respect, his paternalistic
affection and his complete loyalty.

Banning women

Monty's affection for the young men on his personal staff was one thing.
What made this male set-up somewhat suspect, however, was Monty's
absolute refusal to have women in his headquarters. Was he simply behind
the times, as a male chauvinist, in this respect – or did his ban on women
mask, like his later statements on homosexuality in the House of Lords,
an unconscious fear?

The argument that Monty's exclusion of women merely reflected the
traditions of the army as a single-sex organization holds little water.
Monty was no stickler for tradition, especially where it interfered with
professional efficiency. The Women's Army Auxiliary Corps – later, for a
royalist time, Queen Mary's Women's Army Auxiliary Corps – had, after
all, been established in 1917 and throughout the final two years of World
War I women had served with distinction alongside men; indeed, by the
end of World War I some 57,000 women had served in the Corps, which
was eventually disbanded. In 1938 the WAAC had been resurrected as
the ATS – the Auxiliary Territorial Service – in a Territorial Army whose
importance Monty had constantly upheld. Though the ATS proved
initially less popular among volunteers than the Women's Auxiliary Air
Force (WAAF) and Women's Royal Naval Service (WRNS), this was
more because of its 'lesbian' tunic, long Edwardian skirt and regulation
khaki knickers, known as 'passion killers', than an aversion among women
to army service. In June 1941 a new ATS Director, Miss Jean Knox,
hoisted regulation skirts by two inches, redesigned the ATS jacket with
padded shoulders, belt and buckle, and ordered smart Norwegian-pattern
shoes, complete with an apron front. Silk stockings were also permitted,
instead of the old lisle thread ones. As a result ATS recruiting figures shot
up. By March 1942 compulsory military service for women was introduced

into law by proclamation (over protesting male MPs' heads), and by 1943 some 214,420 women were serving in the ATS alone, performing a bewildering array of specialist services from anti-aircraft battery teams to lines-of-communication truck drivers and signallers.[32] By the spring of 1945 even Princess Elizabeth chose to become a subaltern in the ATS, rather than the navy or air force.

For all this, despite the critical manpower shortage of 1941, Monty remained wholly against the intrusion of women into his all-male preserve. When it became clear that ATS women officers and clerks would be trained and would be drafted by the army to take men's positions at his headquarters, Monty – who normally pressed hard for any measures that released trained men to fight, such as Home Guard units taking over static beach and installation defence duties – virulently opposed the measure. As Charles Sweeny's wife later indignantly recalled, Monty, as South-East Army commander, sent what became a virtually open letter to the War Office in 1942 that ran: 'I will not be responsible for the operation of the command if women officers replace men on the staff.'[33]

It was not only his headquarters from which Monty wanted to exclude women. In banning wives from his command areas Monty claimed he wished his men to devote their wartime to raising their professional performance as soldiers, but was this the whole story? As he noted in his memoirs, he did not want men who would sooner or later have to face Germans in battle to 'sink back into the bosoms of their families and pay too much attention to the question of personal comfort and amenities. On this subject I laid down that while officers and men were not allowed to have their wives and families with them, they were to have leave in the normal way so that they could visit their families as often as possible.' He followed this with an explanation of his philosophy: 'that while training was to be hard and tough, when it was over the troops were to return to good billets and good food, with good facilities for hot baths'.[34] It was not, then, a matter of all work and no play in war, as Monty saw the matter, but a case of balance: hard work meriting out-of-hours, off-campus play. The sexual presence of ATS women – whether officers or other ranks – would distract his men, Monty believed, rather than inspire them to fight better, as others believed. (The exception would be nurses, where Monty was adamant that female nursing close to the front helped to save men's lives.)

For Monty, then, the argument was simply one of efficiency – until the efficiency of women army officers, NCOs and other ranks became incontrovertible. When Sweeny's wife later brought up the matter of his 1942 protest letter to the War Office, in a meeting with him in February 1945, Monty's 'response was that he had had more experience since then of the work of the A.T.S.!', Mrs Sweeny recalled his unusually diplomatic answer.[35]

If there was a heterophobic subtext to his exclusionary policy, however, it is unlikely Monty was aware of it – indeed, to judge by his complete openness about his affections for young men it is unlikely he was ever aware of the pattern or significance of his own proclivity as such. Impelled by his homosocial nature to covet attractive, outgoing, masculine young men, he picked them out, encouraged them to serve with him at his headquarters and fell in love with them – rationalizing such behaviour as paternalism, not the product of homosocial affection. By treating such protégés as a benevolent father (in contrast to his less than satisfactory behaviour as a real father), he excused to himself the very power of his affection.

Most interesting of all to the biographer, however, as to the historian of twentieth-century sexuality, is the manner in which Monty justified his attachments: for, as we shall see again and again, Monty now sought consciously or unconsciously legitimization from the young men's mothers – even their wives!

A great affection for the boy

Perhaps the best example of Monty's pattern of attachment, help, loyalty and then justification was his relationship with his Canadian ADC, Trumbull Warren. Having arranged for Warren to go back to Canada for staff officer training, Monty wrote on 25 April 1942 to tell him he was 'very anxious for you to come back over here when your present business finishes, so that I can see you again and help you up the ladder'. He ended, 'Goodbye to you Trumbull, and good luck always. Yrs ever, B.L. Montgomery' adding as a postscript: 'give my kind regards to your lady wife, and daughter'.[36]

Everything was therefore 'above board'; the bishop's son, infused from early childhood with guilt and fear of sin, could live with affections for young men that went way beyond the norm, and in this respect he quickly established a correspondence with Trumbull's wife, Mary, as well as

Trumbull's mother, Mrs Snively, who sent him food parcels for his son David at Winchester College in 1942. About David, however, Monty wrote remarkably little to the mothers in Canada, beyond a mention of his fourteen-year-old's philatelic interest; the subject, instead, was invariably their mutual affection for Trumbull. 'It was a great blow to me when Trumbull left,' Monty confided to Mary Warren on 14 May 1942; 'I am very fond of him and miss him sadly. But he is a very highly efficient officer and will do well; I had to see that he went to the Staff College, even though it meant losing him. He knows that if ever there is anything I can do for him, he has only to ask. And one day I shall hope to meet you. I have never been to Canada and shall come over when we have finished off this war . . . Give my love to Trumbull.'[37]

Shared affection, indeed love, for the young officer was here the compact, Monty relieved to be able to confess the depth of his attachment. 'I can well imagine how you feel about losing Trumbull again,' he wrote to Mary Warren (whom he addressed as 'Mrs Trumbull', refusing ever to use the form Mrs Warren). It was, he claimed, all too understandable that Trumbull, as a young Turk, would 'naturally want to come back here, to the overseas army', and he sympathized with her anxiety, which was replicated on a national scale. 'It is the women who have the hardest burden to bear in war; and especially you in Canada, with your men so far away,' he acknowledged. His help was at hand, however. 'I shall watch over him when he comes back here, and I shall do everything I can to deliver him back safely to you when the war is over. And then I shall come and stay with you both at your home in Canada.'[38]

All this Monty faithfully would do, earning the loyalty of the Warrens to the day Monty died – Warren even arranging to have a private copy made of the film of the funeral of his 'chief', to watch and show to visitors, always choked with tears, at his home. Monty became godfather to the Warrens' daughter Ann, and after one visit to their home in Canada he would write: 'I shall always remember the birthday party, with the children. I have not had one like that since my wife died in 1937. David was then 9 years old and at his Preparatory School.'[39]

That Mary Warren had not repudiated Monty's declarations of affection for her young husband was a mark of generosity and understanding that would cause Monty to hold her dear to the end of his life; indeed, there was nothing he would not do for her in later years – even taking her to tea with the Queen at Windsor.[40] The same was true of Trumbull's mother – who had offered to look after David in Canada in 1942. Monty expressed to Mrs Snively his gratitude for her food parcels for David, especially for the 'honey, candy, etc. as those things are getting scarce in England'; but his real concern, as always in his letters to Mary Warren, was not for David's welfare, but for Trumbull. 'I long to see Trumbull again; you know what a very great affection I have for him,' he would write from the desert to Mary Warren after Alamein;[41] and when he did not hear from him for several months in the winter he became 'very anxious about Trumbull', as he confided to Mrs Snively from Tripoli; 'I wrote to him frequently and could get no answer. Then at last I got a cable from England, and it was a great relief. It made me realise what a great affection I have for the boy; I don't suppose he himself has any idea how fond I am of him. However, he is apparently safe and sound in England and I shall have a letter soon I hope.'[42]

Other famous field commanders in British history are known to have formed deep personal affections for members of their male staff. Such instances do not, of necessity, denote repressed homosexuality, but often reflected the basic need of senior commanders, made lonely by high command, to share trust and emotions with those closest to them in the field. Alan Brooke kept what became a celebrated diary, which he shared with his wife – the only person to whom he could confide, and before whom he could drop his impenetrable mask of asperity, austerity and incisive intellect. Since the death of Betty in 1937 Monty had had no such person, and in choosing young, mostly volunteer or conscripted officers, he did not seek to replicate the intimacy and mutuality of his marriage. He chose them because they were young, debonair, handsome, often recklessly anti-authoritarian, loyal, dependable, efficient and intensely *human*. They represented the youth he himself had lost, or set aside in the grim business of becoming a professional staff officer in World War I; the black sheep who had turned white; the mischief maker who had become a decorated professional. Without ever intending such a destiny, Monty had become a model of military dedication and ruthless professionalism, the greatest trainer of Allied troops of the twentieth century – 'a matchless military trainer' in the words of the Canadian historian, John English.[43]

Yet Monty had become something more, unnoticed by Churchill or a British military establishment still living on its Edwardian privileges: a visionary commander with a belief in youth, and a love of youth. Thus the more important historical question concerning his hand-picked personal and headquarters staff is whether such male–male relationships contributed to, or militated against, professional performance on the field of battle – whether, indeed, such homosocial attachments may be said to have provided the basis for Monty's extraordinary metamorphosis in 1942 from brilliant but socially resented trainer into the foremost British battlefield commander of the century.[44]

Only the test of battle would tell – a test which, despite every obstacle placed in his way by Churchill, was soon to come.

First, however, would come tragic defeat for the very Canadians of whom Monty, as a trainer and field commander, was justly proud.

15

Dieppe

Fiasco

Dieppe spelled disaster – from the beginning. Perhaps no other Allied battle of World War II could be said to have been undertaken for such political rather than military aims; yet this makes the operation, to the historian, all the more intriguing – as well as disturbing, given the tragic loss of life. A battle lasting only nine hours claimed the lives of 1,000 Canadians, with a another 2,000 captured and kept manacled like dogs by the Germans until late 1943.[1] A further 900 casualties were sustained among commandos, Royal Marines and sailors from the 250-craft flotilla that ferried and covered the assault landing, as well as sixty-seven trained pilots who were killed in the 106 Allied planes that were downed by the Luftwaffe, German anti aircraft fire and 'friendly fire' that day.

German losses, by comparison, were small: seventy-five men killed, and forty-eight aircraft lost. In the words of Brigadier Hollis, assistant secretary of the War Cabinet and Chiefs of Staff Committee, the British raid was 'an almost complete failure', with all too many lives 'sacrificed for no tangible result'.[2]

The important word is tangible, however, for the Anglo-Canadian assault on Dieppe on 19 August 1942 achieved two vital if expensive and imperceptible results for the prosecution of the war against the Nazis: firstly, the Dieppe catastrophe put paid to Russian and American demands for a premature second front in 1942; secondly, it taught perhaps the most crucial lesson of World War II to the political and military leaders of the Western Alliance. The commander of the Canadian 2nd Division had assured his assembled officers that such a landing would be 'a piece of cake'. It wasn't. In the word used by Churchill's doctor, who was with him when reports came in of the operation, it was a 'fiasco'.

If the Western Allies were to beat the Germans, they would have to revise radically their approach to modern combat.

Mountbatten the empire builder

For the biographer of Montgomery, Dieppe has an extra significance, for the raid pointed up more sharply than any other operation in World War II the difference between two distinct types of modern Allied inter-service headquarters: one in which the Allied cause came first and battlefield success second; the other, a modern, professional military headquarters dedicated to clear battlefield command first, Allied bonhomie second. Mountbatten's headquarters exemplified the first, Monty's the second.

Since Mountbatten's approach would be very much that adopted by General Eisenhower in North Africa, some months after Dieppe, and in Italy and north-west Europe thereafter, and because Monty's World War II battles would be largely won and lost in his struggle with the Mountbatten/ Eisenhower approach, it may pay to compare them.

Lord Mountbatten had in October 1941 been promoted on the personal whim of the Prime Minister to succeed Admiral Keyes, the Director of Combined Operations who had been hitherto used by Churchill to organize small raids on enemy-held territory, but not to plan or mount large-scale amphibious operations. Lord Mountbatten's new job, Churchill initially decreed, was not only to continue to mount such small raids, but to report to the Chiefs of Staff Committee as an adviser on all combined, or inter-service, operations.

For Captain Mountbatten this was a licence to create a new institution. 'He was a colossal empire builder,' Sir Ian Jacob, Churchill's Assistant Military Secretary, later described[3] – for Mountbatten was determined to succeed where Keyes had failed: namely in making Combined Operations not simply an advisory body to others, but the central agency for amphibious assault warfare in World War II. Churchill, aged almost sixty-eight and surrounded by cronies and sour faces, was impressed by Lord Mountbatten's aristocracy, youth (he was forty-one) and vitality. Thus in March 1942, by Churchillian fiat – 'I cannot have the plans seriously affected'[4] – the Prime Minister unilaterally appointed Mountbatten not only to the grand post of Chief of Combined Operations but also to sit as a fourth chief of staff on the highest professional defence panel in Britain, the Chiefs of Staff Committee!

Sir Dudley Pound, head of the navy, was furious; Sir Alan Brooke, as chairman of the committee, was disbelieving. He never changed his view of Mountbatten as a higher commander in World War II. 'There was no reason for his inclusion in the COS,' he wrote later, 'where he frequently wasted his time and ours.'[5]

Buying off the second front

Churchill, who also liked to waste time on detail and fantasy, did not agree with Brooke's verdict on young Lord Mountbatten. Mountbatten's remit, formulated by Churchill as Minister of Defence and Brooke's boss, thus soon mushroomed from the mounting of raids to advancement of inter-service co-operation on combined operations, and the study of 'tactical and technical developments' in the mounting of 'a full-scale invasion'.[6]

It was the latter aspect that worried Brooke, as pressure grew in 1942 in Britain, America and elsewhwere for a second front in Europe to help draw German pressure off the Russians. While the CIGS was happy for Mountbatten to 'frig about' with raiding parties that were good for national morale, in relation to larger operations he found himself increasingly unhappy over the growing size and questionable professionalism at Mountbatten's headquarters in Richmond Terrace, Whitehall – where in six months a staff of twenty-three increased to more than 400, and where serious invasion studies were inevitably overshadowed and skewed by the excitement and glamour of commando raids.

These two remits – raids and invasion studies – of Combined Operations should never have been run together (and were later separated for the D-Day landings, with a new body, COSSAC, created to mastermind the latter), but in the context of 1942 Churchill was and remained adamant. For political reasons – at home and abroad – he wanted raids and invasion plans to run concurrently; indeed, his greatest strategic-political achievement in 1942 would be that he was able to buy off American preference for a second front in 1942 by damning the Combined Operations plan for a permanent landing in France – Operation Sledgehammer – and substituting instead the 'butcher-and-run' raid on Dieppe, also proposed by Combined Operations, as a larger 'reconnaissance in force', to practise invasion techniques.

It may therefore be argued that Churchill, though he sacrificed so many Canadian lives, saved many tens of thousands of British and American casualties by getting the American President and chiefs of staff to accept a smallish raid on Dieppe in 1942, rather than a major but premature invasion of Europe, Sledgehammer, for which even his military representative in Washington, Field-Marshal Dill, had called. If Sledgehammer, as an invasion, 'ultimately fails tactically', Dill had asked Churchill, echoing General Marshall's view as chief of the US army staff, 'but causes diversion from the Russian front will it [not] have succeeded?'[7] Churchill was not convinced. Dieppe, he argued, risked far fewer lives: 10,000, as he would explain to Stalin in August 1942, rather than 120,000.

The love of piracy

Whatever the politico-strategic difficulties of 1942, Churchill relished raids, which appealed to his schoolboy love of piracy while only imperilling small numbers of men. Mountbatten, mindful of the need to impress his patron, certainly provided such raids: first in December 1941 at Vaagsö, an island off southern Norway, (a 'marked failure' in Churchill's words[8]), then a more successful Combined Operations attack on the Bruneval radar installation in February 1942, followed by the brilliantly successful raid on St Nazaire, which permanently blocked access to the Brittany dry-dock – though resulting in 80 per cent casualties in the process.

Mountbatten's raids were a tonic in an otherwise dismal period of the war on the ground and sea for the Allies – the Germans seemingly successful wherever they strode, from the Caucasus to North Africa, and the Japanese equally so. Since neither the democracies nor the Soviets seemed able, in the first half of 1942, to produce effective forces to meet the Germans in battle, 'even a tiny success lightens up the dark clouds', the naval commander at Portsmouth noted.[9]

Yet there was a world of difference between Drake-like raiding parties and real war. As Monty observed to Goronwy Rees, the young intelligence officer delegated to his headquarters from Home Forces in the spring of 1942, Mountbatten was a very brave man. 'A very gallant sailor. Had

1. (*Above left*) The Tyrant Queen – Monty's mother Maud, née Farrar.
2. (*Above right*) 'Maud insisted on dressing her third son in satin and velvet' –
Monty the renegade.
3. (*Below left*) Bishop Montgomery – Monty's father.
4. (*Below right*) 'A delightful boy, and very beautiful' – Monty's younger
brother Desmond, who died in 1909.

5. 'Rarely has the
Army so fascinated
one of her children'
– parading in
North West India,
1909.

6. 'The safety valve
for English sexual
repression' – India
in the early 20th
century.

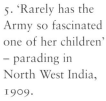

7. 'Once they detrained they were
scarcely more mobile than the warriors
of Agincourt or Crecy' – the battle of
Mons, August 1914.

8. (*Above left*) 'Verdun at its worst was as nothing compared with this' – the Somme, 1916.

9. (*Above right*) 'He ought to have a brilliant future in the Army' – Monty as staff officer, Passchendaele, 1917.

10. (*Below left*) 'The letters are all very much the same; full of protestations of love for their sweethearts.'

11. (*Below right*) 'It is very chilly right now, & it is nice to have someone to keep each other warm' – sleeping soldiers, 1918.

12–13. 'In attempting to quash the "rebellion" in southern Ireland the military was running counter to the will of the nation, however many troops were brought over for the task' – British troops debus (13, *below*), while snipers fire from shelled buildings, Dublin, 1921–2 (12, *left*).

14. 'Though no stickler for drill, he was known to be a fanatic for efficiency and training' – Monty, with his battalion outside Cairo in 1933,
15. (*Inset*) with his son David in Palestine, 1931,

16. and in Palestine, where troops of his division put down the 'Arab Revolt' in 1938–9.

17. 'I thought, dear me, I've met a madman' – Betty Anderson, aged 17, on meeting Monty in 1925.

18. 'The first and only woman, apart from his mother, with whom Monty had a truly profound relationship in his life': Bernard and Betty Montgomery, née Hobart, in India, 1934.

19. 'If there is any mystery in Montgomery's life it probably lies here in these dark months in the winter of 1937' – Brigadier Montgomery after the death of his wife, 1937.

20. 'He'll never see action again' – Monty airlifted on a stretcher from Haifa to Port Said, July 1939.

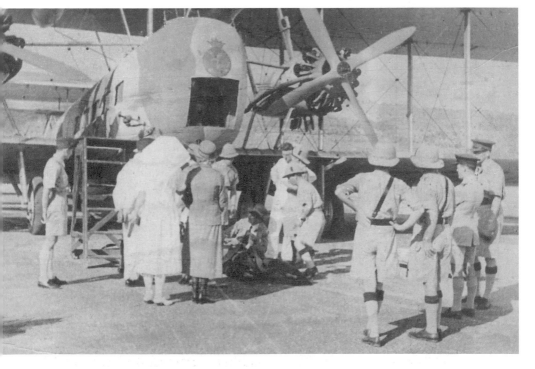

A Disastrous Start to WWII

21. The British Prime Minister, Neville Chamberlain, and BEF Commander, Lord Gort, listen to the ill-fated Gamelin plan, France, 1939.

22. Monty, the first British field general to wear modern battle-dress, with officers of 3rd (Iron) Division, October 1939.

23. Monty's insistence on sexual health and personal hygiene, on and off duty, almost cost him his command, over 'the VD affair' in November 1939.

24. (*Above*) Though Chamberlain crowed that 'Hitler has missed the bus', Monty prepared his division for a fighting, mobile retreat – thereby saving the BEF on 27 May 1940.

25. (*Below*) 'The last scene of Act 1, World War II': Dunkirk, May 1940.

26–28. Denied field command for two years after Dunkirk, Monty set about revolutionizing his Home Forces formations by rigorous professional training, realistic rehearsal – and a new compact between commander and his troops.

29. Winston Churchill (seen here with Monty and the young King Peter of Yugoslavia): 'the embodiment of defiance, but also the man responsible for Britain coming near to losing the war by his military incompetence'.

1942: Fateful Year

30. (*Above*) 'A sop to the Russians and Americans': Canadian catastrophe at Dieppe, August 1942.

31. (*Left*) Rommel leads the Afrika Korps across North Africa to the gates of Cairo.
32. (*Below*) The famed German '88': the greatest tank-destroyer of World War II.

Changing the Team

33. (*Above left*) Churchill sacks his nominee, General Auchinleck, after the fall of Tobruk, August 1942.

34. (*Above right*) Montgomery is finally summoned to take command of the 8th Army, August 1942.

35. 'The two British military chiefs opposing Marshal Rommel's latest thrust': General Sir Harold Alexander and Lieut.-General Montgomery, the *Illustrated London News*, 12 September 1942.

Miracle in the Desert

36–8. 'Monty was able to perform what seemed to so many to be a "miracle" in the summer of 1942: to make jaded, bewildered, sometimes frightened young men believe in themselves once again' – as here, Australians who would help turn the Allied tide (38).

PERSONAL MESSAGE
from the
ARMY COMMANDER

(To be read out to all Troops)

1. When I assumed command of the Eighth Army I said that the mandate was to destroy ROMMEL and his Army, and that it would be done as soon as we were ready.

2. We are ready NOW.

   The battle which is now about to begin will be one of the decisive battles of history. It will be the turning point of the war. The eyes of the whole world will be on us, watching anxiously which way the battle will swing.

   We can give them their answer at once : " It will swing our way."

3. We have first-class equipment ; good tanks ; good anti-tank guns ; plenty of artillery and plenty of ammunition ; and we are backed up by the finest air striking force in the world.

   All that is necessary is that each one of us, every officer and man, should enter this battle with the determination to see it through—to fight and to kill—and finally, to win.

   If we all do this there can be only one result—together we will hit the enemy for " six," right out of North Africa.

4. The sooner we win this battle, which will be the turning point of the war, the sooner we shall all get back home to our families.

5. Therefore, let every officer and man enter the battle with a stout heart, and the determination to do his duty so long as he has breath in his body.

   AND LET NO MAN SURRENDER SO LONG AS HE IS UNWOUNDED AND CAN FIGHT.

   Let us all pray that " the Lord mighty in battle " will give us the victory.

B. L. Montgomery

Lieutenant-General, G.O.C.-in-C., Eighth Army.

23 October, 1942.

El Alamein

39–40. 'There will be no tip and run tactics in this battle; it will be a killing match,' Monty had warned in September 1942, after a successful defence at Alam Halfa; 'the German is a good soldier and the only way to beat him is to kill him in battle'. Monty's personal message to all troops, issued in the hours before the British offensive opened with an 800-gun barrage on the night of 23 October 1942, made clear his determination.

41. The subsequent battle of Alamein became the first decisive Allied victory of World War II, fought in three planned stages: 'the break-in, the dog-fight, and the break-out'. (*Left*) The first German prisoners come in,

42. the deadly infantry 'dog-fight';

43. German artillery shelling in 'one vast minefield'.

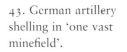

Victory

44. (*Left*) Monty surveys the battle-front from his tank, with his ADC, Capt. John Poston.

45. (*Below*) 'The armour went through as the dawn was breaking,' Monty recorded in his diary; 'the armour finally got clear away and out in the open.'

46. Captain Singer, of the 10th Hussars – who would be killed the following day – brings General Ritter von Thoma, the famed commander of the Afrika Korps, to surrender personally to Montgomery at 10th Army forward field headquarters, 4 November 1942.

three ships sunk under him. *Three* ships sunk under him. [Pause] Doesn't know how to fight a battle.'[10]

Pathological ambition

Churchill's military-political judgement was sounder than Dill's or Marshall's over Sledgehammer – which would undoubtedly have resulted in another Dunkirk at that stage of the war – and his decision to order a 'reconnaissance in force' instead, at Dieppe, in order to placate the Russians was well intended, if completely unnecessary once it was decided by the American and British chiefs of staff to mount landings in north-west Africa rather than the continent of Europe in the autumn of 1942: Operation Torch.

Churchill, however, was by then hoist with his own petard – unable to see beyond Mountbatten's charm and youthful zest. Worse still, Churchill failed to perceive an intrinsic difference between the planning required for piracy and invasion – and nothing the endlessly harrassed chiefs of staff could do could dent Churchill's faith in Mountbatten, once Mountbatten had been made a fourth member of the chiefs of staff, as a vice-admiral and lieutenant general.

Like Lord Gort, Lord Mountbatten was an aristocrat and a man of courage, promoted far beyond his abilities. He had hitherto commanded only a destroyer, with great courage but without much discretion. He had never been required to consider land operations; like Lord Gort he chose poor staff officers, and delegated with total irresponsibility, working from total ignorance. As the Home Forces liaison officer deputed to Combined Operations, Major Rees, afterwards observed, 'No one had as yet considered the problem of deliberately landing in divisional strength in the face of the enemy in one of his most heavily defended areas.'[11] For all its hundreds of staff officers, Combined Operations headquarters was thus as ignorant as ordinary headquarters. As Rees put it, 'all the wisdom and experience of Combined Headquarters was not much more helpful than the ignorance of persons like me'.[12]

Had he been chief of Combined Operations, Monty's approach would have been to organize large-scale exercises and rehearsals, building up experience, lessons, and confidence in invasion command and operation, as he did at 9th Infantry Brigade at Slapton Sands in 1938, at 3 Division before Dunkirk, and V Corps, XII Corps and South-East Army thereafter. But Mountbatten was a very different sort of fish from Montgomery: an elegant, energetic, socially adept dilettante – as the Germans characterized his Dieppe performance – of near-psychopathic personal ambition and resourcefulness in achieving his ends. His concern was not to develop the skills involved in planning, execution and command of steadily larger raids leading towards a real future invasion of Europe, but simply to keep his patron and master, Winston Churchill, sweet on a day-by-day basis by providing piratical 'butcher-and-run' raids, on whatever scale Churchill required. In this tragic way an essentially modest initial plan for a raid on the flanks of Dieppe was magnified for Churchill and the Chiefs of Staff Committee into a possible 'reconnaissance in force' for future invasion – without previous planning, exercises or rehearsal having ever been undertaken in Britain to identify the command and control problems. The lessons of such a 'reconnaissance in force' would, in short, have to be learned against a real, first-class enemy – and, as with the *Scharnhorst* and *Gneisenau* escape, paid for in real blood.

Canadian impatience

Afterwards, Churchill was distraught – the more so since most of the blood spilt was Canadian, not British: a blow to the Empire and the willing contributions of the dominions. Echoes of the Dardanelles went through the Prime Minister's mind, and in the weeks, months and years afterwards he returned again and again to the catastrophe at Dieppe, the little town where he had once courted Clementine, his wife, desperately seeking an explanation of the massacre of so many brave young soldiers.

Mountbatten's former patron, the Canadian Lord Beaverbrook, was even more upset. He never forgave Mountbatten. As a popular-newspaper owner and member of Churchill's government, Beaverbrook had moved mountains to press for a second front in 1942 to help the Russians, yet could not accept the fact that the cost for this public demand had been paid in Canadian, not British, casualties. 'You have murdered thousands of my countrymen. You took those unfortunate Canadian soldiers,' he snarled at Mountbatten. 'They have been mown down in their thousands and their blood is on your hands.'[13]

The blood was and remained on Mountbatten's hands, however much he sought to evade responsibility – which he did for the rest of his days. 'To the end of his life, "Dieppe" was engraved upon Mountbatten's heart, and the name would always raise an instant defensive response, almost as if he was protesting too much,' even his adoring biographer, Richard Hough, recorded.[14]

The failed raid haunted Mountbatten. Nothing had gone right in preparing it, and the business of devising a Combined Operations plan for a pseudo-invasion, then half-handing it over to the army, navy and air-force commanders to carry out, was a nonsense from the start. As Monty later said, had Mountbatten carried out a small Combined Operations raid himself with his own commandos, the chain of planning and command would have been simple and accountable. Monty's 'opinion at the time was that Admiral Mountbatten should have been given overall command of all the forces to be employed in the operation – as [Task] Force Commander. He had the right conception of the correct way to carry it out' – namely, 'to use experienced Commandos and troops from the Royal Marine Division, to land on the flanks and attack the port from the undefended rear as the Japanese did at Singapore and we were to do at Cherbourg in 1944. Mountbatten should have made the plan and issued the orders. He had a high class staff, very experienced in planning raiding operations.' As a raid it was 'right up his street. If it had been done that way, the operation would have been a success – in my personal opinion,' he wrote[15] – gliding over the weakness of Mountbatten's operational command ability and inexperience of his Combined Operations HQ staff, in an attempt to be nice to the new chief of the British defence staff, which by 1962 Mountbatten had become.

Monty's point was that Dieppe had grown from a simple raid into a mock invasion, and no single task force commander had been appointed to carry out such a novel operation of war: 'a reconnaisance in force'. Instead, against Mountbatten's repeated objections, a cumbersome protocol had been followed whereby Mountbatten's headquarters concocted an outline plan, which was then critiqued by what Monty called the 'trinity' of force commanders of the troops, sailors and aircrews who would carry it out, working in conjunction with Combined Operations HQ as specialist advisers. Without an overall task force commander the planning as well as the execution of the 'reconnaissance in force' became a nightmare.

Since the divisional-strength troops eventually chosen for the operation were Canadian, a Canadian major-general, who held command of the

2nd Canadian Division, was selected to be the land force commander in the triumvirate of leaders – a man who had never seen battle, and had never planned or carried out an amphibious assault of any kind! Monty never did find out who was responsible for the choice of Canadians for the operation – 'somebody, I do not know who, decided that the Canadian Army should provide the troops, and the 2nd Canadian Division, under Major-General Roberts, was detailed for the task'.[16] As Monty recalled with retrospective amazement, 'And so it was decided to launch against a defended port in the Atlantic Wall a Canadian Division which had done no fighting, and which was commanded by a Major-General who had never commanded a Division in battle, nor even a battalion. General Roberts was a very nice person; but he was totally inexperienced, was a slow thinker, and was no "ball of fire" in any sense of the word. A very tough guy was needed as divisional Commander, which Roberts was not. This was not the way to approach one of the most difficult operations in war, an opposed landing on an enemy coast – how[ev]er impatient the Canadians were.'[17]

The problem was not simply that Roberts was inexperienced in divisional command, but that he was simply not of sufficient rank, intelligence or personality to decide what was needed – and demand it. Instead, as a junior Canadian general, out of his depth, Roberts was plunged into the chaotic, fevered atmosphere of Richmond Terrace – with predictable results. 'The planning was done at Combined Operations H.Q. in London, and gathered there were planners from G.H.Q. Home Forces, the 2nd Canadian Division, and the three Force Commanders (Navy, Army, Air Force) with all *their* planners,' Monty recalled. 'It would have needed a very good general not to have become bewildered by all the advice that was given – not only by the planners, but also by the Navy and Air Force Commanders.'[18] Roberts was not that man.

Even if Roberts had been a more experienced general, the command set-up would have militated against success. 'It is axiomatic,' Monty declared in retrospect, but with great feeling, 'that the plan must be made by the commander responsible for the battle operation. But there was no *one* commander responsible for this very tricky operation. In fact, there were too many "cooks" employed in the affair and each one had his own very decided views.'[19]

This was Allied fighting by committee, which Monty abhorred, with inexperienced Canadians taking responsibility for the main landings, against Germans whose professionalism Monty had every cause, after

Dunkirk, to respect. How much better would it have been to employ only highly trained commandos and marines. 'The Canadians had been in England since the winter of 1939/40,' Monty noted; 'they had seen no fighting and were very "green"; the soldiery was magnificent material, and so were the regimental officers and brigadiers, but all were totally inexperienced. The senior commanders had no experience in handling troops in battle against a first-class enemy – such as the Germans.'[20]

Since the Canadian 2nd Division would have to come from Monty's area command in South-East Army, Monty inevitably became involved – General Paget, the Home Forces C-in-C, delegating a 'watching brief' to Montgomery that Monty disliked and later bitterly regretted. 'The C-in-C Home Forces at that time was General Paget and in conversation one day I mentioned to him that it was not right to use the inexperienced Canadians for the operation. His view was that they were becoming "impatient" and wanted to go fighting; if they were not allowed to, there would be trouble with the Canadian H.Q. in England under General McNaughton.

'Having expressed my fears, I could do no more but acquiesce; to do otherwise would have been to lower the morale of the Canadian troops, since it was, in the end, agreed that if they wanted to be used for the Dieppe operation their wish would be agreed. And they did want to be used.'[21]

This, as all historians of the operation concur, was very much the case. General Crerar is known to have lobbied Paget, Brooke, Mountbatten and even Churchill to get Canadian units assigned to a major raiding operation. Monty, by contrast, was not keen. As his letters to Trumbull Warren indicated, he felt the business of preparing Canadian units and formations for combat on the battlefield against the Germans was made a hundred times more difficult by virtue of their sensitivity to being placed under a British commander. The troops were tough, there were fine up-and-coming junior officers, but the senior officers were simply not yet good enough to face the Germans in modern battle, in his estimate – and a 'butcher-and-run' raid would only distract them from the task of professional preparation for land battle. Nevertheless, it was not the Canadians' fault, Monty subsequently argued. 'I consider that the responsibility for the reverse, and for the casualties, must lie wholly with us British. When the job was given to G.H.Q. Home Forces, they should never have allowed inexperienced troops to take on the operation. When the buck was passed to me I should have been more emphatic,' he reflected sadly. 'I *did* protest verbally to my C-in-C. I reckon I should have protested vehemently and in writing; this would have been unpopular with the Canadians and possibly have upset their morale.'[22]

This was also true – Monty having been warned in writing by Brooke, as we have seen, to 'go easy' with the Canadians. An objection to using them on the Dieppe quasi-invasion might well have looked as if he had something against them – when his only objection at that stage in the war was the poor standard of their higher commanders. Second-best would simply not do in battle against the Germans.

'I don't blame the Canadian high command,' Monty stated, in a rare moment of retrospective sympathy.[23] In terms of combat with German troops in 1942 the Canadian generals simply 'didn't know what they were in for' – a bloodbath.

Shifting the blame

A specialized raiding operation had been transformed into a mock invasion or 'reconnaissance in force', in response to Churchill's wishes – and the planning history of the battle showed the incompatibility between the two approaches. Mountbatten would later try to shift the blame for the disaster on to Monty and the military force commander, Major-General Roberts, since the initial Combined Operations plan for a small, specialized raid had required radical amendment to include a frontal assault on Dieppe. This was not only historically deceitful of Mountbatten, but self-deceitful; indeed, he never did learn the art of high command rather than PR and fronting.

As a small, piratical, pinprick raid Mountbatten's original Combined Operations plan for a pincer attack on Dieppe by commandos had been appropriate; inflated into a division-strength 'reconnaissance in force' for a real invasion, involving a major landing and evacuation on the same day, before significant German reserves could come into action, the pincer plan of attack became plainly impossible to carry out – as Combined Operations' own military staff pointed out early in April 1942, *before* the Canadians were chosen, or Montgomery brought in. Two such widely separated flank attacks, one six and the other twelve miles distant from Dieppe, mounted by substantial forces of 'normal' soldiers and their supporting artillery and armour, were a non-starter, since the German reserves would have ample time to stop the troops reaching Dieppe, owing to the difficult topography of the area – topography which 'lent itself to [German] delaying action', as the Combined Operations military officer responsible for planning the raid himself later recorded.[24]

The two flanking forces would, the planner recalled, be eighteen miles apart, and subject to defeat in detail. In this circumstance, the infantry of one or other flank might never reach Dieppe in time, and could almost certainly not be counted upon to seize the town and port and re-embark – all by the second tide. It was this impossibility that gave rise to the alternative which Mountbatten's own headquarters then proposed. By landing directly on Dieppe beach with fifty heavily armed Churchill tanks, the invaders would have a reasonable chance of surprising the enemy in the darkness, overrunning the immediately adjacent town and port with infantry, backed by armour, and withdrawing back across the beaches before German reserves, stationed inland, could be brought into serious action. Small landings on the immediate flanks would meanwhile silence enfilading fire.

Literature not history

Combined Operations thus presented the force commanders with a choice: either two widely separated attacks that could never make it to Dieppe with time enough to be re-embarked, or a frontal assault.

No such frontal assault on a port held by the enemy had ever been attempted; indeed, even where attempted by a mix of seaborne assault and behind-the-lines surprise attack by trained long-range desert personnel, at Tobruk and Benghazi in September that year, the raids proved farcical, with many landing craft sunk and almost all participants killed, wounded or captured.[25]

In this sense, the Dieppe mock invasion against Hitler's 'Atlantic Wall' had either to be dropped as an impossible military undertaking, or mounted with all attendant risks. Given the political situation, with Germans driving ever deeper into Russia and the Japanese consolidating their mastery in South-East Asia, the directive from the chiefs of staff for a quasi-invasion assault became to all intents and purposes an order. It was for this reason that General Roberts went along with the force commanders in accepting Combined Operations' alternative choice of a frontal assault landing. He was backed up by his corps commander, General Crerar, his Canadian army commander, General McNaughton, and the personal representative of the C-in-C Home Forces on the planning committee, General Montgomery, once they had conferred over the two alternatives.

Mountbatten's attempt to switch the blame to Monty for this fatal alteration in the plan would begin almost immediately after the disaster, when Churchill demanded an explanation – for Brooke, dining with Mountbatten at Chequers, had made in Churchill's presence a 'very outspoken criticism of the manner in which the Dieppe raid was planned'. Instead of explaining to Brooke (who knew nothing of the detailed planning background) how his own Combined Operations HQ had presented this choice to the force commanders and their military advisers – the choice between defeat in detail, or possible success by surprise – Mountbatten hid behind his erstwhile role of adviser. 'General Montgomery attended all the principal planning meetings,' he claimed (which was untrue), 'and personally supervised the Military Plan while General Roberts was preparing it. I left General Montgomery an absolutely free hand. A telegram to General Montgomery would confirm this,' Mountbatten put in writing to Brooke, threatening to ask Churchill for 'a full impartial inquiry into the planning and execution of the raid and the conduct of all concerned' – his favourite tactic for avoiding criticism.[26]

Brooke, beset by more important problems, backed off – leaving subsequent historians to try to delve behind Mountbatten's repeated veils, omissions and deceits, which extended even to the point of censoring Churchill's draft chapter in his monumental *History of the Second World War*, and persuading him to substitute a largely fictitious account which Mountbatten himself drafted.[27] As Brian Villa, a Canadian historian of the Dieppe tragedy, commented, it was as well that Churchill's Nobel Prize was for literature, not history.

Blaming Monty

Though Mountbatten might retrospectively cajole, charm and entice his former staff into a collective subversion of the record, not all of them would go along with it. In a hitherto unpublished correspondence on the disaster, the Combined Operations officer most closely involved in the military side of the planning, Major Walter Skrine, vehemently objected to Mountbatten's tarring of the force commanders, and of Monty in particular.

Major Skrine's boss, the novelist Lieutenant-Colonel Robert Henriques, was Mountbatten's chief planner. Mountbatten, he later commented, had 'an imperial ambition' and many talents including a quick, logical mind and even swifter intuition, with 'no weakness except a total inability to judge men correctly, whether they were his cronies or subordinates'.[28] As one of Mountbatten's many such misjudgements, however, Henriques had become post-operatively determined to absolve himself, Combined Operations and Mountbatten for the failure of the disastrous raid by claiming that fatal alterations to the Combined Operations HQ plan were made 'after the planning responsibility had passed from C.O.H.Q.'. He also claimed that the army planners working for the land force commander persuaded the navy planners working for the navy force commander to accept a frontal attack, while the naval planners persuaded the army planners to accept a dawn assault, which would ease their problems of navigation in the dark. 'Walter Skrine will know more about it than anybody else,' Henriques wrote to his old boss, Major-General Haydon, who was helping Mountbatten defend himself against the current type-script draft of the 1958 naval staff history of the Dieppe operation. (As First Sea Lord, Mountbatten was determined to avoid exposure, and had begged his former naval force commander, Vice-Admiral Hughes-Hallett, and Major-General Haydon to orchestrate a rebuttal whereby the naval staff historian's version 'might be reworded to put the responsibility for suggesting these changes fairly and squarely where it belongs'.)[29]

Major Skrine, who did indeed know better than anyone within Combined Operations HQ in 1942, would have no truck with this. He pointed out, in a suggested alternative draft for the history, that the original COHQ March 1942 plan for flank landings in brigade (5,000 men) strength was revised by Combined Operations HQ itself 'early in April'. Trained commandos might be able to land six and twelve miles distant from the port, make it into Dieppe and cause havoc, but ordinary infantry would be hard pressed to achieve such success, all in one day. 'Although there were obvious advantages in avoiding a frontal attack against Dieppe town, there were also drawbacks to landing forces on either flank, widely separated,' Skrine recalled. 'The most serious objection was the loss of surprise which must result before the main attack on the town could take place.' The landings would be eighteen miles apart, with potentially significant German forces, fully alerted by the landings, between them. 'To control and coordinate them from the Headquarter Ship, a Hunt Class Destroyer, would not be easy,' Skrine also recalled. 'The country inland – particularly to the West of Dieppe – was enclosed, with one or two small rivers. These were liable to cause delay, especially to tanks, giving the Germans more time to reinforce Dieppe from local reserves.'

Whatever Mountbatten might say in retrospect, the flank attacks, if designed to be more than commando pinpricks, were doomed to fail – especially in the two-tide time-frame envisaged. 'These considerations, among others, led the [Combined Operations] Planners to reexamine the possibility of a frontal assault,' Skrine recalled. 'All available Intelligence in April showed that the [Dieppe] town and neighbouring beaches were only lightly held . . . A further point in favour of a frontal attack, if the leading waves could be landed under cover of darkness, was that there were good prospects of surprising the garrison. The local reserves were some miles inland and not very likely to intervene before we were into the town. Although opinions on this point were divided, H.Q. Combined Operations began to prepare an alternative plan. H.Q. Home Force were associated in this planning from the start, i.e. early in April' – several weeks before the decision to choose Canadian troops for the operation, or to involve Montgomery. On this new basis, the frontal attack was 'to be helped by two subsidiary landings at battalion strength at small beaches, one at Pourville, two miles to the West, and other at Puits the same distance to the east of the town. The main role of these battalions would be to secure the heights which overlooked the main landings and harbour from either flank' – crucial headlands, peppered with caves, which every tourist to Dieppe knew of.

How such a bold frontal assault was to be accomplished in pitch darkness in the few minutes before daylight was unclear. However, a major bombing raid, mounted before the infantry landing, would, it was hoped, 'disorganize the defence, send most of the garrison to ground, or at least distract their attention from small craft approaching the coast in darkness'. Meanwhile the big coastal guns at Varengeville and Berneval, which threatened the assault armada out at sea, would be taken out by parachute and glider troops. 'No serious objections to these ideas were raised either in the Admiralty or in the Air Ministry.'[30]

As Major Skrine noted, a lot depended on the enemy reaction, and there were 'still misgivings at H.Q. Combined Operations, among the military planners, about the intelligence report upon which the frontal attack plan was based'.[31] Since Mountbatten had appointed an old aristocratic buddy of the 1930s, the racing driver and playboy the Marquis de Casa Maury, to be his head of intelligence (in the rank of wing commander, RAF), these intelligence concerns went unmet – indeed, even Mountbatten's official apologist, Philip Ziegler, who did everything in his official biographer's power to help mask Mountbatten's record on Dieppe, could not condone his subject's choice of the marquis, who was widely considered to be 'utterly useless', in the first naval force commander's words. Quoting this, Ziegler could not quite bring himself to agree, but did suggest that failure of COHQ intelligence was the chief cause of the disaster. 'Casa Maury was Mountbatten's man,' he accepted, 'and the shortcomings of his department were ultimately Mountbatten's responsibility.'[32]

Instead of sending in agents or night-time scouts, Casa Maury meanwhile did nothing, relying only on low-level daytime air photographs which showed – thanks to German camouflage – no increase in defensive preparations, especially in the cliff caves of the bay, overlooking the town beach. Thus, inexorably, planning for the disaster had proceeded in April 1942. Finally 'about the third week in April' according to Skrine, 'a formal conference was held at Combined Operations H.Q.'. The chiefs of staff on 30 March had only given Mountbatten licence to plan larger raids such as Dieppe if they were 'agreed by a senior officer of Home Forces from which the troops taking part were to be drawn'.[33] The 18 April conference was therefore a chance to get the 'approval of the Commander-in-Chief Home Forces to the military aspect of the outline plan' submitted by Combined Operations HQ, so that it could then go before the Chiefs of Staff Committee for higher authorization. It was at this conference, attended by General Paget's chief of staff, that the frontal assault in darkness was, Skrine remembered, agreed, in preference to the clearly impracticable, widely separated flanking assaults that would be defeated in detail, and the men all killed or captured. 'The main advantages' of a frontal assault, 'from the Army point of view were:

1. It offered a good chance of surprise.

2. Adequate covering fire for leading waves in the assault could not be provided, in daylight, by Destroyers and low-flying aircraft [hence the crucial importance of selecting beaches on to which infantry close-support tanks could be landed, something that was impossible in the originally planned flanking assaults].

3. There would be a bigger margin of time to reach [adjacent] objective inland and for subsequent re-embarkation.

4. Control of troops and landing craft should be simpler.

5. Fighter cover in daylight could be concentrated over the area of Dieppe.'[34]

On this basis, at another meeting on 25 April at COHQ chaired by Mountbatten and attended by Paget's deputy chief of staff, the draft outline plan was discussed and approved. Neither Montgomery nor the Canadians had yet had any hand in it.

As Skrine wrote to Major-General Haydon, a distinguished Guards officer whom he deeply admired, 'I cannot agree with the suggestion that the frontal attack idea originated in the mind of Monty.'[35] Summarizing, he made it crystal clear for the historical record: 'H.Q. Combined Operations prepared two alternative outline plans for consideration with H.Q. Home Forces before deciding which one should be submitted to the Chiefs of Staff.'[36]

A *watertight* case for Mountbatten

The British chiefs of staff refused, in fact, to give formal consent to the outline plan until mid-May 1942, when they gave guarded approval to the new scheme, though leaving open the timing of night bombing, which would be a matter for Air-Marshal 'Bomber' Harris, who led RAF Bomber Command. Once again, this would be a let-out seized upon by Mountbatten in order to exonerate himself, once the mock invasion had proved disastrous.

In the meantime, with the approval in principle from the chiefs of staff for the outline plan on 13 May 1942, the path became clear for the requisite troops – who had been informally canvassed via Home Forces, Montgomery, McNaughton and Crerar at the end of April – to be formally assigned. It was only at this juncture that Monty, in whose area command the Canadian troops were stationed, was formally appointed by General Paget to be his representative on the detailed military plans.

Sceptical of Mountbatten's experience in mounting operations involving army troops, Monty recommended that the Canadian 2nd Division, nominated by General Crerar for the task, should put their own military team on the detailed plans, with Major Walter Skrine acting as military liaison on behalf of COHQ. He also proposed that an intelligence officer seconded from Home Forces, Major Goronwy Rees, should act as his personal liaison officer with a 'watching brief' on the development of planning.

The frontal-attack plan for Dieppe was clearly never 'Monty's' plan, as Mountbatten later asserted. Nor was Monty – who was mounting progressively larger and more ambitious army exercises leading up to Exercise Tiger, the largest and longest simulated land-battle rehearsal ever conducted in Britain, in June 1942 – able to take more than a monitoring role. The 'planning of the operation had not been in his hands', Rees later recalled, nor was the operation itself; 'its execution equally was not in his hands but in those of the Military, Naval and Air Force Commanders. There was nothing he could do to affect the result, and it would therefore have been a waste of time and effort for him to worry about. Being supremely logical where questions of command were concerned, he did not worry. I almost wished he would,' Rees added – knowing how amateur were the participants, and how hazardous the enterprise was becoming.[37]

Walter Skrine, writing two years before Rees, took the same view. 'I only remember him [Monty] attending one conference at C.O.H.Q., when the Outline Plan was firm and I think had received the blessing of the Chiefs of Staff', Skrine recalled.[38] 'My personal view about Monty's part remains unchanged,' Skrine subsequently wrote, when Hughes-Hallett, Henriques and Haydon had concocted a 'watertight' case for Mountbatten, exonerating COHQ. Once again Skrine protested, reiterating that 'I believe he [Monty] did not come into the picture until after the Chiefs of Staff had approved the [COHQ] plan, as originally conceived, and I do not see how he could be blamed for the subsequent alterations in what was a joint plan.' With McNaughton and Crerar involved, there had indeed been 'too many cooks', but 'Monty lay low throughout', he recalled, having other, bigger responsibilities as South-East Army commander.[39] In this respect Skrine expressed a heartfelt objection to Mountbatten's retrospective attempts to befog the record and redirect accusing fingers: 'I cannot agree that any good purpose will be served by nailing responsibility for vital changes in plan on individuals.' Skrine's recollection was 'fairly clear' – as was his lasting grief for those who died. 'It was the first plan I was put on and I thought of nothing else, day and night, for 2 months. In the years since then, I've often thought about it too, with bitter feelings – I felt in some ways responsible for the advice about the feasibility of landing on the Dieppe seafront, but for a long time couldn't be sure and had difficulty in getting intelligence out of "I" Branch at C.O.H.Q [Casa Maury]. I wasn't allowed [by Maury] to go foraging for it with Home Forces.'[40]

Cancelling heavy bombing support

The most telling and legitimate criticism of Monty would be made by a veteran of Dieppe: a young Canadian company commander in the 'raid', later Brigadier-General Whitaker. Deputed by the C-in-C Home Forces to watch over the detailed military plans drawn up the Canadian military force commander, Monty, in Whitaker's view, did not watch well enough.

Although the operation was eventually cancelled 'for all time' as Monty requested, it was secretly resurrected by Mountbatten in August 1942. Moreover, in its resurrected state – even though by that time Monty had flown out to the Middle East – the 'reconnaissance in force' would reflect virtually every error in command, control and design that had been inherent, if not apparent, in its earlier manifestations.

For Mountbatten, the switch from flank to frontal assault was the biggest, albeit dishonest, stick with which to beat Monty. However there was another, too: the fact that, at a meeting at Combined Operations at Richmond Terrace on 5 June 1942, with Monty himself in the chair as the senior representative of Home Forces (Mountbatten being in America), the issue of night bombing of the dock area by heavy bombers of the RAF, under 'Bomber' Harris, had once again been raised – and the bombing cancelled.

Churchill had told Mountbatten he disliked the idea of flattening Dieppe, where he had once picked blackberries with Clemmie, even though his interdiction on bombing French towns had been lifted with regard to Dieppe. The issue had already been discussed on 1 June 1942, at Combined Operations HQ, with Mountbatten in the chair, and shelved as too contentious. Heavy bombing of the close-support kind envisaged – a new and more frightening Allied form of *Blitzkrieg* – was still unrehearsed and untested; Harris understandably preferred to keep his aircraft for his 'thousand bomber' raids over German industrial cities, not shed their terrible cargoes over innocent French civilians.

Should Monty, at the 5 June meeting, have made heavy bombing a precondition to proceeding, from a military point of view? Later, in his memoirs, Monty thought so, remembering how crucial such bombing became in breaking open the German western flank in Normandy in July 1944 to allow Bradley's and subsequently Patton's armoured forces to burst through – yet forgetting he was in the chair at the conference on 5 June 1942 at Combined Operations, when the planning committee made the fateful decision to do without such heavy bombing, which might have helped demoralize the German defenders. Yet whether such bombing was crucial to the success of the operation was not nearly as clear at the time as it would later appear; nor, on the scientific evidence of the huge bombing raids on Caen in July 1944, would it have had any physical, as opposed to demoralizing, impact on the German defences.[41]

The air-force commander of the Dieppe operation, Air Vice-Marshal Leigh-Mallory, certainly expressed extreme doubt at the 5 June 1942 meeting whether Harris's bombers would even hit the dock area, let alone knock out specific targets such as suspected artillery sites in or on the headlands. Moreover, indiscriminate destruction of buildings in the town, *pace* the record of RAF heavy bombing of German cities, would merely create further obstacles to the progress of the tanks as they came off the beach into Dieppe. In addition, the heavy bombers would only hazard the trip in complete darkness, meaning they would have to leave the area for Britain at the very latest a full hour before the landing even started – thus alerting the German defenders, and giving them time to recuperate (as happened later in the war at Monte Cassino and at Caen). Mountbatten's own naval adviser – chosen to be the naval force commander when the Dieppe raid was eventually mounted – certainly did not believe heavy night bombing was demoralizing enough, or lasted long enough, to warrant the loss of tactical surprise, nor specific enough to hit targets with any accuracy.[42] On balance, Leigh-Mallory recommended doing without heavy bombing, and his fellow navy and army force commanders agreed. Thus the decision was made, by the committee chaired that day by Montgomery, to dispense with heavy bombing completely.

But if the bombing support was cancelled, what would take its place? What artillery – land, air or sea – would support the men as they battled ashore and into Dieppe town, indeed even further inland, beyond the town, where at St Aubin the Canadians were supposed to destroy airfield installations as part of their 'reconnaissance'? In retrospect, this failure was the most egregious deficiency in the plan for Dieppe – and Mountbatten's attempt to shift the blame away from himself and his headquarters is

reprehensible. He had been given the task of studying 'tactical and technical developments' for Combined Operations up to a full-scale invasion of
the Continent. Instead of organizing full-scale exercises with live ammunition, and simulating German defence reactions at Dieppe, he had done
nothing to envision or meet the problem – beyond meekly asking the First
Sea Lord, when dubious heavy bombing was dropped from the plan, if he
might have a naval battleship offshore to lend supporting fire. 'Battleships
by daylight off the French coast? You must be mad, Dickie!' Sir Dudley
Pound is said to have dismissed the verbal suggestion – and the same view
was taken by the Admiralty on the use of naval cruisers.[43]

Instead of insisting, Mountbatten declined to pursue the matter any
further. Worse still, he forbade the naval force commander, Rear-Admiral
Baillie-Grohman – his former boss – to do so either. 'When I protested by
signal and asked if, failing a battleship, we could have one or two cruisers,
the reply was that none was available, and that we must "depend on
surprise"', Baillie-Grohman later recalled.[44] Thus, apart from puny RAF
Hurricanes, armed with cannons, and low-flying Blenheims, operating in
daylight for a few minutes before the alerted Luftwaffe entered the fray,
the 'only gun support for the troops attacking would be from the little
4-inch guns from a few destroyers wallowing about in the sea', Baillie-
Grohman mocked.[45]

But if Mountbatten – after all, a junior naval officer until the autumn
of 1941 – and his staff had failed to 'develop' the necessary fire-support
techniques required for large-scale raids or an invasion, why did a military
commander as experienced and able as Montgomery give his consent to a
plan for a frontal assault on a wide bay overlooked by steep cliffs, potentially bristling with enemy artillery, machine-guns and pillboxes, without
ensuring that these weapons were neutralized by adequate bombing,
air-cannon or naval gun support?

The Monty conundrum

This was the 'Monty conundrum', as Brigadier-General Denis Whitaker
later put it. The Canadian official historian, Colonel Stacey, later pointed
out that *all* 1942 amphibious assault planning suffered this defect, and
that Paget's new Allied Expeditionary Force Planning Committee, which
became in May 1942 the 'Combined Commanders' organization with

General Eisenhower on its panel, proposed an invasion to gain a foothold on the Continent in the Cherbourg area (Operation Wetbob) with almost no covering gunfire save that of 'older destroyers' that the Admiralty might make available.

As far as Dieppe was concerned, meanwhile, the Canadians would have to rely on Casa Maury's COHQ intelligence. This supposed only slight frontal and flanking opposition. Fighter-bomber bombardment was therefore reduced to RAF medium bombers (Blenheims) swooping in to provide support for a bare five minutes of low-level bombing 'before civil twilight', as the landing craft beached. Otherwise the only gunfire support the infantry would have would be from their own Churchill tanks, once landed, plus that of those 4-inch guns of the six Hunt class destroyers scheduled for the operation which could be brought to bear on the coast, while guarding the flotilla from German aircraft and E-boats – guns contemptuously referred to as 'peashooters' by the Canadians. (In the event, the destroyers did not hit a single recorded target during the raid.) Worse still, the COHQ intelligence report on the geology of the Dieppe beach proved flawed, never having been checked. The Dieppe shingle would, in the event, turn out to be several metres deep; most of the heavy Churchill tanks would merely sink in, like stranded whales, to be picked off by German artillery and anti-tank guns as they waddled towards the promenade – not a single tank making it over the concrete wall. It was, in Monty's parlance, 'a dog's breakfast' – yet, until Allied cover was blown, on 7 July 1942 when a German reconnaissance flight discovered the flotilla waiting at anchor off the Isle of Wight, he had done nothing to stop the breakfast. Why?

Yukon I

The Dieppe operation had been scheduled for 21 June 1942, but Monty had insisted, fortunately, upon a dress-rehearsal of the operation first. This exercise, codenamed Yukon, was mounted in June. Its complete fiasco was witnessed by Churchill, Monty, McNaughton, Crerar and senior officers from COHQ (though not by Mountbatten, the operation's progenitor, who was in America).

The débâcle, as the Combined Operations officer, Major Walter Skrine, recalled, certainly served to dampen Canadian over-enthusiasm for the operation. Skrine himself had experienced increasing 'misgiving about the optimism which prevailed throughout the Canadian Div (outside Div H.Q.). They thought it was going to be a piece of cake. Div H.Q. were also too optimistic, and there had been no previous practice in control, from a ship, of the units on shore.' Canadian inexperience was thus being compounded by a gung-ho mentality, after two years abroad without battlefield service. However, the worst nightmare in mounting the dress-rehearsal proved to be the navy's inability to put the men ashore in the right place, at the right time. 'I wasn't happy either about the landing craft crews finding the right beaches in the dark (though that was perhaps none of my business)', Skrine later recalled. He therefore participated in the Yukon rehearsal – 'I landed with the "Pourville" ([which later] landed WEST of Dieppe) Battalion H.Q. We embarked from "Princess Beatrix" in the *dark*. We were almost onto the beach before we could pick up the coast line and I found to my *horror* that there were some houses, just in-shore, when there should have been cliffs! We could do nothing about it at the moment – in time – I remember stopping the men from going into a mine-field which had not been cleared and receiving a tremendous rocket from the Battalion Commander, a moment or so later, for giving orders without his leave! ... The point is that you couldn't see more than a hundred yards.'[46]

Monty, like the other observers of the exercise, was appalled by this and other, even worse, errors of navigation. The tanks arrived an hour late, by which time the infantry would have been slaughtered. As a result, though Mountbatten himself was still in the United States, the scheduled 21 June date for the Dieppe raid was cancelled, and the whole operation postponed until a second exercise – Yukon II – could demonstrate that the navy could land the right troops and tanks on the right beaches, in the dark, at the right time.

Yukon II

The navy couldn't – indeed, this was to prove the bane of Combined Operations throughout World War II, for the Royal Navy never did learn a technique for navigating and landing troops in the dark.

Thus the second Yukon exercise, mounted on 22 June 1942, shifted the landings from nautical twilight to civil twilight, in order to ensure accurate navigation – while surrendering all hope of surprise, and exposing the troops to murderous fire as they attempted to get ashore. Ironically, given the terrible errors of navigation in Yukon I, the second exercise was deemed a success as a result – but condemned almost a thousand Canadians to probable death, since to land in daylight under German machine-gun, artillery and rifle fire was sheer madness. In trying belatedly to rectify the navigational problems (critical for a 250-craft flotilla), the whole business of supporting gunfire had been fatally marginalized; instead of concentrating on gunfire support, the emphasis had switched to traffic control!

No naval gunfire support was rehearsed, nor the means of communication in calling for it – the force commanders relying vaguely on RAF support, which would supposedly be monitored and controlled from a specially equipped separate communications vessel steaming around (and trying to avoid both Luftwaffe and German coastal artillery) offshore.

Ominous reports and discovery

Lord Mountbatten, who had missed the first rehearsal while still in the United States, had attended the second rehearsal, as did Monty and Crerar. Satisfied by what he'd seen, Mountbatten was all for the raid being mounted on the next appropriate tide: 4 July 1942. Speaking to Mountbatten and the three force commanders, Monty had been assured that new radar vessels would improve navigation. Reporting to Paget, he thought the real problem had been lack of 'confidence in the combined plan and in the successful outcome of the operation'. There had been, he said, 'a moment when certain senior officers began to waver about lack of confidence on the part of the troops – which statements were quite untrue. They really lacked confidence in themselves.' What was required, he felt, was 'an infectious optimism which will permeate right down the Force, down to the rank and file'. On balance, he considered the operation 'as planned is a possible one and has good prospects of success', provided the weather was favourable, the raid had average luck, and 'that the navy put us ashore roughly in the right places, and at the right times'.[47]

This was absurdly optimistic – as the battle of Arnhem would also show. In reality, however, Monty was himself becoming more and more anxious about the chances of success by early July 1942. Intelligence was coming through that German forces in northern France were increasing, as Hitler took the threat of a second front more seriously; the political objective of the raid, in helping the hard-pressed Russians, was already being achieved. Why, then, bother to mount it, and risk giving away Allied invasion techniques?

Field-Marshal von Runstedt had been reappointed C-in-C West, and three panzer divisions – 6th, 7th and 10th – as well as a new SS Panzer Corps, comprising the Das Reich and Leibstandart Adolf Hitler divisions, were now under his orders to repel any attack. As the 5,000 assembled troops on the Isle of Wight began to prepare to embark on 2 July 1942, Monty received a 'Martian' (Ultra-based) intelligence report from Home Forces intelligence staff confirming that the highly experienced German 10th Panzer Division – which had captured Boulogne in 1940 and had then served on the Russian front before being re-equipped – had moved to Amiens, only four hours from Dieppe. It was, intelligence now reported ominously, 'at full strength'.

The Dieppe reconnaissance, Operation Rutter, spanning two tides, would take at least twelve hours to complete. In writing to Crerar, Monty had been determined to bolster the morale of 'his' Canadians, facing their first battle against the Wehrmacht. But on 5 July 1942, after Operation Rutter had been postponed for another forty-eight hours because of atrocious weather reports for the French coast, Monty sent an urgent message to Crerar. The 'time ashore' was becoming 'very dangerous', he now warned, 'in view of the presence of a German armoured division at Amiens, which has now been confirmed'.[48] He therefore recommended that if the operation was further postponed by bad weather until 8 July, it should be reduced to a one-tide affair (the form in which it would eventually take place).

Not only did the weather remain too poor for the crucial parachute operations on the coastal gun emplacements, however, but at 6.15 on the morning of 7 July 1942 a German reconnaissance flight of four Focke-Wulf 190 fighter-bombers discovered the flotilla in the Solent and attacked it, hitting the *Princess Astrid*, and also the *Princess Josephine Charlotte*, which was carrying hundreds of sleeping Canadian soldiers on its decks. Though Mountbatten tried to have the men transferred to other craft, any hope of surprise was now gone and, thanks to its discovery and the bad weather, the operation was called off. Hitler was clearly well aware the Allies were preparing some form of attack, for his new directive of 9 July 1942 referred to the 'heavy concentration of ferrying vessels along the southern coast of England';[49] as commander-in-chief of the armed forces and the Wehrmacht, Hitler would, he announced, 'proceed to the West' if the Allies attempted a landing, and would 'assume charge of operations from there', with some thirty-three divisions under his supreme command, plus a further three 'Ersatz' divisions.

The balance of risk had now turned heavily against success. For the Allies to go ahead was tantamount to suicide.

Cancelled for all time

For Monty, cancellation came as a distinct relief. 'I was delighted,' Monty recalled later. 'I had never been happy about doing such a difficult operation with such inexperienced commanders and troops. Bravery alone,' he remarked in a phrase reminiscent of his World War I letter to his mother about Passchendaele, 'is no substitute for military experience.' Five thousand Canadians had been told their destination, as well as countless others who would learn about it from the participants in the days after cancellation – posing an impossible security risk in ever remounting it. 'I wrote a letter to the C-in-C Home Forces, General Paget, and recommended that the operation must never again be contemplated,' Monty stated emphatically.[50]

'This advice was disregarded,' Monty added sadly. Instead, in absolute secrecy 'it was decided to remount the operation. But what was worse, it was put entirely under Canadian command' – cutting him out of the chain of command altogether. Rear-Admiral Baillie-Grohman, who had voiced strong criticisms of the plan in a post-cancellation report, was also cut out – posted to another staff. Even Walter Skrine was 'taken off the operation', as Skrine himself recorded, 'for security reasons'.[51]

Monty was at least exonerated now from responsibility. 'I was now out of it and knew very little about what was going on. I *did* know that the operation was being laid on for some date in August, and again expressed my alarm personally to General Paget. I left England on the 10th August for Cairo to take command of the Eighth Army.'[52]

But if Monty thought that he could thereby discard his historical responsibility for the disaster, he had underestimated Mountbatten's pathological determination not only to get to the top, but to avoid responsibility for anything that did not work. And Dieppe did not work.

Remounting the raid

Why did Mountbatten remount the Dieppe raid, six weeks after its 'permanent' cancellation?

Was it Mountbatten's ruthless personal ambition, as some (including this writer) have suggested: a pathological determination to allow no one to get in his way, or dissuade him from his 'crazy' project? Why did he become so insistent on remounting the operation, knowing that the Germans were now expecting a cross-Channel landing, and that it would never achieve surprise, as Monty warned?

Mountbatten's callousness appalled the survivors. As Captain Whitaker realized during the (literal) post-mortem debriefing, Mountbatten seemed not only indifferent to the terrible loss of life, but dismissive of survivors' criticisms. When General Roberts raised the question of whether the operation had achieved 'tactical surprise' – the very basis on which the frontal attack had originally been planned – Mountbatten retorted that of course the Germans had been 'in a high state of alert', because of the 'condition of weather and tide'. 'My mind reeled,' Whitaker later described. 'So surprise had never been possible? . . . I thought, "What's going on? Yesterday we laid on a raid whose success depended on surprise. Today they tell our military commander that no surprise had been possible anyway? . . . What are they doing to him? To me? To all my friends who are dead on the Dieppe beaches or sitting right now in German prisoner-of-war camps?" The whole raid seemed so incongruous.' He was left wondering, for five decades, '*What is the real story behind Dieppe?*'[53]

Since Mountbatten told so many lies and indulged in so many obfuscations, it is still impossible for historians to know for certain how he managed to get the raid remounted. As the Canadian official historian, Colonel C. P. Stacey, noted in 1960, 'On the circumstances in which the project of the raid was revived about 14 July, and on the reasons for the revival, there is comparatively little written evidence.'[54] Nor did this paucity of historical documentation improve in the following forty years – Mountbatten charming and cajoling his old colleagues during his remaining lifetime into ever-more artful accounts for journalists, writers, historians and film-makers.

Was it, then, psychopathic ambition that led Mountbatten to remount the raid – a sense that, as his naval adviser at Combined Operations later remarked, the abandonment of the Dieppe project, on top of other cancelled Combined Operations projects, 'was rightly felt to be tanta-mount to a defeat'?[55]

Mountbatten certainly seems to have felt his own job as chief of Combined Operations would be on the line if he let slip his last chance to score a major offensive success, rather than the 'pinprick' raids – as Churchill called them[56] – on Vaagsö, Bruneval and St Nazaire. No other large-scale or even small-scale plans drawn up by Combined Operations HQ seemed feasible in 1942; morale among the 400 headquarters staff, not to speak of training school staffs, and many specialist units such as the commandos, was suffering.

However, in getting the raid remounted there was perhaps another, more personal purpose Mountbatten harboured in his once-princely, machiavellian heart – the possibility that he might perhaps be chosen as supreme commander of the full-scale second front, when finally launched.

Second thoughts

Supreme command of the whole cross-Channel second front invasion had become a possibility for Mountbatten in May 1942 when, after witnessing Monty's Tiger exercises in Kent, General Dwight D. Eisenhower visited London on behalf of the US War Department.

Arguing from first principles, Eisenhower had sensibly declared that the primary step in planing an invasion of Europe must be to name a commander. 'In America,' he later recalled telling the British chiefs of staff, 'I have heard much of a man who has been intensively studying amphibious operations for many months. I understand his position is Chief of Combined Operations and I think that his name is Mountbatten. Anyone will be better than none; such an operation cannot be carried out under committee command. But I have heard that Admiral Mountbatten is vigorous, intelligent and courageous, and if the operation is to be staged originally with British forces predominating, I assume he could do the job.'[57]

It was as well for Eisenhower and the free world that such a disastrous appointment was never made – though Mountbatten did, a year later, get supreme command in South-East Asia, to the consternation of many. Certainly Mountbatten's official biographer, Philip Ziegler, considered, like Eisenhower, that Mountbatten would have been well suited for the job of supreme commander for the D-Day invasion. Brooke, fortunately, did not – for Brooke had fought the Germans. How, then, did Mountbatten – who feared Brooke's battle experience and his implacably professional judgement to the point where he would never disagree let alone cross swords with him in Chiefs of Staff Committee meetings – get Brooke to agree to the secret remounting of the Dieppe raid after its 7 July cancellation?

One Canadian historian, after years of study in the available historical records, concluded that Mountbatten must have remounted the raid without chiefs-of-staff approval – particularly as Churchill himself could not later remember having given formal authorization, as Minister of Defence.[58] This, however, was not true. Churchill not only gave his personal authorization to resurrect the raid, as we shall see, but boasted of its importance to Marshal Stalin only days before it took place.

What confused Churchill, in retrospect, was that he remembered having got cold feet at the end of June 1942, just before his 'trial' by censure in the House of Commons and a few days before the cancellation of the original Rutter raid in the second week of July.

The loss of Tobruk, with more than 33,000 British and Commonwealth troops, on 21 June 1942, together with the impending parliamentary debate on his conduct of the war, had caused Churchill, a man of bravado but also compassion, to reconsider the issue of 'expendables' – the word Mountbatten used to describe non-specialist soldiers.[59] Members of Parliament disliked losses where no discernible success was achieved. What if Operation Rutter failed completely? Would a failed raid achieve the primary object of showing genuine British determination to mount a second front? Would a botched landing help persuade Stalin to keep eight million Soviet troops at war with Hitler – thus distracting 260 German divisions from a possible invasion of Britain, and certainly from facing an Allied invasion of the Continent? Would failure at Dieppe also risk turning Americans – as they threatened during discussions about a second front – to pursue a 'Japan first' rather than 'Germany first' strategy, if they witnessed yet another British military disaster? Interestingly, Churchill, privy to Ultra intelligence reports – his daily 'eggs' – had begun to fret at the very moment when Monty also, hearing of the possible arrival of 10th Panzer Division in Amiens, began to have grave doubts about the operation.

Anxious, the Prime Minister had called a small meeting at Downing Street, consisting only of senior Combined Operations personnel: Mountbatten and his naval adviser, 'Jock' Hughes-Hallett. To assist, Churchill also asked General Brooke, the CIGS, and Major-General Ismay, the Prime Minister's chief military assistant (who was also deputy secretary of the War Cabinet and Churchill's representative on the Chiefs of Staff Committee), as well as Brigadier Hollis, Ismay's deputy. The purpose of the meeting on 30 June 1942, four days before the intended mounting of Rutter, was to 'decide whether in the prevailing circumstance it was prudent to go on with it,' as Hughes-Hallett himself recorded.[60] With Mrs Churchill present – showing concern about the high cliffs and headlands overlooking the Dieppe bay on either side, with their numerous caves and concealed gullies – the Prime Minister interrogated Mountbatten and his closest military advisers, asking if they could guarantee success at Dieppe as 'certain'.

History – and up to 10,000, mostly Canadian, servicemen's lives – had hung on the answer.

Brooke's intervention

Young Captain Hughes-Hallett, Mountbatten's forty-year-old head of naval operations at Combined Operations, answered Churchill's question without hesitation, stating truthfully that 'every ship might be blazing within fifteen minutes of the beginning of the engagement'.[61]

This was not, however, what the CIGS, General Brooke, had wished the Prime Minister – who was subject to 'black-dog' depression when things went badly – to hear. Brooke, who had never been an enthusiast for the operation, cut Hughes-Hallett short, saying 'that he thought the question was one of the most unreasonable ones he had ever heard, observing that the object of the operation was precisely to find out whether or not success would result' – and adding that no military leader would ever undertake a real cross-Channel invasion unless such a trial operation was conducted.[62]

Thus it was General Brooke, the most conservative of British generals, who gave his personal imprimatur to Operation Rutter, for reasons one can only guess at, since Brooke never later referred to the mounting of the raid, save to excoriate both the planning and the Combined Operations post-operative report.[63] Yet it is profoundly ironic that the very Prime Minister who had pressed for the raid for reasons of state rather than as a military necessity, had now been brought to question the raid's chances of military success – only to be silenced by the very CIGS who had refused to sacrifice men's lives for political purposes in evacuating Brittany in 1940!

Brooke's crucifix

Brooke's crucifix was his job. As CIGS he had to temper Churchill's penchant for madcap schemes, yet maintain the Prime Minister's self-confidence and morale at a time of continual naval and military misfortune. It was not easy – indeed, no previous CIGS had ever managed it.

Brooke had accompanied Churchill on his recent flight to the United States to persuade Roosevelt to abandon the notion of a 1942 second front, and to pursue instead a 'ring' strategy in Europe, starting in North Africa and slowly tightening the ring as more and more American forces were committed. Brooke also wanted to encourage, not discourage, the Prime Minister on the eve of his 'vote of censure' by Parliament. Moreover, aware that the chiefs of staff were seen as perpetually shooting down new offensive projects, he may have wished 'the professionals' to appear positive and aggressive. Besides, Mountbatten's HQ had come up with nothing better than the Dieppe proposal, beyond the deeply questionable six-divisional Operation Sledgehammer (which would be extremely difficult to mount, reinforce and re-supply in 1942, given the paucity of shipping and landing craft), and an even more questionable operation in northern Norway to protect the PQ convoys supplying Russia from German air attack: Operation Jupiter. Nor did the chiefs of staff – who 'have no ideas and oppose everything,' as the Foreign Office under-secretary Sir Alexander Cadogan noted in his diary a few days later – have any alternative proposals. 'We'd better put an advertisement in the papers, asking for ideas,' Churchill had himself remarked facetiously.[64]

In the end, Brooke reckoned, some sort of bone had to be thrown to the Americans and to the Russians, in terms of a future second front. If the assault did prove a failure, it would at least demonstrate to them, as no words could do, just how difficult a major cross-Channel landing was going to be.

Thus, in the most bizarre of ways, Brooke saved the Dieppe operation from permanent cancellation – and in due course approved its fatal resurrection.

No *alternative*

Brooke's intervention was the turning point in getting Churchill to over-come his fears and give the green light to the resurrection of the Dieppe raid – an intercession Churchill took very much to heart, and which he quoted almost verbatim from memory when defending the disaster before Parliament in September 1942.

Yet the complete cancellation of the Dieppe operation on 7 July 1942, a week later, owing to bad weather and the German attack on the assembled flotilla, had seemed to put a end to all argument and anxiety. How, then, had it been resurrected?

Complete cancellation would leave a major problem for the chiefs of staff, given the lack of feasible alternatives, Mountbatten had recognized. For this reason he had been able, at a Chiefs of Staff Committee meeting held the day before cancellation, on 6 July, to persuade his fellow chiefs of staff to countenance at least the possibility of remounting Rutter at a future date, even if the current operation should be called off owing to continued bad weather.

Thus, in the hours following cancellation on 7 July and the dispersal of many thousands of soldiers, sailors and airmen, with morale plummeting at his Combined Operations HQ – indeed in an atmosphere of 'defeat' for the headquarters itself – Mountbatten made 'the unusual and, I suggest, rather bold proposal that we should remount the operation against Dieppe'.[65]

Far from being cancelled, Mountbatten urged, the operation should, in utmost secrecy, go full steam ahead!

Secret *resurrection*

'Bold proposal' was an understatement. The reaction at COHQ, Rich-mond Terrace, was, as even Mountbatten's official biographer admitted, 'dismay'.[66] Yet, to his certain knowledge, he assured his retinue, the chiefs of staff had no better proposal to offer the Prime Minister – and the international political situation remained critical. Something must be done – and Dieppe was the only thing that could be done.

Next, Mountbatten sought to square the force commanders – indeed, in the subsequent few days he even threatened them with quasi-legal action: a formal inquiry into the reasons behind cancellation that might expose them as cowards, unless they agreed to remount.[67]

Most remained sceptical. Rear-Admiral Baillie-Grohman would not be browbeaten, nor would he withdraw his criticisms of the cancelled operation. Even Leigh-Mallory supported Baillie-Grohman in deploring the lack of an inter-service appreciation of the plan, before it was handed over to force commanders.

It was at this juncture that, in the manner of Machiavelli's prince, Mountbatten became most like the prince he had once been, before the fall of the Battenbergs. Sensing that reluctant COHQ planners and force commanders might torpedo the project in a resurrected form, Mountbatten decided to drop anyone from the scheme who was sceptical or critical. Moreover, to ensure that no one blabbed or gave his game away, Mountbatten used a completely novel approach to the business of British operational planning and command: the insistence on such absolute secrecy that not only would the Germans not learn of the raid's resurrection, but neither would the British.

To achieve this, Mountbatten cut Montgomery out of the revived planning, and removed the naval force commander, substituting one his own staff. Not even his vice-chief of Combined Operations was informed of the revival; virtually all COHQ officers who had been involved in the planning of the original were also kept in the dark – indeed, even Mountbatten's own chief of staff was not told! Nor was Brooke's deputy, the vice-CIGS – in fact not even the deputy Prime Minister was informed, or the Joint Intelligence Agency![68] Under the codename 'Jubilee' the remounted Dieppe operation would be kept so secret that not even the troops themselves would know until the last minute what they were in for.

A fit of military madness

The German Minister of Propaganda, Dr Joseph Goebbels, had written in one of the main German newspapers that an Allied landing on the coast of France would be the product of 'a fit of military madness'.[69] That Mountbatten was able to get away with such a 'crazy' notion, as even the historian of Combined Operations, Bernard Fergusson, called it,[70] seems in retrospect almost incredible.

In the end, Mountbatten's success in getting the Dieppe raid remounted can only be explained in terms of his machiavellian mind, and the context of the time. Brooke, increasingly preoccupied with the problems posed by Rommel, whose German–Italian panzer force had now reached Alamein, only eighty miles from Cairo, was deeply sceptical about a revived Dieppe operation, given German forewarning. However, he had already decided by late June that he would have to go out to Egypt to review the situation in the desert – where the navy had evacuated Alexandria, which was only forty miles from Rommel's front line, and the British administration in Cairo was busy burning files. 'The Middle East situation is about as unhealthy as it can be, and I do not see how it can end,' Brooke had noted in his diary on 28 June 1942.[71]

In terms of Allied military offensive operations in Europe there was no realistic alternative to Dieppe, only operations that were even less likely to succeed, and at far higher cost in life and equipment - as Brooke was painfully aware. The first weeks of July 1942 saw no improvement, especially when, on the 18th, a delegation of top American generals and admirals yet again arrived in London to try and force the chiefs of staff to mount Operation Sledgehammer in 1942. As Harold Nicolson noted in his diary on 22 July: 'The Government are in a difficult position. If they create a second front as a forlorn hope, we shall have another Dunkirk. If they do not do so, they will be accused of letting down the Russians.'[72]

On 23 July, to the relief of General Brooke, Roosevelt backed down over Sledgehammer for 1942. Churchill, however, had then to explain this by telegram to Stalin, along with other, equally disappointing news for the generalissimo. The devastating German attack on Convoy PQ-17 to Murmansk, in which two-thirds of the convoy had been sunk, had forced the Admiralty to halt all further supplies to Russia – a further embarrassment vis-à-vis Stalin. It therefore seemed to Churchill that he would have to explain the situation to the Soviet leader not only in cables but in person, as he had done in June to Roosevelt. There simply was not going to be a second front in 1942, nor would there be further convoys to Russia for the moment.

But if the second front was off, and convoys to Russia were now stopped, what could the Allies do to help Russia? Churchill's crony Lord Beaverbrook was, according to Leo Amery, the Secretary of State for India, still hosting dinner parties for influential members of Parliament to keep pressure on Churchill to open a second front in 1942, 'disregarding all other questions of possibility of another Dunkirk or of feasibility'.[73]

While no one wanted another British defeat, it became imperative for Churchill to keep kicking at Germany, even if only to show Britain was alive.

It was in this context that Churchill, having survived a vote of censure in Parliament, yet stung to the quick by Stalin's furious response on 14 July to the cancellation of convoys to Russia and the probable abandonment of Sledgehammer, made plans to fly to Moscow in person to assure the Soviets that Britain still intended to open a second front 'in due course'. Desperate to have some token of immediate British offensive intentions in Europe to take with him, Churchill therefore encouraged Mountbatten's 'crazy' idea of reviving the cancelled Dieppe operation.

Mountbatten, for all his inability to judge people, had measured the Prime Minister correctly. On 16 July he had, in anticipation, set possible new target dates for the operation: 18–23 August, or alternatively September 1 or 6. The following day, 17 July, he sought to get formal COS permission to remount the operation. Unfortunately for historians – and for Churchill when he came to compose his history of World War II – there was no written record that Mountbatten's suggested minute was formally agreed at the meeting, but Churchill was clearly supportive and re-planning went ahead with COS backing. Three days later, Mountbatten's naval adviser, Hughes-Hallett, was formally approved by the chiefs of staff as the new naval force commander, replacing Baillie-Grohman, who was posted elsewhere. At Mountbatten's request, total secrecy was maintained, denying anyone but a tiny circle of people 'inside knowledge': twenty people in the entire world.

Ignoring warnings

Sadly, Mountbatten's secrecy did not for one moment persuade the Germans to lower their guard on the Channel coast. Instead, it merely avoided any uncomfortable criticism in Britain. Worst of all, it also denied the Canadian troops an opportunity to re-rehearse the raid, in advance of its actual execution – for the men must not suspect a thing, and must be loaded on to landing craft on the evening before the resurrected raid as if going out on another exercise!

Idiocy had now been legitimized, in perhaps the most lethal manner in World War II, as Goebbels had correctly forecast. Even in Britain's most secure committee, the Chiefs of Staff Committee itself, the new Operation Jubilee was referred to only as the 'next big raid', or 'J'. Anyone who objected to Combined Operations requisitions for equipment or personnel was told the secret, unnamed operation had the highest approval – that of the Prime Minister himself.

Admiral Ramsay, the 'saviour' of Dunkirk and currently naval C-in-C Dover, was, like Monty, unimpressed. Ramsay had been appointed naval representative on the recent Combined Commanders organization looking into the planning of a second front under Home Forces; to Mountbatten he expressed in writing his concern that the Germans were not only expecting British raids, but *welcomed* them as excellent pointers to their coastal weaknesses. Why, then, give the Germans what they wanted? 'If it is our intention at some future date to make an attack in force upon the enemy's coast,' Ramsay complained to Mountbatten, 'we are now doing, or proposing to do, our best to make that attack less likely to achieve success.'[74]

Mountbatten ignored the warning; indeed, he was not interested in such niceties. An invasion rehearsal in the summer of 1942 would be a tremendous feather in his cap, and perhaps lead to his appointment either to supreme command of the 1943 invasion of Europe, or at least to Allied chief of staff under an American supreme commander such as General Marshall or even Eisenhower. COHQ was certainly aware, after Rutter's cancellation, of 'a strong rumour that General Marshall was about to be appointed as Supreme Commander in the U.K. and Channel area with Mountbatten becoming his Chief of Staff,' Hughes-Hallett later recalled.[75] Replying to Ramsay's letter on 27 July, therefore, Mountbatten simply reported that 'at the Chiefs of Staff and War Cabinet I was instructed to push on hard with large scale raids'. Moreover, with regard to the 'next big raid', he boasted to Ramsay, he was 'quite confident' he would shortly get the go-ahead, for there were 'political reasons why I feel certain they [the chiefs of staff] will not cancel'.[76]

He was right. Dieppe was becoming a peace offering to Stalin, as Churchill began to make arrangements to visit the dictator in person, in the Kremlin.

All that sort of rot

As July turned into August, Mountbatten was cock-a-hoop, as well he might be. 'Defeat' on 7 July 1942 had been transformed into a victory for COHQ, planning their secret operation in competition with Eisenhower's Combined Commanders group and Paget's Home Forces. In deference to Mountbatten's demand for total secrecy, in fact, the entire second floor of Richmond Terrace was redesignated for force-commander meetings only, and no other COHQ staff allowed on it. Major Skrine, the COHQ planner most closely involved in planning Rutter, later recalled how he was 'told Dieppe was cancelled and was put on other plans for the rest of the summer. I was absolutely astonished to hear about 2 days before it finally took place, that "Dieppe" was "on" again.'[77] In another reference Skrine recollected frankly, 'I was horrified to hear the thing was on . . . I didn't know why it had been remounted or anything about it.'[78]

With only a tiny inner circle of colleagues Mountbatten had managed to resurrect a 'dead' operation involving almost 10,000 men. Apart from his chief of intelligence (who did not even get the German division defending Dieppe right, after six months' preparation!) virtually no one at COHQ was brought into the picture, except for Captain Hughes-Hallett, the new naval force commander. With this handful of men Mountbatten then worked directly with the air-force commander and the military force commander, Major-General Roberts. Meanwhile, General Paget himself, General McNaughton and General Crerar collectively took over Montgomery's watching brief for Jubilee.

The result was catastrophic. Without concerning themselves about the latest intelligence picture or ever re-assessing the raid's chances of success, the secret participants merely revised the old Dieppe plan as a one-tide operation, using commandos instead of paratroops to silence the anti-invasion guns on the wider flanks. No further thought was given to the vital headlands overlooking the main Dieppe beaches, or to the need for an increase in naval gunfire to support the infantry – as Rear-Admiral Baillie had urged, before he was cut out – or gaining more information regarding German beach defences and reserves. As Hughes-Hallett said, in relation to the removal of his predecessor, Baillie-Grohman was preoccupied with the need for ' "appreciations", and all that sort of rot'.[79]

The assault itself was now purely political – no one was interested any longer in its original reconnaissance or military aims; indeed, the aims were often ludicrous, such as the need to collect samples of French bread! This was no longer, in truth, a reconnaissance in force than in perforce. Mountbatten himself was determined to make a newspaper splash, and arranged for no fewer than twenty-five accredited journalists to accompany the raid![80] As Sir Leslie Hollis recalled, Mountbatten was 'able to spend incalculable amounts of public money on projects that took his fancy'[81] – and if the purpose of Dieppe was to boost morale at home and abroad, then publicity was crucial.

Money talked – in all senses. Publicity had already become almost an addiction for Mountbatten, who had immediately taken Hollywood figures like Darryl F. Zanuck and Douglas Fairbanks Jr on to his Combined Operations staff when appointed. The veteran commando, Colonel 'Shimi' Lovat, was dumbfounded by Mountbatten's headquarters, which resembled more a film set than a serious battle-planning centre. It swarmed like a beehive with 'red-tabbed gentlemen', Lovat recalled. 'The bee-hive illusion was enhanced,' he described, 'by busy passages, honeycombed with rooms filled with every branch of the Services, including the powder-puff variety, who looked elegant in silk-stockings.' For the manly Lovat, this heterosexual appearance was belied by a homosexual undercurrent: 'There was said to be,' he added, 'a fair proportion of drones among the inmates.'[82]

What worried Lovat was the unreality of all this – an unreality that would inevitably be paid for in blood, by fighting men facing fighting Germans. 'Signing a pass allowed the visitor, having stated his business, to sit around talking to pretty Wrens, or out on the terrace when it wasn't raining,' he recalled. 'As a port of call Combined Ops was not favoured by the serving officer.'[83]

Was this the future face of Allied war, though – the equivalent of Haig's château headquarters, far removed from the grim reality of the trenches in World War I? Mountbatten's headquarters was certainly a sort of preview of headquarters to come; indeed, a model for Eisenhower's huge, sprawling Supreme Headquarters in Algiers later in 1942, and in London in 1944. Inter-service integration, the bringing-in of American officers, the use of women in executive and staff positions, even the employment of 'drones', were developments of war-winning significance, which Mountbatten pioneered – using his royal blood and wealth (he had married Edwina Ashley, the granddaughter of a multi-millionaire) to overcome service snobbery and Establishment attitudes that had hitherto characterized Britain's miserable performance in World War II.

Blending the three services was one thing – especially as a precursor of Allied, not simply British, planning; but fighting the Germans was another – and in this respect neither Mountbatten nor Eisenhower had a clue, as the Dieppe raid and operations controlled by Eisenhower in the Mediterranean would show. To win the war, the Allies needed inter-service integration at the top, certainly; but they needed also field commanders capable of matching and beating the Germans in battle. As even Mountbatten's most adulatory biographer, Richard Hough, allowed, Mountbatten's 'practice of winning by any means, fair or almost foul' eventually got him to the top – but it did not help him in the most ruthless business of all: beating the enemy. 'He did not win a victory at sea. The enemy frequently damaged his ships, and finally sank him,' Hough concluded. He was handsome and aristocratically inspirational, but the 'fates of war were not on his side'.[84]

The long struggle between two Allied approaches to war, that would soon be epitomized in the very different headquarters of Eisenhower and of Montgomery, was thus prefigured in England in the spring and summer of 1942, as Monty trained his South-East Army in ever-more ambitious battlefield exercises, while Mountbatten responded to the political imperative of the day by secretly remounting a dead and suspect operation through a secret, core team at his headquarters: a major landing in France so disastrous that for the remainder of 1942 Combined Operations would be banned from mounting any raids at all.

Easing the pill

Ironically, it was Joseph Stalin, when Churchill arrived in Moscow to tell him of the forthcoming raid across the Channel, who was sceptical. Churchill had had to carry his 'large lump of ice to the North Pole',[85] as he put it, and reiterate that a second front was not possible in Europe in 1942; but to ease the pill he told Stalin on 12 August that he proposed 'this month', if the weather was favourable, 'to make a raid on a large scale in order to seek information and to test the German resistance. We might lose as many as 10,000 men on this operation,' he boasted to the Communist dictator, 'which would be no more than a reconnaissance.'

Stalin was brutally frank – indeed, he promptly made a grotesque display of insulting the Prime Minister of Britain by ridiculing the country's military efforts. Once again Churchill was forced to justify his military strategy. There would be, he repeated to the dictator on 15 August 1942, 'a more serious raid in August, although the weather might upset it. It will be a reconnaissance in force. Some 8,000 men with 50 tanks will be landed. They will stay a night and a day, kill as many Germans as possible and take prisoners,' he claimed, verbally extending the supposed duration of the operation (in actuality Mountbatten's Operation Jubilee had been reduced to 6,000 soldiers and would only be a nine-hour demonstration, around a single tide, at most). 'The object is to get information and create the impression of an invasion,' Churchill nevertheless reiterated. 'More important, I hope it will call forth a big air battle.'[86]

Stalin was unimpressed, pointing out that, whatever the military rationale of the operation, the Germans would merely broadcast it as the 'failure of a British attempt at invasion'.[87] To this Churchill could only say that the British would counter with their own propaganda: namely, their success in taking German prisoners, and the killing of 'many Germans'.[88]

It seemed a very lame argument, save in respect of Operation Torch – the potentially real invasion of North Africa, for which the Dieppe raid would act as a cover or decoy. If Torch succeeded, Stalin agreed, then 'everybody will understand'.[89]

Dieppe had never been intended as a decoy. Moreover, would the Dieppe operation succeed in 'killing many Germans', without losing too many Canadian and British casualties? Could Mountbatten, so full of bravado, pull it off? Was it now even necessary if the Germans were in any case responding to the mere *threat* of a landing on the Channel coast, while the Combined Commanders now prepared for landings in north-west Africa instead?

Scuppers running with blood

In the context of Churchill's trip to Moscow, and the Prime Minister's feeling that he must make a significant, even sacrificial gesture to Stalin, there was in reality no way in which the revived Dieppe raid could now be halted, save by bad weather or another German sighting. Churchill had given his word to the Russian dictator; indeed, Stalin had, in the end, treated him as a friend, inviting him to sup with him in his private quarters, in the heart of the Kremlin, the literal ogre in his den, talking – to

Churchill's amazement – of 'wiping out' whole sections of the Soviet population such as the kulaks.[90]

In England, meanwhile, Mountbatten had deliberately and effectively excluded any mechanism for a critical appraisal of the Jubilee plan. With Churchill and the CIGS out of the country, and the vice-CIGS not permitted to see the plan or discuss its chances of success, there was no one but the force commanders, and Generals Paget, McNaughton and Crerar – three 'useless generals' – who could halt the march of events. Most significantly, Mountbatten showed not the least interest in likely German reaction. Though German by blood, he was inveterately British by upbringing: a debonair, handsome amateur masquerading as a professional – for the Germans were nothing if not methodical. As the distinguished commander of No.4 Commando, Lord Lovat, remarked, 'the Germans', having observed the Allied flotilla off the Isle of Wight in July, 'got the message, and vigilance continued. Postponement gave the enemy time to strengthen their positions. The assessment of Colonel-General Haase (responsible for coastal defence from Ostend to Normandy) was remarkable. Troops under his command were given "Special Alert" danger periods whenever conditions appeared suitable for Allied landings.'[91] These dates included 10–19 August.

In accordance with this 'Special Alert', General Haase actually organized a divisional anti-invasion exercise at Dieppe on the very day Mountbatten had designated the assault should go in: 18 August 1942. Fortunately, owing to poor weather forecasts, the Allied operation was postponed for that day, and the flotilla only set sail from the Isle of Wight area that night. However, a chance collision with a convoy off Dieppe in the early-morning darkness on 19 August soon put the entire German coastal defence forces at Dieppe back on to maximum alert. The navy then bungled both the approach to the crucial east headland and also the run-in to the main Dieppe beach, causing the tank landing craft to arrive almost thirty minutes late.

In the clear dawn light the Canadian infantry thus disembarked like lambs to the slaughter in front of the seaside town, to be cut down in their hundreds by German machine-guns and concealed artillery in the flanking headlands. Twenty-eight of the Calgary Regiment's fifty tanks were bravely put ashore, but all had difficulty in getting off the deep shingle, were targeted by German anti-tank gunfire, and none was able to penetrate the town or even take out the concealed guns firing at them. Combined Operations intelligence had been lamentably if not criminally inadequate.

Like Monty himself, Major Goronwy Rees had been cut out of the Jubilee replanning and execution of the Dieppe raid, but at the last moment he was permitted, at the request of the Canadian 2nd Division, to witness the operation from HMS *Garth*. Rees was appalled. The destroyer's 4-inch guns were unable to do more than engage a single headland battery, and get hit while laying a lot of smoke. As the hours went by the sight of the Canadian wounded being brought aboard sickened the All Souls Fellow. Many were 'badly wounded, all were suffering from shock and exhaustion. They had the grey, lifeless faces of men whose vitality had been drained out of them; each of them could have modelled for a death mask. They were bitter and resentful at having been flung into a battle far more horrible than anything for which they could have been prepared, and as they came aboard one heard the oaths and blasphemies, the cursings and revilings, with which men speak of leaders by whom they feel that they have been betrayed and deceived. I thought that this is what a beaten army looks like, for no army is beaten until it has lost faith and confidence in those who command it. These men had, at that moment, and it would be a long time before they recovered them again.'[92]

Strangely, Hughes-Hallett, the young naval force commander, experienced no remorse as he made his way back from Dieppe aboard his destroyer-flagship *Calpe*. The 'upper deck was choked with seriously wounded soldiers. I recall a young Ship's Officer asking me whether I had ever believed the history books when they spoke of the "scuppers" running with blood. "If not, lean over the bridge and take a look along the ship's side", he added quietly. I did so and as the ship rolled very gently in a long, lazy swell you could see little red rivulets running down out of each scupper.'[93]

'Morale of returning troops reported to be excellent,' Mountbatten lied to Churchill by telegraphic cypher the next day. 'All I have seen are in great form.'[94] In his diary Mountbatten simply noted: 'Great air battle. Many casualties and some successes.'[95] As his official biographer, Philip Ziegler, admitted, 'The truth in his hands was swiftly converted from what it was to what it should have been.'[96]

It was this aristocratic insouciance that would most rankle in Canada in ensuing years, as the abortive raid was grieved over, picked over, and turned into a national 'Gallipoli'. Canadian lives had been squandered for Allied political purposes – but with the British failing to pick up the historical tab, as Mountbatten, Hughes-Hallett, Paget, McNaughton, Crerar, and a series of other figures connected with the disaster all kept silent or passed the buck.

For Churchill and the chiefs of staff the raid was self-evidently a 'fiasco'; nevertheless, it was 'a lesson to the people who are clamouring for the invasion of France', Brooke growled.[97] He was right. Failure, indeed complete and disastrous failure, had proved far better than any verbal or written argument could have done to the Americans and to the Russians that a second front in 1942 would fail – indeed, for one critical week the American chiefs of staff recommended cancelling the planned landings at Algiers and Oran, inside the Mediterranean, as part of the Torch operation, originally set for 14 October 1942, lest it prove too costly. Churchill was forced to point out to President Roosevelt the difference between the 'steel-bound, fortified coasts of France', exemplified by the Dieppe fiasco, and the 'weak, divided [French] opposition' that would pertain in northwest Africa.[98]

Thus, in its gruesome way, the Dieppe raid achieved its political object. In London the 'magnitude of the repulse and the numbers of casualties served for a time to still the popular, uninformed and vociferous outcry for a Second Front', Sir Leslie Hollis recalled of the Dieppe disaster; 'dead men may tell no tales, but their death was itself a warning'.[99]

A second front could not be launched until the Allies were ready: that is to say, had built up the experience, landing craft, fire-support and the superiority in troops, equipment and generalship that could guarantee success – however hard the Russians were being pressed.

A dilettante exercise

'Lord Louis: Our Tanks Penetrated the Town', ran the deliberately dishonest headline of the *Daily Express* on 21 August 1942, with further lies from Mountbatten that the 'high' losses had been 'expected' – indeed that 'all the men who took part were told and fully accepted the great hazards'. His claims for German aircraft shot down were even more mendacious: 'Luftwaffe lost 273' – six times the actual figure of forty-eight! To cover up the disaster, moreover, the brilliance of Lovat's commando assault on Varengeville was ordered to be played up by Combined Operations, while the slaughter of the Canadians at Dieppe itself was to be kept concealed, as far as possible, lest it affect national morale.

A disaster of such magnitude could not be swept under the carpet, however, especially when the Germans trumpeted their victory with incontrovertible film, photographs and newspaper reports throughout the Third Reich and the occupied countries of Europe.

For the Germans Dieppe was thus a propaganda triumph, as Stalin had warned, and a military vindication of Nazi professionalism. 'Das Oberkommando der Wehrmacht gibt bekannt', ran the special communiqué from Hitler's headquarters already on 19 August 1942: 'The enemy, having landed, was destroyed in close combat at all points and thrown back into the sea.'[100]

That Dieppe was a pathetic political gesture to the Russians, the Germans made contemptuously clear. 'The enemy in making such an attempted landing that served only political purposes and flew in the face of all military reason, has suffered an annihilating defeat. German forces in the West have dealt the dilettante-enterprise an appropriate lesson.'[101]

This was no more than the truth. During the day, the tally of Canadian prisoners had been raised to 2,000, with almost a thousand corpses pictured on the beaches. Luftwaffe losses were reduced to thirty-five. 'All units who took part in the action against the enemy landing performed brilliantly,' the German communiqué announced[102] – pointing out that they had not even needed to commit reserves from outside the local area. Dieppe had provided the German defenders, as Admiral Ramsay had warned Mountbatten, with a wonderful opportunity to test their defensive dispositions – a test which the Germans rightly felt they had passed with flying colours. They had even managed to secure copies of virtually the entire detailed military plan, intelligence summary and naval and military operations orders on captured Canadian officers. As John Campbell, the historian of intelligence relating to the Dieppe raid, remarked: 'the documents and equipment captured at Dieppe presented them [the Germans] with a priceless windfall'.[103]

Though Mountbatten's telegram to Churchill had not spoken of failure, and though he did his best to manipulate press reports in Britain, few were taken in for long. In London the City, as usual, responded with greater caution than tabloid editors – an 'anticlimax' after 'what they had been led to expect', as The Times reported on 21 August. By September most editors had done their sums – and were appalled. 'Dieppe – The Full Story' Picture Post headed its 5 September 1942 edition, acknowledging a 'disappointing setback'. Noting the 'high casualties', it asked: 'Was it worth the price in order to land on enemy-occupied soil for nine hours?' One by one, its editor looked at the grim lessons, in an analysis far clearer and more critical than Combined Operations' own report. In a real invasion, it argued, 'we would surely have to use it [the Allied air weapon] with greater imagination and on a wider scale'. Parachute drops would have to form an essential adjunct to beach landings. A heavily defended seaport could 'be taken quickly only after a devastating bombing attack with all the fury that Bomber Command could muster', it concluded – something which carried severe implications in terms of French civilian casualties, and the subsequent unusability of the port itself. The planners had known this in advance, though – in which case the raid was fatuous as a rehearsal of a potential invasion. Even the grand air battle about which Mountbatten and Leigh-Mallory had crowed was suspect – not only in the number of German planes lost, but in terms of helping the ground forces, whether in attacking German gun emplacements or even distracting their anti-aircraft gunners, who had simply depressed their AA sights and murdered the Canadians as they poured ashore. 'From a military point of view,' *Picture Post* drew the lesson, 'it would be absurd for the German A.A. gunners to have time or ammunition to train their guns on our ground forces . . .'

Thus, though Dieppe had served its political purpose, its military failure had borne out Stalin's insulting contention that the British would not, or could not, fight effectively, even in a small, nine-hour battle: that the British navy had 'lost its initiative' and that the 'British Armies didn't fight either'[104] – in contrast to the American navy and army. Dieppe, in other words, had shown yet again how inept were the British at anything larger than fishing expeditions – and it rankled.

Churchill had boasted to Stalin that there might be 10,000 casualties, but in actuality he never dreamed the operation could be so botched – and the moment he got back to England late in August he was on the retrospective warpath, demanding that Brooke and Mountbatten should 'Explain how the military side of the Dieppe raid was planned.'[105] Later, in December 1942, Churchill declared that 'The time has come when I must be informed more precisely about the military plans. Who made them? Who approved them? What was General Montgomery's part in it? And General McNaughton's part? What is the opinion about the Canadian generals selected by General McNaughton? Did the General Staff check the plans? At what point was the V.C.I.G.S. informed in C.I.G.S.'s absence?'[106] Approached by General Ismay, Mountbatten managed to fob off such inquiries – partly by threatening a formal inquiry himself, which might show blood on everyone's hands. Yet still Churchill could not let go. Eight years after the disaster, following a stroke that affected his memory and when writing his history of World War II, he asked: 'Surely the decision could not have been taken without the Chiefs of Staff being informed. If so why did they not bring it to my attention?'[107]

Churchill might well ask, for the military side of the operation, apart from brilliant flanking raids by trained commandos, seemed almost too sickening to be true: wave after wave of landing craft depositing brave Canadians on to a shore raked by enemy gunfire, like sitting ducks. But Mountbatten refused to take responsibility either for having remounted the raid, or for its execution. He could reasonably claim, by the terms of his directive as chief of Combined Operations, merely to have been the architect and adviser, not the client – despite having his own COHQ man as naval task force commander, and having masterminded the entire revived operation on the second floor at Richmond Terrace. Crucial decisions, such as the agreement to switch from wide flank attacks to a frontal assault on Dieppe's main beach, had been made on the army's behalf, he deceitfully claimed, while the air force had withdrawn its commitment to bomb Dieppe prior to landing without army protest . . . There were, in short, all too many let-outs. In the end, Mountbatten argued, the moral of the story was simple. The Prime Minister had wanted a raid-in-force, and he had got it.

Breaking the rules

'Compromise on this, compromise on the bombing, compromise on every-thing. It's no good!' Monty later commented on Dieppe.[108]

'We learnt many lessons which were of the utmost value to us when the time came to plan the invasion of Normandy,' Monty summed up. 'But I have always considered that we could have gained the information we needed without the loss of all those splendid Canadian soldiers.' As he noted, 'The Canadian Army in England took it very well; they reckoned they had done a good job, and they had. But their losses were terrible. They should never have been asked to take it on.'[109]

'The Dieppe raid,' Monty considered in retrospect, 'is a good example of an operation which broke the rules for the successful conduct of battle. It is clear that it was going to be a very difficult and tricky operation; what was then required was simplicity. But the plan was complicated. The arrangements for inter-communication were inadequate. The troops to be landed for the operation were inexperienced, and had never before fought the Germans. The general was inexperienced. There were too many "cooks" playing with it and no one commander was responsible. In modern war certain factors are vital. Here are a few.

'Simplicity
Good communications
Clear-cut organisation of command and control
Experienced commanders and troops.

'All these were absent . . . Finally, there was no one commander who was responsible.'[110]

Who, then, *was* responsible for the failure, he asked – then struck out his own question, and wrote instead: 'Under such conditions it is too easy to pass the buck. When we invaded Normandy in 1944, Eisenhower was directly responsible for the whole operation. He accepted it. In all operations of war somebody has got to be responsible. He then puts a note on the door of his office:

"The buck stops here." '[111]

To have asked the volunteer soldiers of a dominion country to undertake such a risky operation was, Monty felt, unfair; 'the heroism and bravery displaced at Dieppe was beyond all praise,' he noted, unintentionally using the word he really meant, rather than the intended one. But, he added sadly, 'I reckon we all learnt that to win victories with such men, with the least possible loss of life, they deserved to be put into battle by experienced commanders.'[112]

No more defeats

Neither at the time nor later did Monty question the rationale for the raid – which he rightly took to have been undertaken because of political rather than military reasons. The Russians had needed a sign of seriousness regarding a second front, and so had the Americans. Ergo, a big raid, mounted not for any real military purpose, but to help the Prime Minister. For yet further political reasons, inexperienced Canadians had been chosen to perform the operation, in order to give their government and senior military staffs the sense that they were contributing to the active war effort. But the price of all this was, in combat with a highly efficient enemy such as the Germans, disaster.

The question in the summer of 1942, then, was: how transform continual British military disasters into victory? As Monty later recalled, 'it must be remembered that in 1941, and the first half of 1942, we British were suffering great disasters:

'The defeat in Greece and Crete in 1941.
Shipping losses in the Atlantic.
The loss of the battle cruisers in the Far East in December 1941.
The fall of Singapore in February 1942.
The reverses in the first Burma campaign.
The defeats in the desert by Rommel.
The fall of Tobruk in June 1942.

'I was in England when all these events took place,' Monty reflected. By August 1942, even before the Dieppe operation was secretly remounted, it had already 'become clear to me that we must not suffer any more defeats. I had decided in my own mind that all future operations which took place *under my direct command* must be victories; the British people and the soldiers had had enough of defeat; they deserved successes; I would refuse to launch offensive operations until I was ready and the soldiers had a good and reasonable chance of success. This had become my thinking by 1942, before I took command of Eighth Army.'[113]

Someone, in other words, needed to show the British, and by extension the Americans, that the Germans could be beaten in battle. Monty was convinced he was that man.

Churchill, unfortunately, was not.

BOOK III

ALAMEIN

16

The Desert

The 'Auk' at Alamein

By the summer of 1942 General Sir Claude Auchinleck, the British C-in-C Middle East, was a spent force – indeed, he had shown a veritable genius for appointing the wrong man to command the British 8th Army in the field, then having to sack his nominee and take personal charge of the resultant chaos. He had been sent out to replace General Wavell as C-in-C Middle East in the summer of 1941; thereafter his 8th Army had suffered over 100,000, mostly Commonwealth, casualties – 100 per cent of its original strength – at the hands of General Rommel, who was promoted by a grateful Hitler to the rank of field marshal for outstanding leadership. As Bernard Freyberg, the New Zealand divisional commander, later recorded, 'General Auchinleck was well-known as a bad judge of a man, and he assembled around him a bad staff. I was apprehensive during the whole of this period, because most of us could see it approaching. The "Jock Column" and "Brigade Group", successful with the Italians, were doomed to end in disaster against the Germans, and these were the cause of our failures. It has been argued that our defeats were due to the lack of a good tank. I do not agree . . . The new set-up of the Eighth Army [under Auchinleck] would not work. You could not combine the duties of C-in-C Middle East with command of an army in the desert. The C-in-C should have put in a new commander[, the existing one having] lost his nerve.' Reflecting on Auchinleck's desert command, Freyberg considered Auchinleck's 'scheme', on taking over from General Ritchie towards the end of June, 'was quite fantastic, and would ruin any Army. Auchinleck was completely out of the picture', Freyberg recalled. 'The Army had for the moment disintegrated. The system of command had broken down.' The result of this, and the machinations of Auchinleck's operations staff, meant that, for example, X Corps on one day got 'three separate sets of orders, all of them altering the policy of defence'. Freyberg never even received the change of plan ordering him to retreat from Matruh to Alamein, while 1st Armoured Division, supposedly masking Freyberg's right flank, did. The result was a shambles, including a Balaclava-style ninety-mile charge in reverse, in pitch darkness with 2,800 vehicles, through Rommel's headquarters, back to Alamein – with serious casualties, including Freyberg himself. By the end of July the New Zealand Division's casualties totalled a staggering 9,000 (the entire population of New Zealand was less than 2 million) – 4,300 of them lost in July alone. Questioning his subordinates when he returned to his division from hospital (a fragment of shell had passed clean through his neck), Freyberg found 'that troops had again been dribbled away in penny packets, supporting tanks ordered to leave infantry just when they were most needed, and the latter then left to face the German armour without adequate means to defend themselves'.[1]

Disastrously poor leadership had thus characterized the British way of war. Rommel, outrunning his supplies, had captured Tobruk, but in the end, after a brilliant advance, had been unable to break through the British position at Alamein, the final forty-mile strip of navigable desert between the Mediterranean coast and the impassable Quattara Depression, on his first attempt; he had therefore ordered the cessation of attacks, and had easily repulsed Auchinleck's uncoordinated attempts at counter-attack,[2] while summoning more Axis troops, tanks, artillery, equipment and supplies for a decisive breakthrough assault in August 1942 which would take the Panzerarmee Afrika to Alexandria, Cairo, the Nile and the Suez Canal.

A new commander is needed

Auchinleck – nicknamed the 'Auk' – was a tall, handsome figure, with a lifetime's service in the Indian army. His steadiness and rock-like imperturbability impressed everyone, but after sacking his second nominee, Lieutenant-General Ritchie, and temporarily taking command in the field himself, Auchinleck could clearly not continue both to command 8th Army at Alamein and the whole of the Middle East forces (including Palestine and Persia), centred at GHQ Cairo. A new commander of 8th Army was urgently needed – and it was with this in mind, especially, that

Brooke, as CIGS, had asked Churchill, at the end of July 1942, for permission to fly out to Cairo. In particular Brooke wanted to stop Auchinleck from appointing to the post a third 'dud': his chief staff officer in Cairo, Lieutenant-General T. Corbett. As Brooke later recalled, 'the situation in the Middle East was not improving; and the Auk was suggesting giving the Eighth Army to Corbett.'[3]

Brooke, intending to travel alone, had noted in a letter to his wife that 'the old ruffian [Churchill] is quite jealous that he is not coming with me!'[4] Brooke was speaking too soon. The day before he was due to leave for Egypt, Churchill announced he would go too; they would select the new commander of 8th Army together.

Churchill, a poor picker of men

As a strategist Churchill had no peer. As a picker of men, though, he was, like Auchinleck, far less well endowed. 'Winston wasn't a good judge of character, you know,' even the Prime Minister's loyal Military Assistant, Sir Ian Jacob, later recalled. Nevertheless, as the venerable historian of British intelligence, Ralph Bennett, narrated, Churchill was in the mood for action; he and Brooke 'flew to Cairo on 4 August. Decisions followed swiftly.'[5]

In fact, they didn't. Churchill and Brooke actually arrived after dawn on 3 August 1942, not 4 August, and decisions were certainly not swift. Accompanying the 'British High Command' group into Cairo and then out to view the battlefield at Alamein, Colonel Ian Jacob was an eye-witness to Churchill's four-day intercession over the command of 8th Army – in particular Churchill's insistence on appointing more duds. 'Being so unpredictable himself,' Jacob explained of Churchill, 'he liked dependability and loyalty on the part of others' – 'yes-men'.

Monty, back in England, was *persona non grata*: a no-man.

The quandary

Churchill was in a quandary. Virtually all his command appointments, as Minister of Defence since May 1940, had proved failures or worse. In June 1940, after Dunkirk, he had wanted Lord Gort to command BEF II, and had been amazed to find that no one agreed with him. He had made General Sir Edmund Ironside commander-in-chief of Home Forces – and had then been forced to dismiss him under pressure from his new coalition Cabinet. He had appointed General Dill as CIGS but had overrridden – and ridden over – him until Dill's spirit broke. He had then wanted to rid himself of Dill's successor, General Alan Brooke, but had so far not dared. He had pressed General Wavell into an abortive attempt to hold Greece and Crete against the Germans – thus surrendering the chance to take Tripoli, and secure the northern shores of Africa in 1941. He had then replaced Wavell by Sir Claude Auchinleck in June 1941. Once again he was losing faith in his appointee, as the 8th Army, despite greatly superior numbers of troops and tanks, and access to the highest grade Ultra intelligence, was trounced by Rommel and run back to Alamein. One further offensive would put Rommel in Cairo and Alexandria, only sixty miles from the front line.

In these circumstances, with Roosevelt and Stalin keen to see Anglo-American landings in Morocco and Algeria in October 1942 – Operation Torch – Churchill was in full agreement with the CIGS, General Brooke, that something must be done. But what? Before travelling to Egypt Churchill summoned a cabal of military advisers to meet him in Cairo – Wavell from India, Field-Marshal Smuts from South Africa, General Sir Maitland Wilson from Palestine – and over the subsequent four days they worked over a series of compromise solutions, all of which revolved around the knotty question of who should command 8th Army at Alamein?

Auchinleck's choice: a fathead

Brooke's first thought was to ask Auchinleck's opinion, once they met on the afternoon of 3 August 1942 in Cairo.

Unfortunately, General Auchinleck, as Freyberg noted, was an even worse picker of men than Churchill. The 'Auk' had appointed General Sir Alan Cunningham to command 8th Army, and then had to sack him three months later (under the pretext of 'a nervous breakdown'). He had then appointed his own deputy chief of staff, Lieutenant-General Neil Ritchie – and had had to sack him also, after the disaster at Gazala at the end of June 1942. Auchinleck had then been forced to take personal command of 8th Army in order to hold the front at Alamein – but in doing so had made his deputy chief of staff in Cairo, Major-General Dorman-Smith, his Ludendorff. Dorman-Smith's 'solution' for 8th Army's problems was to break up the army into more brigade groups and 'Jock Columns', on supposedly German lines – leading to a further crisis in morale. Meanwhile, Auchinleck had decided to appoint his Cairo chief of staff, Lieutenant-General Corbett, to command 8th Army – indeed, when Churchill and Brooke arrived at Heliopolis airport, the Prime Minister had been greeted by Corbett, who had explained he would take command of 8th Army as soon as Auchinleck returned from the front: 'I am to succeed him in command of the Army. In fact I have been living with my kit packed for the last week.'[6]

Even Churchill was stunned by Auchinleck's choice of Corbett as his *third* appointee to 8th Army. An Indian army cavalry officer, Corbett had been a chief instructor alongside Monty at Quetta in 1934. In the opinion of Major Bill Williams, who was GSO 2 (Intelligence) in Cairo for several months until he was moved to the desert, Corbett was 'uniquely stupid'.[7] Major-General Freddie de Guingand, who had been DMI in Cairo alongside Corbett, was equally deprecating; he called Corbett 'a complete fathead'.[8]

Listening to Auchinleck, Brooke could only shake his head in amazement. Even as a senior operations staff officer Brooke felt Corbett to be out of his depth. Brooke had, as he later noted, originally offered Auchinleck 'the whole of the Army to choose from for his Chief of Staff' and could not, in retrospect, credit Auchinleck's choice of Corbett in that role – let alone as 8th Army commander to fight Rommel in the crucial battle to defend Cairo!

Brooke therefore made clear his disagreement over Corbett's selection – and was afterwards backed by Churchill, who referred to Corbett as 'a very small, agreeable man, of no personality and little experience'.[9] But if not Corbett to fight Rommel in the field, then who?

Over the past fourteen months Churchill had considered Lord Gort, Sir Bernard Paget, Sir Robert Adam, Sir Maitland Wilson – but never Montgomery.

Churchill's hubris

While Brooke was interviewing Auchinleck, Churchill had been making his own soundings at GHQ with regard to a better choice for command of 8th Army. In particular he heard good things of a forty-three-year-old desert veteran, the commander of XIII Corps at Alamein: Lieutenant-General 'Strafer' Gott – a rifleman who came from the same regiment as Anthony Eden, the Foreign Secretary and former Minister of War. Acting on this hunch, Churchill immediately became determined to appoint Gott.

Churchill's insistence is in retrospect extraordinary, but all too characteristic for a Prime Minister who tended to get 'bees in his bonnet'. As Wavell's and Auchinleck's biographer, John Connell, noted, Churchill's judgement of both men and events was 'impaired' by his lifestyle, impetuosity and controlling character.[10] His doctor had advised him not to make the journey to Egypt and Russia, on account of the altitude at which he would have to fly and the consequent danger of a stroke – not to speak of the danger of being shot down by the Germans, or crashing. But Churchill had been adamant – and in the 'glimmering dawn', with Egypt and 'the silver ribbon' of the Nile below him, where he had fought against the 'natives' almost half a century before at the battle of Omdurman, all Churchill's own fantasies of military command and glory were reignited. 'Now for a short spell I became "the man on the spot". Instead of sitting at home waiting for the news from the front, I could send it myself,' he recorded. 'This was exhilarating.'[11]

It was also dangerously hubristic.

A tantalizing offer

The truth was, just as Auchinleck had sought to fight Rommel through a succession of inferior nominees, so also Churchill saw himself fighting the 'Desert Fox' through his own appointees – having broken all precedent by 'paying a handsome tribute' to the new German Feldmarschall in Parliament: 'We have a very daring and skilful opponent against us, and, may I say across the havoc of war, a great General.'[12] On another occasion Churchill would be heard to exclaim: 'Rommel, Rommel Rommel, what else matters but beating him?'[13]

Once Brooke was done on the afternoon of 3 August, therefore, Churchill himself interviewed General Auchinleck – and became furious when the 'Auk' refused to approve an immediate attack on Rommel's Panzer Army, whoever might be appointed to command the 8th Army.

Brooke had hardly slept aboard his converted bomber aircraft the nights before, and was 'dropping with sleepiness', as he noted in his diary. But Churchill, blessed with the ability to catnap, was fully awake and bent on action. 'Back to the same arguments that the Auk must come back to the Command of M[iddle] E[ast] and leave the Eighth Army,' Brooke noted. 'Exactly what I have always told him from the start. Then he argued strongly for Gott to take over'[14] – an officer Churchill had not even met. As Brooke reflected later, 'It is interesting to note that Winston was already selecting Gott without having seen him.'[15]

Brooke, by contrast, knew Gott, indeed remembered him quite well from before the war. He thought him a 'brilliant' armoured commander – but one who had been out in the Middle East since before the war even began, and was now, according to all accounts, tired, if not jaded by the mounting casualties and constant defeats at the hands of the Germans. Brooke's response was therefore negative.

Baulked by Brooke's arguments, Churchill now turned the tables – suggesting that Brooke himself take command of 8th Army!

Brooke's diffidence

This was a tantalizing offer. Could Brooke have outfought Rommel? It is tempting to think so, since Brooke's command of II Corps in the BEF indicated such great gifts of swift decision, at least in retreat. Moreover, Brooke was an artilleryman – and 8th Army desperately needed a new artilleryman. Yet, in a passage Sir Arthur Bryant omitted from his published version of Brooke's diaries and notes (*The Turn of the Tide*), Brooke noted his own diffidence: namely, that he had never served in the desert before, and would be at a disadvantage, given the rapid build-up of tanks, equipment and troops which Rommel was implementing. 'I shall have a job to convince him that I am unsuitable for the job having never been trained in the desert,' Brooke jotted in his diary.[16]

Gott, however, despite all his desert experience, was even more 'unsuitable', as even his own G2 (Ops) staff officer, Michael Carver, later admitted. 'He was a very tired man at Alamein' – with no practicable idea how to defeat Rommel without suffering more heavy casualties, which he was loath to do.[17] 'I'm the first to agree that he should never have been selected to command Eighth Army,' Carver reflected, 'though I had the greatest affection for him and admiration.'[18]

It is impossible to avoid the inference that Brooke, in listening to reports of Gott's tiredness and lack of tactical conviction, recognized to some degree his own: battered not only by the sleepless nights while flying, but by the interminable hours spent arguing with a Prime Minister/Minister of Defence who belonged to a past century – yet whose wit, rhetoric, feeling for history, sheer strategic brilliance and pulsating determination to attack the enemy never ceased to amaze and inspire.

Pressing for attack

Kept up by Churchill till 1.30 a.m. Brooke finally and gratefully found his bed. Sleep permitted him to think more clearly. When he awoke the next day he felt certain that Montgomery, not Gott, was the right man. After all, Monty had, ten years before, trained his battalion for several years in the self-same desert; moreover, as Brooke had just witnessed, Monty had recently completed in England a major ten-day exercise involving an offensive battle between an armoured army and an infantry army – Exercise Tiger – in order to rehearse extended combat and command involving armoured formations.

To Brooke's relief he found that not only Field-Marshal Smuts but General Auchinleck himself agreed! The notion of Corbett as 8th Army commander-elect was thus consigned to the dustbin – in fact, it was agreed that Corbett should be despatched straight back to India. In his stead, Auchinleck agreed on the afternoon of 4 August 1942, Monty would take command of 8th Army, while the exhausted 'Strafer' Gott would take over 9th Army from General Maitland Wilson, in Persia-Iraq, to head off any potential German breakthrough from the Caucasus. Auchinleck would resume his overall post as C-in-C Middle East.

But if Brooke, as head of the British army, thought he would be able to push through such appointments without difficulties being made by the Prime Minister/Minister of Defence, he was mistaken. In another three-hour session later that afternoon, 4 August, Churchill delivered a strategic overview of the war, and invited Auchinleck, the C-in-C Middle East, to tell the assembled generals and admirals when he proposed to attack Rommel. Not for another six weeks, answered Auchinleck.

'I could see that he [Churchill] did not approve of his replies,' Brooke noted in his diary that night. 'He is again pressing for an attack before Auchinleck can possibly get ready. I find him almost impossible to argue with on this point.' After dinner, things got worse. Far from approving Brooke's decision over Montgomery, as agreed with Auchinleck, Churchill became defiant. 'As I expected, my [day's] work was not approved of !' Brooke recorded, Churchill claiming that Montgomery 'could not possibly arrive in time to hurry on the date of the attack. I told him no one else could. He then pressed for Gott. I told him that I had discussed him with Auchinleck who did not think him up to it, and also that he was tired. I then told him about the project for moving [Maitland] Wilson as too old. He then said I was failing to make use of two of the best men; Gott and Wilson' – neither of whom Churchill knew, but both of whom Anthony Eden had extolled. 'I got even with him this time by suggesting that it was not astonishing that Eden should select old "Green Jacket" officers! . . .'[19]

Thinking back, in later years, Brooke was surprised that Auchinleck should have been prepared to accept Monty, given their earlier mutual animosity in Home Forces – an antagonism he felt would have worked against a Monty–Auk combination, if Auchinleck reverted to his role at GHQ Cairo, and Monty took command of the 8th Army. 'I felt that the Auk would interfere too much with Monty; would ride him on too tight a rein, and would consequently be liable to put him out of his stride.'[20]

Was it this concern, though, that made Brooke, at the time, confront the inevitable: deciding in his own mind that to have Monty in command of 8th Army would inevitably mean moving Auchinleck out of the Middle East?

Ironically, Churchill would take the equal view: that moving Auchinleck to another command would make way for a more dynamic, aggressive general. In Churchill's view, this would best be achieved by appointing his favourite protégé and aristocrat, General Sir Harold Alexander, as C-in-C Middle East, with Lieutenant-General Gott taking over 8th Army under him.

Churchill's brainwave

Even Churchill's preferred decision did not eventuate swiftly or straight-forwardly, for Churchill was a master of psychological manipulation. Brooke had said no to Gott. Barging in on the CIGS as he was getting up on 6 August, three days after their arrival – 'I was dressing and practically naked,' Brooke recorded[21] – Churchill announced he had had a new brainwave. After breakfast he revealed it: Brooke should take over from Auchinleck as C-in-C Middle East, with Monty as his 8th Army com-mander! 'This made my heart race very fast,' Brooke recorded in his diary.[22]

Brooke and Churchill had both flown out to the desert to visit 8th Army headquarters the previous day – and in interviews with numerous commanders and staff officers had formed fresh but still conflicting impres-sions. What was clear to both the CIGS and Prime Minister was that 8th Army desperately needed a new broom. The atmosphere had been depressing, the men they met hard, brave and confused by so many months of defeat, despite having an army that was rarely less than twice the size of Rommel's. Both Churchill and Brooke had met 'Strafer' Gott, but Churchill had flown straight back to Cairo after the desert breakfast near Alamein, while Brooke had spent the entire day visiting 8th Army formations, and having a further, long talk with Gott. As a result Brooke became, like Auchinleck, convinced that Gott was too tired to take com-mand of 8th Army, and had no practicable concept of how to beat Rommel.

Churchill, as was his wont, had felt the opposite. 'I had a long drive alone with Gott, and without making him any offer or suggestion I convinced myself of his high ability, charming simple personality, and that he was in no way tired, as was alleged,' Churchill wrote several days later to his wife Clemmie. 'One knows at once when one can make friends,' he added, in a telling phrase that explained the reason he was such a poor picker of men in contrast to phrases.[23]

Churchill's new brainwave of a Brooke–Montgomery combination, as in the BEF in 1939–40, however, now put Brooke on the spot: forcing Brooke either to assume the task with Monty (a general who, Churchill had said two days before, could not possibly reach Egypt in time to undertake the offensive action Churchill wanted), or to agree to Churchill's alternative solution: Generals Alexander and Gott.

Churchill's tactics showed, as always, remarkable acuity. Brooke was completely wrong-footed – his personal diffidence turning him from an implacable, often surly tiger into a more amenable, even obedient military aide; indeed, Brooke's diary entries and especially his later 'Notes on My Life' evince deep shame at the way he gave in to Churchill's subsequent decisions, once he had said no to his tempting offer – an offer Field-Marshal Smuts also pressed him to accept, promising him 'a wonderful future . . . if I succeeded in defeating Rommel'.[24]

Brooke was certainly torn. He lacked sufficient self-confidence to beat Rommel ('Thanked him for his kindness and told him he really did not know me well enough to be so assured I could make a success of it'[25]), and he had little desire to be demoted from CIGS to become merely C-in-C in Cairo, the butt of Churchill's impatient telegrams demanding premature offensives. Wavell and Auchinleck had both served in that capacity, and been found wanting by the Prime Minister; Wavell had been sacked, and Auchinleck was clearly about to be dismissed. Better to remain, Brooke felt, not only the all-important and universally respected head of the British army but chairman also of the British Chiefs of Staff Committee, out of the public limelight, controlling as best he could the wild schemes and fancies of his generalissimo – as well as spending Sundays with his beloved second wife, Benita, and their children, in the English countryside, watching birds.

Pained at having had to turn down the offer of an historic command, Brooke therefore caved in. By putting Brooke on the spot, the Prime Minister had got his way, once again: Brooke withdrew all objections to the Prime Minister's wishes. Alexander would now be appointed C-in-C in Cairo, 'Strafer' Gott the commander of 8th Army: two 'nice' men, neither of whom had any idea how to command an army successfully in the field against Rommel.[26]

Thus at 8.15 p.m. on the evening of 6 August, the fateful – indeed, for General Gott, fatal – signal was sent to the War Cabinet in London, recording the Prime Minister's decision. Alexander and Gott, two of Britain's most charming generals, were severally informed. For the one it would bring the glory Smuts had rightly prophesied; for the other, an almost immediate, painful death by burning.

Brooke's moment of weakness

How Brooke could have turned down his own chance to 'exercise command in the field', either as 8th Army commander or as C-in-C Middle East, is, for the historian and biographer, one thing.[27] How he can have, against his own better judgement, agreed to the choice of the exhausted 'Strafer' Gott as commander of the 8th Army, under General Alexander, is another matter.

General Alexander had become a master of retreat, in the final days of evacuation of Dunkirk in 1940 and Rangoon in 1942. 'Alex', as he was universally known, had never mounted a major offensive operation as a general, had performed poorly in manoeuvres with armoured formations in England, and had never served in the desert. Gott, by contrast, had served in the desert, but his credentials for beating Rommel were even poorer. As XIII Corps commander under Auchinleck's direct army command, he had ordered the fatal 8th Armoured Division attack against Rommel on 22 July 1942: the 'Balaclava charge' which wiped out an entire British armoured brigade. As one officer in the brigade recalled, the complacent assumption was that 'resistance would be light', and the British tanks were not to advance beyond El Daba – forty miles beyond Alamein! 'There was no attempt at concealment,' the officer narrated, 'and the enemy must have been well aware of our arrival.' Squandering their newly arrived forces on Rommel's anti-tank screen, some 106 British tanks had gone forward; only sixteen survived. The two-hour fiasco 'must have been the most ill-prepared and disgraceful episode of the whole war. There must have been a kind of madness at the Army Command, a feeling that there was a once and for all chance to drive the Axis forces back and that all risks must be taken in the hopes of success. The kindest thing that can be said is that tired men do make mistakes.'[28]

As Brooke knew, Gott had been in the desert too long. He had even confided privately to Brooke his conviction that 8th Army needed 'someone with new ideas and plenty of confidence in them', as Brooke later recalled;[29] 'it's time we had new people out here with new ideas. We've all had enough,' he told his own GSO 2 (Ops).[30] Gott's preference for a 'vast left-hook through Siwa' was not only impracticable, as his GSO 2 told him, but reflected Gott's inherent unwillingness to face up to Rommel again in frontal combat.

Generalissimo Churchill's mind was made up, however; if Brooke would not take command himself, then he, Prime Minister Winston Churchill, would decide who should – and Alexander and Gott were his choices. From Brooke's diary it is clear that Churchill and Smuts, on the afternoon of 6 August, took personal responsibility for the Alexander–Gott 'package' – though not, later, the rap for such idiocy at a critical moment of the war. Brooke, humbled by his refusal to take up Churchill's offer, was meanwhile summoned from a meeting at GHQ Cairo 'by the P.M. to meet him and Smuts and to read their final decision ... Considering everything, this is perhaps the best solution. I accepted it. Alexander is to fly out at once to take over ...'[31]

Casting his mind back to this decision which might well have lost World War II for the Allies, Brooke noted that he had 'very serious misgivings concerning Gott's appointment in his tired state, but was not at that time sufficiently convinced of the disadvantage to oppose the appointment. I may have been weak,'[32] he allowed – for he was, after all, the CIGS and therefore head of the British army.

At a critical juncture of the war, it was another appalling example of British muddle and high-command mismanagement – as a result of which over 100,000 8th Army soldiers had already been killed, wounded and captured since the previous autumn.

An ideal combination

The problem was, to some extent, Ultra – the decoding of high-grade German signals. Being able to read so many secret messages passing between German field commanders and Hitler's OKW and Mussolini's Commando Supremo headquarters, as well as German army–air and supply signals, Churchill was better informed about the enemy than he was about his own British forces! The Germans were constantly complaining about supplies and troops, in an effort to get more sent out to what was, in comparison with the Russian front, a subsidiary theatre. In consequence, the war looked all too often to Churchill a matter of logistics and matériel, not of command and communication – something practitioners and historians of intelligence rarely understood then or, sadly, later.

'Probably no time, except the early weeks of the Normandy landing two years later, saw so much Ultra so densely concentrated upon so short a front as the forty miles from the sea to the Quattara Depression along which the fighting now raged,' historian Ralph Bennett chronicled of July 1942.[33] Despite this information about the enemy, British forces continued to perform miserably on the field of battle. Privy to his Ultra 'eggs' every day, Churchill had reluctantly come to the conclusion that Auchinleck was not up to the business of using his superior forces to defeat Rommel – a reasonable deduction. But by appointing in his place 'charming' officers with whom 'one can make friends', Churchill was doing himself no favours – indeed, he was risking the entire course of the war. As John Connell noted, Churchill's service advisers faced the alternatives 'either of resigning or of complying with instructions which they believed to be dangerous, possibly disastrous'.[34] Attacking the Panzerarmee Afrika at Alamein without a complete overhaul and re-equipping of 8th Army was suicidal, following the disasters of June and July. For telling Churchill this unpalatable truth, Auchinleck was removed.

Churchill was, however, delighted with his replacement choices – imagining, as he wrote soon afterwards to his wife Clemmie, 'that Alexander with his grand capacities for war and Gott with his desert prowess and his hold on the troops would have made an ideal combination'.[35]

They would not. The truth, which neither Churchill nor his official biographer, Sir Martin Gilbert, was ever to realize, was that Alexander had no 'grand capacities for war' – at least, if he had them, nobody could identify them beyond English charm, courage, and Churchill's admiration of an aristocrat.

Generalissimo Churchill

Others certainly held the Hon. General Sir Harold Alexander in less high regard than Churchill. Lieutenant-General Slim, who served as corps commander under Alexander in Burma in the spring of 1942, was later scathing about Alexander's command during the retreat to India. 'I don't believe he had the faintest clue what was going on,' Slim confided to a colleague.[36] Asked why Churchill had such an exaggerated opinion of Alexander, Lieutenant-General Sir Ian Jacob later laughed aloud. 'My dear chap – "Alex" took part in Fowler's Match at Harrow!'[37] – the historic cricket match against Eton, when Fowler, captain of Eton, almost retrieved the game from a seemingly impossible position, and Alexander, as last man in, failed to save it, being caught for 8. *Wisden* designated the match 'without exaggeration' the 'most extraordinary ever played'.[38]

'On top of that,' as Jacob reflected, Alexander had been 'one of the youngest battalion commanders in the First World War. He had the qualities that appealed to Churchill – namely he had terrific courage, he liked to be under fire – and he looked the part' – even though, as Jacob remarked, having served under Alexander for a year as chief of staff after World War II, Alexander 'had no brains'. He 'never once produced a single idea, or suggestion during the entire time I served as his chief staff officer'.[39]

Major-General Eric Sixsmith, who also served under Alexander, was equally frank. 'There's no doubt about it. Alexander was an aristocrat and carried an air of complete confidence in himself. But what, if anything, went on inside his head, is a complete mystery.'[40]

Later, the Oxford don Sir David Hunt – who served as Alexander's head of intelligence – would endeavour to mask the mystery by lauding Alexander as a man with 'an unmistakable flash of genius', blessed by a 'fantastically active mind which was interested in everything from the sciences to the arts but which at the same time could also focus with blinding concentration on the problem before it'.[41] Hunt – who ghosted every word of Alexander's wartime despatches – was certainly blinded by loyalty; his portrait of Alexander is widely thought to have been displaced autobiography.

Hunt was not alone. The narcissist in Churchill, too, saw a fantasy-self in the suave Alexander, the Guards officer almost twenty years younger than himself – and was unworried by Alexander's small brain – indeed in certain respects Alexander's easy, empty-headed personality boded well for Churchill, who became more and more exhilarated at the prospect of being able to stay on in Cairo until the end of August. As the 'man on the spot', generalissimo Churchill could, through Alexander and Gott as his protégés, finally fulfil his dream of commanding, from his armchair, the forthcoming battle, as he had attempted to do during the Battle of Britain,[42] aided by his daily Ultra decrypts.

Time to move on

Churchill's fantasy-self as military commander had very nearly lost his country the Battle of Britain, after losing Norway and very nearly losing the BEF before Dunkirk, and BEF II after Dunkirk, in Brittany. His promotion of Captain Mountbatten had led directly to the fiasco of Dieppe, while his strategic and tactical errors and interference led to the disasters in Greece, Crete and North Africa. He was essential to Britain as the personal embodiment of defiance, in a world rapidly surrendering to the professional superiority of German forces, but he was also responsible for Britain coming near to losing the war by his military incompetence.

Churchill's promotion of Alexander to the job of C-in-C Middle East, however, meant that someone would have to replace Alexander as commander-elect of the Anglo-American northern task force in the forthcoming Operation Torch, targeted at the Algerian coast. For this post Churchill reluctantly agreed to the appointment of Montgomery, and orders to this effect were telegraphed by secret cypher to Whitehall.

It was while watching a major army exercise in Scotland as the guest of General Sir Bernard Paget, therefore, that Monty received, on 7 August 1942, a call from the War Office, telling him of his new northern task force appointment, under General Eisenhower, and summoning him back to London immediately.

In Whitehall that evening Monty was 'given more details' by an unimpressive brigadier. The brigadier, in turn, was unimpressed by Eisenhower, telling Monty 'that the first thing I must do was to get Eisenhower to make a plan for the operation; time was getting on and the Chiefs-of-Staff could not get Eisenhower' – whose chief of staff was still in America – 'to produce his plan,' as Monty later recalled.

'The whole thing did not sound good to me; a big invasion operation in North Africa in three months' time, and no plan yet made. Eisenhower I had barely met; I knew very few American soldiers and did not know how my methods would appeal,' he recalled in his memoirs, thinking of his difficulties with the Canadian generals McNaughton and Crerar. 'The crisis of the war was approaching and great events were to unfold. I was confident of being able to handle any job successfully if I was allowed to put into practice the ideas and methods that had become my military creed, and which by now I was convinced would bring us success in battle against the Germans. I returned to my Headquarters at Reigate hoping for the best; anyway I had now been two years in England – and it was time to move on.'[43]

Near-miss with Patton

Ironically, the other task force commander alongside whom Monty was to serve, under Eisenhower's overall command as C-in-C Allied Force Headquarters (AFHQ), was none other than General George S. Patton. At the American Desert Training Center, despite his age (almost sixty), Patton had impressed everyone by his energy and ambition, as well as his flair for tactical exercises. Indeed, in many ways Patton's self-preparation for modern war was the counterpart of Montgomery's, and from this flowed a similar conviction of the rightness of his own military tenets and beliefs. Just as Monty in England insisted on changing the name of south-eastern command to South-Eastern Army, so Patton in America had bullied colleagues and seniors into seeing that standardization and matériel were but half the American battle, and that there was a need for proper insignia and markings on all 'trucks and vehicles showing the company, regiment, and division to which they pertain . . . To die willingly, as many of us must,' Patton warned the head of American army training, 'we must have tremendous pride not only in our nation and in ourselves but in the unit in which we serve.'[44] Patton was certain he would one day be given the chance to fight against the Desert Fox and 'just to keep my hand in for Marshal Rommel'[45] he was in the habit of shooting at least a hare a day with his ivory-handled revolver.

Certainly there were many points of similarity between these two Allied task force commanders: both considered brilliant by many, mad by some – and intolerable by others. Yet there was, also, an intriguing difference in their military philosophy already at this stage of the war, as they both prepared to serve under General Eisenhower on Torch – a difference that made them, despite all other similarities, as variant as chalk from cheese. For Patton believed that the exercise of command in battle was an art and 'he who tries to define it closely is a fool'[46] – whereas it was Montgomery's deep-seated belief that command *could* be defined, and ought to be; ought to be something so clear, so widely known among his subordinate officers and troops, and so rehearsed, that victory over 'any enemy anywhere' was assured.

Despite this difference, both generals had now proved themselves as trainers and potential army commanders to the point where they had been selected to lead large national forces in Operation Torch – Patton having reported to Eisenhower in London earlier on 7 August 1942, ready to command the Western Task Force landing on the coast of Morocco. 'I am not, repeat not, pro-British,' he noted in his diary – indeed, his American biographer noted the first signs of a 'growing Anglophobia that reached manic proportions'.[47]

Monty arrived too late in the evening to meet Patton that day, but it was arranged they would get together the next day, 8 August 1942. Patton felt the Torch operation in Morocco was 'bad and is mostly political. However, we are told to do it and intend to succeed or die in the attempt.' Typically, Patton was afraid that Montgomery would be given the lion's share of the real fighting – indeed, Patton's diary for 8 August records the complaint he voiced at the conference, namely 'that Northern Task Force was being favored at expense of Western Task Force. Finally got some change . . .'[48]

The concession, however, was not at Monty's expense. Fate had almost thrown both men together – but not quite. For, as Monty shaved at his villa at Reigate early in the morning of 8 August, before leaving to meet Patton and Eisenhower in London, there was another urgent telephone call from the War Office. Orders regarding Torch were cancelled. He was to fly immediately to the Middle East and assume command of the British 8th Army at Alamein – where the army commander-designate had just been shot down and burned to death in a hospital plane, on his way to Cairo for an ill-considered bath and a rest.

Leaving David to a headmaster

For Monty, the summons to the desert was a godsend. 'Instead of carrying out an invasion of North Africa under a C-in-C whom I barely knew,' he later wrote, 'I was now to serve under a C-in-C [Alexander] I knew well and to take command of an Army which was at grips with a German and Italian Army under the command of Rommel – of whom I had heard great things. This was much more to my liking and I felt I could handle that business, and Rommel. So it was with a light heart and great confidence that I made preparations for going to Africa.'[49] His only anxiety, he added, concerned his thirteen-year-old son David, who was at school at Winchester.

On the spur of the moment he decided to ask the headmaster of David's former preparatory school, Amesbury, if he and his wife would take charge of David. Lest they decline for any reason, he put the request in writing rather than telephoning. 'My dear Tom,' he wrote hurriedly to Major Reynolds on the morning of 8 August 1942, 'I have to leave England at very short notice to take charge in a very important place. My destination will appear in the papers in due course. I have been given 8 hours in which to hand over, pack some clothes, and be off. I have not time to see David.' He then gave his step-daughter-in-law Jocelyn Carver's address in Berkshire, and her phone number. 'John Carver is on the Staff in Scotland, and may go anywhere. She (his wife) is not really capable of looking after David's affairs, though it is a very good place for him to go in the holidays whenever he likes.'

This was somewhat patronizing, considering that Monty had for weeks left his dying wife in young Jocelyn's care, and that David now went to stay with her every holiday. However, this was as yet a mild form of Monty's growing, almost pathological urge to reject members of his own family, after Betty died. 'Will you and your lady wife take charge of David for me until I return?' Monty asked the major. 'I would sooner leave him with you than with anyone I know. I am anticipating your acceptance of this task. There is really no one else who could do it. I am sure you will do this. I can never really repay you, but will do my best.'

Monty then enclosed a copy of his will – leaving 'everything I possess' to David – and £200 on account. 'I would like you to pay his school bills, buy his clothes, and in fact be his guardian so long as I am out of England. Give him whatever pocket money you think right. Last term I sent him to Winchester with £2 and gave him another £1 halfway through the term.'

Monty also enclosed David's latest school reports from Winchester. 'There is one thing I want you to watch,' he warned, however. 'His Grandmother is Lady Montgomery, New Park, Moville, Co. Donegal. She is an old lady and quite unable to take charge of anyone. She will want David to go and stay in Ireland for his holidays.

'*On no account is he to go.*

'She is a menace with the young.

'He can have very happy holidays with you, or the Blacklocks, or at

Littlewick Green with Mrs John Carver – this is 3 miles from Maidenhead on the Bath road.'[50]

The malevolence with which Monty referred to his mother raises many questions about Monty's state of mind in the summer of 1942. Whether it was the pressure of war, or his dedication to what he increasingly saw as his historic military vocation, he now saw his elderly mother as a threat – and would increasingly do so as time went on. The tension which seemed to grip him after Dunkirk had never relaxed – and would never now do so, at least not until Lady Montgomery was safely dead. By then Monty had quarrelled savagely at least once with almost everybody who had ever come to mean anything to him, had scandalized his family by his pretensions and his treatment of his mother, had 'insulted and injured' colleagues, seniors, subordinates, friends – and even, in a final irony, turned against the very son David whose custodianship he had, in the summer of 1942 and afterwards, so jealously guarded and apportioned.

All this was, however, in the future. In the meantime, on 8 August, Monty begged the Reynoldses to 'write and welcome' David as 'a No. 2 son'. He himself had written to David, whom he had not consulted in the decision and who might be 'rather upset when he gets my letter'. David was 'all I have left now', and he left him to the Reynoldses. He signed himself 'Monty'. Below this signature he added, somewhat indiscreetly: 'For your special information and not to be spoken about for a day or two, my address will be: HQ 8th Army, Middle East Forces'[51]

Terribly fond of you

Unfortunately, Monty's flight was cancelled that night, owing to bad weather. The following day, 9 August 1942, he wrote again from Reigate to reiterate his almost manic determination that no member of his family be allowed power or even the right to advise over David:

My dear Tom,

I am just off.

In case my letter (the long one) of yesterday did not make it clear, I want to say again that I put David in your complete and absolute charge. If any members of my family chip in and want to advise, see them right off. The sole authority in

EVERYTHING connected with David is yourself; I want you in fact to be his official guardian as long as I am out of England.

If I am killed his legal guardian is then John Carver. But I shall not be killed. Good-bye to you.

Yrs ever

B. L. Montgomery[52]

At Lyneham, weather conditions yet again delayed Monty's journey, and while waiting there he penned a very personal note to his former Canadian ADC, Trumbull Warren, whom he had begun to feel was a son to him as real as, or more real than, David. He explained to Trumbull he was 'off to Egypt to fight Rommel'. This was challenging, but disappointing in that Monty would not be in England when Trumbull returned from his staff training course to rejoin the Canadian army in Britain.

'I am delighted to go, but desolated that I shall miss you,' Monty confided. 'Perhaps we shall meet in the field of battle somewhere. I have at last got rid of Basil Price; it has taken 6 months. He is a very decent chap, but no soldier. Donald has left for Canada, also Gauvran (the French-Canadian A.D.C. who took your place) – both to the Staff College. So I have done my A.D.C.'s well and pushed them up the ladder. Good-bye my friend. Write to me in Egypt. My address will be: H.Q. 8th Army, Middle East Forces. I shall long to hear from you. If anything should happen to me in the contest with Rommel I would like you to know that I am terribly fond of you and often wished you were my own son. Yours always, B. L. Montgomery.'[53]

Such paternalistic expression of affection, at a time when Monty was leaving his real son in the care of an ex-headmaster rather than David's half-brother and his family, and instructing the headmaster to 'see off' any member of the Montgomery family who wanted to help out, raises serious questions about Monty's emotional and mental health at this time. Was he, like General Gordon when summoned to Egypt, verging on madness? Or was he simply driven to the edge of insanity by the lack of professionalism endemic in the British and Canadian armies, and thus able only to find emotional solace through his feelings for his young staff: young officers of whom he grew 'terribly fond', in the 'inverted', 'homoerotic' manner of Thomas Mann: admiring, male–male relationships in which his status as older man, commanding officer and military teacher allowed him to adopt a quasi-paternal attitude of affection, interest

497

and companionship – indeed, to wish he could 'adopt' the young man as his actual son?

Meanwhile, on the evening of 10 August, the skies cleared and Monty, having written to young Trumbull Warren from his heart, was able to leave England. He landed the next morning in Gibraltar, taking off in the evening for Cairo. 'During the journey I pondered over the problems which lay ahead,' he recalled later, 'and reached some idea, at least in outline, of how I would set about the business.'[54]

The question of his own, real son, insofar as Monty was concerned, had been resolved; that of his metaphorical offspring awaited him, in the Middle East. Once again, as so often in his military life, he was taking over a military command upon which he hoped to imprint his own distinctive authority. This time, however, it was at a turning point in World War II.

Playing prima donna

By the time Monty reached Egypt, on 12 August, Churchill and Brooke had flown off to Moscow, but General Alexander was in Cairo – and the outgoing C-in-C, General Auchinleck, also!

This was an awkward and unhappy situation, which Churchill had vainly attempted to avoid by sending his Military Assistant with a personal letter to the 'Auk' on 8 August – having 'learned from past experience that that kind of thing is better done by writing than orally'. In the letter Churchill had explained that he was removing Auchinleck from Middle East and 8th Army command, but was offering him instead – with the full concurrence of the War Cabinet in London – the new Persia-Iraq command he intended to create.

Flying back to Cairo from the desert front at Alamein, Auchinleck had turned Churchill's offer down in a stormy interview with Sir Alan Brooke the next day. Brooke had 'tried to soften the blow as much as I possibly could', but he was not a man to allow Auchinleck to play prima donna. Brooke had himself turned down 8th Army command when offered it by the Prime Minister – indeed, the Middle East Command also – but this was different. Brooke, at least, had proved himself a titan in his job; Auchinleck had proved a failure in his. It was thus, in his view, 'unsoldierly' of Auchinleck to decline.[55]

In truth, Brooke had already entertained second thoughts about offering Auchinleck any further command – Churchill even going so far, the next day, as to write to his wife of the 'Auk': 'He has made a continuous succession of bad choices, each of whom has had to be removed after a disaster and of those that were left I am making a thorough clearance.'[56] Thus when Auchinleck spoke 'like an offended film star', Brooke considered him to be ungrateful and out of touch with the reality of the situation. He felt he had himself turned down Auchinleck's job for the good of his country's cause, whereas Auchinleck was responding like a miffed child. 'In the end I had no alternative but to turn on him and put him in his place,' Brooke later recorded, 'he left me no alternative.' Nor was Brooke one to mince his words when dealing with a difficult subordinate. 'I had to bite him back as he was apt to snarl, that kept him quiet,' he noted with a certain sardonic pleasure.[57]

The 'Auk', so long the highest power in the Middle East, had been brought down to earth. Nevertheless, Brooke's irritation over Auchinleck's petulant response festered, and a few months later, when the question arose of making Auchinleck the C-in-C India, again, he wired to General Wavell: 'I have lost all confidence in him as a commander. He is bad in the selection of men to serve him and has a faulty conception of modern war.'[58]

The wounded lion's den

Whether Brooke's put-down in Cairo made Auchinleck doubly offended – and thus doubly offensive to Monty when he arrived – is a moot point. Auchinleck had, after all, done his best in a difficult struggle against a German commander whose tactical brilliance on the battlefield made desert victory an elusive goal. By taking personal command of 8th Army and counter-attacking Rommel throughout July, however poorly, Auchinleck had sacrificed many brave men's lives but had certainly 'stopped the rot', giving 8th Army time to lick its wounds in early August, regroup and take stock while Rommel brought up more men, tanks and supplies. His pride was therefore deeply hurt by his own dismissal – the more so as it had not been done face to face by the Prime Minister, but by courier and then the abrasive interview with the CIGS. Churchill's letter had informed him that Alexander would be arriving 'almost immediately' and had

directed him to hand over Middle East command 'early next week' – i.e.,
Monday 10 August, or the day after – 'with the utmost smoothness and
efficiency'.[59] Upset by Churchill's refusal to see him face to face, and
mauled in the subsequent acerbic encounter with Brooke in Cairo, Auchinleck now decided to dig in his heels. With Brooke and Churchill out of the
way in Moscow, he approached the handover of 8th Army command to
Montgomery in a deliberately sullen and resentful frame of mind.

Having taken a bath at the Mena House Hotel and breakfasted, and
having sent his personal aide, Captain Spooner, to buy desert clothes on
arrival on the morning of 12 August 1942, Monty was driven to GHQ
to meet Auchinleck in person. The resulting interview, at 10 a.m. in
Auchinleck's map room, was an historical calamity – indeed in some ways
would lead to more bickering between historians than the famous battle of
Alamein, as historians and journalists later took sides. Using an alternative
metaphor, it was as if a distinguished but tiring heavyweight boxer had
fought with and lost to a bantamweight – and for the rest of his life
disputed the verdict.

Auchinleck's warning

Undoubtedly Auchinleck meant well. After all, had he not been the first
man in Egypt to suggest Monty as 8th Army commander – under his own
continuing Middle East command? Was it not Auchinleck himself, after
all, who had created the 8th Army in November 1941 – and who had
saved it from the ultimate catastrophe at the end of June, when it looked
as if Rommel might not only take Tobruk but race through to seize
Alexandria and Cairo also?

Monty, arriving out of the literal blue of the Mediterranean sky, saw it
all differently. For him the 8th Army was no longer Auchinleck's army; it
was an unfortunate Commonwealth army that had been flung back a
thousand miles across North Africa by a victorious German panzer general. Monty was not interested in excuses, long-winded predictions or
warnings: he wanted to shake things up. Thus the interview was as fateful
as with General Lord Gort, the commander-in-chief of Britain's army at
Dunkirk, on 30 May 1940. Just as Monty had then borne away the
impression of a defeated commander, about to order the surrender of the
BEF rearguard under Lieutenant-General Barker, so now his piercing

grey-blue eyes studied, and scorned, the face of the soldier he was to replace as commander of 8th Army.

He remembered how he had succeeded Auchinleck once already, as commander of V Corps in July 1940 – and the furious disagreements they had had when Monty instantly reversed Auchinleck's policy of static beach defence, and had sacked most of Auchinleck's 'useless' personnel. Since those difficult days in Home Forces, under threat of German invasion, Auchinleck's star had risen – but had now finally imploded. He had reaped the harvest of his own inabilities as a commander, after fourteen months of desert campaigning, and as a consequence had been dismissed by the Prime Minister. 'He asked me,' Monty recalled, 'if I knew he was to go. I said that I did.'[60] Yet instead of simply handing over 8th Army to Monty with his blessing, Auchinleck stupidly insisted on briefing Monty on his *own* plans for the 8th Army – whose commander, he began by announcing, he would remain, in defiance of Churchill's orders, until the end of the week!

Brushing away Monty's questions about current British plans for attack, Auchinleck explained the 8th Army was resting and refitting. It had suffered over 100,000 casualties during the past few months – a catastrophic number which meant that, whatever the Prime Minister might say, there could be no question of an immediate British offensive. On the contrary, it was known from British Ultra intelligence that Rommel was building up huge stocks of fuel, ammunition, tanks, troops and supplies for another German panzer offensive, to be launched probably before Roosevelt's promised shipment of 300 American Grant and Sherman tanks arrived and was unloaded at Suez. If Rommel proved successful in this attack, it was imperative that the 8th Army not be allowed to become fragmented and destroyed. As the only coherent, battleworthy British army in the Middle East, contingency plans had therefore been made for part of the army to withdraw up the Nile, the other part into Palestine, barring German access from the south to the oilfields of Abadan, and from the north via the road through Persia and Iraq to the Indian Ocean, which were, in Auchinleck's view, even more important than Egypt. These plans for contingency withdrawal were being prepared personally by one of his subordinates, the deputy chief of the general staff, Major-General John Harding, a former student of Monty's.

'I listened in amazement,' Monty recounted in his memoirs, 'but I quickly saw that he resented any question directed to immediate changes in policy about which he had made up his mind.'[61] For once, Monty remained speechless – though with shock at what he saw as Auchinleck's 'defeatist' stance.

Monty's caricature

Did Monty exaggerate Auchinleck's pessimistic briefing? There can be no doubt, as will be seen, that exaggeration was one of Monty's techniques in dealing with both human and military problems. As a caricaturist does, he would observe intently, sketch an outline in his mind containing all the essentials of the matter under review, and then bring forth an impression, brilliantly clear to all. Often that impression was distorted – even grotesquely so; but in the main it was frank, sincere – and always arrestingly simple.

Monty's caricature of Auchinleck on 12 August 1942 was recorded in his diary. It would remain unaltered for the rest of his life: that of a toppled general, resentful of his fall, and bankrupt of military hope – an image confirmed by contingency plans Monty soon found proliferating both at GHQ and at 8th Army: plans for a possible British withdrawal from Alamein.

No problem

Monty saw no possible reason for withdrawal plans – actual or contingent. Not only were they bad for staff morale, but they were, in his view, unnecessary. He had been rehearsing large-scale military operations for two years in Home Forces. He was a master of training, at every level; of the use of artillery, and the management of reserves, both in defence and attack. From Auchinleck's office he therefore went straight to find his old comrade-in-arms from Dunkirk and Home Forces, General Sir Harold Alexander, the C-in-C-elect. 'During the journey out by air I had considered the problem very carefully. It was clear to me that what was wanted in Eighth Army was a reserve Corps, very powerful, very well equipped, and very well trained. This Corps must be an armoured Corps; it must never hold static fronts; it would be the spearhead of all our offensives,' he later wrote, ignoring the immediate threat posed by Rommel's gathering offensive. 'The Germans had always had such a reserve formation – the Panzer Army – which was always in reserve and was highly trained.

'We had never had one; consequently we were never properly "balanced" and we had never been able to do any lasting good. I came to the conclusion that the formation, equipping, and training of such a reserve Corps must be begun at once and must be a priority commitment.'

In truth, as Field-Marshal Lord Carver later pointed out, Rommel's Afrika Korps – comprising 15 and 21 Panzer Divisions, as well as 90th Light Armoured Division, and Italian armoured and motorized units – was less a reserve corps than the very core of the Panzer Army itself, applied in divisional strength or in smaller units as the tactical situation demanded. But about its training and flexibility Monty was not mistaken. The answer, Monty had decided en route, was to create a British Afrika Korps.

'Immediately on arrival in Cairo on the morning of 12 August, I put the project to General ALEXANDER,' Monty noted in his diary of events in August. 'He agreed, but we had to be very careful as he was not yet C-in-C. It was obviously useless to discuss the matter with General AUCHINLECK or the CGS [Chief of the General Staff, Lieutenant-General Corbett], so I put the question, quietly and unofficially, to the DCGS (Gen. HARDING) and asked him to prepare a paper on the subject and to say definitely whether such a reserve Corps could be formed from existing resources. There were 300 new Sherman tanks due at Suez on 3 September, and these would provide the equipment for the Armoured Divisions.'[62]

What was clear was that, however mistaken as to Rommel's combat command, Monty was completely unfazed by the Panzer Army's impending offensive; it was his own offensive he wished to start preparing.

Conducting the desert war

General Harding remembered the interview well. By 12 August 1942 rumours had begun to circulate about an imminent change in command, so that when, that afternoon, he was sent for by the commander-in-chief, Harding had asked, 'Who is the C-in-C?'

No one seemed sure. In the C-in-C-designate's office Harding found

Monty – characteristically –' sitting in the C-in-C's chair at the desk', while Alex sat on the desk 'drumming his heels. Monty greeted me, introduced me to Alex and explained the posts they had been appointed to.

'"Now you've been out here for some time, John," Monty went on. "You know all the people in these parts; I want you to tell me something about them, who's good and who's no good." And for about an hour he put me through a long questionnaire about all the commanders and formations in the desert at that time down to the brigade level.'[63]

It was clear to Harding who would be conducting the desert war, from now on.

Disagreeable to the enemy

In his diary on the night of 8 August, Brooke had foreseen exactly such a situation. 'I knew that Monty was far better qualified to command the Eighth Army than Alex, and I did not want Alex to be encouraged to interfere with Monty,' he noted.[64] He had been able to convince Churchill of the need to summon Monty immediately, once news of Gott's death had reached Cairo, but he had also taken the time, before flying to Moscow, to warn Alexander in person not to take umbrage at Monty's rude and dictatorial mannner.

Gott's death had shaken Churchill, but once Brooke had overridden his objections, Churchill had swallowed the pill, and had begun indeed to see that Brooke's faith in Monty was not personal but professional. 'In Montgomery, who should be here on Tuesday,' Churchill wrote to his wife Clemmie, 'we have a highly competent, daring and energetic soldier, well-acquainted with desert warfare. If he is disagreeable to those about him,' he now mused, 'he is also disagreeable to the enemy.'[65]

This was the crux of the matter. At last, after three years of disastrous failure, including more than two years as British Prime Minister and Minister of Defence, Churchill had awoken to the brutal fact: war on the modern battlefield against a professional and indoctrinated enemy could not be won by appointing friendly faces.

Serving two masters

Monty was not out to be friendly – indeed, he was completely unafraid to be obnoxious if required. In the desert diary that he now began to write up, he was candid about Auchinleck ('very difficult to deal with'); about Auchinleck's chief of staff ('quite useless'); and Auchinleck's vice-chief of staff ('a menace'). However, in John Harding he had found 'a first-class officer who had been a student under me at the Staff College . . . HARDING seemed to me to be the only officer at GHQ who talked sense, and who obviously knew what he was talking about. The DMO [Director of Military Operations] and DMI [Director of Military Intelligence] were, in my opinion, quite unfit for their jobs.'[66]

This was Monty language – which Harding also spoke and understood. As Harding later memorably recalled of 8th Army and GHQ, 'nobody knew whether they were standing on their arse or their elbow. The army had got completely mucked up: I think the word bewildered describes it better than any other word I can think of.' He certainly had no truck with acolytes and fans of Auchinleck who later claimed 8th Army was poised to win victory in the desert, and that Monty merely stole the mantle of success from its rightful owner. 'The German advance had run out of steam,' he recalled candidly. 'The 8th Army had come to rest where it had come to, and was in a defensive position – more or less on the Alamein position, but it was really more where it had come back to than any organization of the Alamein defensive position as such. Very little had been done to fortify it, as far as I remember.

'As far as the atmosphere in Cairo was concerned . . . Nobody was at all sure – I mean nobody was in any doubt that sooner or later Rommel would resume the offensive, and then it was a matter of conjecture whether the Alamein position would be held or not. And so the Auk decided to have plans prepared for a withdrawal. And these plans were duly prepared. I myself was involved, as DCGS, because I was given the job, in the event of withdrawal taking place, of trying to delay the German advance into the delta by holding a series of canal lines and so on. I had a temporary staff, a small number of staff officers and DRs [despatch riders], on a very temporary and sketchy basis. The plan was that part of the army should withdraw into the delta and should make its escape into Sinai, and the other lot would go down south into the Sudan . . . How far it was widely known I wouldn't like to say – but certainly I knew about it, and took it seriously, because personally I was quite uncertain that the 8th Army on the Alamein position could hold its own against a further offensive by Rommel.'[67]

Typically, Monty wished to hear nothing about withdrawal. 'You see,' Harding recounted, 'one of Monty's great points in his teaching at the Staff College, Camberley, when I was a student there, was that the critical thing in war was to gain and keep the initiative. And I guessed he'd already made up his mind before he arrived on the scene that he would have to fight a major battle in order to get the initiative, and to keep it. And in order to do that he would have to reorganize and revitalize the 8th Army. Those were the things he'd probably made up his mind about; how to do it, he probably kept an open mind about. And this is why he wanted to hear from me personally about the state of the army, the confidence of the various commanders and how he could reorganize the army.'[68]

Harding was quite forthright about the state of the army. 'I remember going through all the formations and telling him about them and about their commanders – that at brigade and divisional level they were very good and efficient and morale was very good. But as a total, no, they were disorganized and they were rattled. They had lost their confidence. And he then asked me, "Well I want to form a *corps de chasse* in order to be able to carry out a major offensive and drive the German–Italian forces out of Egypt and Cyrenaica." And he asked me, he'd got in mind having two armoured divisions and a mobile infantry division and how could this be organized? I said: "And I presume to hold the front at the same time?" And then I said, yes, I thought I could produce a plan to do this.

' "Well, I've got to go now with the C-in-C, General Alexander, to see the ambassador. Can you get on with it for me?" Monty asked. I said yes, if you don't mind it being in my own handwriting I can have it ready in an hour or so. So Monty went off with Alex and I went to my office, where I locked the door and got down to produce those two armoured divisions and mobile infantry division as a main striking force to drive the Axis army out of the desert.'[69]

Ironically, Harding was now serving two masters. Under General Auchinleck's command he had been charged with the preparation of plans for 8th Army's possible withdrawal to the delta, Khartoum and Sinai; for Lieutenant-General Montgomery, plans for a *corps de chasse* in driving Rommel out of Egypt and Cyrenaica!

An amazing state of military affairs

Monty, having seen the ambassador and 'spent the afternoon buying clothes suitable for the desert in August', was delighted by Harding's secret list of formations and units once he saw it: no fewer than three possible armoured divisions and one mobile infantry division with its own armoured brigade. 'Harding produced a plan that looked good and we decided to adopt it,' Monty noted in his diary.[70] However, to plan such a reorganization and to put it into practice were two different things. It was now Wednesday 12 August 1942. Auchinleck had stipulated that the handover of both commands was not to take place before the end of the week, Saturday; moreover, he had made clear that, although Montgomery might in the meantime visit 8th Army, he was to wait until Saturday before assuming command. Were Rommel to attack before then, Auchinleck was emphatic that he himself would resume command of 8th Army in the field, not Monty.

In retrospect it was an amazing state of military affairs, at the cardinal moment in a world war, as Churchill travelled to meet Stalin in Moscow: Churchill's newly appointed Middle East C-in-C and 8th Army commander not only shackled, but driven to feel they could not openly suggest any change of plans or army reorganization for a further three days, lest they upset the outgoing C-in-C, who had been sacked!

Terrified out of his wits

It was in this bizarre situation that Monty asked Alexander's assistant if he could recommend a second personal aide, or ADC, to accompany him to the desert. The recommendation was Gott's ADC, a twenty-three-year-old officer in the 11th Hussars, Captain John Poston MC, an ex-Harrovian armoured-car commander who 'had hardly left school when the war began', but who had been fighting in the desert since 1940, save for one spell in Persia.

Captain Poston had originally been ordered to drive General Gott's car from Alamein to Cairo to be used there during Gott's brief leave before he took formal command of the 8th Army; Poston had thus been spared Gott's tragic fate on his flight back to Cairo, when the air-ambulance, ferrying badly wounded men, had been forced down by German Messer-schmitts and engulfed in flames, with its fuselage door jammed shut.

Poston 'could see I was a lieut-general and he knew I wanted an A.D.C.; but he had never heard of me before', Monty recalled. Explaining who he was, and his new appointment, Monty asked if he would 'come to me as my A.D.C.'. Poston was 'clearly somewhat startled; this was highly secret news, known to very few. He didn't answer at once; he just looked at me, straight in the face. He looked sad; he had just been with Gott, who was known all over the Middle East and was obviously a hero to all young officers. And now his master was dead,' Monty recorded. 'I said nothing, but just waited for his answer: looking into a pair of steady grey eyes. At last he said: "Yes, sir; I would like to come with you." '[71]

In a letter home Poston gave a more shorthand account of the new appointment, describing how he had just driven back from Cairo to XIII Corps to headquarters to collect Gott's personal belongings, passing the burnt-out wreckage of the plane and Gott's grave on his way back to Cairo, when Alexander's ADC suddenly asked 'if I wanted to carry on with the new Army Commander – I said "Yes O.K"!! & went to GHQ at 5 & saw him & all was well. He terrified me out of my wits, but I reckoned I could do it OK. So that was fixed.'[72]

Terrifying or not, it was Monty's first conquest in the Middle East. Leaving Poston to arrange the disposal of Gott's personal belongings, Monty set off to dine with the British ambassador, Sir Miles Lampson, together with Alexander, and also to stay the night at the embassy. Meanwhile, he ordered a car to be ready before dawn the next morning. It was time, he reckoned, to see his new army – on the battlefield.

The Star Chamber

Harding was not alone in his sense of frustration at the way things were sliding in Egypt. 'To me the Auk seemed a defeated man,' the GSO 1 (Plans) at 8th Army under Auchinleck later recalled. 'A man of very great personal stature and integrity who had carried an enormous load, but a defeated man. We used to meet the Auk every night in his [8th Army] caravan about 9 o'clock – just about six of us – to review the day's operations, and to plan the future. Now this was very depressing: there seemed to be very little inspiration and certainly no optimism. Perhaps I was expected to provide it, but I think Winston Churchill talked of 8th Army at that time as "Brave but baffled." I was certainly baffled.'[73]

This was Colonel Charles Richardson, later General Sir Charles Richardson, who was in charge of plans for operations five to seven days in advance. To him, the latter-day references by devotees of Auchinleck to a 'First Alamein' in July 1942 were as specious as they were to Harding. 'I myself had to draw up plans for a withdrawal to Khartoum, and there were others. If you'd spoken to the front-line soldier you'd have got the answer: "there's no question of retreat"; but, the higher up you got, the more the idea of a strategic withdrawal seemed probable,' Richardson confided[74] – having duly drawn up secret plans for a retreat to the Sudan! Of the claims by British historians such as John Connell, Basil Liddell Hart, Roger Parkinson, Correlli Barnett, Philip Warner, Sir Harry Hinsley and others, that Auchinleck's counter-attacks in July 1942 had constituted the battle of 'First' Alamein, Richardson was derisory – for he had been there. 'At the time I certainly was quite unaware that we were "stabilizing". All I was aware of was a chaotic series of attacks scraped together, which to my mind at the time could scarcely have been said to have succeeded. My feeling at that time was that we were improvising reactions, and that this would continue until Rommel would put in a proper attack and that would be the end of it.'[75] As Richardson reflected, 'Long after the war, in the historical process of allocating credit, some writers have attempted to glorify those weeks of piecemeal uncoordinated attacks under the title "The First Battle of Alamein".' Richardson treated this new historians' myth with contempt. 'I can state from my continuous presence as GSO 1 (Plans) throughout those weeks, that no battle entitled to the name "First Alamein" ever took place.'[76]

Richardson had joined Auchinleck at Alamein at the end of June 1942. 'In my own mind, I had no doubt that our situation marked a desperate crisis in the war. If we lost Egypt, the strategic implications were appalling.' Looking at General Auchinleck, he wondered: 'Was this general capable of lifting us out of dire disaster? I thought not. My conclusion was partly influenced by Auchinleck's inability to make effective use of his staff,' he considered, for Auchinleck 'seemed to lack the art of successful delegation, nor did he seem to spend a great proportion of his time visiting his forward commanders, bending them to his will. When I observed him, day after day, sitting in the sand spending long hours staring through binoculars at the distant void horizon I asked myself: "Has he anything left to offer?"'[77]

Richardson felt that Auchinleck hadn't – and was scraping the bottom of an empty barrel for ideas. 'A feature of Auchinleck's method of command had been to hold a daily conference with his principal staff officers in his map lorry every evening about 9 p.m.,' Richardson recalled. 'This was intended to keep the staff fully advised of the C-in-C's intentions. At this conference attended by the BGS (Ops) and the four lieutenant colonels,' Auchinleck's *éminence grise*, a self-appointed supernumerary DCGS from GHQ Cairo, Major-General 'Chink' Dorman-Smith, 'had invariably dominated the discussions, for which there had been neither an agenda nor an established patttern.'[78]

Richardson could hardly credit how the rabbit-toothed Dorman-Smith had managed to jump a rank to major-general with no battlefield or even higher staff experience (he was later dismissed for appalling leadership as a brigadier at Anzio). Richardson had known Dorman-Smith in India and in Palestine. 'His vigorous, restless and inventive mind was continually looking for clever, unconventional and daring solutions to the dire battlefield problems with which Rommel confronted us. Few if any of these solutions were attuned to the capabilities of Eighth Army, which had recently been disastrously defeated. Moreover, Chink was seldom content with pursuing only one solution. Ideas in plenty from the top of his head were liberally distributed, larded with Irish "blarney", to any listeners available in our small group, more particularly, at the "Evening Prayer" session which six of us attended every evening in General Auchinleck's caravan ... The prayer meetings were very depressing; nothing very constructive by way of seizing the initiative ever emerged'[79] – save for Dorman-Smith's proposal, submitted on the back of an envelope, for the next battle, when, as expected, Rommel would attack 8th Army.

About Dorman-Smith's idea Richardson was caustic. 'We all expected Rommel to make one final push in the hope of reaching Cairo. Chink was still in ebullient form, and confided to me the tactical scheme which he had "sold" to the C-in-C; his notes, in a clear round childish hand were on the back of an envelope. I can see them still! This was the theme: on warning of the attack, Eighth Army would withdraw seven miles from their prepared positions. En route, divisions would regroup in two new "Chinklike" varieties of battle group': some taking static roles in 'Defended Observation Posts', situated on the tops of the natural 'pimples' parallel to the coast road, the others fighting 'mobile battles against Rommel's seasoned battle groups (the recent victors of Gazala) in Chink's chosen "killing ground", dominated by the OPs.

'It would be difficult to conceive,' remarked General Richardson, 'a tactical plan more unsuited to the units of the Eighth Army at that time. Depressed by defeat, dismayed by heavy casualties, and disillusioned by the collapse of all their hopes, they were in no mood to leave the comparative security of fixed positions, then marry up with units with whom they had never trained, and emerge without pre-tested radio communications in mobile manoeuvres against an enemy who had proved himself master of this form of fighting.'[80]

Fortunately, Dorman-Smith's days of influence were numbered, even before Monty arrived. When 'Chink' told Richardson that the Prime Minister would be visiting 8th Army the next morning – 5 August 1942 – Richardson 'did not at first grasp its significance' – but Dorman-Smith did.

' "I'm for the Star Chamber tomorrow, Charles," he said, having asked Richardson to his tent for a drink.

' "What do you mean?" I replied.

' "I'm going to be sacked."

'I made a friendly reply, but in my heart thought *"thank God"*.'[81]

The 8th Army desperately needed a new commander, and a new approach to planning and training, as everyone save Dorman-Smith – and later acolytes such as the historian Correlli Barnett – agreed. 'We youngsters felt that the removal of Auchinleck was essential,' Richardson recalled.[82]

De Guingand

Brigadier Freddie de Guingand, who had succeeded 'Jock' Whiteley as chief operations staff officer of 8th Army at the end of July 1942, had loyally commiserated with Auchinleck after he was sacked by courier; indeed, in a charming letter of condolence, de Guingand had called it a victory for 'the old privileged school';[83] in reality, however, he accepted that the army desperately needed 'new blood'. Wise beyond his years, de Guingand therefore warned Auchinleck, as he had warned Mr Hore-Belisha when he was sacked as Minister of War, not to take umbrage and turn down Churchill's Persia-Iraq offer ('this paltry and grimy sop' as Auchinleck's biographer later called it[84]), as 'Chink' Dorman-Smith advised, but to accept Churchill's offer with dignity.

De Guingand's well-meant advice had been rejected – Auchinleck thus remaining in Cairo, in defiance of Churchill's orders, contemplating his future in much the same way as he had recently scanned the seemingly empty desert horizon, while insisting upon hanging on to his two jobs as C-in-C Middle East and 8th Army commander to the last possible moment, before Churchill returned from Moscow.

It was in this way that, to de Guingand's surprise, a signal had come through to 8th Army headquarters on 12 August, from Auchinleck's headquarters in Cairo, instructing de Guingand to meet Lieutenant-General Montgomery at the crossroads outside Alexandria at 7 a.m. the next morning. Was Monty a visitor to the front, or was he now 8th Army commander? De Guingand was apprehensive – wondering whether Monty would keep him in his new job as BGS (Ops).

De Guingand had known Monty since the early 1920s, even served under him on manoeuvres in this selfsame desert in 1933, and had got into Staff College on Monty's personal recommendation. Monty was an ascetic, however, while 'Freddie' – as everyone called the handsome bachelor – was a *bon viveur*. Moreover, as de Guingand also knew, Monty operated the continental command system, where the chief of staff controls *all* the staff, and acts as the commander's veritable deputy in his absence. At a critical moment in the war, if Monty became 8th Army commander, would he not wish to bring in his own trained chief of staff from England?

De Guingand slept badly.

Napoleon and Berthier

Monty almost didn't keep de Guingand on – in fact, he had more or less decided in his own mind that he wouldn't. His first few hours at GHQ Cairo had convinced him that a radical shake-up was needed – and he had been rehearsing such shake-ups ever since Dunkirk: at V Corps, XII Corps, and South-East Army Command. He wanted, for example, his chief gunner at South-East Army, Brigadier Kirkman, to come out immediately, as also Lieutenant-Generals Oliver Leese and Brian Horrocks as fresh corps commanders. He wanted other officers too – in particular his efficient chief of staff at XII Corps, Brigadier Simbo Simpson, currently deputy Director of Military Operations at the War Office.

De Guingand, however, had certain advantages over white-kneed officers in Britain. After serving as Hore-Belisha's Military Assistant in

1939–40, the handsome, debonair and fun-loving de Guingand had become a senior aide to General Wavell in the Mediterranean and Middle East in 1941, and been retained by Wavell's successor, Auchinleck, who made him Director of Military Intelligence in Cairo – despite his lack of intelligence training – and subsequently BGS (Ops), of 8th Army, two weeks before Monty's arrival. He lacked proven skills in running a large operations staff, but his grasp of intelligence – particularly Ultra – and his knowledge of the main *dramatis personae* would, Monty reasoned, be of great potential value.

A few hours in the car with Freddie de Guingand convinced Monty he should at least keep his protégé 'on appro'. As Monty later explained to a colleague, he had 'spotted' de Guingand 'as a very intelligent young officer', when Freddie was 'about 22' and Monty 'about 35'. Monty had been immediately drawn to the young subaltern; indeed, it would have been hard not to have attracted by the effervescent, engaging, blue-eyed young officer, with his infectious sense of humour, his *joie de vivre*, and his lack of respect for 'authority'. 'His life in those days revolved around wine, women, and gambling – in all of which he excelled!!' Monty later recalled with amusement and affection. (Indeed, as Monty noted, de Guingand was just the same, forty years on: 'Wine, women, and gambling – that is still his life!!')[85]

It would be in the role of chief of staff that de Guingand would find his historic métier, Monty later considered – for which, in 1932, there had been an interesting desert rehearsal, not far from Alamein. 'On a Bde. Exercise, I was made to command the Brigade and asked for Freddie as my Brigade-Major. We completely defeated the enemy in the Mena House area!' Monty recollected. 'He revels in responsibility, and accepts it readily,' he went on – but it was the responsibility of backing up a field commander, not as a potential field commander himself. 'He is not a commander in any sense of the word; the highest command he ever held was a platoon,' Monty made clear. 'As a staff officer he was superb in my opinion. As a Chief of Staff he had no equal, again in my opinion. It is difficult to compare him with other Chiefs of Staff, because there were none. I introduced the system when I made him Chief of Staff of the Eighth Army at 6.30 p.m. on the 13th August 1942,' Monty claimed. 'Freddie was in fact, the first proper Chief of Staff in the British Army – and right well did he carry it through. You can take Haig and Kiggell, Gort and Pownall, but they had not the same powers, being merely C.G.S. [Chief of the General Staff]. You would have to go back to Napoleon and

Berthier, to get the comparison,' he maintained without the least embarrassment – and proceeded to illustrate his analogy.

'Berthier was Chief of Staff, as is the continental custom. When Napoleon left Paris, by carriage, to take command of the Army of Italy, in which Berthier was Chief of Staff, he sent orders for Berthier to meet him at a rendezvous some miles from his H.Q. so that they could travel the last miles together and the C-in-C would get an idea of the situation before he took over.

'I did the same with Freddie. I ordered him to meet me outside Alexandria, as you know. And when we arrived at Eighth Army H.Q. I knew pretty well what I was in for.'[86]

Verbal précis

What *was* Monty in for? In his usual fashion, Monty had pushed away the written précis that de Guingand tried to hand over to him. 'I said: "Now, Freddie, don't be silly. You know I never read any papers when I can get the person concerned to tell me himself. Put that bumf away and unburden your soul." He laughed and I saw at once I would now get a first class review of the present situation and the causes of it – with nothing held back. We sat close together with a map on our knees and he told me the story; the operational situation, the latest Intelligence about the enemy, the generals commanding in the various sectors, the existing orders of Auchinleck about future action, his own views about things. I let him talk on. Occasionally I asked a question but only to clarify some point. When he had done there was silence for a moment or two.'[87]

This was undoubtedly one of Monty's great gifts: the ability to listen. The next full moon, in ten days' time, was considered a likely date for Rommel's offensive. Originally it had been thought he would attack in the north, along the coastal road, but the strength of British minefields and prepared positions made this increasingly less likely – suggested, instead, an outflanking move to the south with a very mobile force, while feinting in the north. This, de Guingand explained, would be characteristic of Rommel, and give him tactical surprise, since he could assemble his force in the centre-rear of his positions and withhold the direction of his assault until the final moment.

General Auchinleck's answer, de Guingand explained, had been to prepare a re-hash of 8th Army's defences when defeated at Gazala in June: a system of lightly held forward defence localities (FDLs), and behind them a string of 'boxes' into which the army would retreat if heavily attacked. Behind these boxes there were further proposed lines of defence at Wadi Natrun and the Nile delta. If these could not be held, 8th Army would split into two, one part retreating north into Palestine, the other going south to Khartoum. If, however, 8th Army was successful in countering Rommel's thrust, it was then proposed to mount an offensive in late September, and a training area had already been established where divisions could begin to practise minefield clearance and the like.

Asked what were his personal views on the state of 8th Army, de Guingand expressed his qualms about the current policy of fighting in mobile brigades and battle groups; the lack of co-ordination between army and air force; and the worrying tendency of staff and commanders to 'look over their shoulders'.

It was undoubtedly the uninhibited accounts given first by Harding, then by de Guingand as BGS (Ops) of 8th Army, which set the seal on Monty's intention to 'stir things up' at 8th Army HQ – and it is likely that, as the car 'left the coast road and turned south along a track into the open desert'[88] towards 8th Army headquarters, Monty made his decision to take instant command of the army, ignoring Auchinleck's insistence on remaining army commander until the end of the week.

General waste

A wireless officer in 23rd Armoured Brigade, Major Witherby, later described the desert in the Alamein area. Between Alamein railway station, almost by the sea, and the great, impassable Quattara Depression to the south, stretched a forty-mile expanse, more or less level, but with two commanding shoulders or ridges: the Ruweisat Ridge and Alam Nayil. To the east of the latter, stretching back towards Alexandria like a spinal column, was the Alam el Halfa Ridge. Though the terrain was considered flat when compared with more hilly country, in fact 'much of the country was broken with little hillocks, sand dunes, ravines, some ridges and cliffs. Everywhere there was "camel-thorn" a semi-succulent, growing like gorse and full of chameleons and snails. There were no trees or roads, except the Coast Road, which was bounded by a few Egyptian houses with ruined fig orchards. Away from the road there were occasional signs that barley was cultivated in a scattered way. A track known as the "Barrel Track" led along the Ruweisat Ridge and then to the Coast Road. As part of the defence system, the whole area had been surveyed and large barrels with numbers on them stood on hills to mark the various positions.' Some of the barrels 'had field telephones attached to them. I was at a conference one day beside a barrel when the telephone rang! Someone answered the call & found himself speaking to an equally puzzled German officer.'

Desultory fighting and patrolling had been going on for six weeks, as South African, Indian, Australian, New Zealand and British troops attempted to stop Rommel from breaking through to Cairo and Alexandria. 'The British Army in Egypt seems to have had the strangest generals at this time,' Witherby recalled. 'They cared little for training, paid no regard to the different characteristics of different units, made no allowance for inexperience, made no attempt to impart information and did not learn from their own experience. The bitterness between the New Zealanders and certain other Infantry formations and the Armour seems to have stemmed from the old idea in the old Tank Corps that Tanks could do everything and were independent of other arms. (General Rommel, who seems to have liked making jokes against the Nazi Party, said that they were "pure in race", meaning that they acted on their own, without the co-operation of other Arms.)'

The result was, in Witherby's view, 'the malaise of the time', namely 'poor leadership, poor training, little liaison and the general lack of mutual understanding . . . The constant and apparently pointless moves gave an impression that there was no plan and no one in command. These moves must have used vast quantities of fuel, especially as there were no tracks or roads . . . During this time [before Montgomery's arrival], we tried to get dug in properly using our Engineers and explosives, but usually as soon as we had dug some trenches, orders would come to move! The general waste was fantastic . . .'[89]

The meat-safe

Meanwhile Monty, having heard de Guingand's verbal appreciation, was thoughtful. 'We were quiet now and I was thinking: chiefly about de Guingand,' he later related. De Guingand was well aware his own future hung in the balance. Finally, at 11 a.m. the car drew up at 8th Army HQ on the Ruweisat Ridge, where the acting army commander, Lieutenant-General Ramsden, was waiting.

It was, in the words of Charles Richardson, an 'absurd' HQ, far too far forward, so that it was both within German artillery range and regularly attacked by the German air force, as well as being sited at 'a not very attractive place: an intersection of camel tracks just behind the Ruweisat Ridge, with a liberal supply of camel dung all around, on which Winston Churchill commented when he came there'.[90] More important, it was more than forty miles from Desert Air Force HQ.

'The sight that met me,' Monty recalled in his memoirs, 'was enough to lower anyone's morale. It was a desolate scene; a few trucks, no mess tents, work done mostly in trucks or in the open air in the hot sun, flies everywhere. I asked where Auchinleck used to sleep; I was told that he slept on the ground outside his caravan. Tents were forbidden in the Eighth Army; everyone was to be as uncomfortable as possible, so that they wouldn't be more comfortable than the men.'[91]

Churchill, thinking of Stafford Cripps' love of austerity, had quipped that it would be a great place for him. 'All officers' messes were in the open air,' Monty recalled, 'where, of course, they attracted the flies of Egypt.'[92]

Flies were like miniature vultures, feeding off every living and dead thing. Only the senior officers' dining mess was covered: the proud construct of the chief engineer. An aviary-type frame had been erected, over which mosquito netting had been drawn – thus entrapping the very flies it was meant to keep out. Here Churchill had breakfasted; here Monty was expected to take lunch.

To some extent Auchinleck's spartan life at 8th Army HQ was designed to show officers, men and visitors that 8th Army's high command was not immune to the ordeal the army had been through in its terrible flight from Gazala; perhaps, unconsciously, it was also Auchinleck's personal atonement for the very failure of command that had led to British defeat. Certainly Auchinleck's biographer, John Connell, remarked that 'Rommel fought and worked under the same conditions,' as though this might excuse Auchinleck for imitating him. Yet the fact is that Rommel was in poor health as a result. It was not Rommel's mess conditions that required adoption by 8th Army, Monty felt, but certain of his techniques, such as the intimate use of artillery and anti-tank weapons, and the organization of an armoured corps. Besides, the army staff should stop feeling guilty at their reverses, which no tentless headquarters would mitigate. They should concentrate now on the best way of defeating Rommel and fulfilling the Prime Minister's directive to clear Egypt and Cyrenaica of enemy forces. This would not be effected from a dung-smelling aviary for flies.

'What's this?' Monty barked at de Guingand, 'a meat-safe? You don't expect me to live in a meat-safe, do you? Take it down at once, and let the poor flies out.'[93]

Gratuity

Some days before, Auchinleck had signalled to Brooke how contented he was with Corbett in Cairo ('doing excellently'), with Lieutenant-General Ramsden as commander of XXX Corps ('doing well'), and with Major-General Dorman-Smith ('most valuable').[94]

Monty had met Corbett and Dorman-Smith in Cairo. His interview with Lieutenant-General Ramsden at 8th Army HQ soon confirmed the accounts of de Guingand and Harding – indeed, in response to Monty's blistering interrogation Ramsden revealed the almost incredible, Dorman-Smith-inspired scenario, whereby the entire British front-line defence, south of Ruweisat, would be withdrawn on a codeword 'Gratuity'. Two complete infantry divisions (2nd New Zealand and 5th Indian) would thereupon stream back – the Indian division into 'Army Reserve in the area Ruweisat station', the New Zealanders to 'ALAM HALFA defended locality', covered by armour. Having reached the Alam Halfa area, the New Zealanders would be split up into 'mobile battle groups'.

'The essence of the defensive plan was fluidity and mobility,' Auchinleck had explained his orders, with 1st Armoured Division (which had left the New Zealand Division in the lurch in June) supposedly covering 'the withdrawal of the forward infantry to the ALAM HALFA ridge', which was otherwise virtually undefended. Lest fluidity and mobility in withdrawal be interpreted as defeatism, the orders carried a warning. Nothing in them was to be 'interpreted as a weakening in our intention to hold the present position or as an indication that our efforts have or are likely to fail'.[95]

It was a salutary rider. While the New Zealand and Indian infantry of XIII Corps withdrew, Ramsden's XXX Corps in the north was also to 'thin out' the 'forward zone' and occupy rear 'defensive localities' composed each of 'two infantry battalions, one field battery and one anti-tank battery'. Between these defended localities 'battle groups will counter-attack any enemy who may attempt to attack or outflank our positions'. These so-far unrehearsed battle groups were to be 'controlled by brigade and divisional HQs. Arrangements will be made and recces carried out to enable them to operate rapidly in support of neighbouring Divisions or of 13 Corps,' their orders ran. The battle groups were to be 'organized and trained to act in the above way'.[96]

Perhaps the New Zealand 5th Brigade commander, Howard Kippenberger, best summed up Auchinleck's plans. 'We did not know whether we would fight where we stood, or in the reserve positions,' he remembered, 'or run away.'[97]

It was, in Monty's view, the recipe for yet another British disaster.

Instant action

In his diary for 13 August 1942, Monty recorded how he 'cross-examined General Ramsden, the Acting Army Commander, about the Army plan for a withdrawal if ROMMEL attacked.

'Certain orders had been issued about the withdrawal, but they were very indefinite and no one seemed clear as to exactly what was to be done. There was an air of uncertainty and a lack of "grip". Army HQ was completely out of touch with Air HQ Western Desert.

'It was clear to me that the situation was quite impossible, and, in fact, dangerous,' Monty summarized, 'and I decided at once that I must take instant action. I also decided that it was useless to consult GHQ and that I would take responsibility myself.'[98]

Later biographers of Auchinleck, seeking to cover up the disastrous state of affairs, denied all 8th Army plans for withdrawal – tactical or strategic. Beginning with John Connell in 1959, they would claim that 'An Appreciation of the Situation in the Western Desert', drawn up by Dorman-Smith on 27 July 1942, provided Monty with the blueprint for his battle at Alam Halfa – a twenty-paragraph paper in which Alam Halfa never once appeared![99] Montgomery, Connell claimed, drew up a plan of defence that 'differed in no essential detail from the appreciation of July 27, prepared by Dorman-Smith and approved, readily and willingly, by Auchinleck – Rommel's attack, the measures to deal with it'.[100] The following year, the *enfant terrible* of military history, Correlli Barnett, claimed Monty had put 'his own name to the best of Auchinleck's plans, while assigning to Auchinleck and his officers the blame for the hiatus in leadership and planning for the fortnight-long comings-and-goings of the Purge'.[101] By 1981, twenty years later, it had become almost *de rigueur* to repeat such inanities – the official historian of British intelligence in World War II, Harry Hinsley, extolling Dorman-Smith's Appreciation of 27 July and writing that Auchinleck's 'successors retained his general plan for holding the main Alam el Halfa feature' – never mentioned in the Appreciation! – 'while countering an attempt by Rommel to penetrate in the south'.[102]

Such historians were, sadly, deceiving themselves, often duped and seduced by sacked generals and staff officers who resented Monty's 'take-over' and the new commander's ungentlemanly refusal to mask the true state of affairs in 8th Army. Those officers who stayed on, however, such as de Guingand and Charles Richardson, were emphatic that the detailed plans for withdrawal, fluidity of engagement and *ad hoc* battle groups formed the fatal legacy left by Auchinleck, not 'blueprints' for spurious victory. Indeed, so distressed was Freyberg's stand-in, Brigadier Inglis, that on behalf of the New Zealand Division he had already warned Auchinleck that, after the cock-ups in July, 'he would refuse to take any further part if future arrangements followed the same pattern'.[103]

De Guingand was not surprised at Monty's instinctive response. The whole army looked for leadership, as he knew – a 'craving throughout the army for guidance and inspiration'[104] as one young anti-aircraft artillery officer wrote of this period – and Lieutenant-General Ramsden, as the GOC XXX Corps and acting 8th Army commander certainly did not provide it. In fact, in his appreciation in the car, de Guingand had referred to Ramsden as 'bloody useless', he later recalled – a verdict shared by most officers at 8th Army headquarters at that time.

Ramsden had been a mere battalion commander under Monty in Palestine in 1938–9; it seemed therefore inconceivable that Ramsden should continue as acting 8th Army commander for a further three days while Monty 'waited in the wings' – indeed, in the view of both Churchill and General Brooke, on their visit on 5 August, Ramsden was already above his ceiling as a corps commander, let alone an acting army commander.

It is a mark of Monty's authority that, when he told Ramsden to return immediately to his headquarters at XXX Corps and that he, Monty would take command of 8th Army immediately, Ramsden did not 'belly-ache', but accepted Monty's decision without hesitation or even checking it with

GHQ in Cairo. 'He seemed surprised . . . but he went,' Monty recalled.[105] The new 8th Army commander thereupon sat down to lunch in the open, beneath the baking summer sun.

Savage thinking

Monty had now declared himself de facto commander of the 8th Army; he had to inform GHQ Cairo of this, and to start revitalizing 8th Army from top to bottom. Rommel was building up more and more strength each day; there was not a moment to lose. 'During lunch I did some savage thinking,' Monty later recounted.[106] As soon as lunch was over he issued the first of his historic edicts. The first was a cable to Cairo for a servant:

> *To Mideast from Main A 8th Army*
> Army Commander requires best available soldier servant in Middle East to be sent to Main A Eighth Army at once.

His second cable, to Lieutenant-General Corbett, Auchinleck's chief general staff officer, explained the first:

> *To Mideast from Main Eighth Army*
> For CGS. Lieut-Gen. MONTGOMERY assumed command of Eighth Army at 1400 hrs today.[107]

'I learnt later that the arrival of this telegram made Auchinleck very angry as he had told me not to take over till 15 August,' Monty recorded in his diary. 'Having sent off this telegram to GHQ, I then set out to see my Corps Commanders, so as to be away if any protest came.'[108]

He had now not only taken action, but taken charge.

No surrender

Monty's first visit would be made to the acting commander of XIII Corps – Lieutenant-General Bernard Freyberg, commander of the 2nd New Zealand Division, in the south of the line. Before doing so, however,

Monty gave two more orders. The first was a message to every 8th Army unit, cancelling all army plans and orders for possible withdrawal, however tactical. 'If ROMMEL attacked we would fight him on the ground where we now stood; there would be NO WITHDRAWAL and NO SURRENDER,' Monty noted in his diary.[109] The 8th Army would remain in its existing positions: dead or alive.

Monty's second order was to summon all staff officers at 8th Army headquarters for an urgent conference.

'When, sir?' asked de Guingand.

'Why, this evening of course,' Montgomery replied[110] – and left to see General Freyberg.

Rommel's growing armada

The Egyptian desert resembled in some ways an ocean: 'the Blue' as it was called by the troops; vast, immutable, sown with minefields, subject to dust storms, and without natural features by which to navigate.

Rommel's 'armada', beyond the horizon, could not be seen, but it was there all right, swelling each day. Decrypted Ultra tank returns between 31 July and 3 August had already shown the Afrika Korps massing almost 150 serviceable panzers, as well as almost 100 Italian tanks. More ominously, as in a contest between fleets, the tally of German panzers incorporating the new long-barrelled 75mm gun (which outranged all British tanks) had risen by 2 August to sixty-four – and was still rising. By 10 August, the day Auchinleck left 8th Army headquarters, it was estimated that Rommel commanded, within his German–Italian army, an Afrika Korps of some 37,000 highly trained German troops, fully mobile, boasting 185 medium panzers, 203 guns, and 295 anti-tank guns, including the deadly anti-aircraft/anti-tank '88' – by far and away the best dual-purpose tank-busting weapon of World War II. Rommel's Italian contingent was smaller, numbering 28,700 men and 110 second-class tanks, but it was equipped with a disturbing 240 guns and 270 anti-tank guns. Rommel had, in other words, a front-line Axis army of 65,700 men, 295 tanks, 443 guns and 565 anti-tank guns.

It was Rommel's rate of build-up, however, that was even more alarming. Within the next two days, 8th Army intelligence currently estimated, Rommel would have at his disposal some 200 serviceable Mk III and IV panzer tanks. 'Should the enemy then decide to live by "hunt and peck" supply methods during operations,' the intelligence report ended, 'there can be little else to delay the beginning of his offensive save our own action.'[111]

But what action could 8th Army take? Its remaining medium tanks were not only outnumbered but outgunned, so that offensive action before arrival of the Roosevelt convoy at Suez was potentially suicidal. Fighting a mobile battle, as Auchinleck had instructed his corps commanders to do, was anathema to Monty in these circumstances, for it would be to dance to Rommel's tune: allowing him to lure the 'racially pure' British armour on to Panzer Army's anti-tank guns, and destroy it, as so often before.

'You'll never win a campaign as it is at the moment,' Monty had said of 8th Army to de Guingand in the car.[112] By deciding to create a reserve, armoured corps, he intended to create a new 8th Army. This, however, would take time – which might not be forthcoming if Rommel chose to attack in the next few days. In other words, 8th Army urgently needed a new plan of defence.

Dead or alive

At the XIII Corps headquarters at 3 o'clock in the afternoon of 13 August Monty met Lieutenant-General Bernard Freyberg VC. Freyberg was welcoming, but sceptical. After 9,000 New Zealand casualties, there were no more reserves with which to replenish the division; indeed, it only had two infantry brigades in it. 'I said to him,' recalled Freyberg, '"I want to talk about the control of the New Zealand Forces. I only come under your command for operations, not for discipline or training, and only for operations when the New Zealand Government have given their consent!" I also said to him, "I have had great anxiety in the past with higher commanders who have a mania for breaking up military organisation."'[113] This mania had extended to army and corps commanders, seven of whom had already come and gone in 8th Army. Africa, Freyberg remarked, 'is the graveyard of lieutenant-generals. None of them stay here more than a few months.'[114]

Laughing at the remark, Monty asked Freyberg to tell him what, in his view, was wrong. Freyberg's response – that the infantry had no faith in the armour, which made no effort to integrate its operations with infantry divisions – bore out de Guingand's overview, as did Freyberg's objection to the Auchinleck–Dorman-Smith policy of splitting the army up into 'mobile Battle Groups'. Freyberg's view of Auchinleck's plan for the entire New Zealand Division to leave its prepared positions and retreat into rear 'defended OP areas', in the midst of the forthcoming battle, was caustic. The plan, dreamed up by Dorman-Smith, stank.[115]

Monty told Freyberg not to worry: there would be no mass evacuation to rear positions, and no fragmentation into battle groups. The front line running from the Mediterranean coast through the Ruweisat Ridge and down to Alam Nayil would no longer be a forward defence line: it would be *the* defence line, to be held unto death – as he had already made clear in an order to be distributed to every unit in 8th Army. There would be no mobile withdrawal, or retreat; 8th Army would stand and fight where it stood, to the bitter end. Yes, there was every likelihood Rommel would launch an armoured thrust to outflank 8th Army, Monty acknowledged, passing south of the New Zealand positions on Alam Nayil. Let Rommel just try! As long as the British front line, including the New Zealanders, held firm, Rommel would be unable to press on towards Cairo and Alexandria for fear of becoming entirely cut off; he *must* therefore wheel and try to roll up 8th Army from the rear, as he had at Gazala. Provided that the 'backbone' ridge at Alam Halfa was properly garrisoned, there was nothing to fear: 8th Army would be meeting Rommel on ground of its own choosing. Given well-sited, cohesively controlled artillery and anti-tank guns, and judicious husbanding of 8th Army's own armour, Rommel could, Monty assured him, achieve nothing.

When Freyberg asked what forces would man the Alam Halfa area, currently held by a few hundred infantry troops, Monty retorted it was not a problem: there were plenty of units 'wasting' in the delta – they would be brought up, immediately. The important thing was to look to the front, not backwards: to see that his New Zealand defences were prepared in depth, with proper attention paid to minefields and to cohesive artillery so as to enable the chief gunner to bring the combined weight of divisional, even corps, artillery on any one spot. Auchinleck's policy of mass withdrawals and 'mobility and fluidity' was henceforth redundant.

Once Rommel's attack had been halted, moreover, it would be 8th Army's turn to take the offensive. With its headquarters further north, on the Ruweisat Ridge, XXX Corps would take responsibility for the whole front, while XIII Corps would be withdrawn from the line to train as a highly mobile, armoured break-in corps, similar to the Afrika Korps, in which the New Zealanders themselves would be re-equipped as a light armoured division, on the lines of Rommel's 90th Light Division, and similar to Monty's old 3rd Division, but with an integral brigade of support tanks; indeed, Freyberg would never need to fear he was being sold down the river by British armour again: he would have his own.

Freyberg was both relieved and impressed – indeed 'amazed', as his son later chronicled, for Freyberg 'realised that if Montgomery meant what he said, a new era really had begun'.[116]

Meanwhile, leaving Freyberg to draw up new corps and divisional orders embodying his instructions, Monty finally left XIII Corps HQ and returned to his own dung-spattered 8th Army headquarters on the Ruweisat Ridge, to talk to his staff – for if the troops of 8th Army were baffled and bewildered by the situation in the desert, it was clear the staff were even more confused. It was time, he reckoned, to 'binge' them up.

Gentlemanliness

Outraged by Monty's subsequent boastfulness and lack of magnanimity, a posse of British historians attempted later to cover up the confusion that confronted Monty on his arrival in the desert. They did so not out of stupidity, for the most part, but out of loyalty to the sacked General Auchinleck: a tall, ruggedly handsome, lonely, intelligent, rather wooden individual who was deeply admired for his fortitude.

This historiographical conspiracy of 'Auk-admirers' was understand-able, but historically silly – an attempt to shape history according to their social standards of 'gentlemanliness'. Since Montgomery was not, nor ever sought to be, a 'nice' man, or even a gentleman, he was doomed to perdition at the hands of such historians, for his increasing vanity and lack of magnanimity, once famous, would make him a most unpleasant specimen for historical dissection. As Correlli Barnett (like Monty, a physically small man) put it, Monty's chin was 'on a level with Auchin-leck's decorations';[117] Field-Marshal Sir Gerald Templer – a very tall, imposing, indeed awesome man, who was in many respects an admirer of Monty, remarked that Monty was a 'cocksparrow' beside the majestic figure of the 'Auk' whose jagged, stoic face and large build impressed the irascible Templer.[118] This comparison held good (or bad) for Monty in other respects, as historians saw him. Small in stature and a martinet in behaviour, Monty continually 'stole' the limelight in their eyes, garnering laurels and praise that were often due to colleagues and subordinates. He was arrogant and, like Patton, pathologically boastful. He was, in short, a mega-egoist – whereas men like Alexander and Eisenhower were charming, modest, gentlemanly generals.

How such 'charming' men were supposed to outgeneral ruthless Axis commanders such as Rommel and von Runstedt on the battlefield was not something that such gentleman-admiring historians could easily explain, save with the aid of numbers – men, munitions, airpower: 'brute force' as John Ellis later put it.[119] The Allies, such historians concluded, could only, and did only, win by statistics; in doing so they needed only the charming leadership of men like Alexander and Eisenhower to marshal their numerical superiority – including superior Allied intelligence, benefiting from Ultra.

The dislike of vain men

There was, of course, some truth in this view. The difficulty, however, for such historians was to explain retrospectively why the forces of good manners, despite numerical superiority and Ultra intelligence, had been unable to make headway under 'gentlemanly' commanders in the years before 'arrogant' generals such as Montgomery and Patton came on to the scene – indeed, often after they had done so. The 8th Army had, for example, enjoyed numerical superiority of 'four-to-one' in tanks over Rommel – including a three-month period in which 'the 75mm guns in our tanks (Grants) were superior in anti-tank capability to any guns mounted in the German tanks', according to General 'Pip' Roberts, a tank commander under Cunningham, Ritchie, Gott and Auchinleck. 'Thus the brief advantage over the Germans in tank guns which we had gained was lost by vacillation at the top and failure to understand tank warfare.'[120] Moreover, the 8th Army enjoyed a three-to-two advantage in artillery, and more than parity in the air *prior to* Monty's arrival in the desert, as well as superlative Ultra intelligence – indeed, it was openly, and sarcastically, said in 8th Army in May 1942 that 'Things are getting pretty organised now, they can even tell the date of the next flap.'[121] Such intelligence had certainly helped Auchinleck to restore order in the British line after the rout from Gazala and Tobruk, and to jab back at Rommel's weaker links by pinpointing the locations of Italian units, but Ultra could not, of itself, revitalize a beaten British army – or make it fight cohesively.

What, then, did change 8th Army's fortunes? Was it simply the arrival of Roosevelt's 300 Grant and Sherman tanks in September 1942 that changed defeat into victory, as some historians claimed? In the view of the Auchinleck faction – and of American historians who cursorily dismissed the later triumph of Alamein – it was. A nasty, self-advertising little man had decked himself out, as Barnett described in 1960, in a 'second-hand coat of glory'[122] – a coat meanly stolen from General Sir Claude Auchinleck, victor of 'First Alamein', and his genius-adviser, Major-General 'Chink' Dorman-Smith. Wearing this purloined coat Monty, in a most ungentlemanly way, had then made 'for the top'[123] – being so personally ambitious that he would go on to fight the offensive battle of 'Second' Alamein, as such historians termed it, in October 1942, entirely unnecessarily. As Barnett put it, 'if Montgomery had not fought his battle, Rommel would have been out of Egypt within a month and in Tunisia within three' – thanks to the Anglo-American landings (Torch) at the other end of the Mediterranean. 'The famous Second Battle of Alamein must therefore, in my view,' Barnett opined, 'go down in history as an unnecessary battle.'[124]

How Roosevelt, let alone Stalin or Churchill, would have viewed a British decision to sit back in Egypt, risk losing Malta (which could not be resupplied by convoy without air cover provided from recaptured airfields in Cyrenaica), leave Axis forces in position less than sixty miles from Alexandria, and ask the Anglo-British Torch forces to risk the highly speculative landings in Morocco and western Algeria (where neither French nor German reaction was predictable) with the 8th Army doing nothing, was not something that seems to have entered Barnett's mind – for his target, after lengthy correspondence and 'help' from the still-smarting Dorman-Smith (who had changed his name to O'Gowan after being dismissed in Italy) was the mountebank Field-Marshal Viscount Montgomery of Alamein – and Barnett was not alone.[125]

Captain Stephen Roskill, eminent official naval historian and a later colleague of Barnett at Churchill College, Cambridge, was equally determined to 'nail' the 'military messiah' of North Africa. Thus, two years after publication of Barnett's best-selling squib, *The Desert Generals*, Roskill unwisely sent the manuscript of his latest essay about Montgomery to the warden of Rhodes House, Oxford, Brigadier E. T. Williams, who had been the number two intelligence officer at 8th Army's desert HQ, under Auchinleck, and was subsequently inherited by Monty on 13 August 1942.

Williams, as an Oxford historian, was surprised by Roskill's malevolence. 'In the end your article has an attack on Montgomery's character,' Williams responded, having dealt item by item with Roskill's litany of unpleasant (and often all too true) stories of Montgomery's rudenesses and ill behaviour towards others. 'I am not quite certain what is the point of making it. I suppose I knew his character at the time perhaps better than some,' Williams mused, 'and I think the conclusion, if I may say so, is really rather offensive, don't you, on consideration?

'I am sorry to sound so stuffy about this,' Williams quickly went on. 'I hold your official [naval] war history volumes in very high regard – they are a most remarkable contribution to history. This draft footnote does not seem to me to be of the same temper.'[126]

Chastened, Roskill attempted to defend himself – and in doing so revealed the agenda underlying so much revisionist British historianship of the 1960s and 70s; indeed, underlying most military biography of the period. 'As to the little story at the end,' Roskill wrote back, stung, 'it was hardly an "attack on Monty's character". But as you think it offensive I'll take it out; I think that perhaps, like Monty himself, I have a bit of the gamin in me! And I really don't like vain men; nor believe that the greatest of our generals & admirals were vain in the way that Monty was.'[127]

Roskill was forgetting Horatio Nelson. But Monty had committed the cardinal sin for a Cambridge historian: that of vanity. He was not, therefore, a gentleman.

Mistrust and lack of confidence

The truth was, the 'gentlemen' commanders had tried and had failed, and in doing so had betrayed their troops – just as Haig and his fellow generals had betrayed, for all their 'gentlemanly' qualities, the men under their command in World War I. In 'total war' it was time for players: for professionals, not good British club-men.

As General Richardson – the chief staff officer for plans at 8th Army headquarters under both Auchinleck and Montgomery – later recalled, there had been a 'confusion of purpose endemic' in Auchinleck's plans and orders – and the war diaries of 8th Army and its formations, unavailable to Barnett when he first penned his denunciation of Montgomery's generalship in the desert, provide all too embarrassing justification of Richardson's recall (as Barnett had later reluctantly to admit, when republishing his unchanged 1960 version of the war in the desert, in 1983[128]). But by then Connell and Barnett had infected a whole generation of military historians, official, academic and non-academic.

Far from 'retaining' Auchinleck's plan of defence at Alamein, Monty was aghast at the implications of it – which would, he was certain, have lost Britain the Middle East and the war.

Field-Marshal Carver, who had been GSO2 (Ops) at XXX Corps throughout August 1942, would certainly have no truck with the Cambridge clan, pointing out in 1984 that Hinsley and Barnett were still wilfully deluding themselves. Auchinleck's intended 'mobile battle' was, he re-emphasized, doomed to catastrophe, as everyone serving in the desert at the time knew. 'The operation orders issued at the time – those of 30 Corps written by me – make clear what that [plan of Auchinleck's] was expected to mean,' Carver explained to historians collected at the University of London in 1984, namely 'a collection of brigade "boxes", from which surplus infantry would be sent back to the Nile Delta, based primarily on artillery, disposed in depth between El Alamein and the Delta, between which mobile forces would operate against Rommel's incursions. In case that failed – as a good many people, including notably Freyberg, thought it would – troops were being held back in the Delta to defend it directly, in which event GHQ would push off from Cairo to Palestine.'[129]

There was, in short, extreme scepticism about Auchinleck's plans for defence at Alamein, once Rommel attacked. One young 8th Army major, taken ill and recovering in Cairo in August 1942, recalled the joke circulating among the wounded in his hospital: 'that the battle plan for 8th Army when Rommel attacked was to let him come through. He was to be allowed to advance right up to Cairo, but when he got to the Gezira Sporting Club, on the Nile, the whole of G.H.Q. was to spring to arms and to overwhelm him by sheer weight of numbers. At this time I was told (I do not know if it was true), that there were 80 Brigadiers in the Cairo area.'

This at least showed a British sense of humour. Yet the problem of morale was serious – and seriously, if not mendaciously, underestimated by later historians. 'All round there was a lack of confidence, lack of direction, lack of unity between formations and arms. The Infantry had no confidence in the Armour and vice versa, there was a mistrust between Army and RAF, and lack of co-operation,' one veteran wrote. 'There was a lack of confidence in weapons and too many people were thinking of retreat.'[130]

Another young officer, commanding a Light AA battery, quoted 'one hard-faced infantry sergeant' at this time. ' "Rommel thinks it all out and takes whatever he needs with him. Our lot! Christ, they couldn't organise a piss-up at a brewery!" '[131] The BBC correspondent Denis Johnston, visiting the front at this time, noted the attitude of ordinary soldiers – that 'whenever occasion arises, the British private soldier gets into his slit trench and stays there. This is because he is not interested in the exhibition-ist side of the game. It is not his business, and he sensibly does not want to get killed if he can avoid it. He did not ask to come here, and he intends to go home unless he is unlucky. This attitude has nothing to do with cowardice or bravery. It is just a feeling of indifference to the whole issue.'[132]

Indifference, Monty recognized, was the very quality that would lose Britain the war against the Nazis – who were far from indifferent. The first thing to do, then, after cancelling Auchinleck's plans and meeting the corps commanders, was to inspire the organizational team – the staff of 8th Army headquarters – to pull themselves together. The staff of the brewery 'piss-up' must give Rommel the shock of his life.

An historic address

Arriving late at 8th Army headquarters on the Ruweisat Ridge, Monty found the RAF protective 'air-umbrella' fighters had gone. Yet it was at this camel-dung-smelling army headquarters, within artillery and fighter range of the enemy, that the unknown, white-kneed general from England was to give that evening what would become one of the seminal speeches of military history.

'We thought this "air umbrella" was a very comic thing –' one officer candidly recalled his feeling, 'because we didn't think we were very precious.'[133]

Montgomery did, though. A good staff, well led, was the backbone of a successful army, he felt. Although so close to the front line, 8th Army headquarters was not a mere tactical HQ but contained all the branches of 8th Army's staff, from operations to artillery, engineers to administration, intelligence to plans, signals to staff duties. Some sixty officers therefore stood to attention and saluted. Monty returned the salute, stood on the steps of his predecessor's caravan, bade the gathering to sit in the sand and, in a high, clear and confident voice that rang through the evening stillness of the desert, introduced himself and stated his mission: to end the cycle of British defeat – and defeatism.

'I do not like the general atmosphere I find here,' stated the skinny figure with his foxy, pointed face, high cheekbones and thin, sharp nose jutting beneath his peaked, general's hat. 'It is an atmosphere of doubt, of looking back to select the next place to which to withdraw, of loss of confidence in our ability to defeat Rommel, of desperate defence measures by reserves in preparing positions in Cairo and the Delta.' Such an atmosphere was fatal. 'All that must cease,' Monty now ordered. 'Let us have a new atmosphere.'

And in his high, almost staccato voice, with its weak ('Fwench') R's, he proceeded to tell the staff what he and they were going to do.

The defence of Egypt lies here at Alamein and on the Ruweisat Ridge. What is the use of digging trenches in the Delta? It is quite useless; if we lose this position we lose Egypt; all the fighting troops now in the Delta must come here at once, and will. Here we will stand and fight; there will be no further withdrawal. I have ordered that all plans and instructions dealing with further withdrawal are to be burnt, and at once. We will stand and fight here.

If we can't stay here alive, then let us stay here dead.

The candour and realism of the new army commander came as a shock to those officers who had not met Monty before. Equally, it was clear that the new commander had no intention of being beaten – indeed, had every intention of trouncing Rommel in the coming months, as he explained. Next he gave out the good news, albeit slightly exaggerated:

I want to impress on everyone that the bad times are over. Fresh Divisions from the UK are now arriving in Egypt, together with ample reinforcements for our present Divisions. We have 300 to 400 Sherman new tanks coming and these are actually being unloaded at Suez now. Our mandate from the Prime Minister is to destroy the Axis forces in North Africa; I have seen it, written on half a sheet of notepaper. And it will be done. If anyone here thinks it can't be done, let him go at once; I don't want any doubters in this party. It can be done, and it will be done: beyond any possibility of doubt.

    With his ringing, high-pitched voice piercing the stillness of the desert, Monty's words created an indelible impression – compelling attention. Never once, in fourteen months of Middle East and army command, had Auchinleck ever so addressed his staff. But Monty was by no means finished.

Now I understand that Rommel is expected to attack at any moment. Excellent. Let him attack. I would sooner it didn't come for a week, just to give me time to sort things out. If we have two weeks to prepare we will be sitting pretty; Rommel can attack as soon as he likes, after that, and I hope he does. Meanwhile, we ourselves will start to plan a great offensive; it will be the beginning of a campaign which will hit Rommel and his Army for six right out of Africa.

'But first we must create a reserve Corps, mobile and strong in armour, which we will train out of the line. Rommel has always had such a force in his Africa Corps, which is never used to hold the line but which is always in reserve, available for striking blows. Therein has been his great strength. We will create such a Corps ourselves, a British Panzer Corps; it will consist of two armoured Divisions and one motorized Division; I gave orders yesterday for it to begin to form, back in the Delta.

I have no intention of launching our great attack until we are completely ready; there will be pressure from many quarters to attack soon; I will not attack until we are ready, and you can rest assured on that point.

Meanwhile, if Rommel attacks while we are preparing, let him do so with pleasure; we will merely continue with our own preparations and we will attack when we are ready, and not before.[134]

    Even the sceptical G2 Intelligence, Major 'Bill' Williams – a junior Oxford don in civilian life – found his first impression of hilarity over the missing 'air umbrella' changing to one of reluctant admiration as he listened to Monty speak. Williams had been in intelligence at GHQ Cairo until June, when at de Guingand's prompting he was posted to 8th Army. In both positions he had been primarily responsible for interpreting and relaying to Auchinleck Ultra decrypts of the enemy's most secret signals – and had become frustrated over the use to which this unique intelligence had been put: namely, to plug holes and launch infantry or cavalry attacks that were never co-ordinated, and led so often to tragic and unnecessary deaths. For a desert army to lose more than 100,000 casualties in fourteen months, and still be only sixty miles from Alexandria at the end, was a terrible reflection on 8th Army's leadership – for the soldiers themselves had fought, in the main, with exemplary courage.

'I can remember the address,' Williams related almost forty years later. 'I think we had this rather arrogant view that we'd had rather a lot of generals through our hands, in our day. And this was a new one – but he was talking sense, although in a very sort of strange way: the manner, the phraseology. You've got to remember that the sort of people I'd talk to would be the intelligentsia, so to speak, and this sort of stuff was straight out of school speech-day. And yet . . . I remember it was, it was a feeling of great exhilaration: a feeling that here was somebody who was really going to use his staff. And I remember relating it purely personally to this sort of feeling: well, God, he's the sort of chap who's going to be able to use Ultra, you see. You had this feeling that we kept producing stuff that was out of this world in terms of the amount of information we were getting about the enemy, and somehow it never seemed to get put to any purpose.'[135]

Slightly mad

Speech day, however, was not yet over. 'I want to tell you that I always work on the Chief-of-Staff system,' Monty announced. 'I have nominated Brigadier de Guingand as Chief-of-Staff Eighth Army. I will issue orders through him. Whatever he says will be taken as coming from me and will be acted on at once. I understand there has been a great deal of "belly-aching" out here. By "belly-aching" I mean inventing poor reasons for not doing what one has been told to do.

'All this is to stop at once.

'I will tolerate no belly-aching.

'If anyone objects to doing what he is told, then he can get out of it; and at once. I want that made very clear right down through the Eighth Army.

'I have little more to say just at present,' Monty wrapped up. 'And some of you may think it is quite enough and may wonder if I am mad.

'I assure you I am quite sane,' he claimed. 'I understand there are people who often think I am slightly mad; so often that I now regard it as rather a compliment.' In fact, 'if I am slightly mad,' he remarked (in the same way he had haranged General Dill in the aftermath of Dunkirk, when Dill voiced his fear of imminent German invasion), then there were, as he put it, 'a large number of people I could name who are raving lunatics!!'

He was not mad, it seemed to those present, but strangely, exceptionally, even coldly rational – yet human, at the same time. He knew exactly what he wanted, and wanted their help in getting it done. 'What I have done is to get over to you the "atmosphere" in which we will now work and fight', he summarized; 'you must see that atmosphere permeates right down through the Eighth Army to the most junior private soldier. All the soldiers must know what is wanted; when they see it coming to pass there will be a surge of confidence throughout the Army,' he predicted.

'I ask you to give me your confidence and to have faith that what I have said will come to pass.

'There is much work to be done.

'The orders I have given about no further withdrawal will mean a complete change in the layout of our dispositions; also that we must begin to prepare for our great offensive.'

This brought Monty to the matter of 8th Army's 'absurd' headquarters. 'The first thing to do,' he announced, 'is to move our HQ to a decent place where we can live in reasonable comfort and where the Army Staff can all be together and side by side with the HQ of the Desert Air Force' – a decision that was, in itself, to prove perhaps the most important change in desert warfare in World War II, as Rommel's Panzerarmee war diaries would attest. 'This is a frightful place here, depressing, unhealthy and a rendez-vous for every fly in Africa', he went on; 'we shall do no good work here. Let us get over there by the sea where it is fresh and healthy. If Officers are to do good work they must have decent messes, and be comfortable. So off we go on the new line.

'The Chief-of-Staff will be issuing orders on many points very shortly, and I am always available to be consulted by the senior officer of the staff. The great point to remember is that we are going to finish with this chap Rommel once and for all. It will be quite easy. There is no doubt about it.

'He is definitely a nuisance. Therefore we will hit him a crack and finish with him.'[136]

Monty stepped down. The assembled officers rose and stood to attention.

'It was one of his greatest efforts,' de Guingand would chronicle some years later. 'The effect of the address was electric – it was terrific! And we all went to bed that night with new hope in our hearts, and a great confidence in the future of our Army.'[137]

The army had a new commander; the staff a new chief.

17

The New Line

An insubordinate smile

On the evening of 13 August 1942, the first of the 'new regime' orders went out from 8th Army headquarters to units and formations. A phone call was made to GHQ Cairo, asking for 44th Infantry Division to be sent up immediately, while XIII Corps headquarters sent out an order summoning all 'heads of branches' to begin preparations to receive the fresh division, and to scrap the idea of a mass withdrawal by the New Zealand Division to 'Defended OP' positions.

Instead of withdrawal, the 'following new policy' was to be instigated, 'involving the strengthening of the New Zealand position by an all-round minefield and the addition of a Brigade Group of 44 Division',[1] while the other two brigades of 44 Division would dig in on the Alam Halfa and Khadim Ridge, which Monty had identified as the crucial feature in bringing Rommel's expected attack to a halt – currently defended by only a battalion of weak infantry (fewer than 900 men) without artillery.

The phone call from 8th Army HQ, meanwhile, caused consternation at GHQ in Cairo. Not only had Monty assumed premature command of 8th Army, but was, a few hours later, already demanding reinforcements – in particular a fresh division, only recently arrived from England, unacclimatized to the desert, which Churchill had wanted to see in the front line but which Auchinleck had refused to bring up – since he wanted it for his GHQ 'stop line' around Cairo. So great was the nervousness about a German breakthrough, in fact, that three days before Monty's arrival in the desert, on 10 August, orders had been given that one of 44 Division's brigades was to be held *east* of the Nile river! Similarly, all bridges across the Nile had been reinforced with troop protection and more anti-aircraft units. At first, then, Monty's 'request' was turned down – and only when Monty took the telephone himself and spoke to Major-General Harding was the call taken seriously. Harding consulted Auchinleck. 'Have you asked Alexander? See what he says,' the 'Auk' responded with irritation. Alexander was found talking to the British ambassador, and was told of Monty's request. 'Is that what Monty wants?' he asked. 'Yes,' Harding assured him. 'Well, do it.'[2]

The commander of 44 Division thus received the warning call at 10 p.m. on 13 August – and within hours the division was on its way to Alam Halfa. Meanwhile, having had another talk with de Guingand, Monty retired to one of Auchinleck's desert trucks. 'By the time I went to bed that night I was tired,' he recalled in his memoirs. 'I'm afraid it was with an insubordinate smile that I fell asleep: I was issuing orders to an Army which someone else reckoned he commanded!'[3]

The flight from Egypt

At GHQ in Cairo, meanwhile, Auchinleck's chief staff officer, Lieutenant-General Corbett, had spent the day updating his 10 August orders concerning the possible retreat of GHQ to Sarafand in Palestine. The latest air 'baggage allowances' for officers' evacuation needed to be set, urgently: 75lb for lieutenant colonels and above, but only 60lb for majors and below. Also, a new instruction was necessary, under which four, rather than three, air passages would be required for the anticipated 'flight from Egypt': one for himself as CGS, one for Major-General Dorman-Smith, one for Brigadier Davy, the DMO, and one for Major-General Harding.

But the only flight Corbett would now be making would be to India, and utter obscurity.

New brooms

'I was woken up soon after dawn,' Monty remembered of 14 August 1942, 'by an officer with the morning situation report. I was extremely angry, and told him no one was ever to come near me with situation reports; I did not want to be bothered with details of patrol actions and things of that sort. He apologized profusely and said that Auchinleck was always woken early and given the dawn reports.

'I said I was not Auchinleck and that if anything was wrong the Chief-of-Staff would tell me; if nothing was wrong I didn't want to be told.'[4]

The duty officer was not the only one to be surprised. Straight after breakfast on 14 August 1942 Monty left his headquarters to visit Corps units – where he would acquire his first distinctive desert headgear: an Australian bush hat on which he would, day by day, pin the badges of all the regiments he visited. He wanted to get known by the men – fast. As General Sir Oliver Leese later noted, 'The Army Commander on his first visit to the Australians had gained their confidence by wearing one of their hats. It was all part of his plan to get his personality over to his troops; and when he visited other units nearby he put their regimental badges on his Australian hat. Critics in the clubs in London shook their heads sadly at the idea of a General wearing more than one badge on his hat, but how wrong they were. General Montgomery had only a few weeks to get himself over to the men; for when he went out to North Africa he was unknown to most of his command.'[5]

While Monty examined the vital Ruweisat Ridge defences, comprising the northern and central elements of the British front line, Brigadier de Guingand departed in the opposite direction: to relocate 8th Army headquarters by the sea. When Auchinleck's GHQ liaison officer arrived at 8th Army headquarters at noon from Cairo, therefore, he found the army commander's cupboard bare. Worse still, Monty's staff now flatly refused to co-operate with Auchinleck's proposed 'Deltaforce War Game' for which 8th Army had been requested to provide two staff officers. 'In view of 8th Army's signal U453 timed 0905/14,' the officer reported back to Cairo, 'it is confirmed that no, repeat no, staff officers will be available.' Similarly, Auchinleck's request for a 'Plan of Wadi Natrun defences [on the route to Alexandria] to be given to staff officer who was organizing it' was treated with utter contempt. Colonel Mainwaring, the senior operations officer, 'stated that in view of Eighth Army Commander's new order for "no looking over your shoulder" and "fighting on present position" there is no need for a Wadi Natrun defensive position, therefore there is no action required.'[6]

Monty's address to his staff had evidently done the trick – the staff was behind him. Auchinleck's liaison officer concluded his report with a note about 'future moves'. Neither army commander nor BGS were seen, 'latter being on a recce in the Burg-el-Arab area, neighbourhood of HQ RAF, Western Desert Force. This recce was with a view to moving HQ 8th Army to a site in this locality. The present hope is to move on Sunday 16/8.'[7]

As de Guingand reconnoitred the site for the new army headquarters, Monty carried out a series of blitz visitations. At the 9th Australian Division there was 'general relief and satisfaction' at Monty's 'new policy' – especially the news that 'the formation of battle groups was to cease' immediately, and that the division would fight as a division. 'From the first day of its arrival in the desert, the breaking up of the division and its formations into battle groups with inadequate fire resources and lacking the advantage of the normal system of command and control had been strenuously and continuously opposed,' the division's report on operations at Alamein afterwards chronicled. 'For this reason the new policy was most welcome.'[8]

The same was true of Monty's visit to the 1st South African Division's forward areas. By 2 o'clock he had reached 5th Indian Brigade on the Ruweisat Ridge. Cover was difficult to provide on the rocky, bare ground, but the ridge was obviously the key position in the north – therefore, Monty ordered, it would have to be strengthened by further mines, more dug-in and blasted positions, and the siting of an armoured brigade of Valentine tanks in support, behind the front. Meanwhile, the 'Scheme of withdrawal to MAIN defence and formation of battle groups [was] cancelled', the brigade's war diary recorded.[9]

South of the Ruweisat Ridge were the New Zealanders, whom Monty had visited together with Freyberg on the previous afternoon. As Freyberg's son later noted, before Monty's arrival Freyberg's correspondence and diary entries, where they related to the war in Egypt, 'were gloomy; after it there was a new note of hope and growing confidence'. On 14 August, for example, Freyberg's diary entry ran: 'Went to NZ Div [from XIII Corps HQ] immediately after breakfast. Told them the situation and policy of "New Brooms".'[10]

For General Freyberg, his son considered, Monty's advent was 'the turning point' of World War II.[11] For his part Monty was satisfied that, reinforced by a brigade of 44th Division and with new minefields and gun positions, the New Zealanders would now hold firm at Alam Nayil. The New Zealanders, equally, were impressed by the new army commander – as Brigadier Kippenberger, commander of 5th New Zealand Brigade, later recalled. 'The new Army Commander made himself felt at once,' he described. 'He talked sharply and curtly, without any soft words, asked some searching questions, met the battalion commanders, and left me feeling much stimulated. For a long time we had heard little from Army except querulous grumbles that the men should not go about without their shirts on, that staff officers must always wear the appropriate arm-bands, or things of that sort. Now we were told that we were going to fight, there was no question of retirement to any reserve positions or anywhere else, and to get ahead with our preparations. To make the intention clear our troop-carrying transport was sent a long way back so that we could not run away if we wanted to! There was no more talk of the alternative positions in the rear. We were delighted and the morale of the whole Army went up incredibly.'[12]

The message: 'dig'

The important thing was to make sure the 44th Division got up without delay from the delta, both to reinforce the New Zealanders and garrison the Alam Halfa feature properly. Though new to the desert, the men were not new to Monty. 'The Eighth Army was under new management,' wrote one soldier in the division, W. R. Garrett, a private. 'The new commander was a General Montgomery. He was unknown to the desert veterans but we had served under him in South East England, and a more dedicated leader could not have been chosen. He insisted on all ranks being "put in the picture" as much as possible and the gist of the message on Alam Halfa was – dig.'

This was far from easy, given the hard rock of the Alam Halfa escarpment – yet crucial if the division was to withstand German air, artillery, panzer and infantry attack in the coming days. 'Gradually our situation assumed a shape and meaning,' Garrett recalled. 'We were on the Southern end of a rocky ridge about three hundred feet above the surrounding desert. To the South and West lay a vast yawning wilderness', and on the 'far distant horizon another lonely ridge could be discerned. These ridges bore names on the Army maps that soon became familiar to us and to the world. We were on the Alam Halfa ridge. Beyond was Himeimat ridge. I soon acquired a fascination for Himeimat, akin to a rabbit's fascination for a stoat for thereon we learned sat the dreaded Afrika Korps, looking across the shimmering miles in our direction.'

Himeimat would be the nexus of Rommel's forthcoming offensive. The desert and the work, meanwhile, were pitiless. 'Our rations were bad, corned beef and biscuits and little else served with a sprinkling of sand and garnished with flies. Half a gallon of brackish water for all purposes per man per day. This inevitably led to stomach disorders, a raging thirst and filthy clothes. Above all in terms of torment were the flies. Flies swarmed around us the whole day, seeking moisture in our eyes, mouths and ears. The work was demoralising. Picks and shovels were our only tools and were soon blunted on the unyielding rock. We welcomed the nights and a respite from the torment and toil and sweat. We welcomed the sunrise for its relief from the night's chill. Cuts and abrasions, and there were many, were constantly covered in flies and sand and developed into "desert sores" that festered and refused to heal. If bandaged the flies would penetrate between the folds and search for blood.'[13]

There was certainly no assumption that Rommel could be held. 'Fear would sometimes rise in our hearts as we contemplated our pathetic efforts at fortifying Brigade Headquarters,' Garrett recollected truthfully – work that 'required slit trenches, weapon pits, vehicle and gun positions all of which had to be hewn out of rock.' Garrett's best friend was killed by Stuka divebombers swooping out of the sun – 'writhing and squirming in agony with two stumps smothered in blood and sand where his legs had been severed.' As Garrett chronicled, 'Slit trenches were too shallow, weapon pits inadequate and the situation that would present itself if the 21st Panzer Division loomed over the crest of the ridge on its way to Cairo defied description. In an effort to complete the task in time, Royal Engineeers tried to help with explosives. This had the effect of destroying what little shape or form we had wrested from the rock and adding little to the depth. It all seemed quite hopeless and we despairingly slogged on in our own primitive and painful way.'[14]

This aspect of desert war was one which most armchair-historians all too often ignored, content to see war as a romantic game between gentlemen who were not prey to the cardinal sins of vanity or boastfulness – ignoring Nelson, and his indelible effect on the morale of British 'tars'.

The lowest ebb

British morale had, in the summer of 1942, reached a very low ebb. Correlli Barnett would later claim 'it would be wrong to place too much emphasis on the moral effects produced by the new commander'.[15] Never were the words of a military historian and university teacher more ill-judged! To the ordinary soldier, sent out from an old-fashioned, class-divisive yet democratic and unwarlike country, war was, thanks to the horrific losses on the Somme and at Passchendaele, *not* a game. Churchill was loyally cheered by the officers, but often booed by the soldiers. Indeed, when an 8th Army soldier heard on the radio, a few weeks before Monty's arrival, that Churchill had flown to America, word went round the unit that Sir Stafford Cripps – the left-wing Labour Leader of the House and an increasingly bitter opponent of Churchill's direction of the war – was 'the new Prime Minister'!

Churchill, in short, was far from popular among the men. As one artillery bombardier recorded in his diary, 'This very startling news gave rise to a variety of rumours the worst of which was that Churchill had seen the red light and fled, to be succeeded by Cripps who would hang on until Stalin took over!' – one of a number of rumours that 'mightily pleased the Red element among us who had been advocating a Second Front for a long time as well as decrying Churchill's leadership'.[16]

Thus, among the hardened old 'desert hands', while there was perhaps less fear of combat, there was also greater demoralization about the conduct of the war in general than at home. As Tom Witherby, a wireless officer in 23rd Armoured Brigade – which had been virtually wiped out in Gott's suicidal counter-attack on 23 July in Happy Valley – recalled, 'there were graves everywhere as well as dead crewmen still in their tanks. Flies rose in clouds and eating was difficult. The flies were always on one's hands and arms and knees. The passage of hundreds of vehicles had broken the surface and the dust was terrible. From about two hours after sunrise until midday and from 3 to 6 every afternoon a high wind came up. Rolling dust clouds moved steadily from the North East. Ruweisat Ridge, along which "C" Track ran was now a kind of powder pot, with white dust eighteen inches deep as fine as flour.' Morale was rock bottom.

As Witherby lamented, 'no senior officer ever came to see us', and no one seemed to have any idea how to wrest the initiative from Rommel. 'As far as I remember,' Witherby recalled of the days before Monty's arrival, 'we did not do any training of any kind and had no idea of what we were supposed to be doing or what the plan was. There was a feeling of ill omen and doom and the probability that when the Germans attacked, we would be defeated. The method of the Generals seems to have been to wait until an attack started and then issue Orders accordingly. There was no prior plan or preparation or rehearsal. The troops were supposed to be fully trained, so no further training was needed. Everyone was uneasy. Just a few miles away, over the hill, was the legendary General (now Field

Marshal) Rommel. At any moment he might do something and recent events had shown that this was likely to be unpleasant. Wherever he attacked, we [23rd Armoured Brigade] would have to go and make a counter attack. The "Cavalry Charge" was almost the only manoeuvre that anyone considered.

'No one in Britain or the Middle East seems to have appreciated how good the Germans were,' Witherby felt. The German panzers – especially the Mk IIIs, IVs, and latest Mk IV 'Specials' with their long-barrelled 75mm guns – completely outgunned their British counterparts, as did their mobile, armour-protected 88mm anti-aircraft/anti-tank weapons – yet it was the *combination* of artillery, infantry, panzers and Stuka divebombers, and the synchronized tactics they employed, that made Rommel's smaller, leaner Panzer Army so lethal and so dreaded. As Witherby noted, 'all the weapons outranged those of the Allies and this was used in a standard Battle Drill in which the German soldier first of all pinned down his opponent by fire and then destroyed him at long range without the German soldier himself being placed in equal danger. This system of Battle Tactics enabled an attack to be mounted at short notice without reconnaissance. In effect, the Germans groped or felt their way forward, destroying each defensive position as it was found.'[17]

Where plans were rehearsed, there was a depressing sense of futility and amateurism. Bombardier Challoner, supporting 22nd Armoured Brigade at Dei el Farfa, noted in his desert diary Auchinleck's and Gott's preparations for 'fluid battle', with the brigade 'put on the job of practising moving to various positions which were called "Snipe", "Partridge", "Pheasant", "Grouse" & "Twelvebore"'[18] – English game-shooting terminology that was typical of English cavalry units: units imbued with class-snobbery, refusal to co-operate with other units or formations, hostility towards other arms, and complete lack of imagination as to the cohesive force of a modern army.

Somehow, Monty recognized as he toured the units of 8th Army, he would have to change the hearts and minds of these men: the ordinary soldiers as well as the officers – and it was here that, in the view of soldiers like Field-Marshal Templer, Monty would make his greatest contribution to the winning of World War II.

Harping on Rommel

German professionalism, as Monty suspected even before flying out to Egypt, was symbolized in the figure of Rommel. Auchinleck had sent out a message forbidding British officers to mention Rommel by name: 'I wish to dispel by all possible means [the idea] that Rommel represents something more than an ordinary German general, quite an unpleasant one though, as we have heard from his own officers. The important thing now is that we do not always talk of Rommel when we mean the enemy in Libya. We must refer to "the Germans," or the "Axis powers," or "the enemy" and not always keep harping on Rommel . . . PS. I am not jealous of Rommel.'[19]

To Monty this was silly. Ordinary soldiers would always simplify and invent nicknames; the answer was to concentrate on developing a professionalism of one's own that would match, and eventually overcome, that of the Germans. This would take time, which 8th Army did not have. Therefore, the tactics for meeting Rommel's expected attack must be limited to what the 8th Army could do, and do well. How, though, to persuade the soldiery that such limited tactics would work?

Given the simplicity of the way he intended to fight his first, defensive battle against Rommel, Monty's task was as much a moral one as military. How, overnight, could he raise the morale of a widely dispersed collection of Empire troops – New Zealanders, Australians, Indians, South Africans, Southern Rhodesians, Scottish, Welsh and English: troops who were tired of war, knew the name of the enemy commander but not their own, feared the awesome hitting power of German tanks, artillery and divebombers, and for the most part wished to go home?

Correlli Barnett would later mock Monty's attempts to raise morale by his speeches and visits to the troops as a mere 'publicity' stunt – the 'first British general to project himself to his public (the troops) like a politician or a crooner'[20] – while remonstrating that O'Connor, Wavell and Auchinleck had all 'enjoyed the complete confidence and loyalty of of their men'. Monty's attempts to put himself across to his troops was considered, in this gentlemanly view, to be 'profoundly distasteful' and unnecessary.[21]

Was it unnecessary, though? The fact was, the men of 8th Army did *not* have 'complete confidence' in their generals in the summer of 1942; just the opposite, in fact, following the disasters that had befallen them. A charismatic young naval leader like Mountbatten might address inexperienced Canadian troops, a few days later, on 17 August 1942, and stir them to heady, almost foolhardy self-confidence by his well-meaning (and well-photographed) rhetoric before their doomed attack on the coast of France; but Monty's task in the desert was infinitely more daunting: how to revitalize a demoralized army of 100,000 men, recently defeated in battle and having retreated 800 miles, making them believe in themselves again as an army, and in their ability to win?

Monty's achievement, in this respect, could never be too highly regarded, at least in the opinion of those who had to fight the subsequent battle of Alam Halfa, rather than write about it in the austere comfort of Cambridge college rooms. Major Tom Witherby, for example, returned from hospital to his 23rd Brigade on 17 August 1942, four days after Monty's arrival. 'From Amerya onwards, the aspect of the Desert was so different that I could not have recognized it,' he recalled. '"C" Track, once 200 yards wide and composed of fine dust was now a smooth road running between fenced minefields. The road surface was a kind of "tarmac" made of a combination of sand and sea water. The road, for defensive reasons changed direction frequently and there were neat notices on the fences saying "Please keep off the minefield". All over the Ruweisat Ridge there were neat slit trenches and other fortifications dug into the rock with neat parapets of sandbags. All these had been made with explosives and if one looked around one was sure to see a little puff of smoke as another hole was blasted out by the Sappers ... Everywhere there was a new spirit. One felt that there was at last someone in charge and someone who did not intend to be defeated. The intention was clear. All parts of the Army were to be made as strong as possible. Every post was to have All Round Defence, with its own stores and supplied within itself. We were told that 8th Army had its post at Alamein and that it would fight there and, if necessary, be destroyed there, but "there will be no further retreat, none at all, none".'

Looking back, Witherby was dumbfounded by the transformation. 'It is quite impossible to over emphasize the extent of the change and the speed with which the change took place. Montgomery took command on the evening of August 13th, 1942. I came back on August 17 and the change had already taken place.'[22]

How had Monty managed this?

Intervention by the Almighty

In deciding, immediately upon arrival on 13 August, to scrap Auchinleck's plans for 'fluid' battle, Monty was imposing his will upon the battlefield, based on de Guingand's verbal appreciation and his own military instincts. (De Guingand later confirmed Monty never saw, nor wished to see, Dorman-Smith's or Auchinleck's written appreciations or plans, which he ordered to be destroyed, in much the same way as he had once told his step-son John that he had ordered his letter to be burned, unread, as John had measles!) Monty was simply uninterested in his predecessor's views. '"All great commanders have acted on instinct,"' the historian Ralph Bennett quoted Clausewitz, '"and the fact that their instinct was always sound is partly the measure of their innate greatness and genius".'[23]

Monty's instinct was to be wonderfully confirmed a few days later, by Ultra. As Bennett wrote, this would be one of the supreme moments in the history of intelligence: a case where intelligence was able to back a field commander's instinctive military judgement, formed from a lifetime's experience and dedication to his profession. In the meantime, without Ultra confirmation, Monty had to act upon his own judgement, and this he proceeded to do, with an extraordinary and electrifying decisiveness that infected all around him. Monty's 'military instinct – there was little time for reason and reflection on that crowded day – told him what Rommel would do and how to counter it', Bennett summarized Monty's first day in the desert – and castigated his colleague, Professor Harry Hinsley, for having 'deliberately' sold military historians and the reading public a pack of lies when claiming that 'No basic change was made to Eighth Army's plans following the change of commanders'[24] – a claim so deliberately untruthful that Bennett accused his colleague of 'mischievously mishandl[ing] evidence':[25] the most grievous sin of all for an official historian, working with a sizeable team of assistants for the British government.

In his own independent account of Ultra in the Mediterranean theatre, Bennett was at pains to show not only how remarkable was Montgomery's instinctive military judgement on 13 August 1943, but how, although he took command two days earlier than he was entitled by Auchinleck to do so, it was 'not a moment too soon'.[26] Correlli Barnett had claimed that Monty's signal to GHQ that he was taking over command 'two days earlier than he should have done and in complete disobedience of orders' was 'of no importance militarily' and 'throws a bleak light on his character as a man'.[27] Bennett would have none of Barnett. 'Only three hours after [Montgomery's] address ended on the evening of 13 August,' Bennett pointed out, 'an order from Mussolini was signalled to [Rommel's] desert headquarters: "rapid preparations for a renewal of the offensive" were to be put in hand, the Duce reserving to himself the right to decide when to launch it ... Thirty-six hours after Mussolini's order came the first indication of date: Panzer Army asked the quartermaster's office how much petrol, ammunition, and food it could expect to receive by 25 August.'[28]

The race was on. To prepare 8th Army for a major, co-ordinated Panzer Army onslaught was therefore a matter of the utmost urgency – and had Monty not taken charge prematurely, and had he not immediately ordered the fortification of the the Alam Halfa Ridge, the battle for Egypt would in all probability have been lost. As Bennett pointed out, the Alam Halfa Ridge had not even figured in Dorman-Smith's 'Appreciation'; indeed, Alam Halfa had only been mentioned as one of a number of 'lightly-held' positions in Auchinleck's subsequent army instructions for 'fluid' battle. 'Montgomery sensed the importance of garrisoning Alam Halfa strongly as soon as he reconnoitred the ground ... Auchinleck, who had the authority, did not make it a key defensive position,' Bennett made clear to those who, in the late 1980s, still clung to the Barnett–Hinsley line.[29]

Bennett – who had himself flown out to the desert in the late summer and autumn of 1942 to learn how Ultra was used in the field, and how its effectiveness could be improved – was not exaggerating the timeliness and decisiveness of Monty's change of plan. Tom Witherby, the wireless officer of 23rd Armoured Brigade which had been ordered into suicidal battle on 22 July 1942, was, in retrospect, quite certain that, had 'Strafer' Gott lived, 'we would have been defeated at Alam Halfa and would probably have lost the war'.[30] This was certainly Monty's own view. In his eve-of-Alamein diary in October 1942, Monty penned a scathing indictment not only of the army he had inherited on 13 August, but of the men he held responsible:

The condition of Eighth Army as described above is not overpainted; it was almost unbelievable. From what I know now it was quite clear that the reverses we had suffered at GAZALA and East of it, which finally forced us back to within 60 miles of ALEXANDRIA, should never have happened.

Gross mis-management, faulty command, and bad staff work, had been the cause of the whole thing.

But the final blame must rest on General AUCHINLECK . . .

If changes in the higher command had not been made early in August, we would have lost EGYPT.

Actually, they were made only just in time.

A clean sweep was required in the Middle East, and new Commanders had to be brought in; Commanders who would NOT be influenced by past events, but who would take each situation on its merits and decide on a method suitable to the occasion and to local conditions.

GOTT was to have commanded Eighth Army. I am convinced that this appointment was not sound and might have led to disaster. GOTT was one of the old regime and had been in EGYPT all the war; his tactical ideas were influenced by past events; his plan in 13 Corps for fighting ROMMEL if he attacked in August was very bad and if it had been put into effect I consider the Eighth Army would have been defeated.[31]

On the evidence available today to serious military historians, there is little doubt Monty was right. The chaos produced by the mass exodus of divisions from their forward defence lines, the lingering obsession with mobility (usually backwards), the lack of a proper garrison at Alam Halfa, the dispersion of armour, and the fragmentation of the infantry divisions into battle groups might well have resulted in the greatest British military disaster of the war, leading to another panic in Cairo, and a fighting retreat by Alexander – as he had already conducted in Burma – into Palestine, with others fleeing to the Sudan.

Whether, in such circumstances of British defeat, Roosevelt would have been willing to risk the Torch landings inside the Mediterranean, rather than confining American forces to an invasion of Morocco, as his advisers counselled at the time, is debatable. With 300 Grants and Shermans unloaded at Suez and seized for his own Panzer Army's re-use (Rommel had re-used wherever possible captured British Valentines and even his famed command vehicle was a captured British Stuart tank), Rommel would certainly have been very much master of the Middle East, had he broken through. Malta could not have been re-supplied; starved of fuel and ammunition, the island would inevitably have fallen to Axis invasion, like Crete (and later Leros), giving Hitler and Mussolini's forces complete air and naval control of Mediterranean waters, with consequent improvement in their ability to supply the Panzer Army with men, munitions, tanks, fuel and provisions. Hitler might well have then chosen to mask Stalingrad, as his staff urged, while striking for the oil-wells of Abadan, and with Turkish help achieving a link-up between his forces in the Caucasus and the Axis forces in the Middle East. Certainly this was what Churchill, Brooke, Wavell, Smuts, Auchinleck and others feared. With the unmitigated disaster at Dieppe on 19 August 1942, all hopes of a credible second front in Europe would have collapsed, and the leadership of the United States might well have felt justified in concentrating upon a 'Japan first' strategy, as Admiral King and other senior American commanders were urging the President. Churchill might well have suffered the indignity of a second, and possibly successful, vote of no-confidence in Parliament, resulting in another Minister of Defence, even Prime Minister.

Such counter-factual history is, of course, speculative – but it serves to highlight the strategic as well as local importance of the battle of Alam Halfa: a battle which is so often forgotten or minimalized by historians of World War II. As Major Witherby noted, looking back over the years, the 'Army that the General [Montgomery] took over on 13th August could not possibly have stopped Rommel's German–Italian attack. Montgomery was a giant, Gott was a brave man, but he was tired and he simply did not have the intellectual stature for the Command. I do really feel that the circumstances in which Montgomery appeared at this critical time was one of the rare examples of direct intervention by the Almighty!'[32]

A completely new brain

In one sad sense, Auchinleck's failures were to Monty's advantage – for they encouraged Rommel to make his fateful decision to attack, unaware that there had been a change in British command.

In this way, basing his plan of battle on his experience of fighting the 8th Army over the past year, Rommel gave out his orders on 15 August. Early in July he had had only twenty-five serviceable tanks left, given his 800-mile offensive across the desert; now, despite Auchinleck's counter-offensive jabs, he had 200 German panzers alone, as well as mobile guns, infantry and Italian forces to hold his start-line and give added thrust to the Afrika Korps. The Panzer Army assault, backed by the combined air forces of the Luftwaffe and Regia Aeronautica stationed in the eastern Mediterranean, and using the Afrika Korps as its mailed fist, would smash through the British lines in the southern sector, and prompt a mobile battle – a battle which Rommel, after his succession of victories since the spring, was certain his army would be bound to win, in view of the brave, un-coordinated amateurism of 8th Army. All he needed was sufficient fuel and supplies to keep the Panzer Army going till it reached Alexandria and Cairo.

This plan would be exactly what Monty envisaged – and by laying new minefields at night, ordering defences in the south to be camouflaged – particularly artillery positions – and concealing his new strength between Alam Nayil and Alam Halfa, Monty was able to encourage Rommel in his ill-fated endeavour.

Monty's iron grip was remarkable, as all those at his headquarters later attested. A fed-up, humiliated staff came back to life, confident that the new commander meant business and was going to give his adversary a rude shock. Corps commanders were summoned to a conference at 8th Army headquarters at 0900 hours on 15 August, before Rommel had given out his orders only a dozen miles away, to 'discuss future policy' – and were told to bring 'tracings of minefields laid and projected' for inspection! Freyberg was impressed by Monty's 'speech', and noted in his diary that he agreed with everything the army commander said. Auchin-leck's liaison officer meanwhile reported back to Cairo that evening:

8th Army's defence policy is to stand and fight on present positions, and no withdrawal is to be made. The words 'Army Reserve Position' are being deleted from printed maps.

Defended localities are being considerably strengthened, in both personnel and e.g. fresh minefields.

The new Army Commander attaches particular importance to the holding of the Ruweisat Ridge.[33]

Ramsden's XXX Corps Operation Order No. 72 similarly reflected the Army Commander's new broom:

Introduction
1. All orders and instructions which refer to withdrawal from or thinning out of our present positions are hereby cancelled.

Intention
2. 30 Corps will defend the present FDLs [front line positions] at all costs. There will be no withdrawal . . .

The following day Freyberg addressed the commanding officers of his New Zealand Division, telling them that Auchinleck, Corbett and Dorman-Smith had now gone. 'It has been a clean sweep', he explained, and though he felt personally sorry for the 'Auk', 'there is no doubt it is a good thing to get a completely new outlook on the situation here . . . We have got into a desert complex of moving backwards and forwards. I think it is a very good thing to get a completely new brain on to the thing . . .'[34]

Meantime Monty gave to assembled commanding officers of the rank of lieutenant colonel and above an address similar to his talk to his staff on 13 August. Aged only twenty-two, the acting commander of the Light Anti-Aircraft Regiment's 3rd Battery, Major McSwiney, recalled being summoned to the conference by the sea at Burg-el-Arab – the first he knew of the change of army command. 'There was a mound about ten foot high where a small austere figure stood wearing an open shirt and long shorts, which showed his lilywhite knees. The only insignia of rank for this occasion was his hat, which was a standard General's headgear. About one hundred and fifty officers of Lt Colonel's rank and above, were told to sit down on the sand, whilst this unknown individual began to address us in short high-pitched staccato sentences. "You have been fighting the war by out-of-date methods . . . you are badly trained compared with the enemy . . . I am going to create a new atmosphere . . . the bad old days are over . . . a new era has dawned . . . and finally, If we cannot stay here alive, then let us stay here dead!" I think most of us were strangely impressed, although astonished at his "cocky" attitude – especially as he had not yet even got his knees brown! Within a few days he was seen amongst the forward troops, wearing . . . an Australian felt hat, handing out cigarettes and giving them the same message. Most of them had never seen a Lieut-General before, let alone talked to him. Even my own men were impressed, as he talked to them with sincerity and a total lack of ambiguity, in words they could understand. He predicted (with Ultra to help him!) what Rommel would do next, and how he would deal with it – all of which materialised in the next few weeks.'[35]

Ultra certainly helped the next day, 17 August 1942, when a new decrypt of one of Rommel's signals to Hitler's headquarters arrived at 8th Army headquarters, confirming Monty's instinctive judgement, made four days before: Rommel would shortly launch his offensive in the south, during the period of the full moon on 25 August or thereafter. Thus, when the GSO 2 (Intelligence) at 8th Army excitedly brought Monty the decoded signal, he was amazed at Monty's response. As the twenty-nine-year-old major – still wearing the three crowns of a captain – recalled, it was almost incredible how Monty took the news. Having listened to Williams's report he seemed satisfied that it confirmed his judgement, then moved on to the next battle! Thus, Williams remembered with amazement, Monty 'devoted most of his time that first morning I spent with him' not to discussing the forthcoming German thrust in the south but 'interrogating me about the enemy defences at Alamein. The new Commander of Eighth Army was one battle ahead of the rest of us. Lieutenant-General Montgomery was already devising the offensive which was to make his name.'[36]

Monty's new ADC, Captain Poston, also felt the bristles of Monty's new broom – and was amazed. 'I told you how I originally got the job with poor old Strafer Gott,' Poston wrote to his mother on 25 August, a few days before Rommel attacked. 'I had known [Gott] for quite a time. And I used to see quite a good deal of him when he commanded the 7th Armoured Division – But the new Army Commander is a very nice chap indeed, absolutely ruthless [as] regards people & their jobs. If they don't do it properly or make a mess of it they go. – And a very good thing too, it is what we want a bit more of in this Army. But with the new C in C [Alexander] & Monty all ought to be well & Rommel will have a bit of a sore face if he tries any monkey tricks now. And we will soon have him back again in his proper place & teach him a lesson [not] to take liberties with us out here.'[37]

A most remarkable military appreciation

To fill the role of XIII Corps commander – Gott's former command – Monty had meanwhile insisted on appointing another divisional general from England: his 3 Division protégé, Major-General Brian Horrocks, who arrived at Burg-el-Arab on 15 August, having left his division in Northumberland on the evening of 12 August.

General Alexander, in Cairo, had been charming but vague, almost out of touch, Horrocks related in a confidential account for the official British historian in 1945. 'All he said was: "Monty has some great plan for driving the Germans out of Egypt. I don't know what it is, but you are to take part in it, and I'm letting him get on with it" – that's all he said!'[38]

Corelli Barnett later mischievously twisted Monty's words to make it seem as if, in a 1958 addendum to his controversial, potentially libellous *Memoirs*, Monty accepted Field-Marshal Alexander's version of events in the latter's despatches.[39] In reality Horrocks, arriving at Monty's new headquarters at Burg-el-Arab, still had gained no idea from Alexander what the plan was, or what command he was to have. 'On arrival [15 August] I motored up to [Monty's] Headquarters in the desert, where I spent the first night and where he gave me his appreciation.

'Although he had only been a very short time in Egypt his appreciation was remarkably accurate,' Horrocks related to the official historian immediately after the war. Rommel would probably break through 8th Army's minefields in the south, Monty predicted, then would attempt to sweep around the rear of XXX Corps by seizing the Alam Halfa Ridge. Monty had already summoned 44 Division, and two of its brigades were already digging in on that ridge. The job of XIII Corps was to bar Rommel's passage: by digging-in tanks and guns, and subjecting the Panzer Army to a thorough beating from artillery and aerial bombing – but without allowing his 8th Army armour to take any unnecessary risks. The precious tanks of XIII Corps would be needed later, Monty explained, when 8th Army launched its own offensive. As Horrocks recalled, Monty was most emphatic about this – for he had no intention of fighting an all-out mobile battle until the new American tanks arrived at Suez early in September. 'I will not go into details,' Horrocks explained to the Official Historian, 'except to emphasize the following points':

a) He anticipated that Rommel would make one all-out effort to capture the Delta, and that this attack would be made on the frontage of my Corps, 13 Corps, which was holding the left sector of the Alamein position. He ordered me to defeat the Germans, *but not under any condition to become mauled in the process*, because he was then thinking of his offensive operations. He continually stressed this point afterwards and it is important to consider this when remembering how we fought the battle.

b) In his appreciation he even showed me on a map the area in which he proposed to launch the main attack during the [subsequent offensive] battle of Alamein. Looking back on this conversation the interesting point is that the plan, as outlined by General Montgomery, was adhered to in almost every detail . . .

Looking back still later, in 1960, Horrocks called it 'the most remarkable military appreciation I ever heard',[40] for it seemed incredible that the army commander should be more interested in the future 8th Army offensive than in Rommel's impending thrust, involving over 400 Axis tanks.

Having outlined his plan for XIII Corps' defence at Alam Halfa, Monty then announced that Horrocks would, in the subsequent British offensive battle, command the armoured *corps de chasse*, or X Corps, to be formed in part from XIII Corps formations, and equipped with the new American Shermans. Horrocks was horrified.

'I said "No, no, Sir, it's no good you know." He said, "Why not?" I said, "Well look: I've already commanded an armoured division in England – the 9th Armoured – and I know they'll resent it." You see, I came from a very humble regiment, the old die-hard Middlesex Regiment, and I knew at once that the reaction of the cavalry to me being put in charge of them would be bad. I said "No! For God's sake don't do that! Put [General Herbert] Lumsden in" – because Lumsden was the great hero, he'd won the Grand National [steeplechase], God knows what else, you know what I mean? He was the man. And Monty eventually said, "Yes, I think you're right. I will." '[41]

Monty's subsequent decision, on Horrocks', Alexander's and Alex's chief of staff McCreery's advice, to give command of his *corps de chasse* to General Lumsden – whom he had never met – was one Monty would deeply regret during the coming months. But for the moment at least he was satisfied Horrocks would obey his orders at Alam Halfa, and ensure the crucial defensive battle would follow a simple, well-rehearsed plan.

For Horrocks, however, it was not to be that simple.

A battle of morale

How hard it was to refashion 8th Army's polyglot collection of Empire and Commonwealth forces into a modern, professional, offensive army would be one of the untold stories of World War II. In the meantime, 8th Army had to face Rommel's final attempt at breakthrough. This, then, was Monty's immediate challenge: not only to lay down new policies and principles of modern combat, and to retrain 8th Army to act upon them, but to persuade his men to believe in him.

What Montgomery achieved, in the hours and days after his take-over, was to be, in its way, the equivalent of Churchill's great achievement in 1940, in the dark days following the defeat of the BEF at Dunkirk and the threat of German invasion in the summer of 1940. Military historians have debated the realistic capacity of the German armed forces – naval, air and ground – to mount Operation Sealion, the invasion of England, but its postponement and ultimate cancellation by Adolf Hitler was a decision based as much upon Churchill's rhetoric as upon stubborn RAF resistance in the Battle of Britain. As Len Deighton and Max Hastings have remarked, the RAF did not, in truth, 'win' the Battle of Britain, or even command of the air over Britain in 1940; in fact, Churchill's 'positively mischievous' interventions almost lost Britain the battle.[42] Yet Hitler understood better than anyone in Nazi Germany the power of rhetoric and morale – and in that one respect Churchill had certainly won, Hitler recognized. By his magnificent speeches in Parliament and on the radio, and his many personal visits to airfields, bomb-damaged buildings and formations preparing for invasion, Churchill had ensured the morale of the British people and its defence forces did not break.

Rommel, too, knew the significance of morale. He was suffering high blood pressure and needed a proper rest by August 1942; but when the Commando Supremo agreed to his replacement by one of his subordinates, given the ease with which it was assumed the Panzer Army would smash through to Cairo, Rommel's health miraculously improved. By his great battles at Gazala and Tobruk he had personally made possible the imminent fall of Egypt – and with the build-up of men, panzers and supplies he was not going to sacrifice that pearl to a rival German commander, or allow it to be jeopardized by less than superlative field command.

The subsequent contest between the Panzer Army of Africa and the 8th Army thus became a battle of commanders' wills as much as of tactics – just as it had been between Churchill and Hitler in 1940. Rommel, however, had a highly trained, well-armed, indoctrinated and professionally drilled, mutually co-operating army at his disposal, poised to make a concentrated, all-out attack to breach the British defences at Alamein and race for the Nile, as it had done at Gazala and Tobruk; Monty, by contrast, had inherited a dispirited, beaten imperial army, with poor equipment, poor co-ordination, and loss of faith in its high command. To transform such an army of troops from eight nations, almost overnight, into a new force willing to respond to his will, constituted a veritable 'miracle', in the view of 8th Army veterans – and those armchair-historians who later belittled this achievement were doing history a grave, even deliberate dis service, however understandable their personal 'distaste' for Monty's difficult, ungentlemanly, homosocial, even repressed-homosexual personality.

The task of the serious biographer-historian, in a new millennium, then, is to explain how, on Monty's part, this transformation can have happened – for it was upon Monty's will – his eccentric, misshapen character, his fanatical determination and his deeper motivation – that the military course of World War II now depended, in August 1942, as Field-Marshal Rommel marshalled his Panzer Army at Alamein for the breakthrough to Alexandria and Cairo.

It is time, in short, to explain Monty's psyche at this critical juncture in the history of the Western world; to reconsider not only whether Monty was a repressed 'gay' – in modern, ahistorical parlance – but whether, if he repressed his basic sexuality, it was upon his very homosocial nature that the explanation for his extraordinary performance in the Egyptian desert lay, as, in the days after 13 August 1942, Lieutenant-General Bernard Montgomery – 'shelved' by Churchill since Dunkirk – transformed a beaten force into the most famous and successful British army of the twentieth century.

18

Preparing for Battle

The changing definition of manhood

As Randy Shilts noted in *Conduct Unbecoming*, his groundbreaking history of gays and lesbians in the modern US military, the army's policy towards male–male love has reflected the 'turmoil' of American society's 'changing definition of manhood' in the twentieth century. Anti-gay and lesbian pogroms in the military, he noted, tended to cease whenever there was a war – for the successful prosecution of war demands not the second-best nor the politically correct, but the effective. And in front-line war, since the time of the Greeks, homosocial bonds are the glue which holds together fighting men, and sustains their morale in adversity.

The love of Achilles for Patroclus, just as the legend of the Theban Band of Brothers, symbolized in ancient Greece the importance of male–male love, affection and loyalty in combat – and World War I bore out this imperative. One of the reasons later adduced for the suicidal loyalty of young British officers and men in the trenches of World War I, despite the monstrous callousness of Haig and the High Command, lay in their loving responsibility for each other. Traditionally the 'spoils of war' had included the rape of women; equally, licensed brothels were crucial both as sexual outlets and for the control of sexual disease. Side by side with such hedonism – 'horizontal refreshment' as Monty called it – was, however, the heightened significance of platonic relationships between soldiers in long-drawn-out or bloody combat. 'In times of war even the crudest kind of positive affection between persons seems extraordinarily beautiful,' wrote W. H. Auden – and the beauty of World War I's homoerotic, stoic poetry has, in some ways, never been surpassed.[1]

War and sex

In his pioneering *The Great War and Modern Memory*, Paul Fussell re-examined the phenomenon of homosocial bonding in World War I, leading him to ask whether the lesser poetry of the second war resulted from writers being 'sexually and socially more self-conscious than those of the First? Were they more sensitive to the risks of shame and ridicule? Had the presumed findings of Freud and Adler and Krafft-Ebing and Stekel so diffused themselves down into popular culture that in the atmosphere of strenuous "democratic" uniformity dominating the Second War, one was careful now not to appear "abnormal"?'[2]

Fussell was unsure, though he noted how close the poets of World War I were to the aesthetic movement of the nineteenth century, which had revived the notion of the 'erotic attractiveness of young men', epitomized in poetry from Tennyson to Housman. World War I, with its strange contradiction between horrific, 'publicly-sanctioned mass murder' and 'unlawful secret individual love', lent itself to mass sublimation of sexual instincts. 'Given this association between war and sex,' Fussell argued, 'and given the deprivation and loneliness and alienation characteristic of the soldier's experience – given, that is, his need for affection in a largely womanless world – we will not be surprised to find both the actuality and the recall of front-line experience replete with what we can call the homoerotic.' As Fussell was at pains to point out, he used 'that term to imply a sublimated (i.e., "chaste") form of temporary homosexuality', for 'there was very little' of the 'active, unsublimated kind' at the front.[3]

Most (though not all) sociological/cultural historians agree. Joanna Burke, in her own study of World War I male sexuality, pointed out that intimate male bonding was not confined to public school boys, but that, in the absence of women, 'We must be wary of calling these homoerotic feelings "homosexual",' since in many ways they were merely a 'substitute for the "natural" intimacy between men and women'.[4] In sleep men often 'spooned' together, seeking the closeness and security of heterosexual intimacy they had left at home; 'Hell I think I must close now as my *wife* is in bed (if you can call it so. 1 blanket on the ground not bad eh) & wants me to keep her warm but it is only a Palestine wife, another Sussex boy, & we are both Jacks [men] so there is nothing doing . . . I really must ring off now as my mate keeps saying some nice words which I do not understand, getting cold I suppose. It is very chilly right now, & it is nice to have someone to keep each other warm,' one soldier had written from the trenches in 1917[5] – and little had changed, in this respect, in the Western Desert in 1942. In his seminal study of the 8th Army at Alamein, James Lucas remarked that 'certain pressures' kept the men 'chaste. Homosexual activities were both a military offence and morally repugnant to most soldiers. The only relief was masturbation; silently, at night and followed by feelings of guilt, remorse and shame.'[6] One contributor, an officer, recalled his nostalgia for the brothels of Cairo and Alexandria – Mary's House or Jardin des Fleurs – and the makeshift, all-male life in the desert: 'I notice that friends and buddies in the sections sleep together, two sharing a bed, and one wonders whether they satisfy each other's need in this way – mutual masturbation or whatever. One does have homosexual feelings sometimes up here – they are all such marvelous chaps to soldier with, so patient and humorous, but one cannot entertain the idea; it would be monstrous – the sixth commandment and all that – and Father used to say that that kind of thing was a kind of lunacy, to couple with one's own sex.'[7]

Monty's genius – as Rommel's – would be to see, instinctively and in a manner that had eluded the callous commanders of World War I, that great military leadership in a people's century *could* still be achieved, despite the mechanical, inhumane nature of 'total war', if the commander tapped into this deprived, lonely, womanless, at times homoerotic world of young soldiery, and refashioned it as a source of new personal pride and courage. Examining the 'crushes' of Siegfried Sassoon, Robert Graves and Wilfred Owen, Paul Fussell remarked that 'What inspired such [chaste] passions was – as always – faunlike good looks, innocence, vulnerability, and "charm." The object was mutual affection, protection, and admiration. In war as at school, such passions were antidotes against loneliness and terror.'[8] Joanna Burke agreed, quoting two young men going 'over the top' at the battle of the Somme: 'I looked at Herbert, I could see his lips move – I shouted but I couldn't hear myself at all. I wanted to tell him that we would keep together so I grabbed his hand and we went over together as we had gone to Sunday school, hand in hand.'[9]

Generals Wavell and Auchinleck were both, in all probability, homo-social, if one understands by that term the Thomas Mann picture of Gustav von Aschenbach, the 'invert' in *Death in Venice* who is drawn to male rather than female beauty, and is thus a prey to homoerotic rather than heterosexual desire. At age seventy-five Mann's desires remained almost exclusively of this kind, despite Mann being loyally married and having sired six children; indeed, he noted in his diary his axiom: 'the adoration of "godlike youths" surpasses everything feminine and arouses a desire comparable to nothing in the world'.[10] Such a view was probably replicated in many thousands of cases in the almost exclusively male world of the army, navy or air force.

Certainly this 'adoration' for young people of his own sex would be increasingly true of Monty, even in his eighties – and although we do not have the same wealth of evidence from his early years as we do in the case of Thomas Mann (who was two years older than Monty), the love-affections of the lonely general from 1938 onwards can be documented in considerable detail, thanks to the testimony of his 'love-objects' and his extraordinarily frank and revealing letters to them. 'Impossible,' wrote Mann in his late seventies, 'that any young man could love me';[11] yet Mann still continued to hope – and so, as will be seen, did Monty.

Love, as Fussell recognized, was the key element here, noting that the 'British have a special talent for such passions', instanced in writers from Oscar Wilde to E. M. Forster and J. R. Ackerley. Ackerley had been, like Monty in 1914, a platoon commander, in his case serving in the 8th East Surrey Regiment. In his classic autobiography, *My Father and Myself*, he described how he succeeded in 'sublimating his homosexuality into something purely aesthetic and "ideal"', as Fussell put it – for the war, almost as a matrix to its obscene carnage, heightened unselfish affections rather than lustful self-gratificatory pleasures at home. Indeed in the desert, as at English public schools, aestheticized, idealized affections for fellow males became as much an escape from the adolescent sexual fear of 'real' women as substitute for absent female company, or rehearsal for its eventuality. J. B. Priestley, the novelist, recalled how middle-class English boys, brought up away from home in the monastic, homosocial public schools, 'hailed with relief a wholly masculine way of life uncompli-cated by Woman'[12] – and it was most often these boys who found them-selves the platoon and company commanders in the desert in 1940, watching the men bathing naked in the sea, 'like the old adverts for Pears soap in the 20s, a lot of naked schoolboys frolicking about in an English stream. So one leaves it to wet dreams and sometimes masturbation.'[13]

As such it was these young officers, and the soldiers under their com-mand, to whom Monty had now to appeal, thousands of miles away from home – and it is intriguing to note the extent to which Monty's evangelical energy and success in setting about this task aroused the homophobic dislike of certain later historians.

Generals (later Field-Marshals) Wavell and Auchinleck were also attracted by young men, but were too taciturn and shy to allow their feelings full expression (though Auchinleck settled in Marrakesh after World War II, and ended his days there as a single man with young male servants). By contrast, Monty was, so far as 'love' was concerned, an unembarrassed evangelist, and the ideal of male–male love increasingly dominated his life, giving rise to a sort of demonic – because sexually repressed – energy: an energy that spilled out in his work as a field commander; in his passionate pedagogy as a military educator and trainer; and, increasingly, in his military writings: his urge to put down on paper his unending determination to clarify and simplify the business of modern war on behalf of 'his' men, from his diary and letters to his training notes and famous 'messages' to his troops.

This didactic impulse was not something Monty would ever delegate: for the drive to explain, simplify, inspire and proselytize came not simply fom his mind, but from his homosocial soldier's heart. *He loved young men* – and in the scrubby desert where water was scarce, and the need for a simple bath had led directly to his predecessor's death, the 'mad general' now found a sort of transmuted love: the love of an army in war.

Well-springs of success

To ignore the homosocial aspect of Monty's unique generalship is to miss the well-springs of his success as arguably the greatest – and certainly the most professional – twentieth-century Allied battlefield commander. Though starved of maternal affection, Monty had grown up in an evangelical household, in which love of God, as a male divinity, was *de rigueur*, as were the works of his grandfather Dean Farrar, such as *Eric, or Little by Little*. While Wavell suppressed his feelings in a love of poetry, and even published a collection of verse, *Other Men's Flowers*, Monty was by contrast direct, forthright, extrovert, unabashed. He liked the dashing young ADC he'd inherited from his dead predecessor, the twenty-three-year-old John Poston, and would soon acquire another attractive, blue-eyed young ADC, also a cavalryman: the twenty-two-year-old Johnnie Henderson. He liked the 'boys' to drive him around the desert, sitting always beside rather than behind them. Their youth, bravado and navigational skills touched and impressed him – indeed, it would be John Poston's indefatigable work as a battlefield courier, taking and fetching important messages (as well as impressions) at Alamein which would give Monty – as Henderson remembered – the idea for his famous team of forty liaison officers or 'gallopers' when Allied Land Forces Commander for D-Day and C-in-C 21 Army Group thereafter.

It is important to stress the youth of Monty's new charges (always in their early twenties) for Monty, at age fifty-four, was uncomfortable with people of the same or similar age to himself. Each relationship with his own contemporaries in age and station had to be negotiated, varying between outright personal hostility – as between himself and the 'Auk' – and guarded friendliness, even friendship and trust – as between himself and 'Alex'. Aside from these peer relationships, Monty's exclusive personal interest was in young men: not only because they were able to withstand the rigours of modern battle (air attack, shelling, mortaring, infection, lack of sleep) better than older men, but because they looked to him, and up to him. In that quasi-paternal – even maternal – role he could respond to their need for leadership, guidance, reassurance, confidence, protection and affection.

It was thus this dual experience – the challenge of having to take hold of a baffled, defeated host and shake it into a battle-winning army on the one hand, and the companionship of young men in the remoteness of the Egyptian desert, in an exclusively male environment, on the other – that evoked from Monty not only a simple, clear and feasible battle plan that would deal with Rommel's forthcoming offensive, but something equally significant, historically: a new compact, in a new world war, between an Allied army commander and his troops, a compact based on the strange, heterophobic widower general and young men, no matter how lowly their rank.

Depths of devotion

Monty had depended on young ADCs ever since the BEF campaign. Charles Sweeny, wounded at Dunkirk, was an example. 'Charles was an orphan and possibly it was that fact which drew us close together; he knew the depth of my devotion to him because I had told him of it; he knew that he could call on me for anything he needed, as if I was his father,' Monty wrote in the most public form possible – a signed obituary in *The Times* – after Sweeny was killed, having been one of Monty's most trusted (and happily married) liaison officers, at the end of the war. 'He was an Irish boy with a delightful brogue. There was nothing he liked more than a good argument,' Monty described Sweeny; 'he would "trail his coat" with great skill and, when discussion was started, he would take whichever side was likely to lead to the most heated argument; nothing would shake him from his adopted line of country. He had a very strong character and was utterly incapable of any mean or underhand action; his sense of duty was highly developed, and his personal bravery very great.'[14]

In England between 1940 and 1942 Monty had proved he could arouse the loyalty and faith of a growing coterie of such officers, both personal and staff, who respected his military vision as he rose in rank and command, and whom he helped up the ladder of the army. The challenge now, in the summer of 1942, was to extend the pattern or template of that homosocial, teacher–pupil bond into a relationship with an entire army in the field. And because 8th Army so desperately needed leadership, guidance, reassurance, confidence, protection and affection, Monty was able to perform what seemed to so many to be a 'miracle' in the summer of 1942: to make jaded, bewildered, sometimes frightened young men believe in themselves once again.

To outsiders – particularly Americans, as time went on, and British club or college historians – Monty would appear (and was) braggartly, vain, rude, dogmatic and impossibly self-righteous. But to the men of his adopted tribe, the 'chief', as Trumbull Warren called him, could not, once his predictions of success in battle proved true, do wrong. By then he had become not only their adopted leader, but in the same manner that he adopted their desert clothes, even their headgear, he'd become one of them: an honorary subaltern, NCO, even private. As one corporal remembered of the terrible day when Monty left command of the 8th Army, ' 'E were one of us; and nothing could ever take 'im away. I felt as if I were having me right arm cut off.'[15]

Professionalism is not enough

Years later, Brigadier Sir Edgar Williams would reflect not only on his baptismal meeting as a twenty-nine-year-old captain turned major with the new army commander, but on the nature of the pact that arose between them – for Monty not only applauded the intelligence officer's youth, but soon recognized his talent for intelligence by promoting him to become head of army intelligence in North Africa, in Sicily, in Italy and, ultimately, for the Allied D-Day armies: a heady responsibility for a junior history scholar from Merton College, Oxford.

Monty, however, revelled in the fact that Williams was *not* a regular army officer – licensing Williams to speak openly in a way that regular officers, standing on ceremony and institutional rank, rarely did. 'Did I like him personally? Yes I did,' Williams confessed; 'I liked him very much indeed. He was an exhilarating experience, as the rest of Eighth Army had soon discovered. One was impressed by his sheer competence, his economy, his clarity, above all by his decisiveness. He had made himself the complete professional and he was therefore a quite admirable man to discuss the enemy with, for the Germans, as soldiers, were nothing if not highly professional too.'[16]

As Williams also reflected, after the war, Rommel's legendary status among British troops had owed itself not only to his success in battle; it had become a British excuse for lack of professionalism in co-ordinating the efforts of their own 8th Army – 'our subconscious desire to explain to ourselves our own lack of success'. Rather than face up to the fact that Britain was losing the war by its refusal to meet the professional demands of modern battle, the British had consistently sought to excuse their failures by romanticizing their desert opponent, ignoring the dedicated Nazi and preferring to create in him the image of a mythical North African knight or – as befitted the landowning English upper-middle classes – a 'Desert Fox', as they dubbed him – 'dramatising', as Williams saw it, 'in affectionate fear, a man with much in him to admire: who practised a soldier's hard ethic, blinkered, a-political'.

In this sense, Williams recognized, the British still obstinately refused to accept the notion of total war, even in the darkest hours of World War II – and would be stunned by their later discovery of the Holocaust. It also explained the public's continuing support for Churchill, however resented he was by political colleagues who deplored his pugnacious love of war and his poor prosecution of it; for, despite all his faults, Churchill had, by his mastery of romantic metaphor, been able to maintain a deeply English, even Shakespearean conception of hostilities.

Like Rommel, Monty was imbued by the hard ethic of war; was blinkered, and (at this time) apolitical. To his credit, however, the unknown general recognized on his arrival at Alamein that professionalism was not enough to break Rommel's spell; that the soldiery, composed largely of civilian volunteers and conscripts from so many Allied nations, was not attracted to total war, but – if at all – to the ideals endangered by Axis tyranny. They thus preferred a more personal, quasi-Shakespearean, personality-based war, as their songs and ditties would demonstrate; a war that individualized, sometimes demonized, yet at heart humanized, even romanticized, the struggle in the desert in their eyes. In their own commanders – Generals Wavell, Cunningham, Ritchie, Auchinleck and Gott – they had never found an equivalent to Rommel, and no amount of 8th Army or Middle East publicity could make of such austere, distant commanders the hero the men of 8th Army craved, however hard the GHQ press office tried. Even at the last hour, as Rommel built up his Panzer Army supplies for his final, decisive Axis attack, the British Prime Minister had managed to appoint the wrong man in Gott, and only by the misfortune of his death had the British war machine come up with their least romantic or charismatic commander, flown over from England: a small, unphotogenic, sharp-nosed, foxy-faced general with white knees, drilling blue-grey eyes and, where known at all to the soldiery in Egypt, a reputation for being a martinet – in particular for physical fitness.

Master

The unknown general certainly did not seem the stuff of historic military transformation. And yet, from the moment Monty gave out his orders for all-round fortification of the Alamein–Alam Halfa features, issued his 'no retreat, no surrender' edicts, and began to address not only the staffs and commanders, but also the men of his new army, the transformation became palpable; a transformation that had, at its kernel, an almost Grecian, classical quality: not only in the confrontation between opposing armies camped in the literally deserted landscape of sand and scrub, bordering the blue expanse of the Mediterranean and Aegean seas, but also in this new compact between leader and led: between *erastes*, the mentor, and *eromenoi*, the pupils.

'On the one hand was age, wisdom, and accomplishment; on the other, youth, beauty, and a desire to emulate and excel,' Louis Crompton has written of Greek pederasty: a description that vividly encapsulates Monty's impact on his staff.[17]

Certainly the young Oxford history don who brought Monty the latest intelligence appreciation on 17 August 1942, quickly dubbed Monty with the epithet 'Master' – a name that stuck, among his staff, for the rest of the war. Kit Dawnay, the young Guards officer whom Monty had made his intelligence officer in 3 Division, reflected in his later years on his memories of living with Monty at his various forward headquarters. Dawnay wished, as he wrote, 'above all else to stress the fact that one always had the curious feeling of being taught – and by a great master. In this connection it is interesting to note that he [Monty] was privately and affectionately known by those who worked for him at 8th Army Tac HQ as "Master". There were always new things to be learnt from him . . . It was a quite unforgettable experience.'[18]

Monty's was no grand intellect, yet he was a born teacher – his determination to sort, simplify and impart to others an indelible feature of his personality from the moment he had been put in charge of the training of mountain scouts on the North-West Frontier in the first decade of the century. In the 'fog' of World War I his skill in this area had been both acknowledged and rewarded, as he was given higher and higher promotion as a staff officer. Thereafter, in peacetime, he had sought to integrate those teaching skills into the business of command, with varying results – indeed, had often come close to dismissal for insubordination and high-handedness in relation to the Establishment. But now, in the desert, there was no Establishment to outrage, as Churchill had noted in his letter to his wife Clemmie: only the enemy.

Working as a team

Those 8th Army officers whom he did not like or respect, Monty would simply sack or transfer. The young GSO 1 (Ops) at 7th Armoured Division, for example, recalled that 'We were all pretty sceptical', when Monty made his first appearance at divisional headquarters. 'He was abominably rude,' the officer remembered, 'unnecessarily offensive to some rather elderly gentlemen – including one very highly respected old Territorial gunner called Eustace Smith.'[19]

It was not, however, that Monty wanted, like Churchill, an army of yes men, but that he wanted, without delay, an army that would fight, and fight cohesively, according to tactics he laid down – not 'belly-ache'. By and large such fighters tended to be younger rather than older. 'I've sent for *Jorrocks* – he's very good – enthusiasm, enthusiasm,' he proudly told his staff the day after his arrival[20] – for enthusiasm would be the key to boosting the morale of 8th Army. Commanders who could help him raise morale were both rare and highly prized by him – a quality he came most genuinely to admire in George S. Patton.

In the meantime, however, Monty's own work was only beginning. The affection he bore the young men around him had to be transmitted to an entire army. This time, at least, it was an army undistracted by the proximity of wives and families, or even the fleshpots of Cairo and Alexandria (save on leave). To be sure, it was a recently defeated army, which made his own task the more challenging; but since no previous British commander had been able to impose his will and personality on 8th Army, Monty could hardly do worse than his predecessors, indeed, could only do better – as Patton would, when taking over the defeated US II Corps in Tunisia the following year.

As long as he believed in himself and in his mission, then, Monty had every reason to think he could shake up 8th Army, and make it into a battle-winning rather than losing body of men. As Major Witherby remarked, long after the war, Monty might be a control freak, but he was also a Scrooge in terms of losses, especially lives: 'Everything, both men and weapons, had to be used to the best advantage and with care. In the expenditure of human life, he was a miser'[21] – for in the peculiar way that he had, Monty had immediately adopted the men of the 8th Army as 'his' men, later infuriating 'gentlemen'-historians, but reflecting the simple, homosocial affection he yearned – in the same loneliness that Thomas Mann recorded in his diaries and in his fictions as he grew older – to share and to celebrate, sublimated in a higher cause. In Mann, that cause was literature; in Monty, it was war.

'You do not know me,' he had prefaced his 'adoption' talk to the headquarters staff of 8th Army on the steps of his truck on the Ruweisat Ridge on 13 August 1942. 'I do not know you. But we have got to work together; therefore we must understand each other and we must have confidence in each other. I have only been here a few hours. But from what I have seen and heard since I arrived I am prepared to say, here and now, that I have confidence in you. We will then work together as a team; and together we will gain the confidence of this great Army and go forward to final victory in Africa.'[22]

A simple plan

Sensing that Horrocks might have trouble imposing his authority over the 'belly-aching' brigade and division commanders in XIII Corps, Monty ordered them all to meet him, three days after his arrival, at Alam Halfa – the day *before* Ultra confirmed Rommel's intention to attack in the south.

'I was told to meet the new army commander on Point 110 at Alam Halfa,' the thirty-five-year-old temporary brigadier commanding 22nd Armoured Brigade later recalled. 'I'd never met him before and all I knew about him was he was quite a fire-eater and that he was very keen on physical fitness and everybody in his division in England was on PT. And I said, God if this man comes and tries to put us on PT I shall go bolshie. Because of course we were under tremendous air dispersion wherever we rested – vehicles at least 100 yards from one another – and it was a very trying business going round your regiment, brigade or whatever, and when we came out of the battle the last thing we wanted to do really was PT. And I thought, if this man is obsessed with PT, we're not going to get on awfully well together!'[23]

Nervous about what was in store, Brigadier 'Pip' Roberts arrived 'a little bit early, naturally'.[24] Suffering from 'gyppy tummy, I felt there was just time to disappear over the nearest ridge with a spade and plodding my way back a few minutes later I saw a large cortège arriving at the appointed spot some five minutes ahead of schedule.'[25] Roberts joined them 'and we agreed it must be the point where we were going to meet. And various other people came up, including General Horrocks – he arrived next – one or two more armoured cars came and I wondered when the army commander was coming. And then a man got out of a car with very white knees, clearly he'd not been in the desert long, and wearing an Australian hat with not many badges on it at that time because he'd only just arrived, and I thought it was one of the journalists, you see. So I didn't take a great deal of notice, and then he came up to me and said: "Do you know who I am?" So of course I knew at once who he was! Without any further ado, I said, "Yes, sir," and that's how I first met Monty – on this place where the battle of Alam Halfa was fought.'[26]

There was no mention of PT. The merit of the new army commander, in Roberts' view, was that, whereas in the first half of August there had been a plethora of possible plans 'reminiscent of the situation in the Gazala line some three months earlier in May',[27] once Montgomery arrived there was one plan. 'Before Monty arrived we had a number of different plans. Plan A was this, Plan B was this, Plan C was that, you see. Now when Monty came, there was only one task; to stay on Alam Halfa. All our job was, was to stay there. Immediately the air was cleared, as it were. Everybody knew that we were not moving back, we were fighting here! That is that! Certainly a different atmosphere pervaded, at once. Liddell Hart doesn't agree with me quite on this, but he wasn't there, so he doesn't know. I mean, we all had a very high opinion of Auchinleck, we also had a very high opinion of "Strafer" Gott. But Monty gave as it were a new light on the whole thing: a simple, clear, firm light. And there's not the slightest doubt that if it made a difference to me, naturally it made a difference to the people under me. There's not the remotest doubt about the effect his arrival had.'[28]

Roberts was delighted to have a role he knew he could fulfil, rather than a series of highly dubious possible tasks, whether it was covering the withdrawal of the entire New Zealand Division or a mobile, flank attack on the combined Afrika Korps: 'You see, the defence is much more powerful than the attack, and to be effective in the attack you have to have a preponderance of 3 to 1 or thereabouts – something like that.' With Rommel currently enjoying a 4 to 1 superiority in medium/heavy tanks, Roberts was all too happy to abandon Auchinleck's 'fluid' schemes. 'No, if we were going to stay put like that, fine, we'd stay put. I didn't mind that at all. It was a simple plan. I knew that if we could hold our fire and we stayed put, then we would inflict more casualties than were inflicted on us.'[29]

There was, also, the preciousness of 22nd Armoured Brigade's fifty to sixty tanks to consider. 'We had all the Grant tanks that were left – all the leftovers from all the other units that had gone back to re-equip. Ours was really the only armoured brigade left in the desert – there was another brigade that was left up, called the 23rd Armoured Brigade and they had a few Valentine tanks – these were armed with only a two-pounder gun so they were not at all effective against the German tanks. So I was in the enviable – you might think rather nervous – situation of being in command of virtually the only armoured brigade we had in the desert at that time.'[30]

Monty's memory of the meeting at Alam Halfa was equally vivid – including a run-in with Roberts' divisional commander, the one-armed General Renton. 'During the day [16 August] I met on the southern flank the general commanding the 7th Armoured Division, the famous Desert

Rats. We discussed the expected attack by Rommel and he said there was only one question to be decided: who would loose the armour against Rommel? He thought he himself should give the word for that to happen. I replied that no one would loose the armour; it would not be loosed and we would let Rommel bump into it for a change. This was a new idea to him and he argued about it a good deal.'[31]

An impenetrable position

Renton's senior staff officer, later Field-Marshal Lord Carver, felt Monty had misunderstood Renton, imagining Renton to be a loose cannon in the offensive sense, when in fact the reverse was true – namely, that Renton, saddened by the number of casualties sustained in 'gallant attacks which then achieved nothing', was thinking of withdrawal, not attack. Reflecting on the desert war many years later Carver wondered whether Renton was 'slightly' homosexual; 'a very curious man' who had spent much time with Iraqis and Arabs, and was 'very popular with young men'. Renton was 'imbued with the idea of keeping your forces in being', as Carver put it tartly, 'to take them backwards' – like General Gott before him.[32]

Concerned, meanwhile, that General Renton did not understand his new plan of defence, Monty deliberately removed Roberts' armoured brigade from the Desert Rats Division that evening, and put it directly under Horrocks at XIII Corps. Renton, left with only a light armoured brigade, was furious.

As Horrocks confessed to the official historian, 'this was an untidy picture, as a Brigade should not operate directly under Corps Head-quarters, but I did not want there to be any risk of the Grant tanks being launched into battle by 7th Armoured Division without my order'. Had Renton been allowed to control the 'vital Grant tanks' of 22nd Armoured Brigade, and had he used them as envisaged under the plethora of Auchinleck–Gott plans, Horrocks felt the whole battle would have been in jeopardy: 'As we were outnumbered and out-tanked, if this Brigade was launched head-on at the Germans there was every chance that it would be completely written off; in which case we should really have lost the battle.'[33]

Brigadier Roberts, meanwhile, set to work with a will. The tell-tale British hunting codewords like 'Pheasant', 'Snipe', 'Snippet', 'Grouse',

'Cheeper', 'Gamebirds', 'Hamla', 'Woodcock', were ordered to be torn up; engineers were brought in to blast and bulldoze a series of positions for the Grant tanks on the slopes of Alam Halfa, while a screen of concealed anti-tank gun positions was set up in front of them. On 19 August Roberts confirmed the orders to his 22nd Armoured Brigade in writing, to the effect that '22 Armoured Brigade is to take up an impenetrable position which it is hoped the enemy will attack,' emphasizing that 'the position is a strong one and will resist any enemy tank or other attack', with 'the rear of the position being protected by Fortress "E" [Alam Halfa, garrisoned by 44 Division]'. Moreover, he added, 'the battle positions for armoured regiments are good, give considerable scope for troop commanders' initiative, enable tanks to remain concealed until fire is required and provide good hull-down positions'. In particular, he wanted anti-tank guns 'so sited that not only do they cover their own front but can cover the front of armoured Regiments thereby enabling them to remain concealed until a severe threat develops'. In conclusion he repeated: 'By taking up these positions it is hoped that for once the enemy may have to attack us in good positions of our own choosing.'[34]

This was the crux. The future battle of Alam Halfa was beginning to take shape – almost two weeks before Rommel actually launched his assault.

Churchill's visit

The 8th Army's main headquarters, meanwhile, had moved to Burg-el-Arab alongside the RAF at Desert Air Force headquarters, on the sea. There it was transfigured, becoming almost overnight perhaps the youngest and most professional army staff team of its kind on the Allied side[35] – so much so, in fact, that when the Prime Minister arrived on the evening of 19 August 1942, on his way back from seeing Stalin in Moscow, he could barely credit the change.

Gone, to Churchill's relief, was the 'meat-safe' and the 'liberal supply of camel-dung'. A sea breeze blew in off the shimmering Mediterranean, and the aura of confidence was palpable. Monty gave over his own converted truck, with its small bedroom and office, for the Prime Minister to sleep and work in. 'After our long drive we all had a delicious bathe,' Churchill wrote later, amused by the sight of so many naked bodies. 'All the armies are bathing now at this hour all along the coast,' Monty pointed out, motioning beyond the thousand or so 8th Army soldiers to the western horizon, where unseen German and Italian troops would also be stripping on the sand to plunge into the azure water.[36] Churchill himself 'had no bathing costume and I had some difficulty in keeping the press away as he walked towards the sea in his shirt. He was interested in a group of soldiers in the distance and said how curious it was that they all wore white bathing trunks. I had to explain that no one wore any bathing kit in Eighth Army,' Monty recalled. 'What in the distance looked like white bathing drawers was actually white flesh, which did not get brown because of the khaki shorts!'[37]

Army headquarters was now a hive of orderly activity. Removed from German fighter-range, Colonel Mainwaring, the G1 (Ops), ensured the HQ trucks were now laid out in such a way as to provide an operations courtyard, with maps both inside the lorries and draped outside. Crucially, army and air-force officers now worked side-by-side, sharing intelligence – intelligence which, via Ultra, had now confirmed that Rommel intended to strike in the south, with 25 August as the probable date for the battle.

Churchill's visit was paid on the same day as the doomed Allied cross-Channel raid on Dieppe – news of which Churchill eagerly awaited. But by the cooling beaches bordering the vast Egyptian desert near Alamein, Churchill's primary interest was in the state of the 8th Army under its new commander – and in the same way as the army headquarters staff had been on 13 August, Churchill found himself mesmerized by Monty's authority and confidence.

What astounded Churchill, as it astounded the normally dour British army chief of staff, General Sir Alan Brooke, was the speed with which Montgomery – arriving in the desert on 13 August, a week after their own visit to 8th Army on 6 August – had imprinted his own vision on 8th Army, imposing not only the tactical strategy he intended to adopt, but the kind of professional army he wished 8th Army to become – and his plans for the next-but-one battle. 'Monty's performance that evening was one of the highlights of his military career,' Brooke afterwards related.

He had only been at the head of his Command for a few days, and in that short spell he had toured the whole of his front, met all the senior Commanders, appreciated the tactical value of the various features, and sized up admirably the value of all his subordinate Commanders. He knew that Rommel was expected to attack by a certain date. He showed us the alternatives open to Rommel and the measures he was taking to meet these eventualities. He said he considered the first alternative the most likely one, namely, a penetration of his southern front with a turn northwards into the centre of his position. He explained how he would break up this attack with his artillery, and would reserve his armour to finish off the attack after the artillery had rough-handled it. His armour would then drive Rommel back to his present front and no further. He would then continue with his preparations for his own offensive which were already started. He would attack on the northern part of his front. It would mean hard fighting and would take him seven days to break through, and he would then launch his Armoured Corps (his Corps de Chasse, as he called it) which he had already formed . . . I knew my Monty pretty well by then, but I must confess I was dumbfounded by the situation facing him, the rapidity with which he had grasped the essentials, the clarity of his plans, and, above all, his unbounded self-confidence – a self-confidence with which he inspired all those that he came into contact [with].[38]

Auchinleck, too, had given Churchill an appreciation of the situation and his intentions in the very same operations caravan, but on the Ruweisat Ridge, two weeks before, on 4 August – and had not impressed the Prime Minister or the CIGS. 'Hugh Mainwaring and I virtually heard Winston Churchill [decide to] sack the Auk,' Brigadier 'Bill' Williams later recalled, 'because we stood outside the caravan waiting to be summoned if we were wanted on the ops side or the intelligence side – and Winston gave this astonishing description of what Rommel was doing and said to the Auk: "Well, what are you going to do about that? What's your plan?" I mean, he was incredibly well-briefed, of course he'd got his Ultra, he'd sort of thought it out: Rommel's doing this, what are we going to do? And knowing the Auk . . . the Auk, he wasn't very articulate then. I walked away and I remember Joe Ewart was up there from GHQ and I remember saying to Joe: "Well, we'll get a new army commander now. Who the hell will it be?" '[39]

It had been, at Churchill's implacable insistence, Gott. But now, listening to Montgomery's absolute conviction and clarity, Churchill was bowled over. To the deputy Prime Minister he cabled from Cairo the next day he was 'sure we were heading for disaster under the former regime'.[40] There followed a comparative description that would, in later years, rouse the injured pride of Auchinleck's biographers and other acolytes to sustained fury – for in it they recognized a typical over-simplification by the new army commander, interwoven with Churchill's richer, suppler, and less accusatory language. 'The army was reduced to bits and pieces and oppressed by a sense of bafflement and uncertainty. Apparently it was intended in face of heavy attack to retire eastward to the Delta. Many were looking over their shoulders to make sure of their seat in the lorry, and no plan of battle or dominating will-power had reached the units.'[41]

'About this disagreeable, inaccurate and offensive document the less said the better,' remarked Wavell's and Auchinleck's biographer, John Connell – presumably unaware that Churchill's personal dislike of Montgomery had denied Monty field command for two long years while Churchill's own nominees had stumbled from catastrophe to catastrophe.[42] Offensive or not, the fact remained that Churchill was witnessing with his own eyes a miracle in the desert – a transformation effected in a matter of days by the very man he had obstinately declined to appoint! To the War Cabinet of the United Kingdom, as Prime Minister and Minister of Defence, Churchill was now proud to report that a 'complete change of atmosphere has taken place. The highest alacrity and activity prevails. Positions are everywhere being strengthened, and extended forces are being sorted out and regrouped in solid units. The 44th and 10th Armoured Divisions have already arrived in the forward zone. The roads are busy with the forward movement of troops, tanks, and guns.'[43]

The Prime Minister, like the army, had been won over.

Napoleon's fourgon

Churchill's words echoed the feelings of thousands of ordinary soldiers in the desert. Lieutenant-Colonel Richardson, whose own confidence in Auchinleck in July and August had steadily diminished to the point where he thought renewed British defeat was all too likely, now wrote home: 'The new boss is full of confidence and knows exactly what he wants . . . in marked contrast to the previous regime under which orders had often been regarded as a "basis for discussion".'[44]

On 4 August 1942, on Churchill's first visit to 8th Army headquarters, Richardson had been ashamed. Now he was proud – indeed, when he awoke soon after dawn on 20 August and saw 'the Prime Minister being led by the hand of the Army Commander for a naked dip' he felt profound gratitude to the pudgy, white figure waddling down towards the sea. Churchill's great courage, flying 10,000 miles, often over enemy-held territory, to reorganize the Allied front in the Middle East and to confer personally with Stalin in Moscow, was now at last being matched by the courage and clarity of an 8th Army commander determined to take his army to victory on behalf of that venerated pale figure. 'Monty's devoted attention to the aged Prime Minister,' Richardson recalled later, 'reminded me of a nursemaid carefully leading her charge.'[45]

The *tableau vivant* said it all: at last a new generation was taking over the conduct – and the winning – of World War II, under Monty's firm hand. Nor was this simply a matter of headquarters confidence, for there could be no doubt about Churchill's genuine admiration for what Monty had achieved as he inspected a succession of 8th Army units and formations on 20 August: 44 Division on Alam Halfa, 22nd Armoured Brigade below the ridge, 7th Motor Brigade in the south, and the New Zealanders at Alam Nayil – where Churchill lunched with his old World War I comrade, Lieutenant-General Freyberg, while Monty, for whom a 'place had been kept . . . sat outside in his car eating sandwiches, and drinking his lemonade with all formalities', as Churchill later remembered with amusement.[46]

Montgomery had made it a rule not to 'accept hospitality from any of his subordinate commanders,' Churchill recalled[47] – though Monty's reasoning was more complex. Monty did not wish his commander's eye to be taken off the military ball by concerns about hospitality – though he himself was happy to make an exception, as he would later, again and again, from Tripoli to the Rhine, in Churchill's case, since the Prime Minister's presence in the front line was such a tonic to officers and men, representing different Commonwealth and Allied countries. As Monty's young ADC wrote home, 'it was magnificent to hear Churchill & see him & realise that his voice, manner & all his "idiosyncracies" were not put on'.[48] Taking his own sandwiches and lemonade in his car was for Monty a way of saying he himself would not add to the hospitality burden of an overworked divisional staff, especially with regard to a subject that did not interest him as a dedicated soldier, but which delighted the epicurean Prime Minister – cuisine and beverage.

Napoleon Bonaparte, Churchill later reflected, would at least have had roast chicken from his travelling *fourgon*, while Marlborough . . . Fascinated by great military conflicts and commanders – as a descendant, a historian, a former cavalry officer, a World War I battalion commander and a fighting politician – Churchill had always been enthralled by historical detail. The distinctive eccentricities of military commanders intrigued him – nowhere more potently than now, on his second visit to the 8th Army in August 1942. His mood was now ebullient and instinctive – for in his new certainty of British victory, he saw his carefully laid strategic plans, set out so painfully before Marshal Stalin, taking on a kind of imminent reality. Before flying back to Cairo from Burg-el-Arab on the afternoon of 20 August, therefore, the sixty-eight-year-old insisted on plunging naked once again into the Mediterranean, against his doctor's wishes – and to Montgomery's and Brooke's horror was 'rolled over by the waves' only to emerge 'upside down doing the "V" sign with his legs!'[49]

The smell of victory

Perhaps no single image more encapsulates Monty's achievement in the first seven days of his command of 8th Army in August 1942 than that of Churchill, buff naked, upside down and making a V-for-Victory sign with his white and hairless old legs.

Churchill was transformed, and astonished all those around him by his renewed excitement and energy – even mocking his ailing doctor, Sir Charles Wilson, who had fallen sick. Not even news of the tragic fiasco at Dieppe, as it emerged that day, with its painful toll of brave Canadians, mown down in almost cold blood upon the shingled beach as at Gallipoli, could dent Churchill's exhilaration. 'The Dieppe raid was a great show,' Captain Poston wrote to his mother a few days later, 'a bit expensive perhaps', but 'Churchill was quite pleased with it. He was here when the special signals came through about it & he was damn funny about his stay in Moscow & about Stalin. Things were a trifle difficult to start with but all ended up OK, which is the main thing.'[50]

To Stalin, Churchill had boasted of a major 'reconnaissance in force' that would demonstrate Allied seriousness in preparing for a second front. Dieppe had proved another British catastrophe, but Churchill was oblivious. Like an old but obdurate hunting dog, he had finally picked up, at Alamein, the scent that had eluded him for two long and wearisome years of war: the smell of victory.

Fame and fortune

In Monty's visitors' book, before departing by air for Cairo, Churchill searched for an historical parallel. He had assured the officers and men with whom he talked that the hard times were at an end, and that with Americans and Russians on Britain's side, the war would in time be won. 'I only wish I could do short hand & take down some of the funny things he said,' Monty's ADC reported to his family, for the Prime Minister had not only vividly described Stalin in the Kremlin, but had given 'all the most astounding details' of current strategic planning, including Anglo-American preparations for the Torch landings – secrets which had perforce to be kept from the ordinary officers and men of 8th Army, yet which meant that 'we are not so badly off & that everything [is] not so black as painted by the Press etc, in this war'.[51]

In the end, Churchill found the parallel in his own ancestor, the Duke of Marlborough. 'May the anniversary of Blenheim which marks the opening of the new Command bring to the Commander in Chief of the Eighth Army and his troops the fame & fortune they will surely deserve,' he penned[52] – buoyed not only by the new spirit of confidence rippling through an army that had seemed so baffled and negative just a few weeks before, but by the draft of a special message Monty intended to be read out to every man in the desert, before full moon on 25/6 August.

In addressing men of his old regiment, the 4th Hussars, Churchill had left his own indelible linguistic imprint on one officer, who remembered him saying: 'Gentlemen, you will strike – ah – an unforgettable blow – against the enemy. The corn will be ripe – ah – for the sickle – ah, and you will be the reapers. May God bless you all.'[53] Yet the master rhetorician, so singularly equipped to invent cadences and metaphor, had found himself strangely touched by the simple words of the new army commander – and gave instructions to his Military Assistant, Colonel Jacob, 'that they should be circulated to the Cabinet on his return. They certainly are the most inspiring documents,' Jacob added in his diary, 'and it is quite clear who means to be master in the desert.'[54]

Monty's 'Special Message to Officers and Men of Eighth Army' ran:

1. The enemy is now attempting to break through our positions in order to reach CAIRO, SUEZ and ALEXANDRIA, and to drive us from EGYPT.

577

2. The Eighth Army bars the way. It carries a great responsibility and the whole future of the war will depend on how we carry out our task.

3. We will fight the enemy where we now stand; there will be NO WITHDRAWAL and NO SURRENDER.

Every officer and man must continue to do his duty as long as he has breath in his body.

If each one of us does his duty, we cannot fail; the opportunity will then occur to take the offensive ourselves and to destroy once and for all the enemy forces now in EGYPT.

4. Into battle then, with stout hearts and with the determination to do our duty.

And may God give us the victory.[55]

Churchill's transvestite fantasies

While Monty's special message went to the army printing press, Churchill cabled back to Attlee, his deputy, at home: 'I am satisfied that we have lively, confident, resolute men in command, working together as an admirable team under leaders of the highest military quality' – and added (reflecting the influence of General Brooke), 'It is now my duty to return home as I have no part to play in the battle, which must be left to those in whom we place our trust.'[56]

But did Churchill *really* trust the new army commander, despite his dazzling grip of the situation?

Already on the flight back from Moscow, to Brooke's consternation, Churchill had announced his intention to stay if possible in Egypt, and witness the coming battle. Two other of the Prime Minister's statements on 20 August also suggest that, though Churchill genuinely applauded the new spirit in 8th Army, he either misunderstood or disagreed with Montgomery's tactical plans for the forthcoming battle. 'Trouble with you generals is that you are defensive minded,' he had barked at General Horrocks, on hearing the static plans for XIII Corps at Alam Halfa. 'Why don't you attack? That's the way to win battles, not by sitting down in defence.'[57] Moreover, in his cable to Attlee, Churchill reported that the 'strong line of defence' being developed across the delta from Alexandria to Cairo was 'to give the fullest manoeuvring power to the Eighth Army in the event of its being attacked next week'.[58]

In reality, the delta defence scheme was being undertaken by the newly arrived 51st Highland Division for the very opposite purpose: namely, in order that 8th Army's infantry and supporting armour might remain dug-in at Alamein, leaving 51st Division in the delta to meet any over-ambitious German columns that attempted to by-pass the Alam Halfa ridge – as the division's war diary recorded at the time.

The extent to which Churchill misunderstood his new 8th Army commander is of the greatest historical interest, for it was a misunderstanding that would be mirrored in an almost identical manner in Eisenhower's headquarters two years later, at the height of the battle for Normandy. In both cases Monty held his superiors in a state of awe by his grip on his armies and the utter clarity and simplicity of his tactical forecast; yet somehow, the moment Churchill or Eisenhower left him, they became a prey to their own armchair illusions. Indeed, it is impossible to resist the impression that Churchill tolerated Montgomery, a soldier so unlike his romantic ideal, only so long as Monty produced victories – and was the first to round on ' "your" Monty', as Brooke recalled, whenever victory took longer to achieve than the impatient Prime Minister was prepared to wait.

Brooke, however, managed to steer Churchill away from Egypt, which the prime ministerial party finally left on 23 August 1942. 'I heaved a sigh of relief as I saw his plane take to the air,' Brooke later confided. Monty's transformation of morale in the desert had paradoxically made Churchill more impossible to deal with than ever, even stretching to transvestite fantasies in Gibraltar, on the way back to England. Confined to his house there for security reasons, Churchill 'discussed disguising himself as an Egyptian demi-mondaine . . . so as to be allowed out!' Brooke recalled, leaving him to thank God in his diary that he had 'got him to start from Egypt last night. He had every intention of wriggling out of it if he could. He felt that the Cabinet had given him leave till the 30th and that he should be allowed to stop till then,' Brooke noted on 24 August. 'I knew that he would have given anything to stop on this week so as to be there if Rommel attacks on 25th August.'[59]

Rommel's contempt

At his desert headquarters on the 'other side of the hill' Rommel was equally convinced he would trounce the British in mobile battle, as soon as he could build up sufficient fuel supplies to get him through to Cairo. Obsessed with his own picture of British amateurishness, he paid no attention either to the official British announcement of changes in command on 19 August, or to the changes going on within the British lines – indeed, his lack of reconnaissance by air or infantry patrol in the southern sector of the British front, though intended to lull the British into a false sense of security there, was also a sign of contempt for his opponents.

For months that summer Rommel had benefited from German access to secret signals sent by the American military attaché in Cairo, which had given a wealth of insights into British formation strengths and identifications. That loophole had now been closed, however – as had Rommel's amazing mobile listening centre under Lieutenant Beerbohm, which had intercepted lax British radio traffic on the battlefield, but which had been captured during the fighting in July. Subsequent German intelligence and reconnaissance were, despite Luftwaffe parity with the Desert Air Force, abysmal. Trusting to his remaining aces – his highly trained ground forces, superlative tanks and anti-tank weapons, as well as high morale – Rommel had based his plan on a 'decisive battle . . . to be fought out behind the British front in a form in which the greater aptitude of our troops for mobile warfare and the high tactical skill of our commanders could compensate for our lack of material strength', as he later described.[60]

Rommel's only real concern was the arms race – a race to build up the maximum number of Axis tanks, ammunition and fuel units before the British could be reinforced from Suez. In this respect he was cautiously optimistic. 'The situation is changing daily to my advantage,' he wrote to his wife on 10 August.[61] From German agents in Cairo he knew that a large convoy 'laden with a cargo of the very latest weapons and war material for the Eighth Army would arrive in Suez at the beginning of September'.[62] He therefore made the fatal decision to delay his attack to the very final moment in August, hoping to capture the convoy before the American tanks and munitions could be re-embarked – unaware that every day's grace was manna to the 8th Army under its new commander at Alam Halfa.

Relative strength

Rommel's delay proved the worst mistake of his career. Had he attacked immediately on 15 August he might well have broken through, given the weak 8th Army defences, huge preponderance in German long-barrelled armour and guns, and massive Luftwaffe/Regia Aeronautica air support. It was his caution, paradoxically, which held him back – wanting to build up an even greater striking force. But he failed to see that his advantage was slipping away each day that Montgomery built up his fortifications and prepared his forces for a new kind of defensive battle – and the Royal Navy and Allied air forces attacked his Italian fuel-supply ships.

Whether Rommel was right in referring to the Axis 'lack of material strength' is debatable: it would appear that each side overestimated the other's forces, while underestimating its own. To the British, the German Panzer Mk IIIs and IVs were weapons of ominous power, against which only Grant tanks could compete. The knowledge that, already by 15 August, the Germans possessed well over 200 Mk IIIs and IVs was a matter of considerable disquiet, dominating all 8th Army intelligence reports for the period. The motley array of British Valentine tanks, the single brigade of already ancient Grants – 'Egypt's last hope' as they were nicknamed – and the knowledge that none of the new Sherman tanks would be in line before mid-September was equally worrying.

Fortunately Rommel, in his turn, considerably exaggerated the British forces confronting him. He credited the British XXX Corps at Alamein with a further division still held back in the delta under Alexander (50th Division), and assumed there were two British armoured divisions in reserve behind 7th Armoured Division, south of the New Zealanders – whereas until 27 August there were in the whole of 8th Army only two armoured brigades, one of which was in the north, armed only with two-pounder Valentines, the other below the Alam Halfa Ridge.

In fact, Rommel's armoured superiority now far exceeded the three-to-one ratio deemed necessary for offensive success and, thanks to his urgent appeals for more troops and supplies, the Axis build-up far exceeded that of 8th Army – as the intelligence staff at 8th Army were well aware, having read his decoded signals. By 19 August Major Williams was reporting in his top-secret 8th Army intelligence summary that 'Enemy strength is still growing,' and now included 5,000 élite parachute troops from Crete. By 21 August he reported there had been a 'significant change in the last week'.

The enemy's 'mobile forces have been released from their temporary positional role. He is trying to deny our observation; and he has moved his artillery concentrations further south. His positional infantry, both German and Italian, are now bedded down and anti-tank guns have begun to come up for 164 Div. A definite acceleration of shipping programme is noticeable. There is no reason to believe his supply situation is any longer a strain. The parallel to mid-May begins to be pointed . . . Further information from German parachutists [a euphemism for information based on Ultra decrypts] makes it evident that the stage is almost set.'[63]

In Cairo, Churchill had made a last-minute 'comparison of men, vehicles, weapons, etc. and it was generally agreed that taking one thing and another into account, we were about fifty–fifty with the enemy in the desert', as Churchill's Military Assistant recorded[64] – but this was misleading, since the GHQ comparison was numerical, not qualitative. On paper, 8th Army's tank strength was 478. Of these, however, only seventy-one were, on 22 August, Grants, which possessed six-pounder guns set in an immovable sponson welded on to the main hull, without turret-traverse, making them 'sitting ducks' unless they could manoeuvre the whole tank. The rest of 8th Army's tanks were obsolescent: 117 Valentines, 15 Matildas, 139 Stuarts and 136 deeply unreliable Crusaders. Prone to breakdown and boasting mere two-pounder or 37mm guns, these were helpful against German or Italian infantry, but of no account in armoured combat against German Panzers, or 88s, or captured Russian 76mm anti-tank guns. Indeed, unknown to the British, over 170 of the 234 German tanks now sported long-barrelled 50mm guns and extra frontal armor ('Specials'). A further 26 German tanks were even more powerful: Panzer Mk IV 'Specials', armed with long-barrelled 75mm guns: the most formidable tanks in the desert which could, by their range and shell-power, obliterate any 8th Army tank or armoured vehicle with impunity. Together with the 281 tanks of the Italian armoured divisions, Rommel was expected to put into battle over 500 tanks. His Afrika Korps numbered 'at least 29,000 men, over 100 guns, 200 anti-tank guns and perhaps fifty 88s', Major Williams recorded in his 8th Army intelligence summary on 26 August.[65]

Behind his mask of confidence, even Churchill, once back in London, became at times anxious. 'At any moment Rommel might attack with a devastating surge of armour,' he recalled candidly in *The Hinge of Fate*, recording how, despite his great confidence in his new 8th Army commander, he had quietly hinted to his hostess in Cairo, the British ambassador's wife, that she might be safer with her baby son in the Lebanon.[66]

Only the course of battle would tell.

Pour épater la bourgeoisie

As in England, at 3 Division, V Corps, XII Corps and South-East Army, Monty meanwhile insisted upon rehearsal as the basis of victory. For this he would be excoriated by 'the romantics' – those military historians whose hours of lonely scholarship were brightened by the 'Nelson touch' – the ability of a commander to disconcert the enemy by doing the unexpected in the midst of battle, as Nelson so often did, for example at Copenhagen and the Nile. For historians chronicling World War II only General 'Georgie' Patton would show such genius on the Allied side; and Rommel on the Axis.

The same, historiographically, had been true of the American Civil War, where Lee had drawn the sympathy of historians, while General Grant's tactics were considered heavy-handed and unimaginative. Yet Grant had won the war for the Union, thus helping to cement America as a modern, multicultural democracy.

Monty's battlefield talent was certainly of a different order from that of Rommel or Patton, for it rested upon a quasi-manic sense of order and tidiness, superabundant energy, a rare clarity of mind, absolute dedication to his profession to the exclusion of all other interests, a fanatical insistence upon training and rehearsal, and a strange and growing love of 'his' men – a love which command in the desert finally encouraged him to translate from his personal staff to an entire army.

Having ordered the rehearsal of the defensive role of XIII Corps, on the Alam Halfa position, complete with mock signals and reports in a 'telephone battle' on 21 August (officers were told to 'look up the exercise' during the subsequent battle, as Major Witherby recalled),[67] Monty's own thoughts turned back to the next-but-one battle he would have to fight: his own offensive. To achieve victory with predominantly civilian troops whose democratic ethos was expressed in 'belly-aching' – namely, finding reasons not to do what one was ordered, or only to do it uncooperatively and with ill will – was something which no British army commander had managed to achieve against the Germans or Japanese in three years of total war, whether in Norway, France, Greece, North Africa or the Far East. As in the French army in 1939–40, it seemed that the social problems of an old-fashioned democratic society divided by class and privilege, demoralized by a belated sense of betrayal at the hands of château-bound commanders of World War I, vitiated any attempt at reform.

In small wars of empire, the use of regular army units had obviated or masked these old-fashioned democratic problems in the field; but against the better co-ordinated, more professional, classless forces of Nazi Germany and her allies, British performance had in World War II been abysmal, leading inexorably from Norway and Dunkirk to the surrenders of Singapore and Tobruk – the latter involving the surrender of 33,000 armed troops virtually without a fight, on 21 June 1942. 'Defeat is one thing,' Churchill reflected, 'disgrace is another.'[68] Or, as Major-General de Guingand later wrote, 'democracy had proved itself a poor opponent on the field of battle, when men must lay down their lives'.[69]

In England, Monty had sought to combat this by installing energetic new subordinate commanders, imposing clear objectives in terms of defensive and offensive plans, and by developing a series of training programmes that not only turned civilians into modern combat soldiers, but rehearsed the co-operation of all arms in such a manner that men could see and experience the way in which their role fitted into the larger picture of battle. In attempting this, Monty had met every sort of obstruction, from outraged local property owners to idle GHQ officers in rear headquarters and lieutenant colonels with weak hearts who hated PT. As young Major Goronwy Rees had observed at South-Eastern Army, Monty was admired for his professional dedication, yet was considered, *au fond*, 'a bit mad'. Energetic professionalism, based on meritocracy rather than traditional privilege, was seen as deeply, even subversively, un-British.

In the years before World War I Monty's own wife had scandalized 'society' by 'marrying into trade' – and in many ways, British society hadn't changed a great deal since then. Fossilized by imperial power and the resultant disinclination of the upper and middle classes to sully themselves by doing physical or manual work, imperial British society was all too easy to scandalize. Loyalty, modesty and mediocrity remained, in myriad British social clubs, the greatest of all virtues – whereas Monty was often outrageously immodest and dictatorial. At times, indeed, it seemed as if he acted deliberately *pour épater la bourgeoisie*. As Rees's brigadier, a regular officer, remarked of Monty, 'he likes showing off ' –

a cardinal sin in England. 'And he's always causing trouble,' the brigadier had added. 'Keep your eye out for Monty. He really is a terror.'[70]

To the relief of the GHQ Home Forces brigadier, the 'terror' of South-Eastern Army was now let loose in the desert. But to the brigadier's surprise, the men of 8th Army seemed to take to this 'terror' from the moment he appeared, as if the soldiery had craved the arrival of someone like him – while despising GHQ brigadiers, as in World War I. After years of being thrown into mindless battles by incompetent commanders demanding the same military obedience as in English society at home, a situation had arisen where Monty's eccentricities and social outrage-ousness actually emboldened 'lower-class' soldiers, encouraging them to see themselves no longer as the cheap cannon-fodder of middle- and upper-class Englishmen, intent upon the preservation of their class-privileges as in World War I, but as fellow participants in a struggle against Nazi evil, under the leadership of a figure who inspired men not only to fight for a cause, but for their own pride and self-respect – a leader who *cared* about his troops, not from a distance, but in daily tours to meet and talk with them.

A new form of command

Monty's visits to meet the men were remarkable, indeed unique for a British army commander – and, in the same way as his homosocial affec-tion for his personal staff, they provide us today with a key to understand-ing the phenomenon of Monty's transformation of British morale in the desert in August 1942. To have dictated new battle plans and altered the mindset of his senior commanders and staff in the desert was one thing; to have imbued the men, too, with a new will to fight and to win was another.

When Sir Harold Alexander, on a trip to see Monty at Burg-el-Arab, found that troops were not saluting his car, with its general's pennant, he stopped the vehicle and remonstrated with the soldiers. As the son of an earl, Alexander expected the working classes to tug their forelocks; as a regular Guards officer, especially, he considered saluting an important mark of discipline.

Monty saw things differently. He had spent his entire life, since school, as an infantry officer, learning the trade of a soldier. Leadership was not a matter of privilege, he had come to feel, but of merit; of professionalism and accountability. Officers deserved saluting not as a mark of blind discipline and social respect, but out of respect for the responsibility of command which they bore on behalf of all: the responsibility for the lives and battle-effectiveness of their men in war. Though a brave and most charming man, with impeccable manners, General Alexander was a basically indolent, unimaginative commander, buoyed by an officer-staff who, in a Kiplingesque way, admired him so much that they took virtually the entire responsibility for professional military matters from and for him. This was a traditional, aristocratic form of leadership – the handsome school prefect as admired figurehead – and it certainly made for goodwill in high-command circles, whether in defeat or victory. Ironically, as in the case of Mountbatten, it deeply impressed American staff officers like Eisenhower (though not Patton, who knew something about leadership in the field), and it impressed Churchill – indeed, it impressed Monty, insofar as he recognized the importance of such 'nice' figurehead commanders-in-chief, who could perform the essential role of GHQ buffer against generals being bothered on the battlefield. But as a field commander Monty had no illusions about Alexander – for Monty knew that, no matter how much respect Alexander might arouse among his officer-staff thanks to his impeccable manners and club charm, the majority of modern civilian soldiers would no longer give their wholehearted backing, and if necessary their lives, in the aftermath of World War I, to serve such an aristocrat, in combat with Japanese or Germans. Britain was, at heart, losing the war because of continuing class distinction; Germany was winning it because, under Hitler, it had almost eradicated class differences. Although, by appealing to the values of democracy, Churchill had raised the spirit of the English nation to defend its island, he had singularly failed to make its citizens fight abroad, effectively, in the struggle against an increasingly classless, confident and professional enemy, heady with the wine of conquest.

A modern democratic general, Monty reasoned, must therefore reach beyond the barriers of class and privilege that were holding back Britain's military performance on the field of battle; must win the respect not only of his public-school-educated officers, but of his troops. To achieve this he must either start winning battles, or exercise a new form of command; or both.

Proselytizing

Lieutenant-Colonel Richardson, at 8th Army's new headquarters alongside the RAF, later described the 'new spirit' that Monty created. His first
thought, on seeing the 'slight figure with a pale face and formal uniform'
on the evening of 13 August had been: 'Doesn't look the part'. This had
been followed by amazement at Monty's clarity and self-confidence. 'He
seemed to know his job; certainly he knew what he wanted of his staff,'
Richardson reflected later. But the most extraordinary transformation of
all was, in Richardson's eyes, the change in morale among the troops
themselves by the time the battle of Alam Halfa started: the fact that 'the
fighting men, almost every one of them, had actually seen him and heard
him speak'.[71]

This was the part of Monty's life-story which so enraged military
historians that many of them could not bring themselves to mention it,
or, if they did, only as a retrospective stick with which to beat the
mountebank, and excoriate his behaviour as comparable to that of a
'crooner'. Yet this was in many ways the core of Monty's miracle: a social
key that unlocked the hearts and faith of a whole army – and no one was
more surprised than Monty's own educated, 'middle-class' staff as he
went about this new task.

'At his headquarters, all of us had been amazed, and some even amused
at his behaviour on arrival,' wrote Richardson. 'After a very few days
setting the scene for his first battle, Alam Halfa, he had resolved to see the
soldiers and their officers. No pondering over a multitude of operational
detail, no lengthy conferences with a coterie of advisers, just an intelligence
briefing at 6 a.m.,' he recalled; 'then at 7 a.m. off would go "the circus",
as we cheekily called it: the Army commander in an open Humber staff
car, with one ADC and a supply of cigarettes and magazines. As the
pattern was repeated day after day we had asked Freddie, "What on earth
is he doing?"'

De Guingand's reply was terse: '"Visiting every unit, talking to officers
and soldiers."'[72] 'He goes out the devil of a lot around the army & I
navigate,' Monty's ADC, Captain Poston, described to his family at the
time on 22 August. (The ADC whom Monty had brought out from
England, Captain Spooner, had driven Monty on to a minefield on his first
day at Alamein; he 'knows nothing about the Desert', Poston explained.
'He does the Mess side & that sort of thing.'[73])

The relentless daily visits, in the heat and dust of the desert, involved a psychic strain – the determination to meet and inspire, if possible, every man in his army – that had worn out Monty's opponent, Field-Marshal Rommel. Even de Guingand wondered if Monty was overdoing it. 'But throughout the length of the forty-mile desert front, the soldiers day by day had been assembling round his car. The message,' Richardson recorded, was the same 'as the one he had given to us' – a message of 'utter confidence and a clear indication of the way ahead. Then the cigarettes and magazines [were] dished out by the ADC'.[74]

Far from feeling this to be a PR exercise, the soldiers were amazed that an army commander should feel it important not only to visit their front-line unit commanders, but to speak to them, also. 'He told us everything,' one hard-bitten regimental sergeant major exclaimed after a Monty 'visitation': 'what his plan was for the battle, what he wanted the regiments to do, what he wanted *me* to do. And we will do it, sir. What a man!'[75]

Richardson, desert-hardened and sceptical, was gradually won over by Monty's indefatigable determination to see, hear from, and be seen and heard by the ordinary soldiers – and the extraordinary effect this had on army morale. In this respect, Monty was changing the face of modern war in the democracies, as Harold Macmillan later described. World War I generals had rarely if ever shown themselves in the line. 'Had they done so they would not have authorized the continuous and useless operations at Passchendaele, where 400,000 casualties were incurred to little purpose,' Macmillan wrote. By contrast 'The Second World War was fought by great generals from their caravans . . . They also appeared constantly in the front line, and were well-known to the troops. In this respect, the armies of the Second World War were luckier.'[76]

The historian Barrie Pitt agreed. 'For too long the men of Eighth Army had been expected to endure the hardship of desert life, the heat, the thirst and the boredom,' he wrote in *The Crucible of War: Year of Alamein 1942*, 'then to walk forward into appalling danger, towards death, wounds or captivity, all at the behest of remote Olympian figures whose names they hardly knew, who were rarely seen except as shadowy figures on the back seats of large cars rolling past swathed in dust, who never spoke to them except in reproof for some military solecism such as appearing before them with their shirts unbuttoned, and whose ignorance of military reality they felt had been so often demonstrated by themselves, and paid for in their own blood.'[77]

Monty was determined to change all this – as swiftly as humanly possible. In each case he went out of his way 'to tell them not only that they each had an important part to play in his plan, but what that part was', Pitt described. ' "We are going to hit Rommel for six out of Egypt!" he said, in his high, slightly lisping voice – stressing, however, that this was to be the long-term aim and that the immediate prospect was for a purely defensive, stone-walling battle.' Moreover when, on inspections, he 'walked along the ranks', Pitt recounted, 'he looked deliberately and coolly into every man's eyes so that all felt, in that sudden, surprising moment, the creation of a personal bond. It might not be a bond which everyone welcomed, but whoever found himself looking back into those clear, grey-blue eyes felt irrevocably that military authority could never again lie elsewhere. Here, undoubtedly, was the man in command.'[78]

The diaries, memoirs and letters of desert veterans all attest to the unique impact Monty made on his troops by such personal visits. He did not bother with conventional badges of rank on his shirt, nor did he even wear medal ribbons as Auchinleck, Ritchie and Gott had done. It was as though he wished to reduce command in war to its essence: human intelligence, courage, professionalism, application – and the compact between ordinary soldiers and the personality of the commander. This was something great British commanders from Marlborough to Moore, Wellington to Nelson, had understood – yet which had fallen into disuse in World War I, as Haig watched his forces from afar and relied on his notion of divine inspiration, requiring only remote control of his vast forces.

In so doing, Haig had ruined the very concept of human loyalty for a generation; as Joanna Burke has pointed out, there was not only bitterness as the extent and futility of Haig's bloodbaths were revealed and criticized in later years, but a natural wish by survivors to 'regain their sense of honour and a taste of contentment'.[79] Recognizing this, Monty wished to avoid the taint of failed, old-fashioned 'authority', epitomized in the polish of Haig's brass buckles, and the immaculate turnout of the cavalry lancers who accompanied him. Yet he also needed, as at Quetta, to stand out in the eyes of the men of his new army. He thus deliberately chose the dress of an anti-hero. Visiting the 9th Australian Division he remarked that his general's hat was 'quite the wrong sort of hat to wear – far too warm'; an Australian officer had suggested he 'have one of ours, sir' – and Monty, pinning his general's badge on it ('No badge? – I can't have a hat without a badge'), had begun to change the perception of high command in the desert, adding thereafter the badges of regiments he visited. In this way, without having intended to, he would draw attention to the difference between himself and the previous regime: a new commander with a new message to put across. 'Inevitably, as more and more men saw him and heard what he had to say, the stories began to circulate, the myths accumulate,' Pitt chronicled – for Monty's schoolboy sayings spread through the army like wildfire.[80]

One of the stories had Rommel searching the Afrika Korps for a person who could explain the English cricketing term to 'knock someone for six'. As Pitt noted, 'the methods he used to advertise his presence caused amusement throughout the bulk of the army at first', but it was soon realized that the old officer-club approach to war was over; the gentlemen were out, the players in. 'Shocked disgust' in the Cairo clubs was 'followed by glum acceptance' by the officers[81] – for Monty's was the face of modern leadership, however distasteful to English clubland.

The BBC correspondent Denis Johnston first met Monty on the Alam Halfa Ridge, while looking to interview the Prime Minister. Told he should try the new army commander, Montgomery, he 'walked over to the staff cars, but the only occupant was an Australian officer in a digger's slouch hat, turned up at the side. I stuck my head in the window, and addressed him.

– I say, where do I find the new Army Commander?
– Who?
– His name is Montgomery, I believe.
– I'm the new Army Commander.
– Oh, come, I said. I know he's not an Australian.
His face creased into a bright smile.
– Oh, don't go by my hat, he said. I've just been trying it on. Rather good, don't you think?
– Oh my God! I beg your pardon.
– That's all right, my dear fellow. What can I do for you?'[82]

Rank and privilege by virtue of class was over; professionalism at last was the sole criterion.

Under the spell

Why had no previous 8th Army commander thought to visit and speak to ordinary British and imperial soldiers, beyond sentries and formal parades (which were impossible in or near the front line in the desert owing to the danger of Luftwaffe attack)? 'Through the intervening forty years I have never met anyone who, living through those days, has not admitted that he fell under the spell,' Richardson reflected. 'To me it was an overwhelming contrast to the Auk, staring each day by day at the distant blue and by night meeting with a disheartened and incoherent staff.'

'Some, in studying Monty's activity at that time, have sought to impute an egoistic "cult of personality",' Richardson went on. 'No', he responded categorically, speaking as a veteran of both Auchinleck's and Monty's command in the desert. To his everlasting credit Monty had, as new army commander, 'sensed the bewilderment of the army that he had taken over, and wisely decided that to put that right was for him the highest priority'.[83]

In doing so, Monty enjoyed no advantages of breeding, likeability, charm or physical stature. On his second day in the desert – 14 August 1942 – he had visited the 9th Australian Division, first addressing the senior officers, then going forward to 20th Brigade, where he was given the Australian slouch or 'Digger' hat at Brigadier Windeyer's headquarters. 'Montgomery tried it on without denting it,' the official Australian historian recorded, 'looking rather odd' – so odd, and so interested in headgear that, while he talked with some of the officers there, the divisional commander, General Morshead, took Windeyer aside, anxious lest the new army commander's idiosyncrasies strike Windeyer as eccentric, if not comic. '"This man is really a breath of fresh air,"' he assured him: '"Things are going to be different soon."'[84]

From Windeyer's headquarters Monty was taken to see no-man's land and the soldiers defending Point 24. Monty was still completely unknown to Australian troops, had white knees, and was physically small, indeed almost diminutive, with his pinched, bony face and long, sharp nose – yet in conversation with the men he seemed to strike, as Richardson perceived, an elemental chord that cut right through class-division. Eccentric, stubborn, sometimes menacing in the sharpness of his questioning, he exuded the qualities that soldiers longed for: a genuine interest in their conditions and welfare, a determination to stir things up, a simple vision of how to fight Rommel – and what part the soldiers would play in that fight.

Instinctively the men trusted him, grateful that he had bothered to come to them, and was interested in them. At Point 28 he had, beside his general's badge, first pinned that of the Rising Sun – 'claiming an entitlement to wear it on the ground that his father had been Bishop of Tasmania,' as the Australian official historian recorded.[85]

Monty had, in his way, come full circle – had become, like his father, an evangelist, a missionary among the very Australians his father had visited, baptized, confirmed, wedded, converted, buried. And in that compact, the loyalty that had been soured, indeed poisoned, by the behaviour of Haig and his subordinate commanders in World War I, and by the unending series of ineffectual British commanders in World War II, was, finally, re-created.

Renewal of faith

Monty knew and accepted that he was, from childhood, bound for trouble – and that soldiering was his only means of survival in an English world based on privilege, manners, snobbery, social decorum and sexual hypocrisy. Indeed, when he came to write his own life-story he wanted, initially, to title it *The Sparks Fly Upward*, because, as the writers of the Book of Job put it, 'Man is born unto trouble, as sparks fly upward.'

That he had survived in a hidebound British army in which regimental snobbery parroted English social snobbery, and in which exclusivity, epitomized in the gentleman's club and regimental mess, mirrored the fossilization of the British Empire, was itself a marvel; other troublemakers, including his brother-in-law 'Hobo' Hobart, had not. But his survival in the British army had often hung on a knife edge, and he was roundly disliked by the majority of his superiors, as well as by many of his colleagues. His absolute professionalism, his utter seriousness about teaching the business of war, his ruthless selection – and deselection – of subordinates, his eschewal of alcohol and smoking, his personal isolation from his peers, made him seem profoundly un-English. To such peers he came across like the remorseless new managing director of a failing company: contemptuous of the previous board, brutal in sacking incompetent staff no matter how long or how loyally they had served, and laying down the law about future operations, about management, and about the standard of work he expected, as well as insisting on talking directly to the employees himself, so stunning the whole firm. He was, in other words, a modern manager, with views on leadership and man-management that would in America have made him a millionaire industrialist. Instead, however, he criss-crossed the Egyptian desert, in command of 100,000 men: men living without women, subsisting on half a gallon of water per man per day, eating bully beef and tinned produce, tormented by flies, jaundice, stomach disorders, desert sores that would not heal, and suffering a waning faith in democracy as a means to win the military struggle against Hitler.

Even Stalin, as a ruthless Communist dictator throwing millions of innocent Soviet citizens into the struggle against the German onslaught, had been unable to stop the Wehrmacht, which finally reached the outskirts of Stalingrad in the final days of August 1942. In the desert, ordering the fragmention of 8 Army into mobile armoured units – 'Jock-columns' – as Rommel built up his Panzer Army for its final breakthrough to the Nile, Auchinleck had attempted to articulate a last, despairing hope. No one – apart perhaps from 'Chink' Dorman-Smith, the *éminence grise* who had pressed Auchinleck to adopt such a reorganization of 8 Army – believed it. A new approach had therefore been required, one which would take advantage of Allied strengths, not weaknesses: an approach which would not risk or waste lives, or squander matériel as before.

The squandering was, in retrospect, incredible. According to Barry Pitt, captured British vehicles 'by the end of July [1942] made up 85 per cent of Afrika Corps transport'.[86] Indeed, Rommel's use of captured British artillery guns, anti-tank guns, tanks, fuel, vehicles, and especially anti-vehicle and anti-personnel mines, was one of the most extraordinary features of German ingenuity – and a terrible indictment of British military performance. In one fit of indignation General Dan Pienaar, the commander of the South African Division which finally stopped Rommel's advance at Alamein, had remonstrated with the Desert Air Force that had bombed his men: 'If you've got to bomb my trucks, you might at least hit them. But you missed every bloody one!' Meanwhile, British artillery had shelled him from the rear. 'See here,' Pienaar had continued, 'My father fought the British in the Transvaal, and all I want to know is, what side I'm supposed to be on now. Because if I'm on Rommel's side, say so, and I'll turn round and have him in Alexandria within twelve hours. Just work it out, and let me know as soon as you've decided.'[87]

For Monty's new approach to work – for the 8th Army to apply the cohesive weight of its artillery, its armour and guns, its Ultra intelligence, and its air support against the enemy, rather than its own forces – the problem which Stalin had put his finger upon would, however, have to be faced: how to make the soft, largely frightened citizenry of the world's Western democracies, brought up to value life and individuality rather than blind obedience and sacrifice in the service of a Führer or dictator, fight effectively.

In retrospect, once Monty had achieved the turnaround, the event would come to appear simple, encouraging club-historians and patriots to mock and minimize Monty's contribution to the winning of World War II: the 'very overrated general' of Steven Spielberg's well-meaning movie *Saving Private Ryan*. But for the actual soldiers of 8th Army, and later of the Allied armies who successfully landed on D-Day and fought their way to the Elbe, Monty was far from overrated; to them he was a hero, for all his egoism. As one NCO in the Royal Corps of Signals, J. W. Thraves, recalled, Monty was known only to have served at Dunkirk; 'when he eventually introduced himself to us, we wondered about this thin, ascetic-looking man who, as the desert soldiers used to say, "hadn't even got his knees brown". Once Monty had spoken to us, however, there was a greater feeling of optimism than there had been for months. Officers and NCOs gathered round this little man, as he told us there would be no more withdrawals . . . we were to stay where we were and live or die. Strange that we welcomed these words, but that was the mood of us all – we were fed up with being pushed around.'[88]

Major-General 'Gertie' Tuker, commanding the 4th Indian Division, was even more emphatic. He had felt utter contempt for Auchinleck's strange orders about British soldiers not being permitted to refer to Rommel by name – 'I had them burnt at my H.Q.: they were never circulated or distributed' – and had been infuriated by the lack of confidence in the high command that he'd found in the desert. 'I was just back from Cyprus when Monty arrived,' he recalled. 'I've never seen any sort of men, in an army or a football team, so sick at heart over their leadership as was the 8th Army. When I went out to the Desert I found Dan Pienaar, Freyberg, Morshead – all at loggerheads with Auk.' It was this 'abysmal sense of lost confidence', despite a 'fighting spirit' that was still unbroken, which Monty turned around, in Tuker's recollection. 'All it needed was a man who would give it a plan & hold firm to it.'[89]

Monty was that man – his heart, moreover, in the right place: the soldier's place. Infuriating, demanding, and boastful once successful, he became by his extraordinary leadership the dynamo, the conscience, and the will that would bring them from incessant defeat and military failure to inexorable victory on the field of battle: harnessing their collective spirit in a renewal of faith in democracy and its ability to confound even the most brilliant and evil of racist dictators.

Two-way relationship

The official Australian war historian, Barton Maugham, gave a vivid illustration of Monty's impact on not only the senior officers of the 9th Australian Division at their headquarters, but also the men. 'On another visit to the division made soon afterwards,' Maugham chronicled, 'Montgomery, seeing some gunners beside one of the new [six-pounder] anti-tank guns, asked them what they thought of the gun and was told that they had not fired it; they had been forbidden, they said, to practise with live ammunition because it was so scarce and reserved exclusively for battle use. Within a day or two an order came down from Army Head-quarters that every six-pounder was to fire off half its ammunition stocks in practice. "Unless the men are trained to shoot," said Montgomery's memorandum, "we shall do no good on the day of battle however great the number of rounds we have saved ready for that day."' Maugham even chronicled the story of 51st Highland Division, whose soldiers were forbidden to wear their Highland flashes, or arm-badges, 'because Middle East security forbade formation and unit identifications on dress'. Monty immediately instructed the commander 'to let the men wear their flashes'.[90]

'Other instances could be found,' Maugham reflected – but his point was the same. The 9th Australian Division – already blooded in desert warfare – and the 51st Highland Division – completely inexperienced in war since its re-creation after surrender of the entire original division at St Valéry in 1940 – would be, with Freyberg's New Zealanders, the three infantry divisions that would win the battle of Alamein: and the guts and warrior-tenacity that earned that victory would have, as their undoubted source, the little 'Colonial' troublemaker from Hobart, Tasmania, whose visits to 'his' troops altered the desert agenda. What was clear to all but the college historians of Cambridge was that Monty's methods 'had an extraordinary effect on the Eighth Army, giving it revived hope, a better tone and a new confidence', as Maugham described. 'With an orator's instinct – not with rhetoric but with telling words followed up by action that showed he meant what he said – he told his army the things it wanted to hear, that it would never go back but fight where it stood, that it would surely attack again when ready, but not before, and that tactical methods which had failed – the "boxes" and the small improvised battle groups – would be discarded and the vocabulary signifying them banished.'[91]

In particular, Monty cancelled orders that men were never to be assembled under their commanding officers or sub-unit commanders, owing to the danger of enemy shelling or air attack. 'I consider that if a unit is to be welded into a fighting machine that will fight with tenacity in battle, then it must be assembled regularly and the men addressed personally by their officers,' Monty ordered.[92] His 8th Army would become a new army in which there was a compact between officers and men: a two-way relationship in which commanders, instead of running fragmentary, disparate 'bit and pieces' of an army, now trained and rehearsed their men to carry out their role in a larger plan – and kept them informed how that plan was developing. As a result, Maugham considered, 'No army was ever more confident, none ever had a higher morale, than the Eighth Army when it next attacked.'[93]

'Florence Nightingale'

Correlli Barnett would later dismiss such morale-raising as a mix of 'publicity' – clearly a 'bad' thing in his college book – and 'Florence Nightingale'-type activity.[94] Neither Barnett nor other Auchinleck admirers were interested in the morale of mere footsoldiers. For such armchair military writers, the war must be seen as romantic, and not spoiled by mention of other ranks' cares, fears, inexperience, need of training, or of human concern and military guidance.

Whether mocked later as 'Florence Nightingale', however, or self-appointed 'military messiah', as Barnett sneered,[95] Monty was completely indifferent.[96] It was the lives of his men that had counted, in his book, they who must – and would – win victory over the indoctrinated forces of fascism. And through this new compact, out in the Egyptian desert, he would take care of them: would personally inspire them to achieve great things, and bring as many of them as possible home to their families afterwards. The promise he had given Trumbull Warren's wife and mother would now hold good for an army – which was why, despite his misogynist nature, he would be so admired by women: for he would be as good as his word. He would bring their men home.

The hardest decision

Publicity, Monty would soon discover, could be used as a weapon in this battle to raise morale. Yet to be trusted by civilian soldiers, a battlefield leader needed first to win that trust, not take it for granted as an aristocratic or middle-class right, or buy it in the manner of political votes by clever PR. To win it he had not only to put himself across to his men, but also to deliver. This was something Lord Mountbatten, for example, for all his princely qualities and grasp of modern publicity, had not done at Dieppe. Nor would General Eisenhower, when in November the Torch landings proved initially successful, yet failed to make subsequent headway on the field of battle.

Thus, for all Monty's efforts to create a new spirit in 8th Army, the test of his 'new broom' would be whether his new approach to war worked – a test that was rehearsed in exercises under Lieutenant-General Horrocks[97] – but could only be decided in actual battle at Alam Halfa.

In the context and scale of Monty's later wartime victories, this first defensive battle in August 1942 would not loom very large (something which infuriated Monty's ADC who, writing home, complained at the lack of 'write-up in the papers'[98]), yet its importance would be crucial. It would be the first battle Monty would fight as commander of the 8th Army. Given the imminent arrival of the American supply convoy at Suez, it would be Rommel's last chance of breaking through to Cairo and Alexandria, unless massively reinforced by Hitler.

As it was, the reinforcements Rommel received were worrying to the Allies – indeed, there was considerable tension at 8th Army headquarters as intelligence officers reported the ever-growing strength of Rommel's army at Alamein – which reached 82,000 by the final week of August, backed by a strengthened Luftwaffe slightly outnumbering the RAF, boasting 310 aircraft in North Africa, and further squadrons in Crete.[99] Despite Ultra-directed Allied attacks on Rommel's fuel-supply ships, some fourteen of them, plus thirteen barges and two supply submarines, got through to Tobruk, seven ships and two submarines reached Benghazi, and one ship and one submarine reached Tripoli, while a further submarine made Derna. All panzers got through, 84 per cent of fuel was delivered successfully, and 81 per cent of guns. Moreover, uninterrupted German air transport ensured that considerable numbers of fresh troops were successfully ferried to Alamein: the complete 164th Infantry Division and Ramcke Parachute Brigade in particular, as well as reinforcements for the Afrika Korps divisions, and two replacement Italian divisions, the Bologna Division and the German-trained – and tough – Folgore Parachute Division.

By 15 August 1942 the strength of Rommel's German formations had almost trebled since the July fighting,[100] with 1,000 fresh troops airlifted every day,[101] and 800 new trucks and vehicles. The increase in Axis weaponry was even more forbidding. By 27 August Rommel's tank strength had doubled since the beginning of the month. In addition to 243 Italian medium and 38 light tanks, Rommel could now put into battle no fewer than 234 panzer Mk IIIs and IVs – almost 200 of which were 'Specials', sporting long-barrelled 50mm or 75mm guns, and strengthened by special 20mm armoured 'breastplates' welded on to their fronts, separated from the 50mm-thick frontal chassis by a 100mm gap.[102] No British anti-tank gun could penetrate such armour, whether two- or six-pounder.[103] Moreover, of these 'Specials', the 27 Mk IV high-velocity, armour-piercing models were like Nazi battleships – able to kill any British tank cold at 3,000 yards, three times further than any British tank or anti-tank weapon – as 8th Army was shortly to discover. Rommel's 100 tracked and self-propelled mobile medium-artillery guns, and 200 superlative anti-tank guns – including some 95 captured Russian 76.2 mm guns, 30 of which were self-propelled on Czech tank chassis, and no fewer than 88 of the dreaded, flashless '88s' – dual-role anti-aircraft/anti-tank guns with a horizontal range of 16,200 yards and firing 20 or 21lb armour-piercing and anti-personnel projectiles faster than the speed of sound – were equally lethal. In short, Rommel was fielding the largest and best-equipped panzer army ever to fight in the desert, with the biggest Luftwaffe backing in reconnaisance aircraft, fighters, divebombers and bombers ever seen over North Africa: over 1,000 German and Italian aircraft centred on more than 100 unbeatable Messerschmitt 109bfs and over fifty Italian Macchi MC202s, as well as three groups of 'screaming' Stuka 87s.

It was small wonder, then, that Rommel felt confident – and nervous. He had planned, on a map, the move of each battalion, brigade, division and corps from Alamein to the bridges spanning the Nile at Alexandria and Cairo – with half the Panzer Army turning north to the Suez Canal, the other half south towards Khartoum. Clandestine Egyptian officers assured him they would stage a military uprising to support him, the moment his panzers reached the outskirts of Cairo. 'I hope we shall succeed in bursting open,' he wrote to an old adjutant of his, 'this last gateway barring our path to Egypt's fertile fields.'[104] He had accumulated enough fuel for a seven-day battle – estimated by 8th Army intelligence to be 'an average of about 200 miles of fuel' for all vehicles;[105] his only worry was lest supreme command fail to deliver more – in which case he would have to use captured British stocks, either at Alamein or in Cairo, as General Brooke feared. To reassure him, Kesselring promised to provide an immediate 1,500 tons of fuel from aviation stocks at Alamein, and a subsequent airlift of 700 tons of fuel, with a further 500 tons delivered daily by air, if the promised supply ships did not arrive in time.

Above all, Rommel recognized how critical the battle would be for Germany's hopes of winning the entire war. In Russia the Wehrmacht, in Operation Blue, had seized Sevastopol on 4 July, and Rostov-on-Don on 23 July. The 1st Panzer Army was racing south along the Black Sea, seizing the Crimea and reaching the foothills of the Caucasus by early August, when specially trained Italian and German troops began to scale the mountain passes before the onset of winter. Von Manstein had been made, like Rommel, a field marshal after the fall of Sevastopol; von Paulus, meanwhile, was ordered to take Stalingrad, and by 23 August his forces had reached the Volga north of the city and were fighting in the suburbs. At Hitler's headquarters in the Ukraine there was jubilation. With two giant panzer pincers Hitler seemed within weeks of seizing the world's primary source of oil, in the Middle East. 'A swift strike through the Caucasus,' the historian Richard Overy chronicled, 'opened up the prospect of German domination of the whole Middle East.'[106]

As Overy described, the summer of 1942 saw Hitler at the very height of German military achievement. He had brushed aside Soviet peace feelers the previous autumn, and 'On the face of things, no rational man in early 1942 could have guessed at the eventual outcome of the war';[107] by the summer of 1942 German commanders realized one superhuman effort might win them the war. By seizing Cairo and Alexandria, Germany and Italy would have complete mastery of the Mediterranean, including the final containment of Malta, without which the Allied air forces could not operate in the central Mediterranean. Moreover, with 100,000 tons of new American Sherman tanks and supplies falling into his hands in Suez, vast British stocks of ammunition and fuel, and a supportive Egyptian population and officer-caste intent upon deposing King Farouk, Rommel would be able to form a secure, southern pincer to meet German forces sweeping south from the Caucasus through Persia and Iran, as German divisions had swept through Greece the previous year prior to Operation Barbarossa.

Yet to form this pincer, Rommel *had* to succeed in his offensive – a responsibility which made him literally ill with worry. Suffering from high blood pressure, stomach troubles and a sore throat, he had become so anxious that he had recommended the best panzer general in the Third Reich – General Guderian – to take over his command, and thus clinch the issue, if he was given sick leave. But Guderian was in disfavour with Hitler after insubordinate behaviour the previous winter, before Moscow (he had been sacked as commander of the 2nd Panzer Army in December 1941, after an argument with von Kluge), and it was the insulting OKW suggestion that he promote one of his subordinate generals, General Nehring, if he was so unwell, that had caused Rommel to pull himself together. 'Thereupon,' Ralph Bennett noted, 'Rommel made a sudden recovery.'[108] Once again, Rommel would take responsibility for his own lightning campaign.

When one of his veteran officers, Major Heinz Werner Schmidt, who had been on leave since the capture of Tobruk, appeared at a conference at Alamein, he found Rommel 'a little thinner',[109] but otherwise in fiery form. The Panzer Army commander had ordered the setting up of model British defensive positions, on which Afrika Korps officers could discuss and rehearse their assault techniques, as well as several hundred copies of sketches of the Alamein defences and 'fortifications' of Alexandria;[110] he was aware, as he told his doctor on the day he finally ordered the offensive to begin, that he was launching the 'decisive battle' of the war, from the German point of view – and thus, as Professor Horster recounted his words to the Afrika Korps chief of staff, ' "the hardest decision I have ever had to take. Either the army in Russia succeeds in reaching Grozny [in the Caucasus] and we manage to reach the Suez Canal, or –'.[111]

'Or' was unthinkable – certainly unwritable – for a German army commander, decorated with the Iron Cross with Oak Leaves and recently promoted to the rank of field marshal on the field of battle.

19

Alam Halfa

Big Things at Stake

'Today has dawned at last,' Rommel wrote to his wife Lucie on 30 August 1942, as his forces moved into their assembly positions, preparatory to their moonlight assault. 'It's been such a long wait worrying all the time whether I should get everything I needed to enable me to take the brakes off again . . . As for my health, I'm feeling quite on top of my form. There are such big things at stake. If our blow succeeds, it might go some way towards deciding the whole course of the war. If it fails, at least I hope to give the enemy a pretty thorough beating.'[1]

In the meantime Field-Marshal Rommel had, like his opponent Lieutenant-General Montgomery, issued a special message to be read out to all the men of his Panzer Army, in stirringly personal, almost Nelsonian language:

Today, our army sets out once more to attack and destroy the enemy, this time permanently. I expect every soldier in my army to do his utmost in these decisive days. Long live Fascist Italy! Long live the Greater German Reich! Long live our great leaders![2]

Fearful of the consequences of failure, Rommel had been right to consider Germany's strategic situation in the late summer of 1942, at the very height of its military victories in Russia and North Africa. In retrospect he and Mussolini had only two years to live, Hitler less than three once the Thousand-Year Reich began to tumble. If the much-vaunted Panzer Army did not thrash or even 'destroy' the enemy at Alam Halfa and reach Cairo, Germany would – in view of heroic Russian resistance and Churchill's success in getting Roosevelt to commit America to a 'Europe first' strategy – be doomed. German supremacy on the battlefield was now at stake, and the future of the Third Reich with it. The days, even hours, of Nazi triumph were literally numbered as the moon swelled to fullness, then began to wane. Across the scrub desert was a revitalized 8th Army under a new commander, waiting for the German offensive to begin.

As a captured German general would later comment: 'The war in the desert ceased to be a game when Montgomery took over.'[3]

Will it fall apart?

Two months later, Hitler would send by sea and air an entire German army to Tunisia to try and stop the advancing Allies. Had he given Rommel even a portion of that support in August 1942, he might not have needed to seize Tunisia at all. Preoccupied with the war in Russia Hitler had, however, treated Rommel's desert achievements as excellent propaganda: a German–Italian campaign with enticing possibilities but decidedly subordinate to the war against the Soviet Union, victory in which seemed within his grasp.

In this sense, Churchill's strategic counter-vision had proved amazing. By dint of great courage the ageing Prime Minister had reassured Stalin in person that the Western Allies fully intended to prosecute the war in Europe – in the fullness of time. Starting in North Africa they would build up gradually to a second front in 1943, not 1942 as Stalin hoped. The fiasco of Dieppe had duly demonstrated how inadvisable a premature attempt at continental invasion would be, even with the most enthusiastic of troops. Meanwhile, however, Churchill had shaken up British command in the Middle East with a view to ensuring Egypt was not lost, that Malta could be resupplied (by winning back the Martuba airfields and guaranteeing air cover to the supply convoys), and that the Torch landings would be successful, once French forces in Morocco and Algeria saw that the British and their Allies meant business in the Egyptian desert, and that the Panzer Army was being beaten.

Roosevelt's convoy to Suez, with its several hundred Sherman tanks, was thus the gold that would guarantee strategic victory in the Mediterranean, and thereafter in Europe – as long as Rommel's 515 tanks, backed by 300 highly mobile guns and 1,000 aircraft, did not break through to Cairo in late August and upset the entire Allied applecart, as Rommel had repeatedly done since 1941.

Even Monty's staff were apprehensive. As Lieutenant-Colonel Richardson recalled of the new 8th Army commander, 'we had been impressed with his clear thinking and his amazing confidence; but in many minds, certainly in mine, there lingered doubts: "Is this just a technique, and will it fall apart when we face the crunch with Rommel, still the bogeyman?"'[4]

The battle begins

With hindsight, the bogeyman would have done better to have attacked on 15 August 1942, as he had originally intended, before Montgomery had had time to bring up and dig-in the 44th Division on Alam Halfa, or sow deep minefields in the south. Auchinleck's policy had been to lay not 'too many mines [which] would only limit the ability of Eighth Army's own mobile forces to make a counter-thrust when their turn came', as one staff officer at XIII Corps later noted.[5] Already on 12 August, the day before Monty arrived at 8th Army headquarters, Rommel had had 185 panzer Mk IIIs and IVs fit for combat – and it is certainly debatable whether 8th Army, in its still bewildered state at that time, could have successfully held off the combined weight of a Panzer Army assault.

Fortunately, anxious to stack the maximum number of cards in his favour, Rommel had insisted on sufficient fuel and other supplies being first brought up, and upon the full-moon period. An earlier attack would have permitted his forces to break past the still thin and isolated British minefields while British forces in the south were still scattered, demoralized and looking to the rear. By postponing his assault, however, Rommel hoped to give his troops the chance of breaching British minefields at night under a full moon, when enemy ground forces and aircraft would be handicapped. In order not to arouse British suspicions about the southern *Schwerpunkt*, therefore, he refused to allow more than minimal air reconnaissance over the southern sector, and forbade patrols which might have indicated the location and depth of British minefields. He thus invested his hopes on surprise, power, battle-drill, speed and tactical brilliance on the battlefield – but fatally delayed the kick-off.

Day after day, from 21 August 1942, Horrocks rehearsed and re-rehearsed XIII Corps in telephone signals, movement of reserves, tank, anti-tank and artillery co-ordination. From 14 August engineers had laid, on Monty's instructions, deeper and deeper minefields in the south, as well as dummy ones. Moreover, Monty had tirelessly toured the troops and addressed all senior officers, hammering home his message and his confidence in the inevitable result, not only when Rommel's attack came, but when 8th Army would turn to the offensive thereafter. Thus by full moon on 26 August, 8th Army was ready, the Alam Halfa position fully fortified, and tanks, anti-tank guns and artillery camouflaged and dug in to provide maximum concealment from the enemy – hoping thus to lure the panzers into British gun range, despite their inferiority in reach.

Had Rommel thus attacked on 26 August, he would have received a rude shock; but by waiting for more fuel until 30 August, as the moon waned, he played yet further into Montgomery's hands – for on 27 August a further armoured brigade of sixty-nine reconditioned Grants had finally come into line from the delta, more than doubling Horrocks's tally.[6] Given that no fewer than sixty-seven British tanks would be put out of action by the Panzer Army in the subsequent battle, even in well-defended hull-down defensive mode, the additional support of 8th Armoured Brigade's sixty-nine Grants on 27 August proved for Horrocks providential – and he had ordered a new corps exercise that very day to rehearse their inclusion in the battle plan.

Indeed, so confident was Monty by 30 August that he spent the day finishing and sending out his training programme for 8th Army's next battle, Lightfoot, to take place in the north, and went to bed at 9.30 p.m. Woken by de Guingand in the early hours of 31 August and told that the battle of Alam Halfa had begun – that enemy attacks had been launched in the north and centre as well as the south, and that RAF night-bombers were now in action dropping flares and attacking mobile enemy forces east of Himeimat – Monty merely turned over, and, murmuring 'Excellent, excellent!' went back to sleep![7]

No surprise

Two world-class commanders thus faced each other in the field on 31 August 1942, as General Lee had faced General Grant during the American Civil War. By his prodigious energy, professionalism and tactical genius, Rommel had created in the Afrika Korps and the Panzer Army of Africa a legendary force that took advantage of all the failings of a polyglot opponent, from equipment to tactics. On 29 August he had, in view of his concern that he would not have enough fuel for a long battle in the enemy's rear areas, modified his plan of attack; instead of heading straight for Alexandria and Cairo, he would first seek to 'defeat the enemy in the field'.[8] 'At dawn,' Rommel later chronicled, 'the motorised group was to thrust north up as far as the coast, and then east through the British supply area where a decision was to be sought in open battle. The appearance of our motorised group in the British supply area would probably draw off their motorised forces, and leave them with insufficient to overcome the defence of the 90th Light Division' – whose role was to shield the striking force from being cut off from the Axis supply route in the south. 'We placed particular reliance in this plan on the slow reaction of the British command and troops, for experience had shown us that it always took them some time to reach decisions and put them into effect. We hoped, therefore, to be in a position to present the operation to the British as a *fait accompli*.'[9]

From the start, however, Rommel's plan went wrong. Ultra intelligence had consistently failed to give the date of Rommel's attack, but reconnaissance Hurricanes of 208 Squadron had reported German or Italian transport vehicles forming up on the evening of 30 August, and at 9.45 p.m. Albacore biplanes dropped flares to guide in heavy Wellington bombers. 'We cannot fight successfully on the ground without the closest co-operation of the R.A.F.', Monty had written at the start of his 8th Army Lightfoot Training Memorandum No. 1. 'Without the closest touch between Army and R.A.F. staffs the co-ordination of the Air plan with that of the Army cannot be as effective as it should be, and in emergency may well fail. It involves the whole of the Air plan – the employment of the fighter force for air superiority and protection at the right time and place; the employment of the bomber force and the careful selection of bomber objectives best calculated to assist the military aim; and not least, the careful planning of air reconnaissance without which the close support squadrons for the attack of ground targets cannot operate with maximum efficiency.'[10] Monty's new approach to army–air co-ordination was about to be tested in earnest.

Recovering after the British bombing attack, the Panzer Army set off two hours later, only to run into 'an extremely strong and hitherto unsuspected British mine belt, which was stubbornly defended. Under intense artillery fire, the sappers and infantry eventually succeeded in clearing lanes through the British barrier, although at the cost of heavy casualties and a great deal of time – in many cases it needed three attempts,' Rommel recalled. 'Before long, relay bombing attacks by the R.A.F. began on the area occupied by our attacking force.'[11]

The surprise attack had clearly surprised no one.

Fingerspitzengefühl

'The lead elements of the Panzer Army became firmly wedged in the minefields, exposed to the planes, while sappers worked feverishly to clear lanes ahead of them,' one of Rommel's biographers recorded the frenzied first night of the Panzer Army's attack. 'Trucks, personnel carriers, tanks were hit and began to blaze fiercely. The fires and parachute flares lit the battlefield as bright as day. There were explosions, screams and the rattle of heavy machine-guns ... General von Bismarck was hit by a mortar bomb. Minutes later a British fighter-bomber straddled Nehring's [Afrika Korps] command truck: bomb fragments killed several of his staff, wrecked his radio, and disabled Nehring himelf.'[12]

The Afrika Korps had thus lost its commander before the battle proper had even begun.

Rommel, spending the night at Panzer Army headquarters, recalled that his 'staff spent most of the night on the telephone, with reports pouring in in a continual stream. Even so there remained considerable uncertainty about the situation, although it gradually became clear that things could not have gone altogether as planned.'[13]

This was an understatement – for Rommel had given orders his motorized forces should advance no less than thirty miles east in the moonlight, then strike north towards Burg-el-Arab at dawn!

Such optimism, based on execrable prior German reconnaissance, was a major error for a newly created field marshal (though Monty would commit a comparable error at Arnhem, seventeen days after himself becoming a field marshal), and it is difficult to understand why Generals Nehring, as Afrika Korps commander, von Bismarck (commander of 15th Panzer Division) and von Vaerst (commander of 21st Panzer Division) subscribed to such a bold plan without more accurate information. As Monty had warned in his 1937 'Encounter Battle' article, modern mobile warfare allowed less time to recover from mistakes than in earlier hostilities. Battle plans must therefore be well thought out, and well rehearsed,

using latest intelligence information. If the plan was poor, he had predicted, it would prove difficult, if not impossible, to rectify one's error.

Rommel's pragmatic plan for the final conquest of Egypt fell into this
category. But the very success with which, though vastly outnumbered,
Rommel had thrown back 8th Army at Gazala, snatched Tobruk, and
held on to his gains in July 1942 had blinded Rommel to almost all
battlefield problems save those of supply. He had alienated his air force
by his derision of their efforts and allowed himself to become almost
megalomaniac in his assumptions about the enemy. He had banked on
surprise and speed – and when he found his plan had not worked by dawn
on 31 August, his heart sank, and his famed *Fingerspitzengefühl*, or
military sixth-sense, warned him to stop: not to go on.

Rommel's procrastination

Rommel was right to listen to his instinct. Such was the legendary effect
of his command, however, that he became now a prisoner of his own
reputation. The Afrika Korps chief of staff, Colonel Bayerlein, acting as
corps commander, met Rommel at 8.15 a.m. on the battlefield; he urged
the army be allowed to continue, since both 15th and 21st Panzer Divisions
were at last emerging on the far side of the minefields, after sustaining
significant casualties. Rommel hesitated, telling the Panzer divisions to
halt and wait for new orders, while he thought about the situation.

Without surprise, could he really hope to smash the enemy? Was it a
trap? More even than his decision the day before, this was the hardest
decision of Rommel's life. With luck he might have been by now in a
position to strike up to the sea; instead he was barely emerging from the
enemy's first minefield. What should he do?

If the enemy knew he was coming, there was little point in seeking to
encircle him – he might as well begin the armoured battle immediately, by
seizing the Alam Halfa Ridge and forcing the British to attack *him*,
immediately behind the British front line on the Ruweisat Ridge. Axis air
reconnaissance, however, had shown the Alam Halfa Ridge was now
'heavily fortified', though did not reveal that an entire infantry division
had been brought up from the delta, with artillery, to defend it. Reluctantly
Rommel accepted that 'the battle for the ridge, which was the key to
the Alamein position, would be very severe',[14] but would have to be

undertaken, whatever the casualties. Ordering the army to direct its advance on to Alam Halfa, he asked Field-Marshal Kesselring to put the whole weight of the Luftwaffe and Regia Aeronautica into a *Blitzkrieg* bombing and divebombing attack to support it.

Rommel's procrastination ('C-in-C considers breaking off the battle', his diarist, Corporal Boettcher, recorded at 8.05 a.m.)[15] surprised both Bayerlein and the Panzer Army staff, who detected in it a fatal indecision. In his own memoirs Rommel claimed that the long delay in the minefields 'had given the enemy units in the threatened sectors time to send alarm messages and situation reports back to British Headquarters, and had enabled the British commander to take the necessary countermeasures'[16] – and that it was this that had worried him, not the prospect of a great armoured battle like Gazala. Forced to commit suicide for his passive role in the plot to assassinate Hitler in 1944, Rommel never did learn that 'the British commander' had made up his mind how he would fight the battle as early as 13 August 1942, had ensured that 8th Army rehearse its movements in proper exercises in the intervening weeks – and had simply gone back to sleep when told the battle had begun!

Round two to Rommel

Though he was wrong about the British commander, Rommel's indecision did justice to his professionalism. When should a commander persevere – and when should he accept he has made an error from which he cannot recover? 'A good "kick-off" is essential,' Monty had written in his 8th Army Training Memorandum No. 1 the day before, 'whether acting offensively or defensively; it is becoming increasingly difficult to rectify initial errors.'[17]

Rommel was torn; the specially jewelled field-marshal's baton being held for him in Berlin beckoned, yet he was uncomfortably aware that he had lost the opening round of the battle. His military instincts told him to pull back, his hubris told him to press on, as he had so often done before in unpromising circumstances – and triumphed. There was also the matter of his troops: those tens of thousands of Germans and Italians who had risked and in all too many cases already given their lives and limbs to breach the British minefields (later, it was reckoned that Montgomery had sown 180,000 mines in the area). Certainly Colonel Bayerlein's optimism reflected the legendary courage and ardour of the Deutsche Afrika Korps, which would have felt betrayed if recalled now from the far side of the cruel minefields it had so painfully crossed.

Conversely, that Rommel should so soon have fallen into the 8th Army trap was a tribute, among other things, to Monty's grasp of deception, and of the air weapon. Four years before, in August 1938, in the *Army Quarterly*, Monty had defended his encounter-battle theories against Liddell Hart, while reiterating his vision of the proper tactical use of air power in battle. Reflecting on the great German Spring Offensive of 1918, he remarked that the Allies had done nothing to attack the German concentration of ground forces from the air. The offensive had 'very nearly won the war for Germany', he recalled, whereas, if the entire Allied air forces had been used to attack the concentration, it was possible that the offensive might never have taken place at all. 'The lesson seems to be,' Monty had written, 'that full advantage must be taken of the flexibility of air forces to direct every ounce of power when the decisive moment arrives on to what is then the decisive target. Thus the moment may come for switching off the attacks on the enemy's economic centres and concentrating everything in an overwhelming attack on his assembling armies. The speed at which ground forces can now move suggests that plans for this "switching over" of air effort must be formulated in advance, so that they can be implemented within a few hours.'[18]

The RAF Middle East and Desert Air Force's bombardment of the Axis forming-up positions and rear depots, then the great bombing blitz on Rommel's mobile forces as they tried to force their way through the British minefields in the southern sector towards Alam Halfa on the night of 30–31 August, was Monty's first opportunity as an army commander to put his theories of air-power into effect. While it is true, as strategic historians have pointed out, that the sinking of Rommel's fuel supply ships – by submarines and air attack after decoding Axis signals – sealed the ultimate fate of the Panzer Army once it was ensnared, no single Axis vehicle ran out of petrol in the course of the battle, as Field-Marshal Kesselring, the German theatre commander, afterwards noted. 'Postwar analysis has shown that a great deal more petrol and ammunition reached Libya than was sunk on the way,' Ralph Bennett remarked.[19] Nor did Rommel take the decision to swing up against Alam Halfa for reasons of fuel shortage, given the average 200 miles per vehicle he had amassed; as he wrote in his own account of the battle, it was the loss of surprise, snared within the British minefields, that caused him to decide he simply could not take the risk of a British attack on his lines of communication by extending the reach of his panzer divisions too far beyond 90th Light Division, which was to defend his left flank – just as Montgomery, in the weeks ahead, would have to revise his plan for pushing his armoured *corps de chasse*, in daylight, beyond his infantry break-in at Alamein. By swinging north, straight up to the Alam Halfa heights, Rommel was inviting a 'very severe' battle: but one which, if he seized the ridge, would gain him the 'key to the whole El Alamein position'.[20]

Though later mocked by Hitler, Kesselring and pro-Nazi writers, Rommel's hesitation and subsequent decision to keep his Panzer Army concentrated were therefore signs of instinctive generalship, after a disastrous mistake – though the latter decision, as he knew, could not protect him from the Desert Air Force and British and American bombers operating from Cairo and Alexandria. What had seemed like Luftwaffe superiority in the days before the battle had turned very sour on the night of 30 August – a situation which would only get worse in the ensuing days.

With exemplary courage, then, Rommel's troops moved forward to attack Alam Halfa. It took hours, literally, to refuel and re-arm the Afrika Korps, as well as the Italian Littorio Armoured Division; but at 1 p.m. the assault began. To Monty's chagrin, as he visited his corps commanders, a desert sand storm blew up, masking the German advance. By 3.30 p.m. ground reports duly indicated the panzer divisions were moving northeast, as Monty noted in his diary: the very 'area for which 8th Army layout was designed' – yet hidden by so much swirling sand that the RAF could not get into the air. 'Strong wind was now blowing and the dust was such that the RAF squadrons were unable to take off. This was a tragedy,' Monty recorded. 'From 1200 hours to about 1600 hours two enemy armoured divisions were in and about the RAGIL depression and could not be touched.'[21]

Round two had gone to Rommel.

Peeing in our bags

Eventually, in the late afternoon, the first units of the Afrika Korps saw the Alam Halfa Ridge – like ocean sailors glimpsing land after a storm. Morale in the Korps was second to none: they had, after all, fought their way almost a thousand miles along the shores of North Africa, and felt themselves to be within striking distance at last of the capital of Egypt and the port of Alexandria.

To the officers and men waiting on the ridge, meanwhile, the emergence of the Afrika Korps resembled an armada issuing from a sea mist – hundreds upon hundreds of German tanks and vehicles like a fleet of ships filling the desert. The sight of the German 'battleships' – the long-muzzled Mk IV 'Specials' – struck fear in even the most experienced of British armoured commanders – 'the devil of a gun' as Brigadier 'Pip' Roberts of the 22nd Armoured Brigade put it.

Though Monty had placed 22nd Armoured Brigade directly under Horrocks's corps command, it had been put under operational control of General Gatehouse once further Grant tank reinforcements (8th Armoured Brigade) arrived on 27 August. In consequence it was very nearly lured into the sort of mobile battle Monty wished to avoid.

As Major-General Roberts explained almost forty years later, using tableware to describe the positions: 'You see, the Germans advanced and came up towards Alam Halfa. Now here were we sitting; the Germans came up the [line of] telegraph poles, and when they got there – instead of coming up here they swung away like that!

'Well, my divisional commander was then a man called Alec Gatehouse. And he was sitting further back . . . he could see what was happening too. And here were our forces with all the German Panzers going along like that past our position. And in fact, although Monty says he gave instructions that on no account was the 22nd Armoured Brigade to move its position, at that time Alec Gatehouse said to me, over the air:

' "I don't want you to think we're peeing in our bags here, but you may have to come out of your position and attack him from the rear."

'We did come very near to moving,' Roberts confided. 'So I issued preliminary instructions to people that they'd got to be prepared to move out of their defensive positions – just thinking about it. However at that moment the German tanks stopped and they all turned towards us – just turned, individual tanks, like that, so the situation never arose . . . In fact, we stayed put and it was very effective even though they, the Germans, produced for the first time a long-barrelled 75 mm gun in their Mark IV tank – which was much more effective than our 75 mm gun and it knocked out one squadron of our Grants very efficiently, before we could do anything about it.'[22]

Roberts' description of the advance of the Afrika Korps on the evening of 31 August was to become a classic. It was, he said, like watching 'a snake curl up ready to strike'.[23] Almost ninety German tanks were in the vanguard.

On they come, a most impressive array . . . And now they all turn left and face us and begin to advance slowly . . . I warn all units over the air not to fire until the enemy are within 1000 yards; it can't be long now and then in a few seconds the tanks of CLY [County of London Yeomanry] open fire and the battle is on. Once one is in the middle of a battle time is difficult to judge, but it seems only a few minutes before nearly all the tanks of the Grant squadron of the CLY were on fire. The new German 75-mm is taking heavy toll. The enemy tanks have halted and they have had their own casualties, but the situation is serious; there is a complete hole in our defence.[24]

The deadly Mk IV 'Specials' had knocked out twelve Grants without casualty to themselves.

I hurriedly warn the Greys [the reserve tank regiment] that they must move at all speed from their defensive positions and plug the gap. Meanwhile the enemy tanks are edging forward again and they have got close to the Rifle Brigade's anti-tank guns, who have held their fire marvellously to a few hundred yards. When they open up they inflict heavy casualties on the enemy, but through sheer weight of numbers some guns are overrun. The SOS artillery fire is called for; it comes down almost at once right on top of the enemy tanks. This, together with the casualties they have received, checks them . . .[25]

Roberts' account illustrates the intimate co-operation of hull-down tanks, six-pounder anti-tank guns, field artillery and divisional artillery required to halt a full Panzer advance. As the Royal Scots Greys poured over the crest of Hill 102, 21st Panzer Division began to fall back – though destroying another four Grants as they did so. The 15th Panzer Division, to the right of 21st Panzer Division, had met a similar hail of fire from the hull-down Grants of the 5th Royal Tank Regiment, a regiment of field artillery and the artillery of 44th Division on Alam Halfa. The Afrika Korps had lost twenty-two tanks in all – but more importantly had failed to make any headway in trying to seize the Alam Halfa heights – and had failed to lure the British on to their own famed 88s and anti-tank gun screen.

As Major Carver, a GSO 2 at XIII Corps, and later a field marshal, noted, 'In that hour's battle, on a front of only a few miles, in which certainly not more and probably less than 100 tanks had actually fired their guns at each other, the tide of battle in the desert had turned.'[26]

The swine isn't attacking

Rommel was dumbfounded. Not only could he not believe the manner in which the British armour and artillery had dug itself in, he could not understand why, on past experience, the enemy did not come out and attack him. 'The decisive battle was on no account to become static,' Rommel later explained his battle plan – and his decision, at 4 p.m. on 31 August, to call off the attack on Alam Halfa.

In doing so he hoped to refuel his panzers for a mobile battle the next day, when the 'greater aptitude of our troops for mobile warfare and the high tactical skill of our commanders'[27] would, by tempting out the reluctant enemy tanks, turn the battle to Axis advantage. But if he thought his forces would be allowed to rest for the night, he was grievously mistaken. 'After dusk, the bombers came. It was sheer slaughter,' one of Rommel's biographers described. 'All night long the slaughter went on. Rommel drove out at dawn, 1 September, to watch: the cramped terrain was littered with the wreckage of tanks; many were still burning.'[28]

Rommel could not simply watch his famed Afrika Korps being destroyed by the RAF; Alam Halfa would *have* to be taken, or the battle broken off. The 15th Panzer Division was therefore ordered into the attack again, while 21st Panzer kept the Grants of Roberts' 22nd Armoured Brigade quiet on the left, at Hill 102.

Had the Alam Halfa Ridge been occupied merely as an observation post and lightly defended 'box', and had Rommel been able to lure 8th Army into mobile battle (as Auchinleck had planned to respond), such an Axis attack, on 15 August, might well have succeeded. However, as Rommel later lamented, the Alam Halfa Ridge 'was now heavily fortified; it was also, as we later discovered, held by 44th British Infantry Division, newly arrived from Great Britain',[29] so the Afrika Korps would have had a tremendous battle to wrest the ridge from the enemy, even if individual panzers had broken through Roberts' screen, or lured out his Grants. Monty, however, had warned Horrocks under no circumstances to allow his Grants to get 'mauled' on the German anti-tank screens – and in the clear morning light von Vaerst's 15th Panzer Division merely ran into devastating artillery fire from 44th Division's medium and heavy artillery.

Unable to make headway against the British defences, and with worsening fuel replenishment problems – thanks to British air attack and still incompletely cleared minefield lanes where the Panzer Army had broken through on the first evening – Rommel could only hope that the British armour, that afternoon, would commit its old error: sending unsupported tanks to impale themselves on his anti-tank screens.

The British armour, however, stayed put. As the German 88mm Flak war diarist recorded, Rommel was exasperated: 'The swine isn't attacking,' Rommel complained bitterly to Kesselring.[30]

Wounded, but lethal

Facing Mk IV 'Specials' and 88mm anti-tank guns, the British tanks did well to keep at arm's length – indeed, when Gatehouse ordered the 8th Armoured Brigade with the newly arrived and last serviceable Grant tanks in 8th Army, to work its way round north-west – now that there was little chance of Afrika Korps making for El Hamman – to join up with and support Roberts' 22nd Armoured Brigade, Gatehouse found his Grants were unable to get past von Vaerst's gun-line. The moment they came within range of von Vaerst's 88s, no fewer than seven Grants were picked off – and Brigadier Custance was forced to retire. The moral was clear: with greatly superior tanks and anti-tank weapons, Rommel was a wounded animal, but still lethal.

As Monty had noted in his diary, it was by meeting the enemy on 'ground of its own choosing' that 8th Army had so successfully halted Rommel's attack. Horrocks later recalled how difficult it was 'to restrain the commanders from launching attacks on the Germans',[31] but when 22nd Armoured Brigade lost a further five Grants to 21st Panzer Division's guns, even Roberts saw the merit in holding back. The dog might want to eat the rabbit, as Horrocks had decribed the coming battle to Churchill, but it couldn't. The rabbit had far sharper teeth than the dog – and it knew exactly how to use them.

Stupidity the final flaw

On both sides, armoured commanders and staffs now urged advance; but Rommel and Montgomery were the commanders of the respective armies, and both were aware what was at stake. A false move by the Afrika Korps, and the Panzer Army of Africa was lost; a false move by 8th Army, and – given the ease with which the German Mk IV 'Specials' and 88s could 'brew up' even 8th Army's most powerful tank, the Grant – Rommel could still cause havoc behind 8th Army's front line, despite his growing fuel shortage.

Monty's 8th Army had, it was reckoned, put some fifty-two panzers out of action, but only ten of these were unrepairable. This left Rommel with approximately 160 Mk III and IV panzers, as well as his Italian tanks: a formidable fleet, backed by mobile artillery and anti-tank gunners trained to work hand-in-glove with the panzers – and employing their 88mm anti-aircraft gun in a secondary anti-tank role. Had he had more Grants, Monty could have launched an attack on the neck of Rommel's salient, but he not only lacked such armour, he was, thanks to the War Office, unable to use any of more than a thousand British guns comparable to the dreaded German 88s, sitting in the Middle East.

This was one of the great scandals of the Western Desert, deliberately covered up by all British official historians in the aftermath of World War II. 'The Germans first used their 88 millimetre Anti-aircraft Gun, which is almost identical to the [British] 3.7 inch gun, as an anti-tank in a short action at Halfaya Pass on the Egyptian Cyrenaican border in June 1941 when four of these 88 millimetre guns destroyed eleven out of twelve British Matilda tanks,' a veteran desert AA gunner, Major D. F. Parry, later recalled[32] – a figure which Ian Hogg, a master gunner of the Royal Artillery, increased to ninety British tanks destroyed, 'the majority by the fire of a [single] battery of dug-in 88mm guns'.[33] In fact, according to Major Rudolf Marwan-Schlosser of the 135 Flak Regiment in Africa, Rommel had used 88mm guns to destroy three British light tanks already at Agheila, on the Tripolitanian border, nine days after his arrival in Africa, reversing General Garibaldi's plans for the defence of Tripoli into counter-attack, and using the rallying cry 'Panzers and 88-Flak, Advance!'[34] A 'hollow-charge shell had been provided, capable of holing 165mm of plate at any distance – and the maximum ground range of the 88 was in excess of 16,000 metres! Quite literally,' Ian Hogg noted, 'what it could see, it could kill.'[35]

'The Germans never forgot and the British never remembered,' Parry commented. 'Over a year later at Alamein the destruction caused by the 88 millimetre gun was equally horrific when 75 out of 95 tanks of the 9th Armoured brigade were speedily destroyed with the loss of 230 tank men. Such destruction makes the charge of the Light Brigade at Balaclava pale into insignificance . . . During all this time the men of the Desert Army used the two-pounder anti-tank gun in a hopeless attempt to stop the German tanks while over a thousand 3.7 inch anti-aircraft guns stood silent in the Middle East, on a rare occasion the odd shot was fired at stray enemy aircraft in the vicinity of Alexandria but many never fired a shot in anger during the whole of the war.'[36] Various excuses were later given – the lack of 'optical sights for ground firing'(!), lack of 'anti-tank ammunition'; and the 'gap' such use would create 'in the defences of the Suez canal, a step which was unthinkable'[37] – but they were pathetic. The sheer obtuseness of the British, Major Parry considered as a desert veteran, was in this instance on a par with the loss of Tobruk. Paraphrasing Churchill, he commented, 'Defeat is one thing, disgrace another but stupidity really is the final straw.'[38]

Peter Beale, a Royal Tank Regiment veteran who moved to Australia and became a military historian, found the British failure to use their 3.7-inch anti-aircraft guns – first mooted in 1920, proposed in 1928, specified in 1933, designed in 1934, and first produced in 1938[39] – in the role of tank-killers, as criminal. In *Death by Design* he pointed out that anti-aircraft exercises in Britain up to 1937 had always included the use of such weapons as dual-purpose anti-aircraft and anti-tank guns; but in that year the tradition had stopped. When Churchill raised the subject in 1940 he was told that the use of such weapons in a dual capacity 'had been considered but rejected'.[40]

In the specific case of Britain's magnificent 3.7-inch gun, the failure to use it against tanks was due, Beale claimed, to 'closed minds, small brains, personal vanity or complete inability [of the Royal Artillery and its anti-aircraft establishment] to cooperate with other arms of the services'.[41] Like the story of tank development itself, it was another sorry saga of British bungling and ultimate incompetence.

Without comparable weapons in the desert, then, and without extensive retraining in using the ones they possessed in linked, centrally controlled firepower and in co-operation with other arms, Monty feared the 8th Army would simply revert to its earlier confusions; indeed, at one point in the spring, General Auchinleck had possessed 167 Grants ranged against the Panzer Army, which at that time lacked Mk IV 'Specials' or even Mk III 'Specials', and all the Grants had been lost or had had to be withdrawn. It was not, Monty felt, a risk worth taking; failure would vitiate the very real rise in British morale accruing from a well-fought successful defensive battle.

Sitting tight

Rightly or wrongly, then, Monty chose not to attempt mobile battle, but to sit tight and make Rommel take a pounding – at arm's length.

At the end of his life de Guingand recalled the moment when, as 8th Army chief of staff during the battle of Alam Halfa, he pleaded with Monty in his caravan to counter-attack, striking south through the New Zealand Division's line at Rommel's bottleneck. 'I felt he ought to [deliver a counter-attack] and I persuaded him. He said: "What shall we do now?" – he had me into the caravan. "Rommel's had a hell of a smacking, he's lost a lot of armour, some of his supplies have been blown up by our air force." And I said: "There's a gap here – the New Zealand Division was there – why don't you get the New Zealand Division to have a crack south, try to cut him off?" '[42]

On de Guingand's urging, the attack was in fact attempted. 'On the map it looked an inviting prospect for the British to move south and cut off [Rommel's] retreat,' Freyberg's son recorded. 'The obvious place from which to start such an attack was Bare Ridge', or Alam Nayil. General Horrocks duly 'decided to launch the operation and spent the first days of September trying to persuade Freyberg to mount it with New Zealand troops'. Freyberg, however, refused. 'Less than two months previously the New Zealanders had been overrun by German tanks at Ruweisat and El Mreir, and Freyberg had no intention of exposing his Division to a repeat performance.'[43] Instead, the third brigade of the virgin 44th Division was used, under Freyberg's overall command and against his will; the result was a shambles, with distressing casualties – though de Guingand, like his opposite number Colonel Bayerlein, was dismissive of the difficulties. 'If the New Zealand Division had really been more robust I think we could have achieved big things there, there's no doubt about it,' de Guingand reflected in the evening of life, smoking his pipe.[44]

Basil Liddell Hart agreed; indeed, in an unpublished 'analysis' of the battle which he sent to all and sundry, Liddell Hart not only touted the notion that Monty had 'accepted' Auchinleck's plan of defence at Alam Halfa, but 'missed' a 'great opportunity' of 'trapping the whole Afrika Korps – the core of Rommel's forces – and finishing the war at one bite'.[45]

Colonel Bayerlein meanwhile bombarded Rommel with similar advice, in reverse: to press on, as the Afrika Korps had done in the past with such electrifying results. But Rommel was in the front line – and knew what was possible, and what was not. As one of his biographers wrote, 'That morning Rommel suffered six bombing attacks. The air was unbreathable – hot, acrid with smoke and choked with fine sand. Lethal showers of shattered rock fragments added to the blast and shrapnel effects. "An 8-inch bomb-fragment punched a hole clean through one of the shovels lying on the rim of his slit trench," ' Rommel's diarist recorded. ' "The red hot metal fragment landed on the C-in-C in the trench." '[46]

In his own account Rommel recorded that 'The Afrika Korps continued to be assailed throughout the day by heavy R.A.F. bomber attacks, in the bare and coverless country, with the bomb-bursts frequently intensified by rock splinters, we suffered severe casualties. Seven officers were killed from the Afrika Korps' staff alone ... Swarms of low-flying fighter-bombers were coming back to the attack again and again and my troops suffered tremendous casualties. Vast numbers of vehicles stood burning in the desert. In the afternoon, I shifted my command post, and, in view of the bad supply situation, again considered whether to break off the battle.' The British artillery seemed to be firing ten shells to every German salvo; the German fighters seemed unable to break through the cordons of British fighters protecting the ' "Party Rally" bomber squadrons' (Bostons, in patterns of eighteen aircraft), as Rommel called them.[47]

For his part, two days into the battle, Monty knew his first fight with Rommel had gone miraculously close to plan: that he had only to sit tight, bomb and shell Rommel's over-exposed army, and threaten his rear – giving Rommel no chance for a riposte with his superior armour – and he was bound to win. Egypt had, in fact, been saved; World War II, with concerted American, British and Russian effort, could now be won by the Allies.

The fateful order: retreat

All night long, while Monty slept in his truck at Burg-el-Arab, the Anglo-American air forces kept up their bombing of the Panzer Army – 'relays of aircraft dropping bombs of all sizes,' as Rommel recorded. 'Once again they came crashing round my command post. A vehicle was set alight not ten yards from my slit trench.'[48]

By the third morning of the battle, on 2 September 1942, Rommel decided he had had enough. With dwindling fuel supplies, and Desert Air Force superiority over the battlefield, 'the battle had now reached a stage where material strength alone would decide the issue'. To continue to attack Alam Halfa and Point 102 could lead only to 'a battle of material attrition', in which the Panzer Army, way out beyond its own Alamein defence lines, could only lose its crucial mobile-warfare advantage. Regretfully, therefore, Rommel issued the order he had himself, on the eve of battle, known must spell defeat for Nazi Germany in World War II, as von Moltke had known in 1914 when the Schlieffen plan came to grief: for to fail at Alam Halfa, he knew, was to risk losing the war, given the growing strength of the Allies. As Rommel put it in his reflections on the battle: 'With the failure of this offensive our last chance of gaining the Suez Canal' would be gone. 'We could now expect that the full production of British industry, and more important, the enormous industrial potential of America, which, consequent on our declaration of war, was now fully harnessed to the enemy cause, would finally turn the tide against us.'[49]

Whatever Bayerlein felt, Rommel had no option. The British were refusing to counter-attack. 'Montgomery had attempted no large scale attack to retake the southern part of the line; and would probably have failed if he had,' Rommel noted sanguinely. 'He had relied instead on the effect of his enormously powerful artillery and air force. Added to this, our lines of communication had been subjected to continual harassing attacks by the 7th Armoured Division. There is no doubt that the British commander's handling of this action had been absolutely right and well suited to the occasion, for it had enabled him to inflict very heavy damage on us in relation to his own losses, and to retain the striking power of his own force.'[50]

'We had never before experienced bombing that was anything like last night,' Lieutenant Wilfried Armbruster, Rommel's German-Italian interpreter, noted in his diary. 'Our combat echelon has had many men killed, three Flak 88s were hit and several ammunition trucks.'[51] After breakfast, as yet more British aircraft filled the sky, Rommel signed the fateful order. The Panzer Army would retreat.

The order to retreat

Rommel's decision, on 2 September 1942, was taken badly by the panzer crews and their lorried infantry support troops. 'This morning our drivers bring water forward to us. They tell us that Alam Halfa has been taken and that in two hours we'll be marching on,' the 104th Infantry Regiment chronicler recorded. But the orders were mistaken. 'Already we are thinking of the Nile, the pyramids and the Sphinx, of belly dancers and cheering Egyptians. About 1 p.m. our lorries arrive and we load up. Then we drive off – to the West. To the West?'[52]

It seemed a cruel end to such a magnificent campaign, under their legendary commander. 'That was the end to our dreams of Cairo, the pyramids and the Suez Canal.'[53]

Failure, however, was a fearful word. According to one Italian historian, 'General De Stefanis, commanding the 20th Italian Armoured Corps (Ariete, Trieste and Littorio), informed his divisional officers that the operation must now be considered at an end; it was never intended to be anything more than a demonstration in force. He himself did not seem altogether convinced by the reasons he put forward – which had clearly been dictated from above.'[54]

If the brave, bombed and battered troops were disappointed after three days of battle, however, it was as nothing compared with Field-Marshal Kesselring's reaction when he heard the news later that day – and to the end of his life Kesselring failed to comprehend how Rommel had let victory slip from his grasp. The Six-Day Race – named after the famous bicycle race of that name held in Berlin – 'would have been no problem for the "old" Rommel', he claimed – '*he* would never have called it off when it had already succeeded in outflanking the enemy', he wrote obtusely. Hitler was of the same mind. 'There's no doubt, no doubt at all that he was quite wrong to have called off that offensive, probably under the influence of the sinking of the 4,000-ton tanker. That's Kesselring's view too, and Ramcke shares it. He says, "It was a mystery to us why he didn't go on with it. We had the British on the run again, and we only had to pursue them and knock the living daylights out of them." '⁵⁵ From speaking to Rommel's subordinates Kesselring was certain 'that his troops never understood his order to retreat. Just think – he had already out-flanked the British "last hope" line of defence'.⁵⁶

But Rommel hadn't outflanked anybody – as he was all too painfully aware on 2 September 1942. Like Monty, Rommel's experience in World War I was the basis of his military professionalism; but it was also, as with Monty, the source of his realism. It was not cowardice, weariness, 'psychological reasons' (as Mussolini accused him) or ill-health that made Rommel retreat but concern for the lives of his men. To retreat was possibly to abandon Germany's 'last hope' of winning the war, but there was no option; the battle was lost, and he could only hope to save as many men and weapons as he could.

Moreover, though Kesselring and Bayerlein might continue to fantasize about Cairo, they were failing to interpret the lessons of the battle. The enemy was no longer the same one they had been fighting since 1941; there was new and ominous evidence that the change of British commander had led to a complete change not only in tactics, but in Allied co-operation between services – the very keystone of Germany's own fabled *Blitzkrieg* success since the invasion of Poland. The RAF had always been an air force to reckon with, but had never worked in such close conjuction with British ground forces. Now, however, they were like twins: and therein was spelled the future of warfare. *Blitzkrieg* had been founded upon intimate co-operation between the Luftwaffe and ground forces, especially panzer divisions. Now, belatedly, the British seemed to have understood. Their ground troops had dug themselves in, and appeared impervious to Stuka divebombing attack; meanwhile, despite their numerical and even technical inferiority – since the Messerschmitt 109bf still ruled the skies – the Desert Air Force employed a range of aircraft working in extraordinary unison: biplanes dropping flares for the heavy night-bombers, fighter squadrons protecting the day-bombers, with fighter-bombers mixed between. Moreover, by targeting the Panzer Army's supply columns, the RAF made replenishment a nightmare. 'By maintaining a constant watch on the roads leading to the front he can put a complete stop to daylight supply traffic and force his enemy to drive only by night, thus causing him to lose irreplaceable time,' Rommel reflected. 'But an assured flow of supplies is essential; without it the army becomes immobilised and incapable of action. All this provided us with inescapable conclusions.'⁵⁷

Air-Marshal Barratt, visiting from England, had been present for the first three days of the battle. 'Each evening,' he recorded, Monty had 'had a personal meeting with the AOC [Air Officer Commanding] at which I was present.' Monty 'gave him the clearest possible appreciation of the situation, the information as he knew it, what he intended to do himself, and what he expected the enemy to do. The AOC then said what he could do himself, and a general air plan was agreed upon' – revised each morning 'as a result of events, ground and air, during the night. AVM [Air Vice Marshal] Coningham subsequently informed me that never had he had such a clear and concise exposition of the military situation and needs during his experience in the Western Desert.'[58]

British air power had, in conjunction with the army, finally ended the 'old rules of warfare': namely, the ascendancy of German panzer forces in modern war. By predicting German methods and *Schwerpunkt*, and by his calculated use of air and ground forces, Montgomery had slowed down the business of mobile war. Though blessed with superlative troops, outstanding commanders, formidable equipment and the greatest panzer striking force ever seen in the desert, Rommel had been reduced to impotence. 'Anyone who has to fight, even with the most modern weapons, against an enemy in complete command of the air,' Rommel wrote sadly, 'fights like a savage against modern European troops, under the same handicaps and with the same chances of success.'[59]

In a matter of three days Montgomery had changed the rules of modern warfare – as all but a loyal gaggle of British Auchinleck / Dorman-Smith admirers could later see. Rommel, however, was too restless a soldier to miss the pattern emerging from the proverbial fog (or sands) of war. His legendary tactical skill and the extraordinary superiority of German tank and anti-tank gun crews, and their equipment, meant he could still put up a fight – and would do so again and again over the next two years. But it was a losing game, as he was the first to recognize, below the taunting, haunting heights of Alam Halfa. The enemy had at last pulled himself together, and with the industrial output of Britain and America to back its field commanders, the days of German exploitation of enemy muddle and confusion were over. 'Our feelings at the failure of our offensive can be imagined,' he later wrote.[60] His Nelsonian message of 30 August ('Today our army sets out once more to attack and destroy the enemy, this time permanently. I expect every soldier in my army to do his utmost in these decisive days!') now looked deeply embarrassing, but the lives of his men counted for more than his pride. 'Some very hard days lie behind me,' he wrote to his wife Lucie, two days after his fateful decision to retreat, while still 'hoping that the situation can be straightened out'. He blamed 'supply reasons' for the failure, and 'the superiority of the enemy air force', maintaining that 'victory was otherwise ours'.[61]

It wasn't; the Panzer Army had clearly failed completely in its bid to reach Cairo, and would never have another opportunity, now that the American supply convoy was unloading at Suez. Even his former ADC, Heinz Schmidt, 'developed serious doubts as to whether I should ever, as a soldier, set eyes on the Pyramids'.[62] The overstretched Luftwaffe in Europe and Russia would never be able to spare more echelons for North Africa. The writing was on the wall. Auchinleck and Dorman-Smith had been quite, quite wrong in assuming war would now become a business of battle-groups, Jock-columns and mobility. Rather, the war would become one of organized and professionally directed attrition, in which German mobility, field weaponry and battlefield skill could be cauterized by largely civilian soldiers, lacking a militaristic ethos but serving a democratic cause: a cause characterized by contradictions, inefficiency and argument, yet committed to respect for the individual. The forces of democracy had already thrown up great political leaders in Churchill and Roosevelt. Now, at the eleventh hour, they had thrown up a field commander capable of cutting his brilliant opponent down to size. Rommel's days of panzer glory were over; those of Montgomery, the infantryman, backed by the Allied air forces, were about to begin.

20

After Alam Halfa

The Rommel cult

There were many parallels between Montgomery and Rommel, as Monty's intelligence chief, 'Bill' Williams, later noted. 'Each, an infantryman from a line regiment, served in the First World War and, between the wars, taught at the Staff College and wrote a manual of infantry tactics; each led a division in France in 1940 (but Rommel was already with armour) and was commanding a Corps by 1941. Each in high command was to prove a godsend to the war-correspondent and the cameraman, each to win a victory when his country was most short of victories, and to owe some of his success to the material superiority temporarily to his hand; each to evoke a tremendous morale in those he led, to be served by a brilliant Chief of Staff and to be best when playing a lone hand. Each was primarily a very able professional soldier, a student as well as a practitioner of modern warfare, with a deep interest in his enemy, and no other absorbing occupation.'[1]

Ironically, each would become most famous for his offensive victories – Rommel for the 'Dash to the Wire' in 1941, the 'Cauldron' battles of 1942 including Gazala and the seizure of Tobruk, even for the stunning spoiling attack against the American forces at Kasserine in 1943; Montgomery for the great offensives of Alamein and D-Day – whereas, Williams later mused, it might be that their legendary battlefield prowess, at its most instinctive, was best demonstrated in the art of defence – Rommel in his long retreat from Alamein, Montgomery in the defensive battles of Alam Halfa and Medenine, and in command of American forces in the Battle of the Bulge.

Whatever the tactical truth of this for military historians, both men had now become desert rivals: the fox against the master of the hounds. By defeating Rommel's bid to reach Cairo in 1942 in command of a complete panzer army, Montgomery had saved Egypt, Malta, the Middle East and, it may be argued, ensured the successful mounting of the Torch landings, about which, until 3 September 1942, Roosevelt and his military adviser had entertained grave doubts, refusing to countenance a landing at Algiers. With the failure of Rommel's thrust, however, the entire future of the war in the Mediterranean was turned upon its head – indeed, by 24 September Mussolini was confiding to Rommel that 'the battle in the Mediterranean is for the moment lost. Italy has insufficient shipping to win the battle, particularly as we shall have to face up to an American landing in North Africa next year.'[2]

How far can the outcomes and strategic consequences of such battles, then, be ascribed to the opposing personalities of their commanders? Although in post-war years the 'great men of history' approach to biography became deeply eroded by historians imbued with Marxist, economic, statistical, populist, post-structuralist and other approaches to history, the pendulum began to shift back towards the significance of competing individual leaders as the millennium came to a close. 'The will to win,' wrote Richard Overy in 1995, 'proved inseparable from the ability to fight better' – something that 'had little to do with Gross Domestic Product, even if most soldiers had known what that meant'.[3] In 1999 the biographer of Adolf Hitler, Ian Kershaw, noting the long stream of books and articles that gave pride of place to the historical and economic context of German fascism rather than to the importance of the personality and behaviour of the Führer himself, concluded that a history of modern Germany that overlooked Hitler as a unique personality was myopic. 'No attempt to produce a comprehensive understanding of the phenomenon of Nazism without doing justice to "the Hitler factor" can hope to succeed,' Kershaw considered,[4] for to imagine Germany developing into a police state under Himmler and the SS 'without Hitler as head of government', or Germany entering a general European war by the end of the pacifist 1930s 'under a different leader, even an authoritarian one', or Germany conducting 'out-and-out genocide' under a 'different head of state', was, he maintained, beyond the power of even the most Marxist of historians.[5]

Similarly, the German–Italian successes in North Africa which brought the Panzer Army to the gates of Cairo and Alexandria in the summer of 1942 cannot be fully understood without addressing the will of its German and Italian soldiers, and the military leadership of Erwin Rommel, whose *philosophie de guerre*, his hold on his men, and his use of the weapons at hand (as well as those captured from the British) made him for a time the king of the desert – a role he loved, and which he assiduously cultivated in the best traditions of Third Reich propaganda. As one general later noted, a 'kind of Rommel cult emerged', fanned not only by his victories but by the fact that he 'seldom went anywhere without a posse of personal photographers'.[6] One of his biographers wrote that the 'various tactical headquarters in Africa soon learned that one way to attract his good humour was to station men with cameras at his arrival point – even if they had no film in their cameras'.[7] Thus the German public came to idolize Rommel as the human face of Nazi conquest – something which led to great jealousy among his fellow generals and field marshals, especially those of the old military-aristocratic caste. Erwin Rommel, after all, had no 'von' to his name.

Nor, for that matter, did Hitler.

The business of big ideas

Serious minds in the British army's education directorate had begun to ponder the competition between the political philosophies of the Germans and the British, and had concluded in the weeks after Monty's defensive victory at Alam Halfa that the 'chief reason why we are at a serious disadvantage compared with the Nazis over this business of "big ideas" is that the evil things for which they stand are novel and dynamic, whereas the excellent things for which we claim to be fighting may seem dull and uninspiring'.[8]

Nowhere had this proved more true than on the battlefield. Both the Führer and his favourite field marshal were representative of a class-less modern society that insisted its leaders be 'popular', even adulated – thus bridging the gap between leader and the led. Rommel had seen the virtue of publicity for morale, and saw no reason to be ashamed, since he thought himself a great battlefield general; indeed, had no other interest in life than proving himself as a great field commander. To achieve this, he required troops who would fight effectively, chivalrously as well as courageously, and by his charismatic presence on the battlefield, as well as behind the front lines, he maintained a human loyalty that did him great credit.

Monty also had no 'von' in his name – indeed his reputation was that of an anti-aristocrat: a colonial contemptuous of the idle English gentry whose houses he had gleefully demolished in southern England in 1940. Thereafter, he had scandalized the military hierarchy by his insistence upon performance and fitness, making portly headquarters staff officers go on five-mile runs at the risk of physical collapse. Without reference to his superiors he had sacked almost anyone with grey hair. He meant business, and spared no one, whether in England or upon arrival in the desert. He had toured his units indefatigably in the two weeks before the battle of Alam Halfa, had ordered that 8th Army was to stand or die in its fortified positions, and issued a message saying 'the whole future of the war will depend on how we carry out our task'. Day after day, night after night, Axis and Allied air forces had filled the sky, while the sound of shells, bombs, mortars and explosions had denoted the battle raging in the southern sector of the Alamein line, and on his daily rounds visiting his corps and divisional commanders he was, like Rommel, frequently bombed and strafed. 'During the battle we used to float around the old Desert,' Monty's ADC Captain Poston related afterwards to his mother, '& once got set on by 4 x 109's on the Main Road and were in 3 heavy bombing attacks. One each day of the battle. The first two by 28 & 35 Stukas respectively & the last one, a final effort of theirs to blast their way through by 24 Stukas, 33 x JU 88's & about 40 fighters, very nasty, but all O.K.'[9]

Finally, late on the afternoon of 2 September 1942, the panzers had been reported as pulling back. Victory was in the air, literally and metaphorically. Lieutenant-Colonel Richardson had watched with wonder not only how Brigadier de Guingand now worked with the chief of staff of the Desert Air Force, Air-Commodore George Beamish, but how the new 8 Army Joint Ops Room operated at Burg-el-Arab, hand-in-glove with the RAF. 'In all our dealings with the R.A.F. our motto must be: "United we stand, divided we fall",' Monty had stated in his Training Memorandum No. 1, before the battle began – and the battle had proved the point.[10] 'The battle is going rather well for us at the moment,' Richardson wrote home, 'so much so that the Germans have had to call their advance a "reconnaissance"; of course in actual fact it was a full scale attack by which they hoped to reach Cairo. The RAF have been bombing them day and night and this has been most effective.'[11]

Major Oswald, a GSO 2 at the headquarters, also recalled the sense of amazement. 'Almost nobody moved,' he remembered. 'Now that was a thing that staggered everybody because in every other battle once Rommel was on the loose, people tended to go haywire in all directions trying to pin him down. But here he'd done absolutely everything we wished him to, and run his head against a brick wall. And of course he'd lost 50-odd tanks, vehicles, soldiers – a lot of casualties, all in plain daylight, shelled unmercifully the whole time, bombed from the air and everybody up on the Ruweisat Ridge or at Alam Halfa or in 7th Armoured Division could see this going on: and that was about the biggest morale booster that everybody had – it did everybody a power of good.'[12]

Robert Priestley, a staff officer in 8th Armoured Brigade, was one of those defending the Ruweisat Ridge. 'It was a fascinating battle,' he recalled almost forty years later. 'For the first time since the Germans came into operations in North Africa we were told to do a job we really felt we could do . . . The actual battle went, as far as I could tell, absolutely according to plan. I remember on the second day of the battle visibility was superb – and it very rarely was in the desert. You could see five miles or more quite easily. And we could see the whole of the German army laid out in front of us. I got on a tank with Derrick Mullins, a regimental CO, and we sat there watching the German army being shelled and bombed. And I remember writing home after that battle saying, "All right, this battle's changed the war. Now we shall win. No two ways about it. We shall win." And that confidence never left really.'[13]

Monty's new ADC, who had been in the desert since 1940, also felt that the battle marked a turning point in the war. 'As I told you before,' John Poston proudly wrote to his mother a week after the battle was over, 'if Rommel had the cheek to try to get to Egypt he would get a good hiding & go back with a very sore head. And so he has, & he has also had his Tank strength cut in ½. The news write-up in the papers was so bad that no one thought he had done anything at all. Of course, he got his say in first about the "reconnaissance in Force" & everyone believed it, but in actual fact he made a full-blooded attempt with the whole of the Afrika Korps & an Italian Corps to get Egypt & we, for the first time in this war, met him, fought him, beat him & methodically pushed him back into his old positions with very little loss to ourselves. This was done with great help of the R.A.F., who did magnificent continuous bombing. It is the first time in this war that he has had to admit defeat having taken the initiative & met us on our own ground. It has usually been that, in the end *we* have had to go back, but not this time.'[14]

Lucky stars

Major Witherby was another who felt this to have been the turning point of the war. As Wireless Officer of 23rd Brigade, he had been part of 8th Army's mobile reserve – though painfully aware, from the 'Balaclava' charge in July, how vulnerable his Valentine two-pounder 'peashooter' tanks were to German tank and anti-tank gunfire, especially from the dreaded 88mm dual-purpose anti-aircraft anti-tank guns. The manner in which Monty had transformed the *modus operandi* in 8th Army had already stunned him on his return to the front from hospital in Cairo on 17 August; but the way the battle of Alam Halfa went 'according to plan', two weeks later on 31 August, was to him even more extraordinary. Though Rommel's anti-tank guns and armour, especially the Mk IV 'Specials', had outranged the British tanks and anti-tank guns, they had in turn been outranged by British artillery on Alam Halfa, and by the Desert Air Force. 'Artillery and air bombing was effective even against the German tanks, which had thinner armour at their sides and tops, and it was very effective against infantry in the open, and transport vehicles and guns. The defending units at Alam el Halfa were so positioned that the enemy was constantly under artillery fire, often from several different directions at once. This fire was directed from higher ground, from the air or on pre-arranged targets.' Although the opposing air forces were numerically equal, this was 'not as I remember it', Witherby recalled. 'The impression I had was that the German Air Force (very few Italian planes were present) was more of a guerilla force, making sudden, small scale raids' – raids in which they attracted 'storms of anti-aircraft fire'. As he noted, 10th Armoured Division had two regiments of twenty-five-pounders, while 44th Division disposed of three, and were 'very solidly dug in, the infantry having minefields in front'. Had Rommel managed to break through anywhere, it would not have been for long. 'Artillery from the whole Corps could engage targets as they approached and the artillery was not scattered as the artillery had been in the past but was under one command and was co-ordinated.' There were thus no real 'gaps or flanks, only a solid lump of Army, dug in and with a very strong Air Cover. Each formation was carefully given a task for which it was well suited and within its capacity and almost every formation was in a position to come quickly to the aid of other formations should they need help.' So different was this from any previous experience in the desert, and so crucial was it to halt Rommel at this moment in the war, before 8th Army could be reinforced, that Witherby felt 'most writers do not, in my opinion, give it sufficient weight'. The official history of the Middle East land campaigns, by Major-General Playfair, 'dwells on Rommel's poor health and supply difficulties' – but these were very much the excuses which Rommel gave in his nightly reports to Germany and Italy, decoded at Bletchley Park. 'The truth is that at this time the Battle was altogether astounding,' wrote Witherby as a veteran. 'It was unbelievable.' No ' "all out" German attack' had ever been stopped like that by the British; indeed, '[i]n August 1942 hardly anyone could conceive of the idea of simply stopping the Panzers in their tracks! This was regarded as impossible' – which was why Auchinleck and Dorman-Smith had put their faith in fluid battle.

Witherby vividly remembered the first day of Alam Halfa, as the artillery of 23rd Armoured Brigade thundered and his group of Valentines stood ready to meet 90th Light Division, manning the left flank of the Afrika Korps and providing reconnaissance. 'About this time I met a South African armoured car officer who had been observing at this point before we arrived. I asked him what he thought would happen. He replied that, to judge from previous battles, the Germans would come on all together and get on to the Alam el Halfa Ridge, where they would break up into smaller parties and tear about doing as much damage as they could and finally, they would all join together again and smash us.' As Witherby noted, 'This was not very reassuring, but it was more or less what had happened at Gazala.'[15]

It did not happen at Alam Halfa, however – and Witherby, like thousands of fellow soldiers in 8th Army, thanked his lucky stars – and the new army commander.

Thanks to the Almighty

The new army commander, conversely, thanked his men. On 5 September 1942 Monty distributed a special message to all troops in 8th Army – for the battle of Alam Halfa was to all intents and purposes over, with Rommel's rearguards 'being driven through the Minefield area north of Himeimat. All formations and units, both armoured and unarmoured, have contributed towards this striking victory, and have been magnificently supported by the RAF. I congratulate all ranks of 8th Army on the devotion to duty and good fighting qualities which have resulted in such a heavy defeat of the enemy and which will have far-reaching results. I have sent a message to the AOC Western Desert expressing our thanks to the RAF for their splendid effort.'

Monty had won his first battle against Rommel, and at a special church service in the desert at Burg-el-Arab on Sunday 6 September 1942, gave thanks to the Almighty for 8th Army's deliverance – before continuing with his plans for the next battle.

This would not be so easy, he recognized, yet was vital if the Allies were now to regain the initiative, save Malta and ensure the Torch landings were not seriously opposed by the Vichy French. Not only 8th Army but the whole world must see, for the first time, that the Allies were capable of winning an offensive, all-out battle against the Germans: the battle of Alamein.

Churchill's difficulties

As Ralph Bennett, who was in Cairo at the time, later chronicled, Ultra had helped Montgomery by confirming the rightness of his instinct in fortifying the Alam Halfa Ridge and in his static plan of defence, but it had provided no usable tactical information before or during the battle itself, other than confirming the direction in which Rommel intended to penetrate the British line, and the forces he would use. For their victory over Rommel the men of the 8th Army could legitimately congratulate themselves and their RAF colleagues – and for this, Monty was entitled to take the credit.

The battle of Alam Halfa, Bennett commented, was 'the first unequivocal victory of a British general over Rommel; CRUSADER [Auchinleck's earlier offensive] had turned to dust and ashes in a few weeks, and the mere fact that Rommel could attack again on 30 August was proof enough that "First Alamein" in mid-July was no more than a temporary check.' From the moment, Bennett chronicled, 'when the Axis armour turned back with nothing to show for its efforts but burned-out tanks, Alam Halfa was recognized as an event of great significance, and before Christmas 1942 it could already be seen as the turning point in the African campaign and the foundation on which Montgomery was building a fame greater than that accorded to any other British commander since the outbreak of war.'[16]

For those outside 8th Army and the Middle East, however, it was more difficult to see just how decisive Alam Halfa had been. For reasons of Panzer Army morale, as well as morale at home in Nazi Germany and Italy, Rommel was urged to play down his failure to seize Cairo. He had left behind on the battlefield some thirty-eight unrecoverable panzers and eleven Italian tanks, but the German press – on Rommel's speedy advice, once he saw victory slipping from his grasp on 1 September – had depicted the whole battle as a mere 'reconnaissance in force', in preparation for a supposed major Axis offensive later in the year.

In truth, Rommel had lost the same amount of men and equipment as the Allies had at Dieppe, ten days before – a battle which the Allies, too, had called a 'reconnaissance in force'. In addition to 51 Axis tanks lost at Alam Halfa, the Panzer Army had suffered almost 2,000 German and over 1,000 Italian casualties, had left 33 German and 22 Italian guns behind, 300 German vehicles, 100 Italian vehicles, and 41 aircraft downed, quite apart from damaged tanks and vehicles.

Churchill was pleased, but as generalissimo had other problems which caused him quickly to forget the critical contribution Alam Halfa had made to his rapidly evolving war strategy. Throughout the last days of August and the first days of September 1942 he had felt crushed by the difficulties he was having in persuading the Americans to attack Oran and Algiers as part of Torch – indeed, on the day before Rommel launched his offensive he had told the British chiefs of staff that as the necessary forces 'did not appear to be forthcoming from the United States of America, the conclusion was that there could be no "Torch" '.[17]

The lack of useful Ultra decrypts during the battle of Alam Halfa had also kept the Prime Minister tense and enervated, and on 2 September he had actually summoned the director of military operations, Major-General Kennedy, in some alarm. 'He did not seem to be in very good form,' Kennedy later recalled. Together they had studied the map of Egypt. 'At that moment it appeared to us that Rommel might wish to develop the battle as he had at Gazala. He had got inside our lines, and his most probable course of action seemed to be to attack northwards, in an attempt to destroy our forces piecemeal,' Kennedy remembered. 'The Prime Minister was on tenterhooks, and no wonder. It was a critical moment in the war, and I suspected he was having difficulties with some of his colleagues.'[18]

He was. One particular colleague, the Leader of the House of Commons, Sir Stafford Cripps, remained caustic about the British inability or 'aptitude for handling mechanized forces on a large scale', as Churchill's doctor recalled – and was only with difficulty restrained from resigning from the government. Churchill 'knew that the resignation of the Leader of the House on such an issue as the conduct of the war must lead to a political crisis of the first magnitude', Sir Charles Wilson recalled – as well as the Prime Minister's worried remark: ' "Anything may happen." '[19]

Forgetting the patient explanation of his plan for the Alam Halfa battle which Monty had given at his desert headquarters on 19 August, Churchill hoped upon hope for a British *offensive* triumph at Alam Halfa, not merely an *échec* or riposte to Rommel's foray. His childlike mind went back to his nursery battles with his tin soldiers and cavalry, for he still dreamed of battles of manoeuvre – despite having sacked Auchinleck, the very commander who would have initiated a mobile battle at Alam Halfa. From nervousness about German victory Churchill then astonished Kennedy when, lifting his pudgy 'hand over the German positions, [he] said he hoped our whole line might eventually swing round, pivoting on our left, and so close Rommel in against the depression'.[20]

This was on a par with Hitler, who sacked his chief of staff, Halder, and took personal charge of battlefield tactics from the rear – leading directly to the German disaster at Stalingrad. Yet it is hard not to sympathize with Churchill's dilemma, brought up as he was in an earlier century, distrusting his own generals after the disasters of Gazala and Tobruk, fraught with anxiety over the apparent American refusal to land troops inside the Mediterranean as part of Torch – which would give Hitler time to react by sending troops through Vichy France to Marseilles, and across the Mediterranean to Algeria and Tunisia.

Moreover, while Ultra signals gave no indication of the magnitude of Rommel's failure, Allied decrypts of high-grade Japanese signals to Tokyo from Berlin ('Magic') relayed a German PR version of events, construed for Japanese ears, that was completely at variance with the military facts. On 3 September 1942 the Japanese ambassador actually reported to Tokyo – and thereby, unwittingly, to Washington and London – that the Germans were capturing a 'large number of bunkers' in the outskirts of Stalingrad, and were now 'advancing toward the Caspian Sea and at several points have already reached the railroad which skirts the sea'; indeed, were fighting for the mountain passes east of Mount Elbrus in the Caucasus: the gateway to Persia and the Middle East. This threat from the north was so real that Churchill ordered the chiefs of staff to explore the idea of sending 200 precious tanks to Turkey, to help discourage the

Turks from giving up their neutrality, allying themselves with the Third Reich and permitting free passage across Turkish territory of Nazi forces, from the Caucasus down to the Mediterranean.

But what worried Churchill even more was that the same decrypted Japanese message was being read by Roosevelt. '[T]he progress of the attack is proceeding beyond all expectations,' Ambassador Oshima reported the German version of events. 'Enemy armoured corps have been wiped out [at Alam Halfa] and deep penetration has been made behind the enemy lines. And it appears that the results will be more than we even hoped for.'[21]

The critical test

Fortunately, President Roosevelt had recently sent his former presidential-election opponent, Mr Wendell Willkie, as his personal emissary to Egypt to report back on American military, air force and supply contributions to the Egyptian theatre – especially in view of the 300 American tanks which had been given to the British. Willkie visited Monty's headquarters at Burg-el-Arab on 4 September, and stayed the night with him – indeed, as six American tank crews had been training in Brigadier Roberts' 22nd Armoured Brigade during the battle, Monty even took Willkie to see them and to clamber over some of the Panzer Mk IIIs and IVs which the brigade had 'brewed up': 'dozens of German tanks scattered over the desert', as Willkie afterwards recalled.

They had been captured by the British and blown up at Montgomery's orders. As we would climb up on these wrecked tanks, he would open the food boxes and hand to me the charred remnants of British provisions and supplies which the Germans had taken when they captured Tobruk. 'You see, Willkie, the devils have been living on us. But they are not going to do it again. At least they are never going to use these tanks against us again.'[22]

Willkie's reports, as well as those of American air and military representatives in Cairo, swiftly made it clear to Roosevelt, in the wake of Alam Halfa, that Rommel had not only failed in his last hope of reaching Cairo, but that he had received a severe drubbing:

The wiry, scholarly, intense, almost fanatical personality of General Montgomery made a deep impression on me when I was in Egypt, but no part of his character was more remarkable than his passionate addiction to work . . . Almost before we were out of our cars, General Montgomery launched into a detailed description of a battle which was in its last phases, and which for the first time in months had stopped Rommel dead. No real news of this battle had reached Cairo or been given to the press. The General repeated the details for us step by step, telling us exactly what had happened and why he felt it was a major victory even though his forces had not advanced any great distance. It had been a testing of strength on a heavy scale. Had the British lost, Rommel would have been in Cairo in a few days . . . At first it was hard for me to understand why the General kept repeating in a quiet way: 'Egypt has been saved.' The enemy was deep in Egypt and had not retreated. I remembered the scepticism I had found in Cairo, born of earlier British claims. But before I left the trailer in which General Montgomery had rigged up his map-room, I had learned more about desert warfare, and he had convinced me that something more than the ubiquitous selfconfidence of the British officer and gentleman lay behind his assurance that the threat to Egypt had been liquidated . . . Almost his central thesis was his belief that earlier British reverses on the desert front had resulted from inadequate co-ordination of tank forces, artillery forces, and air power. General Montgomery told me that he had his air officer living with him at his headquarters, and that complete coordination of planes, tanks and artillery had been chiefly responsible for the decisive check to Rommel of the past few days.[23]

For Willkie, after Roosevelt's ominous warning of the possibility of German breakthrough and the anxious rumours he had heard all the way from Washington to Cairo, the picture of this small, beak-nosed army commander, who personalized everything and yet who had such a mastery of military detail, clambering up a wrecked German tank and opening its food boxes to identify British food, was mesmerizing.

Again I was enormously impressed by the depth and thoroughness of General Montgomery's knowledge of his business. Whether it was Corps or Division, brigade, regiment or battalion headquarters he knew more in detail of the deployment of the troops and location of the tanks than did the officer in charge. This may sound extravagant but it was literally true . . . On the way back to General Montgomery's headquarters he summed up what I had seen and heard. He minced no words at all in describing his situation as excellent, and the battle just concluded as a victory of decisive significance. 'With the superiority in tanks and planes that

I have established as a result of this battle, and with Rommel's inability to get reinforcements of materiel across the eastern Mediterranean – for our air forces are destroying 4 out of every 5 of his materiel transports – it is now mathematically certain that I will eventually destroy Rommel. This battle was the critical test.'[24]

Saving Torch

American Baltimores had flown dozens of bombing missions during the battle of Alam Halfa, and the new spirit in 8th Army and the Desert Air Force was now infectious. Even the US Army Air Force Middle East commander, General Brereton, noted in his diary that 'Rommel's bid for Egypt' had failed. 'It was one of the major turning points of the war'.[25]

Satisfied that Rommel had not succeeded in his all-out effort to reach Cairo and Alexandria (the Japanese message of 3 September acknowledged that Rommel 'plans to return to his pre-attack lines'),[26] Roosevelt finally cabled to Churchill on 4 September 1942 to tell the Prime Minister that the Americans would, after all, now countenance landings inside the Mediterranean at Oran and Algiers, as part of Torch in October. 'I am directing all preparations to proceed,' Roosevelt added in commander-in-chief prose, quickly followed by a separate, more personal telegram, bearing the single word: 'Hurrah!'

To this, Churchill replied in three words: 'Okay full blast.'[27]

Alam Halfa had, in effect, not only saved Egypt, but saved the Anglo-American invasion of North-West Africa inside the Mediterranean.

The art of deception

Whatever the Germans might tell the Japanese about their 'reconnaissance in force', there would be no resumption of Axis plans to reach Cairo or Alexandria, let alone a link-up with German forces streaming south from the Caucasus – where the Russian were resisting fiercely. Indeed Rommel, pondering the lessons of his defeat, now wondered whether to pull back to a shorter line, further west, on the Fuka position, that would be easier to defend once 8th Army shifted over to the offensive.

Such a tactical withdrawal was not at all what Monty wished, and it is important to be clear about this, since so much subsequent armchair historiography would miss the point. Monty's prescience in this instance was remarkable, though often ignored by later historians. Already on 5 September Alexander – after reaching 'various decisions' the previous night with Monty – cabled the War Office in London. The text was unmistakably Monty's. 'Consider it most desirable to forestall publicity,' the message ran – and recommended no triumphalism, asking that 'press publicity' should be restricted to 'the following lines: "Enemy attacked our southern flank with whole Panzer Army. After five days' heavy fighting, at times intense, enemy has been driven back by combined efforts all arms, armoured and unarmoured, magnificently assisted throughout by RAF. In spite of every effort, enemy failed to penetrate our main defensive system at any point. Enemy losses in personnel and material have been severe, our own comparatively light."'

Simultaneously at Alamein, Monty asked Wendell Willkie, when he returned to Cairo, to help damp down press accounts of the Alam Halfa battle. The 8th Army commander had 'stopped Rommel', Willkie noted, 'but he was anxious for him not to begin to retreat into the desert before some 300 [sic] American General Sherman tanks that had just landed at Port Said could get into action. He estimated that this would take about 3 weeks. He figured that if he made a formal public announcement of the result of the battle, Rommel's withdrawal might be hastened.'[28]

Rommel must not, in other words, pull back to a more easily defensible position; he must be encouraged to remain at the extremity of his lines of communication. Could Willkie, therefore, address the press, rather than the victorious 8th Army commander? Willkie, as the only civilian witness of the battle, agreed to make, once back in Cairo, a personal statement 'which would not be regarded by Rommel as a sign of aggressive action on his [Montgomery's] part'.[29]

Monty's refusal to comment publicly on the battle, and the strange use of an American politician instead, 'in the language which he [Montgomery] and I had agreed upon in advance', worked wonders. The tidings appeared to be good: Rommel forced to call off his assault – yet the manner of Willkie's announcement so cool as to cause the war correspondents to question whether there had been a victory at all. 'It was the first good news from the British side that these British newspapermen had had in a long time,' Willkie recounted. 'They'd been fooled many times and were wary. The battle line, to their eyes, had hardly sagged, Rommel was still only a few miles from the Nile, while the road to Tripoli, from where we were, seemed long and a little fanciful and the road to Cairo painfully short.'[30]

Thus British and American war correspondents were as misled as Rommel. Even some of Monty's 8th Army officers were aghast at the way the army commander allowed Rommel to occupy not only the old British minefield positions in the south, but even the commanding heights of Himeimat, on the southern side of the Axis penetration. Brigadier 'Pip' Roberts, the commander of 22nd Armoured Brigade, protested at this refusal to contest possession of Himeimat – an opinion he still held almost forty years later. 'I do know that the fact that the Germans had Himeimat was a very severe handicap to us when we came to the main battle of Alamein,' he maintained. 'And I'm thinking of myself because 7th Armoured Division was in the south and had this bloody Himeimat looking right down on us all the time. If we'd taken Himeimat then it would have eased that. From there one saw a very large amount of the battlefield. It was a tremendously useful position – and very difficult to get people off it . . . I think personally it would have been worthwhile having a try, and if it seemed difficult, then give it up. I don't know how much Monty appreciated that it was a tremendous vantage point, looking up the whole of the Alamein line.'[31]

But Monty *did* appreciate its value: a prime piece which, as in a game of chess, he deliberately surrendered in order to keep Rommel at Alamein, at the end of extended lines of communication. It was Monty's opponent, Field-Marshal Kesselring, who afterwards best appreciated the success of Monty's strategy. As German commander-in-chief in the Mediterranean, Kesselring felt in retrospect that Rommel made a strategic error in not preparing a second defence line further back, just as the Germans had in the Hindenburg line in World War I. 'Looking back, I see it was a mistake to remain there [at Alamein],' Kesselring wrote after the war. 'All things considered,' he reflected, 'it would have been better to have retired behind a rearguard to a more easily defended position, for which the Halfaya Pass would have been suitable; or else, under pretence of offering the main resistance from the El Alamein line, to have accepted the decisive battle some twenty miles further west in an area – the so-called Fuka position – which had all the advantages of the El Alamein zone and was better protected on the left wing by the terrain.'

This was written with hindsight, however. At the time, he had been persuaded by Rommel's judgement. Certainly he did not believe the decision to remain at Alamein was a supply one – since a shorter line of comunication would in fact have eased the fuel situation – or a political one, since Rommel's prestige with Hitler was so great, he felt, that 'neither the OKW nor the Commando Supremo would have strongly opposed any serious intention of Rommel to retire to a rear line', with his powerful Panzer striking force intact. 'Rommel had hitherto always found means to get what he wanted. But he believed in the strength of the Alamein line.'[32]

Monty's ruse thus brilliantly succeeded. Rommel stayed.

A hero's welcome – for Rommel

Now that it was shielded behind a demonstrably impregnable line, covered by the Desert Air Force, 8th Army must be refashioned into an offensive force, Monty reasoned: a force capable of smashing through Rommel's defences, clearing Axis forces from Egypt and Cyrenaica, and proving the democracies could and would fight.

If he was to hit Rommel hard in the northern sector of the Alamein front, using infantry and as many as possible of the new Sherman tanks now arriving at Suez, Monty reasoned, he could roll up the entire Axis line from the rear – just as Rommel had hoped to do at Alam Halfa, but from north to south this time.

This, then, was the notion that Monty, soon after his arrival in the desert, had put to his new corps commanders and to Lieutenant-Colonel Richardson, his GSO 1 (Plans), to critique. No one demurred. For the moment, in the aftermath of Alam Halfa, Monty's plan remained unaltered. Richardson's job was to create a deception plan that would misguide Rommel as to the *Schwerpunkt* of 8th Army's attack. By suggesting a main British assault in the south, using dummy positions, vehicles and even a water pipeline to simulate preparations, Rommel was to be urged to hold significant forces in the south, around Himeimat, while 8th Army prepared in secret to smash through the northern line, adjacent to the railway, across the Miteiriya Ridge.

With the hindsight of an historian one can see in the planning of Alamein significant parallels with the greatest Allied battle of World War II: D-Day and the struggle for Normandy. As Rommel would face Montgomery in 1944 behind an Atlantic Wall bristling with guns but too long to defend everywhere in depth, so too at Alamein in 1942 Rommel faced Monty behind deep belts of minefields and strong-points stretching from the

Mediterranean to the impassable Quattara Depression – a forty mile front he could not garrison everywhere in depth, however, no matter how many mines he sowed. Monty thus held the initiative, using elaborate deception measures to confuse his opponent as to the real *Schwerpunkt* of his attack, with growing superiority in air power and the imminent arrival of several hundred Sherman tanks.

Both men now set to work, in 1942, as they would again in 1944: Rommel to fortify his defences, Monty to prepare the break-in weapon. It would become a test of wills, mirrored through the men under their command. Rommel had learned his lesson at Alam Halfa from the way Montgomery had slowed down the 'break-in' by laying extensive mine-fields and blunting the shock value of the assault. By deepening his own minefield belts into two long strips, with lateral belts like rungs on a ladder (thus forming boxes or 'devil's gardens' as they were soon christened), interlacing Italian and German infantry throughout this defensive line, and digging-in his artillery and anti-tank positions, Rommel could hope to slow down the British assault, as he himself had been slowed down on the night of 30 August; this would then leave him time to deal with the British break-in, using his panzer divisions, held back in two main groups, in the north and the south, as a mobile reserve.

Having toured the entire line, having arranged the new interstitching of German and Italian units and brigade groups, having decided the dispo-sition of his armour and artillery, and having given strict instructions for the deepening of the minefields (there would be almost half a million mines laid by the time the battle began) and rehearsal exercises, Rommel then flew on 23 September to Berlin, via Rome, to stay with Goebbels and receive a hero's welcome on 31 September 1942 in the Sportpalast in Berlin. There, recorded for the press by hundreds of Axis cameramen and reporters, he waved the field-marshal's baton given him by Hitler that day at the Reichchancellery, and basked in the Führer's adulatory speech extolling his great desert victories.

What we have, we hang on to

Both Hitler and Mussolini 'agreed' to Rommel's strategy of digging-in at Alamein, then resuming the Axis offensive when 'our troops have been thoroughly provisioned and refreshed and more forces have been sent out to us', as Rommel wrote to his temporary replacement in the desert, General Stumme.[33] 'The Field-Marshal considers a feint or spoiling operation in October is feasible,' he even told Mussolini, 'and, on condition that sufficient supplies are forthcoming, a decisive attack in the winter – though this will be very tough.'[34] To this end Hitler had promised 'the newest and biggest tanks [Tigers], rocket projectors and anti-tank guns', as well as 260mm mortars, multiple rocket projectors and smoke-screen generators. To his friend Kurt Hesse Rommel boasted: 'Give me three shiploads of gasoline for my tanks – and I'll be in Cairo forty-eight hours later!'[35] At a conference with journalists at Goebbels' Propaganda Ministry on 3 October he announced: 'Today we stand just fifty miles from Alexandria and Cairo, and we have the door to Egypt in our hands. And we mean to do something with it too! We haven't gone all that way just so as to get thrown back again. You can take that from me. What we have, we hang on to.'[36] With these famous last words, Rommel flew off to a rest cure with his wife in the Semmering mountains near Wiener-Neustadt.

Doctrine of salvation

Simultaneously, almost six weeks after leaving England, Monty finally wrote on 21 September to Tom and Phyllis Reynolds to thank them for taking over responsibility for his son David – claiming 'there is no one in the whole world I would sooner give David over to' than the prep-school headmaster and his wife.

Having handed David over, Monty showed remarkably little interest in him. 'Tell David that I am very flourishing and enjoyed fighting Rommell [*sic*] – and that I saw him right off,' he instructed the Reynoldses – and recounted in schoolboy language the way Rommel had attacked with 'the whole Panzer Army, plus two Italian Corps, round my southern flank and attempted to destroy my Army; if he had done so, then Egypt was his for the taking'. But Rommel had bitten off more than he could chew. Monty had 'started to wrest the initiative from him on 2nd September and by 6 September I had driven him right back to where he came from, having inflicted heavy losses on him. His losses were such that he is incapable now of staging any offensive that could do me any harm or even cause me any embarrassment. The threat to Egypt has been removed.' He had 'never before faced up in battle to a Field-Marshal', but, he boasted, 'there is no doubt that I won the first round – or won the first game when it was his service. I enjoyed every minute of the battle,' he confided – adding: 'And I fought it in accordance with the doctrine I have been teaching and preaching in England since the Dunkirk days; which makes the victory all the more satisfactory.'

This was the nub: the preacher whose doctrine of salvation had finally been implemented – and had proved effective. He was, he informed the Reynoldses, 'extremely well in health; better than I have been for years. There is no doubt the desert is a very healthy place. I have not had a bath for 4 weeks; I am convinced we all wash and bath far too much!!'[37]

It was clear that Monty was, at last, in his element: the errant schoolboy now reaping the harvest of a lifetime's dedication to the study of warfare in a democracy.

Explaining the battle in advance

'The object of training is success in battle,' Monty had begun his Training Memorandum No. 1 – and it was the failure of the democracies to see the connection between the two which had doomed the Allies to defeat for the first three years of World War II. To train men in a vacuum without a clear idea of the battle they must fight was insane: wasteful of time, effort – and, ultimately, lives.

Training must give men an idea of what was expected of them in battle, and the guidance to prepare themselves for their task. 'Therefore it is necessary for all Commanders to understand clearly the requirements of battle,' Monty's memorandum continued, 'then we can organise our training accordingly. In fact, the approach to training is via the battle' – and in the twenty-seven sections of his memorandum he proceeded to set out the 'fundamentals which will govern the conduct of our battle operations in Eighth Army' – with training 'directed to ensure that we can fight the battle in accordance with these fundamental principles'.[38]

As the years would go by, Monty's insistence on training would irritate military historians who disliked war by precept, while warming to a less structured approach that would permit them, as historians, to 'explain' battles retrospectively. But in a failing democracy Monty knew his task was to 'explain' battle in advance, not afterwards: to clarify warfare for the tens of thousands of men under his new command, after seemingly endless defeat – and in this sense no senior commander in military history had ever approached his job with more didactic skill and determination. Co-operation with the RAF, the 'stage-management of the battle', the efficiency of junior leaders, the initiative and fighting spirit of such officers and their men, the development of battle drills and the importance of information, concentration and tactically advantageous ground led Monty, point by point, to warn against the fallacy behind existing 8th Army methods – in particular the 'splitting up of formations and using isolated brigade groups away from the parent formations, and scattered over wide areas, as a permanent measure'. In his new army book, 'Divisions must fight as Divisions and under their own commanders, with clear-cut tasks and definite objectives', in co-operation with 'artillery centralised under the division's artillery commander, or CRA'. The 'whole essence' of modern tactical methods could be reduced to five imperatives:

Concentration of effort
Co-operation of all arms
Control
Simplicity
Speed of action

Paragraph by paragraph Monty set out his doctrine of modern battle, involving concentration of armour, and the seizing of 'ground which dominates the battle area' – ground that 'must be so important to the enemy that he will be forced to attack our armour on it, i.e. on ground of our own choosing'. With air forces, artillery, infantry, minefield engineers and anti-tank guns co-operating in the seizing and holding of such ground, 8th Army would become a new army to be reckoned with: specializing in night-time operations from 'pitch black dark night' to 'bright moonlight'.

To meet these requirements, Monty stated, commanding officers must now train themselves, their staffs and their subordinate commanders – not only preparing for operations that went according to plan but 'teaching them how to deal with situations that are vague and indefinite; to be mentally robust; to be versatile; to be able to grasp rapidly the essentials of a military problem and to do something about it quickly. Officers must be taught how "lay on the battle" on their own level. They must learn to work on simple and clear verbal instructions, filling in the details by using their military knowledge and their common sense.' It was not enough to delegate training to others. 'Guidance and inspiration must come from above. Therefore Corps, Division, and Brigade Commanders must hold regular discussions and exercises for their subordinates; in this way the doctrine laid down will permeate throughout the formation.'[39]

Alam Halfa had demonstrated the efficacy of this approach to battle; indeed, already on 7 September 1942, eight days after issuing his Training Memorandum No. 1 and in the immediate aftermath of Alam Halfa, Monty drew up a ten-point paper on the 'Main Lessons' of the battle: a document of riveting clarity, and a blueprint for what would become the Monty way of war: tight control by army headquarters; divisions 'fighting as divisions, with definite tasks and clear-cut objectives'; selection of 'dominating ground' that forced the enemy to attack on ground of 8th Army's choosing; infantry trained to hold its ground without armour but with concentrated artillery support; and armoured divisions operating with 'a good screen of anti-tank guns, and concentrated artillery', the fire of which could be 'brought down quickly against any enemy attack'.[40]

This approach had guaranteed success against Rommel in defence at Alam Halfa – but was it enough to guarantee victory in offence? Moreover, could such a victory be won in time to ensure the success of the Torch landings at the other end of the Mediterranean, scheduled now to be launched in early November?

Refusing to be hurried

This was what worried Churchill, after such wearying struggles to get Roosevelt and the American chiefs of staff to back Torch.

Resisting continuing calls for a second front, yet impatient to pave the way in Egypt in order to ensure that the French would not offer more than token resistance to the Torch landings, Churchill now bombarded General Alexander in Cairo with telegrams urging swifter action and an early offensive at Alamein. It was vital, Churchill added, not only to beat Rommel but to reach the Martuba airfields in time to give air support to the next Malta supply convoy in mid-November, if Malta was to continue to hold out. Thus Churchill pressed for an 8th Army attack in late September 1942, hard on the heels of success at Alam Halfa – and was mortified when his 'favourite general' responded in the negative.

Alexander's refusal was immutable – not because of Alexander's obstinacy, but because of Monty's. Monty had promised his staff on the evening of 13 August that he would not be hurried into premature operations. He was as good as his word. However irate the telegrams Churchill sent to Cairo, the new 8th Army commander refused to be bullied into taking unnecessary risks with his men's lives. The strategic reasons for an early British attack were clear to him, as relayed to him at Burg-el-Arab by General Alexander. But certain aspects of the Alam Halfa battle had given Monty cause for concern. Not only had even his most powerful tanks – the Grants – suffered considerable casualties from German panzer and anti-tank gunfire in the battle, but the attempt by Lieutenant-General Freyberg to strike hard at Rommel's lines of communication on the night of 2 November (Operation Beresford) had proved a fiasco – Freyberg first delaying the operation by twenty-four hours by 'belly-aching', then launching the operation with such poor engineering and artillery support that the British infantry units had become stuck in the minefields, had lost cohesion, and many brave men – including the New Zealand brigadier, G. H. Clifton – had been captured, killed or wounded. In offence the luckless infantry brigade from 44th Division had suffered terribly – indeed Beresford had been a complete waste of good men, both veterans and fresh troops. Not only had it failed to discomfit Rommel, but in terms of Monty's plan for an offensive battle at Alamein, Operation Lightfoot, it had shown just how difficult it would be to pierce heavily defended minefields, even at night, and launch the armoured *corps de chasse* into the enemy's rear areas.

The lesson was all too clear to Monty, as it had been since his arrival: without training for modern warfare, the army would fail in offence as it had always failed against German forces. Complete retraining in co-operation was required. Morale alone would not win the battle of Alamein, nor would untested Sherman tanks; the whole army needed to rethink its approach to battle, and start again from scratch.

The role of training in democracy

It is impossible to overstress the importance of such retraining, in fact of training itself as a crucial factor in modern war, indeed of modern Western society. It may be argued that in post-war history training would remain as important a factor as it had become in war: the crucial means by which industrial democracy could work its miracle in competition with communist societies. Faced with the economic dictates of communist dictatorships, the West was forced to modernize its approach to efficiency in order to survive. However reluctantly, Western workforces – managements and workers – had to find a way to demonstrate how company efficiency could co-exist creatively and effectively with democratic individualism. In the Soviet Union, eastern Europe, North Korea, China and other communist states, a theoretical vision of the paramountcy of workers' rights would, paradoxically, deliver poor production and poor societies of near or actual slavery, corruption and ecological disaster, whereas Western democracies, excoriated as capitalist slave-states, accepted the need to modernize, and thereby delivered unequal but widely distributed new wealth in which sufficiently large numbers of people enjoyed individual liberty to think, speak, write, travel, innovate and entertain to the point where, despite all the prognostications of left-wing ideologues, the democratic system survived the Cold War – indeed, triumphed both economically and in military terms.

Monty's own attitude towards the shaping of such a modern society would, as will be seen, later betray the contradictions between his imperialist boyhood and his meritocratic beliefs: at once paternalistic and ruthlessly egalitarian, patriarchal and innovative, racist and yet anti-imperialist. By then, however, he would be, as a famous World War II commander, a figurehead – much as Goebbels had convinced Hitler that Rommel, after the war, should become commander-in-chief of the post-war Wehrmacht. His truly revolutionary work, as a trainer and commander, had been done already in World War II.

Mocked in England as the 'mad general' and for his elaborate 'stage-managing' of large-scale mock battles, Monty had now, in his first battle as an army commander in the field, proved that – even in a new environment, with troops largely unknown to him, and where the enemy was better equipped, drilled and experienced than the British – his vision of 'forward-planning' worked. It was in this respect that thoughtful later commentators such as General Sir David Fraser saw the reward of Alam Halfa as moral rather than material. As General W. G. F. Jackson put it, Alam Halfa 'was a far-reaching psychological victory for the British; not so much over the Axis as over themselves. Montgomery had shown that he knew what he was about and how to do it.'[41]

How to clarify the objective, and train 8th Army to win not only a defensive battle but an offensive one, then, was Monty's next task.

Malingering

To prepare for battle, Monty decreed, 8th Army must rehearse the operation in advance until it knew its lines by heart, with dress rehearsals behind the front using live ammunition, real minefields, and all constituent arms – infantry, artillery, engineers, armour, air – working together. Command and communication procedures – telephone battles, co-operation exercises with RAF staff officers – would also be practised and repractised, as before Alam Halfa. Building on success at Alam Halfa, the battle of Alamein would, he envisioned, turn back the tide of war against those who had begun it, showing the world what the democratic nations could achieve if they applied themselves wholeheartedly, under a leader who had studied the business of modern war, who was a professional to his fingertips, and above all who was determined to end, for all time, the Victorian-Edwardian class and caste divisions that had wrecked the fighting ability of Britain's army.

The revolutionary impact of Monty's new approach to command was recalled by one of his staff officers, William Mather, who had been in the desert since 1940, and was wounded in the summer of 1942. In hospital he had got himself 'fixed up with what I thought was the best job in the army, which was to be brigade major of the 1st Armoured Brigade – which was a very good armoured brigade, and I was only a Territorial [part-time volunteer]. I thought it was a tremendous feather in my hat and I was cock-a-hoop. I was just about to be released from hospital when Monty arrived to take command in the desert.

'And you know, I was rather surprised because I knew he was quite a good soldier, of course, but it didn't mean very much to me. And I thought, how odd, he wasn't desert-worthy, as we used to say, in any way. One of those . . . sort of "Ingleezis" coming out to control the desert sweats who really thought we knew the ways of the desert backwards. So I was really rather surprised, even though we'd been pushed back to Alamein . . .

'I was congratulating myself on getting the job when a new posting came out to me just as I was about to leave hospital. I was to go as a liaison officer to 8th Army headquarters!

'Well, I regarded a liaison officer, even a G2 [Grade 2] liaison officer as a major, as a pretty low form of life compared with being brigade major of the 1st Armoured Brigade. So I went to see the commandant of the hospital and told him – asked him: Can you keep me for another few days until this thing blows over? So he said, Oh yes, fine; and I stayed there for about ten days, thinking that they'd be too impatient, they'd post somebody else to this job.

'Not a bit of it! An order came out [after Alam Halfa] for my arrest! And I realized times had changed!! So I shot off post-haste to 8th Army headquarters, Burg-el-Arab, and I was straightway summoned to Monty. He said: "Mather, you were malingering!"

'I thought, how do you know? And – it was the most extraordinary thing about Monty that he *always* knew what you'd been up to! He was such a rogue himself in many ways that he could see through anybody. *Nobody* could pull a fast one over him, at all. And this was so absolutely apparent that no one bothered after it'd been tried once or twice. Anyway, he said: "Why?"

'So I thought the best thing was to come clean – which people soon realized with Monty. So I said what the position was, that I didn't fancy being a G2 liaison officer instead of being brigade major at 1st Armoured Brigade. And he retorted: "So you think being brigade major at 1st Armoured Brigade is better than a job being one of my liaison officers?"

'I said, "Frankly, yes, sir."

'He said: "Well may I tell you that *I'm destroying the desert trades union*. And the 1st Armoured Brigade's going to become a tank *delivery* regiment!" Similarly with the Bays, the 10th Hussars and the 9th Lancers – he also broke their brigade up!'[42]

Class would be out, meritocracy in.

Getting the old fogies out of their holes

Monty's new ADC, Captain Poston, also felt with Monty's arrival a sea-change taking place in the desert army in which he had served since 1940. 'I have completely turned over a new leaf in life lately,' he wrote to his family soon after Alam Halfa, 'as, remember, the last 3 years I have been in a position to always do as I am told & see hundreds of things that want improvement & be able to do nothing about it. But now all that's changed. I'm now in a position to get things done & put forward some of the ideas & improvements I have thought out in these years.'

Backed by Monty, Poston was determined to 'break that hard Red Tape surface that binds everything in the Army, and attempt to better the Army which is still 2 years behind the times. It makes one unpopular at times pushing in & insisting on things being done, but if you are *firmly* convinced it is correct, you will succeed in the end, & afterwards be respected.' In this way, Poston claimed, he had already got two temporary colonels sacked for lazing in Cairo, to be replaced by 'two new Majors in the desert doing a proper job instead of drawing fantastic allowances in G.H.Q. [Cairo] & drinking all the whisky . . . There is heaps of cleaning up wants doing here & it must be done before we can really succeed in this war.'

One Poston idea was for a hand-held mine detector; another, which was to have an enormous impact on morale in a democratic army, was developed with the head of the 8th Army Film & Photographic Unit, Captain Geoffrey Keating. In Poston's view it was important not only to 'get photos of all the Commanders, etc' but 'lots of single photos of chaps' – ordinary soldiers in 8th Army. These photos 'should be sent home from here to the chap's local papers & published; his parents would love it & so would he be, to think he had been in print. This helps morale, welfare & everything of the chaps here, fighting in difficult conditions, far from home & their parents etc: & all should be done to help them. But G.H.Q. say "No, it is too much trouble."'

To Poston the obstructionism of idle GHQ staff officers and departments (the 600,000 'useless mouths' of which Churchill also complained) was iniquitous. 'Nothing is too much trouble if it is going to better somebody or something,' Poston remarked. 'So, I have concocted an idea with Geoffrey Keating, the head of the branch, to make these chaps think. From time to time we will take photos of single chaps, take their names & addresses & also the name of their local newspaper & send one copy to their parents & one to the paper & ask them to print it & put at the bottom 'Photo by A. F. & P. U.' (Army Film & Photo Unit), M.E.F. Then sooner or later some old idiot in the W.O., or out here, will see this, prick up his old eyes & brain . . . & then, by degrees, it will be taken on. We'll get no kudos,' he added prophetically, 'but the idea will work.'

It did, spectacularly. Meanwhile, as Poston complained, such an initiative required 'very little work', but 'they are too bloody idle. They want to dash off to Shepherds & meet their beautiful girl friends & drink.' To show that the plan could succeed, therefore, Poston proposed to send the photos home himself, to be re-addressed by his parents to local newspapers. 'Otherwise, if the P.O. Officials here see letters with photos continually going to Daily Papers, they will prick their eyes open & we shall have another barrier in our way. Hope this will be O.K. The chaps would love it if they knew they were in print in their local papers at home. Also for the people at home, it would give them a hell of a thrill to see their sons working in the M.E. In this we have the backing of Monty,' he added, 'the Army commander, as I put it to him yesterday & he said O.K. He is all for new ideas & getting the old fogies out of their holes.'[43]

Sweeping the Augean stables

Captain Poston's response to British idleness, bureaucracy and red tape in Cairo was symptomatic of the craving among younger men in 8th Army for a new commander who would create a fresh, positivist, inter-service military culture: not blind or dogged obedience, but open-eyed recognition of the challenge facing the democracies, fighting for a righteous purpose and confident one was contributing to an army in which one's contribution mattered.

Poston himself had left school with minimal qualifications, had worked with horses, then in a hotel, and had finally got a commission in the Royal Tank Regiment – from which he had quickly been encouraged to transfer, once in the desert, to a more 'classy' regiment, the 11th Hussars, who wore smarter uniforms and operated expensive messes. In his simple heart, however, he knew this was all wrong: that Britain would lose the war not because of numbers or even equipment, but in the end because its divided class structure, based on privilege and social élitism, was crippling Britain's efforts on the battlefield; that the fragmentation, the army's 'splitting up into bits and pieces' was symptomatic not only of Auchinleck/Dorman-Smith's misguided, imitative tactics, but symbolic of the dry rot which had so long infected Britain's forces in the Middle East: an antiquated, imperial social snobbery which doomed Britain to defeat, since it forced Britons to fight with one arm tied behind their backs: eschewing, in class-snobbery, the professional co-operation with other arms that had brought Hitler's armies such extraordinary successes. As Alan Moorehead, the Middle East war correspondent, described, it was not Rommel's genius as a commander that had brought the Panzer Army to Alamein,

it had been the genius of the average German soldier for organization. In all its branches the German war machine appeared to have a better and tighter control than our army . . . One saw this talent for organization in all directions. The

Luftwaffe, for example, had a much closer liaison with the ground forces than we, though we made big improvements in this. Time and again, one would note the steady rhythm of a German attack – first the Stukas, then the artillery, then the infantry, then the tanks, then the Stukas following up again.[44]

The British army, by contrast, seemed bogged down by a 'vast tide of paper' and bureaucracy – betraying a profound unwillingness to take responsibility, or show initiative.

Hours and hours were lost each day by men writing things down on bits of paper because it was the system that they should do so, because they would get a 'rocket' if they failed to do so. It is, no doubt, a wise and necessary part of army discipline that forbids a junior officer to approach his colonel directly – he must go through the officer immediately superior to himself. But to many, it has seemed that this system is carried to extremes in the British army, and that the whole question of the relationship between officers and men needs overhauling . . . In the Red army and German army, every officer must first serve in the ranks. Their discipline is far less a matter of manners than in the British army. Men and officers appear to be far more together among the Germans, to understand one another better and therefore to like one another more than in the British army.[45]

Denis Johnston, representing the BBC, found the same problem in Egypt. One central European refugee remarked to him that the British 'always find their enemies more likeable than their friends'.[46] American forces, coming from younger, more vibrant democracies, would not suffer such debilitating handicaps – though, like the Canadians, they would begin combat in the Mediterranean in November 1942 saddled with all too many antiquated or second-rate commanding officers and, inevitably, a fatal inexperience in the tough business of total war. Haig-like World War I-style leadership from rear headquarters would be the besetting problem of such forces – something Monty would do his best to expose and counter, by his own example in 8th Army.

In World War I, the British government eventually had to force Haig to sack his loyal but mediocre staff and commanders, and in World War II Churchill had to exercise the same prerogative. Monty, however, used his own guillotine. Where Wavell, Auchinleck and Alexander 'preferred to accept the army and its system as they found it', and 'commanded by a system of compromises and makeshifts which were adjusted to meet each emergency that came up', as Moorehead described, Monty believed in 'surgery not homeopathy. If a thing was not going right or only partially right, then cut it out altogether; don't try makeshifts and slow drugs; sack the man to blame outright.'[47] As a result, heads quickly rolled. Ramsden, commander of XXX Corps, was sacked after Alam Halfa, and replaced by one of Monty's former Camberley Staff College students: Lieutenant-General Sir Oliver Leese. The commander of the famed Desert Rats, Callum Renton, was also dismissed, to be replaced by another of Monty's ex-Camberley students, Major-General John Harding from Cairo. Under Douglas Wimberley, yet another former Camberley student of Monty's, the 51st Highland Division also came into the front line. A host of brigadiers and colonels meanwhile vanished – such as the CO of a certain unit who, when asked by Monty who trained the officers, answered that this was done by the second-in-command. 'I came across the second-in-command later in the day,' Monty later recalled. 'The poor man denied that he was responsible for training the officers and said that it was done by the CO. I ordered that a new CO be found for the unit at once; it was clear that nobody trained the officers.'[48]

Monty's new broom was sweeping clean the Augean stables – and rather than going down, morale soared.

The rivals

The Axis line at Alamein would be too extended for Rommel to cover in depth throughout, Monty was certain, but the German commander would, as a supreme professional, bring panzer reserves up quickly to beat back any incursions into his line. Surprise, shock and overwhelming weight of initial assault were therefore vital. There was no open flank by which to attempt a battle of manoeuvre, as Rommel had tried at Alam Halfa; it would therefore have to be a battle on almost World War I lines, though supported by Allied aircraft and tanks. Each 8th Army soldier would have to know what was expected of him, and be rehearsed in the performance of his role before the battle commenced – and, even then, be inspired to go on fighting even if things went wrong, or took longer than expected.

As before D-Day, the Rommel style and the Monty style were vividly illustrated by their preparations for the approaching battle, as Monty went round his army, preaching his new gospel, while Rommel, having laid down his defensive policy (lightly held forward positions, main bodies of troops withdrawn to a rear minefield, German–Italian battle-groups formed as fire-fighters to extinguish any penetrations, anti-tank gun lines trained to seal off breakouts, and armoured divisions held back further still, in reserve), left his Panzer Army in Africa and returned to the Third Reich to receive his laurels personally from Hitler, and enjoy a well-earned rest in the mountains with his wife.

Rommel, like Monty, had one son whom he had rarely seen during the war, though he liked to write at length to his wife Lucie, once considered a beauty, but whose long face with deep protruding chin and heavy cheekbones made her look in middle age almost masculine beside Rommel's almost eternally boyish features. Rommel had a small, compact body. The shiny black riding boots and the airman's goggles stretched over his high-peaked officer's cap had come to symbolize, like Nelson's one-armed tunic and black eye-patch, the epitome of drive and bold leadership among the men of the Afrika Korps, the Panzer Army and the German public – indeed, even the men of 8th Army. If commanders like von Runstedt epitomized cold, impersonal, calculating command, in which men were mere pawns to be used and sacrificed in the service of a given military objective, Rommel had come to personify a more human, heroic approach to German command, perceiving – as Hitler had – the need for charismatic leadership if men were to lay down their lives not simply out of duty, but with the sort of faith and inspiration that wins victories – or deprives the enemy of them – even when numerically inferior to that enemy. And the secret here was the same as that which would give rise to Monty's battlefield leadership: the loyalty he inspired among young men.

As one of his biographers quoted, Rommel was 'never happier than when working with young men'.[49] He loved inspecting them, in particular Hitler Youth units, and surrounded himself with attractive and devoted young staff officers. Their loyalty and dedication meant the world to him, as he to them. Like Monty, he thrived on male admiration, and saw in it a compact: that his battlefield skill would, after a lifetime's self-preparation and command experience, bring them the male pride that came with victory, thousands of miles from home, in the otherwise rocky, scrubby, inhospitable conditions of the desert. Long after the unconditional defeat, indeed the devastation of the Third Reich, the exploits and camaraderie of the Afrika Korps would be a source of pride to war veterans – a pride untainted by politics or punitive treatment of conquered peoples.

Rommel's popularity with his troops thus rested on the same intangible yet unique male bond that had animated the loyalty Nelson's 'Jack tars' had felt for their 'little admiral', and which fed likewise on Rommel's legendary victories in the desert. Thus at a personal level Rommel sought, by returning to Germany on 23 September 1942, to avoid the disappointment of his desert charges after the failed 'Six-Day Race', substituting a week of alternative adulation and newspaper coverage in Berlin, for which he was certainly not too ill. Yet he desperately needed to restore his own physical and mental energies for the daunting task ahead – for it was clear to him that Hitler would not send substantial reinforcements to the desert until he could see light at the end of the Russian tunnel. In the Caucasus the 1st Panzer Army under von Kleist had still failed to reach Grozny; by the Volga, von Paulus's forces were still battling to take Stalingrad. The moral for North Africa was clear: Axis hopes of seizing the Middle East were in abeyance. It would be a question now of holding on to Axis gains, until better days to come.

For Rommel personally, this was disappointing but not depressing. His distinctive genius, after all, lay in tactical leadership on the field of battle, at the front, in the thick of combat, where his very presence was a tonic, considered the equivalent of a whole division, so great was the boost to unit and formation morale. The enemy had proved surprisingly successful in the defence of Alam Halfa; now, however, he would once again show the British how much more successful the better-trained Panzer Army, using the Afrika Korps as a mobile reserve, could be in that role.

Monty, meanwhile, relished the challenge of a great offensive battle on the same lines that he'd rehearsed in Exercise Tiger in England in May. But where Rommel could rely on a highly trained, battle-drilled body of men with proven equipment, left to carry out their own training and complete their own defensive preparations, Monty commanded a polyglot Commonwealth army of amateurs – at least in terms of mutual co-operation. His genius would not be in the tactical direction of battle at unit level, but in stage-managing the battle before it took place, in such a way that, no matter what went wrong on the day, the battle would, inexorably, be won. To do this he needed to script the play in advance, make the men learn their lines, ensure proper rehearsal, and personally infect each player with the will to win. Could he do this in six weeks?

Against him he had the most successful panzer army of all time, symbolized by two words – Afrika Korps – and one name – Rommel. In his own favour, however, Monty had short lines of communication to his bases in Alexandria and Cairo; a powerful Desert Air Force backed by

RAF strategic bombers and incoming units of the US Army Middle East Air Force; powerful new American tanks arriving at Suez; new British six-pounder replacement guns for some of the hitherto 'peashooter' Crusader tanks; new six-pounder anti-tank guns arriving in large numbers; air and Ultra intelligence allowing him almost to X-ray the German defensive layout at Alamein as Rommel sowed his 'devil's gardens'; and his own 'miracle' in the desert in the lead-up to Alam Halfa: namely, the response of officers and men to his 'new broom'.

The love of men

'Everyone felt that a new dynamic force had entered into the tired, rather stale, old body of the Eighth Army,' Lieutenant-General Horrocks remarked[50] – and this was almost literally reflected as Monty visited, one by one, the hundreds of British and Commonwealth units after Alam Halfa, on a series of whistle-stop visits to weed and reinvigorate the army as it trained and rehearsed itself for the decisive offensive battle of the war. 'He harangued the army like a prophet. All this might seem like bad form to the officers of the old school, but the troops loved it. Monty had won them over before the battle started,' Moorehead related. 'His shrewdest move of all was to spread the idea that the Eighth Army was an independent striking force, taking its orders from no one. He was their general and he was going to lead them on their own private crusade across Africa.'[51]

However much he might harangue, though, the battle would, Monty became more and more certain, be very tough. Rommel had got nowhere at Alam Halfa, despite superlative leadership, motorized troops, panzers, 88s, weapons . . . Would it be any easier for 8th Army, in reverse? The difficulties encountered by Brigadier Custance's attempt to pass 21st Panzer Division's gun-screen below Alam Halfa, and the complete failure of the New Zealand-led Beresford attack from Alam Nayil against Rommel's lines of communication, only reinforced Monty's conviction that 8th Army must undergo radical retraining, in every echelon and arm, and in co-operation between those echelons and arms. Stalin had claimed the British would not fight; Monty was determined to show that the British would not only fight, but would persevere until they won – as an example to the Allies and to the rest of the world that the Germans could and would be defeated in battle. It was, Monty recognized, not only a matter of organization of resources, and of rehearsal, but of collective will: of imbuing a whole army with his will to win.

Instinctively, for all his great qualities of military professionalism, dissective analysis, clarity of judgement and lightning swiftness of decision, General Brooke had known he could not do this, for he lacked – as his biographer Sir David Fraser acknowledged – the ability to put himself across to ordinary men. As General Paget said of him, he 'had little understanding of the average soldier or day-to-day life of the Regiment or Unit'.

The Under-Secretary of State for War, and later Secretary of State, Sir James Grigg, MP, was even more frank. Brooke 'commanded the admiration and respect of officers, who recognized in him a master of his profession, but rarely did he arouse affection, for he was too insular and rarely offered friendship – regarding subordinates as cogs in the machine'.[52] Brooke had the will to master the tasks he undertook, Fraser felt, but not the fundamental human *need* to earn men's loyalty, affection – and willingness to sacrifice one's life – that were necessary if the men of Rommel's Panzer Army were to be beaten by the British in battle; he was, behind the impassive mask, 'a self-questioning, sensitive man' who had admitted to a colleague, Lieutenant-General Franklyn, who was commanding British forces in Northern Ireland in the summer of 1942, that he did not '*enjoy*' fighting. 'I think Monty does,' Brooke remarked with a mixture of admiration and incomprehension.[53]

Monty did, as his letters to the Reynoldses and to others at the time demonstrated. The prospect of battle, the preparations for it, and the business itself aroused in him the same controlled exhilaration as they did in Rommel. Those historians who later decried Monty's egoism simply missed the point. Battle keyed Monty up, challenging his military intellect, engaging his emotions, promising the summation of a lifetime's self-preparation: the supreme test of his military abilities, and mental and physical resources. In battle men look to their companions for the crucial example of courage, lest they betray their own fear. Thus they share in a collective courage; but they look too to their superior NCOs and officers for the decisions that have to be made: a leadership process that passes from section and platoon commander to company commander to unit commander to brigade commander to divisional commander to corps commander and finally to army commander. Having commanded each of those echelons Monty 'knew his stuff '; what he had to do was to radiate confidence in that knowledge among his subordinate staff, commanders and troops. And to do that successfully he needed to be more than jovial, friendly, charming, intelligent, attractive as a figurehead; needed to radiate not only an enthusiasm for combat, but, in a modern democracy, a love of men.

Inspiration to kill

'I presume you wish to win this war?' Denis Johnston had been asked by his companion, a central European refugee, in Cairo during the 'flap' in July 1942. 'Yet sometimes I wonder with what weapons or by what form of magic you are going to do so.'[54]

It was a fair question, even after Alam Halfa. By October, when the next battle was due to commence, 8th Army would total 195,000 soldiers. Some would, like Monty, enjoy the test of character, determination and courage involved in combat, but most would be fighting as civilian soldiers, as Johnston saw in July, wishing just to do their duty and go home. To fight rather than retreat they required an army commander they could trust to command them wisely: to put them into battle with reasonable chance of success – and survival. They did not need to share his enthusiasm for battle as such, but needed to know that he himself had it, and yet so respected their right to life that, if possible, they would live to tell the tale. It was in this sense that some of Patton's men came to despise him after the 'slapping incidents' in Sicily the following year: the sense of a commander, wonderfully gifted for armoured combat, yet too fanatical in his personal pursuit of glory to care about ordinary civilian-soldiers and their understandable fears.

Field-Marshal Haig had been given an earldom and £100,000 of government taxes for having effectively butchered millions of British, imperial and Commonwealth soldiers under his command on the Western front, concealing casualties both from his men and from his political masters. In Haig's defence, it was afterwards argued that to show care and compassion for his men, as in visiting field hospitals for example, might have weakened him in his determination to continue fighting, and thus resulted in surrender to German military aggression in 1914–18 – as actually happened, it was argued, in France in 1940. This is debatable; certainly, it was the perceived futility and callousness of such mass human sacrifice that explained France's failure to face up to another such bloodletting. What is unarguable, however, is that Monty's unique contribution to democratic military command in the twentieth century would be his demonstration that an army commander *can* care for his men, intimately and compassionately, yet still fight an indoctrinated, fascist, professional enemy in modern war successfully, even where his men lack killing mentality.

German troops, with their strong sense of discipline, initiative, purpose, cruelty and self-abnegation, made formidable battlefield opponents. The American reporter for CBC in Cairo had told the BBC's Denis Johnston it made him despair to hear a British general refer to Rommel as the 'gentleman on the other side'. 'We've got to realise that this is an utterly ruthless thing we're up against': a Nazi state willing to use inhuman methods – 'extreme measures' – to 'complete the conquest of Europe'. 'You realise what that means?' the American had asked, without even knowing the extent of the burgeoning holocaust. 'They've already begun the systematic starvation of Greece, and now there are going to be wholesale massacres of the Jugoslavs. Yet we keep on talking about the enemy as though they were gentlemen!'[55]

For Monty this was the crux. As he wrote some weeks later to General Brooke, 'I am certain that the way to deal with the German is to face up to him in battle, and fight him; it is the only way to deal with him, because then you kill him. The trouble with our British lads is that they are not killers by nature; they have got to be so inspired that they will want to kill, and that is what I tried to do with this army of mine.'[56]

He was telling no more than the truth. By matching the necessity for killing with genuine care for his troops, demonstrated not only in edicts but in indefatigable personal visits, talks, inspections, addresses, training instructions, improvement of leave, news, medical facilities in the field, and insistence – on pain of dismissal – on professional management by officers and staffs, Monty transformed the spirit of 8th Army.

No other British general had ever attempted such a radical approach to modern command in a democratic alliance, and perhaps no other general could have succeeded had he tried. For the source of Monty's battlefield care was undoubtedly homosocial, even homoerotic: at once Greek in the classical quality of an older, experienced man in the role of teacher, educating young men for life and death, yet modern also, in the determination to focus upon, and never lose sight of, the 'human factor', as Monty called it, in an age of total war.

Predicting the course of battle

Alam Halfa had ended Rommel's string of victories in the desert. But if Rommel now used Monty's tactics against 8th Army, what chance did 8th Army have of succeeding, despite its growing superiority in numbers? Against a well-led, well-positioned, well-protected enemy, Rommel had failed to make any dent; how then could 8th Army hope to do better in the same role and the same desert, but in reverse – indeed, against a better armed, better co-ordinated, better equipped enemy, protected by fields sown with hundreds of thousands of anti-personnel and anti-vehicle mines?

Somehow it had to be done. If it succeeded, it would become the model, the example, the archetype for Allied offensive victory, after years of interminable defeat. Like Henry V before Agincourt, therefore, Monty's effort to get out each day among the troops at Alamein was not simply to radiate his infectious self-confidence, but to be infected by their humanity. Not the guns, not the tanks, not the aircraft would be the battle-winning factor, in the end, however 'mathematically certain' he might be of victory, but the fighting faith of serving soldiers in him: that what he said would happen, did happen.

It was vital, then, to tell the truth: to tell them not only his plan of battle in advance, but to predict the very course and duration of the battle from its beginning to its end. No commander in history had ever attempted this. How Monty did so, not only laying down the plan but setting out the way the battle would go *in advance* – even to the number of days it would last, and the numbers of casualties his army would suffer – was to his staff perhaps the most extraordinary evidence of Monty's mastery of the art of leadership, at the very beginning of his career as an army commander in the field. In crucial respects the battle would not, as will be seen, go according to his plan; yet in overall terms, duration, casualties and outcome he would make it do so – bringing victory, a personal knighthood, and fame to the 8th Army: a battle that would go down in history not simply as the turning of the tide of World War II, but for the raising of Allied morale so that, whatever setbacks might come thereafter, confidence in ultimate victory would remain, built upon this seminal battle that had, at its heart, Monty's will, and thus the soldiers' will, to win.

21

Scripting Alamein

Scripting the battle

Having laid down the need to train for battle, Monty thus scripted the battle in advance, just as he had scripted Alam Halfa.

Major Mather remembered the moment vividly. It was 13 September 1942 – six days after the conclusion of Alam Halfa:

'You see, when he wrote the Operation Order for the battle of Alamein it was like a hen giving birth. He walked backwards and forwards on the sands of Burg-el-Arab all day, backwards and forwards, like Napoleon with his head down, his hands behind his back. And we all said: "Master is giving birth."

'And he came back into his caravan and in about four hours – I remember now it was on fourteen sheets of paper – he wrote the whole Operation Order for Alamein. That was it. It wasn't changed, or very few variations were made to it.'[1]

The plan was called 'Lightfoot':[2]

14 September, 1942

LIGHTFOOT
GENERAL PLAN OF EIGHTH ARMY

OBJECT

1. To destroy the enemy forces now opposing Eighth Army. The operations will be designed to 'trap' the enemy in his present area and to destroy him there. Should small elements escape to the West, they will be pursued and dealt with later.

PLAN IN OUTLINE

2. The enemy will be attacked simultaneously on his North and South flanks.

3. The attack on the North flank will be carried out by 30 Corps with the object of breaking in to the enemy defences between the sea and inclusive the MITEIRIYA Ridge, and forming a bridgehead which will include all the enemy main defended positions and his main gun areas. The whole of this bridgehead will be thoroughly cleared of all enemy troops and guns. 10 Corps [*corps de chasse*] will be passed through this bridgehead to exploit success and complete the victory.

4. On the South flank, 13 Corps will:
   a) Capture HIMEIMAT.
   b) Conduct operations from HIMEIMAT designed to draw enemy armour away from the main battle in the North.
   c) Launch 4 Lt Armd Bde round the Southern flank to secure DABA and the enemy supply and maintenance organization at that place, and to deny to the enemy air the use of the air landing grounds in that area . . .

In extraordinary detail the 8th Army commander then laid down, in forty-two precise paragraphs, the strategic, tactical, technical, supply, deception, air, training and morale blueprint for one of the decisive battles of world history – five weeks before the battle commenced.

In many respects Monty's plan was the product of a lifetime's military thinking and experience, from the North-West Frontier of India to the trenches of the Western Front, and the grim education of Dunkirk in May 1940. Out of the chaos of modern *blitzkrieg* warfare a small, beaky-faced misfit had extrapolated the essentials for success in battle. The days of minor desert tactics, Monty felt, were now over. The free world demanded Allied victory, and to obtain that victory, against a seasoned and professional enemy, protected by deep minefields, armed with awesome tanks and artillery and covered by a renowned air force, a new Allied weapon must be forged that would become even more renowned. The task of XIII Corps was to feint in the south while, overnight, XXX Corps smashed passages through the minefields on to the Miteiriya Ridge. That of X Corps – the *corps de chasse* – was to be out beyond XXX Corps by daybreak on the first full day of battle, in massive strength, and to defeat the German armour in the north, before Rommel's southern formations could move to assist. 'All formations and units will at once begin to train for the part they will play in this battle,' Monty ordered.

Time is short and we must so direct our training that we shall be successful *in this particular battle*, neglecting other forms of training. . . The initial break-in attack by 30 Corps, and the initial operations by 13 Corps, and the move forward of 10 Corps to deployment areas, will all be carried out by night with a full moon.

Therefore full advantage must be taken of the September full moon period to practise operating on a moonlit night and actually to rehearse the operations concerned, using similar bits of ground.

There will be a great weight of artillery fire available for the break-in battle. During the training period infantry and other arms must be accustomed to advancing under the close protection of artillery fire and mortar fire.

We must have realism in our training and use live ammunition in our exercises with troops, even if this should result in a few casualties. I will accept full responsibility for any casualties that may occur in this way.

The accurate fire of mortars will be of the greatest value in the break-in battle. No troops can stand up to sustained heavy and accurate artillery and mortar fire without suffering a certain loss of morale; low category troops will be definitely shaken by such fire, and can then be dealt with easily by our own attacking troops.

Tanks that are to work in close co-operation with infantry in this battle must actually train with that infantry from now onwards.

The individual soldier must be given practice so that he will reach a high degree of skill with the weapons he will use in battle.

There is plenty of ammunition available for this purpose. Full use will be made of the [sand] model in preparation for this battle. Every formation headquarters and every unit should have a model of the ground over which it is to operate, and on this model all officers will be instructed in the stage-management of the battle.

Finally all NCOs and men will be shown on the model the part they will play in the battle.

As far as officers and NCOs are concerned the model will be any ordinary piece of ground; the actual place names must not be shown. As the day of attack approaches more information can be disclosed.

No information about our offensive intentions will be disclosed to any officer or other rank who has even the slightest chance of being taken prisoner in a raid; this order will not be relaxed until the morning of D1 day.

I direct the attention of Corps and Divisional Commanders to Eighth Army Training Memorandum No. 1 issued on 31 [*sic*] August 1942. The fundamentals outlined in that memorandum will govern the conduct of our battle operations, and will therefore form the basic background for all our training . . .

There was one further theme Monty wished to emphasize, however, at the end of this fourteen-page blueprint: morale.

MORALE

38. This battle for which we are preparing will be a real rough house and will involve a very great deal of hard fighting. If we are successful it will mean the end of the war in North Africa, apart from general 'clearing-up' operations; it will be the turning point of the whole war. Therefore we can take no chances.

39. Morale is the big thing in war. We must raise the morale of our soldiery to the highest pitch; they must be made enthusiastic, and must enter this battle with their tails high in the air and with the will to win.

    There must in fact be no weak links in our mental fitness.

40. But mental fitness will not stand up to the stress and strain of battle unless troops are also physically fit. This battle may go on for many days and the final issue may well depend on which side can best last out and stand up to the buffeting, and ups and downs, and the continuous strain, of hard battle fighting.

    There will be no tip and run tactics in this battle; it will be a killing match; the German is a good soldier and the only way to beat him is to kill him in battle.

41. I am not convinced that our soldiery are really tough and hard. They are sunburnt and brown, and look very well; but they seldom move anywhere on foot and they have led a static life for many weeks.

    During the next month, therefore, it is essential to make our officers and men really fit; ordinary fitness is not enough, they must be made tough and hard.

42. This memorandum will not be reproduced or copied. It will form the basis of all our plans and preparations for operation 'LIGHTFOOT'.

B. L. Montgomery
Lt. Gen.
G.O.C.-in-C.
Eighth Army

The Oracle

As chief planning officer, Colonel Charles Richardson found the Army Commander's oracular ability amazing:

'At Alamein I was asked, as the planner, to give a figure for the casualties at Alamein, about a fortnight before the battle. And I had to say to Freddie [de Guingand], "I've got no experience on which to base this estimate and there's nothing in the books." So he said, "All right, I'll ask the army commander."

'And Freddie came back the next day, and he said, "Thirteen thousand." Well now that was precisely, within a matter of hundreds, the figure for killed, wounded and missing at the end of the battle!'[3]

Even the old desert 'sweats' were surprised by Monty's *savoir faire la guerre* – and the resulting confidence sweeping the 8th Army.

'It was fascinating because we all used to go down and bathe on the beach before breakfast, all wearing our nothings,' Major Mather recalled, 'and when we were all set the atmosphere was tremendous, because Monty had got a complete grip of the army at once. I mean, he was a professional, much more professional – I mean, we all thought we were professionals, but by Jove he was in a different class!'[4]

Like Rommel, Monty exuded curiosity and interest in his men. This interest was not the *faux* interest of the English aristocratic, seigneurial kind, attempting to impress or palliate subordinates by nice manners and patronizing concern; instead, Monty seemed to respond, instinctively, to the men's dissatisfaction, especially their craving for clear explanation of the purpose for which they were fighting, and means by which they would be successful. He thus radiated energy, confidence – and a driving interest in the 'leaders' and men of his army. One NCO recorded Monty's inspection of his battalion on 20 September in his diary:

The Battalion lines up in companies on an improvised parade-ground by the roadside. The Great Man arrives punctually. His name's Montgomery, and he's only recently reached the Middle East, having been specially sent out from Blighty to shake things up after the summer débâcle. He's supposed to be visiting all Eighth Army units in turn, to size them up and instil a little pep. He proves to be a quiet, severe sort of chap, smallish but tough, with short moustache, pointed features, broody, aggressive grey eyes . . . The inspection lasts a long while, but the General, accompanied by the usual retinue of brass hats, holds it in a steady grip, moving slowly along the ranks, methodically scrutinising each man – up from the boots, then shooting a quizzical glance at the face with sudden upward lunge of his head – stopping every now and then to exchange a word with officers and N.C.O.s, progressing carefully and unhurriedly through the whole parade.[5]

Monty would leave his indelible mark on every soldier he saw. 'Most people feel, to put it mildly, a bit doubtful about the latest G.O.C. [general],' Crimp recorded in his diary the initial response among the 'snootiest' group, the signallers. 'They don't like his new-broom policy and consider his methods extreme,' the NCO noted a few days later, especially when they learned their favourite, but medically suspicious *berka* or Egyptian brothel in Cairo had been closed.[6] Yet once the battalion reached its training grounds, morale soared. A battle was brewing, and each man would have his part to play.

For his part, meanwhile, Monty had not only got to appraise, at first hand, the overall quality of his units, but their leaders. As Major Mather recalled, 'the two things were, that without any effort he virtually knew everybody by name, down to the rank certainly of second-in-command of regiments and brigade majors. I mean, he knew everybody above major, certainly – all senior majors he knew by name – and usually their Christian name and knew all about them. *In the whole of the 8th Army!* It was absolutely fantastic – and without any apparent effort. He would discuss the merits of different people: and he always used to get it right! It was absolutely extraordinary, the way he could sum people up. We called him "The Oracle". Because when you had a problem, you asked Monty. And he knew what the answer was – inevitably he got it right. It was absolutely extraordinary!'[7]

The evening after Monty issued his Lightfoot plan, Major-General Sir Oliver Leese, commander of the Guards Armoured Division in England, arrived to replace Ramsden in command of XXX Corps. Arriving in Cairo on the morning of 15 September he'd breakfasted with Dick McCreery, Alexander's chief of staff, bought some desert clothes, then finally motored in a leisurely fashion to Burg-el-Arab. 'I soon came down to earth,' Leese recalled, 'as the army commander greeted me warmly and then quickly asked me why on earth I had taken so long to get to him!'[8]

Asking Leese to stay overnight in one of his caravans, Monty gave him the exact date and time of the 8th Army's forthcoming offensive – 23 October – and his task: to smash through the enemy's northern defences with four infantry divisions, so that the new 8th Army armoured corps could pass through on to the Miteiriya Ridge and destroy the Afrika Korps.

The next day, at a gathering of all 8th Army corps and divisional commanders, Monty personally went over his 'Lightfoot' plan. Leese was to ensure the break-in area was 'thoroughly cleared of all enemy troops and guns before the armoured brigades begin to move in to them'; Lumsden was to force the enemy to counter-attack X Corps 'on ground of its own choice', astride the enemy's supply route – the Rahman track, running from the sea to the south. No one dissented.

All three corps commanders – Leese, Lumsden and Horrocks – were, however, 'new', having all been divisional commanders only four weeks previously. Moreover, they were all English, which distinctly irritated the Commonwealth divisional commanders – Pienaar, the South African, Morshead, the Australian, and Freyberg, the New Zealander – who saw themselves as being passed over for promotion. Nevertheless, all were impressed by the 8th Army commander's authority, determination and zeal. As before the Alam Halfa battle, the objectives were crystal clear, presented by a general who had now proved himself in battle against the 'bogeyman' Rommel.

It was only after the senior commanders returned to their formations that the true enormity of the undertaking began to sink in – and the problems began.

A tough proposition

Winston Churchill was meanwhile receiving in London his own accurate picture of Axis dispositions – and therefore knew of the ever-deepening belt of German minefields at Alamein. Rommel had waited too long before attacking in August – and had paid the price. Was Monty doing the same? In conversation with his military advisers Churchill began seriously to doubt whether, having delayed his offensive from September to October, Montgomery could possibly now 'blow a hole in the enemy's front', as Churchill signalled to Alexander:

There is a point about the fortifications which the enemy will make in the interval which I should like to put to you. Instead of a crust through which a way can be cleared in a night, may you not find twenty-five miles of fortifications, with blasted rock, gunpits, and machine-gun posts? The tank was originally invented to clear a way for the infantry in the teeth of machine-gun fire. Now it is the infantry who will have to clear a way for the tanks, and it seems to me their task will be a very hard one now that fire-power is so great. No doubt you are thinking about all this and how so to broaden your front of attack as to make your superior numbers felt.[9]

Once again, all Alexander could do was show Monty the signal – which Monty simply ignored. The Prime Minister – an enthusiastic promoter of the use of the first tanks on the Western Front in 1917 – was obviously haunted by past memories, Monty felt. Moreover, his idea of 'broadening the front of the attack' flew against the cardinal principle of concentration that characterized modern military thought.

Yet, in his maddening, illogical and intuitive way, Churchill had put his finger on the nub of the problem – for the task of breaking into Rommel's prepared defences looked increasingly formidable, at least to Oliver Leese.

In his unpublished memoirs, Leese later reflected that, of his five infantry divisions, one (4th Indian) was incapable of offensive action; another (51st Highland, reconstituted after the surrender of the original division at St Valéry in 1940) had never been in battle before; two (2nd New Zealand and 1st South African) were a brigade short and therefore only good for a single attack in the battle; and only one, the 9th Australian, was up to strength and capable of sustained operations:

After the Conference [15 September] my first decision was to see for myself the ground over which I was to do the attack . . .

We were obviously up against a tough proposition. The whole area was quite flat, except for the Miteiriya Ridge which was some 300ft high and which was mostly in German hands. And it stuck out a mile that it was going to be very difficult to conceal our guns, ammunition, tanks and infantry during the concentration prior to the battle . . .

I spent three days in reconnaissance and then I had to decide on the actual point of attack. I had too few Divisions and also too few guns to attack all along my front. I found a certain defilade to cover my right flank about Tel-el-Eisa and I rested my left as best I could on the Miteiriya Ridge.[10]

Contrary to popular legend, Leese was acutely aware that, for a ten-mile-wide break-in, he was short of artillery – 'In point of fact I only had 452 field guns and what was more worrying only 48 medium guns to cover the 30 Corps break-in attack.'[11]

If Leese worried whether he had sufficient infantry and artillery to achieve the break-in, however, he was even more alarmed when he found that his infantry divisional commanders doubted whether the British armour would push through the minefield gaps the infantry made.

Faith and doubt

'When I held my first Corps conference my divisional Commanders listened politely to what I had to say, and then said quite quietly that the Armour would not pass through their gaps in the minefields. I replied that they would of course do so as the Army Commander had issued the order to that effect. The divisional Commanders just repeated again quite quietly their previous opinion that the Armour would not do so.'[12]

The problem was, Freyberg's New Zealanders had been repeatedly let down by the armour in the July attacks; so had the Australians and South Africans. Whether at this stage Monty realized that he had so many doubters is unknown; he made no mention of the problem in either his diary or his memoirs, stating only that GHQ Cairo disliked the idea of a northern thrust and would have preferred to see the conventional inland hook around the south. Others, like the commander of the 4th Indian Division, 'Gertie' Tuker, favoured an attempt in the centre.[13] Yet it seems unlikely that Monty – who, as Major Mather quickly discovered, 'knew everything' – was unaware of such dissension. Treating it as 'belly-aching', however, he ignored it as he had Churchill's objections, and stuck strictly to his masterplan.

Preparations went ahead inexorably. With each day the morale of the troops rose steadily higher. The deception plan in the south, under Colonel Richardson, was destined to become a classic of its kind, guaranteeing – as it would on D-Day in Normandy – complete tactical surprise and German uncertainty about the true *Schwerpunkt*. The artillery plan, meanwhile, was to Monty even more important. The artillery must pave the way for the infantry, then protect it once it had reached its objectives. It must also cover the complicated leapfrog of the armoured corps through, and beyond, the conquered minefield sector. In order that the full, concentrated weight of 8th Army artillery could be brought to bear on the two break-in points, Monty now entrusted the artillery plan to his erstwhile chief gunner at South-Eastern Command, Brigadier Sidney Kirkman, whom he had summoned with Horrocks, but who had had to come out the long way from England.

Like Leese, Brigadier Kirkman stayed his first night in the desert in Monty's guest-caravan. After dinner Monty took him to his map-lorry, explained his plan of battle and instructed Kirkman to see that 'the gunner plan is absolutely as good as it can be – "it's one of the most important factors"', Kirkman recalled Monty's words many years later. 'And I said, "Yes, sir, I understand."'

Recalling the incident almost four decades later, Kirkman felt this to be remarkable: 'I mean if one looks back, almost any other commander in history, having attached importance to an event of that sort, would probably have said, "Is everything going all right – are you happy?" Not a bit of it. He never mentioned it again. I mean, I had plenty of interviews with him, mostly at my request. But between that moment and the Alamein offensive he never again referred to the gunnery plan. He was satisfied that since I was there it would be as good as it could be. There are very few people who have that faith.'[14]

Monty's faith was not misplaced. Indeed, he was quite satisfied that the artillery, like the infantry, would be trained and ready for their role, by the October full moon. The problem, in his view, was the armour. Would it really penetrate beyond the Axis minefields in the north by the first morning of the battle? And if it did, was it to be trusted to remain concentrated and destroy Rommel's armour on ground of its own choosing? Could one realistically hope to create and train a cohesive British armoured corps, akin to the celebrated Afrika Korps, with new tanks about which the crews and maintenance teams knew nothing, in a bare five weeks? Moreover, Churchill's fear of a twenty-five-mile-deep system of fortifications, although exaggerated, was in essence well-founded. On 27 September 8th Army intelligence reported that the Italian Trento Division had been 'sandwiched between German units' and that élite German parachutists were forming 'iron lungs for Italian infantrymen' by being peppered in battalion strengths within the Italian defensive layout.

To test the strength of Rommel's defences, two brigades of the 44th Division carried out an attack on the last day of September – Operation Bulimba. The results were depressing: the troops running into both Ramcke and Folgore parachutists, sustaining heavy casualties, and failing to achieve their object: an ominous sign.

It was clear that, as fast as Monty trained his revived 8th Army for a decisive offensive battle, the African Panzer Army was preparing itself for a decisive defensive one. Vainly, Monty began to insist that the British armoured divisions be prepared to fight their way out of the minefields if resistance proved fiercer and deeper than at first estimated. But could they? More and more, he recognized his plan was overambitious. On 5 October, 8th Army intelligence drew up its latest and most accurate analysis of Rommel's defensive layout, instituted before Rommel left for his cure on 23 September. Using half a million mines, Rommel had ordered the sowing not only of conventional mine belts, but also a system of 'dividing walls' connecting the two main north–south belts at intervals of four to five kilometres, thus forming a series of 'hollow areas'. These hollow areas were intended as 'traps for penetrating troops' who breached the first minefield belt, since they would be forced to move either right or left of the dividing wall, thus 'dissipating the force of the attack'.[15]

This was worrying – though not as much as news that the British armoured commanders were now on the point of open mutiny.

Mutiny in the desert

De Guingand later recalled the circumstances leading up to the 'mutiny' clearly. 'Monty had been called away to give a lecture at the Staff College, Haifa. Lumsden was commander of X Corps, and I thought I'd better go over and listen to what he'd got to say [at a conference of his divisional and brigade commanders].'[16]

In Palestine Monty patiently explained to students exactly how he saw modern armoured operations. 'Some people think that an armoured division operates like a naval fleet. This is not the case,' he emphasized. 'Whatever may be the task of an armoured division, its first step towards achieving success will nearly always be to secure ground which dominates the battle area ... The ground thus occupied should be so important to the enemy that he will be forced to attack our armour on it, i.e. on ground of our own choosing. Having occupied this ground, the heavy armour should be positioned in hull-down positions and be protected by a screen of anti-tank guns dug-in out in front, with artillery control centralised; the light squadrons, accompanied by artillery OPs, should operate towards the enemy and be manoeuvred so as to draw the enemy on to our anti-tank guns and heavy armour, and into areas where he can be dealt with by concentrated artillery fire.'[17]

Meanwhile, at Alamein, to de Guingand's horror, Herbert Lumsden applauded Monty's plan of securing important ground in the forthcoming battle – then declared he would not follow it! ' "Monty's plan – there's one point I don't agree with: that tanks should be used to force their way out of the minefields. Tanks must be used as cavalry: they must exploit the situation and not be kept as supporters of infantry. So I don't propose to do that." After the conference I went up to Herbert,' de Guingand later recalled, 'and I said, "Look here, my dear boy, you can't do this. You know Monty. You must know him well enough – he won't permit dis-obedience to his orders." ' Lumsden, however, was unruffled, telling de Guingand to 'leave that to me'.[18]

Such refusal to obey orders had come to characterize the disparate, Commonwealth units of 8th Army over the past year, and illustrated how little the so-called 'superiority' in arms and men enjoyed by 8th Army really meant to the generals at the time. By late October Rommel's African Panzer Army would muster approximately 100,000 Axis troops, while 8th Army's polyglot strength would rise to almost twice that number. Historians, noting this imbalance, often assumed the numerical ascend-ancy of 8th Army somehow guaranteed Montgomery success. Yet the truth is, 8th Army had enjoyed relatively greater superiority over Rommel in the Crusader operations of November 1941, and again at Gazala in May 1942 – and had been defeated. Herbert Lumsden, supposedly the most experienced armoured commander in the desert, had now been given the first truly armoured reserve corps in Allied battle history, with first-class American Sherman tanks – yet his diffidence over the chances of breaking out through the Axis minefields was becoming known to all the senior commanders of 8th Army and their staff.

'Monty came back the next day and I repeated to him this conference,' de Guingand meanwhile recalled.[19]

What was to be done? Only weeks now remained before 'D' day. The situation was critical. There could be no question of postponing the already-delayed and certainly most important Allied offensive of the war so far, upon whose success the outcome of the Torch landings depended – indeed, upon which was predicated the entire American commitment to the war in the Mediterranean. Failure or defeat at Alamein would, it was generally believed, lead the Vichy French to challenge the Torch landings on their shores in Morocco and Algeria, as well as giving Hitler ample reason to reinforce his German armies in North Africa, concentrating then upon the final capture of Malta – which was only expected to hold out if resupplied by 16 November, when a British convoy was due to sail: ships which could only enjoy air protection if 8th Army recaptured the Martuba airfields, west of Alamein, by that date.

Instinctively, Churchill had recognized the magnitude of Monty's problem. Because the Prime Minister's suggested solution – broadening the attack – was impossible, as well as tactically unsound, Monty had simply ignored it. Now, however, he had to face the fact that Churchill was right: 8th Army was faced with an almost impenetrable line of fortifications. Though he 'whistled in' General Lumsden and reiterated Lumsden's task, Monty knew his words alone would not suffice. Nor would dismissal help; it was simply too late for a wholesale change of armoured commanders, or to start again and completely retrain the British armour for its new role to conform to Lightfoot. The Allied Torch landings and the very survival of Malta were at stake. Reluctantly, therefore, in the light of latest intelligence about the interstitching of German and Italian units, Monty took the only course open to him: he altered his plan.

A killing match

The more Monty thought about the problem, the more he realized that, despite the arrival of so many new anti-tank guns and the imposition of corps artillery programmes under Kirkman, the infantry themselves were at heart nervous of making such a deep penetration into the Axis minefields and gun-lines without tank support. Conversely, the armour was still terrified of being caught in a trap, unable to manoeuvre in the German minefields and picked off like stranded ducks by the dreaded German 88mm guns. Lumsden's personal bravery was unquestioned, but his experience at Gazala had made him reluctant – as Gott had been – once again to risk crippling tank casualties: and this was reflected in his subordinate commanders.

One answer was to close down the *corps de chasse* altogether and allot its armoured divisions to Leese's XXX Corps – a solution which Field-Marshal Carver later felt would have been the wisest course. However, such an armoured infusion would have made the formation far too large for Leese alone, as an as-yet inexperienced corps commander, to handle; indeed, it was questionable whether any British commander at that time had sufficient skill in handling armour to avoid the tanks becoming dispersed and reduced to 'penny-packets'. 'On no account must it become so dispersed,' Monty had warned in his Training Memorandum No. 1, 'that it can be dealt with piecemeal by the enemy.'[20]

The only possible way out, Monty felt, was to alter his Lightfoot plan so that X Corps fought in tandem with XXX Corps, giving the infantry the security they so lacked, while the armour would receive the full benefit of a corps of infantry, replete with artillery and anti-tank guns. In such a scenario there need be no interruption or alteration in the planning: the attacks would go in as arranged. Only, instead of breaking away into the open to engage the Afrika Korps, beyond the German minefields and the 8th Army's infantry, the British armour would work *with* the infantry divisions, indeed use the infantry as bait, to lure the German armour into close combat – for the 8th Army infantry, having broken into the enemy line, would be ordered to undertake further, lateral attacks, north and south, up and down the enemy line: methodically eating away or 'crumbling' the defending Axis troops. The German armour could not possibly watch its defending infantry being so destroyed; would be forced therefore to counter-attack – thus allowing XXX Corps and X Corps to use their superiority in artillery, anti-tank guns and tanks to destroy not only the enemy's infantry, but his armour too.

How this idea came to Monty at this critical moment is a mystery which none of his staff could ever explain, not even his new word for it: 'crumbling'. 'Crumbling' was not a term that existed in the military dictionary. The Afrika Korps had certainly developed its own effective technique for luring British tanks on to its 88mm screen, and its other anti-tank guns, by sending out, as bait, small groups of panzers, which then pulled back. But the notion of striking at the enemy's infantry in order to lure the Afrika Korps on to 8th Army's anti-tank weapons, artillery and tanks was a wholly new concept. It transformed an overambitious 'masterplan'[21] – penetrating the enemy's minefield defences at night and passing an entire armoured corps into the rear of the enemy's line, similar to Rommel's intentions at Alam Halfa – into a much more methodical proposition: a battle involving a massive shock, similar to an invasion; a direct challenge to the integrity of the enemy's line; and then a process of deadly lateral attrition, forcing the enemy to counter-attack.

For this alteration, romantic military historians would never forgive Monty. By contrast, veterans of the desert campaign could only marvel at the way Monty turned an increasingly ominous situation to his advantage: an intriguing example of Monty's underlying realism yet, because it implied that his original concept of a *corps de chasse* was wrong, something for which Monty – who hated ever to admit to having made a mistake – neither claimed nor took the credit he deserved.

A *change of plan*

In his diary, after the battle, Monty recorded the change of plan, but made no mention that it was the 'mutiny' of his armoured commanders which had triggered it. The *corps de chasse*, once passed out beyond the northern bridgehead, had been intended to 'position itself on ground of its own choosing astride the enemy supply routes' – just as Rommel had planned at Alam Halfa. The Panzer Army would be forced to counter-attack the British tanks with its panzer divisions 'which were separated and it was hoped would remain so. Further operations by 10 Corps would depend on how the enemy re-acted to its moves. I hoped that the enemy armoured Divisions would be forced to attack 10 Corps in position,' Monty had written in his original intructions for Lightfoot.[22] It was that part of the plan he now altered.

It was the gradual realization that 8th Army was insufficiently trained that made the alteration necessary, Monty claimed in his diary. After Alam Halfa he had proceeded with the retraining of 8th Army – but had not been impressed by the standard of leadership. Indeed, 'it was becoming apparent that the Eighth Army was very untrained. The need for training had never been stressed; consequently no one ever did any training; most of the commanders were officers who had come to the fore by skill in battle, and because there was no one any better who could be promoted, these officers were not skilled trainers.' There were, Monty candidly considered, 'very few 1st class officers in the Middle East in the higher ranks; most of the No. 1 jobs were filled by second or third rate officers. Here again, AUCHINLECK was to blame; he continually refused to have good men out from England, preferring the second-rate men on the spot whom he knew.'[23]

'By the first week in October I was satisfied with the leadership,' Monty recorded in his diary overview (written on the eve of Alamein); he had had two new corps commanders sent from England, a new head of artillery, and a new tank chief. 'The equipment situation was also good; we had a good heavy tank [Sherman] and it contained a good gun; we had a great weight of artillery and plenty of ammunition; I could concentrate some 400 guns for the operation of blowing the hole in the enemy positions in the North.

'*But the training was not good* and it was beginning to become clear to me that I would have to be very careful, and that I must ensure that formations and units were not given tasks which were likely to end in failure because of their low standard of training.

'The army had suffered 80,000 casualties, and the re-born Eighth Army was full of untrained units.

'The troops had fought a successful defensive battle on 31 August and following days. But this next battle was to be an *offensive battle*, which is a very different proposition. I was determined to have no more failures. The troops in the Middle East had a hard life and few pleasures; they put up with it willingly. All they asked for was success – and I was determined to see that they got it. It was clear that I must so stage-manage the battle that my troops would be able to do what was demanded of them, and I must not be too ambitious in my demands.

'And so, on 6 October, I issued a Memorandum of how I intended to fight the battle.'[24]

The new memorandum was five typescript pages long, written in Monty's unmistakably clear and forthright style. Only twenty-four copies were made: one for each corps commander and divisional commander, one for the Desert Air Force commander, one for the chief gunner, chief engineer, chief administrative officer, head of staff duties, and one for Alexander's chief of staff in Cairo. Marked 'Most Secret' it would become, in its way, the most significant change of plan made by an army commander in North Africa; indeed, it would alter the Allied approach to combat for the rest of the war.

Although the original plan of Lightfoot envisaged very tough fighting, the accent had hitherto been – just like Rommel's at Alam Halfa – on surprise, speed, and the use of massed tanks. Now, only seventeen days from 'D' day, as the launch date for the break-in battle was called, the army commander's new plan envisaged a wholly different sort of battle: a battle of armoured as well as infantry attrition.

Eating the guts out of the enemy

Under the subheading 'The Battle', Monty set out his new approach to the forthcoming contest:

We have great superiority in tanks and in fire-power.

But it is a regrettable fact that our troops are not, in all cases, highly trained.

By doing foolish or stupid things we could lose heavily in the first few days of the battle, and thus negative our superiority.

We must therefore ensure that we fight the battle in our own way, that we stage-manage the battle to suit the training of our troops, and that we keep well-balanced at all times so that we can ignore enemy thrusts and can proceed relentlessly with our own plans to destroy the enemy.

Above all, we must ensure that we keep the initiative; we start with it and we must never lose it; we must make the enemy dance to our tune throughout.

Everything told him that 'the enemy will stand and fight it out. He will have strengthened his defences and I do not want to have serious losses by running our heads into snags. It is particularly important that we should keep well within ourselves, and should not attempt ambitious operations beyond the capabilities of our somewhat untrained troops. Therefore, once we have broken into the enemy positions during the night D/D plus 1 [23/24 October],' Monty laid down, 'we will carry on the battle *at dawn on D plus 1* day as indicated in para 11.'

Paragraph 11 specified the new 'crumbling' basis on which the battle would be fought. Leese's XXX Corps – comprising four infantry divisions – 'will work Northwards from the Northern flank of the bridgehead, using 9 Aust[ralian] Div, and Southwards from the MITEIRIYA ridge using the N.Z., S.A. and 4 Ind[ian] Divisions.' Rommel could not possibly watch these two infantry 'crumbling' operations without responding – but he had insufficient infantry with which to halt the process, so would have to counter it with panzers. This would be X Corps' cue:

The main task of 10 Corps will be to destroy the enemy's armour.

If this is not possible initially, the Corps will be manoeuvred so as to keep the enemy armour from interfering with the 'crumbling' operations being carried out by 30 Corps.

Lumsden's X Corps would thus become a shield for the infantry, not a *corps de chasse* – at least in the early stage of the battle. Moreover, the armoured divisions would be expected to help 'crumble' the enemy:

Opportunity may occur for 10 Corps to assist in these 'crumbling' operations, both in the Northern sector in front of 9 Aust Div, and to the South of the MITEIRIYA ridge on the west flank of the N.Z. Div.

By 'crumbling' Monty meant attacking the enemy, using concentrated artillery, and assaulting day and night. 'I hope that the operations outlined in para 11 will result in the destruction, by a "crumbling" process, of the whole of the enemy holding troops. Having thus "eaten the guts" out of the enemy he will have no troops to hold a front. His Panzer Army may attempt to interfere with our tactics, and may launch counter-attacks; this would be what we want, and would give us the opportunity of inflicting casualties on the enemy's armour.

When we have succeeded in destroying the enemy holding troops, the eventual fate of the Panzer Army is certain – it will not be able to avoid destruction.
To sum up:

a) During the night D/D plus 1 we will break into the enemy positions at the selected places.

b) At dawn on D plus 1 day we will begin the 'crumbling' operations; it is essential to my plans to to begin these operations at dawn.

c) Thereafter we will be ready to take instant advantage of any weakening or 'letting-up' on the part of the enemy; the moment we see signs of this we will leap on him.

d) Throughout it is vital that we should retain the initiative, and keep up sustained pressure on the enemy. He must not have long pauses during which he can recover his balance.

The R.A.F. will help us in this respect.
And we ourselves must shoot the enemy up with artillery from all sides at all times.[25]

Crumbling

Save in a few exceptional circumstances, shock attack at a chosen point and relentless 'crumbling' operations were henceforth to be the basis of Allied fighting – and victory – in World War II, whether British, Commonwealth, American or Russian. It was, in its way, a high tribute to the Wehrmacht: an acceptance that, against such superlative German troops – infantry and armoured – the Allies could, in the end, only hope to defeat or drive back their enemy by a new kind of combat, in which Allied armour worked in planned co-ordination with infantry and air forces to force the enemy, in battle, to commit his reserves, and then relentlessly to annihilate him on ground of Allied choosing. Fantasies of cavalry-style break-out and exploitation were, henceforth, secondary to the winning of the main battle.

No one saw better than Monty the cost and requirement of such an approach to modern battle. 'This battle will involve hard and prolonged fighting,' his new memorandum went on. 'Our troops must not think that, because we have a good tank and very powerful artillery support, the enemy will all surrender. The enemy will not surrender, and there will be bitter fighting,' he warned.

The infantry must be prepared to fight and to kill, and to continue doing so over a prolonged period.

It is essential to impress on all officers that determined leadership will be very vital in this battle, as in any battle. There have been far too many unwounded prisoners taken in this war. We must impress on our officers, NCOs and men that when they are cut off or surrounded, and there appears no hope of survival, they must organize themselves into a defensive locality and hold out where they are. By so doing they will add enormously to the enemy's difficulties; they will greatly assist the development of our own operations; and they will save themselves from spending the rest of the war in a prison camp.

Nothing is ever hopeless so long as troops have stout hearts, and have weapons and ammunition.[26]

Monty's new policy, however, meant training and bringing 8th Army's infantry and armour to such a pitch of determination and enthusiasm that it would be able to sustain its offensive for perhaps ten days or more, involving at least 10,000 casualties – possibly twice that figure. As Field-

Marshal Carver later reflected, this was not something Churchill's nominee, Lieutenant-General Gott, had been willing to countenance – indeed, there probably was, at that moment, no Allied battlefield general willing or able to plan and execute such a battle.

Suddenly, Monty's lifetime of experience, both of training and of battle, made him the ideal commander for such a confrontation in fixed positions. He himself described, in his diary, the enormity of the situation that faced him:

The whole operation was an immense undertaking. We were face to face with the enemy between the sea and the QATTRA Depression; there was no open flank. The enemy was strengthening his defences to a degree previously unknown in the Western Desert.

In introducing his amended plan, he admitted that he did

not think it will be possible to prevent the enemy from finding out that a British offensive is intended at some time. He must know of our growing strength in tanks, artillery, and so on; an Eighth Army offensive is being talked about now in Cairo and other places.

We must therefore obtain tactical surprise, and must try to conceal from the enemy the exact places where the blows will fall and the exact date and time of the blows.

I think that we can do this; in fact, it is essential that we should do so.

Our cover plan [deception] is designed for this purpose.

All the arrangements in connection with the assembly and concentration of troops, and the stage-management of the preliminary arrangements, are designed to hoodwink the enemy as to exactly where the blows will fall. We must not slip up in these arrangements.[27]

Everyone must become a shareholder in the new 8th Army, not only so that he would play his part to the utmost in the coming battle, but so that he would consider its components – secrecy, deception, preparations – a matter of personal honour.

Backwards and forwards to Benghazi

'I am absolutely confident that the next British attack will be a huge success & that we shall finally defeat General Rommel,' wrote one Lieutenant – an ex-chaplain who had been commissioned into an infantry battalion in 8th Armoured Brigade – to his fiancée. 'The air support we are getting now is splendid, our tanks are growing in quality & quantity. Our artillery ditto. I do hope I shall be here to take part in the next big show. I don't want to miss any of it'[28] – indeed, he even 'asked the Colonel if I could get out of going on the instructional course in Palestine, because I was afraid the our big offensive might start some time in the near future, & I might not have been back with the Battalion in time'.[29]

That Monty managed to inspire 8th Army with the will and determination to undertake such a decisive 'killing-match' was, in the end, what would raise him head and shoulders above any other Allied battlefield general in the war so far. Indeed, Field-Marshal Templer would later remark that it was this quality, far more than any tactical ability, which was Monty's true genius, and the reason why he would go down as one of the great captains of history – just as Churchill would for his moral leadership of a beleaguered nation in 1940 and 1941.

The Prime Minister's courage was born of an indomitable spirit, of a lifetime's political struggle, and a deep awareness of the epic nature of history. His confidence, however, was subject to moods of profound depression – his 'dark fears' as his doctor called them – and his night's rest only guaranteed by a 'red tablet'. By contrast, perhaps the most extraordinary facet of Monty's whole character was his infectious, unshakeable self-confidence. If he was mad, as some claimed, then it was a madness that eliminated doubt, exuded confidence and guaranteed his sleep.

This gift of self-confidence Monty now brought to bear in a tireless bid to enthuse and prepare his army for the coming battle. He made it his business to visit virtually every unit of 8th Army, formally and informally. Like his missionary father before him in Tasmania he took his gospel out to the troops. 'It was a great achievement,' Sir Oliver Leese recorded in his unpublished memoirs, 'as day by day his own personality was spreading through the Army, and in the end the battle plan became the personal affair and interest of each man.'[30]

Monty's orders had always borne the unmistakable imprint of his mind – that talent for clarifying complex problems until they appeared to be quite straightforward. Yet, as if to mirror the contradictions of his character, an impish vanity worked increasingly in tandem with his awesome professionalism, striking a bond with ordinary soldiers that would be unique in the history of his country. Churchill was admired, but as his wife Clemmie once said: 'He knows nothing of the life of ordinary people. He's never been in a bus, and only once on the Underground.' His language was rich and eloquent – but after two years of defeat and failure, it aroused as much scepticism as inspiration. The American CBC reporter in Cairo, Winston Burdett, for example, found 'the Old War Horse', as he put it, becoming less and less convincing: 'I dislike the way he uses words to conceal his meaning – rather like an old ham actor whose stuff is wearing a bit thin.'[31] By contrast, Monty's direct, mischievous, schoolboy humour and his evident, almost messianic concern for the welfare of his men began to turn soldierly respect into dynamic loyalty of a new kind. As Moorehead remarked, 'the new general was a man the troops coud understand'.[32] His phrases and sayings swept through an army that had no other diversions or distractions than preparing for the impending battle. And as General Horrocks later emphasized, the bare, scrubby desert, with its absence of civilians or distractions, imparted a classical military quality to the gathering confrontation between the two armies, quite unlike any other theatre of war.

'I have been very busy since I last wrote,' Monty apologized in a letter to the Reynoldses on 6 October – the day he issued his revised plan for Alamein. 'In fact one has no spare time at all; this is probably just as well as there is not a great deal to do in the desert . . . It will be very interesting when I begin to get the *Times*' – adding, with almost unconscious egoism: 'I shall be able to read what the Press said about my appointment.' He was meantime instructing his bank in London to transfer some £500 to the Reynoldses, 'and to keep you always on that mark or thereabouts. Then if anything should happen to me David would be all right for about a year or so; this would tide over the time they always take to wind up one's affairs. Actually,' he assured them, 'I haven't the least intention of letting anything happen to me, and I know it will NOT. But I would like you to have the money and then I needn't bother.'[33]

Meanwhile Monty had, already on 28 September, laid down the system and timing by which officers and men of 8th Army would be informed of the plan of battle. Except for those units furnishing patrols, every man in 8th Army would eventually be told, at least in outline, what the plan was: brigadiers and CREs [engineer commanders] immediately, battalion and regimental commanders on 10 October, company and battery commanders on 17 October, and remaining officers thereafter – officers whose duty was to see that 'all troops' were then properly informed.[34] On 6 October he had amended the date when leave would be stopped, delaying this until 21 October in an effort to avoid alerting enemy agents or intelligence. The aim, however, remained the same.

On Wed 21 October unit commanders will, quietly and without publishing any written orders, stop all further leave. On no account will CO's communicate with leave camps or take any similar action; they will merely stop sending men on leave . . . The reason that can be given is that there are signs that the enemy may attack during the full moon period, and we must have all our men present.

Nor were officers to be permitted to go to Cairo, Alexandria or other delta towns from that date:

A slip-up here might have far-reaching repercussions as it is on that date that regimental officers begin to come into the picture.

Wed 21 October and Thurs 22 October will be devoted to the most intensive propaganda as regards educating the attacking troops about the battle, and to getting them enthusiastic. All ranks must be told that this battle is probably the decisive battle of the war; if we win this battle and destroy the Panzer Army it will be the turning point of the war.

Therefore we will make no mistake about it. We have great superiority over the Germans in artillery and tanks, and the Germans have no conception of what is coming to them in this respect.

We cannot go on with this business of going backwards and forwards to Benghazi.

This time we will hit the German for 6 right out of Egypt and Libya, and will go ourselves to Tripoli and Tunis.

If every officer and every soldier goes into this battle with the determination to win and to kill the enemy, then only one result is possible – and that is complete success.

If every tank crew, and every 6-pdr A[nti].T[an]k. gun team, will hit and disable one enemy tank, then we must win.

If every disabled enemy tank is destroyed at once by the R[oyal]E[ngineers] before it can be towed away, our win becomes all the easier.

These, and other, facts must be got across to the troops in no uncertain voice. They must be worked up to that state which will make them want to go into battle and kill Germans.[35]

The gospel according to Monty

Having altered his tactical policy for the battle in the north, Monty himself seems to have had no doubt about the outcome. As he summarized in his diary relating to the eve of the battle:

As the days passed, it became clear to me that if 30 Corps was successful in blowing the hole, and if 10 Corps could get its leading armoured Brigades out through the gaps unopposed before daylight on D plus 1, then we would have no difficulty in winning the battle. It would merely be a question of time.

There would be much hard fighting, and I was prepared for a real dog-fight to go on for at least a week; but our resources were such that we must win.

I could see that great determination and willpower would be necessary; the enemy would fight hard and there might be many awkward periods; if we wavered at these times we might lose the battle.

The critical essentials would be:

To keep the initiative

To maintain the pressure and proceed relentlessly with the Army plan.

To preserve balanced dispositions so that we need never re-act to enemy thrusts . . .

An essential feature of my plan was that every Commander in the Army, right down to the Lt-Col level, should know my whole plan, how I meant to fight the battle, what issues depended on it, and the chief difficulties the enemy was up against.

I was also determined that the soldiers should go into battle having been worked up to a great state of enthusiasm.

This was essentially an Army battle, fought on an Army plan, and controlled carefully from Army HQ. Therefore, everyone must know how his part fitted in to the whole plan; only in this way could perfect co-operation be assured.[36]

For this reason, apart from daily visits and inspections of units, Monty relied on the technique he'd developed in Home Forces in England, addressing his officers down to lieutenant-colonel level at specially converted gatherings. In England he had done this at post-mortem conferences following an exercise; now he began doing it *before* the battle. Assembling 'all Commanders in each Corps, down to and including Unit Commanders', Monty addressed those from XXX Corps and XIII Corps on

19 October, and from X Corps on 20 October. As one of his staff officers, Major Oswald, later acknowledged, it was this willingness of the army commander to announce openly to his men what he intended to do in the coming battle that astonished even those who admired the way Alam Halfa had been won.

'After Alam Halfa people paid more and more attention,' Oswald related. 'But when he really stuck his neck out before Alamein and said "This is how it's going to go, and what is more, see that every single soldier knows this" – now that's taking a hell of a chance. Because if you're wrong, there's nothing for you to do but remove yourself from the scene . . .

'You could see from the faces of the people who were there, some of whom had long experience of the desert: they said, "By golly, he must be pretty sure – he fairly stuck his neck out. We've never heard anybody say in such detail exactly what's going to happen in the ensuing battle. We've heard generals explaining why we didn't quite manage to win the last one. But here he stuck his head out and he must be jolly certain of himself."

'Now that made a very profound impression.'[37]

Monty, Leese reported in a letter to his wife on 19 October, 'gave a grand Pep talk today to all my Lt-Cols & upwards – in a vast shamiana [tent] made of camouflage & netting – about 200 chaps. He was superb.'[38] 'Corps Conference & address by Army Com[man]d[er] – he inspires confidence,' Brigadier Holworthy, commanding 7th Indian Brigade, noted in his diary the same day.[39] The Commander of 1st Armoured Division, Raymond Briggs, was equally impressed. 'Final conference at Army,' he noted in his diary after the X Corps conference the next day. 'Monty impresses his personality on all C.O.s of Div.'[40] (Twelve months later, in a lecture to the School of Tank Technolgy in England, Briggs remarked: 'It is exemplary of Montgomery's vision that at the Conference at which all Officers down to the rank of Lt-Colonel were acquainted with his plan, that he told them that this battle would not be over in one day, or two days, or even a week. He explained that the several stages would consist of a break-in, a dog-fight, resulting in a break-through, and finally pursuit. That was exactly how it happened.')[41]

Even RAF officers were impressed by Monty's impact on 8th Army. South African Wing-Commander C. M. S. Gardner felt Monty 'put new life and courage into it, and he made it his own. He took over the whole crusader concept, badge [Crusader cross on a shield] and all . . . Perhaps his greatest merit was his insistence on everyone knowing what the plan was, and what his own part was in it. Quite a change from the old method of "never mind what anybody else is doing, we'll tell you all need to know. Don't worry about why, or what it's in aid of. Just do it!" Montgomery's method meant that everybody felt they were important and personally responsible for the success of the plan. And, in the event of disaster, or loss of communications, they knew what to do to make the best of the situation. Perhaps it was easier to use in a static situation like Alamein, but I remember how impressed everyone was with his briefing of all officers down to the rank of Lt. Colonel, before the attack.'[42]

Major 'Bill' Mather was given the task of organizing one of the two senior officer briefings at Amiriya. 'It was absolutely amazing. We were there for two hours . . . He went through it, day by day, and told us how we'd be feeling; how we'd come to a point where we might start to lose hope – and saying but we would carry on.[43] As de Guingand recalled, Monty emphasized again and again the need to retain the initiative, 'and how everyone must be imbued with the burning desire to "kill Germans. Even the padres – one per weekday and two on Sundays!" This produced a roar.'[44]

A hard fight ahead

Monty would begin such addresses by explaining the enemy situation, 8th Army's situation, and his plan of battle, stressing 'how we will fight this battle; we will fight it *our* way and *not* Rommel's way. I want the details of the battle explained to the troops. Every single soldier,' he emphasized, 'must know how the battle will be fought and his part in it; he must understand how the little fight he is to carry out fits into the bigger picture, and how success or failure on *his* part will influence the whole outcome. Once the British soldier knows and understands what is wanted of him and why, he will always do his stuff and will never let down his side; that is my experience.'[45]

The battle, Monty predicted, would have

three definite stages: the break-in to the enemy's positions, the dog-fight, the break out. We will do the 'break-in' on the night of 23 October. The 'dog-fight' will then begin and will involve hard and continuous fighting; our men must be sent into the fight with the light of battle in their eyes and imbued with the burning desire to kill Germans. I believe that the dog-fight battle will become a hard killing-match and will last for 10 to 12 days; therefore our soldiers must be prepared not only to fight and to kill, but to go on doing so over a prolonged period. It will be absolutely vital during this period to retain the initiative and to force Rommel to dance to our tune *all the time*; we must all keep going however tired we may be.

Determined leadership will be very vital in this battle, and especially in the dog-fight.

After the dog-fight battle has gone on for about 10 to 12 days the enemy will crack. Then will come the break-out, and that will lead to the end of Rommel in Africa.

And so you see we will have a hard fight in front of us. But tell the men all about it, work them up to a state of great enthusiasm, and send them into the battle determined to fight, and to kill, and to conquer. Everyone must have faith in the successful outcome of the battle.

Finally, I want to tell all of you, the senior officers of the Eighth Army, that I am completely and utterly confident that we shall win this battle: and in the way I have said.

Tell this to your men.

Let every man know that I have said this.

Let every man know that the result will be *victory*.

And that Victory will be the turning point of the war.[46]

Fighting to fight

As de Guingand later recalled, Monty's proselytizing had a remarkable effect, with the sick rate dropping markedly – in fact, men fighting to be allowed to fight. One NCO in the Rifle Brigade – the motorized infantry formation fighting in the 7th Armoured Division – recorded the return of a wounded company commander in his diary on 19 October. 'Although his convalescence was hardly complete, he insisted, apparently, on coming back for the "big party", as he "couldn't bear to miss the fun". Nobody knows when the "party" is booked to come off. But there's a full moon towards the end of the month.'[47]

As far as possible, while holding the front line at Alamein, every 'break-in' and 'break-out' formation in 8th Army had been ordered to train for its part in the battle, rehearsing co-ordinated minefield clearance, infantry assault, artillery support, anti-tank gunnery and armoured action.[48] 'Training is strenuous, and there are many portents of approaching action,' one Desert Rat signaller noted in his diary on 8 October. 'All the other camps in the area are now filled with infantry, tank and artillery units . . . The anti-tank company has been re-equipped with the latest, and much more formidable, 6-pounder guns, in place of their piddling 2-pounders.' Four days later he noted,

The key word of all present training is 'minefields'. On the desert some miles from the camp there are dummies staked to represent the actual layout of the minefields at the Front. First there's the British, then a space of no-man's land; then the enemy's forward minefield, with his second a short way behind. Three gaps parallel to, and about a thousand yards from, each other have to be made through the three of them. The job of our Battalion is to force these gaps with the aid of sappers and keep them open for the rest of the Armoured Division travelling through after. Each infantry company of the Battalion has to maintain a gap – one platoon to each of its three stages. We've already had several daylight rehearsals, and tonight the process is repeated under conditions of darkness, just as it'll be when the balloon goes up. The task of each company's signal section is to lay cable along its gap, and work telephone stations at each stage. The whole division goes through, one unit at a time – tanks, armoured cars, 25-pounders, Priests [105mm guns on stripped Grant chassis], anti-tanks, ack-ack, ambulances, H.Q., armoured Control-vehicles and the other battalion of infantry . . . The entire procession takes about three hours.[49]

Four hundred mine detectors had been issued to the two northern corps, with 89,000 track-lamps and 120 miles of marking tape. Finally, on 21 and 22 October, the men of the 8th Army were 'let into the secret . . . And, as a result of everything, a tremendous state of enthusiasm was produced. I have never felt anything like it,' de Guingand recorded. 'Those soldiers just knew they were going to succeed.'[50]

We are ready now

On the morning of 23 October 1942 Monty addressed Allied war correspondents at a specially convened press conference, explaining his plan, forecasting the length of the battle, and handing out copies of the 'Personal

Message from the Army Commander' he had, that same day, ordered to be read out by company and platoon commanders to every soldier in the 8th Army. It read:

1 – When I assumed command of the Eighth Army I said that the mandate was to destroy ROMMEL and his Army, and that it would be done as soon as we were ready.

2 – We are ready NOW.

The battle which is now about to begin will be one of the decisive battles of history. It will be the turning point of the war. The eyes of the whole world will be on us, watching anxiously which way the battle will swing.

We can give them their answer at once, 'It will swing our way.'

3 – We have first-class equipment; good tanks; good anti-tank guns; plenty of artillery and plenty of ammunition; and we are backed up by the finest air striking force in the world.

All that is necessary is that each one of us, every officer and man, should enter this battle with the determination to see it through – to fight and to kill – and finally to win.

If we all do this there can be only one result – together we will hit the enemy for 'six', right out of North Africa.

4 – The sooner we win this battle, which will be the turning point of this war, the sooner we shall all get back home to our families.

5 – Therefore, let every officer and man enter the battle with a stout heart and with the determination to do his duty so long as he has breath in his body.

AND LET NO MAN SURRENDER SO LONG AS HE IS UNWOUNDED AND CAN FIGHT.

Let us all pray that 'the Lord mighty in battle' will give us the victory

B. L. MONTGOMERY,
Lieutenant-General, G.O.C.-in-C., Eighth Army.

MIDDLE EAST FORCES
23–10–42[51]

'Many of the war correspondents were rather shaken by the confidence – this bombastic confidence he displayed,' de Guingand remembered. 'They felt there must be a catch in it – how can he be so sure?'[52] To British war correspondents it seemed scarcely possible that an army of such magnitude – almost 200,000 men – could be assembled and launched into battle with complete tactical surprise. Yet such would prove to be the case, helped by the fact that Rommel remained in Austria, having ruled out a British attack before November.

At Alamein, Rommel's Panzer Army subordinates remained equally confident they could hold the line, even if they had given up hope, for the moment, of breaking through to Cairo after defeat at Alam Halfa. The acting African Panzer Army commander, General Stumme, the C-in-C South, Field-Marshal Kesselring, and the chief of operations at Panzer Army HQ, Colonel Westphal, all predicted defeat for the 8th Army if and when they attacked – Westphal writing to Rommel 'that if the British do attack, then we'll be ready and waiting for them. We're all itching to give the enemy a thrashing,' while Stumme had maintained that the British 'are none too happy about it [the impending offensive]. We're going to wipe the floor with the British.'[53]

The complacency of certain senior German commanders was mirrored in the visit of Colonel Liss – chief of western intelligence in Berlin – to the Alamein line on 21 October, and Liss's confident prediction to Berlin, early that evening, that no attack was expected before November. 'He had in mind,' Lieutenant Hans-Otto Behrendt, the temporary German head of Panzer Army Field Interception Intelligence Unit (621 Company), later recorded, 'information' about 'an operation by the Americans and the British scheduled for the beginning of November; this turned out,' he noted, 'to be the major Allied landings in French North Africa'.

If Berlin had become confused over Allied intentions, Behrendt was not, and the Panzer Army was, he recalled, alerted to a possible British attack between 20 and 25 October. In his view, Panzer Army intelligence was not, therefore, 'completely in the dark about the strength and timing of the British offensive', as many British and German writers later maintained; what German intelligence completely failed to divine was 'the axis of thrust and the sectors of attack'.[54] (21st Panzer Division's intelligence report on the battle also recorded that the 'preparations for the attack were observed very early, and did not take our command by surprise at all, even though the main weight of the attack developed in the north, and not in the south, as expected'.)[55]

Behrendt thus refuted Liddell Hart's stubborn claim, widely disseminated, that there was 'no evidence that his [Montgomery's] "deception plan" deceived the enemy effectively'.[56] As Behrendt and the German war diaries and the battle itself would reveal, 8th Army's deception plans, false oil dumps and vehicle build-up in the south, false signals traffic and strict security measures had worked. Monty's belief that he could not 'prevent the enemy from finding out that a British offensive is intended', but that he could achieve 'tactical surprise' over the 'exact places where the blows will fall and the exact date and time of the blows'[57] had been well-founded; no one in the Panzer Army had any idea where 8th Army would assault, nor the exact time, nor the main axis or *Schwerpunkt*.

Everything is set

Liddell Hart, whose nervous breakdown and appeals for appeasement in 1940 were later a deep embarrassment to him, was being churlish by playing down the extraordinary preparations 8th Army had made for the decisive battle. General Leese, for example, later remembered the final hours leading up to the battle. 'I motored slowly round the battlefield talking to as many platoons, gun and tank teams, sapper parties as I could. One went very slowly to keep down the tell-tale dust and as usual one had no windscreen to catch the rays of the sun. The men were quiet and thoughtful – many were writing letters and you often found the Padres giving a last service to their men. Everywhere there was a feeling of expectancy and of high confidence, but a realization of the magnitude of the task that lay ahead. Everyone knew what they had to do and I think that somehow we all realized the terrific issues at stake. The morale of the army was tremendously high and the will to succeed and confidence in their preparedness was evident everywhere.'[58]

The diaries and letters of 8th Army soldiers bear out Leese's account. Writing to his wife at midnight on 19 October Leese had noted the 'glorious moonlight', and the 'tracks we have made & marked with signs & beacons of stones' visible in the moonlight – yet otherwise no indications that some 90,000 men were moving into position for the attack in the north. 'It's wonderful seeing it all gradually come into being,' he recorded proudly. The next day, with his caravan only twenty yards from the sea, he reflected: 'It is queer sitting waiting. I can do no more – and I pray & hope we've done all we can. Everyone is full of confidence – it will be a great relief when it crashes forth. All the events of the last two years seem very small in comparison with this.'[59]

'This is going to be the big "do" – as we have all thought for quite a while,' Lance/Sergeant Bennett of the 64th Medium Regiment recorded in his diary. 'The rough idea is this – on our front the big attack starts – four Divs on a 10–12,000 yd front (they are – N to S, – Aussies (9th), 51st Highland Div, N.Z. Div, 1st S. Africans). At zero hour they will start advancing to a depth of 5–6,000 yds – which should be reached before dawn – they then consolidate their positions and make bridgeheads for the armour. The art[iller]y. on the front is approx 480 guns (incl. 48 Med). Their role will start at zero-20 – when they will concentrate on dangerous H[eavy].B[atterie]'s. At zero hour they will switch to enemy inf. p[o]s[i]t[ion]s. From then on they will be switching continuously backwards and forwards to various targets. They will be firing continuously for 5½ hours. While this is going on in our sector there will be a smaller scale attack in the Southern sector – to get the Himeimat Peaks. All this is the beginning of the big "do" to annihilate Jerry where he is – not to drive him back – and finally to clear him right out of N. Africa.'[60]

If Monty had been able to ensure that even lance sergeants understood his plan, and felt a part of it, he had achieved a miracle. 'We all knew the part we were to play – and what a sense of confidence and purpose that gave to us all,' recalled a sapper in 9th Field Squadron.[61] 'All the guns are in; and the Infantry & Tanks are gradually coming in,' Leese wrote home. 'It's a great feat of concentration. All by night, & everyone concealed by day – dummy vehicles & tanks removed when the right ones come up. I went round some of the area today, & talked to a lot of troops, including some old soldier medium gunners. Full of heart. I saw some of my Highlanders having their pep talk. Their eyes full of fire, they are mad keen for their first battle & go forward between the Australians & the New Zealanders, so they'll have no trouble on their flanks . . . Everywhere you find confidence & good spirits. Please God, our plan is sound. I believe it's good. Like every military operation, it needs a bit of luck.'[62] On his Jeep trips he found 'everyone in tremendous heart. It's very wonderful what an atmosphere [Monty] has created in this short time. He has great force of character, & a great personality.'[63]

De Guingand – whom Monty had sent away for several days' rest in Alexandria – certainly felt sufficiently confident to take three of his colleagues for one last 'slap up' lunch 'with claret and champagne' in Alexandria;[64] Leese himself dined with Monty, after which 'he asked me what I was going to do. I said I was going to look at the [artillery] barrage. He asked what I'd see and what good I'd do; and he then went on to say that there was now nothing further that I could do to influence the battle. My job, he said, was to go to bed early so as to appear fresh in the morning and be able by my appearance to give confidence to the troops. I had then to be on top of my form so as to accept the inevitable shocks of battle; and be able to plan quickly and soundly the next night's attacks.'[65]

Leese agreed – but still stayed up to watch the spectacle.

A formidable enemy

Retiring to his caravan, meanwhile, Monty wrote up his diary. Major Williams had reported that, according to German Sigint signals the night before and wireless interceptions in the field, the enemy appeared to have no suspicion that the battle was about to begin that night. On 1 October the German front-line fighting strength had exceeded 47,000 men, 520 guns, 231 medium panzers and thirty 88mm anti-aircraft / anti-tank guns; that figure had now risen to 53,000 German troops – with 18,000 more currently arriving.[66] Moreover, German panzer strength had now risen to 249 tanks, all of which were 'Specials' with welded extra breastplates[67] – none of which could be knocked out frontally either by British anti-tank guns or by Grants or Shermans. This gave the Panzer Army a combined armoured strength of 548 tanks, or half the British figure. More ominous, though, Axis field and medium guns now totalled 552, with no fewer than 1,063 anti-tank guns! These included almost 300 PAK 38s – a brilliantly simple, light, low-profiled mobile 50mm anti-tank weapon that could penetrate almost five inches of armour at 500 yards; it included also some seventy converted Russian 7.62 anti-tank PAK 36 guns which could penetrate more than four inches of armour at 1,000 yards, and were almost as powerful and as deadly as German 88mm PAK 43s – of which there were now no fewer than eighty-six in the German line, all mounted on four-wheeled armoured trailers, and able to pierce almost seven inches of armour at 2,500 yards. Though the wheel-bogies were generally removed for firing (the gun resting on splayed, outrigger cruciform 'feet'), the 88 could also be fired off its braked wheels – making it a viciously mobile weapon for enfilading fire. And though Italian tanks were inferior to Grants and Shermans, and Italian infantry varied in quality from its crack Folgore parachute division in the south and the hardened Bersaglieri and Trento divisions in the north, its artillery was powerful, peppered with 'semoventi' 90mm self-propelled assault guns that could be used in an anti-tank role, comparable to 88s. Beyond the half a million mines, the troops of the Panzerarmee Afrika had also grown in number: a formidable enemy comprising 108,000 German and Italian troops, a further 18,000 German reinforcements in the process of arriving, and 77,000 Italian troops beyond them in 'rear areas'.[68]

The polyglot 8th Army

Compared with the straightforward German/Italian make-up of the Panzer Army, 8th Army presented a polyglot collection of nationalities, with divisions and brigades from all over the globe: England, Scotland, Wales, Australia, New Zealand, South Africa, India, Greece and Free France, and smaller units and groups from a dozen other countries, from Czechoslovakia and Poland to Canada and the United States – a 'sort of League of Nations army', as Rommel's ADC later sneered,[69] that numbered almost 195,000 men in the forward area now that the 51st Highland Division and reinforcements had been sent up.

In the air, the Desert Air Force, with American day-bombers and fighters under command, was now backed by growing contingents of Middle East RAF and US Army Air Force bomber forces: all in all, ninety-six squadrons.[70] In artillery, morever, Monty could boast a formidable arsenal: 832 British 25-pounders, 52 4.5 and 5.5 calibre guns, 753 six-pounder anti-tank guns, 521 two-pounders, and 24 105mm self-propelled 'Priest' guns. He had, in addition, 205 Grant tanks and 267 Shermans – though the final deliveries were being made that day, and most units had not had time to accustom themselves to them, let alone rehearse with them.[71] A further 105 Crusaders were with forward units, re-armed with six-pounder guns, though still lacking in armour thickness, and notoriously unreliable. This gave 8th Army a total of 577 reasonably competitive tanks: more than double their German counterparts, though not their technical equals. In addition he had 128 Stuarts, 255 Crusaders with 'peashooters' (two-pounder guns) and 196 Valentines, also mounting two-pounder guns, to complete the 8th Army picture – with 'no reserves of equipment' or infantry, however, so that in the case of casualties 'we have to combine two units into one'. 'I would far rather,' Monty commented, 'have a less number of formations with strong reserves in the depots so that they can be kept up to strength in men and equipment' – something which caused him to wonder: 'What will the situation be when I have had 10,000 or 20,000 casualties in the forthcoming operations, and have also lost a lot of tanks?'[72] He would favour, he noted in his diary, 'doing away with' two armoured and two infantry divisions. In that way he would be able (as he did subsequently) to form reserves for the two primary fighting formations he would then keep in 8th Army: an armoured corps and an infantry corps.

If 8th Army lacked the three-to-one ratio which most military theorists felt guaranteed offensive victory – particularly in the flat, scrubby terrain which offered almost no cover whatsoever, and was sown with deep minefields – Monty betrayed no concern about the 'forthcoming battle'; it was the longer-term outlook which concerned him:

And so we come to D day, and everything is set for a great struggle.

The enemy knows we intend to attack, and has been strengthening his defences. On our side we have the initiative and a great superiority in men, tanks, artillery and other material.

We also have an Army in which the morale is right up on the top line; and every officer and every man knows the issues at stake, knows what is wanted, and knows how the battle will be fought and won.

Where he had qualms was in the area of tank command:

The leadership is all right, and the equipment is all right. The training is NOT all right and that is why we have got to be very careful. Having made a successful 'break-in', we must not rush madly into the mobile battle with wide encircling movements and so on; the troops would all get lost.

We must finish up the 'break-in' battle so positioned that we have the tactical advantage, and will be well positioned to begin the 'crumbling' operations which are designed to destroy all his holding troops.

His armour cannot stand back and look on; it will have to counter-attack, and then we can destroy that too.

The 'break-in' battle has been planned accordingly.

There would be much bloodshed, he knew, but it could not be avoided – indeed, in the long run it would, if the battle proved decisive, save lives. He ended gravely:

The battle will be expensive as it will really become a killing match. I consider that the dog fight of the 'crumbling' operations may last for a week, during which time we shall never let go our stranglehold. I have estimated for 10,000 casualties in this week's fighting.

All we need now is average luck and good weather.[73]

Some time after nine o'clock, having made some further notes on the future of the war as he saw it (including North Africa as the springboard to attack Italy while preparing for the eventual second front) Monty went to sleep. He would, he knew, need it.

Not long afterwards, at precisely 9.40 p.m. on 23 October 1942, 8th Army's artillery barrage opened – the biggest of its kind in the war so far. The ground shook, the cloudless black of the night was lit by the flashing of 882 field and medium guns.

'We have started,' Leese wrote to his wife, having retired to his own caravan: '600 guns on a front of about 7 miles'.[74] Twenty minutes later the first infantry crossed the starting line. The battle of El Alamein had begun.

22

Alamein

Trommelfeur

While Monty slept, the Allied air forces bombed German and Italian communication centres, installations, depots and gun emplacements, carefully identified from aerial reconnaissance photographs, while 8th Army artillery attempted to knock out known enemy batteries as well as pounding Axis forward defences. As they did so, teams of specialist sappers, advancing yard by yard behind the infantry, cleared narrow lanes through the minefields by moonlight – paving the way, it was hoped, for the British armour.

'I knew the attack was to start, so I climbed on to a little hillock to watch,' one regimental doctor recalled. 'After nightfall at 9.40 p.m. every gun in the 8th Army fired. The noise a crashing roaring tearing sound was stupendous. There were two searchlights forming a huge "V" over the enemy lines and two Bofors guns firing steadily upward on fixed lines, their tracer shells showing the direction of the attack ... It was like a gigantic firework display and seemed almost unreal. After about twenty minutes the big guns stopped as suddenly as they had started and small arms fire began in the front lines. This lasted for perhaps a further twenty minutes and also stopped quite suddenly. Dead silence. Then the sound of the bagpipes.'[1]

'What a roar,' Sergeant Bennett noted in his diary. 'From then on it was one continuous roar ... The whole time the barrage was on the ground was shaking and our [signals] office trembling.'[2] Major A. Flatow, of the Royal Tank Regiment, recalled how 'The whole Western sky was lit up with reds and blues and greens and white flashes. Even as far away as we were, the ground shook slightly and the bangs and crashes were continuous. From this distance it sounded as if hundreds of kettledrums were being beaten. It lasted hours. An hour later the word was given to advance and we moved towards that noise!'[3]

A. M. Campbell, member of a field ambulance team, had set up an advanced dressing station just inside the British minefield area; 'the noise was indescribable,' he recalled, 'and the wind created by the blast and the shells screaming overhead was terrific and rather fearsome, while the heavens were lit up by the flashes which were almost continuous. There was a rising moon shining over all.'[4]

For the Germans and Italians it sounded the same – *Trommelfeur*, or drumfire – but the noise and light were accompanied by explosions that caused most to cower in their trenches and pray, for the torrent of TNT was soon augmented by carpet bombing from above. 'Soon it was one sheet of incandescence from end to end,' the Italian historian Paulo Caccia-Dominioni, described. 'The clear, starry sky echoed with the thunder of the barrage and was filled with the blinding light of the flares. At the same time bombs rained down on strong-points and defensive positions, on track and cross-roads, on huddling groups of tents and huts . . .'[5]

And this was but the beginning.

The Somme absolved

'We started on enemy batteries, and as far as one can see his retaliation has been checked,' Leese described to his wife. 'I do pray & trust that all goes well with the infantry.'[6]

Behind a series of timed, shifting barrages the forward infantry of four divisions – Australian, Highland, New Zealand and South African – advanced in the north across the British minefield belts, then no-man's land, and into the 'devil's gardens'. Behind them came the mine-clearing sappers, prodding the sand with bayonets and sweeping with mine detectors, while in the south the British 44th Division attempted the same. As soon as the sappers had swept and marked mine-free lanes, two British armoured divisions in the north, and one in the south, were to pass through them in order to take up hull-down positions with anti-tank guns and artillery, and shield the Commonwealth infantry as they 'crumbled' the German and Italian infantry positions – thus forcing the Axis tank forces into counter-attack and gradual annihilation.

'It is a wonderful moonlight night,' Leese described to his wife, 'and on all the tracks the Armoured Corps is moving up to go through. We think we have deceived him, & that he is expecting us to attack in the dark nights in November. I do hope this is right. At any rate he has not interfered with our concentrations & moves. If we have deceived him, it is a wonderful triumph of staff work. I'm going to bed for a short spell, waiting very very anxiously for news.'[7]

The organization, from camouflage to minefield-marking tapes and paraffin lights, telephone signals layout and interdiction of enemy wireless transmission, was certainly unique in British military history. Guns had been covered in hessian, ammunition buried, and 'sun-shades' put over the tanks to resemble trucks, near the front. 'Where Rommel disguised ordinary vehicles as tanks in order to conceal his weakness,' his former ADC, now commanding a special battalion (Special Group 288) at Alamein, recalled, 'Montgomery with laths, canvas, and sacking now transformed formidable new American tanks into innocuous looking transport vehicles to conceal his strength. There was a new Fox in the desert.'[8]

Everything had a name: 'Green', 'Red' and 'Black' infantry lines progressing to 'Oxalic', 'Blue' and 'Mango' objectives in the north, some three to five miles deep inside the Axis lines, and every enemy strongpoint identified and titled, from 'Aberdeen' and 'Stirling' to 'Perth' and 'Dundee'.

'Sun', 'Moon' and 'Star', 'Bottle', 'Boat' and 'Hat' were the coded – and icon-illustrated – minefield lanes for the follow-up tanks, field artillery, anti-tank guns and motorized troops; 'January' and 'February' were the minefields in the south. Hundreds of distinctively red-capped – not helmeted – military policemen were to mark the routes and marshal units, in the moonlight, as they advanced.

That 8 Army's infantry reached, or almost reached, its XXX Corps objectives in the north by first light on day 1 was indeed a triumph – a tribute to the training, morale and courage of the assault divisions. The humiliation of the Somme, with its 57,000 casualties in the first few hours of 1 July 1916 for no gain, had been absolved, this time in a night attack using the combined efforts, weapons and skills not only of an Allied army, but of air forces and navy – since a squadron of ships was standing off the coast, threatening a landing west of Alamein and thus forcing the Panzer Army to keep forces stationed there to meet the danger. Fleet Air Arm Albacores had dropped pathfinder flares over the German lines to guide in the first of the RAF, South African Air Force, Greek and US Army Air Force bombers and fighters that would pound the enemy throughout the battle.

Thus, receiving the first reports at his special Advance Tac HQ on waking on 24 October 1942, Monty had every reason to feel satisfied. The infantry seemed to be through. Now it would be the turn of the armour.

Getting through

The courage of the infantry at Alamein would go down in history, as almost 10,000 assault troops advanced through uncleared minefields and stormed the Axis outposts, trenches, and strong-points in the moonlight with mortars, Bren guns and rifles. The two Axis minefield belts turned out, in places, to be five, six, even seven belts deep. The fighting was merciless – no quarter being given, lest the taking of prisoners slow down the rate of advance before dawn, or the bypassing of defenders leave pockets of resistance that might hold up the leapfrogging companies that followed. The men had been trained to kill, and to kill at night; it was brutal, surgical – and deadly on both sides, the wounded being left where they lay. German Spandaus, stick grenades, 200lb aerial bombs with trip wires, anti-personnel S mines, anti-vehicle Teller mines, barbed wire and mortars – all had to be faced and overcome in the moonlight by the forward infantry, while the sappers cleared lanes behind them for their support weapons and support tanks, prior to the heavy armoured divisions. The S mines were literally lethal: 'When a foot trod on the detonator there were two distinct explosions, The first flung the mine up in the air and the second explosion was at waist height and it spewed out hundreds of ball bearings horizontally,' Corporal Harris, a sapper at Alamein, recalled. 'I felt sorry for the infantry boys. They had to walk across the minefield and take up defensive positions to keep the Jerries off while our lads got to work.'[9]

One New Zealander wrote home, after the battle, that the 'night attack was really grim. Went in that night with 25 in that platoon and reached the objective with twelve . . . At zero hour we began our advance, keeping 200 yards behind the barrage, and as we moved forward we saw the effect of concentrated artillery first. The desert was pockmarked every few feet with shell holes; his wire was blown to bits.' As the men got deeper into the Axis lines, resistance had become fiercer. 'The rotten part about an attack is that it must go on, and if your best mate goes down beside you

you can't stop. It seems hard and callous, but it's unavoidable. The stretcher bearers and the lightly wounded following up attend to them.'[10]

One stretcher bearer recalled the first casualties coming in. 'We feel sick. The remnants of two platoons lie dead or wounded. In the distance one can see a machine gun post. I start sorting the wounded from the dead.' Night-time navigation was, in such circumstances, morbidly straightforward. 'By the dead and wounded lying on the sand we knew we were going the right way. Minefields everywhere. One of our tanks drives onto a mine. A body appears in the flames . . . I can still hear the scream as he falls back into the tank . . . The Germans start to shell our forward positions. Four lads from "D" Company bring in a wounded mate. A shell bursts among them. We go across to give first aid. One of the casualties has both legs and an arm blown off . . . While I stand there he regains consciousness and starts pleading, "Kill me, God, please kill me." I find I am incapable, and with tears in my eyes cover the body with a greatcoat, thinking how small he looks.'[11]

Thus, at the cost of approximately 3,000 casualties, the infantry part of the 'break-in' phase had succeeded in the north. The Allies were through the forward Axis defences, either deep inside the main defensive layout or slightly beyond it, in an eight-mile-wide salient.

The relentless 'killing match' had already begun. Yet it could not proceed to the extended 'dog-fight' or 'crumbling' stage unless the British armour was passed through the minefield lanes on to ground where it could spread out, support the infantry and lure the Axis forces to counter-attack, on to its anti-tank guns. This, sadly, commanders of the armoured divisions would not, or could not, do.

Still on the ridge

'It was dreadful going, the dust, smoke, etc. making one nearly blind', Captain C.B. Stoddart, a young tank commander, described his passage through the Sun, Moon and Star routes – the sappers having cleared first an eight-feet-wide lane wherever there were mines, then widened it to twenty-four feet, and later forty-eight, with two men roped across the gap and advancing on compass bearings behind the New Zealand infantry. Lifted mines were then placed outside the marking tape and oil-lit posts knocked in. 'We were to follow up through the minefields and pass through at first light to meet the enemy armour, make another gap in the enemy gun line and second defences, and let the main British armour through,' he explained to his father after the battle. As he added, sadly: 'In practice it was very different from the theory.'[12]

It was. The young officer's tank belonged to the Warwickshire Yeomanry – one of the three Territorial regiments of 9th Armoured Brigade detailed to support the New Zealand infantry, and help the main armour of General Gatehouse's 10th Division to pass through on to mine-free ground where the tanks and anti-tank guns could manoeuvre and dig in, hull down, to help lure the enemy armour into counter-attack. The Warwickhire Yeomanry's horses had recently been exchanged for tanks, but little else had changed. The regiment had 'spent one day under camouflage putting the finishing touches and then we were led to the post', Captain Stoddart recorded, in preparation for the 'greatest and most difficult steeplechase of our lives.

'We were superbly mounted and you could see the silhouettes of our horses and those of our friends on the right and the left,' Stoddart narrated, using the hunting language of a Warwickshire country squire. 'We had only got the last of our toys four days before, they were still quite strange to many of us and I'm sure during those long night marches we were asking ourselves – How will my squadron make out? How will my troop make out, and how will I myself make out? And I know I thought of many things which I wished we had practised more, or which I felt we had neglected through shortage of time . . .'

This was to be the core of the armoured tragedy at Alamein – lack of higher training. In the pre-dawn darkness, meanwhile, the 'guide found us and led us to the foot of the Miterya [sic] Ridge – our objective – and I will never forget the sight that met us there. A mass of vehicles – toys like ours, a few of those of our friends [Royal Wiltshire Yeomanry], only a very few who had got through on our left – all crammed into a very small space. The order was given to disperse . . . There was almost nowhere to go, and almost at the same moment the German Artillery opened up on us with its full force.' Where his own artillery was, he had no idea – nor had he been trained to ask. 'We stayed where we were for a while and it was no fun but much worse for the infantry who were feverishly digging like mad. In a few minutes we were ordered to go up onto the ridge and engage the enemy guns . . . Suddenly a terrific explosion, I was at the bottom of my toy and it wouldn't go. I soon found out he'd lost a shoe . . .' With little or no attempt at reconnaissance the tank had struck a mine.

'Eventually we both ran to two more horses and got aboard. To cut a long and exhausting story and day short we continued to engage the enemy without making the required gap, and luckily without too heavy losses . . . as darkness fell we were still on the ridge'[13] – the advance having stalled.

Leese, who had been commanding the Guards Armoured Division in England when summoned to the desert, was appalled. As he wrote to his wife on 26 October, '30 Corps attack was a great success. We had casualties, but not so many as I had feared. Everything went most smoothly, and although there were many more mine fields than we feared, we cleared practically all, and I'm convinced the Armour could have come through, & exploited that critical time, immediately after a successful attack.'[14]

What, then, had gone wrong?

Disgrace or wisdom?

General Gatehouse's 10th Armoured Division was supposed to follow up and pass through 9th Armoured Brigade at dawn, establishing itself with tanks and anti-tank guns and artillery several miles beyond the Miteiriya Ridge before the Germans could erect a gun line. His failure to do so was to produce endless controversy among historians in the years that followed.

Field-Marshal Carver, who was GSO 1 of 7th Armoured Division in the south for the first days of the battle before coming under Lumsden's command in the north, reflected forty years later that Monty would have done far better to have trusted his instinct and either made Horrocks the armoured corps commander in the north, leaving Lumsden out of the battle, as he had at Alam Halfa, or made him a mixed infantry-corps commander alongside Leese, splitting the break-in salient into left- and right-hand corps areas. But would Horrocks, still diffident about his humble regimental background, and no more able to break through the Axis minebelts in the south than Lumsden in the north, have been able to reverse the 'armoured rot'?

The British, as Peter Beale pointed out in *Death by Design*, had invented the tank, but then had failed to develop reliable modern mass-produced tanks in time for World War II, or to install powerful and dual-purpose guns and ammunition in them, or to develop co-operative tactics by which to use them effectively: an almost criminal series of failures. Officer cadets at Sandhurst had not been encouraged to go into the tanks, at all; of the cavalry and yeomanry 'gentlemen' who did, 'the experience taught them dash and unflinching courage, but not always the ability to deal intelligently with military problems on the battlefield'. Asked, as he left England for the Middle East with his regiment, whether everything was in order – ammunition, vehicles, other ranks' training, communications – one typical yeomanry colonel responded: 'Dash it George, I don't know anything about any of that – but we've got forty dozen of champagne, well crated, and the pack of hounds is in fine fettle.'[15]

The truth is, Monty's training instructions for the battle were simply not carried out in many of the armoured formations – something Monty ought to have done more to counter. Simply revising Lumsden's role from break-out to leapfrog, on 6 October 1942, did not, of itself, cure the problem for the tanks. The armoured corps was intended to fight a tightly controlled battle of attrition in tandem with the infantry, using its tanks as bait, in intimate co-operation with anti-tank gunners and field, or even medium, artillery, as the Germans had been doing throughout the campaign in the desert; for this sort of battle, unhappily, Lumsden was entirely the wrong man – and his failure to train his formations was to have almost disastrous consequences. 'All three [armoured] divisions had to receive and absorb new infantry brigades,' Michael Carver recorded, with the added problems of new, untested equipment. The 10th Armoured Division's primary armoured brigade, 8th Armoured Brigade, for example, had been told on 12 October it was to get thirty-three new Sherman tanks instead of Grants; fifteen arrived six days before the battle, and the remainder on the day itself. As the officer commanding 10th Armoured Division's motorized infantry brigade later reflected, there had been 'insufficient time to complete any higher training before going into action'. The arrival of sixteen new six-pounder guns to replace eight two-pounders meant that the 'expanded A/Tk Coys [companies] spent most of the time at A/Tk schools learning the drill and technique of the 6 pounder'. As a result, battalion units in the brigade 'only became complete entities shortly before moving up to the battle, and the Bde went into action faced with the problem of learning the higher training, "the hard way" – under enemy fire'.[16]

Without higher training, and struggling to learn the ins and outs of new equipment and organization, the British tank regiments remained 'racially pure', as Rommel mocked. Sadly, even the 1941 so-called 'tank parliament' in England, under Churchill, had produced no effective change in British amateurism – despite the head of the Royal Armoured Corps, General Martel, urging better training establishments, better repair/maintenance units and, above all, 'cooperation between armoured forces and the RAF on a sound footing'.[17]

Churchill had closed down the parliament; the RAF had proved, sadly, as 'racially pure' as the RAC; and the years it would take to develop RAF tank-busting co-operation, in imitation of Panzer–Stuka–88mm co-operation, would become one of the great air-force scandals of World War I – epitomized, when such co-operation finally began to materialize, by the development of the RAF's rocket-firing Typhoon, a strafing aircraft without armour-plating on its underside! Meanwhile, even at Sandhurst in 1942, after a year of British misfortunes in the desert in fighting Rommel, Royal Armoured Corps officer-trainees were denied instruction, Beale recorded, in even the rudiments of 'commanding tanks or learning troop tactics in the field'.[18]

Above all, however, by failing to develop its own 3.7 anti-aircraft gun as a dual-purpose weapon, given its almost identical range, weight of shell, penetration, rate of fire, and size to the 88, the British had stuck their heads in the literal as well as proverbial sand, placing themselves for years at a disadvantage on the battlefield – a place, moreover, where American technology, although it had produced two wonderfully reliable and well-armoured tanks in the Grant and the Sherman, could not rescue the British.

Thus, for better or for worse, Gatehouse's 10th Armoured Division, with its newly acquired Shermans, did not pass through the infantry and yeomanry tank regiments at dawn on 24 October. In Monty's view it was a disgrace; in the view of the British armoured commanders, given the killing power of the German 88s, a sign of worldly wisdom.

Lumsden's lack of pep

'So far as I remember,' Lumsden's chief of operations staff, Brigadier Ralph Cooney, recalled in a letter to the Cabinet Office historian, 'the Wiltshire Yeomanry had run into minefields well covered by enemy anti tank guns on the far side of the Miteiriya Ridge. The New Zealand Division, though they had seized the crest of the ridge and passed leading

Infantry sub-units over it had not cleared all the minefields on the far side. Herbert Lumsden always took a poor view of a tank attack on a minefield even with good artillery support. So I think that [the] New Zealand Division may well have had a feeling that the armour was failing to exploit their success though I feel that they may also have realised that they had not quite succeeded in opening a clear way through the enemy defences which would give the armoured division an adequate start off in a daylight operation.'[19]

For Monty – as would happen again during the D-Day landings in Normandy – the failure of the British armour to strike out and exploit the enemy's confusion on the first day, after a night of brilliant and devastating artillery barrage, was galling. In vain, he tried to put more 'ginger' into Lumsden. He had intended, in his revised battle plan, that 'At dawn on D plus 1 day we will begin "crumbling" operations; it is essential to my plans to begin these operations at dawn', while the enemy was still in shock. His frustration at the lack of 'drive' on the part of the British armoured commanders thus spoke out from every 8th Army signal recorded that day, as well as in his diary.

Already at 5.50 a.m. Monty had sent a message to main 8th Army HQ warning that, while the New Zealand division had 'no a/tk guns or tanks' up, it had got beyond the vital Miteiriya Ridge; the air forces could compound the confusion in the German high command by helping the Australians to begin crumbling immediately on the northern flank of the salient, towards the coast: 'if Aust Div had only slight casualties the Army Commander may decide to attack on coastal sector to clear up that while the going is good. Heavy bomber support will be required.'[20]

In fact the New Zealanders had got the furthest; the Australians, and the Highlanders on their left, had met increasingly fierce resistance – and instead of fighting its way through with tanks to join and pass through the forward infantry line in the salient, Lumsden's right-hand division, 1st Armoured Division, had waited for a safe passage first to be cleared, like belles waiting to go on stage.

The Highlanders, in the middle, had met the toughest opposition and suffered the heaviest casualties of all; although on target alongside the New Zealanders on the left, they were in places only two-thirds of the way through to their objectives in the centre of the break-in salient. As a result, on both left and right sides of the salient, the *corps de chasse* had failed, at dawn, to pass through a single brigade of tanks. As Monty noted in his diary:

On the right, 1 Armd Div could not get out into the open because of the resistance still not overcome by 51 Div.

On the left 10 Armd Div could not cross the MITERIYA [sic] Ridge without heavy casualties owing to heavy fire from enemy artillery and A.Tk guns to the S. West.

This was galling, as the enemy, alerted to the geography of the break-in, could simply pass an anti-tank and artillery cordon of 88 and 7.6 anti-tank guns around it, unless 8th Army forced the enemy to counter-attack with tanks.

I began to form the impression at about 1100 hours that there was a lack of 'drive' and pep in the action of 10 Corps. I saw Herbert LUMSDEN and impressed on him the urgent need to get his armoured divisions out into the open where they could manoeuvre, and that they must get clear of the minefield area. He left me about 1130 hours to visit his Divisions. So far he has not impressed me by his showing in battle; perhaps he has been out here too long; he has been wounded twice. I can see that he will have to be bolstered up and handled firmly.

Possibly he will be better when the battle gets more mobile.

This 'sticky' fighting seems beyond him.[21]

It was beyond most of the British tank commanders of the day, too.

In the inferno

In his analysis of British tank development before and during World War II Peter Beale noted how, in the second half of 1942, the priorities of tank policy were suddenly reversed: the 'normal role' of the tank becoming first and foremost the ability to fire high explosive at enemy personnel: namely, the men manning the enemy's artillery, anti-tank weapons and heavy machine-guns.[22]

This change, Beale suspected, was brought about by the battle of Alamein — and there is little doubt that this was so. The killing ground of Alamein finally proved that, against a first-class, determined enemy, dug-in and armed with superlative weapons such as the 88, the Allies would have to alter their tactics, training and leadership to take out the 88s, not simply panzers. In particular, British armoured units and formations would have to learn the value of concentrated artillery on immediate call via forward fire officers, and to rethink their very role as armour. Pursuit, or *chasse*, would henceforth be a secondary role.

This was a lesson learned, however, in the inferno of Alamein.

A tragedy

For Monty, the failure of the armour to get out of the minefields at dawn on the first full day of the battle and to exploit the enemy's confusion was, and would always remain, a tragedy. General Leese, commanding XXX Corps, privately considered that in missing this opportunity, General Lumsden very nearly lost the battle for 8th Army – indeed, that if Monty had accepted Lumsden's growing defeatism at the end of the first full day (D1), the battle might well have proved a failure, like Rommel's at Alam Halfa – and with equally dire strategic consequences: demoralization of Allied forces in the Middle East, the loss of Malta, rapid build-up of German and Italian forces in North Africa together with improved equipment (such as the Tiger tank), as well as fierce Vichy resistance to the Anglo-American Torch invasions . . .

Monty's – and Leese's – frustration at Lumsden's lack of drive has been refuted by armoured apologists who excuse the poor performance of the British tanks, pointing out the difficulty in getting them through the incompletely swept minefields towards the front, and especially to their vulnerability to German anti-tank weapons, in particular the Panzer Army's dreaded 88s, when they did get out. In the exposed terrain beyond the Miteiriya Ridge, they argue, the British armour could be – and were – picked off like proverbial ducks, to no worthwhile effect.

In terms of individual tanks, this was all too true. Only by co-ordinating their assault tactics with brigade, divisional and corps artillery, even Desert Air Force daylight bombing – which forced the 88s to raise their barrels and give away their positions – could the British armoured divisions have, by combined action, overrun the rear defensive line of the Panzer Army, stopped the enemy from laying fresh minefields, and forced the enemy to begin committing his armour piecemeal, on the first day of battle, while the Axis commander (General Stumme) lay dead on the battlefield, and Rommel was still in Austria.

Lumsden's chief of operations staff accepted that the armour's performance appeared dismal. 'Possibly 10 Armoured Division was a little sticky,' he later confessed. 'It was their first battle. But I doubt if a more experienced formation would have done much better in the circumstances. 1st Armoured Division were up against a similar problem to the north of them and were equally accused of lack of dash.'[23]

They were. Monty's dissatisfaction with Lumsden, as corps commander in control of the two armoured divisions in the salient, certainly grew worse as the hours of 24 October ticked away, and the Germans even began to lay new minefields around the Allied salient in broad daylight, under the protective fire of their own guns: Spandaus, field-guns, anti-tank guns, 15th Panzer Division tanks, and howitzers, while the British armour failed to use its artillery to interdict the enemy, or cover its own advance. 'The armour now had a great opportunity,' Leese wrote in his unpublished account of the battle. 'Rommel had not yet returned from Italy. There was no controlling head and for once the Panzer Corps was fighting piecemeal. General von Stumme had been killed by shell fire . . . and if we could only have broken out during the early morning of the first day, we would have had a good chance to destroy the German armour piecemeal. But by midday on that day it was obvious that the armour had not broken through and to me it was very doubtful whether they could now do so.'[24]

Freyberg had called for a co-ordinated infantry/armour/artillery advance soon after dawn, but could not contact either General Gatehouse, commanding the 10th Armoured Division, or Lumsden! A tactical reconnaissance flight at 9 a.m had reported 'General impression: no movement in any direction'[25] – while Gatehouse's report to Lumsden spoke of 'few of our infantry on South of [Miteiriya] Ridge', and claimed he was 'holding' the ridge with the tank regiments of his 8th Armoured Brigade, and that there was 'much congestion of transport, guns and tanks in NZ area'.

General Leese, visiting the area that morning, was unimpressed by such timidity and lack of determination. At 8 a.m. he had suggested to Lumsden there was even enough space to re-route and bring General Briggs' 1st Armoured Division through the cleared New Zealand 'funnel', in order to outflank the German strong-points holding up the Highland Division in the centre. With the backing of the artillery of both X and XXX Corps, he was certain, it would be possible to penetrate yet deeper into the Axis lines, where there were fewer fixed defences, no minefields, and the infantry could crumble the Axis positions from the flank and even rear.

Had Leese been given overall power of command over the infantry and armoured corps divisions for the break-in phase of the battle, Monty could have reinforced success and outflanked resistance, but with five divisions and two tank brigades already under command in XXX Corps – comprising 90,000 men – this was not humanly possible. Yet to leave Lumsden in command of 8th Army's two armoured divisions in the salient proved a terrible mistake. The performance of a formation, like a unit, reflects the will, determination and professionalism of its commander; Lumsden's weak will as a higher commander was therefore reflected in each link in the downward chain of field command: artillery, engineers, infantry and tank commanders. As Leese reported to Monty, Gatehouse's 'main preoccupation at the moment is to get 10 Armoured Div into position to receive attack from someone else', rather than to expand 8th Army's bridgehead. In frustration, Leese offered to put his entire corps artillery behind Freyberg's New Zealand Division if they would attack that afternoon, under smoke, to help get Gatehouse 'out'. 'Now there is hardly anything happening.'[26]

In Monty's situation, Rommel would himself have now taken charge, driving the panzer divisions forward, probing for the weakest link in the enemy's defences and exploiting it, as he had attempted to do at Alam Halfa; yet Rommel commanded a professionally battle-drilled Panzer Army, which had refined its skills over the previous eighteen months; Monty had been in command of 8th Army for nine weeks, was commanding the often recalcitrant formations of seven different countries – formations which, true to their heritage as old-fashioned democracies, had little notion of 'higher training': namely, the co-ordination of infantry, artillery, armour, anti-tank guns and air forces in battle. Indeed, the state of 8th Army training was, as Monty had noted in his diary, nowhere near that of the Afrika Korps – and even with that famed Korps under his command, out beyond the British minefields at Alam Halfa on 1 September, Rommel had himself failed to make any headway: had hit a wall of enemy air, tank, anti-tank, infantry and artillery fire, forcing him to falter on the first morning of the battle, after the hold up in the British minefields – and within three days to withdraw!

Should Monty have done the same – calling off the battle, sacking Lumsden and the senior armoured generals, and withdrawing to retrain the British armour himself ? To do so, having delayed the British offensive already by a month, was unthinkable. Torch was set for 8 November, in two weeks' time. Somehow he would have to 'kick ass' until the armour began to carry out its assigned role, however unwilling.

Soon after midday on 24 October Monty signalled to both Leese and

Lumsden that it was 'necessary to get the armoured divisions out through 30 Corps final objective before the enemy can ring them in still further'. General Lumsden was to 'meet Gen. Leese at NZ Div HQ and arrange support of 30 Corps artillery to get 10 Armoured Div out through the NZ Div front. The plan must be really properly teed up with adequate artillery support, hence the necessity of starting early, if the operation is to be brought off this afternoon.'[27]

Leese duly met Lumsden at Freyberg's headquarters, but to Leese's dismay Freyberg, after listening to Lumsden's faintheartedness, counselled a *night* attack by the armour, when the infantry tanks would be less conspicuous to German anti-tank gunners. Monty sent a message that 'Army Commander considers it essential to get 10 Armoured Div out this afternoon'[28] – but it was to no avail. The front, won at such terrible cost in infantry blood and courage, was already congealing, ringed-in by local Axis artillery and 88s, leaving 8th Army locked inside a vast minefield salient, where movement outside the cleared areas risked death and destruction from the myriad flowers in the devil's gardens – and into which German and Italian artillery could lob high-explosive shells at will, hitting ammunition lorries, petrol trucks and supply vehicles by the score. Stukas were putting in more and more sorties – as many as thirty divebombing raids were counted that day.

'D day – what is to be the outcome?' Brigadier Hollworthy, commanding one of the weak infantry brigades in 4th Indian Division, just south of the salient, had asked in his diary the previous night. 'I do not expect too much, but keep that to myself'[29] – his diffidence reflecting the bitter experiences of the 'old' 8th Army.

Disturbed that his battle plan was fast disintegrating after such a magnificent infantry effort, Monty told Lumsden yet again he *must* get his right-hand armoured division up and through the Highland Division's front by nightfall, whatever the casualties – 'the main lack of offensive eagerness was in the North', he wrote in his own diary; 'both 9 Aust Div and 51 Div were quite clear that 1 Armd Div could have got out without difficulty in the morning. Lumsden was not displaying that drive and determination that is so necessary when things begin to go wrong; there was a general lack of offensive eagerness in 10 Corps.'[30]

Monty was adamant. This was war; in fact, it was a decisive battle for the Western world. Three thousand brave men had been killed and wounded to get 8th Army this far; the armour *must* now play its full part. 'I therefore spoke to LUMSDEN in no uncertain voice, and told him he must "drive" his Divisional Commanders, and that if BRIGGS and FISHER hung back any more [in the right-hand funnel] I would at once remove them from command and replace them by better men.'[31]

On Leese's orders another infantry attack by 51st Division was launched at 3 p.m., clearing an indisputable passage through the minefields for 1st Armoured Division; at 3.45 p.m. 8th Army headquarters noted that 'in the North 1st Armoured Division is being pressed to push on by Army Commander', whatever the casualties – in fact Briggs, stung by the threat of dismissal, told Fisher, his forward brigade commander, he must break out 'at all costs. Fisher enquired: "Do you mean 'at all costs' literally?" To which Briggs replied: "Yes, I do." '[32]

Within half an hour news came that the forward armoured brigade of 1st Armoured Division had at last 'found a gap and will go through when they have finished mopping up'.[33] 'Adv[ance] of 2 AB rather sticky,' Briggs noted in his diary, 'but application of "ginger" had remarkable effect.'[34] By early evening elements of 1st Armoured Division seemed finally 'out' beyond the forward infantry. 'My application, of "ginger" had worked,' Monty also noted with relief in his diary,[35] for by 5.20 p.m. Fisher's 2nd Armoured Brigade reported itself – erroneously – to be on 'Pierson', the original Lightfoot objective of the Armoured Corps, bounded on the northern extremity by a mild, kidney-shaped elevation known as Kidney Ridge.

As the evening light faded General von Thoma, the Afrika Korps commander – who had temporarily assumed command of the Panzer Army after von Stumme's death that morning – put in the first of the armoured counter-attacks Monty had hoped for, impaling units of 15th Panzer and Littorio Divisions on 8th Army's gun and tank line, and losing twenty-six Axis tanks in the process. The battle, in the right-hand sector of the salient at least, was back on track.

In the left-hand sector, however, there was less good news. Lumsden's 6.45 p.m. signal reporting that Gatehouse's armoured brigade was held up by German minefields 'laid today' below the Miteiriya Ridge infuriated Monty – particularly Lumsden's claim that the minefield was 'covered by guns and M.G's and a force of tanks – probably 21 Panzer'[36] – for 21st Panzer Division, Monty was quite sure, was still way down in the south, guarding against possible breakthrough by Horrocks's XIII Corps. To add insult to injury Lumsden had even signalled that 'location of 24 Armoured Brigade', the second armoured brigade in Gatehouse's division, was 'not known'![37]

Monty knew it was important, however, to remain calm; the battle had only just begun, and Rommel was unlikely to have arrived yet. At Monty's insistence Gatehouse had drawn up plans for a night attack from the Miteiriya Ridge, so that the New Zealand Division would at last be able to start its crumbling operations to the south-west of the salient. Satisfied – given a message from Lumsden that 1st Armoured Division definitely had tanks in action on the Pierson line at 9 p.m. and that the 10th Armoured Division would be out on the same 'shielding' objective by midnight, with its right-hand brigade in supporting distance of 1st Armoured Division's forward regiments – Monty turned in. The first full day of battle was over. With the armour 'out', using cover, its anti-tank weapons and its artillery, the dog-fight could soon begun: the crumbling of Rommel's infantry defences north and south of the salient, luring the Axis armour into abortive counter-attack.

Risking losses

Did Monty underestimate the difficulties faced by his British armoured formations? Lumsden's chief of operations (Lumsden was killed in the Pacific in 1945), Brigadier Cooney, agreed that there were 'many bitter things said by the Infantry Commanders about the armour during these few days', but Cooney blamed this on the 'rather hazy ideas most of these Infantry Commanders had as to the capabilities of armour. They expected the armour to fight and manoeuvre whilst constricted on all sides by minefields covered by anti-tank guns. The armoured commanders usually refused to play this game; when they did they invariably had very heavy losses. The whole plan for the exploitation on the 24th October depended on a clear breach of the enemy defended system on the night 23/24th October. In the event it took eleven days to effect this breach.'[38]

This was a travesty of Monty's revised, 'crumbling' battle plan, though all too true of the attitude of armoured commanders. No mention of 'clear breaches' had been made in 8th Army plans since September, indeed, the armoured commanders had been told to fight their way through if there were hold-ups; it was, once again, the 'racially-pure' syndrome manifesting itself.

The fact was, unless the tanks, their guns and lorried infantry, could debouch from the aptly named 'Bottle' and other minefield lanes, they could not be deployed; to achieve this, they had to be prepared to lift mines – for which they had their own specialist sapper teams, with hundreds of mine detectors and men. They had then to be prepared to work with the infantry divisions and their artillery; and be willing to risk losses – which would save lives later. As Peter Beale commented, 'It is a paradox for a soldier that the more you are prepared to put yourself at risk, the less likely you are to reap the consequences of that risk; the more you are prepared to die the less likely you are to die.'[39] But to reach such a state of battle-readiness, bold leadership is required: leaders driving men to strike hard to attain their objectives whatever the casualties in the opening phase, and thus save greater casualties later. This the Commonwealth infantry commanders and their troops had done, and in a manner that would go down in history. The same could not be said of the British armoured commanders.

In Monty's view – as well as Leese's, and most of the infantry commanders' – the higher tank commanders, by failing to order their regiments to be prepared to take heavy casualties in making their advance through and beyond the 'vast minefield area' of the infantry salient on the first night of battle, had effectively stoppered the armoured corps' own bottle – leaving the massive, concentrated power of two British armoured divisions, with their artillery and lorried infantry, stuck behind, in and around the narrow minefield lanes cleared by the sappers. Resolute leading would have uncorked the bottles containing almost 700 tanks and hundreds of guns, however many were lost in the process; but of resolute leadership there had so far been all too little.

Crisis

Worse was now to come. Monty had given strict instructions he should not be woken in the night except in case of emergency. When he awoke in the early hours of Sunday, 25 October 1942, it was to see the anxious face of his chief of staff, Brigadier de Guingand. It was nearly 3 a.m.

De Guingand explained.

From 'J' reports (wireless interceptions of 8th Army's own signals between commanders and units), it was clear the battle beyond the Miteiriya Ridge – where Gatehouse's 10th Armoured Division was meant to be breaking out with tanks and troops of the New Zealand Division to its assigned objective on the Pierson line – was going badly. An entire column of 'soft-skinned' transport, including ammunition and petrol trucks, had been hit by German bombers, providing an illuminated target for further Axis bombardment; the old and new enemy minefields were proving arduous to clear, and the tank regiments – who disliked night movement – were protesting at their mounting losses, in fact were refusing to go on. Freyberg's own armoured brigade, the 9th, had reached the Pierson line, where it was to provide flank protection for the armoured division's regiments – but the commander of 8th Armoured Brigade, in 10th Armoured Division, had appealed to General Gatehouse as divisional commander to cancel the attack! Lumsden, the corps commander, was not up with Gatehouse, nor were they in telephone or radio communication; Gatehouse had therefore come back eight miles to his main headquarters, inside the old British lines, to telephone Lumsden. As Lumsden had already told Leese he was not keen on the operation, de Guingand felt the situation was getting out of hand; that the battle was in danger of falling apart through lack of determination among the armoured commanders.

Colonel Charles Richardson, who was sharing a tent with de Guingand, vividly recalled the moment. 'I woke up to find Freddie fully dressed and looking worried. "What's going on?" I asked. Freddie replied guardedly: "Things aren't so hot, I'm getting the corps commanders to come and see the Army Commander." '[40]

To de Guingand's great credit as a chief of staff, Richardson felt, he had 'decided the battle had reached a crisis which only the Army Commander could solve, and immediately by telephone convened a conference at Montgomery's Tactical HQ for 3.30'.[41] 'They're coming along at 3.30? I agree with you – quite right,' Monty had told de Guingand. 'I'll be there.'[42]

De Guingand himself described what happened. 'I led the generals along the little path to the lorry. Inside, Montgomery was seated on a stool carefully examining a map fixed to the wall. He greeted us all most cheerfully, motioning us to sit down, and then asked each corps commander to tell his story. He listened very quietly, only occasionally interrupting with a question. There was a certain "atmosphere" present, and careful handling was required. Lumsden was obviously not very happy about the role his armour had been given.'[43]

As Richardson noted, this was a 'diplomatic' understatement; in fact the New Zealand Division's yeomanry tanks had advanced across the Miteiriya Ridge at 10 p.m. on 24 October, with General Freyberg leading the way in his Honey, or Stuart M5 light tank. They were to be followed by Gatehouse's 8th Armoured and 24th Armoured Brigades from 10th Armoured Division, with their infantry and anti-tank guns. Having sustained relatively light casualties on mines, however, Gatehouse's tanks had held back. At 1.40 a.m. on 25 October Gatehouse had referred the decision as to whether to continue to Lumsden – who, miles away from the action, had prevaricated.

Whether it was de Guingand's briefing that misled Monty is difficult to say. According to Monty's own diary he began the conference believing that all was going well in the battle, save on General Gatehouse's sector of the Miteiriya Ridge. At 2.30 a.m., Monty recorded, 1st Armoured Division was 'out in the open' on the right of the salient; on the left of the salient '9 Armd Bde of NZ Div was through the minefield and was planning to move SW in accordance with the ['crumbling'] plan'; while Horrocks's XIII Corps in the far south, near Himeimat, had reported that '7 Armd Div had cleared gaps in the minefield and that the leading Armd Bde was moving West to pass through into the open.'[44]

In contrast to this positive picture, Monty noted in his diary, '10 Corps reported that the break-out of 10 Armd Div was not proceeding well and that minefields and other difficulties were delaying progress. GATEHOUSE had said he did not care about the operation and that if he did get out he would be in a very unpleasant position on the forward slopes of the MITERIYA Ridge; his Division was untrained and not fit for such difficult operations; he wanted to stay where he was. LUMSDEN was inclined to agree with GATEHOUSE.'[45]

By 3 a.m., Monty's diary entry ran: 'it was clear to me that my orders about the armour getting out into the open were in danger of being compromised by the disinclination of GATEHOUSE to leave his hull-down positions on the MITERIYA Ridge. LUMSDEN was agreeing with GATE-HOUSE and some quick and firm action was necessary.'[46]

From Monty's point of view, his entire plan of battle woud be vitiated unless the British armoured divisions got beyond the infantry, and could lure the Axis armour on to their anti-tank weapons. The Miteiriya Ridge was a good defensive position, but this was not Alam Halfa; the ridge did not, in itself, pose any real threat to the integrity of the Axis defensive line at Alamein – particularly when ringed-in by fresh minefields. The armour *must* move beyond the infantry, and provoke the enemy into counter-attack, however many tanks were lost in the process.

Lumsden accepted the need for this – and begged the army commander to speak personally to Gatehouse on the telephone. It was an all-too revealing admission of Lumsden's own weakness of authority, which Monty noted in his battle diary: 'GATEHOUSE wanted to withdraw both . . . Armd Bdes back behind the minefields and to give up all the advantages he had gained; his reason was that his situation out in the open would be very unpleasant and he might suffer heavy casualties. LUMSDEN agreed with GATEHOUSE. The real trouble is that LUMSDEN is frightened of GATEHOUSE and won't give him firm orders.'[47]

Neither Lumsden nor Gatehouse seemed able to understand that, unless the armour got out beyond the minefields, the infantry's 'crumbling' operations on the New Zealand flank would be self-defeating, and the enemy might not be obliged to counter-attack with armour at all. The battle would then come to a halt.

Whatever the casualties, therefore, Monty knew he must keep the initiative, and therefore must step up the pressure. Having berated Gatehouse on the telephone and insisted he 'fight his way out', Monty 'spoke very plainly to LUMSDEN and said I would have no departure of any sort from my original plan and orders; I was determined that the armour would get out from the minefield area and out into the open where it could manoeuvre; any wavering or lack of firmness now might be fatal; if GATEHOUSE, or any other Commander, was not "for it" and began to weaken, then I would replace him in command at once.

'I then issued definite orders [to this effect] to 10 Corps and to 30 Corps.'[48]

De Guingand, both in his post-war account *Operation Victory* and to the end of his life, maintained that without this display of resolution by the army commander, the whole British offensive at Alamein might have foundered: 'Unless it had been made I am firmly convinced that the attack might well have fizzled out, and the full measure of success we achieved might never have been possible. The meeting broke up,' de Guingand declared, 'with no one in any doubt as to what was in the Commander's mind.'[49]

General Leese felt exactly the same: 'There is no doubt in my mind that this Conference cleared any shadow of doubt from anyone's mind as to the Army Commander's intention.'[50]

Intention was one thing, however; actuality another.

A shambles

Monty had once again sent his own ADC, the fearless John Poston, up to the front to bring back a personal report. 'During the opening stages of the battle I had to do close liaison work for Monty,' Poston described in a letter to his family after the battle. 'I used to be out practically all day and sometimes a good deal at night. And often I used to crawl about like a 1918 infantry soldier. Very frightening at times, as Monty used to send me off to find the precise situation on a certain piece of the front. I used to go through with the N. Z. Division in a night attack & return in the morning with the exact situation. There were two of us doing the job, and we had some very exciting times' – which included walking through 'one of the gaps in the minefields and the Huns started a straffe on it. I lay for ½ an hour in a foot of "Talcum" powder sand and thought my last moment had come. Remember, always before I had been in an Armoured Car, but this time I was a "pukka Infantry Wallah"!'[51]

Monty's map was, in this way, as accurate as any in 8th Army. Having got a few more hours' sleep, Monty awoke again at dawn on 25 October, satisfied he had put iron into Lumsden's and Gatehouse's souls. At 8 a.m. he noted with satisfaction in his diary that Gatehouse's right-hand armoured brigade, 24th Armoured Brigade, 'had broken through into the open', indeed, had linked hands with Briggs' 1st Armoured Division to the north, and was now 'alongside the left regiment of 2nd Armoured Brigade on "Pierson"'. Monty's armoured shield was thus 'out', at least at the head of the British salient; over to the left of it, the whole of the 9th Armoured Brigade were 'through the minefield' and ready to support the New Zealand Division's 'crumbling' operations, with one regiment of Gatehouse's 8th Armoured Brigade 'out' to its right, within supporting distance of 24th Armoured Brigade, forming a sort of armoured halo or helmet, beyond the minefields, behind which the infantry could 'crumble' to the north and south, forcing the enemy to counter-attack. 'And so all was now working out well, and we were in the positions we had hoped to have been in at 0800 hours on 24 October,' Monty added. 'It is a good thing I was firm with LUMSDEN and GATEHOUSE last night.'[52]

These were famous last words. 'It is amazing how many weak Commanders we have,' Monty meanwhile reflected. 'At one stage in the battle yesterday the whole of 10 Corps was inactive and doing nothing, waiting for other people to do things. There was no "drive" to get things done, and to get a move on; the whole show had to be galvanized into action, and I had to do this myself. However, all is now well-placed for us to crack along and to keep the initiative; there was a danger yesterday that we might lose the initiative.'[53]

The truth, though, was very different. However crucial the 'removal of doubt' from a psychological point of view, the fact was, 8th Army's armoured offensive, designed to shield the New Zealand Division 'crumbling' operations and lure the Axis armour to counter-attack, was already foundering, at least on the left flank. At 7.15 a.m., under the illusion that Gatehouse had cleared the minefields so that he could pass through the remaining regiments of 8th Armoured Brigade, Monty had confirmed his orders to Lumsden: namely, to 'locate and destroy enemy armoured Battle Groups' and to 'ensure that [crumbling] operations of 2 New Zealand Division South-West from Miteiriya Ridge are not interfered with by enemy armoured forces in the West'.[54] But he was confirming an order that had been overtaken by events in the field – for Gatehouse had sent out no artillery or infantry; indeed, he had already withdrawn *all* units of his 8th Armoured Regiment behind the Miteiriya Ridge, where his lorried infantry brigade was still sheltering. This left the tanks of Freyberg's yeomanry regiments 'out', but alone now, without support from Gatehouse's armoured division's powerful artillery, 250 tanks or 4,000 infantry soldiers. It was, in sum, a shambles.

Among the white tennis balls

Captain Stoddart, in a letter to his father, described how, at 9.30 the previous night, 'we rumbled forward again to start the 48th hour without sleep. We got to the Ridge, passed a mass of burning vehicles – one of the worst sights I have ever seen.'[55] This was the conflagration caused by twenty-two trucks with petrol, oil and ammunition exploding and burning – in some cases 'the charred bodies of their drivers and mates still upright in their cabs, as they had been at the moment when the attack fell on them'.[56] Nevertheless 'We crept forward of the Ridge and through the mines without incident and got to our correct position two miles on without damage at all. Guy [Jackson, troop commander and a Master of the Hounds in England] was beyond all praise.'[57]

Gatehouse's armoured division had made heavier weather of the advance.

On the right of the attack, Gatehouse's 24th Armoured Brigade had found the going equally simple, but in the centre his 8th Armoured Brigade found the business of mine-clearing arduous, and costly in casualties. Only one regiment had initially got through, on to the Pierson line, although the other two eventually joined it – and were then ordered back by Gatehouse!

The situation, for the tank commanders, was certainly menacing. 'Came the dawn and the ground looked frightful,' Stoddart described the situation on the left. 'The Bosche started shooting flares over us, and then came in the 3/4 light the dreaded bouncing, gleaming "white tennis ball", the fastest I've ever seen, shot from the 88mm gun. Very quickly our friends on the left [Staffordshire Yeomanry] started to blow up and catch fire [British tanks, unlike the Germans, did not store their ammunition in fire-retarding bins]. Guy saved us. He called up one squadron leader to ask him what the going was like where he was and Peter Samuel replied it was worse than the Garth country and more wire than the Fernie. Guy put him in a better position. He asked me what it was like where we were and I told it was as flat as a tennis court. He put us all right. The tennis balls came very close to us all and too close to one or two, but Guy manoeuvred us so that we got into a good position for retaliation and could not get into really serious trouble. After this it gradually became lighter, we could see more and a considerable fight ensued against the opposition guns and tanks. We had a battle royal till 3 p.m.'[58]

This was exactly what Monty had intended by his 'crumbling' tactics. As Brigadier Lucas Phillips later chronicled, the two regiments of yeomanry of 9th Armoured Brigade, supported by New Zealand artillery, infantry and smoke, knocked out some thirteen Axis tanks and ten guns, as well as capturing hundreds of Axis infantrymen – beginning the dog-fight process Monty had ordered, and intending, under the brigade's gallant Brigadier John Currie, to advance still further at nightfall on 25 October.[59] Currie had even climbed on to a Warwickshire Yeomanry tank, when his own was hit, and had 'sallied forth' to deal personally with a German battery of 55mm guns, forcing the Germans to abandon their positions! Freyberg, likewise, had criss-crossed the battlefield in his light tank. Currie was therefore disbelieving when he was ordered, on the evening of 25 October, to withdraw all his forces behind the Miteiriya Ridge. Stoddart was, too. 'At 3.30 p.m. we had done well and thought we had the gap and were through,' he wrote to his father. 'I still think so but the order came to withdraw to the Ridge again.'[60]

What, then, had happened?

Bêtes noires

Perhaps the full truth will never be known. What appears to have happened is that Gatehouse, like the commander of his 8th Armoured Brigade, quite simply lost his nerve. As Brigadier Lucas Phillips, the foremost historian of the battle, recorded, Gatehouse had deliberately lied to Lumsden and Montgomery from his headquarters, claiming he could only get one regiment out on to the 'Wiska' Ridge alongside 9th Armoured Brigade, on the Pierson line; in fact by dawn all three of his 8th Brigade regiments, as well as infantry, had got out beyond the minefields; but when the forward regiment, the Staffordshire Yeomanry, suffered a devastatingly accurate early-morning onslaught from 88mm guns, their commander had driven back to the Miteiriya Ridge and in tears had begged Gatehouse to be allowed to retreat. 'Two nights of fighting had cost him thirteen of his fifteen Crusaders, fourteen out of his twenty-eight heavies,' Brigadier Lucas Phillips recounted. 'He was certain to lose more if he stayed out in the open and he asked Gatehouse's permission to withdraw.'[61]

Gatehouse, having lied to Monty about the number of regiments 'out', now disobeyed him; he not only gave Lieutenant-Colonel Eadie permission to retreat, but concealed from Monty the successful advance of the two other regiments of his 8th Brigade. Instead, using Monty's 4.45 a.m. order permitting him to 'retain' them for the moment on the Miteiriya Ridge, he withdrew them from battle, too, leaving the tanks of the New Zealand Division's 9th Armoured Brigade out on the Pierson line, on their own, all day, as Captain Stoddart described to his father.

It was a sorry tale of courage on the part of individual tank commanders, but loss of nerve on the part of the more senior officers. Gatehouse had failed to get either his lorried infantry brigade or his anti-tank guns on to the Wiska line; 'racial purity' had come before multi-culturalism. As the New Zealand official historian, Robin Walker, put it, the armour was perpetuating 'the tradition, established by General Gott (under whom both Lumsden and Gatehouse had served) of giving lip service to the plans but holding to a determination to run the armoured battle its own way'[62] – thus making the armoured divisions the *bêtes noires* of 8th Army's infantry.

The bitter truth

At 10.30 a.m. on the second morning of the battle of Alamein, nine weeks into his new command, Monty began to realize the magnitude of his predecessor Auchinleck's problems – problems which, sadly, the 'Auk' had only made worse by his policy of 'Jock columns', 'boxes', and keeping his formations 'in being'. Monty was informed that Briggs' 1st Armoured Division was *not* on its objective, Pierson – indeed, X Corps now admitted that Fisher's 2nd Armoured Brigade held 'only Eastern end of kidney-shaped feature', the majority of which was occupied by dreaded German 88mm guns. The armoured shield for Monty's northern break-in salient did not, in reality, exist.

The news from the southern end of the Alamein line was even worse. The Free French had failed to capture the Himeimat heights by night, and Horrocks's optimistic report that his second night of assault on the January and February minefields was paying off – that he hoped he would shortly be through into the open where he would force 21st Panzer Division and the Ariete Armoured Divisions to counter-attack – had also proved to be an error; Horrocks's armour had nowhere breached the second-belt minefields; indeed, he had been forced to withdraw 7th Armoured Division and his lorried infantry brigade.

In reality, this was the real crisis of the battle, late on the morning of 25 October, not the 3 a.m. awakening. Shaken, but revealing no signs of anxiety, Monty left at 11.30 a.m. for Freyberg's headquarters in order to ensure that at least the New Zealand Division's 'crumbling' operation was properly set up for the day.

There the bitter truth was at last revealed to him. Gatehouse's 'Sitreps' from 10th Armoured Division had been utterly misleading. In fact no armoured division tanks, anti-tank guns, artillery or infantry whatsoever were out beyond the Miteiriya Ridge, save those of the New Zealander's own support regiment, the Warwickshire Yeomanry. Monty's armoured 'hinge', on the left side of the British salient, did not exist. There was no armoured shield to protect the New Zealanders' 'crumbling' operation. Far from having 'galvanized the whole show into action', as he and de Guingand had thought, Monty's night-time conference and his obsession with keeping to his battle script had only served to frighten Lumsden into resentful silence, Gatehouse into a suppression of the true facts, and Briggs into wildly over-optimistic reports of progress on 1st Armoured Division's front on the right. Further south, Horrocks's XIII Corps' feint had stalled, too.

At a standstill

'The scene of chaos was absolutely unbelievable,' Monty's chief planner, Colonel Richardson, later recalled. 'It was a fundamental difference between the plan and the actual battle that the armour was stopped in the dog-fight area.' The battle '*didn't* go according to plan', Richardson stated categorically ' – and we at his Tactical Headquarters, we thought the battle was going bloody badly for a time!'[63]

At the New Zealand Division headquarters shortly before midday on 25 October, Monty assessed the local situation with Freyberg and then spoke to Leese and Lumsden, who had once again been summoned for a conference. Freyberg, angered by the excessive caution of Gatehouse's armoured brigades, considered it impossible to go ahead now with further 'crumbling' operations that day. In fact, he had no faith that Gatehouse would *ever* break out beyond the Miteiriya Ridge; he therefore advised the army commander to postpone further operations until the evening, and then allow the New Zealand infantry to mount an artillery-supported infantry attack to gain the Pierson line for Gatehouse's armour, on the Wiska Ridge, about 4,000 yards beyond the Miteiriya Ridge. The armour could then follow up and occupy the captured positions. Lumsden agreed.

Monty did not.

In his diary Monty recorded the conference in only the very briefest essentials, and made no mention of the Freyberg–Lumsden proposal – not only because he disliked admitting to failure, but because his rejection of Freyberg's and Lumsden's suggestion was intuitive, and came from the heart as well as the head. Though Monty liked to refer to his military approach as 'scientific' – reducible to principles and systematic knowledge – his own talent for command had a deeper, more personal, more competitive core. From the moment of his arrival in the desert he had personified the German Italian Panzer Army as 'Rommel'. His plan for the battle of Alamein had rested on surprising the enemy – and in his own mind it had worked, not only catching the Panzer Army without its trousers – its commander – but killing the stand-in commander, and by daylight of the first morning of the battle smashing a deep and savage wedge into Rommel's defensive line.

Thereafter, however, the British armour had failed to exploit 8th Army's advantage. Some thirty-eight hours of battle had now passed, and the commander of the Afrika Korps, General von Thoma, acting as temporary commander of the Panzer Army, would now be well aware that the thrust from the Miteiriya Ridge was the principal effort by 8th Army, to judge by counter-attacks with tanks that had begun to build up against the Warwickshire Yeomanry that morning. This was exactly what Monty had hoped would happen – but with Gatehouse's armoured division deployed with artillery on the Pierson line, not the Miteiriya Ridge, too far to support the yeomanry and encourage such attacks!

The New Zealand infantry weapon, Monty was well aware, must be used sparingly, for it was already depleted, following its magnificent performance on the first night of the battle. The 'general situation', Leese recalled, 'was critical. We had failed to break out and the German reserves were still intact. Two of my divisions had started the battle with only two Brigades, reserves capable of sustained action were dwindling, and our armoured ammunition supply would not stand up to a long battle. The South African Division was fought to a standstill and its two brigades were now too weak for further offensive operations. They could of course hold the line. The New Zealanders, who only had two Brigades, were exhausted' – and were wanted, in any case, as a mobile infantry division for the eventual pursuit. 'Only one Brigade of the Indian Division was as yet capable of a sustained attack. Two of the Brigades of the Highland Division had had a good hammering on the first nights of the atack . . . The armour had lost a lot of tanks and had to be re-equipped for any further offensive action.'[64]

Although he wished to keep to his overall battle strategy, Monty felt in his bones he must, if he was to regain the initiative, surprise the enemy. Instead of reinforcing Gatehouse's weakness, he should perhaps exploit his own areas of strength. His British armour had proved a broken reed, as Leese, who had commanded the Guards Armoured Division in England, confided that day in a letter to his wife: 'I'm afraid they've no stomach for a fight, & are not given a lead to have the will to succeed. Sometimes I feel quite ashamed to have been in Armour. All my infantry think nothing of them.'[65] Somehow, Monty felt sure, he must keep von Thoma guessing – and attacking yet again, for a third night from the Miteiriya Ridge would not do that, especially if half-heartedly followed up by the British armour.

He must, in other words, strike elsewhere.

A switch of 180 degrees

'The Army Commander sized up the situation very quickly,' Leese wrote later, 'and made one of his characteristic quick tactical decisions which he so often did in the midst of the heat of a battle.'[66] Freyberg's infantry would undertake no night attack; they would, instead, rest after their tremendous effort. 'Bernard Freyberg has been wonderful,' Leese reported to his wife that night, '& did a grand effort when he personally led his armoured brigade out at night through minefields when all were rattled by the bombing and heavy gunfire on the gaps.'[67] The two brigades of Gatehouse's 10th Armoured Division on the Miteiriya Ridge, Monty now ordered, were to be withdrawn from the battle into reserve. Instead, he decreed, everything would now be thrown into the right-hand sector of 8th Army's break-in, pushing out the 1st Armoured Division shield and starting crumbling operations northwards, to the sea, by the infantry of the 9th Australian Division.

'This really meant a new thrust line or axis of operations, from South to North, a switch of 180 degrees. I hoped that this completely new direction of attack might catch the enemy unawares,' Monty noted in his diary – the decision, duly recorded, dated and signed by the army commander, being attached to the Tactical 8th Army HQ War Diary:

'1. Direction of "crumbling" operations being undertaken by 30 Corps to be changed. 30 Corps to hold Miteiriya Ridge strongly and *not* operate SW from it.

2. Instead 30 Corps to undertake crumbling operations Northwards towards the coast using 9 Aust Div . . .'[68]

The conference at Freyberg's HQ at 12 noon on 25 October 1942 thus marked the first major change, indeed turning point, in the battle. Although Monty's insistence, in the early hours of the morning, on the armour getting out beyond the Miteiriya Ridge would go down in military annals as the mark of his superlative generalship, *pace* de Guingand, it was not. His 'ginger' had *not* worked; the armour had *not* got out on the left, beyond the Miteiriya Ridge, and it was futile to expend further brave New Zealand lives getting it out.

Instead, the New Zealand artillery would, Monty decreed, defend the

New Zealanders *in situ* on the Miteiriya Ridge; meanwhile the Australian infantry, who were proud of their efforts to date and spoiling for more fight, would be asked, that night, to undertake the next major offensive role in the battle.

Rommel takes command

At midnight on 25 October 1942 the Australians duly carried out the first 'crumbling' attack ordered by the army commander, advancing 3,000 yards, taking the vital Point 29, and overrunning a German battalion whose orders showed that no large-scale German counter-attack by the Afrika Korps was envisaged.

Monty's switch of 'crumbling' axis thus proved a complete surprise to the enemy, and the courage of the Australian infantry salutary. However, there was a price to be paid. The casualty figures spoke for themselves. By the next morning, 26 October, Leese's XXX Corps had sustained 4,643 casualties, whereas Lumsden's X (armoured) Corps had suffered a mere 455!

Once again, however, despite the urging of the Australians, 1st Armoured Division failed to push the armoured 'shield' on to the kidney feature in order to help screen the Australian 'crumbling' attacks and entice the Axis armour to counter-attack. In his diary Monty recorded the situation as it was reported to him on the morning of 26 October:

'0600 The attack Northwards by 9 Aust Div was completely successful . . .

0800 1 Armd Div had failed to progress Westwards and North-Westwards.'[69]

The British armour was proving incorrigible. Their navigation was so poor that 1st Armoured Division refused at first to admit they had failed to take the kidney feature, and would not co-operate with the Royal Engineers in surveying-in their positions as the infantry did. Worse still, they had an insufficient grasp of corps artillery co-operation.

What worried 8th Army's intelligence, however, was the Panzer Army – and in particular, its backbone, the Afrika Korps. In his daily intelligence summary for 26 October, Major Williams commented that, following the

British break-in, 'the enemy response has been to wear down our attack piecemeal without committing his main mobile forces for a decisive blow' – a decisive blow that must inevitably be expected. Lumsden had even warned Freyberg that 'Playing with armour is like playing with fire. You have got to go carefully. It is like a duel. If you don't take your time, you will be run through the guts.'[70]

Where, then, would the enemy's 'decisive blow' be delivered, when finally it came? Could the 8th Army salient withstand it, if it came in the north, using air, artillery, anti-tank guns, infantry and long-muzzled Panzers?

The third day of battle, Monday 26 October 1942, would indeed be the fateful day for both armies, for Field-Marshal Rommel had finally resumed command of the German/Italian African Panzer Army – having sent his famous, Napoleonic signal to all Axis formations and units: 'I have taken command of the army again. Rommel.'[71]

Rommel had been telephoned seventeen hours after the battle began, at 3 p.m. on 24 October; he was told the British offensive had started the night before, and that General Stumme was missing, believed captured or dead. He had then waited all night at Wiener-Neustadt airfield while Hitler debated whether to keep him for an armoured operation on the Russian front, or send him back to Alamein. Early on 25 October, having asked for latest news from Egypt, Hitler had decided – but although Rommel had set off at 7.50 a.m. it was only at 11 p.m. on 25 October – i.e., on the third night of the battle – that he had finally arrived at Panzer Army headquarters. As soon as it was light on 26 October he had made his own personal reconnaissance of the northern salient, particularly the new bridgehead – Point 29 – taken by the Australians during the night. In 15th Panzer Division, von Thoma told him, there were, thanks to 'the terrible artillery fire and non-stop RAF bombing attacks',[72] only thirty-one serviceable tanks left out of an original 119, though many could be repaired; meanwhile the British had succeeded in taking 'Hill 28' at midnight, shortly after Rommel's Napoleonic signal, and might quickly launch an armoured attack to break out and sever the army's supply lines by seizing the coast-road area.

There were thus a number of courses open to Rommel, most notably the 'decisive blow' which Lumsden and 8th Army intelligence feared. As Rommel himself later wrote, analysing the battle before his death: 'What we should really have done now was to assemble all our motorized units in the north in order to fling the British back to the main defence line in a concentrated and planned counter-attack.'[73]

But where, exactly, should he have launched such an attack? And why did he not do so?

Rommel's blunder

The truth was, as at Alam Halfa, Rommel was hobbled by his own pre-battle error of judgement. As his former ADC reflected, the two German panzer divisions had been 'split into battle groups in accordance with defensive plans that Rommel had drawn up before he left Africa . . . In this we made a grave blunder. Rommel had intended that the battle groups should exist independently only during the period preceding the anticipated enemy offensive. They were to be concentrated immediately an offensive became definite and its direction was perceived, since only a consolidated force of panzers would prevail against the great tank strength which Montgomery had now built up. Rommel had never dreamed of allowing his Panzers to meet the enemy and be defeated in detail.'[74]

Whether or not this was so, half the Axis armour had certainly been retained in the southern sector, where the main British attack had been feared, and was still there when Rommel arrived; indeed, it would be another day and a half before Rommel summoned 21st Panzer Division artillery and reserves from the south.

In Normandy, two years later, Rommel would find himself in the same situation: 'away from his desk' on the fateful day of enemy attack, and uncertain, thanks to Allied deception measures, whether or not the break-in might be a feint for a more powerful attack elsewhere. As Rommel later explained, once withdrawn from the south, 'our armour could never have returned to the south if the British had attacked there',[75] given the Panzer Army's depleted fuel supplies. Still unsure about the southern front, he thus hung on there for another thirty-six hours of battle – meanwhile putting in the uncoordinated 'piecemeal attacks' in the north which his former ADC claimed he would never have done in Stumme's place.

For Monty this was a godsend. With only half the panzer strength in the north – and their tanks reduced from 119 to 31 by the fighting over the previous two days – Rommel was in no position to 'fling the British back', Monty reckoned, for by now 8 Army had moved so many guns and anti-tank guns into the salient it was doubtful whether even the assembling of the entire Afrika Korps could overrun it. Orders had been given by the Desert Air Force to watch for any concentrations of German armour, so that it could immediately be bombed by heavies and fighter-bombers. In retrospect, by waiting thirty-six hours before collecting his reserve forces, Rommel made the worst error of his military career.

Working like a charm

Monty's deception plan in the south had thus worked beyond all expectation – and the switch in 'crumbling' direction, from the New Zealand side of the salient to the Australian – even with the British armour held back behind the infantry rather than in front – mesmerized Rommel, who could have no idea how reluctant the British armour was to advance.

If Rommel hesitated before concentrating his armour and artillery for thirty-six vital hours, ought he to have, instead, lured the British armour away from the ground their infantry had gained? With considerable honesty, Rommel posed this question in retrospect, wondering whether he 'could have made the action more fluid by withdrawing a few miles to the west and could then have attacked the British in an all-out charge and defeated them in open country. The British artillery and air force could not easily have intervened with their usual weight in a tank battle of this kind,' he reflected, 'for their own forces would have been endangered.'[76]

Once again, however, such retrospective 'what-ifs' were academic; Monty had decided, on 6 October, not to permit a mobile battle by the armoured divisions. Moreover, for Rommel to risk giving up a crucial sector of the Axis defensive line in the north and rely on a mobile battle behind the lines would not only have jeopardized the Axis defensive positions – minebelts, strong-points, high ground – in the south, where the British XIII Corps were already through the first minefield belt and, according to current Panzer Army reports, threatening to burst through the second at any moment, but would have risked open combat with tank forces twice as numerous as his own. Alam Halfa had indicated that the days of wide manoeuvre and easy pickings were over; moreover, the British had new American M4 Shermans – built on the superlative M3 Grant chassis and power unit, but with a new hull top and traversing turret. Given the shortage of Axis fuel supplies, and seemingly continuous Allied air attacks, Rommel had thus felt his safest course was to hold on in the south, and continue the fireman's policy which he had laid down before he left Africa a month earlier. As the military historian Kenneth Macksey wrote in his biography of Rommel, Montgomery's 'scheme of drawing the Axis armour into battle on unfavourable terms to counter local penetrations was working like a charm. Rommel, faced with the steady erosion of his infantry "boxes", had to counterattack to support them.'[77]

As at Alam Halfa, Rommel was thus forced to fight the battle in the way Montgomery dictated. 'Our aim for the next few days,' Rommel recalled, 'was to throw the enemy out of our main defence line at all costs and to reoccupy our old positions, in order to avoid having a westward bulge in our front'. As a result, 'rivers of blood were poured out over miserable strips of land which, in normal times, not even the poorest Arab would have bothered his head about', he acknowledged sadly.[78] He had failed to train his infantry for night attacks with co-ordinated air, artillery and tank support, and was forced therefore to keep counter-attacking at dawn or during the day to 'restore' the night's losses – not to regain the overall initiative. Throwing 15th Panzer, 90th Light and Littorio Divisions as well as Bersaglieri infantry back into the fray on 25 October, with fighter-bombers, Stuka divebombers and protective fighters above, he thus attempted to seize back the lost ground – only to be bombed by RAF and USAAF aircraft as the Axis formations formed up, and shelled by what felt like the whole of 8th Army artillery and anti-tank guns as the Axis forces attacked. Observing the battle for Hill 28 personally, he convinced himself the British 'wished to win through to the area between El Daba and Sidi Abd el Rahman', and brought the Trieste Division north, too, to counter it. German and Italian divebombers were ordered to try and break up the truck columns supporting the threatened break-out, but the Italians sheered away from the vicious anti-aircraft fire, dropping their bombs on their own lines, while the German aircraft pressed on, and were decimated by British fighters and flak. 'Never before in Africa had we seen such density of anti-aircraft fire. Hundreds of British tracer shells criss-crossed the sky and the air became an absolute inferno of fire,' Rommel recorded.[79]

Rommel's counter-attack thus failed miserably, and was called off in the evening. Piecemeal attacks were not the answer, he recognized. It was time to rethink his strategy, and to concentrate his armour for a decisive blow – if he had time.

Preparing decisive blows

Ironically, Monty was thinking the same thing, at the same time. As day three of the battle had dawned on 26 October, he was both encouraged and disappointed. He had estimated for a minimum of 10,000 casualties in the first seven days of the battle. Already, after three nights' fighting, he had reached almost two-thirds of that figure – and these losses were suffered by his finest infantry formations: the New Zealanders, Australians, South Africans and Highlanders. It was important now, Monty felt, not to squander their magnificent achievements, nor to overtax them with casualties. The British salient was secure, the new Australian wedge of 25/26 October driving a further stake into Rommel's northernmost defences. The infantry, Monty decided, must now be given a chance to rest before undertaking further 'crumbling' operations. It was time at last for the British armour, which had sustained only nominal casualties so far, to begin to fight.

At 9 a.m., therefore, on 26 October, Monty issued a new battle directive, which he then gave out personally at a conference of corps commanders held at the headquarters of Morshead's 9th Australian Division at 11.30 a.m. 'After thinking the problem over, I came to the conclusion that 30 Corps needed a short period with no major operations,' he noted in his diary. 'Divisions had been fighting hard since 2200 hours 23 October, and were somewhat disorganized; a period was wanted in which Div areas could be tidied up, and things sorted out.' General Leese was told that, although XXX Corps was to be responsible for defending the bridgehead, it would carry out no major offensive operations for the moment – 'Divisions of that Corps are to be so re-organized and rested that they can conduct major operations in the near future.' In the south, in Horrocks's XIII Corps, the armour of 7th Armoured Division was also to be relieved of offensive tasks. The only offensive action would be conducted, for the moment, by Lumsden's X Corps – whose job was 'to make progress to the West and North West from the Kidney Hill area'. General Lumsden was to concentrate on this 'one hundred per cent', and to stop worrying about the 'security of the bridgehead'.[80]

Lumsden duly returned from this conference to his headquarters to prepare a X Corps plan for a night attack, the object of which would be to push out westwards from the British toehold on Kidney Ridge.

While Lumsden went to 'tee-up' his plan, however, Monty examined the tank casualty figures – which at noon that day showed a combined loss of 239 tanks of all types, mostly on minefields and easily repairable. Together with the very light casualties in officers and men in X Corps it was difficult for Monty to understand the ineffectiveness of the armoured performance so far. The success of 8th Army's 'crumbling' concept had already been reflected in the number of piecemeal counter-attacks put in by Rommel's armour; but it was the infantry of 8th Army that was still having to take the brunt of the casualties. On the right of the break-in salient, a single Australian sergeant had knocked out no fewer than five enemy tanks with his two-pounder anti-tank gun, but there was a limit to the number of further 'crumbling' operations the infantry could be expected to mount in the battle. Half the Afrika Korps had still not been engaged; yet it seemed impossible to make Lumsden understand that the British armour *must* play its part in the battle and pose a threat to Rommel, not simply sit back doing a defensive job that could be done by XXX Corps' own artillery and anti-tank guns, supported by the RAF. Sceptical of Lumsden's zeal for the battle, Monty had therefore told him he wanted to see a copy of his plan of attack, to make sure it was properly tied-in with full corps artillery support.

It was at this point, waiting to see Lumsden's plan at his small tactical headquarters, that Monty decided to check out, first, with his chief gunner, the artillery situation in 8th Army. Brigadier Kirkman clearly recalled the meeting. 'I said to him, "As far as I can find out we can go on with this battle for ten days at the present rate – but we can't go on indefinitely." And Monty replied: "Oh, it's quite all right, absolutely all right, don't worry about ammunition. This battle will be over in a week's time. There'll be no problem." '[81]

Monty's confidence, in view of the 'stickiness' of the British armour, surprised Kirkman. Monty, Kirkman recalled, seemed to have no worries about the eventual outcome of the battle. 'If we fire 150 rounds [in the north] a gun per day, we can continue the battle for three weeks,' Monty noted confidently in his own diary that day.[82] What worried him much more was the amateurishness of his armoured commanders – especially when Kirkman reported that Lumsden was failing to keep in touch with his chief gunner. As Kirkman remembered, 'I said, "The next time you see Herbert Lumsden, I wish you would point out to him that he must keep his corps artillery chief in the picture. He wanders about the country by himself and the corps artillery chief doesn't know what's going on." '[83]

To Monty this was simply exasperating. In his diary he noted at 5 p.m. that day:

I have just discovered that LUMSDEN has been fighting his battle without having his CCRA [corps artillery chief] with him. I have ordered him up at once.

There is no doubt these RAC [Royal Armoured Corps] Generals do not understand the co-operation of all arms in battle. I have had many examples of this since the battle started.

LUMSDEN is not a really high-class soldier.[84]

It was the revelation that Lumsden was not even fighting with his chief of artillery alongside him that caused Monty to abandon even this latest plan for the armour. The British armour had proved 'utterly useless' so far. In such circumstances, what was the point of risking further failure by insisting they play a constructive role in the dog-fight phase of the battle?

It was imperative, Monty felt, not to allow the offensive to peter out into stalemate. Rommel had so far failed to deliver a 'decisive blow'. Perhaps it was time to consider an 8th Army 'decisive blow', rather than pitching Lumsden's armour into the same sort of piecemeal operations that Rommel was conducting.

At 6 p.m. on 26 October, therefore, Monty 'decided to regroup, and re-position, with a view to creating fresh reserves for further offensive action'.[85] Leese recalled the moment well – indeed, was enormously impressed by the army commander's refusal to be put out by the failure of the armour in the battle thus far. Instead of being allowed to feel that the offensive was 'fizzling out', Leese was given a new and crystal-clear challenge: to lock the enemy in close combat with XXX Corps, while the major formations of the 8th Army capable of offensive action were withdrawn from the line, in preparation for a knock-out armoured blow.

'In order to produce a reserve the following moves would take place,' the minutes of Monty's 7 p.m. conference began,[86] recording in detail the wider frontages and side-stepping required to bring the New Zealanders and 10th Armoured Division into reserve, while also enabling the Australians to renew their 'crumbling' operations northwards from the salient towards the sea 'so as to write off all the enemy in his original positions in the coastal sector by getting in behind them', as Monty described his intention in his diary.[87] An hour later General Lumsden's corps headquarters were ordered to drop all orders for attack; instead, Lumsden was made to hand over command of 1st Armoured Division to Leese – and produce plans for an armoured reserve corps, consisting of 'the New Zealand Division and 9 Armoured Brigade, 10 Armoured Division and possibly 7 Armoured Division',[88] brought up from the south, for a concentrated, artillery-assisted armoured assault.

By regrouping his armour Monty would finally ensure Lumsden's X Corps became, at last, the British equivalent of the Afrika Korps, ready to deliver the 'decisive blow' of the battle.

At precisely the same time, 8 p.m. on 26 October 1942, Rommel sent orders for 21st Panzer Division to be ready to move north and rejoin the Afrika Korps, beginning at 9 p.m.[89]

Simultaneously, Rommel and Montgomery were doing the same thing: preparing their 'decisive blows'.

A spectacular mistake

The battle of Alamein was now, unknown to its respective army commanders, churning towards its vortex. Rommel was convinced Montgomery was already breaking out on 26 October, and that he must therefore bring up his southern panzer forces for a concentrated, decisive counter-punch; while Monty was giving up all hope of Lumsden forcing his way on to Kidney Ridge, and had decided, with Rommel only attacking piecemeal, to leave 1st Armoured Division where it was in support of Leese's infantry, and to bring up and concentrate, behind the minefields, all the remaining armour in 8th Army for his eventual decisive blow. 'My general plan is first to reach the coast by a drive Northwards. Then I shall "drive" Westwards along the axis of the road and railway,' Monty noted in his diary. 'During these operations I shall plan to move the armour on my Southern flank [of the salient], holding off the enemy armour and outflanking resistance met frontally.'[90]

Leese's confident opinion that there would be no concentrated panzer counter-attack by the enemy was partly based on his experience of the battle so far, and partly on an appreciation given by the head of 8th Army intelligence, Colonel 'Spud' Murphy. Shortly after the army commander's evening conference on 26 October, Murphy reported the capture and translation of the 'Defensive Policy Plans' of the Italian Trieste Division –

which were to 'wear down' the attack with all means in their power '*without* using concentrated armoured division counter-attacks'. Murphy thus gave the army commander his considered opinion: 'It looks as if this is in fact happening and I do not expect concentrated counterattacks from DAK [Deutsche Afrika Korps] until either our armour has completely broken through or until the infantry have been so weakened that they cannot continue to resist in the Northern sector.'[91]

In fact Murphy was spectacularly mistaken; Rommel, leaving his counter-stroke too late, had made a spectacular mistake.

Death or glory

At 10.45 p.m. on 26 October 21st Panzer Division (less 104 Panzer Grenadier Regiment and Battle Group 39[92]) began its move towards the northern salient, with the HQ section leading along the specially marked Afrika Korps track, following the vehicle pass west of Ruweisat Ridge, northwards to Point 39 and the telegraph track at Point 487. By 3 p.m. the next day, 27 October, the panzers were in action, ramming home the armoured attacks of the rest of the Afrika Korps.

It was too late, however. Monty's insistence that 1st Armoured Division at least push out its armoured shield a little beyond the kidney feature, in order to protect the Australian 'crumbling' operations, had finally borne fruit: for on the night of 26 October Briggs, at his second attempt and supported by the artillery of both X and XXX Corps, claimed he had got his 7th Motor Brigade forward almost 4,000 yards on to the armoured corps' objectives, with '2 KRRC [King's Royal Rifle Corps] on "Wood-cock" & 2 RB [Rifle Brigade] on "Snipe"', as Briggs noted with satisfaction in his diary.[93]

Briggs was wrong, however. The 2nd King's Rifles did not get near the Woodcock position, and 2nd Rifle Brigade were 900 yards off target; nor were these motorized infantry and anti-tank gunners followed up – yet again – by tanks or artillery of 24th Armoured Brigade, as intended by Briggs. Those tanks of 24th Armoured Brigade which did belatedly get forward at 7.30 a.m. – over an hour after 2nd Rifle Brigade had begun to engage enemy tanks at close quarters – immediately opened fire on their own countrymen, the anti-tank gunners of 2nd Rifle Brigade, under Lieutenant-Colonel Vic Turner! Having finally realized their mistake the tanks then turned tail and left Turner's group of 300 men and anti-tank guns completely unsupported for the rest of that fateful day.

Turner was not surprised. He had been warned by a wise South African artillery officer that 'From all the signs, I should think it highly probable that you are in for a death-or-glory affair.'[94]

He was – though in the event it would be glory *and* death for most of them – for Rommel was determined to put in an all-out Afrika Korps attack at dawn, which was to be reinforced by the 21st Panzer Division as soon as their tanks arrived from the south. 'On the 27th,' Kenneth Macksey chronicled,

Rommel took personal control, and threw in a co-ordinated counter-attack employing 21st Panzer and 90th Light Divisions in concentric thrusts aimed at the salient's tip. In conjunction with adjacent elements of 15th Panzer and 164th Divisions, this amounted to the single biggest counterstroke he was to attempt at any time in the battle. But the dive-bombing, intended to support it, suffered the fate of most Luftwaffe interventions in the battle: it was broken up by the overwhelming British fighter defence.

Twenty-four Hurricanes and sixteen American Kittyhawks smashed the German air assault.

So the struggle was waged exclusively as an Army affair, and the indomitable defence of 'Snipe' position by British anti-tank guns guarded by infantry brought the 21st Panzer Division to a halt with heavy tank losses; elsewhere the furious British bombing and their interminable artillery fire held the 90th Light Division at arm's length. Rommel saw it all when, as so often before, he joined the 90th to watch it attack. By nightfall, he knew that his major effort had failed utterly, although he was unaware that this may well have been the turning point in the battle.[95]

At 4.50 p.m. 21st Panzer Division's war diarist was recording reports of '40 dug-in enemy tanks in Minefield L, as well as enemy tanks to the east and north. Heavy anti-tank and artillery fire.' As a result, 'the Panzer attack fails'.[96] In his memoirs, Rommel remembered the fatal day:

Continuous bombing attacks seriously delayed the approach march of the 21st Panzer Division and a third of Ariete . . . Three times within a quarter of an hour units of the 90th Light Division, which had deployed and were standing in the open in preparation for the attack, were bombed by eighteen aircraft. At 15.00 hours our dive bombers swooped down on the British lines. Every artillery and anti-aircraft gun [88mm] which we had in the northern sector concentrated a violent fire on the point of the intended attack. Then the armour moved forward. A murderous British fire struck into our ranks and our attack was brought to a halt by an immensely powerful anti-tank defence [mostly Vic Turner's]. There is, in general, little chance of success in a tank attack over country where the enemy has been able to take up defensive positions, but there was nothing else we could do.[97]

Writing to his wife, he poured out his heart. 'No one can conceive the burden that lies on me,' he wrote to her. 'Everything is at stake and we're fighting under the greatest possible handicap. However, I hope we'll pull through. You know I'll put all I've got into it.'[98]

He did. Time and again the Germans and Italians attacked to try to prevent or smash the presumed British break-out. Even at 12.30 p.m. on 27 October Colonel Murphy refused to believe that the whole Afrika Korps had been committed to battle, obtusely reporting to Monty that 'evidence is against 21 Pz being in the North'. Later in the afternoon, however, the headquarters of 21st Panzer Division was pinpointed, and the violence of the assault on the northern salient thereby explained.

A sticky fight

Monty had begun the day disgruntled by the failure of Briggs' latest attempt to push his armour on to the Pierson line, which had put yet more burden on the infantry, whose casualties were mounting. 'It is clear from the casualty figures,' Monty had noted, 'that we have got to be careful, especially as regards the infantry.'[99] The New Zealanders had no reinforcements in the Middle East, and could be expected to carry out only one more effort; the Highland Division had received 1,000 reinforcements, but 'had had heavy casualties' and had 'suffered heavily in officers, especially in the Co[mpan]y Comd. level'. The South Africans had 'started low in strength and could not now undertake any major offensive operation; no reinforcements were available'.[100] The Australians had also 'had heavy casualties, but there were 4,000 reinforcements in the country' to keep them going. Compared with this, the losses sustained by the British armour appeared minimal, and Monty's frustration, in his diary entry at 8 a.m., had been marked:

My own armour is at present breaking out through the Northern 'funnel'; it is actually out, but its progress Westwards and North-Westwards is very slow.

It is a 'sticky' fight and artillery plays a great part in it.

But the Armoured Div Commanders do not know anything about artillery; they are used to having it decentralised by batteries; there is no CRA [chief gunner] of an Armoured Division who understands how to handle a Div artillery; they have never been trained by their Div Commanders or by the CCRAs of Corps.[101]

The bravery of Lieutenant-Colonel Vic Turner's Rifle Brigade and RHA anti-tank gun crews that day, as well as the adjacent gun-battle between the Afrika Korps and the tanks and artillery of Fisher's 2nd Armoured Brigade, however, heartened the army commander. 'All day the enemy has been attacking the 1st Armd Div which is in the open to the West of the "funnel"; all attacks have been beaten off and there seems no doubt that we have destroyed about 40 tanks,' he recorded with satisfaction in his diary late in the afternoon of 27 October. In the evening he added: 'The one thing we want is that the enemy should attack us. 1st Armd Div have today destroyed 50 enemy tanks (all burning) without loss to themselves.'[102]

General Leese was equally pleased. In a letter to his wife that evening – his forty-eighth birthday – he reported he'd had 'a queer birthday today, but I've a great hope that, though there is a long way to go, we have turned the corner in our battle. It is a hard task as his initial positions were strong – & he has organized in great depth with masses of mines & strong screens of Anti-Tank guns. He has also damaged us a lot with medium & heavy artillery fire . . . Owing to the mass of mines, it has been very difficult to get the Armour out – & when they get a start, they find strong anti-tank gun screens, which the enemy has had time to put out. But today we managed to force on a tank battle – and the enemy lost a number of tanks, and up to date, we have beaten off all enemy counter-attacks with our Infantry and Anti-Tank guns.'[103]

In fact, Turner's anti-tank troop, in one of the most heroic actions of World War II, had 'destroyed or disabled more enemy tanks than had so far been destroyed or damaged in any single unit action', Brigadier Lucas Phillips recounted.[104] 'If he goes on counter-attacking,' Leese meanwhile assured his wife, 'it gives us our opportunity to destroy him – provided we can hold him. So we have come to an interesting stage in our battle. The RAF are wonderful. By day they have complete superiority, & today over ten formations each of 18 bombers went over to bomb tank & M.T. concentrations on our battlefield. It is most inspiring seeing their close order, surrounded by a host of fighters. The latter shot down 24 enemy fighters today, with no loss to themselves.'[105]

Even General Briggs, who had doomed the 2nd Rifle Brigade to fight and die alone on Kidney Ridge – 'Impossible to relieve or replenish,' he noted in his diary[106] – was amazed at Turner's achievement. As he narrated in a subsequent lecture:

From 0300 hours until dusk this one Batttalion, with 13 6-pdr anti-tank guns, together with six anti-tank guns from the Anti-Tank Regiment, withstood eight major attacks varying from 20 to 100 tanks. This action was an epic of the whole war and on it hinged the whole success of the break through at Alamein. Colonel Turner of the Rifle Brigade was awarded the Victoria Cross. In the course of this action 37 enemy tanks were destroyed and 20 more, subsequently recovered, were damaged. Owing to the fact that there was a valley . . . which was commanded by concealed 88mm guns, it was quite impossible to support them by daylight. The decision had to be taken whether it was worthwhile trying to support them at the cost of probably 60 tanks, or whether they should be allowed to fight it out as best they could. I took the decision that the loss of tanks was not justified. Attempts were made to support them by Artillery, by the F[orward O[bservation] O[fficer] who went out in an M3 light tank [Stuart], was lost and has never been seen from that day to this. Two more FOOs were knocked out subsequently.[107]

It was the stalwart defence of Kidney Ridge by Turner's Rifle Brigade unit and anti-tank gunners serving in the Motor Brigade of 1st Armoured Division on 27 October which to some extent restored Monty's plummeting faith in the courage of his British armoured formations. However, his hopes of using the tank reserve force he was amassing to exploit this success were dampened the following morning when he heard that Turner's 2nd Battalion of the Rifle Brigade had been overrun, after dark! Turner and his 300 men had almost single-handedly ruined Rommel's Afrika Korps offensive – and Briggs had failed to get a single man, gun or tank through to reinforce Turner, or fortify his position with more guns, even under cover of dark. The few survivors had had to retreat during the night, unsupported by either 2nd or 24th Armoured Brigade, or 133 Lorried Infantry Brigade; moreover 24th Armoured Brigade had inadvertently run into a minefield, causing further heavy losses, after a running battle in the morning, to their tanks – '24 Armed Bde had suffered considerable casualties owing to mishandling by KENCHINGTON', Monty noted testily at 7 a.m. on 28 October.[108]

The 133 Lorried Infantry Brigade, sent from Gatehouse's 10th Armoured Division, had failed even more miserably; it had attacked Wimberley's Highlanders rather than the enemy, had then got lost, knocked out three 88mm guns and crews, and finally surrendered its forward infantry battalion to a German–Italian counter-attack! As its commander, Brigadier A. W. Lee, described to the official British historian, their wireless sets were hopeless for desert work, and the better ones were 'mounted in unarmoured 15 cwt. trucks, most of which were only 2 wheel drive'.[109] Lumsden and Gatehouse had assured Lee 'that all he had to do to take *Woodcock* and *Snipe* was to "walk through", but that he would be given ample artillery support and that the two armoured brigades would be up at first light'.[110] Brigadier Lee, like Turner, felt his brigade was 'sold down the river', as he put it, by the armoured commanders, who had taken no measures to clarify the puzzling topology of the area, with its ridges, defiles and shallow depressions, and failed 'to understand the limitations of Inf[an]try formations under their command, and what they could and could not be expected to do'.[111]

Reflecting on the fury of Rommel's counter-attacks in the Kidney Ridge area, however, Monty could only welcome the fact that Rommel was finally playing into his hands in the way he had predicted before the battle. However haphazard the British baiting attacks, Rommel's Afrika Korps, in direct contradiction of 8th Army's intelligence assessment, was now irrevocably committed to the fight.

But if Briggs could not even reach and rescue, let alone support, the few hundred infantry and artillerymen of his own Rifle Brigade on the Kidney Ridge because of the fear of 88mm guns, would the new 8th Army armoured reserve he had begun to assemble be able to advance westwards from the Australian salient, any more than it had beyond the Miteiriya Ridge?

Yet again, Monty felt he would have to alter his plan, as he had altered Lightfoot. Having locked the Afrika Korps in combat around the Australian sector, he must find a way of breaching the German gun-line – for the lesson of Alamein was that the anti-tank gun was now queen of the desert.

While pondering the best axis of attack, Monty now decided to quietly withdraw 1st Armoured Division and 24th Armoured Brigade, and add them also to his *corps de chasse*, ready for the *coup de grâce* – aware, in his heart, that clearing a path for his British armour would, once again, have to be achieved by the PBI – the 'poor bloody infantry'.

A change of plan

Dawn on 28 October 1942 saw the battle of Alamein entering day five. At 8 a.m. Monty recorded the results of his conference with Lumsden and Leese – at which he ordered the complete withdrawal of Lumsden's armoured corps headquarters, troops and tanks from the current battle, and the handing over to General Leese of all offensive operations. 'We now have the whole of Panzer Army opposite the Northern funnel,' Monty explained. While keeping Rommel's panzers committed in the Australian sector, Leese was now to prepare an 8th Army *infantry* attack, through Rommel's gun-line, towards the main supply route to the west of Alamein station – indeed, the New Zealander infantry were to be put back into the battle, rather than be withdrawn into the armoured reserve corps under Lumsden:

I explained that after 9 Aust Div operation tonight, the next operation would be a 'drive' NW by 30 Corps to get SIDI RAHMAN; I then wanted to launch armoured cars South-West from that place, to get across the enemy supply routes and to prevent rations, petrol, water, etc. from reaching the forward troops.

The NZ Div would be used for this operation, but it was now very weak.

In truth, Freyberg was reluctant to use his New Zealand infantry, after the punishing casualties they had already taken, trying to get the British armour 'out'. 'I will lead any infantry you like,' Freyberg told Monty, 'but I will not take my New Zealanders into another assault.'[112]

'I often think some people fail to grasp the extraordinary confusion which existed in the battle area in the north,' Monty later recalled. The eventual operation 'was actually carried out by two British infantry brigades and a British armoured Brigade – and not by New Zealanders as so many imagine, although it was led by Freyberg. He refused to do it, and I had to bribe him brigade by brigade!! It took me some hours to complete the bribery.'[113] According to Brigadier Lucas Phillips, Monty 'told

Freyberg that he could have 9th Armoured Brigade again', to support the New Zealanders, 'but Freyberg shook his head; it was a matter for infantry. Montgomery then offered him a British infantry brigade as well, but he still shook his head, although Montgomery could see that he was clearly "weakening". "Very well, Bernard, I'll give you two infantry brigades."'

Freyberg finally gave in. ' "I could see," Montgomery said afterwards, "that the old warhorse was itching to fight again. This sort of show was very much his cup of tea and I knew he was the right man for it." '[114]

Summoning Horrocks from XIII Corps at 11 a.m., Monty explained his intention, and together they agreed on infantry formations which could be spared in the south if XIII Corps' sector was thinned out and became a purely defensive front. About his divisional commanders, Monty was, in his diary, quite emphatic:

Easily my best fighting Divisional Commander is FREYBERG, and then MORSHEAD.

I am therefore going to fight the battle for the present with 30 Corps, and have placed one Arm[oure]d Div under command of 30 Corps.[115]

The NZ Div will be used to 'drive' along the coast towards SIDI RAHMAN and beyond. To keep the NZ Div up to strength and to enable it to operate offensively, British Inf Bdes in turn will be put into it:

    First: 151 Bde (DLI) [50 Div]

    Second: 131 Bde (Queens) [44 Div]

    Third: Greek Bde

[These infantry brigades would all have to brought round from Horrocks's southern front.]

This will enable 2 NZ Div to keep going. As each Inf Bde in turn becomes exhausted, so it will rejoin its own Division in 13 Corps and the next Bde will come up.[116]

If Leese could do this, the battle of Alamein would inexorably be won – by the infantry, in a self-replenishing battering ram.

As Monty saw it, the enemy's non-motorized infantry would not be able to get away from this ram, while 8 Army's armoured cars could break out and harry Rommel's supply route along the coast, behind the lines. This would still leave Monty with the remaining two armoured divisions for his *corps de chasse* – 1st and 7th – and his motorized New Zealand Division, which could then be launched to 'finish off' any pockets of enemy resistance; a task which he hoped would not, this time, be beyond the armour.

Such was the confident new plan Monty gave out at midday on 28 October. He had not, however, reckoned on the political repercussions thousands of miles away in England.

The blood-red carpet

To his staff and his commanders Monty allowed nothing but confidence to show – he retired to bed at the same time each night and exuded optimism by day. Thus, while Rommel made himself increasingly ill with anxiety, Monty appeared quite unruffled each morning at breakfast. He was not relaxed, as General Sir Charles Richardson later made clear. 'I don't think relaxed is the right word because his style in fact was very taut. Of course there was never any hurry, no flap and that sort of thing, and this was really due to his iron self-discipline – his professional approach to the art of command – rather than to a relaxed style.

'His philosophy really went like this: that a commander must radiate confidence at all times – that was his great expression: "radiate confidence". And if he couldn't control his emotions and conceal his fears, then he shouldn't be a commander at all! So in order to preserve the nervous energy to carry out that bit of self-discipline, he would have a very orderly regime of sleep and rest and diet and so on.

'Now secondly, a commander must personally control the battle throughout; and in order to be able to do that he must plan it so that he remains in balance – what he called "poise" ("always retain poise"), and he would personally encourage his subordinates – visit them, and control the battle by word of mouth personally.'[117]

Behind his mask of confidence, however, Monty was far from satisfied with the way the battle had gone since the break-in on the first night. In withdrawing the armour of Lumsden's X Corps he was not so much steering the great armoured steamroller of 8 Army, as so many commentators afterwards saw the battle, as bowing to the failure of such a steamroller! Lumsden had warned that tanks could not cut their way through gun-lines – and he had been proved right. Rommel had found the same, too. For armour to punch its way forward, new techniques would be required, involving intimate co-operation with RAF ground-attack fighters, artillery and infantry. This would take time and training; in the meantime the infantry of seven Allied nations would have to carry the torch.

This was not at all what Monty had planned; in withdrawing his armour from the main battle Monty was, in effect, abandoning the policy he had originally laid down for the battle – that of an armoured shield with which to protect the infantry's 'crumbling' attacks and draw upon itself the German armoured counter-attacks; instead, he was now, finally, reverting to an inexorable infantry-style battle that would entail even heavier infantry casualties than he had anticipated, while keeping his main armour in reserve, merely to 'mop up' and pursue, once the infantry had rolled out a carpet.

The carpet, sadly, would be blood-red before it was fully unrolled.

Spreading rumours of British failure

Meanwhile, counting the cost of his abortive counter-attacks, Rommel began to fear the inevitability of defeat. On the morning of 28 October, after another night of savage bombing, and with the RAF blitzing his armour as it formed up for further counter-attacks, he had written to his wife: 'The battle is raging. Perhaps we will survive in spite of all that goes against us. If we fail it would have grave consequences for the entire course of the war, for in that case North Africa would fall to the British almost without a fight. We are doing our utmost to succeed, but the enemy's superiority is tremendous and our own resources very small. If we fail, whether or not I survive the battle will be in God's hands. The lot of the vanquished is hard to bear. I have a clean conscience, as I have done everything to gain a victory and have not spared my own person. Should I remain on the battlefield I would like to thank you and our boy for all the love and joy you have given me in my life. My last thought is of you. After I am gone, you must bear the mourning proudly.'[118]

The capture of a British map showing Montgomery's intended drive north-west from the Australian salient had confirmed Rommel's feeling that the critical moment of the battle had arrived – though he had mistakenly thought Montgomery was about to launch an all-out *armoured* attack. Accordingly, 'the whole of the Afrika Korps had to be put into the line', Rommel recorded in his memoirs, with the last panzer, artillery, anti-tank and German infantry units of 21st Panzer Division brought up from the south. 'Any soldier who fails or disobeys,' he ordered, 'is to be courtmartialled regardless of rank'[119] – for this was, as he put it in a message to all commanders, 'a battle for life or death'.[120]

Ironically, it was at this moment that rumours of British, rather than German, failure began to infect 10 Downing Street. Winston Churchill, combining the offices of Prime Minister and Minister of Defence, had assumed the British armour would remain 'out' until it had destroyed the Axis armour. Now, according to latest reports coming in, Monty was withdrawing the whole of X Corps!

Quite who began to spread the rumour that this withdrawal implied grievous losses, even retreat, was for years unknown. Eventually, from the unpublished portion of Field-Marshal Brooke's diary, it became clear who the culprit was: none other than Foreign Secretary Anthony Eden – in London! On the evening of 28 October 1942 Eden went to 10 Downing Street 'to have a drink with him [Churchill] and had shaken his confidence in Montgomery and Alexander and had given him the impression that the Middle East offensive was petering out!!' Brooke noted in utter exasperation the following day, 29 October. 'Before I got up this morning I was presented with a telegram which PM wanted to send Alexander. Not a pleasant one!'[121]

Brooke managed to hold back the unpleasant telegram, but at Eden's insistence the British Minister of State in Cairo, Richard Casey, was ordered by cable to go straight up to the Alamein front and report back – a sad reflection of Eden's conspiratorial and meddling faithlessness.

Essential to break through somewhere

While Eden conspired, Monty prepared for his next infantry blow, which would precede Freyberg's assault. As on the first night of Alamein, Leese arranged a full XXX Corps artillery barrage, on the night of 28 October, to start the Australian Division on a series of fierce new 'crumbling' operations northwards to the sea.

'At about 21.00 hours a tremendous British drum-fire started to pound the area west of Hill 28,' Rommel recorded. 'Soon hundreds of British guns concentrated their fire into the sector of the 2nd Battalion, 125th Regiment, north of Hill 28. The British launched their assault at 22.00

hours. The weight of this attack was something quite exceptional.' For six hours the Australians advanced, mercilessly. 'No one can conceive the extent of our anxiety during this period,' Rommel wrote. 'That night I hardly slept and by 03.00 hours was pacing up and down turning over in my mind the likely course of the battle, and the decisions I might have to take.'[122]

Throughout the battle the Allied air forces and the Royal Navy had kept up their pressure on Rommel's fuel supply – as during Alam Halfa – and by mid-morning on 29 October, after news of yet another sinking, Rommel was clear he must prepare for withdrawal to Fuka 'before the battle reached its climax'.[123] To him 'It seemed doubtful whether we would be able to stand up much longer to attacks of the weight which the British were now making, and which they were in any case still able to increase. It was obvious to me that I dared not await the decisive break-through but would have to pull out to the West before it came. Such a decision, however, could not fail to lead to the loss of a large proportion of my non-motorized infantry, partly because of the low fighting power of my motorized formations and partly because the infantry units themselves were too closely involved in the fighting.'[124]

At 2.45 p.m. that day his aide noted in his diary: 'C-in-C enlarges over lunch on his plan to prepare a line for the army to fall back on at Fuka when the time comes, now that the northern part of the Alamein line is no longer in our hands.'[125] To his wife Rommel confessed in his daily letter: 'I haven't much hope left. At night I lie with my eyes open, unable to sleep for the load that lies on my shoulders.'[126]

For Monty there had been no such sleep-problem since the second night of the battle. Nevertheless the responsibility for ensuring victory weighed equally heavy. The battle, on 29 October, had reached day six. One medium regiment gunner noted in his diary: 'Am told a Hun prisoner said that the fighting here is far more intense than in Russia!'[127] From the tally kept of enemy tanks and guns destroyed, as well as mounting numbers of prisoners, Monty knew how the situation must look to Rommel; equally, however, the heavy casualties sustained by the Australians and the damage done to their support tanks on minefields, made him chary about asking too much of Morshead's men. In his diary for Thursday 29 October he noted that the 'attack of 9 Aust Div made good progress and some 200 prisoners were taken', but that the Australians 'got hampered by minefields and did not reach the railway as I had hoped'. Disappointed but concerned not to expend further human life until the Australians had had time to sort out their positions and reorganize their artillery and tank support, he postponed their next 'crumbling' operation. 'The new front is being re-organized and the attack will be resumed tomorrow night, i.e. Friday, 30 October, when I hope the Australians will reach the sea and clean up the whole area.'[128]

It was at this juncture, while preparing for a renewed infantry offensive to the sea, prior to a Freyberg-led infantry advance along the coast road, that Monty for the first time in the battle was made aware of the political pressure being brought to bear from London. At 11.50 a.m. on 29 October he was informed that Churchill's own son-in-law, Duncan Sandys, would pay a visit to his headquarters the next day; meanwhile, General Alexander himself suddenly appeared with the Minister of State in Egypt, Richard Casey, bearing a disturbing telegram from Churchill. In this, the Prime Minister pointed to the imminent Allied landings in North-West Africa (Torch), and painted an optimistic (though illusory) picture of their prospects – namely, that the French would assist the Allies in Tunisia and perhaps even rise up in Vichy France. 'Events may therefore move more quickly, perhaps considerably more quickly, than had been planned,' Churchill signalled[129] – urging that everything now be done to expedite a victory by 8th Army.

De Guingand recalled the deputation in his book *Operation Victory*: 'I was taken aside by Casey, who asked me whether I was quite happy about the way things were going.'[130] So alarmed was Casey, in fact, by the apparent stalemate and the withdrawal of the entire *corps de chasse*, that he showed de Guingand a signal to London he'd drafted, preparing Churchill for a possible reverse. Brigadier Williams remembered the moment quite clearly. 'I had a curious sort of truck which had a shelf-cum-bench in it, and Freddie brought Casey into it and we sat on this bench. I talked to Casey and told him the enemy point of view – and then suddenly there was this business of Casey mumbling away that he ought to go and prepare a signal to warn Winston that things weren't going well, and Freddie having this incredible burst of temper, saying: "For God's sake don't! If you do, I'll see *you're drummed out of political life*!"' – a threat which greatly amused young Major Williams, since de Guingand evidently had 'no appreciation that he [Casey] wasn't in political life anyway!'[131]

In his memoirs Monty claimed to have been too busy to bother about what signal Casey eventually sent. However, the evidence of his diary confirms that, on the contrary, he took the pressure from Casey and Churchill very much to heart. ' "Torch" is on 8 November,' Monty noted.

'It is becoming essential to break through somewhere, and to bring the enemy armour to battle, and to get armoured cars astride the enemy supply routes. We must make a great effort to defeat the enemy, and break up his Army, so as to help "Torch". I have therefore decided to modify my plan,' he concluded[132] – and set down his new intention.

Rather than driving the New Zealanders in a self-replenishing infantry battering ram through the left flank of the Australian 'thumb' (as it was soon nicknamed at 8th Army headquarters) and along the coast road to Sidi Rahman, he would ask the Australians to continue their assault towards the sea in the far north, but instead of exploiting it, he would put all his reserve forces into a surprise, *Blitzkrieg* infantry-cum-armoured attack *westwards* from the Kidney Ridge area, across the Rahman track. This hole would be blown by Freyberg, and would be some three miles deep; through it Monty would pass his entire armoured corps and two armoured car regiments:

The Armd Car Regts will be launched right into open country to operate for four days against the enemy supply routes.

The two Armoured Divisions will engage and destroy the DAK.

This, in effect, is a hard blow with my right, followed the next night with a knock-out blow with my left. The blow on night 31 Oct/1 Nov will be supported by some 350 guns firing about 400 rounds a gun.

I have given the name 'SUPERCHARGE' to the operation.[133]

Thus, instead of being held back in reserve until Leese's XXX Corps had smashed an infantry path all the way through the Axis forces along the coast, Lumsden's armoured corps was once again being asked to take part in an assault capacity – this time as part of 'a knock-out blow'.

Whether the armour would perform any better than it had in the battle so far, however, remained to be seen. Leese was hopeful, as he told his wife, but not overly confident with regard to the armour. 'We launch next a further attempt to break the Armour through what we hope are the last main enemy minefields.' Reflecting on the battle so far, he wrote: 'This battle will be argued for many years, as to whether the Cavalry might have got through as a result of initial break. We had deceived & surprised the enemy – & I feel there was a chance. All our infantry feel that. I've been very definite with Herbert [Lumsden], and I trust they will really make a big effort, if we can get another break-in. Bernard [Freyberg] is doing the break, so there is a grand chance. The enemy is beginning to feel our shelling, bombing and general pressure, but I think the battle is not yet over by a large margin yet.'[134]

He was right.

Political pressure

Two years later, in Normandy, Monty would face the same pressure from Churchill – whose ear had been bent by Eisenhower and others, frightened of stalemate. Meanwhile at Alamein, on 29 October, Monty's soldierly instinct was to smash his way in a self-replenishing thrust with infantry and artillery, behind the Australians, on to and along the coast road, however long it might take and however many casualties this would entail. Certainly this was what Rommel feared. In his memoirs Rommel recalled that his army 'had been so badly battered by the British air force and artillery that we could not now hope to stand up for long to the British break-through attempt, which was daily or even hourly expected'.[135]

Given the strategic hopes vested in Torch, an accelerated victory at Alamein seemed vital – and it was this necessity that had caused Monty to alter his plan for Supercharge. Ultra decrypts, moreover, indicated Rommel was becoming 'critically' short of fuel – in which case a British armoured thrust inland, through the desert and hopefully through Italian defences, might be able to encircle, even cut off, the German panzer units better than a direct, methodical assault along the coast road. For good or ill, Monty therefore noted in his diary that 'at 1100 hours on 29 October I changed my plan and decided to attack further to the south, because I had learnt that 90 Light Div was in [the Australian] area, also that the enemy is very short of petrol'.[136]

Military historians would hail this as the decisive moment of the battle of Alamein. But if truth be told, Churchill's signal and the necessity of speeding up the conclusion of the battle in the interests of Torch was to produce a tantalizingly slow finale to one of the decisive battles of human history – indeed threatened, at one moment in the following days, to squander it.

The dope

John Poston, Monty's ADC, had been used as a personal liaison officer from the very start of the battle, for Monty was dissatisfied by the situation reports and telephone conversations with commanders; he wanted a 'personal impression' of the way the battle was going in certain sectors. The twenty-three-year-old Poston thus became Monty's eyes and ears around the front. 'Army Comd (Monty) sent ADC (Poston. 11.H[ussars]) with personal congratulations on handling of Div,' General Briggs recorded in his diary on 29 October, proud of Lieutenant-Colonel Turner's stalwart defence of Kidney Ridge but unaware how deeply disillusioned Monty had become with the performance of the armour. For his part Poston was aware – and reported back – just how confused and difficult the fighting was, in the heat, smoke and seemingly endless expanse of sand, as he braved mines, shells and bombs to get through. 'I used to go to the Armoured Brigades & forward Regiments to see what was going on,' he afterwards described to his family. ' "Kidney Hill", perhaps you have heard of it, had many awful moments for me! One day though, two of us were forced to the ground in far too shallow a slit trench for 20 minutes, & during the time one of Jerry's 210mm shells landed about 6 yds away, rolled over & lay there like a great fish, & we were just too staggered to move, & in the end just crept away like two naughty chickens!

'Another time,' Poston related, 'I was driving along & saw chaps running like hell, so leapt out of the Jeep, ran 10 yds & flung myself in the sand. It was Jerry doing one of his frightening Fighter Bomber [Stuka] raids. The bomb fell, & at the end I had no Jeep, one landed on the bonnet & that was that! . . . There was quite a bit of sniping by the Huns from derelict tanks, & one day I was marking my map by a tank, luckily covered by it, but the chap who was giving "the dope" had his head & shoulders above the back of it, suddenly flopped down dead from a sniper. It was awful but one grows used to it.'[137]

The 8th Army's casualties were mounting – but Ultra, at least, began to provide a welcome indication that Rommel's nerve was cracking. Rommel's situation day report to OKW (the Wehrmacht high command) for 28 October had been decrypted at Bletchley Park in England, and forwarded both to Churchill in London and to Montgomery at Alamein late in the evening of 29 October. The report described the situation as 'grave in the extreme', with fuel stocks at a critically low level and German tank strength down to eighty-one. Moreover, very strong British forces appeared to be preparing to break through in the north, via Sidi Rahman.[138] Excited, Churchill summoned Brooke at 11.30 p.m. on 29 October and showed him Rommel's message. 'He had a specially good intercept he wanted me to see and was specially nice,' Brooke recorded in his diary. Referring to the Middle East, Churchill now asked: 'Would you not like to have accepted the offer of Command I made to you and be out there now?'[139]

After Churchill's ignorant tirade earlier that morning, this *volte-face* was galling to Brooke. Time and again Brooke had had to keep his cool, driven to distraction by Churchill's changes of mood and mind; but he was mollified, however, when Churchill went on to say how grateful he was that Brooke had elected to stay and serve him in London. Brooke and Churchill each retired to bed, much relieved.

Postponement

All day on 30 October the RAF bombed the German lines, as the Australians prepared for the second stage of their infantry assault, due to kick off at 10 p.m. 'The attack of 9 Aust Div went in under a terrific artillery fire,' Monty noted noted in his diary. 'My caravan at my Tactical H.Q. shook all night.'[140]

At 6 a.m. the next morning, day eight of the battle, Monty recorded that the Australian assault had been 'a great success. By dawn over 400 prisoners had been taken, all Germans, and the attack had reached the coast. The rest of 164th German Division were trapped and will not be able to escape.'[141]

He was speaking too soon. Rommel had hoped, after the lull on 30 October, to pull 21st Panzer Division into mobile reserve, to be replaced by the Italian Trieste Division. Taking personal charge of the counter-attack from a new command post by the mosque at Sidi Abd el Rahman, he detailed von Thoma, the commander of the Afrika Korps, to assemble everything he had to rescue the 125 Infantry Regiment, cut off by the Australian advance – and the battlefield became, once again, an inferno. Reconnaissance aircraft spotted the German panzers moving, and both the Desert Air Force and RAF went into battle on 8th Army's behalf, attacking the panzers as they collected.

Certainly, if Monty wished he had held to his intention to break out from the Australian sector, given the apparent success of the Australian night attack, such thoughts must have been quickly erased by the fierceness of the German counter-attacks throughout 31 October. 'Some 18 German tanks were rushed down the road and broke through, and have joined the Germans that are cut off,' Monty noted at 6 p.m.;[142] however not even the rugged Australians could seal off the pocket.

The rivers of blood spilled that day threatened to become a sea. Able to glimpse but not reach the coast, the Australians were able only to hold the coast road and railway – to which they clung tenaciously despite everything Rommel did to dislodge them that day and the next. Some of the most savage fighting of the battle occurred as ground was taken, lost, and retaken on both sides. Leese recalled the heroism of the Australians with enduring admiration:

The Australians . . . established a very difficult salient beyond Point 29 [Thompson's Post] which they held against continuous Panzer counterattack. If the front of that Division had been penetrated during their four-days' ordeal, the whole success of the 8th Army plan could have been prejudiced. As it was, they suffered over 5000 casualties, but they beat off all enemy attacks . . . They drew on their front most of the Panzer Corps of which they destroyed a great part with their anti-tank guns. It was a magnificent piece of fighting by a great Division, led by an indomitable character, Leslie Morshead.[143]

Rommel, having personally directed the panzer and infantry counter-attacks against the Australians with the Afrika Korps commander at his side wrote to his wife the next day: 'It's a week since I left home – a week of very, very hard fighting. It was often doubtful whether we'd be able to hold out. Yet we managed it each time, though with sad losses. I'm on the move a lot in order to step in wherever we're in trouble. Things were very bad in the north yesterday morning [31 October],' he confided, 'although it was all more or less cleared up by the evening'[144] – causing him to wonder why Montgomery did not now commit his British armour.

Why, Rommel asked in a retrospective analysis of the battle, had the British not thrown in 'the 900 or so tanks, which they could safely have committed on the northern front, in order to gain a quick decision with the minimum of effort and casualties. In fact, only half that number of tanks, acting under cover of their artillery and air force, would have sufficed to destroy my forces, which frequently stood immobile on the battlefield.'[145]

Liddell Hart, inadvertently, provided the answer to Rommel's question in 1958 when, reviewing the battle, he noted how the British tank 'commanders and troops became bitterly critical about the continued attempt to push a mass of tanks through such a narrow breach under the enemy's concentrated fire, and felt that the battle was becoming a "Passchendaele-with-armour".'[146] Thus, to the end of his life, Rommel failed to appreciate the failure of the British armour to co-operate with infantry, artillery and air forces in the confined spaces of such a battle – compelling Monty to withdraw X Corps from the fighting entirely, and to allocate it behind Freyberg's human and artillery battering ram – an acknowledgement that the British could only win the battle by the use of infantry forces, not armour.

However, even the launching of Commonwealth and Allied infantry was becoming, after the casualties of the first week's fighting, a test of faith in Monty's powers of battlefield leadership on behalf of his 'League of Nations' army. Operation Supercharge, as Monty titled it, promised to do what the armour would not – but even that operation had, sadly, to be postponed. To Monty's consternation, Freyberg informed Leese he needed more time to set up his attack, given the confusion of the battlefield and the exhaustion of the troops.

The Australians were fighting to the death in the north; yet without Freyberg, Monty was clear, the 'knock-out blow with my left' might fail, given the fierceness of Axis resistance. Judging by experience, Lumsden's X Corps could not be counted upon to pass through unless all resistance had been extinguished. Monty had no option, therefore, but to accept a twenty-four-hour postponement – wrecking the advantage of right–left surprise.

Such was the price of democracy, in combat with the forces of the dictators. The art of battlefield – rather than theoretical – command, Monty was learning, lay not in fine tactics, but in shaping the battle so that the weaknesses of democracy – the relative lack of martial spirit, and the friction inherent in the attempt to co-ordinate the forces of so many coalition countries – did not completely destroy the chance of victory. It was becoming, in other words, a test of patience as well as resolve.

Supercharge

The situation on the desert battlefield was certainly fantastically confused
– so confused in fact that the chief of staff of the New Zealand Division
and the G1 (Plans), 8th Army, were told to go and identify all units on the
ground and, by authority of the army commander, order those not
involved in Supercharge to withdraw to the rear immediately![147]

Refusing to use his own New Zealand brigades, Freyberg was adamant
he would need to use two for the break-in, with more to follow. Tynesiders
of 151 Brigade from 50 Division, in the south, were brought up for the
attack, but in order to make sure of success Freyberg also asked for a brigade
of Highlanders from General Wimberley's division, who knew the ground.
The artillery, however, expressed reservations about having first to support
the Australians in the north, then Freyberg's attack further south and
towards the west, in what would be the first creeping barrage of World War
II in the desert; thus the operation was set for 1 a.m. on 2 November.

Monty remained unfazed by the delay. Intelligence had confirmed that
'90 Light Div and 21 Panzer Div are both up North in the SIDI RAHMAN
area, and that all the troops up in that area are German';[148] this reassured
him that his knock-out blow would this time succeed, as long as the
armour followed up without delay.

Preparations resembled those of 23 October. As the hours of Sunday 1
November – day nine of the battle – ticked away, General Leese wrote
home to England: 'We are having the hell of a dog fight. The Boches is
fighting hard. He knows he's done, if he is beaten' – for defeat at Alamein
would spell the end of the Axis forces in North Africa. 'Tonight we are
going to have another try to get our armour out. I do trust & hope we
shall succeed this time. If we can bring on another armoured battle, we
can finish him off. It's all a matter of who can stick it longest . . . If only
we can make a good hole tonight, it will be grand. The RAF has been
first class and we have been bombed very little, in comparison with the
pounding we have given him. The shelling has been very heavy on our
side – and quite enough by him, as he has more heavy and medium artillery
than us.' In haste, just before 4 p.m., he ended: 'I must go to a conference
with [Monty]. It will be wonderful if tonight comes off.'[149]

Monty had personally written out the order for Supercharge, the final
stage of the battle, on 30 October, before accepting Freyberg's plea for
postponement. 'We know from all sources of intelligence that the enemy

is in a bad way, and his situation is critical,' Monty had written in the final paragraph of his original directive – a euphemism for Ultra. 'The continued offensive operations of Eighth Army and the R.A.F. have reduced him to such a state that a hard blow *now* will complete his overthrow.'[150]

In the privacy of his diary, however, he admitted the twenty-four-hour delay, 'gives an advantage to the enemy';[151] equally he knew, as he later revealed, 'that there were doubts in high places about SUPERCHARGE, and whisperings about what would happen if it failed. These doubts I did not share and I made that quite clear to everyone,' he related; it had to succeed.[152]

The personal letters Monty wrote that evening bear out his patient confidence – though whether he would be able to round up the Panzer Army's mobile forces, given the possibility that Rommel might withdraw to Fuka, was another matter. To the commandant of the Staff College Monty wrote that he was 'in the middle of a terrific battle with Rommell [*sic*]. I would like to lecture to the Staff College about it! I hope to defeat him in a few days time. So far it has been a complete slogging match, carried on in an enormous minefield.'[153] Owing to mines, shelling and bombing he had had to abandon his staff car and move around the battlefield in a Grant tank – leading to his latest headgear, a black beret of the Royal Tank Regiment, with his general's badge alongside that of the RTR. 'In the latter stages of this battle the Army Commander came up every day to see me in a tank. I think it was then that he first wore the famous Beret with two badges,' Leese recalled later. 'His drive up had a most heartening effect on the troops.'[154]

To the Reynoldses, acting as David Montgomery's guardians, Monty wrote in similarly confident vein, remarking that Rommel was 'resisting desperately. I hold the initiative. But it has become a real solid and bloody killing match. I do not think he can go on much longer. I am dealing him a terrific blow in the very early hours of tomorrow 2nd Nov and it may well knock him off his perch. I hope so.'[155] Whether the British armour would or would not follow through, he was unsure – and remained resigned to the possibility that he would have to order yet more attacks by his dwindling infantry. To his boss and mentor, Sir Alan Brooke, he described the battle and its approaching climax:

I have managed to keep the initiative throughout and so far Rommel has had to dance entirely to my tune; his counter-attack and thrusts have been handled without difficulty up to date. I think he is now ripe for a real hard blow which may topple him off his perch. It is going in tonight and I am putting everything I can into it; I think we have bluffed him into where it is coming. I hope to loose two regiments of Armd Cars into open country where they can manoeuvre. If everything goes really well there is quite a good chance we may put 90 Light Div and 21 Panzer Div both in the bag. But battles do not go as one plans, and it may be that we shall not do this. We have got all the Germans up in the north in the Sidi Rahman area, and I am attacking well south of that place. There will be hard and bitter fighting as the enemy is resisting desperately and has no intention of retiring.

I am enjoying the battle, and I have kept very fit and well. It is getting chilly now, especially at night, and I have taken to 4 blankets at nights. Tonight's battle I have called 'Supercharge' and I enclose a copy of my orders for it. If we succeed it will be the end of Rommel's army.

Reviewing his subordinates he considered that 'Oliver Leese has been quite first class; so has Horrocks, but he is away in the south and has little to do.' Lumsden, charged with the armoured break-out from Freyberg's break-in, was another matter:

Lumsden has been very disappointing; he may be better when we get out into the open. But my own view is that he is not suited for high command, but is a good fighting Div Commander. He is excitable, highly strung, and is easily depressed. He is considerably at sea in charge of a Corps and I have to watch over him very carefully. The best of the lot is Oliver Leese, who is quite first class. Freyberg is superb, and is the best fighting Div Comd I have ever known. He has no great brain power and could never command a Corps. But he leads his Division into battle, going himself in front in a Honey tank with two other Honies in attendance. The only way to find him during a battle is to look for a group of 3 Honey tanks in the NZ area; that will be Freyberg!!

My great task is to keep morale high and spirits up.

I believe that the attack we launch tonight may just do the trick. I am placing great reliance on the Armd Cars, and if I can launch them into enemy rear areas the morale and material damage they will do will be immense.

I hope you are keeping fit.

Yours ever

Monty[156]

With this, Monty retired to bed and went to sleep.

Just after 1 a.m. on 2 November 1942, day ten of the battle, the combined guns of two British corps thundered: a shattering and ominous herald of the major British attack most Axis troops in the north of Alamein had feared must, eventually, come.

Creeping barrage

0100 Attack went in under a creeping barrage on a front of 4000 yds fired by over 300 25-pdrs. It was probably the first creeping barrage ever used in EGYPT. The attack was a complete success.

Thus ran Monty's initial diary entry for 2 November 1942.[157]

Wellington and Albacore bombers added to the conflagration. Fifteen thousand shells were fired over four and a half hours. The headquarters of the Afrika Korps was hit, and von Thoma injured; telephone lines were destroyed, and short-wave radio transmissions jammed to disrupt signals. When Rommel went forward in the early morning he found the infantry positions which 8th Army had attacked to the south-west of the coastal sector, in the dark, had been overrun on a 4,000-yard-wide front, and the British armour was threatening to break out.

The Highlanders, on the left-hand side of the advance, had carried out a model night-attack that took them not only on to their target, but so deep into the Axis tank laagers the infantry had begun dropping grenades into tank turrets. Opposition was stronger on the right, however – the passage of the Durham Light Infantry 'rough and bloody', as Brigadier Lucas Phillips recorded; yet virtually all objectives were secured. One Durham infantryman recalled being cheered on in half-whispers by Australians. 'One slapped me on the back and whispered, "Sic em for me, Limey". I got the queer feeling we were going to a dangerous sort of football match. The continuous growling of the guns and whining of the shells seemed unreal . . . It was pitch black and freezing cold. There was scores of empty slit -trenches but most of them held enemy dead.'

Even the controversial Woodcock position on Kidney Ridge had finally fallen to troops of the 133 Lorried Brigade, on the left flank, and a Maori battalion (28th) of New Zealanders had linked the Tynesiders and Australians on the right.[158] Promptly at 5.45, Freyberg had laid down, the Crusader, Grant and Sherman tanks of his supporting 9th Armoured

Brigade were to move behind another creeping barrage on to 'Recluse': the Rahman track. An hour later, at 6.45 a.m., Lumsden's corps was to pass through the two armoured brigades of Briggs' 1st Armoured Division – 2nd and 8th Brigades – on to the Tell-el-Aqqaqir Ridge.

In many respects it was a carbon copy of the opening phase of Lightfoot, with the same timed artillery barrage, the same infantry assault in the darkness, the same follow-up by support tanks of 9th Armoured Brigade, paving the way for sappers, motorized infantry, anti-tank guns, artillery and heavy tanks of the main Armoured Division.

Sadly, however, it followed exactly the same pattern as on the night of 23 October.

The armour fails to get out

In the letter he penned to his wife Margaret the next day, General Leese confided his profound disappointment. 'Our break through attack on Sunday was magnificent. The Infantry did 4000 yds behind a barrage & my armour [123 tanks of 9th Armoured Brigade, attached to the New Zealand Division] followed it up another 2000 yds in the dash. It was not so difficult as our first night. The Armour then again failed to get out.'[159]

In his unpublished memoirs, Sir Oliver Leese was more caustic. 'The attack [by XXX Corps] exceeded all expectations,' he wrote. 'The effect of the tanks of the 9th Armoured Brigade [the New Zealand support brigade] moving along the lanes in rear of the infantry was devastating to the enemy morale; and neither infantry brigade had even to mop-up. By dawn all objectives were captured and the 9th Armoured Brigade were on the Tell-el-Aqqaqir feature.

'Once again there seemed to be a chance for the Armour to break out. Two Armoured Car Squadrons of the Royals had got out but the armour was again unable to get beyond our FDLs [front line]. The 9th Armoured Brigade themselves had had a great success but they had had many casualties and were forced to withdraw.

'Once again it was up to the infantry soldier. I almost said: "as usual".'

It was, indeed, another tragedy: presaging the battle of Tell-el-Aqqaqir, and the true climax of the battle of Alamein.

Before daylight

As on 24 October, the problem was impending daylight. Twenty-nine of 9th Armoured Brigade's tanks had failed even to reach the front line – one squadron having taken the wrong fork, and having had to return, delaying the Warwickshire Yeomanry by a crucial half hour before sun-up. These thirty minutes were – as had happened at Dieppe, two months before – to mark the difference between success and suicide.

'The advance of the armour was too slow,' Freyberg noted in his own account of the battle, 'and at 0500 hours I gave orders to press on with the Divisional Cavalry carriers in front, and not wait for the ground to be swept for mines.' As a result of 9th Armoured's delay, Freyberg stated, however, 'The barrage to cover the advance of 9 Armoured Brigade to their final objective had to be postponed for half an hour, i.e. to 0615 hours. This was a great pity. Had we had another hour's darkness 9 Armoured Brigade might have got through before first light.'[160]

Instead, the brigade of yeomanry tanks emerged in the dawn light, watched by dozens of alert 88mm and 7.62cm gunners, as well as other German and Italian artillery officers. The subsequent charge by 9th Armoured Brigade was later likened to that of the Light Brigade at Bala-clava. Monty had told Freyberg he would accept 100 per cent casualties in order to burst through the 'bulge' to the Rahman track; Briggs' 1st Armoured Division would then pass through and position itself on the Aqqaqir high ground, perhaps even cutting off 21st Panzer Division in the north, but certainly forcing Rommel either to counter-attack with his remaining armour, or run away – leaving his non-motorized formations to be captured.

There was no wireless communication, however, between the three yeomanry regiments of 9th Armoured Brigade; worse still, their anti-tank guns did not get through. The result, as dawn broke, was lethal.

'All the bounds were called after packs of hounds,' Captain Stoddart recounted. 'We knew what to expect and that at any moment the sun would come up . . . I gave all my crew a sip of whisky and we were off. Very slowly at first in the half light. Nothing happened for a few minutes and then hell was let loose. The by this time well-known and dreaded "white tennis balls" again came leaping and bounding at us from the darkness and from every direction. I was the first of the whole Regiment to be hit . . . We were very nearly run over by our own friends and Jerry was shooting hard and it was not yet properly light . . .'

German tanks now joined the fray. Stoddart crawled over to another disabled Sherman where, finding that the radio was working, he attempted to radio his commanding officer. As he described to his father, 'My name on the air was "Charlie". So I called up: "Charlie' – What do you what me to do?" etc. I was answered in English by a German who said, "Charlie, you have been very quiet lately, I hope you haven't been in trouble, but isn't it nice to see all your beautiful new toys going up in smoke – over!" '[161]

As General Bayerlein later remarked, 'the German forces were given, in the form of the 88 Pak-Flak gun, a weapon which, in the multiple uses to which it could be put, was envied but never matched. It contributed decisively to German successes, even though it was considered by the English to be "unfair" because of its muzzle size and velocity'. As Rommel put it, the 88 was the very 'backbone' of the Panzer Army in Africa.[162]

Brigadier Currie, to show an example to his yeomanry tank commanders, had insisted on standing on the outside of his own tank during the charge. He led a charmed life; his tanks quickly overran the forward 50mm guns of the German and Italian positions, but as they raced beyond the Rahman track – distinguished by its telegraph poles – the dawning light had silhouetted the tanks, and they were engaged by dug-in 88s on the Tell-el-Aqqaqir Ridge as well as by forward panzers of 15th Panzer Division, emerging from the morning mist. According to the German formation war diaries, Rommel had ordered German artillery and infantry 'feint' attacks to be carried out early on the morning of 2 November 'to divert the enemy forces in the north',[163] where the Australian 'thumb' threatened to reach the sea with the next British offensive; thus the Germans had already been preparing for their morning spoiling action when news of the British offensive had come through.

Instead of attacking, the Germans had found themselves attacked: their forward troops shattered by murderously concentrated shelling in the night, followed by enemy infantry advance. Infantry positions held by Panzer Grenadiers and Bersaglieri alike were simply wiped out by the Highlanders and Tynesiders, yet the professionalism of the Afrika Korps, especially in its use of anti-tank guns and artillery, had not become legendary without reason. The 21st Panzer Division had been alerted at 2.17 a.m. by the Afrika Korps headquarters of an attack, and had been ready to fight at 4.30, once the *Schwerpunkt* became clear. The 15th Panzer Division was aware its front had been penetrated by 3 a.m. 'The enemy may have broken through the Bersaglieri,' it reported to Afrika Korps at 3.10, and contact had been 'lost'. By 3.15 Afrika Korps ordered 21st Panzer Division to 'push through' and 'restore the situation. Its advance will be of decisive importance.' Meanwhile, 15th Panzer Division was to prepare to beat off the attack on its front. 'The enemy must be destroyed. Keep in line communication with 21 Pz Div as long as possible.' At 3.40 a.m. Rommel's chief of staff 'gave orders for 15 and 21 Pz Div to attack immediately. Speed was essential. General von Vaerst was to lead the attack', as von Thoma could not be reached at his Tactical HQ. Von Vaerst, reconnoitring the position 'thought the situation did not look too good', Afrika Korps reported to Rommel. 'The 88mm AA guns on the Otto track were probably holding their positions. The infantry seems to have been overrun.'[164]

Thus, as the sun rose inexorably over the desert on 2 November 1942 – day ten of Alamein – there was still no mercy for the troops of either side.

The battle of Tell-el-Aqqaqir

In trying to smash a path through to the Aqqaqir Ridge, Brigadier Currie had lost 75 of his 94 tanks, and 230 of his 400 men. As Brigadier Lucas Phillips described, Currie looked at the devastation of his brigade and the guns they had overrun; 'As far as the eye could see lay the terrible record – tank after tank burning or wrecked, the smoke of their burning mingled with the cold mist, the crimson shafts from the eastern sky tincturing all objects with the hue of blood. Only here and there could he see a tank still defiantly shooting it out with the more distant guns and the tanks of the Afrika Korps. He was very angry, very bitter. In fulfilment of his orders, he was ready to sacrifice all if Fisher's brigade had been there to crash through whatever ragged breaches he had torn in the enemy's wall of guns.'[165] But Fisher had not been there.

In Leese's view, had 1st Armoured Division pressed on the heels of the self-sacrificing Brigadier Currie, the battle might then have been won by weight of numbers, with concentrated artillery fire focused by the forward artillery observers of the armoured regiments, as well as RAF attacks keeping the two Panzer divisions apart. Again and again Freyberg signalled to Leese to urge on 1st Armoured Division, but without avail. When the commander of the leading regiment of Fisher's brigade reached Currie, Currie called him up on to his tank.

'Well, we've made a gap in the enemy anti-tank screen, and your brigade has to pass through bloody quick,' Currie declared. The Lancers' colonel, Gerald Grosvenor, surveying the scene of destruction and smoking hulks, answered: 'I have never seen anything, sir, that looks less like a gap.'[166]

Fisher was, unfortunately, already two and a half miles behind Currie when 9th Armoured Brigade made its fateful yeomanry attack; indeed, it was 7 a.m when Grosvenor reached Currie, in broad daylight. By then, with 21st Panzer Division moving to join up with the 15th, it was too late for 2nd and 8th Armoured Brigades to force their way through.

General Briggs was adamant, after the war, that the leading brigade of his armoured division was right to refuse to go forward; 'The plain truth is that armour cannot charge concealed or semi-concealed guns just behind a crest & get away with it. These have to be dealt with methodically by stalking, H[igh] E[xplosive] fire and artillery concentrations, & this takes time. If [Fisher's] 2nd Armoured Brigade had been closer up, the story would have repeated itself.'[167]

Rightly or wrongly Fisher thus held back in the blazing morning sunlight, and the great slugfest of 2 November took place, with hundreds upon hundreds of tanks, anti-tank guns and artillery guns hammering away at each other in a three-mile-square area east of the Rahman track – while between them the infantry, which had cleared the way forward to this point, sheltered as far as possible in slit trenches as the battle raged. One artillery signals sergeant supporting the New Zealand Division, noting in his diary the number of tanks that had passed along 'Boomerang Track', remarked: 'I did not imagine we had so much armour out here.'[168]

Monty, however, was determined to force a gap, and ordered Leese to put in yet another infantry assault through the south-west corner of the salient on to the 'Skinflint' ridge; meanwhile, bypassing Lumsden, he gave direct orders to Briggs to switch the 8th Armoured Brigade to that area, ready to exploit the gap. 'I will take care of that,' he snapped, when Briggs' chief of staff voiced his concern about the vulnerability of the northern flank.[169]

Briggs attempted to concur with the army commander's order, but by then almost all Brigadier Custance's regiments in 8th Armoured Brigade were fighting fiercely, and both Fisher and Custance were confident they were knocking the guts out of the two panzer divisions and their gun-lines.

They were. The great tank battle that had been the original objective of

Monty's Lightfoot plan had, by accident, finally come to pass. Von Thoma reckoned he was holding back the enemy advance east of the crucial Otto, or Rahman, track; yet in doing so the Panzer Army took a mortal pounding. Briggs had trained his tank commanders to use indirect fire, lobbing shells from hull-down positions where the tank commanders operated as observation officers to their own crews, peeping over the ridges of dunes and defiles. The artillery were using 'Priests' – massive 105mm guns mounted on Grant chassis – and the RAF were being asked to bomb the support echelons visible behind the panzers. Armoured cars were beginning to exploit local gaps in the Axis line, while naval parties were attacking the coast, just behind the German lines, forcing Panzer Army headquarters to look in two directions. Co-operation between all arms was, finally, becoming the order of the Allied day.

By 5.30 p.m. on 2 November Rommel was signalling to von Thoma: 'Enemy too strong. I have seen 40 knocked out tanks myself. Our losses high. Enemy outflanking formations individually.' The Afrika Korps, he reckoned, 'will have 30–35 tanks at the most tomorrow. The enemy in the front line alone has a fourfold superiority. The gaps are closed, but very thinly held. If the enemy attacks again the line will not hold. Every fresh attack opens a fresh hole. No reserves.'[170]

The result was inescapable: 'Withdrawal necessary.'[171] The 8th Army had won.

Retreat

German and Italian infantrymen not locked in combat began retreating that very night. To his wife, Rommel wrote of 'the end' and to OKW he radioed at 7.50 p.m. on 2 November his famous admission of defeat:

After ten days of extremely hard fighting against overwhelming British superiority on the ground and in the air the strength of the Army is exhausted in spite of today's successful defence. It will, therefore, no longer be in a position to prevent a new attempt to break through with strong enemy armoured formations which is expected to take place tonight or tomorrow. An orderly withdrawal of the six Italian and two German non-motorized divisions and brigades is impossible for lack of MT [motor transport]. A large part of these formations will probably fall into the hands of the enemy who is fully motorized. Even the mobile troops are so closely involved in the battle that only elements will be able to disengage from the enemy . . . The shortage of fuel will not allow of a withdrawal to any great distance. There is only one road available and the Army, as it passes along it, will almost certainly be attacked day and night by the enemy air force.

In these circumstances we must therefore expect the gradual destruction of the Army in spite of the heroic resistance and exceptionally high morale of the troops.[172]

Did the message mean Rommel was withdrawing; was seeking permission to withdraw; or was standing fast and expecting to be annihilated? Not until the early hours of the next day, 3 November, did Rommel's follow-up report reach OKW, in which he retrospectively announced his orders for the retreat of the Axis infantry, to begin at 10 p.m. on the night of 2 November.

These two messages were decoded at Bletchley Park in England, and were in Brooke's hands (and Monty's) by midday on 3 November, as Brooke ecstatically recorded in his diary:

Whilst at lunch I was called up by DMI [Director of Military Intelligence] and informed of the two recent intercepts of Rommel's messages to GHQ and Hitler in which he practically stated that his army was faced with a desperate defeat from which he could only extricate remnants![173]

In his 'Notes on My Life' Brooke wrote: 'It can be imagined what the receipt of this message . . . meant to me. I dared not yet allow myself to attach too much importance to it, but even so felt as if I were treading on air the rest of that day.'[174]

Even Monty's own staff, given the failure of the British armour to break out in Supercharge, were surprised by the defeatism of Rommel's signals. Morale among 8th Army units was becoming paper thin; indeed, for many of those sheltering from the hail of shells and bullets survival was of more concern than victory. 'I shall never as long as I live forget 2 November, 1942,' one Highlander recalled.

It was the longest day of my life. Never was I more pleased to see the sun go down that day and be thankful to be still alive . . . We had to stay put from the moment the tanks went through us until the sun set. The shelling and mortaring were unceasing, heavy and accurate. All day long we expected every minute to be our last . . . Apart from many wounded, some of whom died later from wounds received, we had 48 officers and men killed outright. By the time the sun did eventually set, the horizon was filled with 'brewed-up' tanks, mostly Shermans . . . Eventually, the remaining tanks withdrew for the night and we were left alone, constantly expecting a Jerry counterattack . . . We didn't think at the time that Jerry was beaten.[175]

The decoding of Rommel's increasingly despairing messages thus gave new heart to those listening to reports of the battle at 8th Army head-quarters. 'This Ultra message reached us extremely quickly,' Charles Richardson recalled. 'Being somewhat sceptical of the army commander's optimistic view of events, I shall never forget the elation of myself and of Bill Williams.'[176]

Ultra was soon confirmed by air reconnaissance. Rommel's diarist noted that by evening 'countless trucks and tanks of the Littorio armoured division, packed with troops, are visible on the road as they make their individual ways back. Afrika Korps reports that Littorio is no longer under officer-control – it has just burst at the seams. Elements of it are in full flight'[177] – and the same was reported of the Trieste Motorized Division. 'Just before dinner – about 5 o'clock – we heard that Jerry was pulling out,' Sergeant Bennett recorded in his diary. 'Personally I do not believe it is a full scale retreat – although some chaps are very optimistic – but there seems to be no doubt that there is some sort of movement on foot – the RAF have reported it. At any rate it is good news.'[178]

For 8th Army, it was. Hitler, however, was flabbergasted.

Victory or death

Rommel's second report, announcing his order to retreat, was only given to Hitler at 9 a.m. on 3 November, when he awoke. Threatening to have the duty officer shot for withholding it, Hitler sacked General Warlimont, who 'is snug asleep, while Rommel is appealing to me'[179] and immediately countermanded the retreat – dictating his equally famous signal that Rommel was to fight to the death at Alamein:

With me the entire German nation is watching your heroic defensive battle in Egypt, with well-placed confidence in your leadership qualities and in the courage of your German and Italian troops. In your present situation nothing else can be thought of but to hold on, not to yield a step, and to throw every weapon and every fighting man who can still be freed into the battle . . . You can show your troops no other road than to victory or death.[180]

Mussolini despatched a similar signal, via his chief of the Italian high command, Marshal Cavallero: 'Duce considers it imperative to hold present front at all costs.'[181]

Rommel was hurt and ashamed – especially by the implication that he was running away. He was, he recalled, 'completely stunned, and for the first time during the African campaign I did not know what to do'[182] – claiming that, without Hitler's countermand, he might still have rescued his Army:

Looking back, I am conscious of only one mistake – that I did not circumvent the 'Victory or Death' order twenty-four hours earlier. Then the army would in all probability have been saved, with all its infantry, in at least a semi-battleworthy condition.[183]

This, however, was moonshine. Hitler's countermand was only decoded at Rommel's Panzer Army headquarters at 1.30 p.m. on the afternoon of 3 November – by which time, behind a rearguard of artillery and motorized units, those troops who could get away were already on the move; indeed, had been on the march for more than fifteen hours, as Rommel had directed. They could not, and were not, stopped – rather, the RAF reported increasing, not decreasing Axis movement westwards.

How, in these circumstances, Rommel could have hoped to save even a 'semi-battleworthy' army, while Montgomery's air, artillery, infantry and tanks hammered at the final doors of the keep of Rommel's Alamein castle, is hard to understand. Leese's infantry attack by the Highlanders south-westwards on to Skinflint, on the afternoon of 2 November, had paved the way for an armoured night assault by Lumsden's X Corps. This unhappily proved no better, indeed worse, than the daytime advance of the armoured formations, as Briggs himself acknowledged. 'Night attack by 7 Mot Bde,' Briggs noted in his diary the assault he'd put in. '2RB & 7RB NOT successful. Strength of opposition not well gauged.'[184]

Poorly gauged or not, the attacks made it impossible for Rommel to pull out his guns or grenadiers – indeed, the constant pressure so threatened the Italian/German line that Rommel had been forced to throw in his entire motorized and armoured reserves in order to prevent a rout, even before receiving Hitler's order.

Rommel's armour and artillery were now attempting to hold back a flood. Already a whole regiment of South African armoured cars were causing havoc as far west as Daba, British and American aircraft of the Desert Air Force were mercilessly bombing the retreating infantry columns – yet the British armour failed to get through.

With Lumsden's armoured break-out still stalled, Monty had to ask Leese at 9 a.m. on the morning of 3 November, yet again, to use the infantry brigades he had in hand to undertake yet another infantry attack 'in order finally to push out the armour', as Leese recalled.

Exhausted, Leese decided to make three separate infantry assaults, beginning late that afternoon, the first of which was to be carried out by the 1st Gordons supported by a battalion of tanks, in the evening, west of Tell-el-Aqqaqir.

'Today we seemed almost ringed in again by Anti-Tank guns, though we were easily through the minefields,' Leese wrote to his wife that evening. It seemed a tragedy.

As the evening attacks were mounted, Leese became more hopeful. 'Then it suddenly became clear that we had beaten him,' he wrote to his wife, 'and that he was going back. Whether we can break out and cut him off remains to be seen. If we can do so tomorrow we shall cut off thousands of men. It all depends on our success at daylight tomorrow. I hope it will come off. It's been a terrific fight. I have had over 8000 casualties in the Corps. We have taken over 5000 prisoners so far in the Corps, and there are a great number of German dead. It is a hard war here, and victory can only be had at a high price, but it is wonderful if we have driven him out of this defended area ... All my divisions have done jolly well. The Australians have suffered most. By their continual efforts on the coast, they drew the enemy to the north, & thus made possible the break in the centre. The Highlanders have been grand, and have learnt a lot about war. The South Africans did their attack well. They were too short initially in numbers to do much more. The New Zealanders have been grand. Bernard [Freyberg] is magnificent. We hope he may cut off the enemy tomorrow by a bold mobile move. It's grand to have done it so far.'[185]

Once again, however, Lumsden's X Corps fouled up – leading to heart-breaking Scottish casualties on 3 November. 'Three or four hours before the attack was due to go in, 10 Corps informed us that their armour was 2000 yards beyond the Sidi Rahman track and were therefore in possession of our objective,' Leese recalled in his unpublished memoirs. To avoid shelling Lumsden's tanks, Leese therefore cancelled the corps' artillery barrage ahead of his attack, making do with smoke. 'Just before zero hour the armour informed us that in actual fact they were still 2000 yards short of the Sidi Rahman track. It was too late to do anything; the attack went in unsupported and failed.'[186]

Whether Hitler's 'Victory or Death' order was taken seriously at the front is unclear. Major von Luck, commanding a panzer reconnaissance battalion, claimed that Rommel 'decided to pass on to his commanders the Fuehrer's order to hold fast; the men, however, were not to be informed'.[187] David Irving gave a contrary version, Rommel telephoning the Africa Korps commander and insisting, 'You have got to instil this order into your troops: they are to fight to the very limit.'[188]

Either way, German rearguard troops fought with their customary determination. The commander of the 51st Highland Infantry Division, Major-General Douglas Wimberley, had pleaded with Leese to withdraw any of Lumsden's tanks, 'if there were any there', and to 'let my attack go in properly under a Barrage. The position was, as we had reported, strongly held, not a sign of our tanks was to be seen, but plenty of enemy ones,' Wimberly recounted later. 'The Gordons made little progress, and lost a lot of men; I felt it had been sheer waste of life and was sick at heart. Worst of all, thinking that it was an advance rather than an attack, the Gordons put a number of their Jocks on the top of the tanks, to be carried on them forward to the objective. I saw the tanks, later, coming out of action, and they were covered with the dead bodies of our Highlanders. It was an unpleasant sight and bad for morale.'[189]

Leese was mortified by this waste of human life – and furious with Lumsden's staff. 'I had learnt a lesson never again to cancel an artillery programme. Armour can always be moved quickly off any area at will by R/T [radio]. An artillery programme once decided on,' he later reflected, 'must be allowed to run.'[190]

Monty too drew the lesson; and though historians scoffed at later artillery programmes which proved unnecessary – as during the first Allied landings on the mainland of Europe at Reggio the following year – Monty himself remained unrepentant. An infantryman's courage depended on his loyalty to his commander: and no good commander should abuse that loyalty simply to save shells.

Wimberley, meanwhile, was so distraught that, when Leese explained that the armour reported that it was *still* unable to gain the Tell-el-Aqqaqir feature, and that a *further* Highland infantry attack would be necessary to take it, Wimberley broke down. 'I was so sick at heart at being overruled regarding not firing my barrage for the Gordon attack that I must have shown it over the phone, unmistakably,' he recalled. 'I remember Oliver [Leese] said over the phone, "Surely now you, Douglas, of all people are not going to lose heart." '[191]

Wimberley did not. Argyll and Sutherland Highlanders and an infantry brigade from 4th Indian Division, under command, were ordered, once again, to pave the final path for Lumsden's armour. At last, at 2.30 a.m. on Wednesday 4 November 1942, by the light of the waning moon, Brigadier 'Pasha' Russell's 5th Indian Brigade advanced in perfect order behind a creeping barrage, with medium artillery pounding known centres of resistance, and clearing a path for X Corps, some five miles deep, taking out anti-tank guns, mortar pits and strong-points as they went.

At 6.15 a.m. a battalion of Argyll and Sutherland Highlanders, in a separate attack, began making for its objective: Point 44, at the heart of the Tell-el-Aqqaqir feature – only to find that the Germans had already pulled out.

At 6.30 a.m. Monty recorded in his diary:

The armour went through as the dawn was breaking; it got clear away and out into the open, 1 and 7 Armd Divs leading. We had at last passed our armoured formations into the enemy rear areas, and into country clear of minefields, and into country where they could manoeuvre.

The armoured cars raced away to the West, and were directed on FUKA and BUQQUSH.

I ordered the 2 NZ Div, with 4 Light Armd Bde under command, to move out SW, get on to the FUKA track and move with all speed to secure the FUKA bottleneck.[192]

A wave of exhilaration went through the whole of 8th Army. After twelve days and thirteen nights of battle, Rommel's army was smashed, as Monty had predicted – to the day.

23

The Lessons of Alamein

The capture of von Thoma

Alamein was the first offensive battle won by the democracies against a German-led army in World War II; more than half the Panzerarmee Afrika was killed, wounded or captured – 55,000 casualties in an army than had numbered 108,000 at the start of the battle;[1] 'anything that did not reach the road and race off westwards was lost,' Rommel recorded.[2]

The fact that the battle was won, in the end, by perseverance and dogged determination made it all the more moving a victory. 'We've got so many prisoners we hardly know what to do with them,' Lieutenant Potts, the former chaplain, wrote to his fiancée. 'Things are pretty decent now though we had a mighty tough battle for the first 13 days of the offensive. Some of our best fellows are gone, killed or wounded, but we are in high spirits now & hope it will soon all be over. In all this I have not even mentioned that I love you.'[3]

Shortly before his death Major-General de Guingand reflected how 'Democracy had shown itself a poor opponent on the field of battle, when one must be willing to lay down one's life',[4] but Alamein changed that perception – for the Allies as much as for the Germans. The battle demonstrated that, with determined leadership, modern training and better co-operation between services, arms and nations, as well as improved equipment, the Allies could – and would – go on to win the war. 'I believe that our tactics will be a classic for night attacks,' Leese wrote proudly to his wife in the aftermath, adding: 'I feel that "The Battle of Egypt" is the first phase of the great Allied offensive.'[5]

It was. While the Führer was now urged by Field-Marshals Rommel and finally Kesselring to relent over his suicidal order ('The Führer must be crazy,' Rommel had been heard to say[6]), Winston Churchill was free to dictate the messages he had dreamed of. 'I send you my heart-felt congratulations on the splendid feat of arms achieved by the Eighth Army under the command of your brilliant lieutenant, Montgomery, in the Battle of Egypt,' Churchill began by cabling Alexander – moving swiftly on to the prime ministers of the Commonwealth.

At Alamein, shortly after midday on 4 November, the commander of the Afrika Korps was captured, still carrying out Hitler's order to the letter, directing Afrika Korps operations on the northern flank of the British break-out from his own *Kampfstaffel*, or command group. Seeing his tank hit, his chief of staff, Colonel Bayerlein, ran away on foot as fast as his legs would carry him. David Irving, in his biography of Rommel, branded von Thoma a traitor to the Nazi cause for surrendering rather than dying, and several German authors have also contended that von Thoma intended to be captured, but Major Oswald, in charge of Montgomery's Tactical HQ, later well remembered the circumstances of von Thoma's capture, and his soldierly bearing when brought before the 8th Army commander that afternoon:

'A traitor? Nonsense, of course he wasn't. I've heard it said that he was pretty suicidal. But he was a very experienced officer. He'd commanded the Afrika Korps throughout the battle, had commanded the Condor Legion in the Spanish Civil War and was probably one of Germany's leading experts on the use of armour. He was rather a fine-looking chap. I thought he preserved a very soldier-like demeanour – after all, his truck had been shot from under him in the heart of the battle, he'd had a pretty good dusting, and had been brought straight before the army commander.'[7]

Oswald was correct, as Trooper Lindsay of the 10th Hussars recorded. Acting as observation fire officer for B Squadron, Captain Grant Singer's vehicle had been spotted and pierced by a 50mm armour-piercing shell. Informed by Singer, Shermans of B Squadron 10th Hussars opened fire on the Panzer Mk III which had hit Singer's Dingo scout car. 'The enemy machine began to burn, and when the dust from the bombardment had cleared a hand could be seen waving a white cloth. A single figure appeared. The remainder of the crew had been killed.'[8]

The figure was the commander of the Afrika Korps. Captain Singer – who was himself killed the following day – brought von Thoma straight back to Monty's headquarters.

Monty, bare-headed and wearing a light-coloured pullover without insignia of rank over his desert shirt and cotton trousers, greeted his adversary's salute by staring intently into his gaunt eyes. Studying von

Thoma's face he saw the bearing not of a politically motivated Nazi, nor of a traitor, but that of a soldier: a fellow professional. Disregarding the possible publicity or even the political consequences, Monty told him he wished him to dine in his headquarters mess that evening, as his personal guest, before going into captivity. Von Thoma could scarcely refuse. In his diary Monty noted:

General VON THOMA, the Commander Africa Corps, was a prisoner at my HQ and he dined with me in my mess. He is a very nice chap and was quite willing to talk about past events. We discussed the battle in Sept. when ROMMEL attacked me, and we discussed this present battle.

I doubt if many Generals have had the luck to be able to discuss with their opponent the battle that has just been fought.[9]

More than any other episode during the battle, this image of the 8th Army commander on the evening of possibly the most historic British/Commonwealth victory of World War II is the most revealing. While Churchill sought Brooke's approval to ring the church bells of Britain and frantically despatched telegram after telegram to the heads of state of the Allied Nations – to Roosevelt, Stalin, Fraser, Curtin and others – the mountebank Bernard Montgomery, still casually dressed, sat beneath the camouflaged canvas of his mess-tent and, as soon as the meal was over, had the table cleared and a map of the Egyptian desert produced.

'Now, tonight my forces are approaching Fuka – what do you think about that? Come on, what would you do, von Thoma?' Monty harangued his 'luckless opponent', as Oswald later recalled.[10] But von Thoma would give nothing away.

Absolutely smashed

In Cairo on 1 November the BBC reporter Denis Johnston, starved of news, had noted in his diary: 'Front probably bogged down in another stalemate. Every sign of usual ballsup starting.'[11] On 4 November, however, he was taken to 8th Army headquarters, where the head of 8th Army intelligence announced, sceptically, that Monty would give a press conference at his Tactical HQ the following morning to announce 'complete victory'.

There, by the beach, standing beside the commander of the Desert Air Force, Monty delivered, on 5 November, his historic announcement. 'Enemy who can get away are in full retreat,' Johnston noted in his diary. 'Rommel absolutely smashed. Von Thoma, Commander of the Afrika Korps, captured . . .'[12]

In England, shortly before midnight on 4 November, the BBC announcer had already advised listeners 'not to switch off, as at midnight we are giving the best news we have heard for years', Harold Nicolson noted in his diary. 'Then it comes. It is Alexander's communiqué: the Germans are in full retreat in Egypt . . .'[13]

As 8th Army commander Monty's task was now to direct the pursuit of Rommel's fleeing Panzer Army. General Lumsden was ordered to race across the desert and crush Rommel's retreating survivors against the sea, while Freyberg, in a wider sweep, stopped the Fuka escape-route. This manoeuvre by the *corps de chasse* soon proved a lamentable failure – as Leese had feared. 'They don't impress me much,' he confided to his wife. XXX Corps' casualties would total 8,875, compared with 2,886 in X Corps. 'I'm terribly proud of my Infantry Corps and my Army Tanks, but qua Armour I pray & hope that the GAD [Guards Armoured Division, still in England] will have a very different spirit to the Armour here.'[14]

Thus, though he left most of his infantry and weapons behind on the battlefield, Rommel did, at least, manage to get almost half his Panzer Army away, with vehicles racing four abreast along the coast road – which, by an unfortunate error of judgement by the veteran Desert Air Force commander, Air Vice-Marshal Coningham, the RAF and USAAF, despite vast bomber forces, were not ordered to block. Meanwhile, Horrocks took the 30,000 remaining Axis troops prisoner and 'tidied up' the chaos of the battlefield, with its thousands of corpses, smoking tanks, and hundreds of thousands of mines.

Completely crippled

Despite his disappointment with his armoured formations and the RAF in pursuit mode, Monty was moved by the perseverance with which the 8th Army had won through to victory in the battle. His very first act, as the tanks of the *corps de chasse* chased after Rommel, was to visit General Morshead, the commander of the 9th Australian Division, to thank him personally for what the Australian troops had done to achieve a successful outcome in the battle. A week later, on 12 November 1942, 'A Personal Message from the Army Commander' was also printed 'To be Read Out to All Troops' in 8th Army, especially those held back around the charred wreckage of the battlefield. Each man had been given his task in the battle; to each one, Monty was determined to voice his gratitude, and explain the magnitude of their achievement:

When we began the battle of Egypt on 23 October I said that together we would hit the Germans and Italians right out of Africa.

We have made a very good start and to-day, 12 Nov., there are no German and Italian soldiers on Egyptian territory except prisoners.

In three weeks we have completely smashed the German and Italian Army and pushed the fleeing remnants out of Egypt, having advanced ourselves nearly 300 miles up to and beyond the frontier . . . The prisoners number 30,000, including nine Generals.

The amount of tanks, artillery, anti-tank-guns, transport, aircraft, etc., destroyed or captured is so great that the enemy is completely crippled.

This is a very fine performance and I want, first, to thank you all for the way you responded to my call and rallied to the task. I feel that our great victory was brought about by the good fighting qualities of the soldiers of the Empire rather than by anything I may have been able to do myself.

Secondly, I know you will all realise how greatly we were helped in our task by the R.A.F. We could not have done it without their splendid help and co-operation. I have thanked the R.A.F. warmly on your behalf.

Our task is not finished yet; the Germans are out of Egypt but there are still some left in North Africa. There is some good hunting to be had further to the West, in Libya; and our leading troops are in Libya ready to begin. And this time, having reached Bengasi and beyond, we shall not come back . . . As in all pursuits some have to remain behind to start with; but we shall all be in it before the finish.[15]

They would be – for Alamein was but the beginning of the Allied march to Berlin. Yet Monty would not have been Monty if he had not, almost immediately, begun to draw up, as was his didactic wont, the lessons, while they were still fresh in his mind. 'We are very apt in the British Army,' he had noted in his diary, 'to become immersed in details without *first* being clear as to the main fundamentals on which all the details hang; it is these broad fundamentals which governed the whole battle and formed the basis of the victory.'[16] And in his relentlessly analytical way, he proceeded to clarify them.

The Ten Commandments

Monty's *philosophie de guerre*, in launching his offensive, had rested on three phases of battle: the break-in, the dog-fight, and the break-out. The same approach, in time, would be adopted in planning the D-Day landings and the battle of Normandy in 1944. Meanwhile, to carry out these three phases, his experience of Alamein had taught him that an army and its commander should observe Ten Commandments:

1. Careful planning of the break-in battle to give tactical advantage over the enemy – the *Schwerpunkt*.

2. Rapid switching of the thrust line as opposition becomes too stiff on any one axis.

3. Deception.

4. Rapid re-grouping and collecting of reserves after the break-in battle.

5. Maintaining the initiative, involving continous new thrusts with centralized artillery support.

6. Concentrating the fire of artillery

7. Ensuring of tactical surprise at every stage.

This led him to number 8, perhaps the greatest lesson for the democracies, namely the relation of plans to what could be expected of the men:

8. A Commander must so plan and conduct his battle that his operations will be in keeping with the standard of training of his troops. I had an untrained Army, due to Auchinleck and his regime, and I had to be very careful what I did with it. Commanders especially did not know how to fight a good enemy in a real dog-fight; they had been used to dispersion, and to battle-groups and tip and run tactics. The

training of Commanders by their superiors was unknown; there had been no firm doctrine of war on which to base training.

Nor, did he feel, was enough attention paid to the selection of the fighting teams: the leaders who must guide and drive their men into battle, and through to the end of it.

9. Determined leadership is vital, and nowhere is this more important than in the higher ranks. Other things being equal the battle will be a contest between opposing wills.

Generals who become depressed when things are not going well, and who lack the drive to get things done, and the moral courage and resolution to see their plan through to the end, are useless in battle. They are, in fact, worse than useless – they are a menace – since any lack of moral courage, or any sign of wavering or hesitation, has very quick repercussions down below.

An army, like any successful organization, needed not only leaders, but good staff officers. His final lesson therefore concerned the staff – and the spirit within the army:

10. To win battles you require good Commanders in the senior ranks, and good senior staff officers; all of these must know their stuff.

You also require an Army in which the morale of the troops is right on the top line. The troops must have confidence in their Commanders and must have the light of battle in their eyes; if this is not so you can achieve nothing.[17]

By these means, Monty had made certain of victory – and would do so again, he was sure, whatever happened in the pursuit of Rommel's smashed up remnants, or in Torch, or on the second front when launched. Others, including Rommel, might label this brute force[18] – but brute force had been applied in World War I, and had made the price of victory horrific, indeed ultimately self-defeating for the democracies. Alamein, however, was brute force applied relentlessly, yet with constant variations, to a chosen *Schwerpunkt* until the enemy cracked – and under Monty's command, it had worked.

No Allied general had hitherto found a way to handle German armoured attack in World War II, let alone mount a successful Allied counter-attack. Alamein showed how blunt still was the instrument of Allied armoured warfare; but with a new approach to training, planning and co-ordination between arms, the battle had proved victory over the Nazis could be – and would be – won. As Rommel's son Manfred later recalled, Rommel 'knew it was all over after Montgomery's breakthrough at El Alamein in North Africa';[19] the Germans were bound to lose the war.

The fundamentals

'I have now fought Rommel twice,' Monty meanwhile wrote to Sir Alan Brooke on 10 November 1942; 'the first time he attacked me and I saw him off; the second time I attacked him and smashed him up.

'There is much to be learnt from these two battles, and together I think they form the material for a very short and quite small pamphlet on the "Conduct of Battle." This might be given to all Generals, and perhaps Brigadiers, and would be a good doctrine for the whole Army. The two battles were fought on very definite lines. This last one was planned to take the form it did take, and there is no doubt it was too much for Rommel. But I have not time to write it out just yet.

'I believe that unless the Army in England can be given some very clear doctrine, in which the basic fundamentals stand out like beacons, we shall have many failures.'[20]

They would – from Kasserine to Anzio. Such exhortations to study the lessons of battle, and to learn from them, evinced Monty the inveterate teacher as well as battlefield commander. Colleagues and allies would sometimes mock – as when General Patton attended Monty's 'teach-in' or study week at Tripoli several months later and delivered his famous judgement: 'I may be old, and I may be stoopid, but it just don' mean a thing to me!' But to those who knew his life and career, Monty's unending search to simplify, to draw lessons, to train and to teach, were the very characteristics that made him so distinctive as a modern military commander.

In a country riven by class-distinction, upper-class indolence, working-class obstructionism and middle-class confusion, Monty had brought a new sense of common purpose, and clarified the means by which to achieve that purpose. As General Strawson – not a Monty admirer – later wrote:

What mattered about Montgomery was his clarity, his conviction, his confidence, together with his thoroughness and his determination to see an unromantic conclusion – victory for *his* army. It was by mastering the mechanics of the set-piece battle that Montgomery set the seal of his authority on the Eighth Army, the Prime Minister and the country. His sense of certainty, his simple eloquence, the obvious grip he exerted over his subordinates and, through them, over the soldiers, his flamboyant press conferences and personal signals to Churchill – all these things illustrated the power of his leadership. Some disliked what they saw as vanity and showmanship, but on the whole people loved it, from the private soldier up to the Prime Minister.[21]

It was, justly, the battle of Alamein which was credited with the 'turning of the tide' of World War II by German commentators as well as British; yet in military terms the battle itself was only the first, messy, and certainly bloody manifestation of a new Allied approach to warfare on the part of the democracies. For this reason, as much or more than its strategic contribution to the war effort, Alamein was crucial to the morale of the free world. No one who lived in Britain, the Commonwealth or even the occupied countries of Europe would ever forget the moment when the news of Rommel's defeat came through. From civilians in factories to resistance workers in occupied Europe, the sense of a change in the fortunes of democracy was palpable.

Alamein thus became a symbol for the free world, and the enslaved world, as much as a military achievement in its own right: a symbol of Allied determination and combined effort in defeating the Nazis.

The battle itself had underlined the need for co-operation between all arms, and the combination of army and air, and even the navy through the landing of forces behind the enemy front lines. This was the shape of democratic battle to come. Two long years after Dunkirk, the Desert Air Force had been persuaded to mount armour-piercing cannons on two of its ninety-six squadrons; the advent of the 'tank-buster' (and anti-tank gun buster) was finally approaching. A seventeen-pounder anti-tank gun was at last being produced which, in 1943, would finally have a hitting power similar to the 88. The very role of armour in modern warfare was in question, for it was becoming clear that Allied tanks – save in certain exceptional cases – would contribute more to Allied victory by co-operating with infantry than by attempting to remain 'racially pure'. This had proved true at Alamein, would do so again at Stalingrad in the coming weeks – and would characterize Allied offensive operations in Europe for the rest of World War II, with only occasional 'break-outs' when the enemy resistance had been flattened.

Alamein, though often later derided as a battle in the mould of World War I, was thus, in truth, the proving ground of modern warfare on the part of the democracies in World War II. Its lessons in leadership, tactics, weapons and co-operation were legion: and it was Churchill's 'little man on the make' who had made it happen, after the bitter defeats of 1940, 1941 and 1942. By ensuring the RAF fought hand-in-glove with the 8th Army, Monty had altered the nature of modern warfare in the democracies. But his greatest influence had been on the battlefield itself, where his approach to teambuilding, training, morale and command had revolutionized the performance of the Allies. In the grim business of toughening men to be willing to fight well and, if necessary, to die for their country and cause, a new team spirit needed to be inculcated, Monty had judged, based on a more professional approach to warfare and an implacable determination on the part of all soldiers to win, in order to go home with the pride of having done their duty, to the best of their ability. General Leese, especially, was awed by Monty's achievement in this respect. 'His plan of action depended on the Army fighting as one great team with one common purpose directed by him,' Leese later reflected; 'and if he was to succeed, he must impress his personality on the Army in the short few weeks before the great Battle started.'[22]

That Monty had managed to do this in such a short period of time was to Leese the mark of Monty's greatness, however much criticism Monty suffered in later years. The battle plan for Alamein, Leese recalled with admiration, had become the 'personal affair and interest' of every single soldier. 'What a lesson to some parts of industry,' he reflected in post-war, union-ravaged England. 'Could not the employers and the Trades Unions in some of our basic industries get closer together and somehow work out a scheme, which would enable their affairs to make one concerted effort towards true National co-operation?'[23]

As before the war, and throughout the first disastrous years of the war, this proved impossible in post-war Britain – which made Monty's achievement, in retrospect, the more extraordinary. Author after author would play down or denigrate Monty's leadership. Not only did Auchinleck acolytes feel duty-bound to do so, but non-military historians waded in, too. Churchill's admiring biographer, Martin Gilbert, concocted a narrative in which charming General Alexander, as Churchill's favourite general, had made all the tactical decisions in the battle, while Churchill's bitterly critical biographer, Clive Ponting, saw the battle as a disaster: 'a slogging match in which British casualties were, proportionately, as high as on the Somme. In the battle which began on 23 October the British lost six times more men killed and wounded than the Germans and Italians and over 600 tanks compared with the enemy's 180.'[24]

It became clear that, as the battle receded into distant memory, it looked all too easy, or too costly. Yet no other Allied field commander, even Patton, had managed to cut through the hierarchies, class-consciousness and snobberies of multi-ethnic formations, arms and units as Monty managed to do at Alamein. 'I saw that army. It was a broken, baffled army, a miserable army. I felt for them with all my heart,' Churchill recalled his first trip to Alamein early in August 1942; three months later, on 6 November, he was basking in 8th Army's reflected glory – though admitting to the luncheon party at 10 Downing Street that he had first appointed General Gott, not Montgomery . . .[25]

Given the courage and professionalism of German troops, it had become essential to motivate Allied soldiers – whether from Australia, New Zealand, South Africa, Southern Rhodesia, India, Greece, France, Scotland, England or America – to pull together. This the little 'outsider', 'the mountebank', the former 'colonial', had done, making himself known to his new army as a commander who knew his stuff, had a clear idea of how he wished to fight Rommel, and saw combat as a team effort, in which *every man* could play his part, and feel proud in doing so.

Monty's inclusivity had inspired 8th Army to fight as it had never fought before – indeed, as no Allied army had ever fought in World War II. No other Allied commander – whatever idle historians might infer later in loyalty to Auchinleck and others – could have mounted or won such a battle: the decisive battle of World War II which smashed the Panzer Army, saved Malta, paved the way for Allied success in invading Morocco and Algeria on 8 November 1942, and provided the lessons on which almost all subsequent Allied battlefield success was based. 'A terrible lot, including French public opinion, hinged on it,' Leese confided in a letter to his wife on 7 November,[26] as the survivors of Rommel's once-proud Afrika Korps fled towards the Egyptian border; indeed, Hitler's first act, on hearing of the Torch landings, was to beg Maréchal Pétain and the Vichy government to join Germany by declaring war on Britain and the United States. Pétain declined – compelling Hitler to occupy Vichy France and despatch German forces to counter the Allied advance in Tunisia, where all but a handful would be lost.

'I do hope the Morocco venture will go well tomorrow. My only doubt,' Leese confided to his wife, meanwhile, 'is that so many of the troops have never been under fire before . . .'[27] Given the almost six months it would take the Anglo-American forces to capture Tunis, it was a wise concern. Fighting the Germans was no easy matter.

Professionalism, determination, and the lifelong dedication of a teacher had made it possible for Monty to begin the transformation of 8th Army in the desert in 1942, but there was still a long way to go before the 'League of Nations' army would match the Panzer Army in professionalism. In the meantime, though, the die was cast: and the agent making it gel was something impossible to define, yet which pulsed through the army in a manner previously unknown: a devotion to and identification with 'his' men which had enabled Monty to convince the soldiery of a 200,000-man army that they mattered, and would win.

They did: and in that strange, homosocial bond there was created the faith that guided a legendary 8th Army in the desert – an invincible army which turned the tide of war, and by its proud example spelled the inevitable end of Nazi dreams of conquest and racial extermination.

Notes

Preface

1. E. Homberger and J. Charmley, eds., *The Troubled Face of Biography*, 1988, p. 9.
2. Nigel Hamilton, *Monty: The Making of a General 1887–1942*, 1981; *Monty: Master of the Battlefield 1942–1944*, 1983, and *Monty: The Field-Marshal 1944–1976*, 1986.
3. Lucien Trueb: 'Monty's Little Swiss Friend', in T. E. B. Howarth, ed., *Monty at Close Quarters: Recollections of the Man*, 1985, p. 128.
4. Da Vinci had been arraigned in court, as a young man, for sodomy, but the case was not proven (see A. Richard Turner, *Inventing Leonardo: The Anatomy of a Legend*, New York 1993/London 1995, p. 13). Aware of this, and interpreting a childhood dream or fantasy recorded by da Vinci, *Leonardo da Vinci, a Memoir of his Childhood*, published in 1910, became Freud's celebrated *coup* in the realm of biography, impeaching contemporary life-writing for 'silently passing over its subject's sexual activity or sexual individuality' and denouncing conventional biographers for their 'discretion or prudery' while revealing the great Renaissance artist and scientist not only to have been a repressed homosexual, but linking da Vinci's profound, though often unfinished, creativity to his repressed sexuality (S. Freud, *Leonardo da Vinci, a Memoir of his Childhood*, 1910, Norton edition [*Leonardo da Vinci and a Memory of His Childhood*] 1964, p. 16). Though Freud's methodology was duly shown to be deeply flawed and the domain of biography did not as a result become the promised colony of the Vienna Psychoanalytic Society as he had predicted to C. G. Jung in 1909 ('the domain of biography, too, must become ours' – Peter Gay, *Freud: A Life for Our Time*, 1988, p. 268), his argument stuck. Marcel Duchamp's pastiche of the *Mona Lisa*, with an elegant, pencil moustache and goatee, in 1919, said it all: Leonardo was essentially gay – albeit, for the most part, sublimated.
5. For example, 'Talk of Alexander and of Others Too', the *Guardian*, 8 June 1995: 'The history of world warfare teems with accounts – some apocryphal, some firmly based – of warriors whose gaiety extended beyond their humorous moments. These include Alexander the Great, most of the army of ancient Sparta, Julius Caesar, Frederick the Great, Richard the Lionheart, Lord Kitchener, Earl [*sic*] Montgomery of Alamein, and Earl Mountbatten of Burma.'

6. 'Viscount Montgomery Talks to College', *The Cheltonian*, Summer 1959, p. 61.

7. Quoted in Alan Moorehead, *Montgomery: A Biography*, 1946, p. 83.

8. Letter, B. L. Montgomery to Denis Hamilton, 22.12.58, papers of Sir Denis Hamilton.

9. Drew Middleton, 'Monty, Hard to Like or Ignore', *New York Times*, 25 March 1976.

10. Paul Fussell, *The Great War and Modern Memory*, 1975, p. 272.

11. Samuel Johnson's visionary statement of the ideals of biography, published in *The Rambler* 250 years ago, maintained that biography, more than history, has the opportunity of helping us, as individuals, to live more fulfilling lives – *The Rambler*, no. 60, Saturday, 13 October 1750, in Samuel Johnson, *The Rambler*, vol. 1, ed. W. J. Bate and A. B. Straub, New Haven, 1969. For this to happen, Dr Johnson warned, the biographer must have the courage to tell the life 'really as it was' – *Boswell's Life of Johnson*, ed. George Birkbeck Hill, rev. edn L. F. Powell, 1934, vol. II, p. 155. 'If nothing but the bright side of characters should be shewn,' he cautioned, 'we should sit down with despondency, and think it utterly impossible to imitate them in *any thing*.' Even the sacred writers, he noted, 'related the vicious as well as the virtuous actions of men; which had this moral effect, that it kept mankind from despair, into which they would naturally fall, were they not supported by the recollection that others had offended like themselves'; Powell, *Boswell's Life of Johnson*, vol. IV, p. 53. By 'act of imagination', he exhorted modern biographers, they should present narratives that would enable people to witness, at one remove, the 'joys and calamities of others', 'however fictitious' the techniques. In this way, empowered by the biographer, readers would be able to project themselves on to such characters: 'placing us, for a time, in the condition of him whose fortune we contemplate'. As Johnson noted, 'Our passions are therefore strongly moved, in proportion as we can more readily adopt the pains or pleasures proposed to our minds, by recognizing them as once our own'; *The Rambler*, no. 60, op. cit., p. 319.

12. Ibid.

1 Born Unto Trouble

1. H. David, *On Queer Street: A Social History of British Homosexuality, 1895–1955*, 1997.

2. *The Memoirs of John Addington Symonds*, ed. Phyllis Grosskurth, 1986, p. 94.

3. A. Chalfont, *Montgomery of Alamein*, 1976, p. 8.

4. *The Memoirs of John Addington Symonds*, ed. Grosskurth, p. 112.

5. Ibid., p. 87.

6. Brian Montgomery, *A Field Marshal in the Family*, 1973, p. 110.

7. Ibid., p. 81.

8. Ibid., pp. 91, 110, 107.

9. Ibid., p. 110.

10. Ibid., p. 79.

11. F. Farrar, *Eternal Hope, 5 Sermons*, 1878.

12. Case XVII in Havelock Ellis' *Sexual Inversion* of 1897, reprinted in *The Memoirs of John Addington Symonds*, ed. Grosskurth, p. 287.

13. *The Memoirs of John Addington Symonds*, ed. Grosskurth, p. 186.

14. Ibid., p. 117.

15. Brian Montgomery, *A Field Marshal in the Family*, p. 20.

16. Ibid., p. 21.

17. B. L. Montgomery, *Memoirs*, 1958, p. 18.

18. Ibid., p. 19.

19. Ibid., p. 111.

20. 'Wellington', ms draft in 'Napoleon/Wellington', May–June 1969, Lord Montgomery Deposit, Box 36, Imperial War Museum (IWM).

21. 'Early drafts: chapters 1 to 12', Lord Montgomery Deposit, Box 27, IWM.

22. B. L. Montgomery, *Memoirs*, p. 17.

23. Moorehead, *Montgomery*, p. 27.

24. Ibid., p. 26.

25. Brian Montgomery, *A Field Marshal in the Family*, p. 74.

26. Ibid., p. 63.

27. Moorehead, *Montgomery*, p. 26.

28. Ibid., p. 27.

29. B. L. Montgomery, *Memoirs*, p. 18.

30. A. L. Rowse, *Homosexuals in History: A Study of Ambivalence in Society, Literature and the Arts*, 1977, p. 148.

31. Ibid., p. 155.

32. John E. Mack, *A Prince of Our Disorder: The Life of T. E. Lawrence*, 1976, p. 440.

33. See Phillips Sale no. 30,968, Item 370, ' "Edward Shaw" and his nephew "Ted": The Penitent Rituals of Lawrence of Arabia' – twelve typed letters by T. E. Lawrence, using an assumed name, to Mr Sid Abrams, swimming instructor at the Southampton Baths: Books, Maps & Manuscripts catalogue for 30 June 2000 sale, 101 New Bond Street, London.

34. Mack, *A Prince of Our Disorder*, p. 438. 'The taboo against intimacy with women was', Mack points out, 'always intense for Lawrence' (ibid., p. 440). See also P. Knightley and C. Simpson, *The Secret Lives of Lawrence of Arabia*, 1969; J. Wilson, *Lawrence of Arabia: The Authorised Biography of T. E. Lawrence*, 1989.

35. M. Asher, *Lawrence: The Uncrowned King of Arabia*, 1998, p. 370.

36. See, for example, J. N. Lockman, *Scattered Tracks on the Lawrence Trail – 12 Essays on T. E. Lawrence*, 1996.

37. Asher, *Lawrence*, p. 292.

38. Letter, T. E. Lawrence to Mrs C. Shaw, 18.9.25, in *The Letters of T. E. Lawrence*, ed. Malcolm Brown, 1988, p. 290.

39. R. Hyam, *Sexuality and Empire: The British Experience*, 1990, p. 58.

40. T. E. Lawrence, *Seven Pillars of Wisdom: A Triumph*, 1962, p. 28.

2 Bad Boy

1. Chalfont, *Montgomery of Alamein*, p. 28.
2. Hyam, *Sexuality and Empire*, p. 57.
3. Brian Montgomery, *A Field Marshal in the Family*, p. 92.
4. Ibid., p. 115.
5. B. L. Montgomery, *Memoirs*, p. 18.
6. Moorehead, *Montgomery*, p. 27.
7. Ibid., p. 29.
8. Ibid., p. 26.
9. 'Early drafts: chapters 1 to 12', Lord Montgomery Deposit, Box 27, IWM.
10. Moorehead, *Montgomery*, p. 28.
11. Ibid., pp. 28–9.
12. Montgomery, *Memoirs*, p. 17.
13. Interview with Field-Marshal Lord Carver, November 1999.
14. Moorehead, *Montgomery*, p. 30.
15. Chalfont, *Montgomery of Alamein*, p. 36.
16. Hyam, *Sexuality and Empire*, p. 182.
17. 'A Pauline in the earliest days of the 20th Century', typescript dated 11.1.68, Lord Montgomery Deposit, Box 36, IWM.
18. Ibid.
19. Ibid.
20. Moorehead, *Montgomery*, p. 34. See also B. L. Montgomery, *Memoirs*, p. 22: 'My father had always hoped that I would become a clergyman ... and I well recall his disappointment when I told him that I wanted to be a soldier.'
21. Moorehead, *Montgomery*, p. 34.
22. Montgomery, *Memoirs*, p. 22.
23. Mack, *A Prince of Our Disorder*, p. 33.
24. Montgomery, *Memoirs*, p. 22.
25. Ibid.
26. 'A Pauline in the earliest days of the 20th Century'.
27. V. Musgrave, *Montgomery, His Life in Pictures*, 1947, p. 14.
28. Ibid.
29. 'Viscount Montgomery Talks to College', *The Cheltonian*, Summer 1959, p. 61.
30. 'A Pauline in the earliest days of the 20th Century'.
31. Ibid.
32. Ibid.
33. Quoted in B. L. Montgomery, *Memoirs*, p. 21.
34. Ibid., p. 22.
35. Ibid., p. 20.
36. Musgrove, *His Life in Pictures*, p. 14.
37. B. L. Montgomery, *Memoirs*, pp. 23–4.
38. Moorehead, *Montgomery*, pp. 28, 33.

39. Ibid., pp. 27, 31.

40. 'Viscount Montgomery Talks to College', *The Cheltonian*, Summer 1959, p. 61.

41. Quoted in N. Hamilton, *Monty: The Man Behind the Legend*, 1987, p. 114.

42. Quoted in Moorehead, *Montgomery*, p. 30.

43. 'Early drafts: chapters 1 to 12' (phrase later struck out), Lord Montgomery Deposit, Box 27, IWM.

44. Brian Montgomery, *A Field Marshal in the Family*, p. 136.

45. Ibid., p. 137.

46. B. L. Montgomery, *Memoirs*, p. 19.

47. Ibid., p. 25.

48. Ibid., p. 26.

49. Mrs Warrington, quoted in Brian Montgomery, *A Field Marshal in the Family*, p. 16.

50. Ibid.

51. An ardent imperialist, Churchill had favoured full British annexation of Afghanistan 'right up to the Russian border' rather than mere retaliatory action against dissident tribesmen's raids. Instead he had had to content himself with the chance of proving his bravery in British 'punitive' operations, followed by withdrawal. 'Being in many ways a coward – particularly at school', Churchill admitted at the time to his brother Jack, ' – there is no ambition I cherish so keenly as to gain a personal reputation for courage.' The righteousness of the cause, he confessed to his mother, was in many respects irrelevant. 'I do not care for the principles I advocate,' he confided, 'as for the impression which my words produce & the reputation they give me. This sounds terrible,' he realized. 'But you must remember we do not live in the days of Great Causes.'

52. B. L. Montgomery, *Memoirs*, p. 27.

53. Hyam, *Sexuality and Empire*, p. 122.

54. Ibid., p. 123.

55. Ibid., p. 130.

56. Ibid., p. 133.

57. Mack, *A Prince of Our Disorder*, p. 79.

58. Ibid., pp. 97, 99.

59. 'Monty', unpublished memoir by Brigadier Clement Tomes, 1958, quoted in Hamilton, *The Making of a General*, p. 53.

60. Moorehead, *Montgomery*, p. 16.

61. Ibid., pp. 46–7.

62. Ibid., p. 43.

63. B. L. Montgomery, *Memoirs*, p. 28.

64. Moorehead, *Montgomery*, p. 39.

65. Robert Graves, *Goodbye to All That* (1929), 1960.

66. B. L. Montgomery, *Memoirs*, p. 29.

67. Moorehead, *Montgomery*, p. 44.

68. B. L. Montgomery, *Memoirs*, p. 30.

69. Ibid.

70. Moorehead, *Montgomery*, p. 44.
71. Ibid., p. 45.
72. Ibid., p. 44.
73. Ibid., p. 47.
74. Mack, *A Prince of Our Disorder*, p. 97.
75. J. Masters, *Bugles and a Tiger*, 1956, p. 153.
76. Moorehead, *Montgomery*, p. 47.
77. Mack, *A Prince of Our Disorder*, p. 88.
78. *The Memoirs of John Addington Symonds*, ed. Grosskurth, pp. 267-8.

3 The Great War

1. World War I Letters Album, BLM 1/1, IWM, annotation, p. 2.
2. Ibid., annotation, p. 1.
3. Ibid., annotations, p. 1.
4. Ibid., letter of 30.7.14, from Sheppey Union, Minster, Kent.
5. World War I Letters Album, BLM 1/2, IWM, letter of Sunday, 2.8.14.
6. World War I Letters Album, BLM 1/2, IWM.
7. Niall Ferguson, ed., *Virtual History*, 1997, pp. 269-73.
8. Ibid., p. 260.
9. Ibid., p. 246.
10. M. Howard, *Studies in War and Peace*, 1970, p. 103.
11. Paul Crook, *Darwinism, War and History: The Debate over the Biology of War from the 'Origin of Species' to the First World War*, 1994, p. 64.
12. E. F. M. Durbin and John Bowlby, *Personal Aggressiveness and War*, 1939, p. 26.
13. World War I Letters Album, BLM 1/2, IWM, letter of 2.8.14.
14. Ferguson, *Virtual History*, p. 273.
15. Ibid., p. 276.
16. World War I Letters Album, BLM 1/4, IWM.
17. Ferguson, *Virtual History*, p. 275.
18. World War I Letters Album, BLM 1/3, IWM, Minster, 5.8.14.
19. World War I Letters Album, BLM 1/5, IWM.
20. World War I Letters Album, BLM 1/7, IWM, letter of Sunday, 9.8.14.
21. Ibid.
22. World War I Letters Album, BLM 1/9, IWM.
23. World War I Letters Album, BLM 1/8, IWM, letter of 11.8.14.
24. World War I Letters Album, BLM 1/10, IWM, letter of 15.8.14, Strensall Camp, York.
25. World War I Letters Album, BLM 1/13, IWM, letter to 'My dear Father', 22.8.14.
26. R. Holmes, *Riding the Retreat*, 1995, p. 78. Churchill would feel the same way, hoping in 1915 to lure America into the war on the side of the Allies by

inciting German U-boats to sink the *Lusitania* (with the loss of 128 American lives), and again in World War II, while Monty himself would later make a similar dictum about American involvement in a third world war in Europe, should it ever arise – adding that he himself would shoot the American, if necessary. It was not numbers that counted in securing military aid and alliance, but the emotionally symbolic significance of dead nationals in order to attain public support for involvement.

27. Ibid., p. 26.

28. H. von Moltke, *Erinnerungen, Briefe, Dokumente 1877–1916*, 1922, p. 384, quoted in C. Barnett, *The Swordbearers*, 1963, p. 91.

29. Quoted ibid., p. 34.

30. Lyn Macdonald, *1914: The Days of Hope*, 1989, p. 122.

31. War Diary, 1st Battalion Royal Warwickshire Regiment (RWR), Royal Warwickshire Regimental Museum, Warwick.

32. J. E. Edmonds, *Military Operations. France and Belgium, 1914*, vol. I, 3rd edn, 1933, p. 141.

33. Ibid.

34. B. L. Montgomery, *Memoirs*, p. 32.

35. World War I Letters Album, BLM 1/23, IWM, letter of Sunday, 27.9.14.

36. World War I Letters Album, BLM 1/9, IWM, letter of 14.8.14, Strensall Camp, York.

37. Quoted in Brian Montgomery, *A Field Marshal in the Family*, p. 159.

38. B. L. Montgomery, *Memoirs*, p. 32.

39. Arthur Osburn, *Unwilling Passenger*, 1932, quoted in Holmes, *Riding the Retreat*, p. 207.

40. Brian Montgomery, *A Field Marshal in the Family*, p. 160. Lt-Col Elkington, who would have been shot had he been of lesser rank, made a spectacular atonement: he joined the Foreign Legion, winning the Croix de Guerre and the Médaille Militaire. He was subsequently reinstated in the British army and awarded the DSO.

41. World War I Letters Album, BLM 1/23, IWM, letter of 27.9.14.

42. Ibid.

43. Ibid.

44. A. von Kluck, *The March on Paris and the Battle of the Marne 1914*, 1920, p. 121.

45. Ibid., pp. 137–9.

46. World War I Letters Album, BLM 1/23, IWM.

47. Ibid.

48. World War I Letters Album, BLM 1/18, IWM.

49. World War I Letters Album, BLM 1/19, IWM.

50. World War I Letters Album, BLM 1/22, IWM.

51. Ibid.

52. World War I Letters Album, BLM 1/23, IWM.

53. Ibid.

54. World War I Letters Album, BLM 1/24, IWM, letter of Tuesday, 29.9.14.

55. Ibid.
56. World War I Letters Album, BLM 1/23, IWM, letter of 27.9.14.
57. B. L. Montgomery, *A History of Warfare*, 1968, pp. 22–3.
58. World War I Letters Album, BLM 1/24, IWM, letter of Tuesday, 29.9.14.
59. Ibid.
60. Ibid.
61. World War I Letters Album, BLM 1/25, IWM, annotation, p. 17.
62. World War I Letters Album, BLM 1/25, IWM, letter of 2.10.14.
63. World War I Letters Album, BLM 1/28, IWM, annotation, p. 20.
64. B. L. Montgomery, *Memoirs*, p. 33.
65. War Diary, 1st Battalion, RWR.
66. Ibid.
67. B. L. Montgomery, *Memoirs*, p. 33.
68. Account for Royal Warwickshire Regiment, quoted in a letter from Norman Cliff to the *Observer*, 7 April 1968.
69. B. L. Montgomery, *Memoirs*, p. 34.
70. 'Monty' – unpublished memoir by Brigadier Clement Tomes, 1958, Nigel Hamilton Research Papers, IWM.

4 The Somme and After

1. Tomes, 'Monty'.
2. Ibid.
3. Ministry of Defence, Confidential Personnel Records.
4. C. Barnett, *Britain and Her Army*, 1970, p. 379.
5. World War I Letters Album, BLM 1/31, IWM, annotation p. 22.
6. Brian Montgomery, *A Field Marshal in the Family*, p. 164.
7. Copy in World War I Letters Album, BLM 1/31, IWM, p. 23.
8. World War I Letters Album, BLM 1/40, IWM, annotation to letter to Maud, 2.4.16.
9. Montgomery, *Memoirs*, p. 35.
10. World War I Letters Album, BLM 1/35, IWM, letter to Maud, 11.2.16.
11. Ibid.
12. World War I Letters Album, BLM 1/36, IWM, letter to Maud, 22.2.16.
13. World War I Letters Album, BLM 1/38, IWM, letter to Maud, 7.3.16.
14. World War I Letters Album, BLM 1/36, IWM, letter to Maud, 22.2.16.
15. World War I Letters Album, BLM 1/32, IWM, History of the 104th Infantry Brigade.
16. Ibid.
17. World War I Letters Album, BLM 1/38, IWM, annotations, p.32.
18. G. De Groot, *Douglas Haig, 1861–1928*, 1988, p. 208.
19. Ibid., p. 209.
20. Ibid., p. 223.

21. World War I Letters Album, BLM 1/41, IWM, letter to Maud 10.4.16.
22. World War I Letters Album, BLM 1/30, IWM, annotations, p. 22.
23. World War I Letters Album, BLM 1/43, IWM, letter to Maud, 7.5.16.
24. World War I Letters Album, BLM 1/42, IWM, letter to Maud, 26.4.16.
25. De Groot, *Douglas Haig*, p. 244.
26. Ibid., p. 234.
27. Ibid., pp. 225, 234.
28. Gerald De Groot, for example, believes Haig's 'original plan' was for a 'breakthrough' (see summary, ibid., p. 275) on the Somme, while Denis Winter claims that 'Haig's correspondence leaves no doubt' that Haig intended a 'feint' attack on the Somme, followed two weeks later – after German reserves were committed on the Somme – by 'the big attack' or 'breakthrough' at Ypres (D. Winter, *Haig's Command, A Reassessment*, 1991, p. 50). That neither the hundreds of thousands of British troops nor historians had or have any real idea of what Haig intended – and search for clues in his 'correspondence' – is perhaps the most tragic reflection on the battle.
29. Quoted in Winter, *Haig's Command*, p. 60.
30. De Groot, *Douglas Haig*, p. 238.
31. Winter, *Haig's Command*, p. 45.
32. De Groot, *Douglas Haig*, p. 245.
33. R. Prior and T. Wilson, *Command on the Western Front: The Military Career of Sir Henry Rawlinson 1914–18*, 1992, p. 155.
34. De Groot, *Douglas Haig*, p. 249.
35. Ibid., p. 251.
36. Ibid.
37. J. Laffin, *British Butchers and Bunglers of World War One*, 1989, p. 68.
38. Quoted ibid., p. 70.
39. Ibid., p. 69.
40. De Groot, *Douglas Haig*, p. 252.
41. 'Memorandum on Policy for the Press', issued on 26 May 1916, quoted ibid., p. 242.
42. World War I Letters Album, BLM 1/47, IWM, letter to Maud, 4.7.16.
43. Laffin, *British Butchers*, p. 73.
44. Winter, *Haig's Command*, p. 307.
45. De Groot, *Douglas Haig*, p. 252.
46. Ibid., p. 253.
47. Ibid.
48. Winter, *Haig's Command* p. 254.
49. Letter to J. E. Edmonds, Official Australian Historian, quoted ibid., p. 253.
50. De Groot, *Douglas Haig*, p. 235.
51. Ibid., p. 252.
52. Ibid., p. 255.
53. Laffin, *British Butchers*, p. 69.
54. World War I Letters Album, BLM 1/47, IWM, letter to Maud, 4.7.16.
55. Ibid.

56. J. Keegan, *The First World War*, 1998, p. 311

57. E.g., B. Bond and N. Cave, eds., *Haig: A Reappraisal 70 Years on*, 1999, containing essays by a group of the foremost British military history writers and teachers of World War I studies as a self-confessed 'pro-Haig' apologia – with just a solitary index entry for 'casualties' in the entire 270-page work.

58. World War I Letters Album, BLM 1/48, IWM, annotation to Letter to Maud, 23.7.16.

59. World War I Letters Album, BLM 1/49, IWM, letter to Maud, 12.7.16.

60. Haig's OAD91, quoted in Winter, *Haig's Command*, p. 307.

61. World War I Letters Album, BLM 1/48, IWM, letter to Maud, 23.7.16.

62. M. Ferro, *The Great War, 1914–1918*, 1973, p. 81.

63. 3,080 men were sentenced to death for shirking combat, both to terrorize them and frighten their compatriots. Of them 346 were actually executed – though the 'survivors' were psychologically traumatized. See N. Ferguson, *The Pity of War*, 1998, p. 346.

64. Norman Dixon, *On the Psychology of Military Incompetence*, 1976, pp. 378–9.

65. Laffin, *British Butchers*, p. 99.

66. De Groot, *Douglas Haig*, p. 262.

67. Ibid., p. 256.

68. B. L. Montgomery, *A History of Warfare*, p. 470.

69. Laffin, *British Butchers*, p. 88.

70. De Groot, *Douglas Haig*, p. 276.

71. Laffin, *British Butchers*, p. 88–9.

72. See 'The Death Instinct: Why Men Fought', in Ferguson, *The Pity of War*, pp. 339–66.

73. Howard, *Studies in War and Peace*, p. 101.

74. World War I Letters Album, BLM 1/48, IWM.

75. Fussell, *The Great War and Modern Memory*, p. 192.

76. Ibid.

77. Ibid.

78. B. L. Montgomery, '1914/18 War', Montgomery Papers, IWM.

79. World War I Letters Album, BLM 1/51, IWM, letter to Maud, 27.7.16.

80. War Diary, 104th Infantry Brigade (WO 95/2482), PRO.

81. World War I Letters Album, BLM 1/52, IWM, letter to Maud, 6.8.16.

82. Ibid.

83. World War I Letters Album, BLM 1/53, IWM, letter to Maud, 10.8.16.

84. World War I Letters Album, BLM 1/54, IWM, letter to Maud, 17.8.16.

85. Ibid.

86. World War I Letters Album, BLM 1/55, IWM, letter of 27.8.16.

87. De Groot, *Douglas Haig*, p. 265.

88. Ibid.

89. War Diary, 104th Infantry Brigade (WO 95/2482), PRO.

90. De Groot, *Douglas Haig*, p. 275.

91. B. L. Montgomery, *A History of Warfare*, p. 471.

92. B. L. Montgomery, '1914/18 War'.
93. Winter, *Haig's Command*, pp. 225–57.
94. De Groot, *Douglas Haig*, p. 275.
95. Laffin, *British Butchers*, p. 94.
96. De Groot, *Douglas Haig*, p. 274.
97. Winter, *Haig's Command*, p. 66.
98. B. L. Montgomery, '1914/18 War'.
99. De Groot, *Douglas Haig*, p. 276.
100. W. Churchill, *The World Crisis*, 1927, pp. 187–91.
101. De Groot, *Douglas Haig*, p. 258.
102. Ferguson, *The Pity of War*, pp. 305–6.
103. Letter, D. H. Lawrence to Catherine Carswell, 9.7.16, in David Roberts, *Minds at War: The Poetry and Experience of the First World War*, 1996, p. 201.
104. Ferguson, *The Pity of War*, p. 361.
105. C. Coker, *War in the Twentieth Century: A Study of War and Modern Consciousness*, 1994, p. 162.
106. Keegan, *The First World War*, p. 388.
107. De Groot, *Douglas Haig*, p. 335.
108. Ibid., p. 336.
109. Ibid., pp. 336–7.
110. Ibid., p. 338.
111. War Diary, IX Corps (WO 95/835), PRO.
112. Ibid.
113. World War I Letters Album, BLM 1/63, IWM, letter of 9.10.17.
114. De Groot, *Douglas Haig*, p. 336.
115. Ibid., p. 344.
116. Ibid., p. 346.
117. Keegan, *The First World War*, p. 393.
118. Ibid., p. 395.
119. B. L. Montgomery, *Memoirs*, pp. 35–6.
120. World War I Letters Album, BLM 1/64, IWM, letter to Maud, 8.11.17.
121. De Groot, *Douglas Haig*, p. 353.
122. Ibid., p. 376.
123. War Diary, IX Corps (WO 95/837), PRO.
124. Ibid.
125. De Groot, *Douglas Haig*, p. 382.
126. Ibid.
127. Ferguson, *The Pity of War*, p. 316.
128. World War I Letters Album, BLM 1/65, IWM, annotation.
129. World War I Letters Album, BLM 1/65, IWM, letter to Maud, 3.9.18.
130. War Diary, 47th Division (WO 95/2705), PRO.
131. B. L. Montgomery, *Memoirs*, p. 36.
132. War Diary, 47th Division (WO 95/2705), PRO.
133. Ibid.
134. World War I Letters Album, BLM 1/65, IWM, letter to Maud.

135. World War I Letters Album, BLM 1/66, IWM, letter to Maud, 28.10.18.

136. J. Hussey, 'Portrait of a Commander-in-Chief', in Bond and Cave, *Haig: A Reappraisal*, p. 28.

137. J. H. Johnson, *1918: The Unexpected Victory*, 1997, p. 166.

138. World War I Letters Album, BLM 1/66, IWM, letter of 28.10.18.

139. World War I Letters Album, BLM 1/67, IWM, letter of 7.11.18.

5 Peace

1. De Groot, *Douglas Haig*, p. 407.

2. Ibid.

3. Ibid., pp. 277–8.

4. Winter, *Haig's Command*, p. 332.

5. De Groot, *Douglas Haig*, pp. 277, 407.

6. Ibid., p. 303.

7. George Orwell, *Collected Essays II*, 1968, p. 77.

8. Fussell, *The Great War and Modern Memory*, p. 197.

9. 'C.N.', *The Making of an Officer*, 1916, p. 14.

10. Ibid., p. 67.

11. Ibid., p. 61.

12. B. L. Montgomery, *Memoirs*, p. 36.

13. World War I Letters Album, BLM 1/68, IWM, letter to 'My darling Mother', 18.8.19, General Headquarters, British Army of the Rhine.

14. Ibid.

15. World War I Letters Album, BLM 1/68, IWM, annotations, p. 61.

16. Brian Montgomery, *Monty: A Life in Photographs*, 1985, p. 5.

17. B. L. Montgomery, *Memoirs*, p. 39.

18. Brian Montgomery, *A Life in Photographs*, p. 179.

19. Interview with Colonel P. J. Gething, 21.8.78.

20. *Owl Pie*, Christmas 1920.

21. A. P. Herbert, *The Secret Battle* (1919), 1982 edn, p. 130.

22. Ibid., Introduction, p. xii.

23. A. J. P. Taylor, *The First World War*, 1966, p. 140.

24. Dixon, *On the Psychology of Military Incompetence*, p. 94.

25. B. L. Montgomery, *Memoirs*, p. 38.

26. Letter, B. L. Montgomery to Major A. E. Percival, 14.10.23, Percival Papers (P18, file 4/2), IWM.

27. The British army had fifty-one battalions stationed in Ireland by early 1921: B. Bond, *British Military Policy Between the Two World Wars*, 1980, p. 18.

28. Letter, B. L. Montgomery to Major A. E. Percival, 14.10.23, Percival Papers (P18, file 4/2), IWM.

29. Diaries of Sir Peter Strickland, IWM.

30. Ibid.

31. Douglas Wimberley, 'Monty, A Personal Memoir', unpublished ms, 1980, IWM.

32. Papers of Sir Peter Strickland, IWM.

33. Letter, B. L. Montgomery to Major A. E. Percival, 14.10.23, Percival Papers (P18, file 4/2), IWM.

34. Quoted in Brian Montgomery, *A Field Marshal in the Family*, p. 182.

35. Diary of Sir Peter Strickland, 11.7.21, IWM.

36. History of the 6th Division in Ireland, Strickland Papers, IWM.

37. Diary of Sir Peter Strickland, 17.5.22, IWM.

38. Ibid., 11.7.21.

39. Quoted in Brian Montgomery, *A Field Marshal in the Family*, pp. 182–3.

40. Letter, B. L. Montgomery to Major A. E. Percival, 14.10.23, Percival Papers (P18, file 4/2), IWM.

41. Ibid.

42. Percival lectures, Percival papers, IWM.

43. Col. Commandant Tom Barry to Ewan Butler, in Ewan Butler, *Barry's Flying Column*, 1971, p. 37.

44. Yigal Allon inscription on photo, 1948, Liddell Hart Centre for Military Archives, King's College, London (LHCMA).

45. A. Danchev, *The Alchemist of War*, 1998, p. 61.

46. Ibid., p. 71.

47. Ibid.

48. Ibid.

49. Ibid.

50. B. L. Montgomery, *Memoirs*, p. 40.

51. D. Fraser, *And We Shall Shock Them*, 1983, p. 80.

52. Bond, *British Military Policy*, pp. 24–5.

53. Fraser, *And We Shall Shock Them*, p. 80.

54. Lawrence, *Seven Pillars of Wisdom*, p. 395.

55. Letter, Kaiser Wilhelm to von Bülow, 31.10.05, in B. H. Liddell Hart, *History of the First World War*, 1970, p. 12.

56. M. Gilbert, *Churchill*, vol. IV, *1917–1922*, 1975, p. 451.

57. Ibid.

58. Quoted in Bond, *British Military Policy*, p. 29.

59. M. Carver, *The Seven Ages of the British Army*, 1984, p. 198.

60. Bond, *British Military Policy*, p. 35.

61. Carver, *Seven Ages of the British Army*, p. 197.

62. Bond, *British Military Policy*, p. 36.

63. B. Liddell Hart, *Memoirs I*, 1965, p. 55.

64. Ibid.

65. Letter, B. L. Montgomery to B. Liddell Hart, 16.7.24, Liddell Hart Papers, LHCMA.

66. Bond, *British Military Policy*, p. 35.

67. Liddell Hart, *Memoirs*, p. 55.

68. Letter, B. L. Montgomery to B. Liddell Hart, 16.7.24, Liddell Hart Papers, LHCMA.
69. Letter, B. L. Montgomery to Brigadier Sir Edgar Williams, 7.9.62, Montgomery Ancillary Collections, Box 21, IWM.
70. F. de Guingand, *Operation Victory*, 1947, p. 167.
71. The *Antelope*, January 1925, quoted in Hamilton, *The Making of a General*, p. 175.
72. F. de Guingand, *From Brass Hat to Bowler Hat*, 1979, p. 1.
73. Interview with Major-General R. C. Macdonald, 24.4.78.
74. Brian Montgomery, *A Field Marshal in the Family*, p. 192.
75. Ibid.
76. Diary of Training, 'A' Company, 1st Battalion Royal Warwickshire Regiment, 1928. The original was purloined and auctioned anonymously in 1978, when it was purchased by the Imperial War Museum.
77. Quoted in Hamilton, *The Man Behind the Legend*, p. 42.
78. Interview with Lady Michelmore, 10.4.78.
79. Ibid.
80. Ibid.
81. Brian Montgomery, *A Life in Photographs*, p. 35.
82. Letter, Lady Michelmore to author, 20.2.78.
83. Lady Michelmore interview.
84. Chalfont, *Montgomery of Alamein*, p. 32.
85. Brian Montgomery, *A Life in Photographs*, p. 47.
86. World War I Letters Album, BLM 1/57, IWM, annotation, p. 49.
87. World War I Letters Album, BLM 1/56, IWM, letter of 28.8.16.
88. Ibid., annotation, p. 46.
89. Brian Montgomery, *A Life in Photographs*, p. 57.
90. Hamilton, *The Man Behind the Legend*, p. 42.
91. Ibid.
92. Ibid.

6 Marriage

1. Liddell Hart, *Memoirs*, p. 64.
2. Hamilton, *The Man Behind the Legend*, p. 41.
3. Diary of Training, 'A' Company, 1st Battalion Royal Warwickshire Regiment, 1928, IWM.
4. Interview with Brigadier J. P. Duke, 17.8.78.
5. Diary of Training, 'A' Company, 1st Battalion Royal Warwickshire Regiment, 1928, IWM.
6. Liddell Hart, *Memoirs*, p. 55.
7. Ibid.
8. 'B. L. Montgomery', personal file, Ministry of Defence.

9. B. L. Montgomery, *Memoirs*, p. 41.

10. 'B. L. Montgomery', personal file, Ministry of Defence.

11. Hamilton, *The Man Behind the Legend*, p. 42.

12. Ibid.

13. Brian Montgomery, *A Field Marshal in the Family*, p. 196.

14. B. L. Montgomery, *Memoirs*.

15. D. Fraser, *Alanbrooke*, 1982, p. 93.

16. Ibid., p. 83.

17. Brooke left in 1927, while Lieutenant-Colonels Giffard and O'Connor joined the staff as instructors.

18. Michael Carver, *Harding of Petherton*, 1978, p. 39.

19. Interview with Lieutenant-Colonel John Carver, 3.3.78.

20. R. Davenport-Hines, *Sex, Death and Punishment: Attitudes to Sex and Sexuality in Britain since the Renaissance*, 1990, p. 10.

21. Second reading, Sexual Offences Bill, House of Lords, Hansard, vol. 266, 11 May–2 June 1965, cols 645–7.

22. Ibid.

23. Ibid., 15 June–8 July 1965, col. 342.

24. B. L. Montgomery, *Memoirs*, p. 42.

25. Hyam, *Empire and Sexuality*, p. 7.

26. Davenport-Hines, *Sex, Death and Punishment*, p. 134.

27. H. Daley, *Small Cloud*, 1987, p. 48.

28. Hyam, *Empire and Sexuality*, pp. 11–12.

29. Lieutenant-Colonel John Carver interview.

30. Quoted in Andrew Birkin, *J. M. Barrie and the Lost Boys*, 1979, p. 60.

31. Brian Montgomery, *A Field Marshal in the Family*, p. 202.

32. Lieutenant-Colonel John Carver interview.

33. Ibid.

34. Interview with Lady Herbert, 1.12.77.

35. Lieutenant-Colonel John Carver interview.

36. Ibid.

37. Brian Montgomery, *A Field Marshal in the Family*, and Olive, Lady Hamilton, personal recollection, May 1978.

38. Interview with Colonel R. O. H. Carver, 18.9.80.

39. Brian Montgomery, *A Field Marshal in the Family*, pp. 206–7.

40. Danchev, *The Alchemist of War*, p. 89.

41. Ibid., p. 85.

42. Ibid., pp. 85–6.

43. Ibid., p. 93.

44. Ibid.

45. Ibid., p. 94.

46. Ibid., p. 95.

47. Ibid., p. 82.

48. Ibid., p. 216.

49. Mack, *A Prince of Our Disorder*, pp. 440–41.

50. Interview with Lieutenant-Colonel John Carver and Mrs Jocelyn Carver, 3.3.78.
51. Hamilton, *The Man Behind the Legend*, p. 40.
52. Lady Michelmore interview.
53. Hamilton, *The Man Behind the Legend*, p. 43.
54. Colonel R. O. H. Carver interview.
55. Hamilton, *The Man Behind the Legend*, p. 43.
56. Lieutenant-Colonel John Carver interview.
57. Colonel R. O. H. Carver interview.
58. Lieutenant-Colonel John Carver interview.
59. B. L. Montgomery, *Memoirs*, p. 41.
60. Lieutenant-Colonel John Carver interview.
61. B. L. Montgomery, *Memoirs*, p. 42.
62. Hamilton, *The Man Behind the Legend*, p. 40.
63. Lieutenant-Colonel John Carver interview.
64. Ibid.
65. Colonel R. O. H. Carver interview.
66. B. L. Montgomery, *Memoirs*, p. 41.
67. Tomes, 'Monty'.
68. Ibid.
69. Liddell Hart Papers, LHCMA.
70. Brian Montgomery, *A Field Marshal in the Family*, p. 211.
71. Ibid., p. 212.
72. Ibid.
73. Tomes, 'Monty'.

7 In Command

1. Liddell Hart, *Memoirs*, p. 55.
2. Interview with Colonel P. B. I. O. Burge, 11.4.78.
3. World War I Letters Album, BLM 1/69, IWM.
4. World War I Letters Album, BLM 1/70, IWM.
5. World War I Letters Album, BLM 1/72, IWM.
6. World War I Letters Album, BLM 1/73, IWM.
7. World War I Letters Album, BLM 1/74, IWM.
8. Lieutenant-Colonel John Carver interview.
9. Moorehead, *Montgomery*, p. 75.
10. Ibid., pp. 76–7.
11. Colonel P. B. I. O. Burge interview.
12. Brian Montgomery, *A Field Marshal in the Family*, p. 215.
13. Moorehead, *Montgomery*, p. 76.
14. Quoted ibid., p. 74.
15. Quoted ibid., p. 83.

16. Colonel P. B. I. O. Burge interview; letter to author, 27.3.78.

17. Major G. R. H. Bailey, 'Recollections of Monty', unpublished manuscript.

18. Lady Herbert interview.

19. B. L. Montgomery, *Memoirs*, pp. 42–3.

20. Interview with Major G. R. H. Bailey, 8.3.78.

21. Bailey, 'Recollections of Monty'.

22. Colonel P. J. Gething interview.

23. 'B. L. Montgomery', personal file, Ministry of Defence.

24. Ibid.

25. Colonel P. J. Gething interview.

26. Interview with Major-General Sir Francis de Guingand, 7.5.78.

27. 'B. L. Montgomery', personal file, Ministry of Defence.

28. Colonel P. J. Gething interview.

29. Ibid.

30. 'B. L. Montgomery', personal file, Ministry of Defence.

31. Bond, *British Military Policy*, p. 138.

32. Interview with Major Neil Holdich, 16.8.78.

33. B. L. Montgomery, *Memoirs*, p. 19.

34. Colonel P. B. I. O. Burge interview.

35. Major Neil Holdich interview.

36. Colonel P. B. I. O. Burge interview.

37. Major Neil Holdich interview.

38. Colonel P. B. I. O. Burge interview.

39. Ibid.

40. Ibid.

41. General Hans von Seeckt, *Thoughts of a Soldier*, 1930.

42. Ibid., p. 107.

43. Colonel P. B. I. O. Burge interview.

44. Ibid.

45. Ibid.

46. 'B. L. Montgomery', personal file, Ministry of Defence.

47. Interview with Colonel R. A. N. Davidson, 8.3.78.

48. Brigadier J. P. Duke interview.

49. 'B. L. Montgomery', personal file, Ministry of Defence.

50. Brigadier J. P. Duke interview.

51. Ibid.

52. Quoted in Martin Samuels, *Command or Control: Command, Training and Tactics in the British and German Armies, 1888–1918*, 1995, p. 280.

53. Interview with Major-General Eric Sixsmith, 17.4.79.

54. Interview with Brigadier 'Tochi' Barker, 25.3.80.

55. C. Barnett, *The Desert Generals*, 2nd edn, 1983, p. 267.

56. Brian Montgomery, *A Field Marshal in the Family*, p. 227.

57. Letter, B. L. Montgomery to Brigadier Sir Edgar Williams, Montgomery Ancillary Collections, Box 21, IWM.

58. Quoted in de Guingand, *Generals at War*, 1964, p. 170.

59. 'Monty and Betty Montgomery' – recollections prepared by Colonel Alan Davidson, 8.3.78.
60. Brigadier 'Tochi' Barker interview.
61. Lieutenant-Colonel John Carver interview.
62. Ibid.
63. Colonel P. B. I. O. Burge interview.
64. Brian Montgomery, *A Field Marshal in the Family*, p. 226.
65. Ibid., p. 229.
66. Ibid., p. 225.
67. Interview with General Sir Dudley Ward, 22.2.78.
68. 'B. L. Montgomery', personal file, Ministry of Defence.
69. Colonel R. A. N. Davidson interview.
70. Major-General Eric Sixsmith interview.
71. Ibid.
72. Brigadier 'Tochi' Barker interview.
73. Letter, B. L. Montgomery to Mary Connell (copy), 14.1.53, Lord Montgomery Deposit, Box 1, IWM.
74. Ibid.
75. Interview with Viscount Montgomery, 30.8.78.
76. Colonel R. A. N. Davidson interview.
77. Viscount Montgomery interview.
78. Letter, B. L. Montgomery to Mary Connell (copy), 14 January 1953, Lord Montgomery Deposit, Box 1, IWM.
79. Lieutenant-Colonel and Mrs John Carver interview.
80. Interview with Mrs Jocelyn Carver, 3.8.78.
81. Colonel R. A. N. Davidson interview.
82. Letter, B. L. Montgomery to Major A. E. Percival, 14.10.23, Percival Papers (p. 18, file 4/2), IWM.
83. Bond, *British Military Policy*, p. 208.
84. Ibid., p. 216.
85. B. L. Montgomery, *Memoirs*, p. 49.
86. Colonel R. A. N. Davidson interview.
87. General Sir Dudley Ward interview.
88. Lieutenant-Colonel and Mrs John Carver interview.
89. Ibid.
90. Ibid.
91. Letter, Betty Montgomery to Jocelyn Tweedie, communicated by Mrs Jocelyn Carver.
92. Colonel P. B. I. O. Burge interview.
93. 'B. L. Montgomery', personal file, Ministry of Defence.
94. Ibid.
95. B. Liddell Hart, *Europe in Arms*, 1937.
96. Letter, B. L. Montgomery to B. Liddell Hart, 22.5.37, LHCMA.
97. Danchev, *The Alchemist of War*, p. 190.
98. C. Barnett, *The Collapse of British Power*, 1984, p. 502.

99. Danchev, *The Alchemist of War*, p. 191.
100. Liddell Hart, *Europe in Arms*, p. 143.
101. Chamberlain to Liddell Hart, 8.3.37, LHCMA, 1/159.
102. Letter, B. L. Montgomery to B. Liddell Hart, 22.5.37, ibid.
103. Ibid.
104. J. R. Colville, *Man of Valour*, 1972, p. 56.
105. Ibid., pp. 56, 64.
106. Ibid., p. 56.
107. Ibid., p. 62.
108. Ibid.
109. Ibid., pp. 67–8.
110. Ibid., p. 86 and elsewhere.

8 The Death of Betty

1. Letter communicated by Mrs Jocelyn Carver.
2. B. L. Montgomery, 'The Problem of the Encounter Battle as Affected by Modern British War Establishments', *Royal Engineers Journal*, September 1937.
3. Letter, B. L. Montgomery to B. Liddell Hart, of 17.9.37, Liddell Hart Papers, LHCMA.
4. 'Recollections of General Sir Frank Simpson', recorded by Eugene Wason for Sir Denis Hamilton, 1978.
5. Ibid.
6. The 2nd Queen's, 2nd Middlesex, 1st KOSB and, replacing the 1st Green Howards that November, the 2nd Lincolnshire Regiment.
7. Lieutenant-General Sir Frederick Morgan, *Peace and War*, 1961, p. 129.
8. 'Recollections of General Sir Frank Simpson'.
9. Fraser, *And We Shall Shock Them*, p. 8.
10. Ibid., p. 12.
11. 'Recollections of General Sir Frank Simpson'.
12. Ibid.
13. Fraser, *And We Shall Shock Them*, p. 8.
14. 'Recollections of General Sir Frank Simpson'.
15. Ibid.
16. Ibid.
17. 'B. L. Montgomery', personal file, Ministry of Defence.
18. Ibid.
19. 'David Montgomery's Life', Lord Montgomery Deposit, Box 1, IWM.
20. B. L. Montgomery, *Memoirs*, p. 43.
21. Mrs Jocelyn Carver interview.
22. Ibid.
23. B. L. Montgomery, *Memoirs*, p. 42.
24. Mrs Jocelyn Carver interview.

25. Letter of 9.10.37, communicated by Mrs Jocelyn Carver.
26. Letter of 15.10.37, communicated by Mrs Jocelyn Carver.
27. B. L. Montgomery, *Memoirs*, p. 44.
28. Viscount Montgomery interview.
29. Moorehead, *Montgomery*, p. 89.
30. B. L. Montgomery, *Memoirs*, p. 44.
31. Moorehead, *Montgomery*, p. 89.

9 Post-Mortem

1. 'Recollections of General Sir Frank Simpson'.
2. B. L. Montgomery, *Memoirs*, p. 44.
3. Moorehead, *Montgomery*, p. 90.
4. B. L. Montgomery, *Memoirs*, p. 44. Final sentence deleted in published version, original in 'Early drafts: Chapters 1 to 12', in Lord Montgomery Deposit, Box 30, IWM.
5. Ibid.
6. Brian Montgomery, *A Field Marshal in the Family*, pp. 237–8.
7. Moorehead, *Montgomery*, pp. 68, 70.
8. Lieutenant-Colonel John Carver, 'Reflections on Bernard and Betty Montgomery', unpublished manuscript communicated to the author by Lt-Col J. Carver.
9. Letter, Lieutenant-General Wilson to General Wavell, 10.11.39, quoted in K. Macksey, *Armoured Crusader*, 1967, p. 171.
10. Iverach Macdonald, *The History of the Times*, vol. V, 1984, pp. 44–5.
11. Letter of 21.10.37 (first section dated 19.10.37), communicated to the author by Colonel R. O. H. Carver.
12. Ibid. (second section).
13. B. L. Montgomery, *Memoirs*, p. 45.
14. Moorehead, *Montgomery*, p. 89.
15. Brian Montgomery, *A Field Marshal in the Family*, p. 236.
16. 'Recollections of General Sir Frank Simpson'.
17. John Connell, *Wavell: Scholar and Soldier*, 1964, p. 204.
18. 'Instructions for individual training issued by me as Brigadier, Comdg 9th Inf Bde', Aug. 1937–Jan. 1938, BLM 11, IWM.
19. Morgan, *Peace and War*, p. 128.
20. B. L. Montgomery, *Memoirs*, p. 45.
21. Viscount Montgomery interview.
22. Mrs Jocelyn Carver interview.
23. Letter, B. L. Montgomery to Mary Connell (copy), 14.1.53, Lord Montgomery Deposit, Box 1, IWM.
24. 'Instructions for individual training issued by me as Brigadier, Comdg 9th Inf Bde', Aug. 1937–Jan. 1938, BLM 11, IWM.
25. *Kingsbridge Gazette*, 8 July 1938.

26. Ibid.

27. Morgan, *Peace and War*, p. 130.

28. One copy of the 170-page report survives at the Staff College, Camberley.

29. *The Britannia Magazine*, summer term, 1938.

30. Connell, *Wavell*, p. 201.

31. Ibid., p. 200.

32. Morgan, *Peace and War*, p. 130.

33. B. L. Montgomery, *Memoirs*, p. 46.

34. Wording as per manuscript in 'Early drafts: Chapters 1 to 12', Lord Montgomery Deposit, Box 30, IWM.

35. B. L. Montgomery, *Memoirs*, p. 46.

36. Ibid.

37. BLM 13/5, IWM.

38. Ibid.

10 Breaking Down

1. 'B. L. Montgomery', personal file, Ministry of Defence.

2. Connell, *Wavell*, p. 204.

3. Ibid., p. 197.

4. Miscellaneous War Office file (WO 216/111), PRO.

5. Letter of 1.1.39, Miscellaneous War Office file (WO 216/111), PRO.

6. Ibid.

7. Letter of 6.1.39, Miscellaneous War Office file (WO 216/111), PRO.

8. 'B. L. Montgomery', personal file, Ministry of Defence.

9. Ibid.

10. Ibid.

11. Ibid.

12. 'David Montgomery's Life', January 1953, Lord Montgomery Deposit, Box 1, IWM.

13. Lady Michelmore interview.

14. Ibid.

15. 'B. L. Montgomery', personal file, Ministry of Defence.

16. Ibid.

17. Dwight D. Eisenhower, *Crusade in Europe*, 1948, p. 2.

18. 'Recollections of General Sir Frank Simpson'.

19. Ibid.

20. Viscount Alanbrooke, 'Notes on my Life', published in part in A. Bryant, *The Turn of the Tide*, 1957. MS preserved in Brooke Papers, LHCMA.

21. 'Recollections of General Sir Frank Simpson'.

11 Dunkirk

1. Letter of 1.1.39 to General Adam, Miscellaneous War Office file (WO 216/111), PRO.

2. 'Memoirs – Early Drafts: Chapters 1–12', Lord Montgomery Deposit, Box 30, IWM.

3. Ibid.

4. Lieutenant-Colonel G. M. B. Gough, 2nd Lincolnshire Regiment, 'What Did You Do Grandpa?', typescript 83/32/1, IWM.

5. Ibid.

6. Bryant, *Turn of the Tide*, p. 51.

7. Charles Burdick and Hans-Adolf Jacobsen, eds., *The Halder War Diary, 1939–1942*, 1988, p. 65.

8. Ibid.

9. Colville, *Man of Valour*, p. 155.

10. 'Memoirs – Early Drafts: Chapters 1–12', Lord Montgomery Deposit, Box 30, IWM.

11. B. L. Montgomery, *Memoirs*, p. 52.

12. Ibid., p. 56.

13. Lord Bridgeman, letter to Field-Marshal Montgomery, 25.8.52, BLM 22, IWM.

14. Interview with Field-Marshal Sir Gerald Templer, 27.4.79.

15. B. L. Montgomery, *The Path to Leadership*, 1961, p. 41.

16. Alanbrooke Diaries, LHCMA.

17. 'Personal Memorandum – Discipline', 13.10.39, Sint Sixtusabdij Deposit, IWM.

18. Gough, 'What Did You Do Grandpa?'

19. David Irving, *Hitler's War*, 1977, p. 53.

20. B. L. Montgomery, *The Path to Leadership*, p. 126.

21. Bryant, *Turn of the Tide*, p. 82 and Alanbrooke Diaries, LHCMA.

22. Bryant, *Turn of the Tide*, p. 83.

23. B. L. Montgomery, *The Path to Leadership*, p. 126.

24. Bryant, *Turn of the Tide*, p. 82.

25. Entry of 23.11.39, Alanbrooke Diaries, LHCMA.

26. LHCMA.

27. Quoted in Brian Montgomery, *A Field Marshal in the Family*, pp. 253–4.

28. Fraser, *Alanbrooke*, p. 142.

29. B. L. Montgomery, *The Path to Leadership*, p. 126.

30. Brian Montgomery, *A Field Marshal in the Family*, pp. 254–5.

31. B. L. Montgomery, *Memoirs*, p. 60.

32. Bryant, *Turn of the Tide*, p. 83.

33. Fraser, *Alanbrooke*, p. 162.

34. Dixon, *On the Psychology of Military Incompetence*, p. 94.

35. Bryant, *Turn of the Tide*, p. 82.

36. Fraser, *Alanbrooke*, p. 146.

37. B. L. Montgomery, *Memoirs*, p. 58.

38. Ibid.

39. War Diary, HQ 3rd Division, September 1939–June 1940 (WO 167/218), PRO.

40. Ibid.

41. 3 Div. Training Exercise No. 2, 16.12.39, BLM 16/2, IWM.

42. B. L. Montgomery, *Memoirs*, p. 59.

43. 3 Div. Training Exercise No. 3, 7–8.3.40, BLM 17/19, IWM.

44. Ibid.

45. Alanbrooke Diaries, LHCMA.

46. Letter of 11.4.40, Sint Sixtusabdij Deposit, IWM.

47. Ibid.

48. Lady Herbert interview.

49. 'Personal Memorandum for Brigadiers and Officers Commanding Units of Div Troops', 29.4.40 (Annotated: 'Issued because I felt sure a German attack was imminent'), BLM 15/10, IWM.

50. B. L. Montgomery, *Memoirs*, p. 61.

51. Klaus Maier et al., eds., *Das deutsche Reich und der zweite Weltkrieg*, vol. II, 1979, p. 283.

52. Fraser, *Alanbrooke*, p. 151.

53. Sir Robin Dunn, 'The First Round' (1940), 94/41/1, IWM.

54. Ibid.

55. Ibid.

56. Interview with Lieutenant-Colonel C. P. Dawnay, 23.8.78.

57. Gough, 'What Did You Do Grandpa', 83/32/1, IWM.

58. Bryant, *Turn of the Tide*, p. 98.

59. War Diary, II Corps, G. Ops (WO 167/148), PRO.

60. War Diary, GHQ BEF, May 1940 (WO 167/27, 28, 29 and 31), PRO.

61. Ibid.

62. War Diary, 3rd Division Signals (WO 167/222) PRO.

63. Bryant, *Turn of the Tide*, p. 99.

64. Ibid., p. 101.

65. Alanbrooke Diaries, LHCMA.

66. Bryant, *Turn of the Tide*, p. 102.

67. Ibid., p. 91 and Alanbrooke Diary, LHCMA.

68. Colville, *Man of Valour*, p. 190.

69. Ibid., p. 196.

70. B. Liddell Hart, ed., *The Rommel Papers*, 1953, p. 22.

71. Dunn, 'The First Round'.

72. Ibid.

73. War Diary, GHQ BEF, May 1940 (WO 167/27, 28, 29 and 31), PRO.

74. J. R. Colville, *The Fringes of Power: Downing Street Diaries 1939–1955* (entry for 18 May 1940), 1985, p. 135.

75. Ibid.

76. Letter, Lieutenant-General Oliver Leese to Margaret, Lady Leese, 19.5.[40], Leese Papers, IWM.

77. Ibid.

78. Gamelin had also examined, on 19 May, the possibility of using Dunkirk and the Channel ports for evacuation of the northern armies, but the French Admiralty considered the possibilities of successful evacuation to be remote, and only considered a plan to reinforce the northern armies, rather than evacuating them – Maier et al., *Das deutsche Reich und der zweite Weltkrieg*, p. 291.

79. B. Bond, ed., *Chief of Staff: The Diaries of Lt-General Sir Henry Pownall*, vol. I, 1972, p. 323.

80. Letter, Lieutenant-General Oliver Leese to Margaret, Lady Leese, 'Later', 19 [5.40], Leese Papers, IWM.

81. Colville, *The Fringes of Power*, p. 137.

82. J. Colville, *Man of Valour*, p. 213.

83. Alanbrooke Diary, LHCMA.

84. Dunkirk Diary of Lieutenant-Colonel O. A. Archdale, 78/52/1, IWM.

85. BLM 19/2, IWM.

86. B. L. Montgomery, *Memoirs*, p. 66.

87. Ironically, it was this very officer – then Lieutenant-Colonel Kinzel – who would surrender to Field-Marshal Sir Bernard Montgomery on behalf of the German Northern Armed Forces on 4 May 1945 at Lüneburg Heath.

88. B. L. Montgomery, *Memoirs*, p. 66.

89. B. L. Montgomery, *The Path to Leadership*, p. 126.

90. Archdale, Dunkirk Diary.

91. Ibid.

92. Bond, *Chief of Staff*, vol. I, p. 352.

93. Ibid.

94. Ibid.

95. All quoted in M. Egremont, *Under Two Flags*, 1997, pp. 164–6.

96. Bryant, *Turn of the Tide*, p. 138.

97. Lieutenant Colonel C. P. Dawnay interview.

98. Gough, 'What Did You Do Grandpa?' 'On 27 May the Belgian army capitulated, exposing the northern flank of the British and French in the cut-off northern army group. By a brilliant march at night, the British blocked this flank' – C. Barnett, *Britain and Her Army*, 1970, p. 430.

99. Bryant, *Turn of the Tide*, p. 143.

100. B. L. Montgomery, *History of Warfare*, p. 502.

101. Bryant, *Turn of the Tide*, p. 145.

102. War Diary, GHQ BEF (WO 167/27, 28, 29 and 31), PRO.

103. Bryant, *Turn of the Tide*, pp. 146–7.

104. B. Horrocks, with Eversley Belfield and Major-General H. Essame, *Corps Commander*, 1977, p. 10.

105. Letter of 8.9.98 from Father Alphonse, Archivist, Sint Sixtusabdij, Westvleteren, IWM.

106. BLM 19/2, IWM.

107. Horrocks, *A Full Life*, 1960, p. 102.
108. Gough, 'What Did You Do Grandpa?'
109. Bryant, *Turn of the Tide*, p. 151.
110. Lieutenant-Colonel C. P. Dawnay interview.
111. Bryant, *Turn of the Tide*, p. 146.
112. B. L. Montgomery, *The Path to Leadership*, pp. 127–8.
113. Horrocks, *A Full Life*, p. 85.
114. B. L. Montgomery, *The Path to Leadership*, p. 128.
115. Horrocks, *A Full Life*, p. 85.
116. B. L. Montgomery, *The Path to Leadership*, p. 128.
117. Dunn, 'The First Round'.
118. Ibid.
119. 'Special Order of the Day,' 3 Division, 30.5.40 in BLM 19, IWM.
120. B. L. Montgomery, *Memoirs*, p. 63.
121. Letter, Lieutenant-General Oliver Leese to Margaret, Lady Leese, 30.5.42, Leese Papers, IWM.
122. L. F. Ellis, *The War in France and Flanders 1939–1940*, 1953, p. 234.
123. See Gort's 'Summary of Events: Flanders Campaign 10 May – 3 June, 1940', sent to Major-General B. L. Montgomery, 22.6.40, BLM 21/1 and 2, IWM.
124. War Diary, GHQ BEF, 30 May 1940 (WO 167/27, 28, 29 and 31), PRO.
125. Bryant, *Turn of the Tide*, p. 120.
126. BLM 19/2, IWM.
127. Letter of 25.8.52, BLM 22/2, IWM.
128. Ibid.
129. Letter, Lieutenant-General Oliver Leese to Margaret, Lady Leese, 30.5.42, Leese Papers, IWM.
130. War Diary, GHQ BEF (WO 167/27, 28, 29 and 31), PRO.
131. Ellis, *The War in France and Flanders*, p. 234.
132. War Diary, GHQ BEF (WO 167/27, 28, 29 and 31), PRO.
133. Ibid.
134. B. L. Montgomery, *Memoirs*, p. 64.
135. BLM 19/2, IWM.

12 In the Aftermath of Dunkirk

1. Bryant, *Turn of the Tide*, p. 169.
2. Ibid., p. 172.
3. Ibid.
4. Letter of 24.6.40, BLM 20/3, IWM.
5. Dunn, 'The First Round'.
6. B. L. Montgomery, *Memoirs*, p. 67.
7. Explanatory 'Note' dated August 1963, BLM 19/1, accompanying 'Itinerary of Events', May–June 1940, BLM 19/2, IWM.

8. Ibid.

9. B. L. Montgomery, *Memoirs*, p. 67.

10. Ibid.

11. Letter of 5.6.40, BLM 19/4, IWM.

12. BLM 19/3, IWM.

13. Bryant, *Turn of the Tide*, p. 159.

14. BLM 19/3, IWM.

15. Colville, *Man of Valour*, p. 230.

16. Bryant, *Turn of the Tide*, p. 339; Colville, *Man of Valour*, p. 245.

17. Colville, *Man of Valour*, p. 235.

18. Ellis, *The War in France and Flanders*, p. 327.

19. Letter of 25.8.52, BLM 22/2, IWM.

20. 'Only a madman would give a Corps to Barker' – ibid.

21. B. L. Montgomery, *The Path to Leadership*, p. 24.

22. Colville, *The Fringes of Power*, p. 177.

23. *The Black Book*, Reichssicherheitshauptamt, 01/5 (4–15).091, IWM.

24. General Ismay was Churchill's Military Secretary.

25. Colville, *The Fringes of Power*, pp. 166–7, entry for 19.6.40.

26. Ibid., p. 186.

27. Ibid. p. 167, entry for 20.6.40.

28. B. L. Montgomery, *Memoirs*, p. 69.

29. Ibid.

30. Ibid.

31. Ibid.

32. Colville, *The Fringes of Power*, p. 122.

33. Chalfont, *Montgomery of Alamein*, p. 218.

34. B. L. Montgomery, *Memoirs*, p. 70.

35. Letter of 14.5.46 in 'Montgomery' file, Liddell Hart Papers, LCHMA.

13 Home Forces

1. Lord Montgomery Deposit, Box 4, IWM.

2. Lieutenant-Colonel C. P. Dawnay interview.

3. Ibid.

4. See A. Danchev, *Very Special Relationship: Field Marshal Sir John Dill and the Anglo-American Alliance 1941–44*, 1986, p. 5.

5. Ibid.

6. Fraser, *Alanbrooke*, p. 177.

7. Ibid.

8. Letter of 5.8.40, BLM 20/4, IWM.

9. B. L. Montgomery, *Memoirs*, p. 70.

10. General Thorne 'thought the German left wing could be held in the Ashdown Forest, but he did not see what could prevent the right wing advancing

through Canterbury to London, especially if his only trained and equipped Division (the 3rd) was to be moved away to Northern Ireland. The P.M. promised that this should not be done' – Colville, *The Fringes of Power*, p. 180, entry for 30.6.40.

11. War Diary, 3rd Division (WO 167/220), PRO.

12. Horrocks, *A Full Life*, p. 94.

13. War Diary, 3rd Division (WO 167/220), PRO.

14. Chalfont, *Montgomery of Alamein*, p. 120.

15. B. L. Montgomery, *Memoirs*, p. 68.

16. Ibid.

17. Fraser, *Alanbrooke*, p. 187.

18. S. Gresty, 'My Last 7 Days with the British Expeditionary Force, May–June 1940', 90/26/1, IWM.

19. Speech in the House of Commons, 4.6.40, Hansard.

20. John Connell, *Auchinleck*, 1959, p. 149.

21. Ibid., p. 157.

22. Letter to VCIGS, 29.6.40, quoted in Connell, *Auchinleck*, p. 156.

23. H. Winton, *To Change an Army: General Sir John Burnett-Stuart and British Armoured Doctrine, 1927–1938*, 1988, p. 148.

24. 'Notes on 4th Division', 25.7.40, BLM 25/30, IWM.

25. 'Notes on Portsmouth Area', 25.7.40, BLM 25/29, IWM.

26. Ibid.

27. 'Notes on 50th Division', BLM 25/31, IWM.

28. Connell, *Auchinleck*, pp. 162–3.

29. Letter of 5.8.40, BLM 20/4, IWM.

30. Connell, *Auchinleck*, p. 163.

31. Letter of 6.12.58 to F. de Guingand, De Guingand Papers, IWM.

32. B. L. Montgomery, *Memoirs*, p. 71.

33. National Press Club Speakers Series, Washington, DC, 8.4.97.

34. Field-Marshal Sir Gerald Templer interview.

35. B. L. Montgomery, *Memoirs*, pp. 72–3.

36. Ibid., p. 73.

37. Ibid., p. 71.

38. 'First Senior War Staff Course, 1940', 25.10.40, BLM 24/3 and 4, IWM.

39. Ibid.

40. Ibid.

41. Connell, *Auchinleck*, p. 162.

42. Alanbrooke, Diary entry 7.12.40, Alanbrooke Papers, LHCMA.

43. G. Rees, *A Bundle of Sensations*, 1960, p. 150.

44. War Diary, HQ V Corps (WO 166/249), PRO.

45. World War I Collection, ART 1172, IWM.

46. B. L. Montgomery, *Memoirs*, p. 72.

47. Letter of 7.5.41, Dawnay Papers, IWM.

48. Peter Fleming, *Invasion 1940*, 1957, and Kenneth Macksey, *Invasion*, 1980, pp. 141–2.

49. Operation Instruction no. 25 dated 2.5.41, War Diary, HQ XII Corps (WO 166/344) PRO.

50. Dawnay Papers, IWM.

51. War Diary, HQ XII Corps (WO 166/344) PRO.

52. Ibid.

53. Ibid.

54. Rees, *A Bundle of Sensations*, p. 132.

55. Ibid., p. 133.

56. Headquarters, South-Eastern Command (WO 199/2623), PRO.

57. Ibid.

58. John A. English, *The Canadian Army and the Normandy Campaign: A Study of Failure in High Command*, 1991, p. 126.

59. Ibid., p. 135.

60. Ibid., p. 127.

61. Ibid., p. 131.

62. Headquarters, South-Eastern Command (WO 199/2623), PRO.

63. 2.1.42, Headquarters, South-Eastern Command, (WO 199/2623), PRO.

64. Ibid.

65. Ibid.

66. Ibid.

67. Bryant, *Turn of the Tide*, p. 310.

68. Fraser, *And We Shall Shock Them*, p. 202.

69. Bryant, *Turn of the Tide*, p. 311.

70. Ibid.

71. Letter of 8.1.42, BLM 20/5, IWM.

72. World War I Letters Album, BLM 1/64, IWM, annotation to letter of 8.11.17, p. 55. In a private letter to his former ADC and Canadian military assistant, Lieutenant-Colonel Trumbull Warren, Monty was, in his old age, even more excoriating. He had, he wrote to Warren, received the review of a new biography of McNaughton. 'If ever a man was unfit to command in the field it was Andy [McNaughton], and I said so to Alanbrooke in no uncertain voice . . . The same is true of Harry Crerar. What I suffered from that man!'; letter of 1.1.69, Warren Papers, IWM.

73. Letter of 27.6.42, Warren Papers, IWM.

74. Letter of 25.4.42, ibid.

75. Letter of 1.6.42, ibid.

76. Letter of 25.4.42, ibid.

77. Horrocks, *A Full Life*, p. 99.

78. 'Montgomery of Alamein', BBC recording of 24.9.58.

79. Letter to Mary Warren, 2.6.42, Warren Papers, IWM.

80. Letter to Trumbull Warren, 2.6.42, ibid.

81. 'SE Army, Exercise Tiger, Final Conference, Remarks of Army Commander, 4 June 1942', BLM 26/1, IWM.

82. Merle Miller, *Ike the Soldier, as They Knew Him*, 1987, p. 359.

83. M. Blumenson, *Mark Clark*, 1984, pp. 57–8.

84. Miller, *Ike the Soldier*, p. 359.

85. S. Ambrose, *Eisenhower the Soldier, 1890–1952*, 1984, p. 130.

86. Ibid., p. 129.

87. Ibid., p. 130.

88. Ibid., p. 150.

89. Miller, *Ike the Soldier*, p. 359.

90. Ambrose, *Eisenhower the Soldier*, p. 151.

91. Rees, *A Bundle of Sensations*, p. 133.

92. T. Parrish, *Roosevelt and Marshall*, 1989, p. 255.

93. A. Wedemeyer, *Wedemeyer Reports!*, 1958, p. 105.

94. D. D. Eisenhower Diary, 6.4.42, quoted in Ambrose, *Eisenhower the Soldier*, p. 151.

14 Personal Relations

1. See, *inter alia*, Danchev, *Very Special Relationship*, p. 66.

2. 'Recollections of General Sir Frank Simpson'.

3. Ibid.

4. Colville, *The Fringes of Power*, p. 189.

5. Sweeny Papers, IWM.

6. Letter of 18.6.41, ibid.

7. 'Recollections of General Sir Frank Simpson'.

8. Rees, *A Bundle of Sensations*, p. 133.

9. 'Recollections of General Sir Frank Simpson'.

10. Rees, *A Bundle of Sensations*, p. 133.

11. 'Recollections of General Sir Frank Simpson'.

12. D. J. Potter, *Fiasco: the Breakout of the German Battleships*, 1970, p. 124. Despite wartime censorship, British newspapers, led by *The Times*, were so excoriating that Churchill was forced to set up the only judicial inquiry 'ever held into the conduct of a battle'. The tribunal's report, although predictably a whitewash ('a collector's piece of officialese and double talk') was kept secret for the rest of the war. The deputy Prime Minister drew a veil over the incident in Parliament on 18 March 1942, claiming that 'The general findings do not reveal that there were any serious deficiencies either in foresight, co-operation or organization.' This was the very opposite of the truth – since almost '700 fighters and bombers – the entire force at the disposal of the RAF – had been flung into the battle without success because they were too late and completely unco-ordinated. Thirteen brave young Fleet Air Arm pilots had been sent uselessly to their deaths. Twenty-seven young sailors had been killed and eighteen seriously wounded aboard the destroyer *Worcester*,' Potter pointed out – 'a piece of pitiful heroism which need never have happened if the Navy had brought in bigger ships.' As neither the press nor members of Parliament were satisfied, Churchill read out an Admiralty document drawn up a week before the escape, predicting its possibility, but ignoring the

failure to rehearse for such an eventuality. 'I have read this document to the House because I am anxious that Members should realize our affairs are not conducted by simpletons and dunderheads as the comic papers try to depict,' Churchill claimed. Potter, *Fiasco*, pp. 201, 212, 206.

13. Lieutenant-Colonel John Carver interview.

14. 'Recollections of General Sir Frank Simpson'.

15. English, *The Canadian Army*, pp. 128–9.

16. Rees, *A Bundle of Sensations*, p. 131.

17. Ibid., p. 135.

18. Ibid., p. 148.

19. Letter of 20.8.40, Dawnay Papers, IWM.

20. Letter of 20.9.40, ibid.

21. Ibid.

22. Letter of 5.10.40, Sweeny Papers, IWM.

23. Ibid.

24. Letter of 8.11.40, Dawnay Papers, IWM.

25. Letter of 26.12.40, Dawnay Papers, IWM.

26. Undated letter (November 1941), Dawnay Papers, IWM.

27. Letter of 11.3.42, Warren Papers, IWM.

28. Rees, *A Bundle of Sensations*, pp. 136–7.

29. Ibid., p. 136.

30. Undated letter, handwritten on reverse of letter from Trumbull Warren to Montgomery of 13.3.64, Warren Papers, IWM. The officer's name was Michael Carver (though no relation to Betty Montgomery's family). Carver not only became CIGS, in due course, but a field marshal – one of many young Turks Monty would 'push up the ladder' in his career.

31. Letter of 25.4.42, Warren Papers, IWM.

32. R. Terry, *Women in Khaki*, 1988, p. 135.

33. Mrs Margaret Sweeny, typescript memoir. Sweeny Papers, IWM.

34. B. L. Montgomery, *Memoirs*, pp. 73–4.

35. Mrs Margaret Sweeny, typescript memoir, Sweeny Papers, IWM.

36. Letter of 25.4.42, Warren Papers, IWM.

37. Letter of 14.5.42, ibid.

38. Letter of 27.6.42, ibid.

39. Letter of 20.11.54, ibid.

40. Letter of 15.2.57, ibid.

41. Letter of 24.11.42, ibid.

42. Letter of 10.1.43, ibid.

43. English, *The Canadian Army*, p. 125.

44. In this connection, an outstanding example of personal affection outweighing professional judgement and standard of efficiency is to be found in the case of Admiral Beatty, a discreet but active adulterer in the Nelsonian mode who, according to his biographer Stephen Roskill, not only sought adulterous sex off the battlefield, but chose and formed a considerable attachment to the twenty-seven-year-old Ralph Seymour, making Seymour his flag lieutenant on his flagship,

despite a marked lack of signals expertise – a wholly disastrous affection, as Roskill pointed out, which led to Beatty's failure to trap Admiral von Hipper's battle fleet by the Dogger Bank in December 1914 through badly worded signalling: S. Roskill, *Admiral of the Fleet Earl Beatty, The Last Naval Hero*, 1980, p. 103. (Lady Beatty did not share her husband's feelings for Seymour. Thus when, after World War I, Seymour fell in love with the niece of Beatty's wife, the unfortunate young man was driven to suicide by the opposition of the rich and whim-driven Lady Beatty – ibid., p. 316.)

15 Dieppe

1. The sentence 'Wherever possible, prisoners' hands will be tied to prevent the destruction of their documents' was found by the Germans in captured Canadian orders for the Dieppe engagement. As a result, British and Canadian soldiers taken at Dieppe were tied on 8 October 1942, and kept tied or handcuffed until 22 November 1943, after Red Cross intervention – C. P. Stacey, *Six Years of War*, 1957, pp. 396–7.
2. J. Leasor, *War at the Top*, 1959, p. 218.
3. Interview with Lieutenant-General Sir Ian Jacob, 18.5.79.
4. P. Ziegler, *Mountbatten*, p. 169.
5. Lord Alanbrooke, 'Notes on My Life', Brooke Papers, LHCMA.
6. Ziegler, *Mountbatten*, p. 156.
7. J. M. A. Gwyer and J. R. M. Butler, *Grand Strategy*, 1964, p. 632.
8. B. Villa, *Unauthorized Action: Mountbatten and the Dieppe Raid*, 1988, p. 105.
9. Ibid., p. 188.
10. Rees, *A Bundle of Sensations*, p. 149.
11. Ibid., p. 144.
12. Ibid.
13. T. Driberg, *Beaverbrook: A Study in Power and Frustration*, 1956, p. 291.
14. R. Hough, *Mountbatten: Hero for Our Time*, 1980, p. 154.
15. 'Note by Field-Marshal Montgomery on the Dieppe Raid: August 1962', Lord Montgomery Deposit, IWM.
16. Ibid.
17. Ibid.
18. Ibid.
19. Ibid.
20. Ibid.
21. Ibid.
22. Ibid.
23. Ibid.
24. Major Walter Skrine, 'Amended Draft' for Dieppe, Haydon Papers, IWM.
25. Julian Thomson, *War Behind Enemy Lines*, 1998, pp. 86–98.
26. Letter of 31.8.42, CAB 127/24, PRO.

27. Villa, *Unauthorized Action*, pp. 24–41.

28. Quoted in Brereton Greenhouse, *Dieppe, Dieppe*, 1992, p. 150.

29. Letter, Mountbatten to Major-General Charles Haydon, 16.7.58, Haydon Papers, JCH 2/7–8, IWM.

30. 'Alternative draft for Paragraph 3 and Note on Various Alterations to the Outline Plan made by the Force Commanders Subsequently', drafted by Walter Skrine, August 1958, Haydon Papers, IWM.

31. Ibid.

32. Ziegler, *Mountbatten*, p. 194.

33. Henriques to Haydon 'Alternative re-draft of Para 3', August 1958, Haydon Papers, IWM.

34. Letter to Major-General Haydon, 18.8.58, Haydon Papers, IWM.

35. Ibid.

36. 'Second Alternative Draft for Paragraph 3', 'Origin of the Plan', 'A draft of Walter Skrine', August 1958, Haydon Papers, IWM.

37. Rees, *A Bundle of Sensations*, p. 157.

38. Letter to Major-General Haydon, 17.8.58 Haydon Papers, IWM.

39. Letter to Major-General Haydon, 14.10.58, Haydon Papers, IWM.

40. Ibid.

41. Report no. 14, in Terry Copp, ed., *Montgomery's Scientists: Operational Research in Northwest Europe*, 2000, pp. 20–1, and 99–106.

42. Captain Hughes-Hallett, 'After-action Report by Naval Force Commander of *Jubilee*, 30 August 1942, Para 8 of lessons learned, including the need for far more effective methods of supporting the troops': 'The methods whereby effective support can be given are not considered to include night bombing' – quoted by Hughes-Hallett in his unpublished memoirs, vol. II, p. 197, Hughes-Hallett Papers, 67/70/1, IWM.

43. Ziegler, *Mountbatten*, p. 189.

44. D. Whitaker and S. Whitaker, *Dieppe: Tragedy to Triumph*, 1992, p. 147.

45. Ibid.

46. Letter to Major-General Haydon, 31.8.58, Haydon Papers, JCH 2/7–8, IWM.

47. Letter of 1.7.42, quoted in Stacey, *Six Years of War*, p. 335.

48. Whitaker and Whitaker, *Dieppe*, p. 172, quoting letter of 5.7.42, National Archive of Canada.

49. Stacey, *Six Years of War*, pp. 350–1.

50. 'Note by Field-Marshal Montgomery on the Dieppe Raid: August 1962', Lord Montgomery Deposit, IWM.

51. Letter to Major-General Haydon, 17.8.58, Haydon Papers, IMW.

52. 'Note by Field-Marshal Montgomery on the Dieppe Raid: August 1962', Lord Montgomery Deposit, IWM.

53. Whitaker and Whitaker, *Dieppe*, pp. xiv–xv.

54. Stacey, *Six Years of War*, p. 340.

55. J. Hughes-Hallett, 'The Mounting of Raids', *Journal of the United Services Institution*, November 1950.

56. Villa, *Unauthorized Action*, p. 304.

57. D. D. Eisenhower, *Crusade in Europe*, 1948, p. 75.

58. Villa, *Unauthorized Action*.

59. Q. Reynolds, *Dress Rehearsal: The Story of Dieppe*, 1943, p. 265.

60. J. Hughes-Hallett, unpublished memoirs, vol. II, p. 165, Hughes-Hallett Papers, 67/70/1, IWM.

61. Villa, *Unauthorized Action*, p. 90 and J. Hughes-Hallett, unpublished memoirs, vol. II, p. 165, Hughes-Hallett Papers, 67/70/1, IWM.

62. Villa, *Unauthorized Action*, p. 90.

63. Of the Combined Operations report Brooke told Mountbatten he was 'very disappointed with the paucity of ideas' – Ibid., p. 23.

64. D. Dilks, ed., *The Diaries of Sir Alexander Cadogan OM, 1938–1945*, 1971, p. 461.

65. Ziegler, *Mountbatten*, p. 190, quoting BBC TV interview, 19.8.72.

66. Ibid.

67. Villa, *Unauthorized Action*, p. 196.

68. F. Hinsley et al., *British Intelligence in the Second World War*, vol. II, 1981 pp. 695–704.

69. Goebbels writing in *Das Reich*, quoted in M. Balfour, *Propaganda in War 1939–45*, 1979, p. 279.

70. B. Fergusson, *The Watery Maze: The Story of Combined Operations*, 1961, p. 173.

71. Bryant, *Turn of the Tide*, p. 417.

72. Nigel Nicolson, ed., *Harold Nicolson, Diaries and Letters, 1939–1945*, 1967, p. 236.

73. J. Barnes and D. Nicholson, eds., *The Empire at Bay: The Leo Amery Diaries 1929–1945*, 1988, p. 821.

74. DEFE 2/306, PRO.

75. Villa, *Unauthorized Action*, p. 192.

76. DEFE 2/306, PRO.

77. Letter to General Sir Charles Haydon, 20.8.58, Haydon Papers, JCH 2/7–8, IWM.

78. Villa, *Unauthorized Action*, p. 198, quoting CBC 'Close-Up: Dieppe' broadcast 9 September 1962.

79. Ibid., p. 195.

80. Ibid., p. 23.

81. Leasor, *War at the Top*, p. 135.

82. Lord Lovat, *March Past*, 1978, p. 238.

83. Ibid.

84. Hough, *Mountbatten*, 1980, pp. 270–1.

85. W. S. Churchill, *The History of the Second World War*, vol. IV, *The Hinge of Fate*, 1951, p. 428.

86. Record of meeting with Stalin on 15.8.42, quoted in M. Gilbert, *Road to Victory: Winston S. Churchill 1941–1945*, 1986, p. 198.

87. Ibid.

88. Ibid.

89. Ibid.

90. Churchill, *History of the Second World War*, vol. IV, pp. 447–9.

91. Lord Lovat, *March Past*, p. 278.

92. Rees, *A Bundle of Sensations*, pp. 170–1.

93. Hughes-Hallett, unpublished memoirs, vol. II, p. 191, IWM.

94. Gilbert, *Road to Victory*, p. 211.

95. Ziegler, *Mountbatten*, p. 191.

96. Ibid., p. 701.

97. Lord Moran, *Winston Churchill: The Struggle for Survival*, 1966, p. 73.

98. Telegram of 27.8.42, quoted in Gilbert, *Road to Victory*, p. 219.

99. Leasor, *War at the Top*, p. 218.

100. 'Der gelandete Feind wurde im Nahkampf überall aufgerieben und ins Meer geworfen' – H. Wamper, *Dieppe: Die Beährung des Küstenwestwalles*, 1943, p. 9.

101. 'Der Feind hat bei diesem, nur politischen Zwecken dienenden, aber jeder militärischen Vernunft hohnsprechenden Landungsversuch eine vernichtende Niederlage erlitten. Die deutsche Macht im Westen hat dem dilettantenhaften Unternehmen die gebührende Abfuhr erteilt' – Sondermeldung, late evening 19 August, Aus dem Führerhauptquartier, 19.8.42 – ibid.

102. 'Alle an der Abwehr der feindlichen Landung beteiligten Verbände der Deutschen Wehrmacht haben sich hervorragend geschlagen' – ibid., p. 12.

103. John P. Campbell, *Dieppe Revisited: A Documentary Investigation*, 1993, p. 96.

104. Gilbert, *Road to Victory*, p. 192.

105. Letter, Mountbatten to Brooke, 31.8.42, CAB 127/24, PRO.

106. 21.12.42 to Ismay, Ismay II/3/244a, LHCMA.

107. August 1950, Ismay II/3/252a, LHCMA.

108. Interview for CBC 'Close-Up: Dieppe', broadcast 9 September 1962, quoted in Villa, *Unauthorized Action*, p. 246.

109. 'Note by Field-Marshal Montgomery on the Dieppe Raid: August 1962', Lord Montgomery Deposit, IWM.

110. Ibid.

111. Ibid.

112. Ibid.

113. Ibid.

16 The Desert

1. P. Freyberg, *Bernard Freyberg VC: Soldier of Two Nations*, 1990, p. 381.

2. Sometimes called the battle of First Alamein.

3. 'Notes on My Life', in Bryant, *Turn of the Tide*, p. 432.

4. Fraser, *Alanbrooke*, p. 280.

5. R. Bennett, *Ultra and Mediterranean Strategy 1941–1945*, 1989, p. 139.

6. Churchill, *History of the Second World War*, vol. IV, p. 412.

7. Interview with Brigadier Sir Edgar Williams, 20.12.79.

8. Sir Francis de Guingand interview.

9. 'Operation Bracelet', unpublished diary of August/September 1942 by Sir Ian Jacob, communicated to author.

10. Connell, *Auchinleck*, p. 305.

11. Churchill, *History of the Second World War*, vol. IV, p. 412.

12. Lord Ismay, *Memoirs*, 1960, p. 272.

13. Sir Ian Jacob, diary entry, 8.8.42, quoted in Connell, *Auchinleck*, p. 710.

14. Bryant, *Turn of the Tide*, p. 439.

15. 'Notes on My Life', ibid., also Fraser, *Alanbrooke*, p. 282.

16. Fraser, *Alanbrooke*, p. 282.

17. Letter, Lieutenant-Colonel R. M. P. (later Lord) Carver to J. A. J. Agar Hamilton, 14.6.50, communicated to the author by Field-Marshal Lord Carver.

18. Interview with Field-Marshal Lord Carver, 14.1.81.

19. Bryant, *Turn of the Tide*, p. 441.

20. Ibid., p. 442.

21. Diary entry of 6.8.42, ibid., p. 444.

22. Ibid.

23. Letter of 9.8.42, in Gilbert, *Road to Victory*, p. 168, and M. Soames, *Speaking for Themselves: The Personal Letters of Winston and Clementine Churchill*, 1998, p. 467.

24. Diary entry, 6.8.42, in Bryant, *Turn of the Tide*, p. 446.

25. Ibid.

26. Alexander had never served in the desert; Gott's only idea of going 'right round' Rommel's forces via Siwa, in order to avoid heavy casualties, was dismissed even by his GSO 2, partly on grounds of the terrain, and in part because of the impossibility of giving air cover: Field-Marshal Lord Carver interview.

27. 'By accepting it I should definitely be taking a course which would on the whole help the war least', Brooke rationalized in his diary – his French-English showing signs of his exhaustion – Diary entry of 6.8.42 in Bryant, *Turn of the Tide*, p. 445.

28. T. Witherby in A. McKee, *El Alamein: Ultra and the Three Battles*, 1991, p. 77.

29. 'Notes on My Life', in Bryant, *Turn of the Tide*, p. 443.

30. Field-Marshal Lord Carver interview.

31. Diary entry in Bryant, *Turn of the Tide*, p. 446.

32. Diary entry, ibid., p. 448.

33. Bennett, *Ultra and Mediterranean Strategy*, p. 131.

34. Connell, *Auchinleck*, p. 305.

35. Letter of 9.8.42, in Gilbert, *Road to Victory*, p. 168.

36. Lieutenant-General Sir Ian Jacob interview.

37. Ibid.

38. N. Nicolson, *Alex: The Life of Field-Marshal Earl Alexander of Tunis*, 1973, pp. 19–20.

39. Lieutenant-General Sir Ian Jacob interview.
40. Major-General E. F. Sixsmith interview.
41. D. Hunt, *A Don at War*, 1966, pp. 118–19.
42. 'Such interventions as he made were indeed positively mischievous' – 'Churchill and the Battle', in Len Deighton and Max Hastings, *Battle of Britain*, 1989, rept. 1999, p. 218.
43. B. L. Montgomery, *Memoirs*, p. 77.
44. *The Patton Papers*, vol. II, ed. Martin Blumenson, 1972, p. 82.
45. Ibid.
46. Ibid.
47. Carlo D'Este, *Patton: A Genius for War*, 1995, p. 419.
48. *The Patton Papers*, vol. II, ed. Blumenson, p. 82.
49. B. L. Montgomery, *Memoirs*, p. 78.
50. Reynolds Papers, IWM.
51. Ibid.
52. Ibid.
53. Warren Papers, IWM.
54. B. L. Montgomery, *Memoirs*, p. 79.
55. Fraser, *Alanbrooke*, p. 288.
56. Letter of 9.8.42, in Gilbert, *Road to Victory*, p. 168.
57. Fraser, *Alanbrooke*, p. 288.
58. Ibid.
59. Churchill, *History of the Second World War*, vol. IV, p. 422.
60. B. L. Montgomery, *Memoirs*, p. 94.
61. Ibid.
62. Diary Notes 12.8.42–23.10.42: 'Review of the Situation in Eighth Army from 12 Aug to 23 Oct 42', BLM 27/1, IWM.
63. Interview with Field-Marshal Lord Harding, 23.5.79.
64. Fraser, *Alanbrooke*, p. 286.
65. Letter of 9.8.42, in Gilbert, *Road to Victory*, p. 168.
66. Diary Notes 12.8.42–23.10.42: 'Review of the Situation in Eighth Army from 12 Aug to 23 Oct 42', BLM 27/1, IWM.
67. Field-Marshal Lord Harding interview.
68. Ibid.
69. Ibid.
70. Diary Notes 12.8.42–23.10.42: 'Review of the Situation in Eighth Army from 12 Aug to 23 Oct 42', BLM 27/1, IWM.
71. B. L. Montgomery, *Memoirs*, p. 96.
72. Letter no. 45, 22.8.42, Poston Papers, IWM.
73. Interview with General Sir Charles Richardson, 7.11.79.
74. Ibid.
75. Ibid.
76. C. Richardson, *Flashback*, 1985, p. 105.
77. Ibid., p. 102.
78. C. Richardson, *Send For Freddie*, 1987, p. 68.

79. Richardson, *Flashback*, p. 103.

80. Ibid., pp. 107–8.

81. Ibid.

82. Ibid., p. 109.

83. Ibid., p. 71.

84. Connell, *Auchinleck*, p. 714.

85. Letter, B. L. Montgomery to 'Bill' Williams, Papers of Sir Edgar Williams, IWM.

86. Ibid.

87. B. L. Montgomery, *Memoirs*, p. 97.

88. Ibid.

89. C. T. Witherby, 'Alam el Halfa', typescript memoir, 78/61/1. IWM.

90. General Sir Charles Richardson interview.

91. B. L. Montgomery, *Memoirs*, p. 99.

92. Ibid.

93. De Guingand, *Operation Victory*, p. 139.

94. General Auchinleck to CIGS, quoted in Connell, *Auchinleck*, pp. 678–9.

95. War Diary, Eighth Army HQ, August 1942 (WO 169/3910, 3915, 3916), PRO.

96. Ibid.

97. H. Kippenberger, *Infantry Brigadier*, 1949, p. 191.

98. Diary Notes 12.8.42–23.10.42: 'Review of the Situation in Eighth Army from 12 Aug to 23 Oct 42', BLM 27/1, IWM.

99. Appendix One in Connell, *Auchinleck*, p. 937. In a letter to Fred Majdalany on 26 May 1965, the historian John North recounted how he had shown Monty a copy of the Dorman-Smith memorandum, 'reprinted in the Auk's despatch'. Monty had 'remarked quite spontaneously, "Never seen this before". Nor was he interested. Nor, incidentally, did a copy of this document ever come to light in Eighth Army files. The Official History for the period ignores it . . . There's no mention of the Alam Halfa ridge in the D-S Memo' – Majdalany Papers, 86/70/1, IWM.

100. Connell, *Auchinleck*, pp. 717–18.

101. Barnett, *The Desert Generals* (1983 edn), pp. 257–8.

102. Hinsley et al., *British Intelligence in the Second World War*, vol. II, p. 409.

103. Freyberg, *Freyberg VC*, p. 383.

104. Major J. M. McSwiney, typescript memoir, p. 107, 97/36/1, IWM.

105. B. L. Montgomery, *Memoirs*, p. 100.

106. Ibid.

107. War Diary, Eighth Army HQ, August 1942 (WO 169/3910, 3915, 3916), PRO.

108. B. L. Montgomery, *Memoirs*, p. 100.

109. Diary notes 12.8.42–23.10.42: 'Review of the Situation in Eighth Army from 12 Aug to 23 Oct 42', BLM 27/1, IWM.

110. De Guingand, *Operation Victory*, p. 136.

111. War Diary, Eighth Army HQ, 'I' Section, July–December 1942 (WO 169/3937), PRO.

112. De Guingand, *Operation Victory*, p. 136.

113. Freyberg, *Freyberg VC*, p. 384.

114. Moorehead, *Montgomery*, p. 120.

115. In a paper Monty drew up to help Churchill counter a libel suit by Dorman-Smith after World War II, Monty noted of Dorman-Smith: 'I taught him at the Staff College. Regarded him then as eccentric. Later got in touch with other eccentric and far seeing soliers; theoretical; no practical balance; balmy [*sic*].' Major-General Graham, according to notes Monty made after speaking to him, considered Dorman-Smith 'A lunatic. Interfered at Army H.Q. A menace', while Brigadier E. T. Williams told Monty of Dorman-Smith's 'Brainwaves. Memoranda to Auk. Auk would send them to Freddie [de Guingand] to investigate: thus interfering with all the day-to-day work. Regarded by Eighth Army H.Q. as a menace. ["]Bits and pieces["] true. Divisions broken up.' – 'BLM's Comments on Maj-Gen Dorman-Smith and other papers, 1953–4, arising out of Dorman-Smith's intention to sue Churchill for libel over a statement regarding the state of the Eighth Army in 1952', BLM 57/8, IWM.

116. Freyberg, *Freyberg VC*, p. 385.

117. Barnett, *The Desert Generals* (1983 edn), p. 257.

118. Field-Marshal Sir Gerald Templer interview.

119. J. Ellis, *Brute Force*, 1990.

120. G. P. B. Roberts, *From the Desert to the Baltic*, 1995, p. 89.

121. Ibid., p. 67.

122. Barnett, *The Desert Generals*, p. 266.

123. Ibid.

124. Ibid., p. 272.

125. 'He was distinguished and enormously vivid . . . [S]itting in the library that first morning, one had the feeling of equality': Correlli Barnett on Dorman-Smith, quoted in Lavinia Greacen, *Chink: A Biography*, Foreword by Correlli Barnett, 1989, p. 330. 'A second writer got in touch [with Dorman-Smith]: John Connell . . . Emboldened by the two new friendships, Chink . . . Accepted an invitation to attend a Military Commentators' Circle meeting in London at which Auchinleck was to attend . . . and here he met a third writer, R. W. "Tommy" Thompson. Thompson was to become a more malleable disciple than Barnett and Connell' – ibid., pp. 330–1.

126. Letter, Brigadier E. T. Williams to Stephen Roskill, 9.5.62, Papers of Sir Edgar Williams, IWM.

127. Letter, Stephen Roskill to Brigadier E. T. Williams, 12.5.62, Papers of Sir Edgar Williams, IWM.

128. Barnett, *The Desert Generals*, p. 303.

129. Field-Marshal Lord Carver, 'Monty – Forty Years On', a public lecture in the Department of War Studies, King's College, London, 8 March 1984.

130. C. T. Witherby, 'The Voyage of the Eighth Armoured Division', 1942, 78/61/1, IWM.

131. Major J. M. McSwiney, typescript memoir, p. 115, 97/36/1, IWM.

132. D. Johnston, *Nine Rivers from Jordan*, 1953, p. 38.

133. Brigadier Sir Edgar Williams interview.
134. Cabinet Papers (CAB 106/654), PRO.
135. Brigadier Sir Edgar Williams interview.
136. Cabinet Papers (CAB 106/654), PRO.
137. De Guingand, *Operation Victory*, pp. 136–7.

17 The New Line

1. War Diary, 8th Army HQ, August 1942 (WO 169/3910, 3915, 3916), PRO.
2. Field-Marshal Lord Harding interview.
3. B. L. Montgomery, *Memoirs*, p. 103.
4. Ibid., p. 103.
5. Unpublished memoirs, Papers of General Sir Oliver Leese, IWM.
6. War Diary, 8th Army HQ, August 1942 (WO 169/3910, 3915, 3916), PRO.
7. Ibid.
8. 14 August entry, reconstruction of Alamein chronology for British Official War History, quoting 9 Australian Division Report on Operations 23 October–5 November 1942, CAB 106/780, PRO.
9. 14 August entry, reconstruction of Alamein chronology for British Official War History, quoting 5 Indian Brigade (WD 853/1/3), CAB 106/780, PRO.
10. Ibid.
11. Freyberg, *Freyberg VC*, p. 386.
12. Kippenberger, *Infantry Brigadier*, p. 196.
13. W. R. Garrett, 'A Private Viewing', typescript memoir, 93/19/1, IWM.
14. Ibid.
15. Barnett, *The Desert Generals*, p. 258.
16. Louis Challoner, Desert Diary, P479, IWM.
17. Witherby, 'Alam el Halfa'.
18. Challoner, Desert Diary.
19. R. D. Law and C. W. H. Luther, *Rommel*, 1980, p. 164.
20. Barnett, *The Desert Generals*, p. 267.
21. Ibid.
22. Witherby, 'Alam el Halfa'.
23. Bennett, *Ultra and Mediterranean Strategy*, p. 145.
24. Hinsley et al., *British Intelligence in the Second World War*, p. 409.
25. Bennett, *Ultra and Mediterranean Strategy*, p. 146.
26. Ibid., p. 140.
27. Barnett, *The Desert Generals*, p. 258.
28. Bennett, *Ultra and Mediterranean Strategy*, p. 140.
29. Ibid., pp. 144–5.
30. Witherby, 'Alam el Halfa'.
31. Diary Notes 12.8.42–23.10.42: 'Review of the Situation in Eighth Army from 12 Aug to 23 Oct 42', BLM 27/1, IWM.

32. Witherby, 'Alam el Halfa'.

33. War Diary, 8th Army HQ, August 1942 (WO 169/3910, 3915, 3916), PRO.

34. Freyberg, *Freyberg VC*, p. 386.

35. Major J. M. McSwiney, typescript memoir, 97/36/1, IWM.

36. E. T. Williams, 'Gee One Eye, Sir', in T. Howarth, ed., *Monty at Close Quarters: Recollections of the Man*, 1985, p. 22.

37. Letter no. 46, 25.8.42, Poston Papers, IWM.

38. Interview, 1945, CAB 106/654, PRO.

39. Barnett, *The Desert Generals*, pp. 238, 330. In his despatches, Alexander described Auchinleck's plan as being one in which 8th Army 'was to hold as strongly as possible the area between the sea and the Ruweisat Ridge and to threaten from the flank any enemy advance south of the ridge from a strongly defended position in the Alam el Halfa ridge. General Montgomery, now in command of Eighth Army, accepted this plan in principle, to which I agreed.' This summary was 'quite untrue', as Monty pointed out to the Minister of War in 1962. Casting his mind back to the time when Alexander published his despatches he recorded: 'I remember at the time I was fed up with the whole affair and realised it was quite useless to have an argument about it. Hence my minute dated 12–11–47. I had had a preliminary skirmish with [Alexander] on the subject in Quebec in September 1947, when I was in Canada as C.I.G.S. I never understood the words: "General Montgomery accepted this plan in principle." What plan? Perhaps you can tell me,' he suggested to the Minister of War. 'I would much like to meet the man who gave me any plan in Cairo on the 12th August 1942 – except the one outlined to me by Auchinleck that the Eighth Army must be kept "in being", and that if in danger of being overrun it must be withdrawn. The truth is that there was no plan for the action of the Eighth Army to base its defensive action on the Alam Halfa ridge. As soon as I took command on the 13th August, I reconnoitred the ground with my Chief of Staff and at once saw the vital importance of that ridge – which was undefended!!! That was the first time the word "Alam Halfa" had ever been mentioned to me. We made the battle plan at Eighth Army HQ, based on holding firmly from that ridge northwards and having a mobile flank in the south. I then told Alexander what I proposed to do. He agreed. He himself at that time had not even seen the ground.' As John North, the historian who ghostwrote Alexander's 'so-called Memoirs', revealed in 1965, Alexander had been at pains to be nice to his predecessor, Auchinleck, in retrospect, but in truth had no more written his own 'Memoirs' than he had his own 'Despatches', having got North to do the former, and his former chief of intelligence, David Hunt, to do the latter. 'The controversial passage concerning the plan in the Alex despatch was written by the present High Commissioner in Cyprus [Sir David Hunt],' North confided. 'He reads Horace for relaxation ... Alex, in Canada at the time, carelessly or not caring – or remembering – let it go when the original TS, with various other amendments, was submitted to him by the W[ar] O[ffice].' Military historiography had thus been subjected to the unending British obsession with being 'nice' – or, as North put it, giving 'Auchinleck the benefit of the doubt': a well-meant gesture by the indolent Alexander, which years later

licensed Barnett and other historians – notably R. W. Thompson in 1967 – to parade Monty's supposed 'theft'.

40. Horrocks, *A Full Life*, p. 107.
41. Interview with Lieutenant-General Sir Brian Horrocks.
42. Deighton and Hastings, *Battle of Britain*, p. 218.

18 Preparing for Battle

1. Fussell, *The Great War and Modern Memory*, p. 270.
2. Ibid., p. 280.
3. Ibid., p. 271.
4. Joanna Burke, *Dismembering the Male: Men's Bodies, Britain and the Great War*, 1996, pp. 24, 133.
5. Ibid., p. 135.
6. James Lucas, *War in the Desert: The Eighth Army at Alamein*, 1982, p. 55.
7. Ibid., p. 57.
8. Fussell, *The Great War and Modern Memory*, p. 272.
9. Burke, *Dismembering the Male*, pp. 136–7.
10. A. Heilbut, *Thomas Mann: Eros & Literature*, 1995, p. 14.
11. Ibid.
12. Quoted in Fussell, *The Great War and Modern Memory*, pp. 273–4.
13. Lucas, *War in the Desert* p. 57.
14. Quoted by C. P. Dawnay in Howarth, *Monty at Close Quarters*, pp. 17–18.
15. 'Monty – In Love and War', directed by Jeremy Bennett, BBC Television, 1987.
16. Quoted in Howarth, *Monty at Close Quarters*, p. 28.
17. Louis Crompton in C. Summers, ed., *The Gay and Lesbian Literary Heritage*, 1995/7, p. 343.
18. Dawnay in Howarth, *Monty at Close Quarters*, p. 18.
19. Field-Marshal Lord Carver interview.
20. Richardson, *Flashback*, p. 110.
21. Witherby, 'Alam el Halfa'.
22. Cabinet Papers (CAB 106/654), PRO.
23. Interview with Major-General G. P. B. Roberts, 8.1.80.
24. Ibid.
25. Roberts, *From the Desert to the Baltic*, p. 94.
26. Major-General G. P. B. Roberts interview.
27. Roberts, *From the Desert to the Baltic*, p. 93.
28. Major-General G. P. B. Roberts interview.
29. Ibid.
30. Ibid.
31. B. L. Montgomery, *Memoirs*, p. 104.
32. Field-Marshal Lord Carver interview.

33. Letter, Lieutenant-General Sir Brian Horrocks to British Official Historian, 1945 (CAB 44/992), PRO.

34. War Diary, 22nd Armoured Brigade HQ, August 1942 (WO 169/4251), PRO.

35. Colonel Mainwaring, G1 (Ops) was thirty-six, Colonel Richardson, G1 (Plans) was thirty-six, Colonel Belchem, G1 (Staff Duties) was thirty-one and Major Williams, G2 [later G1] (Intelligence) was twenty-nine.

36. Churchill, *History of the Second World War*, vol. IV, p. 462.

37. B. L. Montgomery, *Memoirs*, pp. 105–6.

38. 'Notes on My Life' in Bryant, *Turn of the Tide*, p. 478.

39. Brigadier Sir Edgar Williams interview.

40. Churchill, *History of the Second World War*, vol. IV, p. 465.

41. Ibid., pp. 465–6.

42. Connell, *Auchinleck*, p. 718.

43. Churchill, *History of the Second World War*, vol. IV, p. 466.

44. Richardson, *Flashback*, p. 110.

45. Ibid.

46. Churchill, *History of the Second World War*, vol. IV, p. 465.

47. Ibid.

48. Letter no. 45, 22.8.42, Poston Papers, IWM.

49. Bryant, *Turn of the Tide*, p. 480.

50. Letter no. 46, 25.8.42, Poston Papers, IWM.

51. Ibid.

52. Churchill, *History of the Second World War*, vol. IV, p. 466.

53. Recounted by Captain C. B. Stoddart, in Cabinet Papers (CAB 106/793), PRO.

54. Jacob, 'Operation Bracelet'.

55. Diary Notes 12.8.42–23.10.42: 'Review of the Situation in Eighth Army from 12 Aug to 23 Oct 42', BLM 27/1, IWM.

56. Churchill, *History of the Second World War*, vol. IV, p. 467.

57. Lieutenant-General Sir Brian Horrocks interview.

58. Churchill, *History of the Second World War*, vol. IV, p. 465.

59. Bryant, *Turn of the Tide*, p. 485.

60. Liddell Hart, *The Rommel Papers*, p. 274.

61. Ibid., p. 263.

62. Ibid., p. 269.

63. War Diary, 8th Army HQ, 'I' Section, August 1942 (WO 169/3911), PRO.

64. Jacob, 'Operation Bracelet'.

65. War Diary, 8th Army HQ, 'I' Section, August 1942 (WO 169/3911), PRO.

66. Churchill, *History of the Second World War*, vol. IV, p. 465.

67. Witherby, 'Alam el Halfa'. See also Roberts, *From the Desert to the Baltic*, p. 96.

68. Churchill, *History of the Second World War*, vol. IV, p. 344.

69. De Guingand, *From Brass Hat to Bowler Hat*, p. 10.

70. Rees, *A Bundle of Sensations*, p. 132.

71. Richardson, *Flashback*, p. 125.

72. Ibid.

73. Poston Papers, Letter no. 45, 22.8.42, IWM.

74. Richardson, *Flashback*, pp. 125–6.

75. V. Peniakoff, *Popski's Private Army*, 1957, p. 211.

76. Harold Macmillan, *Winds of Change 1914–1939*, 1966, pp. 92–4

77. B. Pitt, *The Crucible of War: Year of Alamein 1942*, 1982, p. 216.

78. Ibid.

79. Burke, *Dismembering the Male*, p. 23.

80. Pitt, *Crucible of War*, p. 217.

81. Ibid., p. 216.

82. Johnston, *Nine Rivers from Jordan*, p. 44. (Monty thereupon arranged the interview with Churchill for Johnston.)

83. Richardson, *Flashback*, p. 126.

84. Barton Maugham, *Tobruk and Alamein*, 1966, p. 610.

85. Ibid.

86. Pitt, *Crucible of War*, p. 219.

87. Johnston, *Nine Rivers from Jordan*, pp. 16–17.

88. J. W. Thraves, North Midland Corps Signals (TA), typescript memoir, 98/3/1, IWM.

89. Letter, Major-General 'Gertie' Tuker to Major-General Raymond Briggs, 20.1.61, Briggs Papers, 99/1/1, IWM.

90. Maugham, *Tobruk and Alamein*, p. 611.

91. Ibid.

92. Ibid., p. 622.

93. Ibid., p. 611.

94. Barnett, *The Desert Generals*, pp. 267–8.

95. Ibid., pp. 249ff.

96. 'I cannot remember anything about the Corelli [*sic*] Barnett book. He is, of course, entitled to his opinion. The two who could tell him most about the condition of the Eighth Army in July/August 1942 would be Churchill and Alanbrooke – neither of whom he seems to have consulted. See Churchill's telegram to the War Cabinet of 6 August 1942 in Vol 4 of his war memoirs, in which he stresses the need for "a drastic and immediate change in the High Command" and talks of "vehement action to animate the whole of this vast but baffled and somewhat unhinged organization." I am sure that if Corelli Barnett had been in command at Alamein he would have done much better than I did!' – Letter, B. L. Montgomery to C. D. Hamilton 31.8.60, in Papers of Sir Denis Hamilton.

97. See C. E. Lucas Phillips, *Alamein*, 1962 (1973 edn), p. 77.

98. Letter of 14.9.42, Poston Papers, IWM.

99. Hinsley et al., *British Intelligence in the Second World War*, p. 142.

100. Maugham, *Tobruk and Alamein*, p. 623.

101. D. Irving, *The Trail of the Fox: The Life of Field-Marshal Erwin Rommel*, 1977, p. 185.

102. Hinsley et al., *British Intelligence in the Second World War*, pp. 412, 712.

103. Ibid., p. 713.

104. Irving, *The Trail of the Fox*, p. 186.

105. GSI GHQ MEF Weekly Review of the Military Situation, up to 1800 hrs 31.8.42 (CAB 106/780), PRO.

106. R. Overy, *Why the Allies Won*, 1995, p. 67.

107. Ibid., p. 15.

108. Bennett, *Ultra and Mediterranean Strategy*, p. 147.

109. J. Strawson, *El Alamein*, 1981, p. 64.

110. Bennett, *Ultra and Mediterranean Strategy*, p. 146.

111. Liddell Hart, *The Rommel Papers*, p. 275.

19 Alam Halfa

1. Liddell Hart, *The Rommel Papers*, p. 275.

2. Irving, *The Trail of the Fox*, p. 191.

3. Quoted in Chalfont, *Montgomery of Alamein*, p. 156.

4. Richardson, *Flashback*, p. 111.

5. Quoted (unattributed) in A. Stewart, *Eighth Army's Greatest Victories, Alam Halfa to Tunis 1942–1943*, 1999, p. 58.

6. By 31 August 8th Army had a total of 164 fit Grants on the battlefield: WD 104/1/1278, in CAB 106/780, PRO.

7. De Guingand, *Operation Victory*, p. 146.

8. Kriegstagebuch, Panzerarmee Afrika, Appendices, 29 August 1942, in Law and Luther, *Rommel*, p. 171.

9. Liddell Hart, *The Rommel Papers*, p. 274.

10. WD 106/3/930–6, in CAB 106/780, PRO.

11. Liddell Hart, *The Rommel Papers*, p. 274.

12. Irving, *The Trail of the Fox*, p. 191.

13. Liddell Hart, *The Rommel Papers*, p. 276.

14. Ibid., p. 277.

15. Irving, *The Trail of the Fox*, p. 192.

16. Liddell Hart, *The Rommel Papers*, p. 276.

17. WD 106/3/930–6, in CAB 106/780, PRO.

18. B. L. Montgomery, 'The Major Tactics of the Encounter Battle', *Army Quarterly*, August 1938.

19. Bennett, *Ultra and Mediterranean Strategy*, p. 151.

20. Liddell Hart, *The Rommel Papers*, p. 277.

21. Diary Notes 12.8.42–23.10.42: 'Review of the Situation in Eighth Army from 12 Aug to 23 Oct 42', BLM 27/1, IWM.

22. Major-General G. P. B. Roberts interview.

23. Quoted in Stewart, *Eighth Army's Greatest Victories*, p. 64.

24. Roberts, *From the Desert to the Baltic*, p. 100.

25. Ibid.

26. Michael Carver, *El Alamein*, 1962, p. 56.

27. Liddell Hart, *The Rommel Papers*, p. 274.

28. Irving, *The Trail of the Fox*, p. 192.

29. Liddell Hart, *The Rommel Papers*, p. 277.

30. Quoted in R. Walker, *Alam Halfa and Alamein*, 1967, p. 180.

31. Sir Brian Horrocks, Letter to the British official historian, 1945 (CAB 44/ 992), PRO.

32. Major D. F. Parry, '8th Army – Defeat and Disgrace', unpublished memoir, 83/24/1, IWM.

33. Ian Hogg, *The Guns of World War II*, 1976, p. 57.

34. R. F. Marwan-Schlosser, *Rommels Flak als Pak: Das Flak-Regiment 135 als Rückgrat des Deutschen Afrikakorps*, 1991, pp. 10–11. The Germans had secretly designed the Krupps 88mm gun in Sweden, long before Hitler became Chancellor, developed it as soon as Hitler came to power, and had been using it in a dual AA/ field-gun role since the Spanish Civil War, when it demolished lightly armoured tanks with ease – P. Chamberlain and T. Gander, *Anti-Aircraft Guns*, 1975, p. 20. The British-built Vickers 3.7 anti-aircraft gun was designed in 1934, prototyped in 1936, went into production in 1938, was one and a half times the weight of its German counterpart (9,325 kg to 6,861 kg), and endowed with a carriage so complicated and unwieldy it could not initially be used (ibid., p. 50). The 88 was used as an officially designated (i.e., not improvised) dual-purpose assault weapon in the Dunkirk campaign ('Procedure for the Attack of Fortified Defensive Positions', German army training manual of 1939: 'assault detachments, closely followed by anti-tank and 88mm guns, will be thrust through any gap in the defensive front' – Hogg, *The Guns of World War II*, pp. 55–6) with anti-tank as well as anti-aircraft ammunition, to significant effect – yet the British took no note, continuing to produce two-pounder 'peashooter' anti-tank guns which could not penetrate 50mm armour at 1,000 yards, while only manufacturing six-pounders in any quantity when Rommel had already run riot in North Africa. Even then the British six-pounders could not pierce Panzer 'Specials' frontally, or match the range and deadly accuracy of the 88s, which could target a British tank several miles away.

35. Hogg, *The Guns of World War II*, p. 56.

36. Parry, '8th Army – Defeat and Disgrace'.

37. Hogg, *The Guns of World War II*, p. 58.

38. Parry, '8th Army – Defeat and Disgrace'.

39. Ian Hogg, *Allied Artillery of World War Two*, 1998, p. 99. M. M. Poston, in Poston et al., *Design and Development of Weapons*, 1964, gave first 'mooting' of the 3.7-inch gun as 'c.1920', first specification 1933, first pilot delivery 1936, and first gun produced as 1938: a process lasting eighteen-years: pp. 284, 348, 355, 357, 368.

40. P. Beale, *Death by Design: British Tank Development in the Second World War*, 1998, p. 110.

41. Ibid., p. 113.

42. Sir Francis de Guingand interview.

43. Freyberg, *Freyberg VC*, p. 392.
44. Sir Francis de Guingand interview.
45. B. H. Liddell Hart, 'Analysis of Alamein – Montgomery's Conduct of the Battle', dated November 1958 and sent to, among others, Major F. Majdalany, 20.8.64: Majdalany Papers, 86/70/1, IWM.
46. Irving, *The Trail of the Fox*, p. 193.
47. Liddell Hart, *The Rommel Papers*, p. 279.
48. Ibid., p. 280.
49. Ibid., p. 283.
50. Ibid., p. 284.
51. Irving, *The Trail of the Fox*, p. 193.
52. Ibid.
53. Ibid.
54. P. Caccia-Dominioni, *Alamein 1933–1962: An Italian Story*, 1966, pp. 153–4.
55. Irving, *The Trail of the Fox*, p. 194.
56. Quoted ibid., p. 194.
57. Liddell Hart, *The Rommel Papers*, p. 285.
58. Barratt Report, 27 August–9 September 1942, PRO AIR 37/760.
59. Liddell Hart, *The Rommel Papers*, p. 285.
60. Ibid., p. 287.
61. Ibid., p. 282.
62. Heinz W. Schmidt, *With Rommel in the Desert*, 1951, repr. 1980. p. 171.

20 After Alam Halfa

1. E. T. Williams, draft review of D. Young, *Rommel*, 1950, Papers of Sir Edgar Williams, IWM.
2. 'Erinnerungsprotokoll über den Empfang beim Duce in Rocca della Caminata um 11 uhr', 24.9.42, AL 1349/2, IWM.
3. Overy, *Why the Allies Won*, p. 324.
4. I. Kershaw, *Hitler, 1889–1936: Hubris*, 1998, p. xxix.
5. Ibid., p. xxvii.
6. Irving, *The Trail of the Fox*, p. 6.
7. Ibid.
8. Directorate of Army Education, Booklet i, November 1942, quoted in Overy, *Why the Allies Won*, p. 283.
9. Letter no. 49, 14.9.42, Poston Papers, IWM.
10. WD 106/3/930–6, in CAB 106/780, PRO.
11. Richardson, *Flashback*, p. 112.
12. Interview with Major-General M. St John Oswald 22.4.80.
13. Interview with Major Robert Priestley.
14. Letter no. 49, 14.9.42, Poston Papers, IWM.

15. Witherby, 'Alam el Halfa'.
16. Bennett, *Ultra and Mediterranean Strategy*, pp. 142–3.
17. Gilbert, *Road to Victory*, p. 220.
18. J. Kennedy, *The Business of War*, 1957, p. 268.
19. Lord Moran, *Winston Churchill: The Struggle for Survival*, p. 75.
20. Kennedy, *The Business of War*, p. 267.
21. B. Lee, *Marching Orders, the Untold Story of World War II*, 1995, p. 69.
22. W. Willkie, *One World*, 1942, p. 4.
23. Ibid., p. 6.
24. Ibid, pp. 8–10.
25. L. H. Brereton, *The Brereton Diaries, 3 Oct 1941–8 May 1945*, 1976, p. 152.
26. Lee, *Marching Orders*, p. 69.
27. Gilbert, *Road to Victory*, p. 226.
28. Willkie, *One World*, p. 11.
29. Ibid.
30. Ibid., p. 12.
31. Major-General G. P. B. Roberts interview.
32. A. Kesselring, *The Memoirs of Field-Marshal Kesselring*, 1953, p. 133.
33. Irving, *The Trail of the Fox*, p. 197.
34. 'Erinnerungsprotokoll über den Empfang beim Duce in Rocca della Caminata um 11 uhr', 24.9.42, AL 1349/2, IWM.
35. Irving, *The Trail of the Fox*, p. 198.
36. Ibid.
37. Letter of 21.9.42, B. L. Montgomery to Tom and Phyllis Reynolds, Reynolds Papers, IWM.
38. WD 106/3/930–6, in CAB 106/780, PRO.
39. Ibid.
40. Diary Notes 12.8.42–23.10.42: 'Review of the Situation in Eighth Army from 12 Aug to 23 Oct 42', BLM 27/1, Montgomery Papers, IWM.
41. W. G. F. Jackson, *The North African Campaign 1940–1943*, 1975, p. 274.
42. Interview with Sir William Mather. 23.01.80.
43. Letter no. 49, 14.9.42, Poston Papers, IWM.
44. A. Moorehead, *African Trilogy (The End in Africa)*, 1998, pp. 409–10.
45. Ibid.
46. Johnston, *Nine Rivers from Jordan*, p. 51.
47. Moorehead, *African Trilogy*, p. 520.
48. B. L. Montgomery, *Memoirs*, p. 113.
49. Irving, *The Trail of the Fox*, p. 87.
50. Stewart, *Eighth Army's Greatest Victories*, p. 79.
51. Moorehead, *African Trilogy*, p. 521.
52. Fraser, *Alanbrooke*, p. 282.
53. Ibid., p. 287.
54. Johnston, *Nine Rivers from Jordan*, p. 5.
55. Ibid., p. 51.
56. Letter of 27.11.42, B. L. Montgomery to General Alan Brooke, Alanbrooke

Papers, 14/61, LHCMA. Patton, too, found difficulty in inculcating a more homicidal instinct in his American troops.

21 Scripting Alamein

1. Sir William Mather interview.
2. In order to preserve security and mislead the enemy, codenames for major operations were deliberately kept mundane – a professional requirement at variance with the Prime Minister's penchant for resounding titles, such as 'Overlord'.
3. General Sir Charles Richardson interview.
4. Sir William Mather interview.
5. R. L. Crimp, 'The Overseas Tour of a Conscript Rifleman: A Four Years' Diary', entry of 20.9.42, 96/50/1, IWM.
6. Ibid., entry of 23.9.42.
7. Sir William Mather interview.
8. General Sir Oliver Leese, unpublished memoir, Oliver Leese Papers, IWM.
9. Churchill, *History of the Second World*, vol. IV, p. 528.
10. Leese, unpublished memoir.
11. Ibid.
12. Ibid.
13. Briggs Papers, 89/1/1, IWM.
14. Interview with General Sir Sidney Kirkman, 16.4.80.
15. War Diary, 8th Army HQ, 'I' Section, August 1942 (WO 169/3911), PRO.
16. Major-General Sir Francis de Guingand interview.
17. Address to Middle East Staff College, Haifa, 21.9.42, in Belchem Papers, IWM.
18. Major-General Sir Francis de Guingand interview.
19. Ibid.
20. WD 106/3/930–6, in CAB 106/780, PRO.
21. '10 Corps will be passed through this bridgehead [in the north] to exploit success and complete the victory' – Lightfoot: General Plan of Eighth Army, 14.9.42, BLM 28/3, IWM.
22. Diary Notes 12.8.42–23.10.42: 'Review of the Situation in Eighth Army from 12 Aug to 23 Oct 42', BLM 27/1, IWM.
23. Ibid.
24. Ibid.
25. Lightfoot: Memorandum no. 2, 6.10.42, BLM 28/5, IWM.
26. Ibid.
27. Diary Notes 12.8.42–23.10.42: 'Review of the Situation in Eighth Army from 12 Aug to 23 Oct 42', BLM 27/1, IWM.
28. Letter, Captain C. Potts to Miss P. Stubbs, 9.9.42, Con shelf and 92/28/1, IWM.
29. Letter, Captain C. Potts to Miss P. Stubbs, 7.10.42, ibid.

30. Leese, unpublished memoir.

31. Johnston, *Nine Rivers from Jordan*, p. 49.

32. Moorehead, *African Trilogy*, p. 521.

33. Letter of 6.10.42, B. L. Montgomery to Tom and Phyllis Reynolds, Reynolds Papers, IWM.

34. 'Lightfoot, No. 1 Memorandum by Army Commander', 28.9.42, BLM 28/4, IWM.

35. Ibid., with dates amended by Montgomery in accordance with 'Lightfoot Memorandum No. 3' of 6.10.42, BLM 28/6, IWM. It is interesting to compare this with Patton's address to officers of 45th Division before the Sicily landings the following year: 'When we land against the enemy,' Patton told them, 'don't forget to hit him and hit him hard . . . You must kill him. Stick him between the third and fourth ribs. You will tell your men that. They must have the killer instinct. Tell them to stick him. He can do no good then. Stick them in the liver. We will get the name of killers and killers are immortal': J. Burke, *An Intimate History of Killing*, 1999, p. 183.

36. Diary Notes 12.8.42–23.10.42: 'Review of the Situation in Eighth Army from 12 Aug to 23 Oct 42', BLM 27/1, IWM.

37. Major-General M. St John Oswald interview.

38. Letter, Lieutenant-General Oliver Leese to Margaret, Lady Leese, 19.10.42, Box 2, Leese Papers, IWM.

39. Diary of Major-General A. W. W. Holworthy, entry of 19.10.42, 91/40/2, IWM.

40. Diary no. 1, 14.12.40–18.4.43, entry of 20.10.42, Briggs Papers, 91/1/1, IWM.

41. 'El Alamein and El Hamma', 2.11.43, Briggs Papers, 91/1/1, IWM.

42. C. M. S. Gardner, 'Come and Fly with Me', typescript, 99/23/1, IWM.

43. Sir William Mather interview.

44. De Guingand, *Operation Victory*, p. 161.

45. 'Extract from Address to Senior Officers of Eighth Army by General Montgomery before the battle of Alamein', Lord Montgomery Deposit, Box 29, IWM.

46. Ibid.

47. Crimp, 'The Overseas Tour of a Conscript Rifleman', entry of 19.10.42.

48. See Carver, *El Alamein*, pp. 79–80.

49. Crimp, 'The Overseas Tour of a Conscript Rifleman', entry of 8.10.42.

50. De Guingand, *Operation Victory*, p. 161.

51. B. L. Montgomery, *Memoirs*, pp. 127–8.

52. De Guingand, *Operation Victory*, p. 163.

53. Irving, *The Trail of the Fox*, pp. 201–2.

54. H.-O. Behrendt, *Rommel's Intelligence in the Desert Campaign*, 1985, p. 198.

55. Appendix 55 in Extracts from 21st Panzer Division War Diary appendices, 16.10.42–15.12.42, AL 926/4, IWM.

56. Liddell Hart, 'Analysis of Alamein'.

57. 'Lightfoot Memorandum No. 2 by Army Commander', 6.10.42, BLM 28/5, IWM.

58. Leese, unpublished memoir.

59. Letter, Lieutenant-General Oliver Leese to Margaret, Lady Leese, 20.10.42, Box 2, Leese Papers, IWM.

60. Diary of F. T. Bennett, 64th Medium Regiment, 4.6.42–17.2.43, 88/12/1, IWM.

61. G. N. Giddings, 'Opa's War Years 1939/46', 93/4/1, IWM.

62. Letter, Lieutenant-General Oliver Leese to Margaret, Lady Leese, 20.10.42, Box 2, Leese Papers, IWM.

63. Air mail letter, Lieutenant-General Oliver Leese to Margaret, Lady Leese, 22.10.42, ibid.

64. Richardson, *Send For Freddie*, p. 94; *Flashback*, p. 119.

65. Leese, unpublished memoir.

66. 'Estimate of the German Strengths in Egypt, 1st Oct 42 – Most Secret', copy in Briggs Papers, 91/1/1, IWM.

67. Hinsley et al., *British Intelligence in the Second World War*, p. 715.

68. Lucas Phillips, *Alamein*, p. 123.

69. Schmidt, *With Rommel in the Desert*, p. 164.

70. D. Richards and H. Saunders, *Royal Air Force 1939–1945*, vol. II, *The Fight Avails*, 1953, p. 233.

71. See Carver, *Alamein*, p. 81.

72. Diary Notes 12.8.42–23.10.42: 'Review of the Situation in Eighth Army from 12 Aug to 23 Oct 42', BLM 27/1, IWM.

73. Ibid.

74. Air mail letter, Lieutenant-General Oliver Leese to Margaret, Lady Leese, 23.10.42, Box 2, Leese Papers, IWM.

22 Alamein

1. Ian Mackay, 'Fighting Fit: The Story of a Regimental Medical Officer in World War II', 94/8/1, IWM.

2. Diary of F. T. Bennett.

3. Major A. F. Flatow, 'A Personal Narrative of El Alamein', typescript memoir, 99/16/1, IWM.

4. Quoted in P. Warner, *Alamein*, 1979, p. 105.

5. P. Caccia-Dominioni, *Alamein*, p. 210.

6. Air mail letter, Lieutenant-General Oliver Leese to Margaret Lady Leese, 23.10.42, Box 2, Leese Papers, IWM.

7. Ibid.

8. Schmidt, *With Rommel in the Desert*, p. 173.

9. Lucas, *War in the Desert*, pp. 117–18.

10. E. M. Scott, ibid., p. 169.

11. Ibid., p. 172.

12. Letter, C. B. Stoddart to his father, undated (late 1942), CAB 106/793, PRO.

13. Ibid.
14. Air mail letter, Lieutenant-General Oliver Leese to Margaret, Lady Leese, 25.10.42, Box 2, Leese Papers, IWM.
15. Beale, *Death by Design*, p. 177.
16. Major-General A. W. Lee to Colonel Law, 30.4.47, CAB 106/793, PRO.
17. Beale, *Death by Design*, p. 166.
18. Ibid., pp. 177–8.
19. Letter, Brigadier R. Cooney to Brigadier Harry Latham, 8.3.49, CAB 106/793, PRO.
20. War Diary, 8th Army Tactical HQ, October 1942, WO 169/3911, PRO.
21. Alamein Diary, BLM 28/1, Montgomery Papers, IWM.
22. Beale, *Death by Design*, p. 96.
23. Letter, Brigadier R. Cooney to Brigadier Harry Latham, 8.3.49, CAB 106/793, PRO.
24. Leese, unpublished memoir.
25. War Diary, 8th Army Tactical HQ, October 1942, WO 169/3911, PRO.
26. Walker, *Alam Halfa and Alamein*, p. 301.
27. War Diary, 8th Army Tactical HQ, October 1942, WO 169/3911, PRO.
28. Ibid.
29. Ibid., entry of 23.10.42, 91/40/2, IWM.
30. Alamein Diary, BLM 28/1, IWM.
31. Ibid. Monty recorded 2,483 casualties in XXX Corps for the first night of the battle, but the figure was probably higher.
32. Lucas Phillips, *Alamein*, p. 207.
33. War Diary, 8th Army Tactical HQ, October 1942, WO 169/3911, PRO.
34. Diary entry of 24.10.42, Briggs Papers, 99/1/1, IWM.
35. Alamein Diary, BLM 28/1, IWM.
36. War Diary, 8th Army Tactical HQ, October 1942, WO 169/3911, PRO.
37. Ibid.
38. Letter Brigadier R. Cooney to Brigadier Harry Latham, 8.3.49, CAB 106/793, PRO.
39. Beale, *Death by Design*, p. 183.
40. Richardson, *Send for Freddie*, p. 96.
41. Ibid.
42. Ibid.
43. De Guingand, *Operation Victory*, p. 200.
44. Alamein Diary, BLM 28/1, IWM.
45. Ibid.
46. Ibid.
47. Ibid.
48. Ibid.
49. De Guingand, *Operation Victory*, p. 200.
50. Leese, unpublished memoir.
51. Letter no. 54, 2.12.42, Poston Papers, IWM.
52. Alamein Diary, BLM 28/1, IWM.

53. Ibid.

54. Ibid.

55. Letter, Captain C. B. Stoddart to his father, CAB 106/793, PRO.

56. Lucas Phillips, *Alamein*, p. 223.

57. Letter, Captain C. B. Stoddart to his father, CAB 106/793, PRO.

58. Ibid.

59. Lucas Phillips, *Alamein*, p. 234.

60. Letter, Captain C. B. Stoddart to his father, CAB 106/793, PRO.

61. Lucas Phillips, *Alamein*, p. 230.

62. Walker, *Alam Halfa and Alamein*, p. 310.

63. General Sir Charles Richardson interview.

64. Leese, unpublished memoir.

65. Letter, Lieutenant-General Oliver Leese to Margaret, Lady Leese, 25.10.[42], Box 2, Leese Papers, IWM.

66. Leese, unpublished memoir.

67. Letter, Lieutenant-General Oliver Leese to Margaret, Lady Leese, 25.10.[42], Box 2, Leese Papers, IWM.

68. War Diary, 8th Army Tactical HQ, October 1942, WO 169/3911, PRO.

69. Alamein Diary, BLM 28/1, IWM.

70. Lucas Phillips, *Alamein*, p. 231.

71. D. Fraser, *Knight's Cross*, 1998, p. 373; Irving, *The Trail of the Fox*, p. 201.

72. Liddell Hart, *The Rommel Papers*, pp. 305–6.

73. Ibid., pp. 307–8.

74. Schmidt, *With Rommel in the Desert*, p. 176.

75. Liddell Hart, *The Rommel Papers*, p. 308.

76. Ibid.

77. K. Macksey, *Rommel: Battles and Campaigns*, 1979, p. 151.

78. Liddell Hart, *The Rommel Papers*, p. 306.

79. Ibid., p. 307.

80. War Diary, 8th Army Tactical HQ, October 1942, WO 169/3911, PRO.

81. General Sir Sidney Kirkman interview.

82. Alamein Diary, BLM 28/1, IWM.

83. General Sir Sidney Kirkman interview.

84. Alamein Diary, BLM 28/1, IWM.

85. Ibid.

86. War Diary, 8th Army Tactical HQ, October 1942, WO 169/3911, PRO.

87. Diary entry, Monday, 26.10.42, Alamein Diary, BLM 28/1–6, IWM.

88. War Diary, 8th Army Tactical HQ, October 1942, WO 169/3911, PRO.

89. '20.00 *Uhr. Befehl vom DAK: in 1 Stunde Abmarsch der Div. nach Norden in den Raum um Pkt 39*' – Kriegstagebuch Nr 8 der 21 Panzer-Division von 1.10–31.12.42, AL 926/1, IWM. (A warning order bringing the northern Kampfgruppe of the division under DAK command for possible action in a new sector had been recorded at 13.10 hours.)

90. Entry of Tuesday 27.10.42, Alamein Diary, BLM 28/1, IWM.

91. War Diary, 8th Army HQ, 'I' Section, October 1942, WO 169/3911, PRO.

92. Entries of 26-28.10.42, Kriegstagebuch Nr 8, 21 Panzer Division von 1.10–31.12.42, AL 926/1, IWM.

93. Diary entry of 26-27.10.42, Briggs Papers, 99/1/1, IWM.

94. Major R. A. Wyrley-Birch, in Lucas Phillips, *Alamein*, p. 271.

95. Macksey, *Rommel: Battles and Campaigns*, pp. 151–3.

96. Kriegstagebuch Nr 8 (see n. 89).

97. Liddell Hart, *The Rommel Papers*, pp. 309–10.

98. Letter, Field-Marshal Erwin Rommel to Lucie Rommel, 27.10.42, ibid., p. 309.

99. Alamein Diary, BLM 28/1, IWM.

100. Entry of 27.10.42, ibid.

101. Ibid.

102. Ibid.

103. Letter, Lieutenant-General Oliver Leese to Margaret, Lady Leese, 17.10.[42], Box 2, Leese Papers, IWM.

104. Lucas Phillips, *Alamein* p. 296.

105. Letter, Lieutenant-General Oliver Leese to Margaret, Lady Leese, 17.10.[42], Box 2, Leese Papers, IWM.

106. Entry of 27.10.42, Briggs Papers, 99/1/1, IWM.

107. Letter, General R. Briggs to B. Liddell Hart, 3.2.50, Briggs Papers, 99/1/1, IWM.

108. Alamein Diary, BLM 28/1, IWM.

109. Letter, Brigadier A. W. Lee to Lieutenant Colonel M. E. Laws, 30.4.47, CAB 106/793, PRO.

110. Lucas Phillips, *Alamein* p. 299.

111. Letter, Brigadier A. W. Lee to Lieutenant Colonel M. E. Laws, 30.4.47, CAB 106/793, PRO.

112. Lucas Phillips, *Alamein*, p. 330.

113. Letter, B. L. Montgomery to F. Majdalany, 17.4.65, Majdalany Papers, 86/70/1, IWM.

114. Lucas Phillips, *Alamein*, p. 330.

115. Briggs' 1st Armoured Brigade was withdrawn to reorganize for the new break-in operation, while its defensive positions were taken over by Gatehouse's 10th Armoured Division, under the command of Leese's Corps.

116. Alamein Diary, BLM 28/1, IWM.

117. General Sir Charles Richardson interview.

118. Law and Luther, *Rommel*, p. 195; Liddell Hart, *The Rommel Papers*, p. 310; Irving, *The Trail of the Fox*, p. 204.

119. Irving, *The Trail of the Fox*, p. 204.

120. Liddell Hart, *The Rommel Papers*, p. 311.

121. Alanbrooke Diary, Alanbrooke Papers, LHCMA.

122. Liddell Hart, *The Rommel Papers*, p. 312.

123. Ibid.

124. Ibid.

125. Irving, *The Trail of the Fox*, p. 206.

126. Liddell Hart, *The Rommel Papers*, p. 312.

127. Entry of 29.10.42, Diary of Lt.-Colonel W. D. McClure, 94/47/1, IWM.

128. Entry of Thursday, 29.10.42, Alamein Diary, BLM 28/1, IWM.

129. Signal to Alexander, with additional paragraph 'for you and Montgomery alone': Churchill, *History of the Second World War*, vol. IV, p. 535.

130. De Guingand, *Operation Victory*, p. 206.

131. Brigadier Sir Edgar Williams interview.

132. Entry of Thursday, 29.10.42, Alamein Diary, BLM 28/1, IWM.

133. Ibid.

134. Letter, Lieutenant-General Oliver Leese to Margaret, Lady Leese, dated 29.10.[42], (possibly 30.10.42), Box 2, Leese Papers, IWM.

135. Liddell Hart, *The Rommel Papers*, p. 314.

136. Entry of Thursday, 29.10.42, Alamein Diary, BLM 28/1, IWM.

137. Letter no. 54, 2.12.42, Poston Papers, IWM.

138. Hinsley et al., *British Intelligence in the Second World War*, p. 441. The figure related to fit tanks, which rose again in number to 102 by 1 November: ibid., p. 445.

139. Bryant, *Turn of the Tide*, p. 513.

140. Alamein Diary, BLM 28/1, IWM.

141. Entry for 30.10.42–31.10.42, ibid.

142. Ibid.

143. Leese, unpublished memoir.

144. Liddell Hart, *The Rommel Papers*, p. 316.

145. Ibid., pp. 339–40.

146. 'The (2nd) Battle of Alamein', November 1958, Majdalany Papers, 86/70/1, IWM.

147. Richardson, *Flashback*, p. 122.

148. Alamein Diary, BLM 28/1, IWM.

149. Letter, Lieutenant-General Oliver Leese to Margaret, Lady Leese, 1.11.[42], Box 2, Leese Papers, IWM.

150. Alamein Diary, BLM 28/1, IWM.

151. Entry of Saturday, 31.10.42, ibid.

152. B. L. Montgomery, *Memoirs*, p. 136.

153. Letter, B. L. Montgomery to Major-General Godwin-Austen, 31.10.42, The Royal Warwickshire Regimental Museum.

154. Leese, unpublished memoir.

155. Letter, B. L. Montgomery to Tom and Phyllis Reynolds, 1.11.42, Reynolds Papers, IWM.

156. Letter, B. L. Montgomery to General Sir Alan Brooke, 1.11.42, Alanbrooke Papers, LHCMA.

157. Alamein Diary, BLM 28/1, IWM.

158. Lucas Phillips, *Alamein*, p. 348.

159. Letter, Lieutenant-General Oliver Leese to Margaret, Lady Leese, 3.11.[42] Box 2, Leese Papers, IWM.

160. Freyberg, *Freyberg VC*, pp. 405–6.

161. Letter, Captain C. B. Stoddart to his father, CAB 106/793, PRO.

162. Marwan-Schlosser, *Rommels Flak als Pak*, p. 5.

163. Afrika Korps to 164 Division 1900 hrs, AL 834/2/2, IWM.

164. Ibid.

165. Lucas Phillips, *Alamein*, p. 356.

166. Ibid., p. 362.

167. Major-General R. Briggs to Brigadier C. E. Lucas Phillips, undated letter, Briggs Papers, 99/1/1, IWM, and Lucas Phillips, *Alamein*, p. 360.

168. Diary of F. T. Bennett, 2.11.42, 88/12/1, IWM.

169. Lucas Phillips, *Alamein*, p. 367. For Monty to intervene directly was not unusual. Briggs' Crusader tank had a field telephone, linked to Corps, 'which in turn had a line to Tac Army HQ', as Briggs recalled, since 'Corps had a switch-board so Army Tac HQ could be linked to any division by line' – letter, Briggs to Lucas Phillips, Briggs Papers, 99/1/1, IWM.

170. C-in-C to corps commander, 1730–1800 hrs, 2.11.42, DAK Messages, AL 834/2/2.

171. Ibid.

172. Irving, *The Trail of the Fox*, pp. 209–10.

173. Alanbrooke Diary, Alanbrooke Papers, LHCMA.

174. Bryant, *Turn of the Tide*, p. 516.

175. Lucas, *War in the Desert*, p. 238.

176. General Sir Charles Richardson interview.

177. Irving, *The Trail of the Fox*, p. 211.

178. Diary of F. T. Bennett, 3.11.42, 88/12/1, IWM.

179. Irving, *The Trail of the Fox*, p. 211.

180. Liddell Hart, *The Rommel Papers*, p. 321.

181. Irving, *The Trail of the Fox*, p. 209.

182. Liddell Hart, *The Rommel Papers*, p. 321.

183. Ibid.

184. Entry for 3.11.42, Briggs Diary, Briggs Papers, 99/1/1, IWM.

185. Letter, Lieutenant-General Oliver Leese to Margaret, Lady Leese, 3.11.42, Box 2, Leese Papers, IWM.

186. Leese, unpublished memoir.

187. H. von Luck, *Panzer Commander*, 1989, p. 95.

188. Irving, *The Trail of the Fox*, p. 212.

189. Major-General Douglas Wimberley, unpublished memoir, communicated to the author by General Wimberley.

190. Leese, unpublished memoir.

191. Wimberley, unpublished memoir.

192. Alamein Diary, BLM 28/1, IWM.

23 The Lessons of Alamein

1. Lucas Phillips, *Alamein*, p. 394; 30,000 Axis troops were taken prisoner, 10,724 of them German.

2. Liddell Hart, *The Rommel Papers*, p. 326.

3. Letter Lieutenant C. W. K. Potts, 1st Battalion, The Buffs, to Miss Pamela Stubbs (later Mrs Potts), (?)6.11.42, 92/28/1, IWM.

4. De Guingand, *From Brass Hat to Bowler Hat*, p. 10.

5. Letter, Lieutenant-General Oliver Leese to Margaret, Lady Leese, 7.11.42, Box 2, Leese Papers, IWM.

6. Irving, *The Trail of the Fox*, p. 214.

7. Major-General M. St John Oswald interview.

8. Lucas, *War in the Desert*, p. 256.

9. Alamein Diary, BLM 28/1, IWM.

10. Major-General M. St John Oswald interview.

11. Johnston, *Nine Rivers from Jordan*, p. 72.

12. Ibid., p. 73.

13. Nicolson, *Diaries and Letters, 1939–1945*, entry of 4.11.42, p. 259.

14. Letter, Lieutenant-General Oliver Leese to Margaret, Lady Leese, 9.11.42, Box 2, Leese Papers, IWM.

15. Message of 12.11.42, BLM 28/1–6, IWM.

16. 'Main Lessons of the Battle', The Battle of Egypt 23 Oct. 1942–7 Nov. 1942, BLM 28/1–6, IWM.

17. 'Main Lessons of the Battle', 10 Nov. 1942, BLM 28/2, IWM.

18. Irving, *The Trail of the Fox*, p. 208.

19. J. Steinhoff et al., *Voices from the Past*, 1989, pp. 365–6.

20. Letter, B. L. Montgomery to General Sir Alan Brooke, 10.11.42, Alanbrooke Papers, 14/61, LHCMA.

21. John Strawson, *Churchill and Hitler*, 1997, p. 360.

22. Leese, unpublished memoir.

23. Ibid.

24. C. Ponting, *Churchill*, 1994, p. 389.

25. Nicolson, *Diaries and Letters, 1939–1945*, entry of 4.11.42, p. 259.

26. Letter, Lieutenant-General Oliver Leese to Margaret, Lady Leese, 7.11.42, Box 2, Leese Papers, IWM.

27. Ibid.

Sources

The Full Monty is based on primary and secondary research work originally conducted in the compilation of the three volumes of my official *Monty* biography, published in 1981, 1983 and 1986 (listed in the bibliography below). The entire corpus of research materials – including all interviews conducted for the official biography – was deposited and catalogued, on completion, in the Imperial War Museum in London, and is available to scholars through the IWM's Department of Documents. In addition, I have used a number of fresh manuscript, unpublished and published documents in compiling *The Full Monty*. These documents and publications have been individually listed in the endnotes. For ease of overall reference, however, the following summary of manuscript and printed book sources relating to *The Full Monty* may be useful.

Janet Foster and Julia Sheppard's *British Archives: A Guide to Archive Resources in the United Kingdom* (London, 1995) is an excellent preliminary guide. Robin Higham's *World War II in Europe, Africa and the Americas, with General Sources: A Handbook of Literature and Research* (London, 1997), *Official Military Historical Offices and Sources* (London, 2000) and *A Guide to the Sources in British Military History* (London, 1972) are all worthy guides – as well as Gerald Jordon's supplement: *British Military History: A Supplement to Robin Higham's Guide to the Sources* (New York, 1988).

Manuscript sources

The main manuscript sources in Britain relating to Field-Marshal Montgomery are the Imperial War Museum in Lambeth, London (IWM); Royal Warwickshire Regimental Museum, Warwick (RWRM); the Public Record Office in Kew, Surrey (PRO); the Liddell Hart Centre for Military Archives in King's College, Strand, London (LHCMA); National Army Museum, London (NAM); Southampton University (SA); RAF Museum, Hendon (RAFM); and Churchill College Archives, Cambridge (CCA).

The primary holdings in the United States are the National Archives in Washington, DC (NA); the US Army Center of Military History, Washington,

DC; US Army Military History Institute, Carlisle, Pennsylvania (MHI); and Eisenhower Presidential Library, Abilene, Kansas (DDEL); as well as the Manuscript Division of the Library of Congress, Washington, DC (LC). In Canada, National Archives of Canada, Ottawa (NAC).

IWM holdings include: Montgomery Papers (IWM collection, International Thomson Organization Collection, Lord Montgomery Deposit), and Montgomery ancillary and other collections. The ancillary collections include selected Montgomery-related papers of John Ackroyd, G. Astley, R. F. K. Belchem, F. J. Bellenger, Alan Brooke, Arthur Bryant, C. Chavasse, Major A. W. Cheyne, Francis de Guingand, P. B. Earle, James Gunn, John Harding, J. R. Henderson, J. F. V. Hernu, F. L. Hughes, Oliver Leese, Carol Mather, Major John North, Roy Plomley, John Poston, Tom and Phyllis Reynolds, Frank Simpson, Lucien Trueb, Trumbull and Mary Warren and Edgar Williams. Letters include those bought and donated by Sir Denis Hamilton, written by George Erskine, W. V. Griffin and Norman Scorgie; also photocopies of BLM's letters to Clementine Churchill, Mary Churchill, Colin Coote, Louis Mountbatten, Noel Ritchie, 'Manny' Shinwell, and D. N. Wimberley.

Other IWM collections that relate to Montgomery and which have been used in the writing of *The Full Monty* include: Raymond Briggs Papers, Percival Papers, Strickland Papers, Haydon Papers, Majdalany Papers, Quentin Reynolds Papers, F. T. Bennett Papers, W. D. McClure Papers, C. W. K. Potts Papers, Col. J. G. M. B. Gough Papers, Robin Dunn Papers, O. A. Archdale Papers, S. Gresty Papers, Charles and Margaret Sweeny Papers, A. F. Flatow Papers, Ian Mackay Papers, G. N. Giddings Papers, R. L. Crimp Papers, C. M. S. Gardner Papers, A. W. W. Holworthy Papers, C. T. Witherby Papers, D. F. Parry Papers, J. M. McSwiney Papers, Louis Challoner Papers, W. R. Garrett Papers and copies of the German War Diaries.

RWRM holdings include Regimental War Diaries, *The Antelope*, Montgomery collection, Tomes collection, etc.

PRO holdings include Prime Minister's Papers, Cabinet Office official history papers, British formation and unit war diaries, Harold Alexander Papers and 'Mary' Coningham reports.

LHCMA holdings include Alanbrooke Papers, John Kennedy Papers, Hastings Ismay Papers, Liddell Hart Papers, 'Freddie' de Guingand Papers, Chester Wilmot Papers and Ironside Papers.

NAM holdings include Ironside Papers and Templer Papers.

SA holdings include Mountbatten Papers.

RAFM holdings include Tedder Papers and Robb Papers.

CCA holdings include Tedder Papers, Ronald Lewin Papers and Stephen Roskill Papers.

NA holdings include US formation and unit war diaries.

MHI holdings include Bradley Papers and Forrest Pogue interviews.

DDEL holdings include Eisenhower Papers, Walter Bedell Smith Papers, Harry C. Butcher Papers and Kay Summersby Papers.

NAC holdings include Stacey Papers, Crerar Papers and Guy Simonds Papers.

Bibliography

The best and most useful essayistic introduction to published Montgomery sources, with a full bibliography, is Colin F. Baxter's *Field Marshal Bernard Law Montgomery 1887–1976: Selected Bibliography* (Westport, CT, 1999). This is the most comprehensive and up-to-date Montgomery bibliography in print. Meanwhile, the following is a list of published works used in the writing of *The Full Monty*.

Alexander, H., *The Alexander Memoirs*, London, 1962.
Ambrose, S., *Eisenhower the Soldier, 1890–1952*, London, 1984.
Asher, M., *Lawrence: The Uncrowned King of Arabia*, London, 1998.
Balfour, M., *Propaganda in War 1939–45*, London, 1979.
Barnes, J. and Nicholson, D., eds, *The Empire at Bay: The Leo Amery Diaries 1929–1945*, London, 1988.
Barnett, C., *Britain and Her Army 1509–1970: A Military, Political and Social Survey*, London, 1970.
—— *The Desert Generals*, 2nd edn, London, 1983.
—— *The Swordbearers*, London, 1963.
Baxter, C., *The War in North Africa, 1941–1943: A Selected Bibliography*, Westport, CT, 1996.
Beale, P., *Death by Design: British Tank Development in the Second World War*, London, 1998.
Behrendt, H.-O., *Rommel's Intelligence in the Desert Campaign*, London, 1985.
Belchem, D., *All in the Day's March*, London, 1978.
Bennett, R., *Ultra and Mediterranean Strategy 1941–1945*, London, 1989.
Birkin, Andrew, *J. M. Barrie and the Lost Boys*, London, 1979.
Blumenson, M., *Mark Clark*, London, 1985.
Blumenson, M., ed., *The Patton Papers*, vol. II, New York, 1972.
Bond, B., *British Military Policy Between the Two World Wars*, London, 1980.
Bond, B., ed., *Chief of Staff: The Diaries of Lt-General Sir Henry Pownall*, vol. I, London, 1972.
Bond, B. and Cave, N., eds, *Haig: A Reappraisal 70 Years on*, London, 1999.
Brereton, L. H., *The Brereton Diaries, 3 Oct 1941–8 May 1945*, New York, 1976.
Brett-James, A., *Conversations with Montgomery*, London, 1984.
Brooks, S., ed., *Montgomery and the Eighth Army: A Selection from the Diaries, Correspondence, and other Papers of Field Marshal the Viscount Montgomery of Alamein, August 1942 to December 1943*, London, 1991.
Bryant, A., *The Turn of the Tide*, London, 1957.
Burdick, Charles and Jacobsen, Hans-Adolf, eds., *The Halder War Diary 1939–1942*, Novato, CA, 1988.
Burke, Joanna, *An Intimate History of Killing*, London, 1999.
—— *Dismembering the Male: Men's Bodies, Britain and the Great War*, London, 1996.
Butler, Ewan, *Barry's Flying Column*, London, 1971.

'C.N.', *The Making of an Officer*, London, 1916.

Caccia-Dominioni, P., *Alamein 1933–1962: An Italian Story*, London, 1966.

Campbell, John P., *Dieppe Revisited: A Documentary Investigation*, London, 1993.

Carver, Michael, *El Alamein*, London, 1962.

—— *Harding of Petherton*, London, 1978.

—— *The Seven Ages of the British Army*, London, 1984.

Chalfont, A., *Montgomery of Alamein*, London, 1976.

Chamberlain, P. and Gander, T., *Anti-Aircraft Guns*, London, 1975.

Chandler, A. D., ed., *The Papers of Dwight David Eisenhower: The War Years*, Baltimore, 1970.

Churchill, Winston, *The History of the Second World War*, vol. IV, *The Hinge of Fate*, London, 1951.

—— *The World Crisis*, London, 1927.

Coker, Christopher, *War in the Twentieth Century: A Study of War and Modern Consciousness*, London, 1994.

Colville, J. R., *The Fringes of Power: Downing Street Diaries 1939–1955*, London, 1985.

—— *Man of Valour*, London, 1972.

Connell, John, *Auchinleck*, London, 1959.

—— *Wavell: Scholar and Soldier*, London, 1964.

Copp, Terry, ed., *Montgomery's Scientists: Operational Research in Northwest Europe*, Waterloo, Ontario, 2000.

Crook, Paul, *Darwinism, War and History: The Debate over the Biology of War from the 'Origin of Species' to the First World War*, Cambridge, 1994.

Daley, H., *Small Cloud*, London, 1987.

Danchev, A., *The Alchemist of War*, London, 1998.

—— *Very Special Relationship: Field Marshal Sir John Dill and the Anglo-American Alliance 1941–44*, London, 1986.

Davenport-Hines, R., *Sex, Death and Punishment: Attitudes to Sex and Sexuality in Britain since the Renaissance*, London, 1990.

David, Hugh, *On Queer Street: A Social History of British Homosexuality, 1895–1955*, London, 1997.

D'Este, Carlo, *Patton: A Genius for War*, London, 1995.

De Groot, Gerard J., *Douglas Haig, 1861–1928*, London, 1988.

De Guingand, F., *From Brass Hat to Bowler Hat*, London, 1979.

—— *Operation Victory*, London, 1947.

Deighton, Len and Hastings, Max, *Battle of Britain*, Ware, 1999.

Dilks, D., ed., *The Diaries of Sir Alexander Cadogan OM 1938–1945*, London, 1971.

Dixon, Norman, *On the Psychology of Military Incompetence*, London, 1976.

Driberg, T., *Beaverbrook: A Study in Power and Frustration*, London, 1956.

Durbin, E. F. M. and Bowlby, John, *Personal Aggressiveness and War*, London, 1939.

Edmonds, J. E., *Military Operations. France and Belgium 1914*, vol. I, 3rd edn, London, 1933.

Egremont, M., *Under Two Flags*, London, 1997.

Eisenhower, D. D., *At Ease*, New York, 1967.

—— *Crusade in Europe*, London, 1948.

Ellis, J., *Brute Force*, London, 1990.

Ellis, L. F., *The War in France and Flanders 1939–1940*, London, 1953.

English, John A., *The Canadian Army and the Normandy Campaign: A Study of Failure in High Command*, London, 1991.

Farrar, F. W., *Eternal Hope, 5 Sermons*, London, 1878.

Ferguson, Niall, *The Pity of War*, London, 1998.

Ferguson, Niall, ed., *Virtual History*, London, 1997.

Fergusson, B., *The Watery Maze: The Story of Combined Operations*, London, 1961.

Ferro, Marc, *The Great War 1914–1918*, London, 1973.

Fleming, Peter, *Invasion 1940*, London, 1957.

Fraser, D., *Alanbrooke*, London, 1982.

—— *And We Shall Shock Them*, London, 1983.

—— *Knight's Cross*, London, 1998.

Freud, S., *Leonardo da Vinci and a Memory of His Childhood* (1910), New York, 1964.

Freyberg, P., *Bernard Freyberg VC: Soldier of Two Nations*, London, 1990.

Fussell, Paul, *The Great War and Modern Memory*, London, 1975.

Gay, Peter, *Freud: A Life for Our Time*, New York, 1988.

Gilbert, M., *Churchill, A Life*, London, 1991.

—— *Churchill*, vol. IV, *1917–1922*, London, 1975.

—— *Road to Victory: Winston S. Churchill 1941–1945*, London, 1986.

Graves, R., *Goodbye to All That* (1929), London, 1960.

Greacen, Lavinia, *Chink: A Biography*, Foreword by Correlli Barnett, London, 1989.

Greenhouse, Brereton, *Dieppe, Dieppe*, Montreal, 1992.

Gwyer, J. M. A. and Butler, J. R. M., *Grand Strategy*, London, 1964.

Hamilton, Nigel, *Monty: The Making of a General 1887–1942*, London, 1981.

—— *Monty: Master of the Battlefield 1942–1944*, London, 1983.

—— *Monty: The Field-Marshal 1944–1976*, London, 1986.

—— *Monty: The Man Behind the Legend*, Wheathampstead, 1987.

Heilbut, A., *Thomas Mann: Eros & Literature*, New York, 1995.

Herbert, A. P., *The Secret Battle* (1919), Oxford, 1982.

Hinsley, F. H. et al., *British Intelligence in the Second World War, Its Influence on Strategy and Operations*, vol. II, London, 1981.

Hogg, Ian, *Allied Artillery of World War Two*, Marlborough, 1998.

—— *The Guns of World War II*, London, 1976.

Holmes, R., *Riding the Retreat*, London, 1995.

Homberger, E. and Charmley, J., eds., *The Troubled Face of Biography*, London, 1988.

Horrocks, B., *A Full Life*, London, 1960.

Horrocks, B., with Belfield, E. and Essame, H., *Corps Commander*, London, 1977.

Hough, R., *Mountbatten: Hero for Our Time*, London, 1985.

Howard, Michael, *Studies in War and Peace*, London, 1970.

Howarth, T. E. B., ed., *Monty at Close Quarters: Recollections of the Man*, London, 1985.

Hunt, D., *A Don at War*, London, 1966.

Irving, David, *Hitler's War*, London, 1977.

—— *The Trail of the Fox: The Life of Field-Marshal Erwin Rommel*, London, 1977.

Ismay, Lord, *Memoirs*, London, 1960.

Jackson, W. G. F., *The North African Campaign 1940–1943*, 1975.

Jewell, D., ed., *Alamein and the Desert War*, London, 1967.

Johnson, J. H., *1918: The Unexpected Victory*, London, 1997.

Johnston, D., *Nine Rivers from Jordan*, London, 1953.

Keegan, John, *The First World War*, London, 1998.

Kennedy, J., *The Business of War*, London, 1957.

Kershaw, I., *Hitler, 1889–1936: Hubris*, London, 1998.

Kesselring, A., *The Memoirs of Field-Marshal Kesselring*, London, 1953.

Kippenberger, H., *Infantry Brigadier*, London, 1949.

Kluck, A. von. *The March on Paris and the Battle of the Marne 1914*, London, 1920.

Knightley, P. and Simpson, C., *The Secret Lives of Lawrence of Arabia*, London, 1969.

Laffin, J., *British Butchers and Bunglers of World War One*, Gloucester, 1988.

Law, R. D. and Luther, C. W. H., *Rommel*, San Jose, 1980.

Lawrence, T. E., *The Letters of T. E. Lawrence*, ed., Malcolm Brown, London, 1988.

—— *Seven Pillars of Wisdom: A Triumph*, Harmondsworth, 1962.

Leasor, J., *War at the Top*, London, 1959.

Lee, B., *Marching Orders, the Untold Story of World War II*, New York, 1995.

L'Etang, Hugh, *The Pathology of Leadership*, London, 1969.

Lewin, R., *Montgomery as Military Commander*, London, 1971.

Liddell Hart, B. H., *Europe in Arms*, London, 1937.

—— *History of the First World War*, London, 1970.

—— *Memoirs*, London, 1965.

—— *The Real War 1914–18*, London, 1930.

Liddell Hart, B. H., ed., *The Rommel Papers*, London, 1953.

Lovat, Lord, *March Past*, London, 1978.

Lucas, James, *War in the Desert: The Eighth Army at Alamein*, London, 1982.

Lucas Phillips, C. E., *Alamein*, London, 1973.

Luck, Hans von, *Panzer Commander*, New York, 1989.

Macdonald, Iverach, *The History of the Times*, vol. V, London, 1984.

Mack, John E., *A Prince of Our Disorder: The Life of T. E. Lawrence*, London, 1976.

Macksey, Kenneth, *Armoured Crusader*, London, 1967.

—— *Invasion, The German Invasion of England, July 1940*, London, 1980.

—— *Rommel: Battles and Campaigns*, London, 1979.

Macmillan, Harold, *Winds of Change 1914–1939*, London, 1966.

Maier, Klaus et al., eds., *Das deutsche Reich und der zweite Weltkrieg*, vol. II, Stuttgart, 1979.

Marwan-Schlosser, R. F., *Rommels Flak als Pak: Das Flak-Regiment 135 als Rückgrat des Deutschen Afrikakorps*, Wiener Neustadt, 1991.

Masters, J., *Bugles and a Tiger*, London, 1956.

Maugham, Barton, *Tobruk and Alamein*, Canberra, 1966.

McKee, A., *El Alamein: Ultra and the Three Battles*, London, 1991.

Miller, Merle, *Ike the Soldier, as They Knew Him*, New York, 1987.

Montgomery, B. L., *Memoirs*, London, 1958.

—— *The Path to Leadership*, London, 1961.

—— *A History of Warfare*, London, 1968.

Montgomery, Brian, *A Field Marshal in the Family*, London, 1973.

—— *Monty: A Life in Photographs*, Poole, 1985.

Moorehead, A., *African Trilogy (The End in Africa)*, London, 1998.

—— *Montgomery*, London, 1946.

Moran, Lord, *Winston Churchill: The Struggle for Survival*, London, 1966.

Morgan, Frederick, *Peace and War*, London, 1961.

Musgrave, V., *Montgomery, His Life in Pictures*, London, 1947.

Nicolson, Nigel, *Alex: The Life of Field-Marshal Earl Alexander of Tunis*, London, 1973.

Nicolson, Nigel, ed., *Harold Nicolson, Diaries and Letters, 1939–1945*, London, 1967.

Orwell, George, *Collected Essays*, vol. II, *My Country, Right or Left*, London, 1968.

Overy, R., *Why the Allies Won*, London, 1995.

Parrish, T., *Roosevelt and Marshall*, New York, 1989.

Peniakoff, V., *Popski's Private Army*, London, 1957.

Pitt, B., *The Crucible of War: Year of Alamein 1942*, London, 1982.

Ponting, C., *Churchill*, London, 1994.

Poston, M. M. et al., *Design and Development of Weapons*, London, 1964.

Potter, D. J., *Fiasco: the Breakout of the German Battleships*, London, 1970.

Prior, R. and Wilson, T., *Command on the Western Front: The Military Career of Sir Henry Rawlinson 1914–18*, Oxford, 1992.

Rees, G., *A Bundle of Sensations*, London, 1960.

Reynolds, Q., *Dress Rehearsal: The Story of Dieppe*, New York, 1943.

Richards, D. and Saunders, H., *Royal Air Force 1939–1945*, vol. II, *The Fight Avails*, London, 1953.

Richardson, Charles, *Flashback*, London, 1985.

—— *Send For Freddie*, London, 1987.

Roberts, David, *Minds at War: The Poetry and Experience of the First World War*, Burgess Hill, 1996.

Roberts, G. P. B., *From the Desert to the Baltic*, London, 1995.

Roskill, S., *Admiral of the Fleet Earl Beatty, The Last Naval Hero*, London, 1980.

Rowse, A. L., *Homosexuals in History: A Study of Ambivalence in Society, Literature and the Arts*, London, 1977.

Samuels, Martin, *Command or Control: Command, Training and Tactics in the British and German Armies, 1888–1918*, London, 1995.

Schmidt, Heinz W., *With Rommel in the Desert* (1951), London, 1980.

Seeckt, General Hans von, *Thoughts of a Soldier*, London, 1930.

Soames, M., *Speaking for Themselves: The Personal Letters of Winston and Clementine Churchill*, London, 1998.

Stacey, C. P., *Six Years of War*, Ottawa, 1957.

Steinhoff, J. et al., *Voices from the Past*, Washington, DC, 1989.

Stewart, A., *Eighth Army's Greatest Victories, Alam Halfa to Tunis 1942–1943*, London, 1999.

Strawson, J., *Churchill and Hitler*, London, 1997.

—— *El Alamein*, London, 1981.

Summers, C., ed., *The Gay and Lesbian Literary Heritage*, London, 1995.

Symonds, J. A. S., *The Memoirs of John Addington Symonds*, ed. Phyllis Grosskurth, Chicago, 1986.

Taylor, A. J. P., *The First World War*, London, 1966.

Terraine, J., *The Right of the Line*, London, 1985.

Terry, R., *Women in Khaki*, London, 1988.

Thompson, R. W., *Dieppe at Dawn: The Story of the Dieppe Raid, 19 August 1942*, London, 1962.

—— *The Montgomery Legend*, London, 1967.

Thomson, Julian, *War Behind Enemy Lines*, London, 1998.

Turner, A. Richard, *Inventing Leonardo: The Anatomy of a Legend*, New York, 1993/London, 1995.

Villa, B., *Unauthorized Action: Mountbatten and the Dieppe Raid*, Toronto, 1988.

Walker, R., *Alam Halfa and Alamein*, Wellington, New Zealand, 1967.

Wamper, H., *Dieppe: Die Beährung des Küstenwestwalles*, Berlin, 1943.

Warner, P., *Alamein*, London, 1979.

Wedemeyer, A., *Wedemeyer Reports!*, New York, 1958.

Whitaker, D. and Whitaker, S., *Dieppe: Tragedy to Triumph*, London, 1992.

Willkie, W., *One World*, New York, 1942.

Wilson, J., *Lawrence of Arabia: The Authorised Biography of T. E. Lawrence*, London, 1989.

Winter, Denis, *Haig's Command: A Reassessment*, London, 1991.

Winton, H., *To Change an Army: General Sir John Burnett-Stuart and British Armoured Doctrine, 1927–1938*, London, 1988.

Ziegler, P., *Mountbatten*, London, 1985.

Index

NOTE: A number of entries comprise two paragraphs, the first a chronologically ordered index of events and the second an alphabetically ordered list of topics.